'Professor Lu Zhouxiang has done an excellent job in bringing together a range of essays – both general and focused on particular states, regions, and themes – concerned with nationalism in both East and South-East Asia. This will be of value to the general reader by virtue of its breadth of coverage. It will also help historians and social scientists in the field to contextualise their own findings in light of similar work by other specialists.'

John Breuilly, Professor, *London School of Economics and Political Science*

'Nationalism is one of the most powerful and important factors to shape Asia, one of the most dynamic areas in the world, and understanding it is crucial for scholars and the wider world alike. Combining syntheses of deep research with strong explanatory frameworks, this handbook will be essentially reading for all scholars of nationalism and ideology.'

Rana Mitter, Professor, *University of Oxford*

'This handbook is invaluable guide to nationalism in East and Southeast Asia. It offers a comprehensive survey of the field and is an essential work of reference for scholars of nationalism.'

Gerard Delanty, Professor, *University of Sussex*

THE ROUTLEDGE HANDBOOK OF NATIONALISM IN EAST AND SOUTHEAST ASIA

This handbook presents a comprehensive survey of the formation and transformation of nationalism in 15 East and Southeast Asian countries.

Written by a team of international scholars from different backgrounds and disciplines, this volume offers new perspectives on studying Asian history, society, culture, and politics, and provides readers with a unique lens through which to better contextualise and understand the relationships between countries within East and Southeast Asia, and between Asia and the world. It highlights the latest developments in the field and contributes to our knowledge and understanding of nationalism and nation building. Comprehensive and clearly written, this book examines a diverse set of topics that include theoretical considerations on nationalism and internationalism; the formation of nationalism and national identity in the colonial and postcolonial eras; the relationships between traditional culture, religion, ethnicity, education, gender, technology, sport, and nationalism; the influence of popular culture on nationalism; and politics, policy, and national identity. It illustrates how nationalism helped to draw the borders between the nations of East and Southeast Asia, and how it is re-emerging in the twenty-first century to shape the region and the world into the future.

The Routledge Handbook of Nationalism in East and Southeast Asia is important reading for those interested in and studying Asian history, Social and Cultural history, and modern history.

Lu Zhouxiang is an Associate Professor within the School of Modern Languages, Literatures and Cultures at National University of Ireland Maynooth, Ireland.

THE ROUTLEDGE HANDBOOK OF NATIONALISM IN EAST AND SOUTHEAST ASIA

Edited by Lu Zhouxiang

NEW YORK AND LONDON

Designed cover image: Indonesian Flag Flying On Independence Day,
Bali. Ian Trower / Alamy Stock Photo

First published 2024
by Routledge
605 Third Avenue, New York, NY 10158

and by Routledge
4 Park Square, Milton Park, Abingdon, Oxon, OX14 4RN

Routledge is an imprint of the Taylor & Francis Group, an informa business

© 2024 selection and editorial matter, Lu Zhouxiang; individual chapters, the contributors

The right of Lu Zhouxiang to be identified as the author of the editorial material, and of the authors for their individual chapters, has been asserted in accordance with sections 77 and 78 of the Copyright, Designs and Patents Act 1988.

All rights reserved. No part of this book may be reprinted or reproduced or utilised in any form or by any electronic, mechanical, or other means, now known or hereafter invented, including photocopying and recording, or in any information storage or retrieval system, without permission in writing from the publishers.

Trademark notice: Product or corporate names may be trademarks or registered trademarks, and are used only for identification and explanation without intent to infringe.

Library of Congress Cataloging-in-Publication Data
Names: Lu, Zhouxiang, editor.
Title: The Routledge handbook of nationalism in East and Southeast Asia / edited by Lu Zhouxiang.
Description: New York, NY: Routledge, 2023. | Includes bibliographical references.
Identifiers: LCCN 2023003520 (print) | LCCN 2023003521 (ebook) | ISBN 9780367629205 (hbk) | ISBN 9780367629212 (pbk) | ISBN 9781003111450 (ebk)
Subjects: LCSH: Nationalism—East Asia. | Nationalism—Southeast Asia. | East Asia—Politics and government. | Southeast Asia—Politics and government.
Classification: LCC DS517.13 .R69 2023 (print) | LCC DS517.13 (ebook) | DDC 320.54095—dc23/eng/20230421
LC record available at https://lccn.loc.gov/2023003520
LC ebook record available at https://lccn.loc.gov/2023003521

ISBN: 978-0-367-62920-5 (hbk)
ISBN: 978-0-367-62921-2 (pbk)
ISBN: 978-1-003-11145-0 (ebk)

DOI: 10.4324/9781003111450

Typeset in Bembo
by codeMantra

CONTENTS

List of Figures — xi
List of Tables — xii
List of Contributors — xiii
Acknowledgements — xxiii
Abbreviations — xxiv

    Introduction: The arrival of the age of nationalism and nation states — 1
    Lu Zhouxiang

PART I
Theoretical considerations — **15**

1 Applying classic and contemporary nationalism theories to East and Southeast Asia today — 19
   Tina Burrett

2 Decolonialising Southeast Asian nationalism — 35
   Claire Sutherland

3 An alternative origin of nationalism in the East: The emergence of political subjectivity under the non-Western-centric world order — 48
   Atsuko Ichijo

4 The clash of empires, the rise of nationalism, and the vicissitude of Pan-Asianism in East Asia and Southeast Asia — 60
   Yongle Zhang

5 Post-colonialism, nationalism and internationalism in
  East and Southeast Asia 74
  Peter Herrmann

6 Traditional colonialism, modern hegemonism, and the
  construction of Asian nations 89
  Feilong Tian

PART II
East Asia: The roots, growth, ingredients, expressions, and contestation of national discourses **101**

7 Chinese nationalism in late Qing times: How to (not) change a
  multi-ethnic empire into a homogenous nation-state 108
  Julia C. Schneider

8 Nationalism in China towards a non-Western-centric history of ideas 122
  Zhiguang Yin

9 Nationalism, national salvation and the development of female
  hygiene in the Republic of China era 138
  Meishan Zhang

10 Between a rock and a hard place: The changing Taiwanese identity
   and rising Chinese nationalism 151
   Yitan Li

11 China's digital nationalism 167
   Florian Schneider

12 The dream of a strong country: Nationalism and China's Olympic journey 181
   Lu Zhouxiang

13 Conflict in Xinjiang: Nationalism, identity, and violence 196
   Arabinda Acharya and Rohan Gunaratna

14 'Dear Asian friends, we want to build peace'; Rightwing nationalism,
   internationalism, and Honda Koei's teaching about the
   Asia-Pacific War, 1965–1973 213
   Yoshiko Nozaki

15 Nationalism, history, and collective narcissism: Historical revisionism
   in twenty-first-century Japan 234
   Sven Saaler

16 Abe's feckless nationalism 250
    Jeff Kingston

17 Commercial nationalism and cosmopolitanism: Advertising
    production and consumption of (trans)national identity in Japan 267
    Koji Kobayashi

18 Nation, nationalism and identity discourses in North
    Korean popular culture 280
    Udo Merkel

19 Taekwondo: A symbol of South Korean nationalism 295
    Udo Moenig

20 South Korea's postdevelopmental nationalism 308
    Charles R. Kim

21 The emergence of calculated nationalism in South Korea
    in the twenty-first century 325
    Gil-Soo Han and David Hundt

22 The birth and transformation of Japanese-Korean nationalism 337
    Masaki Tosa

PART III
Southeast Asia: Ethnic and religious diversity, local rivalries, and political resistance 353

23 Nationalism, colonialism and decolonisation in Southeast Asia: The
    rise of emancipatory nationalism 361
    Stefan Eklöf Amirell

24 Comparative nation-building in the borderlands between China,
    Myanmar, and Thailand 375
    Enze Han

25 Nationalism, ethnicity, and regional conflict in twenty-first-century
    Southeast Asia 388
    Arabinda Acharya

26 The making of Hoa identity: Migrants, nationalism and
    nation-building in post-colonial Vietnam 404
    Zhifang Song

27	Writing nationalism in post-reform Vietnam: Portrayals of national enemies in contemporary Vietnamese fiction *Chi P. Pham*	416
28	Populist nationalism in Philippine historiography *Rommel A. Curaming*	429
29	Buddhist nationalism in Burma/Myanmar: Collective victimhood and ressentiment *Niklas Foxeus*	441
30	Nationalism in colonial and postcolonial Myanmar: Solidarities, discordance, and the crisis of community *Maitrii Aung-Thwin*	459
31	Competing nationalisms: Shifting conceptions of nation in the construction of Indonesia in the twentieth century *Joshua Kueh*	473
32	A journey through Cambodian nationalism: Political, elite and popular *Kimly Ngoun*	488
33	Xāt Lao: Imagining the Lao nation through race, history and language *Ryan Wolfson-Ford*	504
34	Different streams of Malay nationalism from the late colonial to contemporary eras *Ahmad Fauzi Abdul Hamid and Azmi Arifin*	519
35	Singapore's national narrative: Ripe for renewal *Michael D. Barr*	534
36	Exclusion and inclusion: Melayu Islam Beraja and the construction of Bruneian nationalism and national identity *Asiyah Kumpoh and Nani Suryani Abu Bakar*	549
37	Nationalism in transition: Construction and transformation of Rai Timor *Takahiro Kamisuna*	561
38	The routinization of charisma in Thai nation construction: A Weberian reading of Thai royalism, nationalism, and democracy *Jack Fong*	576

Index   *595*

FIGURES

5.1	Formational development between inclusion and exclusion	80
5.2	Purpose enhancement	80
10.1	Taiwanese/Chinese identity (1992/1906~2020/2012)	155
10.2	Taiwan independence vs. unification with the Mainland (1992/1906~2020/2012)	155
19.1	Park Chung Hee (centre) during the military coup, 1961	297
19.2	The victorious ROK Army Taekwondo Team, 1973: Taekwondo became part of South Korean military training	300
22.1	*Garasu no kamen* (*Glass Mask*) by Suzue Miuchi	343
22.2	Pirated version of *Garasu no kamen*	343
38.1	Prince Narisara Nuwattiwong's 1887 painting "Queen Suriyothai Elephant Combat" depicting the queen (center with weapon) defending King Maha Chakkraphat (right with weapon) from the Burma's Viceroy of Prome (left with weapon) before she was slain (public domain)	579
38.2	The 1593 elephant combat between Mingyi Swa (left with weapon) and Naresuan (right with weapon). In Thai accounts, the former is slain by the latter in the duel. Based on a Siamese painting from the seventeenth–eighteenth century (Collection of Maurice Collis, public domain)	580
38.3	The "Ruling Monarchs" postcard printed by Rotary Photographic Co Ltd. in 1908. Chulalongkorn is first at the top left (public domain)	585
38.4	Khrong Chandawong (right) and Thongphan Suthimat (left) being led to their execution by firing squad (Baker and Phongpaichit 2005, 174)	590

TABLES

10.1	Main economic indicators	160
10.2	US-China-Taiwan military expenditure as a percentage of government spending, 2000–2017	161
15.1	Main triggers for historical revisionists and their reactions	241
29.1	Changes of Christian, Buddhist, and Islam communities between 1973 and 2014	453

CONTRIBUTORS

Ahmad Fauzi Abdul Hamid is a Professor of Political Science, School of Distance Education, Universiti Sains Malaysia (USM), Penang, Malaysia. He has held Visiting Fellowships with the S. Rajaratnam School of International Studies, Nanyang Technological University, Singapore (2008–2009); the ISEAS-Yusof Ishak Institute, Singapore (2015–2016); the Southeast Asia Regional Centre for Counter-Terrorism, Ministry of Foreign Affairs, Kuala Lumpur (2020), the Faculty of Social Sciences and Humanities, Universiti Malaysia Sarawak (2021–2022), and was Scholar-in-Residence, Oxford Centre for Islamic Studies, United Kingdom (2021). Trained as a political scientist at the universities of Oxford, Leeds and Newcastle, United Kingdom, his research interests lie within the field of political Islam in Southeast Asia. Ahmad Fauzi is the editor-in-chief of *Kajian Malaysia: Journal of Malaysian Studies* and an editorial board member of *KEMANUSIAAN: The Asian Journal Humanities*, both published by USM Press.

Nani Suryani Abu Bakar is a Lecturer at the History and International Studies Programme, Faculty of Arts and Social Sciences, Universiti Brunei Darussalam, Brunei. She obtained her BA in Education at Universiti Brunei Darussalam (1997), MA (2001) in Modern History, and PhD (2006) in East Asian Studies from Leeds University, UK. Her field of study is the political history of Brunei and Malaysia in particular, and Southeast Asia in general. She also has special interest in the socio-economic history of Brunei.

Arabinda Acharya is an Associate Professor and Senior Research Advisor at the Rabdan Academy in Abu Dhabi (UAE), and a Visiting Professor at National Chengchi University, Taiwan, and XIM University, India. Before that, he was with the National Defense University in the USA, and the S. Rajaratnam School of International Studies, Nanyang Technological University, Singapore. He is also the Director of the Centre for Peace and Development Studies, India. Acharya holds a PhD in International Relations from Deakin University, Australia. His areas of specialization include regionalism and human security, political violence and terrorism (as listed in the United Nations Roster of Global Experts), maritime security, and cyber security. His recent publications include *South China Sea Developments and Implications for Freedom of Navigation* (World Scientific, 2021), *Whither Southeast Asia Terrorism* (Imperial College Press, 2015), *Ten Years After 9/11: Rethinking the Jihadist Threat* (Routledge,

2013), *The Terrorist Threat in Southern Thailand: Jihad or Quest for Justice* (Potomac Books Inc., 2013), and *Ethnic Identity and National Conflict in China* (Palgrave Macmillan, 2010).

Stefan Eklöf Amirell is a Professor of Global History at Linnaeus University. He is also the director of the Linnaeus University Centre for Concurrences in Colonial and Postcolonial Studies and a former president of the Swedish Historical Association (2016–2022). His research interests include political culture in maritime Southeast Asia, treaty-making and diplomatic history in colonial Southeast Asia, United States imperial expansion, and piracy in world history. He is the author of *Indonesian Politics in Crisis: The Long Fall of Suharto, 1996–1998* (NIAS Press, 1998), *Power and political culture in Suharto's Indonesia: The Indonesian Democratic Party (PDI) and the Decline of the New Order, 1986–98* (Routledge, 2003), and *Pirates of Empire: Colonisation and Maritime Violence in Southeast Asia* (Cambridge University Press, 2019).

Maitrii Aung-Thwin is an Associate Professor of Myanmar/Southeast Asian History at the National University of Singapore. His current research is concerned with nation-building, identity, public history, infrastructure, and Buddhist networks in South and Southeast Asia. His publications include *A History of Myanmar since Ancient Times: Traditions and Transformations* (with Michael Aung-Thwin 2013), *The Return of the Galon King: History, Law, and Rebellion in Colonial Burma* (2011), and *A New History of Southeast Asia* (with Merle Ricklefs et al, 2010). Assoc Prof Aung-Thwin served on the Association of Asian Studies Board of Directors (USA) and he is currently a trustee of the Burma Studies Foundation (USA), and editor of the *Journal of Southeast Asian Studies*.

Azmi Arifin is a Senior Lecturer of Malaysian Political History, School of Humanities, Universiti Sains Malaysia (USM). He obtained his BA and MA from USM, and his PhD in Malaysian Historiography from Universiti Kebangsaan Malaysia (UKM) in 2006. His recent works include *Nasionalisme dan Revolusi di Malaysia dan Indonesia: Pengamatan Sejarah* [Nationalism and Revolution in Malaysia and Indonesia: An Historical Observation] (2006); *Sejarah Malaysia: Wacana Kedaulatan Bangsa, Kenegaraan dan Kemerdekaan* [Malaysian History: Discourse on Nation, Citizenship and Independence] (2016); and *Di Sebalik Tabir Sejarah Malaysia 1945–1957* [Behind the Scenes of Malaysian History 1945–1957] (2016).

Michael D. Barr began researching Singapore history and politics while a student at the University of Queensland in the 1990s. Since then, he has written or edited seven books related to Singapore, along with another 40 journal articles and book chapters. His commentaries and/or opinion columns have appeared in print in *The Economist, Australian Financial Review, Financial Times, Wall Street Journal,* and *Nikkei Asian Review*, and have been broadcast on BBC TV, ABC TV, and ABC Radio. His most recent books include *Singapore: A Modern History* (2019; 2020), *The Limits of Authoritarian Governance in Singapore's Developmental State* (2019), and *Singapore's Ruling Elite: Networks of Power and Influence* (2014). Michael is enjoying an active retirement as an Associate Professor of International Relations (Academic Status) at Flinders University, Deputy Editor of *Asian Studies Review*, and a Fellow of the Australian Academy of the Humanities.

Tina Burrett is an Associate Professor of Political Science at Sophia University, Japan. Her recent publications include 'Charting Putin's Shifting Populism in the Russian Media 2000–2020' *Politics and Governance* (2020) and 'Journalism in Myanmar: Repression, Reporters and the Rohingya', *The Routledge Companion to Political Journalism* (2021). She is also the author of

Television and Presidential Power in Putin's Russia (Routledge, 2011) and co-editor of *Press Freedom in Contemporary Asia* (Routledge, 2019, with Jeff Kingston), *Japan in the Heisei Era* (1989–2019): *Multidisciplinary Perspectives* (Routledge, 2022, with Noriko Murai and Jeff Kingston) and *The Routledge Handbook of Trauma in East Asia* (Routledge, 2023, with Jeff Kingston). She writes for *The New Internationalist* and other media publications and has worked in the UK, Japanese and Canadian parliaments. Her chapter was completed during at visiting fellowship at Clare Hall, Cambridge University (2021-2022).

Rommel A. Curaming, PhD, is a Senior Assistant Professor and Programme Leader (Chair) at the History and International Studies Programme of the Universiti Brunei Darussalam. He completed PhD in Southeast Asian Studies at the Australian National University and MA degrees from the National University of Singapore and University of the Philippines-Diliman. His research focuses on various aspects and cases of knowledge production and consumption in/on Southeast Asia, particularly Indonesia, the Philippines and the Malay World. He published in international journals such as *Critical Asian Studies, South East Asia Research, Time and Society, Philippine Studies, Inter-Asia Cultural Studies,* and *SOJOURN*, among others. His most recent publications include the book *Power and Knowledge in Southeast Asia: State and Scholars in Indonesia and the Philippines* (Routledge, 2020).

Jack Fong, PhD, is a Professor of Sociology at California State Polytechnic University, Pomona. As a political, urban, and existential sociologist, his research interests centre on social systems that experience systemic crises and how such dynamics change self and society. His recent publications and sociological imaginations examine social progress and regress from a perspective informed by Nietzschean philosophy. He is the author of *Employing Nietzsche's Sociological Imagination: How to Understand Totalitarian Democracy* (Lexington Books, 2020), *The Death Café Movement: Exploring the Horizons of Mortality* (Palgrave Macmillan, 2017) and *Revolution as Development: The Karen Self-Determination Struggle Against Ethnocracy (1949–2004)* (BrownWalker Press, 2008).

Niklas Foxeus, Associate Professor (Docent), is currently a Research Fellow and Senior Lecturer at the Department of History of Religions, ERG, Stockholm University. He received his PhD from that department with a dissertation about Burmese Buddhist esoteric congregations (2011). He has conducted research within projects about the encounter between Buddhism and capitalism (2013–2015), Buddhist nationalism, tensions between Buddhists and Muslims (2015–2020), and currently about doctrinal forms of Burmese Buddhism (2020–).

Rohan Gunaratna is a Professor of Security Studies at the S. Rajaratnam School of International Studies, Nanyang Technology University, and Head of International Centre for Political Violence and Terrorism Research, Singapore. He received his Masters from the University of Notre Dame in the US where he was a Hesburgh Scholar and his doctorate from the University of St Andrews in the UK where he was a British Chevening Scholar. A former Senior Fellow at the Combating Terrorism Centre at the United States Military Academy at West Point and at the Fletcher School of Law and Diplomacy, Gunaratna conducted field research in Indonesia, Thailand, Philippines, Sri Lanka, Bangladesh, Kashmir, Pakistan, Afghanistan, Uzbekistan, and other conflict zones. He is the author and editor of 12 books, including *Inside Al Qaeda: Global Network of Terror* (Columbia University Press). He also serves on the editorial boards of the journals *Studies in Conflict and Terrorism* and *Terrorism and Political Violence*.

Contributors

Enze Han is an Associate Professor at the Department of Politics and Public Administration at the University of Hong Kong. His research interests include ethnic politics in China, China's relations with Southeast Asia, and the politics of state formation in the borderland area between China, Myanmar, and Thailand. He is the author of *Asymmetrical Neighbours: Borderland State Building between China and Southeast Asia* (Oxford University Press, 2019) and *Contestation and Adaptation: The Politics of National Identity in China* (Oxford University Press, 2013).

Gil-Soo Han is a Professor of Communications and Media Studies in the School of Media, Film, and Journalism, Monash University, Australia. His research interests include media, ethnicities, religion, health and nationalism. His recent publications include *Funeral Rites in Contemporary Korea: The business of death* (Springer, 2019), *Nouveau-riche Nationalism and Multiculturalism in Korea: A Media Narrative Analysis* (Routledge, 2016) and *Korean Diaspora and Media in Australia: In Search of Identities* (University Press of America, 2012).

Peter Herrmann is a Social Philosopher with an academic background in sociology, political science, economics, and jurisprudence. He is a member of the European Academy of Science and Arts and member of the Beyt Nahrin Mesopotamian Academy of Sciences and Arts (BEN-MAAS). He is affiliated with the world of teaching and research, chasing for answering the Faustian question "what holds the world together at its core". His recent positions span from the Max-Planck Institute for Social Law and Social Policy, Germany over the Faculty of Economics and Sociology at University of Lodz, Poland to his current position as a Research Fellow at the Human Rights Centre, School of Law at Central South University, China. His recent publications include *Is There Still Any Value in It? Revisiting Value and Valuation in a Globalising Digital World* (Nova Science Publishers, 2019) and *Right to Stay – Right to Move* (Vienna Academic Press, 2019).

David Hundt is an Associate Professor of International Relations in the School of Humanities and Social Sciences, Deakin University, Australia. His main areas of interest include political economy, economic development, and international relations in the Asia-Pacific region. He has a particular interest in the history and politics of the Korean peninsula. His recent publications include *Varieties of Capitalism in Asia: Beyond the Developmental State* (Palgrave Macmillan, 2017) and *Korea's Developmental Alliance: State, Capital and the Politics of Rapid Development* (Routledge, 2009).

Atsuko Ichijo is an Associate Professor in the Department of Criminology, Politics and Sociology, Kingston University, UK. Her research interest is in the field of nationalism studies and is the author of 'Kokugaku and an alternative account of the emergence of nationalism of Japan' (2020, forthcoming) *Nations and Nationalism*; 'The articulation of national identity in early twentieth century East Asia: Intertwining of discourses of modernity and civilisation' (2018) *Asian Studies Review*, Vol. 42, Issue 2, pp. 342–355; *Food, National Identity and Nationalism* (Palgrave, 2016, with Ronald Ranta); *Nationalism and Multiple Modernities: Europe and Beyond* (Palgrave, 2013). *The Emergence of National Food: The Dynamics of Food and Nationalism*, which she has co-edited with Venetia Johannes and Ronald Ranta, is published by Bloomsbury in 2019. She is a member of the editorial team of *Nations and Nationalism* and a book series editor of 'Identities and Modernities in Europe' series (published by Palgrave).

Contributors

Takahiro Kamisuna is a PhD candidate at the Centre of Development Studies, the University of Cambridge. He holds a Master's of International Public Policy (Valedictorian) from Osaka University in Japan and an MSc in Comparative Politics from the London School of Economics and Political Science. His recent paper on East Timorese nationalism won the Pattana Kitiarsa Prize (2020) at the Association of Asian Studies. His article, "Beyond Nationalism: Youth Struggle for the Independence of East Timor and Democracy for Indonesia", appeared in the *Indonesia* journal published by Cornell University's Southeast Asia Program.

Charles R. Kim is Korea Foundation Associate Professor of Korean Studies at the University of Wisconsin-Madison. He is a cultural historian with interests in nationalism, media, and memory in Cold War/post-Cold War Korea. His first book, *Youth for Nation: Culture and Protest in Cold War South Korea* (University of Hawai'i Press, 2017), explores the formation of early South Korean nationalism through two key historical developments: the April 19th Students Revolution of 1960 and the rise of authoritarian leader Park Chung Hee in 1961. He is a co-editor of *Beyond Death: The Politics of Suicide and Martyrdom in Korea* (University of Washington Press, 2019).

Jeff Kingston is a Professor of History at Temple University Japan. His recent monographs include *Japan in Transformation 1945–2020* (2021), *The Politics of Religion, Nationalism and Identity in Asia* (2019), and he edited *Critical Issues in Contemporary Japan* (2019), *Press Freedom in Contemporary Japan* (2017) and co-edited *Japan in the Heisei Era* (2022), *Press Freedom in Contemporary Asia* (2020) and *Japan's Foreign Relations with Asia* (2018). He also wrote *Nationalism in Asia: A History Since 1945* (2016) and edited *Nationalisms in Asia Reconsidered* (2015). His current research focuses on transitional justice and the politics of memory.

Koji Kobayashi is an Associate Professor in the Center for Glocal Strategy at Otaru University of Commerce, Japan, and Adjunct Senior Lecturer at Lincoln University, New Zealand. His research interests include globalisation, media, marketing and nationalism as they relate to sport and recreation. His work appeared in journals such as *Sociology of Sport Journal*, *International Review for the Sociology of Sport*, *Sport in Society*, *Leisure Studies*, *Managing Sport and Leisure*, *International Journal of Cultural Studies* and *Consumption Markets and Culture*. He is a co-editor of the special issue on Asian Sport Celebrity in the *International Journal of the History of Sport*, which was then turned into a book published by Routledge in 2021. His recent publications include a book chapter in *Challenges of Globalization and Prospects for an Inter-Civilizational World Order* edited by Ino Rossi (2020). He is a member of the Editorial Board for *Communication and Sport*.

Joshua Kueh is a Reference Librarian for Southeast Asia in the Asian Division of the Library of Congress, covering topics on Indonesia, as well as Brunei, Malaysia, Philippines, Singapore, and Timor Leste. He received his doctorate in trans-regional history from Georgetown University, specializing in topics related to empires in Southeast Asia. His research interests include subjects connected to migration and the state, inter-communal relationships, narratives of empire, and trade networks in Southeast Asia. More recently, he has been learning about Malay manuscripts and printing in Southeast Asia. His research has appeared in the *Journal of the Malaysian Branch of the Royal Asiatic Society* and *Philippine Studies: Historical and Ethnographic Viewpoints*.

Contributors

Asiyah Kumpoh is an Assistant Professor at the Faculty of Arts and Social Sciences, Universiti Brunei Darussalam, Brunei. Her current research and publications focus on conversion narratives, the Brunei Dusuns and the historical evolution of religion, culture and ethnic identity in Brunei Darussalam and Southeast Asia. Among her latest publications are *The Bruneian Concept of Nationhood in the 19th and 20th Centuries: Expression of State Sovereignty and National Identity* (with Nani Suryani Abu Bakar, *Brunei Museum Journal* 2021, 79–84) and *Globalisation, Education and Reform in Brunei Darussalam* (Palgrave Macmillan, 2021, co-edited with L.H. Phan, R. Jawawi, K. Wood and H. Said).

Yitan Li, PhD, is the Chair and Professor of Political Science and Director of Asian Studies at Seattle University. He holds a PhD in Politics and International Relations from the University of Southern California. His research focuses on international relations, foreign policy analysis, international conflict and security, international political economy, comparative politics, and Chinese and East Asian politics. He has published recently in *Applied Economics, Asian Affairs, Asian Perspective, Canadian Journal of Political Science, Foreign Policy Analysis, Fudan Journal of the Humanities and Social Sciences, International Studies Perspectives, Journal of Chinese Political Science, Journal of Contemporary China, Journal of East Asian Studies, Journal of Territorial and Maritime Studies, Nationalism and Ethnic Politics,* and *Political Research Quarterly*. His recent book (co-authored with Scott Gartner, Chin-Hao Huang, and Patrick James) is entitled *Identity in the Shadow of a Giant: How the Rise of China is Changing Taiwan*. He is currently serving as the editor of the *Journal of Chinese Political Science*.

Udo Merkel, PhD, is an Independent Critical Scholar with extensive international experience. He holds various degrees from British and German universities in the Social Sciences, Sport Sciences and Educational Studies. Over the last 30 years, he worked at universities in Europe (Germany and England), Latin America (Argentina and Brazil) and South-East Asia (South-Korea). He has a keen academic interest in the critical, social-scientific analysis of international events and the sports industry, i.e. the sociology, politics and economics of hosting and participating in mega events, in particular sports events, and he has published widely in this area. After visiting North Korea twice for research purposes, he has produced several papers on the socio-economic, cultural and political significance of festivals and spectacles in this country paying particular attention to the role of events as a foreign policy and diplomatic tool. After leaving the University of Brighton at the end of 2020 due to the UK's exit from the EU, he is now based in Spain and can be reached via udo1merkel@aol.com.

Udo Moenig, PhD, is an Associate Professor at the Department of Taekwondo, Youngsan University in Yangsan, South Korea. He has a PhD in Physical Education, and teaches and researches in the areas of martial arts and Asian studies. He was appointed as the first foreigner in Korea to teach taekwondo at a university. He researched, lectured, and published extensively in the fields of Asian Studies, martial arts, and sports. He has practical experiences in martial arts for over 40 years.

Yoshiko Nozaki is a Professor in the Faculty of International Social Sciences at Gakushuin University, Japan, and Associate Professor Emerita at the State University of New York at Buffalo. She earned her MA and PhD at the University of Wisconsin-Madison. She has authored, co-authored, and/or edited several books, including *Natural Science Education, Indigenous Knowledge, and Sustainable Development in Rural and Urban Schools in Kenya: Toward Critical Postcolonial Curriculum Policies and Practices (*Sense Publishers, 2014); *What U.S. Middle*

School Students Bring to Global Education: Discourses on Japan, Formation of American Identities, and the Sociology of Knowledge and Curriculum (Sense Publishers, 2010); *War Memory, Nationalism, and Education in Postwar Japan, 1945–2007: The Japanese History Textbook Controversy and Ienaga Saburo's Court Challenges* (Routledge, 2008); and *Struggles over Difference: Curriculum, Texts, and Pedagogy in the Asia-Pacific* (SUNY Press, 2005). She is a recipient of American Educational Research Association Division B Outstanding Book Award (twice in 2006 and 2009).

Kimly Ngoun, PhD, is a University Educator, Researcher, Editor, and Language Interpreter. Currently, he is the Chief Editor and Publication Director at the Asian Vision Institute (AVI), a Phnom Penh-based think tank. He holds a PhD in Political Science from the Australian National University (2017), a Master of Arts in Southeast Asian Studies from Chulalongkorn University (2007), and a Bachelor of Education majoring in Teaching of English as a Foreign Language (BEd, TEFL) from the Royal University of Phnom Penh (2003). Before joining AVI, he had more than ten years of work experience as a senior lecturer of English and International Studies at the Royal University of Phnom Penh and two-year experience as a Khmer-English interpreter and translator at the Extraordinary Chambers in the Courts of Cambodia (ECCC). Kimly published original research articles in the *Journal of Contemporary Asia*, *Journal of Southeast Asian Studies*, and *South East Asia Research*. He also co-edited three books.

Chi P. Pham, PhD, is a Research Fellow at the Institute of Literature, Vietnam Academy of Social Sciences, Hanoi, and Alexander von Humboldt Postdoctoral Fellow at the Institute of Asian and African Studies, University of Hamburg, Germany (2019–2022). She received her first PhD degree in Literary Theory from Vietnam Academy of Social Sciences, Hanoi, and her second PhD degree in Comparative Literature from University of California, Riverside. She has written numerous essays on Vietnamese literature and culture for both academic and non-academic publications, in both Vietnamese and English. Her recent publications include *Literature and Nation-building in Vietnam: The Invisibilization of the Indians* (Routledge, 2021), *Revenge of Gaia: Contemporary Vietnamese Ecofiction* (Penguin Random House, 2021, co-edited with Chitra Sankaran), *Ecologies in Southeast Asian Literatures: Histories, Myths and Societies* (Vernon Press, 2019, co-edited with Chitra Sankaran and Gurpreet Kaur), and *Aesthetic Experience in Ramayana Epic* (Hanoi National University Press, 2015).

Sven Saaler is a Professor of Modern Japanese History at Sophia University in Tokyo. After earning a PhD in Japanese Studies and History from Bonn University, he was successively a lecturer at Marburg University (1999–2000), head of the Humanities Section of the German Institute for Japanese Studies (DIJ) (2000–2004) and associate professor at The University of Tokyo (2004–2008). He is also a member of the steering committee of the National Institutes for the Humanities (NIHU). He is the author of *Politics, Memory and Public Opinion* (2005) and *Men in Metal: A Topography of Public Bronze Statuary in Modern Japan* (2020) and co-author/co-editor of *Pan-Asianism in Modern Japanese History* (2007), *The Power of Memory in Modern Japan* (2008), *Pan-Asianism: A Documentary History* (2011), *Mutual Perceptions and Images in Japanese-German Relations, 1860–2010* (2017), and the *Routledge Handbook of Modern Japanese History* (2018).

Florian Schneider, PhD, Sheffield University, is a Senior University Lecturer in the Politics of Modern China at the Leiden University Institute for Area Studies. He is a managing editor of *Asiascape: Digital Asia*, director of the Leiden Asia Centre, and the author of three books: *Staging China: The Politics of Mass Spectacle* (Leiden University Press, 2019), *China's*

Digital Nationalism (Oxford University Press, 2018), and *Visual Political Communication in Popular Chinese Television Series* (Brill, 2013, recipient of the 2014 EastAsiaNet book prize). In 2017, he was awarded the Leiden University teaching prize for his innovative work as an educator. His research interests include questions of governance, political communication, and digital media in China, as well as international relations in the East-Asian region.

Julia C. Schneider is a Lecturer in Chinese History at the Department of Asian Studies at University College Cork, Ireland. She holds a joint PhD in Modern Sinology from Ghent and Göttingen Universities and an MA in Classical Sinology from Heidelberg University. From 2014 to 2019, she was an Assistant Professor at the Department of East Asian Studies, Göttingen University. Her book *Nation and Ethnicity*, published in 2017 by Brill, won the Foundation Council Award of Göttingen University. Her research interests include historiography, history of ideas, and ethnohistory in Qing and Republican times as well as Jurchen and Manchu studies. She has published in journals such as *Journal of Asian History* and *Global Intellectual History*.

Claire Sutherland is a Professor of Politics in the Department of Social Sciences at Northumbria University in Newcastle, United Kingdom. Claire has a long-standing interest in nationalism and nation-building – understood as how states construct nationhood to maintain their legitimacy – and museum representations of the nation in selected Southeast Asian and European cases. She has published widely on aspects of nationalist ideology and its relationship with cosmopolitanism, citizenship and migration, among others. Her current interests include theorising beyond the nation through a maritime lens, and looking at how structural racism and colonial legacies connect with nationalism. Claire is the author of *Reimagining the Nation: Togetherness, Belonging and Mobility* (Policy Press, 2017), *Nationalism in the Twenty-First Century: Challenges and Responses* (Palgrave, 2011) and *Soldered States: Nation-building in Germany and Vietnam* (Manchester University Press, 2010).

Zhifang Song is a Lecturer in Anthropology at the University of Canterbury, New Zealand. He holds a BA (Hebei Normal University), MA (Beijing Foreign Studies University) and a PhD (University of Southern California). Zhifang's research interests include kinship and family (especially changes under the conditions of modernity and postmodernity), visual anthropology, Societies in East Asia, economic development and rural ecology, religion and modernity, and globalization and transnational flow of people and ideas. His research appears in *The Palgrave Handbook of Ethnicity* (2019) and journals, including *American Anthropologist* and *The Asian Journal of Humanities and Social Studies*.

Feilong Tian, PhD, is an Associate Professor within the Law School of Beihang University, China. He obtained his PhD and MA in Law from Peking University, China and BA in Law from Nanjing University, China. His research interests include Constitutional Law, Political Theory, Administrative Law and the Hong Kong and Macau Basic Law, and he has published extensively in these areas. His recent publications include *Hong Kong's New Order* (Hong Kong OrangeNews Press, 2022), *The Chinese Political Constitution* (City University of Hong Kong Press, 2017), *Observations on Hong Kong's Political Reform – Perspectives of Democracy and Rule of Law (The Commercial Press, 2015),* and *The Principles of Political Constitution on China's Constitutional Transformation (Central Compilation & Translation Press, 2015).*

Masaki Tosa is a Professor of Cultural Anthropology in the School of Asia 21 at Kokushikan University, Japan. He is the author of numerous articles and books on pop culture, nationalism, religion, and media in East Asia. His recent publications include *Gazing at the Peripheries of Korean Society* (Iwanami, 2012), and as an editor and contributor, *Sport Nationalism in East Asia* (Mineruba, 2015). His current research interests are focused on multi-sited ethnography of national identity in East Asia.

Zhiguang Yin, PhD, is a Professor in International Politics at the Fudan University, China. His research interest lies mainly in the area of Chinese modern intellectual and legal history, ethnic minority policy, nineteenth-twentieth century history of international relations, and Sino-Middle Eastern relations. His current project investigates the Chinese interactions with the Afro-Asian nations in the 1950s and 1960s. It is particularly interested in the transnational dissemination/reception of mass cultural products in shaping the general public's encounter, experience and imagination of Third World Internationalism. His most recent monographs include *A New World: Afro-Asian Solidarity and the PRC's Imagination of Global Order* (Contemporary World Press, 2022) and *Politics of Art: The Creation Society and the Practice of Theoretical Struggle in Revolutionary China* (Brill, 2014). His articles appear in English and Chinese academic journals such as *European Journal of International Law*, *History*, *Turkish Journal of Sociology*, and *Kaifang Shidai* (Open Times).

Ryan Wolfson-Ford is a Southeast Asia Reference Librarian at the Asian Division, Library of Congress and received his PhD in Southeast Asian History at the University of Wisconsin-Madison in 2018. His research interests include the Lao elite, palm leaf manuscripts and intellectual and political history. He has conducted archival research in Laos, Thailand, France and the United States. He was a lecturer of Asian history at Arizona State University for the 2019–2020 academic year. His publications include articles in peer-reviewed journals (*Journal of Southeast Asian Studies*, *South East Asia Research*) and a book chapter in an edited volume entitled *Monarchies and Decolonisation in Asia*.

Meishan Zhang holds a BA in Museum Studies and Archaeology (2013) at Nankai University, China, an MA in Museum and Gallery Studies (2014) at the University of St. Andrews, U.K., and a PhD in History (2021) at Trinity College Dublin, Ireland. Her research interests lie in the areas of modern Chinese history, gender history, and the development of Western medicine in China in the late 19th and early 20th centuries. Her current research explores the sweeping social changes in the city of Republican Shanghai by investigating the production and adaptation of Western medical materials for women.

Yongle Zhang is an Associate Professor in the School of Law at Peking University, China. He received his PhD in political science from the University of California, Los Angeles in 2008. He works on constitutional history, history of international relations and international law, as well as intellectual history, with a focus on themes like state building and constitutional change, empire and international law, political ethics and legal ethics, and political party and political representation. He is the author of a trilogy: *Remaking An Old Country: 1911–1917* (Peking University Press, 2011, 2016), *The Rivalry of Nations: Kang Youwei and the Decay of the Vienna System* (The Commercial Press, 2017), and *Shifting Boundaries: A Global History of the Monroe Doctrine* (SDX Press, 2021).

Lu Zhouxiang is an Associate Professor within the School of Modern Languages, Literatures and Cultures at National University of Ireland Maynooth. He received his PhD from University College Cork, Ireland in 2011. His research interests include nationalism, national identity, Chinese history, sport history, and cultural history. His recent publications include *Chinese National Identity in the Age of Globalisation* (Palgrave Macmillan, 2020), *A History of Shaolin: Buddhism, Kung Fu and Identity* (Routledge, 2019), and *Politics and Identity in Chinese Martial Arts* (Routledge, 2018).

ACKNOWLEDGEMENTS

I wish to thank Max Novick at Routledge for giving me the opportunity to take on this challenging and exciting project. I am grateful for the contributions of Udo Merkel, Martin Shiels, and Peter Herrmann, who helped in proofreading and providing editorial inputs and advice on the manuscript. I would also like to express my gratitude to all the contributors for their enthusiasm, effort, and devotion during the three-year journey of producing this book. As a Chinese proverb puts it, 'A single tree does not make a forest; one string cannot make music' (独木不成林，单弦不成音). Together, we have created a small but diverse forest of knowledge and a short but thought-provoking tune of scholarship.

ABBREVIATIONS

AASC	Afro-Asian Solidarity Conference
ABIM	Angkatan Belia Islam Malaysia
ABIM	Angkatan Belia Islam sa-Malaysia
ACC	Asian Cultural Council
ACC	Asian Culture Center
AFPFL	Anti-Fascist People's Freedom League
AI	Artificial Intelligence
AIIB	Asian Infrastructure Investment Bank
AIRF	Arakan Rohingya Islamic Front
AMANAH	Parti Amanah Negara/National Trust Party
AMCJA	All-Malayan Council of Joint Action
API	Angkatan Pemuda Insaf/Aware Youth Corps
ARNO	Arakan Rohingya National Organization
ASDT	Timorese Social-Democratic Association
ASEAN	Association of Southeast Asian Nations
ASG	Abu Sayyaf Group
AWAS	Angkatan Wanita Sedar/Aware Women Corps
BA	Barisan Alternatif/Alternative Front
BNBCC	British North Borneo Chartered Company
BPP	Border Patrol Police
BRI	Belt and Road Initiative
BRICS	Brazil, Russia, India, China and South Africa
CCP	Chinese Communist Party
CGP	Center for Global Partnership
CIA	Central Intelligence Agency
CPP	Cambodian People's Party
CPP	Communist Party of the Philippines
CSD	Collective Self-defense
DAP	Democratic Action Party
DI	Darul Islam
DK	Democratic Kampuchea

Abbreviations

DMZ	Demilitarized Zone
DPJ	Democratic Party of Japan
DPP	Democratic Progressive Party
DPRK	Democratic People's Republic of Korea
DPW	Department of Public Welfare
DRV	Democratic Republic of Vietnam
ETIM	East Turkistan Islamic Movement
EU	European Union
GAHT	Global Alliance for Historical Truth
GAISF	General Assembly of International Sports Federation
GAM	Gerakan Aceh Merdeka/Free Aceh Movement
GANEFO	Games of the Newly Emerging Forces
GATT	General Agreement on Tariffs and Trade
GCBA	The General Council of Buddhist Associations
GCSS	The General Council of Sangha Sammeggyi
GE	General Election
GEACPS	Greater East Asia Co-Prosperity Sphere
GERAKAN	Parti Gerakan Rakyat Malaysia/Malaysian People's Movement Party
GLCs	Government-linked Companies
HM	Hizbul Muslimin
HM	Hizb-ul-Mujahideen
ICAPP	International Conference of Asian Political Parties
ICC	International Coordinating Committee
IMF	International Monetary Fund
IMU	Islamic Movement of Uzbekistan
IOC	International Olympic Committee
IRK	Islamic Religious Knowledge
ISA	Internal Security Act
ISIS	Islamic State of Iraq and Syria
ITF	International Taekwondo Federation
IV	Indische Vereeniging/Indies Association
IVS	Indonesisch Verbond van Studeerenden
JI	Jemaah Islamiyah
JIM	Jemaah Islah Malaysia
JOC	Japan Olympic Committee
KCIA	Korean Central Intelligence Agency
KMM	Kesatuan Melayu Muda/Young Malays Union
KMT	Nationalist/Kuomintang
KOSTRAD	Army Strategic Reserve
KPA	Korean People's Army
KRIS	Kesatuan Ra'ayat Indonesia Semenanjung/Union of Peninsular Indonesians
KSSM	Kurikulum Standard Sekolah Menengah/Secondary School Standard Curriculum
KTA	Korea Taesudo Association
LDP	Liberal Democratic Party
LPDR	Lao People's Democratic Republic's
LRA	Law on Regional Autonomy

Abbreviations

MCA	Malayan Chinese Association
MCD	Modernity-Coloniality-Decoloniality
MCP	Malayan Communist Party
MIB	Melayu Islam Beraja/Malay Islam Monarchy
MIC	Malayan Indian Congress
MILF	Moro Islamic Liberation Front
MN	Muafakat Nasional/National Concord
MNLF	Moro National Liberation Front
MNP	Malay Nationalist Party
MOE	The Ministry of Education
MTA	Mong Tai Army
MTMIB	Majlis Tertinggi Melayu Islam Beraja
NAM	Non-Aligned Movement
NDF	National Democratic Front
NLD	National League for Democracy
NPA	New People's Army
OECD	Economic Co-operation and Development
OPM	Organisasi Papua Merdeka/Free Papua Organization
PAP	Peoples' Action Party
PAPF	People's Armed Police Force
PAS	Islamic Party of Malaysia
PASPAM	Persaudaraan Sahabat Pena/Brotherhood of Pen Friends
PH	Pakatan Harapan/Pact of Hope
PIJAR	Centre for Information and Action Network for Democratic Reforms
PKI	Indonesian Communist Party
PKI	Partai Komunis Indonesia/Indonesian Communist Party
PKM	Partido Komunista ng Pilipinas/Communist Party of the Philippines
PKMM	Parti Kebangsaan Melayu Malaya
PKMS	Singapore Malay National Organisation
PKR	Parti Keadilan Rakyat/People's Justice Party
PMIP	The Pan-Malayan Islamic Party
PN	Perikatan Nasional/National Alliance
PP	Pantayong Pananaw
PPP	Purchasing Power Parity
PR	Pakatan Rakyat/People's Pact
PRB	Partai Rakyat Brunei/People's Party of Brunei
PRC	People's Republic of China
PRD	Partai Rakyat Demokratik
PRM	Parti Rakyat Malaysia/ Malaysian People's Party
PRRI	Revolutionary Government of the Republic of Indonesia/Pemerintah Revolutioner Republik Indonesia
PSI	Partai Sarekat Islam
PSP	Progress Singapore Party
PTA	Parent-Teacher Association
PUTERA	Pusat Tenaga Ra'ayat
RCEP	Regional Comprehensive Economic Partnership Agreement
RH Law	Reproductive Health Law
RLG	Royal Lao Government

ROC	Republic of China
ROK	Republic of Korea
ROV	Republic of Vietnam
RPF	Rohingya Patriotic Front
RSO	Rohingya Solidarity Organization
SBKRI	Surat Bukti Kewarganegaraan Republik Indonesia/Indonesian Citizenship
SIPRI	Stockholm International Peace Research Institute
SIRD	Strategic Information and Research Development Centre
SLOOC	The Seoul Olympic Organizing Committee
SMID	Indonesian Student Solidarity for Democracy
SOAS III	Sultan Omar Ali Saifuddien III
SPN21	21st Century National Education System
SPRIM	Solidaritas Perjuangan Rakyat Indonesia untuk Maubere
SSRC	Social Science Research Council
TIP	Turkistan Islamic Party
TITP	Technical Intern Training Program
TTA	Taiwan Travel Act
UBD	Universiti Brunei Darussalam
UDT	Timorese Democratic Union
UMNO	United Malays National Organisation
UN	United Nations
UNPKO	UN Peacekeeping Operations
USDP	Union Solidarity and Development Party
UWSA	United Wa State Army
VOC	Vereenigde Oost-Indische Compagnie
WPK	Workers' Party of Korea
WTF	World Taekwondo Federation
WUC	World Uighur Congress
WUKO	World United Karate Organization
XUAR	Xinjiang Uygur Autonomous Region

INTRODUCTION

The arrival of the age of nationalism and nation states

Lu Zhouxiang

Nationalism emerged in the late eighteenth century and became a powerful political force that spread around the globe and shaped the modern world. Nationalism is a concept with multiple meanings and can be analyzed as 'an ideology, a movement, the process of "nation" and "nation-state" building, and an individual's political orientation' (Dekker and Malova 2003, 345). Most scholars see nationalism as a global political movement and have developed different theories to explain the phenomenon from a wide range of perspectives and levels (Weiss 2003). For example, Eugen Lemberg defined nationalism from a sociological perspective as 'a system of ideas, values and norms, an image of the world and society which makes a large social group aware of where it belongs and invests this sense of belonging with a particular value' (cited in Alter 1994, 8). He emphasized that shared origins, character, language and culture, or common subordination to a given state power nourished national consciousness; the philosopher and social anthropologist Ernest Gellner suggested that nationalism was 'a theory of political legitimacy.' It was a product of modern societies' need for cultural homogeneity and was 'the consequence of a new form of social organization, based on deeply internalized, education-dependent high cultures, each protected by its own state' (Gellner 1983, 48); the political scientist Benedict Anderson (1983) advances the theory that a nation is a socially constructed community, imagined by the people who perceive themselves as part of that group. The convergence of capitalism and print media in the eighteenth and nineteenth centuries contributed significantly to the development of a nationalism that was able to unite people from different classes to fight and sacrifice for such a limited imagining; the historian Elie Kedourie (1960) saw nationalism as a doctrine invented in Europe which 'holds that humanity is naturally divided into nations, that nations are known by certain characteristics which can be ascertained, and that the only legitimate type of government is national self-government.' In the past century, nationalism became a major political driving force and has made national self-determination the foundation of the modern international order (Kedourie 1960, 9).

This wide range of definitions, approaches, and analytical focuses from different disciplines and perspectives clearly reflect the diversity and complexity of nationalism. In a nutshell, nationalism is a thought and ideology based on the concept of nation. As historian Peter Alter (1994, 5) noted, 'in nationalism, the nation is placed upon the highest pedestal; its value resides in its capacity as the sole, binding agency of meaning and justification.' Karl

W. Deutsch (1979, 301), a political scientist, also observed that 'nationalism is a state of mind which gives "national" messages, memories, and images a preferred status in social communication and a greater weight in the making of decisions.' In short, a nation can be regarded as the building block of nationalism, and nationalism is a doctrine and discourse about the character, interests, rights, and duties of nations. To individuals, national consciousness and nationalism emerge 'whenever they felt that they belong primarily to the nation, and whenever affective attachment and loyalty to that nation override all other attachments and loyalties' (Alter 1994, 9). For communities and societies, nationalism frequently leads to organized social movements and political parties, economic practices, revolutions, and wars that are aimed at furthering the alleged aims, ideology, and interests of nations.

The formation of sovereign states and embryonic national consciousness

From a historical perspective, the term 'nation' is considerably more archaic than 'nationalism.' According to Greenfeld (1992), the Latin word *natio* is the origin of the modern word nation. It means someone born and carried derogatory connotations. In Rome, the title *natio* was often given to a group of foreigners who came from the same geographical region. In the Middle Ages, the feeling of 'the same origin' evoked a sense of national consciousness in university students who came from geographically or linguistically related regions. Furthermore, the word nation was endowed with a new meaning which referred to their country of origin. By the late thirteenth century, the meaning of nation had transformed into a 'community of option' and 'a political, cultural and then social elite' (Greenfeld 1992, 5). In the following centuries, alongside the rise of sovereign states and nation states, particularly in Europe, the term 'nation' continued to experience a steady semantic transformation and eventually evolved into the sense in which it is understood today. Accompanying 'nation,' the term 'nationalism' first appeared in a work by the German philosopher and theologian Johann Gottfried Herder in 1774. Herder's understanding and interpretation of nation were profoundly cultural instead of political. He believed that nations were organically formed entities with a unique and shared language and distinct cultural properties, and each national culture should thrive for peaceful coexistence with others (Miller 1998; van den Bergh 2018). However, in contrast to Herder's observations, when 'nationalism' entered into general linguistic usage in the mid-nineteenth century, it developed into a concept dominated by politics (Shafer 1972).

The historian Ernest Renan (1882, 9) has argued that nations, in the modern sense of the term, 'are something fairly new in history.' 'Classical antiquity had republics, municipal kingdoms, confederations of local republics and empires, yet it can hardly be said to have had nations in our understanding of the term.' Generally speaking, nations, nationalism, nationalist ideologies, and the system of nation states are recent in date and novel in character (Smith 2000). Their formation advanced with the rise of early centralized sovereign states in Western Europe from the fifteenth century onward. There are four complex set of reasons, i.e. changing contexts, that explain this significant development. Religion, social structure, language and military reforms all played an important role in this process.

First, transformations in religious identity contributed to the formation of the sovereign state and national consciousness. Medieval civilization in Europe was governed by the all-pervasive concept of the Christian God. Christianity dominated the region and the Vatican claimed authority over the whole Christian world. During this period, 'God's will was sufficient to explain all phenomena. The service of God was seen as the sole legitimate purpose of all human enterprise' (Davies 1996, 430). Individual identity, popular culture, philosophy, way of life, and the political system were all based on, and framed by, Christian ideas, norms, and values.

Introduction

To all loyal Christians, the Pope was the supreme spiritual leader of the Christian world. They identified themselves as subjects of God rather than subjects of kings. As Stavrianos (1975, 201) noted, 'mass allegiance to a nation was, during those centuries, unknown. Instead, most men (sic) considered themselves to be first of all Christians, second, residents of a certain region such as Burgundy or Cornwall, and only last, if at all, Frenchmen or Englishmen (sic).'

The late Middle Ages saw a crisis in Christendom. With the fall of the Christian Byzantine Empire and the Holy Roman Empire, the Vatican could no longer maintain its supreme authority over its dependencies (Davies 1996, 383). The transformation of the power structure between kings and the Papacy resulted in the consolidation of royal authority and changed the spiritual image to which people had allegiance. Consequently, the notions of 'subject to the king' and 'subject to the kingdom' began to prevail.

The power struggle between royalty and the Papacy can be dated back to the thirteenth century when a fundamental conflict broke out between Edward I (King of England) and the church over Pope Boniface VIII's bull, *Clericis laicos* (1296). The latter prevented the secular states of Europe from appropriating church revenues without the permission of the Vatican. France and England were the only two countries that resisted these Papal claims, while other secular authorities generally accepted the bill. Subsequently, the rivalry between Philip IV of France and the Papacy ended with the death of Pope Boniface VIII and resulted in the proscription of the Knights Templar at the beginning of the fourteenth century. The new Pope, Clement V, was a weak spiritual leader, while Philip IV established a centralized royal power to rule France. The transformation in religious identity made Christianity a vehicle for the construction of centralized royal power and contributed to the formation of a sovereign France. As Greenfeld (1993, 95) observed:

> the election of France and the immediate relationship between the kingdom and God, was manifested first and foremost in the king. From an exemplary son of the universal church, the king became the focus of a new Christian cult, and France – a church in its own town.

In England, King Henry VIII was the driving force for separating the English Church from the Vatican. He introduced the first Act of Annates in 1532 to cut the financial payment to Rome. One year later, the Act of Appeals 1533 curtailed Rome's ecclesiastical jurisdiction. This was followed by the Act of Supremacy in 1534 which abolished Papal authority in England. Thereafter, the king became the Supreme Head of the Church of England, and the religious image and the political image were combined into one (Davies 1996). With the rise of the king's power, England began transforming into a sovereign state. A collective identity based on the Kingdom of England started to emerge among the growing numbers of English Protestants.

Second, the transformation of social structures stimulated the emergence of sovereign states and national consciousness. Medieval Europe was based on feudalism. People were under the rule of feudal lords and kings. The Pope and the Emperor claimed the authority over all feudal kingdoms. Religion functioned as a vehicle for uniting all the smaller kingdoms, principalities, duchies, counties, and cities into a united political entity. In this political entity, rulers of kingdoms and feudalities distributed their land to nobilities, who distributed their land among their vassals. The existence of countless self-governing manors led to a decentralization of state power. Feudal lords owned everything on their land, including their peasants, crops, and village(s), taxed the people, had their own military forces, and became the ever-present leaders for those cultivating their fields. In this period, the Emperor, the Pope, and the kings were spiritual leaders far away from everyday life of the ordinary people. People gave allegiance to the feudal lords who had the real power. Therefore, the sense of nation remained vague and obscure, while localism and other forms of territorialism were dominant. As Davies (1996, 382) states, 'medieval Europeans were conscious of belonging to their native village or town…They were aware of belonging to a body of men and women who acknowledged the same feudal lord; to a social estate, which share the same privileges.'

Hugh Seton-Watson (1977, 18) has argued that the essence of the social order of Medieval Europe was linked to the mutual obligations between social groups, guaranteed by law and by institutions. The rulers endowed certain rights to the upper class and formed the feudal system. People were connected vertically in hierarchical subordination. Davies (1996, 516) describes how 'social groups were defined by their function, by the legal restrictions and privileges which were imposed in order to facilitate that function, and by their corporations.' In such social systems, nobility and landowners obtained their wealth from serfs and farmers. Power struggles occurred between the central power (the monarchy) and the social elites, such as churches, nobles, feudal lords, and land owners, indicating that there was not always a balance between these forces.

The emergence of organized merchants and manufacturers in developing urban centers formed a new socio-economic force which undermined existing power relations and structures. Urban capitalism, which coexisted with a landowner-directed agriculture based on serfdom or tenantry, began to change the social and economic structures of Europe. The rising petty bourgeoisie, city burghers, and small landowners boosted the eclipse of the older feudal system and strengthened centralized royal power. Alliances between the two social groups benefited each other. On the one hand, the king gained support from the bourgeoisie, which led to a weakening of the church and the territorial feudal lords, and consolidated and strengthened centralized power structures. On the other hand, the bourgeoisie benefited from the newly established social order and laws which allowed them to profit from the booming free market and industry. Consequently, the claims and interests of new social groups began to form the basis for the legitimacy of the monarchy. The transformation of social structures, accompanied by the emergence of new norms and values, slowly changed people's views, norms and values, and gave rise to new concepts such as individualism, competition, the achievement principle, division of labor, and others. The new social groups were 'bound together by horizontal ties of solidarity and no longer linked only vertically in hierarchical subordination' (Seton-Watson 1977, 18). Political consciousness began to emerge among these rising social groups which, in turn, gave birth to an embryonic form of national consciousness.

Third, the rise of the vernacular languages of nations in Western Europe aided the construction of national consciousness, distinctiveness, and identity. In the era of the Roman Empire, Latin functioned as the vehicle for the promotion of Christianity and the building of the empire. Following the collapse of the Roman Empire, Charlemagne and the Papacy utilized Latin as a vehicle to bind disparate ethnic groups together (Slavitt 1999). During the Middle Ages, Latin was the language of the church, universities, and courts, and also served as the medium of exchange in all intellectual life. As John A. Armstrong (1982, 281) has noted, 'throughout the Romance region, the requirement of precision in legal and theological affairs was met by the persistence of Latin as the sole elaborated code of the learned.'

With the decline of the Vatican and the strengthening of royal power in France, England, and (what was later to become) Germany, the use of Latin began to diminish and a clear internal linguistic division took shape. In England, the Anglo-Saxon dialects came together with French in the fourteenth century in the new English language. Under King Edward III, the Pleading in English Act 1362 made English the official language of the law courts and the parliament. From then on, English began to be widely used among all social groups and became a building block for an embryonic English national consciousness (Seton-Watson 1977, 29). In France, Latin began to decline after Philip IV made French the language of royal edicts in Northern France in the thirteenth century (Asher and Simpson 1994). In 1539, the Ordinance of Villers-Cotterets, signed into law by Francis I, made French the official language of the country. Then in 1629, Louis XIII promulgated the Code Michaud that made French the compulsory language for the registration of baptisms, marriage, and burials. Thereafter, French came to be widely used among all the social classes and became an important symbol of French identity (Greenfeld 1992, 99). In the German-speaking parts of Europe, priest and theologian Martin Luther nailed his *Ninety-Five Theses* to the door of the Castle Church in Wittenberg in 1517 and declared that religion should rest on each individual's faith and comprehension of the Bible (Marshall 2017). The event triggered the Protestant Reformation. Subsequently, Luther's German translation of 'The New Testament' and the complete Bible, published in 1522 and 1534, respectively, made the Bible more accessible to ordinary Germans and facilitated the rise of the modern German language and literature, as well as laid the seeds for a German identity (Schaff 1910).

Fourth, the military revolution, i.e. advances in warfare technology and strategies, contributed to the rise of sovereign states and national consciousness. Davies (1996, 519) states that 'the modern state without the military revolution is unthinkable. The road from the arquebus to absolutism, or from the maritime mortar to mercantilism, was a direct one.' The late Middle Ages saw the move from cold weapons to firearms and explosives. The invention of the musket and artillery changed the way war was fought. The increasing demand for firearms also stimulated the growth of modern industry and mercantilism. Modern warfare gave rise to trained standing armies with professional skills and strict discipline (Smith 1977), and these standing armies consolidated the royal power and gave kings an 'incomparable political instrument for reducing the power of the nobles and for forcing their subjects to obey' (Davies 1996, 519).

This military revolution led to the fall of the nobility and the rise of new social groups. The social and political functions of the nobility were weakened as military careers were now offered to talent from all social classes (Thomson 1972). Manufacturers who produced firearms and civilians who served the standing army gained functional significance. The alliances between the new social groups and the royalty allowed the king to further weaken the power of the feudal lords.

As the importance of religious authority and regional feudal lordships continued to decline, new social groups and centralized royal power dominated the early sovereign states of Western Europe. In England, a national consciousness emerged as people began to show their loyalty to the king – the incarnation of the monarchy and the centralized sovereign state (Greenfeld 1992, 74). The doctrine of the 'Divine Right of Kings' was developed in the late sixteenth century in order to consolidate the monarch's supreme authority, to instill obedience, and to make all social ranks religiously and morally obliged to obey the royalty. This doctrine also dominated France. The kings of France were portrayed as the incarnate essence of society and the 'State,' and French identity transformed from an 'essentially religious into a political one' (Greenfeld 1992, 112).

To conclude, the formation of the sovereign state and the prevalence of the Divine Right of Kings in the fifteenth and sixteenth centuries nourished embryonic national consciousness which was based on 'a notion of an emotional attachment to a landscape, a dynastic state or a ruler' and an ideology consolidating the political unification of the monarchy (Alter 1996, 6).

The emergence of nation states, national identity, and nationalism was a slow, non-linear and incremental process, initiated and driven by several factors that led to the transformation of 'loyalty to the monarch' into 'loyalty to the state,' and eventually into 'loyalty to the nation'.

The rise of nation states and nationalism

In the seventeenth and eighteenth centuries, social and political transformations became increasingly conducive to the rise of nation states and nationalism. The royal authority began to be seen as a barrier to the new social groups. The rising petty bourgeoisie, privileged city dwellers, the city burghers, and landowners demanded more economic and political freedom, and opposed the restrictions and heavy taxes imposed by the monarch. Their claims eventually developed to be one of the most important factors behind the English and the French Revolutions, which resulted in the demise of royal power and the formation of modern nation states (Hobsbawm 1988, 105).

In England, James I's strong belief in the 'Divine Right of Kings' caused severe conflicts between the monarch and the parliament and resulted in the English Revolution of the mid-seventeenth century. According to Guizot, Marx, and Engels, the English Revolution marked a significant stage in the shift from feudalism to capitalism. The gentry who dominated the parliament were 'bourgeois' modernizers who were determined to maximize their profit margins. Those who supported the king were 'feudal' traditionalists more interested in preserving their power, status, and authority (Stone 1985, 44–45). As the parliament became the servant of the bourgeoisie, 'Parliamentary statutes, speeches, and pamphlets separated the issue of nationality from the issues of religion and the English Crown and clarified the meaning of national identity' (Greenfeld 1992, 77). The Revolution drew more people into political action and extended national consciousness to 'new geographical areas and lower social levels,' and made the nation the primary object of people's loyalty (Hill 1970, 265; Lefebvre 2005). After the English Civil War (1642–1651), the monarch no longer functioned as a major host for national consciousness, and England began its transformation from a sovereign state to a nation state.

The French Revolution (1789–1799) was another milestone in the rise of the bourgeoisie as it marked the beginning of the transition of France from a sovereign state into a nation state. Most scholars describe the French Revolution as the result of the clash between the old feudal noble class and the emerging capitalist bourgeois class (Lefebvre 2005). During the French Revolution, 'various social, political and intellectual developments found powerful expression in radical politics' (Hutchinson and Smith 1994, 7). Led by the bourgeoisie, people from around the country 'transcended regional, corporate and religious barriers and joined together as the people of a state, as a political nation' (Alter 1994, 56–57). Consequently, the power transferred from the monarchy to the nation, and the concept of nation state replaced the monarch's sovereign state as the source of identity (Greenfeld 1992, 166).

The French Revolution constructed French identity in several different ways. First, a primary level education system was established to foster patriotism and promote French as a standardized language. Second, print media such as newspapers, booklets, and journals were used to promote the radical social and political changes and propagandize the idea of the nation and nation state. Third, new symbols of the French nation, such as the national flag, national songs, and national day, were created (Stavrianos 1975). As Kohn (1944, 20) has observed, the French Revolution infused the idea of nationalism and created 'a consciousness in which all citizens could share' – 'the masses were no longer in the nation, but of the nation.'

Introduction

Since the emergence of early examples of European nationalism, represented by the revolutions of England and France, 'nationalism has been understood as a political movement born by broad sections of society which declares attachment to the nation to be the supreme bond' (Alter 1994, 56). Following the French Revolution, Napoleon's expansionist policies provoked reactions in England, Spain, Germany, Poland, and Russia. It intensified and 'diffused the civic ideas of national autonomy, unity and identity across Europe' (Hutchinson and Smith 1994, 7). After the defeat of Napoleonic France, the Congress of Vienna (1814–1815) was held by the major European powers to redraw the geopolitical map. However, the Congress ignored the national and liberal impulses of small nations, and so stimulated their resistance. Thereafter, nationalism became the driving factor in the rising tide of independence movements in Europe. The Greeks, under the Ottoman rule, declared independence in 1821 and achieved it in 1829. The Belgian Revolution of 1830 led to the establishment of an independent Belgium free from Dutch rule. Independence movements were also launched by Italian, German, and Irish nationalists.

From the late eighteenth and early nineteenth centuries onward, print media, the growth in literacy, and the greater social communication and growing economic contacts between different social classes increased the distribution of new political ideas. It helped people to slowly embrace their national symbols and norms, and supported certain political organizations (Hutchinson and Smith 1994, 27–28). An increasing proportion of populations began to 'perceive themselves as members of a particular nation. They identified with its historical and cultural heritage and with the form of its political life, and endowed existence with meaning both in the present and the future' (Alter 1994, 9).

In summary, the modern form of nationalism can be understood as 'both an ideology and a political movement which holds the nation and the nation state to be crucial indwelling values' (Alter 1994, 8), and as a vehicle for mobilizing and assembling people under a united front for a common, primarily political goal. It was the forces that emerged from various political and economic interests, combined with an ethnic, cultural, and religious consciousness, that bonded people into one 'imagined community' or 'nation.' Nationalism encapsulated these forces and united people under a single banner, creating a sense of pride, belonging, and commitment to the perceived common interest of the nation. The essence of nationalism is the power struggle between interest groups. On the macro level, that is often demonstrated through the rivalry between countries, nations, or alliances of nations. On the micro level, rivalries and conflicts between religious groups, ethnic groups, social classes, or political and military groups are the most visible forms of such power struggles.

As people sought to establish territorial political entities corresponding to their group identity combined with their desire for fundamental political and economic changes, nationalism became the dominant political doctrine within Europe and beyond (Armstrong 1982, 4). In 1776, the United States declared independence from the British Empire. In the first half of the nineteenth century, European colonies in Central and South America – most of which were under Spanish rule – rose in rebellions that gave birth to Haiti (1804), Columbia (1810), Paraguay (1811), Argentina (1816), Chile (1818), Mexico (1821), Costa Rica (1821), Peru (1821), Brazil (1822), Bolivia (1825), and a host of other independent nation states.

In the first half of the twentieth century, nationalism and national rivalries triggered the First World War (1914–1918) and the Second World War (1939–1945). In the 1940s and 1950s, following the Second World War, more than 25 nations declared independence. In the following decades, the growth of nationalism among the oppressed nations of the Western powers' colonies in Asia, Africa, Central America, and Oceania gave rise to an even greater number of newly independent nation states. At the same time, nationalists from different ethnic and religious backgrounds launched separatist movements in Burma, Canada, China, India, Indonesia, Iran, Iraq, Lebanon, Spain, Sri Lanka, Turkey, the former Yugoslavia, and many other countries across the world.

While globalization and technology are facilitating the integration of humanity, nationalism is, on the contrary, still constructing and reinforcing both the physical and psychological borders between nations. In 2022, the number of independent states around the world has reached 195, and there is little doubt that the figure will continue to grow in the future. In addition to dividing the world into fragments, nationalism has generated tensions and conflicts across the globe. The Cold War and the arms race, in particular between NATO and the Warsaw Pact countries, the Israeli-Palestinian conflict, the Indonesian Genocide, the Indo-Pakistani wars, the Iran–Iraq War, The Troubles in Northern Ireland, the Islamic State movement, the Russia-Ukraine war, and the recent trade war between China and the United States have all witnessed the continuous impact of nationalism on world politics, economics, and international relations.

Studying nationalism and nation building in Asia

Pierre van den Berghe argued that nationalism is 'an extension of kinship selection and "nepotism" which has become salient in the modern world because of large-scale population movements, colonialism and conquest' (Hutchinson and Smith 1994, 48). Together with the rise of nationalism and the emergence of independent nation states across the five continents, the twentieth century saw the transformation of the international system. Asia gradually gained independence from Western hegemony and colonization, and moved from an enforced wallflower existence at the periphery toward a central position in a new global constellation. Since the late twentieth century, led by China, India, Indonesia, Japan, Malaysia, Saudi Arabia, Singapore, South Korea, Turkey, and Vietnam, Asia's fast growing economic, cultural, and political influence has made it an important player in the age of globalization. Against this background, nationalism in Asia has become an increasingly discussed and debated topic.

As the largest continent in the world, Asia encompasses 48 countries and is home to nearly 60 percent of the world's population. Current studies on nationalism in Asia have been challenged by the region's geographical, social, and cultural diversity and complexity. A handful of published works have tried to examine nationalism in Asian countries from a comparative perspective, each providing case studies on several countries in East, Southeast, South, Central, or West Asia (Emerson et al. 1942; Ball 1952; Holland 1953; Kennedy 1968; Kedourie 1974; Kang 1979; Breuilly 1993; Leifer 2000; Reid 2009; Rozman 2012; Omelicheva 2014; Kingston 2016). Most research has focused on individual countries in the region, notably the major economic powers, including China (Dittmer and Kim 1993; Unger 1996; Hughes 1997; Zhao 2004; Schoppa 2011; Mitter 2020), India (Chatterjee 1986, Bhatt 2001; Pandey 2002; Chatterji et al. 2019), Iran (Cottam 1979; Ansari 2012), Indonesia (Legge 2011; Arianto, et al. 2018), Japan (Iida 2002; McVeigh 2003; Shimazu 2009; Wilson 2013), South Korea (Robinson 1988; Shin 2006; Kal 2013), and Turkey (Kieser 2013; Al 2019).

Some have studied the construction of national identity and nationalism in the first half of the twentieth century, when many Asian countries were transforming from having been Western powers' colonies or semi-colonies into independent nation states (Kahin 1952; Duiker 1976; Gould 2010; Narangoa and Cribb 2011; Sato 2015; Boshier 2017). Others have examined the development and transformation of nationalism in Asia since the mid-twentieth century in the context of the Cold War, the Vietnam War (Duiker 1994), civil war (South 2005; Epkenhans 2016), diplomacy (Gries 2004), the spread of democracy (Corbridge and Harriss 2000; Connors 2002; He 2017; Bertrand 2021), modernization (Zheng 1999; Dönmez and Yaman 2019), and globalization (Starrs 2012; D'Costa 2012). Others have analyzed the relationships between ethnicity (Bulag 1998; Bertrand 2004; Findley 2010; Han 2013; Yaghoubian 2014; Sheikh 2018), religion (Farhadian 2005; Yu 2005; Walton and Hayward 2014; Shani and Kibe 2019; Kingston 2019), and nationalism.

In addition, an increasing number of scholars have started to explore the issue from social, cultural, and technological perspectives by identifying and analyzing the role of language (Simpson 2007), education (Vickers 2005; Nozaki 2008), literature (Tsu 2005), popular and traditional cultures (Guo 2004; Lei 2006; Menon 2012; Surak 2012; Daniels 2013; Benesch 2014), film and television (Muhlhahn and Haselberg 2012; Gorfinke 2017), gender (Blackburn and Ting 2013), sport (Zhouxiang and Hong 2014; Merkel 2014), food (King 2022), the internet (Mengin 2014; Schneider 2018), and other social and cultural institutions in the construction of national identity and nationalism in Asian countries.

Generally speaking, in the field of nationalism studies, Asia is still a novel topic and underresearched continent which needs to be explored further. Unlike existing literature that either offers case studies on several Asian nations, or gives an in-depth analysis of a specific country, this Handbook intends to provide readers with both a holistic and detailed view of Asian nationalism. Instead of covering the whole of Asia, it focuses solely on East and Southeast Asia, and covers 15 countries: Burma, Brunei, Cambodia, China, East Timor, Indonesia, Japan, Laos, Malaysia, North Korea, South Korea, Singapore, Thailand, the Philippines, and Vietnam.

Written by a team of international scholars from different academic backgrounds and disciplines, the book presents a comprehensive and multi-disciplinary survey of the formation and transformation of nationalism in the context of Asian culture, politics, economy, and society. It explores a diverse set of topics, including theoretical considerations on nationalism and internationalism; the formation of nationalism and national identity in the colonial and postcolonial eras; the relationships between traditional culture, religion, ethnicity, education, gender, technology, sport, and nationalism; the influence of popular culture on nationalism; and politics, policy, and national identity.

In short, this Handbook illustrates how nationalism helped to draw the borders between East and Southeast Asian nations, and how it is re-emerging in the twenty-first century to shape the region and the world into the future. It intends to highlight the latest developments in the field and contribute to our knowledge and understanding of nationalism and nation building. It also offers new perspectives on studying Asian history, society, culture, and politics, and provides readers with a unique lens through which to better contextualize and understand the relationships between countries within East and Southeast Asia, and between Asia and the world.

While the chapters in this Handbook offer the latest insights, it is worth emphasizing that the research must be as dynamic as the field of research itself; we can compare our subject matter to geological formations where shifts that are, at first glance, limited in range and scope contribute to wider ranging and unpredictable shifts in the geosphere. Here, this applies to economic, political, and socio-cultural changes. As we are facing unimaginable challenges in the age of globalization, it is of utmost importance that we (a) provide such up-to-date research as is contained in this present Handbook, and (b) use it for future research, not least research that aims to find well-informed and differentiated answers to the questions arising around the dynamic relationship between globalization and nationalism.

I hope that the topics and views in this volume will further stimulate interdisciplinary research and debate on nationalism, nation building, and identity construction and discourses in Asia in both the historical and modern contexts, while disseminating knowledge and scholarship to a wider audience.

References

Al, Serhun. 2019. *Patterns of Nationhood and Saving the State in Turkey: Ottomanism, Nationalism and Multiculturalism*. Abingdon: Routledge.

Alter, Peter. 1994. *Nationalism*. 2nd Edition. London: Edward Arnold.

Anderson, Benedict. 1983. *Imagined Communities: Reflections on the Origin and Spread of Nationalism*. London; New York: Verso.

Ansari, Ali M. 2012. *The Politics of Nationalism in Modern Iran*. Cambridge: Cambridge University Press.

Armstrong, John A. 1982. *Nations before Nationalism*. Chapel Hill: The University of North Carolina Press.

Asher, R. E., and J. M. Y. Simpson. 1994. *The Encyclopedia of Language and Linguistics*. Oxford: Pergamon Press.

Ball, W. MacMahon. 1952. *Nationalism and Communism in East Asia*. Melbourne: Melbourne University Press.

Benesch, Oleg. 2014. *Inventing the Way of the Samurai: Nationalism, Internationalism, and Bushidō in Modern Japan*. Oxford: Oxford University Press.

Bertrand, Jacques. 2004. *Nationalism and Ethnic Conflict in Indonesia*. Cambridge: Cambridge University Press.

Bertrand, Jacques. 2021. *Democracy and Nationalism in Southeast Asia*. Cambridge: Cambridge University Press.

Bhatt, Chetan. 2001. *Hindu Nationalism Origins, Ideologies and Modern Myths*. Abingdon: Routledge.

Blackburn, Susan, and Helen Ting, eds. 2013. *Women in Southeast Asian Nationalist* Movements. Singapore: National University of Singapore Press.

Boshier, Carol Ann. 2017. *Mapping Cultural Nationalism: The Scholars of the Burma Research Society, 1910–1935*. Copenhagen: NIAS Press.

Breuilly, John. 1993. *Nationalism and the State*. 2nd Edition. Manchester: Manchester University Press.

Bulag, Uradyn E. 1998. *Nationalism and Hybridity in Mongolia*. Oxford: Clarendon Press.

Butterfield, Herbert. 1965. *The Origins of Modern Science, 1300–1800*. London: Free Press.

Chatterjee, Partha. 1986. *Nationalist Thought and the Colonial World: A Derivative Discourse*. London: Zed Books.

Chatterji, Angana P., Thomas Blom Hansen, and Christophe Jaffrelot, eds. 2019. *Majoritarian State: How Hindu Nationalism is Changing India*. Oxford: Oxford University Press.

Connors, Michael Kelly. 2002. *Democracy and National Identity in Thailand*. Abingdon: Routledge.

Corbridge, Stuart, and John Harriss. 2000. *Reinventing India: Liberalization, Hindu Nationalism and Popular Democracy*. Cambridge: Polity.

Cottam, Richard W. 1979. *Nationalism in Iran: Updated Through 1978*. Pittsburgh: University of Pittsburgh Press.

Daniels, Timothy P. 2013. *Building Cultural Nationalism in Malaysia: Identity, Representation and Citizenship*. Abingdon: Routledge.

Davies, Norman. 1996. *Europe: A History*. Oxford: Oxford University Press.

D'Costa, Anthony P., ed. 2012. *Globalization and Economic Nationalism in Asia*. Oxford: Oxford University Press.

Dekker, Henk, and Darina Malova. 2003. "Nationalism and Its Explanations." *Political Psychology* 24 (2): 345–376.

Deutsch, Karl Wolfgang. 1979. *Tides among Nations*. New York: Free Press.

Dittmer, Lowell, and Samuel S. Kim, eds. 1993. *China's Quest for National Identity*. Ithaca: Cornell University Press.

Dönmez, Rasim Özgür, and Ali Yaman. 2019. *Nation-Building and Turkish Modernization: Islam, Islamism, and Nationalism in Turkey*. Lanham: Lexington Books.

Duiker, William J. 1976. *The Rise of Nationalism in Vietnam: 1900–1941*. Ithaca: Cornell University Press.

Duiker, William J. 1994. *Sacred War: Nationalism and Revolution in a Divided Vietnam*. New York: McGraw-Hill.

Emerson, Rupert, Lennox A. Mills, and Virginia Thompson. 1942. *Government and Nationalism in Southeast Asia*. New York: International Secretariat, Institute of Pacific Relations.

Epkenhans, Tim. 2016. *The Origins of the Civil War in Tajikistan: Nationalism, Islamism, and Violent Conflict in Post-Soviet Space*. Lanham: Lexington Books.

Farhadian, Charles E. 2005. *Christianity, Islam and Nationalism in Indonesia*. Abingdon: Routledge.

Findley, Carter V. 2010. *Turkey, Islam, Nationalism, and Modernity*. New Haven: Yale University Press.
Gellner, Ernest. 1983. *Nations and Nationalism*. Cornell University Press.
Gorfinke, Lauren. 2017. *Chinese Television and National Identity Construction: The Cultural Politics of Music-Entertainment Programmes*. Abingdon: Routledge.
Gould, William. 2010. *Hindu Nationalism and the Language of Politics in Late Colonial India*. Cambridge: Cambridge University Press.
Greenfeld, Liah. 1992. *Nationalism: Five Roads to Modernity*. London/New York: Harvard University Press.
Gries, Peter Hays. 2004. *China's New Nationalism: Pride, Politics, and Diplomacy*. Berkeley: University of California Press.
Guo, Yingjie. 2004. *Cultural Nationalism in Contemporary China*. Abingdon: Routledge.
Han, Enze. 2013. *Contestation and Adaptation: The Politics of National Identity in China*. Oxford: Oxford University Press.
He, Baogang. 2017. *Nationalism, National Identity and Democratization in China*. Abingdon: Routledge.
Hill, Christopher. 1970. *God's Englishman: Oliver Cromwell and the English Revolution*. New York: Dial Press.
Hill, Christopher. 1985. *The Collected Essays of Christopher Hill*, Volume 3. Brighton: Harvester Press.
Hobsbawm, Eric. 1988. *The Age of Capital, 1845–1875*, London: Cardinal.
Holland, William L., ed. 1953. *Asian Nationalism and the West*. New York: The Macmillan Co.
Hong, Fan, and Lu Zhouxiang, eds. 2015. *Sport and Nationalism in Asia – Power, Politics and Identity*. Abingdon: Routledge.
Hughes, Christopher. 1997. *Taiwan and Chinese Nationalism: National Identity and Status in International Society*. Abingdon: Routledge.
Iida, Yumiko. 2002. *Rethinking Identity in Modern Japan: Nationalism as Aesthetics*. Abingdon: Routledge.
Kahin, George McTurnan. 1952. *Nationalism and Revolution in Indonesia*. Ithaca: Cornell University Press.
Kal, Hong. 2013. *Aesthetic Constructions of Korean Nationalism: Spectacle, Politics and History*. Abingdon: Routledge.
Kang, Tia S., ed. 1979. *Nationalism and the Crises of Ethnic Minorities in Asia*. Westport: ABC-CLIO.
Kedourie, Elie. 1960. *Nationalism*. London: Hutchinson.
Kedourie, Elie, ed. 1974. *Nationalism in Asia and Africa*. Abingdon: Frank Cass.
Kennedy, Joseph. 1968. *Asian Nationalism in the Twentieth Century*. London: Palgrave Macmillan.
Kieser, Hans-Lukas. 2013. *Turkey Beyond Nationalism: Towards Post-Nationalist Identities*. London: I.B. Tauris.
Kingston, Jeff. 2016. *Nationalism in Asia: A History since 1945*. Hoboken: Wiley-Blackwell.
Kingston, Jeff. 2019. *The Politics of Religion, Nationalism, and Identity in Asia*. Lanham: Rowman & Littlefield.
Michelle T. King, ed. 2022. *Culinary Nationalism in Asia*. New York: Bloomsbury Academic.
Kohn, Hans. 1944. *The Idea of Nationalism: A Study of Its Origins and Background*. New York: Macmillan.
Kohn, Hans. 1967. *Prelude to Nation-State: the French and German Experience, 1789–1815*. Princeton: D. Van Nostrand Company, Inc.
Lefebvre, Georges. 2005. *The Coming of the French Revolution*. Princeton: Princeton University Press.
Legge, J.D. 2011. *Intellectuals and Nationalism in Indonesia*. Sheffield: Equinox Publishing.
Lei, Daphne P. 2006. *Operatic China: Staging Chinese Identity across the Pacific*. London: Palgrave Macmillan.
Leifer, Michael, ed. 2000. *Asian Nationalism*. Abingdon: Routledge.
Marshall, Peter. 2017. *1517: Martin Luther and the Invention of the Reformation*. Oxford: Oxford University Press.
McVeigh, Brian J. 2003. *Nationalisms of Japan: Managing and Mystifying Identity*. Lanham: Rowman & Littlefield.
Mengin, Francoise, ed. 2004. *Cyber China: Reshaping National Identities in the Age of Information*. London: Palgrave Macmillan.
Menon, Jisha. 2012. *The Performance of Nationalism: India, Pakistan, and the Memory of Partition*. Cambridge: Cambridge University Press.
Merkel, Udo. 2014. "The Politics of Sport and Identity in North Korea." *The International Journal of the History of Sport – Special Issue: The Politics of Sport and Identity is Asia* (edited by Fan Hong and Lu Zhouxiang) 31 (3): 376–390.

Miller, David. 1998, "Nation and Nationalism." In *Routledge Encyclopedia of Philosophy*, ed. Edward Craig. London: Routledge, Taylor and Francis, accessed September 6, 2022, https://www.rep.routledge.com/articles/thematic/nation-and-nationalism/v-1/sections/the-evolution-of-nationalism. doi:10.4324/9780415249126-S039-1.

Mitter, Rana. 2020. *China's Good War: How World War II Is Shaping a New Nationalism*. Cambridge, MA: Harvard University Press.

Muhlhahn, Klaus, and Clemens von Haselberg, eds. 2012. *Chinese Identities on Screen*. Münster: LIT Verlag.

Narangoa, Li, and Robert Cribb. 2011. *Imperial Japan and National Identities in Asia, 1895–1945*. Abingdon: Routledge.

Nozaki, Yoshiko. 2008. *War Memory, Nationalism and Education in Postwar Japan, 1945–2007*. Abingdon: Routledge.

Omelicheva, Mariya Y., ed. 2014. *Nationalism and Identity Construction in Central Asia: Dimensions, Dynamics, and Directions*. Lanham: Lexington Books.

Pandey, Gyanendra. 2002. *Remembering Partition: Violence, Nationalism and History in India*. Cambridge: Cambridge University Press.

Patunru, Arianto A., Mari Pangestu, and M. Chatib Basri, eds. 2018. *Indonesia in the New World: Globalisation, Nationalism and Sovereignty*. Singapore: Yusof Ishak Institute.

Rafi Sheikh, Salman. 2018. *The Genesis of Baloch Nationalism: Politics and Ethnicity in Pakistan, 1947–1977*. Abingdon: Routledge.

Reid, Anthony. 2009. *Imperial Alchemy: Nationalism and Political Identity in Southeast Asia*. Cambridge: Cambridge University Press.

Renan, Ernest. 1990 [1882]. "What Is a Nation?" In *Nation and Narration*, edited by H. Bhabha, 8–22. Abingdon: Routledge.

Robinson, Michael Edson. 1988. *Cultural Nationalism in Colonial Korea, 1920–1925*. Seattle and London: University of Washington Press.

Rozman, Gilbert. 2012. *East Asian National Identities*. Palo Alto: Stanford University Press.

Sato, Shigeru. 2015. *War, Nationalism and Peasants: Java under the Japanese Occupation, 1942–45*. Abingdon: Routledge.

Schaff, Philip. 1910. *History of the Christian Church*. New York: Charles Scribner's Sons.

Schneider, Florian. 2018. *China's Digital Nationalism*. Oxford: Oxford University Press.

Schoppa, R. Keith. 2011. *Revolution and Its Past: Identities and Change in Modern Chinese History*. Abingdon: Routledge.

Seton-Watson, Hugh. 1977. *Nations and States*. London: Methuen Young Books.

Shafer, Boyd G. 1972. *Faces of Nationalism: New Realities and Old Myths*. New York: Harcourt Brace Jovanovich.

Shani, Giorgio, and Takashi Kibe, eds. 2019. *Religion and Nationalism in Asia*. Abingdon: Routledge.

Shimazu, Naoko, ed. 2009. *Nationalisms in Japan*. Abingdon: Routledge.

Shin, Gi-Wook. 2006. *Ethnic Nationalism in Korea: Genealogy, Politics, and Legacy*. Redwood City: Stanford University Press.

Simpson, Andrew, ed. 2007. *Language and National Identity in Asia*. Oxford: Oxford University Press.

Slavitt, David R. 1999. "The Decline and Fall of Latin (and the Rise of English)." *The World & I* 14 (10): 18.

Smith, Adam. 1977. *An Inquiry into the Nature and Causes of the Wealth of Nations*. Chicago: University of Chicago Press.

Smith, Anthony D. 2000. *The Nation in History*. Oxford: Wiley-Blackwell.

South, Ashley. 2005. *Mon Nationalism and Civil War in Burma: The Golden Sheldrake*. Abingdon: Routledge.

Starrs, Roy, ed. 2012. *Nations under Siege: Globalization and Nationalism in Asia*. London: Palgrave Macmillan.

Stavrianos, L. S. 1975. *The World since 1500: A Global History*. New York: Prentice-Hall.

Stone, Lawrence. 1985. "The Bourgeois Revolution of Seventeenth-Century England Revisited." *Past and Present* 109 (11): 44–54.

Surak, Kristin. 2012. *Making Tea, Making Japan: Cultural Nationalism in Practice*. Palo Alto: Stanford University Press.

Thomson, George Malcolm. 1972. *Sir Francis Drake*. New York: William Morrow & Company Inc.

Tsu, Jing. 2005. *Failure, Nationalism, and Literature: The Making of Modern Chinese Identity, 1895–1937*. Palo Alto: Stanford University Press.
Unger, Jonathan. 1996. *Chinese Nationalism*. Abingdon: Routledge.
Uzer, Umut. 2016. *An Intellectual History of Turkish Nationalism: Between Turkish Ethnicity and Islamic Identity*. Salt Lake City: University of Utah Press.
van den Bergh, Godfried van Benthem. 2018. "Herder and the Idea of a Nation." *Human Figurations: Long-term Perspectives on the Human Condition* 7 (1) (May), accessed October 15, 2022, http://hdl.handle.net/2027/spo.11217607.0007.103.
Vickers, Edward, ed. 2005. *History Education and National Identity in East Asia*. Abingdon: Routledge.
Walton, Matthew J., and Susan Hayward. 2014. *Contesting Buddhist Narratives: Democratization, Nationalism, and Communal Violence in Myanmar*. Honolulu: East-West Center.
Weiss, Hilde. 2003. "A Cross-National Comparison of Nationalism in Austria, the Czech and Slovac Republics, Hungary, and Poland." *Political Psychology* 24 (2): 377–401.
Wilson, Sandra, ed. 2013. *Nation and Nationalism in Japan*. Abingdon: Routledge.
Yaghoubian, David. 2014. *Ethnicity, Identity, and the Development of Nationalism in Iran*. Syracuse: Syracuse University Press.
Yu, Xue. 2005. *Buddhism, War, and Nationalism: Chinese Monks in the Struggle against Japanese Aggression 1931–1945*. Abingdon: Routledge.
Zhao, Suisheng. 2004. *A Nation-State by Construction: Dynamics of Modern Chinese Nationalism*. Palo Alto: Stanford University Press.
Zheng, Yongnian. 1999. *Discovering Chinese Nationalism in China: Modernization, Identity, and International Relations*. Cambridge: Cambridge University Press.
Zhouxiang, Lu, and Fan Hong. 2014. *Sport and Nationalism in China*. Abingdon: Routledge.

PART I

Theoretical considerations

The concepts of the 'nation state', 'national identity' and 'nationalism' first emerged in Western Europe and the Americas in the late eighteenth and early nineteenth centuries before they spread to East and Southeast Asia as part of Western colonization and imperialist expansion. Many of the existing and most influential theories of nationalism were developed by Western scholars – notably Hans Kohn (1944), Ernest Gellner (1983), Eric Hobsbawm (1983, 1990), Elie Kedourie (1960), Karl W. Deutsch (1953), Miroslav Hroch (1968, 1971), Anthony D. Smith (1971, 1986, 1991) and John Armstrong (1982) – and make explicit reference to Europe, with Benedict Anderson's 'Imagined Communities' (1983) and Chatterjee's 'Derivative Discourse' (1986) being two of the few exceptions. Tina Burrett's opening chapter offers a critical analysis of the major classical and contemporary theories of nation formation, national identity discourses and nationalist ideology. She discusses more recent approaches to the study of nationalism from the perspectives of constructivist and complexity theories with examples from contemporary East and Southeast Asian societies. Burrett convincingly points out that existing theories of nationalism that had been developed by Western scholars offer a useful base and starting point for understanding nationalism in contemporary Asia, but that new dynamics and divergences, accelerated by globalization, require new and different approaches. As the meaning and content of nationalism depend on social context and thus change over time, the factors underpinning, informing and feeding nationalism must be analyzed and explained with reference to the specific local context. Her contribution highlights the importance of a relativist approach as the changes in one region are not only shaping developments in other regions but also have immediate repercussions in their own region. While this has always been the case, today's globalization encourages and speeds up such developments, if for no other reason than due to what we may call the 'acceleration of history'.

For a long time, nationalism was primarily understood and interpreted through the Western canon 'in which many academics and students have been and continue to be educated' (Sutherland 2023, 35). In recent years, there has been a growing call for decolonizing curricula, adopting anti-racist pedagogies and decentralizing the colonial legacy by upending the intellectual ascendancy of modernity/coloniality to incorporate multiple perspectives. Claire Sutherland's chapter on 'Decolonialising Southeast Asian Nationalism' reveals that such a decolonial approach is particularly beneficial to the critical study of nationalist ideologies, and can also be linked to critiques of the conceptualization of Southeast Asia itself as an artifact of area studies. Decolonializing involves a thorough and challenging engagement with the imperial trappings of the Western canon. It also entails questioning what makes canonical knowledge legitimate, the erasures and inequalities bound up with it and the structural racism that perpetuates it. Sutherland explores the theory, methodology and pedagogy of decoloniality in relation to the study of Southeast Asian nationalism, and concludes that decoloniality needs to refuse Eurocentric frameworks of canonical knowledge and resist belittling perspectives of the 'other' as 'methodologically, this entails looking beyond the nation or nation-state as a unit or category of analysis' (Sutherland 2023, 44).

Atsuko Ichijo's contribution further challenges the in-built Eurocentrism in existing social and political theories on nationalism by offering possible alternative origins and expressions of nationalism in a non-Western context. Ichijo (2023, 52) first defines nationalism as 'societal self-understanding with the nation as its basic unit' and a 'form of human self-reflexivity', before analyzing this 'self-understanding' process through the cases of China's Song dynasty (960–1279), the Imjin War (1592–1598) between Japan and Korea, and the rise of Kokugaku in eighteenth-century Japan. She points out that in each of these three cases, crises triggered societal self-understanding, collective self-reflection and the act of collectively imagining a nation. Arguably, based on slightly modified definitions that offer a different theoretical frame for interpretation, she suggests that alternative forms of nationalism and national consciousness have existed in East Asia long before the nineteenth century.

Before the arrival of Western colonial powers, a Sino-centric, multi-layered tributary system operated in East and Southeast Asia for centuries as a form of trade and diplomacy. In general, there was a distinct lack of cultural or inter-state competition in the region. Yongle Zhang's chapter on 'The Clash of Empires, the Rise of Nationalism, and the Vicissitude of Pan-Asianism in East and Southeast Asia' deals with these two issues. He shows how the invasion of Western powers in the nineteenth century resulted in the collapse of the Sino-centric tributary order and reduced East and Southeast Asian kingdoms to colonies and semi-colonies. As the center of the tributary system, China was carved up by the imperialist powers before achieving re-integration and revival, and ultimately recognition and (economic) blossoming, in the twentieth century. At the same time, Japan slowly completed its transformation into a modern nation state and became a new colonial/imperialist power, and the only Asian one. Driven by a nationalism that reflected the duality of resisting Western powers and oppressing Asian neighbors, Japan developed the idea of the Greater East Asia Co-Prosperity Sphere to legitimize and, more importantly, justify its imperialist and colonial expansion. Many East and Southeast Asian nations, however, drew on and adopted the communist, anti-capitalist understanding of nationality and internationalism in their struggle for independence and liberation. Zhang emphasizes that rich legacies of internationalism in East Asia and Southeast Asia have the potential to promote international cooperation and, in so doing, prevent extreme forms of nationalism in the region.

Zhang's chapter is complemented by Peter Herrmann's contribution which presents a methodological framework for a better understanding Asian nationalism, postcolonialism and internationalism. Herrmann asserts that postcolonialism is, not least, a setting that largely depends on what it claims to overcome, namely economic and cultural colonialism, nationalism and even internationalism – which could be understood as a new form of colonialism. The topic is especially relevant for this time and space, insofar as construction and reconstruction play a major role, utilizing changing global constellations and, in turn, also influencing these constellations.

In the last chapter of this section, Feilong Tian offers a comprehensive analysis of the relationships between traditional colonialism, modern striving for and achieving hegemony, and Asian nationalism. Tian points out that the history of modern Asia has become part of the colonial history of Eurocentrism. Powered by a common law, transnational financial and trade structures, the English language and a maritime geopolitical system, the traditional British colonial rule played an instrumental role in shaping East and Southeast Asia during the colonial and postcolonial periods. After the Second World War, the United States developed a keen interest in Asia and slowly established a more rigorous global system. Its main ingredients were the principles of the US-American legal system, the institutionalization of US dollar hegemony and the sanctions system, overseas military bases and (corresponding) security cooperation arrangements, technology, ideology and US-American popular and consumer culture. Tian argues that Asian nationalism and pan-Asian regionalism are the main forces resisting both traditional colonialism and the new US-American hegemony. According to Tian, the future of Asia depends on its unity and self-development, and the skillful juggling of nationalism, pan-Asian regionalism and globalism. The 'Belt and Road Initiative' and the idea of a 'Community of Shared Future for Humankind' could potentially play a constructive role in promoting peace and prosperity in Asia and beyond.

The reader may find that some of the contributions in this section seem to show different, or even opposing, arguments. For example, Sutherland criticizes 'Eurocentric' approaches, and Ichijo 'modernist' ones. However, Zhang's chapter is based on a modernist approach, while Tian asserts that Asian nationalism was a specific intellectual and political consequence of European colonialism, and thus, to some extent, shaped by Eurocentric views and concepts.

It is important to reiterate that most of the past and current research on the nation state, nationalism and national identity, by both Western and Asian scholars, is primarily based on a Western or 'modern' definition and understanding of these concepts, from both linguistic and socio-political perspectives. From the very beginning, we are dealing with a Western political concept and a nation state framework passively and/or actively adopted by Asian countries during the process of imperialist expansion, colonization, decolonization and modernization in the past two centuries. We can criticize Eurocentric and modernist approaches, but in the end, all discussion is still based on Western intellectual foundations- even the endeavour to critical reflect on the nature and contents of knowledge, the way it was gathered and disseminated.

There may be a need to modify the definition of nationalism when applying it to East and Southeast Asia due to the different socio-economic, political and cultural contexts, but the question then is: Are we still discussing the same civic-political idea infused by the French Revolution, that 'the masses were no longer in the nation, but of the nation'? Or the Chinese Revolution version: 'The people became the masters of their own country'? A more feasible approach is therefore not to abandon classical and contemporary theories of nationalism developed by Western scholars, but to use them in a critical and constructive manner – the key is to take into consideration the specific local Asian context, especially cultural, political, economic, ethnic, religious and legal factors. Only by doing so can we achieve a more comprehensive and unbiased understanding of the origins, development and manifestation of nationalism in Asian countries.

Overall, the contributions in this section clearly show an urgent need for revisiting fundamental methodological, conceptual and theoretical issues, which will inevitably lead to a discussion of the essence, multi-faceted nature and versatile appearance of modern nationalism in a global context from today's perspective and practice.

References

Armstrong, John. 1982. *Nations before Nationalism*. Chapel Hill: University of North Carolina Press.
Anderson, Benedict. 1983. *Imagined Communities: Reflections on the Origin and Spread of Nationalism*. London; New York: Verso.
Chatterjee, Partha. 1986. *Nationalist Thought and the Colonial World: A Derivative Discourse*. London: Zed Books.
Deutsch, Karl W. 1953. *Nationalism and Social Communication*. Cambridge, MA: MIT Press/New York: John Wiley & Sons, Inc.; London: Chapman & Hall.
Gellner, Ernest. 1983. *Nations and Nationalism*. Ithaca: Cornell University Press.
Hroch, Miroslav. 1968. *Die Vorkämpfer der nationalen Bewegung bei den kleinen Völkern Europas. Eine vergleichende Analyse zur gesellschaftlichen Schichtung der patriotischen Gruppen*. Prague: Universita Karlova.
Hroch, Miroslav. 1971. *Obrození malých evropských národů: Národy severní a východní Evropy*. Prague: Universita Karlova.
Ichijo, Atsuko. 2023. "An Alternative Origin of Nationalism in the East: the Emergence of Political Subjectivity under the Non-western Centric World Order." In *The Routledge Handbook of Nationalism in East and Southeast Asia*, edited by Lu Zhouxiang, 48–59. Abingdon: Routledge.
Kedourie, Elie. 1960. *Nationalism*. London: Hutchinson.
Kohn, Hans. 1944. *The Idea of Nationalism: A Study of Its Origins and Background*. New York: Macmillan.
Hobsbawm, Eric and, Terence Ranger, eds. 1983. *The Invention of Tradition*. Cambridge: Cambridge University Press.
Hobsbawm, Eric. 1990. *Nations and Nationalism since 1780: Programme, Myth, Reality*. Cambridge: Cambridge University Press.
Smith, Anthony D. 1971. *Theories of Nationalism*. New York: Harper & Row.
Smith, Anthony D. 1986. *The Ethnic Origins of Nations*. Oxford: Basil Blackwell.
Smith, Anthony D. 1991. *National Identity*. London: Penguin Books.
Sutherland, Claire. 2023. "Decolonialising Southeast Asian Nationalism." In *The Routledge Handbook of Nationalism in East and Southeast Asia*, edited by Lu Zhouxiang, 35–47. Abingdon: Routledge.

1
APPLYING CLASSIC AND CONTEMPORARY NATIONALISM THEORIES TO EAST AND SOUTHEAST ASIA TODAY

Tina Burrett

Introduction

It has become a trope among commentators to argue that nationalism is resurging in the first quarter of the twenty-first century. But in East and Southeast Asia, where the majority of modern states were born from nationalisms fermented by war, anti-colonial or other emancipatory struggles, nationalist pulses never went away. This chapter introduces some of the key classic and contemporary theories of nationalism as tools for explaining how nationalist ideas and movements have shaped East and Southeast Asia. In applying such a large body of literature to such a vast geographic area, this chapter is inevitably selective and should be read as an overview.

Classic nationalism theories written in the last three decades of the twentieth century still have much to offer in explaining nationalisms in East and Southeast Asia today. These twentieth-century texts tend to focus on national political elites, economic systems or cultural symbols and myths as the main explanatory factors behind the rise of nationalism. More recent scholarship, borrowing from constructivism, complexity theory and globalisation studies, draws attention to the peer-to-peer and transnational dynamics underpinning nationalism, elements largely missing in classic theories. Theorists working in the constructivist school also bring greater diversity to our understanding of national identity, helping us to see how gender and social class may lead individuals to perceive the nation and nationalism differently from dominant groups within their national community.

This chapter begins by revisiting classic definitions of the nation and by discussing what makes it distinct from other collective entities and identities, specifically the state and ethnic groups. The second section analyses the relevance for Asia today of nationalism scholarship from the late twentieth-century, a fertile period for theoretical innovation. These theories fall into three broad schools—focusing on cultural, political or economic factors as the main drivers of nationalism. The most significant theorists working in each school are presented, in turn, with their ideas applied to examples from East and Southeast Asia. The final section discusses how insights from constructivism and complexity theory are expanding and challenging classic theories of nationalism in light of the accelerating pace and influence of globalisation in Asia and elsewhere.

In classic theories, the character of different nations and nationalisms is often presented as dichotomous—civic verses ethnic nationalism, majority verses minority and/or mass-led verses elite. But in reality, nationalism is frequently driven by a blurring of seemingly contradictory factors, manifesting in complex ways. The final section of this chapter, while introducing readers to contemporary nationalism theories, also analyses how these contradictions appear in Asian nationalisms today. Throughout its analysis, this chapter applies theoretical debates to the functions and goals of nationalism in Asia, including nation building, development, democratisation, state legitimisation, national autonomy, geopolitical manoeuvring and integration into the global economy. In conclusion, it argues that the rich body of nationalism theories should be treated as a typology for analysing the equally varied aims and origins of specific cases of nationalism in East and Southeast Asia (Breuilly 2001). When combined with knowledge of specific historical, social and political contexts, theories can illuminate why particular varieties of nationalism come to dominate in certain settings and times (Calhoun 1997, 8).

Key concepts

In the world today, the nation, state and nationalism are central to political legitimacy, personal identity and organisation of the international system. We live in a world of *states*, defined as sets of autonomous decision-making institutions with sovereignty and a monopoly on coercion within demarcated territorial borders. The world is also divided into *nations*, named groups of people with a shared historic homeland, a common culture and collective myths and memories. Unlike most religions, for example, nations also make claim to a specific territory they call 'home'. The existence of nations necessitates division of the world into 'us' and 'them'. *Nationalism* is an ideological movement aiming to attain or maintain autonomy, solidarity and identity on behalf of a group of people deemed by at least some of its members to constitute an actual or potential nation (Smith 2000, 1). Nationalist ideologies are differentiated from other collective belief systems and identities by their temporal and spatial claims and their emphasis on loyalty to the nation above all else. Nationalist movements look to the past to demonstrate the presence of the nation throughout time. Nations are bound together by their shared sacrifices in the past—real or imagined—that create a present-day solidarity and a desire to continue a common life in the future (Renan 1994). Nations can correspond with a specific *ethnicity*, a group of people bound by shared cultural attributes that distinguish them from other groups, such as a common language, ancestry or other social signifiers. Equally, ethnicity may not be the foundation of national identity, as in the case of multi-ethnic immigrant states such as Singapore, where civic symbols like the constitution and flag, alongside behavioural norms and values, denote belonging (Ortmann 2009). In other words, the nation and nationalism are highly subjective concepts. As Seton-Watson states, all we can say 'is that a nation exists when a significant number of people in a community consider themselves to form a nation' (1977, 5).

Classic nationalism theories

Ethnosymbolist and cultural approaches

Ethnosymbolism is a school of nationalism studies stressing the importance of symbols, myths, memory, rituals, values and traditions in the formation and persistence of nations and nationalism (Ozkirimli 2010, 143). Theorists in this school argue that the continuity of ethnic identities and nations is more significant than the changes they undergo over the *longue durée* (Armstrong 1982). They thus focus on the symbolic boundaries—words, signs, language, dress, etc.—separating nations from their neighbours (Smith 2009, 23). Ethnosymbolists stress three common principles. First, modern nations cannot be understood without considering the pre-existing ethnic communities on which they are based. Second, understanding the origins and persistence of nations requires an analysis of collective cultural identities over many centuries. Third, myths of origin, cultural symbols, cults of heroes, memories of golden ages and attachments to homelands all play an important role in the self-definition and endurance of national identities (Smith 2000, 12–13).

John Armstrong, one of the first ethnosymbolists, begins his analysis by underlining the long gestation of modern nations and nationalism. For Armstrong, evidence of ethnic consciousness can be found among ancient civilisations. Modern nations are the most recent manifestation of ethnic identities stretching back centuries, and in some cases millennia (Armstrong 1982, 2). Armstrong argues that ethnic groups define themselves not based on their own features, but by reference to strangers. Group identity is based on a comparison with those excluded from membership. This allows for changes in the cultural and demographic composition of the group, providing that a boundary is maintained with 'others' (Armstrong 1982, 4–5). Armstrong therefore focuses his attention on the symbolic boundaries ethnic groups use to differentiate themselves from others rather than on intra-group characteristics. For him, 'myth, symbol, communication, and a cluster of associated attitudinal factors are usually more persistent than purely material factors' in acting as 'symbolic boarder guards' differentiating group members from outsiders (Armstrong 1982, 6–9). For this reason, nationalism often involves symbolic goals, such as official status for the nation's language or protection for important historic sites.

Anthony D. Smith shares Armstrong's contention that modern nations are formed around pre-existing ethnic groups over a long time span. Unlike Armstrong, however, Smith sees more change than continuity between modern nations and their premodern forbearers. For Smith, nationalism and nations are mostly modern, even if they are based on pre-existing ethnic ties. Although not absolute, there are strong differences between nations and the ethnic groups that precede them, though a few nations may be able to point to considerable continuities from the medieval era. The Japanese, for example, are able to trace their cultural heritage back to dynastic periods and to premodern ethnic communities (Smith 2000, 13–14).

Smith draws a definitional distinction between nations and pre-modern ethnic groups, which he calls *ethnie*. The latter are defined by six main attributes (Smith 1991a, 21–22):

1 a collective proper name
2 a myth of common ancestry
3 shared historical memories
4 one or more differentiating elements of common culture
5 an association with a specific homeland
6 a measure of solidarity (at least among elites)

Most of these attributes are subjective, suggesting that the *ethnie* exists in a fluid rather than fixed state. Smith identifies war, exile, enslavement, an influx of immigrants and religious conversion as factors generating the most fundamental changes in ethnic identities. Yet, even in the face of radical transformations, a sense of common ethnicity remains remarkably durable (Smith 1991a, 26). The Chinese, for example, have been subject to conquest by the

Mongols, Europeans and Japanese; yet, a distinctive Chinese ethnic identity persisted and, at times, received a new lease on life under conditions of subjugation.

In his classic *National Identity*, Smith defines the nation as 'a named human population sharing an historic territory, common myths and historical memories, a mass, public culture, a common economy and common legal rights and duties for all members' (1991a, 14). How and why a nation emerges depends on the type of ethnic community that precedes it. Smith identifies two main types of ethnic community that have formed the basis for modern nations (leaving aside immigrant nations such as Singapore and Australia). The first type is 'lateral' *ethnies*, which are composed of elites such as aristocrats, clergy, bureaucrats, merchants and military officers. This ruling class lacks a broad base in society and has little cultural affinity with the lower classes over whom they rule. The second type is 'vertical' *ethnies*, a broader inter-class community sharing a common culture. The Aryans of India are an example of the lateral type, while Sikhs represent the vertical (Smith 2000, 14).

Early Western European nations tended to be based on lateral *ethnies*. Unlike in most other places and times, Western European upper-class *ethnies* were able to create strong territorial states by incorporating periphery regions and the middle classes of subordinate *ethnies* into their cultural orbit (Japan and Han China are rare non-Western examples). The main drivers of this process, which Smith calls 'bureaucratic incorporation', were the emerging institutions of the state. New state institutions and infrastructures were used to diffuse elite culture downwards and to link distant periphery regions to the core. The nations formed by vertical *ethnies* tend to be communities under colonial rule or other forms of subjugation. In these cases, the role of the state apparatus is less significant, as the bureaucracy is controlled by colonial powers. Here, indigenous intellectuals play a key role in mobilising the formerly passive masses behind a route to modernisation that rejects foreign ways in favour of a rediscovered set of native cultures, myths and histories. Smith calls this process 'vernacular mobilisation' (1991a, 52–65). Examples of vernacular mobilisation by intellectuals and professions include the Burmese and Indonesians, who managed over time to transform their *ethnie* from a dominated people into a politically independent nation.

John Hutchinson (1987) also highlights the significance of long-term cultural factors in explaining the rise of nationalism. His work distinguishes two parallel kinds of nationalist movement, one political and oriented towards sovereignty, the other cultural and concerned with the moral regeneration of the ethnic community. In the latter movements, nationalist intellectuals are critical to the process of defining and reviving the ethnic community through the rediscovery of myths, symbols and memories. Many cultural-nationalist movements form under colonial rule, to protect the nation's distinct and ancient culture from the threat posed by foreign powers. But Hutchinson argues that while political nationalists seek an independent state to protect the nation, cultural nationalists are more concerned with establishing a strong cultural community (2013, 76). In the first place, theirs is a moral enterprise to regenerate the nation from within and from below, by appealing to the memory of a golden age. Promoting the idea of regeneration, these movements continue to appear after independence and even within states never subjected to colonial rule. Hutchinson argues that cultural nationalists present populations with new maps of identity, combining the virtues of historical tradition and modern progress at times of crisis when established identities are shaken (2013, 86). The right-wing nationalism that has risen in Japan since its economic bubble burst in the early 1990s, exemplifies this nostalgia for a mythicised golden age. Japanese nationalists glorify the pre-war era when Japan was a powerful empire, contrasting this period with what they term present-day decline and degeneration (Guthmann and Rots 2017, 222).

Critics of ethnosymbolism argue that it is not difficult to find nationalism in the pre-modern era if one defines the nation as broadly as Armstrong and Smith. Theorists such as Walker Connor (1994) and Brendan O'Leary (1997) accuse Smith of conflating ethnic groups and nations. Connor also criticises Smith for failing to address what percentage of a given people must acquire national consciousness to transform a group from an *ethnie* to a nation (Connor 1990, 99). Smith's lateral and vertical models of nation formation both suggest that elites develop national consciousness before the masses. For Connor, evidence of national consciousness among the elite is not sufficient to confer nation status on an ethnic group, a view Smith opposes (Connor 1994, 40; Smith 2008, 6). Whether or not mass consciousness is essential to the definition of a nation is a point of contention. Hastings (1997) and Greenfeld (2003) argue that it is not necessary for the masses to be conscious of it for the nation to exist, while Breuilly (2001) agrees with Connor in rejecting this claim. For modernist theorists, it is not until modern political and economic processes like capitalism, industrialisation, bureaucracy and democracy emerge in the eighteenth century, forcing elites to 'invite the masses into history', that nations and nationalism emerge (Nairn 2003, 328).

Economic approaches

The most celebrated modernist theorist, Ernest Gellner (1964), argues that the birth of modern, industrial, capitalist societies made nationalism a necessity. He begins his thesis by distinguishing between three stages of human society: the hunter-gather, agro-literate and industrial. For Gellner, nationalism is a political concept, maintaining that the national and political unit should correspond (1983, 1). In the hunter-gather phase, there are no states and therefore no need for nationalism, which seeks a political home for the national culture. In agro-literate societies, the masses are engaged in agricultural production, divided into small local cultures and communities. Above the masses, a small elite of clergy, bureaucrats, merchants and aristocracy use culture to separate themselves from the common people and possess no incentive to impose their way of life on the peasantry (Gellner 1983, 9–12). But in industrial societies, the masses must become socially mobile, literate and culturally homogeneous to fulfil the needs of a growth-oriented, technologically advanced economy. Changes in the economy necessitate context-free communication and cultural standardisation. As technology evolves, workers must be able to develop the skills needed to perform new occupations (Gellner 1996, 106–108). Only the state has the resources to establish a public education system guaranteeing cultural homogeneity and access to standardised knowledge. Public education brings the state and culture together to turn peasants into workers (Gellner 1983, 35).

Gellner argues that it is state-sponsored nationalism, transmitted via public education to meet the needs of the industrial economy that engenders nations. Nationalism invents nations and not vice versa. But industrial societies are not always able to absorb all cultures within their borders into the nation. Industrialisation, especially in its later stages, gives rise to new conflicts. Labour migrants flock to industrial cities, bringing them into competition with existing inhabitants for jobs and services. When migrants resemble current residents culturally and physically, class conflict ensues. But if newcomers differ in appearance, religion or language, competition can take the form of ethnic conflict. Resentments develop on both sides and can lead to demands for secession as newly conscious nations seek their own state to house their distinct culture (Gellner 1983, 60–75). Recent examples from Asia include the Uyghur in China and the Rohingya in Myanmar.

Conflict in Asia, specifically the 1970s wars in Indochina, inspired Benedict Anderson's influential *Imagined Communities* (2006). These wars proved to Anderson the power of nationalism to trump the allure of political ideologies, particularly socialism. In arousing such deep attachments, Anderson argues that nations and nationalism have more in common with kinship and religion than with ideology (Anderson 2006, 5). Therefore, Anderson defines the nation as an 'imagined political community'—imagined as both limited and sovereign. It is imagined because even members of the smallest nations will never know the majority of their compatriots. It is imagined as limited because all nations have boundaries outside which other nations lie. And it is imagined as sovereign because nations were born during the Enlightenment, when the legitimacy of monarchs and religion were in decline and nations aspired to be free and self-governing (Anderson 2006, 6–7).

According to Anderson, the receding of religious and dynastic communities from the seventeenth century provided the space in which nations could emerge. The nation replaced religion in providing a kind of immortality, by establishing a link between the dead and unborn generations. Another major factor contributing to the rise of nations was the invention of print capitalism that displaced Latin as the common language of Europe's elites. By the sixteenth century, the Latin market was saturated and more books were being produced in vernacular languages. Mass printing led to the standardisation of vernacular languages and the creation of vernacular reading publics. Novels and later newspapers published in standard vernaculars allowed readers who would never meet to imagine themselves as members of the same national community (Anderson 2006, 26–36). Rising literacy rates, in conjuncture with the diffusion of capitalism and communications technology, led to new demands for linguistic unification, spreading nationalism across the globe.

Similarly to Benedict Anderson, Tom Nairn begins his theorising from the position that 'nationalism represents Marxism's greatest historical failure' (Nairn 2003, 317). For Nairn, the roots of nationalism can be found in the uneven development of the global capitalist economy since the end of the eighteenth century (2003, 323–324). Unlike Gellner, Nairn does not argue that nationalism is a product of industrialisation per se, but rather that it is the result of the international system of capitalist exploitation and inequality. Capitalism spread unevenly across the world through the mechanism of imperialism. The activities of a set of 'core' imperialist countries enmeshed the 'periphery' part of the world into the capitalist system through violence and domination. Exploitation by foreign powers stirred resistance among periphery elites. Outclassed in terms of military and economic resources, the only thing native elites had on their side was numbers. To win independence from colonial powers required appealing to the masses for support. Complicating matters for local elites, few wanted to reject the progress brought by Western technologies along with ejecting their Western overlords. This meant crafting a populist, cross-class national identity, strongly differentiated from the foreign forces of domination on the grounds of culture. The 'development nationalism' of Indonesia's Soekarno, for example, blended celebration of indigenous culture with a native form of Marxism known as *Marhaenism* that promised social justice, individual freedom and an end to colonial and capitalist exploitation (Anderson 2002, 5). Periphery elites like Soekarno had to invite the people into history and write the invitation card in the language and culture of the masses (Nairn 2003, 327–328).

Michael Hechter's theory of nationalism also involves colonialism, but within rather than between states. His concept of 'internal colonialism' refers to the unequal exchange between regions of a country—owing to market forces or government policies—resulting in uneven distribution between the core and periphery. The term is also used to refer to periphery regions that are both economically disadvantaged and culturally distinct from the core of the state (Hechter 1999, xiv). A good example is the Philippines, where economic grievances motivate rebellion against the state by culturally distinct provinces, particularly the

Moro insurgency in Southern Mindanao (McDoom et al. 2019, 927). Hechter argues that in pre-industrial societies, economic and cultural differences between the core and periphery are unimportant, as these regions are practically isolated from each other. Under industrialisation, core-periphery contact increases. If industrialisation brings a general increase in wealth and welfare that sees core and periphery becoming more economically equal, the cultural differences between regions are not socially meaningful. But, Hechter argues, industrialisation rarely leads to increased equality and harmony between core and periphery. Rather, groups in the core seek to entrench their advantages by institutionalising the existing system of stratification. Economic decisions tend to be made in the core to its own benefit, leading the periphery to lag behind. The most prestigious and powerful positions go to members of the core, a system Hechter calls the 'cultural division of labour' (1999, 7–9; 1978, 294–295). The cultural division of labour leads individuals to identify with their core or periphery group, resulting in the development of distinctive ethnicities. The separate group identities that developed between supporters of Thailand's red and yellow shirt movements are a case in point. Supporters of the red shirt movement were drawn mainly from rural and working-class populations in the northeast of the country, while the yellow shirts represented the urban middle classes in the south and west (Fuller 2013).

Hechter argues that for group solidarities to emerge, inequality between core and periphery must be seen as part of an unjust pattern of collective oppression. Further, there must be adequate means of communication between members of the oppressed group. If there are clear cultural differences between groups, for example, language or religion, the greater the probability that the periphery will develop a separate collective solidarity rather than integrating into the national society (Hechter 1999, 42–43). The indigenous people of Vietnam's Central Highlands—with religious and linguistic traditions distinct from the rest of Vietnam—provide a good example to illustrate Hechter's theory (HRW 2004).

Several commentators, however, point out that facts on the ground do not uphold Nairn and Hechter's emphasis on economic exploitation as the genesis of nationalism. The strongest nationalist movements sometimes develop in the wealthiest regions of a state, for instance, in Hong Kong within China (Ozkirimli 2010, 121–123). Similarly, several commentators have cast doubt on Gellner's assertion that industrialisation is always the starting point for the spread of nationalism. Examples include nationalist movements in pre-industrial Burma and the Philippines. Furthermore, some nationalist movements reject modernisation—including industrialisation—for example, the Khmer Rouge in Cambodia (Ozkirimli 2010, 130–131). Anderson's theory that nationalism replaces religion is also called into question by the facts (Greenfeld 1993, 49). In contemporary Indonesia, nationalism is reinforcing religious identities and institutions. Owing to these counter examples, fellow modernists such as John Breuilly (2001) caution against grand theories, arguing that many different preconditions can spark the spread of nationalism—including political as much as economic factors.

Political approaches

Theorists focusing on political changes—including the growth of the bureaucratic state and mass enfranchisement—compose another subcategory of modernists. John Breuilly is a key proponent of nationalism belonging in the political sphere. For him, nationalism is strictly a political movement aimed at seizing, legitimating and sustaining state power. Rather than offering a general theory, Breuilly constructs a framework for studying nationalism in its various forms (Breuilly 1993, 1). Seeking to understand the different functions played by nationalism in pursuit of state power, Breuilly develops a typology of nationalisms that he then uses to analyse comparative case studies. Breuilly classifies nationalist movements along two axes; one, whether the movement controls or opposes the state, and two, the movement's political goals. He identifies three nationalist political goals: (1) nationalist movements may seek to break away from the state (separation), for example, the Kachin and Shan independence movements in Myanmar; (2) they may seek to reform the state in a nationalist direction, as was the case with the 1868 Meiji restoration in Japan; and (3) nationalists may aim to unite with other states (unification), evident in China's ambition regarding Taiwan (Breuilly 1993, 9).

Breuilly further identifies three functions of nationalist ideology for opposition movements. First, *coordination*, meaning the use of nationalist ideas to establish a common cause among elites that may have divergent interests in opposing existing state powers. The Kuomintang in early twentieth-century China, for example, sought to bind together military, bureaucratic and economic elites. Second, *mobilisation*, using nationalist ideology to gain support from groups currently excluded from the political process—General Aung Sung's appeal to non-Burman minorities to join his independence movement being a case in point. Finally, *legitimacy*, meaning justification of the movement's goals both to the state it opposes and to foreign governments. Western governments' enthusiasm for Tibetan independence, for instance, is bound up with the Dalai Lama's advocacy of his cause (Breuilly 1993, 381–388).

Political legitimacy is also central to Eric Hobsbawm's understanding of nationalism. Hobsbawm contends that nations, nationalism, national symbols and histories are deliberately socially engineered (Hobsbawm and Ranger 1983, 13). Many ceremonies and symbols that seem old in origin are in fact quite recent 'invented traditions' (Hobsbawm and Ranger 1983, 1). By invented tradition, Hobsbawn means a set of practices seeking to 'inculcate certain values and norms of behaviour by repetition, which automatically implies continuity with the past' (ibid). Hobsbawm argues that the nation itself is an invented tradition. Despite being modern, nations make claims to historical continuity to establish political legitimacy and cement social unity (Hobsbawm and Ranger 1983, 12). But the appearance of historical continuity is largely the product of invention. For example, many supposedly age-old Japanese traditions—group harmony, martial arts and industrial paternalism—turn out to be modern, just as the rituals and rules of sumo, Japan's 'ancient' national sport, are mostly twentieth-century creations (Vlastos 1998, 1).

Hobsbawm identifies two processes of invention, the adaption of old traditions to new situations and the invention of new traditions. The former occurs in all societies, while the latter is found largely in societies undergoing rapid transformations when it becomes vital to stem social fragmentation. Inventing traditions was one strategy used by the founders of North Korea to maintain loyalty to the new regime after the Korean War (Jackson et al. 2021). As seen elsewhere, the introduction of mass primary schooling, national monuments and public ceremonies were three tactics employed by North Korean authorities to consolidate national identity, collective solidarity and loyalty to the state (Hobsbawm and Ranger 1983, 271–272). In another example, following the end of communism in Mongolia, Genghis Khan has been reinvented as a national hero. In 2012, the Mongolian government designated 14 November—traditionally the first day of winter—as Khan's birthday and a public holiday. In 2006, a gigantic statue of Khan was unveiled near the capital Ulaanbaatar.

The Mongolian state's celebration of Genghis Khan also illustrates Paul Brass' theory of the instrumental nature of nationalism (1991). Instrumentalists argue that nationalism is created and sustained by competing elites to mobilise public support behind their economic and political interests. National identities and symbols are continually reconstructed owing to the changing needs of political elites in their struggles to control resources. The changing nature of the struggle between competing nationalist elites in Taiwan is a good example. Since democratisation, Taiwanese civic nationalists have increased their calls for independence in the context of electoral competition with ethnic nationalists who stress cultural ties and accommodation with China (Hughes 2019). Brass further argues that ethnic conflicts do not arise from cultural differences, but from the wider political and economic contexts shaping elite competition. Depending on the political and economic environments, elites may choose to play up or down differences with other nations or ethnic groups. For example, in recent years, it has become domestically political expedient for governing elites in Japan and South Korea to emphasise their differences, leading to a series of clashes over historical, trade and territorial issues (Deacon 2021).

Critics argue that instrumentalists fail to account for the role of non-elites in shaping nationalisms. Such criticism could equally apply to Hobsbawm as well as Brass. Breuilly complains that theories focusing on elite manipulation do not explain why the masses make sacrifices for the nation that serve elite interests rather than their own. The masses are not a passive audience for nationalist discourse from above, but rather have their own reasons to support the nationalist cause. Critics further contend that Brass' theory does not explain why elites choose nationalism to mobilise the masses, rather than appealing to class or other identities (Ozkirimli 2010, 128–129). Ethnosymbolists such as Smith also take issues with the assertion that elites have a free hand in deciding the content of national identity. Assessing Hobsbawm's theory of 'invented traditions', Smith argues that the past acts as a constraint on elite construction of the nation. The masses will only accept a new tradition if it is shown to connect with the group's past (Smith 1991b, 356–357).

Contemporary nationalism theories

Constructivist approaches

In the new millennium, theorising on nationalism has witnessed a revival, with a new generation of scholars drawing on constructivist ideas from a broad spectrum of disciplines. Constructivists hold that power is simultaneously ideational and material and that identities are constructed through social interaction (Finnemore and Sikkink 2001). While earlier constructivists, such as Anderson, focused on elites and political institutions in the formation of nationalism, the role of the masses remained largely veiled. The recent 'everyday nationalism' approach brings the masses back into the picture, while at the same time challenging the excessive institutionalism and invisibility of dominant ethnicities in classic theories (Fox and Miller-Idriss 2008a). Adherents of this approach argue that the problematising of nationalism around mobilisation and changing outcomes has led many scholars to focus on elites and ethnic minorities who are easier to identify and observe than the masses and majorities (Kaufmann 2004). A focus on *change* means that there have been few works examining what allows some nations and national identities to remain *stable* (Wimmer 2013). Goode and Stroup argue that this tendency has been exacerbated by a persistent theoretical dichotomy between civic and ethnic nations (2015, 3). In brief, a civic national identity defines national loyalties in terms of state institutions, thus collapsing the distinction between nationality and citizenship. In contrast, ethnic nations are defined by primordial ties, most often in terms of perceived common kinship (Kohn 1994). As a result, civic nations tend to be portrayed as tolerant and pluralist, while ethnic nations are presented as the opposite. Nations are often inaccurately described as civic when the interests and identity of the majority population become institutionalised by the state as universal rather than ethnic. A focus on institutions and top-down identity formation thus disguises discrimination against minorities and conceals the ethnic politics of majorities (Goode and Stroup 2015, 4).

Everyday nationalism is an approach for observing how ethnicity and nationhood are manipulated and reproduced by the masses of 'ordinary people doing ordinary things' (Fox and Van Ginderachter 2018, 547). The crucial methodology innovation made by this approach is to replace *individuals* (usually elites) and *groups* (nations/ethnicities) with ethnic or nationalist *practices* as units of analysis, allowing enquiry into areas neglected by classic texts (Goode and Stroup 2015, 8). Research focuses on exposing the ways that ordinary people infuse everyday routines with ethnic or nationalist content. How 'ordinary people think the nation, talk the nation, enact the nation, perform the nation, consume the nation —and of course reject, resist, ignore, and avoid the nation—all in ways that contribute to the reproduction and legitimation— or dismantling and undermining—of national forms of belonging' (Fox and Van Ginderachter 2018, 546). Ethnographic observation is the preferred methodological approach to understanding these everyday social practices, the 'micro-interactional moments' that shape and maintain ethnic identity on a daily basis (Fox and Miller-Idriss 2008b, 575).

The lens of everyday nationalism allows scholars to consider overlooked influences on national identities and ethnic boundaries, including transnational and market forces, both accelerated by late stage globalisation. Canonical theorists such as Gellner demonstrate how state attempts at economic modernisation result in cultural standardisation and common national identity. But the private sector increasingly influences ethnic boundaries as much as the state by shaping cultural consumption. 'Ethno-preneurs' sell ethnicity as a commodity, and in so doing adapt, change and invent ethnic practices to appeal to consumer preferences (Comaroff and Comaroff 2009). For instance, ethno-preneurs may promote ethnic tourism as a means of economic and/or cultural survival. In Southwest China, local government initiatives have established ethno-tourism sites showcasing minority cultures as a mean of development. Mengqi Wang's study of one such project in a Buyi village demonstrates how tourism changed villagers' everyday language and the ways in which they express and interpret their ethnicity (2012, 449). In another example, efforts by the Chinese state to exploit Tibet as a domestic ethnic tourism destination are changing Tibetan notions of what is morally right and authentic within their own culture. Tibetans have refused to celebrate their own cultural festivals and are using civil disobedience to protest Chinese political and economic exploitation. In 2009, many Tibetans refused to participate in *Losar* (New Year) celebrations and in 2007 declined to wear traditional fur-trimmed robes for an annual horse festival that had become a tourist attraction, despite being fined up to 3,000 yuan (Saxer 2012, 77).

An everyday-nationalism approach may also reveal how consumer choices influence citizens' feelings of ethnic belonging and understanding of the nation. Economic behaviour may be invested with nationalist meaning, for example, buying brands associated with one's ethnic group (e.g. kosher or halal food); supporting tariffs against imported goods; starting a business that sells commodified ethnic commodities or boycotting chains deemed 'unpatriotic' or culturally 'inauthentic' (Edensor 2002). Responding to the popularity of Japanese food overseas, for example, Japan's government set up an organisation—the so-called 'sushi police'—to reclaim *washoku* as the cultural property of the Japanese nation. In 2013, they also led a successful effort to have Japanese cuisine certified by UNESCO as intangible cultural heritage (Farrer and Chuanfei 2021, 13). Discerning the ethnic significance of consumer practices, however, requires great care, as motivations for such choices may be determined by nationalist principles, but equally by convenience or necessity. Ethnographic observations or interviews may be required to unearth the otherwise unspoken motivations behind economic preferences (Goode and Stroup 2015, 13).

Constructivist scholars in international relations have drawn attention to the influence of transnational norms and communities on national identity, factors rarely considered by classic nationalism theorists who tend to focus on the nation as the unit of analysis (Rissen-Kappen et al. 1999). Although a recent discussion on the relationship between globalisation and the nation often sees the former as an *emerging* threat to the latter, globalisation and the external world have long influenced national identities. In turn, ethnic and national collectivities have been important agents and accelerators of regional and global networks, processes sped up by new communications technologies in the twenty-first century (Hutchinson 2011). Katherine Verdery, for example, demonstrates how the transnationalising of democratic norms has prompted nationalist politics that simultaneously reterritorialises and deterritorialises collective boundaries (Verdery 1998). This phenomenon is at work in contemporary Thailand, where in widespread protests, the Thai people are demanding the right to define their nation for themselves, challenging traditional autocratic nationalist conceptions based on the military, monarchy and religion (Selway 2020). Thai elites emphasise the nation's uniqueness to justify a lack of democracy, but protestors define themselves as part of a trans-Asia democratic movement. Indeed, the Thai protesters forming of the Milk Tea Alliance (along with pro-democracy activists in Hong Kong, Taiwan and Myanmar) shows that they see their demands as transnational (BBC 2021). The symbols adopted by protesters—drawn from Harry Potter, the Hunger Games and Japanese anime—further demonstrate the influence of transnational cultural on these movements.

Complexity theory approaches

In recent years, scholars have applied complexity theory—the concept that complex social phenomena emerge from seemingly uncoordinated individual acts—to enhance our understanding of nations and nationalism. The theory holds that social phenomena, like nations, cities or markets, are complex systems whose whole represents more than the sum of its parts (Urry 2005). Complexity theorists argue that researchers should focus on the network properties of nations to better comprehend how nationalism emerges from below; why it may gestate in small circles for long periods then suddenly explode; why it is often contagious; and why local variation in the content of national identity strengthens rather than weakens the nation's power to mobilise (Kaufmann 2017, 6).

Complexity theorists challenge the vertical elite-diffusion model of nationalism that envisions the nation as a network of individuals connected via elite nodes. Rather, they argue that peer-to-peer networks are as or even more important in the construction and replication of nations. Complexity theorists conceive of the nation as horizontally constructed, with the content of national symbols existing everywhere and nowhere: like a forest, the nation lives as a complex whole, emerging from the interaction of individuals, groups and institutions (Malesevic 2013). Yves Déloye perceives national identity as spreading along 'various, ambiguous lines' based on largely unconscious processes, without easily identifiable actors (2013, 616–17). Inhabiting a space with national styles of architecture, watching national sports, buying national brands—all matter more than participating in occasional state-sponsored nationalist activities like national holidays. These banal microsocial practices create a dense series of associations between things, acts, spaces and forms of representation to offer countless ways of expressing national identity (Edensor 2002). Only by aggregating everyone's individual perspectives can national identity be revealed.

Anthony Cohen's (1996) concept of 'personal nationalism' echoes this idea. A nation's history, literature, music, landscapes, language and food are social building blocks used by individuals to construct their personal national identity. Although individuals may interpret these social phenomena differently, it is by sharing them that common attachment to the nation is created. Complexity theory therefore draws attention to how gender, religion and lifestyle can refract the national image. It further clarifies how individuals' national identities may switch from symbol to symbol as they move from the periphery to the capital or overseas—journeys that change perception of the nation (Kaufmann 2017, 20). Individuals identify deeply but differentially with national symbols across space and time. Difference energises rather than detracts from nationalism, as this 'crowdsourced nationalism' allows civil society rather than state elites to direct national identity (Surowiecki 2004).

Complexity theorists challenge Anderson's notion of the nation as an 'imagined community' in which individuals who never meet are nonetheless conscious of belonging to the whole unit. They contend that members need not agree on a common set of boundaries, myths or memories for the nation to act in unison. Birds fly in unison without imagining the whole flock or agreeing a direction of travel. This may explain why nations with highly contested memories remain united. For example, Japan's WWII legacy and current peace constitution hotly divide domestic opinion without undermining national identity (Saaler and Schwentker 2008).

Where classic nationalism theory tells the story of premodern localism giving way to homogenous nationalism, complexity theory sees local cultures as active agents in the co-production of nations. This is essential as nation-states are often distant and abstract and must be woven into the micro-solidarities that generate emotional attachment to the nation (Kaufmann 2017, 14). Once locales come to think of themselves as intertwined with the nation, localism can strengthen rather than undermine national identity. The Gwangju region of South Korea—site of the famous pro-democracy demonstrations brutally crushed by the military on 18 May 1980—provides an illustrative example. The military dictatorship that ruled South Korea for 30 years came predominantly from the Gyeongsang region and ruthlessly discriminated against Gwangju. Even after democratisation in the late 1980s, for the majority of Koreans, Gwangju remained negatively imagined as the 'city of blood' owing to the 1980 uprising (Shin 2004, 622). But the Gwangju Biennale festivals held between 1995 and 2002 transformed the image of the city by commemorating the 18 May protests in art. Today, Gwangju is an important *national* symbol of popular democracy, resistance and justice (Shin 2004, 626). Local Gwangju identity and national Korean identity thus became mutually reinforcing.

Complexity theorists further challenge assumptions about the linear spread of nationalist ideas, recasting understanding in terms of tipping point dynamics. Classic theories consider nationalist ideas to spread smoothly from elites to the masses. Not only do these theories fail to consider peer-to-peer dynamics; they ignore why nationalist ideas diffuse in some fertile situations but not in others. Classic theories see nationalism as a vaccine injected into the body of the nation from the top. But complexity theory perceives nationalism as a virus, with the more who become infected with nationalist ideas creating more vectors for its spread, until a tipping point is reached (Brubaker 1996; Kaufmann 2017). Individuals are more likely to be converted to a cause if approached through multiple social connections. Hence, the success of nationalist causes is only in part explained by its intrinsic appeal. Nationalist movements are doomed to fail until they reach the critical mass necessary to start a chain reaction of mobilisation. Herding behaviour is important, as less committed individuals need to be convinced that their peers are also engaged before they will endorse a movement

(Kaufmann 2017, 18). The wider geographic spread and social participation in Hong Kong's 2019 pro-democracy protests compared to protests in 2014 are an example of tipping point dynamics at work (Ng 2020; Lee 2020).

The spread of nationalism can also be accelerated to a tipping point by internal or external stimuli, for example, a change in regime, the switch from an imperial to vernacular language or the introduction of new communications technologies (Eriksen and Jenkins 2007; Laitin 1998; Hroch 1985). Nationalist agitation and secession may create role models that embolden other groups to seek self-determination. Similarly, ethnic and nationalist violence often begets yet more violence—both at the inter- and intra-state level (Horowitz 2001; Forsberg 2014). A feedback loop of violence, for example, was evident in Myanmar in the 1990s, when the state faced multiple ethnic insurgencies involving the Kachin, Arakanese, Karen and other minorities (Forsberg 2008).

Conclusion

As globalisation continues to impose massive social and economic transformations on Asian societies, it is unlikely that the allure of nationalism will decline soon. Growing social fragmentation and economic disparity strengthens the appeal of nationalism as a tool to bind the nation and legitimate the state. A rise in the uneven distribution of political power, both between and within states, adds fuel to ethnic and national rivalries. At the same time, developments in communication technologies are breaking down barriers between media producers and consumers, giving ordinary citizens greater ability to challenge elite discourse on national identities and values (Gurevitch et al. 2009). Transnational networks and the external world increasingly shape the identity of nations and nationalism. Indeed, nationalism is one manifestation of globalisation, providing ethnic and national collectivities with coherence in a world of fragmentation and unpredictable change (Hutchinson 2011).

Under the influence of globalisation, the study of nationalism in Asia is becoming more urgent and more complex. Existing theories of nationalism, conceptualised largely with reference to Europe since the eighteenth century, offer a good starting point for understanding nationalism in contemporary Asia. But new dynamics and divergencies accelerated by globalisation require new approaches. Adding to the classic view, constructivism and complexity theory draw attention from elites to the masses and from centres to the periphery, highlighting the importance of everyday nationalism, tipping points and the multivocal nature of nationalism. Taken together, classic and contemporary theories demonstrate that the meaning and content of nationalism depends on social context and changes over time. Why nationalism comes to prominence in some settings, for some groups, in some periods is contingent on a wide range of factors that can only be explained with reference to the local context. The factors underpinning nationalism should, therefore, be studied individually for each nation. Even then, theories pertaining to a particular nation must be revised frequently, as national identity is an evolving discourse. Understanding the range of nationalisms in today's East and Southeast Asian societies, therefore, requires reference to multiple theories and approaches.

Acknowledgement

This chapter draws on the author's 2015 publication 'East Is East and West Is West? Applying Theories of Nationalism to Asia', in *Asian Nationalisms Reconsidered*, edited by Jeff Kingston, 7–20. Abingdon: Routledge. The author is grateful to Yuhki Komano and Sunny Mizushima for their research support for this chapter. This chapter was written at Clare Hall, University of Cambridge where the author was a fellow and with support from the Japan Society for the Promotion of Science (JSPS).

References

Anderson, Benedict. 2002. "Bung Karno and the Fossilization of Soekarno's Thought." *Indonesia* 74 (October): 1–19.
———. 2006. *Imagined Communities: Reflections on the Origin and Spread of Nationalism*. Third Edition. London: Verso.
Armstrong, John. 1982. *Nations before Nationalism*. Chapel Hill: University of North Carolina Press.
BBC. 2021. "Milk Tea Alliance: Twitter Creates Emoji for pro-Democracy Activists." *BBC News*. 8 April. https://www.bbc.co.uk/news/world-asia-56676144 (accessed 18 September 2021).
Brass, Paul. 1991. *Ethnicity and Nationalism: Theory and Comparison*. London: Sage.
Breuilly, John. 2001. "The State and Nationalism." In *Understanding Nationalism*, edited by Montserrat Guibernau and John Hutchinson, 32–52. Cambridge: Polity.
Brubaker, Rodgers. 1996. *Nationalism Reframed: Nationhood and the National Question in the New Europe*. Cambridge: Cambridge University Press.
Calhoun, Craig. 1997. *Nationalism*. Buckingham: Open University Press.
Cohen, Anthony P. 1996. "Personal Nationalism: A Scottish View of Some Rites, Rights, and Wrongs." *American Ethnologist* 23 (4): 802–815.
Comaroff, John, and Jean Comaroff. 2009. *Ethnicity Inc*. Chicago: Chicago University Press.
Connor, Walker 1990. "When Is a Nation?" *Ethnic and Racial Studies* 13 (1): 92–103.
Connor, Walker. 1994. *Ethnonationalism: The Quest for Understanding*. Princeton, NJ: Princeton University Press.
Deacon, Chris. 2021. "(Re)Producing the "History Problem": Memory, Identity and the Japan-South Korea Trade Dispute." *The Pacific Review* 35 (5): 789–820.
Déloye, Yves. 2013. "National Identity and Everyday Life." In *The Oxford Handbook of the History of Nationalism*, edited by John Breuilly, 615–634. Oxford: Oxford University Press.
Edensor, Tim. 2002. *National Identity, Popular Culture and Everyday Life*. Oxford: Berg Publishers.
Eriksen, Thomas, and Richard Jenkins. 2007. *Flag, Nation and Symbolism in Europe and America*. Abingdon: Routledge.
Farrer, James, and Wang Chuanfei. 2021. "Who Owns a Cuisine? The Grassroots Politics of Japanese Food in Europe." *Asian Anthropology* 20 (1): 12–29.
Finnemore, Martha, and Kathryn Sikkink. 2001. "Taking Stock: The Constructivist Research Program in International Relations and Comparative Politics." *Annual Review of Political Science* 4 (1): 391–416.
Forsberg, Erika. 2014. "Transnational Transmitters: Ethnic Kinship Ties and Conflict Contagion 1946–2009." *International Interactions* 40 (2): 143–165.
Fox, Jon E., and Cynthia Miller-Idriss. 2008a. "The 'Here and Now' of Everyday Nationhood." *Ethnicities* 8 (4): 573–576.
Fox, Jon, and Cynthia Miller-Idriss. 2008b. "Everyday Nationhood." *Ethnicities* 8 (4): 536–563.
Fox, Jon E., and Maarten Van Ginderachter. 2018. "Introduction: Everyday Nationalism's Evidence Problem." *Nations and Nationalism* 24 (3): 546–552.
Fuller, Thomas. 2013. "Economic Realignment Fuels Regional Political Divisions in Thailand." *The New York Times*. 3 December. http://www.nytimes.com/2013/12/04/world/asia/thailand-protests-reflect-searing-divisions-of-changing-country.html?pagewanted=all (accessed 15 September 2021).
Gellner, Ernest. 1964. *Thought and Change*. London: Weidenfeld and Nicolson.
———. 1983. *Nations and Nationalism*. Ithaca, NY: Cornell University Press.
———. 1996. "The Coming of Nationalism and Its Interpretations: Myths of Nation and Class." In *Mapping the Nation*, edited by Gopal Balakrishnan, 98–145. London: Verso.
Goode, J. Paul, and David R. Stroup. 2015. "Everyday Nationalism: Constructivism for the Masses." *Social Science Quarterly* 96 (3): 717–739.
Greenfeld, Liah. 1993. "Transcending the Nation's Worth." *Daedalus* 122 (3): 47–62.
———. 2003. *The Spirit of Capitalism Nationalism and Economic Growth*. Cambridge: Harvard University Press

Gurevitch, Michael, Stephen Coleman, and Jay Blumer. 2009. "Political Communication: Old and New Media Relationships." In *Media Power in Politics*. Sixth Edition, edited by Doris A. Graber, 45–56. Washington, DC: CQ Press.

Guthmann, Thierry, and Aike Rots. 2017. "Nationalist Circles in Japan Today: The Impossibility of Secularization." *Japan Review*, no. 30: 207–325.

Hastings, Adrian. 1997. *The Construction of Nationhood: Ethnicity, Religion and Nationalism*. Cambridge: Cambridge University Press.

Hechter, Michael. 1978. "Group Formation and the Cultural Division of Labor." *American Journal of Sociology* 84 (2): 293–318.

———. 1999. *Internal Colonialism: The Celtic Fringe in British National Development*. Second Edition. New Jersey: Transaction Publishers.

Hobsbawm, Eric, and Terence Ranger. 1983. *The Invention of Tradition*. Cambridge: Cambridge University Press.

Horowitz, Donald. 2001. *The Deadly Ethnic Riot*. Berkeley: University of California Press.

Hroch, Miroslav. 1985. *Social Preconditions of National Revival in Europe*. First Edition. Cambridge: Cambridge University Press.

HRW. 2004. "Vietnam: Violence against Montagnards during Easter Week Protests." *Human Rights Watch*. 14 April. https://www.hrw.org/news/2004/04/14/vietnam-violence-against-montagnards-during-easter-week-protests (accessed 10 September 2021).

Hughes, Christopher R. 2019. "Revisiting Taiwan and Chinese Nationalism: Identity and Status in International Society." In *Taiwan Studies Revisited*, edited by Dafydd Fell and Hsin-Huang Michael Hsiao, 63–74. Abingdon: Routledge.

Hutchinson, John. 1987. *The Dynamics of Cultural Nationalism*. Abingdon: Routledge.

———. 2011. "Globalisation and Nation Formation in the Longue Durée." In *Nationalism and Globalisation: Conflicting or Complementary*, edited by Daphne Halikiopoulou and Sofia Vasilopoulou, 84–98. Abingdon: Routledge.

———. 2013. "Cultural Nationalism". In *The Oxford Handbook of the History of Nationalism*, edited by John Breuilly, 75–95. Oxford: Oxford University Press.

Jackson, Andrew David, Codruta Sîntionean, Remco Breuker, and CedarBough Saeji. 2021. *Invented Traditions in North and South Korea*. Honolulu: University of Hawaii.

Kaufmann, Eric. 2004. *Rethinking Ethnicity: Majority Groups and Dominant Minorities*. Abingdon: Routledge.

———. 2017. "Complexity and Nationalism." *Nations & Nationalism*, 23 (1): 6–25.

Kohn, Hans. 1994. *The Idea of Nationalism: A Study in Its Origins and Background*. New Brunswick: Transaction Publishers.

Laitin, David. 1998. *Identity in Formation*. Ithaca, NY: Cornell University Press.

Lee, Francis. 2020. "Solidarity in the Anti-Extradition Bill Movement in Hong Kong." *Critical Asian Studies* 52 (1): 18–32.

Malesevic, Sinisa. 2013. *Nation-States and Nationalisms: Organization, Ideology and Solidarity. Cambridge*. Cambridge: Policy Press.

McDoom, Omar Shahabudin, Celia Reyes, Christian Mina, and Ronina Asis. 2019. "Inequality between Whom? Patterns, Trends, and Implications of Horizontal Inequality in the Philippines." *Social Indicators Research* 145 (3): 923–942.

Nairn, Tom. 2003. *The Break-Up of Britain: Crisis and Neo-Nationalism*. Champaign: Common Ground.

Ng, Mee Kam. 2020. "The Making of 'Violent' Hong Kong: A Centennial Dream? A Fight for Democracy? A Challenge to Humanity?" *Planning Theory & Practice* 21 (3): 483–494.

O'Leary, Brendan. 1997. "On the Nature of Nationalism: An Appraisal of Ernest Gellner's Writings on Nationalism." *British Journal of Political Science* 27 (2): 191–222.

Ortmann, Stephan. 2009. "Singapore: The Politics of Inventing National Identity." *Journal of Current Southeast Asian Affairs* 28 (4): 23–46.

Ozkirimli, Umut. 2010. *Theories of Nationalism: A Critical Introduction*. Second Edition. Basingstoke: Palgrave Macmillan.

Renan, Ernest. 1994. "Qu'est-Ce Qu'une Nation?" In *Nationalism*, edited by John Hutchinson and Anthony D. Smit, 17–18. Oxford: Oxford University Press.

Rissen-Kappen, Thomas, Steve Ropp, and Kathryn Sikkink. 1999. *The Power of Human Rights: International Norms and Domestic Change*. Cambridge: Cambridge University Press.

Saaler, Sven, and Wolfgang Schwentker. 2008. *The Power of Memory in Modern Japan*. Folkestone: Global Oriental.

Saxer, Martin. 2012. "The Moral Economy of Cultural Identity: Tibet, Cultural Survival, and the Safeguarding of Cultural Heritage." *Civilisations* 61 (1): 65–81.

Selway, Joel. 2020. "Thailand's National Moment: Protests in a Continuing Battle over Nationalism." *Brookings*. 2 November. https://www.brookings.edu/blog/order-from-chaos/2020/11/02/thailands-national-moment-protests-in-a-continuing-battle-over-nationalism/ (accessed 14 September 2021).

Seton-Watson, Hugh. 1977. *Nations and States: An Enquiry into the Origins of Nations and the Politics of Nationalism*. Abingdon: Routledge.

Shin, HaeRan. 2004. "Cultural Festivals and Regional Identities in South Korea." *Environment and Planning D: Society and Space* 22 (4): 619–632.

Smith, Anthony D. 1991a. *National Identity*. London: Penguin Group.

———. 1991b. "The Nation: Invented, Imagined, Reconstructed?" *Millennium – Journal of International Studies* 20 (3): 353–368.

———. 2000. "Theories of Nationalism Alternative Models of Nation Formation." In *Asian Nationalism*, edited by Michael Leifer, 1–20. Abingdon: Routledge.

———. 2008. *The Cultural Foundations of Nations: Hierarchy, Covenant and Republic*. Oxford: Blackwell.

———. 2009. *Ethno-Symbolism and Nationalism: A Cultural Approach*. Abingdon: Routledge.

Surowiecki, James. 2004. *The Wisdom of Crowds: Why the Many Are Smarter Than the Few and How Collective Wisdom Shapes Business, Economies, Societies, and Nations*. New York: Doubleday.

Urry, John. 2005. "The Complexity Turn." *Theory Culture & Society* 22 (5): 1–14.

Verdery, Katherine. 1998. "Transnationalism, Nationalism, Citizenship, and Property: Eastern Europe since 1989." *American Ethnologist* 25 (2): 291–306.

Vlastos, Stephen. 1998. *Mirror of Modernity: Invented Traditions of Modern Japan*. Berkeley: University of California Press.

Wang, Mengqi. 2012. "The Social Life of Scripts: Staging Authenticity in China's Ethno-Tourism Industry." *Urban Anthropology and Studies of Cultural Systems and World Economic Development* 41 (2): 419–455.

Wimmer, Andreas. 2013. *Ethnic Boundary Making: Institutions, Power, Networks*. Oxford: Open University Press.

2
DECOLONIALISING SOUTHEAST ASIAN NATIONALISM

Claire Sutherland

Introduction

Nationalist ideology often attempts to establish a given nation's *longue durée*, understood as distant origins that can be traced far back through calendrical time and are made manifest through deeply rooted culture and belonging to the land. These narratives of national longevity are variously employed to shore up state legitimacy and popular solidarity, or fuel nativism, chauvinism, exclusionary 'Othering' and hierarchies of belonging (Back and Sinha 2012). The notion of *longue durée*, however, has historiographical origins and methodological implications, which can help to distinguish different strands of meaning linking decolonialising to nationalism, and specifically Southeast Asian nationalism. Decolonialising, in turn, involves deep and challenging engagement with the imperial trappings of the Western canon, in which many academics and students in both (previously) colonising and colonised countries have been and continue to be educated. Decolonialising entails questioning and 'unravelling' (Saini and Begum 2020, 217) what makes canonical knowledge legitimate, the erasures and inequalities bound up with it and the structural racism that perpetuates it. In so doing, the extent to which so-called 'Western civilisation' has been intertwined with and often dependent on economic, intellectual and sociocultural contributions from erstwhile colonies can be identified, traced and brought to the fore, together with other unacknowledged systems of thought and sources of knowledge. That is, decolonialising pays attention to positionality, power differentials and the 'loss, mutilation and marginalisation of bodies of knowledge' (Gopal 2021, 20). As such, it should be reparative.

Following Walter Mignolo, decoloniality involves recognising the 'intimacies' among continents, which Lisa Lowe (2015, 21) defines as 'the circuits, connections, associations, and mixings of differentially laboring peoples.' This also means unravelling received notions of chronological, linear time, not only in critiquing nationalism, but also methodological nationalism, understood to mean taking the nation-state for granted as a category of analysis (Sutherland 2016b, 2020). Without idealising a precolonial past or creating new boundaries in place of those it breaks down, decolonialising work should equally target 'native tyrannies and nationalist elites' (Gopal 2021, 10) as well as colonial rulers, and the collaboration between them. More positively, it should seek to reframe and retell history that incorporates different perspectives and make space for equal dialogue between them, highlighting the contribution of racialised and other minorities in creating Europe's cultural identity and the condition of global modernity. This is particularly applicable to the critical study of nationalist ideology because, as Joseph Roach (1996, 6) points out, 'the relentless search for the purity of origins is a voyage not of discovery but of erasure.' In addition, decolonial thinking can also be linked to critiques of the conceptualisation of Southeast Asia itself as an artefact of area studies (Walker and Sakai 2019).

Tariq Jazeel (2017) notes that the postcolonial has developed its own disciplinary canon in the Western academy in a way that decolonial thinking has not and cannot, given its critique of establishment structures like academia. All the more surprising, then, is that since the Rhodes must Fall student movement spread to Oxford University from South Africa in 2016, this radical theoretical perspective is having an impact on many British university campuses, among others. It has led to demands that academics across the disciplinary spectrum decolonise their curricula, adopt anti-racist pedagogies in the classroom, and decentre the colonial legacy by upending the intellectual ascendancy of modernity/coloniality to incorporate multiple perspectives. To be clear, this does not mean replacing Western canonical knowledge, but rather enriching it, contextualising it and challenging it to withstand a range of new critiques, in the spirit of rigorous enquiry that defenders of rational modernity themselves hold dear. At the same time, however, the link between decolonial theory and pedagogic practice is not always clearly articulated or at the forefront of university initiatives, which rightly focus on implementing practical measures. The three parts of this chapter, devoted to theory, methodology and pedagogy, respectively, consider each of these aspects of decoloniality in relation to the study of Southeast Asian nationalism.

Decolonial theory

According to one of its foundational scholars, Aníbal Quijano (2008, 181), decolonial theory is based on 'the social classification of the world's population around the idea of race, a mental construction that expresses the basic experience of colonial domination.' This posits that Eurocentrism, capitalism and racism have proven more durable than colonialism itself, permeating societies and dominant knowledge systems to this day. Quijano models a homogenising social system of white supremacy emanating from Europe, beginning with the colonisation of the Americas and leading to a racialised hierarchy of slavery, serfdom and waged labour. He demonstrates how the economic power of capital has been co-constitutive of European modernity, also understood to include the bourgeois family, the nation-state and Eurocentric rationality (Quijano 2008, 193). Although the racialised stratification of black Africans, indigenous inhabitants, *mestizos* and European whites did not take the same form in Asia as in the Americas, parallels can certainly be drawn with the colonial organisation of Chinese, Malay and Indian labour in British Malaya, and the ethnic hierarchies between French, Vietnamese, Khmer and Lao in the colonial administration of French Indochina, for example. In comparable ways, non-Europeans were lumped together into broad categorisations of indigenous or indentured peoples, whose chief characteristics were deemed to be cultural inferiority and so-called 'backwardness.' This was understood to mean a lesser degree of advancement along a chronological continuum of development and progress than Europeans and led to a mutually reinforcing duality, which persists today in the broad terms of 'the West' and 'the Rest' (Walker and Sakai 2019, 6).

Extermination, exclusion and discrimination were the tools used to constrain and control colonial relations between racialised groups, and, according to Quijano (2008), these antecedents created power differentials that still characterise South and Central American democratic systems today. Quijano contends that as a result, many black and Indian citizens there have never been accorded full citizenship, in the sense of equal, non-discriminatory access to its rights and duties. This is certainly not confined to South America, since one enduring legacy of colonialism has been to spread racialised prejudice across the globe. Walter Mignolo (2008, 248), another foundational member of the Modernity-Coloniality-Decoloniality (MCD) school of thought, considers modernity and coloniality to have been co-constitutive phenomena for the last 500 years, ever since the establishment of transatlantic commerce in the early sixteenth century. He draws attention to Quijano's distinction between colonialism and the continuing 'coloniality of power forced on non-European cultures that have remained silenced, hidden and absent' (Mignolo 2008, 240). This leads to Mignolo's (2008, 247) definition of decolonisation as 'to produce, transform, and disseminate knowledge that is not dependent on the epistemology of North Atlantic modernity.'

In a much-cited essay, Eve Tuck and K. Wayne Yang (2012) point out that decolonisation is not a metaphor, but an existential matter of land restitution for the indigenous inhabitants of settler colonies, such as those of North America, Australia and New Zealand. Consequently, Stephen Legg (2017, 347) suggests that we 'think not of "decolonising" (unacquiring colonies), despite how clearly useful it has been to many scholars and activists, but of "decolonialism" (challenging the practices that made colonies and which sustain colonial durabilities).' That is, decolonialising is about upending learned but deeply embedded thought patterns that posit 'Western civilisation' as superior and more advanced, and thus the most appropriate epistemic frame through which to view every other world culture. This critique cannot come from within, but must stand outside the coloniality of power in order to retrieve erased and absent knowledge. Mignolo (2008, 256) does not advocate cultural relativism, however, but rather what he calls 'diversality,' or a network of knowledge systems. As he noted in a piece co-authored during a visiting scholarship at City University of Hong Kong, 'different colonial experiences have resulted in **diverse** (post) colonial situations and decolonial options' (Lee, Liang and Mignolo 2015, 187; emphasis in original).

Decolonialising scholarship encompasses a variety of approaches beyond the MCD movement to which Quijano and Mignolo belong. These range from Dipesh Chakrabarty's *Provincialising Europe*, though Kuan-Hsing Chen's *Asia as Method*, to Prasenjit Duara's *Circulatory Histories* (Goh 2020). Though not explicitly decolonial, Heonik Kwon's *The Other Cold War* (2010) and Tim Harper's history of *Underground Asia* (2020) arguably also present decolonial perspectives, in that they decentre the narrative from the hegemonic Superpowers and imperial metropole, respectively. Decolonialising should be attuned to how nationalism, not least Southeast Asian nationalism, has replicated colonial modes of racialising its citizens according to a hierarchy of belonging, such as when Southeast Asian seafaring communities around Malaysia, Indonesia, Sabah and the southern Philippines are 'tabulated into grids' (Tagliacozzo 2009, 111), or ethnic minorities like the Cham are essentialised as timeless and folkloric (Taylor 2008, 16).

Cynthia Chou (2006, 128) has shown how Singapore and Indonesia aim to sedentarise and classify the sea-dwelling Orang Suku Laut according to a mainstream ethnic category, such as Malay, within their respective nation-state systems. Similarly, 'Vietnamese anticolonial nationalism itself mirrors colonial modes of racial differentiation in the abjection of the nation's racial other' (Nguyễn-võ 2018, 331) with regard to the Cham and Vietnam's other ethnic minorities. It is not alone in Southeast Asia. For instance, colonialism and Bamar nationalism together have helped fuel ethnic separatism in Myanmar (Cockett 2015, xii). Elsewhere, Stefan Ehrentraut (2011, 799) has underlined 'the vulnerability of those who reside inside Cambodia but outside the conceptual Cambodian nation.' The same 'non-belonging' extends to Muslim Thai brides moving to Malaysia to be with their husbands and Malay Muslims residing in Thailand without ever being able to access 'true Thainess' in the eyes of the law (McCargo 2011). Conversely, Sumit Mandal (2014, 818) documents how some Malays are challenging Malaysia's dominant ethnonationalist *Bumiputera* narrative by (re)discovering their Arab heritage, thereby undermining notions of Malay purity that are 'politically correct but historically flawed' (Ahmad 2014, 24).

To take yet another example, Thomas Mullaney (2021, online) has argued that the People's Republic of China's initial strategy was 'to recognise ethnic diversity into irrelevance [...] to preempt threats of local nationalism,' until the policy of 'celebration and neutralisation' was overtaken by the pressures of social inequality and ethnic scapegoating. In other words, decolonialising involves holding both colonialism and nationalism to account for oppression (Nguyễn-võ 2018, 333). There are moments of solidarity between oppressed peoples; what unites them within a decolonialising project is that in dismantling hierarchies of knowledge and power, 'epistemic justice leads to social justice' (Serrano-Muñoz 2021, 7). And yet, the incommensurability of their struggles lies in the distinctiveness of each nationalist project, its (anti-)colonial context and the erasures inherent in the creation of the imagined community (Anderson 1991).

Gavin Walker and Naoki Sakai (2019, 3; emphasis in original) argue that predefining areas like Southeast Asia as objects of study serves to reinscribe the Western gaze and the hierarchies of knowledge that gave rise to area studies in the first place; 'the integrity of this unity does not derive from the needs and demands of the population inhabiting the area but rather from the strategic conditions of those who catalogue data and produce knowledge about it *at a distance*.' That is, they explicitly link area studies as an interdisciplinary academic field to Eurocentric 'othering' and colonial control. In this context, distance refers not to physical presence but rather to an intellectual separation between specialist and indigenous knowledge, thereby cementing the supposed superiority of 'expert' approaches. It is precisely such theoretical and methodological presumptions that decolonial scholars seek to question, not only in terms of spatiality but also temporality.

The historian Fernand Braudel, a member of the French *Annales* school of thought, used the concept of *longue durée* in his magisterial work *The Mediterranean and the Mediterranean world in the Age of Philip II* (1995, 23), defining it as 'the slow unfolding of structural realities.' In an even wider-ranging history of Pacific peoples, Patrick Vinton Kirch (2002, 3) later took up Braudel's 'elegant metaphor of history as a ceaseless progression of waves of different amplitude [...] the longest of these the *longue durée*.' At the same time, nationalist ideologues and some ethno-symbolist scholars advocate for the *longue durée* of the nation, seeking to establish its antiquity and continuity so as to shore up its legitimacy. References to waves and the sea's materiality can also be used to evoke a form of oceanic thinking, one that disrupts the chronological spacetime of modernity and – by extension – nationality, thereby offering a way of thinking through decoloniality.

There is indeed a tendency for authors to reach for maritime images in countering myths of national exceptionalism and national spacetime narratives of bounded territoriality and chronological longevity (Sutherland 2020). For example, Vilashini Cooppan (2019, 396–7) evokes 'the forward lines and coming-back-round curves, the creeping links and perforating breaks, the eddies and the swells, the liquid peaks and the valleys in the very shape' of what she calls oceanic spacetime, as opposed to 'Eurochronology' or the calendrical time that structures 'imagined communities' (Anderson 1991). In turn, oceanic spacetime holds the promise of other ways of thinking and being, extending not only but also to national identity, in contrast to the rigid 'grids of empire' and their traumatic legacy (Cooppan 2019,

397). Part familiar critique of the implacable, onward march of progress, part imaginative engagement with the materiality of the sea, Cooppan's oceanic spacetime echoes human geographers' efforts to theorise wet ontologies and the so-called Hypersea (Steinberg and Peters 2015; Peters and Steinberg 2019), which can be used to destabilise static understandings of national identity and belonging.

In the East Asian context, coloniality, modernity and nationalism have been presented as a mutually reinforcing conceptual triad (Barlow 2012, 625). Decolonial scholars would argue that the construction of national identity and the consolidation of nation-state borders are central facets of the coloniality of being and mind, which refer to how people identify and how they relate to others in the world, respectively. Linked to this, Tessa Morris-Suzuki (2019, 213) notes that area studies approaches to regions like East and Southeast Asia chime with Braudel's understanding of civilisations as rooted in the natural conditions surrounding them. In other words, this forms the spatial counterpoint to the temporal conception of *longue durée*, both of which are reflected in national spacetime (Sutherland 2020). Appropriately enough, then, the decolonial scholars Ramón Grosfoguel, Boaventura de Sousa Santos and Aníbal Quijano chose a special issue of the Fernand Braudel Centre's Review to lay out their critique. Both Grosfoguel (2006) and de Sousa Santos (2006) began by situating their critical analysis of coloniality in the context of a *longue durée* lasting several centuries. For her part, Morris-Suzuki proposed 'liquid area studies,' focusing on human interaction and exchange through trade and travel, as a means of escaping Braudel's rather static determinism. Using maritime links as an example of how people located at great distance could be connected much more strongly and meaningfully than close neighbours living in segregated zones, Morris-Suzuki (2019, 214) draws attention to the protean nature of cultural areas, thereby subverting nationalist narratives of bounded continuity and longevity.

Morris-Suzuki notes that migration can be posited as the norm rather than the exception and be constitutive of identity, which is also a key insight of migration studies (Anderson 2019; see also Sutherland 2020). This flips a fundamental element of both nationalist ideology and the nation-state system on its head and therefore chimes with a decolonialising approach. For example, Nicolas Weber (2019, 80) draws attention to how 'exile is an intrinsic and indefectible part of the Cam [Cham] identity,' thereby refocusing analysis away from the Vietnamese conquest of the Champa empire and towards its lasting legacy for the Cham diaspora across Southeast Asia and the rest of the world. To take another example, Yến Lê Espiritu (2017, 483) invokes Braudel's concept of *longue durée* to describe the palimpsest of Pacific colonial history. Yet in her analyses of the Vietnam War, she chooses to refocus her studies on the refugees who passed through the United States's Pacific territories and their inhabitants, rather than on a conflict between nation-states. Indigenous and refugee perspectives 'constitute a radical otherness that cannot be easily dismissed or assimilated to national belonging paradigms,' thereby subverting nationalist narratives (Espiritu 2017, 485). In other words, Espiritu depicts a *way* of living 'Other-wise' (Shilliam 2015, 8), as opposed to the essentialised Other that serves to constitute the limits of the nation.

Espiritu's analysis spanning Southeast Asia and the Pacific provides a further illustration of how creating connections and conversations between artificially delineated 'areas,' themselves products of colonial knowledge, is a form of decolonialising practice that emphasises relationality and fluidity over bounded identities (see also Nguyễn-võ 2018; Serrano-Muñoz 2021). As Edward Said (1999, online) once put it; 'I occasionally experience myself as a cluster of flowing currents. I prefer this to the idea of a solid self, the identity to which so many attach so much significance.' In the same way, oceanic thinking can offer a way of decentring and disrupting national and colonial categories. Reframing national spacetime in this way allows for the recovery of temporal 'hauntings' such as those discussed in Pheng Cheah's *Spectral Nationality* (2003) and Heonik Kwon's *Ghosts of War in Vietnam* (2008), among others (Sutherland 2016a). Positing mobility rather than native rootedness as the norm upends received notions legitimising 'national history' and the nation-state construct. Deterritorialising the concept of the nation also enables 'methodological denationalism' (Anderson 2019). The next section focuses on how decolonial methodologies can help retrieve other ways of experiencing the nation.

Decolonial methodologies

Decolonial thinking is one theoretical lens which can be used to disrupt national imaginaries, whether that be ideologically or methodologically, though it is by no means the only possible approach to this in relation to Southeast Asia or elsewhere (Duncan 2004; Tran and Reid 2006; Horstmann and Wadley 2006; Tagliacozzo et al. 2015). For example, Keith Taylor (1998) not only stepped outside methodological nationalism but also avoided considering Southeast Asia as an 'area.' His *History of the Vietnamese* (Taylor 2013, 3) rejects nationalist historiography, eschewing anachronistic projections of contemporary Vietnamese nationhood back through time and 'an internal logic of development leading to the present.' Instead, Taylor adopted what he called elsewhere a 'surface orientation,' which opens up the 'possibility of imagining Asian surfaces as something other than parts of nations' (Taylor 1998, 973). Taylor explicitly placed the fluidity of human experience at the centre of his approach and rejected the teleological inevitability of the nationalist project. After all, the borders of Indochina and Vietnam remained fluid in the minds of the Vietnamese (erstwhile Indochinese) Communist Party for much of the 1930s and 1940s (Goscha 1995). Similarly, Tim Harper (2020) traces the intersecting stories of early twentieth-century Asian revolutionaries on a global scale, charting the ebb and flow of their anti-imperialist activities and chronicling the astonishing variety and vitality of their relationships and ideas. Despite this bewildering array of potential ideological avenues, nationalism eventually prevailed with its own system of marginalising racial and other minorities in the name of national unity, but this was by no means a foregone conclusion.

Though a rather unwieldy term in itself, Bridget Anderson's (2019, 41) concept of methodological denationalism builds on the scholarship of transnationalism, mobilities, borders and decolonialism in challenging, not assuming 'difference between state differentiated categories.' As Anderson's survey of the literature across several social sciences demonstrates, it is defined in opposition to taking the nation-state for granted as a category of analysis and projecting it back through calendrical time, the same principle on which nationalist ideology itself is predicated (Anderson 1991; Sutherland 2016b). Dipesh Chakrabarty (2000, 153) notes how Rabindranath Tagore distinguished between two forms of nationalism, one historicist and one poetic, that was 'outside of historical time' (see also Chatterjee 2005; Sutherland 2020). Similarly, Meera Ashar examines how both Tagore and M.K. Gandhi were hostile to the idea of the nation as a concept derived from a European historical imaginary. Applied to an Asian society, Tagore believed that this understanding of nationhood was '*not the outcome of its own living*' (cited in Ashar 2015, 256; emphasis in original).

Echoes of a decolonial 'ethos of living other-wise' (Shilliam 2015: 8) resonate down the decades. This does not mean to be 'Othered' in relation to the imperial centre, or the wholesale adoption of nationalist principles as a counterweight to the nationalism of the colonial powers. Rather, it recalls Gandhi and Tagore's critique of nationalism in 'refuse(ing) the colonial conceit that European knowledge traditions hold supreme interpretive authority over the varied cosmologies and cultures of humanity' (Shilliam, 2015: 8). Tim Harper shows that nationalism was but one current of anti-colonial thought among a maelstrom of ideas, also highlighting silences and erasures. For example, he uses Singapore's early twentieth-century coroner's reports to draw attention to the anonymous human flotsam struck down by misery, murder or causes unknown; 'a sombre, almost silent counterpoint to the colony's self-mythology of migrant opportunity, free enterprise and benevolent government' (Harper 2020, 68). While imperial agents' reactions to the anti-imperialists' tactics form part of Harper's account, they neither shape nor drive the narrative. This is arguably a decolonialising approach, insofar as it neither frames its analysis from the imperial centre nor uses methodological nationalism, but rather seeks to capture some of the fluidity and mobility of resistance movements on their own terms.

Moving from the humanities to the social sciences, Meera Sabaratnam's critique of International Relations as a discipline centred on an imagined Western subject offers a number of practical decolonising methodologies premised on critical dialogue. These are designed to reframe received ideas 'which naturalise forms of historic inequality between communities and people' (Sabaratnam 2011, 784). They include demonstrating enduring hierarchies between formerly colonised and colonising powers as part of 'a deeper challenge to the colonial system of thinking' (Sabaratnam 2011, 787). This serves to restore agency and make space for alternative perspectives by countering foundational myths of European civilisation's exceptionalism and superiority over other civilisations, which are part and parcel of Europe's history of development. Related to this is a critique of binary thinking, epitomised in the dichotomy between the civilised and 'savage'. This was central to justifying imperialism and *The White Man's burden* (Kipling, 1899), and arguably the developmentalist paradigm. Sabaratnam argues instead for a focus on the connections and relationships between civilisations, and the insights they have to offer, without assuming Europe to be a central reference point. Making space for alternative views 'that are not simply imitations of secular nationalism' (Sabaratnam 2011, 792) embeds the study of nationalism in a more dialogic, holistic context, and can open up entirely different ways of conceiving and organising political relations.

Decolonial methodologies are also attuned to the fact that field research can be actively harmful to its 'subjects' in reproducing hierarchies of knowledge and power if the researcher is assumed to be an outside 'expert' looking in; the 'ways in which scientific research is implicated in the worst excesses of colonialism remains a powerful remembered history for many of the world's colonized peoples' (Smith 2021, 1). Academics trained in the Anglo-American tradition find themselves trying to undo the oppositional, binary modes of thinking and debating they may have internalised, and which have clear antecedents in the colonial project (Singh 2018, 9), in favour of more flexible, conversational approaches. Contrary to 'extractive' data-gathering methods that subordinate the subject to the researcher's 'will to know,' such as giving an interview, these privilege the quality of relationships with research participants over answering research questions, and position participants as the primary audience rather than relying on entrenched academic hierarchies for legitimation (Bhattacharya 2019, 197). To delimit, 'discover' and explain according to disciplinary frameworks is to dominate a subject, and so relinquishing a claim to authoritative academic expertise also means ceding control over it (Singh 2018, 18). Indeed, as one of the '10 Ds' of decolonising, Ndlovu-Gatsheni (2021, 884) lists 'dedisciplining.' This also extends to language; writing in vernacular languages is another key strategy for *Decolonizing the Mind* (Ngugi Wa 1986).

Decolonising curricula, knowledge systems and institutional structures is all about subverting developmentalist thinking predicated on linear chronology and some sort of path of moral and civilisational perfectability. With regard to nationalism studies, Ashar (2015, 262) questions whether Asian anti-colonial nationalists necessarily accepted the developmentalist premise of progress and perfectability when they took up this cause, or rather saw it first and foremost as a means to end oppression. Certainly, neither can be assumed. Likewise, any decolonialised political enquiry into contemporary nationalist movements must be mindful of the legacies of empire (in colonising and colonised countries alike) and avoid falling into the trap of methodological nationalism (Sutherland 2016b). Similarly, 'comparative politics needs to critically assess its commitment to the state as the (endogenous) unit of comparison' (Shilliam 2021, 118). The next section turns to how this work is being undertaken, starting with the Western universities that did so much to entrench the modernity/coloniality paradigm in the first place.

Decolonial pedagogy

Walter Mignolo (2013, 4) states unequivocally that 'there is no modernity without coloniality.' Furthermore, there is no coloniality without racialised hierarchies of power, the legacies of which continue to play out across institutions and disciplines today. Asian studies are no exception (Palat 2000). Decolonialising practice is deeply personal and self-reflective in that it challenges the Western-centric canon on which much academic knowledge is built and from which many scholars derive their claim to expertise. This can be profoundly destabilising, as erasures come to light and glaring gaps in the coverage of education systems suffused with colonial assumptions and intellectual arrogance are laid bare. Decolonialised thinking entails initiating real dialogue between different worldviews and dismantling and rebalancing racialised hierarchies of knowledge, as reflected in university curricula and colonially inflected notions of which parts of the world are worthy of study. It seeks to avoid reinscribing the trauma of colonial ascendancy, or *Unthinking Mastery* (Singh 2018).

As Syed Farid Alatas (2015, 192) observes, decolonialising the social sciences in general requires regarding non-Europeans not as objects of study but as 'sources of sociological ideas and theories' in their own right. For example, a chapter in his co-authored textbook *Sociological Theory beyond the Canon* (Alatas and Sinha 2017) introduces the renowned Filipino author and nationalist Jose Rizal as a theoretician too, reading his novels as sociological critiques of colonialism's material and intellectual manifestations. The textbook sets out to correct Eurocentric and androcentric biases in teaching sociology by placing the works of Marx, Durkheim and Weber in the context of their erasures of non-Western contributions to the field and Orientalist assumptions. It provides a corrective to this by also covering the fourteenth-century C.E. philosopher and social theorist Ibn Khaldun, the nineteenth-century social reformer Florence Nightingale and the twentieth-century religious scholar Said Nursi, among an international range of thinkers.

Alatas and Sinha (2017, 2) present their work as 'a new form of legitimating the classics, by revealing their timeless qualities, notwithstanding their various conceptual, methodological and ideological limitations.' The authors are careful to note that Eurocentrism is not limited to Western scholars and Western scholars are not necessarily Eurocentric. They aim to prepare students to be critical of 'intellectual imperialism,' wary of applying theories based on European experience to other parts of the world, and aware of ongoing academic dependency on the West as the higher education sector's global powerhouse, which continues to dominate access to resources for teaching, technology and research (Alatas 2015, 196, 199). As such, *Sociological Theory beyond the Canon* could be a useful introductory primer for undergraduate study of Southeast Asian nationalism.

As a counterpoint to this approach, Beng-Lan Goh draws on the work of Prasenjit Duara and Kuan-Hsing Chen to transcend colonially inflected, developmentalist and nationalist framings of Asian politics and society in favour of interregional social scientific theory and methods. Drawing on East, South and Southeast Asian 'historical circulations and cultural imaginaries' (Goh 2020, 102–103), this is a decolonialising project that challenges universalising claims and identifies alternative resources for bringing about social renewal in Asian interdependence. As a basis for the comparative study of Southeast Asian nationalisms, it sets itself apart from area studies, understood as the application of 'Western concepts to Asian material, or demonstrating complete and authoritative knowledge about a place' (Niranjana cited in Goh 2020, 105), instead situating its critique from within an explicitly inter-Asian intellectual tradition. It seeks to transcend binary logics, de-emphasise Euro-America as a source of knowledge and compare different Asian cultural manifestations alongside colonialism and nationalism as key influences on contemporary (Southeast) Asia, all of which chime with decolonialising work.

Embedding the study of Southeast Asian nationalisms in this conceptual framework complements and complicates comparative analyses by bringing in additional interregional perspectives. Methodologically and pedagogically, this entails combining 'multiple regional elements within a knowledge category aimed at building critical alliances to expand one's limited frame of reference' (Goh 2020, 107). So, at the same time as distancing itself from nationalist framings as part of a decolonialising move, this approach can potentially shed new light on Southeast Asian nationalism as an object of study. As previously noted, interpreting events through Asian cosmologies has both an ethical and an analytical dimension, in that developing new normative models and imaginaries focuses on different Asian paradigms of time and space that co-exist with capitalist modernity (see Kwon 2010; Cheah 2003; Chatterjee 2005).

Anglo-American higher education's traditional emphasis on critical enquiry cannot deflect charges of hypocrisy unless it turns that critical enquiry on itself. All this because the legacy of colonialism continues to shape the life experiences of students and staff through what they experience and learn there, depending on the hierarchies of race, class, gender, (dis)ability and other characteristics mediating that experience. As Lowe (2015, 7) puts it:

> colonial divisions of humanity—settler seizure and native removal, slavery and racial dispossession, and racialized expropriations of many kinds— are imbricated processes, not sequential events; they are ongoing and continuous in our contemporary moment, not temporally distinct nor as yet concluded.

Resistance within the academy to decolonialising knowledge and institutions on the grounds of freedom of speech is conservative (with a small c). That is, it seeks to preserve the *status quo*. Even though hypocrisy could be seen as one of the defining features of colonial modernity, the widespread Black Lives Matter protests following George Floyd's killing in Minneapolis in May 2020 and the greater visibility of anti-Asian racism – both during the COVID pandemic and following assaults and murders of Asian-Americans in early 2021 – have highlighted these ongoing 'divisions of humanity' (Elfrink 2021; Guardian 2021). That President Joe Biden felt able to condemn these attacks as 'Un-American,' however, elides the fact that anti-Asian discrimination has a long pedigree in U.S. history stretching back to the 1850s, as embodied in the 1882 Chinese Exclusion Act (Yam 2021; McKeown 2008). On the contrary, nationalism is a vehicle for racism and inequality as much as emancipation and liberty, whether that be in the United States, Southeast Asia or anywhere else (Stovall 2021).

Conclusion

Decolonial scholars try to be attuned to the 'continual hum' (Ashar 2015, 263) of colonial categories in contemporary discourse, not least the legacy of Empire in nationalist politics. If the nation is indeed a product of modernity, then a decolonialising approach would take this to mean that it is also inextricably linked to coloniality. Exploring the interconnectedness of capitalist modernity, colonialism and nationalism in the Southeast Asian context is by no means new, and adopting a decolonial approach does not equate to searching for precolonial alternatives to nationhood and the nation-state (Ho, 2013). To do so would replicate the kind of essentialising analyses of non-Western identity and belonging that decoloniality seeks to escape. Ways of living 'Other-wise' (Shilliam 2015, 8) can also bring perspectives, insights and even cosmologies to the fore that continue to exist and evolve alongside capitalist modernity (Chatterjee 2005). Rather than 'anachronistic survivals, or as the representations of a more authentic and pristine past, they are to be seen as a cluster of responses to the onslaught of capitalism, their traditions and cultures representing *not* a transhistorical primordial "essence," but the symbolic resolutions of political struggles' (Palat 2000, 129; emphasis in original).

Decolonialising work can be profoundly unsettling for those educated in the Western canon, as it challenges the validity or completeness of received knowledge and thus the basis of academic expertise and professional identity. Decoloniality recognises colonialism's enduring legacy in the academy and seeks to subvert it by refusing Eurocentric frameworks of canonical knowledge and resisting belittling perspectives on the 'Other.' Methodologically, this entails looking beyond the nation or nation-state as a unit or category of analysis, perhaps by privileging the fluidity of oceanic thinking over the cartographic certainties of delineated borders and calendrical time. Any perceived homogeneity or putative continuity to national identity quickly breaks down as racialised and minoritised hierarchies of belonging are brought to the fore and nationalisms are examined for the colonial categories they reproduce, the voices they erase and the subordination they demand in the name of putative 'imagined community' solidarity. Instead, stepping outside the bounds of national spacetime can bring with it the freedom to conceptualise other forms of being together, whether in spirit or in person, and other ways of imagining identities that are better attuned to human co-existence. This also extends to validating different perspectives on the homelands that may be of symbolic importance to nationalists but have nonetheless been relentlessly exploited throughout capitalist modernity to the current point of exhaustion and overheating.

References

Ahmad, A. T. 2014. *Museums, History and Culture in Malaysia*, National University of Singapore Press; Singapore.
Alatas, S. F. 2015. 'Doing Sociology in South East Asia,' *Cultural Dynamics* 27 (2): 191–202.
Alatas, S. F. and Sinha, V. 2017. *Sociological Theory beyond the Canon*, Palgrave Macmillan; London.
Anderson, B. 1991. *Imagined Communities*, London; Verso.
Anderson, B. 2019. 'New Directions in Migration Studies: Towards Methodological De-Nationalism,' *Comparative Migration Studies* 7 (1): 36–49.
Ashar, M. 2015. 'Decolonizing What? Categories, Concepts and the Enduring "Not Yet",' *Cultural Dynamics* 27 (2): 253–265.
Back, L. and Sinha, S. 2012. 'New Hierarchies of Belonging,' *European Journal of Cultural Studies* 15 (2): 139–154.
Barlow, T. 2012. 'Debates over Colonial Modernity in East Asia and another Alternative,' *Cultural Studies* 26 (5): 617–644.

Bhattacharya, K. 2019. '(Un)Settling Imagined Lands: A Par/Des(i) Approach to De/Colonizing Methodologies,' in *The Oxford Handbook of Methods for Public Scholarship*, edited by Leavy, P., 175–208, Oxford University Press; Oxford.
Braudel, F. 1995. *The Mediterranean and the Mediterranean World in the Age of Philip II, Volume 1*, University of California Press; Berkeley, LA and London.
Chakrabarty, D. 2000. *Provincializing Europe*, Princeton University Press; Princeton, NJ.
Chatterjee, P. 2005. 'The Nation in Heterogeneous Time,' *Futures* 37: 925–942.
Cheah, P. 2003. *Spectral Nationality*, Columbia University Press; New York.
Chou, C. 2006. 'Borders and Multiple Realities: The Orang Suku Laut of Riau, Indonesia,' in *Centering the margin: Agency and narrative in Southeast Asian borderlands*, edited by A. Horstmann and R. Wadley. Oxford: Berghahn.
Cockett, R. 2015. *Blood, Dreams and Gold: The Changing Face of Burma*, Yale University Press; New Haven and London.
Cooppan, V. 2019. 'Time-Maps: A Field Guide to the Decolonial Imaginary,' *Critical Times* 2 (3): 396–415.
De Sousa Santos, B. 2006. 'Between Prospero and Caliban: Colonialism, Postcolonialism, and Interidentity,' *Review (Fernand Braudel Center)* 29 (2): 143–166.
Duncan, C., ed. 2004. *Civilizing the Margins: Southeast Asian Government Policies for the Development of Minorities*, Cornell University Press; Ithaca, NY and London.
Ehrentraut, S. 2011. 'Perpetually Temporary: Citizenship and Ethnic Vietnamese in Cambodia,' *Ethnic and Racial Studies* 35 (4): 779–798.
Elfrink, T. 2021. 'New York Man Charged with Hate Crime in Asian American Attack that Bystanders Watched without Helping,' *The Washington Post*, 31 March, https://www.washingtonpost.com/nation/2021/03/30/asian-american-attack-newyork-condo/, accessed 19 April 2021.
Espiritu, Y. L. 2017. 'Critical Refugee Studies and Native Pacific Studies: A Transpacific Critique,' *American Quarterly* 69 (3): 483–490.
Goh, B.-L. 2020. '"Inter-Asia as Method" and Radical Politics,' in *The Oxford Handbook of Comparative Political Theory*, edited by Jenco, L., Idris, M. and Thomas, M, Oxford University Press; Oxford.
Gopal, P. 2021. 'On Decolonisation and the University,' *Textual Practice*, 35 (6): 873–899.
Goscha, C. 1995. *Vietnam or Indochina? Contesting Concepts of Space in Vietnamese Nationalism 1887–1954*, Nordic Institute of Asian Studies; Copenhagen.
Grosfoguel, R. 2006. 'World-Systems Analysis in the Context of Transmodernity, Border Thinking, and Global Coloniality,' *Review (Fernand Braudel Center)* 29 (2): 167–187.
Guardian. 2021. 'Authorities Name All Eight Victims in Atlanta Spa Shootings,' 20 March, https://www.theguardian.com/us-news/2021/mar/19/atlanta-spa-shootings-victims-named, accessed 19 April 2021.
Harper, T. 2020. *Underground Asia*, Allen Lane; Milton Keynes.
Ho, E. 2013. 'Foreigners and mediators in the constitution of Malay sovereignty', *Indonesia and the Malay World* 41 (120): 146–167.
Horstmann, A. and Wadley, R. 2006. *Centering the Margin: Agency and Narrative in Southeast Asian Borderlands*, Berghahn; New York.
Jazeel, T. 2017. 'Mainstreaming Geography's Decolonial Imperative,' *Transactions of the Institute of British Geographers* 42 (3), 334–337.
Kipling, R. 1899. 'The White Man's Burden,' http://www.kiplingsociety.co.uk/poems_burden.htm, accessed 14 July 2021.
Kwon, H. 2008. *Ghosts of War in Vietnam*, Cambridge University Press; Cambridge.
Kwon, H. 2010. *The Other Cold War*, Columbia University Press; New York.
Lee, V., Liang, H. and Mignolo, W. 2015. 'Globality and the Asian Century,' *Cultural Dynamics* 27 (2): 185–190.
Legg, S. 2017. 'Decolonialism,' *Transactions of the Institute of British Geographers* 42: 345–348.
Lowe, L. 2015. *The Intimacies of Four Continents*, Duke University Press; Durham, NC.
Mandal, S. 2014. 'Arabs in the Urban Social Landscapes of Malaysia: Historical Connections and Belonging,' *Citizenship Studies* 18 (8), 807–822.
McCargo, D. 2011. 'Informal Citizens: Graduated Citizenship in Southern Thailand,' *Ethnic and Racial Studies* 35 (4): 833–849.
McKeown, A. 2008. *Melancholy Order: Asian Migration and the Globalisation of Borders*, University of Columbia Press; New York and Chichester.

Mignolo, W. 2008. 'The Geopolitics of Knowledge and the Colonial Difference,' in *Coloniality at Large: Latin America and the Postcolonial Debate*, edited by Jáuregui, C., Dussel, D. and Moraña, M., 225–258, Duke University Press; Durham.

Mignolo, W. 2013. 'Imperial/Colonial Metamorphosis: A Decolonial Narrative, from the Ottoman Sultanate and Spanish Empire to the US and the EU,' in *The Oxford Handbook of Postcolonial Studies*, edited by Huggan, G., 1–21, Oxford University Press; Oxford.

Morris-Suzuki, T. 2019. 'Liquid Area Studies: Northeast Asia in Motion as Viewed from Mount Geumgang,' *Positions: Asia Critique* 27 (1): 209–239.

Mullaney, T. 2021. 'How China Went from Celebrating Ethnic Diversity to Suppressing It', *The Guardian*, 10 June, https://www.theguardian.com/commentisfree/2021/jun/10/china-celebrating-diversity-suppressing-xinjiang-communist-party, accessed 28 June 2021.

Ndlovu-Gatsheni, S. J. 2021. 'The Cognitive Empire, Politics of Knowledge and African Intellectual Productions: Reflections on Struggles for Epistemic Freedom and Resurgence of Decolonisation in the Twenty-First Century,' *Third World* Quarterly 42 (5): 882–901.

Ngugi Wa, T. 1986. *Decolonizing the Mind: The Politics of Language in African Literature*. Oxford: James Currey.

Nguyễn-võ, T. H. 2018. 'Articulated Sorrows: Intercolonial Imaginings and the National Singular,' *Canadian Review of American Studies* 48 (3): 327–351.

Palat, R. A. 2000. 'Beyond Orientalism: Decolonizing Asian Studies,' *Development and Society* 29 (2): 105–135.

Peters, K. and Steinberg, P. 2019. 'The Ocean in Excess: Towards a *More-than-Wet* Ontology,' *Dialogues in Human Geography* 9 (3): 293–307.

Quijano, A. 2008. 'Coloniality of Power, Eurocentrism, and Social Classification,' in *Coloniality at Large: Latin America and the Postcolonial Debate*, edited by Jáuregui, C., Dussel, D. and Moraña, M., 181–224, Duke University Press; Durham.

Roach, J. 1996. *Cities of the Dead: Circum-Atlantic Performance*, Columbia University Press; New York.

Sabaratnam, M. 2011. 'IR in Dialogue. But Can We Change the Subjects? A Typology of Decolonising Strategies for the Study of World Politics,' *Millennium* 39 (3): 781–803.

Said, E. 1999. 'On Writing a Memoir,' *London Review of Books*, 21 (9), https://www.lrb.co.uk/the-paper/v21/n09/edward-said/on-writing-a-memoir, accessed 9 June 2021.

Saini, R. and Begum. 2020. 'Demarcation and Definition: Explicating the Meaning and Scope of "Decolonisation" in the Social and Political Sciences,' *The Political Quarterly* 91 (1): 217–221.

Serrano-Muñoz, J. 2021. 'Decolonial Theory in East Asia? Outlining a Shared Paradigm of Epistemologies of the South,' *Revista Crítica de Ciências Sociais* 124: 5–26.

Shilliam, R. 2015. *The Black Pacific*, Bloomsbury; London.

Shilliam, R. 2021. *Decolonizing Politics*, Polity; Cambridge and Medford, MA.

Singh, J. 2018. *Unthinking Mastery*, Duke University Press; Durham and London.

Smith, L. T. 2021. *Decolonizing Methodologies*, 3rd Edition. Zed; London.

Steinberg, P. and Peters, K. 2015. 'Wet Ontologies, Fluid Spaces: Giving Depth to Volume through Oceanic Thinking', *Environment and Planning D* 33 (2): 247–264.

Stovall, T. 2021. *White Freedom*, Princeton University Press; Princeton.

Sutherland, C. 2016a. 'Inviting Essential Outsiders in: Imagining a Cosmopolitan Nation,' *European Review of History* 23 (5/6), 880–896.

Sutherland, C. 2016b. 'A Post-modern Mandala? Moving beyond Methodological Nationalism' *HumaNetten* 37: 88–106 (online).

Sutherland, C. 2020. 'Stop the Clock! Taking the Nation Out of Linear Time and Bounded Space,' *Time and Society* 29 (3): 727–749.

Tagliacozzo, E. 2009. 'Navigating Communities: Race, Place, and Travel in the History of Maritime Southeast Asia,' *Asian Ethnicity* 10 (2): 97–120.

Tagliacozzo, E., Siu, H. and Perdue, P. 2015. *Asia inside out: Connected places*, Harvard University Press, Cambridge, MA, and London.

Taylor, K. 1998. 'Surface Orientations in Vietnam: Beyond Histories of Nation and Region,' in *Journal of Asian Studies* 57 (4): 949–978.

Taylor, K. 2013. *History of the Vietnamese*, Cambridge University Press; Cambridge.

Taylor, P. 2008. 'Minorities at Large: New Approaches to Minority Ethnicity in Vietnam,' *Journal of Vietnamese* Studies 3 (3): 3–43.

Tran, N. T. and Reid, A., eds. 2006. *Vietnam: Borderless Histories*, University of Wisconsin Press, Madison.

Tuck, E. and Yang, K. W. 2012. 'Decolonization Is Not a Metaphor,' *Decolonization: Indigeneity, Education & Society* 1 (1): 1–40., K. W. 2013. *A History of the Vietnamese*, Cambridge University Press; Cambridge.

Vinton Kirch, P. 2002. *On the Road of the Winds: An Archaeological History of the Pacific Islands before European Contact*, University of California Press; Berkeley, Los Angeles and London.

Walker, G. and Sakai, N. 2019. 'The End of Area,' *Positions: Asia Critique* 27 (1): 1–30.

Weber, N. 2019. '"Moving in an Endless Single Line": Memory, Exile and History in Cam Diaspora's Narrative Poems', *Sojourn: Journal of Social Issues in Southeast Asia* 34 (1): 76–109.

Yam, K. 2021. 'Biden Says Hate Crimes against Asian Americans are 'un-American' and That They "Must Stop",' *NBC News*, 12 March, https://www.nbcnews.com/news/asian-america/biden-calls-hate-crimes-against-asian-americans-wrong-it-s-n1260753, accessed 19 April 2021.

3
AN ALTERNATIVE ORIGIN OF NATIONALISM IN THE EAST

The emergence of political subjectivity under the non-Western-centric world order

Atsuko Ichijo

Introduction

The conventional account of the origin of nationalism is that it was born in the West and spread to the rest of the world as the West became dominant. This view has been most clearly stated by Elie Kedourie in his celebrated *Nationalism* originally published in 1960:

> Nationalism is a doctrine invented in Europe at the beginning of the nineteenth century. It pretends to supply a criterion for the determination of the unit of population proper to enjoy a government exclusively its own, for the legitimate exercise of power in the state, and for the right organization of a society of states. Briefly, the doctrine holds that humanity is naturally divided into nations, that nations are known by certain characteristics which can be ascertained, and that only legitimate type of government is national self-government. ... These ideas have become firmly naturalized in the political rhetoric of the West which has been taken over for the use of the whole world. ...
>
> *(Kedourie 1993: 1)*

This neatly highlights a couple of key aspects of the conventional understanding of nationalism: (a) that it is the most powerful normative principle globally ordering the political world and (b) that it is embedded in an international system (no nationalism without a society of states). More fundamentally, the quotation clearly identifies the Western centricity found in the majority of contemporary political and social theories as Shmuel Eisenstadt (2000, 2001, 2005a, 2005b) has repeatedly pointed out. In other words, nationalism as the fundamental principle of ordering the political world is seen to have been born in the West and to have spread to the rest of the world to become the global norm. This is because the fundamental expectation in contemporary social sciences is that the rest of the world would eventually converge with the Western model, perhaps because of diffusion, or perhaps because of imposition of ideas and processes through colonialism and imperialism (Ichijo 2013).

The current chapter aims to critically examine consequences of the in-built Western centricity in social and political theories on our understanding of nationalism, in particular, regarding its origin and spread. This chapter contends that the conventional, Western-centric account of nationalism is not as accurate as it could be, since it neglects the role of agency and subjectivity in the non-Western parts of the world by adopting a diffusionist view of the spread of nationalism. The diffusionist view holds that nationalism was born in the West and spread to the rest of the world because of the rise of the West. According to this view, non-Western parts of the world are a passive recipient of ideas and technologies from the West, and they learn to emulate what the West has gone through to join the modern, advanced world. This chapter challenges the validity of the diffusionist account, and therefore the assumption of Western centricity behind it, by investigating the case of East Asia where we can observe phenomena which bear striking qualitative similarity to nationalism but which emerged before East Asia was incorporated into the Westphalian order in the nineteenth century. If we can ascertain that these phenomena are indeed cases of nationalism, then the diffusionist account would be invalidated.

The problem: the assumption behind the diffusionist view

The Western centricity found in Kedourie's formulation of nationalism does not simply stem from the fact that his view is state-centric and articulated in an environment which was conditioned by the idea of Westphalian order. Benedict Anderson (1991), another giant in the study of nationalism, does not focus on the modern state. Rather, he examines worldviews and consciousness and sees nationalism as cultural artefacts. In terms of the origin of nationalism, he argues that nationalism as a political model was first developed in the Americas, not in Europe. However, nationalism emerged in the Americas under European colonial rule and its emergence was conditioned by what was taking place in Europe: the collapse of holy and dynastic cosmology ushering a new conception of time, the rise of print capitalism which helped elevate the vernacular as the main means of imagining the nation, and the rise of the modern, administrative state which sent Creole officials to far-flung corners of their territories to help establish the shape of their shared community. Nationalism might have first emerged in the Americas, but it emerged within the context conditioned by social change that was taking place in Europe.

The claim that nationalism originated in Europe in itself is not problematic, as it could be just a statement of fact. However, in conventional views of nationalism, the European origin of nationalism thesis is, more often than not, coupled with the diffusionist account about its spread – that nationalism born in Europe spread to the rest of the world where such an idea was unknown. Again, stating that the idea of nationalism was not known in non-Western parts of the world in itself could just be a statement of fact. What is problematic is what usually follows: non-Western societies which had not been aware of nationalism simply absorbed and adopted it when the West brought it to them because they did not have agency to do otherwise under the emerging Western hegemony.

The problem here can be described from a different angle in reference to Anderson's work. As it is widely known, Anderson is puzzled with the appeal of nationalism which, in his view, cannot be explained by either Marxism or liberalism and proposes to treat 'nationality', 'nation-ness' or 'nationalism' as 'cultural artefacts of a certain kind' (Anderson 1991: 4). He then proceeds to suggest:

> The creating of these artefacts towards the end of the eighteenth century was the spontaneous distillation of a complex 'crossing' of discrete historical forces; but ... once created, they become 'modular', capable of being transplanted, with varying degrees of

self-consciousness, to a great variety of social terrains, to merge and be merged with a correspondingly wide variety of political and ideological constellation.

(Anderson 1991: 4)

Anderson's idea of the modularity of the nations and nationalism is not fully developed but he makes a further mention to it in *Imagined Communities*:

… (in the age of nationalism that followed the American and French revolutions) the 'nation' proved an invention on which it was impossible to secure a patent. It became available for pirating by widely different, and sometimes unexpected hands. ….

(Anderson 1991: 67)

… twentieth-century nationalisms have, as I have been arguing, a profoundly modular character. They can, and do, draw on more than a century and a half of human existence and three earlier models of nationalism. ….

(Anderson 1991: 135)

What emerges from these excerpts is nationalism in the form of 'neatly packaged artefacts, and abstract object, being transplanted to flourish in different socio-historical contexts' (Ichijo 2019: 5). In this view, the agency of people of non-Western societies is not denied; after all, they 'pirate' the cultural artefact called nationalism drawing from various histories. However, the format of imagining a nation has already been fixed. Partha Chatterjee has famously objected: 'If nationalisms in the rest of the world have to choose their imagined community from certain "modular" forms already made available to them by Europe and the Americas, what do they have left to imagine?' (Chatterjee 1993: 5). In Anderson's account of the origin and spread of nationalism, people of non-Western society are not necessarily seen as a passive recipient of Western-derived ideas and they are seen as an active participant in adapting the modularised idea into their own context. Nonetheless, the extent to which they can exercise their agency and subjectivity is limited as what to imagine is already prescribed by the West.

The problem with the diffusionist account, as the current chapter sees it, is that it is deeply Western-centric. The Western centricity the current chapter is concerned with can be found in various dimensions. For instance, Kedourie's account has that nationalism as one of the most important principles of organising politics in the modern world was born in the West and it became the global norm along with the rise of the West. While the rise of the West and imposition of Western standards across the world can be seen as historical facts, Western hegemony has been justified in reference to the idea of progress and being modern. This suggests a worldview that non-Western parts of the world were generally inferior to the West, and perhaps more benignly, a general assumption in social sciences that societies across the world would eventually converge with the Western model. This type of Western centricity that Eisenstadt (2000) as well as many postcolonial theorists, including Chatterjee (1993), have been challenging is also found in the study of nationalism. In Anderson's account, Western centricity is found in the idea of modular nationalism in that the way a nation is imagined has been articulated and fixed by those in the colonial Americas and Europe, and people of non-Western societies can only exercise their agency and subjectivity in transplanting the idea and making it their own. In other words, there is only one way of conceptualising the nation which was formed by those in the West and there is no possibility of a different way of thinking about the nation.

Having identified the problem, this chapter moves on to offer an alternative account of the origin and spread of nationalism drawing from East Asian experiences. This chapter first provides a conceptual framework to investigate nations and nationalism in a less Western-centric manner and investigates three case studies: Song China, the Great East Asian War and Chosŏn Korea, and the rise of Kokugaku in Tokugawa Japan.

The conceptual framework: what is the nation and nationalism?

Before embarking on a search for an alternative account of the origin and spread of nationalism, we first need to refine our conceptual framework. As this chapter has been arguing, the conventional theories of nations and nationalism are Western-centric, which means the concepts used in them are naturally limited by socio-historical conditions peculiar to the West. Applying these concepts directly to non-Western parts of the world would inevitably produce findings that are in line with the conventional views.

In this context, this chapter problematises the largely structural nature of conventional definitions of nations and nationalism. As it has been discussed elsewhere, conventional, structure-oriented explanations of nations and nationalism are by definition conditioned by how Western societies have developed (Ichijo 2013). If nationalism as 'a political principle, which holds that the political and the national units should be congruent' (Gellner 1983: 1) is a societal response to shift to an industrial society, logically speaking, without industrialisation there is no nationalism. The Marxist take on nationalism that it is a by-product of the emergence of bourgeois society which is an inevitable phase in the development of history (Hobsbawm 1990) can be seen as an attempt to understand history from a universalist perspective, but it still draws from Western experience. When nationalism is understood to be a function or property of the modern state as in the case of Anthony Giddens (1985) or John Breuilly (1982), the modern state in question is typically understood to be embedded in the Westphalian order, a uniquely Western environment which has now globally prevailed. In exploring the origin of nationalism in non-Western parts of the world, relying on a structure-oriented conceptual framework is not useful.

Taking a cue from Eisenstadt's work on multiple modernities, this chapter proposes to overcome this problem by adopting an agency-focused framework. Briefly, Eisenstadt argues that in order to counter Western centricity and its teleological tendency that are built in conventional theories of modernity, one needs to shift focus to the agency of human beings. Modernity, according to Eisenstadt (2000: 2), should be seen as 'a story of continual constitution and reconstitution of the multiplicity of cultural programs'. He then advocates focusing on 'some distinct shifts in the conception of human agency' in order to understand modernity in a way that is liberated from Western centricity by paying attention to an 'intensive reflexivity' and 'an emphasis on the autonomy of man' (Eisenstadt 2000; 2001). Shifting the focus of our attention from structurally defined characteristics to human agency, or more plainly, workings of human mind, or different categories of human thought (Grosby 2019) has the potential to make social science enquiries more universalistic as the working of human mind is reasonably assumed to be universal.

Applying Eisenstadt's suggestion to the study of nations and nationalism would mean adopting a more culture-oriented approach. Notwithstanding the problems with the assumption behind modular nationalism, Anderson's (1991) approach to nations and nationalism is useful as it is based on individuals' consciousness and behaviour (Smith 1998: 131–142): it is about how people make sense of the world when old orders collapsed, and when new technology makes it possible to share thoughts with a larger number of people. In a similar vein,

Liah Greenfeld, who sees nationalism not as a product of modernity but as a constituent part of modernity, suggests that nationalism is a style of consciousness, and argues that nationalism 'locates the source of individual identity within a "people", which is seen as the bearer of sovereignty, the central object of loyalty, and the basis of collective solidarity' (1992: 3). In the case of Greenfeld's work, reference to sovereignty needs careful consideration when applied to the non-Western context, but the basic idea that nationalism is about arranging individuals' identity in reference to a collectivity is less constraint by specific socio-historical conditions, which, in turn, is a more useful approach to the examination of nations and nationalism in non-Western parts of the world.

As discussed in more detail elsewhere, this chapter proposes to understand nationalism as 'societal self-understanding with the nation as its basic unit' (Ichijo 2013: 39), a form of human self-reflexivity. In other words, nationalism is a particular style of workings of human mind trying to address some existential questions, including where they are from, what they are doing and where they are going in reference to the nation.[1]

Armed with this understanding, we will investigate three non-Western cases to test the validity of the diffusionist account of nationalism.

The case of the Song dynasty (960–1279)

The Song dynasty which arose after several decades of civil strife in China following the collapse of the Tang dynasty in 907 attracted the attention of historians, in particular, those of Meiji Japan. Among them, Naitō Konan (1866–1934) is well-known for his view that the the Tang-Song transition marks the transition from the medieval to modern periods in China (Naitō 2015). While Naitō cannot be categorised as in the anti-Western camp in establishing the discipline of history in Japan, his suggestion certainly represents a rejection of a blanket imposition of periodisation of history based on European experiences (Fogel 1984). In this regard, Naitō's work has affinity with the idea of multiple modernities. While Naitō did not focus on the idea of 'China', or Chinese nationalism for that matter, he saw in Song China the foundation of Chinese Republicanism that emerged in the early twentieth century which he supported (Fogel 1984). In Naitō's mind, there was an important rupture between the Tang dynasty and the following Five Dynasties and Ten Kingdoms Period on the one hand and Song China on the other: the collapse of aristocratic dominance coupled with the rise of dictatorial rule and the rise of popular class in politics, economics and culture (Naitō 2015). From the current chapter's perspective, Naitō appears to argue that the liberation of individuals, albeit quite a limited one from the twenty-first-century perspective, in many spheres of life took place in Song China. The liberation of individuals, or commoners, involves an increase in the degree of agency they could exercise, which, in turn, could lead to the emergence of a different societal/collective self-understanding.

Other scholars have directly engaged with the issue of national consciousness and nationalism in the Song dynasty. Their work is, interestingly, embedded in Song China's relations with its neighbours – international relations, in other words. This is interesting as conventional accounts of nations and nationalism are clearly embedded in the framework based on the Peace of Westphalia (1686). Nationalism does not exist without the international, and if the articulation of who the Chinese were was carried out in reference to Song China's international relations, what was articulated bears qualitative similarity to the conventional view of nationalism. This points to another possible weakness in the conventional diffusionist account which is premised on the spread and acceptance of the Westphalian convention in order for any society to have nationalism.

Broadly following Anderson's 'imagined community' thesis, Nicolas Tackett (2017) argues that Chinese national consciousness first emerged among the *shidafu* (literati) class in the Northern Song era (960–1127). He substantiates his claim using numerous surviving court chronicles, collected works of individuals, 'embassy travelogues, annotated maps and geographic gazetteers' (Tackett 2017: 23) – a consequence of the rapid expansion of woodblock printing, an equivalent to the rise of print capitalism, in the Song era – as well as poems and archaeological findings. According to him, there are a number of factors which facilitated the formation of national consciousness in China in the eleventh century. First of all, there was profound social change – the decline of old aristocracy which led to the rise of new literati class that was relatively meritocratic because it was governed by the centralised civil servant exam, a factor which has been pointed out by Naitō. In Tackett's view, this represents something similar to the collapse of the old cosmic order in Europe. As touched upon above, there was also the rapid expansion of woodblock printing which made more or less simultaneous sharing of knowledge including imagination possible.

Not very much in line with Anderson's argument, but in agreement with other scholars as seen below, Tackett also thinks that fundamental change in Song China's understanding of so-called 'international relations' was important. He argues the fact that the relationship with its north-eastern neighbour, Liao (907–1125), was one of those between equals which represents a fundamental shift in political elite's conception of China from a universalistic/civilisational empire to a homogeneous, ethno-cultural polity, which he likens to a modern nation-state. Furthermore, during the course of the Northern Song era, the Chinese state, which had been already centralising and bureaucratic in the Weberian sense, enhanced its surveillance and record keeping capabilities, thus strengthening the 'modern' nature of the polity.

Tackett's arguments are backed up by surviving documents. That *shidafu* officials sent to Liao on fairly regular diplomatic missions (performing what Anderson said Creole officials did in various corners of the Americas) felt solidarity with the Han Chinese officials of Liao, their counterpart, suggests that there was an imagined community built on writings – learning of classics as well as contemporary writings. The officials who were sent to Liao would produce reports fixing the border between Northern Song and Liao at various levels while enhancing the idea of ethno-cultural 'Han' people rather than cosmic 'Hua' people. They naturalised the landscape, in particular, Yan Mountains as the border between Song and Liao, thus transforming the idea of unbounded sovereignty ('All under Heaven') in the Tang era to a more bounded understanding of sovereignty. At the same time, they became aware that the boundary of the state (Northern Song) did not coincide with that of the nation (Han people), introducing what appears similar to irredentism.

As touched above, Tackett pays particular attention to Northern Song's interaction with Liao. In Tackett's view, the strengthening of national consciousness among Northern Song *shidafu* was facilitated by their interaction with Liao which was consciously showing off their Khitan ethnicity at state occasions such as receiving embassies form Song and maintained a multicultural policy to deal with their diverse population. The boundary between us (the 'Han' people) and them (the Khitans) did not emerge in a vacuum but was socially produced and maintained in the context of an inter-state relationship which developed in a context unique to East Asia.

More forcibly than Tackett, Ge Zhaguang (2017) argues that the emergence of 'China' consciousness in Song China represents an origin of nationalist ideology and places his argument directly in the discussion of Song China's relationship with its neighbours, i.e. its international relations. Agreeing with Tackett, Ge takes the view that by the establishment of the Song dynasty, the fundamental idea of 'All under Heaven' putting China at the centre of the world as the only civilised entity had been hollowed out. At this point, China found itself 'among equals' rather than at the apex of hierarchy as Morris Rossabi and his collaborators have argued (Rossabi 1983). The Song elite, grasping the fundamental shift in their relationship with their neighbours from the classical times, reassessed the situation and redefined what used to be understood as barbarians in their surroundings as enemy states with which it had to form more clearly defined relationships: the borders had to be defined unambiguously and they needed to be maintained; the residency of foreigners needed to be more strictly controlled; the movement of knowledge in the form of personnel and books had to be banned in order to reduce the potential national security risk. Ge (2017) identifies the emergence of 'China' consciousness in poetry, contemporary commentaries and scholarly writing: more and more efforts were made to distinguish what was Chinese from what was barbarian in clothing, rites and other aspects of life and to conserve what was deemed to be Chinese amid deepening concern about permeation of foreign/barbarian influence in China. With mounting concern over the basis of legitimacy of China, which was not based on blood but culture, which, in turn, was seen to be eroded by foreign influence, scholar-officials were engaged in serious discussions about the orthodoxy of China. What Ge's work describes is an intense collective self-reflection, perhaps limited to the literary class, about who the Chinese were mainly in response to geopolitical change.

These works suggest that nationalism as a societal self-understanding placing the nation at the centre had emerged in Song China before the Sino-centric world had a full collision with the Westphalian order in the nineteenth century. In short, the case of Song China serves as a piece of evidence that the diffusionist theory is not accurate about the origin and spread of nationalism.

The Great East Asian War/the Imjin War (1592–1598)

The Great East Asian War (1592–1598), otherwise known as the Imjin War or the Japanese Invasion of Korea, was a violent power struggle involving Chosŏn Korea, Japan and Ming China spanning over six years and mobilising in excess of 300,000 combatants. As the contemporary War of the Spanish Armada, by far the largest military conflict in Europe in the sixteenth century, involved about 50,000 soldiers, it was evidently the largest war in the sixteenth-century world (Swope 2020; Haboush 2016). While the conflict is relatively unknown to Western scholarship, it had remained a pivotal moment in East Asian peoples' memory until World War II.

As the conflict is relatively unknown, a brief description of the event is necessary. The Great East Asian War started in 1592 with the invasion of Chosŏn Korea by Japanese troops sent by Toyotomi Hideyoshi, the war lord who was about to pacify and unify Japan torn by a century of civil war. Hideyoshi's true motive is still debated (Swope 2020) but it is conventionally held that intent on conquering Ming China, Hideyoshi lobbied Chosŏn Korea to support his ambition to invade China originally, then India later, in the 1580s. Chosŏn Korea declined to join Hideyoshi's enterprise and was invaded by Hideyoshi's forces while distracted by domestic division. The invading forces advanced fast since the Korean side was ill prepared and within two weeks of the landing, they took Seoul, and the court fled to north, to Kaeson initially, then on to Pyongyang and then to Ûiju. In the meantime, the Ming counterforce arrived, and the Japanese forces were driven back to Seoul. The first phase of the war lasted till 1596 followed by a doomed peace negotiation, and the second phase started in 1597. The invasion was eventually called off by the council of elders who took over the running of Japan when Hideyoshi passed away in 1598. Korea suffered a great deal from the war with 'perhaps 20 percent of its populace dead and its agriculture and infrastructure devastated. Many Korean buildings and treasures were destroyed or looted. Tens of thousands of Koreans were carried back to Japan as slaves' (Swope 2020: 113). The Sō family of Tsushima acted as a go-between to negotiate postwar settlement from 1599, and the relationship among Chosŏn Korea, Japan and Ming China was restored by 1608.

While many international relations scholars focus on the fact that the Great East Asia War, the greatest military conflict in the sixteenth century, globally speaking, has not attracted much attention in the study of how world orders have emerged and developed, JaHyun Kim Haboush (2016) is interested in another side of the War: as a catalyst for the emergence of nationalism in Korea. Challenging the conventional view of Korean nationalism that it was imported from the West together with colonialism, Haboush puts forward a thesis that the discourse of the Korean nation first arose during the Great East Asian War among leaders of civilian voluntary army ('the Righteous Army') that engaged with guerrilla warfare in the absence of the Korean Royal Army, and who needed 'a vision of the land and the people for which the volunteers should fight and risk their lives' (Haboush 2016: 3). This vision of the Korean nation was enriched by other ideas during the Great East Asian War and continued to develop during the Manchus' attacks on Chosŏn Korea in 1627 and 1636–1637. Haboush argues that the idea of Korea 'as a sacred and inviolable land of Koreans and Korean culture' (2016: 39) emerged in earnest in the face of fast advancing enemy, the invading Japanese forces, and its emergence and development was facilitated by four factors: the deep trauma caused by wars, a certain type of local, civilian elite, scholar-officials, trained in the Confucian tradition, the dual linguistic spaces based on classical Chinese and vernacular Korean and the postwar availability of commemorative channels (2016: 14–21). According to Haboush, both the Great East Asian War and the Manchu invasion left the Koreans deeply traumatised since in the sixteenth century, Korea was intent on transforming itself to a 'small China', a society marked and distinguished by civil culture, and the Japanese invasion was not anticipated. When Manchus ran over the country, being trampled by other barbarians left Koreans deeply humiliated. The deep and acute collective trauma facilitated the sharpening of a sense of being Koreans and what Korea was. Koreans during and after the Great East Asian War were therefore engaged with self-reflection at the societal level well before the arrival of Western colonialism. Furthermore, in the Great East Asian War, because the Royal Army melted away, it was left to the local, civilian elites who were not trained in military matters and who had no obligation to engage with military conflict, to volunteer to defend the country and to extol others to join. The fact that civilian officials were compelled to take up arms added the impetus to the articulation of who the Koreans were and what Korea was. The local scholar-officials mobilised their classical training to spell out the moral obligation for all to fight against the advancing enemy making sense of the world in reference to their civilisational background. While these elites were trained in classical Chinese, they issued their appeals in vernacular Korean, which enabled them to co-opt oral traditions in extolling ordinary Koreans to join the Righteous Army (Haboush 2016: 73–92). In Andersonian terms, the Koreans were invited to join the enterprise of imagining who the Koreans should be and what the country should be in the vernacular drawing from their Confucian background. In the postwar period, the experiences of wars were repeatedly visited collectively to sharpen the contour of the nation that had been defined. Thus, the idea of the Korean nation defined by ethnicity, culture and civilisation was firmly established, according to Haboush, by the mid-seventeenth century.

Haboush's analysis which draws from letters, appeals and literary work from the time of the Great East Asian War convincingly shows that some Koreans were engaged with collective reflection on who they were producing societal understanding of themselves. They were imagining themselves as an entity which they have to defend with their own life, a point Benedict Anderson was puzzled about when he started to look into the power of nationalism. Admittedly, it is difficult to claim that this was a mass phenomenon but those who were engaged with thinking about the Korean nation and producing explanation as to who they were, where they came from and where they were going did not have to wait for the model of imagination originally created in the Americas; they did not have to be told what to imagine. The case of the Great East Asian War and the emergence of Korean nationalism show, in other words, that the diffusionist account of the spread of nationalism is not fully convincing.

The rise of Kokugaku in Tokugawa Japan in the eighteenth century

In the study of nationalism, the case of Japanese nationalism is often seen as an epiphenomenon of the country's modernisation/Westernisation and it is seen as a case of diffusion of nationalism *par excellence* (Breuilly 1982: 206–210). The standard narrative would be faced with fast-expanding Western hegemony in the nineteenth century, lower-ranking samurais of peripheral domains under Tokugawa Shogunate (those whose upward social mobility was heavily curtailed by the 'establishment', the equivalent to the frustrated intellectuals in Kedourie's account) decided that the only way forward was to stage a coup so as to open the country and to catch up with the West. Nationalism was one of the ideas and practices Japan imported from the West in order to avoid colonisation by them. For those who engineered regime change from old-fashioned Tokugawa Shogunate to a modern, centralised Meiji state, nationalism was about developing the country by introducing the fruits of industrialisation, strengthening the military so as to defend their border and nurturing loyalty to the idea of Japan represented by the semi-divine emperor. Nationalisation of the Japanese was pursued through standard measures, including compulsory primary education and conscription. The Japanese case thus described is in line with most of modernist views of nationalism: it is a function of industrialisation (Gellner 1983), capitalist development (Hobsbawm 1990) or the modern state-building (Giddens 1985; Breuilly 1982).

One feature of the Japanese case is that it is often seen as 'exceptional'. As seen in John Breuilly's assessment, compared to the Chinese and Turkish cases, 'the Japanese case can be regarded as a case of successful reform nationalism' (Breuilly 1982: 218), which makes the Japanese case stand out. However, from the current chapter's perspective, what is relevant is that it is seen as a case of diffusion, that the Japanese learned of nationalism as part and parcel of modernisation, and they adopted the formula developed by the West to imagine who they were and acted on the fruits of collective reflection.

However, the current chapter contends that the conventional modernist account of nationalism of Japan is not fully accurate. From this chapter's perspective that nationalism is societal self-understanding centred on the nation, the nationalism of Japan can be traced back to earlier periods. It has been argued that the idea of Japan as a divine country, certainly a form of collective imagination about the country, could be traced back to the two failed attempts to invade Japan by Mongols in the late thirteenth century (Satō 2006); the current chapter focuses on the rise of Kokugaku (国学), a nativist school of thought (or National Learning) which arose in eighteenth-century Japan to demonstrate that a collective self-understanding of who the Japanese were and what Japan was arose before the arrival of the Western model of nationalism as Tokugawa Japan was largely isolated from the rest of the world. While scholars of Edo Period, including Kokugaku scholars, were aware of the existence of the West and other parts of the world, the transmission of idea was heavily censored by the Tokugawa government and what Kokugaku scholars engaged in terms of thinking about who the Japanese were and what Japan was could not have been exogenously induced.

Among the specialists, there is still no consensus as to what Kokugaku is. Some including Harry Harootunian (1988) and Peter Nosco (1990) regard Kokugaku as a form of nativism, a strand of thought to support and protect the native people's interest over and against outsiders', in particular that of immigrants. Thomas McNally (2016) rejects this claim and argues that Kokugaku should be seen as a form of exceptionalism, a pattern of thought to see a group of people particularly distinct. From the perspective of sociology of knowledge, Randal Collins (1998) sees a clear parallel between Kokugaku and Romanticism, which he understands as a reaction against the rise of neo-Confucianism in Tokugawa Japan in the case of former and the Enlightenment in the case of latter. Collins is therefore arguing that qualitatively similar development in thought took place in Japan and Western Europe at around the same time without interaction between the two. One of the problems about establishing the identity of Kokugaku stems from the fact that Motoori Norinaga (1730–1801), widely seen as having established Kokugaku as a distinct school of thought, never used the term 'Kokugaku' but described what he was engaged with as 'the study of the old way' (Ichijo 2020). For the purpose of this chapter, Kokugaku is understood to be a school of learning that emerged in eighteenth-century Japan which focuses on studying Japanese classical texts such as *Man'yōshū*, an anthology of poetry compiled in the late eighth century and *Kojiki*, 'Record of Ancient Matters', compiled in 712 instead of Buddhist sutras and Chinese classical text in search of authentic Japan. Pioneers of Kokugaku include Keichū (1640–1701), a Buddhist monk who specialised in the study of Japanese poems and who was commissioned by Tokugawa Mitsukuni (1628–1701), one of the most powerful and prominent retainers and a blood relation of the contemporary shogun, to prepare a thorough commentary on *Man'yōshū*; Kada no Azumamaro (1669–1736), who articulated the contour of what is now known as Kokugaku in opposition to Confucianism and Buddhism; Kamo no Mabuchi (1697–1769), who studied *Man'yōshū* to develop sharp critique of neo-Confucianism and advocated the superiority of the ancient Japanese language as 'natural'; and Motoori Norinaga, who commented on *Kojiki* and the *Tale of Genji* to suggest that *mono no aware* (the movement of the heart as it feels) as the essence of Japanese literature.

The rise of Kokugaku is relevant to this chapter because it was a radical challenge to the prevailing intellectual climate of Tokugawa Japan where a universalistic school of neo-Confucianism called Cheng-Zhu school was the officially designated orthodoxy. In contrast to Cheng-Zhu school which was concerned with the exploration of universal principles and their manifestation in life and politics, Kokugaku was focused on pursuing the question of 'what is Japan?'. Kokugaku scholars were occupied with uncovering the uncontaminated 'essence' of Japaneseness through the study of ancient Japanese texts because they were seen to have been produced before foreign influences, such as Buddhism and Confucianism, were firmly established in Japan. Upon close reading of these presumably pristine texts, they argued that

> Japan in antiquity was a country where perfection in every respect of life – human behaviour, governance, order – was realised naturally through the "true heart". Human beings were simply good, and life was effortlessly harmonious because the ancient ways of Japan, the expression of the true hart, prevailed.
>
> *(Ichijo 2020: 273)*

And, according to them, this is the state where the Japanese and Japan should aspire to go back to in order to overcome a wide range of social and political crises they were experiencing, as these problems were induced by the occlusion of the true heart due to foreign influences.

Eighteenth-century Kokugaku was indeed an intensive, collective self-reflection about who the Japanese were in response to the perceived social and political problems. The explanation and diagnosis of the problems were given in reference to the newly discovered authentic Japaneseness and the course of action to overcome those problems was proposed. This is clearly an exercise of human agency to produce societal/collective understanding of the world, and it is explained in reference to the essence of the Japanese nation. In the eighteenth century, Japan's contact with the West was severely limited and Kokugaku scholars were engaged with an intense, collective self-reflection without following a formula formed by the Creole officials in the Americas. This suggests that the diffusionist account of the spread of nationalism does not accurately describe what some of eighteenth-century Japanese experienced.

Conclusion

Inspired by the critique of in-built Western centricity in social and political theories articulated in the theory of multiple modernities, this chapter questions the conventional diffusionist account of the spread of nationalism which holds that nationalism was invented in the West and exported to the rest of the world as the West's hegemony spread all over the globe. This chapter's main objection is directed to the implication of such Western centricity: that people in non-Western parts of the world did not have political subjectivity and that they became 'modern' because they were taught to be so by the Westerners. According to the conventional theories of nationalism, albeit in an exaggerated format, there was no nationalism in East Asia before the nineteenth century when the Westphalian order finally prevailed over the Sino-centric order which had been in place for centuries: East Asians under the Sino-centric order were not true subjects of history because they did not know how to be so.

Having calibrated the definition of nationalism as 'societal self-understanding with the nation as its basic unit' (Ichijo 2013: 39), a form of human self-reflexivity, this chapter investigated three cases in which there are written records of intensive, collective self-reflection that took place before the full collision with the West: the Song dynasty of China, the Great East Asian War and the rise of Korean nationalism and the rise of Kokugaku in Tokugawa Japan. In each of the cases, there is evidence that efforts to produce a societal self-understanding in the face of various crises were made suggesting that the act of collectively imagining a nation took place before the nineteenth century. Granted none of the cases can be described as mass phenomena, and if the criteria to ascertain the existence of nationalism are that it is a mass phenomenon, none of the cases would fit the bill. However, as the aim of this chapter is to challenge the in-built Western centricity in conventional theories of nationalism, this critique would not be applicable.

When the focus of analysis is shifted to human agency or the workings of human mind, something that should be more universal than the experience of industrialisation or the collapse of Judeo-Christian cosmology, for instance, we can observe cases of nationalism in the non-Western context well before the nineteenth century. Nationalism, in other words, is not a Western invention which the rest of the world had to learn. Acknowledging this is yet another small step towards shaking off prevailing Western centricity in contemporary social and political theories.

Note

1 The affinity between nationalism thus defined and religion has been discussed in depth by Steven Grosby (see, for instance, 2019).

References

Anderson, Benedict. 1991. *The Imagined Communities: Reflections on the Origin and Spread of Nationalism (revised edition)*. London: Verso.
Breuilly, John. 1982. *Nationalism and the State*. Manchester: Manchester University Press.
Chatterjee, Partha. 1993. *The Nation and Its Fragments: Colonial and Postcolonial Histories*. Princeton: Princeton University Press.
Collins, Randal. 1998. *The Sociology of Philosophies: A Global Theory of Intellectual Change*. Cambridge, MA: Harvard University Press.
Eisenstadt, Shmuel. 2000. "Multiple Modernities." *Daedalus* 129: 1–29.
Eisenstadt, Shmuel. 2001. "The Civilisational Dimension of Modernity: Modernity as a Distinct Civilisation." *International Sociology* 16 (3): 320–340.
Eisenstadt, Shmuel. 2005a. "Modernity in Socio-Historical Perspective." In *Comparing Modernities: Pluralism versus Homogeneity*, edited by Eliezer Ben-Rafael and Yitzhak Sternberg, 31–56. Leiden: Brill.
Eisenstadt, Shmuel. 2005b. "Collective Identity and the Constructive and Destructive Forces of Modernity." In *Comparing Modernities: Pluralism versus Homogeneity*, edited by Eliezer Ben-Rafael and Yitzhak Sternberg, 635–653. Leiden: Brill.
Fogel, Joshua. 1984. *Politics and Sinology: The Case of Naitō Konan (1866–1934)*. Cambridge, MA: Council on East Asian Studies, Harvard University.
Ge, Zhaguang. 2017. *Here in 'China' I Dwell: Reconstructing Historical Discourses of China for Our Time*. Leiden: Brill.
Gellner, Ernest. 1983. *Nations and Nationalism*. Oxford: Blackwell.
Greenfeld, Liah. 1992. *Nationalism: Five Roads to Modernity*. Cambridge, MA: Harvard University Press.
Grosby, Steven. 2019. "Once again, nationality and religion." *Genealogy* 3 (3): 48. doi:10.3390/genealogy3030048.
Haboush, JaHyun Kim. 2016. *The Great East Asian War and the Birth of the Korean Nation*. New York: Columbia University Press.
Harootunian, Harry. 1988. *Things Seen and Unseen: Discourse and Ideology in Tokugawa Nativism*. Chicago, IL: Chicago University Press.
Hobsbawm, Eric. 1990. *Nations and Nationalism since 1780: Programme, Myth, Reality*, Cambridge: Cambridge University Press.
Ichijo, Atsuko. 2013. *Nationalism and Multiple Modernities: Europe and Beyond*. London: Palgrave Macmillan.
Ichijo, Atsuko. 2019. "The Origin of Nationalism: A Review of Literature." *Studies on National Movements* 4: 1–9.
Ichijo, Atsuko. 2020. "Kokugaku and an Alternative Account of the Rise of Nationalism of Japan." *Nations and Nationalism* 26 (1): 263–282.
Kedourie, Elie. 1993. *Nationalism (fourth, expanded edition)*. Oxford: Blackwell.
Naitō, Konan. 2015. 中国近世史 (*The Early Modern History of China*). Tokyo: Iwanami Shoten.
Nosco, Peter. 1990. *Remembering Paradise: Nativism and Nostalgia in Eighteenth-Century Japan*. Cambridge, MA: Council on East Asian Studies, Harvard University.
Rossabi, Morris, ed. 1983. *China among Equals: The Middle Kingdom and Its Neighbors, 10th-14th Centuries*. Berkeley, CA: University of California Press.
Satō, Hiroo. 2006. 神国日本 (*The Divine Country, Japan*). Tokyo: Chikuma Shobo.
Smith, Anthony. 1998. *Nationalism and Modernism*. Abingdon: Routledge.
Swope, Kenneth. 2020. "Ming grand strategy during the Great East Asian War, 1592–1598." In *East Asia in the World: Twelve Events That Shaped the Modern International Order*, edited by Haggard, Stephan and Kang, David, 108–128. Cambridge: Cambridge University Press.
Tackett, Nicolas. 2017. *The Origins of the Chinese Nation: Song China and the Forging of an East Asian World Order*. Cambridge: Cambridge University Press.

4
THE CLASH OF EMPIRES, THE RISE OF NATIONALISM, AND THE VICISSITUDE OF PAN-ASIANISM IN EAST ASIA AND SOUTHEAST ASIA

Yongle Zhang

Introduction

In East and Southeast Asia, although proto-nationalist consciousness had existed since ancient times, nationalism, defined as the idea and pursuit of the integration of the political and cultural boundaries of a nation, is the product of modern times, arising from the collision between local peoples and Western colonialism as well as inter-imperial conflicts.

Since the nineteenth century, the theoretical paradigm of "from empire to nation-state" (Esherick et al. 2006) has deeply influenced the historical narrative of many East and Southeast Asian intellectuals. According to this narrative, industrialized Western countries were perceived as well-organized nation-states. Although empire as a loose form of political rule prevailed in many non-Western regions, the influence of European nation-states encouraged many nations controlled by empires in non-Western regions to develop self-consciousness leading to modern nationalism. However, this paradigm ignores the fact that the building of nation-states and empires was a synchronous process in the West from the fifteenth century. For example, Spain began to colonize the external world soon after Castile and Aragon formed a composite monarchy in the fifteenth century, while the Netherlands began to colonize Southeast Asia immediately after its independence from Spain in the late sixteenth century. The colonial empires tried to build a homogeneous citizenship in their metropolises, while using different laws to govern the subjects of their colonies.

It has been more than five centuries since European colonists first entered East and Southeast Asia. Historically, there had been a tributary system centered on China in East and Southeast Asia. In the tributary system, the Chinese emperor accepted tribute from the rulers of tributary polities as a symbol of loyalty, and usually sent more generous gifts in return. Since the gifts in return were a fiscal burden on China, the Chinese emperor often limited the number of tributary states and frequency of their tribute. This kind of gift exchange was itself also a form of trade and diplomacy (Takeshi 2008, 12–26). This political relationship also opened a space for trade between the different states. In addition to the tributary order centered on China, some stronger regional regimes, such as the Kingdom of Annam, the Kingdom of Siam, and Kingdom of Myanmar, also demanded tribute from weaker local rulers, thus forming a multi-layered tributary system. The Southeast Asian tributary system is often described as the "Mandala system" – regional political centers demanded loyalty from surrounding weaker rulers and often caused the vassals of other regional powers to shift allegiances. Lesser rulers might pay tribute to several greater regional powers simultaneously (Shaddick 2011), while rulers in different ranks of the regional hierarchy might also pay tribute directly to the Chinese emperor. In such a regional system, the political boundaries were usually flexible, and the courts of rulers were often ethnically diverse.

By the nineteenth century, European colonists had successfully established footholds in Southeast Asia and destroyed or subjugated some local regimes that had paid tribute to China, including Malacca, the Samboja Kingdom, Sumatra, and Brunei. However, they had not systematically reshaped the political order in the Indochinese Peninsula, let alone in East Asia. For example, the Dutch colony in Taiwan had been expelled by Ming loyalist Zheng Chenggong in the seventeenth century. In the nineteenth century, the industrial revolution greatly increased the military ascendancy of the Western colonial empires, accelerating the disintegration of the traditional regional order. On the eve of the First World War, only three major pre-colonial regimes maintained their independence in East and Southeast Asia – China, Japan, and Siam.

Two types of conflict between empires provided a focus for the growth of nationalism. The first was the conflict between the colonial maritime empires and the regional empires. In the nineteenth century, the colonial empires brought the Korea, Ryukyu, and Vietnam kingdoms into their spheres of influence by declaring them independent states through international treaty, thus cutting off their traditional political ties with China. As a new colonial empire, Japan imitated the Western powers and selectively used Western international law to undermine the tributary system. After being separated from the tributary system by the colonial empires, nationalists in Korea, Vietnam, and other countries not only rebelled against the colonists but also attempted to weaken their traditional political and cultural ties with China. As the center of the tributary system, China was thus reduced from an empire to a semi-colony.

The second was the conflict between the colonial empires themselves. After the Congress of Vienna (1814–1815), the system of "concert of powers" was adopted in Europe by the great powers to resolve their conflicts and prevent popular revolutions. This system was also used to settle conflicts in their colonies. Western colonial empires jointly maintained a hierarchical international order that regarded the Asian colonies and semi-colonies as either "semi-civilized" or "barbarous". The concert of powers greatly reduced conflicts between colonial empires in their colonies. However, from the mid-nineteenth century, the spread of nationalism was accelerating The First World War destroyed the concert of Europe, and the post-war Versailles-Washington system did not build a stable alternative. The conflicts between colonial empires became increasingly fierce, providing fertile ground for the development of nationalism. Japan's reaction to the Western powers inspired many nationalists across Asia. Many Asian leaders visited Japan where they learned of Western nationalism from Japanese sources and were inspired by the discourse of Pan-Asianism in their struggle against Western colonialism.

More importantly, the conflict between colonial empires created vulnerable points in the imperialist system that facilitated the rise of nationalist movements. In 1899, the Philippines took advantage of the war between Spain and the United States to establish a republic. Their resistance to the subsequent conquest by the United States encouraged nationalist passions in Asia. In 1905, Japan defeated Russia in the Russo-Japanese War, which led to the 1905 Russian Revolution. The Persian Constitutional Revolution began shortly afterward.

In 1908, the Young Turk Revolution began in the Ottoman Empire. In 1911, the republican/nationalist revolution broke out in China.

Lenin (1963) discussed the influence of Asian revolution in a series of works. In his *Imperialism, the Highest Stage of Capitalism*, written in 1916, Lenin expounded the idea of launching a revolution against the weakest link in the chain of imperialism. After the October Revolution, the Bolsheviks advocated national self-determination as a universal principle. In contrast, American President Wilson's support for national self-determination mainly applied to the European territory of the empires defeated in the First World War and ignored their colonies. The Communist International supported self-determination for all the oppressed nations of the East and communist parties in many countries were to play a key role in the struggle for national independence. Although the communist movement aimed to transcend nationalism, its anti-imperialist and anti-colonial aims exerted enormous influence on nation building and state building in Asia.

Traditional empires, colonial empires, and the communist movement: the regional conditions for the rise of nationalism

Modern European nationalism emerged in an inter-state system in which many states of the similar size and strength co-existed without a mutually recognized superior authority. In the nineteenth century, influenced by nationalism, dynastic rulers in Europe began to rebrand themselves as the representatives of the nation. Although the European powers recognized each other as equal nation-states, they were committed to jointly safeguarding the myth of the superiority of European civilization in the colonies. Only a few non-Western countries, such as China, the Ottoman Empire, Japan, and Persia, were recognized as semi-civilized countries, while other indigenous peoples were usually classified as barbarous or savage.

Nonetheless, there was a traditional regional order in pre-colonial East and Southeast Asia. In China, for more than 2,000 years, the historic convention was that once a ruler could firmly control the Central Plains, they would have the legitimacy to demand subordination from surrounding political rulers. Chinese emperors formed differing relations with these rulers according to differing geographical, political, and cultural distance. The boundless "all-under-heaven" (天下), characterized by a series of political concentric circles centered on the "son of heaven" (天子), was the scope of rule claimed by the emperor. There was no absolute internal/external distinction in this understanding of the political order. The emperor paid more attention to the rulers and regimes closer to the center and was indifferent to more remote regions as long as the tranquility of the empire was unaffected. The Qing emperors inherited this traditional spatial order and regarded themselves as the center of all-under-heaven. Even after the first Opium War, the Qing court still regarded the Western powers as barbarians who should pay respect to the Celestial Kingdom according to China's traditions.

After the second Opium War, the Qing government was forced to change its position. In 1858, the Treaty of Tianjin allowed foreign envoys to stay in Beijing. In 1861, the first official permanent diplomatic agency, the Office for the General Management of Affairs Concerning the Various Countries, was established and, in 1864, supported William Martin's translation and publication of Henry Wheaton's *Elements of International Law*. In treaties with other countries in the nineteenth century, the Qing government usually signed the name of the state as Zhong Guo (中国), Zhong Hua (中华), The Great Qing State (大清国), or The Great Qing Empire (大清帝国). To recognize China as only one state among equals was an important sign of the decline of the tributary system.

In the second half of the nineteenth century, Japan and the Western powers together accelerated the destruction of the tributary system. During the Meiji Restoration, Japan actively appropriated Western international law to force the Ryukyu Kingdom, which had paid tribute to both China and the Satsuma Domain of Edo Japan, to end its tributary relationship with China. Japanese officials argued that under international law, a state could not recognize two overlords at the same time. However, in the Balkans at that time, several political entities recognized both the Ottoman Empire and Russia as overlords at the same time, and international law did not dispute this practice (Carty and Nijman, 2018). Henry Wheaton's *Elements of International Law* also recorded this practice (Wheaton 1916; Kármán and Kunčević, 2013). Using this questionable interpretation of international law, Japan forced Ryukyu to stop paying tribute to China, then transferred Ryukyu affairs from the jurisdiction of the Ministry of Foreign Affairs to the Ministry of Internal Affairs, and finally annexed Ryukyu. In 1876, Japan signed the first unequal treaty with Korea, which recognized Korea as an independent state. The intention of Japan was to separate Korea from the tributary system as an isolated state without any protection from Beijing. To counterbalance Japan, the Qing diplomat Li Hongzhang allowed several Western powers to sign treaties with Korea. Nonetheless, after the First Sino-Japanese War (1894–1895), Japan established its dominance over the Korean kingdom and ultimately annexed Korea in 1910.

In the process of annexing Vietnam, France took a similar approach. Initially, in 1874, France signed a treaty with the Kingdom of Vietnam that recognized the King as an independent power subordinate to no other state. Then, in 1884, France declared Vietnam its protectorate. China recognized the new reality in the following year in a new Sino-French treaty. Vietnam was completely stripped out of the tributary system and became a French colony.

As part of the Russo-British "Great Game" in Central Asia, Britain tried to separate Tibet from China and establish a buffer zone between its colonies and Russia. Russia, in turn, regarded Mongolia as within its sphere of influence. Following the outbreak of the 1911 Revolution, Britain and Russia supported separatist movements in Tibet and Outer Mongolia, respectively, encouraging the rise of nationalism in these areas. Tibet eventually remained in China, while Outer Mongolia became independent in 1945 and was under the influence of the Soviet Union until the end of the Cold War.

In the second half of the nineteenth century, nationalism soared in Europe, with Italy and Germany becoming unified nation-states, and began to limit the concert of powers. Colonized peoples witnessed the rise of nationalism in the colonial metropolises and were encouraged to develop anti-imperialist and anti-colonial sentiments. For example, Chinese nationalists thinker Liang Qichao and Communist leader Li Dazhao had traveled and studied in Japan and Vietnamese Communist leader Hồ Chí Minh had studied in France.

The weakening of the colonial empires in inter-imperial conflicts provided favorable conditions for the rise of nationalism in their colonies. The First World War had broken the agreement between the great powers to jointly maintain the myth of the civilized states. Short of manpower, the colonial empires used troops raised from their colonies in Europe. This mobilization contributed to the spread of nationalism in the colonies. The war also highlighted the weakest link in the chain of imperialism when the Bolsheviks launched the October Revolution in Russia. After the October Revolution, Lenin announced the policy of national self-determination and supported the independence of a series of nationalities in Russia as well as the independence of oppressed nations in the colonial empires. To compete with the Bolsheviks, President Wilson announced his *Fourteen Points*, which included supporting the independence of various nations within the German, Austro-Hungarian,

Ottoman, and Russian Empires. After the First World War, several new nation-states emerged in Europe, which greatly encouraged the national independence movements in the colonies.

The First World War weakened the old European powers but strengthened Japan and the United States. After the Meiji Restoration, Japan continued to develop its colonial empire. In the process, it clashed with the Western empires and its Pan-Asianism gained increasing significance. Japanese Asianist thinkers argued that Asia, then colonized by the white race, had a shared destiny for the yellow race and that, as the first nation in Asia equal to the Western powers, Japan should lead the other Asian nations in resisting the white oppressors. For this reason, Japan encouraged nationalist movements in East and Southeast Asia.

Many Asian political elites had lived or traveled in Japan and were influenced by Japan's Asianism. For example, Vietnamese nationalist Phan Bội Châu visited in 1905 to seek Japan's support. He met Liang Qichao, Sun Yat-Sen, Zhang Taiyan, and other Chinese political elites in Japan. At the time, he called on Vietnamese intellectuals to study in Japan. In 1907, the Burmese nationalist Sayadaw U Ottama visited Japan. In China, the abolition of the imperial examination system in 1905 encouraged many from the Chinese elites to study in Japan in the interests of their own social mobility and they were influenced there by Japanese intellectual movements, including nationalism.

To weaken the Qing Dynasty and China, Japan supported China's anti-Manchu nationalism to a certain extent. For example, China's anti-Manchu revolutionary organization, the China Revolutionary Alliance, was supported by the Japanese *Kokuryū-kai* (Black Dragon Society), which aimed to colonize the Heilongjiang River Basin and Siberia. Consequently, Japan became an overseas base of the anti-Manchu revolution. In the process, anti-Manchu revolutionaries were also influenced by Japan's Pan-Asianism. During the invasion of China, Japan also encouraged Manchu and Mongolian nationalist forces to create pro-Japanese puppet regimes, including the puppet Manchukuo regime from 1932 to 1945, and the puppet regime in Inner Mongolia from 1933 to 1945. The Japanese need to dismember China stimulated academic research in Japan. Many Japanese scholars limited the idea of China to the so-called "China proper" and regarded Manchuria, Mongolia, Xinjiang, and Tibet as independent regions or at least as regions entitled to secession.

Japanese elites had long aspired to occupy Southeast Asia. In 1896, two Filipino nationalists, Jose A. Ramos and Doroteo Cortes, went to Japan to seek support. Umeya Shokichi, a Japanese in Hong Kong, supported Emilio Aguinaldo, leader of the Filipino independence movement. In 1899, when Aguinaldo asked for Japanese armed support, Shokichi contacted the Japanese army through Sun Yat-Sen who organized a shipment of weapons to the Philippines, but the ship sank in a storm. Konoe Atsumaro, a Japanese politician, founded the Oriental Youth Association, which supported Philippine independence. The association attracted many young people from across Asia. During the Second World War, the Filipino nationalist José Paciano Laurel chose to cooperate with Japan and was elected the president of the Second Republic of the Philippines in 1943.

The Japanese government initially collaborated with the French colonial authorities in Japanese-occupied Vietnam rather than support anti-French nationalist forces, with the exception of their long-term support for Caodaism. Later, after the removal of the French regime, Japan supported the emperor Vua Bảo Đại, who was unpopular among the people and was resisted by Vietnamese nationalist forces due to his pro-French record.

Similarly, Japan took advantage of some Burmese nationalists, such as Ba Maw, Aung San, and U Nu, to work against the British and declared Myanmar independent in 1943.

However, the Communist Party of Myanmar resisted Japan. Later in the war, Myanmar's political elites turned against Japan and signed the British-Myanmar treaty in 1947 to gain British recognition of its independence. Ibrahim HJ Yaacob, leader of the Malay Youth Association, who advocated for independence from Britain, also chose to cooperate with the Japanese. However, the Japanese colonial regime later dissolved the Malay Youth Association, and some members of the organization joined the resistance led by the Communist Party.

As the only major independent country in Southeast Asia, Thailand signed an alliance with Japan in 1941 and expanded its territory during the war. Thai opposition forces supported the Allies and the Thai government later shifted to the Allied side.

In 1942, Japan occupied Dutch Indonesia and released Indonesian nationalist leaders Sukarno from prison and Mohammad Hatta from exile. Both chose to cooperate with the Japanese. During its rule, Japan promoted Pan-Asianism in Indonesia and left weapons for Indonesian nationalists when withdrawing after the war, which made it difficult for the Dutch to reestablish control over the country.

In the early nineteenth century, the United States sold opium to China on a large scale. In 1844, the two countries signed the unequal Treaty of Wanghia. In the second half of the nineteenth century, the United States forced open Japan and Ryukyu with warships, seized the Philippines from Spain, and promoted the Open Door Policy in China. In the Russo-Japanese War, the United States supported Japan and encouraged it to follow an "Asian Monroe Doctrine" after the war to counterbalance the European powers in the region. The support of the United States encouraged Japan's ambition to invade China. After the First World War, the United States did not support the independence of the colonized peoples of Asia but by transferring German colonial rights and interests in the Shandong Province of China to Japan, it stimulated a strong nationalist movement in China.

After the Second World War, the United States did encourage national independence in many areas colonized by Japan. However, such support was always conditional on its own national interest. For example, the United States supported Indonesia's independence from the Dutch, Malaysia's independence from Britain, and allowed Filipino independence from its own control. But in Korea and Vietnam, where it saw the possibility of communists taking power, it fostered local pro-Western movements and sent troops to intervene directly. After the Second World War, the collective security system established by the United States in East and Southeast Asia in the name of anti-communism eroded the autonomy of its allies. The United States did not end colonialism; instead, it replaced traditional colonialism with a new type of informal empire in Asia that is still well and vigorous today.

Finally, it is worth mentioning that the Communist International also supported the national independence movements in the Western powers' Asian colonies. A series of communist parties were established and became major forces in national independence movements in the region. In China, the Comintern helped found the Communist Party of China (CCP) and reorganize the Kuomintang (the Nationalist Party), with the two parties uniting under the banner of anti-imperialism to jointly launch the Northern Expedition in 1926. The Communist Party of Korea, founded in 1925, was recognized and supported by the Communist International. The Comintern also led the founding of the Communist Party of Indochina. Many members of the party, including Ho Chi-Minh, had been active in China for a long time, and many had joined the CCP.

In the first half of the twentieth century, the communist movement combined nationalism with internationalism. On the one hand, the communist parties of all countries strived for national liberation and social revolution; on the other hand, they supported each other in their struggles. In Southeast Asia, some nationalists had cooperated with Japanese colonialists to fight against the Western colonists, but the communist parties preferred to oppose both Japanese and Western colonists.

In 1943, the Comintern was dissolved. After the victories of the anti-imperialist and anti-colonial movements, many nations were established under the leadership of their own communist parties. In time, the ruling communist parties of different countries began to develop national characteristics. For the Chinese Communist Party, the Soviet Union showed an increasingly obvious hegemonic tendency and, consequently, the two countries broke apart in the 1960s.

The jurisdiction of pre-colonial local rulers and the boundaries of the colonial empires inspired the boundaries of many post-colonial nations. For example, Indonesia reverted to a pre-colonial jurisdiction and annexed East Timor in 1976. In Vietnam, formally a secondary tributary center in the pre-colonial period, the Communist Party of Indochina attempted to establish an Indochinese Union after their successful reunification war by invading Laos and Cambodia.

To highlight their national uniqueness, many new nation-states tried to weaken their traditional cultural ties with China following independence. Both North Korea and South Korea promoted Hangul (the Korean alphabet) and eliminated the use of Chinese characters. In Vietnam, Latin phonetic characters created by French missionaries were officially adopted in place of Chinese characters.

In defining the characteristics and boundaries of a nation, ethnic minorities were at risk of alienation by the majority. Immigrants from ethnic minorities under colonial rule often became the target of nationalists. A common nationalist narrative in newly independent nations depicted both Westerners and Chinese as the "other". In Indonesia, because there were many Chinese in the Communist Party of Indonesia, the Suharto regime appropriated both anti-communist and nationalist sentiments to slaughter hundreds of thousands of Chinese. In Malaysia, the exclusion of Chinese led to Singapore's independence in 1965. In the Philippines, Vietnam, Myanmar, Laos, Cambodia, and other countries, there were also significant anti-Chinese incidents. King Vajiravudh of Thailand had even published a pamphlet calling the Chinese "Jews of the Orient" (Vajiravudh 1917). Similarly, the Rohingya people in Myanmar, descended from Muslim immigrants during the colonial period, were attacked by nationalists.

Such depictions of the other often shape national identity. For nations deeply influenced by Chinese culture, such as Vietnam and Korea, it was a basic strategy of nation building to weaken the influence of China. Inevitably, as China has become increasingly important to its neighbors through new economic opportunities in recent decades, this narrative, and the status of overseas Chinese and Chinese culture, has undergone further transformation.

From semi-colony to colonial empire: the formation of Japanese nationalism, Asianism, and the Greater East Asia Co-Prosperity Sphere

Japanese nationalism was unique in Asia in that it imitated Western imperialism and colonialism in colonizing its neighbors but at the same time claimed to be uniting the oppressed Asian nations in resistance to the West. There was an element of "missionary nationalism" to this approach. When Japan focused on coordinating its ambitions with the West, its nationalism emphasized that Japan had taken the lead in civilization by learning from the West and so had a special responsibility to educate and enlighten its Asian neighbors;

when confronting the West, it criticized and opposed Western colonialism and tried to build regional hegemony in the name of liberating Asian peoples.

In 1853, American warships had forced Japan to open to the world and many Western powers then forced Japan to sign unequal treaties. In the second half of the nineteenth century, Japan was regarded by the Western powers as a semi-civilized state without full sovereignty. However, Japan's strength increased rapidly through political and economic reform and industrialization. Japan not only won the First Sino-Japanese War but also defeated Russia in the Russo-Japanese War and was recognized as a member of the family of nations by Western powers. Before the First World War, Japan was the only non-Western country that was really accepted by the club of colonial empires. At the same time, Japan had started its own colonial expansion by annexing Ryukyu and Korea, and then invading China and Southeast Asia.

During the Meiji period, many Japanese intellectuals insisted that Japan was a state built upon a single nation – the Yamato Nation. In fact, it was not until the Tokugawa Shogunate that Japan brought Hokkaido, home to the indigenous Ainu people, under its jurisdiction. Effective rule of Hokkaido by Japan was only established in the Meiji period. Many Japanese in the Meiji period regarded Hokkaido as a colony much as the British did India. The Ryukyu people did not belong to the Yamato nation either and were subject to a policy of forced assimilation after the annexation by Japan in 1879.

From the outset, the Meiji government adopted Western culture and customs. In 1883, when the Rokumeikan (Deer Cry Pavilion) opened in Tokyo, Japanese Foreign Minister Inoue Kaoru and some diplomats tried to imitate Western customs and entertain high-ranking officials from Europe and the United States. They were regarded as the vanguard of the Europeanization School. Meanwhile, in 1879, the Meiji government promulgated *The Great Principles of Education* in the name of the emperor to promote Confucianism and loyalty to the emperor. This policy of the Meiji government caused two different reactions from the public.

The first was the School of Europeanization, represented by Fukuzawa Yukichi. In 1873, Fukuzawa, together with Nishi Amane, Nishimura Shigeki, and others, established *Meirokusha* (Meiji Six Society) and launched the *Meiroku Zasshi* magazine, which introduced Western thought and culture, and fiercely criticized Confucianism. Fukuzawa's masterpiece *An Outline of A Theory of Civilization* published in 1875 expressed his recognition of the Western theory of the hierarchy of civilization, in which Western countries were regarded as the most civilized; Turkey, China, Japan, and other Asian countries were regarded as semi-civilized; and African and Australian indigenous peoples were regarded as barbaric (Fukuzawa 2009, 17). Fukuzawa associated Confucianism with despotism and believed that the Confucian emphasis on internal moral virtue did not conform to the spirit of civilization. He advocated that to gain equal status with the great powers, Japan should be transformed by the example of Western civilization. He translated the concept of *Kokutai* (国体), which the Meiji government attached great importance to, into "nationality". The concept of Kokutai originated in China. In the late Edo period, it was associated with the national system centered on the emperor. The Meiji government promoted the concept of Kokutai through the constitution of 1889 and the educational edict of 1890. The emperor's *Bansei-Ikkei* (unbroken Imperial line), the emperor's status in the Shinto religion, and the relationship between the emperor and ministers, were all included in Kokutai. From the outset, Fukuzawa understood Kokutai as nationality, distinguishing the vitality of the nation from that of the monarchy. He argued that a common colonial strategy was to destroy indigenous people but preserve their monarch and that, therefore, the ruler was not essential to the vitality of the nation.

Fukuzawa's admiration for Western civilization internalized the Western colonial mentality. In *An Outline of a Theory of Civilization*, he argued that the contemporary world could be called the world of trade and war, "War is the art of extending the rights of independent governments, and trade is a sign that one country radiates its light to others" (Fukuzawa 2009, 235). On a journey to Europe, having seen how the British controlled their colonies, Fukuzawa expressed his admiration for them and wished that one day Japan could rule India and China as the British did (Wakamori et al. 1990). He was also an important representative of the "Good-bye Asia" movement. He criticized China and Korea as two bad neighbors hurting the Western impression of Japan since all the three countries were grouped together in the concept of Asia. To preserve Japan's image, Fukuzawa proposed that Japan should leave Asia and join with the Western powers in dealing with these two bad neighbors (Fukuzawa 1960, 240). After the outbreak of the First Sino-Japanese War, Fukuzawa organized a society to raise money for military expenses and vigorously praised the war as a righteous war of civilization against barbarism (Fukuzawa 1960, 500).

The second response comes from the *Kokusui Shugi* (the School of National Essence), which opposed Europeanization. The theorists of Kokusui Shugi advocated maintaining the independence of Japanese culture and emphasized the selective absorption of Western culture while respecting traditional Japanese culture. *Kokusui* in Japanese was often translated as "national character" or "national spirit". Among the major theorists of Kokusui Shugi, Shiga Shigetaka argued that Japan's national essence came from its unique geography and the customs, landscape, and living habits of the Yamato people. For Shiga, the backwardness of the Japanese was due not to the lack of Europeanization but the distortion of their quintessence during Japan's historical development. Miyake Setsurei regarded the Eastern and Western civilizations as parallel and completely independent regional cultural systems that could be integrated into a new distinctly Japanese philosophy.

In terms of political views, most of the Kokusui Shugi theorists advocated constitutional monarchy with the cabinet system and believed that the royal family should not bear political responsibility directly. In terms of foreign relations, many belonged to the intellectual wave of early Asianism. Shiga stressed that Japan should join with China and other Asian neighbors to meet the challenges of the Western power. At the same time, he expressed regret that Japan had given up its occupation of Taiwan in 1874. Miyake Setsurei regarded Japan as "Britain of the East". He stressed that since China was powerless, and European powers could not effectively manage Asia, Japan should take on the responsibility of leading Asia. The theorists of the Kokusui Shugi discussed four directions for Japanese colonization: colonization of Hokkaido; migration to the Hawaiian Islands; expanding Japan's influence in Taiwan, the Philippines, the islands of Southeast Asia, and Australia; and extending Japanese influence to Manchuria and Mongolia through the Korean Peninsula.

The Meiji government adopted a highly pragmatic approach. It continued to learn from the West to ensure that Japan would be regarded as a "civilized state" while resolutely defending the hierarchical order of society with the emperor at the top. When the First Sino-Japanese War broke out, the views of the Kokusui Shugi School and the School of Europeanization converged as both supported Japan's invasion of Korea and China. The School of Europeanization had always criticized the traditional values of Chinese civilization and Asian culture, but argued that Japan, after a process of self-reform, had reached civilized status and was entitled to play a leading role in East Asia. Although the Kokusui Shugi School emphasized the value of traditional Asian culture, they argued that the baton of civilization had been transferred from China to Japan and that Japan must take the lead in the struggle of Asia against Western expansion.

In 1897, a group of political elites led by Takayama Chogyū, Inoue Tetsujirō, and Takatarō Kimura established the "Great Japan Association" and launched the *Nihonshugi* journal to promote the "Japanese Doctrine". After the victory over China in the First Sino-Japanese War, the Japanese Doctrine was used to explain and advocate Japan's supremacy and provide legitimacy to the empire's colonial expansion.

After the First Sino-Japanese War, the Triple Intervention of Russia, Germany, and France was a blow to the Japanese elites. The complexity of the situation in East Asia forced the Japanese government to repair its relationship with China. Japanese nationalists also suspended the idea of partitioning China, popularized during the First Sino-Japanese War, and assisted the Meiji government to court China by emphasizing "Asia in one" and "the friendship between Japan and the Qing". In 1897, Miyake Setsurei, Kuga Katsunan, Tsuyoshi Inukai, and Etō Shinpei jointly established the East Asia Association and invited Chinese political exiles like Kang Youwei and Liang Qichao to join. In 1898, Konoe Atsumaro initiated The Common Culture Association focusing on the study of China. In October 1898, financed by the Japanese government, the two associations merged into the East Asia Common Culture Association with Konoe as its president. The Association set up branches and published journals in China, hoping to forge an alliance between the two countries.

In November 1898, when Konoe met Kang Youwei, the leader of the Chinese reformers in exile, he expounded the Asian Monroe Doctrine, "The contemporary Oriental issue is not simply an Oriental issue. It has become a world issue. European powers are competing in the East for their own interests. East Asia is for the East Asians. The East Asian people must have the power to solve the problem independently. The same is true of Monroe Doctrine in America. As a matter of fact, the obligation to realize the Asiatic Monroe Doctrine in the East Asia falls on the shoulders of our two nations" (Konoe 1968, 195). This idea could be traced back to a famous paper published by Konoe in early 1898, which argued that there would be a final war between the yellow race and the white race, and that Japan would lead the yellow race.

In 1900, the Japanese government participated in the suppression of the Boxer Rebellion as a member of the Eight-Power Allied Forces. While the Japanese government worked with the Western powers in suppressing China to ensure that it gained from the expedition, it continued to promote Pan-Asian discourse on "the same language, the same racial origin" and "fraternity".

In 1904, Shigenobu Okuma, who as the prime minister had promoted the 1902 alliance between Britain and Japan, delivered a speech "On the Peace in East Asia" at Waseda University. He responded to the ongoing war between Japan and Russia, saying that it was a war between civilization and barbarism with Japan representing constitutionalism' and Russia representing despotism. Considering Japan's status in East Asia, Ōkuma argued that Japan was the only country qualified to guide China, Japan should treat China based on the friendship of shared culture and blood, and the peace-making conditions of the ongoing war should also ensure Japan's status as "the pillar of peace in East Asia" (Ōkuma 1907, 101–123). The speech, regarded in Tokyo as the articulation of the "Okuma doctrine", explained the Russo-Japanese War from the perspective of race and civilization, and clearly expressed Japan's vision of its sphere of influence.

Japan's victory in the war was widely interpreted as a defeat of the white race by the yellow race. The establishment of Japan's sphere of influence in Southern Manchuria was also interpreted by the theorists of the Asian Monroe Doctrine, such as Kodera Kenkichi, as a step toward preventing China, part of the yellow race, from falling to the European powers.

In 1914, Ōkuma, who had formed a cabinet for the second time, declared war on Germany under the banner of maintaining peace in East Asia. When European powers transferred their attention from East Asia to Europe to fight the war, Ōkuma proposed *The Twenty-One Demands* to China. Some demands were very similar to the hegemonic demands of the United States on Latin American countries. In 1915, after Yuan Shi-kai announced the Hongxian Monarchy, Ōkuma's cabinet decided to eliminate Yuan from China's central government. A series of anti-Yuan movements emerged in China, including the second Manchu-Mongolian Independence Movement promoted by Kawashima Naniwa and the Royalist Party in northeast China, the third revolution led by Sun Yat-Sen, and the National Protection Army led by Cai E and Liang Qichao. These movements were supported to various degrees by the Japanese. After Yuan's death, China was carved up by local warlords, making it easier for Japan to build up its power and influence in the country.

Japan's China policy during the First World War resulted in severe criticism from Ikki Kita who argued that the policy to preserve China was incompatible with the Anglo-Japanese Alliance. Under the alliance, Japan acted as a lackey of British imperialism, participating in the Banking Consortium, carrying out economic aggression against China with Western countries, and providing loans to the warlords in the north rather than the revolutionary forces that sought China's self-preservation. Kita exposed the hypocrisy of Ōkuma's Asian Monroe Doctrine and demanded that Japan truly practice an Asian Monroe Doctrine by abandoning the British, supporting Chinese revolutionaries in the south, and protecting the yellow race against Western imperialism (Kita 1921, 242).

At the 1919 Paris peace conference, the Japanese demanded that racial equality be included in the Covenant of the League of Nations, forcing Wilson to make concessions and agree to transfer German privileges in China's Shandong Province to Japan. Article 21 of the Covenant of the League of Nations, which made concessions to the Monroe Doctrine, was regarded by the Japanese delegation as recognition of Japan's special regional interests (Burkman 2008, 79). When the League of Nations was founded, Japan won a permanent seat on the League Council. However, Japan's Asian Monroe Doctrine was soon attacked by the Western powers. The Washington Conference of 1921–1922 ended the Anglo-Japanese Alliance and forced Japan to give up some military and political interests in Shandong. The great powers strengthened their common domination of China and restrained Japan's claim of special interests there.

Japan had a tradition of cooperation with the Western powers but under constant threat from the West support for the Asian Monroe Doctrine became more significant in the Japanese military. While the Washington Conference suppressed Japan's Asian Monroe Doctrine, the world economic crisis of 1929–1933 brought new opportunities for its application. On 18 September 1931, the Japanese Kwantung Army attacked China's Northeastern Army in Fengtian Province, and soon occupied Northeast China. The following year, the puppet Manchukuo regime was established with the last Qing emperor Puyi as its head. The general assembly of the League of Nations ruled that the Manchukuo regime was illegal and so, in 1933, Japan withdrew from the League of Nations. Japan also withdrew from the Five-Power Treaty and the London Naval Treaty, abandoning the agreed limitations of the Versailles-Washington System on the Japanese Navy.

Japan launched an all-out war against China in 1937. The following year, the concept of a Greater East Asia Co-Prosperity Sphere (GEACPS) was put forward by two military officers, Hideo Iwakuro and Kazuo Horiba. In 1940, the cabinet issued the *Basic Outline of National Policy* proposing to build "a new order of Greater East Asia with the Japanese Empire as the core and the firm integration of Japan, Manchuria and China as the backbone" and "establish an economic cooperation sphere covering the whole of Greater East Asia". Japan's foreign minister, Yōsuke Matsuoka, promoting the concept of the GEACPS, asked the question, if the United States could rely on the Monroe Doctrine to claim its dominant position in the Western Hemisphere so as to maintain the stability and prosperity of the American economy, why could Japan not do the same thing in Asia? (Iriye 1975, 133). Japanese militarists advocated the so-called *Ōdō* (the kingly way) and announced that Asia should be "liberated" from Western colonists, and that a regional order under Japanese leadership should be established. The scope of the GEACPS designated by the cabinet of Fumimaro Konoe extended to East Siberia in the north, to British India in the west, and to the South Pacific Ocean.

From the Asian Monroe Doctrine to the GEACPS, Japanese political elites refined their political discourses based on the United States' Monroe Doctrine. They also tried to take international law to build a system of East Asian international law to legitimize the GEACPS. The German jurist Carl Schmitt's theory of *Großraum* (great space) influenced Japanese jurists such as Kaoru Yasui (Professor of University of Tokyo), Masatoshi Matsushita (Professor of Rikkyo University), and Shigejirō Tabata (Associate Professor of Kyoto University). They carefully studied the Monroe Doctrine and Großraum theory and adapted them to Japanese Asianism. Schmitt's criticism of the universalism of international law and his concept of regional Großraum as an intermediate spatial unit between the global order and the nation-state seemed to meet the practical needs of Japan's GEACPS.

Schmidt emphasized the exclusion of external interference and the role of the dominant nation in Großraum but offered little discussion on its internal configuration, thus making room for Japanese jurists to develop the theory. Shigejirō Tabata argued that an East Asian international law needed to go beyond the principle of absolute equality of States in modern international law. For him, the GEACPS was not a union of equal states based on free will and international treaties but "the connection of destiny beyond free will". Member states of the GEACPS would not have the right to arbitrarily withdraw from the sphere. Matsushita specifically pointed out that the internal principle of the GEACPS was a combination of unequal states. The dominant state was responsible for maintaining the co-prosperity sphere as the leading state. It should exercise its rights and obligations under international law, but if any member states could not fully exercise their rights and obligations, the leading state should act for them. The leading state here is the Japanese equivalent of Schmitt's concept of *Reich*. This interpretation can be seen as an expression of Japanese fascism in the field of international law. Although it claimed to transcend nation-state, its core was deeply nationalistic.

From the tension between the School of Europeanization and the School of Kokusui Shugi in the early Meiji period to the invention of an East Asian international law for the GEACPS, Japanese nationalism demonstrated the duality of resisting Western colonialism in the name of the weak and imitating Western colonialism against the weak. The School of Europeanization was eager to learn from the Western "civilized nations" and aspired to be recognized as an equal by them. They believed that the neighboring Asian countries should be transformed according to the Japanese adaptation of the Western standard of civilization. The School of Kokusui Shugi emphasized that Japan should define its own national spirit and emphasized the identity of Asia as a power base for Japanese leadership. After the First Sino-Japanese War and the Russo-Japanese War, Japan's main ideological schools formed a high degree of consensus on the country's external expansion. After the First World War, the pressure of the Washington Conference on Japan, the economic predicament of Japan, and the rise of the domestic military power prompted Japan to abandon its concert with the

West and openly launch its expansion under the banner of liberating Asia from the Western colonists. It had taken decades for this missionary nationalism to evolve into the colonial imperialism that brought disaster to Asia.

Conclusion

As in other regions of the world, division and conflicts between different ethnic groups existed in pre-colonial East Asia and Southeast Asia. However, the nationalist consciousness to seek the uniting of cultural and political boundaries on national lines only came into being after Asian peoples met with Western colonialists. The Western powers colonizing Asia were characterized by the duality of nation-state and colonial empire: their metropolises were committed to the building of homogenous nation-states while governing their indigenous colonial subjects as separate and lesser peoples. Colonial empires attacked the pre-colonial tributary system, pretending to recognize the autonomy of many local rulers before subduing them to absorb them into their empires. In confrontations between colonial empires, all used nationalism as a means to weaken each other. While the concert of great power in the nineteenth century suppressed national independence movements, with the weakening of the concert, national independence movements could no longer be restrained. Different political conditions led to different forms of nationalism in different nations. In Southeast Asia and Japan, two distinct types of nationalism emerged.

The first type emerged in those nations that were completely colonized. Their nationalism was aimed at the colonial suzerain, sometimes using the power of another colonial empire, such as Japan, against them. At the same time, those nations might also inherit the borders defined by the colonial powers. We can see these features in Malaysia, Indonesia, and the Philippines. Similarly, the French colonial jurisdiction of the Union of Indochina provided a blueprint for Vietnam's expansionism after its reunification in 1975.

The second type applies primarily to Japan, who had risen from a semi-colony to a colonial empire through internal reform on the Western model. In building a strong official nationalism, Japan imitated Western colonialism. In its expansion into the territories of its Asian neighbors, Japan appealed to the rhetoric of liberating Asia from Western imperialism and colonialism. There were some similarities between Siam and Japan. Both maintained independence in the face of Western invasion. Siam promoted internal reform by imitating the Southeast Asian colonies of Western powers and created an official nationalism by constructing an image of Westerners and Chinese as the other of the Thai nation. The kingdom briefly annexed some British and French colonies through cooperation with Japan during the Second World War but reverted to the Allied side in the later stages of the war.

In the movement for national independence and liberation in East and Southeast Asia, communism played an important role in the struggle against colonialism and imperialism. The communist theory of nationality also exerted enormous influence on the nation building of many countries in the region. As communist internationalism gradually faded during the Cold War, the nationalist dimension of the communist movement became more significant.

However, the history of the region also contains resources beyond extreme nationalism. In 1955, representatives of 29 Asian and African countries and regions held the Asian-African Conference in Bandung, Indonesia. For the first time, Asian and African nations deliberated on their own future without the intervention of colonial empires. This is an important internationalist moment. On 1 January 2022, with the formal implementation of the Regional Comprehensive Economic Partnership (RCEP) Agreement, a new regional order of free trade in East Asia and Southeast Asia was established, and political cooperation among countries based on economic cooperation further strengthened. Hopefully, this move to establish a further mechanism of coordination will help consolidate the achievements of anti-imperialist and anti-colonial revolutions and build a common regional identity that constrains extreme nationalism.

References

Burkman, Thomas W. 2008. *Japan and the League of Nations: Empire and World Order, 1914–1938*, Honolulu: University of Hawai'i Press.
Patrick Sze-lok Leung, and Anthony Carty. 2018. "The Crisis of the Ryukyus (1877–82): Confucian World Order Challenged and Defeated by Western/Japanese Imperial International Law." In *Morality and Responsibility of Rulers: European and Chinese Origins of a Rule of Law as Justice for World Order*, edited by Anthony Carty and Janne Nijman, 360–385. Oxford: Oxford University Press.
Esherick, Joseph W., Hasan Kayali, and Eric Van Young, eds. 2006. *Empire to Nation: Historical Perspectives on the Making of the Modern World*. Lanham: Rowman & Littlefield.
Fukuzawa, Yukichi. 2009. *An Outline of a Theory of Civilization*. Translated by David A. Dilworth and G. Cameron Hurst III. New York: Columbia University Press.
Fukuzawa, Yukichi. 1960. *Complete Works of Fukuzawa Yukichi, Vol. 10*. Tokyo: Iwanami Shoten.
Fukuzawa, Yukichi. 1960. *The Complete Works of Fukuzawa Yukichi, Vol. 14*. Tokyo: Iwanami Shoten.
Kármán, Gábor and Lovro Kunčević, eds. 2013. *The European Tributary States of the Ottoman Empire in the Sixteenth and Seventeenth Centuries*. London: Brill.
Kita, Ikki. 1921. *An Informal History of the Chinese Revolution*. Tokyo: Seikishobou.
Lenin, Vladimir. 1963. *Imperialism, the Highest Stage of Capitalism, Lenin's Selected Works, Volume 1*. Moscow: Progress Publishers.
Manggala, Pandu Utama. 2013. "The Mandala Culture of Anarchy: The Pre-Colonial Southeast Asian International Society." *Journal of ASEAN Studies* 1 (1): 1–13.
Miwa, Kimitada. 1975. "Japanese Images of War with the United States." In *Mutual Images: Essays in American-Japanese Relations*, edited by Akira Iriye, 133. Cambridge, MA: Harvard University Press.
Ōkuma, Shigenobu. 1907. "On Peace in East Asia." The Editorial Department of Waseda University ed. *Collection of Ōkuma Shigenobu's Speeches*, 101–123. Tokyo: Waseda University Press.
Shaddick, Edwina Hui May. 2011. *Lao Sovereignty and the Return of the Mandalas*. Singapore: Singapore Management University
Takeshi, Hamashita. 2008. *China, East Asia and the Global Economy*. London and New York: Routledge.
The Editorial Board of Konoe Atsumaro's Diary, ed. 1968. *Konoe Atsumaro's Diary. Vol. 2*, 195. Tokyo: Kajima Institute Publishing.
Vajiravudh, King of Siam. 1917. *The Jews of the Orient*. Bangkok: Siam Observer Press.
Wakamori, Taro, et al. 1990. *The Story of Japanese History*. Tokyo: Kawade Shobō Shinsha.
Wheaton, Henry. 1916. *Wheaton's Elements of International Law*. London: Stevens & Sons.

5
POST-COLONIALISM, NATIONALISM AND INTERNATIONALISM IN EAST AND SOUTHEAST ASIA

Peter Herrmann

Introduction

By merging the different terms and concepts brought together in the title, we face a dilemma, widely known as the Böckenförde dilemma. For Böckenförde, a German jurist specialising in constitutional law, the problem consisted in the productive tension between the secular state and religious faith systems. On the one hand, he considers them mutually exclusive; on the other hand, however, he points out that the modern secular state depends in the last instance on the faith system which the very same state claims to have overcome.

This contribution is concerned with a similar dilemma: here, we are dealing with a tension between nationalism and supranationalism, with colonialism and internationalism located in-between. The different concepts are said to overcome each other, while at the same time each depends on the ongoing existence of the other. Putting this into a formula, we may say that nationalism was necessary to overcome colonialism, i.e., to establish a post-colonial system, whereas the underlying spirit was actually an internationalist claim, transcending a notion of an autarkic nation – aiming for full recognition on the international scale contradicts in some way the notion of autarky.

Or in simple terms: to achieve supranational standing, a strong nation state is needed, but successfully achieving this standing tends to undermine the nation state. The same is true for the relationship between colonialism and nationalism.

The fundamental thesis of this contribution is that we are stuck using terms and concepts that sway back and forth between objective historical realities and the social constructs of utopian communities. To overcome this limitation, some basic notions of quantum theory are borrowed, giving us a more creative – and daring – method of coping with the objective laws of history. This also means that we have to commence the analysis by looking at the elementary forms from which the concrete constellations can be approached – underlining here that what follows has to be understood as fundamental research dealing with methodological issues, and only marginally immediately applicable.

Realities – a construct

We must keep in mind that we are in all cases dealing with social constructs or imagined communities (Benedict Anderson). In simple terms, we may say that in the first case – post-colonialism – we are dealing with a socio-legal dimension; in the second case – nationalism – a socio-psychological construct; and in the third case – internationalism – a socio-economic entity. In all three, of course, this is a matter of emphasis, not exclusivity. It must be critically noted that we are moving in a kind of cage, the centrality of nation suggesting some kind of inevitable given or, using Heidegger's terminology, the *ens certum* – that which is certain and cannot be questioned. It is remarkable that this certainty has established itself during such a historically short period of time.

In the light of post-colonialism, it makes sense to begin with the country as a relevant point of reference. Countries, enveloped in the form of the state, can be seen as legal entities acting as states (and as sub-units: public kindergartens, public transport facilities, etc.) with the status of full agency in the system defined by law, with the exclusive power of defining and executing national law (legislature). This is in line with Max Weber's definition of the state as the sole legitimate power holder. It does not have any meaning as an imagined community, and on the international stage is in principle 'valid without citizens'; however, while such a state does not require any kind of demos or subjects, it nevertheless defines its citizens – i.e., no citizenship without a passport.[1] This definition is concerned with belonging, and also with rights and duties. While not exclusively, citizenship is today closely linked to nation/nationality, which can be understood as a concept under which identity is established.

Nation and nationality are important points of reference for people, allowing them to identify with the system, i.e., the country. In turn, the country as a legal entity accepts some form of responsibility for its citizens, now defined as members of the thus established identity. The nation state is then understood as a merger of the two entities – country and nation – establishing a geographical and economic entity that is able to act (based on its legal status) and willing to act (bound by its socio-economic frame of action). Interestingly, this is inherently contradictory – the aim of establishing this identity is not autarky, but rather to position it in relation to other states.

Consequently, we must switch methodologically from the analysis of entities as nation states, and their relationship to each other, to the analysis of relationalities. The elementary forms of these complex structures are potentially changing all the time; they are in fact only defined by their relative position and when the relation changes, they change as well. In very bold terms, this can be understood if we look at the role and position of class in international wars: depending on the state of a war, each class takes a new position.

This means that we are dealing with liquid entities, and that it is the indeterminacy that makes an entity most suitable for such a constellation – the relevant slogan is "if it does not exist already, make it exist by specifying the framing". Another aspect emerges from looking at the specific constellation, i.e., by aiming at understanding the relationality from the perspective each viewer takes. In very simple terms: of course, it matters whether I am citizen, applying for citizenship or not interested in citizenship.

Some methodological challenges

In fact, a fundamental problem of social science is that today a kind of mechanical thinking still prevails. In Aristotle's thinking, for instance, the most fundamental difference is that between stasis and dynamics; a moving cause is needed to transpose stasis into dynamics, into movement. Humans, understood as supreme beings, are taken as this cause. It is not only supremacy of humans but also supremacy of movement that is in this way set as something that must be aimed for, without considering first the substantial side.

In other words, movement and dynamics as the superior state of society:

> The overwhelming success of the way of thinking in natural science and the resulting control of natural, and in its wake, social processes made natural science the real science in the public consciousness. Other disciplines also emulated its example. For sociology, psychology and economics, for example, it became – at least implicitly – a guiding principle by which these disciplines partly judged themselves or by which they were judged from the outside.
>
> *(Goernitz 1999: 57)*

However, reality is stronger than theory. While the main task of theory is seemingly to reduce complexity, bringing order from chaos, reality permanently challenges theory simply by the fact that the increasing precision of theoretically based cognition results in increasing recognition of faults and shortcomings. Somewhat metaphorically, we can say that it needed an apple to fall on Isaac Newton's head to allow Albert Einstein to detect that the movement depends on the – changing – position of the observer. From here, it is only a small, though in hindsight necessary, step for Niels Bohr to suggest:

> What is it that we humans depend on? We depend on our words … Our task is to communicate experience and ideas to others. We must strive continually to extend the scope of our description, but in such a way that our messages do not thereby lose the objective or unambiguous character … We are suspended in language in such a way that we cannot say what is up and what is down. The word 'reality' is also a word, a word which we must learn to use correctly.
>
> *(Bohr [1934] 1977, 17)*

Of course, and particularly when the cup holding our tea smashes to the ground, it is difficult to accept that gravity does not actually exist (see the reflections by Kleban 2021). Or again with Niels Bohr: "Isolated material particles are abstractions, their properties on quantum theory being definable and observable only through their interaction with other systems" (Bohr 1928: 581). In addition, at the very moment of the manifestation of structures, they change their character, establishing themselves as new independent entities.

This is a long-winded introduction aiming at opening an urgently needed different view on post-colonialism, nationalism and internationalism. So far, we can summarise in this way: (1) we are looking at topics in social science – different dimensions of nationality/nationhood, and also the region and its specific definition in concrete perspectives – and while we establish in this way a procrustean bed of institutions and enforceable legal rules, we fail to recognise that these tools are permanently changing their character. (2) Overcoming its inherent limits, social science has made the same step as natural science, moving from mechanical understanding of relations to relationality, defined by indeterminableness and determined regularity, moving the real world towards a more complex approach with the core dimensions of processuality and relationality (or one could also say: time and space).

To greatly simplify, and looking directly at the topic, national, international and supranational systems are permanently changing; paradoxically, in several cases, this means that these systems remain as they are, because the people living in the systems think that they cannot change anything, despite the fact that the entire universe around them, and even their internal structure, has changed fundamentally. It is about living and making policies in castles in the air – castles that once stood on firm ground which in different ways has been removed. One problem is that the needed change requires not least a revisiting and possibly a revoking of the terms we are used to, without having clear alternatives.

Complexity as a common thread

Goethe's Faust speaks of wanting to "see what holds the earth together in its innermost elements". This idea implies (i) that such an inner bond exists, and (ii) that it is intrinsic and cannot be changed. Two pathways for this search can be made out: looking for an exact analysis, a matter of mathematically definable structures; and looking for a spiritual bond, one which emerges from human activities.

One can reformulate this in the light of different schools of thought or academic disciplines – in broad terms, for instance, economics versus political economy, mechanical physics versus quantum physics, clinical psychology versus gestalt-therapy, geography versus geopolitics. The social side follows, by and large, the dichotomy of an individualist-separatist approach – a socially led unfolding approach, considering the social as the ground from which the individual actively evolves and establishes him/herself. This is validated by looking at the institutional systems which human beings erect as an organisational framework: tribes, cities, states, international organisations and the like.

The Treaty of Westphalia is still generally seen as the foundation for the modern state as an actor on the international agenda. At the time a hugely progressive step, it is increasingly a fetter, caught in a limited understanding of the process of socialisation. One can say that it is an institutional replication of individualism, politically and economically expressed by methodological nationalism. Such a short-sighted interpretation is easily seen as mistaken or even malicious; this assumption overlooks, however, that we are dealing with a specific reality, and interpretation can only be a reflection of this reality.

Looking back, the modern nation state was established very much as a bulwark against such praxis of societal bonds characterising the feudal system. The cornerstones were military force and a modern, tax-based finance system. While this did not happen overnight, it can be presented in a nutshell as follows, taking the words from Benno Teschke's research in The Myth of 1648:

> Demand for additional resources affected taxation ... leading to the transition from feudal "domain state" to the modern "tax state"... In the modern tax state, "the 'private' resources of the ruling power were exceeded in value by the 'public' revenues derived from a system of general taxation" (Ormrod 1995: 123, Braun 1975). This passage from fiscal personalism, in which there was no real distinction between royal private income and public revenue (le roi faut vivre du sien), to fiscal institutionalism is held to have been consummated by the centralising monarchy, which extended its fiscal supremacy over the entire realm. In this process, new modes of fiscality operated by new public institutions were invented and enforced against the autonomous powers of the nobility and the privileges and immunities of the clergy, leading to fiscal uniformity and institutional centralisation (Ormrod 1995: 124–7) ... The most important innovation was the shift from feudal military and financial assistance and inelastic, indirect taxation to generalised, elastic direct taxation.
>
> *(Teschke 2011: 120)*

A thorough reading makes clear that this was a process of socialisation, though at the time it was much criticised as the advance of a ruthless individualism, threatening the integrity of society – the aristocracy, rich landlords and other 'nobles' were very much seen as landesvater, fathers/patrons of the land, a pattern that still persists.

Behind the mindset, the foundation firm enough to carry the different edifices are, different of what is commonly understood under the catch-all term 'capitalism'. It is important to be aware that such a foundation can only be found on a meta-level, the actual 'design' of the edifices being too varied to allow more. With Fernand Braudel, a functional approach is proposed:

> Every task, once allocated in the international division of labour, created its own form of control and that control articulated and governed the form taken by society … In every case, society was responding to a different economic obligation and found itself caught by its very adaptation, incapable of escaping quickly from these structures once they had been created. So if society took a different form here or there, it was because it represented a solution or perhaps the solution, "which was best suited (other things being equal) to the particular types of production with which it was confronted".
>
> *(Braudel 1984: 62)*

This goes far beyond commodity production, being a matter of production of life; the term 'production' actually gains an entirely new meaning.

From here, we can consider space-time as a relevant variable, supposing that every space and every time are specifically interwoven with their juxtaposition, emanating as regime – nationally, internationally and globally. From Fernand Braudel (1987: 30), we can borrow the distinction between the three planes of time: the longue durée, the time of episodes and the time of events. Each plane grasps a different depth of the anchoring (the fashion of the day does not last long and is quickly forgotten). This complex relationality could be characterised as follows:

> The longue durée interlinking with the temps allongée, and these planes of history interacting in both respects, the regional and the national, but in addition as criss-cross relationship, i.e., the long-term regional plane directly relating to the national dimension of the temps allongée – and of course, in the very long run even the long-term dimension is undergoing some alteration.
>
> *(Herrmann 2020)*

We can now take a next step and consider space-time as a relevant variable. Supposing that every space and every time are specifically interwoven, presuming that historical development follows specific historical laws, we witness a transcription of the vague rules governing regimes into legal, obligatory norms. Regimes are understood as:

> as sets of implicit or explicit principles, norms, rules and decision-making procedures around which actors' expectations converge in a given area of international relations. Principles are beliefs of fact, causation and rectitude. Norms are standards of behaviour defined in terms of rights and obligations. Rules are specific prescriptions or proscriptions for action. Decision-making procedures are prevailing practices for making and implementing collective choice.
>
> *(Krasner 2009: 113)*

This is one of the standard definitions from international relations, applied here without reference to the international aspect.

Juridification, then, means to reach at clear definitions, but also clear mechanisms of sanctioning. Importantly, even if we see this process as one of tying up the terms and conditions, the process of juridification and the subsequent implementation are never fixed, but always a matter of 'struggle for law' (Jhering, 1879; Holmes, 1897; Pashukanis, 1924).

Bringing order into things

The following will elaborate some further methodological questions relevant to East and Southeast Asia. Trying to classify countries in the region today is nearly impossible. The reason for this is simple: the commonly used terms of 'developing country', 'emerging economy' and 'threshold country' are extremely biased.

On the one hand, of course all countries are developing – is it not the very nature of societies that they are not static? And would not even stasis within a developing world mean development, elements partly stemming against the rest? Indeed, the question is not least about the direction of development.

Furthermore, the common use of the term is pejorative, suggesting one and only one correct form of and goal for development, and that any country or unit not yet moving in that direction must accept and follow the one hegemonic pattern, allowing for national derivations only in as far as they are necessary to secure the achievement of the ultimate goal. The other terms are equally pejorative or over-generalised, not allowing meaningful orientation.

On the other hand, arguments can be easily turned around. Do we not classify countries as static, rigidly caught in a status quo, if we consider 'developing' as an attribute that applies only to some countries? Finally, any use of the prefix 'post' suggests that such qualifications are only possible as matters of distinction, apparently without their own value. Although it is correct that making history depends on what was and is, it also has its own value, derived from utopias, visions and anticipated potentials.

More relevant than working towards a classification and/or attribution is an attempt to look for a qualification of the processuality. To achieve this, below I bring together different analytical layers, focusing on socialisation. We arrive at two presentations, the first concerned with extension of inclusion as a contradictory process, the second looking at socialisation as an extension of the depth of appropriation.

Obviously, today's societies are more inclusive than their predecessors. Slavery was constitutive in the early stages of societal development, but although it still exists, it is not elementary in character. However, at certain breaking points, we find an 'impediment' that prepares the predecessors emerging for a new formation. We can say that the stage of real exclusion (locating something, some people, some groups literally outside of society) has been overcome by (i) importing the excluded, i.e., establishing mechanisms of social exclusion, and (ii) successively overcoming that exclusion, striving for more inclusive patterns (with a very broad brush, e.g., slaves becoming second-class citizens, with successive development then elevating them to full citizens), while the ruling classes sustain their hegemonic position. Environmental questions are not addressed, as they are considered marginally relevant; they may later determine the agenda, but the original agenda of the Anthropocene remains unchanged and is even strengthened by claiming that a sustainable restructuring is underway.

Processes of inclusion/exclusion/re-inclusion are different from case to case, sometimes starting from the dissolution of an original entity, sometimes commencing from separate parts, moving to integration – as we are dealing with a multi-stage process, there exist a multitude of options.

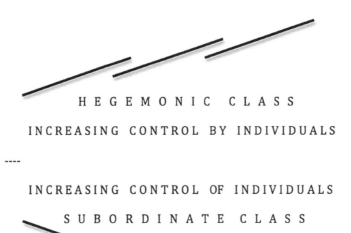

Figure 5.1 Formational development between inclusion and exclusion

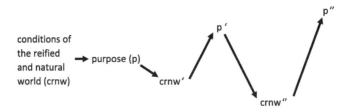

Figure 5.2 Purpose enhancement

We can move further, looking at the mechanisms that are substantially backing the process. Socialisation is seen as a process standing on two legs: the first, aiming at increasing comfort, understood as congruence between living human beings and the reified and natural world; and the second, the individual and collective decisions concerning this relationship – deepening the relationship will deepen the understanding, and vice versa.

The general and generic organisation of life by relating to others and relating to the environment changes both sides and deepens our relation to the world we live in. For example, instead of eating raw meat, humans learn to cook it, making it more digestible. This means, in turn, that the concrete purpose is refined and extended: instead of domesticating animals and preparing more elaborate and healthy meat dishes, we find nowadays in many regions a move towards veganism, which, lived by a majority, would have implications that can hardly be imagined.

A new society rather than a new nation

Only now have we arrived at a point that allows us to approach the question of post-colonialism, nationalism and internationalism in a new way. The focus is on China. Presented is a vision that reflects real trends, though it is unlikely to become soon reality. Nevertheless, it is a useful intellectual exercise, possibly contributing to moving towards new steps of polity-making.

The thesis is that our main concern should not be analysing the (South-East) prospect in the light of what we have – the nation state and the various relations of inequality, independence, dependence and oppression. Instead, and without denying those givens, we have to focus on the challenges society faces today. Let us begin by briefly touching upon the present mainstream debate and the challenges they propose.

The victory that did not happen

Francis Fukuyama suggested – presenting a Western-biased optimist interpretation of history – the end of history. The book of this title was published in 1992, giving a more or less immediate response to the developments in the socialist countries. He suggested not only that conflicts between main adversaries would no longer determine international relations, but furthermore, and more importantly, that this end was a victory of the supposed 'better reality'. However, this did not reflect reality; on the contrary, a new confrontation emerged, and new war strategies were presented. As much as the so-called war on terror had been an aggressive strategy towards an external enemy, it had also been a war within national borders, much of it culminating in the year of the pandemics.

> In the UK and the United States, 2020 was experienced not just as a public health emergency or a major recession, but as the culmination of a period of escalating national crisis, summarised by the words Trump and Brexit. How could countries that once boasted of global hegemony and that were undisputed leaders in matters of public health fail so badly to manage the disease? It must reflect a deeper malaise … Perhaps it was their common enthusiasm for neoliberalism? Or the culmination of a process of decline stretching over many decades. Or the insularity of their political cultures?
>
> *(Tooze 2021: 25 f)*

It will not come as a surprise that we find a weird amalgamation bringing together aggressive foreign policy, racism, nationalism, closure of borders and nationalist autarkic orientations; one can never be sure whether the concrete mix is stirred by aggressively exclusionary hatred or by pragmatic opportunism.

Taking globalisation seriously

It is fair to say that the unifying link is provided by the exacerbation of developments that are counter-intuitive. Mentioning some of the main issues means pointing at the same time at major challenges ahead. While Tony Blair said in 2005:

> I hear people say we have to stop and debate globalisation. You might as well debate whether autumn should follow summer.
>
> *(Blair 2005)*

it seems now that actually both may and should be questioned. Climate change, with all its foreseeable and unforeseeable consequences, is at the top of the agenda, questioning if the regularity that still persists will exist in the future; and the firm conviction stated by Blair in the same speech, that globalisation:

> is replete with opportunities, but they only go to those swift to adapt, slow to complain, open, willing and able to change. Unless we own the future, unless our values are matched by a completely honest understanding of the reality now upon us and the next about to hit us, we will fail. And then the values we believe in become idle sentiments ripe for disillusion and disappointment.
>
> *(Blair, 2005)*

sounds today like a naïve conviction of sandbox economics.

While the amount of data globally collected and processed reaches within hours dimensions that the human brain does not deal with during a lifetime, the necessary mechanisms of coordinating informed decisions remain limited, so that we must deal with a data surplus that works like a black hole: the surplus produced enters another round, again and again, the only purpose being its own reproduction. What is reproduced is not even a placeholder for something, i.e., money, a share, an investment bond; does not even represent a computer, fountain pen, car or bowl of rice. It solely presents, instead, a tool for speculation – while meaningful for the individual as a means of speculation, it is from a macroeconomic perspective the brushwood to light the pyre on which capitalism has climbed.

While states remain formally the main polities, decision-making power has gone astray: large corporations, the corporate sector and individuals occupying government functions; self-declared philanthropists emerging as world health ministers; social networkers becoming Pandora-like opinion leaders; sober financial strategists becoming self-enthroned policy manipulators of supposed liberation; ex-bookshop managers growing to become universal managers of a 'total market', and even of the universe – reigning over space and aiming at a new singularity for themselves and then for humankind; singers acting as idols for politicians, making heavy donations in order to motivate them to follow in their footsteps.

While nationality is still the main reference for defining polities, it is in many instances no longer relevant. Looking at migration, we find on the one hand mass movements hitting the poorest regions and the poorest segments of the population extremely hard; on the other hand, we find a global elite measured in wealth, education or cultural reputation. Nationality does not play a role anymore.

While we are aware of the beat of the wings of a far-away butterfly (Lorenz, 1963), we do not know how to stop it, nor do we know how to control its consequences. Furthermore, the repercussions present another set of unforeseeable events in global relationships and thus also another space for cooperative action.

While we are aware of the need to think and act strategically, much is left to short-termism, oriented along election campaigns and the need to decide how to repair the damage that could have been avoided or limited by strategic orientations. This is linked not least to the reorientation of small-scale action, space and time, providing fields of real influence and/or parochialism.

Southeast Asia – pre-world society

It is difficult or even impossible to set priorities, especially when considering the present methodological approach. With some justification, however, we may take digitisation as a focal point, as we find links from various fields coming together. Digitisation reaching out, and the way it does (or does not), is an important aspect in the overall shape of socialisation.

In a nutshell, digitisation is an important aspect of shaping individual lives and the handling of complex national, international and global relationships, even by way of defining the relevant parameters. It is *definiens* and *definiendum* at the same time.

We should not forget that this is a late phenomenon, the roots of which can be found at a very early stage of social development. In 1689, Gottfried Leibniz elaborated in his article *Explication de l'Arithmétique Binaire* the foundation for the modern understanding. Digitisation and artificial intelligence are parts of efforts to formulate everything in a way that makes it calculable and controllable. Mathematisation, numerification and much later digitisation are expressions of such trends, complemented by the fundamental humanist ideas or ideologemes, presuming the rational being; Gauss and Humboldt, representing two different approaches to measuring the world, finding a common expression in Kant's categorical imperative, are cornerstones (see Kehlmann 2006).

This is the onset of the contractualist approach to interpreting society and the relationship between its members, the citizens. The result, as a reflection of persisting interests and power structures, is a simple and very simplifying understanding of reality: human relationships rest on the binary code of jurisprudence – and if they are not yet doing so, they are moving towards such normalisation, standardisation and finally juridification.

Although such thinking is most pronounced in trade and other commercial relations, it is the general zeitgeist of modernity. Like a purchasing contract, we find social contracts and constitutions alike designed by way of two parties relating to each other according to ex-ante defined criteria; if a third party is involved, it is as mediator. Today, however, this pattern has changed in a far-reaching way and binarisation/numerification have been, at least in some areas, replaced by more advanced means.

However, as shown in Figures 5.1 and 5.2, we are witnessing a development characterised by an increasingly controlled inclusion and extension of purposes, with two possible consequences. The first is the continuation of the given patterns of the traditional nation state and the developmental model, which is very much that of Western modernisation. Pronouncedly, it was presented by Rostow through his model of five stages of development (Rostow 1960). One of the problems with this is that it basically asks everybody to stand on their tiptoes, while forgetting that then nobody can see better. In other words, it initiates a motion of endless growth without putting in place mechanisms of control that are suitable to maintain quality. Political control is translated into complete social management; economic growth is about increased commodity production, independent of its use value; financial instruments are detached from the financial system, so technically complicated that they cannot be fully understood anymore, let alone controlled – now following their own rules, emerging as self-running.

We can say that the entire system is suffering from a threat of permanent surplus production, resulting in ever larger absurdities for individuals and society as a whole (Herrmann/Yudina 2021). In other words, we are witnessing an inappropriate appropriation, a decoupling of technical feasibility and meaning. This is in part also inherent in notions of postcolonialism and the traditional models of development – that there is this one model considered correct and applicable to all.

An alternative pathway is, by the same means, to make use of the possibilities and opportunities that are given, setting data collection, data processing and data use in the wider context of quantum theoretical achievements. Allowing a non-mechanical application means we can actually look at new societal models, going beyond the four pillars that are dominant today – nation states, separation of powers, growth of commodity production and comparative (it would be more correct to say competitive) advantage. On various occasions, critiques of the different issues have been raised, from a general critique of the principles to practical concerns. A common denominator of all critiques is the need for a historical perspective – what at some point in history has been good, i.e., appropriately working, is not necessarily so under changed circumstances. Such a broad point can then be translated into a critique of the modus operandum.

One of the problems in all cases is that alternatives are not clear-cut. This means we must work with:

- the analysis of existing general trends, in part as a matter of extension/prolongation,
- the analysis of existing projects,
- possible visions and
- theoretical reflections concerning the role of the state and its possible transformation.

General trends have already been presented, albeit painted with a broad brush: the move of digital technology/digitisation and artificial intelligence to qualitatively new levels, giving control away to the instruments but also allowing the extension of control, subject to "control of the instruments, limiting the control by the instruments" (Gumbrecht 2021); migration as a movement that goes far beyond the question of refugees, concerning spatial, temporal, educational, qualificational and vocational matters; and surplus production to such an extent that it ends in a 'black hole', as mentioned above – it should be added that this black hole has as its reverse an increasing impoverishment in material and immaterial terms.

On another occasion (Herrmann 2016), I characterised the challenges we are all facing by highlighting the following five 'New Giants':

- the complexity of government and the limited scope of governance,
- the individualisation of problems and their emergence as a societal threat,
- abundance of knowledge and its misdirection towards skills,
- societal abundance versus inequality of access and
- over-production of goods – the turning of goods into 'bads'.

This provides us with a platform for moving the debate further, looking at potentials for Southeast Asian countries and the region – going beyond the simple prolongation of the traditional thinking of statehood and nationality to face the challenge of finding a positive solution to the questions humankind as a whole has to answer; moving together or not being able to find a planetary answer; and continuing to shift problems along the verge of self-destruction, as the speech by Mia Amor Mottley from Barbados, addressing the General Assembly of the United Nations, underlined:

> Three years ago when I made my maiden speech I indicated from this very podium and told the international community that the world appeared awfully similar to what it looked like a hundred years ago. Barbados made that position clear. Regrettably we have not come to say we told you so but we have come to say that the needle has not moved and that we have not seen sufficient action on behalf of the people of this world … The answer … is that we have the means to give every child on this planet a tablet and we have the means to give every adult a vaccine and we have the means to invest in protecting the most vulnerable on our planet from a change in climate, but we choose not to.
>
> *(Mottley 2021)*

Belt and Road Initiative and BRICS

We could look at many examples of new patterns of governance. ASEAN is one; various shifts in the finance and banking sector are another; to some extent, new forms of managing global value chains and professional self-regulation are another. Going beyond any regional reference, one could also mention the World Wide Web consortium. It is important to note that the focus of the contributions to this volume can only be understood if they are reflected upon against the background of the wider set of changes taking place globally.

Here there is only space for a brief look at two of them, namely the Belt and Road Initiative (BRI) and BRICS, chosen not least due to the (mostly negative) resonance they receive from many Western powers.

It would be more appropriate to speak of the BRI, also known as the New Silk Road, as 'one challenge – one goal', for its structure is as new as it is far-reaching in its ambitions. In brief, it is the political economy of mutual advantage, establishing as a guideline the principle of comparative need. As such, it stands against the traditional developmental economics, the Ricardian postulate of comparative advantage, and also against newer approaches that argue for value chains.

What is truly remarkable – and criticised or welcomed, depending on one's political perspective – is the fact that this is a rather radical shift, bringing the 'political' back into political economy, to develop a setting that is not mainly exchange-based but rather cooperation-based. Speaking of cooperation-based rather than cooperation-oriented is meaningful, highlighting that cooperation is the point of departure, not a means to an end.

This brings us back to the earlier suggestion of 'one challenge – one goal'. The point of departure is indeed (i) the insight that we face a constellation which is, albeit possibly in different ways, of concern to the participants, (ii) the insight and will to deal with this constellation as one that requires and allows intervention, instead of working towards extraction in order to gain the most from it, and (iii) the emphasis on the need to pool resources rather than maximise outcome. The obvious problem is the conditions under which participants cooperate, requiring strong political mechanisms to ensure that the track is not left.

BRICS is the intergovernmental organisation concerned with cooperation between Brazil, Russia, India, China and South Africa (the latter only joining in 2010). Should we say that it is an experiment? It is bits of some very different things: regional cooperation, though there is no region involved; a political association, though the politics of the participating countries could hardly be more different; a group set up for economic cooperation, though the countries are extremely different when it comes to mode of production, available resources and mechanisms of regulation; a think tank, though it does not have a defined profile in terms of topics/issues; an institution, though it lacks a formal constitution.

It is remarkable that it was founded during a UN-General Assembly (61st UNGA, 2006), as this suggests a large dissatisfaction; and indeed the first summit in 2009 highlighted the wish to give a stronger voice to their countries. In the following years, it became clear that the aim – though not made entirely explicit – was not least to repel the dominant role of the US, especially the quasi-war via the dollar-hegemony (see Mahbubani, 2020: 89).

Conclusion

BRI and BRICS: it is an open question how these will develop, from the perspective of real development. The latter in particular is evidence of the need for a complex methodology, that of a jigsaw with gaps and fitting parts that change during the process of mounting. As an action at least in part provoked by the Western centre and in particular the US, the setting changes with every new step of each actor – and we have to emphasise that we are not only dealing with two actors. Rather, the 'old centre' and BRICS are each one actor *and* multiple actors, and there are third parties on the playing field – countries not belonging to either of these two groupings and playing a role in the strategic consideration of each of the main players. Much as in chess, we also have to include the fact that every single piece is also able to decide in relative independence, even to decide to leave the board – but not, however, to leave the arena.

None of this is in principle new. However, new is (i) the direct and outspoken link between agencies, (ii) the accelerated speed of the (inter)action and (iii) the awareness of the other players, and with this the need to think and act strategically.

> Such complex interactions are like a person walking through a maze where the walls rearrange themselves as the person moves through it. New steps have then to be taken to adapt to the walls of the maze that change in response to each person's walk through the maze. Complex systems theory involves studying the consequences of the dynamic and partially unpredictable interactions between elements making up any system.
> *(Urry 2016: 60)*

When we talk about the wings of the proverbial butterfly causing a tornado at the other end of the world, we often forget that the butterfly is affected twice: first by the initial movement and then by the repercussions of the tornado. The surest way for it to lose control is to follow rigidly its original course.

In the present context, this would mean to follow the traditional course from colonialised country to post-colonialist state, aiming to build a strong nation state, strong enough to gain an influential or even dominant position on the international level. From a short- or mid-term perspective, this may be useful; however, from a long-term perspective, it does not solve the actual problems behind colonialism – superpowers depending on regaining and maintaining their predominant position in processes of colonialisation. We should not understand colonialisation only in the traditional sense, but should add dependencies as part of value chains, externalisation of environmental burdens and the like.

A *perpetuum mobile* is well-known to be impossible; the same goes for a *perpetuum externum abusionem*, i.e., the endless externalisation of exploitation. This is even more the case when pursued with the claim, and need, of the exterior to develop according to the same pattern – low-wage countries compete with the need for eternal sales markets, the development of external markets also results in demand for political emancipation and the endless processes that develop paradoxically result in a growing blockage if the concepts and criteria are not changed, sometimes fundamentally.

This piece has hopefully made clear that today's tasks in the political sphere are as different from what we have faced hitherto as the challenges that confront us. 'Tasks in the political sphere' must be taken as carefully chosen wording, needing further consideration. The commonly used distinction between, and even separation of, polity, politics and police lacks viability – we must revisit the separation of powers, seen as an indispensable mainstay of modern communities since Montesquieu.

It should also be clear that the framework within which we act (allowing that non-action is a form of action) has changed: global and local, institutional and informal, societal and social, public and private, these are the main categories that need to be revisited in theory and practice. Adding to the major challenges of polity-building is the size of China and

Southeast Asia, which must make us alert to both the new opportunities and the huge dangers. The self-sacred open societies of the West have obviously failed to deliver; postcolonialism should be understood as prelude to an entirely new chapter of world history and geopolitics (Brunnhuber, 2021).

Note

1 Or equivalent document, usually with limited validity, in particular limiting travel. It deserves mentioning that the passport as we know it today is only a late invention, while 'freedom to travel' is an old utopia, mentioned by Thomas More, for instance, who also speaks about passports.

References

Blair, Tony. 2005. "Leader's Speech, 2005." Accessed November 9, 2021. www.britishpoliticalspeech.org/speech-archive.htm?speech=182.

Bohr, Niels. 1928. "The Quantum Postulate and the Recent Development of Atomic Theory." *Nature* 121: 580–590.

Bohr, Niels (quoted in: *Philosophy of Science*, volume 37 (1934): 17, and in Newton, Roger Gerhard). 1997. *The Truth of Science: Physical Theories and Reality*. Cambridge, MA: Harvard University Press.

Braudel, Fernand. 1984. *Civilization and Capitalism, Volume 3: The Perspective of the World*. Translated by Siân Reynolds. London: Williams Collins Sons & Co Ltd./New York: Harper & Row.

Braudel, Fernand. 1987. *Grammaire de civilisations*. Paris: Flammarion, 2002.

Brunnhuber, Stefan. 2021. "Open Societies versus Autocratic Experiments or Why the Latter Are Parasitic, Cannibalizing and Self-Limiting." *Cadmus* 4 (4): 216–225.

Goernitz, Thomas. 1999. *Quanten sind anders. Die verborgene Einheit der Welt*. With a preface by Carl Friedrich von Weizsaecker. Heidelberg/Berlin: Spektrum Akademischer Verlag.

Goethe, Johan Wolfgang von. 1808. *Faust Part I* translated by A.S. Kline, 2003. Accessed October 23, 2021. www.poetryintranslation.com/PITBR/German/FaustIScenesIVtoVI.php#Scene_IV.

Gumbrecht, Hans-Ulrich. 2021. "Mein kleiner Roboter und ich: Wie ich ein Smartphone kaufte und zu verstehen begann, was mich von den unter Dreissigjährigen unterscheidet [My little robot and me: How I bought a smartphone and began to understand what makes me different from the under-thirties]." *Neue Zuercher Zeitung*, 11 November.

Herrmann, Peter. 2016. "From 5 Giant Evils to 5 Giant Tensions – The Current Crisis of Capitalism as Seedbed for Its Overturn – Or: How Many Gigabytes has a Horse?" (Seminar 'Continuidad y Cambios en las Relaciones Internacionales' at ISRI (Instituto Superior de Relaciones Internacionales Raúl Roas García), Habana.

Herrmann, Peter. 2020. "The Transformation That Could Not Happen – or: There Won't Be a Clear Answer as Long as We Ask the Wrong Question." Working Paper 18, International Association on Social Quality, Amsterdam.

Herrmann, Peter and Maria Yudina. 2021. "Social Narcissism – How Society Pushes Us To Overestimate Our Capacities, Leaving Many Behind." *Living Standards of the Population in the Regions of Russia* 17 (3): 382–388.

Holmes, Oliver Wendell Jr. (1897). *The Path of Law*. Auckland: The Floating Press, 2009.

Jhering, Rudolph von. 1879. *The Struggle for Law*, with an Introduction by Albert Kocourek. Translated from the fifth German edition by John J. Lalor. Chicago: Callaghan & Co., 1915.

Kehlmann, Daniel. 2006. *Measuring the World*. New York: Pantheon.

Kleban, Matthew. 2021: "Astrophysicist Janna Levin explains Gravity in 5 Levels of Difficulty." *Wired*. Accessed August 22, 2021. https://youtu.be/QcUey-DVYjk.

Krasner, Stephen D. 2009. "Structural Causes and Regime Consequences: Regimes as Intervening Variables." In *Power, the State, and Sovereignty. Essays on International Relations*, 113–128. London/New York: Routledge.

Lorenz, Edward N. 1963. "Deterministic Nonperiodic Flow." *Journal of the Atmospheric Sciences* 20 (2): 130–141.

Mahbubani, Kishore. 2020. *Has China Won? The Chinese Challenge to American Primacy*. New York: Public Affairs. Hachette Book Group.

Mottley, Mia Amor. 2021. "Barbados – Prime Minister Addresses United Nations General Debate, 76th Session (English)." Accessed October 9, 2021. Automatic transcript, edited by Peter Herrmann. www.youtube.com/watch?v=wz_lDnay3H8.

Pashukanis, Evgeny Bronislavovich. 1924. "The General Theory of Law and Marxism." In *Selected Writings on Marxism and Law*, edited by Piers Beirne and Robert Sharlet. Translated by Peter B. Maggs. Foreword by John N. Hazard. London: Academic Press, 1980.

Rostow, Walt Whitman. 1960. "The Stages of Economic Growth: A Non-Communist Manifesto." Cambridge: Cambridge University Press.

Teschke, Benno. 2011. "The Myth of 1648. Class, Geopolitics, and the Making of Modern International Relations." New York: Verso. With reference to Ormrod, William Mark. 1995. "The West European Monarchies in the Later Middle Ages." In *Economic Systems and State Finance*, edited by Richard Bonney, 123–160. Oxford: Oxford University Press.

Tooze, Adam. 2021. "Shutdown: How Covid Shook the World's Economy." London: Allen Lane.

Urry, John. 2016. "What Is the Future?" Cambridge/Malden: Polity Press.

6
TRADITIONAL COLONIALISM, MODERN HEGEMONISM, AND THE CONSTRUCTION OF ASIAN NATIONS

Feilong Tian

Introduction

From "community" to "union", the history of Europe since World War II is the history of European countries overcoming war and internal division to achieve unity and development. In the European Union (EU), European countries enjoy collective security, a common market, a common currency, the EU law and a balanced order of sovereignty and EU governance, thus to a certain extent realizing Kant's ideal of "perpetual peace" within Europe (Kant, 1795/2011). Although the EU still has important defects or even crises in its "strategic autonomy" (Habermas, 2011), and lacks the ability to review and balance the global hegemony of the US as a result of the rebuilding of Europe after World War II, the cultural and institutional construction of EU integration is a miracle compared to other continents.

In comparison with Europe, Asia's strategic autonomy is more problematic. Where is Asia? Will Asia think for itself? Can Asia achieve unity? What is the basis of Asia's autonomy? Considering Asia's history of colonization and fragmentation, and the reality of being subject to European and American hegemony, the cultural and political unity of Asia is a huge problem that Asian countries have to face and must struggle to solve.

How can Asia become a culturally and politically conscious community of historical destiny? This is a necessary stage and a major test for Asian various nationalities to move towards modern political maturity. Twenty-first-century Asia, in addition to suffering from overly pronounced internal pluralism and conflict and the complex legacy of traditional colonialism, is also under the systemic domination of a "new kind of hegemony", that of the US – "US global power is exercised through a global system clearly designed by itself" (Brzezinski, 1997).

The various regional armed conflicts and trade disputes that have occurred since the end of the twentieth century have allowed us to perceive the power and destructiveness of the hegemony of this "global system". The withdrawal of US troops from Afghanistan in September 2021 marked a critical failure of US democratic globalization and the political return of Taliban Islamism (Ding, 2021; Qian, 2022). However, it did not mean the disappearance of US hegemony in Asia. The US is trying to establish a tighter Asian hegemonic system in the form of an Asian version of NATO. Although Asian countries have long perceived and judged the oppressive nature and dominant power of US hegemony, it has been difficult to form a united community mechanism to effectively counteract it culturally and politically. The US has penetrated the shield of nationalism of Asian countries and the net of intra-Asian united communalism, with its powerful security and financial trade system.

Historically, Asian nationalism was a specific intellectual and political consequence of European colonialism. The systematic jurisprudence of the nation-state and of sovereignty matured in the early modern period in Europe, providing a systematic philosophy of the state and a paradigm of international law for European nations caught up in religious and feudal wars of suzerainty. Since the Peace of Westphalia in 1648, nationalism has gradually spread from Europe to the rest of the world along the path of colonialism, with the colonized peoples of Asia thus acquiring powerful ideological weapons and words of struggle against colonialism.

From early nationalism in Europe to the right to national self-determination in the twentieth century, nationalism began to be universally accepted by Asian peoples in their struggle for salvation and survival, and national democratic revolutions with the intent of modern nation-building took place in a wide region of Asia; the political consequences were the decolonization of Asia and the independent liberation of Asian peoples. Nationalism in Asia formed a kind of shield against colonialism, national sovereignty was legally transformed into state sovereignty and the modern Asian political map was gradually formed.

However, nationalism is a double-edged sword, and Asian countries at the forefront of the national liberation struggle and modernization process have imitated to a certain degree the Western powers through aggression towards and oppression of their Asian neighbours, leading to disorder in the region. Japanese imperialism, from the *Datsu-A Ron* to the ideological and political line of the Greater East Asia Co-Prosperity Sphere, is a typical example. The Japanese model did not bring about "coexistence and co-prosperity" in Asia, but rather a brutal, bloody and turbulent intra-Asian war.

The nationalism and political states established in Asia in the course of resistance to colonialism need to be tempered by the introduction of universal values that transcend nationalism, and require the peaceful and democratic construction of a common cultural and political order in Asia – through a healthy and constructive pan-Asianism and the strategic wisdom of China's contemporary Belt and Road Initiative, "A Community of Shared Future for Mankind" (Tian, 2018) exists.

Answering the fundamental question "Where is Asia?" requires examining the impact of pan-Asianism, and overcoming the hegemonic impulses and the normative limits of national sovereignty that have emerged from it. While resisting colonialism with nationalism, there is also a need to temper nationalism with a communitarian pan-Asianism, and to establish mutual trust in history and culture and interchange of economic interests in the Asian multilateral region (Pang, 2001), so as to gradually promote Asia's strategic autonomy, cultural self-confidence and joint self-improvement in a regional integrated governance structure. As China's value proposition and institutional initiative for Asian and global issues, the "Community of Shared Future for Mankind" is not only a continued struggle against traditional colonialism, but also a legitimate counterweight to the new US hegemony and a reasonable restraint on Asian nationalism, and can serve as a common conceptual basis and a practical path for multilateral cultural and political cooperation and governance among Asian nationalities and countries.

Eurocentrism and traditional colonialism: the British Empire and its influence on Asia

On July 1, 1997, Hong Kong was returned to China, bringing an end to a British colonial stronghold in Asia. On the day of the handover ceremony, Chinese nationalism and pride were at its peak, but Prince Charles, present at the ceremony, wrote in his diary: "Such is the end of Empire, I sighed to myself".

That is right. The empire on which the sun never set was a worldwide achievement of British global colonialism, which had occupied a wide range of Asian territories and implemented a fruitful colonial rule. British colonial rule was different from earlier Spanish and Portuguese colonial rule, as well as from the colonial models of other European powers. It pursued a deep colonial rule in the sense of fine governance, so that the British colonies continued to depend on Britain for their culture, institutions and trade systems even after they became independent. John Darwin's book *Unfinished Empire* (2013) systematically examines the historical construction of the British imperial colonial system and its far-reaching influence, which can partly explain the inherent dependence of many Asian countries and regions on the British colonial legacy.

In Hong Kong, this far-reaching influence has been perpetuated and kept in the form of "one country, two systems" (Liu, 2015), with Hong Kong's common law and its mechanism of foreign judges being the most important symbols. In Singapore, this far-reaching influence has also lived on in the legal system and the operation of the judiciary, despite the significant "decolonization" of the legal field by the government of former Prime Minister Lee Kuan Yew, including the abolition of juries and wigs, and reforms to improve judicial efficiency. Singapore's rule of law model is characterized by a combination of Eastern culture and English common law, which Yossi Raja (2012) calls the "authoritarian rule of law". Similarly, the Indian legal and political system was profoundly influenced by the British colonial legacy, and the higher education, cultural values and political thinking of its elites continued to be significantly influenced and dominated by London.

British colonization of Asia was one of the most profound and successful models in the realm of traditional colonialism. Many other European countries also colonized Asia, leaving a varying cultural and institutional legacy.

In the case of China's coastal and frontier regions, Macau was colonized by Portugal for centuries, Taiwan was colonized by the Dutch and Japanese, and Xinjiang, Tibet and the northeast were partially colonized by British, Russian and Japanese powers. However, China was a sovereign country with a relatively consolidated political system, and colonialism failed to consistently penetrate China's shield of sovereignty shield; China lost part of its territory and sovereignty in the areas of justice and trade, and was reduced to a semi-colonial state.

India became a complete British colony, a complex historical process interspersed with British, French and Portuguese colonial wars and the resistance struggles of the Indian native states and the Indian nation. The Indian National Revolt of 1857–1859 was a direct conflict between British colonialism and Indian nationalism, resulting in the abolition of the East India Company's proxy colonial rule and the introduction of direct British rule. The countries of Southeast Asia have suffered from colonialism throughout modern times, with the Dutch, Portuguese, Spanish, French, British and Americans colonizing the region one after another, engaging in plunder and war.

In contrast to East and Southeast Asia, central and western Asia also experienced the aggression and domination of the British, French and other European colonial powers. The

Belt and Road Initiative proposed by China seeks to promote connectivity and common development in the Asian region through the revival of the Silk Road. In his book *The Silk Roads* (2017), Peter Frankopan examines the multilateral, plural and colonial impact of the Silk Road from the perspective of colonial and global history. Its influence and legacy as a range of routes travelled not only by ancient merchants from China and the West, but also by modern Western colonizers, cannot be ignored. Reviving the Silk Road as a path of peaceful development entails facing various political, religious, cultural and economic conflicts caused by colonialism, imperialism and nationalism in Asian countries.

Traditional colonialism, especially British colonialism, is characterized by the universalism of modernity and globalization, an important background and qualifying factor for the construction of Asian autonomy in the post-colonial era. British colonization and globalization relied on the systematic construction and refinement of maritime civilization based on the Scottish Enlightenment, whose core elements include the following.

First, a common law based on the British rule of law tradition and the judicial skills to build a uniform legal system covering all colonies. This maintained its consistency after decolonization, rooted in its judicial centrality and the universalism of de-sovereignty and de-nationalization, but a large amount of "London legislation" was applied to the colonies generally or specifically, establishing Britain's colonial prerogatives and special interests as a sovereign state.

Second, the international financial and trade system, based on British financial and industrial capital, established a system of economic domination over the colonies, which were reduced to a source of raw materials and a dumping market for commodities, and the colonial industrial structure had to adapt to the monopoly interests of the British Empire and the vested interests of the capitalist groups.

Third, British culture and its powerful output mechanism back in London became the centre of study and a cultural mecca for the elites of the colonies.

Fourth, the maritime geopolitical system – by establishing colonies in major sea ports, trade hubs and land ports around the world, Britain was able to separate and control the Asian region and expand its colonial interests by taking advantage of the conflicts within the region, establishing a maritime colonial model that was different from the land colonial model. They incorporated the ports and land colonies into a huge system of overseas colonial empire, using the military, trade and culture to carry out geopolitical expansion and domination, with the aim of limiting and weakening Asian countries in the relevant geopolitical regions, causing long-term political division and regional conflicts. The "divide and conquer" approach to colonial retreat by the British perpetuated and even intensified the contradictory elements of the old geopolitics, thus perpetuating British post-colonial influence, such as the partition of India and the frequent ethnic and religious conflicts in Southeast Asia.

The construction of a new hegemonic system in the age of globalization

The colonization and domination of Asia by traditional colonialism centred on European power and typified by British power resulted in a vast region of Asia that remained strongly dependent on Britain in terms of its cultural, political and economic and trade systems. However, the Eurocentric colonial era was largely ended by the two world wars in the first half of the twentieth century, in which the colonies were also involved. These gave rise to two trends of thought.

First, the decline of European civilization, i.e., the loss of its civilizing aura due to its civil war and violent character, as typified by Spengler's *The Decline of the West*, and the emergence of the colonies' questioning and reflection.

Second, the rise of decolonized nationalism and even pan-Asianism in the Asian region, in which nationalism denies the legitimacy of colonial rule and seeks political independence in the form of national self-determination. Pan-Asianism, in turn, is an aspect of the regional expansion of Asian nationalism, a more systematic self-integration and confrontation with colonial imperialism.

However, the decline of traditional colonialism and the independence of Asian countries did not mean the end of Western regional dominance, and the new hegemonic system led by the US replaced traditional colonialism to regain control over Asia. This type of hegemonic system is a rejection of the British colonial imperial system and its major institutional legacy, with both the technical legacy of traditional British colonization and new features.

The system's underpinnings include:

1. The modelling and globalization of US law – that is, legal transplantation and assistance in legal reform and modernization in a wide range of Asian regions. This came in the form of a written US-style constitution superimposed on common law, one which not only consolidated the legal traditions of former common law colonies, but also came to penetrate and control the legal culture. Rule of law reforms modelled on the US law are proliferating in Asian countries; this kind of legal globalization is more systematic and dominant than ever before.
2. The globalization and institutionalization of dollar hegemony. This is the hegemonic financial system of the US dollar as the world's reserve currency and sanctioning tool, established through the post-World War II Bretton Woods system and the SWIFT system. Asian countries that do not comply with this system face severe financial sanctions and suffer a huge loss of economic sovereignty and development interests.
3. The institutional constraints of widespread US military bases and security cooperation agreements around the world. In place of British territorial colonies, the US military bases have been established throughout Asia, and the US military hegemony has been constructed through bilateral or multilateral security agreements. These military bases and security agreements constitute an institutional tool for the US intervention in Asia and the advancement of geopolitical objectives, as well as an updated iteration of the legitimacy and institutional techniques of traditional colonialism.
4. The US establishment of patent and knowledge superiority in advanced technology, and its instrumentalization of sanctions. Through advanced education, personnel training, military-civilian integration, capital venture investment and global control of scientific and technological intelligence, patent control and high-tech information monopoly, the US has built a scientific and technological hegemony over all other countries and transformed the relevant knowledge and patent advantages into tools for export control and cut-throat sanctions.
5. The globalization of US democratic and entertainment cultures. The US uses its political system, value system, lifestyle and popular culture as templates to export to the world, and it establishes a large number of civil society projects and funds NGOs to implement the globalization of American democracy. It also uses Hollywood, Facebook, Twitter and other cultural mechanisms to transmit American culture and values to the outside world, and uses its strong soft power to achieve global cultural and ideological leadership.

Due to this "global system" that is characteristic of the new US hegemony, and the relative solidity of these core elements of hegemony, it is extremely difficult to reflect on and combat the nationalism or regionalism of US hegemony, and it is difficult to gather a solid political consensus and take concerted collective action even within and among Asian countries. With this new type of hegemony, the US achieves geopolitical control over "Eurasia" in order to achieve two US interests, namely "maintaining unique US global power in the near term and gradually transforming that power into institutionalized global cooperation in the future" (Brzezinski, 1997).

The US attaches great importance to the institutionalization of its global hegemony, including its hegemony over Asia, and the mechanisms by which it operates. Perry Anderson (2017), in *The H-Word: The Peripeteia of Hegemony*, defines the US hegemony as "a global empire built through military treaties and open markets" and further points out the hegemonic use of international organizations in the global system: "International institutions are first and foremost strategic tools to enforce the will of the US".

Of course, there is also a certain critical dimension to the European perspective of American hegemony beyond understanding and acceptance, such as Carl Schmitt's very perceptive, sensitive, ideologically critical and clear discussion of the decline of the European public law (international law) order and the ascent of American liberal imperial hegemony. In *Nomos of the Earth*, he reminds European countries and the world that the US brings not only so-called freedom, but also hegemony.

This US hegemony has largely absorbed and ended the worldwide influence of Europe, and has taken over as the new systemic dominant force in Asia. We can see a glimpse of US hegemony in the US-Japan Security Treaty, the US-Philippines Defense Treaty, the US military presence in the South China Sea, the US military cooperation with Singapore, the US strategic cooperation with India, the 20-year US occupation of Afghanistan and even the recent US security assistance agreement with Nepal. Under the US hegemony, Asia is still not autonomous, and Asian unity still faces serious threats and disadvantages.

Resistance from Asia: nationalism and pan-Asianism

Whether it is the traditional colonialism of Eurocentrism or the new hegemonic system dominated by the US, both are in fact a kind of pan-colonialism in which external forces dominate, control, dismantle and reconstruct Asia. The means and manifestations of control and domination keep changing, but the essence of control and domination remains the same. The historical construction of the West in Asia, however culturally and institutionally self-contained, has thus always been oppressive and unequal in its political relations, interrogating and impacting the Western system of domination.

The two basic types of resistance in Asia are nationalism and regionalism. The emancipation of national independence in Asia, whether through socialism or capitalism, has been a process entailing the nationalization of ideas and political integration. Regionalism, however, represents a certain political maturation of Asian nationalism, one which sustains resistance against the Western system through a systemic mindset and approach.

That is why Asian countries need both nationalist self-improvement and regionalist solidarity. The political-philosophical and constitutional embodiment of nationalism is the principle of national sovereignty, a new principle that has certainly brought about complex boundary demarcation disputes and territorial disputes among Asian countries, but also constitutes a juridical shield against Western intervention and domination.

Traditional colonialism deeply colonized Asia territorially, culturally and institutionally, divided Asia geographically and politically according to a strict Orientalist logic, and established a "Near Middle East Far East" cognitive framework centred on Europe. It carried out the colonial separation of spheres of influence, trade system construction and cultural-institutional transformation of Asia, resulting in Asia's spiritual dependence on European and American colonial heritage and its psychological submission and strategic obedience to European and American hegemony in the post-colonial period. The colonial culture, the colonial system and the Euro-American hegemonic system have inherently hierarchical and exploitative characteristics, thus inflicting lasting mental domination and deprivation on the Asian peoples.

The adaptation to the Western system will produce mixed results, with some peoples developing faster and integrating more smoothly, while others do so more slowly and with more difficulty; regardless of the specific level of development, they all face an open question: Can Asia have its own cultural values and modernization path? This is the historical and spiritual root of pan-Asianism in the recent history of Asia.

Under the stimulation of Western colonialism, there is a widespread nationalist urge and a pan-civilizational quest for unity and self-improvement in non-Western regions, such as the Great Asianism proposed by the founder of the Republic of China Sun Yat-sen in 1924, the pan-Africanism promoted by Ghanaian political leader Kwame Nkrumah, the pan-Arabism promoted by Egyptian President Gamel Abdul Nasser and the pan-Asianism promoted by countries such as China and India. These approaches, facing together the racial oppression and exploitation of interests by Western colonialism, seek common historical and cultural roots in an attempt to build a closer regional community in order to gain equal status and discourse in the global system.

Admittedly, pan-Asianism or Greater Asianism has been seriously distorted and abused, turning into the Greater East Asia Co-Prosperity Sphere of Imperialist Japan during World War II and the East Asian Unionism promoted by the Japanese-controlled regime established by Wang Jingwei in Shanghai. This has led to considerable stigmatization of this idea and movement. The fundamental moral flaw of East Asian Unionism lies in the loss of national sovereignty and dignity, the loss of national subjectivity, the loss of the ethics of equality that should characterize regionalism and its degeneration into a national surrenderism subservient to Japanese militarism. Pan-Asianism will be a short-lived monstrosity if it only aims at a single peace and fails to uphold equality and dignity.

In contrast to Wang Jingwei, both Mao Zedong's *On the Protracted War* (1938) and Chiang Kai-shek's *China's Destiny* (1943) were political lines with a kernel of nationalist legitimacy, thus standing firm and stable. Japan's Greater East Asia Co-Prosperity Sphere, in contrast, was a mishmash of over-inflated nationalism, imperialism and the crude Asian version of the Monroe Doctrine, establishing not a community of equality and mutual assistance among Asian countries, but Japanese imperial hegemony in imitation of that of European and American powers, thus directly opposing the awakened nationalism of Asian countries and becoming a world enemy due to its fascist core. Its ultimate failure was inevitable.

After World War II, pan-Asianism regained momentum in the context of decolonization and national independence of Asian countries, and in 1947 Indian Prime Minister Nehru advocated a new Asian community at the Asian Conference: "We are not targeting any country. Our vision is to promote peace and progress around the world". Nehru systematically addressed Indian nationalism in his book *The Discovery of India*, but this conference revealed a new pan-Asian tendency.

The agenda for Asian unity was further accelerated with the establishment of the new China in 1949. In 1954, Chinese Premier Zhou Enlai visited India and Burma and put forward the Five Principles of Peaceful Coexistence: mutual respect for each other's territorial integrity and sovereignty; mutual non-aggression; mutual non-interference in each other's internal affairs; equality and cooperation for mutual benefit; and peaceful co-existence. These were the fruit of international law borne by pan-Asianism, recognized and supported by Asian countries and the wider Third World. The Bandung Conference of 1955 was a high point of neo-pan-Asianism; the ten principles for the conduct of international relations adopted there were an extension and development of Zhou Enlai's Five Principles.

The Non-Aligned Movement, founded in Belgrade in 1961, also had elements of and contributions from pan-Asianism. In 1974, Deng Xiaoping expounded the "three worlds division" theory in the UN General Assembly, clarifying the nature of the struggle in the world system, the level of struggle and the law of solidarity in the Third World; the reasonable elements of pan-Asianism were absorbed into it.

But since World War II, pan-Asianism has been suppressed by the Western capitalist camp, which scorns the Asian spirit of self-improvement, solidarity and collective action embedded in pan-Asianism and criticizes Asian nationalism and pan-Asianism through liberalism and globalism. Vijay Prasad (2022) argues that "the various tentacles of US imperialism in Asia and the hostile environment of the Cold War undermined any possibility of a revival of Pan-Asianism". However, he also acknowledges and even pursues a new pan-Asian movement: "Opening a serious dialogue on a new and progressive pan-Asianism is useful". This can be seen as acknowledgement and expectation by Indian scholars of the legacy of pan-Asian cooperation between India and China.

Contemporary pan-Asianism has a tendency to multilateralize. China's Belt and Road Initiative and "A Community of Shared Future for Mankind", with their rational elements of pan-Asianism; the active construction of China's relations with ASEAN; India's economic, trade and foreign policy in South Asia, as well as its conflict and cooperation variations with China – these all bear the marks of the former pan-Asianism. Even in the context of strategic competition between China and the US, there is still room for the possibility of strategic rapprochement and cooperation (Ma, 2020). Asia calls for deep cooperation and unity.

Pan-Asianism has the historical basis and political legitimacy of a regional community that is anti-hegemony, anti-intervention and in favour of joint self-improvement, and is also a rational development of the democratization of regional governance and the multilateralization of international relations. In a twenty-first-century context, the discussion of Asian nationalism and the common destiny and autonomy of Asia cannot be separated from an objective, retrospective evaluation and transformation of the twentieth-century pan-Asianism movement and trend of thought.

In short, in the long colonial history of Asian domination, the traditional colonialism of Eurocentrism was the foundation, producing a strong cultural and institutional influence, and was succeeded by the new hegemonic system led by the US in the era of globalization. This system has gradually realized the re-domination of Asia through a global system approach.

Asian nationalism and pan-Asianism are the ideological results of resistance to European colonialism and new types of hegemony, along with positive institutional attempts and limitations. They constitute a rational ideological resource and philosophical basis for the construction of Asian unity, self-improvement and autonomy, and a rational basis for a rational regionalist structure for achieving peace, security and common development in Asia.

Legal Orientalism and the construction of an independent Asia: the case of Singapore

In terms of history, diplomacy and political thinking, Asian autonomy has been eroded and dominated by traditional colonialism and the new US hegemony, and its systemic impact and negative legacy cannot be countered and eliminated in the short term. In terms of legal order, a kind of legal Orientalism (Ruskola, 2013) modelled on Anglo-American law still has an enveloping effect on Asian countries.

The construction of Asian autonomy cannot be achieved without the decolonization of the thought pattern of rule of law and legal systems. Of course, this process is a legal reconstruction under the principles of nationalism and sovereignty. It does not mean a "legal reversion" of Asian countries, but rather a re-synthesis based on their own civilization, sovereignty and experience of modernization.

We can use the decolonization of law in Singapore as an example of Asian law reclaiming its autonomy and rejecting an ideological legal Orientalism. A former British colony, it has adopted the English common law and its judicial system, with judicial links with the regions where common law is applied, such as mutual citation of precedents and interaction in legal education and exchange of jurisprudence.

After independence in 1965, Singapore embarked on a process of systematic decolonization. It has taken a path of judicial autonomy: on the one hand, selectively inheriting the British institutional heritage and maintaining Singapore's organic ties with the Western world; on the other hand, systematically legislating on issues of national security and public order to clear the legal and judicial spheres. It has created systematic national security and public order legislation in order to clean up elements of the legal and judicial system that endanger the nation's interests, and to promote the autonomy of Singapore's common law.

Overall, Singapore has embarked on an aggressive and effective decolonization of the judiciary against external interference and judicial dependence, which has provided critical support for national sovereignty, security and development interests. Its judicial decolonization experience includes the following main aspects:

First, a group of legal reformers led by the Cambridge Townsmen Association in England was critical to, and effective in, reforming English law. The key figures in Singapore's legal reforms were Lee Kuan Yew, Yeo Bang Hsiao and Eddie Barker – respectively, Prime Minister, Chief Justice of the Supreme Court and Law Minister. They shared a common Cambridge law study experience and an inherent understanding and critique of English law, a strong consensus on Singapore law and judicial reform, and a specific grasp of the flaws and shortcomings of English law in their careers as lawyers. Judicial decolonization has proceeded smoothly, with a high degree of leadership consensus.

Second, a combination of substantive and symbolic reform to several institutions of English law established rationalized, autonomous jurisprudence and legal beliefs in Singapore. Rather than developing a transitional dependence and obsession with English law, Singapore has tailored it to its own needs. Under the leadership of Lee Kuan Yew and others, the country has successively abolished the jury system, the judge wig system and procedural redundancy, improving the legal precision of the judicial fight against crime, the approachability of judges and the efficiency of judicial trials. This process has also reformed the original common law judges' bad habits of using procedure and precedent to delay trials, shirk responsibility and bypass the law.

Third, legislation has been created, with public order as the core value, to rectify the possible damage of English law on Singapore's sovereignty, security and development interests, and to firmly establish legal and judicial sovereignty. This rule of law system has long been criticized in the West as authoritarian, largely due to the systematic legislation in the area of public order led by Lee Kuan Yew and others, which limited the legal arrangements left over from English law and the room for intervention by outside forces.

Such legislation includes the *Vandalism Act*, the *Newspaper and Printing Presses Act*, the *Legal Profession Act* and the *Maintenance of Religious Harmony Act*. The most recent public order legislation includes the *Public Order Act* of 2009 and the *Foreign Interference (Countermeasures) Act* of 2021, which provide stricter legal definitions and penalties for internal threats and external interventions in the area of public order. These laws are based upon national sovereignty backed by nationalism and serve as a counter-balance to the original colonial law.

The founding fathers of Singapore sought a better balance between public order and freedoms. The criticism of Singapore's legal authoritarianism is unfocused and over-liberal, and misunderstands the value of public order in Eastern cultures. The rule of law in Singapore has evolved into a bridge between Western and Eastern legal cultures, and the experience of Singapore's legal reconstruction may offer much to other Asian countries and regions, such as Hong Kong.

Fourth, Singapore severed its dependence on English law in terms of judicial practice, strengthened the patriotic identity and judicial confidence of judges, and advanced the process of judicial autonomy. Due to the profound influence of colonialism, certain colonizing measures and arrangements inevitably still exist in the Singaporean system, including judges' continued reliance on and attachment to English law. The power of final adjudication is still in principle linked to the British Privy Council, while English law is still invoked and applied in Singapore, and Singaporean common law education is still British-influenced.

The Lee Kuan Yew government did not implement complete decolonization across the board, but rather made effective choices and qualifications to ensure that the legacy of English law served Singapore, but not to the detriment of national security. Measures include political vetting and patriotic education for Singaporean civil servants, to ensure that law enforcers identify with Singaporean values and legal sovereignty; strict criteria and procedures for the selection of judges, to support patriotic judges in the independent exercise of judicial power; presidential decisions on whether to refer cases to the British Privy Council and to terminate such referrals in concrete practice; the enactment of the *Application of English Law Act* to restrict the application of English law in Singapore; legal education and judicial personnel training that focuses on autonomy and the quality of local education.

These autonomy and localization measures safeguarded Singapore's judiciary from being weakened and marginalized during the decolonization process, while maintaining its fundamental position and influence in the regions where common law was applied. It is a special political wisdom to distinguish between what should be conserved, what should be restricted and what should be abolished in the colonial legal system.

Fifth, the cultural confidence and cultural identity of Singapore's "Asian values" have effectively supported the decolonization of justice at the values level. As the primary legislator of Singapore's founding, Lee Kuan Yew introduced the Asian values concept as a normative criticism of Western culture, arguing that the political and legal systems of Asian countries should be based on these. This cultural trust and self-identification with the law and the judiciary has been important to the sweeping series of reforms that have decolonized Singapore's judiciary.

It is impossible to decisively carry out a real decolonization of justice if a country continues to culturally degrade itself with an Orientalist vision and to emulate Western culture and institutions. The "Asian values" expressed by Singapore's political leader and his legal reforms can be seen as a combination of Asian nationalism and pan-Asianism.

Tune into the future: Asia and the building of a community of shared future for mankind

In the overall interest of Asian modernization, Asia's united self-improvement is a path that can be universally discussed, attempted and accepted as a legitimate strategy for Asian peoples to cope with post-colonial hegemony. Nationalism and pan-Asianism are powerful ideological and institutional weapons for Asian peoples and nations seeking self-improvement and unity. We must be wary of the egomaniacal and hegemonic mimetic impulses of nationalism and pan-Asianism, and of any denial and dismantling of both from the European and American camps. Nationalism is the basic shield against hegemony, and pan-Asianism is the systemic structure for constructing a genuine multilateral order. Both have a counter-hegemonic and anti-interventionist nature and function, and thus are bound to become the target of Western hegemony's suppression.

The future of Asia depends on Asia's united self-improvement. The US has the US-Mexico-Canada Agreement and the Monroe Doctrine. Africa has pan-Africanism and the African Union. Arab countries have the Arab League, Latin American countries have the Latin American Common Market and Southeast Asian countries have ASEAN. These regional organizations were born out of different political motives, communication of interests and cultural backgrounds, but share a common protective function and goal: to create an ideological and organizational mechanism based on nationalism and regionalism, seeking equal identity and mutually recognized juridical status.

Regionalism, in its rationally constructed sense, should be based on the principles of peaceful development, equality and mutual benefit, opposing hegemony and external intervention, combating internal bullying and inequality, organically coordinating regionalism, nationalism and globalism, and promoting long-term peace and the common development of all countries around the world.

Asia is the most complex continent in the world, and the construction of modernity and regional wholeness in Asia is an academic and political undertaking that is far from complete. Asia has long been blocked by internal barriers, dominated by Western colonization, provoked into confrontation by geopolitical conflicts and competing interests, and divided by overly diverse and scattered cultures, religions and ethnicities. Whether it is the pan-Asianism of the twentieth century, the "Asian values" of Lee Kuan Yew and others, the East Asian modernity discussed in Asian academia or the "Community of Shared Future for Mankind" newly proposed by China, all try to think about the common destiny of Asia, the connotations of modernity and the possibility of unity, based on the historical roots of Asian culture. Asia's independent thinking, joint self-improvement and common development are the core for the restructuring of the global order in the twenty-first century.

References

English-language references

Anderson, Perry. 2017. *The H-Word: The Peripeteia of Hegemony*. London: Verso.
Brzezinski, Zbigniew. 1997. *The Grand Chessboard: American Primacy and its Geostrategic Imperatives*. New York: Basic Books.
Darwin, John. 2013. *Unfinished Empire: The Global Expansion of Britain*. New York: Bloomsbury Press.
Frankopan, Peter. 2017. *The Silk Roads: A New History of the World*. New York: Vintage Books.
Habermas, Jürgen. 2011. *Zur Verfassung Europas: Ein Eaasy*. Berlin: Suhrkamp Verlag.
Kant, Immanuel. 2011. *Perpetual Peace*. San Diego: The Book Tree.

Linton, Henry. *Is HK Judiciary Sleepwalking to 2047?* Hong Kong: Sherriff Books.
Mahbubani, Kishore. 2020. *Has China Won? The Chinese Challenge to American Primacy*. New York: Public Affairs.
Nehru, Jawaharlal. 2004. *The Discovery of India*. Deli: APH Publishing Corp.
Paxson, Frederic L. 2017. *The New Nation*. North Charleston: CreateSpace Independent Publishing Platform.
Rajah, Jothie. 2012. *Authoritarian Rule of Law: Legislative, Discourse and Legitimacy in Singapore*. Cambridge: Cambridge University Press.
Ruskola, Teemu. 2013. *Legal Orientalism: China, the United States and Modern Law*. Cambridge, MA: Harvard University Press.
Schmidt, Carl. 2011. *Der Nomos der Erde im Völkerrecht des Jus Publicum Europaeum*. Berlin: Duncker & Humbolt GmbH.
Spengler, Oswald. 2021. *The Decline of the West*. London: Arktos.

Chinese-language references

Chiang, Kai-shek 蒋介石. 1943. 中国之命运 (*China's Destiny*). Nanjing: Cheng Chung Books.
Ding, Long 丁隆. 2021. "阿富汗塔利班的意识形态转型" (Ideological Transition of the Afghan Taliban). 现代国际关系 (*Contemporary International Relations*), no. 12: 10–17, 33, 57.
Du, Weiming 杜维明. 2001. 东亚价值与多元现代性 (*East Asian Values and Pluralistic Modernity*). Beijing: China Social Sciences Press.
He, Li 何理. 2010. "毛泽东关于三个世界划分理论与二十世纪七十年代中国外交战略调整" (Mao Zedong's Theory on the Division of Three Worlds and Adjustments to Chinese Diplomatic Strategy in 1970s). 中共党史研究 (*CPC History Studies*), no. 4: 14–21.
Li, Zhenzhong 李振中. 1992. "纳赛尔与泛阿拉伯主义" (*Nasser and Pan-Arabism*). 阿拉伯世界 (*Arab World Studies*), no. 3: 11–14.
Liu, Zhaojia 刘兆佳. 2015. 一国两制在香港的实践 (*The Practice in Hong Kong of One Country, Two System*). Hong Kong: The Commercial Press.
Lv, Yuanli 吕元礼. 2002. 亚洲价值观：新加坡政治的诠释 (*Asian Values: An Interpretation of Singaporean Politics*). Nanchang: Jiangxi People's Publishing House.
Mao, Zedong 毛泽东. 1964. 论持久战 (*On Protracted War*). Beijing: People's Publishing House.
Pang, Zhongying 庞中英. 2001. "中国的亚洲战略：灵活的多边主义" (China's Asia Strategy: Flexible Multilateralism). 世界经济与政治 (*World Economics and Politics*), no. 10: 30–35.
Qian, Xuemei 钱雪梅. 2022. "美国与塔利班：谁能改造阿富汗?" (US vs. Taliban: Who Can Transform Afghanistan?). 文化纵横 (*Beijing Cultural Review*), no. 1: 38–47.
Sang, Bing 桑兵. 2015. "解读孙中山大亚洲主义演讲的真意" (Interpreting the True Meaning of Sun Yat-sen's Great Asianism Speech). 社会科学战线 (*Social Science Front*), no. 1: 95–116.
Shu, Yunguo 舒运国. 2014. "泛非主义与非洲一体化" (Pan-Africanism and African Intergration). 世界历史 (*World History*), no. 2: 20–37+157–158.
Swaran Singh, Zhang, Guihong 斯瓦兰·辛格、张贵洪. 2012. "亚洲多边主义：政治实践与理论贡献" (Asian Multilateralism: Political Practice and Theoretical Contributions). 国际观察 (*International Review*), no. 2: 30–36.
Tian, Feilong 田飞龙. 2018. "人类命运共同体：探索科学社会主义实践新路" (A Community of Shared Future for Mankind: Exploring New Approaches of Scientific Socialism Practice). 科学社会主义 (*Scientific Socialism*), no. 4: 22–27.
Vijay Prashad 维贾伊·普拉萨德. 2022. "亚洲的团结可能吗？" (Is Unity in Asia Possible?). *Guancha Syndicate*, April 23, 2022. https://www.guancha.cn/VijayPrashad/2022_04_23_636392.shtml
Wu, Jianjie 吴剑杰. 1997. "从大亚洲主义走向世界大同主义——略论孙中山的国际主义思想" (From Greater Asianism to World Cosmopolitanism: A Brief Discussion of Sun Yat-sen's Internationalist Ideology). 近代史研究 (*Modern Chinese History Studies*), no. 3: 185–208.
Zheng, Yongnian 郑永年. 2016. 中国崛起：重估亚洲价值观 (*The Rise of China: Reassessing Asian Values*). Beijing: The Oriental Press.

PART II

East Asia

The roots, growth, ingredients, expressions, and contestation of national discourses

Part II of this handbook explores the origins, development, constituents, manifestations, and contestation of nationalism in China, Japan, North Korea, and South Korea through diverse perspectives and approaches.

In pre-modern times, China did not see itself as a country but a *Tianxia* (meaning the world, literally 'under heaven'). The ideological core of this cultural entity was Confucianism in conjunction with Tianxiaism. The latter suggested that China was the only true civilization in the world and that its cultural superiority remained unchallenged. The Qing dynasty's defeat in the two Opium Wars (1840–1842 and 1856–1860) forced the Chinese to re-evaluate their relationship with foreign powers and redefine the meaning of Tianxia. The country's enlightenment thinkers and reformists were convinced that salvation would only be achieved when people showed their loyalty to a modern nation state instead of submitting to an emperor or a culture-bound empire. In order to achieve this goal, they introduced the Western concepts of nation, nation state, and nationalism to the broader public. Against this context, we may ask if we can speak of a 'tamed nationalism', striving for a favorable position in relation to the Tianxia instead of evolving with its own expansionist or separatist visions.

Julia C. Schneider's chapter deals with this question and offers an introduction to early Chinese nationalism. It examines Chinese intellectuals' conceptualizations of the nation and the nation state, their models and roots, as well as the political history, and shows how important aspects of nationalism, such as constitutionalism, national elections, and synchronization of administrative systems, were introduced by reforms in the late Qing era. Schneider also discusses the limitations of early Chinese nationalism, outlining how the proto-democratic features of the nationalists' modern nation state, the Republic of China (ROC), quickly declined, and how the Republic fell into crisis soon after its founding in 1912.

In the first half of the twentieth century, in response to foreign aggression and against the background of the two World Wars, anti-imperialism, militarism, and Social Darwinism prevailed in China, giving rise to a very distinct version of nationalism that focused on and stressed national survival, national unity, and national strengthening. Zhiguang Yin's chapter reviews the striving for and the emergence of modern Chinese national unity in the context of the country's anti-imperial and anti-colonial revolution. He pays particular attention to the applications of nationalism and its associated concepts outside the European historical and socio-political contexts in which they were developed. Yin points out that the transition and dissemination of ideas were far from being a simple and smooth story of intellectual transfusion or even diffusion. Particularly, the spread of nationalism from the dominant Western powers to the oppressed peoples of Asia ignited a process of contestation in which generations of intellectuals began to aspire to a future for their own nations through rewriting, cross-pollinating, interpreting, adapting, criticizing, and resisting those discourses that justified Western dominance.

Meishan Zhang's contribution investigates the influence of nationalism on nation building and modernization with particular reference to the establishment and development of the modern female hygiene system in the ROC era (1912–1949). Zhang traces the historical roots of the active participation of the political and medical agencies with the goal of strengthening the country and 'race'. She points out that nationalism helped to reshape the female body into a national body, turning women into a hope for national salvation and revitalization, particularly due to their role in nurturing the next generation. During this transformation process, women's voices and experiences, although limited, began to emerge in public discussions.

After the Civil War, the Communists established the People's Republic of China (PRC) on the mainland. The Chinese Nationalists Party (KMT) and its government retreated to Taiwan and remained there as the ROC. Against the background of the Cold War, the PRC was recognized by socialist countries led by the Soviet Union, while the ROC (Taiwan) was supported by the Capitalist bloc headed by the United States. Both claimed to be the sole representative of China, which came to be known as the 'Two Chinas' situation. Following the famous ping-pong diplomacy of 1971, the United Nations recognized the PRC as the sole government representing China. In subsequent years, more than 110 countries switched their recognition from the ROC to the PRC. Yitan Li's chapter traces the changing Taiwanese identity in the ROC and rising nationalism in the PRC over the past decades. He argues that Taiwan is stuck between a rock and a hard place when it comes to moving forward. On the one hand, the Taiwanese identity is becoming increasingly different from the mainland Chinese identity, moving Taiwan further down the path of becoming a distinct nation state. On the other hand, rising nationalism in mainland China, buttressed by the PRC's rising economic and military power, keeps Taiwan in the PRC's orbit – a centripetal force that pulls Taiwan ever closer to unification with the mainland, peacefully or otherwise. Li concludes that Taiwan is eager to maintain its unique social structures, national identity, and political system based on decades of democratization. At the same time, Taiwan is now facing a hard choice between drifting further away from or returning to the mainland.

The next chapter, written by Florian Schneider, focuses on contemporary nationalism in the PRC. It introduces and discusses four key concepts: techno-nationalism, online nationalism, cyber-nationalism, and digital nationalism. He investigates how Chinese organizations, algorithms, and users generate feedback loops through their interactions on the internet. He then explains how these networked processes create a nationalism that, as an emergent property, powerfully affects politics, but is not under the control of any single actor, group, or organization. Schneider further argues that this kind of digital nationalism is likely to shape Chinese domestic politics and international affairs for the foreseeable future. In addition, the digital networks of Capitalist platforms that seek to commodify culture and monetize attention continue to affect politics everywhere.

Nationalism is a concept dominated by politics (Breuilly 1993, 1). Its development is reinforced by economic, cultural, linguistic, and/or other kinds of national aspirations; hence, these less-dominant elements are assigned an auxiliary function in the consolidation of national consciousness (Alter 1994). Sport is one of these national aspirations. Lu Zhouxiang's chapter on 'The dream of a strong country' studies the role of sport and the modern Olympic movement in the construction of Chinese nationalism. His chapter makes an important contribution to the wider debate on sporting patriotism and its influence on people's perception of the strength of a nation, national confidence, and self-esteem. Zhouxiang argues that, for a long time, sport was seen as one of the few areas where China could achieve excellence, shine in glory, and defeat developed Western countries. However, after decades of rapid economic development, there are many other areas from which China can derive recognition, self-esteem, pride, and self-confidence. Today, rather than just focusing on the political significance of Chinese 'tracksuit ambassadors', i.e. successful athletes and teams, there is more of a focus on their personalities and individuality. However, as long as athletes compete for their country and under their national flags, it will be impossible to separate sport and the Olympics from the influence of politics and nationalism.

Ryan (1997, 157) stated that

> ever since the start of the age of nationalism at the end of the eighteenth century, there have been tensions between the concepts of the state and the nation. Where the political borders of the state and the cultural boundaries of the nation do not coincide, as is the case with the vast majority of so-called nation-states, friction develops between the principles of territorial integrity and national self-determination.

As early as the late nineteenth century, Chinese enlightenment thinkers and revolutionaries understood that nationalism might lead to ethnic conflicts within China, thus posing a major threat to political stability and national unity. Enlightenment thinker Liang Qichao therefore developed the theory of 'Big Nationalism' and 'Small Nationalism' to cope with this complex issue. According to this theory, every ethnic group in China, such as the Han, the Zhuang, the Miao, the Manchus, the Mongols, the Tibetans, the Uyghur, and the Hui, have their own 'Small Nationalism', while 'Big Nationalism' united all ethnic groups together to stand against imperialist powers. Soon after the establishment of the ROC in 1912, state leaders, nationalists, and intellectuals promoted 'Big Nationalism' together with the idea of 'Five Races under One Union', which meant that the five major ethnic groups in China would unite under the Republic, to create and reinforce a sense of national unity among all ethnic groups. Despite this, 'Small Nationalism' was growing among the Uyghur, the Tibetans, and the Mongols, and eventually gave birth to the Uyghur independence movement in 1933 and led to the establishment of the Mongolian People's Republic in 1945.

Following the establishment of the PRC in 1949, continuous efforts were made by the Communist regime to cultivate 'Big Nationalism' among all ethnic groups. Although the Hui, Manchu, Zhuang, Yi, Miao, and other ethnic minorities have maintained a relatively harmonious relationship with the Han majority, the rising 'Small Nationalism' among the Uyghur has led to tension and conflicts in Xinjiang. Arabinda Acharya and Rohan Gunaratna's chapter offers a comprehensive analysis of nationalism, identity, and violence in Xinjiang. It points out that in Xinjiang, China faces the conundrum of bridging the gap between the center and the periphery, which has become complicated by the unique set of needs and interests of the Uyghur as they are eager to protect and preserve their culture and identity. Over the years, Beijing has implemented policies of assimilation supplemented with force and general repression. The Uyghur consider these aggressive attempts at integration an attack on their religion and culture which has led to concerns of dilution or even outright destruction of their identity. Acharya and Gunaratna argue that extremism and terrorism are frequently caused by marginalization and repression, perceived or otherwise. This becomes more aggravated where the identity of a particular population is at stake. They suggest that the way to establish an enduring peace in Xinjiang is for the government to empathize with challenges to Uyghur identity and address associated concerns in a democratic and non-violent way.

Moving on to Japan, Yoshiko Nozaki first discusses the relationship between war memory, education, and nationalism and examines the writing and teaching of Japanese historian and educator Honda Koei about the Asia-Pacific War (1931–1945) in the late 1960s and early 1970s. Nozaki points out that a modern nation state governs its people in part by creating and disseminating narratives and discourses of the nation. One important site of such efforts is the education of younger generations in schools, especially teaching history in classrooms. Despite government pressure to diffuse right-wing nationalist narratives in the education sector, Honda – a junior high school teacher, then – took a critical, internationalist approach to teach about the war from the perspectives of its Asian victims. It was epoch-making because, prior to his practice, the issue of the war atrocities Japan committed had been rarely addressed directly in classrooms. Honda's students learnt about Japan's past wrongdoings and were asked to write letters to 'Asian junior high school friends'. They underwent a quiet struggle, but managed to articulate new forms of identities with an inclination toward building peace. In that process, they spoke as 'we', the Japanese – a reaffirmation of the imaginary, fixed national boundaries. However, a large number of parents were rather reluctant to support Honda's history lessons because they were concerned about their children's apologies for Japan's war crimes and feelings of shame. Nozaki concludes that Honda's case shows some inherent complexity, contradiction, and uncertainty in the formation of national identity at grassroots levels in a society where nationalism and internationalism compete.

Sven Saaler turns the focus to contemporary Japan by offering a critical analysis on historical revisionism – a highly contested form of nationalism that has developed in the country in the late twentieth and early twenty-first centuries. He argues that historical revisionism emerged as a result of the growing critical analysis of Japanese history, in particular of Japan's wartime past; and a perceived series of 'insults' to the honor of the nation, including apologies for past 'injustices'. He views the aggressive rhetoric employed by Japanese historical revisionists in this context as symptomatic of a collective narcissism. Saaler concludes that historical revisionism poses a danger to world peace and raises concerns that, without remedial measures, a repetition of the history of the first half of the twentieth century may not be avoided.

Jeff Kingston further discusses Japan's nationalism and historical revisionism by examining how former Prime Minister Abe Shinzo promoted a right-wing nationalist agenda that involved revising the Japanese Constitution and rewriting Japan's wartime history. To demonstrate the nature of Abe's nationalism, Kingston also examines his record on immigration, territorial disputes, alliance with the United States, freedom of expression, and the 2020 Tokyo Olympics. He points out that during Abe's long tenure, he transformed the political discourse on Japan's shared history with Asia and targeted those favoring more contrite and critical perspectives on the wartime and colonial past. Kingston argues that there is evidence to claim that there was a reemergence of reactionary nationalism and patriotic boosterism during the Abe era. It appears that this was a top-down phenomenon that did not ignite grassroots support. In the end, Abe's 'flawed record and policy shortcomings diminished his legacy, and limited his ability to transform national identity and nurture ardent nationalist sentiments' (Kingston 2023, 264).

In 1995, the sociologist Michael Billig made a major contribution to the field of nationalism studies by introducing the concept of 'banal nationalism' which implies less visible and taken-for-granted forms of nationalism in everyday life that is 'constantly "flagged" in the media through routine symbols and habits of language'. According to Billig, nationhood and nation states are reproduced from day to day through small familiar reminders that operate mindlessly beyond the level of conscious awareness. The signs of nationalism are everywhere but are often overlooked. Nevertheless, they are constantly shaping and reinforcing people's sense of national identity. Advertising is one of the channels that banal nationalism is regularly conveyed to individuals in an unnoticed manner. In the last chapter on Japan, Koji Kobayashi analyzes the production and consumption of (trans)national identity through Japanese advertising in the contemporary era. It explains how nationalism is commercially reproduced through the insularity of the Japanese advertising industry and the centrality of local cultural intermediaries, and reveals how such production is variously operated through complex relationships among a range of actors and organizations, including governments, corporations, NGOs, advertising agencies, and consumers. Kobayashi (2023, 276) concludes that Japanese advertising 'has remained in serving as a main vehicle of nation-centric ideas, views and sentiments due to the insularity of their domestic industries and the centrality of Japanese actors and organizations within the context of cultural production', and 'this form of commercial nationalism through everyday consumption and embodiment of national identity is powerful in normalizing and naturalizing the homogeneity of Japanese ethnicity, culture and identity'.

The next four chapters in this section look at nationalism in the two Koreas, the Democratic People's Republic of Korea (DPRK) in the North and the Republic of Korea (ROK) in the South, divided along the 38th parallel since 1948. In the past seven decades, two distinctively different world views, socio-economic systems, national identities, and nationalism have emerged on the divided peninsula and shape the everyday life of the divided Korean people. Udo Merkel's chapter discusses the contribution of public celebrations, commemorations, ceremonies, anniversaries, and other festivities to nation building and identity construction in North Korea. He shows in great detail that the North Korean rulers have developed an extensive set of cultural tools specifically for nation building purposes that help its citizens to make sense of who they are as a nation against the wider context of the political and ideological conflicts between the two Koreas. At the same time, the country's rulers, half-heartedly, also promote a pan-Korean identity that emphasizes the strong ethnic ties and common cultural heritage of the Korean people – a balancing act that 'keeps the issue of reunification in the public discourse without the need to engage in complex and difficult political negotiations' (Merkel 2023, 293).

According to Eric Hobsbawm (1983, 1), nation and nationalism are constructed by 'invented traditions' that include 'a set of practices, normally governed by overtly or tacitly accepted rules and of a ritual or symbolic nature, which seek to inculcate certain values and norms of behavior by repetition, which automatically implies continuity with the past'. The process includes the adaptation and, often, modification of old traditions and institutions, and the deliberate invention of new traditions with the purpose of creating order and unity. North Korea's public ceremonies, commemorations, and festivals have been created and promoted by all three Kim governments to legitimize its power and promote national unity. Over the course of time, these 'invented traditions' became unique symbols, suitably tailored discourse, and 'collective group self-presentations' of the socialist nation state, through which nationalism became a substitute for social cohesion.

Udo Moenig continues to analyze Korean nationalism through the lens of 'invented traditions' by exploring the historical formation of taekwondo, a form of martial arts that was declared the 'national sport' of South Korea by its government in 1971. He observes that the formation of taekwondo into a relatively uniform entity happened during the turbulent decades after Korea's liberation from Japanese colonial rule in 1945. Influenced by the surging nationalism and militarism of the time, taekwondo was promoted by Park Chung Hee's military regime (1960–1979) as an ideological and political instrument for controlling the population during its drive for spiritual, moral, and cultural restoration of the Korean nation. Moenig (2023, 305) noted:

> Today, the Korean taekwondo community and the public often regard taekwondo as a "national property"; therefore, expecting extraordinary privileges in decision making, controlling rights, and development direction. These sentiments are compounded by still lingering nationalistic attitudes in regards to taekwondo's origins and history.

After decades of industrialization and modernization, South Korea has developed into one of the most affluent and developed countries in Asia, which has, in turn, brought pride and confidence to the Korean people and led to the transformation of Korean nationalism. Charles R. Kim's chapter studies South Korea's 'postdevelopmental nationalism' (1980s–present) and celebrates the country's accomplishments in the areas of industrialization, democratization, technological advancement, and cultural innovation. He points out that postdevelopmental nationalism evolved out of the older developmentalist nationalism of the nation building era (1948–1980s), and it is produced and reproduced by influential actors and agencies in the government, journalism, the entertainment industry, and mainstream academia, as well as by ordinary citizens. As a hegemonic discourse, it is not a singular doctrine, but a set of common-sense assumptions and narratives about Korean history, its modern trajectory, its current place in the world, and its desired direction for future advance. Kim highlights that postdevelopmental nationalism is not only premised on collective South Korean national unity, but also supports the perpetuation of domestic socio-economic inequalities and inequities.

Gil-Soo Han and David Hundt's chapter continues discussing the development and shape of contemporary South Korean nationalism focussing on generational differences. They introduce the idea of 'calculated nationalism' and illustrate how this strain of nationalism has influenced South Korea's treatment of ethnic minorities, changed younger people's views of reunification, and reshaped Korean-Japanese relations. It reveals that unlike the older generations who were willing to limit their personal gain in solidarity with the effort to build an affluent Korean society, the younger generations of South Korea are more reluctant to make personal sacrifices for the greater good. They tend to prefer calculating personal benefit over contribution to the whole society and national development.

Masaki Tosa (2023, 337) argues that 'there is no safe terrain to objectively analyse one country's nationalism by detaching it from the other'. Korean nationalism is primarily born out of the Japanese occupation and colonization between 1910 and 1945 and the subsequent division of South Koreans' sense of who they are as a nation has been continuously shaped and reinforced by the tense relationship and rivalry between South Korea and Japan. The latter has found its expression in several political conflicts and diplomatic rows and even includes territorial disputes. Using Liah Greenfeld's 'nationalism trilogy' as the theoretical framework, Tosa's chapter studies the birth and transformation of 'Japanese-Korean nationalism'. It points out that throughout the second half of the twentieth century, Korean nationalism experienced complex interactions with Japanese nationalism, and that criticizing one side usually contributes to supporting the other. The two countries

> have engaged in sibling rivalry, precisely because they share the same macroscopic process from the collapse of the traditional society to the birth of a nation in the premodern-colonial situation, to the collective mobilization and economic growth, and finally to the prevalence of madness. The love-hate relationship is a root metaphor that represents this whole process.

Tosa (2023, 350) warns that nationalism may push the human mind to extremes – either total denial or narcissistic assertion – and 'the situation may worsen in the future unless the subjective projection of nationalism is objectified in a multidimensional perspective'.

The chapters in the second part of this handbook clearly confirm one of the truisms in the academic field of nationalism studies: the phenomenon of nationalism and related concepts such a national identity (discourses) is a rather complex and multifaceted social construction that can only be fully understood against its specific socio-historical, economic, political, and cultural context. That also means that, like societal developments, the sense and narratives of the nation are never fixed and/or permanent as it changes over time adjusting to new circumstances and/or in response to social and political forces that seek to revise and/or modify how a nation sees itself. As the following chapters cover several countries in East Asia, one might be tempted to engage in a comparative analysis identifying and analyzing commonalities and differences. The readers may reflect on the magnitude and extent of differences and heterogeneity, which supports what has been argued before: a high degree of cultural and political relativism is required to understand the idea of the nation, nationalism, and the prevalent national identity discourses in the East Asian context.

References

Alter, Peter. 1994. *Nationalism*. 2nd Edition. London: Edward Arnold.
Billig, Michael. 1995. *Banal Nationalism*. Thousand Oaks: Sage Publications.
Breuilly, John. 1993. *Nationalism and the State*. 2nd Edition. Manchester: Manchester University Press.
Merkel, Udo. 2023. "Nation, Nationalism and Identity Discourses in North Korean Popular Culture." In *The Routledge Handbook of Nationalism in East and Southeast Asia*, edited by Lu Zhouxiang, 280–294. Abingdon: Routledge.
Moenig, Udo. 2023. "Udo Taekwondo: A Symbol of South Korean Nationalism." In *The Routledge Handbook of Nationalism in East and Southeast Asia*, edited by Lu Zhouxiang, 295–307. Abingdon: Routledge.
Hobsbawm, Eric. 1983. "Introduction: Inventing Traditions." In *The Invention of Tradition*, edited by Eric Hobsbawm and Terence Ranger, 1–14. Cambridge: Cambridge University Press.
Kingston, Jeff. 2023. "Abe's Feckless Nationalism." In *The Routledge Handbook of Nationalism in East and Southeast Asia*, edited by Lu Zhouxiang, 250–266. Abingdon: Routledge.
Kobayashi, Koji. 2023. "Commercial Nationalism and Cosmopolitanism: Advertising Production and Consumption of (trans) National Identity in Japan." In *The Routledge Handbook of Nationalism in East and Southeast Asia*, edited by Lu Zhouxiang, 267–279. Abingdon: Routledge.
Ryan, Stephen. 1997. "Nationalism and Ethnic Conflict." In *Issues in World Politics*, edited by Brian White, Richard Little and Michael Smith, 157–178. London: Palgrave.
Tosa, Masaki. 2023. "The Birth and Transformation of Japanese-Korean Nationalism." In *The Routledge Handbook of Nationalism in East and Southeast Asia*, edited by Lu Zhouxiang, 337–352. Abingdon: Routledge.

7
CHINESE NATIONALISM IN LATE QING TIMES
How to (not) change a multi-ethnic empire into a homogenous nation-state

Julia C. Schneider

Introduction

Elie Kedourie (1960[1961], 9) defined nationalism as a "doctrine that holds that humanity is naturally divided into nations, that nations are known by certain characteristics which can be ascertained, and that the only legitimate type of government is national self-government". Kedourie himself did not believe that this doctrine was factually correct though:

> Humanity is not naturally divided into 'nations'; the characteristics of any particular 'nation' are neither easily ascertainable nor exclusively inherent in it; while to insist that the only legitimate type of government is national self-government is capriciously to dismiss the great variety of political arrangements to which men have given assent and loyalty.
>
> *(Kedourie 1971, 28)*

Today, scholars of nationalism mostly agree with Kedourie (Breuilly 1982; Gellner 1983; Anderson 2006[1983]; Hobsbawm 1990). The interesting fact though is that many nationalists continue to cling to, and many states still officially adhere to, the doctrine of nationalism in their images of the nation and the nation-state (Wimmer 2006; Kumar 2006). This makes the study of nationalism a relevant endeavour until the present day.

Imaginary ideas of the nation can also be found among early Chinese nationalists, by which I refer to a loose group of men who discussed and published texts on nationalism in the last two decades of the Manchu Qing Dynasty (1636/1644–1912). Liang Qichao, Zhang Taiyan, Kang Youwei, Sun Yat-sen, Yang Du, Zou Rong, Liu Shipei and Wang Jingwei, to name only the most well-known ones, argued for the existence of a natural Chinese nation, defined by clear, objective characteristics and the right of this nation to self-government as opposed to being ruled autocratically by Manchu, i.e. foreign, emperors.

Confronted with the increasing fragmentation of the Qing Empire, many late imperial Chinese thinkers concurred that the empire had to become a nation-state to survive. They perceived the Qing Empire as weak, regarding both internal and external threats. Internally, the Taiping, Panthay, Nian, Miao and other rebel groups had competed for supreme power for decades. Externally, the Qing's weakness stood in painful opposition to the strength of Western imperialist states (Opium Wars and unequal treaties) and of imperialist Japan (First Sino-Japanese War and Treaty of Shimonoseki). The acknowledgement of this situation led many thinkers to engage with politics. They merged their Chinese understandings of the world, such as the concepts of "All-under-Heaven" (*tianxia* 天下) and "Great Unity" (*datong* 大同), with political theories and doctrines recently imported from the West, such as nationalism, republicanism, constitutionalism and liberalism, in order to find ways to empower the Qing Empire.

Their solution ideas differed, sometimes profoundly, as they followed different ideological trajectories and interpreted the fundamental idea of the naturalness and primordialism of nations in different ways. The Qing Empire was a vast territory, inhabited by heterogenous peoples whom even the most enthusiast nationalist could not easily construct as a naturally united, homogenous nation. To overcome the discrepancy between the multi-ethnic (multi-cultural, multi-lingual, multi-religious, etc.) Qing Empire and the imagined homogenous nation, or, as Benedict Anderson famously wrote, to stretch "the short, tight, skin of the nation over the gigantic body of empire", Chinese nationalists followed different strategies (Anderson 2006[1983], 86).

A smaller group of Chinese nationalists, among them Liu Shipei and Wang Jingwei, aimed at establishing an exclusively Chinese nation-state in the borders of the 18 Chinese provinces, also called China proper (Liu 1997[1903]; Wang 1905). Zou Rong even argued that "all Manchus residing in China shall be driven out or killed" as "China is the China of the Chinese", though it remains unclear what exact territory he had in mind (Zou 1999[1903], 36; see also Laitinen 1990, 92f.). However, their ideas came to be overrun by—or rather grinded down and stealthily integrated into—the empire-to-nation concept of nationalism.

Chinese nationalists are often divided into revolutionaries and reformists, the former wanting to overthrow the Qing, the latter being open to a constitutional Qing monarchy. However, this differentiation becomes blurred if one uses images of the Chinese nation and nation-state as a criterion of differentiation. Although Liang Qichao, Kang Youwei and Yang Du were reformists, and Zhang Taiyan and Sun Yat-sen revolutionaries, they shared the image of the nation as homogenously Chinese and of the nation-state in the borders of the Qing Empire. The revolutionary-reformist distinction is therefore not used here as it does not do justice to the ways in which the approaches of late imperial nationalists overlapped. Moreover, some changed their opinion over time, meandering between the two poles of revolution and reform.

In order to bring the complement of conceptual and political histories—and its protagonists—to the fore, I discuss the two main aspects of late Qing Chinese nationalism in this chapter. First, I introduce the conceptualisations of the nation and the nation-state in the Chinese intellectual discourse of late Qing times. Second, I explain how the political aspects of nationalism were put into practice during the same time.

Chinese concepts of the nation

Terms

Nationalism, that is, Western conceptualisations of the nation, was new to the Chinese discourse and was mainly transmitted via the Japanese discourse in late Qing times. Chinese neologisms for "nation" and related terms were in fact Japanese neologisms, as was the case for many political theories travelling from the West to Japan and further during that time (Bastid-Bruguière 2004).

At first, there were no standardised and clearly defined terms for "nation" in Chinese. For example, Liang Qichao translated "people" (German *Nation*) as *minzu* 民族 (Japanese *minzoku*, lit. "ethno-people"), emphasising an ethno-centric definition; "nation" (G. *Volk*) as *guomin* 國民 (J. *kukkomin*, lit. "state-people"), emphasising a state-related definition; and "state" or "nation-state" (G. *Staat*) as *guojia* 國家 (J. *kokka*, lit. "state-family") (Liang 1983d[1903], 71–72). Moreover, *minguo* 民國 (J. *minkokku*, lit. "people-state") was used to translate "nation-state (of the people)", or "republic", implying a constitutional system (Zhang 1984c[1907]).

Accordingly, there were two terms for nationalism. First, *guojiazhuyi* 國家主義 (J. *kokkashugi*) or "state-nationalism" (also "nation-statism", Karl 2002, 15) assumed that state or empire borders defined who belonged to the nation, no matter if the inhabitants of that state were ethnically homogenous. Second, *minzuzhuyi* 民族主義 (J. *minzokushugi*) or "ethno-nationalism" assumed that ethnic identity defined who belonged to the nation. Ethno-national identity was usually based on presumedly objective characteristics, for example, "place, blood relation, physical appearance, language, script, religion, customs and way of living" or "same blood relation, language and script, place of living, customs, religion, and spirit and physique" (Liang 1983d[1903], 75; Wang 1905, 1, 1–2).

State- and ethno-nationalism resemble Hans Kohn's well-known binary typology of civic and ethnic nationalism (Kohn 1948). Kohn claimed that Western states such as France, the United States and the United Kingdom were civic nations with supra-ethnic principles, such as Enlightenment, liberalism and cosmopolitanism, whereas ethnic nations in Central and Eastern Europe, Asia and Africa were socially and politically underdeveloped and thus clung to "traditional ties of kinship" (Kohn 1948, 331). Scholars later criticised the artificiality as well as the moralistic undertone of Kohn's Western-centric typology. Moreover, a clear distinction between civic and ethnic nations is impossible, as civic and ethnic national principles usually overlap (Özkırımlı 2010, 37). This comes to the fore in Chinese conceptualisations of the nation as well.

In the Chinese discourse on nationalism, *guojiazhuyi* was quickly abandoned in favour of *minzuzhuyi*. In turn, minzuzhuyi prima facie lost its ethnic component and is usually translated back into English as "nationalism" and not "ethno-nationalism". By shifting from a broader nationalist discourse, meandering between state- and ethnicity-related concepts, to a more limited, singular concept, Chinese nationalists nativised nationalism. In fact, they had been following their own agenda from the start. Torn between state-nationalism and ethno-nationalism, they wished for the large Qing territory with a homogeneous Chinese nation. The solution was to use both definitions, but hide one within the other. On the one hand, Chinese nationalists conceptualised the Chinese nation-state as a state formed, governed and inhabited by the Chinese ethno-nation (*minzu*). On the other hand, this Chinese nation-state (*guojia*) was territorially defined by the Qing Empire which Chinese thinkers had become to understand as "China" over the course of the nineteenth century (Mosca 2011). Again, we are reminded of Anderson's image of the "short, tight, skin" of the homogenous Chinese ethno-nation that Chinese nationalists intended to stretch over "the gigantic body" of the heterogenous Qing Empire (Anderson 2006[1983], 86). Like in other multi-ethnic empires, Chinese nationalists intended to do this stretching by assimilating the non-Chinese Qing subjects into Chinese citizens, at least rhetorically.

Non-Chinese peoples living in the People's Republic of China are today mostly referred to as non-Han (Chinese) people (*fei Han minzu* 非漢民族) or minority nationalities (*shaoshu minzu* 少數民族). I prefer to use the term non-Chinese to emphasise that the Chinese thinkers this chapter focuses on generally agreed that peoples who were not ethnoculturally Chinese could not immediately become equal citizens of China as a nation-state. Moreover, by using non-Chinese and Chinese instead of non-Han and Han Chinese, I wish to point out that Han Chinese imposes an artificial difference between Han Chinese and Chinese which is de facto non-existent. An Uyghur can be a citizen of China, and therefore a Chinese citizen, but the expression Uyghur Chinese as an equivalent to Han Chinese is not commonly used. The inverse conclusion shows that even without the prefix Han, Chinese refers to the dominant people regarding language, culture, politics and population share and non-Chinese peoples are not even tacitly included in this term.

To legitimise the inclusion of non-Chinese regions that had been conquered by the Manchus and their allies during the first half of the Qing Dynasty, many Chinese nationalists adopted the idea of the nation as a "more-than-local ethnic" group (Akzin 1964, 46). Liang Qichao famously considered individual nationalist sentiments of local ethnic groups as "lesser nationalism" (*xiao minzuzhuyi* 小民族主義) (Liang 1983d[1903], 75–76), which was separatist and thus negative, hindering empowerment of the nation. Therefore, he intended to strengthen the nationalist sentiment of a "more-than-local ethnic" group. This "greater nationalism" (*da minzuzhuyi* 大民族主義), as Liang called it, was considered the most advantageous solution for the Chinese as well as the non-Chinese people (Liang 1983d[1903], 76). The "non-Chinese people", by which I refer to non-(Han) Chinese people living in the Qing Empire here, would profit from Chinese superiority as soon as they became integrated by assimilation.

Liang does not give details what Chinese superiority and assimilation of non-Chinese in fact mean. However, the essay wherein he refers to these ideas is his well-known analysis of the Swiss nationalist thinker Johann Kaspar Bluntschli, and we can thus approach Liang's ideas by referring to Bluntschli's conceptualisation of superior nations that bring about the "nationalisation" of people of "mental inequality" (Bluntschli 1886, 109, 86). Bluntschli assumed that the superiority of certain nations lies in their "education, mind, and power" as well as "their ideas and institutions" (ibid., 109, 84). His definition of superior nations was based on a Eurocentric racist understanding of humanity, and he included only the "European-Aryan nations" like the Prussians, French and English into this groups (ibid., 89). Only these people had the right "to become [...] the political leaders of the other nations of the earth, and so to perfect the organization of mankind" (ibid., 89–90). Liang transferred Bluntschli's concept to East Asia, supposing that the Chinese nation was to Asia what the Aryan nations were to Europe. He presented the concept of greater nationalism as a natural and inevitable sentiment that just needed to be unearthed in order to strengthen the Chinese nation (Liang 1983d[1903], 76). Disregarding and downplaying their non-Chineseness, Liang's concept of "greater nationalism" implied that the non-Chinese people were indeed part of a greater Chinese nation (*Zhonghua minzu* 中華民族) (ibid., 76; Liang 1983e[1905], 2; Zhang 1984c[1907], 252–256). Even if some of them were not entirely homogenous with the Chinese nation yet, they would become so over time by assimilation, either passively as Liang and Yang Du claimed, or actively promoted by the state as Zhang Taiyan suggested (ibid., 257; Liang 1983d[1903], 76; Yang 1986[1905], 374).

Culturalism and nationalism

The first sinologist who addressed the topic of Chinese nationalism was Joseph Levenson. Levenson published a study of Liang Qichao wherein he formulated his now famous thesis that in the transitional period from Qing to Republican times (1912–1949), culturalism "shaded off into" nationalism (Levenson 1953, 109). Culturalism refers to understandings of Chinese identity and the position of the self and the other in the world (Schneider 2020b). Levenson argued that culturalism which had been "the dominant Chinese view of their identity and place in the world" for one or even more millennia was replaced by nationalism (Townsend 1992, 97). For many decades, Levenson's "culturalism-to-nationalism" thesis remained the state of the art. However, in 1992, James Townsend argued that culturalism was a rather limited, elitist idea of Chinese identity and not as universally or popularly accepted as Levenson claimed. Further, he argued that culturalism actually did not disappear with the advent of nationalism, but was integrated into it (ibid.; see also Schneider 2017b).

John Fitzgerald too argued that the validity of a culturalist Chinese worldview is limited to the nineteenth century. He claimed that rather than being the predecessor and opposite of nationalism, nascent culturalism in the nineteenth century was the first phase of nationalism, a proto-nationalism (Fitzgerald 1995, 79). Fitzgerald referred to Partha Chatterjee's "theory of [three] stages in the constitution of nationalist discourse" in India: departure, manoeuvre and arrival (Chatterjee 1986, 43). The parallels that Fitzgerald identifies in the nationalist discourses in India and China are particularly interesting with regard to the first stage, "departure". During the proto-nationalist stage of "departure", Indian thinkers assumed that "the superiority of the West lies in the materiality of its culture [...]. But the East is superior in the spiritual aspect of culture" (ibid., 51). Indian proto-nationalists sought to combine these two superiorities in a "cultural synthesis" to achieve "true modernity" (ibid.). Fitzgerald puts Chatterjee's stage of "departure" in India in relation to nineteenth-century Chinese culturalism, which was also "profoundly concerned with the preservation of the nation" by cultural synthesis (Fitzgerald 1995, 80). In both cases, native culturalism was a proto-nationalist, elitist imagination of identity, aimed at transforming popular consciousness.

Certain culturalist ideas of identity, however, existed well before the nineteenth century, and Chinese culturalism thus seems to be more than a preliminary stage of nationalism. In particular, the two above-mentioned concepts of the All-under-Heaven and Great Unity strongly impacted Chinese conceptualisations of identity, of self and other in imperial times. They are discussed in the next section, and it suffices to say here, that no matter if we take culturalism as an older or younger concept, the Chinese discourse on nationalism was at first deeply embedded into the culturalist discourse, and finally absorbed it. Chinese concepts of the Chinese nation have always included a culturalist aspect, serving a two-fold purpose. First, it legitimises "Chinese rule over non-Chinese peoples as well as non-Chinese rule over the Chinese"; and second, it determines which culture the Chinese nation adheres to and at the same time offers the possibility for non-Chinese people to become part of the nation by acculturation and assimilation according to the greater nationalism paradigm (Townsend 1992, 113).

Western and Chinese roots

Chinese conceptualisations of the nation were based on Western theories and doctrines. Republicanism and constitutionalism as well as social Darwinism, historicism and racism constituted important parts of Chinese nationalism, just like in Western nationalisms. At the same time, Chinese nationalism was complemented by native culturalism, most importantly the above-mentioned concepts of All-under-Heaven and Great Unity (Schneider 2020b). Many Chinese nationalists used culturalism to moderate their ethnic definition of the Chinese nation. According to the concepts of All-under-Heaven and Great Unity, China was imagined as unitary, similar to the nationalist idea of a nation's homogeneity. Both concepts moreover offered solutions to the factual problems of ethnic inhomogeneity by claiming the possibility of unidirectional change of non-Chinese people, their "assimilation" (*tonghua* 同化) to the Chinese, or "sinicisation" (*Huahua* 華化, *Hanhua* 漢化). Applied to the concept of nationalism, this means that non-Chinese people can become part of the Chinese nation by assimilation. Liang Qichao and Yang Du thought of the assimilative process as passive and unconscious, inevitable and quasi-natural; Zhang Taiyan supported a more active and conscious approach according to which non-Chinese people could be merged into the Chinese nation by state-led measures within 20 years or so (Liang 1983d[1903], 76; Yang 1986[1905], 369–370; Zhang 1984c[1907], 257).

By embedding Chinese culturalism into nationalism, the image of Chinese superiority could be upheld, at least in East Asia. Particularly, the All-under-Heaven concept, as outlined by John K. Fairbank (1970[1968]), supports a mono-cultural in contrast to a multi-cultural understanding of human civilisation, or, as Levenson famously put it, "I think; therefore I am Chinese" (Levenson 1953, 110). There is but one culture, which the Chinese people (or rather, their elite) happen to have achieved first. If non-Chinese people begin to "think", they cannot help but adopt that very same culture as that is the only culture available. This idea of Chinese superiority, inherent in culturalism, left a deep and lasting imprint on Chinese understandings of nationalism, particularly regarding nationalist approaches to non-Chinese people.

Another crucial aspect of Chinese nationalism is its relation to historiography. In Europe in the eighteenth and nineteenth centuries, history as a scholarly discipline emerged simultaneously with nationalism, and historians were often complicit in the nation-building agenda, telling their respective nation's history to help legitimising nationalist aims (Kumar 2006, 7). They mostly adhered to the theory of historicism which assumes a teleological development of nations in prefixed, progressing steps, albeit in different pace. European historians mostly used a three-fold model of periodisation (antiquity, middle ages, modernity).

Parallel to the development of the Chinese discourse on nationalism and in fact closely related, Chinese thinkers began to merge native concepts of history with Western historicism, inspired by Japanese historians like Kuwabara Jitsuzô and Ukita Kazutami (Duara 1995; Moloughney & Zarrow 2011). Many Chinese thinkers and historians would set out to force Chinese and Asian history into the straitjacket of European periodisation, adapting it to their new understanding of national history (Schneider 2017b, 298). Last but not least, Chinese nationalists included social Darwinist and pseudo-scientific racist concepts into their understanding of the nation and its history. These concepts helped to continue and manifest the image of China, both as state and as culture, as one of the most continuous, unique and centralised entities in East Asia and even the world (Liang 1983b[1902], 74; Zhang 1984c[1907], 253).

Historicism, racism and social Darwinism helped nationalists to locate Chinese and non-Chinese people on the teleological timeline of historical progress and to support the culturalist assumption of Chinese superiority with arguments considered scientific. According to these theories, Chinese people's customs, political-administrative system, religious beliefs and way of living were clearly more progressive than and therefore superior to those of the non-Chinese people.

These theorisations were particularly helpful to find a solution to the "nationality question" which had haunted reformist and revolutionary thinkers in the early twentieth century, particularly in multi-ethnic empires such as Russia, Austria-Hungary and the Qing Empire. The nationality question basically asked what was to become of smaller groups of people, or "nationalities", in the global process of nation-building, when empires became nation-states. According to the theory of nationalism, every nation had the right to establish its own nation-state with a government that represented the nation. However, many revolutionary thinkers, even if they did not belong to the majority people who either already held the political power as in Russia or intended to hold it in a future nation-state like the Chinese, did not want to grant that right to every ethnic group. They raised arguments why smaller groups of people were in fact not nations, but "nationalities", "minorities" or "ethnicities" who did not have the right to establish their own nation-states (Luxemburg 1976[1908–1909]; Lenin 1977[1925]; Stalin 1953–1954[1913]). It is interesting that socialists like Luxemburg, Lenin and Stalin and nationalists like Bluntschli, Liang Qichao and Zhang Taiyan alike agreed that minority peoples lacked historical progress and thus basic abilities that were indispensable for a nation, for example, a strong national sentiment and the ability to govern and administer themselves. Therefore, they all agreed that minority peoples could only profit from being merged into larger nations and become part of their nation-states. They assumed that "majority" peoples, or nations, had a quasi-naturally given and thus inherent ability to lead minority peoples towards developmental progression and raise them to a higher level of history.

Merging minority peoples into a majority nation was supposed to prevent future attempts of minority peoples to separate from the majority nation. Accordingly, Chinese nationalists who identified themselves with the majority Chinese nation denied non-Chinese minority people like Manchus, Mongols, Tibetans and Turkic Muslims to found their own nation-states and instead claimed that the future Chinese nation-state was supposed to include all regions of the Qing Empire.

Nationalism in practice

Homogenisation and synchronisation

What does the Chinese answer to the nationality question mean in practice? On the one hand, it assumes a statist territorial image of the Chinese nation. According to most late Qing nationalists, the territory of the nation-state they had in mind comprised all regions of the Qing Empire: Inner and Outer Mongolia; Inner and Outer Tibet; Inner Manchuria which was included in the province-prefecture-county system in 1907 and divided into three provinces, namely Fengtian (Mukden), Jilin (Kirin) and Heilongjiang; East Turkestan and Dzungaria which were included in the province-prefecture-county system in 1884 and merged into one province, Xinjiang; and the 18 Chinese provinces. These diverse regions bring the multi-ethnic composition of the Qing Empire to the fore, which was further increased by dozens of diverse non-Chinese indigenous peoples. By assuming that all these regions and peoples would become the Chinese nation-state, early Chinese nationalists automatically implied that the multi-ethnic populations of the Qing Empire were to become a Chinese nation despite their different languages, religious beliefs and ideologies, customs and ways of living, political-administrative systems, etc.

While the territorial image of the nation-state was a statist one, the Chinese nation-state was also embedded into a decisively Sino-centric hegemonic image of the Chinese ethno-nation. The diversity of the Qing Empire's population, also reflected in its multiple political-administrative systems (Schneider 2020b), was to be dissolved and all regions were to be synchronised following the Chinese model of state administration, the province-prefecture-county system, also called "prefectural" (*junxian* 郡縣, also *chün-hsien*) system.

As outlined above, the differences were supposed to be overcome by the assimilation of the non-Chinese peoples into the Chinese nation.

Attempts to homogenise national populations and to synchronise national administrations often go hand in hand with nation-building processes. In nationalist thinking, synchrony and homogeneity are considered to be important pre-conditions for a nation-state's stability. This understanding comes to the fore in different strategies of synchronisation and homogenisation in many world regions during the last one-and-a-half centuries or so. Nationalist homogenisation can be achieved by "the break-up of multinational arrangements" and the erection of new nation-state borders between people considered to be different nations (Hall 2006, 38). However, particularly in the first decades of the twentieth century, nation-states founded in the borders of multi-ethnic empires attempted to achieve homogenisation of their populations by strategies of acculturative education, forced assimilation or even ethnic cleansing. In many states, also in the People's Republic of China, such strategies continue to be applied until today.

The Qing as a constitutional monarchy

Apart from theorising how to homogenise the multi-ethnic populations of the Qing Empire and how to synchronise its divers political-administrative systems, Chinese nationalists discussed about the general political system that should replace the Qing autocratic monarchy. For most nationalists, and also for Chinese nationalists, a constitution and elected parliament representing the nation were necessary ingredients for a powerful nation-state. This had already come to the fore during the Hundred Days' Reform in the summer of 1898.

The young Guangxu Emperor Zaitian had ascended the throne as a three-year-old toddler in early 1875 on the suggestion of his aunt, the Empress Dowager Cixi, who became regent until his coming-of-age. The Guangxu Emperor's official reign time lasted from 1875 to 1908; de facto, he reigned less than ten years though, from 1889 (his coming-of-age) until autumn 1898 (the end of the Hundred Days' Reform). During this time, he showed increasing interest in political reforms in other countries, above all the Meiji Reforms in Japan. At the same time, reformer Kang Youwei and other "Confucian radicals" were developing reformist ideas to overcome the Qing Empire's military, political and economic weaknesses which were presented all too clearly in the Qing's defeat in the First Sino-Japanese War (1894–1895) (Zarrow 2005, 13). The reformers particularly stressed the necessity of a constitutional monarchy supported by popular nationalism and patriotism.

In 1898, Kang Youwei and his disciple Liang Qichao had the opportunity to discuss their ideas with the emperor in person. Following their secret meetings, the emperor issued edicts to facilitate reforms of education and the imperial examination system. He also intended to establish new offices in the areas of commerce, industry and agriculture, and to abolish sinecures. Although Empress Dowager Cixi has often been described as a money-wasting and power-obsessed anti-reformist, she actually seems to have been quite satisfied with the reforms. Only when the Guangxu Emperor began to dismiss influential officials and replace them with men close to him did Cixi stage a coup to prevent a coup against herself. The emperor was put under house arrest for the rest of his life, the reformers, so they were caught, were executed, and the reformist edicts withdrawn. Kang and Liang managed to escape to Japan, and it was probably due to their partial narrative of the Hundred Days' Reform that the degree of its reformism has been exaggerated, especially when compared to the reforms that Cixi and her government issued after the Boxer Rebellion in 1901 (Zarrow 2005, 15–19).

In fact, when Cixi introduced her reformist agenda, the "New Policy", from 1901 onwards, the Hundred Days' Reform clearly served as a model. Even if the New Policy's main purpose "was to recentralise political and military authority" which had become increasingly disintegrated since the Taiping Rebellion, it introduced a new school and education system, abrogated the imperial examination system, and reformed the bureaucracy (Rhoads 2000, 142). In 1908, Cixi issued the "Outline of an Imperial Constitution" (*Qinding xianfa dagang* 欽定憲法大綱). This first and last Qing constitution, patterned on the Meiji constitution, limited the emperor's autocratic power and introduced the election of representative assemblies on local, provincial and national levels. Already in 1908, local assemblies were elected. By 1909, nearly all provinces had voted for their provincial assemblies. Although the Qing constitution had not been established by a Consultative Assembly, the New Policy was largely in accordance with what Kang Youwei and other reformist nationalists had had in mind in 1898.

The beginning of the end

However, the fate of the Qing Empire took a turn for the worse when the Guangxu Emperor and Empress Dowager Cixi died on two consecutive days in late 1908. Before her death, Cixi had determined her grand-nephew Puyi as the new emperor. When he ascended the throne, the Xuantong Emperor Puyi was not even three years old. His father Zaifeng, Prince Chun, brother of the late Guangxu Emperor, became regent.

At first it seemed as if Prince Chun would fully continue Cixi's New Policy. Provincial elections were continued, and Prince Chun convened the first meeting of a Consultative Assembly in Beijing in 1910. However, the elections and appointments of the Consultative Assembly's members brought a hotly debated issue of late Qing rule to the surface: the priority of the Manchus. The Consultative Assembly consisted of a "lower house", designated by the provincial assemblies and the Senate or "upper house", appointed by the emperor (or his regent). Each had 100 members. However, representatives of Manchus were granted extra seats in the provincial assemblies, and the electorate-elected ratio was such that "the Manchus were greatly overrepresented within China proper" (Rhoads 2000, 135). Also in the upper house, Manchus were overrepresented. The regent appointed 38 Manchus (and 46 Chinese). Moreover, the Manchu representatives were generally from the imperial family or with hereditary titles.

The final nail in the coffin of Prince Chun's government was his choice of cabinet members. The cabinet was created in May 1911 to replace the traditional offices of the Grand Council and the Grand Secretariat. Not only did Prince Chun choose former Councillors and Secretaries as new cabinet members, but 9 of 13 cabinet members, including the new Prime Minister, were imperial princes. Consequently, Prince Chun's cabinet was severely criticised by Chinese reformers as the "imperial kinsmen's cabinet" (ibid., 168).

In hindsight, it is difficult to know if Prince Chun's decision to "reimperialize" the Qing government and his failure to follow Cixi's plans to diminish Manchu priority were the main reasons for the anti-Manchu, anti-Qing revolts that broke out in late 1911 or just speeded up the decline of the Qing Dynasty (ibid., 171). Probably, it had been too little too late already when Cixi introduced the New Policy in 1901. Either way, Prince Chun offered the revolutionaries the final legitimation to overthrow the last dynasty that ruled China.

When the Xinhai Revolution broke out in autumn 1911, Prince Chun had to ask Yuan Shikai for help. When he assumed regency in 1908, Prince Chun had dismissed Yuan, a high-ranking Qing official, as he was becoming too powerful. Now, Yuan agreed to help the Qing against the revolutionaries only after Prince Chun offered him a high official post. At the same time, several officials advised the regent to dissolve his cabinet and install a new prime minister who would form a cabinet without interference from the Qing court. Finally, and under threat from different parties at court, Prince Chun agreed to the proposed political reforms. Unsurprisingly, Yuan Shikai was elected the new prime minister in November 1911 and immediately began to extend his power, starting with replacing regent Prince Chun with Empress Dowager Longyu, widow of the Guangxu Emperor.

However, Yuan Shikai's appointment and the hastily issued reforms could not stop the anti-Qing revolution. In many cities, the revolutionaries turned against the Manchus who "faced the very real prospect of racial annihilation" (ibid., 173). In Wuchang, Xi'an, Taiyuan, Zhenjiang, Fuzhou and Nanjing, hundreds of Manchu families were massacred (ibid., 187–200). Arguing that only a new republican government could ensure the Manchus' safety, the revolutionaries used the carnage to force the court into abdication. Finally, Empress Dowager Longyu gave in. On January 1, 1912, the Republic of China was proclaimed under the provisional presidency of famous revolutionary leader Sun Yat-sen. The last Qing Emperor formally abdicated on February 12, 1912. In exchange for his help in bringing about the Qing abdication and avoiding a lengthy civil war, Yuan Shikai demanded the presidency. On February 14, Yuan Shikai was elected the president, replacing Sun Yat-sen.

First national elections for the provincial assemblies were held in winter 1912/1913, "the only occasion when various Chinese political parties competed for the votes of a substantial nationwide electorate with considerable freedom from bureaucratic manipulation or coercion" (Young 2008[1983], 222). However, it is important to remember that the electorate encompassed only 4–6 per cent of the population as solely men of at least 25 years, meeting certain education and property conditions, were allowed to vote (Bandeira 2020, 21). Still, this was indeed the closest a Chinese nation-state on the mainland got to democratic elections for a long time. When it appeared that the electors favoured the newly founded Kuomintang (KMT) and KMT party leader Song Jiaoren openly criticised Yuan Shikai, the president diminished the (proto-)democratic character of the Republic. With Song Jiaoren's assassination in March 1913 on Yuan Shikai's order, the short Chinese (proto-)democratic interlude was already over. In early 1914, Yuan dissolved the Republican Constitutional Assembly.

Concluding remarks

In the previous section, I have discussed how a constitutional system with representative government bodies (parliament, assemblies) was introduced already in Qing times and how it came to an end under the Republican government. It remains an open question, if the nationalist reformers and revolutionaries, who were all proponents of constitutionalism, would have been better off with a slowly reforming constitutional monarchy than with a republic that finally plunged into civil war and chaos under the anti-democratic regimes of Yuan Shikai, the Beiyang and other warlords, and Chiang Kai-shek.

Moreover, Chinese nationalists like many early twentieth-century reformers all over the world supported constitutionalism and democratic elections only to a limited degree. They did not aim at granting the right to vote to the whole population, but only an exclusive selection of men was supposed to exercise full citizenship rights. All others had to wait until they were educated enough, rich enough, or until their gender was no longer considered to be a major obstacle against civil rights.

In late Qing times, many non-Chinese people were among those automatically excluded from the right to vote for their representatives, although Chinese nationalists "anticipating that constitutional and parliamentarist movements among Mongols, Tibetans, and Turki could lead to the separation of the respective regions, [...] hoped that parliamentary representation, albeit limited, would be an instrument against centrifugal tendencies" in non-Chinese regions (Bandeira 2020, 15). There were several reasons why Mongols, Tibetans and Turkic Muslims were not allowed to vote. Chinese nationalists argued that first, Tibet, Mongolia and Xinjiang were sparsely settled; organising elections would create logistic problems. This argument might have been valid to a certain degree in case of Mongolia and Tibet which had not been integrated into the province-prefecture-county system. However, Chinese nationalists did not differentiate between Mongolia and Tibet on the one hand, and Xinjiang—which had been made a province already in 1884—on the other. Second, many Chinese nationalists plainly claimed that Mongols, Tibetans and Turkic Muslims were inferior and backwards, and thus not ready to elect representatives and have provincial assemblies (ibid., 19). Therefore, Chinese nationalists agreed with the Qing court that Mongol, Tibetan and Turkic Muslims representatives should only be imperially appointed members of the upper house. Although officially there were two seats for Xinjiang in the lower house, they remained vacant as there were nearly no voters or potential candidates anyway due to the rigid rules (ibid., 22). Consequently, there were 12 Mongol, one Tibetan and one Turkic Muslim representative in the upper house, all from noble background.

The limited system of constitutional monarchism in final Qing years was a reflection of two different layers of power-politics and indeed a clash of two power ideals. On the one hand, there was the upper house. This was a continuance of Qing "simultaneous rule" in that it took the interests and influences of the "constituencies" of the empire into account, Manchu and Mongol nobles and Chinese scholar-officials occupying more prominent positions compared to Tibetans and Turkic Muslims (Crossley 1999, 14). On the other hand, there was the lower house which was a reflection of the culturalist-nationalist concept the Chinese reformers had of the Chinese nation and its non-Chinese inhabitants.

The history of the Republic of China is often told as a success story wherein the Chinese state kept most of the Qing territory intact (Esherick 2006). In view of the clash of two power ideals manifested in the Qing-style constitutionalism, however, one can also tell a history of collapse and disintegration (Bulag 2006). Mongol and Tibetan noblemen were already disillusioned by the marginal role they were supposed to play on national level under a constitutional Qing monarchy. When it became likely that the Qing monarchy was doomed, they anticipated their equally marginal role in a future Chinese nation-state. On December 29, 1911, one day after Empress Dowager Longyu had indirectly agreed to the abdication of the Xuantong Emperor, the Jebtsundamba Khutughtu, highest Buddhist notable in Mongolia, was elected as the theocratic leader and became the Holy Khan (*Bogd Khan*) of Mongolia (Bulag 2006, 265).

Mongolia was only the first region that broke from "the gigantic body" of the Qing Empire, because the "skin of the nation" was too short and too tight to fit for all imperial constituencies (Anderson 2006[1983], 86). Over time, a number of states emerged from the Qing Empire, most importantly the Republic of China, whose successor state is on Taiwan today; the Bogd Khanate of Mongolia (1911–1919 and 1921–1924), the Mongolian People's Republic (1924–1992) under Soviet patronage and the Republic of Mongolia (1991–today); Manchukuo (1932–1945) and the Mongol Border Land (1939–1945) under Japanese control; and de facto independent Tibet (1913–1950). Moreover, also the Chinese-inhabited regions of China proper as well as Xinjiang were often not controlled by a Republican government, apart from a few years of centralised dictatorship under Chiang Kai-shek before the Communists threatened his position. Only under Communist rule from 1949 onwards did a Chinese central government begin to establish a more or less stable rule over the former Qing regions except Outer Mongolia (and Taiwan, which, however, had never been under Qing rule completely and became a Japanese colony after the First Sino-Japanese War in 1895).

This stability, however, comes at a high price for many, not only, but particularly the non-Chinese people who have been conceptualised as "minority nationalities", but otherwise remain conceptually inferior nationalities from a Chinese nationalist perspective. This is the legacy of early Chinese nationalist thinking and its mixed roots in Chinese culturalism and Sino-centrism as well as Western racism, historicism and social Darwinism.

Reference

The year dates in square brackets after the publication date indicate when the text was first published.

English-language references

Akzin, Benjamin. 1964. *State and Nation*. London: Hutchinson.
Anderson, Benedict. 2006. *Imagined Communities: Reflections on the Origin and Spread of Nationalism*. Revised ed. (first ed. 1983). London: Verso.
Bandeira, Egas Moniz. 2020. "Late Qing Parliamentarism and the Borderlands of the Qing Empire—Mongolia, Tibet, and Xinjiang (1906–1911)." *Journal of Eurasian Studies* 11 (1): 15–29.
Bastid-Bruguière, Marianne. 2004. "The Japanese-Induced German Connection of Modern Chinese Ideas of the State: Liang Qichao and the Guojia Lun of J. K. Bluntschli." In *The Role of Japan in Liang Qichao's Introduction of Modern Western Civilization to China*, edited by Joshua A. Fogel, 105–124. Berkeley: Institute of East Asian Studies, University of California Berkeley, Center for Chinese Studies.
Bluntschli, Johann K. 1886. *Allgemeine Staatslehre*. In *Lehre vom modernen Staat*, vol. 3. Stuttgart: Verlag der J. G. Cotta'schen Buchhandlung.
Breuilly, John. 1982. *Nationalism and the State*. Manchester: Manchester University Press.
Bulag, Uradyn E. 2006. "Going Imperial: Tibeto-Mongolian Buddhism and Nationalisms in China and Inner Asia." In *Empire to Nation: Historical Perspectives on the Making of the Modern World*, edited by Joseph W. Esherick, Hasan Kayalı, and Eric Van Young, 260–295. Lanham: Rowman & Littlefield Publishers.
Chatterjee, Partha. 1986. *Nationalist Thought and the Colonial World: A Derivative Discourse?* Tokyo: Zed Books.
Duara, Prasenjit. 1995. *Rescuing History from the Nation: Questioning Narratives of Modern China*. Chicago: University of Chicago Press.
Esherick, Joseph W. 2006. "How the Qing Became China." In *Empire to Nation: Historical Perspectives on the Making of the Modern World*, edited by Joseph W. Esherick, Hasan Kayalı, and Eric Van Young, 229–259. Lanham: Rowman & Littlefield Publishers.
Fairbank, John K. 1968. "A Preliminary Framework." In *The Chinese World Order: Traditional China's Foreign Relations*, edited by John K. Fairbank, 1–19. Cambridge, MA Harvard University Press.
Fitzgerald, John. 1995. "The Nationless State: The Search for a Nation in Modern Chinese Nationalism." *The Australian Journal of Chinese Affairs* 33: 75–104.
Gellner, Ernest. 1983. *Nations and Nationalism*. Oxford: Blackwell.
Hall, John A. 2006. "Structural Approaches to Nations and Nationalism." In *The SAGE Handbook of Nations and Nationalism*, edited by Gerard Delanty and Krishan Kumar, 33–43. London: SAGE.
Hobsbawm, Eric John. 1990. *Nations and Nationalism since 1780: Programme, Myth, Reality*. Cambridge: Cambridge University Press.
Karl, Rebecca E. 2002. *Staging the World: Chinese Nationalism at the Turn of the Twentieth Century*. Durham, NC: Duke University Press.
Kedourie, Elie. 1961. *Nationalism*. Revised ed. London [et al.]: Hutchinson.
———. 1971. *Nationalism in Asia and Africa*. London: Weidenfeld & Nicolson.
Kohn, Hans. 1948. *The Idea of Nationalism: A Study in Its Origins and Background*. New York: Macmillan.
Kumar, Krishan. 2006. "Nationalism and the Historians." In *The SAGE Handbook of Nations and Nationalism*, edited by Krishan Kumar and Gerard Delanty, 7–20. London: Routledge.

Laitinen, Kauko. 1990. *Chinese Nationalism in the Late Qing Dynasty: Zhang Binglin as an Anti-Manchu Propagandist*. London: Curzon Press.

Leibold, James. 2007. *Reconfiguring Chinese Nationalism: How the Qing Frontier and Its Indigenes Became Chinese*. New York: Palgrave Macmillan.

Lenin, Vladimir Ilyich. 1977[1925]. "Theses on the National Question." (Written in 1913). Translated by George Hanna. In *Lenin Collected Works*, vol. 19, 243–251. Moscow: Progress Publishers. Accessed online: *Marxists Internet Archive*. 13 August 2021. https://www.marxists.org/archive/lenin/works/1913/jun/30.htm.

Levenson, Joseph R. 1953. *Liang Ch'i-Ch'ao and the Mind of Modern China*. Cambridge, MA: Harvard University Press.

Luxemburg, Rosa. 1976[1908–1909]. "The National Question." In *The National Question: Selected Writings by Rosa Luxemburg*, edited by Horace B. Davis, vol. 19, 243–251. New York and London: Monthly Review Press. Accessed online: *Marxists Internet Archive*. 13 August 2021. https://www.marxists.org/archive/luxemburg/1909/national-question/index.htm.

Moloughney, Brian, and Peter G. Zarrow, eds. 2011. *Transforming History: The Making of a Modern Academic Discipline in Twentieth-Century China*. Hong Kong: Chinese University Press.

Mosca, Matthew W. 2011. "The Literati Rewriting of China in the Qianlong-Jiaqing Transition." *Late Imperial China* 32 (2): 89–132.

Özkırımlı, Umut. 2010. *Theories of Nationalism: A Critical Introduction*. Second Edition. Basingstoke: Palgrave Macmillan.

Rhoads, Edward J. M. 2000. *Manchus and Han: Ethnic Relations and Political Power in Late Qing and Early Republican China, 1861–1928*. Seattle: University of Washington Press.

Schneider, Julia C. 2017a. "Missionizing, Civilizing, and Nationizing: Linked Concepts of Compelled Change." In *New Religious Nationalism in Chinese Societies*, edited by Cheng-tian Kuo, 89–115. Amsterdam: Amsterdam University Press.

———. 2017b. *Nation and Ethnicity: Chinese Discourses on History, Historiography, and Nationalism (1900s–1920s)*. Leiden: Brill.

———. 2020a. "When the World Shrinks: Chinese Concepts of Culture, Identity and History in the Early Twentieth Century." *Global Intellectual History*, Special issue "Worldviews in Twentieth-Century Chinese Historiography": 1–23.

———. 2020b. "A Non-Western Colonial Power? The Qing Empire in Postcolonial Discourse." *Journal of Asian History* 54 (2): 311–340.

Stalin, Joseph. 1953–1954[1913]. "Marxism and the National Question." In *J. V. Stalin Archive: Collected Works*, vol. 2. Moscow: Foreign Languages Publishing House. Accessed online: *Marxists Internet Archive*. 13 August 2021. https://www.marxists.org/reference/archive/stalin/works/1913/03.htm.

Townsend, James R. 1992. "Chinese Nationalism." *The Australian Journal of Chinese Affairs* 27: 97–130.

Unger, Jonathan, and Geremie Barmé. 1996. *Chinese Nationalism*. Armonk, NY: M.E. Sharpe.

Wimmer, Andreas. 2006. "Ethnic Exclusion in Nationalizing States." In *The SAGE Handbook of Nations and Nationalism*, edited by Delanty, Gerard and Kumar, Krishan, 334–344. London: SAGE.

Young, Ernest P. 2008. "Politics in the Aftermath of Revolution: The Era of Yuan Shih-k'ai, 1912–16." In *The Cambridge History of China. Vol. 12, Part 1: Republican China, 1912–1949*, edited by John K. Fairbank, 208–255. Cambridge: Cambridge University Press.

Zarrow, Peter G. 2005. *China in War and Revolution, 1895–1949*. London: Routledge.

Zou, Rong 鄒榮. 1999[1903]. "The Revolutionary Army." Translated by Stephen C. Angle and Marina Svensson. *Contemporary Chinese Thought* 31 (1): 32–38.

Chinese-language references

Ge, Zhaoguang 葛兆光. 2014. 何為中國：疆域、民族、文化與歷史 (*What Is China? Border, Ethnicity, Culture and History*). Xianggang: Niujin daxue chubanshe.

Liang, Qichao 梁啟超. 1983. 飲冰室合集 (*Collected Works from the Icedrinker's Studio*), 文集 (*Collected Essays*) & 專集 (*Collected Monographs*). Beijing: Zhonghua shuju.

———. 1983a[1902]. "新史學" (Renewal of Historiography). In 飲冰室合集, 文集 (*Collected Works from the Icedrinker's Studio*), vol. 4, 1–32. Beijing: Zhonghua shuju.

———. 1983b[1902]. "亞洲地理大勢論" (General Developments of Asia's Geographical Conditions). In 飲冰室合集, 文集 (*Collected Works from the Icedrinker's Studio, Collected Essays*), vol. 10, 69–77. Beijing: Zhonghua shuju.

———. 1983c[1902]. "中國地理大勢論" (General Developments of China's Geographical Conditions). In 飲冰室合集, 文集 (*Collected Works from the Icedrinker's Studio, Collected Essays*), vol. 10, 77–101. Beijing: Zhonghua shuju.

———. 1983d[1903]. "政治學大家伯倫知理之學說" (Teachings of the Great Political Scientist Bluntschli). In 飲冰室合集, 文集 (*Collected Works from the Icedrinker's Studio, Collected Essays*), vol. 13, 67–89. Beijing: Zhonghua shuju.

———. 1983e[1905]. "歷史上中國民族之觀察" (Reflections on China's Ethnicities in History). In 飲冰室合集, 專集 (*Collected Works from the Icedrinker's Studio, Collected Monographs*), vol. 41, 1–13. Beijing: Zhonghua shuju.

Liu, Shipei 劉師培. 1997[1903]. "讓書" (Book of Expulsion). In 劉師培全集 (*Complete Works of Liu Shipei*), vol. 2, 1–17. Beijing: Zhongguo zhongyang dangxiao chubanshe.

Wang, Hui 汪晖. 2004. 现代中国思想的兴起 (*The Rise of Modern Chinese Thought*). Beijing: Sanlian shudian.

Wang, Jingwei 汪精衛. 1905. "民族的國民" (An Ethnic Nation) 民報 *(The People's Journal)* 1–2: 1–31, 1–23.

Yang, Du 楊度. 1986[1905]. "金铁主义说" (On the Doctrine of Gold and Iron). In 扬度集 (*Works of Yang Du*). Changsha: Hunan renmin chubanshe.

Zhang, Taiyan 章太炎. 1984. 章太炎全集 (*Complete Works of Zhang Taiyan*). Shanghai: Shanghai renmin chubanshe.

———. 1984a[1900]. "訄書初刻本" (Book of Urgency, First Edition). In 章太炎全集 (*Complete Works of Zhang Taiyan*), vol. 3, 1–106. Shanghai: Shanghai renmin chubanshe.

———. 1984b[1904]. "訄書重訂本" (Book of Urgency, Revised Edition). In 章太炎全集 (*Complete Works of Zhang Taiyan*), vol. 3, 113–348. Shanghai: Shanghai renmin chubanshe.

———. 1984c[1907]. "中華民國解" (Explaining the Zhonghua Nation-State). In 章太炎全集 (*Complete Works of Zhang Taiyan*), vol. 4, 252–262. Shanghai: Shanghai renmin chubanshe.

8
NATIONALISM IN CHINA TOWARDS A NON-WESTERN-CENTRIC HISTORY OF IDEAS

Zhiguang Yin

Introduction

Is there a Chinese nationalism? The application of the terminology in itself is an ontological attempt to comprehend a complex socio-political phenomenon with a concept which is burdened by its own cultural and historical baggage. In a Foucauldian sense, this act of naming, whether being called as Chinese nationalism or nationalism in China, is a manifestation of power, an extension of boundary of one *épistémè* over another. The practical benefit of having this universal concept to depict configurations of certain socio-political and cultural behaviour and thinking is obvious. In the case of 'nationalism', it helps to depict a common process starting from Europe and then across the world since the early nineteenth century, aiming at state-making, rights to self-government and excise the right organisation of a society of states in the name of a unity of a certain population (Kedourie 1961, 9–10). As researchers observe that unlike other 'isms', nationalism suffers from a 'philosophical poverty' (Anderson 2006, 5). Nevertheless, this does not stop researchers and public media from applying this concept normatively to depict the phenomenon of national independence movement across the world. In a sense, the apparent universality of nationalism only exists in the formative application of this word, based on the assumption that there is a received common understanding of nationalism. It is, explained by Ernest Gellner, a necessary component of modernity and the most salient principle of political legitimacy (Gellner 1964, 147–178; Gellner 1983, 6–7).

Nationalism is more of a doctrine than a philosophical 'ism'. In the European context, nationalism retrospectively provides legitimacy to a union against European territorial empires and transnational religious authority. It depicts a sovereign status established in the Peace of Westphalia among European protestant nations. It connects to the modern European notion of sovereignty which is fundamentally an extension of private land ownership. By emphasising the exclusive right to a piece of land by its inherited residence with the same ethnic origin, a modern European nation-state sovereignty came into existence (Moore 2003, 3–4). In today's discussions of nationalism, such an ethno-centric exclusive right to land ownership forms an underlining, but largely unspoken criteria. Consequently, the application of nationalist rhetoric is constantly risking of reenforcing the imagination that the world is nothing but an 'inherently fragmented space' (Oakes 2008, 61).

The ethno-centric ideal of nationalism, however, can rarely translate into a political reality (McGarry and O'Leary 1993, 10–16). Instead, it usually has a blurry line with racism and xenophobia. Since the late nineteenth century, we can often see ethno-centric nationalism being used to justify expansionism or ethnic cleansing in Europe. In this sense, nationalism and imperialism in the modern European historical context form the 'opposite sides of the same coin' (Mayall 2003, 108).

Further problems occur when we try to apply this concept to understand the state-making history outside Europe. Scholars have already pointed out the problem of using this Eurocentric view of nationalism to appropriate the anti-colonial nationalist movements in the Third World (Chatterjee 1993, 5). Consequently, recent scholarship has proposed a 'Third-World nationalism', or an 'anticolonial nationalism' to mark the socio-political differences which could lead the development of the Third World national independence movements to a different historical trajectory (Goebel 2015, 12–16; Manela 2009). The need to use attributive modifiers shows that nationalism is far from being a normative concept. It is at best a term used to depict a state-making process and a flawed justification of its result. However, it does not stop researchers from applying this term to understand the historical transformation of China from a universal empire to a modern state. To scholars of International Relations, China is a 'civilization pretending to be a nation-state' (Pye 1992, 1162). The underlining assumption in this claim is that both 'civilization' and 'nation-state' consist of a set of attributes which make these notions what they are. Today's scholarship has been constantly battling against the Western-centrism in our academic and popular narratives. However, some of our fundamental lexicon remains to be essentialist and Western-centric.

Existing scholarship has already pointed out that the emergence of nationalism in China at the turn of the nineteenth and twentieth centuries was closely associated with global anti-colonial movements. It should be understood as a process of 'concept-formation and intellectual reorientation' (Karl 2002, 5–9). Therefore, this chapter looks at nationalism and its associated concepts such as nation-state, and sovereignty with a particular attention to their applications outside the European historical and socio-political contexts in which they were formed. It takes a historical materialist approach to the study of idea and looks at the formation of a modern Chinese national unity in the context of twentieth-century Chinese revolution. It does not want to repeat a postcolonial problematic, trying to discover the subjectivity of the non-Western world by 'provincializing Europe' (Chakrabarty 2000). Instead, this chapter is interested in a story of entanglement, in which the meaning of nationalism in the non-Western world emerges through the long history of anti-imperial and anti-colonial domination. To borrow the expression of the Afro-Asian Solidarity Conference (AASC) in Cairo in 1957, the discussion of the rise of nationalism in the non-Western world is about the 'breaking free' from the 'imperialist monopoly' of modern ideas.

How do we understand such a monopoly of ideas? The modern political knowledge formed in the historical context of nineteenth-century global expansion of colonialism and nation-state world order is exercising its Foucauldian power of discipline. As Lydia H. Liu indicates, the transnational moving of concepts is far from being merely a creation of 'equivalent synonyms' in different languages (Liu 1995, 3–10). The transnational travel of ideas was far from being a simple story of intellectual transfusion or even diffusion. Particularly in the case of the spread of 'nationalism' from the dominant to the oppressed, it ignites a global process in which generations of intellectuals begin to aspire the future of their own nations through rewriting, crossbreeding, interpreting, adapting, criticising, and resisting those discourses of dominance.

Minzu and *Minzu Zhuyi*: an etymology

In modern Chinese, the term *minzu* (民族) indicates a two-fold connotation. On the one hand, it means 'ethnicity', which defines the racial difference in a biological taxonomic sense. On the other hand, it is similar to the use of 'nation' in Marxist texts, which, as a political concept, strongly emphasises the broader historical connection among social groups. Comparing to the implications of this word rooted in Western cultural and historical experiences, 'nation' follows a drastically different path in China. Such a variation not only appears in the formation and practice of ethnic policy in People's Republic of China (PRC), but also exists in its historical transformation in the late nineteenth century when China as an empire was struggling to cope with the rapidly changing global order featured with the expansion of European legal principles.

A common understanding is that the Chinese terms *minzu* and *minzu zhuyi* (民族主义, nationalism) in their modern senses have a strong Japanese influence. Recent studies also show that German missionary Karl Friedrich August Gützlaff (郭士立, 1803–1851) had already used the word *minzu* in the periodicals and books he published in Chinese in the early 1830s (Huang 2017, 70–73). According to Huang Xingtao's research, the early use of *minzu* in Chinese is close to the German concept of *Nation*, which signifies a naturally occurred unity of people. The word *min* (民) in Chinese refers to the general public, whereas *zu* (族) focuses on the gathering of families or tribes. Until the late nineteenth century, *minzu* in Chinese texts was used almost exclusively in this sense (Jin and Liu 2008, 531).

From the First Sino-Japanese War in 1895 to the late 1910s, reformist intellectuals began to use *minzu* more closely to its contemporary connotation. In 1896, *Shiwu Bao* (时务报, Current Affairs), a Chinese periodical in Shanghai edited by Wang Kangnian (汪康年, 1860–1911) and Liang Qichao (梁启超, 1873–1929) published a Chinese translation of a Japanese newspaper article on 'Turkish Empire'. The article was translated by a long-term collaborator of Liang Qichao, Japanese sinologist Kozyo Satakichi (古城贞吉, 1866–1949). It mentions six '*minzu* under the governance of the Turkish Empire', including 'Tuerqi ren, Alabiya ren, Xila ren, Yaerminiya ren, Lamu ren, and Yaerbaniya ren (literally means Turkish people, Arabic people, Greek people, Armenian people, Romani people, and Albanian people)'. The article claims that '*minzu* of ancient state' (古国民族, *guguo minzu*) does not understand the 'art of leadership and rule' (统御之道, *tongyu zhidao*), and has to rely on tribal and religious unity to govern. However, other *minzu* under its rule have been under the influence of cultural and material development of Western Europe. Consequently, they began to demand 'self-rule' (自主) (Kozyo 1896, 24).

This text draws a distinction between the old and the new *minzu*. The former relies on tribal and religious ties to build its political unity, whereas the latter, although not clearly stated in the article, forms its political agency under the influences of the West European material and cultural progresses. The story about the Ottoman Empire being the 'sick man of Europe' was widely known by the then Chinese reform-minded intellectuals. Particularly after 1895, the possibility that China could be broken up by European powers and the rising Japan became an eminent concern to Chinese intellectuals and officials. It is particularly intriguing to notice that this early use of *minzu* has very little ethno-centric implication. Surely, it refers to unity of people with a similar ethnic background, in which case the Chinese notion '*ren*' (人, people) was used. However, it can also be used in the context such as '*guguo minzu*' which indicates a political unity formed under different principles of governance (*tongyu zhidao*). A unity can form or dismantle as a result of politics rather than ethnicity. Ethnicity as the foundation of tribalism, which is recognised as a form of political unity, is backwards and no match for the advanced West European nations. Hence, it needs to be transformed.

The Chinese word resembling the ethno-centric notion of nation, or more specially 'race', is '*zhong*' (种). In an article published in *Zhejiang Chao* (浙江潮, Tidal Wave in Zhejiang), a periodical published in Japan by Chinese overseas students, '*minzu zhuyi*' (民族主义, nationalism), is defined as 'unifying same *zhong* and alienating different *zhong* to build a state for the *minzu*' (Yuyi 1903, 3–7). However, in the early 1900s, terminologies used to elaborate the notion of nationalism were in flux. Liang Qichao, for example, considers nationalism as a rejection to the 'freedom of invasion'. It deters 'other *zu* from invading us', and 'us from invading others'. Hence, nationalism is 'the fairest principle in the world'. It is a modern state theory which began 'at the turn of 18th and 19th centuries'. Liang refers to the *Déclaration des droits de l'homme et du citoyen de 1789* as one of the intellectual foundations of nationalism with a focus on its advocacy of '*guomin duli*' (国民独立, literally independence of national people) in the world (Liang 1999a, 459). Comparing to the article in *Zhejiang Chao*, which focuses on nationalism sustaining the rise of main European powers, Liang Qichao's attention was on nationalism being a force of mobilisation in the anti-imperialist and anti-colonial movements among the small and weak nations. He combed through historical events such as European resistances against Napoleonian expansionism, Irish independence movement, Anglo-Boer War, and anti-Spanish resistance in Philippines as examples to argue that nationalism could be a force to deter 'new imperialism' (新帝国主义) and promote equality among states around the world (Liang 1999a, 459–460). Liang was more interested in nationalism being a force to facilitate 'equality' (*pingdeng*, 平等) among nations. Such an equal status could only be achieved if people across the world with the 'same ethnic, linguistic, religious, and customary backgrounds could organise themselves into autonomise, well-structured governments, working toward the public good and defending themselves from other nations' (Liang 1999b, 656).

Undoubtedly, Japanese intellectual discussions had a tremendous impact on the development of modern notions of nation and nationalism in Chinese. In comparison, the Japanese ethno-centric view on *minzu* functions as the justification for the Japanese to lead the 'yellow race' in competition for dominance against the 'white race'. However, it is clear that from an early stage, Chinese discussions on *minzu zhuyi* were more interested in taking it as a state theory, providing the *volonté Générale* capable of unifying individuals into a collective, from which a modern state could emerge. Only after this transformation, can China be a 'nation-state' and Chinese people be the 'master' of 'building their own nation into a full-fledged member of the modern world' (Unkown 1903, 11–12; Yuyi 1903, 5). Consequently, the Chinese discussions of *minzu,* from its inception, were largely associated with envisioning of a new world order featuring with national self-determination (*zizhi*, 自治) and equality.

Nationalism and the imagination of a new world order

Being treated as a state theory, Chinese discussions of nationalism have always been closely associated with its imagination of a new world order. Transferring China from a universal empire into a modern state also means taking China out of the traditional Confucius *tianxia* (literally means, everything under the heave) order and resituating it in a modern inter-state order. Therefore, in early discussions of nationalism, *minzu* and *shijie* (世界, the world) often appear together. Expressions such as '*zhonghua minzu*' (中华民族, Chinese nation), '*shijie minzu*' (世界民族, world nations), '*minzu guojia*' (民族国家, nation-state), and '*shijie guojia*' (世界国家,

world states) are regularly seen in discussions forming crucial contexts for us to understand the connotations and implications of the Chinese understandings of nation and nationalism.

A common misconception about nationalism is that it always risks of leading towards Chauvinism. The foundation of such a misconception is the premise that only dominance by a hegemonic power could constitute the optimal situation for ensuring and maintaining an open and stable world economy. The decline of one hegemon means confrontations and conflicts, and will always lead to the rise of another (Gilpin 1975; Gilpin 1981; Keohane 1980, 131–162; Keohane 1984; Kindleberger 1987). Based on this premise, nations in the non-Western world established during the wave of the anti-imperial national independence movement in the late nineteenth and early twentieth centuries could only replicate the European historical experience and go on a path of either expansionism or self-destruction (Kedourie 1961). A state will either strive to become a regional or global hegemon and success or being placed under the dominance of a rising hegemon.

This Eurocentric and teleological view of the world order is reenforced by cases such as the rise of Japan in the late nineteenth century. The Japanese understanding of *minzoku* (民族) also combines the notion of people and race. A crucial component in the forming of Japanese understanding of *minzoku* was the civilisation theory with a twist of state-centrism. In 1875, Fukuzawa Yukichi (福沢諭吉, 1835–1901) introduced the Civilisation as a singularity into Japanese. His *Bunmeiron* (文明論) depicted in his widely circulated book *Bunmeiron no Gairyaku* (文明論之概略, An Outline of a Theory of Civilization, 1875, hereafter refers as *Outline*) aims to provide a path for Japan in the time of great transformation to become a 'civilised nation' (文明国) like the 'most civilised nations in Europe and the United States of America'.

Fukuzawa's categorisation of civilisation as the 'civilised', the 'semi-civilised', and the 'savage' has a subtle but crucial difference from its Western source. The civilisation theory popular in the then Euro-American world was deeply rooted in the study of ethnography. The three-tier division was a categorisation of the world's people. This ethno-centric view of civilisation can be understood as the *raison d'état* of an empire. It always emerges when an empire is on an expansionist trajectory, providing justification for the domination of one race over the others. The standard of civilisation forms the foundation for the justification of a European expansionism.

However, to Fukuzawa, his vision of transforming Japan into a 'civilised nation' would not work with such an ethno-centric view of civilisation placing the White race at the top of human civilisation and evolution. Therefore, Fukuzawa downplayed the centrality of race in his version of civilisation theory. Instead, he placed *kuni* (国, state) rather than 'people' as the fundamental unit to evaluate the level of development. In this way, the hierarchical order only denotes the different levels of development of state. A semi-civilised state could transform into a civilised one if applying the modernisation model proved to be useful by the success of the civilised Western countries. Unlike the ethno-centric civilisation theory, which suggests the other races need to be enlightened by the White race, the Japanese take on civilisation theory gives importance to self-transformation through reform and learning.

To Fukuzawa, for Japan as a 'state in the East' (東洋の一国), the source for modernisation comes from teachings offered by '*seiyō bunmei*' (西洋文明, Western Civilisation) (Fukuzawa 1962, 770). This notion of modernisation by transforming Japan less like an Eastern nation but more like a European state was later coined famously as 'leaving Asia and joining Europe' (脱亜入欧) (Sukehiro 1998, 30–97; Zachmann 2011, 53–60).

By the early 1880s, Fukuzawa began to actively express the idea that 'Asia should work together to fend off the Westerns' bully and invasion'. This marks the emergence of his civilisation theory that has matured into a pan-Asian geopolitical strategy later known as '*Nihon meishu-ron*' (日本盟主論, literally means Japan as the leader in the union) (Zhou 2014, 29–41).

Although in the late nineteenth century, Chinese intellectuals were attracted to both the pan-Asian ideal and discourses of nationalism (Saaler and Szpilman 2011, 20–26). However, instead of accepting the statist narrative of Japan being the leader of the Asian yellow race, the Chinese elites were particularly interested in the idea that Asia could work together to fend off the growing Western penetration. The US occupation of Philippines in 1898 and the Anglo-Boer War in 1899 were two major global events reminding the Chinese about the real possibility of China being broken up by the Western expansionism. Growing number of Chinese elites also quickly became disillusioned of the Japanese rhetoric of 'the Orient for the Orientals' (東洋は東洋人の東洋なり) and the unity of the yellow race in the Orient based on shared cultural identity (*Dōbun,* 同文, literally means same language) and the ethnic relationship among the Asian races (*Dōshu* 同種, literally means same ethnicity). In 1894, during the First Sino-Japanese War, Japanese expedition force conducted a massacre at Port Arthur (in Chinese *lvshunkou,* 旅順口). The killing lasted for four days, leaving more than 20,000 Chinese unarmed service men and civilians dead. This atrocity was among the first widely reported massacres in Western media in modern history. When the news about the massacre appeared in the US media, Japan turned from the 'light of civilization' in the 'darkness of the Far East', to just another 'Asian barbarian'. As the *Kansas City Journal* observed, '[t]he barbarities perpetrated by the civilized Japanese at Port Arthur are just as revolting as if they had been committed by the uncivilized Chinese' (Dorwart 1973, 697–701). Fukuzawa was extremely upset by the American media reaction towards the Japanese action at Port Arthur. He continued to defend that the Japanese military action in China was a war to advance world civilisation by eliminating the backward forces. China should be thankful for the Japanese as a civilising leader. He also condemned the reports of massacre as false, which originated from the long-lasting bias and arrogant disbelief towards the fact that a 'backward nation could transform itself into prosperity' (Dong 2014, 107–09).

It did not take very long for the intellectuals from other Asian nations to realise that the Japanese idea of Asianism was firmly centred on the Japanese domination of Asia. Dr Sun Yat-sen once warned Vietnamese anti-colonial revolutionary Phan Bội Châu (1867–1940) that Japan was interested in 'power' (*qiangquan,* 强权) rather than 'humanity' (*rendao,* 人道). Therefore, Japan would not be a reliable ally in the cause of global anti-colonialism (Liu 2011, 72). Instead of relying on the hierarchical civilisation theory, Chinese intellectuals were more interested in seeing Asia as a union against imperialism. In 1898, *Qingyi Bao* (清议报, *The China Discussion*), a reformist periodical published in Yokohama by Liang Qichao, Mai Menghua (麦孟华, 1875–1915), and Ou Jujia (欧榘甲, 1870–1911), published a short article titled 'New Monroeism from the Far East' (《极东之新木爱罗主义》). It claims to be a translation of a news article published in the U.S. The article calls the New Monroeism as a 'new imperialism excised by the US and Britain to dominate the world'. Such a new imperialism is different from the 'Roman imperialism' as it calls for 'justice and peace, self-determination and rule of law'. The international order under such a new Monroe doctrine is 'under the governance of an international arbitral institution, jointly led by Britain, the U.S.A. and Netherland'. This world order advocates 'open door policy' and 'free trade'. It will also prevent the colonial expansion of European powers in China and 'take China under the joint protection provided by the U.S.A., Britain and Japan' (Kataoka 1899, 21).

There are no further comments associated with this article, showing how the Chinese reformists think about the 'new imperialism' from the U.S., Britain, and Japan. However, other texts published in the same period by intellectuals in the inner circle of these Chinese reformist thinkers are helpful in piecing together a comprehensive picture of Chinese attitude towards Asianism. One of the significant features is that the ethno-centric view among Euro-American advocates of social Darwinism such as Benjamin Kidd and Walter Bagehot was either omitted or altered in Chinese translations and introductions of their works.

A famous interpretation of Benjamin Kidd comes from Liang Qichao, which focuses on the importance of cooperation in the national progression. In Liang's reading, Christianity, which Kidd placed in a crucial position in his narrative, was omitted. Instead, Liang elaborates on the general function of 'religion' in 'combating against the inherited evil of mankind', 'promoting the unification of different groups', and 'serving the future interests of the entire mankind' (Liang 2001, 424). Liang believes that Kidd's theory moves a step further from the natural selection theory of Charles Darwin. Although a single organism can perish, the development of the entire species is eternal. Liang therefore argues that 'death' serves an important evolutionary function if 'each individual could die for the benefit of the entire race and the current generation of a race would die for the future generation'. In this sense, death becomes a form of sacrifice, which aims to 'give birth to the future'. Different from the Western reception of Benjamin Kidd, Liang believes that it is the philosophical thinking about death that establishes Kidd as a 'revolutionary figure in the development of evolutionism'.

To Liang Qichao, Kidd's discussion on the relation between individual and society is intriguing. Liang argues that within a species group, the number of individuals who hold the spirit of 'sacrificing now in exchange for a better future' determines the group's level of evolution. He believes that the path of evolution is always forward-looking. The past and present are merely 'gateway to the future'. Therefore, Liang suggests that Kidd is reminding readers not only to focus on seeking for the well-being now but also think about the 'bigger picture for the future'. To Liang, 'nation' is a present-facing institution which is only responsible for looking after the interests of a certain group. 'Society', however, beholds the future general well-being of the entire human kind. However, Liang did not envision a clear solution for humankind's transformation from fragmented nation to a universal global society. He simply rejects Herbert Spencer's conviction which argues for the destined abolishment of national boarder and arrival of a cosmopolitan world. In Liang's reading, by embodying presence with future-looking destiny, Kidd manages to save the present from its temporality. This makes Kidd's thought more valuable. Chinese intellectuals should also respond to this development and recognise that any discussions about the present must have a future-facing purpose. Only by doing so, we can then transcend from the nineteenth century, an 'era focusing only on the present existence' (现在主义之时代) and make the 'thinking about current society, nation, and morality' more 'meaningful and valuable' (Liang 2001, 426–427). Through Liang's interpretation, Kidd's justification for Anglo-Saxon global economic and military expansionism became a philosophical enquiry of a series of more dialectic and universal relations, namely life and death, presence and future, nation and society, individual and community.

Most Chinese intellectuals in the early twentieth century show concerns about imperialism. In 1901, *Kai Zhi Lu* (开智录, Enlightenment Recording) published an article titled 'On the Development of Imperialism and the Future of the twentieth Century World'. The author suggests that the Afro-Asian cooperation against imperialism will reshape the course of the twentieth-century historical development. The author takes imperialism as an 'expansionism (膨胀主义)', an 'ism advocating territorial acquisition (版图扩张主义)', a 'militarism (侵略主义)', and a 'Dick Turpinism (狄塔偏主义)'. The rise of imperialism leads to an 'era when liberty decays'. Imperialism began in the late nineteenth and early twentieth century when 'the European powers recovered from revolutions'. It feeds upon the 'inequality of national powers across the global'. The author, using the pseudonym Zi Qiang (自强, literally means self-strengthening), specifies that imperialism refers to the 'expansionist global doctrine of Britain, the USA and Germany'. It is different from the 'territorial expansionist policy that Russia and France always embraced'. Japan should also be viewed differently, as it 'merely follows the European powers'. The author emphasises that combating against imperialism should rely on 'waving the flag of self-reliance and liberty, encouraging national people's spirit of independence and love of freedom'. The resistance against imperialism and the pursuit of national independence and self-reliance (自由自主) will have the momentum, which is 'tens and hundreds of times larger than the one driving the European revolutions', and eventually transform 'Asia and Africa' into a 'big battlefield of the twentieth century' (Unknown 1985, 178–184).

Such a criticism against imperial world order and an awareness of achieving independence through some forms of cooperation among the weak and the small nations can be spotted at the time across many Third World intellectuals. Probably to the surprise of the nineteenth-century Anglo-Saxon imperial elites, the hierarchical world order they envisioned based on the dichotomy between centre and peripheral, advanced, and backward, developed and underdeveloped achieved its 'universality' in their most unintended manner. The empire and its knowledge become the 'Other' in the 'peripheral' and 'semi-peripheral' world. By writing back against and writing through the imperial knowledge, the broader Third World creates its own modernisation experience and modern world view.

Nationalism in the context of internationalism: a communist narrative

In the Manifesto of the Communist Party of China (CCP) passed in the First National Congress of the CCP in July 1921, it states that any individual 'regardless of gender and nationality' can join the party. The only existing copies of this document are the Russian version archived by the Communist International and an English version found in Chen Gongbo's (陈公博, 1892–1946) monography *The Communist Movement in China*. A Chinese translation of the document is now in the Museum of Chinese Revolutionary History (中国革命历史博物馆) in Beijing, in which the word 'nationality' is translated as '*minzu*' (民族). The common translation of 'nationality' in contemporary Chinese is '*guoji*' (国籍). It is unclear which Chinese expression was used in the original Chinese copy. However, this is a meaningful ambiguity. It indicates the basic Marxist understanding of the 'national question' (in Chinese 民族问题, *minzu wenti*). On a normative level, the communist ideal of a transnational and trans-class unification of the world is not compatible with nationalism which divides the world into mutually excluding fragments. However, in practice, national liberation movements against the imperialist global order played a crucial role in facilitating the communist revolution across the world.

When Karl Marx was completing the Communist Manifesto, the modern nation-state recognition was also spreading across Europe with the rising national revolutions in 1848 (Connor 1984, 5–7). In the Manifesto, the word '*Nationalität*' (and the relating words such as *Nationalen* and *Nation*) is used to indicate the political unity of people with the same consanguineous relation. Such a political unity is also related to the geographic condition of people's place of residence. Being isolated in their own physical space forms the condition of '*lokalen und nationalen Selbstgenügsamkeit und Abgeschlossenheit*' (local and national seclusion and self-sufficiency) among different nations. However, this was transformed by the bourgeoisie need for a world market. The condition of fragmentation and isolation turned into a 'universal inter-dependence of nations'. This also transforms the intellectual creations of individual nations into '*Gemeingut*' (common property). It is under such a complexity of inter-connectiveness that the 'national one-sidedness and narrow-mindedness' was shattered. To Marx, the destiny and nature of a nation are associated with the world order shaped by the changing method of production. The hierarchical relation between the civilised '*Länder*' (state) and uncivilised and semi-civilised states was a global manifestation of a domestic exploitive relation generated in the process of the bourgeoisie 'need of a constantly expanding market for its production'.¹

When translating Marx's German text, we can see three inter-connected words being used to form the complex notion of *minzu* in Chinese. The word '*das Land*' and the suffix '*-völkern*' were used to indicate the territorial affiliation of a group of people with legal responsibilities and rights. When discussing the relationship between different groups of people and their historical development, the Manifesto uses the word '*Nation*'. The German text of the Manifesto uses '*Land*', '*Volk*', and '*Nation*' to describe the complexity of the formation and transformation of nation. It states that the development of the method of production terminated the fragmented status of population, capital, and means of production. The 'loosely connected provinces', consequently, have to relinquish their differences and form a united, singular nation, or in German, '*eine Nation*'. We could understand the global order based on nations formed during the development of the bourgeoisie methods of production as a *World System*. However, in its English translation, some of the crucial differentiations are missing. For example, when translating '*die Bauernvölker*', the English text reads as 'nations of peasants'. The connotation of 'people' as a political unity expressed in the German word '*Volk*' is absent in the English text.

To Marx, forming of a singular '*eine Nation*' fits the interest of the bourgeoisie. It is a world order with a clear hierarchy, in which the bourgeoisie occupies the centre and the proletariat as the peripheral. In the context of nineteenth century, the hierarchical order was countries ruled by the bourgeoisie (*den Bourgeoisvölkern*) extending their dominance to the pre-industrial agricultural countries (*die Bauernvölker*). Such a hegemonic unity needs to be demolished through the 'national liberation' (*der nationalen Befreiung*). It is a resistance against the bourgeois hegemonic socio-political order (*Gesellschaftsordnung*) rather than a rejection of the inter-connected status of all nations. Eventually, through the unity of 'working men of all countries' (*Proletarier aller Länder*), a new world order could come into being.

The Chinese communists develop their understanding of *minzu* in the dynamic of national liberation and internationalism. Li Dazhao (李大钊, 1889–1927), one of the founding fathers of the CCP, was among the first to understand Chinese national liberation in this context. In 1912, Li Dazhao and his colleagues at the Peiyang Law and Politics Association (北洋法政学会) translated Nakajima Hata's (中島端, 1859–1930) *The Destiny of China Being Divided* (支那分割の運命) with annotations and commentary. In the commentary, Li and his colleagues considered Japanese 'Asian Monroeism' (亚洲孟罗主义) as the equivalent of 'pan-Asianism' (大亚细亚主义), which was 'merely a synonym of Japanese ambition of dominating Asia' (Li 1999, 479). To Li Dazhao, ideas for regional domination in the forms of 'Pan…ism' are fundamentally 'in conflict with democracy'. It is 'nothing more than the cant term for despotism' (Li 1959, 109). Regional domination in forms of 'pan-Europeanism', 'pan-Americanism', 'pan-Asianism', 'pan-Germanism', and 'pan-Slavism' are all selfish hegemonic ambitions, seeking to subjugate other people (Li 1959, 105).

In comparison, Li Dazhao proposed his own 'New Asianism' (新亚细亚主义) as a counter argument to the Japan-centric pan-Asianism. Li considered that 'pan-Asianism' was not aiming to promote national self-determination. Instead, it was 'an imperialism aiming to absorb the small and weak nations' (Li 1959, 119). A true Asianism, according to Li Dazhao, should come from a unified action against imperialism. All the Asians under oppression should work together, striving for 'justice (*gongli*, 公理, literally means truth acknowledged by the public) and equality (*pingdeng*, 平等)', even 'at the cost of armed resistances' (Li 1959, 120).

Through 'New Asianism', Li Dazhao has envisioned a spatial order which does not involve hegemonic domination of space. Instead of having a dominating power filling the geopolitical 'void', Li believes that the national independence movements in Asia will transform the nations formerly dominated by hegemonic powers. Only with self-determined nations filling up the space of Asia can a true union of equality could form. This will then turn Asia into a 'larger union' on equal footing with Europe and America, leading the world into a 'federation of equals' that could 'advance the wellbeing of humankind' (Li 1959, 12).

Li Dazhao believes that the future of Asianism is the union of the world. It should not be understood as a regionalism or even narrow-minded nationalism which opposes the ideal of 'globalism' (*Shijie zhuyi*, 世界主义). Different from the state-centric view in Japanese pan-Asianism, Li Dazhao sees the future of China in the context of a broader liberation of all oppressed Asians. Our 'common enemy' is 'hegemony' (*qiangquan*, 强权). Our 'common friend' is 'justice' (*gongli*) (Li 1959, 280). Mao Zedong (毛泽东, 1893–1976) expressed a similar opinion. In a letter to Zhang Guoji (张国基, 1894–1992), who at the time was already living in Singapore, Mao states that Hunan people living abroad should take the position of 'globalism', which 'wishes the best for ourselves and others as well'. It is different from 'colonialism' which 'based the wellbeing of one nation over the sacrifice of the others' (Pang et al. 2002, 71). These early discussions on the relation between Chinese revolution and a transformation of the global order form the foundation for the later discourses sustaining the imagination of an Afro-Asian solidarity order in the PRC.

Li's depiction of a new 'Asianism' adds another layer to the complexity of this transnational diffusion of ideas in modern time. It entails an innovative understanding of the dialectic relation between nationalism and internationalism (or in Li Dazhao's word 'globalism'), reminding us that concepts as such could only acquire their limited universality in certain socio-historical contexts. In this case, it reminds us that the contradiction between nationalism and internationalism is only true in the European historical context. In the non-European world, the nationalist agenda of independence would only be possible when it became a transnational movement. Mao gave a clearer narrative of this dynamic. He claims that instead of 'transforming the Orient', it is better to think about 'transforming China and the world'. The focus on the world (*shijie*, 世界) clarifies that 'our proposition is for the world', and the 'beginning of our transformative practice starts from China' (Pang et al. 2002, 75). Revolutionary leaders and progressive intellectuals in Asia came to this understanding when they began to understand that hegemonic powers were already operating on a global level. To the CCP, liberation as a transformation for the oppressed world only gains its momentum in the modern history of anti-imperialism (Mao 1983, 148). It is a 'part' of a global transformation associated with the historical development of imperialist warfare and anti-imperialism across the world (Mao 1983, 147–55). Henceforth, liberation could not just be a nationalist transformation. It is, by nature, a universal mission rooted in the shared experience of suffering from the imperialist hegemony among the world's peoples, particularly peoples from what is later known as the 'Third World nations'. This narrative of a shared historical experience caused by the nineteenth-century global expansion of imperialism consequently becomes the foundation for the understanding and practices of sovereignty among the Third World nations.

Nationalism in Chinese revolution

In its early years, the CCP had made a distinction between 'modern national liberation movement' and 'primitive national xenophobia'. During its debate against the statists in Xinshi group (醒狮派, literally awakened lion school), the CCP considered the state-centric nationalism as a 'nationalism of the bourgeoisie' which only 'interests in liberation of one nation' (Xiao 1925). During the same period, the Fourth National Congress of the CCP passed a resolution on national liberation movement, stating that the 'policy on assimilating Mongolians and Tibetans' in China is hegemonic politics similar to the 'pan-Turkism in Turkey'. It is 'oppressing the small and weak nations in the name of national glory'. Instead, 'the nationalism of the proletariat' emphasises on the right of self-determination. It is a 'nationalism of equality' (Tongzhanbu 1991, 32). Therefore, instead of focusing on the tension between the right of secession and policy of assimilation, the CCP advocates the right of self-determination among different ethnic groups in China under the political goals of achieving the liberation of 'Chinese nation as a whole' (中国整个的民族) and the 'unification of China' (Agency 1980, 2).

The CCP's understanding of nationalism also contained the early reformists' focus on establishing political subjectivity of *guomin* (国民, national people) through actions of liberation and reform. This element became more pronounced after the 1927 party purge when the CCP was driven underground and became active in the rural and remote areas. At the time, the so-called base-areas (根据地) under the CCP control were located in areas with great ethnic diversity. The economic development in these inland areas was also significantly belated comparing to the coastal cities. In this context, the CCP began to acknowledge that liberation cannot be a top-down one-size-for-all initiative. Instead, it needs to recognise the socio-economic diversity among regions. In this sense, recognising the 'right of self-determination of the Manchurian, Mongolian, Hui, Tibetan, Miao, and Yao people' is to recognise that areas populated by these ethnic groups should have the right to determine the pace and policy of liberation suitable for their own regional socio-economic conditions. Recognising the right of self-determination does not mean the absence of a unified party leadership. The CCP is clear that the territorial unification and the establishment of a 'people's sovereignty' within the territory inherited from the Qing Empire have always been the goal for liberation and national self-determination. In the 1928 party manifesto, the CCP emphasised the party leadership in conducting works in different ethnic regions. It states that 'an ethnic minority work office needs to be established in party regional headquarter'. This is to make working among 'the proletariat from other ethnic groups' easier, as when working in these regions, 'ethnic minority languages need to be used'. However, all works need to be 'under the supervision and guidance of the local party headquarter' (中共中央统战部 1991, 88).

In practice, particularly during the war against the Japanese invasion from 1931 to 1945, the communist revolutionary agenda of creating a proletarian state and eventually a communist world order is embedded in the language of achieving a national liberation against imperialism. To both the Nationalist Party (Guomindang, 国民党) and the CCP at the time, *Zhonghua minzu* (the Chinese nation) was an 'oppressed nation' (被压迫民族). No ethnic groups in China could be isolated from the reality of Japanese invasion. Since the Second United Front beginning in 1937, the CCP had always been developing the notion of nationalism based on Dr Sun Yat-sen's narrative. The Chinese national liberation as a whole and the equality among all ethnic groups within China were the two cornerstones in the CCP's understanding of nationalism in this period. To the CCP, the goal of national liberation could be jeopardised by the external influence of imperialism trying to drag China into the imperialist conflicts by allying with a certain imperialist country. It could also be negatively impacted by internal factors such as the hegemonic Han Chauvinism, selfishness of certain classes, and collaborative elements in China to protect their own interests by sacrificing the national interest (*minzu liyi*, 民族利益) (Zhou 1941). In the context of imperialist invasion, cooperation and unification are the only way to safeguard the nation. Chinese nationalism and internationalism are 'not in conflict against each other'. Internationalists could only 'achieve the goal of Chinese independence and liberation' by 'firmly excise Chinese nationalism'. At the same time, Chinese nationalists must 'sympathise and cooperation with internationalist movement, in order to overthrow the hegemony of imperialism and achieving real national equality on the global stage'. Only by then, the 'Chinese nation can be thoroughly liberated'. In this sense, the notions that 'nation is supreme' (民族至上) and 'state is supreme' (国家至上) are 'revolutionary' in all colonies, semi-colonies, and weak and small nations under invasion. Whereas in 'all the capitalist states, such notions are counter-revolutionary' (Zhou 1941).

The CCP considers that the nationalist agenda of independence would only be possible when it became a transnational movement in the non-European world. Liberation as a transformation for the oppressed world only gains its momentum in the modern history of anti-imperialism (Mao 1983, 148). It is a 'part' of a global transformation associated with the historical development of imperialist warfare and anti-imperialism across the world (Mao 1983, 147–55). Liberation does not only mean gaining the Westphalian sovereignty (Krasner 1999, 73–104). Without the capabilities 'which enable governments to be their own masters', states could at most be recognised as possessing the 'negative sovereignty' (Jackson 1993, 27). Jackson also uses the term negative sovereignty to describe a formal legal condition of a state enjoying the freedom from external interference. It resonates with Krasner's categorisation of the Westphalian sovereignty. Henceforth, liberation could not just be a nationalist transformation. It is, by nature, a universal mission rooted in the shared experience of suffering from the imperialist hegemony among the world's peoples, particularly peoples from what is later known as the 'Third World nations'. This narrative of a shared historical experience caused by the nineteenth-century global expansion of imperialism continues to influence the PRC's nation-building narratives and foreign conducts with the Third World nations since 1949.

This idea that sovereignty could only emerge through an act of liberation by the people against all forms of oppression, foreign, and domestic alike is deeply rooted in the modern Chinese experience of social revolution. It was given constitutional status in the Common Programme of the Chinese People's Political Consultative Conference (hereafter refers as the Common Programme) in 1949. As the first constitutional document of the PRC, it proclaims at the beginning that the 'glorious triumph of the Chinese people's liberation war and the people's revolution' marked the 'end of an era under imperialist, feudalist and crony capitalism in China'. With the establishment of the PRC, an old nation of China is made anew. Its hallmark is the transformation of the 'Chinese people' from being oppressed into the 'master of the new society and the new nation' (Conference 1992, 1). All its state power 'belongs to the people' (Conference 1992, 4).

The Common Programme pays more attention to defining the centrality of the people in all the state institutions. Such a position is not received as a form of empowerment but as a result of their own revolutionary struggle. This notion is reflected in the narrative of the 1949 Common Programme. It defines the newly formed nation in the historical dynamics of socio-political transformation. The 'will of the people' to establish the PRC is a consensus reached through this historical process and becomes the political foundation of the new nation (Conference 1992, 1). History does not stop with the establishment of the new republic, with the territorial transference between the old rulers and the new sovereign. The protection of the territorial sovereignty by the 'military force of the people' is certainly a major responsibility of the newly formed government (Conference 1992, 3).

However, it is more important for the new regime to carry out the missions of the people's sovereign and 'strive for independence, democracy, peace, unity, prosperity and strength of China' (Conference 1992, 2). The means of achieving this mission is by 'developing new democracy people's economy', 'transforming China into an industrial nation', promoting the 'public morality' (*gongde* 公德) among the 'national people' (*guomin* 国民), and 'defending the perpetual peace of the world' and 'friendly cooperation among peoples of all nations' (Conference 1992, 3–4). Until the recently 2018 Amendment, the Chinese Constitution has always maintained this historical approach and placed the history of revolutionary struggle of the Chinese people since 1840 at the central of its source of law (Agency 2018).

The PRC's understanding of the Afro-Asian solidarity reflects its own domestic experience of liberation through revolution. It is viewed as a segment in a long history of the ongoing struggle for national and social liberations in the Third World, which stretches back to the early twentieth century and forms the post-WWII Afro-Asian and later the Tricontinental solidarity movement.

This solidarity movement embodied the hope for a new world order envisioned by the former colonised world. It challenges the traditional Eurocentric diplomacy that resonates on the notion of the balance of powers. The newly formed nations and nations seeking for independence were actively pursuing a democratic and equal international order that did not discriminate against the weak and poor nations. The confidence in the possibility of achieving such an idealistic global order contextualises the nation-building practices in many of those nations. To the PRC, this international call for an egalitarian global order signifies a historic moment in which the weak nations could unite and make their own fate.

As Zhou Enlai stated in his Bandung Speech in 1955, with more and more 'Afro-Asian nations freeing themselves from the constraint of colonialism', the 'Afro-Asian region' has transformed tremendously. The Afro-Asian peoples' rising awareness of 'regaining control of their own fates' after a 'long struggle' against colonialism symbolised that 'yesterday's Asia and Africa' being made anew. The common historical experience of suffering and struggle enables the Afro-Asian peoples to envision their *volonté générale* to achieve 'freedom and independence', and to 'change the socio-economical backwardness caused by the colonial rule' (Zhou 1990, 112–114). In this long historical process of transformation, the Afro-Asian peoples have developed a sense of 'empathy and solicitude' that enable the Afro-Asian nations to peacefully coexist and achieve 'friendly cooperation' (Zhou 1990, 120).

The historical narrative in Zhou's Bandung speech contextualises the proposal of Five Principles of Peaceful Coexistence recognised in the Final Communique of the Afro-Asian Conference. Sovereignty does not only convey principles of non-intervention and territorial integrity; it also exists in the context of the recognition of a set of collective international responsibilities. These responsibilities, as coined in the Final Communiqué of the Asian-African Conference of Bandung, are 'recognition of the equality of all races and … all nations large and small', 'promotion of mutual interests and co-operation', and using 'peaceful means' 'in conformity with the Charter of the United Nations' to settle 'all international disputes' (Collective 1955).

Conclusion

In the closing remark at the Afro-Asian Peoples' Solidarity Conference, Guo Moruo, the chairman of the Chinese Delegation, gives sincere regards to the Egyptian people, as they 'defeated the joint imperialist aggression' (Guo 1958, 187–191). Guo quotes Mao's words and says 'unity is power'. The imperialists have 'a consistent policy of dividing us', hoping to 'conquer us one by one'. Hence, we need to 'unite together' (Guo 1958, 190). The final declaration of the conference takes the similar line and suggests the capability of 'solidarity and mutual support among the Afro-Asian people' is key in defeating imperialist order and achieving perpetual peace of the world (Agency 1958, 219).

Comparing to the hegemonic view, which sees the world space as empty void being filled by dominant powers, the world order coming from the oppressed believes that the world space should be filled by the liberated people. The former believes that global stability comes from the balance of powers, whereas the latter envisions a world federation formed by the autonomous people through acts of liberation.

The image of an international unity against imperialism was deeply intertwined in the PRC's domestic exercises of nation-building. The knowledge about the 'struggles' in the Third World helped the Chinese general public to image the Chinese national liberation in the context of a major transformation of the global order. The genesis of the PRC in this context is more than just a creation of a Westphalian sovereign. It is seen as a step towards a creation of a new world order and ultimately the liberation of humankind. It is also situated in the creation of a new time, in which the transformation of the world from 'old' to 'new' is happening.

Note

1 All German, English, and Chinese texts of the Manifesto are based on Marxists Internet Archive. Chinese: https://www.marxists.org/chinese/marx/01.htm; English: https://www.marxists.org/archive/marx/works/1848/communist-manifesto/ch01.htm#007; and German: https://www.marxists.org/deutsch/archiv/marx-engels/1848/manifest/0-einleit.htm. Last accessed 28 October 2021.

References

English-language references

Anderson, Benedict. 2006. *Imagined Communities, Reflections on the Origin and Spread of Nationalism.* London: Verso.
Bowden, Brett. 2009. *The Empire of Civilization, the Evolution of an Imperial Idea.* Chicago: The University of Chicago Press.
Chakrabarty, Dipesh. 2000. *Provincializing Europe: Postcolonial Thought and Historical Difference.* Princeton, NJ: Princeton University Press.
Chatterjee, Partha. 1993. *The Nation and Its Fragments, Colonial and Postcolonial Histories.* Princeton, NJ: Princeton University Press.
Collective. 1955. *Final Communiqué of the Asian-African Conference of Bandung.*
Connor, Walker. 1984. *The National Question in Marxist-Leninist Theory and Strategy.* Princeton, NJ: Princeton University Press.
Dorwart, Jeffrey M. 1973. 'James Creelman, the "New York World" and the Port Arthur Massacre', *Journalism Quarterly* 50: 697–701.
Gellner, Ernest. 1964. *Thought and Change.* London: Widenfeld and Nicolson.
———. 1983. *Nations and Nationalism.* Oxford: Blackwell Publishing.
Gilpin, Robert. 1975. *U.S. Power and the Multinational Corporation: The Political Economy of Foreign Direct Investment.* New York: Basic Books.
———. 1981. *War and Change in World Politics.* Cambridge: Cambridge University Press.
Goebel, Michael. 2015. *Anti-Imperial Metropolis, Interwar Paris and the Seeds of Third-World Nationalism.* Cambridge: Cambridge University Press.
Jackson, Robert H. 1993. *Quasi-States: Sovereignty, International Relations and the Third World.* Cambridge: Cambridge University Press.

Karl, Rebecca E. 2002. *Staging the World: Chinese Nationalism at the Turn of the Twentieth Century*. Durham, NC: Duke University Press.

Kedourie, Elie. 1961. *Nationalism*. London: Hutchinson & Co. Publishers Ltd.

Keohane, Robert O. 1980. 'The Theory of Hegemonic Stability and Changes in International Economic Regimes, 1967–1977', in *Change in the International System*, edited by Ole R. Holsti, Randolph M. Siverson, and Alexander L. George, 131–162. Boulder, CO: Westview Press.

———. 1984. *After Hegemony: Cooperation and Discord in the World Political Economy*. Princeton, NJ: Princeton University Press.

Kindleberger, Charles P. 1987. *The World in Depression, 1929–1939*. Harmondsworth: Pelican Books.

Krasner, Stephen D. 1999. *Sovereignty: Organized Hypocrisy*. Princeton, NJ: Princeton University Press.

Liu, Lydia H. 1995. *Translingual Practice: Literature, National Culture, and Translated Modernity – China, 1900–1937*. Stanford, CA: Stanford University Press.

Manela, Erez. 2009. *The Wilsonian Moment: Self-Determination and the International Origins of Anticolonial Nationalism*. New York: Oxford University Press.

Mayall, James. 2003. 'Nationalism and Imperialism', in *The Cambridge History of Twentieth-Century Political Thought*, edited by Terence Ball and Richard Bellamy. Cambridge: Cambridge University Press.

McGarry, John, and Brendan O'Leary. 1993. 'Introduction: The Macro-Political Regulation of Ethnic Conflict', in *The Politics of Ethnic Conflict Regulation*, edited by John McGarry and Brendan O'Leary. London: Routledge.

Moore, Margaret. 2003. 'Introduction: The Self-Determination Principle and the Ethics of Secession', in *National Self-Determination and Secession*, edited by M. Moore. Oxford: Oxford University Press.

Oakes, Timothy, and Patricia L. Price, eds. 2008. *The Cultural Geography Reader*. London and New York: Routledge.

Pye, Lucian. 1992. 'Social Science Theories in Search of Chinese Realities', *China Quarterly* 132: 1161–1170.

Saaler, Sven, and Christopher W. A. Szpilman. 2011. 'Introduction: The Emergence of Pan-Asianism as an Ideal of Asian Identity and Solidarity, 1850–2008', in *Pan-Asianism, A Documentary History*, edited by Sven Saaler and Christopher W. A. Szpilman. Lanham: Rowman & Littlefield Publishers, Inc.

Seeley, John Robert. 1914. *The Expansion of England, Two Courses of Lectures*. London: Macmillan and Co., Limited.

Sukehiro, Hirakawa. 1998. 'Japan's Turn to the West. Modern Japanese Thought', in *Modern Japanese Thought*, ed. by Bob Tadashi Wakabayashi, 85. Cambridge: Cambridge University Press.

Zachmann, Urs Matthias. 2011. 'The Foundation Manifesto of the Kōakai (Raising Asia Society) and the Ajia Kyōkai (Asia Association), 1880–1883', in *Pan-Asianism, A Documentary History*, edited by Sven Saaler and Christopher W. A. Szpilman, 53–60. Lanham: Rowman & Littlefield Publishers, Inc.

Chinese-language references

Agency, Xinhua News 新华社. 2018. 中华人民共和国宪法 (The Constitution of the People's Republic of China).

———. 1958. '亚非人民团结大会宣言: 告世界人民书' (Declaration of the Afro-Asian People's Solidarity Conference: An Open Letter to Peoples of the World), in 亚非人民团结大会文件汇编 (*Collection of Documents of the Afro-Asian People's Solidarity Conference*). Beijing: Shijiezhishi Chubanshe.

———. 1980. '中国共产党第六次代表大会底决议案' (The final resolution of the Sixth National Congress of the CCP), in 六大以来: 党内秘密文件 (*Since the Sixth National Congress: Secret Documents of the CCP*), ed. by 中.S.o.t.C.C. Party. Beijing: Renmin Chubanshe.

Conference, Chinese People's Political Consultative 中国人民政治协商会议. 1992. 中国人民政治协商会议共同纲领 (*Common Programme of the Chinese People's Political Consultative Conference*), in 建国以来重要文献选编 (*Collection of Key Documents since the Founding of the People's Republic of China*), ed. by 中.C. Archive). Beijing: Zhongyang Wenxian Chubanshe.

Dong, Shunbo. Jul. 2014. '论福泽谕吉对旅顺大屠杀事件的评论' (Fukuzawa Yukichi's comments on the Port Arthur Massacre). Sheke Zongheng (*Social Sciences Review*) 29: 107–109.

Fukuzawa, Yukichi. 1962. '蘭学事始再版序' (Forward for the Reprint of The Origin of Dutch Studies), in 福沢諭吉全集 (*The Complete Works of Fukuzawa Yukichi*). Tokyo: Iwanami shoten.

Fukuzawa, Yukichi 1875. 文明論之概略 (*An Outline of a Theory of Civilisation*) Tokyo: Fukuzawa Yukichi.

Guo, Moruo 郭沫若. 1958. '中国代表团团长郭沫若的发言' (Speech of Guo Moruo, the Chairman of the Chinese Delegation), in 亚非人民团结大会文件汇编 (*Collection of Documents of the Afro-Asian People's Solidarity Conference*). Beijing: Shijiezhishi Chubanshe.

Huang, Xingtao. 2017. 重塑中华: 近代中国"中华民族"观念研究 (*Reshaping Zhonghua: The Concept of 'Zhonghua Minzu' in Modern China*) Hong Kong: Joint Publishing.

Jin, Guantao & Qingfeng Liu. 2008. 观念史研究: 中国现代重要政治术语的形成 (*Studies in the History of Ideas: The Formation of Important Modern Chinese Political Terms*). Hong Kong: Chinese University of Hong Kong.

Kataoka, Tsuruo. 1899. '极东之新木爱罗主义' (New Monroeism from the Far East). 清议报 (*The China Discussion*) 2.21.

Kozyo, Satakichi. 1896. '土耳其论' (On Turkey). Shiwu Bao (*Current Affairs*) 11.

Li, Dazhao. 1959. 李大钊全集 (*Selected Works of Li Dazhao*) Beijing: Renmin Chubanshe.

———. 1999. '支那分割之命运驳议' (Against the Destiny of China Being Divided), in 李大钊全集 (*Complete Works of Li Dazhao*), ed. by S. Zhang, L. Han, S. Zen, Z. Li, L. Yan, W. Chen, Z. Zhou, R. Yang, J. Guo, J. Zhao, R. Du, H. Wang, Z. Xie, Z. Deng, H. Zhang, and W. Zhu. Shijiazhuang: Hebei Jiaoyu Chubanshe.

Liang, Qichao. 1999a. '国家思想变迁异同论' (The transformation of State Theory, similarities and differences), in 梁启超全集 (*The Complete Works of Liang Qichao*), ed. by P. Zhang. Beijing: Beijing Chubanshe.

———. 1999b. '新民说' (On the new Citizen, 1902), in 梁启超全集 (*The Complete Works of Liang Qichao*), ed. by P. Zhang. Beijing: Beijing Chubanshe.

———. 2001. '进化论革命者颉德之学说' (Introducing Bejamine Kidd, a Revolutionary Thinker on Evolutionism), in 饮冰室文集点校 (*Collection and Anotation of Liang Qichao's Works*). Kunming: Yunnan Jiaoyu Chubanshe.

Liu, Xianfei. 2011. '东游运动与潘佩珠日本认识的转变' (The Changes in Phan Boi Chau's Understanding of Japan after the Movement of Traveling about Japan). Dongnanya Yanjiu (*Southeast Asian Studies*) 69–73.

Mao, Zedong 毛泽东. 1983. '新民主主义论' (On New Democracy), in 毛泽东集 (*Collected Writings of Mao Tse-Tung*), ed. by M. Takeuchi. Tokyo: Hokubōsha.

Pang, Xianzhi, Hui Feng, Xu Yao, Futing Zhao, and Zhengyu Wu, eds. 2002. 毛泽东年谱, 1893–1949 (*The Annotated Chronicle of Mao Zedong, 1893–1949*). Beijing: Zhongyang Wenxian Chubanshe.

Tongzhanbu, Zhonggongzhongyang, ed. 1991. 民族问题文献汇编 1921.7–1949.9 (*Collection of Documents on National Questions, from July 1921 to September 1949*). Beijing: Zhonggongzhongyang Dangxiao Chubanshe.

Unknown. 1985. '论帝国主义之发达及廿世纪世界之前途' (On the Development of Imperialism and the Future of the 20th Century), in 近代中国史料丛刊三编·第十五辑·清议报全编 (*Collection of Modern Chinese Historical Documents, Volume 3, Number 15, Complete Collection of Qingyi Bao*), ed. by 沈云龙. Taipei: Wenhai Chubanshe.

Unkown. 1903. '国家学上之支那民族观' (View on Chinese Nation from the point of State Theory). 游学译编 (*Translations of International Studies*) 11: 11–23.

Xiao, Chunv 萧楚女. 1925. '显微镜下之醒狮派' (*The Awakened Lion School under Microscope*). 中国青年 (The Chinese Youth).

Yuyi. 1903. 民族主义论 (On Nationalism). Zhejiang Chao (Tidal Wave of Zhejiang) 1.

Zhou, Enlai 周恩来. 1941. '民族至上与国家至上' (Nation Supremacy and State Supremacy). 新华日报 (*Xinhua Daily*), Part 1, June 15, Part 2, June 22.

———. 1990. '在亚非会议全体会议上的发言' (Speech delivered to the *Plenary Session of the Bandung Conference*), in 周恩来外交文选 (*Collection of Zhou Enlai's works on Foreign Affairs*), ed. by 中华人民共和国外交部 & 中共中央文献研究室. Beijing: Zhongyang Wenxian Chubanshe.

United Front Work Department 中共中央统战部 (ed.) 1991. 民族问题文献汇编 1921.7–1949.9 (*Collection of Documents on National Questions, from July 1921 to September 1949*). Beijing: Zhonggongzhongyang Dangxiao Chubanshe.

Zhou, Songlun. 2014. 文明「入欧」与政治「脱亚」—福泽谕吉「文明论」的逻辑构造 (Civilisation 'Joining Europe' and Politics 'Leaving Asia': The Logic Structure of Fukusawa Yukichi's 'Civilisation Theory'). Ershiyi shiji (*Twenty-First Century*) 142: 29–41.

9
NATIONALISM, NATIONAL SALVATION AND THE DEVELOPMENT OF FEMALE HYGIENE IN THE REPUBLIC OF CHINA ERA

Meishan Zhang

Introduction

Nationalism in the Republic of China era is a fusion of traditional Chinese Sinocentrism (华夏中心主义) rooted in the national blood and modern Western nationalism. This combination is a new world outlook and national consciousness that accompanied people 'opening their eyes to see the world', as well as repeated military failures. At the beginning of the twentieth century, the constitutionalists represented by Liang Qichao (梁启超) and the revolutionaries led by Sun Yat-sen (孙中山) gradually formed a consensus on establishing an independent, democratic and unified multi-ethnic country through continuous debates and attempts to establish a nation-state. 'National Salvation' (救亡图存) and 'Strengthening the Nation and the Race' (强国保种) became the most resounding slogans for government reforms and social movements in the late Qing and the Republic of China eras (Zheng 2007, 5; Mitter 2002, 44). Women, considered by reformers as the mothers of 'new citizens' and the leading cause of the country's backwardness, were under re-examination of their significant role in building a modern and unified state. Furthermore, the women's liberation movements in other countries and the introduction of Western obstetrics and gynaecology reinforced initiating a modern female hygiene system that would support the state ideology by reducing infant mortality and enhancing women's vitality.

In the late 1800s, Liang Qichao clearly stated in 'On education for women' that the goal of education for women was to 'better serve both the husband and the children, make a harmonious and orderly home and give birth to high-quality races' (Liang 1897). Women's mission in the country still inherited Confucianism and was embedded in their responsibilities towards the family and the next generation. Intellectuals of the May Fourth Movement (五四运动) and the New Culture Movement (新文化运动) were committed to liberating women from these family shackles. Adopting Western women's lifestyle as a model, they advocated that women should dedicate themselves to their country with independent personalities in the political economy and their social life and individuality (Chen 1916). In terms of administrative measures, establishing a health system for female hygiene based on

Western biomedicine and public health theories and practice became the leading way to turn the female body into a national body through political intervention (Rogaski, 2004).

Among the rich literature on nationalism in China, Frank Dikötter put forward the concept of 'racial nationalism' for the first time on the basis of the two nationalisms previously highlighted by the socialist John Hutchinson, namely 'political nationalism' and 'cultural nationalism'. He discovered that racial nationalists portrayed the nation as a pseudo-biological entity united by ties of blood during this period (Dikötter 1996). During the Republic of China era, the exploration of, and vision for, optimizing race was very significant. The image of a robust mother served as a powerful symbol of a strong race. Yet, there remains no structured study devoted to the institutional construction around women's health under the discourse of racial nationalism.

This chapter focuses on the performance, characteristics and limitations of the establishment and development of female hygiene in the wave of nationalism during the Republic of China era. By presenting the construction of the female hygiene system around childbirth technology, this chapter traces the historical scenes of the active participation of the political and medical forces in China with the ultimate goal of national salvation. Continuing with Dikötter's point of view that the core of nationalism in this era was to strengthen the country and race, I, the author, argue that it was due to this strong demand that women's health issues began to encourage the embracing of Western medicine and the female body becoming a national body in the Republic of China era. While women were criticized as being a drawback to the country, they were becoming the hope for future revitalization, due to their role of nurturing the next generation.

The adoption of Western medicine in China

Recognition of Western culture as an advanced civilization by the Chinese ruling class only began in the late Qing Dynasty. When China's national strength weakened, especially after the failure of foreign wars in the second half of the nineteenth century, the Sinocentrism disintegrated. Chinese scholar-bureaucrats were forced to recognize the degree of development of Western civilization and even later regarded Western civilization as a social model (Liu 2017, 122).

After the Opium War, the Qing government introduced Western technology and culture on a large scale in an official form for the first time: the Self-Strengthening Movement/ the Westernization Movement (洋务运动) with slogans such as 'Changing Chinese ways through foreign ways' (用夷变夏) and 'Learn from the foreigners to resist the foreign powers' (师夷长技以制夷). The most important contributions of the Westernization School (洋务派) to the dissemination of Western medicine lay in the translation of Western medicine concepts, sending international students to study abroad and setting up Western-style medical schools. Under the discourse of the emerging nation-state, the legal system, medical treatment, living habits and daily necessities, and even clothing related to the female body were reconstructed with the image of strong and educated women in the Western world as a model (Zhang 2018, 406).

As well as the adaptation of a more universal concept of hygiene, the Chinese authorities had been investing in overseas student projects since the late Qing Dynasty. Witnessing Japan's successful example of replacing the Japanese HAN prescription medicine based on Chinese medicine with the German medical system, under the advocacy of reformists in China's late Qing Dynasty, Chinese medical students flowed to mainly Japan (Ai 2010).

They became an essential medium in the trend of Western medicine and public health practice flowing to China.

In addition, the spread of Western medicine in China also benefited from missionaries and colonialism. Medical missionaries and colonial governments had been introducing and localizing hospitals and their public health facilities in treaty ports, such as Shanghai and Guangzhou, since the mid-nineteenth century (MacPherson 1987). In 1902, Dr. Mary H. Fulton founded the Hackett Medical College (广东女医学堂) for Women in Guangzhou, the capital city of Guangdong Province (Lin 2015, 64). Together with its affiliated hospital, the David Gregg Hospital for Women and Children (道济医院), it served as a medical centre to mainly diagnose and treat women and children at an early stage (Zhou 2010, 199). On the one hand, the philanthropic medical activities carried out by these missionaries and colonial governments had created a certain degree of trust in Western medicine among the Chinese people. On the other hand, those medical facilities in concession areas and treaty ports became templates for the Chinese obstetrics and gynaecology institutions initiated later (Zhou 2008).

To conclude, the development process of medicine in the early twentieth-century China transited 'from the age of gods to the age of experimentation, then entering the age of science' (Chen 1981, 257). The adoption of Western medicine and the construction of a female hygiene system in China were inseparable from the national endeavour in China and the medical development in the United States, Europe, Japan and other countries.

The rise and fall of the nation is the responsibility of every woman

The late Qing Dynasty was when the concept of modern nationalism in China began to form and knowledge of female hygiene began to spread. The national idea in the late Qing Dynasty was still in the transition period from the feudal concept of 'Tianxia' (a China-centred world天下) to the modern notion of 'a multi-ethnic unified country'. In 1902, Liang Qichao formally put forward the idea of a 'Chinese nation' (中华民族). In his articles 'On the General Trend of Changes in Chinese Academic Thought' (论中国学术思想变迁之大势) and 'Observation of Chinese Nations in History' (历史上中国民族之观察), he discussed issues such as 'whether the Chinese nation is a single nation and whether there is a most important ethnic group' (Liang 1902; 1905). In his 1907 article 'Discourse on the Ideology of Gold and Iron' (金铁主义说), Yang Du (杨度) clearly stated that the difference between the 'Chinese nation' and other nations lies in culture (Yang 2008, 213). The development of nationalism at this time was stimulated by Western nationalism and the introduction of Western culture promoted formation of the self-consciousness of Chinese culture in the world.

When the reformers learn from the so-called advanced Western system and culture, they incorporate Western medicine into their reformation ideas. The article 'Prosperity and Power Begin with Hygiene' (富强始于卫生论) in the *Zhixin Bao* (知新报), a journal of the reformist faction, states:

> If you want to govern the world, you must start your own country; if you want to govern a country, you must start by strengthening the people; if you want to strengthen the people, you must start by strengthening your body. Western medicine is very prosperous, and it is close to entering the Dao.

(Liu 1897)

Liang Qichao had taken the liberation of women as an essential link to national salvation, in stating, 'the rise and fall of the nation is the responsibility of every woman' (Liang, 1897). To enable women to assume their responsibilities to their country, he proposed banning foot binding, promoting women's education, banning early marriage and advocating women's rights, but he did not include establishing a female health system (Huang 2004, 88).

However, as an increasing number of people were accepting the missionary hospital's promotion of birth delivery in China, there were some reflections on the high risk of the traditional birth delivery method. In 1898, the *Universal Bulletin* (万国公报) published 'A Letter from Suzhou' (苏州来稿), which used as an example the author's wife's death during childbirth, condemning the traditional midwife, and calling for the promotion of Western birth delivery techniques (Anonymous 1898, 1). At the beginning of the twentieth century, there were already some small clinics and obstetrics classrooms established by some squires who supported Western medicine along the southeast coast (Zhu 2013, 84).

Despite there being very few officially supported institutions for female hygiene, the most influential were the hospitals and medical schools established by Yuan Shikai (袁世凯) in the name of the local government. In 1907, China's first female student studying abroad, Jin Yunmei (金韵梅), an expert in gynaecology, returned to China from the United States and was hired by Yuan Shikai to establish the Beiyang Women's Medical Bureau (北洋女医局) and Changlu Women's Medical School (长芦女医学堂) in Tianjin. Students in the midwifery class of the Changlu Women's Medical School worked as interns at the Beiyang Women's Medical Bureau, creating a midwife training model that combined clinical practice and midwifery class teaching in an officially sponsored Western-style gynaecological hospital (Gao 2014).

In the late Qing Dynasty, nationalism and knowledge of women's health were discussed and reshaped in the national crisis and in the exchange of Chinese and Western cultures. They were still in the awakening stage of exploring the country's road to strengthening. Many discussions were conducted among the folk and intellectuals, despite the lack of official discourse and concrete institutional measures. However, these discussions were breakthrough and provided the basis for public opinion on the formal formation of nationalism and establishment of the female hygiene system during the Republic of China era.

Female body and the strength of the nation

The establishment of the Republic of China marked the first Republic regime in Chinese history. The revolutionaries represented by Sun Yat-sen were more systematic in discussing nationalism and female hygiene as part of the construction of a modern country. On January 1, 1912, Sun Yat-sen clearly announced the founding policy of the 'Five Races Under One Union' (五族共和) in the 'Inaugural Address of the Provisional President' (临时大总统就职宣言书):

> The foundation of the country lies in the people, and it integrates the Han, Manchu, Mongolian, Hui and Tibetan regions as one country; the Han, Manchu, Mongolian, Hui and Tibetan ethnic groups as one person. It is called the unity of the nation.

From this, the Chinese nation and the Republic of China gradually became the concept of unity (Sun 1982, 2).

Driven by the May Fourth Movement, modern Chinese nationalism joined the wave of the national liberation movement after the First World War. Resisting imperialist oppression and realizing national self-determination became the theme of this period (Zheng 2013, 6). Following the May Fourth Movement, Sun Yat-sen's 'Three Principles of the People' (三民主义) added content related to opposing imperialist aggression and enhancing China's international status. In 1924, he pointed out in the 'Outline of National Government Founding' (国民政府建国大纲) that 'the government should resist foreign aggression and power and, at the same time, revise the treaties of various countries to restore our international equality and national independence' (Sun 1986, 127). Sun Yat-sen's 'nationalism' also created a discussion of the population issues that encouraged fertility. He believed that the slowdown in China's population growth was very dangerous to the future of the Chinese nation (Cui and Yao 1986, 35).

In addition, Sun Yat-sen's 'Three Principles of the People' also put forward requirements for the quality of the race and proposed improvement and progress in science and health (Editor 1912). Women's health was also placed under the discourse of 'strengthening the country and protecting the race' and became part of the contents of the administrative construction of an independent country.

Under the tone established by the 'Three Principles of the People', the Beiyang period (1912–1928) was when China transitioned from a feudal system to Republican politics. Despite the frequent wars among warlords, the Beiyang government aimed to catch up with other developed countries. It promulgated regulations on the development of natural science and Western-style education. In terms of education, the government enacted the Order of Medical Specialized Schools (医学专门学校令) on November 22, 1912. This regulation stipulated the content of medical education based on Western medicine and completely excluded traditional Chinese medicine from the education system (Luo 2016, 31). Regarding the health system, the government continuously adjusted its health administrative functions. The female body became partially liberated in the discourse of nationalism and as a target of government intervention. These measures to improve women's physical health included the banning of foot binding and waist girdling and launching of 'the Campaign of Heavenly Breast' (天乳运动). The new image of a woman as 'the mother of the nation' (国民之母) had also prompted the government to incorporate reproductive activities into its administrative management (He 2016, 226). When establishing administrative facilities, midwives were included in the management, which belonged to the Ministry of Internal Affairs (内务部) and then the Department of Health under the Ministry of Health (卫生部下设的卫生司). During this period, reformers had already begun legislative attempts to regulate midwives.

In 1913, the Department of the Capital's Police (京师警察厅) of Beiyang government issued 'The Provisional Ban of Traditional Midwives' (京师警察厅暂行取缔产婆规则) (Editor 1918). However, according to this regulation, all midwives could obtain a business licence by registering with the government; hence, the management effect of midwives was not significant (Editor 1926).

Despite there remaining many deficiencies in the administrative strength, female hygiene knowledge had become a hot topic in popular periodicals represented by the '*Women's Magazine*' (妇女杂志). Medical journals and columns gradually developed an argument that the female body was the foundation of the country, and that women should be helped to build a new self-identity from a scientific perspective. Many journals guided women in body management with Western medicine knowledge on the one hand and connected female hygiene with advanced and powerful countries on the other. As a result, obstetrics had gradually become a specialized knowledge and trend (Zhu 2013, 85). These newspapers called on midwives to have medical expertise and 'reliance on specialist doctors with knowledge of Western medicine' in all aspects of childbirth hygiene (Chen 1919, 60). In the article

'China Should Train Midwives Today' (中国今日宜培养助产士), it was proposed that opening up the midwifery industry and cultivating professional midwives should be viewed as 'the essential plan of China's race preservation today, and the good method of strengthening the country' (Chen 1916, 9).

In the early days of the Republic of China, the government and intellectuals established an independent and free multi-ethnic country as the direction of their nation-building. Through the voice of national self-determination, they explored the administrative system belonging to China. Female hygiene, still inheriting the tradition of the late Qing Dynasty, remained in the context of a strong country and a robust race. Discussions on women's health in periodicals and newspapers provided a specific mass basis and public opinion support for the innovation of birth delivery technology and rise of the modern midwife industry.

National rejuvenation and the construction of a female hygiene system

In 1927, Chiang Kaishek (蒋介石) led the National Revolutionary Army to victory. Almost all of the major provinces of China's eastern seaboard were under the control of the nationalists (Mitter 2002, 50). This geographically nearly unified situation provided an opportunity for national administrative construction. Regarding nationalism, the demand for 'rejuvenation' was apparent. In terms of responsibility for the country, this demanded endeavours from both the government and the 'new citizens' (新国民), especially women.

In the institutionalization of female hygiene, the Republic of China government focused its human and financial resources on reforming delivery methods. In addition to the fact that the financial strength was still unable to support comprehensive reforms, the high maternal and infant mortality rate rose to become a major social crisis related to the survival of the nation. Meanwhile, the Darwinian theory of evolution and 'race improvement with hygiene' (卫生强种说) was spreading prevailingly among intellectuals. Healthy infants were expected as 'new citizens' and the hope of national rejuvenation (Zhang 2009, 94). Healthy mothers and safer reproductive processes were viewed as the guarantees of healthy babies. However, compared with European and American countries, China's maternal mortality and infant death rates made healthcare reformers extremely anxious. Qu Jun (瞿骏), who continuously wrote about reproductive issues in *Funü shibao* (妇女时报), estimated that 3,330,000 mothers and infants had died during childbirth in 1926 in China (Judge 2015, 117). Lin Zhongda (林仲达) estimated that in 1932, the maternal mortality rates in Japan, Germany and the United States were 33%, 51% and 71%, respectively, while the mortality rate in China was as high as 176% (Zhao 2014, 43). The revealed discrepancy between idealized metaphysical cosmology and the harsh reality opened the door to the possibility of the Western delivering practice entering the orthodoxy.

While the high maternal and infant mortality rates had prompted Chinese reformers to modify and regulate the pregnancy and childbirth process, examining the leading causes of maternal and infant deaths determined the focus of childbirth reform. According to Zhang Gong (张弓)'s estimation of the maternal and infant deaths in Shanghai's Hongqiao District, postpartum infections were the leading cause of maternal death, accounting for 69% of all deaths, and tetanus was the primary cause of death in infants (Zhang 1933, 4). Medical specialists believed that the main reason for those tragedies was improper disinfection of the traditional midwife during the delivery process. This led to the traditional midwives who undertook the task of family delivery without knowledge of sterilization becoming a threat to the lives of mothers and babies. Whether or not these survey results reflected objective conditions or were exaggerated due to the intention of eradicating traditional midwives, the primary goal of constructing female hygiene based on Western medicine could not avoid challenging the dominance of indigenous reproductive customs.

Holding the ideal of strengthening the country and the race, while facing the realities mentioned above, the Nanjing National Government's measures for childbirth reform were divided into the following three categories: school-based education and professionalization of midwives, the legislation and institutionalization of midwifery practice, and the governmental guidance on women's health.

In 1928, the nationalists established China's first Ministry of Health (卫生部) (Baum 2020, 5). As the Ministry of Health was being established, the plan for maternal and child health concentrated on four areas: expanding Western-style medical education, supervising and managing modern and traditional midwives, setting up maternal and child health institutions, and conducting research on maternal child health issues (Yang 1941, 283). On January 23, 1929, the Ministry of Health and the Ministry of Education (教育部) co-founded the Central Midwifery Education Committee (中央助产教育委员会). Participants in the meeting, including officials from the Ministry of Health and the Ministry of Education, as well as heavyweights in the medical field, such as Liu Ruiheng (刘瑞恒), Wu Zhenchun (吴振春), Jin Baoshan (金宝善), Yang Chongrui (杨崇瑞) and Yan Fuqing (颜福庆), decided to establish the First Midwifery School in Peking as a national model for public and private midwifery schools.

On October 16, 1929, the Peking National First Midwifery School (北平第一助产学校) opened. Liu Ruiheng, the Deputy Minister of Health, wrote an inscription for the school 'Make the offspring healthy and the country strong' (健种强国), and Jin Baoshan, the director of the Department of Health Care of the Ministry of Health (卫生部保健司), wrote the inscription 'A powerful country and race reply on mother and child, and it is benevolence to take care of the body in the right way'. These inscriptions reflect the great responsibility of the midwifery industry for the path of the Republic of China government to make the country more robust and also reflect the ultimate goal of the government's strong support for the midwifery industry (Wang 2014, 485). With an exceptional lineup of teachers, the school cultivated more than 450 undergraduates majoring in midwifery in its 25 years of existence. It also organized on-the-job training, research classes and other projects throughout the year to provide midwifery talents across the country (Wang 2014, 487).

Referring to the First Midwifery School template, Yang Chongrui founded the National Second Midwifery School (国立第二助产学校) in Nanjing in 1933. Under the promotion of Yang Chongrui and the demonstration of national midwifery schools, provincial and municipal midwifery schools were launched across the country (Xia 2007, 37).

Regarding midwives' management, the Nanjing Nationalist Government issued a series of regulations to bring midwives who were initially free agents into the national health administrative power. In 1928, the Ministry of Health promulgated the 'Chinese Midwives Rules' (助产士条例), which first formed the certification system for Western-style midwives. The regulations stipulated that midwives must receive domestic or foreign midwifery education, have relevant midwifery experience or pass the state-sponsored midwife exam to obtain a midwife certificate and conduct midwifery business. Second, midwives were obligated to report the identity and status of the baby and undertake the task of birth statistics. In addition, the business of midwives could not exceed the scope of normal delivery, while only obstetricians had the authority to advise the mother on dystocia (The Ministry of Health 1996, 628).

From 1929 to 1949, the number of qualified midwives registered nationwide increased substantially, from 385 in 1929 to 3,694 in 1937 and, by 1949, the number rose to over 10,000

(Yip 1995, 134; 166; Zhu 1988, 119). Although the number of modern midwives had been proliferating, Yang Chongrui estimated that China needed more than 100,000 midwives to cater for the basic needs of women and infants. In addition to the shortage in number, the distribution of Western-style midwifery services in urban and rural areas was very uneven. These midwives were mainly concentrated in urban areas that could afford their wages and accepted a higher degree of Western medical knowledge. However, in some urban areas, due to people's distrust of the new birth delivery method, there was a dilemma that midwives had 'nothing to do' and traditional midwives remained in control of childbirth-related events (Anonymous 1948, 1). For instance, according to Yang Chongrui's surveys, as many as 40,000 traditional Chinese midwives were trusted by families as their pregnancy acquaintances. The development time of the Western medical education in China was far shorter than in Western countries, and China was also unable to train and provide enough professional midwives to replace the midwives in a short period (Guo 1935, 1).

Therefore, when Chinese public health experts with a Western education background, represented by Yang Chongrui, formulated the female hygiene system, they believed that it was impossible to copy the Western medical system completely while confronting the aforementioned unique national conditions in China and encountering the obstacles in promoting Western-style midwifery. They regarded the transformation of traditional midwives as medical education content and a policy of professionalizing the industry in parallel with cultivating new-style midwives (Philips 2006, 182).

As the previous attempts to ban traditional midwives were showing little success, the Nanjing National Government adjusted how it dealt with traditional midwives, by replacing 'banning' with 'reform'. In 1928, the Ministry of the Interior of the Nanjing National Government (内政部) promulgated the Management Rules for Traditional Midwives (管理接生婆规则) (Cheung and Mander 2018). The rules confirmed the legal status of traditional midwives by issuing licences and regulating their business behaviour. For example, midwives were not allowed to use the services of professional physicians, such as surgical operations and obstetric operations, during the delivery process. They could only perform measures such as disinfection and cutting the umbilical cord. The rules stipulated that the local government officials should set up midwifery training classes to provide 'scientific' training for traditional midwives (The Ministry of Interior 1996, 629). According to the above regulations, in 1928, the Health Bureau of Beiping Special City (北平特别市卫生局) established the Midwife Training Centre (产婆讲习所) (later renamed the Midwife Training Class 接生婆训练班) and the registered old midwives were required to obtain hygiene training here (Editor 1935, 33). The main aspects of the training were cleaning and disinfection methods, delivery methods, umbilical cord tying and cutting methods, suspended animation and resuscitation methods, nursing methods of puerpera and concise human anatomy. When the training period expired, a licence would be issued after passing the test, and a birth basket was added for each person containing birth attendance equipment and medicine. One of the advantages of the birth basket was in considering that many retrained midwives would be illiterate; graphical representation was provided with the products (He 2016, 133).

According to the *Health Bimonthly* (卫生半月刊), as of 1935, 145 traditional midwives had graduated from such training classes (Editor 1935, 33). Although the number of graduates was far fewer than the number of traditional midwives who conducted this business, the retraining model in Peking had set an example for other cities across the country.

Following Beiping's example, the Shanghai government also carried out a reform of midwives in response to the 'Regulations for Midwives'. In 1928, the Shanghai Municipal Health Bureau cooperated with the Zhongde Midwife School (中德助产学校) to start a midwife training class. The training team instructed on basic modern midwifery practice and hygienic standards. Each training course lasted for three months with 50 or 60 students enrolling (Yu 1940, 2). The Health Bureau stipulated that the midwives participating in midwife training classes should, themselves, purchase midwifery supplies for their internships. The birth basket was a necessary set of tools for retrained midwives and the birth baskets used by Beijing-trained midwives were recommended (Editor 1930, 15).

There were still many problems in the training classes for traditional midwives in terms of actual implementation. The most obvious drawback was the quickness of these training courses, which was reflected in the lack of class hours and oversimplification of the teaching content (Zhu 2015, 159). For example, in the Hebei Qinghe Midwife Training Class (河北清河产婆训练班), the training period was only two weeks of two and a half hours each day (Editor 1935, 1). In the 1934 'Shanghai Health Bureau's Regulation of Setting up a Training Class for traditional midwives' (上海市卫生局训练产婆简章), the purpose of the course arrangement was to enable the midwives to obtain concise obstetric knowledge and understand the methods in the shortest period of time (Shanghai Health Bureau 1934, 143).

Considering that the education level and deep-rooted concept of delivery of the traditional midwives made it difficult for them to digest knowledge of physiology and pathology, the training class focused on teaching basic operations, such as disinfection and cutting the umbilical cord. As a result, there was a massive imbalance between the knowledge taught in the training class and the clinical operation (Fujian Government 1936, 582). The local government's eagerness to accomplish the targets, the lack of educational resources and the backwardness of the traditional midwives resulted in limitations of the childbirth reform.

The reform of delivery technology also pushed women from the private sphere to the public space. The government built low-cost or free medical facilities in order to attract people resistant to the new birth delivery method, due to economic difficulties and unfamiliarity with Western medicine. From the 1920s, some public hospitals had cooperated with the government to provide free beds and promoted new birth delivery methods in cities and villages (Huang 2005, 30).

Obstetric education and obstetric institutions had also increased the procedures of prenatal and postnatal examinations, hospital observation and isolation before childbirth, thereby increasing the safety of mothers and babies and strengthening the government's control of women's pregnancy and childbirth body and the baby's birth status. In this way, Western medicine was able to bring females into a new wave of nationalism in the name of strengthening the country and the race.

It is worth mentioning that the government and medical reformers also made efforts in propaganda when facing the problem of popularizing and promoting Western medicine knowledge. In the health campaigns hosted by local governments, both maternity and infant health exhibitions and healthy baby competitions were common forms of engaging people. Childbirth was no longer a woman's personal affair, but a public matter to construct people's patriotic and healthy new national identity.

Conclusion

From the late nineteenth century to the end of the Republic era, Western medical culture, nationalism and the wars of aggression entered China together. The crisis of national subjugation brought about by the failure of several wars forced the traditional Sinocentrism to 'shrink' into modern nationalism. Both the constitutionalists and the revolutionaries gradually reached a consensus on establishing an independent, democratic and unified multi-ethnic country through continuous debates and attempts to establish a nation-state. As a result, 'National Salvation' and 'Strengthening the Nation and the Race' became the main themes for government reforms and social movements during this period. The liberation of women and the legitimization of Western medicine, in the discourse of nationalism and pursuit of a powerful nation, were incorporated into the management of the government in the form of a female hygiene system.

Following the establishment of the Republic of China Sun Yat-sen's 'Three Principles of the People' became the founding thought. In the 'Three Principles of the People' discussions about encouraging fertility, advocating Western medicine and liberating women guided the health administrations of the Beiyang government and the Nanjing government. During the Beiyang period, from 1912 to 1928, a medical education system and a health administration based on Western medicine were initially established. The female body was partially liberated due to government intervention. During this period, government-issued norms for midwifery behaviour, although ineffective, had set a precedent for professionalization of the female hygiene system and the midwifery industry.

In 1927, the Nanjing Nationalist Government came into power and took control of most of China's territory. The core of nationalism was to meet the demand for 'rejuvenation', which highlighted the responsibilities of both the government and the 'new citizens', especially women. Therefore, the institutionalization of female hygiene involved an unprecedented number of policies and personnel.

Faced with high maternal and infant mortality rates, in establishing female hygiene with a focus on childbirth, the government now perceived women's health and reproductive behaviour as going beyond inheriting the family's lineage and promoted the mission of national salvation. Measures for childbirth reinforced school-based education and the professionalization of midwives, the legislation and institutionalization of midwifery practice, and the governmental guidance on women's health.

After the September 18th Incident (九一八事变), especially after the North China Incident (华北事变), and the July 7th Incident (七七事变), the increasingly aggravating national and ethnic crisis promoted an upsurge of modern Chinese nationalism. The idea that all ethnic groups in China formed a multi-ethnic community was being increasingly accepted by people of all ethnic groups in the country (Zheng 2006, 12).

However, Japan's aggression towards China in 1937 was a fatal blow to the midwifery industry. Following the July 7th Incident, beacon flames spread everywhere and some of the midwifery schools were destroyed in war zones, some were suspended and some had to move away. There are very few workers who can recite and stabilize (Gong 1940, 14).

> There were more than 30 midwifery schools before the war. By 1940 about 1/5 of them were directly destroyed by the enemy and about 1/4 of them were at a standstill as they were close to the war zone. Another 1/10 moved to the inner land but were unable to provide classes, and now there are only around 10 schools, which are struggling to continue classes in difficult circumstances.
>
> *(Wang 1940, 15)*

Unfortunately, the civil war between the nationalists and the Communist Party after the victory of the Anti-Japanese War made the restoration of female hygiene more difficult.

To conclude, during the construction of the female hygiene system, the reshaping of women's roles, in responding to the country's call for national salvation, was intertwined with the health facilities they could access. As a result, the main implementation of this system was concentrated in, and restricted to, urban areas with relatively advanced medical conditions. With both women's social responsibilities and their well-being considered in a society's concerns at an unprecedented scale, the impact of this system was more far-reaching than merely an increase in the popularity and prevalence of Western medicine. It transformed the female body into a national body, while laying the foundation for a mediated Chinese form of modern obstetrics and gynaecology system, which the communist government adopted after 1949. During this transformation, women's voices and their personal experiences, although limited, began to emerge in public discussions. A few women, such as Yang Chongrui, even entered the decision-making level of the health system, setting a benchmark for women's participation in the institutional construction of a nation-state.

References

English-language references

Baum, Emily. 2020. "Medicine and Public Health in Twentieth-century China: Histories of Modernisation and Change." *History Compass* 18 (7): 1–11.

Cheung, Ngai Fen and Rosemary Mander, 2018. "Table 3.1 Midwifery Policies of the Nationalist Government of China, 1911–1949." *Midwifery Policies in China*. London: Routledge.

Dikötter, Frank. 1996. "Culture, "Race" and Nation: The Formation of National Identity in Twentieth Century China." *Journal of International Affairs* 49 (2): 590–605.

Judge, Joan. 2015. *Republican Lens: Gender, Visuality, and Experience in the Early Chinese Periodically Press*. Berkeley: University of California Press.

Lin, Shing-ting. 2015. "The Female Hand: The Making of Western Medicine for Women in China, 1880s–1920s," PhD thesis, Columbia University.

Mitter, Rana. 2002. "Contention and Redemption: Ideologies of National Salvation in Republican China." *Totalitarian Movements and Political Religions* 3 (3): 44–74.

Philips, Tina. 2006. "Building the Nation through Women's Health: Modern Midwifery in Early Twentieth-Century China," PhD thesis, University of Pittsburgh. https://d-scholarship.pitt.edu/9563/1/phillipst_etd2006_1.pdf.

Rogaski, Ruth. 2004. *Hygienic Modernity: Meanings of Health and Disease in Treaty-Port China*. Berkeley: University of California Press.

Yip, Ka-che. 1995. *Health and National Reconstruction in Nationalist China: The Development of Modern Health Service, 1928–1937*. Ann Arbor, MI: Association for Asian Studies.

Zhang, Shaoqian. 2018. "Shaping the New Woman: The Dilemma of Shen in China's Republican Period." *Dao* 17 (3): 401–420.

Chinese-language references

Ai, Zhike 艾智科. 2010. "晚清的中西医汇通思想及其走向" (The Thought of Combining Traditional Chinese and Western Medicine in the Late Qing Dynasty and Its Trends). 历史档案 (*Historical Archives*) 2: 120–125.

Anonymous. 1898. "苏州来稿: 请广行西法收生以解产厄说" (A Letter from Suzhou: Please Widely Practice to Solve the Problem of Childbirth). 万国公报 (*Universal Bulletin*), January: 1–2.

Anonymous. 1948. "妇婴卫生是民族健康的基石" (Maternal and Infant Health is the Cornerstone of National Health). 医潮 (*Medical Journal*) 10: 1.

Chen, Bangxian 陈邦贤. 1981. 中国医学史 (*History of Chinese Medicine*). Taibei: Taiwai Shangwu Yinshuguan.

Chen, Duxiu 陈独秀. 1916. "孔子之道与现代生活" (The Way of Confucius and Modern Life). 新青年 (*The New Youth*), 2 (4): 1–7.

Chen, Yao Xiping 陈姚樨屏. 1916. "中国今日宜养成产婆论" (China Today Should Cultivate Midwife). 妇女杂志 (*Women's Magazine*) 2 (4): 9.

Chen, Yuan 陈垣. 1919. "北京保安产科医院序" (Beijing Bao'an Obstetrics Hospital). 光华卫生报 (Guanghua Weisheng Bao) 4: 60.

Cui, Lin, and Yao Minhua 崔林, 姚敏华. 1986. "孙中山人口思想研究——纪念孙中山诞辰一百二十周年" (Research on Sun Yat-sen's population thought——commemorating the 120th anniversary of Sun Yat-sen's birth). 人口研究 (*Population Research*) 10 (6): 35–40.
Editor. 1912. "孙中山先生谈话" (Mr. Sun Yat-sen talks). 民主报 (*Minzhu Bao*), June 26, 1912.
Editor. 1918. "产婆限期领照" (Midwife to Get a License in Limited Time). 晨钟报 (*The Morning Bell*), August 31.
Editor. 1926. "旧式产婆" (Old style midwife). 晨报 (*Morning Post*), October 13.
Editor. 1930. "卫生局拟设产婆训练班" (Health Bureau Plans to Set up Midwife Training Classes), 申报 (*Shenbao*), February 10: 15.
Editor. 1935. "北平第一助产学校五年来工作概况" (An Overview of the Work of Peiping the First Midwifery School in the Past Five Years). 卫生半月刊 (*Health Bimonthly*) 3: 33–37.
Editor. 1935. "河北省乡村卫生工作鸟瞰" (A Bird's-Eye View of Rural Health Work in Hebei Province). 公共卫生月刊 (*Public Health Monthly*) 1: 1.
Fujian Government 福建省政府. 1936. "福建省会训练及管理接生婆办法" (Measures for the Training and Management of Midwives in the Capital of Fujian Province). 福建省政府公报 (*Fujian Government Gazette*) 582.
Gao, Xi 高晞. 2014. "卫生之道与卫生政治化—20世纪中国西医体系的确立与演变 (1900–1949)" (The Establishment and Evolution of Western Medical System in China in the 20th Century). 史林 (*Historical Review*) 5: 91–102, 189.
Gong, Xuhui 龚旭辉. 1940. "助产职业之检讨" (Review of Midwifery Profession). 浙江省立杭州高级护士助产职业学校校刊 (*Zhejiang Provincial Hangzhou Senior Nurse Midwifery Vocational School Journal*) 1: 14.
Guo, Renji 郭人骥. 1935. "今日助产士的修养" (The Training of Midwives Today). 上海市惠生助产学校重建新校落成纪念特刊 (1935) (*Shanghai Huisheng Midwifery School Reconstruction and New School Completion Commemorative Special Issue*) 1.
He, Jiangli 何江丽. 2016. 民国北京的公共卫生 (*The Public Health of Beijing during the Republic of China*). Beijing: Beijing Normal University Press.
Huang, Qinglin 黄庆林. 2005. "国民政府时期的公医制度" (The Public Medical System in the Period of the National Government). 南都学坛 (*Academic Forum of Nandu*) 1: 30–31.
Huang, Yanli 黄嫣梨. 2004. "梁启超与近代妇女解放" (Written Statement on Re-understanding Liang Qichao). 文史哲 (*Journal of Chinese Humanities*) 3: 88–90.
Jin, Guantao 金观涛. 2017. "百年来中国民族主义结构的演变" (The Evolution of Chinese Nationalist Structure over the Past Hundred Years). 二十一世纪 (*Twenty-First Century*) 15: 65–72.
Liang, Qichao 梁启超. 1897. "论女学" (On Education for Women). 时务报 (*The Chinese Progress*), April 12.
Liang, Qichao 梁启超. 1897. "倡设女学堂启" (Announcement of Establishing the Girls' School). 时务报 (*The Chinese Progress*), November 15.
Liang, Qichao 梁启超. 1902. "论中国学术思想变迁之大势" (On the Major Trend of Changes in Chinese Academic Thoughts). 新民丛报 (*Xinmin Congbao*) 3, 5, 7, 9, 12, 16, 18, 21, 22.
Liang, Qichao 梁启超. 1905. "历史上中国民族之观察" (Observation of Chinese Nations in History). 新民丛报 (*Xinmin Congbao*) 65, 66.
Lin, Zhongda 林仲达. 1932. "国难声中之儿童教养问题" (The Problem of Children's Education Amid the National Crisis). 东方杂志 (*The Eastern Miscellany*) 29 (7): 6.
Liu, Ming 刘明. 2017. "西学东渐与晚清"三代观"的变迁" (The Eastward Spread of Western Culture and the Change of the View of "Three Dynasties""). 武汉大学学报人文科学版 (*Journal of Wuhan University (Arts & Humanity)*) 4: 122–130.
Liu, Zhenlin 刘桢麟. 1897. "富强始于卫生论" (Prosperity and Power Begin with Hygiene). 知新报 (*Zhixinbao*), November 11.
Luo, Wei 骆威. 2016. "南京国民政府时期的高等教育立法" (*Higher Education Legislation in the Period of Nanjing National Government*). Nanjing: Nanjing University Press.
Shanghai Health Bureau. 上海卫生局. 1934. "修正上海市卫生局训练产婆简章" (Amendment to the Shanghai Municipal Health Bureau's Guide to Training Midwives). 上海市政府公报 (*Gazette of Shanghai Municipal Government*) 143.
Sun, Yat-sen. 1982. "中华民国临时大总统就职宣言书" (Inaugural Address of the Provisional President). In 孙中山全集 (*The Complete Works of Sun Yat-sen*), edited by 中国社会科学院近代史研究所中华民国史研究室 (Edited by the Research Office of the History of the Republic of China, Institute of Modern History, Chinese Academy of Social Sciences); 中山大学历史系孙中山研究室

(Sun Yat-sen Institute Department of History, Sun Yat-sen University); 广东省社会科学院历史研究室 (History Research Office of Guangdong Academy of Social Sciences) 2: 2. Beijing: Zhonghua Book Company.

Sun, Yat-sen. 1986. "国民政府建国大纲" (Outline of National Government Founding). In 孙中山全集 (*The Complete Works of Sun Yat-sen*), edited by 中国社会科学院近代史研究所中华民国史研究室 (Edited by the Research Office of the History of the Republic of China, Institute of Modern History, Chinese Academy of Social Sciences); 中山大学历史系孙中山研究室 (Sun Yat-sen Institute Department of History, Sun Yat-sen University); 广东省社会科学院历史研究室 (History Research Office of Guangdong Academy of Social Sciences) 9: 127. Beijing: Zhonghua Book Company.

The Ministry of Health, Republic of China 民国卫生部. 1996. "助产士条例" (Chinese Midwives Rules). In 中国卫生法规史料选编 (1912–1949.9) (*Medical Laws and Legislation (1912–1949.9)*) edited by 陈明光 Chen Mingguang, 628. Shanghai: Shanghai Medical University Press.

The Ministry of Interior, Republic of China 民国内政部. 1996. "管理接生婆规则" (Management Rules for Traditional Midwives). In 中国卫生法规史料选编 (1912–1949.9) (*Medical Laws and Legislation (1912–1949.9)*) edited by 陈明光 Chen Mingguang, 629. Shanghai: Shanghai Medical University Press.

Wang, Qin 王琴. 1940. "助产教育的重要" (The Importance of Midwifery Education). 浙江省立杭州高级护士助产职业学校校刊 (*Zhejiang Provincial Hangzhou Senior Nurse Midwifery Vocational School Journal*) 1:15–16.

Xia, Junsheng 夏俊生. 2007. "杨崇瑞开拓中国妇幼卫生事业" (Yang Chongrui Pioneered the Cause of China's Maternal and Child Health). 炎黄春秋 (*Yanhuang Chunqiu*) 8: 36–39.

Yang, Chongrui 杨崇瑞. 1941. "中国妇婴卫生工作之过去与现在" (Past and Present of Maternal and Infant Health Work in China). 中华医学杂志 (*Chinese Medical Journal*) 27 (5): 283.

Yang, Du 杨度. 2008. "金铁主义说" (Discourse on the Ideology of Gold and Iron Yang). In 杨度集 (*Collected Writing of Yang Du*), edited by 刘晴波 (Liu Qingbo), 213. Changshai: Hunan remin chubanshe.

Yu, Songjun. 1940. 中德高级助产职业学校十五周年纪念册 (The 15th Anniversary Book of Zhongde Senior Midwifery Vocational School), *Shanghai Municipal Archives* Q235-3-464: 2.

Zhang, Gong 张弓. 1933. "中国之母性的保护问题" (The Protection of Motherhood in China). 女声 (*Woman's Voice*) 1 (16): 4.

Zhang, Zhongmin 张仲民. 2009. "出版与文化政治: 晚清的"卫生"书籍研究" (*Publishing and Cultural Politics: A Study of Books on "Hygiene" in the Late Qing Dynasty*). Shanghai: Shanghai Bookstore Publishing House.

Zheng, Dahua 郑大华. 2006. "中国近代民族主义的形成、发展及其他" (The Formation, Development and Others of Nationalism in Modern China). 史学月刊 (*Journal of Historical Science*) 6: 10–13.

Zheng, Dahua 郑大华. 2007. "论中国近代民族主义的思想来源及形成" (On the Ideological Origin and Formation of Modern Nationalism in China), 浙江学刊 (*Zhejiang Academic Journal*) 1: 5–15.

Zheng, Dahua 郑大华. 2013. "中国近代民族主义与中华民族自我意识的觉醒" (The Chinese Modern Nationalism and the Self-Awareness of Chinese Nation). 民族研究 (*Ethno-National Studies*) 3: 1–14.

Zhou, Chunyan 周春燕. 女体与国族: 强国强种与近代中国的妇女卫生 (1895–1949) (*Women's Hygiene in Modern China (1895–1949)*). Gaoxiong: Liwen Cultural Group.

Zhou, Yanping 周燕萍. 2008. "民国时期上海市妇幼卫生档案简介" (A Brief Introduction to Shanghai Maternal and Child Health Archives in the Republic of China). https://www.archives.sh.cn/dazn/ztzn/201203/t20120313_5590.html.

Zhu, Chao 朱潮. 1988. 中外医学教育史 (*History of Chinese and Foreign Medical Education*). Shanghai: Shanghai Medical University Press.

Zhu, Meiguang 朱梅光. 2013. "取缔抑或养成: 近代国人关于旧式产婆出路之争" (Being Prohibited or Being Cultivated—The Debate of Modern Chinese on Traditional Midwives' outlet). 安徽史学 (*Historiography Research in Anhui*) 4: 82–88.

Zhu, Meiguang. 朱梅光. 2015. "职业重塑: 民国旧式产婆训练班研究" (Remolding Career: on Traditional Midwife's Training Schools in the Republic of China). 四川师范大学学报 (*Journal of Sichuan Normal University*) 42 (3): 157–163.

10
BETWEEN A ROCK AND A HARD PLACE

The changing Taiwanese identity and rising Chinese nationalism

Yitan Li

Introduction

The Taiwan Strait has been a flashpoint for potential conflict for decades. With the rise of the People's Republic of China (PRC) and the gradual decline of the dominance of the United States (US) in the region, further exacerbated by the deteriorating US-China relations, the likelihood of a crisis in the Taiwan Strait has increased significantly. Since 1949, the Republic of China (ROC) on Taiwan and the PRC have undertaken two completely different paths of development. Taiwan has become a multi-party democracy, whereas China remains a highly economically developed one-party state. The distinct political trajectories in Taiwan and China have created two vastly different social experiences. These different social experiences have led to the formation of distinct identities and nationalisms on each side of the Taiwan Strait.

This chapter traces the changing Taiwanese identity in Taiwan and rising nationalism in China. It argues that the domestic and international challenges the PRC faces have increased the likelihood of diversionary nationalism, a kind of nationalism that elites could use to divert public attention away from internal problems toward external crises. Taiwan is stuck between a rock and a hard place as a way of moving forward. On the one hand, the Taiwanese identity is becoming increasingly distinct from the Chinese identity on the Mainland, moving Taiwan further down the path of becoming a distinct nation-state – a centrifugal force moving away from China's center of gravity. On the other hand, rising nationalism in China buttressed by China's rising economic and military power keeps Taiwan in China's orbit – a centripetal force that pulls Taiwan ever closer to the unification with the Mainland, peacefully or otherwise. The contention then lies between what the future would look like in this potential hybridity of Taiwanese democracy and Chinese authoritarianism. Taiwan, supported by the international community, would likely resist the gravitational pull by China. However, China is now powerful enough to overcome such resistance. Taiwan faces a hard choice between drifting further away from and returning to the Mainland.

This chapter unfolds in the following sections after this introduction. In the first section, a brief history of the Taiwan issue will be provided. The second section traces the changing Taiwanese identity and explains why this new identity is different from the Chinese identity on the Mainland. The third section examines the rising nationalism in China and how this rising nationalism has kept Taiwan in China's orbit and increasingly more so. The final section, before the conclusion, synthesizes the centrifugal and centripetal forces and explains why Taiwan is stuck between a rock and a hard place due to the increasing likelihood of diversionary nationalism.

The Taiwan issue: a brief history

After the Chinese Communist Party (CCP)-led troops defeated the Nationalist/ Kuomintang (KMT) troops in the Chinese Civil War, the PRC was founded in 1949 and the KMT government fled to Taiwan. This led to what is now known as the "Taiwan Issue". The governments on the two sides of the Taiwan Strait have viewed the Taiwan issue differently. The PRC claims that after the KMT lost the Chinese Civil War, the ROC ceased to exist; and that Taiwan has always been a (lost) province of China. Thus, the PRC became the only China. The ROC argues that the KMT's retreat to Taiwan was a relocation of the ROC government from Nanjing to Taipei. The ROC never ceased its existence (Blanchard and Hickey 2012). As a matter of fact, until the United Nations (UN) Resolution 2758 on October 25, 1971, the ROC had occupied the China seat on the UN Security Council. The ROC government on Taiwan has had effective sovereign control over Taiwan since the KMT's resettlement.

Beijing has always considered Taiwan as part of the PRC and an inalienable Chinese territory. The ultimate goal of the PRC government is to reunite the country under the PRC. Taipei's views about cross-Strait relations have changed over time. When the KMT first arrived in Taiwan, the KMT government firmly believed that there was only one China – the ROC. And the goal of the ROC government was to return to the Mainland and reunify the country under the ROC. However, the ROC has gradually given up its goal of returning to the Mainland and its territory claims over the entire Chinese Mainland. Today's government in Taipei only claims effective jurisdiction over the island of Taiwan and several small offshore islands.

This complex and ambiguous relationship in the Taiwan Strait created conditions for the "1992 Consensus", a result of a historic meeting in Hong Kong between the semi-official representatives of the PRC and ROC governments. The "1992 Consensus" states that there is only "one China", but each side of the Taiwan Strait is allowed to interpret what that "one China" means. To Beijing, the one China means the PRC and to Taipei the ROC. The two sides have been able to operate through this ambiguity and maintain functional interaction since 1992, particularly under the KMT rule. Things started to change after the Democratic Progressive Party (DPP) became more dominant in Taiwan's politics, especially after the DPP won the presidential election in 2000 for the first time. The DPP is generally speaking more pro-independence and has not accepted the "1992 Consensus" (Rigger 2011; Roy 2003; Porsche-Ludwig and Chu 2009). I now turn to the discussion of Taiwan's identity change, which is both endogenously and exogenously linked to how people in Taiwan view cross-Strait relations.

The changing Taiwanese identity

Since 1949, the two political entities separated by the Taiwan Strait have maintained two different political systems. The PRC remains a one-party authoritarian system. In Taiwan, the KMT was the only and dominant political party between the 1940s and 1980s. The KMT government operated under the martial law for 38 years. When the martial law was finally lifted on July 15, 1987, it started to create a more pluralistic political environment for opposition parties to emerge. The pro-independence DPP began to grow as a viable challenger to the dominant KMT. Over time, Taiwan gradually evolved into a multi-party electoral democracy. Direct presidential elections took place in 1996 (KMT win), 2000 (DPP win), 2004 (DPP win), 2008 (KMT win), 2012 (KMT win), 2016 (DPP win), and 2020 (DPP win). China's one-party political system and Taiwan's democratization have created two different socialization experiences for their respective citizens, leading to distinct identities across the Taiwan Strait.

During the early decades of separation, Taiwan had an upper hand in economic and military superiority. However, things started to change as mainland China continued its economic rise. In spite of the "cold war" at the moment, there is no question that there has been a strong and clear convergence of economic relations across the Taiwan Strait. In recent years, such convergence has gradually shifted into an asymmetrical scenario in which Taiwan is increasingly more dependent on the Mainland. However, there has not been a clear path toward political convergence between the two.

One possible explanation for the lack of political convergence is that Taiwanese identity matters (Li 2014; Liu and Li 2017, 263). Lepesant (2018, 65) argues that the "'identity of the state' is subject to diverging forces and it can evolve with time". As the older generations of pro-mainland Chinese gradually fade away, the younger generations re-shape their identity into something uniquely Taiwanese as a result of their distinct social experience.

The PRC often stresses the fact that identity comes from antiquity, shared history, language, and culture, so the Taiwanese identity should be no different from the mainland Chinese identity. Lucian Pye (1997, 209) argues that the Chinese people see themselves as a civilization-state – one that is bound by a "sense of culture, race, and civilization, not an identification with the nation as a state". If the Chinese identity is civilizational based on language, familial norms, and the structure of social relationships, the Chinese would consider the Taiwanese who are from the same civilization as from the same state (Jacques 2012). Moreover, the overwhelming majority (over 90% on each side) of both the Taiwanese in Taiwan and Chinese in mainland China are Han Chinese (Brown 2004). The Han-dominated ethnic identity makes the majority of people in Taiwan and China belong to the same nation. Therefore, Taiwanese are Chinese.

Other scholars focus more on the social aspects of identity formation. For example, a recent stream of literature suggests that identity can be formed and solidified through a common socialization process and identity can also be updated when the socialization process changes (Brown 2004). Since the 1996 presidential election, the trend of Taiwanese identifiers has increased and the trend of Chinese or dual-Chinese identifiers has decreased significantly. People who identify as Taiwanese are more likely to vote for the DPP, whereas people who identify as Chinese or both Chinese and Taiwanese are more likely to vote for the KMT (Tsai 2007).

Taiwan has experienced several waves of identity changes (Li 2014). Looking at the issue of identity from a broader perspective, for instance, Inglehart (1981, 880–900) argues that as the middle class moves from materialism to post-materialism, the "new class" experience value changes as they go through a shared socialization process. New identities may be formed during this socialization process. Taiwan's economic and political transformation in the past several decades has followed the modernization pattern very closely. As the middle class gradually emerged in the 1980s and 1990s, Taiwan began to experience an increased desire for democracy. Although it may be hard to build a common identity among all groups in Taiwan (Shih and Chen 2010), democratization in Taiwan helped to fuel the socialization process that created the new Taiwanese identity.

At the same time, however, China has taken a different path, which can be characterized as rapid economic growth through state capitalism coupled with continued rigidity in its political system. This path, in turn, has created a different socialization process as compared to the one found in Taiwan. And it has created a different identity for the mainland Chinese, one that is becoming increasingly nationalistic and sees the return of Taiwan as an integral part of restoring China's historical glory. And the longer Taiwan and mainland China remain separated from each other, the more distinct their respective social experiences will become.

The people of Taiwan perceive a complex range of identities. For example, Zhong's (2016, 336–352) research suggests that the majority of Taiwanese people do not identify themselves with the mainland Chinese state, although they still associate themselves with the Chinese nation. Moreover, from the perspectives of the native Taiwanese, the "ROC is regarded as a foreign colonial regime" (Chiung 2018, 56). In recent years, systematic de-Sinicization and Taiwanization processes have occurred in Taiwan. Some are government-led efforts, such as modifying history textbooks to emphasize the aboriginal culture, language and history, promoting local dialects, changing "China Post" to "Taiwan Post", etc. Others are citizen-led efforts, such as putting "Republic of Taiwan" stickers on passports to cover "Republic of China", preference for local dialects over mandarin Chinese, etc. (Lynch 2006; Liu and Li 2017, 263).

The formation and consolidation of Taiwanese identity do not appear to be solely associated with the pro-independence green camp, currently led by the Tsai Ing-wen government. The uniqueness of Taiwanese identity is shared by younger generations of Taiwanese across the party spectrum, including people who identify as KMT. Even the pro-status quo president Ma Ying-jeou proclaimed the "three noes" policy – no unification, no independence, and no use of force in his presidential inaugural address in May 2008 (Goodspeed 2008). Taiwan's democratization has enabled the production of a new Taiwan-centered historiography that emphasized the two diverging historical trajectories of Taiwan and China, the promotion of competing political discourses and the emergence of several forms of Taiwanese nationalism (Wang 2005, 69–70, cited in Lepesant 2018, 66). We have seen the construction of a unique "Taiwan experience", which includes the shared "economic miracles", "political successes (constitutional government reformation)", and a "modern democratic nation unifying both moral culture and material civilization" (Maehara 2018, 90). From Taiwan's perspective, the question of to whom Taiwan belongs has taken a constructivist turn (Wendt 1992). Generally speaking, the KMT government has maintained stronger ties with the mainland China. KMT supporters tend to identify more strongly with the Chinese identity or the dual-Taiwanese and Chinese identity. Whereas the DPP supporters tend to emphasize the Taiwanese identity derived from the unique Taiwanese social and political experiences. Taiwan's identity formation and domestic politics are both endogenous and exogenous to each other.

According to the National Chengchi University's Election Study Center data, the percentage of people who identify themselves as Taiwanese has increased from 17.6% in 1992 to 64.3% in 2020, whereas the percentage of people who identify themselves as Chinese has decreased from 25.5% to 2.6%. And the percentage of people who identify themselves as both Taiwanese and Chinese has also decreased from 46.4% to 29.9% (see Figure 10.1). Figure 10.2 shows that, as of December 2020, the largest three groups of people regarding the independence and unification stances are those who want to "maintain status quo, decide at a later date" (28.8%), "maintain status quote indefinitely" (25.8%), and "maintain

Between a rock and a hard place

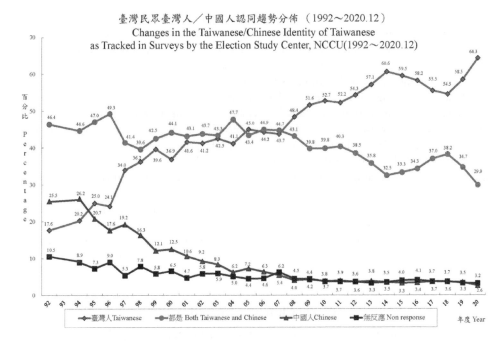

Figure 10.1 Taiwanese/Chinese identity (1992/1906~2020/2012)

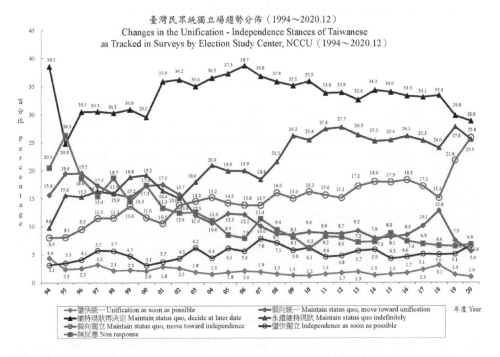

Figure 10.2 Taiwan independence vs. unification with the Mainland (1992/1906~2020/2012)

status quo, move towards independence" (25.5%). "Unification as soon as possible" (1%) and "maintain status quo, and move towards unification later" (6.6%) were among the least preferred options. Since the outbreak of COVID-19 and the passing of Hong Kong's new national security law in late June 2020, the percentage of people in Taiwan who identify as Taiwanese has increased further from 58.5% to 64.3% year to year.

These numbers suggest that identity plays a crucial role in Taiwanese people's position on independence vs. unification. Tsai Ing-wen capitalized on the Taiwanese identity issue and won the re-election with a landslide in 2020 in spite of her poor economic performance. Tsai ran on the slogan "Today's Hong Kong, Tomorrow's Taiwan", referring to Beijing's unwillingness to ensure democratic values in Hong Kong (Sobolik 2019). Thus, any possible future unification with the mainland would mean the end of Taiwan's hard-earned democracy.

Lepesant (2018, 78–79) argues that further economic integration with the mainland is seen as a threat to Taiwan's economy as it increases Taiwan's dependency on China, whereas increased human contacts have not bridged the gap separating the two populations – they have only empathized the differences in "values, world visions, behaviors, divergences in language, centers of interest and life styles that create a 'we Taiwanese' identification distinct from a 'they Chinese' identification".

Rising Chinese nationalism

If there is one thing that is most deeply embedded in China's national glory, it is the future return of Taiwan to the Mainland. Many believe that the "Chinese dream" to restore its historical glory cannot be realized without a full national unification. As Yan (2001, 34) points out, "the Chinese regard their rise as regaining China's lost international status rather than as obtaining something new" and "the Chinese consider the rise of China as a restoration of fairness rather than as gaining advantages over others". For China to regain its international statues as a true world power, it must resolve the most nationalistic problem – the Taiwan issue. And nationalism will likely play a deterministic role in the future of cross-Strait relations.

What is nationalism?

What does nationalism mean in the Chinese context? "In Chinese, nationalism can be rendered as either aiguo-zhuyi 爱国主义 – the ism (zhuyi 主义) of loving the state (爱国), or as minzu-zhuyi 民族主义 – the ism of the people's clan (民族)" (Carlson et al 2016, 425). "Nationalism" is sometimes used interchangeably with the term "patriotism". Chen (2020, 80) argues that "patriotism taps the affective component of one's feelings toward one's country. It assesses the degree of love for and pride in one's nation, encouraging loyalty to the nation-state", whereas "nationalism is constituted by love for, pride in, and loyalty to the nation, it also includes negative comparisons of other countries relative to one's native country". In the context of the Taiwan issue, Chinese nationalism can be characterized by "a sense of national pride, national loyalty, national devotion, and national superiority" (Carlson et al. 2016, 425). It reflects China's determination to both regain control over Taiwan and regain its national superiority to cleanse the "century of national humiliation".

Types of nationalism

There are different types of nationalism. Broadly speaking, nationalism can be top-down or bottom-up (Zhao 2004). Top-down or elite nationalism is usually initiated by the government. Clausen (1998, cited in Chen 2020, 80) describes top-down nationalism as "fueled by 'authoritative discourses' conducted in education and the main national media under official control to appeal to the desire for a national identity". "A top-down approach focuses on the state or media as leading characters in cultivating nationalism by campaigns or education" (Anderson, 2006, cited in Chen et al 2019).

Popular nationalism, however, is driven by the mass public. As a bottom-up approach, it "emphasizes ordinary people's role in constructing nationalism through daily conversation about belonging and self-categorization" (Billig, 1995, cited in Chen et al. 2019). They are "spontaneous responses…rather than state manipulation" (Gries 2004, cited in Chen 2020, 80).

There's a particular type of nationalism that is especially relevant for cross-Strait relations – diversionary nationalism, which derives from the diversionary literature of war. Diversionary theory argues that, when in trouble at home, leaders may have incentives to use crises overseas to divert attention away from domestic problems (Coser 1956; Levy 1989). These domestic problems could be a weak economy, low approval ratings, or personal/political scandals (Ostrom and Job 1986; Brulé, 2006). The main reason is that when a troubled leader pursues actions addressing an international crisis, domestic audience may be expected to "rally-around the flag" to lend support to the leader (Ostrom and Simon 1985; Morgan and Anderson 1999; Morgan and Bickers 1992; James and Rioux 1998; Ostrom and Job 1986; Levy 1989; DeRouen 2000). The elites hope that the general public could forget about the real "problem" at the moment; and the leader would enjoy an increased approval or support and a changed focus on the dialog and policy agenda.

In the context of cross-Strait relations, it is highly likely that when Mainland leaders face domestic pressures, economic or political, Taiwan is used as the perfect "scapegoat". "The diversionary theory of nationalism therefore contends that states generate nationalism in their citizens to defuse the ticking bomb of economic inequality" (Solt 2011, 822).

> The diversionary perspective asserts that political elites widely recognize economic misery as a useful tool for mobilizing people against its supposed causes. States can cunningly foster nationalist sentiments to respond to the sense of insecurity triggered by high levels of economic inequality. Hence, nationalism serves states' interests by diverting attention from high levels of economic inequality.
>
> *(Chen 2020, 77; Solt 2011)*

In the case of cross-Strait relations, reasons for instigating diversionary behaviors do not necessarily have to be economic and the means of diversion do not have to be military actions or conflicts. They can be non-military means, such as strong verbal rhetoric (Li et al 2009). As China continues to rise, it has faced pressures both domestically and internationally, creating ample potential scenarios for China's leaders to incite diversionary nationalism.

Trend of Chinese nationalism

Has nationalism been rising in China? With the exception of a few scholars (see Johnston 2016/2017 and Chen 2020 for examples of exceptions), the overall view is that Chinese nationalism has become more "assertive" or "aggressive" (Wong 2020). Moreover, Chinese nationalism has clearly been rising. Several interesting changes have occurred. First, Chinese nationalism has shifted from top-down elite nationalism to bottom-up popular nationalism. Chen et al. (2019, 12) explain that previous studies on online agenda-setting in China have generally suggested the image of a powerful government. For instance, Luo (2014) found that it is the government, not the public, that sets the online agenda, while Jiang (2014) found that the public has limited power to set the agenda, as the government maintains strict control on the boundaries of expression.

(cited in Chen et al. 2019, 530)

This trend has been changing. Zhao (2013) sees the shift as a "strident turn".

> This strident turn is in part because the government is increasingly responsive to public opinion as the average Chinese find a growing number of ways such as the social media to express [t]he[i]r nationalist feelings and put pressure on foreign-policy makers. But more importantly, this turn is due to the convergence of Chinese state nationalism and popular nationalism.

(Zhao 2013, cited in Carlson et al. 2016)

The Chinese government is becoming more responsive to popular nationalism in the internet age. Chen et al. (2019, 12) find that the internet breaks down the "hierarchical structure of information distribution and challenges the legitimacy of the top-down model of national building". However, the Chinese government still has effective control over how it wants nationalism to spread.

Second, the primary audience of Chinese nationalism has shifted from foreign to domestic. Wong (2020) argues that "the target audience of nationalistic rhetoric has drastically shifted from a mixed audience, including both foreign states and domestic populaces, to primarily the domestic population". Weiss (2020) points that China's "wolf warrior diplomacy" approach has appeased Chinese nationalists at home, but has had limited appeal abroad. Beijing considers the Taiwan issue an internal matter. Speaking the language of nationalism bodes well to China's domestic audience. This is perhaps the most significant linkage between Chinese diversionary nationalism and cross-Strait relations, as the elites in Beijing may be using the Taiwan issue as a diversion away from domestic and international challenges they face.

Chinese nationalism appears to be gaining strengths even at a faster pace during the Xi-Trump era. "In their critique of Chinese foreign policy under Xi Jinping, Orville Schell and Susan Shirk (2019, 9) describe a sense of 'nationalist triumphalism' in the Xi era whereby 'China's assertiveness increased markedly in both international and domestic domains, and… has provoked a growing backlash in the United States and around the world'" (Albertoni and Wise 2021, 52). After a year of sharp contrasts of how the two countries have battled COVID-19, the effective measures taken by the Chinese government to get the coronavirus under control and return lives to normal and the clear ineffectiveness and inability of the US's government to do the same have strengthened China's confidence in its own political system. Such confidence coupled with rising anti-China strategies and policies by foreign governments, especially the deterioration of US-China relations, has led to increased levels of Chinese patriotism and nationalism.

Analysis and synthesis

If identity in Taiwan has shifted away from a clear preference for unifying with the Mainland and Chinese nationalism has been rising, have the odds of the Mainland forcing Taiwan to unification increased? Evidence suggests that the challenges mainland China faces today has increased such odds.

China's rise and major challenges Beijing faces

The rise of China has been a widely debated topic. China's rise needs to be placed in a geopolitical context, particularly the role Taiwan plays in US-China relations. Ample discussions have emerged in recent years revolving around the issue of China's rise and the potential implications for US-China relations. For example, Martin Jacques (2012) in *When China Rules the World*; Michael Pillsbury (2016) in *The Hundred-Year Marathon*; Graham Allison (2017) in *Destined for War*; and more recently Kishore Mahbubani (2020) in *Has China Won?*, all, in one way or another, attempt to address China's rise and contemplate what the world would look like when China becomes powerful enough to challenge the US supremacy. Scott Gartner, Chin-Hao Huang, Yitan Li, and Patrick James (2021) in *Identity in the Shadow of a Giant* specifically address how the rise of China has been changing Taiwan.

While China's rise was a gradual process, it has picked up speed in recent years. It moved from a very backward country to the second largest economy in a mere 30 years' time. The beginning of China's rise can be traced back to the late 1970s, when the government, led by Deng Xiaoping, decided to implement a series of reforms to open China's doors. Particularly in the last decade, China's capacities have increased to the point where China now has clear superiority over Taiwan and the potential to challenge the US in the region. Table 10.1 shows that in 1991, Taiwan's GDP per capita with Purchasing Power Parity (PPP) was $9,136, more than eight times the size of the Mainland's ($1,099). By 2017, mainland China's overall GDP with PPP ($23,300,783 million USD) was almost 40 times the size of Taiwan's ($574,940 million USD). Mainland China went through periods of rapid economic rise. China's growth has slowed down in recent years. As China reaches a level of saturation in its domestic growth, the Chinese government needs to maintain a similar level of economic growth to keep China's economic engine running and ensure the party's legitimacy. Recently, China has taken several steps to further expand its power.

As China's domestic economy slows down, it needed to find new ways to keep its economy growing. One of such ways was the promotion of the "Belt and Road Initiative" (BRI). BRI is China's effort to revitalize the ancient "Silk Road" (belt) and the creation of a new maritime trading route (road) linking China through Southeast Asia and South Asia to Africa and the Middle East through infrastructure and investment projects. BRI is part of Beijing's greater plan to integrate China's internal markets with those of its neighbors and create a "community of common destiny" (Greer 2018). China also launched the Asian Infrastructure Investment Bank (AIIB) in 2014, a system largely seen as an alternative to the "Washington consensus" dominated banking and investment system. Both the BRI and AIIB are designed to outsource China's domestic growth stagnation and promote China's influence in the region and beyond and weaken Washington's efforts to contain China (Cai 2018; Greer 2018; Dollar 2015). However, there has been an increasing level of resistance to and criticism of China's BRI by several countries, for instance, in the case of Sri Lanka and Malaysia (Dipanjan 2019; Abi-Habib 2018).

In terms of China's military rise, China has been using a combination of traditional power projection strategy and lessons learned from the US-Soviet Cold War arms race. For power projection, China has gradually reduced the PLA's land-based powers and re-directed resources and emphasis to the Air Force and Navy, on track to turn China into a "blue water" military power. For instance, China launched its first aircraft carrier – the Liaoning in

Table 10.1 Main economic indicators

	GDP growth (annual %)			GDP per capita, PPP (current international $)			GDP, PPP (current international $) in million USD		
Year	China	US	Taiwan	China	US	Taiwan	China	US	Taiwan
1990	3.9	1.9		$987	$23,954		$11,19,938	$59,79,589	
1991	9.3	−0.1	8.36	$1,099	$24,405	$9,136	$12,64,767	$61,74,043	$1,87,314
1992	14.2	3.6	8.29	$1,268	$25,493	$10,778	$14,77,498	$65,39,299	$2,23,159
1993	13.9	2.7	6.8	$1,462	$26,465	$11,251	$17,22,420	$68,78,718	$2,35,140
1994	13.1	4.0	7.49	$1,669	$27,777	$12,160	$19,88,673	$73,08,755	$2,56,404
1995	10.9	2.7	6.5	$1,869	$28,782	$13,129	$22,52,436	$76,64,060	$2,79,224
1996	9.9	3.8	6.18	$2,071	$30,068	$13,650	$25,21,268	$81,00,201	$2,92,665
1997	9.2	4.5	6.11	$2,277	$31,573	$14,040	$28,01,135	$86,08,515	$3,03,737
1998	7.8	4.4	4.21	$2,459	$32,949	$12,840	$30,53,459	$90,89,168	$2,80,369
1999	7.7	4.7	6.72	$2,664	$34,621	$13,819	$33,37,894	$96,60,624	$3,04,171
2000	8.5	4.1	6.42	$2,933	$36,450	$14,941	$37,03,735	$1,02,84,779	$3,31,452
2001	8.3	1.0	−1.26	$3,227	$37,274	$13,448	$41,04,067	$1,06,21,824	$3,00,450
2002	9.1	1.8	5.57	$3,552	$38,166	$13,750	$45,47,550	$1,09,77,514	$3,08,875
2003	10.0	2.8	4.12	$3,961	$39,677	$14,120	$51,03,705	$1,15,10,670	$3,18,590
2004	10.1	3.8	6.51	$4,455	$41,922	$15,388	$57,74,280	$1,22,74,928	$3,48,479
2005	11.4	3.3	5.42	$5,093	$44,308	$16,532	$66,39,272	$1,30,93,726	$3,75,769
2006	12.7	2.7	5.62	$5,884	$46,437	$17,026	$77,13,674	$1,38,55,888	$3,88,589
2007	14.2	1.8	6.52	$6,864	$48,062	$17,814	$90,45,939	$1,44,77,635	$4,08,254
2008	9.7	−0.3	0.7	$7,635	$48,401	$18,131	$1,01,13,837	$1,47,18,582	$4,16,961
2009	9.4	−2.8	−1.57	$8,374	$47,002	$16,988	$1,11,48,547	$1,44,18,739	$3,92,065
2010	10.6	2.5	10.63	$9,333	$48,375	$19,278	$1,24,84,967	$1,49,64,372	$4,46,105
2011	9.5	1.6	3.8	$10,384	$49,794	$20,939	$1,39,57,939	$1,55,17,926	$4,85,653
2012	7.9	2.2	2.06	$11,351	$51,451	$21,308	$1,53,31,823	$1,61,55,255	$4,95,845
2013	7.8	1.7	2.2	$12,368	$52,782	$21,916	$1,67,88,028	$1,66,91,517	$5,11,614
2014	7.3	2.6	4.02	$13,440	$54,697	$22,668	$1,83,36,440	$1,74,27,609	$5,30,519
2015	6.9	2.9	0.81	$14,450	$56,444	$22,400	$1,98,14,259	$1,81,20,714	$5,25,562
2016	6.7	1.5	1.51	$15,531	$57,589	$22,592	$2,14,11,542	$1,86,24,475	$5,31,281
2017	6.9	2.3	3.08	$16,807	$59,532	$24,408	$2,33,00,783	$1,93,90,604	$5,74,940
2018			2.6			$25,000			$5,89,369

2012 by retrofitting a Soviet-era decommissioned aircraft carrier – the Varyag. In December 2019, China commissioned its first home-built aircraft carrier – the Shandong (Pickrell 2019; Rajagopalan 2019). China established its first overseas naval base in Djibouti in 2017 (Headley 2018). PLA Air Force also revealed its J-20 stealth fighter in 2018 (Joe 2018). China also learned lessons from the former Soviet Union's failure during the Cold War. As Pillsbury (2016) points out, China has been consciously not to replicate the "U.S.-style system of power projection, as the Soviets did", because it would be too expensive and too revealing of China's intentions to challenge the US. Data from the Stockholm International Peace Research Institute (SIPRI) show that China has maintained a sizable percentage of its government spending on military expenditure (see Table 10.2).

Table 10.2 US-China-Taiwan military expenditure as a percentage of government spending, 2000–2017

Year	US	China	Taiwan
2001	9.0%	11.98%	11.0%
2002	9.7%	11.87%	11.1%
2003	10.6%	11.63%	10.6%
2004	11.3%	11.58%	10.6%
2005	11.4%	10.98%	10.2%
2006	11.3%	10.96%	10.1%
2007	11.1%	10.54%	10.5%
2008	11.3%	8.38%	10.9%
2009	11.2%	8.09%	10.3%
2010	11.7%	7.64%	10.2%
2011	11.8%	6.79%	10.2%
2012	11.4%	6.55%	10.5%
2013	10.6%	6.54%	10.0%
2014	9.9%	6.58%	10.1%
2015	9.4%	6.1%	10.6%
2016	9.0%	6.0%	10.4%
2017	8.8%	6.1%	10.5%

China has also become much more assertive in the South China Sea. "Since 2014, China has done extensive and fast land reclamation for 3,000 acres", such as "making artificial islands and building airstrips, ports, radar facilities, solar arrays, lighthouses, and other supporting facilities on them", and has had several flare-ups involving "land grabbing" and/or "defending and strengthening the maritime features it currently controls" (Zhang and Li 2018, 83–102).

As China matures in its labor-intensive manufacturing sector, its growth is gradually slowing down. As the cost of labor becomes more expensive and new capital harder to obtain, growth now hinges more upon China's ability to develop technological innovation (Wan 2007). This is a common problem described as the "middle income trap" (Kharas and Kohli 2011; Peerenboom 2014). Almost all the countries that went on to become advanced economies broke out of the middle income trap by moving out of labor-intensive manufacturing sector and into the technology sector. China's most obvious policy shift in that direction has been its "Made in China 2025" strategic plan. "Made in China 2025" aims at moving China into advanced manufacturing, a sector dominated by high-income, developed countries such as the US (Hopewell 2018). To achieve this goal, China has required foreign companies to hand over their technology, in many cases through a joint-venture business structure, in order to access China's market. China has also intensified its efforts to acquire technology from overseas. This strategy has irritated the US, especially the former Trump administration.

Recently, China has met several domestic and international challenges. The most prominent ones are the protests in Hong Kong, the outbreak of the coronavirus, and the Trump administration's resistance to China's rise.

First, the massive protests against the "Hong Kong Extradition Bill" showed the tension between Hong Kong's freedom and civil liberties and the central government's heavy-handed approach to manage Hong Kong's affairs. The protests in Hong Kong also cast doubts in China's commitment to the "one country, two system" framework, which is the cornerstone for managing future relations with Taiwan.

Second, the COVID-19 pandemic is a reminder of the vulnerability of the global interdependence system. The global economy and international travel came to a sudden halt. Global supply chain and trade were interrupted. China faces the domestic pressure of economic slowdown. It also faces the external pressure of decreasing demands, supply chain relocation out of China by major global companies and the shortage of imported energy sources. To alleviate the pressure of decreasing external demand for China's exports, China has proposed a "dual circulation" model that would redirect external demand of Chinese goods to internal consumption. China's domestic economic pressure could be a potential source of diversionary nationalism. In the context of rising US-China tensions, chances of using Taiwan as a scapegoat are increasing.

Finally, pressure from the US has increased significantly. President Barack Obama, through his then Secretary of State Hillary Clinton, first expressed the need for an "Asian Pivot" to deal with the rise of China in the 2011 Foreign Policy article "America's Pacific Century" (Clinton 2011). Allison (2017) reignited the debate about the "Thucydides Trap". US-China tensions are bound to rise, although it may not necessarily be in the form of balance of power (Chan 2012; Chan 2019). President Donald Trump took the US to a much more direct and confrontational level by engaging China in full-blown trade wars (Wong and Koty 2019) and suppressing China's "Made in China 2025" initiatives.

Increasing volatile US-China-Taiwan relations

With regard to Taiwan, the Trump administration maintained a strong US-Taiwan relationship. One of the very first controversial issues Trump had to deal with was an unprecedented decision to take a congratulatory yet protocol-breaking telephone call from Tsai Ing-wen on December 2, 2016, breaking the tradition of not having any direct communication between the US and Taiwanese presidents since relations were severed in 1979 (Phillips et al 2016). Trump insisted that it was nothing but an ordinary phone call of congratulations. However, evidence suggests that the call had been planned with work months in the making and was designed to show a tough opening line with China (Gearan et al 2016).

Another development was the passage of the Taiwan Travel Act (TTA) by the 115th Congress in 2018. The TTA allows high-level active US and Taiwanese officials to visit each other (van der Wees 2018). Some analysts believe that these activities are a bad idea, as it is "flawed", "unnecessary", "provocative", and a poke in China's eye (Hickey 2018). Trump dispatched his Secretary of Health and Human Services Alex Azar to visit Taiwan in August 2020 – the highest-level US official to visit Taiwan in four decades. The visit was strongly condemned by Beijing.

The Trump administration also continued with weapon sales to Taiwan. The US's approval for a $330m arms sale to Taiwan is viewed as a sign of Washington's support for the government in Taipei amid rising Chinese pressure on the island (White and Hille 2018). All signs point to the fact that the Trump administration did everything it could to suppress China's rise.

Since President Joseph Biden took office, there have not been any clear signs of improvement in the strained US-China relations. The Biden administration seems to have been following Trump administration's policies on China. The extraordinary diplomatic clash during the high-level talk between the two governments' officials on March 18, 2021 in

Anchorage signals tough times ahead (Gaouette et al 2021). The Biden administration still does not have coherent and effective policies to deal with China (Ge and Chen 2021).

Facing domestic and international pressures and as Taiwan drifts further away from a path of unification with the Mainland, Beijing has clear and increased incentives to take advantage of the rising nationalism to act toughly on Taiwan.

Conclusion

The confluence of changing identity in Taiwan and rising nationalism in mainland China has made cross-Strait relations unpredictable and volatile. Social experiences in Taiwan continue to solidify the unique Taiwanese identity on the island. Chinese nationalism continues to rise, particularly diversionary nationalism. Beijing's ability to manage its internal and external challenges will determine the CCP's legitimacy essential for the country's stability and the viability of the Chinese alternative to Western democracy. "Nationalism in contemporary China serves as a powerful instrument in impeding public demand for democratic change" (Tang and Barr 2012, cited in Carlson et al 2016, 439). For Xi Jinping, it is not necessarily about individual crises he faces, but how the accumulation of crises and pressure might affect China's overall political stability and the CCP's legitimacy. From the perspective of popular nationalism, "The public reaction to the 1996 Taiwan Strait crisis shows not only the salience of the Taiwan issue but also a public expectation that Beijing would take a tough stance on Taiwan" (Ohlendorf 2014, 476). As China continues to rise, pursues the "Chinese Dream" of national glory and unification, and faces domestic and international challenges, Beijing would be expected to take a tougher approach to solve the Taiwan problem sooner rather than later. Domestic and international challenges Beijing faces have increased the likelihood of diversionary nationalism in mainland China. Chances of Taiwan being used as a pressure release point have increased significantly. War is never desirable. But the desire and need for national unification on the part of mainland China have put Taiwan between a rock and a hard place. The difficult choice Taiwan may have to make is between maintaining its unique social identity and political system based on decades of democratization process and being forced to be reunited with the mainland China.

References

Abi-Habib, Maria. 2018. "How China Got Sri Lanka to Cough Up a Port." *New York Times* (Online). New York Times Company, last modified June 25, 2018, https://search.proquest.com/docview/2058629760.

Albertoni, Nicolás and Carol Wise. 2021. "International Trade Norms in the Age of Covid-19 Nationalism on the Rise?" *Fudan Journal of the Humanities and Social Sciences* 14 (1): 41–66.

Allison, Graham T. 2017. *Destined for War: Can America and China Escape Thucydides's Trap?* Boston, MA: Houghton Mifflin Harcourt.

Anderson, Benedict R. O'G. 2006. *Imagined Communities Reflections on the Origin and Spread of Nationalism*, edited by Benedict R. O'G Anderson, American Council of Learned Societies. Rev. ed. London: Verso.

Billig, Michael. 1995. *Banal Nationalism*. London: Sage.

Blanchard, Jean-Marc F., and Dennis Van Vranken Hickey. 2012. *New Thinking about the Taiwan Issue*. Politics in Asia Series. Abingdon: Routledge.

Brown, Melissa J. 2004. *Is Taiwan Chinese?* Berkeley: University of California Press.

Brulé, David. 2006. "Congressional Opposition, the Economy, and U.S. Dispute Initiation, 1946–2000." *Journal of Conflict Resolution* 50 (4): 463–483.

Cai, Kevin G. 2018. "The One Belt One Road and the Asian Infrastructure Investment Bank: Beijing's New Strategy of Geoeconomics and Geopolitics." *Journal of Contemporary China* 27 (114): 831–847.

Carlson, Allen R., Anna Costa, Prasenjit Duara, James Leibold, Kevin Carrico, Peter H. Gries, Naoko Eto, Suisheng Zhao, and Jessica C. Weiss. 2016. "Nations and Nationalism Roundtable Discussion on Chinese Nationalism and National Identity." *Nations and Nationalism* 22 (3): 415–446.

Chan, Steve. 2012. *Looking for Balance: China, the United States, and Power Balancing in East Asia*. Stanford, California: Stanford, CA: Stanford University Press.

Chan, Steve. 2019. "More than One Trap: Problematic Interpretations and Overlooked Lessons from Thucydides." *Journal of Chinese Political Science* 24 (1): 11–24.

Chen, Rou-Lan. 2020. "Trends in Economic Inequality and its Impact on Chinese Nationalism." *Journal of Contemporary China* 29 (121): 75–91.

Chen, Zhuo, Chris Chao Su, and Anfan Chen. 2019. "Top-Down or Bottom-Up? A Network Agenda-Setting Study of Chinese Nationalism on Social Media." *Journal of Broadcasting & Electronic Media* 63 (3): 512–533.

Chiung, Wi-vun Taiffalo. 2018. "Languages under Colonization." In *Changing Taiwanese Identities*. 1st edition, 39–63. Abingdon: Routledge.

Clausen, Søren. 1998. "Party Policy and National Culture: Towards a State-Directed Cultural Nationalism in China." In *Reconstructing Twentieth-Century China: State Control, Civil Society and National Identity*, edited by Kjeld E. Brodsgaard and David Strand, 253–279. Oxford: Clarendon Press.

Clinton, Hillary. 2011. "America's Pacific Century." *Foreign Policy* 189: 56–63.

Coser, Lewis A. 1956. *The Functions of Social Conflict*. Glencoe, IL: Free Press.

Derouen, Karl. 2000. "Presidents and the Diversionary use of Force: A Research Note." *International Studies Quarterly* 44 (2): 317–328.

Dipanjan, Roy Chaudhury. 2019. *China's BRI Comes under Severe Criticism on its Fifth Anniversary International-News]*. New Delhi.

Dollar, David. 2015. "China's Rise as a Regional and Global Power - the AIIB and the 'One Belt, One Road'." *Horizons* (No. 4). https://www.brookings.edu/opinions/the-aiib-and-the-one-belt-one-road/.

Gaouette, Nicole, Kylie Atwood, and Jennifer Hansler. 2021. "Extraordinary Diplomatic Clash Signals Tough Times Ahead for the US and China." *CNN Wire Service*, March 20, 2021. https://search.proquest.com/docview/2503041158.

Gartner, Scott Sigmund, Patrick James, Chin-Hao Huang, and Yitan Li. 2021. *Identity in the Shadow of a Giant*. Bristol: Bristol University Press.

Ge, Jianhao and Dingding Chen. 2021. "Can China-US Relations Improve during the Biden Administration?" *Diplomat*, May 3.

Gearan, Anne, Philip Rucker and Simon Denyer. 2016. "Trump's Taiwan Phone Call was Long Planned, Say People Who were Involved." *The Washington Post* (Online), last modified Dec 5, 2016, https://search.proquest.com/docview/1845683365.

Greer, Tanner. 2018. "One Belt, One Road, One Big Mistake." *Foreign Policy*, last modified December 6, 2018, https://foreignpolicy.com/2018/12/06/bri-china-belt-road-initiative-blunder/.

Gries, Peter Hays. 2004. *China's New Nationalism: Pride, Politics, and Diplomacy*. Berkeley: University of California Press.

Goodspeed, Peter. 2008. "Taiwan's Three no's; Island's Ma Ying-Jeou Strengthens Ties with China." *National Post*, Jun 16, 2008. https://search.proquest.com/docview/330724262.

Headley, Tyler. 2018. "China's Djibouti Base: A One Year Update." *The Diplomat*, Dec 4, 2018.

Hickey, Dennis V. 2018. "Taiwan Travel Act: Bad Idea?", last modified Jan 29, 2018, accessed August 8, 2021, https://www.chinausfocus.com/foreign-policy/taiwan-travel-act-bad-idea.

Hopewell, Kristen. 2018. "What Is 'Made in China 2025' – and Why Is It a Threat to Trump's Trade Goals?" *The Washington Post*, http://login.proxy.seattleu.edu/login?url=https://search-proquest-com.proxy.seattleu.edu/docview/2034140909?accountid=28598.

Inglehart, Ronald. 1981. "Post-Materialism in an Environment of Insecurity." *The American Political Science Review* 75 (4): 880–900.

Jacques, Martin. 2012. *When China Rules the World: The End of the Western World and the Birth of a New Global Order*. 2nd edition. New York: Penguin Press.

James, Patrick and Jean Sebastien Rioux. 1998. "International Crises and Linkage Politics: The Experiences of the United States, 1953–1994." *Political Research Quarterly* 51 (3): 781–812.

Jiang, Ying. 2014. "'Reversed Agenda-Setting Effects' in China Case Studies of Weibo Trending Topics and the Effects on State-Owned Media in China." *Journal of International Communication* 20 (2): 168–183.

Joe, Rick. 2019. "China's Stealth Fighter: It's Time to Discuss J-20's Agility." *The Diplomat*, last modified December 07, accessed February 17, 2019, https://thediplomat.com/2018/12/chinas-stealth-fighter-its-time-to-discuss-j-20s-agility/.

Johnston, Alastair Iain. 2017. "Is Chinese Nationalism Rising? Evidence from Beijing." *International Security* 41 (3): 7–43.

Kharas, Homi and Harinder Kohli. 2011. "What is the Middle Income Trap, Why do Countries Fall into it, and how can it be Avoided?" *Global Journal of Emerging Market Economies* 3 (3): 281–289.

Lepesant, Tanguy. 2018. "Taiwanese Youth and National Identity under Ma Ying-Jeou." In *Changing Taiwanese Identities*. 1st edition, 64–86. Abingdon: Routledge.

Levy, Jack S. 1989. "The Diversionary Theory of War: A Critique." In *Handbook of War Studies*, edited by Manus I. Midlarsky. Boston, MA: Unwin Hyman.

Li, Yitan. 2014. "Constructing Peace in the Taiwan Strait: A Constructivist Analysis of the Changing Dynamics of Identities and Nationalisms." *Journal of Contemporary China* 23 (85): 119.

Li, Yitan, Patrick James, and A. C. Drury. 2009. "Diversionary Dragons, Or "Talking Tough in Taipei": Cross-Strait Relations in the New Millennium." *Journal of East Asian Studies* 9 (3): 369–398.

Liu, Frank C. S. and Yitan Li. 2017. "Generation Matters: Taiwan's Perceptions of Mainland China and Attitudes towards Cross-Strait Trade Talks." *Journal of Contemporary China* 26 (104): 263.

Luo, Yunjuan. 2014. "The Internet and Agenda Setting in China: The Influence of Online Public Opinion on Media Coverage and Government Policy." *International Journal of Communication (Online)* 8: 1289.

Lynch, Daniel C. 2006. *Rising China and Asian Democratization: Socialization to "Global Culture" in the Political Transformations of Thailand, China, and Taiwan*. Stanford, CA: Stanford University Press.

Maehara, Shiho. 2018. "Lee Teng-Hui and the Formation of Taiwanese Identity." In *Changing Taiwanese Identities*. 1st edition, 87–92: Routledge.

Mahbubani, Kishore. 2020. *Has China Won? The Chinese Challenge to American Primacy*. 1st edition. New York: Public Affairs.

Morgan, T. C. and Christopher J. Anderson. 1999. "Domestic Support and Diversionary External Conflict in Great Britain, 1950–1992." *The Journal of Politics* 61 (3): 799–814.

Morgan, T. C. and Kenneth N. Bickers. 1992. "Domestic Discontent and the External Use of Force." *The Journal of Conflict Resolution* 36 (1): 25–52.

Ohlendorf, Hardina. 2014. "The Taiwan Dilemma in Chinese Nationalism: Taiwan Studies in the People's Republic of China." *Asian Survey* 54 (3): 471–491.

Orville, Schell and Susan, Shirk. 2019. "Course Correction: Toward an Effective and Sustainable China Policy." *Center on US-China Relations, Asia Society*. https://asiasociety.org/center-us-china-relations/course-correction-toward-effective-and-sustainable-china-policy.

Ostrom, Charles W. and Brian L. Job. 1986. "The President and the Political use of Force." *The American Political Science Review* 80 (2): 541–566.

Ostrom, Charles W. and Dennis M. Simon. 1985. "Promise and Performance: A Dynamic Model of Presidential Popularity." *The American Political Science Review* 79 (2): 334–358.

Peerenboom, Randall. 2014. "China and the Middle-Income Trap: Toward a Post Washington, Post Beijing Consensus." *Pacific Review* 27 (5): 651–673.

Phillips, Tom, Nicola Smith, and Nicky Woolf. 2016. "Trump's Phone Call with Taiwan President Risks China's Wrath." *The Guardian*, December 3. https://search.proquest.com/docview/1845461290.

Pickrell, Ryan. 2019. "China just Added a 2nd Aircraft Carrier to its Rapidly Growing Navy.", last modified December 17, accessed February 10, 2020, https://www.businessinsider.com/china-adds-second-aircraft-carrier-to-its-rapidly-growing-navy-2019-12.

Pillsbury, Michael. 2016. *The Hundred-Year Marathon: China's Secret Strategy to Replace America as the Global Superpower*. 1st edition. New York: St. Martin's Griffin.

Porsche-Ludwig, Markus and Ching-peng Chu. 2009. *The Political System of Taiwan*. 1st edition. Baden-Baden: Nomos Publishers.

Pye, Lucian W. 1997. "Chinese Democracy and Constitutional Development." In *China in the Twenty-First Century: Politics, Economy, and Society*, edited by Itoh, Fumio and Daigaku, Aoyama Gakuin, 205–218. Tokyo: United Nations University Press.

Rajagopalan, Rajeswari Pillai. 2019. "China's Second Aircraft Carrier: A Sign of PLA Naval Muscle?" *The Diplomat*, December 26, 2019.

Rigger, Shelley. 2011. *Why Taiwan Matters: Small Island, Global Powerhouse*. Lanham: Rowman & Littlefield.

Roy, Denny. 2003. *Taiwan: A Political History*. Ithaca, NY: Cornell University Press.

Shih, Cheng-Feng, and Mumin Chen. 2010. "Taiwanese Identity and the Memories of 2–28: A Case for Political Reconciliation." *Asian Perspective* 34 (4): 85–113.

Sobolik, Michael. 2019. "Today, Hong Kong. Tomorrow, Taipei." *The Diplomat*, Sep 24, 2019.

Solt, Frederick. 2011. "Diversionary Nationalism: Economic Inequality and the Formation of National Pride." *The Journal of Politics* 73 (3): 821–830.

Tsai, Chang-Yen. 2007. *National Identity, Ethnic Identity, and Party Identity in Taiwan*. Maryland Series in Contemporary Asian Studies. Baltimore: University of Maryland.

van der Wees, Gerrit. 2018. "The Taiwan Travel Act in Context." *The Diplomat*, March 19.

Wan, Ming. 2007. *The Political Economy of East Asia*. Washington, DC: Sage.

Wang, Fu-chang. 2005. "Why Bother about School Textbooks? An Analysis of the Origin of the Disputes over Renshi Taiwan Textbooks in 1997." In *Cultural, Ethnic, and Political Nationalism in Contemporary Taiwan*, edited by John Makeham and A-chin Hsiau, 55–59. New York: Palgrave Macmillan.

Weiss, Jessica Chen. 2020. "China's Self-Defeating Nationalism: Brazen Diplomacy and Rhetorical Bluster Undercut Beijing's Influence." *Foreign Affairs*, July 16.

Wendt, Alexander. 1992. "Anarchy Is What States Make of It: The Social Construction of Power Politics." *International Organization* 46 (2): 391–425.

White, Edward and Kathrin Hille. 2018. *US Agrees $330m Arms Sale to Bolster Taiwan Defences*. London: The Financial Times.

Wong, Brian. 2020. "How Chinese Nationalism Is Changing: Chinese Nationalism used to Be Aimed at both Domestic and Foreign Audiences. Not Anymore." *The Diplomat*, May 26.

Wong, Dorcas, and Alexander Chipman Koty. 2019. "The US-China Trade War: A Timeline." (February 25, 2019). https://www.china-briefing.com/news/the-us-china-trade-war-a-timeline/.

Yan, Xuetong. 2001. "The Rise of China in Chinese Eyes." *Journal of Contemporary China* 10 (26): 33–39.

Zhang, Enyu and Yitan Li. 2018. "Rival Partners? Cross- Strait Relations after the Permanent Court of Arbitration Ruling over the South China Sea Disputes." *Journal of Territorial and Maritime Studies* 5 (1): 83–102.

Zhao, Suisheng. 2004. *A Nation-State by Construction Dynamics of Modern Chinese Nationalism*. Stanford, CA: Stanford University Press.

Zhao, Suisheng. 2013. "Foreign Policy Implications of Chinese Nationalism Revisited: The Strident Turn." *The Journal of Contemporary China* 22 (82): 535–553.

Zhong, Yang. 2016. "Explaining National Identity Shift in Taiwan." *The Journal of Contemporary China* 25 (99): 336–352.

11
CHINA'S DIGITAL NATIONALISM

Florian Schneider

Introduction

In 2016, Taiwanese singer Chou Tsu-yu from the multi-national girl band Twice is forced to issue a tearful apology to her mainland Chinese fans after online commentators had identified her holding a miniature flag of the Republic of China (ROC) that governs Taiwan; the outrage that ensued online over her waving this symbol of Taiwanese autonomy threatened to end her career and cost the parent company Twice its lucrative mainland audience.

In 2019, in the wake of the Hong Kong protests, the NBA manager Daryl Morey posted an image on his Twitter account that supported the protesters, leading to an angry and swift online backlash, boycotts, and cancelled games; the NBA had to issue an apology to the citizens of the People's Republic of China (PRC).

In 2020, during the early phases of the COVID-19 pandemic, a Danish broadsheet published a satire of the PRC flag, replacing the five golden stars with viral particles. Chinese online outrage culminated in a flood of memes that mocked the Danish flag, and more generally the Danes. China's ambassador to the country warned Denmark that it risked losing the respect of the Chinese people (see Schneider 2021a on this case).

As these examples illustrate, falling foul of angry Chinese nationalists on the internet can have dire consequences, whether for individual, companies, or states. Online vitriol seems ubiquitous, in digital China, and it often shapes current affairs and international relations in toxic ways. At times, such nationalist sentiments spill into the streets, for instance, during the protests that shook many Chinese cities during the 2012 Sino-Japanese dispute over islands in the East China Sea (Gries et al. 2016), or they lead to discrimination against foreigners in China, for instance, during the COVID-19 pandemic (see Chris Hughes' contribution in Woods et al. 2020). The groundwork for such behaviours is often laid in online forums, social media platforms, and chat apps. And in those spheres, nationalism is a constant feature of political discourse.

This chapter explores the workings of China's digital nationalism. In what follows, I will outline what digital nationalism is, how it operates in China, and what makes its dynamics special. At first glance, digital nationalism may simply seem to be popular nationalism expressed on the internet. Popular nationalism is indeed a crucial input to digital nationalism, so much so that the digital dimension can appear merely like an extension of popular sentiments that play a role elsewhere in Chinese politics, for instance, during nationalist street protests or commercial boycott activities. However, as this chapter will show, digital nationalism has its own dynamics, whether in China or elsewhere. It is driven by the interconnected activities of organizations, technologies, and users, and these activities generate digital nationalism as the emergent property of complex information and communication networks.

To explain these processes, this chapter first discusses conceptual issues related to socio-technological interactions in digital systems. This chapter then proceeds by introducing the three inputs into China's digital nationalism: the organizations in digital China's political economy, the algorithms and interfaces that govern interactions on the PRC internet, and the internet users who engage with each other and with nationalist discourses online.

How digital nationalism works

The observation that online forums have become home to often aggressive nationalist expressions and activities has led to several key terms that describe the phenomenon. Most notably, this includes online nationalism or internet nationalism (Breslin & Shen 2010), cyber-nationalism (Jiang 2012; Leibold 2016; Wu 2007), techno-nationalism (Platin & De Seta 2019; Qiu 2010), and digital nationalism (Mihelj & Jiménez-Martínez 2020; Schneider 2018a). These concepts are often used interchangeably, and they frequently refer simply to popular nationalism expressed online. While this can be a convenient shorthand, it risks overlooking, or collapsing, the complexities that unfold when ideologies and community sentiments become mediated through digital technologies. In this section, I will tease apart these processes and distinguish between four dimensions of nationalism in digital societies: techno-nationalism, online nationalism, cyber-nationalism, and digital nationalism. I propose definitions for these terms and describe how each operates, respectively, through policy, discursive practices, social practices, and socio-technical dynamics.

Techno-nationalism: nationalist policy and cyber-sovereignty

A crucial foundation for nationalism in digitally contexts is how the institutions of the nation-state create the legal and political frameworks for national media ecosystems to function. These activities might best be called 'techno-nationalism': the use of state policy to create and maintain digital systems for national use. A techno-nationalist agenda allows nation-states to introduce and oversee the physical infrastructures that make internet communication possible, for instance, through the construction and regulation of fibre-optic connections or wireless network towers. It also drives governments to regulate the internet and its related technologies, whether indirectly through policy frameworks that govern digital commercial activities or through direct intervention into communication practices in the form of censorship or propaganda.

China is a prominent example of techno-nationalist politics (Schneider 2018a, ch.8). The construction of the so-called 'Great Firewall', and of a media ecology that uses homegrown digital services instead of multi-national platforms, is informed by a geo-political and geo-economic outlook that extends the logic of territorial sovereignty to digital realms. This emphasis on 'cyber-sovereignty' is certainly not unique to the PRC (Shklovski & Struthers 2010, Goode 2021), but the Chinese government has been particularly vocal about its sovereignty framework (Creemers 2020). Indeed, the idea of cyber-sovereignty today informs all aspects of PRC digital politics, from the regulation of the domestic market to the promotion of regulatory principles in international contexts like the Belt and Road Initiative (Shen 2018) or global internet governance more broadly (Creemers 2016). It is before this backdrop that we need to understand nationalist expressions and activities on the PRC internet.

Online nationalism: nationalist discourses in online spheres

A sizable body of empirical media and communications scholarship has examined the nationalist discourses that groups, organizations, and individual internet users produce in forums and on social media (Feng & Yuan 2014, Jiang 2012, Shen & Breslin 2010, Schneider 2018b, Wu 2007), and it is these discourses that might most appropriately be called 'online nationalism'. The outrage against Taiwanese singer Chou for waving the ROC flag is as much an expression of online nationalism as angry vitriol against NBA manager Morrey for supporting Hong Kong protesters. But online nationalism also incorporates the creation and posting of images, emojis, videos, and other digitally native contents that contribute to nationalist discourses. The memes that Chinese online users created to criticize the Danish broadsheet for its insensitive COVID-satire are an example of Chinese online nationalism.

At this level of analysis, the question tends to be how an increasingly diverse range of actors deploys, and possibly alters, the building blocks of nationalism online, and how the resulting discourses relate to more traditional forms of nationalist expressions, for instance, in legacy media like newspapers, radio, and television, at cultural sites like museums or mass events, or in political contexts like official documents, parliamentary debates, or the speeches of leading politicians. These 'offline' discourses remain important, especially where they set public agendas, frame current affairs, or legitimate policies and institutions, so an important issue in the study of online nationalism is how online and offline discourses interact.

That said, it bears keeping in mind that human activities do not neatly divide into online and offline behaviours; in our ubiquitously digital societies, the two realms of human activity are intimately linked. Media formats 'converge' online (Jenkins 2006); for instance, when a politician's speech is filmed, digitized, edited, and then posted on a video sharing platform. Consumers of such contents may access them online, but they are still tethered to the material world. They have physical, bodily reactions to their online engagements. They pay their hard-earned wages for access to certain media contents. And they relay their responses to people they know through face-to-face interactions. Our everyday feelings, physical activities, and social dynamics in material space are overlaid by a stratum of data flows into which we dip at many moments of our day, and this is also true for how internet users express community sentiments like nationalism.

Cyber-nationalism: digitally enabled nationalist activism and mobilization

The definition of online nationalism that I have provided here highlights how nationalist dynamics unfold through discursive practices on the internet, but it does not yet tell us much about the social practices that are tied to these discourses. This is where the concept of cyber-nationalism becomes useful. Cyber-nationalism shall here describe the strategic use of computer technologies ('cyber') in the service of nationalist projects. When nationalists mobilize to flood a discussion with online vitriol, when they organize street protests through their social media networks, when they coordinate their protest activities through chat apps, or when they finance their endeavours through e-commerce, they engage in cyber-nationalism.

In that sense, cyber-nationalism is a particular strand of cyber-activism: a digitally enabled form of socio-political mobilization. Where online nationalism describes nationalist representations and discourses, cyber-nationalism describes mobilization and practice. These two dimensions are related, and they often overlap: any nationalist activism is informed by nationalist discourses, and it, in turn, contributes to those discourses. A good example of this connection are the consumer boycotts that often accompany Chinese public anger at foreign brands for perceived offences against the Chinese nation. The backlash against the NBA in 2019 produced a great deal of online nationalism, in the form of social media commentary, but it also spilled over into cyber-activism aimed at shutting down NBA games in China and shaming anyone associated with American basketball. Analytically, however, it can be helpful to distinguish these processes and ask how they interact in specific cases. When online anti-Japanese sentiments lead to street protests, then it is because nationalist actors have tapped into social networks for activist coordination and mobilization.

Digital nationalism: the socio-technical systems behind contemporary nationalism

In both online nationalism and cyber-nationalism, technology provides the medium or vehicle through which actors express themselves and act. Digital technology effectively increases, diversifies, and makes more visible who can contribute to public discussions and activities about the nation. Nationalism relies on what scholars of technology call the 'affordances' of the medium, that is: the 'latent cues in environments (…) that hold possibilities for action' (Parchoma 2014, 360). Indeed, when Benedict Anderson (1983/2006) famously explored the origins of 'imagined communities' like the nation, he focused strongly on the affordances of media technologies like the printing press, as well as on the political economy of print capitalism that created those affordances. It is these technological affordances and political economy dynamics that the term digital nationalism is meant to capture.

Digital nationalism refers to the nationalist discourses and practices that emerge as actors interact with each other through socio-technical systems. In this sense, digital nationalism describes the overarching framework within which online nationalism and cyber-nationalism play out. Studies of digital nationalism then also frequently incorporate discursive and social practices online, minimally as empirical cases, but they draw attention to the chains of interactions between organizations, technical systems, and people that generate nationalism in our inherently complex contemporary societies.

This is why digital nationalism is not simply an extension of nationalism to online forums. Digital nationalism possesses dynamics that profoundly alter the rationale of nationalism itself. Once nationalism becomes filtered through digital systems, it behaves in new and at times unexpected ways. When discourses and social practices move through digital systems, they become part of complex socio-technical networks in which people and algorithms interact. Take the example of the official smartphone app that promotes Xi Jinping thought, an application called 'Study (Xi), Strong Country' (Xue Xi Qiang Guo), but colloquially referred to as 'Xi's little red app' (Zhong 2021): the app itself is a form of infrastructure, and its interface design and algorithm shape how users interact with its contents. At the same time, the app communicates statements that fall into the category of 'online nationalism', so: contributions to the nationalist discourse in online spheres. But the app also mobilizes Chinese Communist Party (CCP) members around certain policies, using a gamified point system to nudge them towards the state's techno-nationalist agenda. All levels of digitally mediated nationalism come together in this context, generating a digital nationalism that can have unintended side-effects. For instance, users frequently 'game' the system by letting videos run in the background or flipping through content without paying attention, simply to gain more points. Such externalities are typical for digital nationalist dynamics, which are an example of complex networked processes.

The complexity of these networks matters. It generates what network scholars have called 'emergent properties': outcomes that are more than the sum of their parts (Monge & Contractor 2003, 233; Morçöl & Wachhaus 2009, 46). To fully appreciate how digital nationalism behaves, as an emergent property, it is important to understand two crucial parts of complex networked processes: resonance and variability (see Hollnagel 2012). Resonance refers to feedback loops between interconnected activities. These can be human activities, such as making statements about the nation, reading the news, or connecting with an acquaintance online. They can also be technological interactions, for instance, when algorithms filter data, curate content on a social media feed, or assess the level of interaction that a digital artefact generates. Each activity has its own outcome, its 'output', which, in turn, serves as an input to some other activity: for instance, interaction with an online post may cause an algorithm to assess it as highly relevant, which pushes it onto a social media feed, leading a user to read the piece and leave a comment, and so on. Importantly, the links through which interactions run are non-linear (Morçöl & Wachhaus 2009, 49). They double back on each other to generate feedback loops, and this means that a change in one activity can have layered and often delayed effects on the output of another. In other words, these interactions create resonance within the system.

In a system characterized by resonance, the 'variability' of outcomes can become unpredictable, so much so that a sudden even minor amplitude variation in one activity can have extreme effects that shake the entire system. A useful example is how seemingly 'banal', low-key nationalist expressions serve as an input to commercial websites and social media platforms, which facilitate their spread because of the traffic they generate. Online nationalism then builds up over time, leading to long-term effects that generate sudden bursts of variance elsewhere in the system, such as unanticipated cyber-nationalist activism in the face of a perceived offence against the nation. In that sense, digital nationalism has a 'temperature' that is affected by a series of complex interconnections and couplings 'upstream'. Under certain conditions, a change in one activity can filter through chains of socio-technical interactions to radically affect the amplitude of nationalist temperature. This is how sudden and surprising nationalist outbursts 'emerge' from the complexity of networks that had ostensibly transported relatively benign 'low temperature' patriotic undercurrents (Schneider 2021b). The result is not necessarily in the interest of the authorities, as occasional CCP condemnation of commercialized patriotism illustrates (Wang 2021).

In practice, China's networks feature three types of activities that interact to generate such outcomes. These are organizational, algorithmic, and user activities, and I will go through each, in turn.

The organizational inputs into China's digital nationalism

China's digital nationalism is in no small part affected by the activities of organizational actors, specifically organizations in two realms of the political economy: official agencies under the auspice of the CCP or the PRC state, and commercial actors like the large media and technology conglomerates that provide the infrastructure and much of the content of digital China.

Official actors: how the Party and the state contribute to digital nationalism

In China's digital nationalism, one centrally important input is the official establishment. State and party institutions promote an official version of nationalism, replete with party-approved symbols and rituals. This 'state-led nationalism' (Zhao 2004) is meant to promote citizens' attachment to the state and inspire unity, pride in China and its achievements, and an overall 'rational patriotism'. To achieve this end, state-led nationalism relies on a narrative that collapses China's past into 5,000 years of continuous history, frames China's tumultuous entry into modernity as the outcome of foreign aggression during the so-called 'century of humiliation', and presents Chinese current affairs as a success story in which the party has guided the nation along a 'road to revival' that will ultimately lead to unification, prosperity, and international recognition (Cohen 2002; Callahan 2010).

Much of this contemporary state-led discourse is not originally digital. It dates to the 1980s, and it became a particularly important part of the CCP's legitimation strategies after the fall of the Soviet Union and the events on Tiananmen Square in 1989 (Hughes 2006). Since then, it has been promoted through 'patriotic education' (Wang 2012), state media (Zhao 2008, 168), museums and exhibitions (Denton 2014), and official propaganda campaigns such as the one that celebrated the China Dream under Xi Jinping in 2013 (Sun 2019). However, the internet and especially its mobile version have become such a universal source for information in China that the CCP had to update its propaganda strategies to remain relevant and effective.

In part, this has meant simply digitizing official materials and placing them on China's web, for instance, by encouraging state media to post their reporting online, by creating online archives to flank the efforts of museums and important patriotic sites, or by launching dedicated government websites to relay the official position on current affairs issues like territorial disputes (Schneider 2018a). At that level of engagement, the authorities essentially treat China's digital networks as an 'info-web' and use the central position that their institutions maintain within those networks to inject the 'correct' (read: officially approved) symbols and statements into discourses about the nation, its leaders, and their sovereignty (Schneider 2016).

Simultaneously, the authorities have rolled out communicative efforts that increasingly use the affordances of the medium to their advantage. This has meant creating entirely new digital communication platforms like the state-run search engine China Search (ChinaSo.com) or the mobile solution for studying Xi Jinping thought mentioned earlier. It has also meant changing the strategies for engaging with citizens, at least in part. Traditional CCP propaganda relays official positions and flags the ideological buzzwords (or tifa) of the day (Qian 2012), which frequently makes the messaging appear wooden, even patronizing. While such traditional propaganda continues to play an important role in China's political communication, it is today accompanied by contents and styles that aim to persuade rather than dictate.

The party has realized that it needs to be persuasive if it wants its interpretation of nationalism to attract China's tech-savvy internet users, especially its youths. To rejuvenate its outreach, propaganda leans heavily on pop-cultural references, especially those familiar from Japanese animation, manga, and gaming (or 'AMG' culture). This is visible in the way the Chinese Communist Youth League has moved its activities to digital spheres (Guo 2018): on popular social media and video sharing platforms like Sina's Weibo, Bilibili, or Douyin (the Chinese version of Tik Tok), the Youth League produces original content steeped in internet memes, and it promotes content designed by private actors such as social media influencers and content creators. Good examples include the way the Youth League has pushed nationalist content created by domestic online commentator LexBurner, cartoonist Wuheqilin, or animation artists Lin Chao (creator of the popular nationalist anime 'Year Hare Affair'; see Guan & Hu 2020). In many ways, official attempts to promote nationalism are a public-private partnership between the authorities and entrepreneurs who are able to make a living with their nationalist products. Yet where such private actors promote a hollowed-out nationalism that does not involve official oversight, they are quickly shut down. This then also explains the seemingly contradictory phenomenon of state and party officials criticizing commercial actors for 'selling' patriotism (Wang 2021); in digital China, nationalism may sell well, but it has to be sold on the party's terms.

Another important dimension of official efforts to promote and 'guide' nationalism is the way the authorities manipulate online discussions. The party and state employ dedicated influence operators, and these paid commentators talk up the party, appeal to nationalist sentiments, and discredit critics online. Collectively, they have become known as China's 'fifty-cent army' (wu mao dang), based on the debatable assumption that they receive 50 cents (five 'mao') for each comment they leave online (Han 2018: ch.5).

Not all online defenders of the official position are necessarily paid for their interventions into public discussion. Many are private citizens driven by genuinely held beliefs about the nation and the need to uphold its dignity, and so the party and state can rely on a sizable 'voluntary fifty-cent army' of internet users (ibid.: ch.7) who are willing to swamp online discussions with nationalist commentary. This again illustrates how official governance augments its state and party activities with the actions of private individuals who are not necessarily associated with the establishment.

Public-private collaboration also extends to regulatory issues. The party and state's attempts to 'guide public opinion' are not limited to online propaganda efforts. They also encompass censorship of unwanted expressions. Much of this censorship relies on state action, for instance, blocking foreign services like Facebook or YouTube, or arresting and trying individuals who have infringed upon the PRC's laws and regulations for online conduct. However, the authorities outsource much of the day-to-day regulation of online discourses to private actors, creating a 'public-private nexus' (Creemers 2018) that operates at three tiers: the corporate level, the level of group and thought leaders, and the level of individual users.

The first tier of the governance effort focuses on the corporations that run China's platforms. These companies rely on licences to operate in China's market, and they need to conform with state guidelines on opinion guidance if they want to remain in business. This means that much of the censorship on platforms like Sina Weibo, Weixin, Bilibili, or Douyin is enforced by moderators who work for the respective company.

The companies then hand down the pressure for regulation to a second tier: opinion leaders and group moderators. For instance, anyone who runs a social group on Tencent's chat app Weixin is personally responsible for the behaviour of the group members and can lose their platform privileges or even their account in cases of misconduct. This means that these power users are under constant pressure to civilize the discussions they oversee, for example, by repeatedly reminding group members of community guidelines or ejecting members from the forum if they voice potentially controversial views.

Finally, the companies and the group moderators each pass on the responsibility for managing platform expressions to the individual users themselves. This third governance tier relies on self-regulation. Faced with the constant threat of having their posts removed, the views of their content throttled, or their accounts deleted, users have strong incentives to self-censor. The pressure is particularly high for streamers and bloggers who rely on platform feeds for their income, but small-time users are also affected: in a country where social media platforms like Weixin are no longer a service but an essential infrastructure for everyday life (Platin & De Seta 2019), having one's account closed effectively removes the user from their social circle and impedes their access to everything from ride-sharing to payment services to e-commerce. It is not hard to see how these measures would inspire self-regulation and conformity.

These governance strategies are of course not limited solely to issues of nationalism, but the degree to which the authorities have approved nationalism as the go-to framework for interpreting politics makes it potentially hazardous to question nationalist assumptions online, both for individuals and for platform providers.

Commercial actors in China's digital political economy

The Chinese state and the CCP are crucial actors in China's digital ecosystem, but they do not provide the most popular platforms and services that citizens use on an everyday basis. In fact, many of the official offers are minor players compared to the commercial alternatives that dominate the capitalist landscape of digital China (Hong 2018). Those alternatives come from China's internet and technology giants, most importantly the 'BAT', an acronym that stands for Baidu, Alibaba, and Tencent. Baidu runs China's largest commercial search engine, one of its most prominent Wikipedia-like online encyclopaedias, and China's dominant map and location service, but it is also a powerhouse in artificial intelligence (AI) research. Alibaba is famous for its e-commerce platforms, specifically Taobao and AliExpress, but it is further involved in financial technology, AI, surveillance, social engineering, and video entertainment. Tencent is originally a video game publisher and vendor, but it also runs the hugely influential chat app Weixin along with its many essential everyday-life functionalities. These three conglomerates are flanked by numerous other influential companies, such as Sina, which runs the microblogging service Weibo (Sullivan & Sapir 2013), or ByteDance, the enterprise behind Douyin/Tik Tok (Zhang 2021). Together, these corporate actors design and manage online communication within the PRC, and they do so according to the logic of what scholars call the 'platform economy' (Kenney & Zysman 2016).

Digital China is fundamentally a capitalist economic system. As such, it relies on the ability of enterprises to extract value from digital interactions. Much like capitalist media conglomerates in the US or elsewhere, it does so by commodifying content, mining and selling data, and generally monetizing and exploiting the activities, interactions, and labour of users (also known as 'digital labour', 'free labour', or 'playbour'; see the contributions in Scholz 2013). This has profound effects on how actors behave. In an environment where the scarce commodity is time, digital spheres become an 'attention economy' (Bueno 2017): an economic system in which the priority is to attract as much cognitive engagement as possible. Particularly effective strategies include using simplistic, one-sided issues as 'click-bate' and appealing to strong emotions, especially outrage and fear. Nationalist discourses reliably produce these requirements, and so there is a strong incentive for content producers and anyone who wishes to be seen on China's internet to frame their concerns in nationalist terms.

Importantly, the commercial rationale of platforms and their attention economy develops its own dynamics due to the way actors assess their success at generating attention that can be monetized, for instance, through advertising revenues, subscriptions, or micro-transactions. The platforms measure attention and interaction through metrics like page views, 'likes', and other numerical indicators, which can, in turn, skew the logic that informs content production. The issue is not whether users absorb, process, enjoy, or even internalize specific content; these aspects of media consumption become negligible. What matters are the communicative strategies that generate engagement, good or bad. To truly make content go viral, an aggressive style or exaggerated frame of reference can be extremely effective, and so the commercial rationale of digital China generates strong incentives for nationalist expressions.

Digital designs and algorithmic mechanics

The incentive structures in China's digital economy are the outcome of feedback loops between organizations and individuals, but those loops are enabled through, and mediated by, digital technology. The capitalist incentives in China's media environment are problematic on their own, but they become truly powerful because of the way digital measures such as clicks, likes, and shares are algorithmically relayed through the system.

In digital networks, it is no longer just people who interact; users engage in social, political, and economic activities through digital interfaces, which are coupled to algorithmic processes. Importantly, technological designs are by no means innocent in the making of these interactions. They are not neutral contraptions that users can wield to whichever end they choose. This is succinctly captured by Malvin Kranzberg's (1995, 5) dictum that 'technology is neither good nor bad; nor is it neutral'. Artefacts have politics (Winner 1980; see also Woolgar & Cooper 1999), and those politics are built into them by design.

This is not to say that technology and its designs rigidly define how users interact, but they generate the 'functional and relational aspects which frame, while not determining, the possibilities for agentic action in relation to an object' (Hutchby 2001: 444). This is precisely the technological 'affordance' mentioned earlier: digital designs create a range of plausible and practical possibilities for how users can deploy them. In networked socio-technical processes, technological artefacts like search engines, social media platforms, and web resources are part of our interaction chains and shape our behaviours, so much so that they function like 'actors' (Latour 2005).

Much like elsewhere in the world, and as outlined above, Chinese digital designs are strongly driven by commercial and regulatory rationales that produce their own 'media logic' (Chadwick 2013). In the Chinese case, that logic combines an authoritarian suspicion of unregulated collective activity with a commercial incentive to have users generate viral content that can be monetized. Chinese interfaces and backend processes anticipate these demands and guide users into patterns of behaviour that promise to maximize profit while minimizing political risk.

Take the example of how social media providers like Tencent of Sina designed their algorithms to control public debate: the main news feeds do not show posts chronologically but based on often obscure algorithmic choices that balance popularity (likes, shares, comments), personal preferences (user histories), commercial incentives (sponsored content and advertising), and political considerations (conformity with official regulation). Much like on Facebook, these systems benefit from viral engagement, and few things generate such viral engagement like the fear or anger accompanied by nationalism, which turns nationalism into a privileged topic in algorithmically curated feeds.

Similar dynamics operate in many online forums, especially those that rank comments based on the degree of interaction they produce. This is true for many news comments sections, but it is also the case in seemingly more innocuous settings. Take the online encyclopaedia Hudong Baike as an example (Schneider 2018a, 176–181) – a direct competitor to Baidu's encyclopaedic service. Until a major relaunch of its site in 2019, Hudong allowed users to comment on entries and each other's posts, and it then showcased those discussions by presenting the five most popular comments. On topics that touched on national sovereignty or identity, the most popular comments were frequently the most chauvinistic. This is not to say that there were no nuanced interventions and alternative views; such comments also existed, but they could only be accessed by clicking through and expanding the various comment threads. Defaults are powerful (most users only ever use and view default options), and so the knowledge aggregator's design choices contributed to the impression that nationalism was both the most popular and most appropriate lens through which to view China and its role in the world.

Other cases of design bias are more subtle. Nationalism can often appear banal, in online contexts, for instance, when a search engine like Baidu returns the simplified character script used in mainland China (rather than the traditional script used in Hong Kong, Taiwan, and many diaspora communities abroad), or when it produces results that default to domestic PRC contexts, sources, or perspectives. These outcomes are not generated by individual people with a nationalist agenda; they are produced by a combination of design and algorithmic choices that privilege common denominators among users, such as a physical location that common sense would suggest as the user's 'homeland'. However, common sense is never natural, nor is it neutral. It is commonly shared knowledge created by communication, and it is precisely the seemingly self-evident insistence on the national context, with its nationalist references like flags, colour-schemes, emblems, and so on, that normalizes that context as the default for political action (see also Billig 2009). The defaults of the platforms seamlessly interact with the defaults of political assumptions, creating and reinforcing an algorithmically generated comfort-zone. In other words, digital interfaces, algorithms, and biases produce the very sense of 'homeland' in the first place.

User-generated discourse and practice

This chapter has so far discussed the organizational and technological actors that create inputs into the complex socio-technical systems that constitute digital China, but a third set of actors is largely still missing from this picture: the individual users. Due to the technological affordances of the medium, internet users are not merely consumers, they are producers of content, or 'produsers' (Bruns 2006).

Users who create and spread nationalist statements online likely do so for a host of reasons, most of which are difficult to explore empirically. Online nationalists might be motivated by state funding, by commercial rationales, by conviction, or by the wish to make themselves intelligible in the readily available vernacular of nationalist discourse. In fact, we know relatively little about the people behind online nationalism. One assumption is that popular nationalism is driven by 'angry youths' (Rosen 2009), which have moved online to become what is commonly called 'little pinks' (Wu et al. 2019; see also Fang & Repnikova 2018 for a critique); others have questioned whether it is really young people who are most nationalist in contemporary China (Johnston 2016).

Regardless of who precisely fuels nationalism in China, or why, their interactions with the socio-technical systems of digital China generate widespread references to the community of the nation. These processes sit on top of contemporary community sentiments more broadly, for instance, imagined communities built around popular cultural appreciation. Indeed, the Chinese case illustrates how the social practices from one digitally imagined community translate to the context of another: the Chinese internet socializes its users into a digital cultural environment characterized by idol worship, ubiquitous fandom practices, and conspicuous pop-culture consumption, generating what Zhang (2016) calls 'fandom publics'. Many internet users take the lessons they have learned from these fandom publics and apply them to other contexts, such as when they perform their role as Chinese citizens. Liu Hailong (2019) and his colleagues have shown how contemporary popular nationalism in China today draws from fandom patterns. They call the result 'fandom nationalism', to reflect how nationalist activities in digital China rely on many of the communicative and mobilization strategies familiar from the way fans behave online.

Chinese fandom publics frequently initiate 'flame wars' and 'meme wars', in which fan groups attack each other online in support of celebrities or in attempts to defend their interpretations of cultural franchises. The debates that ensue on such occasions are often highly toxic, not to mention deeply political, for instance, when fans go head-to-head over their understandings of 'correct' gender roles and sexuality. A high-profile case in 2020 was the vicious disputes over homo-erotic fan depictions of beloved television actor Xiao Zhan. In cases such as these, fan groups tend to be highly organized, to the point that they describe their own community mobilization and activism in militaristic terms like armies, invasions, and battles for commanding heights.

Fans frequently organize in this fashion to flood online forums, social media pages, or microblogging hashtags in attempts to drown out statements that offend their sensibilities. Perceived antagonists are mocked relentlessly, usually through the kind of crude memes familiar from online satire, which is known as e'gao in Chinese (Gong & Yang 2010). In extreme cases, internet users investigate their perceived enemies through crowd-sourcing, a practice known as the 'human flesh search engine' (Herold 2011), and then publish their identities online. This 'doxing' then frequently leads to severe forms of harassment.

All these practices have become part of the toolbox that nationalists use online to defend China against perceived enemies, domestic or foreign (Liu 2019). For example, in 2016, nationalist users swamped the Facebook page of Tsai Ying-wen with angry insults, after the Taiwanese public had elected the liberal, independence-leaning politician as the president of the ROC. But fandom nationalism also targets perceived traitors of the nation at home, for instance, Olympic athletes who do not measure up to the high expectations of the nationalists, intellectuals like the author Fang Fang who dare to criticize state policy like China's COVID-19 management, and celebrities that are suspected of being sympathetic to causes such as Hong Kong or Taiwanese autonomy.

In all such cases, and much like in fandom conflicts, the strong antagonisms and crude shouting matches leave little room for nuance, discussion, or even reconciliation. This is not to say that there are no counter-movements: internet users with more liberal sensibilities frequently dismiss crude nationalist commentators on China's internet as 'pink maggots', 'fifty-centers', 'cyber red guards', and 'patriotraitors'. The meaning of nationalism is clearly a site of strong contestations in digital China. Nevertheless, the viral dynamics of loud, nationalist viewpoints frequently drown out dissent and create what psychologists call a 'spiral of silence' (Noelle-Neumann 1993): a dynamic in which those who disagree with the dominant narratives no longer dare to speak out. This is then part of why it is so difficult to assess how widespread aggressive nationalism truly is in China. The loud and highly visible online nationalism that emerges from Chinese digital networks may not represent the majority, but it is effective at setting the agenda and framing Chinese politics, all while silencing alternative discourses.

Conclusion

This chapter has explored how digital nationalism works in China. It made the case that nationalism in digital spheres develops unique dynamics, and that we should view those dynamics as consisting of legal and policy frameworks (what I have called 'techno-nationalism'), discursive practices ('online nationalism'), social mobilization ('cyber-nationalism'), and socio-technical systems ('digital nationalism'). In the Chinese case, political and commercial actors collaborate to create profitable and politically acceptable spheres for online interactions, which users then enter to engage in all manner of activities. With official actors strongly lacing these environments with the symbols and discourses of state-led nationalism, users pick up these building blocks of community sentiment and often revamp them for their own purposes. Due to the complex feedback loops that characterize these interactions in commercially driven and technologically mediated networks, nationalism becomes an emergent property that can take on a life of its own. It can turn on foreigners and compatriots alike, in ways that are not under any single actor's control.

Understanding these dynamics is crucial. China's digital nationalism is set to shape Chinese domestic politics and international affairs for the foreseeable future. But it is also a cautionary tale. It illustrates what happens when powerful political actors set nationalism as the primary parameter for political discourse, and when private groups and citizens run with these parameters to make sense of politics. This is then a much broader issue that is bound to affect politics anywhere that community sentiments are filtered through the digital networks of capitalist platforms that seek to commodify culture and monetize attention – which is to say everywhere.

References

Anderson, Benedict. 1983/2006. *Imagined Communities* (3rd ed.). London & New York: Verso.
Billig, Michael. 2009. *Banal Nationalism* (9th ed.). London: Sage.
Breslin, Shaun, and Simon Shen. 2010. "Online Chinese Nationalism'. *Chatham House Asia Programme Paper ASP PP 2010/03*, retrieved 9 August 2021 from: https://www.chathamhouse.org/sites/default/files/public/Research/Asia/0910breslin_shen.pdf
Bruns, Axel. 2006. "Towards Produsage: Futures for User-Led Content Production." In *Proceedings Cultural Attitudes towards Communication and Technology 2006*, edited by Fay Sudweeks, Herbert Hrachovec, and Charles Ess, retrieved 9 August 2021 from http://eprints.qut.edu.au/4863/1/4863_1.pdf.
Bueno, Claudio C. 2014. *The Attention Economy: Labour, Time and Power in Cognitive Capitalism*. London & New York: Rowman & Littlefield.
Callahan, William A. 2010. *China—The Pessoptimist Nation*. Oxford: Oxford University Press.
Chadwick, Andrew. 2013. *The Hybrid Media System—Politics and Power*. Oxford: Oxford University Press.
Cohen, Paul. 2002. "Remembering and Forgetting: National Humiliation in Twentieth-Century China." *Twentieth-Century China* 27 (2): 1–39.
Creemers, Rogier. 2016. "Recognizing China's Internet Governance despite Its Foundational Opposition to Western Values." *China US Focus*, retrieved 15 December from https://www.chinausfocus.com/society-culture/recognizing-chinas-internet-governance-despite-its-foundational-opposition-to-western-values.
Creemers, Rogier. 2018. "Disrupting the Chinese State: New Actors and New Factors." *Asiascape: Digital Asia* 5 (3): 169–197.
Creemers, Rogier. 2020. "China's Conception of Cyber Sovereignty: Rhetoric and Realization." In *Governing Cyberspace: Behavior, Power, and Diplomacy*, edited by Dennis Broeders and Bibi van den Berg, 107–142. Lanham: Rowman & Littlefield.
Denton, Kirk A. 2014. *Exhibiting the Past—Historical Memory and the Politics of Museums in Postsocialist China*. Honolulu: University of Hawai'i Press.
Fang, Kecheng, and Maria Repnikova. 2018. "Demystifying 'Little Pink': The Creation and Evolution of a Gendered Label for Nationalistic Activists in China." *New Media and Society* 20 (6): 2162–2185.
Feng, Miao, and Elaine J. Yuan. 2014. "Public Opinion on Weibo: The Case of the Diaoyu Island Dispute." In *The Dispute over the Diaoyu/Senkaku Islands: How Media Narratives Shape Public Opinion and Challenge the Global Order*, edited by Thomas A. Hollihan, 119–140. New York: Palgrave Macmillan.

Goode, J. Paul. 2021. "Artificial Intelligence and the Future of Nationalism." *Nations and Nationalism* 23: 363–376.

Gong, Haomin, and Yang Xin. 2010. "Digitized Parody: The Politics of Egao in Contemporary China." *China Information* 24 (1): 3–26.

Guo, Shaohua. 2018. "'Occupying' the Internet: State Media and the Reinvention of Official Culture Online." *Communication and the Public* 3 (1): 19–33.

Guan, Tianru, and Hu Tingting. 2020. "The Confirmation and Negotiation of Nationalism in China's Political Animations – A Case Study of *Year Hare Affair*." *Continuum* 34 (3): 417–430.

Gries, Peter. 2004. *China's New Nationalism—Pride, Politics, and Diplomacy*. Berkeley: University of California Press.

Gries, Peter, Derek Steiger, and Tao Wang. 2016. "Popular Nationalism and China's Japan Policy: the Diaoyu Islands protests, 2012–2013." *Journal of Contemporary China* 25 (98): 264–276.

Han, Rongbin. 2018. *Contesting Cyberspace in China: Online Expression and Authoritarian Resilience*. New York: Columbia University Press.

Herold, David K. 2011. "Human Flesh Search Engines: Carnivalesque Riots as Components of a 'Chinese Democracy'." In *Online Society in China: Creating, Celebrating, and Instrumentalising the Online Carnival*, edited by David K. Herold and Peter Marolt, 127–145. Abingdon: Routledge.

Hollnagel, Erik. 2012. *FRAM: The Functional Resonance Analysis Method: Modelling Complex Sociotechnical Systems*. Farnham & Burlington, VT: Ashgate.

Hughes, Christopher R. 2006. *Chinese Nationalism in the Global Era*. Abingdon: Routledge.

Hong, Yu. 2017. *Networking China: The Digital Transformation of the Chinese Economy*. Urbana: University of Illinois Press.

Hutchby, Ian 2001. "Technologies, Texts and Affordances." *Sociology* 35 (2): 441–456.

Jenkins, Henry. 2006. *Convergence Culture: Where Old and New Media Collide*. New York & London: New York University Press.

Jiang, Ying. 2012. *Cyber-Nationalism in China. Challenging Western Media Portrayals of Internet Censorship in China*. Adelaide: University of Adelaide Press.

Johnston, Alastair Iain. 2016. "Is Chinese Nationalism Rising? Evidence from Beijing." *International Security* 41 (3): 7–43.

Kenney, Martin, and John Zysman. 2016. "The Rise of the Platform Economy." *Issues in Science and Technology* 32 (3): 61–69.

Kranzberg, Melvin. 1995. "Technology and History: 'Kranzberg's Laws'." *Bulletin of Science, Technology & Society* 15 (1): 5–13.

Latour, Bruno. 2005. *Reassembling the Social — An Introduction to Actor Network Theory*. Oxford: Oxford University Press.

Leibold, James. 2016. "Han Cybernationalism and State Territorialization in the People's Republic of China." *China Information* 30 (1): 3–28.

Liu, Hailong, ed. 2019. *From Cyber-Nationalism to Fandom Nationalism: The Case of Diba Expedition in China*. Abingdon: Routledge.

Mihelj, Sabina, and César Jiménez-Martínez. 2020. "Digital Nationalism: Understanding the Role of Digital Media in the Rise of 'New' Nationalism." *Nations and Nationalism* 27 (2): 331–346.

Monge, Peter R., and Noshir S. Contractor. 2003. *Theories of Communication Networks*. Oxford: Oxford University Press.

Morçöl, G. and Wachhaus, A. 2009. "Network and Complexity Theories: A Comparison and Prospects for a Synthesis." *Administrative Theory & Praxis* 31 (1): 44–58.

Noelle-Neumann, Elisabeth. 1993. *The Spiral of Silence: Public Opinion, Our Social Skin*. Chicago, IL: The University of Chicago Press.

Parchoma, Gale 2014. "The Contested Ontology of Affordances: Implications for Researching Technological Affordances for Collaborative Knowledge Production." *Computers in Human Behavior* 37: 360–368.

Platin, Jean-Christophe, and Gabriele De Seta. 2019. "WeChat as Infrastructure: The Techno-Nationalist Shaping of Chinese Digital Platforms." *Chinese Journal of Communication* 12 (3): 257–73.

Qian, Gang. 2012. "Watchwords: The Life of the Party." *China Media Project*, retrieved 9 August 2021 from http://chinamediaproject.org/2012/09/10/watchwords-the-life-of-the-party/.

Qiu, Jack L. 2010. "Chinese Techno-Nationalism and Global WiFi Policy." In *Reorienting Global Communication: Indian and Chinese Media beyond Borders*, edited by Michael Curtin and Hemant Shah, 284–304. Urbana, IL: University of Illinois Press.

Rosen, Stanley. 2009. "Contemporary Chinese Youth and the State." *The Journal of Asian Studies* 68 (2): 359–369.
Schneider, Florian. 2016. "China's 'Info-Web': How Beijing Governs Online Political Communication about Japan." *New Media and Society* 18 (11): 2664–2684.
Schneider, Florian. 2018a. *China's Digital Nationalism*. New York & Oxford: Oxford University Press.
Schneider, Florian. 2018b. "Mediated Massacre: Digital Nationalism and History Discourse on China's Web." *Journal of Asian Studies* 77 (2): 429–452.
Schneider, Florian. 2021a. "COVID-19 Nationalism and the Visual Construction of Sovereignty during China's Coronavirus Crisis." *China Information* 35 (3): 301–324.
Schneider, Florian. 2021b. "Emergent Nationalism in China's Sociotechnical Networks: How Technological Affordance and Complexity Amplify Digital Nationalism." *Nations and Nationalism* 28 (1): 267–285.
Scholz, Trebor, ed. 2013. *Digital Labor: The Internet as Playground and Factory*. Abingdon: Routledge.
Shen, Hong. 2018. "Building a Digital Silk Road? Situating the Internet in China's Belt and Road Initiative." *International Journal of Communication* 12: 2683–2701.
Shen, Simon, and Shaun Breslin, eds. 2010. *Online Chinese Nationalism and China's Bilateral Relations*. Lanham: Lexington.
Shklovski, Irina & Struthers, David M. 2010. "Of States and Borders on the Internet: The Role of Domain Name Extensions in Expressions of Nationalism Online." *Policy & Internet* 2 (4): 107–129.
Sun, Zhen. 2019. "Utopia, Nostalgia, and Femininity: Visually Promoting the Chinese Dream." *Visual Communication* 18 (1): 107–133.
Sullivan, Jonathan & Eliyahu V. Sapir. 2013. "Strategic Cross-Strait Discourse: A Comparative Analysis of Three Presidential Terms." *China Information* 27 (1): 11–30.
Wang, Lei. 2021. "Mashang ping: 'tonggao aiguo' bu shi aiguo, shi yi zhuang liuliang shengyi" [Immediate Criticism: 'Published Patriotism' Is Not Patriotic, It Is a Business in Traffic]. *The Paper*, retrieved 15 December 2021 from https://www.thepaper.cn/newsDetail_forward_14716236
Wang, Zheng. 2012. *Never Forget National Humiliation—Historical Memory in Chinese Politics and Foreign Relations*. New York, NY: Columbia University Press.
Winner, Langdon. 1980. "Do Artifacts have Politics?" *Daedalus* 109 (1): 121–136.
Woods, Eric Taylor, et al. 2020. "COVID-19, Nationalism, and the Politics of Crisis: A Scholarly Exchange." *Nations and Nationalism* 26 (4): 807–25.
Woolgar, Steve, and Geoff Cooper. 1999. "Do Artefacts Have Ambivalence? Moses' Bridges, Winner's Bridges and Other Urban Legends in S&TS." *Social Studies of Science* 29 (3): 433–449.
Wu, Jing, Li Simin, and Wang Hongzhe. 2019. "From Fans to 'Little Pink': The Production and Mobilization Mechanism of National Identity under the New Media Commercial Culture." In *From Cyber-Nationalism to Fandom Nationalism: The Case of Diba Expedition in China*, edited by Liu Hailong, 32–52. Abingdon: Routledge.
Wu, Xu. 2007. *Chinese Cyber Nationalism: Evolution, Characteristics, and Implications*. Lanham, MD: Lexington Books.
Yang, Guobin. 2020. "Performing Cyber-Nationalism in Twenty-First-Century China: The Case of Diba Expedition." In *From Cyber-Nationalism to Fandom Nationalism: The Case of Diba Expedition in China*, edited by Liu Hailong, 1–12. Abingdon: Routledge.
Zhao, Suisheng. 2004. *A Nation- State by Construction: Dynamics of Modern Chinese Nationalism*. Stanford, CA: Stanford University Press.
Zhao, Yuezhi. 2008. *Communication in China – Political Economy, Power, and Conflict*. Lanham & Plymouth, MI: Rowman & Littlefield.
Zhang, Weiyu. 2016. *The Internet and New Social Formation in China: Fandom Publics in the Making*. Abingdon: Routledge.
Zhang, Zongyi. 2021. "Infrastructuralization of Tik Tok: Transformation, Power Relationships, and Platformization of Video Entertainment in China." *Media, Culture, & Society* 43 (2): 219–236.
Zhong, Raymond. 2019. "Little Red App: Xi's Thoughts Are (Surprise!) a Hit in China." *The New York Times*, February 14, retrieved 9 August 2021 from 2https://www.nytimes.com/2019/02/14/technology/china-communist-app.html.

12
THE DREAM OF A STRONG COUNTRY
Nationalism and China's Olympic journey

Lu Zhouxiang

Introduction

Nationalism is a concept dominated by politics. Its development is reinforced by economic, cultural, linguistic and/or other kinds of national aspirations; hence, these less dominant elements are assigned an auxiliary function in the consolidation of national consciousness (Alter 1994). Sport is one of these national aspirations. As Cronin (1999, 51) observes:

> Sport is, and always has been, inextricably linked to the forces of nationalism and identity... It is a form of national popular culture, a forum for the creation, expression or maintenance of senses and ideals of identity, a form of business, and a central point of focus for groups within and outside any given society or nation.

In the last 20 years, a considerable amount of research has been conducted by historians, social scientists and political scientists in order to examine the relationship between sport and nationalism. These studies have revealed that sporting nationalism accompanies other forms of nationalism – linguistic, civic, ethnic, cultural and religious – and often functions as a galvanizing or motivating force in nationalist movements. It serves a wide range of political objectives, such as 'enhancing prestige, securing legitimacy, compensating for other aspects of life within their boundaries and pursuing international rivals by peaceful means' (Bairner 2001, 18). Nevertheless, the relationship between sport and nationalism needs to be explored further. Using historical narratives and a qualitative research approach, this chapter aims to understand the role of the modern Olympic movement in the construction of Chinese nationalism, and discusses the wider debate on sporting patriotism and its influence on people's perception of national confidence and self-esteem, as well as on the country's sporting policy and practice.

Liu Changchun's one-man Olympics

Since the mid-nineteenth century, sport has been consistently interwoven with Chinese nationalism. After the two Opium Wars, influenced by an embryonic nationalism concerned with defending China against foreign powers and restoring the 'Celestial Empire', the Qing court introduced and promoted Western military gymnastics as part of the Self-Strengthening Movement (1861–1895), in an attempt to enhance the country's military power. At the turn of the century, Western sport and physical education were advocated by intellectuals, reformers and nationalists eager to achieve national salvation by transforming China into a powerful, modern nation state. Thanks to their efforts, sport was promoted as a means of cultivating new citizens and widely accepted as a basic approach to 'preserving the nation' (保国) and 'preserving the race' (保种). In the 1900s, both traditional Chinese martial arts and Western sports were used by Han Chinese nationalists in their plans to overthrow the Manchu regime. Sports schools and societies became places where revolutionaries built up their power and contributed to the success of the 1911 Revolution (Luo 2008).

The establishment of the Republic in 1912 heralded a new era. A modern nation state took shape, and the political foundation for Chinese nationalism had been laid. Focusing on anti-imperialism and national survival, the government trumpeted military citizenship education as the guiding philosophy of the education system, and sport and physical education were promoted in order to consolidate national unity, cultivate patriotism, improve the health and physique of the people and aid national defence. At the same time, international sporting events such as the Far Eastern Championship Games and the Olympic Games were introduced to China and soon came to be regarded as important vehicles for winning international recognition and fostering a sense of national identity and unity.

In 1932, China sent its first athlete to the Los Angeles Olympics, prompted by Japan's attempt to gain legitimacy for its invasion of Chinese territory by sending a team from its puppet state Manzhouguo (满洲国 – Manchuria) to the US. On 17 June, 1932, *Taidong Daily*, a newspaper backed by the Japanese authorities, announced that two athletes from northeastern China – the country's best sprinter Liu Changchun (1909–1983) and top middle-distance runner Yu Xiwei (1909–1980) – would represent Manzhouguo at the Olympics. Upon hearing the news, Liu Changchun issued a public denial in *Dagong Daily*:

> What the puppet regime's newspaper reported is a lie. As the offspring of the Yellow Emperor of the Chinese nation, as a Chinese person, I will never represent the puppet Manzhouguo state at the 10th Olympic Games!
>
> *(Liu 1980, 221)*

With the support of Zhang Xueliang (1901–2001), President of Northeast University, and Hao Gengsheng (1899–1975), Inspector for Physical Education in the Ministry of Education and Chairman of the China National Amateur Athletic Federation (CNAAF), Liu and Yu decided to compete for the Republic of China at the Los Angeles Olympics. However, Yu was unable to join the Chinese team due to the Japanese authorities' interference. A special ceremony was held at Shanghai Port on 8 July, 1932 for the three-man national squad, which consisted of Liu Changchun, his coach Song Junfu (1897–1977) and team leader Shen Siliang (1896–1967). More than 400 people attended. Foreign Minister Wang Zhengting (1882–1961) handed the national flag to Liu. The team was sent off with cheers and chants of 'Long Live the Republic of China!'

That day a Shanghai newspaper published a picture of Lord Guan Yu (the Chinese God of War) holding a broadsword and standing on a boat, blessing the country's first Olympic squad. *Dagong Daily* commented, in a patriotic tone:

> This time, our great Chinese athlete travels tens of thousands of miles to attend the [Olympic] event alone. The country is suffering. We hope our countrymen can strive

forward bravely [like Liu Changchun], so that our future generations can be freed from suffering and pain.

(Song 2021)

The decision to send Liu Changchun to the Olympics was based on politics and nationalism. Hao Gensheng explained that participating in the Olympics could:

> Stop the Japanese attempt to legalize the Manchurian puppet state.
> Push Chinese sport into a new era, raise the Republic of China's national flag at the Olympics and set an example for future generations.
> Allow us to communicate with young people from all over the world.
> Allow us to observe and learn from the Games, in order to gain an awareness of the weaknesses of Chinese sport.
> [Tell the story of] Liu Changchun, [who] is from northeastern China; he is suffering due to the Japanese invasion of Manchuria. We can take this opportunity to tell the world about Japan's crime in China.
>
> *(Tang 1999, 214)*

The Chinese delegation arrived in Los Angeles on 29 July, 1932. The next day, Liu Changchun marched in the opening ceremony with the Chinese national flag. On 31 July, he competed in the men's 100-metre preliminaries but failed to qualify for the final. The team then attended the World Youth Debate Convention in Los Angeles, where Song Junfu took the opportunity to deliver a speech in English condemning the Japanese invasion of China.

Back in China, Liu was regarded as a national hero competing for the country's pride and dignity. People began to pay attention to the role of sport in diplomacy, and in winning recognition from the international community and building up national confidence. Shen Siliang (1933, 7) observed:

> It was an amazing experience for the whole world that China's national flag and the Chinese delegation appeared in the Olympic stadium... Although we only sent one athlete to participate in the Games, the objective is clear. We want to show our spirit to the world. The waving of the Chinese national flag tells the world that China is still sustained by youth and vigour and will compete against the superpowers in sport. It shows that China will never give up and will never let the superpowers carve it up.

China's presence at the 1932 Olympics impressed state leaders. Four years later, the KMT government decided to send a large delegation to the Berlin Olympics. Trials were held to select elite athletes from each province, and training camps were established (Ministry of Education 1948). In total, 69 Chinese athletes participated in the Berlin Games, with a martial arts team included in the delegation in order to showcase traditional Chinese culture.

Although the national team failed to win a medal, the trip was considered to have been valuable from political and diplomatic perspectives. It was widely believed that participation in the Berlin Olympics had further consolidated national consciousness and enhanced China's international status. Winning a medal was a secondary matter (Xu 2008, 47).

After 1936, drained by the Second Sino-Japanese War (1937–1945) and the subsequent Civil War between the Communists and Nationalists, the government's attention was drawn away from the Olympics. With limited funding and resources, the CNAAF still managed to send athletes to the 1948 London Olympics, but this ill-prepared and poorly organized team failed to win a medal (Dong 1980, 11). Nevertheless, this demonstrated China's motivation to stay engaged with the world and to compete with foreign powers. By participating in the three Olympic Games in 1932, 1936 and 1948, the modern Chinese nation state established its position in the world and thus further fostered a sense of national unity among its people.

Two Chinas

The year 1949 saw the end of the Civil War and the partition of China. The Communists Party launched the People's Republic of China (PRC) in Beijing, while the Nationalist Party and its government retreated to Taiwan and have remained there as the Republic of China (ROC). The Communists adopted the policy of 'claiming a mandate to rule China by virtue of the nationalist quest for greatness and modernization' (Zhao 2004, 210). The main objective was to build China into a strong country, restore its rightful position in the world and revive the national confidence and self-respect that had been lost. In order to achieve this, Beijing initiated land and economic reforms. By the mid-1950s, the country had succeeded in tackling the problems of nation building and economic underdevelopment (MacFarquhar 1997).

Economic recovery and the establishment of a stable political system coincided with calls for the realization of one basic element of Chinese nationalism – self-strengthening. Soon after the establishment of the PRC, the Korean War (1950–1953) had reinforced the other element of Chinese nationalism – anti-imperialism. To secure the northeastern border and defend the Socialist bloc against the Capitalist powers, Beijing sent the People's Volunteer Army to assist North Korea and fought the United States to a standstill. The Chinese people were convinced that the 'War to Resist US and Aid Korea' (抗美援朝) marked the first victory of China over foreign aggressors since the 1840s. It ended the so-called 'hundred years of humiliation' (百年国耻) and was regarded as a turning point in Chinese history that symbolized the revival of China, further boosting nationalism and patriotism.

In such an atmosphere, sport was inevitably linked to the power of the nation. Throughout the 1950s and 1960s, sport and physical education continued to be promoted by the government as efficient ways to train strong bodies for the country. Policy-makers also saw high-level sport as a vehicle for enhancing national self-esteem, and an elite sport system was established to produce high-performance athletes. The objective was to win medals at international sporting events and help the 'New China' (新中国) to achieve international recognition and reinforce domestic unity. Sporting success soon came to be regarded as one of the PRC's most important achievements in socialist modernization and was portrayed as a symbol of national revival.

In a world divided by the Cold War, participating in the Olympics was no longer a simple sporting matter but a serious political and diplomatic issue. In 1952, the Olympics took place in Helsinki, Finland. This marked the beginning of the political conflict between Communist China and Nationalist China (Taiwan), which came to be known as the Two Chinas issue. Both wanted to be the sole representative of China at the Olympics and announced that they would not go to the Games unless their counterpart was expelled.

When the International Olympic Committee (IOC) decided to invite both sides to the Games, Taiwan withdrew in protest. Beijing received the IOC invitation just one day before the Games were due to commence, but still sent a national team of 40 athletes to Helsinki. Although they missed most of the competitions and did not win any medals, Premier Zhou Enlai (1898–1976) praised their participation as a great victory in international politics. Consequently, a centralized sport system was established to meet the country's political and diplomatic demands. Elite sport was promoted to inspire the people, build up national confidence and serve the goal of catching up with the Western powers, namely the US and the UK.

While an elite sport system was established to produce athletes for the Olympics, the diplomatic battle between the PRC and the ROC continued. In 1956, the IOC invited both to participate in the Melbourne Olympics with the team names of Peking – China and Formosa – China. However, when the ROC delegation arrived in the Olympic Village on 29 October, the PRC flag was accidentally raised and members of the team dragged it down (Zhang 2010). This incident soon turned into a political dispute. Journalists from mainland China who urged the Organizing Committee of the Games to issue an explanation and apology were expelled from the Olympic Village. Consequently, the PRC withdrew from the Games (Tang 1999).

Over the following two years, the PRC still hoped that the IOC would expel Taiwan. However, the IOC did not have any intention of doing so; it aimed to convince Beijing that it was better for the two Chinese Olympic committees to co-exist. Finally, the PRC withdrew from the IOC in 1958. This decision was deeply rooted in Cold War politics and diplomacy. As Sports Minister He Long (1896–1969) explained:

> We must stick to our principles and stances. We cannot do anything that may damage the honor of our motherland. We are a great socialist country, and no one can isolate us! We have friends all over the world! Despite being blocked and isolated by imperialist countries for almost ten years, our country has still achieved rapid development. I believe there will be a day when they will invite us back to the international sports family. China has one quarter of the world's population and no one can ignore this.
> *(Editorial Department of 'Biography of Contemporary Chinese Figures' 1993, 518)*

In subsequent years, the ROC continued to participate in the Olympic Games as 'Taiwan'. Driven by a defensive strain of nationalism triggered by the Sino–Indian border conflict, the Sino–Soviet split and the Vietnam War, the PRC allied with the Non-Aligned Movement (NAM) member states and used the Games of the Newly Emerging Forces (GANEFO) of 1963 to win support from, and build up its relationship with, newly independent nations in Asia, Africa and Latin America. By doing so, the PRC successfully established its position as one of the leading powers in the third world and changed an international political landscape mainly shaped by the Western capitalist bloc, led by the US, and the Eastern socialist bloc, led by the Soviet Union.

However, all efforts to build China's national confidence and international influence through sport were suspended when the Cultural Revolution started in 1966. Not until the early 1970s was the sporting system revived as an aspect of Beijing's diplomacy with Western countries, a sea change triggered by the famous Ping-Pong Diplomacy which began in 1971 (Lu 2016).

In the 1970s, an increasing number of Western countries shifted diplomatic recognition from the ROC to the PRC. In 1979, the United States officially recognized the PRC as the sole legal government of China. Later that year, the IOC reached a resolution that the Chinese Olympic Committee (PRC) in Beijing would be the representative of China. The Chinese Olympic Committee (Taiwan) in Taipei would attend the Olympic Games under the name of Chinese Taipei. In February 1980, Beijing sent its national team to the XIII Winter Olympics held in Lake Placid, New York. This ice-breaking journey marked the re-emergence of the PRC in the Olympic Movement.

Nationalism and the Olympic strategy

The period after the Cultural Revolution entailed 'the continuation of intensive efforts to rebuild the country and to make up for the self-inflicted damage of the tragic decade from

1966 to 1976' (Rodziński 1991, 432). Deng Xiaoping's 'reform and opening up' policy was implemented to achieve the goal of modernization, and the transition to a free market economy paved the way for individual freedoms. At the same time, alongside academic criticism of the Cultural Revolution and of extreme left-wing ideology, interest in liberalism, individualism and Western democracy increased (Ma 1998). Western Studies flourished. University students abandoned Russian and turned to learning English; Western literature, arts, music, TV and cinema, condemned as 'poisonous weeds' (毒草) during the Cultural Revolution, were reintroduced to the general public; Western food, drinks, clothes and lifestyle became symbols of the rich, developed capitalist countries, regarded as fashionable, luxurious and embodying an 'advanced Western culture' (先进的西方文化).

By the end of the 1980s, Western influence had reached almost every corner of Chinese society. The prosperity of the highly developed Western countries, especially the US, the UK, France and Germany, shocked and impressed many Chinese. When they turned their gaze back to China, the illusion of a great and strong socialist country suddenly collapsed. Consequently, a new strain of nationalism focused on national revival began to rise, triggering inordinate expectations and demands for modernization and Westernization.

According to Hobsbawm (1992, 143), interest in sport can be viewed as symbolic in the context of national struggle. It offers people an opportunity to consolidate their identity through competition against other nations. International sporting contests, which pit nation against nation and generate feelings of patriotism and jingoism, are by their nature a medium for the expression of identity, nationalism and politics. As Edwards (1984, 172) observed:

> [The] embellishment of outstanding sports performance with the trappings of patriotism occurs in all societies. Nowhere is sport politics more clearly evident than in modern international sports. Here, world-class athletes and other sports personnel emerge as little more than political foot soldiers, frontline troops in assorted cultural and ideological struggles camouflaged under the pageantry of international competitions.

Being the natural unit of international sports competitions, nation states are eager to promote their self-images and international reputations, and boost the morale of their people, through sport (Leiper 1987, 331). Therefore, each national team is loaded with symbolism and functions as the carrier of national prestige. Elite athletes' performances signify nothing less than national survival for large numbers of people in many different societies (Hoberman 2004). There is no doubt that their success contributes to consolidating a sense of national dignity and encourages patriotism. This has made sport 'the most popular form of nationalist behaviour as the masses of people become highly emotional in support of their national team' (Kellas 1998, 21).

Throughout the 1980s, Chinese nationalism was expressed intensely at international sporting events, notably the Olympics. While China had fallen far behind highly developed Western countries in terms of the economy, technology and national construction, Chinese people could feel a sense of confidence restored through the defeat of Western competitors. The country's sporting success was regarded as evidence of ideological superiority and a totem of national revival. For example, after the national table tennis team won seven gold medals at the 1981 International Table Tennis Championships in Yugoslavia, thousands of people in Beijing and Shanghai took to the streets to celebrate the success, chanting 'Long live China!' The editor of *Sport Daily* concluded:

> The relationship between sport and nationalism has never been so tight. The influence of sport on people's minds and lives has never been so strong. The contribution of sport to the development of socialist culture and ethics has never been so important.
>
> (Editor 1982)

Alongside economic and political reforms, and influenced by nationalism, sport in China underwent a significant transformation. The Sports Ministry developed a new sports policy in line with the goals for reform set forth in the 'Four Modernisations' (四个现代化) of agriculture, industry, science and technology, and national defence. According to the new strategy, both mass sport and elite sport were to be promoted. However, elite sport was set as the main focus.

Sports Minister Wang Meng explained the reasons behind this decision:

> China is still a poor country and restricted in the amount of money it can invest in sport. Elite sport is also an effective way to boost China's new image on the international stage. Therefore, the solution is to bring elite sport into the existing economic and administrative system, which could assist in the distribution of some of the nation's limited resources to medal-winning sports.
>
> (Wang 1982, 150)

It was hoped that sporting success would bring pride, confidence and hope to the Chinese people, all needed in the new era of reform and opening up (Rong and Zhang 1984).

Based on this strategy, the Sports Ministry drafted a blueprint for the development of elite sport in the 1980s and 1990s. The short-term plan required the national team to place in the top six at the 1984 Olympics. The long-term plan required China's elite sport athletes to reach world-class levels by the end of the 1980s (Hao 2006, 11). Deng Xiaoping wrote an inscription in 1983 to show his support for this elite sport-first policy: 'Enhance the Level of Performance, Win Honour for the Country!' (提高水平, 为国争光)

The strategy was first tested at the 1984 Olympic Games. Fifty-two years after Liu Changchun had represented China at the 1932 Olympics, Chinese athletes landed in Los Angeles again, with the absence of the Soviet Union and other Eastern European countries giving them an opportunity to shine. The national team won 15 gold medals and finished fourth in the medal tally.

This success excited many Chinese people. In Los Angeles, overseas Chinese supported the national team with a silk banner emblazoned with big Chinese characters that read: 'You make Chinese people feel proud and elated! You represent the spirit of the Chinese nation!' (Shan and Liu 2008). On their return to Beijing, the Olympic squad was welcomed at the airport by representatives of the central government and received a congratulatory telegram from the State Council: 'You have achieved great success at the Olympics, and this victory has helped to construct China's spirit and confidence. It has inspired the Chinese people on their march toward modernisation' (Hao 2008, 89).

Encouraged by the success, the central government issued 'A Notification about the Further Promotion of Sport' in October 1984 (Tan 2005, 416). The relationship between sport, politics and nationalism was highlighted as follows:

> Sport has a close relationship with health, the power of the nation and the honour of the country. It plays an important role in promoting political awareness, achieving modernisation targets, establishing foreign relations and strengthening national defence. Therefore, the Party and the people have recognized the importance of sport in our

society and will develop sport in China further… The remarkable achievement in sport, especially the success at the 1984 Olympics, has restored our self-confidence and national pride. It has stimulated a patriotic feeling among all the Chinese, both at home and abroad, and enhanced China's international influence.
(Central Committee of the Communist Party of China 1984)

Following this line of thought, the Sports Ministry produced an Olympic Strategy in 1985, aiming to improve China's international image by transforming the country into a leading sports power. Consequently, the famous Juguo Tizhi (举国体制) was instituted to promote elite sport. Based on the professional training and selection system launched in 1963, a well-organized and tightly structured three-level pyramid system was developed to meet the needs of the elite sport-first strategy (Sports Ministry 1993, 107), with more and more funding and resources channelled into Olympic sports.

Criticisms of gold medal fever

In the 1980s, China entered a period of enlightenment that 'culminated in an intensified cultural passion – a soul-searching discussion, led by the educated elite, about China's history, culture and future' (Zhao 2004, 136). Intellectuals began to search for the cause of China's failures during the Mao era. Many of them blamed traditional Chinese culture and called for the 'adoption of Western culture and models of modernisation to regenerate China' (Zhao 2004, 132). In the late 1980s, a group of intellectuals led by Su Xiaokang took anti-traditionalism to an extreme and proclaimed that 'Chinese culture must be thoroughly and entirely destroyed', placing their hopes for China entirely in the introduction of Western culture.

This pro-Western movement reached its peak with the airing of the TV series *River Elegy* (河殇) in 1988, which portrayed China as an ancient, declining civilization. It called for the abolition of the traditional Chinese culture, ideology and political system, and urged the adoption of the 'Blue Ocean Civilization' of the West. The pursuit of Western Studies and the widespread influence of Western culture, individualism and liberalism gave rise to radicalism (Chen 1997). This led to pro-democracy demonstrations in Tiananmen Square in June 1989, which was initiated by patriotic students who believed that national salvation and revival could only be achieved through complete political reform and Westernization (Zhao 2004).

The call for reform also reached the field of sport. Leading academics and senior policymakers publicly questioned and debated the sensitive issue of whether millions should be spent on the pursuit of Olympic medals or on the improvement of people's health and the promotion of sport at grassroots level (Wu 2002, 351–352). The debate reached a critical level when Zhao Yu, a former professional cyclist turned writer, published an article entitled 'The Dream to Be a Strong Country' that criticized the sporting system and the Chinese people's inordinate expectations. He argued that gold medals had become a heavy burden and would bring disaster down on the country, and recommended that the state pay more attention to mass sport, because a strong country depends on healthy citizens rather than a few elite athletes (Zhao 1988).

Zhao Yu's article received many responses from the media, the general public and some state leaders. More than 30 newspapers republished it. The *Guangming Daily* and *Wenhui Daily* praised the article as a 'breakthrough in sports literature' (Zhong 2007). The *People's Daily* commented:

> Mass sport has been neglected for a long time and put aside. Sport in China has focused on competitions and gold medals, and there is a deep misunderstanding of sport in

contemporary China. We should not ignore this problem, and should change our way of thinking and carry out real reforms. Zhao Yu's criticism and warnings have inspired many. It is an expression of honesty and real patriotism.

(Zhong 2007)

When the 1988 Olympics took place in Seoul, South Korea, Chinese athletes performed far below expectations, with the gold medal tally falling from 4th in 1984 to 11th. Seeking a reason for this 'failure', Zhao Yu's criticism was cited. The *People's Daily* commented that the truth of the matter lay in 'The Dream to Be a Strong Country' (Zhong 2007). *Literature Daily* stated: 'The results of China's performance at the 1988 Olympics have exposed the crisis in Chinese sport... The gold medal dream has been smashed. The true value of "The Dream to Be a Strong Country" is now realized' (Zhong 2007).

Zhao Yu subsequently interviewed Sports Ministry staff and national team athletes for a new article entitled 'The Defeat in Seoul' that further explored the causes of China's failure at the 1988 Olympics. He again harshly criticized the elite sport system and questioned the Olympic strategy (Zhao 1988). However, these criticisms soon came to be overshadowed by a new nationalism that emerged in the early 1990s.

The Olympics and China's rise

Entering the 1990s, Chinese nationalism was transformed by a series of international incidents, notably the Yinhe Incident in 1993 and the US intervention in the Taiwan Strait Confrontation of 1995–1996 (Hillman 2004). By the mid-1990s, 'much of the growing discontent in China was vented as a vigorous resentment toward the supposedly renewed Western – primarily American – attempt to "contain" China' (Liu 2001, 206).

A 1996 book entitled *China Can Say No* strongly expressed this anti-Western/anti-American sentiment. It recalled the nation's past colonial subjugation and presented a parallel between the tragic past and China's international dilemma in the present, symbolizing a change of trend in thought among nationalists and the intelligentsia.

That same year, Samuel Huntington's *The Clash of Civilizations and the Remaking of World Order* was published in China and became a bestseller among the intelligentsia. It proposed that cultural and religious identities would be the primary source of conflict in the post-Cold War world, that the rise of Asia and other non-Western nations would become a potential threat to the West and that the world order would be reshaped by 'fault line conflicts' between civilizations. This book convinced many of the validity of 'containment' and lent support to the nationalist sentiment expressed in *China Can Say No*.

The 1999 NATO bombing of the Chinese Embassy in Belgrade, Yugoslavia further strengthened this new strain of nationalism. The incident caused the deaths of three Chinese journalists, and demonstrations against the US and the UK took place in major Chinese cities. Many people questioned not simply why NATO had bombed the embassy, but also whether this meant that China was still a weak country that could be easily bullied by Western powers, as in the nineteenth century. In anger and sorrow, many concluded that 'a backward country will be bullied' (落后就要挨打).

Following closely on the heels of the embassy bombing came a 2001 mid-air collision between a US Navy EP-3 surveillance plane and a PLA Navy interceptor fighter jet near Hainan Island in 2001, with the nationalistic reaction aroused even more powerful. When the American crew was eventually released by the Chinese authorities, an outraged Chinese public protested against the US and accused Beijing of weakness and kowtowing to the West.

In short, the major focus of Chinese nationalism from the 1990s onwards has been criticism of 'Western containment of China's rise' (西方遏制中国崛起). Strengthening China and protecting its sovereignty remain the main focus. A strong sense of national pride and self-confidence has also emerged, as China has grown into one of the world's leading economies and becomes an increasingly important player in world affairs.

To revive Chinese civilization and assure the rise of China has become the ultimate goal of contemporary Chinese nationalism, and competing against developed countries in the West has been a major facet of this mission. This determination, generated by both the ruling politicians and the general public, has strengthened the 'gold medal fever' and resulted in the consolidation of the elite sport system.

With the growth of the Chinese economy, the government's budget for sport increased dramatically and the elite sport-first strategy was reinforced. Great efforts were made to accomplish the goal of winning Olympic medals. In 1995, the Sports Ministry issued the 'Strategy of Winning Glory at the Olympics' (奥运争光计划) to emphasize the political importance of elite sport. It stated: 'The athletes have written a glorious chapter in Chinese Olympic history. Elite sport has been utilized to show the achievements of China's reform and opening-up and has inspired the whole nation' (Sports Ministry 1995).

The 'Strategy of Winning Glory at the Olympics' and the Juguo Tizhi have led to continuous success on the international sports stage. From the 1992 Barcelona Olympics to the 2008 Beijing Games, Chinese athletes climbed the gold medal ladder at record speed. In 1996, the national squad's performance at the Atlanta Olympics (16 gold, 22 silver, 12 bronze medals) inspired many and tightened the connection between sport, patriotism and nationalism. When the team returned to Beijing, President Jiang Zemin welcomed them and remarked:

> During the Games, Chinese athletes developed the spirit of patriotism, collectivism and revolutionary heroism. You followed the spirit of sportsmanship, solidarity and struggle, overcame so many difficulties and achieved so many successes. You have won great honour for your motherland. Your spirit of struggle has created an image of a hardworking and progressive China and shown the world the Chinese people's determination to revive the Chinese nation. You are fine sons and daughters of the Chinese people! (Liu 1996, 4)

The country's leading sports journal, *New Sport*, published a special feature on the Atlanta Olympics and encouraged all Chinese people to study the athletes' 'sporting spirits' – 'the motherland first' (祖国至上), 'solidarity and friendship' (团结友爱), 'professional dedication' (敬业奉献), 'scientific integrity' (科学求实), 'law abidance' (遵纪守法) and 'hard work' (艰苦奋斗) – and use them to aid the 'Four Modernisations' (Liu 1996, 4).

Olympic success continued into the twenty-first century, as did cultivation of the 'sporting spirits'. At the 2000 Sydney Olympics, the Chinese team for the first time ranked third in gold medals and total medals. Chinese media praised this 'historical breakthrough' (历史性突破) and highlighted its political significance. A commentator concluded: 'There is no doubt that China's sporting success reflects its great achievements in economic, political and cultural developments… sport is a mirror which reflects a nation's rise and fall… Chinese athletes' power comes from one source – the powerful Chinese national consciousness and patriotism… the spring of the great revival of the Chinese nation will arrive soon' (Fang 2000).

In 2004, China sent a big delegation of 203 athletes to the Athens Olympics. With 32 gold medals, the Chinese team came second to the US. The shining star was Liu Xiang, who took gold in the men's 110 m hurdles and thus became the first Chinese man to do so in track and field – bringing to mind Liu Changchun at the 1932 Olympics. He was also the first Asian male gold medallist in an Olympic sprint event (Editor 2004a). At the end of the Games, a *People's Daily* editorial again linked sporting success to national revival:

> When a country is powerful, its sport will flourish. The Chinese athletes' excellent performance on the Olympic stage is inevitable proof of our great achievements in economic reform and modernisation… The achievements at the Games have shown China's ability to stand proudly and independently among the other nations of the world… Chinese athletes will make more contributions to realising China's great revival.
>
> *(Editor 2004b)*

The 2008 Olympics saw the eruption of China's new nationalism. In total, 11,028 athletes from 204 countries and regions took part in the Games, with China beating the US to first place in the gold medal count. Many Chinese people believed that hosting the Beijing Olympics and the Chinese athletes' excellent performance demonstrated China's capability and position in the world. It coincided with China's remarkable economic achievements and was seen as powerful evidence of 'the rise of China' (中国崛起) and 'the great revival of the Chinese nation' (中华民族伟大复兴). Journalist Zheng Zhaokui (2008) commented: 'The 2008 Olympics is a coming-of-age ceremony for the 30 years of reform and opening up. The success of hosting the Games indicates that the dream of being a strong country is getting closer and closer'.

The sports patriotism debate

Surprisingly enough, despite the booming nationalism and patriotism expressed before and during the Beijing Olympics, the Games became the starting point for a shift in public perspective. Many intellectuals and journalists began to criticize gold medal fever, and there were strong calls for reformation of the sporting system. They believed that government's sport policy was at odds with the real Olympic spirit and that the state should focus on mass sport and people's fitness, rather than gold medals and the 'face' (面子) of the nation. A commentator argued:

> We feel proud that China won so many gold medals at the Olympics. However, the 'Gold Medal Champion, the Pride of China' slogan should not be advocated. We need a clear mind to rethink this issue from different perspectives. We are still far away from being a real global sporting power… Promoting mass sport and improving the physique of the people should be the new mission of Chinese sport.
>
> *(Qing 2008)*

Criticism of the elite sport system and gold medal fever continued in 2009, further triggered by the 2010 Asian Games in Guangzhou, China. More than 10,000 athletes from 45 countries and regions competed and Chinese athletes put on a dazzling display, dominating with 199 golds and topping the gold medal table for the eighth consecutive time (Gilmour 2010). This dominance was described by many Chinese commentators as a monopoly. Yang Ming, a journalist from the state-owned Xinhua News Agency, published an editorial entitled 'Some Thoughts on "No More Challengers"' to criticize what he saw as China's macabre gold medal fever. He argued:

> In recent years, we have over-emphasized gold medals and neglected the nature of sport. Sport belongs to the people. It should be used to improve people's health and physique. Unfortunately, we forgot this. Elite sport has dominated people's minds… During the past twenty years, China's elite sport has advanced, but at the cost of a decline in people's

fitness levels! Yes, we captured the world title at the 2008 Beijing Olympics. Now we have secured the Asian title again. What a mockery! I suggest that China send amateur players/college students to the next Asian Games and end the country's dominance in the Games.

(Yang 2010)

Yang Ming's article triggered a nationwide debate on elite sporting policy. Wei Jizhong, President of the Fédération Internationale de Volleyball, criticized Yang's suggestion of having amateurs represent China at the Asian Games. However, he agreed that the government should not put too much emphasis on gold medals, and made two recommendations: first, the government should reduce its investment in elite sport and let this depend more on the market and society. Second, the government should promote mass sport by providing more facilities and improving physical education at school (Editor 2010).

Another article, from the China News Service, commented: 'Some of Yang Ming's arguments are radical... However, his criticisms will push forward China's transformation from a global sporting power to a leading country in both elite sport and mass sport. It will benefit Chinese sport and, more importantly, facilitate the transformation of Chinese society' (Weng 2010).

In addition to criticism of gold medal fever, the Guangzhou Asian Games provoked a discussion on the relationship between sport and patriotism, and stimulated a new way of thinking – the idea of freeing sport from politics and having it serve the all-round development of society (Zhao 2010).

In general, the debate led to public calls for the promotion of sport for the masses. According to an online survey conducted by Yahoo China, the majority of Chinese internet users believed that the government should focus more on the development of mass sport and provide more resources, facilities and services to meet the demands of ordinary people (Yahoo 2012). The traditional 'Win Honour for the Country' idea is now challenged by many Chinese, especially the younger generations born since the 1970s.

Faced with mounting criticism from the media, academia and the general public, the government began to revise its sports policy and turn its attention to mass sport, and a strategy of pushing sport towards the market and having its fate depend on society's interests. A 'National Fitness Regulations' decree was issued in August 2009 to guide this reform (Editor 2009). Two years later, the Sports Ministry issued the 'Action Plan for the National Fitness for All Programme 2011–2015' to guide the development of mass sport. Former Sports Minister Yuan Weimin explained:

We should not put too much emphasis on gold medals. The time to win honour for the country through sporting success has passed. We have accomplished the old mission. Now we are going to set a new target: to improve people's physique and quality of life through sport. Promoting mass sport should be the priority.

(Zhao and Wang 2009)

Conclusion

In first half of the twentieth century, influenced by social Darwinism and militarism triggered by the two world wars, and fanned by anti-imperialism and nationalism, Chinese people believed that sport could help the country to recover its strength and win international recognition. In this period, the Olympic Games was an important vehicle for nation building and identity construction, giving birth to the first generation of Chinese Olympians competing for the country's honour and dignity.

Following the establishment of the PRC in 1949, sport and physical education were promoted by the Sports Ministry and its local commissions to train healthy and strong citizens. Sporting success became a symbol of achievements in socialist modernization. However, due to the 'Two Chinas' issue, the PRC withdrew from the Olympic movement in 1958, returning only in 1980. From then on, in the context of reform and opening up and the launch of the 'Four Modernisations', Chinese nationalism created a strong desire to achieve sporting success and create something that the whole nation could be proud of.

China's international status and national strength came to be measured by its sporting success, and each Olympic Games became a place where the Chinese people could witness the glory of their country and experience a sense of unity as a great nation. China, which had lost almost every war it was involved with in the nineteenth and first half of the twentieth century, began to strive to be victors in any kind of international competition, especially the Olympics.

From the late 1980s, intellectuals began to question the country's elite sport-first policy and morbid expectations of sporting success. Criticism of gold medal fever resumed after China topped the gold medal table at the Beijing 2008 Summer Olympics. This suggests that an increasing number of Chinese people are now moving away from extreme sports nationalism.

For a long time, sport was seen as one of the few areas where China could achieve excellence, shine in glory and defeat developed Western countries. However, after decades of rapid economic development, there are many other areas from which China can derive recognition, self-esteem, pride and self-confidence. The high-speed train network, the space station, rising technology giants like Huawei and Tencent, and achievements in industrialization, urbanization, modernization and poverty alleviation have all become new sources of pride and inspiration.

Today, rather than just focusing on the political significance of Chinese 'tracksuit ambassadors', i.e. successful athletes and teams, there is more of a focus on their personalities and individuality. Chinese Olympians that have shot to fame include not only gold medal winners but also those with notable personalities – such as swimmer Fu Yuanhui, who went viral for her colourful interviews and over-the-top facial expressions, and high jumper Zhang Guowei, who became well-known for his dance moves during competitions and his funny posts on social media. However, as long as athletes compete for their country and under their national flags, it will be impossible to separate sport and the Olympics from the influence of politics and nationalism. A better solution is therefore to encourage people to achieve a better understanding of elite sport and guide sporting nationalism in a positive direction, one that is more tolerant and open-minded.

Acknowledgement

Some parts of this chapter are taken from the author's co-authored monograph (with Fan Hong) *Sport and Nationalism in China* (Routledge, 2014).

References

English-language references

Alter, Peter. 1994. *Nationalism*. London: Edward Arnold.
Bairner, Alan. 2001. *Sport, Nationalism and Globalization*. Albany: State University of New York Press.
Cronin, Mike. 1999. *Sport and Nationalism in Ireland: Gaelic Games, Soccer and Irish Identity since 1884*. Dublin: Four Courts Press.
Editor. 2004a. "Brave Liu Xiang Did It! Chinese Fans Jubilant." *China Daily*, August 28.
Edwards, Harry. 1984. "Sportpolitics: Los Angeles 1984 – The Olympic Tradition Continues." *Sociology and Sport* 1 (2): 172–183.

Gilmour, Rod. 2010. "What the Asian Games and China's Dominance Tell Us about the London 2012 Olympics." *Telegraph*, November 30.
Hillman, Ben. 2004. "Chinese Nationalism and the Belgrade Embassy Bombing." In *Nationalism, Democracy and National Integration in China*, edited by Leong H. Liew and Shaoguang Wang, 65–84. Abingdon: Routledge.
Hoberman, John. 2004. "Sportive Nationalism and Globalization." In *Post-Olympism? Questioning Sport in the Twenty-First Century*, edited by John Bale and Mette Krogh Christensen, 177–188. New York: Berg Publishers.
Hobsbawm, Eric. 1992. *Nations and Nationalism since 1780: Programme, Myth, Reality*. Cambridge: Cambridge University Press.
Kellas, J. G. 1998. *The Politics of Nationalism and Ethnicity*. Basingstoke: Palgrave Macmillan.
Leiper, J. M. 1987. "Politics and Nationalism in the Olympic Games." In *The Olympic Games in Transition*, edited by Jeffrey O. Segrave and Donald Chu, 329–344. Champaign, IL: Human Kinetics.
Liu, Jun Toming. 2001. "Restless Chinese Nationalist Currents in the 1980s and the 1990s: A Comparative Reading of *River Elegy* and *China Can Say No*." In *Chinese Nationalism in Perspective: Historical and Recent Cases*, edited by C. X. George Wei and Xiaoyuan Liu, 205–231. London: Greenwood Press.
Lu, Zhouxiang. 2016. "Sport and Politics: The Cultural Revolution in the Chinese Sports Ministry, 1966–1976." *International Journal of the History of Sport* 33 (5): 569–585.
MacFarquhar, Roderick, ed. 1997. *The Politics of China: The Eras of Mao and Deng*. Cambridge: Cambridge University Press.
Rodziński, Witold. 1991. *The Walled Kingdom*. London: Fontana Press.
Tan, Tien-Chin. 2008. *Chinese Sports Policy and Globalization: The Case of the Olympic Movement, Elite Football and Elite Basketball*. Loughborough: Loughborough University.
Xu, Guoqi. 2008. *Olympic Dreams: China and Sports, 1895–2008*. Cambridge, MA: Harvard University Press.
Zhao, Suisheng. 2004. *A Nation State by Construction*. Palo Alto, CA: Stanford University Press.

Chinese-language references

Central Committee of the Communist Party of China 中共中央. 1984. "中共中央关于进一步发展体育运动的通知" (Notification on the Further Promotion of Sport), October 5.
Chen, Xiaoming 陈晓明. 1997. "「文化民族主義」的興起" (The Rise of "Cultural Nationalism"). 二十一世紀 (*Twenty-First Century*) 39: 35–45.
Dong, Shouyi 董守义. 1980. "奥林匹克旧事" (Old Stories about the Olympics). In 体育史料, 第二辑 (*Historical Materials for Sport, vol. 2*), edited by 体育文史资料编审委员会 (Committee of Historical Materials for Sport), 11–14. Beijing: People's Sport Press.
Editor. 1982. "为精神文明建设作出新贡献" (Contribute to the Development of Socialist Culture and Ethics). *China Sports Daily*, January 1.
Editor. 2004b. "五星红旗我为你骄傲" (I am Proud of the Five-Starred Red Flag). *People's Daily*, August 30.
Editor. 2009. "专访体育总局局长刘鹏: 促进全民健身活动开展" (Interview with Sports Minister Liu Peng: Facilitate the Development of Sport-for-all). *Xinhua News Agency*, September 7. http://www.gov.cn/jrzg/2009-09/07/content_1411128.htm.
Editor. 2010. "中国体育12个焦点问题, 魏纪中杨明展开激烈辩论" (12 Key Issues of Chinese Sports, Wei Jizhong and Yang Ming Had a Fierce Debate). 天府早报 (*Tianfu Morning Post*), November 30. https://sports.sohu.com/20101130/n278006185.shtml.
Editorial Department of《当代中国人物传记》丛书编辑部 (Biography of Contemporary Chinese Figures). 1993. 贺龙传 (*Biography of He Long*). Beijing: Contemporary China Press.
Fang, Yan 方焰. 2000. "评论: 中华民族伟大复兴的报春花" (Commentary: Spring Flower for the Great Revival of the Chinese Nation). *China News*, October 2. https://www.chinanews.com.cn/2000-10-02/26/49328.html.
Hao, Qin 郝勤, ed. 2006. 体育史 (*The History of Sport*). Beijing: People's Sport Press.
Hao, Qin 郝勤, ed. 2008. 中国体育通史, 第六卷, 1980–1992 (*The History of Sport in China Vol. 6, 1980–1992*). Beijing: People's Sport Press.
Liu, Changchun 刘长春. 1980. "我国首次参加奥运会始末" (The First Time Our Country Participated in the Olympics). In 体育史料 (*Historical Materials for Sport*), edited by 体育文史资料编审委员会 (Committee of Historical Materials for Sport), 221–228. Beijing: China Book Press.

Liu, Ji 刘吉. 1996. "弘扬中华体育健儿精神" (Promote the Spirit of Chinese Athletes). 新体育 (*New Sport*) 11: 4–5.

Luo, Shiming 罗时铭, ed. 2008. 中国体育通史, 第三卷, 1840–1926 (*The History of Sport in China Vol. 3, 1840–1926*). Beijing: People's Sport Press.

Ma, Licheng 马立诚. 1998. 交锋三十年 (*30 Years of Confrontation*). Beijing: Contemporary China Press.

Ministry of Education 民国教育部, ed. 1948. "第十一届世界運動會之參加" (Participating in the 11th World Games). In 第二次中国教育年鉴 (*The Second Yearbook of Chinese Education*), edited by 民国教育部 (Ministry of Education of the Republic of China), 1312–1317. Shanghai: Shangwu Press.

Qing, Xiang 庆祥. 2008. "奥运金牌大国的崛起与反思" (Rethink the Rise of China as a Major Olympic Power). *Sina Blog*, August 23. http://blog.sina.com.cn/s/blog_52e9bd8d0100akvp.html.

Rong, Gaotang, and Caizhen Zhang 荣高棠, 张彩珍. 1984. 当代中国体育 (*The History of Contemporary Chinese Sport*). Beijing: China Social Science Press.

Shan, Xu, and Fang Liu 山旭, 刘芳. 2008. "一个来自中国的电话改变1984年奥运会" (A Phone Call from China Changed the 1984 Olympics). 瞭望东方周刊 (*Observe the East Weekly*), August 26.

Shen, Siliang 沈嗣良. 1933. "第十届世界运动会和初次参加的我国" (At the 10th Olympic Games, Our Country Participated for the First Time). 体育研究与通讯 (*Sports Studies and News*) 1 (January): 7–14.

Song, Yan 宋燕. 2021. "接力, 不断向前奔跑" (Relay, Keep Running Forward). Xinhua, August 2. http://www.xinhuanet.com/comments/2021-08/02/c_1127721620.htm.

Sports Ministry 国家体委. 1993. "关于下发《国家体委关于体育体制改革的决定（草案）》的通知" (Notification on the Issuing of the "Sports Ministry's Decision on the Reform of the Sport System (Draft)"). In 中国体育年鉴1949–1991精华本, 下册 (*Yearbook of Chinese Sport 1949–1991, Vol. 2*), edited by 中国体育年鉴编辑委员会 (Editorial Team of the Yearbook of Chinese Sport), 107. Beijing: People's Sport Press.

Sports Ministry 国家体委. 1995. "奥运争光计划纲要1994–2000" (Strategy for Winning Medals at the Olympics 1994–2000), July 6.

Tan, Hua 谭华, ed. 2005. 体育史 (*The History of Sport*). Beijing: Higher Education Press.

Tang, Mingxin 湯銘新. 1999. 我國參加奧運滄桑史1896–1948 (*China and the Olympic Games 1896–1948*). Taipei: 中華台北奥林匹克委員會 Olympic Committee Press, 1999.

Wang, Meng 王猛. 1982. "王猛同志在1980年全国体育工作会上的工作报告" (Comrade Wang Meng's Report at the 1980 National Sports Conference). In 体育运动文件选编 1949–1981 (*Sports Policy Documents 1949–1981*), edited by 国家体委政策研究室 (Sports Ministry Policy Research Centre), 145–253. Beijing: People's Sport Press.

Weng, Yang 翁阳. 2010. "新华炮轰警醒中国 - 真正讽刺的是唯金牌论" (Xinhua Wakes Up China – First in the Gold Medal Tally, What a Mockery). *China News Network*, November 16. http://yayun2010.sina.com.cn/o/2010-11-16/13285312221.shtml.

Wu, Shaozu 伍绍祖, ed. 2002. 中华人民共和国体育史 (*The History of Sport in the People's Republic of China*). Beijing: China Book Press.

Yahoo. 2010. "投票: 您支持谁? 人民日报还是新华社?" (Opinion Poll: Who Do You Support? People's Daily or Xinhua News Agency?). *Yahoo Sport*, November 19, 2010. http://sports.cn.yahoo.com/ypen/20101119/91839.html.

Yang, Ming 杨明. 2010. "'一骑绝尘' 引发的思考" (Some Thoughts on "No More Challengers"). *Chengdu Business Daily*, November 15.

Zhang, Luping 张路平. 2010. "广州亚运会该卸下政治负担" (The Guangzhou Asian Games Should Unload the Political Burden). *QQ News*, October 13. http://sports.qq.com/a/20101013/000500.htm.

Zhang, Qixiong 張啟雄. 2010. "「法理論述」vs.「事實論述」:中華民國與國際奧委會的會籍認定交涉" (Law versus Facts: Negotiation on the Republic of China's seat in the IOC). 臺灣史研究 (*The History of Taiwan*) 17 (2): 81–129.

Zhao, Lingmin 赵灵敏. 2008. "奥运年的中国民族主义" (Chinese Nationalism in the Year of the Olympics). 南风窗 (*Nan Feng Window*) 15: 1–3.

Zhao, Renwei, and Jingyu Wang 赵仁伟, 王镜宇. 2009. "后奥运时代: 中国体育改革何去何从" (The Reform of Chinese Sport in the Post-Olympic Era). 半月谈 (*Bimonthly Talk*), December 11.

Zhao, Yu 赵瑜. 1988. 兵败汉城 (*The Defeat in SEOUL*). Beijing: China Social Sciences Press.

Zhao, Yu 赵瑜. 1988. 强国梦 (*The Dream To Be a Strong Country*). Beijing: Zuojia Press.

Zheng, Zhaokui. 2008. "北京奥运 中国崛起丰碑" (The Beijing Olympics, Monument to the Rise of China). https://www.chinanews.com.cn/olympic/news/2008/08-25/1359395.shtml.

Zhong, Weizhi 仲伟志. 2007. "1988: 强国梦" (1988: The Dream to be a Strong Country). 经济观察报 (*Economic Observer*), August 10.

13
CONFLICT IN XINJIANG
Nationalism, identity, and violence

Arabinda Acharya and Rohan Gunaratna

Introduction

Much of the current scholarship on the subject deals with the violence involving the Uighur in Xinjiang as a minority religious or political issue. There are differing perceptions of the conflict. While Beijing claims that the Uighur fight for a separate Muslim homeland is terrorism, a number of assessments regard this conflict as a result of repression and excessive human rights violations by the state or as a ruse by China to crush dissent. Though a few scholars implicate ethnicity or religion, or both, as causal factors in the conflict, the precise role of ethnicity or religion in shaping a distinct identity or nationalism (Uighur identity or Uighur nationalism) or the hardening of the same vis-à-vis the state is usually overlooked. Some have also discussed national identity and, more specifically, the formation and evolution of such an identity shaping the grass-root conditions that have sustained a 'low-level' insurgency and sporadic violence in Xinjiang (Gladney 2004a). However, these studies have not considered the role of religion, especially Islam, as one of the building blocks of a competing nationalism and identity that marks the distinction between the Uighur and the Han-Chinese. Additionally, analysis grounded in theory is generally absent from most literature on the conflict in Xinjiang.

This chapter makes two arguments. First, that political violence and terrorism encompass tensions involving the defense not only of basic rights but also of identities. Thus, the roots of the conflict in Xinjiang lie in the perceived or real threat to the minority identity of the Uighur, which is largely due to Beijing's suppressive policy toward these groups in the name of national integration. For the Uighur, China's nation-building process has posed a serious threat to the development and reproduction of their identity, triggering a growing desire to protect the same from complete extinction.

Second, the Xinjiang issue could be transforming itself from a separatist conflict to one which is a contestation for an equitable stake in the development and economic prosperity, along with a struggle to preserve indigenous identities. This is derived from the nature and the scale of the incidents, especially after the 2008 Beijing Olympics, and from an assessment of the capability of the Uighur groups, including the East Turkistan Islamic Movement (ETIM), also going by the name the Turkistan Islamic Party (TIP), which China accuses of being responsible for most of the violence in Xinjiang. Incidents of violence since 2009 reflect anguish and discontent at a local level more than organized acts of terrorism. ETIM exists and operates mostly outside China – mainly in Pakistan. The group has very limited resources and personnel, and scant support in Xinjiang to be a credible threat to China on its own. Groups like the Islamic Movement of Uzbekistan (IMU) and Al Qaeda support the cause of ETIM. But these groups have priorities and problems of their own separate from the Xinjiang issue. There is no indication that any of the other overseas Uighur organizations, including the World Uighur Congress (WUC), is inclined or capable of carrying out terrorist attacks in China. Thus, Beijing errs in continuing to see the discontent at the local level as a separatist or terrorist issue, which ultimately leads the Uighur to perceive the government response as demonic and extreme, fueling the cycle of distrust and violence.

In this chapter, Uighur nationality and Uighur identity are being used interchangeably.

International relations theory and conflict

Despite being a stage for recurrent violence and even terrorism with transnational dimensions, the sources and implications of the conflict in Xinjiang remain under-studied in the wider literature of international relations. This is not, however, unique to the Xinjiang conflict. Most of the Cold War literature on conflict is focused on superpower rivalry or on the territorial and demographic predicament of the post-colonial states, particularly the lack of alignment between the territorial boundaries and ethnic composition of new 'nation-states', and the concern for regime survival which underpinned these states' quest for 'national security' (Ayoob 1995). These explanations, however, remained grounded in the realist literature, focusing on the state and paying little attention to ideational elements, especially issues of national and group identities and their impact on the conflict (Acharya and Acharya 2006). Traditionally, realism has paid far less attention to internal conflicts than to regional or interstate conflicts. It tends to ignore domestic political systems and the ethnic and cultural identities which underpin many conflicts, such as the ones in Southern Thailand, Southern Philippines, Xinjiang, and in many other parts of the world.

Liberalism, which is more concerned with explaining the conditions of peace than the causes of conflicts, is also mostly focused on regional conflicts. From a domestic political perspective (one of the key tenets of liberalism), conflicts like the one in Xinjiang may be due to constraints that trap domestic political elites into seeing any challenge to their authority as a challenge to the state itself. Leaders in this situation often experience what Kalevi Holsti (1996) calls the 'state strength dilemma', in which, rather than seeking to resolve the conflict by providing opportunities for political participation or economic development, there is a tendency to use force as a means to achieve national integration (Poe et al. 2002).

A different explanation comes from the constructivist school which implicates culture and identity in promoting both conflict and cooperation. Here, the focus is on contested national identities as a source of dispute and conflict. Thus, the roots of the Xinjiang conflict could be in the identity dissonance that sustains itself due to state policies that feed the grievances and the perception of marginalization among the Uighur.

Identity dissonance is most acute in societies where sizable minorities with different ethnic, religious, or linguistic roots live. Here, minorities concern over their share in the political space, control of resources, and protection of their identities often contribute to conflicts (Gurr 2001). There is also a strong and positive correlation between ethnic conflict and ethnic nepotism measured by ethnic heterogeneity (Vanhanen 1999), as with religious polarization and internal conflict (Reynal-Querol 2002). With religious polarization, conflicts tend to be protracted as there can be a perception that the conflicting issues are indivisible and not amenable to settlement through negotiations (Svensson 2007). In respect of Xinjiang, for example, Islam could be said to be at the root of the hardening of the Uighur identity that has manifested in violence against the Han-Chinese and the state.

Issues involving identity are further aggravated where national integration or state consolidation is at stake. National identity is often defined in terms of 'the dominant group's [the majority] values and culture, with other groups on the periphery tending to be left out' (Snyder 2000). Domination, as Snyder points out, works if the power of the dominant group is so overwhelming as to preclude rational resistance or when it is tolerated by those who are deprived of power yet decide that being second-class citizens is better than being first-class rebels. In an ethno-nationalist or religious context, identity conflict and strife are the outcomes when domination fails or is not tolerated by the minority community.

State consolidation also impacts the existing state, society, and institutional structures and arrangements that affect minorities, which, in turn, can invoke uncertainty and perception of threat among the minorities. This is especially problematic when ethnic or religious minorities are seen as potential threats to national integration by the ruling elite, who are invariably drawn from the majority community (Winichakul 1994).[1]

In Xinjiang, the conflict is thus rooted in the perceived injustice arising out of unfulfilled minority needs and interests that has resulted in incomplete integration. Beijing's failure to address minority group's fundamental needs, provide space for participation in governance, and ensure an equitable distribution of resources and benefits (Lederach 1978, 8) also feeds the perception of injustice, leading, in turn, to the identity dissonance which is driving and sustaining the conflict.

A human security perspective

A concomitant perspective emerges from the human security discourse – looking at the 'individual' or a particular social group as against the 'state' per se. Emphasis on the individual is not new; in fact, it was one of the dominant security discourses before September 11, 2001 (9/11) terrorist attacks in the United States of America. At the core of the debate was the tension between the 'security of the state' and the 'security of the individual'. Though not mutually exclusive, 'security for whom?' was at the heart of the pre-9/11 security debates. For the traditionalists, the focus was on the state, security of which is indivisible and commensurate with national survival (including protection of its sovereignty and territorial integrity), force projection, and capabilities. Proponents of human security argued, however, that security is reducible to an objective referent and set of threats; what was really threatened is not an abstraction like 'the state' but the material well-being of the individual (Meyers 1993, 12). Hence, the emphasis was on more general threats to human existence and ways to overcome them.

The concern for human security grew out of a campaign to limit the salience of state security vis-à-vis the rights of the individual. One of the key arguments of the proponents of the human security discourse was that the state is not a good or sufficient provider of human security. From a human security perspective, the focus on state security conveys 'a profoundly false image of reality', causing states to 'concentrate on military threats' and ignoring 'other and perhaps even more harmful dangers', thus 'reducing [individual's] total security' (Ullman 1983, 129). An extreme manifestation of this discourse was the argument that the state is, in fact, a threat to the security of the individual. Therefore, the proponents of human security emphasized the need to substitute the state as the referent object of security with the 'individual', to be accomplished by limiting state activities and widening the range of people's choices and the means to pursue those choices in a safe environment. Here, the emphasis was on the individual or, in a broader sense, on societal security, as against the security of the state. The focus was on internal and long-term structural sources of instability, the costs of violent conflict, social problems, and human health and welfare, tackling which would strengthen the capability of societies to deal with conflicts in a more comprehensive and effective manner.

But 9/11 exposed the limitations of the human security discourse. The scale of response required to cope with security concerns involving post-9/11-era terrorism was beyond the competency of any agency except the state. The state was very much back at the center of security and public policy discourse. This was manifested in aggressive policies to hunt down terrorists with almost disproportionate use of force, as seen in Afghanistan and Iraq. Several countries also used public angst against terrorism to equate indigenous anti-state discontent with terrorism and justify extreme measures against those involved. Beijing's attempt to put the Uighur resistance in the broader context of the global conflict and justify hard-hitting measures against those involved should be seen in this context.

Identity and security

A human security perspective comes from the fact that political violence and terrorism encompass tensions involving the defense not only of basic rights but also the well-being of ethnic and religious groups and especially their national and religious identities (Giddens 1990; Shaw 1994). According to this school of thought, ethnic conflicts and terrorism, particularly those involving identity, 'always [occur] in conjunction with the denial of basic human rights' (Buzan 1991). In other words, ethnic conflict is more likely to occur when basic rights are systematically violated by the state (Callaway and Harrelson-Stephens 2006). These discourses suggest a 'causal link' between ethnic conflict or terrorism and violations of human rights – understood as 'political and civil', 'security', and 'subsistence rights' (Clarke 2008, 272).

The relationship between human security and identity, and ethnic conflict and terrorism is explained, to a great extent, by the scholars of the Copenhagen School. Barry Buzan (1991) identified five security elements – military, political, economic, societal, and environmental – each of which, either individually or collectively, has the potential to threaten state security. Later, modifying the typology, Ole Waever, Buzan, and others proposed a duality of state and societal security, instead of five sectors of state security. According to these scholars, societal security is a referent object of state security in its own right, and both societal and state securities are related to the issue of 'survival'. The survival of the state relies on the 'maintenance of its sovereignty', whereas the survival of the society depends on the 'maintenance of its identity' (Waever et al. 1993, 24–25). State security is generally concerned with protecting the sovereignty of the state from external threats, while societal security concerns situations where societies perceive a threat in terms of identity (ibid.). The existence and development of identity lie at the heart of the concept of societal security and distinguish it from that of state security. As Michael Clarke (2008, 273) noted, 'If a state loses its sovereignty, it will not survive as a state, while if a society loses its identity, it will not survive as a society'.

Society is about the 'self-conception of communities and individuals identifying themselves as members of a community'; it is 'fundamentally about identity' (Waever et al 1993, 24). According to Waever et al (ibid., 25), the key to society is the set of ideas and practices that 'identify individuals as members of a social group'. In other words, societies are constituted by a sense of social identity, where its most 'basic social identity' is what enables its members to consider themselves as 'one sector' where the state is to be used. As Buzan, Waever, and de Wielde (1997, 2) put it, societies are 'politically significant ethnic/national and religious groups' which are able to manifest themselves as 'distinct referent objects of security'.

Societal identity is usually defined along several dimensions – language, religion, culture, and history. The identity of a particular social group is often produced by comparison with the dominant identity value of another. Some societies may need 'others' to remind themselves of their own self-identity. 'Who we are' can often mean 'who we are not' (Roe 1999, 194). At any given point in time, only one, or a few, of these dimensions will be the 'dominant identity value' or identity marker for a given society (Roe 2005). For example, in Xinjiang, Islam has been a dominant Uighur identity value as it distinguishes the Uighur from the Han-Chinese, who are traditionally Confucian and Buddhist. In other words, it is Islam, not ethnicity alone, which has shaped the Muslim identity vis-à-vis the Han-Chinese. But for the country as a whole, the 'dominant identity value' can be something other than religion or ethnicity. Here, concerns for state consolidation, protection of territorial integrity, and preservation of national sovereignty can outweigh narrow considerations of ethnicity, religion, or language. Nevertheless, such considerations – ethnicity, religion, or language – constitute the fault lines that may generate conflicts involving minorities.

The key question that the Copenhagen School scholars are criticized for is whether identity is 'solid and constant' or whether it is a process, 'fluid and changing' (ibid., 42). This is what Helena Lindholm (1993), for example, characterizes as the debate between 'constructivism' and 'culturalism'. The argument is that identities are socially constructed, but once constructed they can be regarded as 'temporarily fixed' for a certain period of time until they are 'reconstructed' again (Roe 1999, 193). Identities are constructed by people and groups through numerous processes and practices; they can be recognized as objects in the sense that most members of the group adhere to and behave in accordance with such processes and practices. However, they are relative in terms of time. Societal identities are objective, while they are in a dynamic process.

Threats to identity

How is a given individual's or society's identity threatened? There is no easy answer as it is difficult to distinguish a 'perceived threat' from what can be objectively assessed as threatening. Often, real threats may not be 'accurately seen', whereas perceived threats may not be real, but still have real effects (Waever et al. 1993, 43).

There are nevertheless a number of ways to identify threats to individual or societal security which are relevant in the context of the Xinjiang conflict. First, a particular society can feel threatened when there is a perception that its 'we' identity is being put in danger or when its ability to sustain its essential character or reproduction of that identity is at risk. What underscores the notion of societal security is the ability of a society to sustain its essential character under changing conditions and against actual or possible threats to this ability (Clarke 2008, 272). Besides 'sustainability', it focuses on acceptable conditions for the 'evolution' of societal identities, including traditional patterns of language, culture, association, religion, and national customs among others (ibid., 273).

Threats to the reproduction of a society can occur through the sustained application of 'repressive measures' against the expression of the identity. For instance, if the organizations for reproducing language, religion, and culture are forbidden to operate, identity will not be inherited by the next generations (Roe 1999, 195). In this respect, threats to an identity can range from the 'suppression of its expression' to the 'interference' with its ability to 'reproduce itself' (Yuchao and Dongyan 2006, 25). In practice, these threats may occur where there are prohibitions or restrictions on the use of language, names, and dress; closure of places for education and worship; and even the killing or deportation of members of the particular society.

Second, policies and practices of governance can bring different ethnic, religious, cultural, and linguistic groups to loggerheads. In many cases, it has been found that the desire of particular minorities to protect their identities often comes into conflict with the demands of loyalty to the state dominated by the majority group. It is the contradiction in these two desires that constitutes the root cause of conflicts with ethnoreligious connotations. Except for rare situations where a minority group has a monopoly on power, most minorities are in a disadvantageous position vis-à-vis the majority in their respective states (ibid., 25). They may be at risk of political marginalization, economic deprivation, forced assimilation, cultural oppression, physical oppression, and even genocide (ibid.).

In many cases, significant sections of the relevant national minorities do not perceive their current political status as 'legitimate', which is the reason why some ethnic minorities demand national self-determination and may even resort to terrorist activities under particular circumstances (Connor 2002, 37). Such a demand can be a reaction to the nation-building process, which is seen as an exercise of state power dominated by the majority to build a national identity (Yuchao and Dongyan 2006, 26). In a state-building process, assimilation is often a national demand, and the rights and interests of minorities are compromised as they are subordinated to the dominant political entity (ibid.). Clearly, some policies and commitments to nation-building can be perceived as not only violations of human rights but also threats to identity. It is the real or perceived threats to identity that generate discontent among disadvantaged minorities. Thus, the conflict involving the Uighur is a manifestation of threats to identity rather than just human rights violations (ibid., 52).

Although ethno-nationalist and minority conflicts are usually rooted in the perception of threat and marginalization, such perceptions are not always the primary generators of conflict. Conflicts in which the rights and political/social viability of particular communities are central issues are not evidence of ethnic chauvinism or of hatred for 'the other'. But 'identity conflicts emerge with intensity when a community, in response to the unmet basic need for social and economic security, resolves to strengthen its collective influence and to struggle for political recognition' (Regehr 2007). Such conflicts are reflections of a more fundamental political and social distrust, borne out of a community's experience of economic inequity, political discrimination, and human rights violations (ibid.).

The distrust which has now led to militancy in Xinjiang is rooted in neglect, military repression, official insensitivity to local concerns, and forcible attempts to impose uniformity of social behavior on the Uighur. Moreover, there has always been a clash between the cultural values of the dominant group and the religio-cultural identity of the subordinate one. Protests and violence in Xinjiang can be seen as manifestations of a social movement by the Uighur competing against the state and the majority community, which they perceive as a threat to their Islamic and Uighur identities.

Against this background, this chapter will now examine how the conflict in Xinjiang is more of an issue of identity dissonance than a terrorist threat as commonly perceived and aggressively peddled by Beijing. The aim is to deconstruct the claim that the Xinjiang issue is inextricably linked to transnational terrorism, which justifies hard-hitting measures by the state. It will also demonstrate that unrest and violence in Xinjiang may be the outcome of grievances at a local level that could be addressed with more nuanced measures than Beijing's largely ineffective and counter-productive current responses.

Construction of the Uighur identity

The early years

It is held by most Chinese historians that Islam was introduced to China in AD 651, during the Tang Dynasty (AD 618–907) (Shoujiang and Jia 2004; Guanglin 2005). This was 18 years after the death of Prophet Mohammed, during the Caliphate of Uthman ibn Affan, the third caliph of Arabia Othman (AD 644–656). Development and spread of Islam during all the dynasties in China followed periods of positive and negative responses from respective rulers, with the Ming Dynasty (AD 1368–1644) being seen as the 'golden age of Islam in China' (Rahman 1997), and the most difficult period being during the Qing Dynasty (AD 1644–1911) (Israeli 2002, 8). When the Qing Dynasty was overturned in 1911, the Republic of China announced that the country belonged equally to the Han, Hui (Muslim), Man (Manchu), Meng (Mongol), and Zang (Tibetan) peoples. The authorities allowed further autonomy in the northwestern regions with significant Muslim populations, and large areas came under control of Muslim warlords, leading to frequent intra-Muslim and Muslim-Han conflicts.

A new wave of Islamization in China occurred during the Republican period (1912–1949). Wahhabi-inspired reform movements, known as the Yihewani in Chinese (from Ikhwan), became popular in some parts of China. The most prominent of the movements at that time was the Xinjiao (new school) led by a Chinese Muslim named Ma Wanfu (1849–1934) (Berlie 2004, 29). The Islamic reforms at that time were noted for their critical stance toward both traditionalist Islam and Sufism. Due to increased interaction between Chinese and Middle Eastern Muslims, Chinese Muslims began to reevaluate their traditional ideas of Islam, which led them to unify under the concept of the Islamic Ummah. Several associations were founded nationwide by Muslim intellectuals educated in these new schools. These included the Chinese Muslim Mutual Progress Association (Beijing, 1912), the Chinese Muslim Educational Association (Shanghai, 1925), the Chinese Muslim Association (1925), the Chinese Muslim Young Students Association (Nanjing, 1931), the Society for the Promotion of Education among Muslims (Nanjing, 1931), and the Chinese Muslim General Association (Jinan, 1934) (ibid., 34). These organizations had considerable social effects during the decades of turmoil in China following the Communist revolution and became the foundation stones for the construction of a distinct Muslim identity, especially in areas that came to be dominated by the Uighur in China's northwest.

Having won the civil war against the Nationalists, the Chinese Communist Party (CCP) declared the establishment of the People's Republic of China (PRC) on October 1, 1949. In the early years of the PRC, Beijing proclaimed that the political rights and religious freedom of all nationalities were equally protected. The CCP attempted to avoid any conflict with Muslims in the interests of stabilizing the domestic situation and developing relations with Muslim countries in the international arena (Israeli 2002, 288–289). Following the CCP's political-administrative structures, the Islamic Association of China (Zhongguo Yisilanjiao Xiehui) was founded in 1953 as an organization for regulating Islamic practices (ibid.).

The CCP's policies toward Muslims were generally moderate and tolerant in the first decade of the People's Republic. However, these were followed by periods of harsh ideological and political oppression of Muslims and other religious minorities during the Great Leap

Forward (1958–1961) and the Cultural Revolution (1966–1976). The oppression of religious leaders and the destruction of mosques by the Red Guards caused increasing grievances among Muslims. Revolts against the government broke out in many areas where Muslims were concentrated. Since the advent of Deng Xiaoping's reform and opening up program (gai ge kai fang) in 1979, there has been a considerable moderation of the religious policies. Muslims were allowed more rights and freedom, such as going on the pilgrimage (Hajj), and mosques were reopened and reconstructed in urban and rural areas. Growing manifestations of an 'Islamic revival' are evident in the Muslim communities of contemporary China (ibid.).

Going forward

The PRC comprises 56 officially recognized nationalities (minzu), including the Han-Chinese who are the majority. Islam is the religion of ten of the 55 minority groups. The largest of the ten Muslim groups is the Hui – descendants of Central Asian, Arabian, and Persian Muslim immigrants who intermarried with Han-Chinese and have largely integrated into Chinese society. The second largest Muslim group forms the majority of the residents of Xinjiang Uygur Autonomous Region (XUAR), comprising the Uighur, Kazak, Dongxiang, Kirgiz, Salar, Tajik, Uzbek, Baoan, and Tatar. In fact, the ethnic classification of this group is a challenge; it is difficult to distinguish these traditionally nomadic and agriculturalist people in clear terms. The languages used by these groups belong to the eastern or Altay branch of the Turkic family. The commonality in the languages among different sub-groups indicates their ties with Central Asian Turks (Millward and Perdue 2004, 33). Unlike the Hui, the majority of whom speak Chinese, are scattered throughout China and are deeply influenced by Chinese culture, the Turkic Muslims are very different from the Han-Chinese in terms of language, culture, religion, and historical experience. These groups have retained their unique dress, customs, language, culture, and most significantly, their faith (ibid.). The largest group among them is the Uighur (Uyghurs, or Weiwuer 维吾尔 in modern Chinese).

Islamic identity among the minority nationalities in China is far older than the ethnic concepts recognized by the Chinese government. Like any other Muslim minority residing in non-Islamic states, China's Muslims have faced a series of issues in terms of their identity. The identity of China's Muslims is closely related to the millennial existence of Islam in a China dominated by the Han-Chinese. China's national integration policies have also put considerable stress on minorities. Beijing's policies toward the Muslim minorities have been presented in various forms over different periods of time. The conflict between the state's attempts at assimilation and Muslim's desire for the protection of their identities has presented a persistent threat to the ethnic harmony and public security of the PRC.

The emergence of ethnic conflict in Xinjiang is closely related to the formation of Uighur identity, which is a twentieth-century phenomenon (Gladney 1996, 446). The Uighur had originally practiced Buddhism (Samolin 1964, 73; Gladney 2004a, 210–214; Millward and Perdue 2004, 40–43).[2] The Buddhist Uighur resisted conversion to Islam until the Islamization of the Tarim Basin between the tenth and sixteenth centuries (Gladney 2004a, 210). Due to the displacement of the Buddhist Uighur, the term Uighur disappeared from historical records for centuries (Rudelson and Jankowiak 2004, 299). The modern Uighur, as a single ethnic nationality, integrates a number of different Muslim Turkish peoples from the oases where the dispersed population migrated (Moneyhon 2004, 6). But even though 90 percent of the indigenous inhabitants of Xinjiang are called Uighur, there are a number of sub-groups that maintain their primary loyalties not to the collective whole of their ethnic group but to their tribes and oases. Therefore, the term Uighur, representing the ethnicity of the people of Turkic origin, does not provide a uniform identity (ibid.). As Rudelson and Jankowiak (2004, 299, 303) noted, the identities of Xinjiang's Turkic groups, especially the Uighur, are 'inherently weak' and 'in constant flux', making them vulnerable to assimilation. Moreover, the process of distinguishing ethnic groups by 'officially designated identities' (Gladney 2004b, 102) has contributed to the particularity and complexity of the Uighur identity.

Though Islam is an essential aspect of Uighur identity, it is not the only source of Uighur confrontation with the Chinese state. To some extent, the people recognized as Uighur Muslims emerged out of opposition to other nationalities, especially the Han-Chinese (Gladney 2004a, 210). After 1949, the salience of Islamic identity was reinforced by government policies that aimed at the integration of all nationalities under the dominance of the Han-Chinese. Uighur consider China's nation-building process an aggressive attempt at total assimilation of their Islamic religion and Turkic culture. The term 'Sinicization' is frequently used to refer to China's attempts at integration. As Erkin Alptekin, the former president of the WUC, once stated, 'the Chinese want to replace us with their own people as colonists, and assimilate those of us who remain, wiping out our culture' (Schwartz 2004).

One of the ways to confront the myriad challenges to identity is to emphasize those ethnic, religious, linguistic, and cultural characteristics that differentiate the minority from the dominant community (Fuller and Lipman 2004, 339). Given the sociopolitical oppositions with which the Uighur were confronted, it is not surprising that Islam became an important 'cultural marker' of Uighur identity (Gladney 2004a, 218). As Denise Helly (1985, 107) argued, Islam has played a critical role as a 'unifying ideology' of resistance, rather than a 'pure resurgence of Islamic orthodoxy'. Mosque attendance and Islamic education, for example, became essential ways for the Uighur to strengthen the distinctions in their identities vis-à-vis the Han-Chinese. Islam also contributed to the hardening of the Uighur identity relative to the Han-Chinese, in particular, and to the state as a whole.

Government policies and Uighur identity

The identity of Muslims in China has evolved in the course of continuous interaction between Islam and Chinese society over 1,300 years. This interaction has enabled the majority of the Muslims, especially the Hui, to generally integrate into Chinese society and live in apparent harmony with the Han majority. The Uighur, however, consider China's nation-building process, especially its policy of integration, as a serious threat to their identity, which has triggered violent reactions. The disparity between Beijing's policies and the political demands of the Uighur has further highlighted the essential role of Islam for Muslims in Xinjiang. Over time, Islam has become the rallying point in this battle of contested identities.

Since 1949, Beijing has made efforts to consolidate 'the unity and cooperation' among the various nationalities in the country (*Zhongguo de Shaosu Minzu Zhengce jiqi Shijian* 1999). Accordingly, the government has gradually established its political and military control over Xinjiang. Under the preferential policies adopted by the CCP and the central government, Xinjiang's economy developed, and the living standards of the people in the region generally improved. Relations between the Han and the Uighur people were harmonious in general but deteriorated due to radical sociopolitical policies toward the Muslim minorities starting with the 'Hundred Flowers Campaign'. The campaign, which encouraged open criticism of and diversity of views on important sociopolitical issues (Worden et al. 1987), resulted in widespread criticism of the CCP by people from all walks of life. More specifically, minority communities expressed their discontent against the dominance of Han-Chinese officials in autonomous governments and demanded greater autonomy, and even independence, for their respective autonomous regions (Millward and Tursun 2004, 92–94). This led to a reversal of the 'open-minded' stance which was replaced by the hard-line Anti-Rightist policy (*fanyou douzheng*) of 1957. The CCP launched severe crackdowns on the opposition, who were regarded as anti-revolutionaries and rebels. Many Muslim officials, especially the Uighur, came under attack for their 'local nationalism'. Thousands of non-Han political elites were removed from office and dispatched to labor camps for 'thought reform' (ibid.). The Anti-Rightist campaign marked the beginning of ideological intolerance and political oppression of religious and ethnic minorities.

During the Great Leap Forward period, the CCP fully abandoned the gradualist approach to minority matters and launched the religious reform movement, with a distinct anti-Islamic stance. The 'complete blending of all the nationalities' was considered by the party as critical to 'continued socialist construction' in regions where ethnic minorities were concentrated (ibid.). The Chinese Muslim Association was abolished in 1958. The Islamic Institute was closed, and the formal study of Islamic literature and law was banned (DeAngelis 1997). Islamic and other religious organizations across China were shut down and their publications stopped. The government promoted Chinese in education, while the languages of the minorities were sidelined (Minglan 2001). The destruction of Uighur education, for example, was reflected by the frequent changes in writing systems in Xinjiang. In 1956, the Cyrillic alphabet was introduced by the government in Xinjiang to replace the Arabic alphabet, which had been used by the Uighur for hundreds of years. In 1960, the Cyrillic alphabet was replaced by a modified Latin alphabet (ibid.).

The minority policies of the CCP focused on immediate and total assimilation during the Cultural Revolution as well (Gladney 1995, 372). Under the extreme left policies, religion was especially suppressed, so were minority languages and cultural traditions. The Uighur in Xinjiang, like other Muslim minorities throughout China, saw their religious texts and mosques destroyed, their religious leaders persecuted, and individual adherents punished (DeAngelis 1997, 161). Reflecting on the measures, an article in the *Izvestiya*, a Russian periodical, commented that the ultimate goal of China's nationalities policy was 'the complete liquidation of national characteristics and distinctions' (Gladney 1995, 374).

To some extent, Deng Xiaoping's reform and opening program (*gaige kaifang*) restored minorities' rights by providing opportunities 'to preserve or reform their own customs and ways' (Israeli 1981, 901). A number of mosques were rebuilt and reopened, while some received state funds for repairs. Muslims were allowed to practice their faith, and classical and devotional Islamic literature was printed and distributed, subject to legal restrictions. Islamic schools at all levels were reopened. Religious festivals were allowed to be observed with the full holiday allowance. Almsgiving (*zakat*) was permitted again under the condition that the funds were used to support Islamic instruction, mosques, and the poor (DeAngelis 1997, 163). In 1984, the central government reintroduced the Arabic script for the Uighur. The Uighur written language was allowed for popular publications. They were also allowed to use local vernacular in their radio and television broadcasts.

Several preferential policies were also implemented to improve the economies in minority autonomies (*Constitution of the People's Republic of China*).[3] In Xinjiang, the government invested in infrastructure, such as building energy and transport networks, in order to create better conditions for economic development and provide more job opportunities for the local population. State policies also encouraged minority people to develop individual businesses and private trading began to flourish due to liberalized regulations.

Though socioeconomic incentives were considered a long-term antidote against separatist aspirations, in the case of Xinjiang, the economic improvement contributed to greater tensions between the Uighur and the Han-Chinese. One reason for Uighur dissent was the rapid growth in Han-Chinese migration into Xinjiang. The migration of millions of Han-Chinese into Xinjiang dramatically transformed the demographic structure of the region, which was considered by indigenous Muslims as a serious threat to their religion and culture as it was to their socioeconomic development. The official policy was to attract qualified professional, technical personnel, and agricultural workers from all over the country to engage in infrastructure and other development projects in Xinjiang. The PRC claimed that this policy was designed to promote economic development and stability in Xinjiang rather than demographic change. There were also large inflows of self-initiated migrants who competed in the region's labor market (Howell and Fan 2011).

Most of these Han-Chinese migrants settled down permanently in the main cities in northern Xinjiang, particularly in Urumqi, and on state farms all over the region. This is very evident from the demographic changes in the region. In 1949, the total population of Xinjiang was 4.33 million, of whom 75.9 percent were Uighur and only 6.7 percent were Han-Chinese (*Kua shiji de Zhongguo renkou – Xinjiang fence* 1982). The 2010 census puts the Han-Chinese population at 8.74 million – 40.1 percent of the total of 21.8 million in Xinjiang. Though the exact number of Uighur in Xinjiang (as per 2010 census) is not available, it is estimated to be about 10.4 million, representing 47.7 percent of the total population of the region. Even though the Han-Chinese are still a minority in the region, their population grew from 6.7 percent in 1949 to 40.1 percent in 2010, whereas the Uighur population shrank from 75.9 percent to 47.7 percent during the same period.[4] As Iredale et al. (2001) put it, this represents the largest demographic change to occur in a major region of China since 1949.

There was also pronounced inequality between the Han-Chinese and Uighur people in terms of their respective share in socioeconomic development. From the Uighur perspective, the migration of the Han-Chinese to XUAR has limited the employment of the local Uighur because the majority of them do not speak Mandarin Chinese and few are as well educated as the Han-Chinese immigrants. Though state-orchestrated Han-Chinese migration to Xinjiang ceased in the 1980s, these migrants continue to receive priority over minorities in employment (ibid.; Sun and Fan 2011; Weimer 2004; Pannell and Schmidt 2006). As a result, the Han-Chinese nearly dominate trade and commerce and usually have well-paying jobs and higher-ranked positions in the government, the party, and the military in XUAR (Bhattacharya 2003, 369). The Uighur also see how the Han-Chinese residents live in newer neighborhoods and have access to schools with better teachers and facilities (ibid.). This has led to a sense of injustice and anti-Han-Chinese and anti-government feelings among the Uighur. The attacks since 2009, whether in XUAR or outside, were manifestations such as frustration and feelings of marginalization.

Moreover, many Uighur believe that the presence of vast numbers of Han-Chinese, who are not Muslims, has posed a serious threat to their religious identity. They are worried that their descendants will be drawn away from the traditional path of Islam by the 'atheism' and 'materialism' of the Han-Chinese migrants.

The discontent among the Uighur is thus an outcome of an expression of intense bitterness against Beijing's policies toward its minorities, especially its intolerance of Islam (Rahman 1997, 53), combined with the growing disparity in socioeconomic development vis-à-vis the Han-Chinese. The Uighur believe that their freedom of association and expression, particularly involving religious issues, has been limited by Beijing's distinctly hostile policies toward minority communities. They are dissatisfied with Beijing's regulations governing mosque construction, Islamic publications and media, the content of religious education, exit requirements for pilgrimages, and the arrests and interrogation of Imams and the Ulema deemed to be 'subversive'. Similarly, the industries and infrastructural projects that tap Xinjiang's enormous gas, oil, and mineral deposits are seen as exploitation of the local resources to the detriment of the local population (Yom 2003) due to the dominance of the Han-Chinese in such ventures. As Bovingdon (2004) argues, the persistence of inequality between the Han-Chinese and Uighur has fueled ethnic-based conflicts and separatist movements in the region.

To a great extent, the radical policies against Muslim minorities reflected the 'sharpened assimilationist' agenda embraced by the CCP and the state (Millward 2007, 263). Unfortunately, the state remained oblivious to the fact that these policies produced results which were exactly opposite to what was intended. In increasing numbers, the Uighur rallied around their religion as a core element in their struggles for rights and even independence. Islam became a unifying force for the Uighur. Decades of social turbulence and harsh treatment of Muslims worsened the relationship between the Muslim minorities and the Han-Chinese majority. In particular, Uighur opposition to the Han-Chinese and the state began to be manifestly radical and violent. For the Uighur, violence was seen to be the only mode of political praxis that could actively, frequently, and aggressively contest Chinese authority while powerfully reaffirming their societal identity (Yom 2003).

Unrest in Xinjiang and Beijing's response

Since the early 1990s, Uighur opposition to Beijing has manifested in waves of violence. The first wave was marked by the Baren incident in 1990, followed by unrest and bombings between 1991 and 1993. The second wave manifested in Yining in 1997, which triggered a series of bombings in Urumqi, Khotan, Korla, and Kashgar in 1997 and 1998. The third and most recent one was the ethnic clash in Urumqi in July 2009, reportedly killing 197 people, including both Han-Chinese and Uighur. The deadliest rioting was in August and September 2009 following syringe attacks on Han-Chinese civilians and police in Urumqi. The years 2011 and 2012 also witnessed bouts of violence in the region, though on a lesser scale.

The Chinese response to the unrest in Xinjiang continues to reflect insensitivity and arrogance. The 'strike hard' (*yanda*) campaign against what the official establishment describes as the 'three evil forces' of 'terrorism, separatism, and splittism' was characterized by a huge military deployment, followed by killings, arrests, and swift executions. Even though the East Turkistan militants are too few, disorganized, and dispersed to pose any real threat to Chinese control over Xinjiang, Beijing's response has been disproportionately aggressive. This is not discounting the fact that the government has made significant investment to better economic conditions in the region. But the ruling elite's aggressive demeanor, overreaction to any form of protests, and high sensitivity and low threshold to any criticism of the responses to the unrests in the region have aggravated the situation.

According to some analysts, China's 'religious policy is primarily a policy of control' (Lap-Yan 2006). The priority that the Chinese government places on economic development and the tools that it employs to ensure national stability are seen to be trampling the identity – cultural, religious, and ethnic – of the Uighur as a minority community. For example, plans to relocate residents of 'Old Kashgar' to new housing estates were perceived to be a threat to Uighur identity. While the authorities claimed that this would improve their quality of life, the Uighur considered this as an attack on their cultural heritage and a well-orchestrated state attempt to break up their communities as the project involved the destruction of ancient Islamic architectural sites (Tharoor 2009). The attacks in Kashgar on July 31, 2011 were triggered by the demolition of traditional Uighur houses in the center of the old city. In the words of Henryk Szadziewski of the Washington-based Uyghur Human Rights Project, 'This is the Uighurs' Jerusalem. By destroying it, you rip the soul out of a people' (Tharoor 2009).

Several attacks outside the XUAR were either claimed by Uighur militant organizations or attributed to them by the Chinese but denied by the alleged organizations. Many of the militant organizations, like ETIM and TIP, and their leaders operate outside of China, and most have little or no control over the Uighur population in the XUAR. The dynamics changed a bit with the involvement of groups like Al Qaeda and the Islamic State of Iraq and Syria (ISIS). For example, some of the attacks outside the XUAR during the months leading up to the 2008 Beijing Olympics, like the March 8, 2008 attempted hijacking of flight CZ6901, involved elements from Pakistan (Elegant 2008), while attacks on March 1, 2014 at Kunming railway station in Yunan province involved 'Sunni extremists' belonging to a single terrorist cell who were on their way to wage jihad outside of China (*VOA News* 2014). Nevertheless, these and other attacks further hardened Beijing's policy of repression against the Uighur in the XUAR – 'to de-emphasise Uyghur ethnicity and try to instill a greater sense of "Chineseness"' (AFP 2014). As a column in the Economist asserted, 'China, which prefers to play down the role of its policies in Xinjiang in generating discontent, has long sought to discredit its Uygur critics by linking them to terrorism' (T.P. 2014). Many Uighur from the XUAR had reportedly been attracted to the so-called Caliphate claimed by ISIS and went to serve the ISIS. Understandably, their activities were entirely outside of China and the possibility of the return of these entities to the XUAR is remote.

Protests or acts of terrorism?

Despite what some analysts describe as the 'transnationalization' (Gladney 2004a, 112–118) of their ethnoreligious identity, which makes the Uighur particularly susceptible to radical ideas that are at the root of much of terrorist violence in many other parts of the world, the Islam practiced by the Uighur remains substantively moderate. This explains why extremist groups like ETIM have not been able to establish a firm foothold in Xinjiang, which is evident from the lack of sophistication in attacks, particularly during and after the 2008 Olympics. This is despite the fact that ETIM has received advanced training in terrorist tradecraft under the tutelage of the IMU and Al Qaeda.

The majority of the violent incidents in Xinjiang that Beijing has characterized as acts of terrorism do not appear to be carried out by organized entities with high skill sets and transnational support networks. For example, in August 2008, the perpetrators drove a dump truck into a group of People's Armed Police Force (PAPF) officers during the morning exercise and used knives and a handgun. In August and September 2009, a group of Uighur stabbed civilians and police officers in Urumqi with hypodermic syringes which were rumored to carry HIV or anthrax (subsequently found to be untrue). In July 2011, two Uighur drove a vehicle into a Han-Chinese crowd, following it up with knife attacks. In 2012, attacks were carried out with knives. These attacks do not reflect centralized planning and control or tactical sophistication, which are hallmarks of organized and group-based resistance.

Moreover, it is evident that much of the violence in the region is stemming from the divide between Han-Chinese and the Uighur communities, with the Uighur acting out their anger and frustration against the Han-Chinese and the state. Increasing Han-Chinese migration into Xinjiang, forced relocation of Uighur to other parts of the country, and the widening gap between the Han-Chinese and Muslim minorities in terms of socioeconomic development has reinforced the sense of marginalization that has produced widespread discontent among the Uighur. The Uighur see the Han-Chinese usurping political and economic opportunities in the region. The Han-Chinese see the Uighur as an ungrateful race that, despite pro-minority policies of the government, such as exemption from the one-child policy and heavy economic investment in the region, continue to be rebellious and often violent. Such divergent perceptions have polarized both communities and led to hostility and violence in recent years. This has been made even more complicated because Beijing continues to conflate extremist ideology with particular religious practices, cracking down on both at the same time. Attempts to voice discontent are construed as anti-state actions, and the ensuing military response is often highly disproportionate.

Conclusion

In Xinjiang, China faces the conundrum of bridging the gap between the center and the periphery, which has become complicated by a unique set of needs and interests of a minority community that is fiercely attempting to protect its identity. Over the years, Beijing has implemented policies of integration supplemented with force and general repression. The Uighur consider these aggressive attempts at integration an affront to their religion and culture, which has led to concerns of dilution or even outright destruction of their identity.

As discussed earlier, the perception of a threat to the identity of a given social group can undermine its overall security. Threats to identity can manifest in many forms. One is the inability of a given minority to sustain its essential character due to policies of the majority that are perceived to be deliberately hostile. In the case of the Uighur in Xinjiang, for example, Beijing's attempt to dilute the demography of the region through sponsored migration of Han-Chinese is seen as a hindrance to the sustainability of the essential character of Muslim identity.

Similarly, the use of repressive measures, together with limited autonomy and lack of opportunity for political expression, has hindered conditions that facilitate the evolution of societal identities. This, in turn, is seen as limiting the ability of the given minority to reproduce itself. As discussed earlier, if the minority community is inhibited in its ability to reproduce its distinct language, religion, and culture, there will be a concern that their identity will not be inherited by the next generation. Most of the policies of the government – introduction of standard Mandarin Chinese in the education system, restrictions on cultural and religious practices, and demolition of ancient homelands, to name a few – are being seen as clear attempts to wipe out the Uighur identity.

China's repressive campaigns might have reduced the number and scale of violent incidents in the short run, but the root of ethnic tension and Muslim opposition to the state has not been eliminated. History clearly illustrates that Islamic identity, especially a convoluted perception of the same, is a 'potential instrument of political destabilization' (Newby 1988, 947) among Muslim communities under a non-Muslim government. The threat from more organized entities like ETIM or, for that matter, Al Qaeda or ISIS, is of limited consequence, at least at present. In additional to Islamic nationalism represented in the present day, the political concept of Pan-Turkism which dates back to the 1880s also impacts the Xinjiang region uniquely. Pan-Turkism advocates for a culturally and nationally unified Turkic people. While this idea may seem utopic to some, the hope of an actualized Pan-Turkic nation has driven some of the actions of separatist Uighurs. Beijing needs to appreciate that extremism and terrorism often take root due to marginalization and repression – perceived or otherwise. This becomes more aggravated when the identity of a particular population is at stake.

Beijing also needs to distinguish local, ethnic, or religious grievances from terrorist motivation. It must be able to recognize protests which are against specific grievances reflecting anguish and discontent at a local scale and that can be easily resolved without disproportionate use of force. The situation in Xinjiang has not and does not portend to be a problem of massive proportions. The way to establish enduring peace is for the government to empathize with challenges to Uighur identity and address associated concerns.

Acknowledgment

Some parts of this chapter are taken from the authors' co-authored monograph (with Wang Pengxin) *Ethnic Identity and National Conflict in China* (Palgrave Macmillan, 2010).

Notes

1 A similar analogy can be drawn from the conflict in Southern Thailand where ethnicity has been at the root of a historical sense of vulnerability among Siamese rulers.
2 The term Uighur was first used to identify Turkic nomadic societies practicing shamanism and Manichaeanism in Mongolia. Later, it referred to the name for a sedentary oasis society practicing Buddhism. It was also used as a linguistic designation to distinguish one branch of Old Turkish. Chinese originally used Uighur and later Hui Hu for all Turkic Muslims.
3 This was laid down in the constitution, which proclaimed that "the state gives financial, material and technical assistance to the minority nationalities to accelerate their economic and cultural development." *Constitution of the People's Republic of China*, Article four (Beijing: National People's Congress, 1982).
4 The statistics for 2010 are compiled from different communiqués of the National Bureau of Statistics of China. Though the population of Han-Chinese is available in official communiqués, the same for the Uighur is difficult to come by. The number of the minority population in Xinjiang in 2010 is the sum of the same population in 2000 (8.3 million) and number by which this population has increased (2.9 million) between 2000 and 2010. See "Communiqué on Major Data of the Xinjiang Uygur Autonomous Region in 2010 the sixth national census [1]," *Xinjiang Uygur Autonomous Region Bureau of Statistics*, May 6, 2011.

References

AFP. 2014. "Crackdown after China Killings may Backfire, Say Experts." March 2. https://www.thefreelibrary.com/Crackdown+after+China+killings+may+backfire%2c+say+experts.-a0360245381
Acharya, Amitav, and Arabinda Acharya. 2006. "Kashmir in the International System." In *Kashmir New Voices, New Approaches*, edited by W. Pal Singh Sidhu et al. London: Lynne Rienner Publishers.
Ayoob, Mohammed. 1995. *The Third World Security Predicament: State Making, Regional Conflict and the International System*. Boulder, CO: Lynne Rienner.
Berlie, Jean A. 2004. *Islam in China: Hui and Uyghurs between Modernization and Sinicization*. Bangkok: White Lotus Press.
Bhattacharya, Abanti. 2003. "Conceptualising Uighur Separatism in Chinese Nationalism." *Strategic Analysis* 27 (3): 357–381.
Bovingdon, Gardner. 2004. *Autonomy in Xinjiang: Han Nationalist Imperatives and Uyghur Discontent*. Washington, DC: East-West Center.
Buzan, Barry. 1991. *People, States and Fear: An Agenda for Security Studies in the Post-Cold War Era*. London: Harvester Wheatsheaf.
Buzan, Barry, Ole Wæver, and Jaap de Wilde. 1997. *Security: A New Framework for Analysis*. Boulder: Lynne Rienner.

Callaway, Rhonda L., and Julie Harrelson-Stephens. 2006. "Towards a Theory of Terrorism: Human Security as a Determinant of Terrorism." *Studies in Conflict and Terrorism* 29 (7): 773–796.

Clarke, Michael. 2008. "China's 'War on Terror' in Xinjiang: Human Security and the Causes of Violent Uighur Separatism." *Terrorism and Political Violence* 20 (2): 271–301.

Connor, Walker. 2002. "Nationalism and Political Illegitimacy." In *Ethnonationalism in the Contemporary World*, edited by Daniele Conversi. Abingdon: Routledge.

DeAngelis, Richard C. 1997. "Muslims and Chinese Political Culture." *The Muslim World* 87 (2): 151–168.

Elegant, Simon. 2008. "China's Curious Olympic Terror Threat." *Time*. March 10.

Fuller, Graham E., and Jonathan N. Lipman. 2004, "Islam in Xinjiang." In *Xinjiang. China's Muslim Borderland*, edited by S. Frederick Starr. London and New York: M.E. Sharpe.

Guanglin, Zhang. 2005. *Islam in China*. Beijing: China Intercontinental Press.

Giddens, Anthony. 1990. *The Consequences of Modernity: Self and Society in the Late Modern Age*. Cambridge and Stanford: Polity Press/Stanford University Press.

Gladney, Dru C. 1995. "Islam." *Journal of Asian Studies* 54 (2): 371–377.

Gladney, Dru C. 1996. "Relational Alterity: Constructing Dungan Hui, Uygur, and Kazakh Identities across China, Central Asia, and Turkey." *History and Anthropology* 9 (2): 445–477.

Gladney, Dru C. 2004a. *Dislocating China: Muslims, Minorities and Other Subaltern Subjects*. London: C. Hurst & Co. Ltd.

Gladney, Dru C. 2004b. "Chinese Programme of Development and Control: 1978–2001." In *Xinjiang. China's Muslim Borderland*, edited by S. Frederick Starr. London, New York: M.E. Sharpe.

Gurr, T.R. 2001. *People versus States: Minorities at Risk in the New Century*. Washington, D.C.: United States Institute of Peace Press.

Helly, Denise. 1985. "The Identity and Nationality Problem in Chinese Central Asia." *Central Asia Survey* 3 (3): 99–108.

Holsti, Kalevi J. 1996. The State, War and the State of War. Cambridge: Cambridge University Press.

Howell, Anthony, and Cindy Fan. 2011. "Migration and Inequality in Xinjiang: A Survey of Han and Uyghur Migrants in Urumqi." *Eurasian Geography and Economics* 52 (1): 119–139.

Iredale, Robyn R., et al., 2001. *Contemporary Minority Migration, Education, and Ethnicity in China*. Cheltenham, UK: Edward Elgar Publishing.

Israeli, Raphael. 1981. "The Muslim Minority in the People's Republic of China." *Asian Survey*, 21 (8): 909–919.

Kua shiji de Zhongguo renkou – Xinjiang fence, 1994. The Population of China Towards the 21st Century: Xinjiang Volume Beijing: Zhongguo tongji chubanshe, 1994.

Lap-Yan, Kung. 2006. "National Identity and Ethno-religious Identity: A Critical Enquiry into Chinese Religious Policy with Reference to Uighurs in Xinjiang." *Religion, State and Society*. 34 (4): 375–391.

Lederach, John Paul. 1997. *Building Peace: Sustainable Reconciliation in Divided Societies*. Washington, DC: United States Institute of Peace Press.

Lindholm, Helena. 1993. "Introduction: A Conceptual Discussion." In *Ethnicity and Nationalism: Formation of Identity and Dynamics of Conflict in the 1990s*, edited by Helena Lindholm. Gothenburg: Nordnes.

Meyers, Norman. 1993. *Ultimate Security: The Environmental Basis of Political Stability*. New York: W. W. Norton & Company.

Millward, James A. 2007. *Eurasian Crossroads: A History of Xinjiang*. New York: Columbia University Press.

Millward, James A., and Peter C. Perdue. 2004. "Political and Cultural History through the Late 19th Century." In *Xinjiang: China's Muslim Borderland*, edited by S. Frederick Starr. New York: M. E. Sharpe.

Millward, James A., and Nabijian Tursun. 2004. "Political History and Strategies of Control, 1884–1978." In *Xinjiang: China's Muslim Borderland*, edited by S. Frederick Starr. New York: M. E. Sharpe.

Moneyhon, Matthew D. 2004. "Taming China's 'Wild West': Ethnic Conflict in Xinjiang." *Peace Conflict, and Development: An Interdisciplinary Journal* 5 (5): 2–23.

Newby, L. J. 1998. "The Begs of Xinjiang: between Two Worlds." *Bulletin of the School of Oriental and African Studies* 61 (2): 278–297.

Pannell, Clifton W., and Philipp Schmidt. 2006. "Structural Change and Regional Disparities in Xinjiang, China." *Eurasian Geography and Economics* 47 (3): 329–352.

Poe, S.C., C. N. Tate, and D. Lanier. 2000 "Domestic Threats: The Abuse of Personal Integrity." In *Paths to State Repression: Human Rights Violations and Contentious Politics*, edited by C. Davenport. Latham, MD: Rowman and Littlefield.

Rahman, Yusuf Abdul. 1997. "Islam in China 650–1980 CE." *Islam Awareness*. http://www.islamawareness.net/Asia/China/islchina.html

Regehr, Ernie. 2007. "It's Not Really a Matter of Hate." *Disarming Conflict*. http://www.igloo.org/disarmingconflict/itsnotre/.

Reynal-Querol, Marta. 2002. "Ethnicity, Political Systems and Civil Wars." *Journal of Conflict Resolution* 46 (1): 29–54.

Roe, Paul. 1999. "The Intrastate Security Dilemma: Ethnic Conflict as a 'Tragedy'?" *Journal of Peace Research* 36 (2): 183–202.

Roe, Paul. 2005. *Ethnic Violence and the Social Security Dilemma*. Abingdon: Routledge.

Rudelson, Justin, and William Jankowiak. 2004. "Acculturation and Resistance: Xinjiang Identities in Flux." In *Xinjiang. China's Muslim Borderland*, edited by S. Frederick Starr. London, New York: M.E. Sharpe.

Samolin, William. 1964. *East Turkistan to the Twelfth Century: A Brief Political Survey*. The Hague: Mouton & Co.

Shaw, Martin. 1994. *Global Society and International Relations*. Cambridge: Polity Press.

Schwartz, Stephen. 2004. "Beleaguered Uyghurs: Oppressed Minority, Terrorist Recruits, or Both?" *Weekly Standard* 9: 39. http://www.uyghuramerican.org/articles/59/1/Beleaguered-Uyghurs-Oppressed-minority-terrorist-recruits-or-both.html.

Shoujiang, Mi, and You Jia. 2004. *Islam in China*. Beijing: China Intercontinental Press. 2004.

Snyder, Jack. 2000. *From Voting to Violence: Democratization and Nationalist Conflict*. New York: W. W. Norton & Company.

Sun, Minjie, and Cindy Fan. 2011. "China's Permanent and Temporary Migrants: Differentials and Changes, 1990–2000," *The Professional Geographer* 63 (1): 1–21.

Svensson, Isak. 2007. "Fighting with Faith: Religion and Conflict Resolution in Civil Wars." *Journal of Conflict Resolution* 51 (6): 930–949.

Tharoor, Ishaan. 2009. "Tearing Down Old Kashgar: Another Blow to the Uighurs." *Time*, July 29. http://www.time.com/time/world/article/0,8599,1913166,00.html.

T.P. 2004. "Terror in Kunming." *The Economist*, March 3. https://www.economist.com/analects/2014/03/03/terror-in-kunming.

Ullman, Richard. 1983. "Redefining Security," *International Security* 8 (1): 129–153.

Vanhanen, Tatu. 1999. "Domestic Ethnic Conflict and Ethnic Nepotism: A Comparative Analysis." *Journal of Peace Research* 36 (1): 55–73.

VOA News. 2014. "Train Station Attackers Were Trying to Leave China for Jihad." March 5, 2014. https://www.voanews.com/a/train-station-attackers-were-trying-to-leave-china-for-jihad-official/1864422.html.

Waever, Ole, B. Buzan, M. Kelstrup, and P. Lemaitre. 1993. *Identity, Migration, and the New Security Agenda in Europe*. London: Pinter.

Wiemer, Calla. 2004. "The Economy of Xinjiang." In *Xinjiang. China's Muslim Borderland*, edited by S. Frederick Starr. London, New York: M.E. Sharpe.

Winichakul, Thongchai. 1994. *Siam Mapped: A History of the Geo-Body of a Nation*. Chiang Mai: Silkworm Books.

Worden, Robert L., Andrea Matles Savada, and Ronald E. Dolan. eds.1987. "Policy toward Intellectuals." In *China: A Country Study*. Washington, DC: GPO for the Library of Congress. http://countrystudies.us/china/72.htm.

Yom, Sean L. 2003. "Uighur flex their muscles," *Asia Times*, January 23, 2003. http://www.atimes.com/china/DA23Ad01.html.

Yuchao, Zhu, and Blachford Dongyan. 2006. "Ethnic Disputes in International Politics: Manifestations and Conceptualizations." *Nationalism and Ethnic Politics* 12 (1): 25–51.

"*Zhongguo de Shaosu Minzu Zhengce jiqi Shijian*." National Minorities Policies and its Practice in China. Beijing: Information Office of the State Council of PRC, 1999. English translation at http://lt.china-office.gov.cn/eng/zt/zfbps/200405/t20040530_2910831.htm.

Zhou Minglan. 2001. "The Politics of Bilingual Education in the People's Republic of China since 1949." *Bilingual Research Journal* 25 (1–2): 147–171. https://www.tandfonline.com/doi/abs/10.1080/15235882.2001.10162788

14
'DEAR ASIAN FRIENDS, WE WANT TO BUILD PEACE'

Rightwing nationalism, internationalism, and Honda Koei's teaching about the Asia-Pacific War, 1965–1973

Yoshiko Nozaki

Introduction

In the past several decades, notably through its textbook screening system, the Japanese government has (more or less constantly) attempted to whitewash Japanese war atrocities that were perpetrated during the Asia-Pacific War (1931–1945)[1] from rightwing nationalist perspectives. One of the state efforts, or its *de facto* censorship of school textbooks, has focused on descriptions of war suffering within/out Japan; however, internationally it is the removal of war atrocities Japan caused in Asia and Pacific that has become well known. Because of this, international audiences have often assumed that Japanese teachers have never been able to teach about the war from critical, internationalist perspectives. In fact, however, a tradition of such critical, internationalist teaching has existed in the face of challenges of governmental pressures and societal attitudes hesitant to fully support it.

A modern nation-state governs its people in part by creating and disseminating narratives. One important site of such efforts is education of younger generations in schools, especially teaching history (and social studies) in classrooms. After all, education that takes place between teachers and students is one of the most effective ways to promote a national narrative, and to make and remake certain identities into the national identity. However, as Raymond Williams reminds us, the actual processes of identity ('consciousness' in his term) formation needs to be understood as complex and flexible (Williams 1980, 38–40), and so it is important to examine closely and carefully the process(es) of identity formation at local sites—in this chapter, history lessons in classrooms.

Benedict Anderson (1983) has argued that a nation is a cultural artifact constructed historically and politically by narratives of nation and that modern educational systems play a powerful role in shaping and disseminating such narratives. In history education in schools, narratives are ubiquitous, and some narratives of nation constitute part of 'official knowledge' (Nozaki & Inokuchi 2000)—the knowledge that the state sanctions, directly or indirectly, and diffuses through the schools it controls (Apple 2000).

Narratives invite people to form certain identities. Official narratives of nation, however, do not always—or universally—produce the intended official national identity. As some critics in postcolonial studies have argued, national narratives—and so the actual national identity that is formed—are always unfinished, ambiguous products that require constant writing and narrating, and so they often involve contradictions and incoherence. Moreover, counter-narratives can and do emerge to disturb the officially prescribed boundary of the imagined national community (Bhabha 1990), and oppositional or alternative forces would try to spread the counter-narratives. It follows that rivalry national narratives compete in a society, and such a competition, or struggle, can take place 'vertically' from the powerful (e.g., the state) to the people as much as 'horizontally' through the everyday 'interactions of individuals, groups, and institutions,' in which actors (e.g., schoolteacher) at local, grassroots levels may serve as important 'nodes' (Kaufmann 2016, 7). An empirical question arises here: What happens when a schoolteacher introduces to his/her students counter-narratives that attempt to cross that imaginary—but official—national boundary, and what kinds of identities emerge as a result?

This study takes an in-depth look at history education about the Asia-Pacific War taught by Honda Koei (1933–1995), a Japanese historian and educator. In the late 1960s and early 1970s, as a junior high school social studies teacher, he broke new ground by teaching about the Asia-Pacific War from the viewpoints of its Asian victims.[2] It was epoch-making because, prior to his practice, the issue of the war atrocities Japan committed had been rarely addressed directly in classrooms. Honda's history lessons put into practice from 1965 to 1973 involved various learning activities, including his students writing letters to imaginary Asian friends and conducting research on the damage the war caused. While meeting with a considerable degree of criticism and ambivalence on the part of the students' parents, Honda's practice resulted in the publication of a series of volumes, including one entitled *Bokura no Taiheiyo Senso* [The Pacific War, as We View It].[3] Although his practice has long inspired many Japanese educators, from elementary school to university, who attempt to counter the nationalist interpretation of the war through education, it also highlights many difficulties confronting postwar Japanese critical, internationalist teaching about the war.

A historical context: narrating the nation in postwar Japan, 1950s–1960s

In Japan during the mid-1950s, conservatives and rightwing nationalists who seized the state sought to impose as official knowledge their narrative of the Asia-Pacific War, one that represented the war in a 'positive' light. The positive light in practice meant telling nothing about the damages, sufferings, and victims, domestic or foreign, of the war. The Ministry of Education (MOE) began to use its textbook screening system (*kyokasho kentei*) to censor school textbooks. For example, as early as 1952, the MOE disapproved a history textbook for high schools authored by historian Ienaga Saburo (1913–2002) on several grounds, including one that too much space had been given to the war and its aftermath. The ministry suggested that the entire description be dropped because students had experienced the events themselves. Although the text was approved in the next year with no changes, it met a more severe censorship in the early 1960s, which led Ienaga to bring court challenges—the first lawsuit was filed against the Japanese government in 1965, and the second lawsuit was filed against the MOE in 1967 (Nozaki 2008, 32–48). (As discussed below, Honda would testify for Ienaga in the first lawsuit.)

In these years, the MOE also objected strongly to texts that referred to the wartime suffering of people in Korea, Nanjing, Hiroshima, Nagasaki, or elsewhere. In addition, the state changed the textbook adoption system in ways that made texts with small market shares unprofitable, which led to the discontinuation of some critical and internationalist texts and the increase of the state's influence on the market and texts. Because of the Cold War—or, more precisely, a series of military conflicts in Asia—these state actions met no objection from Japan's Asian neighbors (for further discussion, see Nozaki 2008; Nozaki & Inokuchi 2000).

Throughout the 1950s and early 1960s, the Japanese ordinary people's discourses on the war were mixed, and some remained silent (Yoshida 1995, 78–104).[4] Despite the state's strong rightwing nationalist revisionism, the history textbook authors attempted to include updated and/or verified accounts of historical events, resulting in some contradictions and incoherence. For example, most texts still included a passage, however brief, on Chinese resistance to Japanese imperialism, and another on the US atomic bombing and its aftermath, because it was simply impossible to narrate the nation's defeat otherwise. In addition, many texts depicted Emperor Hirohito exclusively as a peacemaker who ended the war, without ever, of course, addressing the question—why didn't he stop the war at the outset? (see also Nozaki 2008, 66–68).[5]

It should be noted that public views on the war also reflected Japan's postwar history. For one thing, the issues of Japan's war responsibility were obscured internationally and nationally, as the emperor not only escaped the prosecution of the Tokyo Tribunal but also remained on the throne, reinventing himself as the symbol of a peaceful Japanese nation. For another, no matter how much of a 'liberation' the US-led occupation was, people still felt that the nation was 'occupied.' Thus, when the occupation ended in 1952, there was a sudden growth of grassroots nationalism everywhere, though this by no means involved a (re)glorification of the war. Scars from the war—for some physical and for others mental—were still too fresh and painful for the ordinary Japanese to examine that period critically, and the official narrative of the war did not seem to encompass many people's war experiences (Yoshida 1995; Dower 1999). Above all, local actors who had played leadership roles in the war efforts continued to take active roles, but now in speaking of 'democracy' (Yoshimi 1987; Nagahama 1984). The change in their language did not involve changes in their values, inclinations, and styles of being (see also Gluck 1993, 76–79). In other words, at grassroots levels, nationalism was renewed and everyday forms of imperialism and fascism with affection for the emperor were still alive.

A transformation began to take place in the late 1960s, and continued into the 1970s, as Japanese began to recognize the damages the Asia-Pacific War had caused Asian countries and peoples (Yoshida 1995, 106–164). This was due largely to the Japanese rethinking of their own war experiences in light of the Vietnam War, which allowed them to realize the two facets of their own war experience—that they were simultaneously victims and victimizers. The US war planes and bombers flying from Okinawa to Asia, and the US military presence in other Japanese cities, reminded the Japanese of their own past aggression against Asia, and media reports of Vietnamese civilian sufferings, often with vivid photographs, reminded them of their own war suffering (Yoshida 1995, 129–131). Public views on the war became more clearly divided into three groups: those who saw it wrong, just, and inevitable (Yoshida 1995, 125).[6]

In this context, counter-narratives of the war began to emerge and disturb the officially constructed boundaries of the imagined community. Various grassroots oral history projects recorded the accounts of ordinary Japanese war experiences (e.g., US air raids on many cities [Saotome 1971], US atomic bombings of Hiroshima and Nagasaki, and the Battle of Okinawa [Okinawa-ken 1975]), and some municipal governments (e.g., Okinawa Prefecture), not the

Japanese government, funded some of these projects.[7] In 1971, journalist Honda Katsuichi, having been 'impressed by US media coverage of the Vietnam War, especially on atrocities committed by the US forces,' began to report in a similar manner on Japan's wartime wrongdoings in China (Honda 1972, 4–5).[8] Around the same time, Emperor Hirohito's visits to Europe (September to October, 1971), which met in many places with resentment, triggered historian Inoue Kiyoshi's interest in conducting serious scholarly research on the active role of the emperor in the drive to war, and he later published a volume that was the first scholarly work on the topic (Inoue 1975). In terms of school textbooks, Ienaga had a victory in his second lawsuit at the Tokyo District Court in 1970s, which compelled the MOE to relax its criteria for textbook screening (Nozaki 2008, 41–48).

These developments inspired progressive teachers to include counter-narratives of the war in their lessons from critical perspectives[9]; however, the issue of the Japanese war atrocities was seldom taught in schools, and there were several reasons for that: a new framework for critical examination on the war was clearly still in formation and 'facts' were still in the process of discovery; the parents of school-age children were the generation of the war years, who had participated, willingly or not, in the Japanese war effort; and the conservative and rightwing nationalists, if not ultra-nationalists, succeeded in formation of the dominant power bloc at the national level (see also Murai 1994, 418–419). History education about the war became a contested site for narrating the nation, and critical teachers such as Honda experienced its difficulties, contradictions, and uncertainties.

Honda Koei and his teaching about the war in the late 1960s

Honda Koei was born in 1933 and raised in poverty. In 1945, he was a junior high school student mobilized to construct an air base near his school in Muroran, Hokkaido—a northern city with a major military port. He was an ordinary boy, a product of the time who believed in the Japanese Empire, and Japan's defeat in the Asia-Pacific War caused him to experience a sensation in which 'the "divine nation Japan" inside me began to come crashing down' (Honda 1994c, 20).

Although his parents, father a carpenter and mother a peddler, wanted him to get a job after high school graduation, he decided to go on to college and entered Waseda University, a private university in Tokyo. He took various part-time jobs, struggled to make ends meet, fell ill, but managed to excel at the university. He was a brilliant student of history, and his research on the Kabasan Incident—a radical political uprising that took place in 1884 in Japan—was highly regarded in academic circles for its close examination of local primary sources and contribution to a new understanding of the event. He published several journal articles as an undergraduate student, but it was teaching history that he found most challenging, and when he graduated in 1956, he became a social studies teacher at a junior high school in Tokyo (for his childhood and college days, see Honda 1994c, 13–85). While busy with gathering and studying teaching materials (Honda 1967, 1), he continued to write and publish about history education in relation to his teaching practices.

In planning his history lessons, Honda had two curriculum ideas: taking international perspectives (in his words, 'emphasizing world history'), and allocating more lesson time to modern/contemporary history (Honda 1973, 11). In the mid-1960s, Honda became interested in teaching about the Asia-Pacific War from the perspectives of its Asian victims, and so he conducted library research to find teaching materials but found no good data (in part because the Japanese government had conducted no study or survey on such matters officially) (Honda 1973, 35). School textbooks, given the state's *de facto* censorship, contained almost no material on the topic. According to Honda, no junior high school history textbooks authorized by the MOE contained descriptions of Japanese war atrocities—except one text that referred to Korean forced laborers (as Honda testified in Ienaga Saburo's first lawsuit at the Tokyo District Court) (Kyokasho Kentei Sosho o Shiensuru Zenkokurenraku-kai 1991, 872).

In 1965, when he was teaching history to eighth-graders, Honda encountered an issue of *Chuo Koron*, a monthly general opinion magazine, at a bookstore. The issue featured a series of articles concerning Japanese war atrocities as represented in textbooks of various Asian countries. It also included several translations of actual textbooks from Thailand, China, the Philippines, Burma, Indonesia, and South and North Korea (Yamamoto 1965, 84–92; Niijima 1965, 93–97; Ozawa 1965, 97–101). Honda made a handout for his classes, entitled 'How People of Asia View the Pacific War,' including several quotes from the translations.

At first, Honda attempted to use the handout before starting his lessons on the war, having his students read and discuss it. However, when they reacted with silence (reactions ranged from speechlessness to moans), he understood that the information was too shocking for his students and decided not to press them to discuss it but to revisit it later. After studying the war for several weeks, Honda again had his students direct their attention to the handout and asked them to write a letter to 'friends in junior high schools in Asia.' Writing a letter in this context meant writing not a real letter, but an essay. However, we should note, it placed his students in a certain imaginary boundary in which they had to speak and write as members of a nation, 'Japanese.'

The students wrote rather long letters, spelling out their thoughts 'unceasingly.' According to Honda, the common theme was one of apology, with the students asking their imaginary Asian friends to understand that not all Japanese wanted the war (Honda did not refer to the exact number of students who spoke this way). More than several students also pointed out that responsibility for the war lay with those who supported emperor-centered imperialism and fascism. Some students wrote that Japan was reborn and successful after the war and expressed their desire to help Asian countries. A few others referred to a continuation of wars in Asia (i.e., Korea and Vietnam) and hoped to join with their Asian friends to eliminate war. Honda felt that his students' hearts ached because of Japanese wartime atrocities and that they 'wrote with all their heart' (Honda 1973, 38–39).

Three years later, in 1968, Honda again taught the history of the Asia-Pacific War to another cohort of eighth-graders.[10] This time he provided the handout only at the end of his lessons—just before his students were to write a letter to their Asian friends. In their letters, most of his students stressed the point that Japan was now different from its past and had become a peaceful nation. They cited the renunciation of war expressed in Article 9 of the 1946 constitution as the basis for the new, peaceful Japan. Honda noticed, however, that the letters were more abstract than those written in 1965, and that they showed less recognition of Japan as the aggressor in the war (Honda 1973, 39–40).

He also noticed that several students wrote that Japan had also experienced hardships, and others stated that the war had been inevitable. A few suggested that perhaps the textbooks depicted Japan in a worse light than it deserved, and another few even suggested that the Asian textbooks were telling lies. These views dismayed Honda (as such language did not appear in 1965). However, he also realized that these were similar to what adults with little knowledge of the war (or of Asian experiences of the war) might say. He took a lesson from this teaching practice and thought, 'the task of education is to *extinguish* these views one by one' (emphasis added by the author) (Honda 1973, 41). One may be surprised at his choice of term 'extinguish' here; it could imply brainwashing. Of course, in a less extreme sense, it could mean raising a critical consciousness. Although his later practices suggest that he did not mean the former, he never elaborated on his choice of this terminology.

An attack on Honda: conservative intellectuals and the MOE

Honda testified for Ienaga in the first textbook lawsuit in the Tokyo District Court. As mentioned above, Ienaga mounted two court challenges to the state's *de facto* censorship of textbooks in the late 1960s. Honda was asked, perhaps because he was a schoolteacher actively involved in history education and was a known figure among historians as he belonged to several historical associations. In June 1969, Honda gave his testimony in court, reporting on his 1965 and 1968 teaching practices, and stated that teachers must teach the real facts of the war in order to allow students to 'acquire a deep understanding of peace,' but that very few history textbooks for junior high schools, because of the textbook screening, wrote about the reality of sufferings inflicted upon Asian countries and people by the war (Kyokasho Sosho o Shiensuru Zenkokurenrakukai 1991, 870–871).

According to Honda, his testimony upset the MOE, and it had no compunctions about undermining Honda. In its July 1969 newsletter, *Monbu Jiho*, the monthly journal of the MOE, the Ministry featured several articles that supported its position in the textbook lawsuits. One of them was a transcription of a round-table talk involving three famous conservative critics—Onabe Teruhiko of Ochanomizu Women's University, Fukuda Tsuneari (a well-known literary critic), and Kosaka Masataka of the University of Kyoto. Though the purpose of the round-table talk was to critique Ienaga, the three critics attacked Honda at length, calling his teaching 'wrong peace education' ('Zadankai' 1969, 16–18). Onabe stated that Honda assumed that students would become peace-loving Japanese if he taught the facts, i.e., Japan's wrongdoings, and argued that that was 'too simplistic.' He also accused Honda of 'bending the historical facts' in order to promote peace. Kosaka asserted that Honda's teaching was wrong not only as history education but also as peace education. Fukuda questioned the validity of Honda's data, arguing that, because students often write what pleases their teacher, he found in Honda's practice 'a teacher ... looking into Narcissus' mirror' ('Zadankai' 1969, 17).

These conservative intellectuals did have a point: the difficulty of education, from a critical perspective or not, and the danger of teachers imposing their ideology. They were, however, not self-reflective on their own ideology at all. For example, their argument fundamentally contradicted the way the state had imposed its official narrative upon schools, teachers, and students—particularly in its use of textbook screening processes to achieve *de facto* textbook censorship. Moreover, although they accused Honda of bending the facts, they actually misrepresented Honda's style of teaching and reporting on his practice. While Honda deliberated and selected actual contents of his lessons (as all teachers do), he took care to present verifiable facts to his students. Importantly, even though he testified against the state, he reported on the diverse voices of his students—from those (re)presenting critical, internationalist views on the war to those more or less leaning toward the state's nationalist position.

'Dear Asian junior high school Friends ...': letters of the 1971–1972 classes

During the 1971–1972 school year, Honda again taught history to eighth-graders (three classes, in total 109 students). He completed his lessons on the Asia-Pacific War by the end of February 1972, and March was final exam time (the Japanese school year ends in March), but because Honda had to travel on school business during that time, instead of giving an exam, he had his students write letters to junior high school friends in Asia.[11] The students used the full class period (45 minutes) to write their letters, and the result, Honda found, was 'overwhelm[ing].' As he put it: '[E]very line of every student ... was full-spirited, written wholeheartedly' (Honda 1973, 74). Honda did not cite the specific phrases and statements that moved him so deeply, nor did he state what precise differences he noticed between these letters and those written by his students in 1965 and 1968.

We can speculate, however, on the themes and language that moved Honda by examining the language of letters contained in subsequent publications. The first such publication came out at the end of March as a booklet that the students themselves made by mimeographing all of the letters.[12] According to Honda, publishing the booklets was his students' idea. One day in class he asked his students, 'What should we do with these fine letters from your hearts?' One of the students replied, 'I thought [we] were actually going to mail [them] to Asia, because [they were] "letters to junior high friends in Asia." Isn't that so?' Honda replied, '[T]o mail them, we should make a booklet [of mimeographs].' When he added that he would not be able to do so because of his busy schedule at the end of school year, the students told him that they would do it by themselves (Honda 1973, 74–75).

It is possible that some of the students felt pressured by Honda and the other students who wished to do the project (in fact, one student later wrote that she felt 'led' by Honda). Therefore, some contemporary critics are at least partially justified in criticizing Honda for exerting an influence, even if it was unconscious (Murai 1996, 96–107). However, those students who were reluctant did not speak up, even though Honda's style of teaching clearly encouraged students to express opposing views. The mimeographed booklet, entitled *Ajia no Chugakusei no Tomo eno Tegami* [Letters to Junior High Friends in Asia], appeared at the end of March (all the letters would be republished later in *Bokura no Taiheiyo Senso* [Honda 1973, 78–194]).

*****

I would like to take a moment to give an analysis of the letters of the 1971–1972 classes. In *Bokura no Taiheiyo Senso*, 108 letters were included without alteration, and classified into five groups, with each group given a heading (and each letter a sub-heading using some phrase from the letter). The first group, with a heading 'What Should I Do Now?' (30 letters), contained letters revealing students' shock at learning about Japanese war atrocities. The second group, with a heading 'War Itself Is the Worst of All' (17 letters), addressed the nature of war in general and of the Asia-Pacific War specifically. The third group, 'Japan Is Different from What It Was in the Past' (21 letters), contained references to a contemporary 'peace-loving Japan.' The fourth group, 'Who Was the Ringleader of the War?' (14 letters), included discussions on war responsibility. And the fifth group, 'Toward Peace in Asia' (26 letters), was marked by arguments for building peace in Asia. The headings (and sub-heading) indicate Honda's thoughts (and so analysis) on the letters, but he did not give many explanations or such an analysis—his style was just to collect and arrange.

In my analysis, each letter articulated and linked several topics and themes. The most frequent statement in the letters was one expressing a desire for peace (or no more war); approximately, 50 percent of the students wrote for peace (or were against war). Statements of apology also appeared frequently, but with some differences in wording: approximately 10 percent of the students spoke in a direct, straightforward manner using phrases such as 'I apologize ...' and 'Please forgive us ...,' while another 20-plus percent spoke in a more subtle manner, using phrases such as 'I feel sorry ...' and 'It may be no use to apologize, but ...'

'Shame' was another term that appeared often: approximately 17 percent of the students spoke of it, though the actual phrases they used varied, including 'I'm ashamed,' 'I feel it shameful to be a Japanese,' and 'I feel wartime Japan was shameful.' Expressions closely related to the sense of shame (e.g., 'I'm disappointed at Japan,' 'I came to dislike my own country,' and 'I lost my pride') appeared in another 10 percent of the letters. In addition, approximately 15 percent of the students discussed the issue of who should be held responsible for the war, though they did not arrive at any consensus. Some (about 5 percent) thought the emperor was responsible; some (about 4 percent) thought the emperor was not responsible. Others placed responsibility on the government, the military, imperialists, and/or Japanese citizens.

The most salient feature of these letters was the students' attempt to find meaning in being part of a nation, of Japan and Japanese, and their feelings seemed to remain uncertain at best. For example, a letter Honda placed in the fifth group began by introducing the writer: 'Dear junior high students in Asia: Hello, everybody! I'm ... living in Tokyo, Japan.' Immediately following this introduction, he expressed an apology and a feeling of shame:

> I have heard that you learn at your school about the inhumanity [committed] by the Japanese during the Pacific War. I think I must apologize for that as a Japanese.... The attitude of Japanese toward Asia at that time was to have no hesitation about murdering tens of millions of people as if they were killing insects, and [no hesitation about] randomly looting the things they needed to support themselves. And if [Asian] people did not obey, they were all massacred. I feel ashamed as a child of such a Japanese [nation].... [Y]ou perhaps bear a grudge against Japanese, but please do not hate us. [I] think the Japanese government should go to Asian countries with the emperor and apologize.
>
> *(Honda 1973, 187–188)*

Note that the phrase 'I think I must apologize ...' shows a little uncertainty about apologizing to his imaginary Asian friends. He positioned himself as a Japanese—as part of the nation—and therefore he felt ashamed. However, he did not wish 'us' to be hated because of past Japanese war atrocities. Instead, he saw the government and the emperor as the ones who really needed to apologize (though, as the phrase 'I think' indicates, he stopped short of outright assertion).

The young writer continued by expressing 'our' desire to 'make friends with you, and, together, ... build a future world without war' (Honda 1973, 188). However, it seems he was not sure that 'our' proposal would be accepted. As he put it:

> [I] think [I] ought not to say 'forget about the things before,' but, together with you, let's do our best to let the day of true peace in which no wars exist come. Let's make [sure] that kind of tragedy never happens again. What do you think of us? We are worried about it. However, it's not the way that human beings of the same kind [i.e., you and us] feud. Please, from now on, let's join hands and build a fine world. So long!
>
> *(Honda 1973, 188)*

He spoke of his desire that the people cross national boundaries and work toward a peaceful future. This was his vision of the future national identity. However, understanding Japan's past aggressions, he could not help recognizing that the nation's history was part of its identity. As indicated in the wording '[I] ought not to say,' he knew that his imaginary Asian friends probably would not 'forget' and might refuse to work together. He wondered what 'you think of us,' indicating the uncertainty and ambiguity he felt when imagining who 'we' are and who 'we' can be.

Students' conducting research by visiting foreign embassies

Had it ended with the mimeographed booklet, the 1972 project would not have been so original, because making a commemorative collection of student writings in March (i.e., at the end of school year) was—and still perhaps is—common practice in Japanese schools. However, the students also proposed another project—visiting foreign embassies, presenting the booklet of their letters, and conducting interviews about war damage. The students formed 18 groups, with each group taking responsibility for two or three countries during the spring break (at the end of March) and several holidays in April and May. In total, they visited 35 embassies, including the embassies of Korea, China, Vietnam, the Philippines, Australia, New Zealand, and the United States. In addition, a group of students visited the Japanese government.

According to Honda, by visiting the embassies, the students learned about international differences in culture, customs, and economic status.[13] The students also learned about the severity of political situations in some countries. For example, when they telephoned the Thai embassy to make an appointment, the students were told that the embassy would not answer 'such political questions.' Similarly, when a group telephoned the South Vietnam embassy, they were told that 'junior high schoolers do not have to know that,' and when some called the Cambodian embassy, a woman in the office told them, 'We cannot take time for you, because our country … has been invaded, so the embassy has been short-handed and busy.'[14] The students were treated very kindly at the Chinese embassy (of the Republic of China, Taiwan), but felt that the officers made too many negative comments about communism.[15] At the South Korean embassy, they were also treated kindly, though they felt that the officer was worried about saying something inappropriate.

In April, the students compiled the information each group had obtained, and together they reached the (tentative) conclusion that approximately 18.82 million people had died in East Asia because of the war.[16] By this time, the students had become ninth-graders, and Honda continued to teach them social studies (though the subject matter area shifted from history to civics, including economics and politics). During the weeks of student research, the principal of the school received three telephone calls: one from a concerned mother, another from the South Korean embassy, and one from the Japanese police. The calls were not made to praise the students' project; rather, in retrospect, they were indicative of widespread ambivalence among various segments of society with respect to critical, internationalist teaching about the war that attempted to see it from Asian victims' viewpoints. Honda and his colleagues (*and* his students) were about to encounter considerable parental criticism.

Parental responses

Honda first sensed reservations among the students' parents when he finished a regular meeting of a grassroots educational movement in April 1972. Several mothers came to speak to him about the mimeographed booklet, and when Honda asked for their opinions on it, they all said that they had been 'completely absorbed in reading' it. However, their views were not entirely positive. While they said that they appreciated it because it gave them a chance to discuss their wartime experiences with their children ('for the first time' as one mother said), they were not satisfied with the focus of the letters. As one mother put it: 'Well, [I wonder] if it is one-sided to [tell] only the story that [Japan] attacked [Asian countries] and did terrible things. The booklet does not write about *us*' (emphasis added). And, according to Honda, all of the mothers agreed with her (Honda 1973, 196).

The mimeographed booklet raised questions about whose knowledge should be taught in schools, how it should be taught, and who should decide. Honda thought, 'it might be impossible' to teach as he did 'without having any negative reaction from parents,' and that it would be important to include parents' views on the war. As he put it:

> [T]he important thing for instructors would be how to respect such negative parents' opinions and how to use them in order to facilitate students' learning not by dismissing such opinions but by incorporating them into lessons.
>
> (Honda 1973, 333–334)

In short, he was willing to take multiple perspectives into his teaching. However, it is not clear whether he had a given strategy in mind to deal with diverse views, including those adversarial to his critical, internationalist views, on the war. Rather, it appears that he was about to enter a pedagogically uncertain territory.

At the beginning of May, Honda assigned his students the task of 'Let's Learn from Parents' War Experiences': interviewing their parents about their experiences during the war and writing down their stories and, separately, asking them to write comments on the student letters, if possible. Ninety-three students (out of 109) were able to obtain written comments from one or both of their parents. Honda took the level of parental participation as a sign of 'serious[ness],' even though their comments included sharp criticism of the project. Honda included 56 parental comments in the later volumes (Honda 1973), and he classified the comments into three groups: 13 comments (largely negative) under the heading 'No Apology Is Necessary'; 25 comments (ambivalent) under 'The Scars from the War Cannot be Condemned'; and 18 comments (largely positive) under 'Our Experience That [We] Do Not Want to Repeat.'

Because he omitted comments to avoid creating duplicates, we cannot know the exact ratio of positive to negative parental comments. However, it is likely that a large number of parents were upset because they found the students' letters overwhelmingly apologetic. For example, one parent wrote:

> [This] is just like a volume of repentance about *Daitoa Senso* [the Great East Asian War]. What do kids who do not know the war have to repent for? It would be right to admit frankly, as one thing in history, the atrocities the old Japanese forces committed, but [I] suppose it would also be true that [the war] became one of the beginning points of liberation for the colonies ...
>
> (Honda 1973, 198)

Not all of the students wrote direct apologies—in fact, the most frequent topic in the students' letters was the desire for peace; thus, some of the parents' reactions were based more on their perceptions than on the facts. One reason that parents may have perceived the letters this way was because they felt, consciously or not, that it was controversial to admit to the war as an aggression against Asian nations and apologize for it—since there was still (shared) sense of limit to what could be said about the war. However, it also seems that parents felt uneasy about opening up a space to confront all of the unresolved issues of the war, the nation's past, and their lived experiences. One mother, whose war time experience was of displacement, fleeing to her grandparents' place and helping with agricultural work there, stated, '[I] wonder if [our kids] would distrust [us] parents who experienced the war, so I have a little bit of uneasy feeling' (Honda 1973, 201–211).

Other parents, however, evaluated the letters much more positively. As one mother put it:

> [Reading] this collection of essays, I—as one who received the education of the old days—feel keenly how free today's education is. [We] all feel reluctant about learning the ugly acts ... of [our own] country; however, [we] need to know the facts and understand the war itself.
>
> *(Honda 1973, 223)*

Knowledge of Japanese war atrocities evoked bitterness about Japan's war efforts even among the parents who had positive views about Honda's teaching. One parent, who had been an 18-year-old *kamikaze* squad member at the time of Japan's defeat, stated that he had experienced the war and had criticized the misery it brought, but he realized that his criticism had been in terms of 'our experience as victims.' The letters enabled him to 'come to see the other side of the war.' This caused him more frustration than it settled. As he put it:

> Thinking of [the pilots who] took off for *kamikaze* attacks just before the defeat, and thinking that [I] would not have been able to have this peaceful family [I have now] if the war had continued for another two or three days, I feel that [my] genuine belief of the time—because of that [I] endured destitution and danger exposed—was betrayed. Having come to know the facts through the textbooks of [other] Asian countries, once again the anger and regret come back to me against Japan's acts in which it had taken any means necessary to achieve the aims [of the war].
>
> *(Honda 1973, 218–219)*

One may wonder what kinds of stories these parents told their children in terms of their war experiences. In *Bokura no Taiheiyo Senso*, Honda included the parents' wartime stories, by setting five themes ('soldiers going to the front,' 'air raids,' 'student mobilization and Spartan education,' 'people's lives during the war,' and 'aftermath of the war') and extracting passages and lines that fit in each theme (in other words, he chose not to present each parent's story in its entirety). He did not explain how he identified these themes and why he decided to present them by theme, not by person. Whatever Honda's intentions were, the parents' war experiences were particular and polymorphous (e.g., where they were, whether they were with or without their parents, and what they were doing) (Honda 1973, 229–246).

Some of the fathers were in the military, undergoing training inside Japan or sent to various battlefields, including mainland China, Taiwan, Mutanchiang in Manchuria, Lingayen Gulf in the Philippines, and Bougainville Island in Papua New Guinea. Some of them were detained in Siberia and elsewhere after Japan's defeat. Those remaining in Japan (in Tokyo or other prefectures such as Saitama, Chiba, and Hiroshima) experienced air raids; however, the exact events related differed: running this way or that to make their escape from fire; seeing burnt-out dead bodies, houses, and neighborhoods; or the loss of grandparents, parents, friends, and/or schoolteachers. Other stories were about being mobilized to work in the rice fields, eating frogs, producing airplane components in a factory, being evacuated from home without parents, receiving military training in schools, or surviving severe hunger and poverty during and after the war. Every story had distinctive specificities, and as such it would have been difficult to make a single narrative of war experience out of the parental stories.

More parental criticism

In late May, Honda again encountered criticism when he and his colleague asked parents at a Parent-Teacher Association (PTA) meeting for support to print a professionally typeset version of the mimeographed booklet. Honda thought that they would easily win the support they desired, but instead they were met with an awkward silence. Eventually, a parent in charge of the meeting spoke up, saying, '[We] understand well the efforts of teachers, so it's really difficult to say [this], but why do the students do nothing but apologize so much?' Again, there was an awkward silence and a chilly atmosphere, until the same parent spoke again: 'Representing the voices of many mothers, I say what is difficult to say. [We] wonder if [our children] will become people with servile spirits.' Honda's colleague tried to persuade the parents by stating that the students wrote such letters because Japan brought so much damage to Asia, but the atmosphere did not seem to change (Honda 1973, 317).

In the end, Honda was able to get the support he desired because of one parent who put in a few good words to help him; the parent had asked those who opposed the idea if they had looked at Honda's handout that had triggered the whole project in the first place by introducing the descriptions of the war from Asian textbooks. Most of them had not seen it. The implication was that they might have criticized Honda unfairly. Honda apologized for having failed to distribute the handout to the parents and proposed a new title for the volume, *Taiheiyo Senso o Kangaeru* [Thinking about the Pacific War]. He also stated that it would contain not just the students' letters, but also the parents' comments. Honda felt that the real cause of parental opposition was not that they had not seen the handout, but the position the letters took (which regarded Japanese as the aggressor, rather than as the victim), but he made no further argument (Honda 1973, 318–319).

The typeset volume came out in late June and raised some media interest in the following months. In particular, the *Mainichi Shinbun,* one of the major Japanese newspapers, featured the volume favorably in its morning edition on August 15—the day Japan commemorates as the 'end' of the war (not the 'defeat').[17] The coverage was a half-page in length and consisted of an illustration drawn by a student, a photo of some students doing the project, an interview with the principal, and excerpts of writings by students and parents ('Ajia no Tomo e' 1972). A television station also contacted the school to feature the project on its educational program; the school principal was not enthusiastic but left the decision up to Honda and his colleagues. Honda declined the invitation because when one of his colleagues consulted with a group of parents, the parents reacted negatively. In short, Honda was not able to overcome parental opposition to, and ambivalence about, critical, internationalist teaching about the war from the viewpoint of Asian victims.

'We speak up again': student responses to parental criticism

During the summer holidays of 1972, Honda gave his students an assignment: to write an essay on the typeset volume. Honda chose 14 essays that he saw as presenting the theme 'We Speak Up Again,' and included them in a later volume (Honda 1973). The essays showed that when faced with the parents' criticisms, some students adjusted their positions. One student stated that he changed his mind 'a little,' because his parents 'suffered like people in Asia suffered at that time.... [O]rdinary Japanese participated in the war not because they wanted to, but because they were forced to' (Honda 1973, 347). Another student, while still feeling the letters had been written from their hearts, noted that students had developed 'a fixed way of thinking' about the war, and believed that the reason so many students apologized was because Honda had 'only exposed [to us] too much' about 'the inhumane acts Japan committed against Asian countries' (Honda 1973, 349). To be sure, this student had a somewhat faulty memory in criticizing Honda's lessons, as his lessons included a variety of topics aside from Japanese war atrocities (e.g., the Great Depression, Western powers in Asia, the rise of fascism in Germany and Japan, resistance in Japan, the Battle of Okinawa, and the US atomic bombings) (for further discussion on his contents and materials to teach the unit concerning the Asia-Pacific War, see Honda 1973, 48–71).

Others argued against the parents' criticisms, and some of the arguments were quite articulate. For example, one student thought their 'parents' comments were very interesting,' but felt it was 'a little wrong' that some parents argued that there is 'no need to apologize like that to Asian countries because Japan also suffered considerable damage.' He presented this argument:

> [W]e wrote letters of apology not to the countries that caused injury to Japan but to Asian countries that were dragged into the war because they were colonies at that time. In addition, it was Japan that started the war, so [I] think it's natural to apologize. In my view, because those [Japanese] people [who lived during] that time experienced great hardship, they still cannot see the war objectively even now.
>
> (Honda 1973, 358–359)

Another student wrote to counter a parental suggestion that the students should have a more forward-looking manner toward their Asian friends, rather than repentance. He stated:

> A forward-looking manner would [only] emerge from someone looking back, i.e., by reflecting on Japan's having done wrongs in the past as well as inheriting its good deeds [of the past]. [I'm] sure that if we think through things quickly in a forward-looking manner, it will result in repeating the wrongs.
>
> (Honda 1973, 356–357)

However, making this point did not mean that he had no empathy for the parents' feelings. He noted that 'it's natural' for the parents to 'give first place [in their thoughts] to those [Japanese] victims,' since the parents' stories about war experiences made him 'really understand' the hardship and sufferings they went through. While he was critical of the arguments that exempted ordinary Japanese entirely from responsibility for the war, he concluded that: 'We should build a peaceful world, learning from the experiences of our fathers and mothers' (Honda 1973, 245–247).

The 1972 Japan-China Joint Statement: apology or no apology?

On September 25, 1972, Prime Minister Tanaka Kakuei visited the People's Republic of China, the first step toward officially ending the war with China (the two countries would sign a Peace Treaty in 1978). Tanaka went to China despite strong objections from his own party, the Liberal Democratic Party (LDP, Japan's ruling party since 1955),[18] and the Ministry of Foreign Affairs. At the conclusion of Tanaka's visit, Japan and China issued the Sino-Japanese Joint Declaration that recognized the People's Republic of China as the only legitimate government of China (see also He 2009). The declaration also included a line stating that Japan 'feels keenly' its responsibility for the heavy damage it caused to the Chinese people through the war and that it 'reflects deeply' (*hansei*) on that responsibility ('Nihon-seifu' 1972). It was the first official 'apology' Japan made to China, but it was undermined after Tanaka returned to Japan. In a Diet session held on November 7, Tanaka avoided defining the war as aggression, stating, '[F]rom my current position I cannot say if it can be definitely concluded that the past war was an aggression' ('Shugiin' 1972, 44; see also Yoshida 1995, 139–138).

The apology also stirred a debate over history textbooks. Since the mid-1950s, the MOE had whitewashed textbook descriptions of the war, and, as a result, school textbooks in the late 1960s and early 1970s carried almost no references to Japanese war atrocities, and very little in the way of critical reflection on the war. Following the joint statement, the Education Minister stated in a Diet session that '[Japanese] people should know fully about the war with China, reflect on it, and keenly feel the responsibility' for the war, and that compulsory and adult education should enable them to do so ('Kyokasho' 1972, 23). However, Ministry officials were divided between those who thought minor changes would suffice and those who felt it necessary to shift the perspective from which the war was presented ('Kyokasho' 1972, 23).

Honda incorporated these developments into his teaching by distributing a handout reprinting the Joint Declaration and some newspaper articles about the history textbook debate. His students overwhelmingly supported Japan's apology to China: 95 students (out of 107) said that it was good that Japan apologized to China; eight students said that it was not yet a full apology; and four students said that Japan should not have apologized. Concerning the textbooks, most of his students were angry because they felt that their textbooks had told them 'lies' and that the future textbook revisions would be too late for them. In Honda's view, his lessons 'had nothing in need of correction,' but, because he had not expected his students' anger, he made no further argument. Had he done so, he would have had a good opportunity to discuss with his students the nature of the official knowledge represented in school textbooks and how it was shaped by the power of the state (and the politics of the time).

Graduation and continuation

In the spring of 1973, following the US withdrawal from Vietnam, the geo-political contour of Asia underwent significant changes. The lives of Honda's students were changing as well—they were graduating (the ninth grade is the end of compulsory education). Before they left, Honda asked for their comments on his lessons and teaching methods, and some of the pros and cons of his pedagogical approach came to light. Although the majority of his students appreciated the handouts, discussion opportunities, and many activities, including not only writing letters and visiting embassies but also other activities they did, one student found his lessons difficult to follow because Honda often did not use textbooks (Honda 1973, 397). Another student, who thought he became good at explaining opposing views because of Honda's approach, stated that 'in the first semester after entering the junior high, I felt Mr. Honda was left-leaning,' and that Honda's attempt to impose 'socialist views' on his students resulted in their having a 'backlash' against socialism, so he asked Honda 'not to do that from now on' (Honda 1973, 398).

Some suggested that Honda should have made his views more explicit. For example, when Honda had his students discuss issues in social studies class, he typically refrained from expressing his own views because he thought his taking sides would discourage students from expressing their ideas freely; some students felt that he should have been more open, however. One student wrote, 'it is not fair to have only students express their opinions' and continued:

> Is it the reason [you] cannot express [your] opinion that [you] would be found fault with, if it were known to people of the rightwing? Or I wonder if [you are] told not to teach about things of the left because both the MOE and the [local] education board are rightwing.... There is such a thing as freedom of thought and beliefs, and don't [you] ... have a bad conscience [for not practicing it]?
>
> *(Honda 1973, 386)*

The writer suggested that before their graduation, Honda should distribute a handout stating his positions on the issues debated throughout his social studies lessons and give students the opportunity to ask him questions.

Because his classes were essentially finished at that point, Honda did not agree to the suggestion. He also felt that this particular student wanted a last-minute promotion of leftwing views, and he believed that giving 'one great speech' of his own would not change the views held by the majority of students who remained fairly conservative, even after three years of Honda's teaching (Honda 1973, 387). The students graduated at the end of March 1973, and in August the volume *Bokura no Taiheiyo Senso* was published by a commercial press (Honda 1994b, 416). The volume included all of the materials contained in the previous publications and added the students' comments on parental criticisms and Honda's lessons. As he later reflected, the 1971–1972 teaching practice made him aware that students' active learning and thinking can generate knowledge 'far beyond the frameworks of teachers' (Honda 1994b, 416).

In 1975, three years after their graduation, Honda had an opportunity to have a discussion on history education (and social studies) with four students of the 1971–1972 cohort. They were more or less in agreement on their appreciation for Honda's lessons with many handouts. One of them, recalling that he had criticized Honda's selection of the teaching materials before, expressed his desire to have multiple perspectives in teaching about the war. As he put it:

> I want social studies teachers to take democracy very seriously. There are people who oppose war ... and there are people who like wars. Having such [a variety of] people is democracy. It is important not to ignore this aspect, to maintain neutrality, and to have the [historical] data [used in class] be multi-faceted—this will be a way that makes students think.
>
> *('Seitotachi' 1975)*

Honda continued to teach social studies at the same school but left there in April 1977 to become secretary-general of *Rekishi Kyoikusha Kyogikai* [History Educationalist Conference in Japan], a nationwide association of history educators. He began teaching part-time in several universities, and in April 1983, became a tenured professor at Miyagi Education University, a national university with a solid reputation for its educational research and teacher education.

At one point in 1975, meeting another round of controversy, Honda began articulating a problem of education: it is insufficient that teachers just teach history from within their frameworks, they must let students grow (to think and act for themselves), but it is uncertain who the students would become and what they would do if they really started growing. When a teacher has a controversy over his/her history teaching and students' growing in unexpected ways, it is difficult to 'settle right or wrong.' He suggested the importance of making clear 'the extent to which students' views on history developed' through their education. In the late 1980s, he stated, 'I have tackled that difficult problem ever since. I wish to find a way out soon, but [I do not know] when, and for the time being I'm still pursuing [it]' (Honda 1994b, 420–421). As late as 1993, Honda was still tackling it (Murai 1996, 108–110). Honda died in 1995, leaving the unresolved problem with us. In a contemporary theoretical sense, Honda's problem is about the contradiction, ambiguity, and uncertainty in the process of history education and the formation of national identity among students.

Conclusion

Narratives of nation are powerful tools that can involve people in a shared sense of national identity to allow them to believe in the *homogeneity* of who 'we' are, where 'we' come from, and where 'we' should go. In these narratives, as Hein and Selden (2000, 3) write, 'major wars are defining moments in forging and sustaining national identities,' as they imaginarily construct the national boundary and divide the world into 'them' and 'us' (Nozaki & Inokuchi, 1998). As a historical representation, teaching history concerning the issues of war—with accounts of heroism as well as of war atrocities and crimes against humanity—is impossible without telling some narratives and/or using some narrative forms (White 1987).

In the mid-1950s and 1960s, the Japanese state took a strong hand in its textbook screening to make the rightwing narratives of the Asia-Pacific War into official narratives and imposed them upon its schools. In the mid-1960s, the struggle over national narratives moved to the public arena when historian Ienaga initiated his court challenges against the state. In this context, Honda took critical, internationalist perspectives, taught about the issues of war from the viewpoints of its Asian victims, and asked his students to write letters to their (imaginary) junior high school friends in Asia. Because he brought oppositional narratives to his history lessons, it should come as little surprise that Honda's teaching was controversial. At the national level, the state and the conservative intellectuals who supported the state's efforts launched a negative/misinformation campaign to discredit his practice. However, Honda did not get shaken, perhaps because it was expected—as Honda was one of the progressives in the first place, and he testified for Ienaga.

What Honda did not anticipate was the controversy that took place at his school. He (and his colleagues) found a large number of parents uneasy about their children's apologies and feelings of shame as expressed in their letters, and reluctant to support his practice. This is not to suggest that these parents were fully in accord with the rightwing nationalist perspectives. The parents did not object to everything; as they stated, they were 'completely absorbed' in reading the volume of student letters and appreciated it because it offered them the opportunity to discuss their own wartime experiences with their children for the first time. However, they also wondered if the accounts of the war (re)presented in the volume were one-sided, feeling that their experiences were not included—as one mother stated, it 'does not write about us.'

It appears that part of the parental criticism stemmed from their (long-cherished) desire to have their stories/memories heard. It may also have been an expression of their grievance against the postwar hegemonic power, including not only the Japanese state that evaded its responsibility for the sufferings of ordinary people and remained indifferent to the issues of Japanese civilian causalities[19] but also the leaders and elites of the wider society who, more or less, accepted the government position to constitute the norms for what could be said and taught about the war.[20] The problem was that most of the parental perspectives remained, if not monolithic, limited; when they talked about their war experiences, they mostly focused on their sufferings, which was perhaps reasonable,[21] though their stories rarely expressed empathy with 'other' people's sufferings in Asia and elsewhere. In other words, there was no discussion to see how what happened to 'us' and what happened to 'them' were structurally related and intertwined in the pursuit of aggressive war. Honda attempted to incorporate the parental voices in his practice; however, he did not seem well prepared to deal with them.[22]

Honda's project required that the students work seriously on their identity formations in relation to their views on history (and the world). In particular, they underwent quite a struggle to write letters to their imaginary Asian friends, as well as to understand their parents' criticisms, but they managed to express their views. Most of them were remarkably mature and insightful in moving through the process. However, many of their parents would have preferred it, if their children had not had to go through it. The parents who resented Honda's teaching were (probably) correct in their argument that the children bore no responsibility for war crimes committed before their birth, but perhaps they missed the important point. Younger generations have the right to know their nation's past to prefigure new forms of identities that grow out of the past but depart from it in significant ways. To borrow Terry Eagleton's terms, the students should be allowed to 'go somehow all the way through [the alienation of national identity] and out the other side' (though, I should also mention, Eagleton hints that that could be 'an impossible irony') (1990, 23–24).

The students' struggle can be seen as a movement for the freedom to be fully human, which requires 'double optics.' As Eagleton puts it:

> [It] necessarily be caught up in the very metaphysical categories it hopes finally to abolish; and any such movement will demand a difficult, perhaps ultimately impossible double optics, at once fighting on a terrain already mapped out by its antagonists and seeking even now to prefigure within that mundane strategy styles of being and identity for which we have as yet no proper names.
>
> *(Eagleton 1990, 24)*

The students were indeed 'caught up in the very metaphysical categories'— 'Japanese' and 'Asian nations,' while wanting to be 'fully human' so that they could see the world from multiple perspectives, or, at least, be able to comprehend the two sides of the war—the sufferings of their parents as well as of the Asian peoples. Unquestionably, the students underwent the struggle, but did they emerge somewhere on the other side where they were able to overcome the captivity by those metaphysical categories?

We should note a contradiction that took place in Honda's critical, internationalist practice. His teaching seems to have fixed, rather than deconstructed, binary categories of 'Japanese nation' and 'other (Asian) nations.' As a result, it constituted one form of Japanese national identity, with some inclination toward peace building. When the students expressed their wish to build a peaceful world with their Asian neighbors, they wrote as 'we,' and a good number of them also apologized as 'Japanese.' They needed to become a Japanese—a member of nation, even if it was an 'imagined community'—in order to apologize. Their calls for friendship and peace building remained restrained by the national boundaries set by that imaginary. The dilemma here is that Honda's teaching did not result in a formation of identity that transcends, or overcomes, the fixed national boundaries. In other words, nationalism and internationalism are no different in their effects/outcomes, as both presuppose, construct, and/or reinforce national boundaries in their imaginaries.

We also note that, in Honda's practice, although it was perhaps not what he intended, some uncertain, ambiguous identities were produced that did not converge upon the right-leaning or left-leaning ideologies. Honda brought to his classes counter-narratives—narratives that opposed the state's official narratives—and in so doing opened the classroom up to become an arena where those narratives compete. Did Honda wish his students to uphold the oppositional narratives and form a critical, internationalist identity? Honda's writings suggest he did—and if so, his teaching remained imperfect, as the students' letters and comments revealed rather a complexity and contradiction in the formation of their identities. The counter-narratives Honda introduced did not necessarily produce oppositional consciousness, just as the state's official narratives did not always result in the intended rightwing nationalist identities. In the process of Honda's teaching and his students' learning about the war, the emerging identities remained more or less unfinished and ambiguous—they manifested both hopes and uncertainties to become something new.

In my view, Honda fell short of the double optic, in that he never questioned his and his students' identity as 'Japanese,' however critical and internationalist he was. He appreciated—or was 'overwhelm[ed]' by, in his words—those letters in which students apologized 'wholeheartedly' as 'Japanese.' The binary categories of 'Japanese/aggressors' and 'Asians/victims' were so natural (and perhaps emotionally loaded) for him that he did not see the need to deconstruct the binary in order to (re)articulate a position from which students could narrate the ways that the sufferings of Asian peoples and those of their parents were structurally related and intertwined in the work of empire. Of course, 'double optics' could be 'ultimately impossible,' as Eagleton himself suggests. In any case, imperfection and contradiction are something educators learn to live with, and Honda did it precariously, honestly, and with commitment.

Notes

1 In postwar Japan, the war that resulted in Japan's defeat in 1945 has been called by different names. Japanese historians now often use *Ajia-Taiheyo Senso* [the Asia-Pacific War]—which appears in the title of this chapter. The name officially used during the late war years was *Daitoa Senso* [the Great East Asian War], which was replaced by *Taiheiyo Senso* [the Pacific War], which was coined and promoted by the United States and became popular within Japan. Some historians forged the name *Jugo-nen Senso* [the Fifteen-Year War]; others *Nicchu Senso* [the China-Japan War]. In everyday lives, it has been referred to simply 'that war' (*ano senso*) or 'the previous great *war*' *(sakino tai-sen)* (Nozaki 2008, 6–7, 49–50).
2 In Japanese education, the junior high school subject 'social studies' consists of three sub-subject matters: geography, history, and civics. A social studies teacher often teaches all three sub-subjects to the same cohort of students over three years.
3 The Japanese term 'bokura' means 'we,' generally used by young males, and 'bokura no' means 'our.' It is undeniable that the book title is masculine by today's standard. By the title, though a literal translation is 'Our Pacific War,' Honda signified that the book is about his students' views on the Pacific War.
4 Yoshida (1995) argues that a 'double standard' in dealing with the issues of war responsibility was established in the early 1950s by which, internationally, the Japanese government admitted its responsibility for the war and aggression (to a very limited extent) by accepting the Tokyo Tribunal's decisions, but within the nation it ignored—'sealed' in Yoshida's term—the questions of war responsibility. Because of this double standard, there was a (shared) sense of limit to what

could be said about the war among the Japanese. In the 1980s, this standard began to change, but the debate has continued to exist today.
5 The rightwing nationalists promoted the view of the emperor as an innocent peacemaker during the war, while discrediting the Tokyo Tribunal. However, since the Tokyo Tribunal did not prosecute the emperor, discrediting it would lead to the denial of view of him as innocent. This has been one of the logical failures of rightwing nationalist discourse.
6 In the 1967 nationwide survey, 17.1 percent of 2,402 respondents (over 20 old) agreed that Japan 'did a wrong thing' by conducting the war with China; in the 1972 survey 26.4 percent of 2,369 respondents agreed. The number of those who saw the war as 'just' because Japan acted in its national security remained more or less the same, at 9.7 percent in 1967 and 8.4 percent in 1972. Those who saw it as 'inevitable' because the country had no choice but to enter into it increased, from 35.9 percent to 46.6 percent. Those who chose 'do not know' or gave no response decreased, from 29.4 percent to 13.9 percent. My interpretation of the data differs somewhat from that offered by Yoshida (1995).
7 A research project funded by the Okinawa Prefecture was launched to publish two volumes of the records of Okinawans' personal accounts of their experiences in the Battle of Okinawa. The initial planning of the project began around 1965, actual research activity began in 1967, and the results were published in the early 1970s as a part of a series entitled *Okinawa Kenshi* [Okinawa Prefectural History].
8 Honda Koei and Honda Katsuichi are two different individuals. In this chapter, when referring to the latter, his full name is used.
9 Gluck (1993, 70–79) identifies four agents ('custodians of the past' in her terminology) that have shaped versions of Japanese war memories: progressive intellectuals, conservative intellectuals, the popular media, and individual memories of ordinary citizens. As Gluck suggests, a good diversity and fluid relationships have existed among the progressives.
10 It is common in Japanese junior high schools to have a teacher teach the same cohort for three years (from admission to graduation). A social studies teacher often teaches geography for the seventh-graders, history for the eighth-graders, and civics for the ninth-graders. That is, he/she usually teaches history at three-year intervals.
11 Not having an exam at the end of the semester is not common in current Japanese junior high schools. However, in the 1960s and 1970s, some teachers were able to do so, as Honda's other teaching practice records indicate.
12 The booklet, consisting of approximately 100 pages, contained all the letters of all three classes. It accompanied three separate mini-booklets containing the letters from each class.
13 For example, students learned that some countries had only a room as their office (Portugal), while other had a big building (Germany). Some countries had a long break at lunch (Italy and Afghanistan); some observed the Easter break; and some did not allow young people to visit them (the United States, the United Kingdom, and the USSR).
14 The United States and South Vietnamese's incursion into Cambodia began in April 1970.
15 At this point, Japan did not have diplomatic relations with the People's Republic of China, even though it had gained the right to membership of the United Nations in October 1971. Interestingly, when the students returned to visit the Taiwan embassy again during the summer, they felt that they were treated with some suspicions. The US President Nixon visited China in February 1972, and Japan's Prime Minister Tanaka Kakuei in September 1972. After Tanaka's visit to China, the students somehow understood the reason(s) for the suspicions at the Taiwan embassy.
16 The students' finding had some value because little research existed on the topic around the time. The Japanese state has never officially studied the damage caused by the war inside and outside Japan.
17 In Japan, the defeat in the war (*haisen*) has been called 'the end of the war' (*shusen*). It is a euphemism and still common to use today.
18 The LDP is still Japan's ruling party (as of September 2022), though it was out of power twice, 1993–1994 and 2009–2012.
19 The only exception was the provision of very limited compensation for Okinawan victims and atomic bombing victims.
20 There is little doubt that the Tokyo Tribunal was a 'tribunal of the victors,' and as such it had biases (Minear 1971). However, it is also important to examine the ways the postwar Japanese state used the decisions for its benefit. The Tokyo Tribunal did not consider 'prosecution of Japanese

war leaders for war crimes committed against their own people' (Tanaka 1996, 134), so the state conveniently ignored that issue.

21 On the memories of repatriates from Manchuria (who had gone there as 'settlers' for reclamation), Gluck (1993, 77) states: 'The nation, which had roused them to do the work of empire, now repudiated the entire endeavor, leaving their personal pasts beside the postwar point.... [I]t was not until the 1970s that individual Manchurian memoirs began to flood into public view ....' I would argue that, given the fact that their voices had been suppressed for more than two decades, it was not too unreasonable that they wanted to talk about their sufferings when they were allowed to speak. Many parents of Honda's students (and their voices) can be viewed more or less in a similar light.

22 Some may wonder why Honda was so unprepared. One answer might be that Honda's practice was very new, so it was difficult to know its outcome beforehand. However, I suspect, because the state efforts for disseminating rightwing national narratives were quite anachronistic and vernacular, the progressives with oppositional ideas—Honda was one of them—tended to assume, wishfully or not, that 'ordinary people' were on their side. They tended to underestimate the degree and range of hesitation and ambivalence that existed among ordinary people toward telling their children about the Japanese war atrocities from critical, international perspectives. Moreover, however 'people-centered' the progressives tried to be, they were 'elites' who wished to promote their kind of national narratives to construct a certain national identity.

References

English-language references

Anderson, Benedict. 1983. *Imagined Communities: Reflections on the Origin and Spread of Nationalism*. London: Verso.

Apple, Michael W. 1992. *Official Knowledge: Democratic Education in a Conservative Age*. Abingdon: Routledge.

Bhabha, Homi K. 1990. "Dissemination: Time, Narrative, and the Margins of the Modern Nation." In *Nation and Narration*, edited by Homi K. Bhabha, 291–322. Abingdon: Routledge.

Dower, John W. Dower. 1999. *Embracing Defeat: Japan in the Wake of World War II*. New York: W.W. Norton & Company.

Eagleton, Terry. 1990. "Nationalism: Irony and Commitment." In *Nationalism, Colonialism, and Literature*, edited by Terry Eagleton, Fredric Jameson, and Edward W. Said, 23–39. Minneapolis: University of Minnesota Press.

Gluck, Carol. 1993. "The Past in the Present." In *Postwar Japan as History*, edited by Andrew Gordon, 64–95. Berkeley: University of California Press.

He, Yinan. 2009. *The Search for Reconciliation: Sino-Japanese and German-Polish Relations since World War II*. Cambridge: Cambridge University Press.

Hein, Laura. & Mark Selden. 1999. "The Lessons of War, Global Power, and Social Change" In *Censoring History: Citizenship and Memory in Japan, Germany, and the United States*, edited by Laura Hein & Mark Selden, 3–50. Armonk: M.E. Sharpe.

Kaufmann, Eric. 2017. "Complexity and Nationalism." *Nations and Nationalisms* 23 (1): 6–25.

Minear, Richard. 1971. *Victors' Justice: The Tokyo War Crime Trial*. Ann Arbor: The Center for Japanese Studies, the University of Michigan.

Nozaki, Yoshiko. 2008. *War Memory, Nationalism, and Education in Postwar Japan, 1945–2007*. Abingdon: Routledge.

Nozaki, Yoshiko, and Hiromitsu Inokuchi. 1998. What U.S. Middle Schoolers Bring to the Classroom: Student Writing on the Pacific War. *Education about Asia*, 3 (3): 30–34.

Nozaki, Yoshiko and Hiromitsu Inokuchi. 2000. "Japanese Education, Nationalism, and Ienaga Saburo's Textbook Lawsuits." In *Censoring History: Citizenship and Memory in Japan, Germany, and the United States*, edited by Laura Hein and Mark Selden, 96–126. Armonk: M. E. Sharpe.

Tanaka, Yuki. 1996. *Hidden Horrors: Japanese War Crimes in World War II*. Boulder: Westview Press.

White, Hayden. 1987. *The Content of the Form: Narrative Discourse and Historical Representation*. Baltimore: John Hopkins University Press.

Williams, Raymond. 1980. "Base and Superstructure in Marxist Cultural Theory." In *Problems in Materialism and Culture*, 38–40. London: Verso.

Japanese-language references

Honda, Koei. 1967. *Kin/gendaishi o Do Oshieru ka* (*How to Teach Modern and Contemporary History*). Tokyo: Meijitosho.
Honda, Koei. 1973. *Bokura no Taiheiyo Senso* (*The Pacific War, as We View It*). Tokyo: Hatonomori Shobo.
Honda, Koei. 1994a. *Honda Koei Chosakushu, Dai 1-kan* (*The Writings of Honda Koei, Vol. 1*). Tokyo: Rukku Inc.
Honda, Koei. 1994b. *Honda Koei Chosakushu, Dai 2-kan* (*The Writings of Honda Koei, Vol. 2*). Tokyo: Rukku Inc.
Honda, Koei. 1994c. *Honda Koei Chosakushu, Hokan* (*The Writings of Honda Koei, Supplemental Volume*). Tokyo: Rukku Inc.
Honda, Katsuichi. 1972. *Chugoku no Tabi* (*A Journey in China*). Tokyo: Asahi Shinbunsha.
Inoue. Kiyoshi. 1975. *Tenno no Senso Sekinin* (*The Emperor's War Responsibility*). Tokyo: Gendaihyoronsha.
Kyokasho Kentei Sosho o Shiensuru Zenkoku-renrakukai. 1991. *Ienaga Kyokasho Saiban Chisai-hen: Dai 1-ji Sosho-hen III* (*Ienaga Textbook Lawsuit at the District Court Edition: The First Lawsuit Edition, Vol. 3*). Tokyo: Rongu Shuppan.
"Kyokasho no Chugoku: Hansei to Jijitsu Do Oshieru ([China in School Textbooks: How to Teach about 'Facts' and 'Reflection']." September 30, 1972. *Mainichi Shinbun*, 23.
Murai, Atsushi. 1994. "Bokura no Taiheiyo Senso to Heiwa Kyoiku" (*The Pacific War, as We View it* and Peace Education). In *Honda Koei Chosakushu, Dai 1-kan* [*The Writings of Honda Koei, Vol. 1*], edited by Koei Honda, 415–422. Tokyo: Rukku Inc.
Murai, Atsushi. 1996. *Gakuryoku kara Imi e: Yasui, Honda, Kutuumi, Suzuki Kaku Kyoshitsu no Moto-seito no Kikitori kara* (*From Academic Achievement to Meaning: from the Interviews with Former Students of Classes of Yasui, Honda, Kutuumi, and Suzuki*). Tokyo: Sodobunka.
Nagahama, Isao. 1984. *Nihon Fashizumu Kyoushiron: Kyoshi-tachi no 8-gatsu 15-nichi* (*On Japanese Facisum and Schoolteachers: Schoolteachers' August 15th*). Tokyo: Akashi Shoten.
"Nihon-seifu to Chuka-jinmin-kyowakoku-seifu no Kyodoseimei (the Sino-Japanese Joint Declaration)." September 29, 1972. Retrieved from https://www.mofa.go.jp/mofaj/area/china/nc_seimei.html
Niijima, Atsuyoshi. 1965. "Chugoku no Kyokasho ni Miru Nicchu Senso" (The Sino-Japanese War, as Represented in Chinese Textbooks). *Chuo Koron* 936 (October): 93–97.
Okinawa-ken, ed. 1975. *Okinawa-kenshi Dai 10-kan Kakuron-hen 9 Okinawasen Kiroku 2* (*Okinawa Prefectural History, Vol. 10, Specifics 9, Record on the Battle of Okinawa 2*). Okinawa: Okinawa-ken
Ozawa, Yusaku. 1965. "Nanboku-chosen no Kyokasho ni Miru Nihon (Japan as Represented in Textbooks of North and South Koreas). *Chuo Koron* 936 (October): 97–101.
Saotome, Katsumoto. 1971. *Tokyo Daikushu:Showa 20-nen 3-gatsu 10-ka no Kiroku* (*The Great Air Raid of Tokyo: A Record of March 10th, 1945*). Tokyo: Iwanami Shoten.
"Seitotachi to Kataru Senso to Shakaika Kyoiku: Haisen 30-nen Zadankai, Sono 1" (Discussion on the War and Social Studies Education with Students: A Round-Table Talk Thirty Years after the War, Part 1]. 1975 August. *Rekishichiri Kyoiku* 240.
"Senso o Wabiru: Ajia no Tomo e Chugakusei ga Bunshu (Apologizing for the War: Junior High Students Making a Collection of Essays to Friends in Asia)." August 15, 1972. *Mainichi Shinbun* 17.
"Shugiin Yosan Iin Kaigiroku, Dai 70-kai Kokkai (House of Representatives Budget Committee Records, the 70th Diet)." November 7, 1972, no. 4: 44. Retrieved from https://kokkai.ndl.go.jp/#/detailPDF?minId=107005261X00419721107&page=44&spkNum=321&current=-1
Yamamoto, Tatsuro. 1965. "Tonan Ajia Shokoku no Kyokasho ni Miru Taiheyo Senso" (The Pacific War, as Represented in Textbooks in Southeast Asian Countries). *Chuo Koron* 936 (October): 84–92.
Yoshida, Yutaka. 1995. *Nihonjin no Sensokan: Sengishi no nakano Henyo* (*The Japanese Views on the War: Changes in the Postwar History*). Tokyo: Iwanami Shoten.
Yoshimi, Yoshiaki. 1987. *Kusanone no Fashizumu: Nihon Minnshu no Senso Taiken* (*Grassroots Fascism: War Experiences of Japanese People*). Tokyo: Tokyo Daigaku Shuppannkai.
"Zadankai: Kyokasho Saiban" (A Round-table Talk: Textbook Lawsuits). 1969, June. *Monbu Jiho* 1104: 10–32.

15
NATIONALISM, HISTORY, AND COLLECTIVE NARCISSISM

Historical revisionism in twenty-first-century Japan

Sven Saaler

Introduction

What are the core facets of nationalism? Previous interpretations have focused on the role of a common culture or language (Weber 1976), racial or ethnical kinship (Connor 1994), citizenship (Greenfeld 1993), and the influence of print capitalism (Anderson 1983) and tradition (Hobsbawm and Ranger 1983). Others have pointed out that the emergence of nationalism is closely related to the processes of industrialization (Gellner 1983) and mass mobilization for war (Giddens 1985; Mosse 1990; 2001 and many others). While most scholars agree that nationalism is a modern phenomenon, some point to the premodern roots of the nation and of national culture. Taking a middle-of-the-road approach, Anthony Smith has shown that nationalisms, while modern products, depend on myths and symbols that sometimes have premodern origins (Smith 2004). All of these commentators acknowledge the centrality of a historical narrative and national memory in constituting national identity. As early as the 1840s, John Stuart Mill pointed out that while the "feeling of nationality may have been generated by various causes" such as

> race and descent, … community of language and … of religion, … the strongest of all is identity of political antecedents: the possession of a national history, and consequent community of recollections; collective pride and humiliation, pleasure and regret, connected with the same incidents in the past.
>
> *(Mill 1958, 229)*

It is important, at this point, to distinguish between history as an academic discipline and what Mill calls "recollections," or historical memory, as we would call it today (see also Smith 1999; 2004; Saaler 2020). The rise of the nation-state in the nineteenth century to become the most common global form of political organization went hand in hand with the emergence of history as a scholarly discipline. From the outset, the two were closely associated. Nation-states employed historians at national universities and other institutions, and these historians provided the state with the "national histories" they needed to legitimize this new form of political organization. Yet, as history developed into a truly academic discipline, the contradiction between scientific inquiry into the past, on the one side, and the often counterfactual or at least distorted historical *memory* of the nation—sometimes also called "public history"—on the other, became increasingly explicit and more difficult to bridge. While dispassionate academic inquiry resulted in critical analysis and examination, multi-faceted interpretations, and diverse images of the nation's past, national narratives for political and public consumption require simplicity, cohesion, uniformity, and, above all, an unalloyed sense of glory or triumphalism.

Many nineteenth-century historians chose to provide state institutions with the legitimizing and aggrandizing narratives they required, even though historians were aware that this dimension of their job was unscientific. The catastrophic events of the first half of the twentieth century, however, caused major changes in the ways professional historians conducted their work. The majority now agreed on the necessity of intellectual independence from national or state-related institutions. They also formed a broad consensus on the need for a certain degree of objectivity in creating a meaningful account of a given historical subject.

In recent decades, however, the rise of "historical revisionism" and of "post-truth" approaches to history, closely related to the global resurgence of nationalism from the 1990s, has triggered a renewed emphasis on national narratives reminiscent of nineteenth-century approaches. Despite the ignorance of—and disinterest in—scholarly methodology and procedure by the revisionist camp, these simple narratives of grandeur and glory have a strong appeal to mass audiences. Their success lies in their ability to arouse emotions and feelings of belonging and pride.

But there is one further factor that helps explain the recent growth of narratives of historical revisionism: the phenomenon of "collective narcissism." Related to the concept of "the narcissism of small differences" described by Sigmund Freud (1991, 131) in the early twentieth century, a growing body of scholarship since the 1990s has pointed to the connection between collective narcissism and various forms of ethnocentrism, narrowly framed versions of nationalism, and "blind patriotism" (cf. Brown 1997; Staub and Lavine 1999; Bizumic and Duckitt 2008; Golec de Zavala et al. 2009; 2019; Golec de Zavala and Lantos 2020). While most nationalists consider their own nation to be unique, collective narcissists describe their nation as *uniquely* unique—and thus exceptional as well as superior to all others. As Wilber Caldwell (2006, 2) writes in *American Narcissism*, "feelings of national exceptionalism are a universal characteristic of nationalism; and historically embedded national superiority myths and self-serving notions of universal mission fuel the growth of potent varieties of nationalism."

The connection between nationalism and collective narcissism—as well as historical revisionism—has been ignored until very recently. As recently as 2013, two political scientists wrote that, "little attention has been given to the possibility of narcissistic identification with the nation and its possible negative consequences for international relations" (Cai and Gries 2013, 122). Furthermore, as a summary of previous studies of collective narcissism shows (Golec de Zavala et al. 2019, 48–50), Japan has rarely been included in research on this subject (with the notable exceptions of Warren and Caponi 1996 and Iwabuchi 2002), even though deep-seated convictions about Japanese exceptionalism and uniqueness are widely acknowledged—in Japan and elsewhere[1]—and have been the subject of many studies over recent decades (Dale 1986; Befu 1987; Aoki 1990). As I argue in this chapter, it is hardly possible to understand certain forms of Japanese nationalism—and in particular historical revisionism—without referring to the concept of collective narcissism.

In what follows, I argue that in Japan the rise of historical revisionism as a form of collective narcissism since the 1990s was triggered by two major factors: the growing critical analysis of Japanese history, in particular of Japan's wartime past; and, linked with this, a perceived series of "insults" to the honor of the nation, including apologies for past "injustices" (on the emergence of historical revisionism in Japan, see Saaler 2005; 2014; 2016a). While this reaction was at first largely directed at domestic opponents such as historians and politicians, in recent years foreign scholars and even whole nations have also become targets of Japanese historical revisionists. While some might not consider "historical revisionism" an especially worrying phenomenon, I argue that its aggressive character reveals the danger that nationalist discourses pose to world peace and suggest that without remedial measures, a repetition of the history of the first half of the twentieth century cannot be avoided.

Historical revisionism as a global phenomenon

Before addressing the Japanese case, I want to emphasize that historical revisionism is a global phenomenon and by no means limited to Japan. While Holocaust denialism is probably the best-known example, recent assaults on critical interpretations of colonialism and imperialism or attempts to limit critical discussion of the history of slavery—or even present slavery in a favorable light—belong to the same category of discourse. Denialist attitudes toward war crimes, atrocities, and genocide are particularly provocative forms of revisionism, increasingly leading to frosty international relations and diplomatic friction. In many authoritarian states, laws are being passed to prohibit the publication of critical interpretations of the nation's past.

Both Holocaust denial and the exoneration of colonialism and slavery are linked to racist ideologies of white supremacy. This explains why Holocaust denialists come not only from Germany, but also from the UK and the US. Their aim is to defend the "honor" of the "white race" by either denying that the Holocaust happened or deflecting some of the blame onto the Jews themselves. One of the most famous examples is British writer David Irving, whose revisionist approach entailed the relativization of the Holocaust and downplaying the role of Hitler, whom he considered a great leader. His case received global attention in the late 1990s, when he sued the American sociologist Deborah Lipstadt for libel after she had characterized him as "one of the most dangerous spokespersons for Holocaust denial" (Lipstadt 1994, 181). The court eventually established that he had shown denialist tendencies and Lipstadt won the case in 2000 (see Evans 2002).

But while Irving was familiar with the methodology of historical research (though he often ignored it and even falsified or twisted his own findings), historical revisionism has gained popularity among people who have never practiced history or trained as historians. Particularly troubling is the embrace of this ideology by a certain type of politician–populist nationalists like former US President Donald Trump. These politicians are characterized by strongly anti-intellectual tendencies and constantly attack what they call "liberal" or "leftist" scholars, accusing them of defaming "our great Nation." In his speeches, Trump exposes the aggressive character of a historical revisionism driven by a collective narcissism marked by all the features discussed above. Take, for example, a speech he gave on 4 July 2020:

> Against every law of society and nature, our children are taught in school to hate their own country and to believe that the men and women who built it were not heroes but that were villains. The radical view of American history is a web of lies, all perspective is removed, every virtue is obscured, every motive is twisted, every fact is distorted and

every flaw is magnified until the history is purged and the record is disfigured beyond all recognition. This movement is openly attacking the legacies of every person on Mount Rushmore. They defiled the memory of Washington, Jefferson, Lincoln and Roosevelt. Today we will set history and history's record straight.

(Trump 2020)

While there is too much to unpack every element of this diatribe here, most readers would accept that historians do not think in binary oppositions such as hero vs. villain, that few professional historians would constantly—and undetected by other scholars in the field—distort facts, and that even historians who identify as "radical" would, in the larger academic community, have no choice other than to adhere to accepted standards and follow established procedures.

Trump's reference to "every law of society and nature" suggests that he embraces—or at least is attempting to instrumentalize—the widespread belief that the nation is a "natural" principle of human organization. As Ernest Gellner wrote in 1983:

> nationalism tends to treat itself as a manifest and self-evident principle, accessible as such to all men, and violated only through some perverse blindness, when in fact it owes its plausibility and compelling nature only to a very special set of circumstances, which do indeed obtain now, but which were alien to most of humanity and history. It preaches and defends continuity, but owes everything to a decisive and unutterably profound break in human history. It preaches and defends cultural diversity, when in fact it imposes homogeneity (...).
>
> *(Gellner 1983, 123–125)*

The fact that Trump's "nationalism" is motivated, at least in part, by white supremacism, confirms Gellner's emphasis on nationalism's tendencies toward homogenization rather than respect for diversity. But what has most likely upset Trump here—like other politicians influenced by collective narcissism in their approach to national history—is that historians, as discussed in the introduction, are no longer perceived to be providing simple narratives that serve the political needs of the state or the ruling elite, as they did in the nineteenth century. In the twenty-first century—in the light of the world wars and state-sponsored massacres, genocide, and institutionalized torture that marked the first half of the twentieth century—mainstream historians value objectivity and multiple perspectives as guiding principles. Certainly, in some countries, World War II created new narratives of national pride and grandeur, such as that of "the greatest generation" in the US. But as sociologist Zygmunt Bauman has shown in his seminal work *Modernity and the Holocaust*, it was the worship of the nation, working in combination with the "efficiency" of modern bureaucracies, that brought about the systematic exclusion of minorities, their dehumanization and demonization and, eventually, mass extermination (Bauman 1989, chapter 4).

Against this bleak background, history as an academic discipline (as well as the other social sciences) began to look for alternative approaches to the nation and nationalism. Emphasizing the importance of objectivity, British historian E. H. Carr argued in 1961 that historians need to be aware of the need for impartiality in their work—notwithstanding "the impossibility of total objectivity" (Carr 1961, 163).

In an age in which large corporations provide funding for research in the natural sciences which promise results that serve their needs—for example, studies funded by the sugar industry "proving" that sugar is not unhealthy, or research funded by an automobile maker showing that its vehicles are better for the environment than those of its competitors—history has surely retained a better track record in terms of the objectivity of research results. As Carr has pointed out, the binary opposition between "sciences" and "history" that is often proposed is fundamentally flawed, as history is closely akin to many of sciences in terms of procedure and the presentation of research results (ibid., 110).

Taking issue with the postmodern critique that all historical narratives are equally "constructs," Richard Evans has powerfully emphasized that while objectivity has its limits, not only do postmodernist claims fail to do justice to the concrete reality of instances of violent victimization (Evans 2000, introduction and chapter 4), they also overestimate the degree to which historians can interpret the sources and other evidence on which they base their conclusions (ibid., ch. 4 and passim). And, more importantly, the idea that "anything goes" in the construction of national narratives becomes a convenient excuse for falsifying, distorting, or denying historical facts—under the pretext that all narratives are mere constructs and are therefore all equally real, or unreal. The reality vs. narrativity debate can at times take on bizarre dimensions—as in a Bank of America study that concluded that there is a 50% possibility that we are living in a Matrix, referring to the 1999 movie starring Keanu Reeves (Furedi 2016). While it is impossible to prove that this is *not* the case, for the professional historian this kind of discussion appears nihilistic—despite the Greek philosopher Plato raising the same issues regarding perceptions and representations in his "cave allegory," 2,500 years before the emergence of postmodernism.

Be that as it may, the appearance of the term "alternative truth," declared Word of the Year by *Oxford Dictionaries* in 2016, is sufficient proof that non-scholarly and falsified versions of history have caught the popular imagination—at least in society at large (like the idea that we might live in a Matrix). As Richard Evans (2020) has pointed out in his most recent book, this also includes conspiracy theories. For professional historians, the popularity and currency of these "alternative truths" are worrying. There is no doubt that historians make mistakes. Their writings are constantly being debated, revised, and sometimes even proven wrong and rejected by the community of scholars. But my point here is that this is exactly what academia is all about. The slow (and never-ending) process of building knowledge and gradually furthering our understanding of the past, based on agreed procedures, is fundamentally different from the "post-truth" approach of historical revisionism. Its proponents—most of whom have no academic training as historians and do not hold academic positions, at least in the field of history—have no problem denying established facts, falsifying evidence (see Evans 2002), or concocting conspiracy theories of the most obscure and bizarre kind to "explain" the past (see Evans 2020). Being guided by their raw emotions, rather than a sincere desire to search for truth, they have no interest in negotiating or modifying their ideas through robust debate and research, as professional historians do. They ignore new results presented by historians and will rarely, if ever, admit that they might have been wrong. Their emergence can be accounted for by the close association between historical revisionism and collective narcissism, the subject to which I turn next.

Historical revisionism and collective narcissism

Nationalism is a highly ambivalent ideology. While some scholars have emphasized its importance for the cohesion and integration of modern societies, others have focused on its divisive character. Leaving aside the obvious problems such as the exclusion of minorities, the increasing polarization of political and societal debates in recent decades has shown how divisive nationalism can be. Even in Japan, often considered an ethnically "homogeneous" society with a high degree of social "uniformity," critical scholars and journalists have been marginalized and, on a rhetorical level, excluded from the collective of the nation. While Japan is often portrayed—and misunderstood—as a particularly "harmonious" society, the rhetorical weapons deployed in this context are highly aggressive and can spark violent language and behavior. Japanese writers and politicians who dare to critique the status quo—all the way up to former prime ministers—have been dubbed "traitors to the nation" (*baikokudo*), "anti-Japanese" (*han-nichi*), and "human scum" (*ningen no kuzu*) (for citations, see Saaler 2016a; 2016b).

This polarization and rhetorical exclusion as a reaction to criticism or a perceived refusal to recognize national "greatness" is symptomatic of collective narcissism. In recent years, this concept has become an influential analytical tool to explain the virulence of nationalism, its role as a source of inter-group enmity, and the prevalence of hate speech and violence against outside groups as well as domestic opponents (for an overview of the development of the concept, see Golec de Zavala et al. 2019). Previous research, however, has largely ignored the overlap of collective narcissism with the strategies of populists, who also tend to claim that they alone understand the nation and its history, that they alone are the "true" representatives of the nation, and that those who criticize "the nation" as they perceive it are traitors or at best anti-social elements (see Müller 2016).

Collective narcissism has been defined as "an in-group identification tied to an emotional investment in an unrealistic belief about the unparalleled greatness of an ingroup"—an investment so excessive that it is "difficult to sustain" (Golec de Zavala et al. 2009, 1074). It is especially likely to "flourish in social contexts that emphasize the group's greatness and uniqueness," as Golec de Zavala et al. (2009) have emphasized. To be sure, this applies to many kinds of groups, including soccer clubs or religious groups. In his analysis of "great power discourse" in the twenty-first-century US and China, Linus Hagström (2021) has, however, pointed out that collective narcissism is an essential element of the "quest for greatness" among the major powers, and therefore the concept is highly relevant in international relations (ibid. 2; see also Golec de Zavala et al. 2019, 58; Brown 1997, 662f).[2]

Collective narcissism is thus an essential concept to help us understand the continuing tensions between nations that harbor delusions of "greatness." This *belief* in exceptional greatness feeds an unwillingness to accept negative aspects of one's nation's past (or present), resulting in friction with other nations that also believe themselves to be pre-eminent. According to previous research, collective narcissism leads to self-aggrandizing attitudes toward the nation, but also to authoritarian tendencies as well as support for military aggression (Golec de Zavala et al. 2009; 2019, 42). Collective narcissists generally are "prejudiced towards outgroups that are construed as threatening to the ingroup's privileged position" (ibid., 46). Their beliefs can be a source of prejudice and violence against minorities, as in the case of anti-Semitism (Golec de Zavala and Cichocka 2012). Allied to the connection between collective narcissism and anti-Semitism is the suggestion that collective narcissists are particularly receptive to conspiracy theories (Golec de Zavala et al. 2019, 51; Cichocka et al. 2015, passim). While individual narcissism manifests an exaggerated degree of personal self-esteem, the problematic character of collective narcissism lies in its confrontational and aggressive attitudes to the Other and the potential to trigger clashes between whole nations, including military conflicts (Cai and Griess 2013).

Some commentators argue that in cultures with a strong sense of collectivism, collective narcissism maybe the source of individual narcissism (rather than vice versa), with the latter stemming "from the reputation and honor of the groups to which one belongs" (see Warren and Caponi 1996). The authors of a multinational study that includes Japan conclude that individuals who hold strong collectivistic views of the nation often show signs of "exhibitionistic narcissistic personality disorder" (in the US) and "closet narcissistic personality disorders" (in Japan and Denmark) (ibid., 77f).

Whatever the precise links may be, due to its aggressive character, collective narcissism is to be expected a risk factor in contemporary societies. The collective narcissist requires constant validation of what s/he perceives as the pre-eminence of his or her ingroup, reacts aggressively to criticism of this ingroup, and retaliates "with excessive hostility in situations that require a stretch of imagination to be [even] perceived as a threat or deliberate provocation" (Golec de Zavala and Lantos 2020, 275). Donald Trump's 2020 speech cited above shows just how virulent such a reaction can be.

Apart from the influence of collective narcissism, this aggressive behavior might also be linked to the concept of *thymos*, or "spiritedness," which Francis Fukuyama (2018) has analyzed in his book *Identity*. "Thymos," Fukuyama writes, "is the part of the soul that craves recognition of dignity; isothymia is the demand to be respected on an equal basis with other people; while megalothymia is the desire to be recognized as superior" (ibid., pos. 81).

As I will show in the next section, Japanese historical revisionists are characterized by the confrontational and aggressive attitudes defined by scholars of collective narcissism. They also share many of the characteristics of Donald Trump—including their tendency to megalothymia. Abe Shinzō, a former prime minister and well-known historical revisionist, has been called "Trump before Trump" by none other than Steve Bannon, the infamous founder of the right-wing news website Breitbart (Osaki 2017). Like their American counterparts, Japanese historical revisionists are highly sensitive to criticism of their collective—the nation of Japan—and react aggressively to what they perceive as disrespect toward "Japan" or sectors of the Japanese nation. Their ideas are both domestically divisive and threaten Japan's relations with its neighbors—the former victims of Japanese wars and colonial rule. In the next section, I examine the factors that trigger the narcissist reactions of Japan's historical revisionists and what effects their behavior has.

Historical revisionism in twenty-first-century Japan

What are the triggers that incite Japanese historical revisionists to attack domestic enemies and outside groups, and how are these reactions manifested? Who are the protagonists of the revisionist movement, and how do they launch their attacks on critics and their views on Japan's colonial and wartime past? According to my research, the main triggers for historical revisionists and their reactions are as follows (for a more detailed analysis, see Saaler 2005; 2016a; 2016b; Hashimoto 2015).

Most, if not all, of these perceived "insults" and the reactions to them can be explained by one or more of the characteristics and thought patterns of collective narcissists, as defined by Golec de Zavala (2011, 310):

- It really makes me angry when others **criticize** my group.
- I insist upon my group getting the **respect** that is due to it.
- I wish other groups would more quickly recognize the **authority** of my group.
- Not many people seem to fully understand the **importance** of my group.
- The true **worth** of my group is often misunderstood.
- My group deserves **special treatment**.
- If my group had a major say in the world, **the world would be a much better place**.

Table 15.1 Main triggers for historical revisionists and their reactions

Trigger (perceived insult)	Reaction	Example for trigger (T) and reaction (R)
Critical analysis of Japan's wartime past, in particular claims that the Asia-Pacific War (1931–1945) was a war of aggression, an unjust war, or a simply "bad war."	Justification, whitewashing and glorification of the war, for example, by interpreting it as a "war of Asian liberation" or even a "holy war."	T: postwar works of Japanese historians. R: publishing revisionist articles and books; establishment of a Prize for the best "Article on the True View of Modern History" (APA 2021).
Apologies for the Asia-Pacific War that imply that it was a war of aggression.	Justification, whitewashing and glorification of the war in counter-statements.	T: statements by prime ministers Hosokawa Morihiro and Murayama Tomiichi, 1993–1995. R: numerous counterstatements, culminating in the 1995 "Declaration for Asian Nations' Symbiosis" (Saaler 2005, 75f).
Claims that Japanese soldiers, airmen and sailors died "in vain" (*mudajini*) or "died like dogs" (*inujini*), sacrificed by a reckless military leadership or an irresponsible government.	Emphasizing the glorious character of the war and the "heroic sacrifice" of the soldiers.	T: Fujiwara (2001). R: Public statements and lobbying by revisionist groups and groups affiliated with the Yasukuni Shrine.
Claims that Japanese colonial rule of Taiwan and Korea was unjust, unfair, or exploitative.	Emphasizing Japan's contributions to the modernization of its former colonial territories, for example, the building of railroads and the promotion of industrialization.	T: Complex historiographical controversy. R: Simplistic and one-sided assessments of Japanese colonial rule as "beneficial" (cf. Caprio 2010).
Claims that the Japanese state organized a system of wartime brothels behind the frontlines and was involved in procuring young girls and women to serve as forced prostitutes or "comfort women" (*ianfu*).	Denial, relativization, or minimization of Japan's war crimes; defaming the victims of war crimes and shedding doubt on the credibility of oral testimonies.	T: Writings by Korean, Chinese and Japanese historians as well as historical exhibitions and statements by Korean and Chinese politicians and activists. R: Cf. Yamaguchi (2020); Saaler (2021a).
Claims that Japanese military units committed atrocities, including the Nanjing Massacre (1937/1938).	Ditto.	T: Writings by Chinese and Japanese historians as well as historical exhibitions and statements by Chinese politicians and activists. R: Cf. Kasahara 2007.

(Continued)

Table 15.1 (Continued)

Trigger (perceived insult)	Reaction	Example for trigger (T) and reaction (R)
Claims that challenge the territorial integrity of Japan—for example, Chinese claims that the Senkaku Islands are Chinese "territory" or Korean claims that the Liancourt Rocks are Korean "territory."	Presenting future war scenarios involving China (and Korea) and lobbying for enhanced military preparedness, an increase in military expenditure, and a revision of Japan's "peace constitution."	T: Chinese and Korean territorial claims. R: Nakamura (2012).
Any criticism of Japan coming from Chinese or Korean sources.	Anti-Korean or anti-Chinese hate speech, focusing on contemporary problems in Korean or Chinese politics and society.	T: All of the above. R: See analysis below.

One could possibly add the claim "My group has a monopoly on truth," because these mindsets do not allow any kind of constructive debate.

But who are Japan's historical revisionists and why are they so easily upset when confronted with critical views of the nation's history? Naturally, an individual's personal background has a part to play. Previous research has identified "undermined self-esteem" and "frustrated personal entitlement" as a major factor behind the adoption of nativist views (Golec de Zavala and Lantos 2020, 276). We could probably add megalothymia to the list.

The kind of revisionism espoused by Abe Shinzō is clearly based on personal factors—namely the reputation of his grandfather, as Abe himself explains in his book *Towards a Beautiful Country* (Abe 2007). Abe's grandfather Kishi Nobusuke was a career bureaucrat in the Japanese puppet state of Manchukuo in the late 1930s and later a minister in the wartime cabinet of Tôjô Hideki, playing an important role in empowering Japan to fight an extended war which would cost the nation millions of lives. (Around 90% of Japan's war dead perished in the last 18 months of World War II, including all victims of aerial bombings.) After the war, Kishi was arrested as a war criminal and spent several years in prison. Never brought to trial, he re-emerged as a politician, financed by prewar drug dealer Kodama Yoshio and the CIA (see Williams 2020; Weiner 2007, chapter 12). In his book, Abe rejects accusations that his grandfather was a war criminal and asserts that he was only serving the nation and the emperor (Abe 2007, 70–72). In so arguing, Abe reveals his belief that his family history and the wartime history of Japan are intertwined, leading to a collective narcissism influencing—if not dominating—his views on the nation's history. For him, the rehabilitation of wartime history is necessary to restore the family honor.

An exaggerated attachment to the nation can also be a result of a change in political allegiances. Some of Japan's most notable historical revisionists are intellectuals or scholars who started their careers in fields unrelated to history, but were influenced by Marxist methodology in their academic work. Some of them even joined the Japanese Communist Party. In the 1960s, however, partly as a result of the violence that marked the 1968 student movement, a number of intellectuals "converted" to nationalism and, in an attempt to expunge their earlier allegiances, came to hold extreme nationalist views, relentlessly attacking any criticism of the nation by the political left. Two examples of historical revisionists who have traveled this route are professor of education Fujioka Nobukatsu, one of the leaders of the revisionist movement from the late 1990s, and Itō Takashi, one of the few historians to associate himself with the movement (see Saaler 2005).

Others are mostly "in it for the money," perhaps combined with a vague enthusiasm for contemporary Japan, leading them to the simplistic conclusion that Japan cannot have possibly done wrong in the past. Prominent members of this group include two foreign revisionists, youtuber Tony Marano (aka Texas Daddy) and lawyer and former TV entertainer Kent Gilbert. Both have written books and regularly contribute to right-wing periodicals (see Saaler 2016a; 2016b). Most recently, a US-based scholar was recruited by Japan's revisionist circles not only to attack the comfort women's narratives, but also to address other highly sensitive issues (cf. Curtis 2021).

Certain periodicals have developed into important platforms for historical revisionism; obviously for their publishers, profit is an important consideration.[3] From the 2000s onward, the biweekly journal *Sapio*, with a print run of 120,000 copies at its peak, frequently ran articles justifying the Asia-Pacific War as a "war of Asian liberation." It even claimed that Japan should re-establish the Greater East Asian Co-Prosperity Sphere—the group of countries colonized or occupied during the war—but argued that "this time" Korea should be excluded because "everybody hates Korea," and that China should also be left out (*SAPIO*, 3 October 2010, cover). While *Sapio* was discontinued in 2018 after several years of declining sales, monthly journals such as *Rekishitsū* or *WiLL*, the latter with a print run of 100,000 copies,[4] have stepped up to fill the void and have raised the stakes by surpassing its predecessor in the aggressiveness of its tone. Considering the reaction of mainstream scholars to the aggressive stance taken by *Sapio* in the 2000s and 2010s (see Saaler 2005), the fact that it disappeared because its tone was too *moderate* might sound counter-intuitive to contemporary observers, but proves the point that Japan is not the harmonious society we often imagine it to be and that discussions about politics and history are increasingly polarized.

Most of the contributions to *Rekishitsū* or *WiLL* are not finely crafted articles, but rather transcripts of discussions (*taidan*), usually between two or three participants, which are characterized by a highly emotional tone, a lack of evidence—and often logic—in the presentation of the arguments, and a strong anti-intellectual bias. While critical interpretations of national history are the staple content of academic journals, the revisionists writing in these journals do not bother attempting to find fault with scholarly arguments by presenting new evidence or pointing out logical fallacies. Rather, they typically deploy the handy tools of "alternative truths" or "conspiracy theories" to defend their collective against perceived attacks. Unsurprisingly, the content of *WiLL*, in particular, is highly repetitive and replays the same debates—the topics listed at the beginning of this section.

WiLL and its sister journal *Hanada* have been empowered by its affiliations with long-time prime minister Abe Shinzō, who has contributed pieces or taken part in interviews which are reproduced in these journals. Abe's successor, Suga Yoshihide, also wrote articles for *WiLL* during his time as the Cabinet Secretary of the Abe administration (Suga 2019). The inclusion of contributions by sitting or former prime ministers gives this embodiment of twenty-first-century nationalism and the platform in which is it presented a disturbing degree of relevance and significance in the Japanese political scene. In his contributions, Abe has never shied away from using the aggressive language identified by scholars of collective narcissism (see Abe and Hyakuta 2013). In July 2021, for example, he reacted to criticism of the Tokyo Olympics continuing to be scheduled despite the ongoing corona pandemic as "anti-Japanese" (*han-nichi*) (Abe and Sakurai 2021, 39). Illustrating the divisive and populist character of Abe's brand of nationalism, he named the mainstream newspaper *Asahi*

Shinbun and the Japanese Communist Party as culprits. Two of *WiLL*'s writers used the same language, but extended the "anti-Japanese" label to all "liberals" (Takahashi and Kadoda 2021). Again, personal motives and collective narcissism are connected here: Abe undoubtedly regarded criticism of the Olympics as an attack on Japan's national honor, but also as an attack on his personal record of achievement—the bid for "Tokyo 2020" was won in 2013, during his tenure as the prime minister.

Abe not only empowers *WiLL* as a platform for revisionism, but also his interview partners—journalist Sakurai Yoshiko, in the case of the article cited above, and novelist Hyakuta Naoki, who is well-known for his anti-Chinese and anti-Korean hate speech. In this respect, he follows Watanabe Shōichi, a scholar of premodern English literature, whom Abe has referred to "my teacher," even though he never formally studied under Watanabe. In a 2012 article in the journal *Rekishitsū*, Watanabe made the sweeping claim that "all Korean national heroes are terrorists" (Watanabe 2012, 30). Drawing on the biographies of Korean independence fighters, he pronounced them all "guilty" of anti-Japanese activities during the era of Japanese colonial rule (1910–1945). Lacking any appreciation of the larger context of anti-colonial movements in the first half of the twentieth century, and in particular immediately after World War I, Watanabe fails to see this phase of Japanese-Korean history in any context other than his narrow understanding of the nation-state, which, at the time, was simultaneously an empire—the Empire of Japan. Tellingly, his article formed part of a special section of the November edition of *Rekishitsū* titled "Anti-Korean Typhoon."

War crimes are another subject to which historical revisionists react with particular belligerence. When testimonies of the 1937/1938 Nanjing Massacre were registered in UNESCO Memory of the World in 2015, influential historical revisionist Takahashi Shirô, writing in *Rekishitsū*, has discredited the massacre as "fake" (*detarame*) (Takahashi 2015), as many revisionists had done before him (most notably, Tanaka Masaaki, cf. Tanaka 1987). The building of statues dedicated to the "comfort women" in Korea, the US, and various European states has probably triggered more reaction from historical revisionists—along with the Abe government, as well as the succeeding Suga administration—than any other history-related issue in the early twenty-first century. These responses included insulting the elderly victims as well as slighting the Korean "national character," a highly questionable concept to begin with (see Saaler 2018). In particular, historical revisionists have cast doubt on the authenticity—or even truthfulness—of the testimonies of former comfort women, often adding ethnic slurs such as "all Koreans are liars" and "lying is a special skill of Koreans" (see Saaler 2021a for citations).

In 2020, the mayor of Nagoya, Kawamura Takeshi, well-known for denying the Nanjing Massacre, was involved in a campaign to unseat Aichi Prefecture governor Ōmura Hideki, because the latter had lent his support for an exhibition that included an artist's interpretation of a comfort women statue. The recall motion failed to gather sufficient support, falling short of the required 860,000 signatures. Scandalously, many of the 435,000 signatures the campaigners gathered proved to be forgeries and the campaign manager—though not mayor Kawamura, who was only deeply involved as a supporter of the campaign—was later arrested (*Asahi Shinbun*, 16 February 2021). While this case shows that historical revisionism lacks broad support in Japanese society, it also reveals how far narcissism-driven revisionists will go to defend the "honor" of their nation against perceived threats and insults—while eventually, through their dishonorable actions, clearly damaging Japan's international reputation.

Especially notable for his obscurantism and anti-intellectualism among the contributors of *WiLL* and similar revisionist journals is Mabuchi Mutsuo, a former diplomat. With regard to World War II, he claims that the US, not Japan, was the aggressor and that the US forced Japan into the war (Mabuchi 2016). Recycling anti-Jewish conspiracy theories, he also claims that the Russian Revolution was a scheme hatched by "American Socialists," or "Jews from the finance capital families on Wall Street" (ibid., 37). According to Mabuchi, it was also a Jewish conspiracy that drove Japan into war—supposedly against its will—with the US (ibid.). In a 2020 article, Mabuchi further claims that "the Jewish international finance capital" was responsible for preventing the re-election of US President Donald Trump (Takayama and Mabuchi 2020, 121).

These and similar diatribes would not deserve attention were they not appearing in publications with six-figure circulations, and if prime ministers did not endorse these journals by adding their authority to their line-up of authors. The belligerent rhetoric, the self-contained character of the conspiracy theories they promote, and the anti-intellectual bias, which is widespread among populists and their followers, are all elements of what some observers are calling the "culture wars" of the twenty-first century.

Conclusion

Historical revisionism is one of the more grotesque and, at the same time, dangerous forms of nationalism to have developed in the late twentieth and early twenty-first centuries. Although the writing and rewriting of history always has been an integral part of nation-building, the merger of historical revisionism with the recourse to "alternative truth" and the increasing anti-intellectual tendencies of the movement, as well as the influence of racist ideologies, all demonstrate that it has morphed into a self-contained and aggressive movement that is unwilling to engage in dialogue. Reacting aggressively to perceived threats; spreading conspiracy theories and insulting opponents rather than engaging in dialogue; criticizing, falsifying, and even deconstructing rival interpretations and theses, Japanese historical revisionists are clearly showing signs of collective narcissism.

Emerging as a political movement in the 1990s, with long-time prime minister Abe Shinzō as one its most influential advocates, historical revisionism has become a powerful reactionary force. Although the Liberal Democratic Party (LDP) considers itself a "conservative" party, its close association with historical revisionism indicates that it has mutated into a reactionary organization, advocating nineteenth-century ideologies. Its aim is not to preserve any of the achievements made by Japan and the Japanese over the last 75 years, but rather to return Japan to the nineteenth century.

This trend was evident, for example, in Prime Minister Abe's support for kindergarten in Osaka, in which children aged 3–6 (!) were made to memorize and recite the 1890 Imperial Rescript on Education in order to familiarize them with the emperor-centered ideology of nineteenth-century Japan. Abe had supported the kindergarten with financial donations and, for a time, his wife Akie held the post of "honorary director," encouraging the owner to name a yet-to-be-built elementary school the "Abe Shinzō Memorial School." Due to irregularities in the way the kindergarten owner purchased the land for the school from Osaka Prefecture (at a nearly 90% discount from regular land prices; see McNeill 2021) and the ensuing scandal, it was never built. But the story illustrates the growing influence of historical revisionist and reactionary thought in Japanese society, which, in many ways, mirrors similar developments in other countries around the globe.

Readers who value the positive aspects of nationalism rather than seeking to be critical of its negative impacts might be tempted to view this author as underestimating the importance of the integrative functions of nationalism and the fact that national identity, as some have put it, "fulfills a fundamental human need" (Caldwell 2006, 151; see also Fukuyama 2018). But this is hardly the case with narcissist-driven forms of nationalism—or possibly any form of nationalism, given that human societies existed and thrived long before nationalism (see Gellner 1983, cited above). To be sure, nationalism has secured liberation from foreign domination, colonial rule, and oppression by narrow political or social elites. In the twenty-first century, however, nationalism is no longer a liberating force. The power of state surveillance and indoctrination has made it, above all, a tool to mobilize the population against anything considered a threat—whether external or internal. The rise of xenophobic forms of nationalism over the last few decades and the often-lamented "drift to the right" in the politics of many countries are clear evidence of these tendencies.

The most worrying aspect of the spread of a narcissism-driven nationalism are the implications for foreign policy (see Cai and Gries 2013). As Golec de Zavala (2011, 312) argues, "studies confirm that collective narcissists react with *retaliatory hostility* towards other groups whose actions or opinions undermine the in-group's idealized image." The provocative activities of historical revisionists, which have undone many of the positive achievements of the reconciliation policies of the 1980s and 1990s (see Saaler 2021a) and created new obstacles, are a textbook example of the aggressive character of collective narcissism outlined by Golec de Zavala and others. The constant escalation in revisionist polemics is most evident in the rhetoric: since 2013, revisionists no longer speak of historical discussions or even a "history problem" (*rekishi mondai*)—right-wing politicians and pundits now use the expression "history war" (*rekishisen*) to describe the controversies involving Japan and other Asian nations, and have increased their efforts to sanitize the narrative of Japan's role in World War II (Saaler 2021b).

However, since the early 2000s, groups of historians from Japan, Korea, and China have come together to demonstrate that the "history war" is not an academic phenomenon. They have published books that express a shared understanding of East Asian history, demonstrating that although differences will always remain, the respect for objectivity which underscores the way that academic historians conduct their work allows at least a minimum consensus to emerge regarding a shared past.[5]

Which of the two camps will prevail in Japan remains to be seen but, for the foreseeable future, nationalism driven by collective narcissism—including its specific manifestation of historical revisionism—will remain "a factor contributing to the escalation of intergroup conflicts, an independent and unique predictor of retaliatory aggression and prejudice, as well as a core belief driving divisive political choices undermining democratic political systems" (Golec de Zavala et al. 2019, 38).

Postscript

After the completion of this manuscript, former Prime Minister of Japan, Abe Shinzō, was assassinated on 8 July 2022. I decided not to make any revisions to this chapter, partly due to the production schedule of this volume, but mainly because I could not observe any change in Abe's views between submission of this chapter and his death. Certainly, Abe's several contributions to the journal *WiLL*, including his last article published in the issue that went on sale on 24 June 2022, give no indication of any change in his views.

I thank the anonymous readers as well as Jeff Kingston and Bucky Sheftall for comments on an earlier version of this chapter.

Notes

1 While Japanese discourses of national uniqueness and exceptionalism are sometimes considered unique to Japan, there is an abundant literature discussing parallel phenomena in other nations. See, for example, Caldwell (2006, 143–144) and Lipset (1996) for the case of the US.
2 See also the January/February 2018 issue of the journal *Foreign Affairs*, which features a series of six articles on "How Nations Confront the Evils of History."
3 For an analysis of the phenomenon of internet right-wing activism, which is not unrelated to the publications analyzed here, but operates on a somewhat different level, see Hall (2021).
4 For publication numbers, see the website of the Japan Magazine Publishers Association, https://www.j-magazine.or.jp/user/printed/index/44
5 These textbooks, authored by multinational groups of historians and educators, are now available in English. See, for example, Fuchs et al. (2018); this two-volume work is available as a free download from the Georg-Eckert-Institute for International Textbook Research at http://www.gei.de/de/publikationen/eckert-expertise/ee-einzelband/news/detail/News/eckhardt-fuchs-tokushi-kasahara-sven-saaler-hg-a-new-modern-history-of-east-asia.html

References

English-language references

Anderson, Benedict. 1983. *Imagined Communities: Reflections on the Origin and Spread of Nationalism*. London: Verso.
Asahi Shinbun. 2021. "Police to probe Aichi governor recall petition for alleged fraud." *Asahi Shinbun*, 16 February, online. https://www.asahi.com/ajw/articles/14194747 (accessed 15 July 2021).
Bauman, Zygmunt. 1989. *The Modernity and the Holocaust*. Cambridge: Polity.
Bizumic, Boris and John Duckitt. 2008. "'My group is not worthy of me': Narcissism and ethnocentrism." *Political Psychology* 29: 437–453.
Brown, Andrew D. 1997. "Narcissism, Identity, and Legitimacy." *The Academy of Management Review* 22 (3): 643–686.
Cai, Huajian, and Peter Gries. 2013. "National Narcissism: Internal Dimensions and International Correlates." *PsyCh Journal* 2: 122–132.
Caprio, Mark. 2010. "Neo-Nationalist Interpretations of Japan's Annexation of Korea: The Colonization Debate in Japan and South Korea." *Asia-Pacific Journal/Japan Focus* 8/44 (4) (1 November 2010). https://apjjf.org/-Mark-Caprio/3438/article.html. Accessed: 20 October 2021.
Carr, Edward H. 1961. *What is History?* London: Vintage Books.
Caldwell, Wilber W. 2006. *American Narcissism. The Myth of National Superiority*. New York: Algora Publishing.
Cichocka, Aleksandra, Marta Marchlewska, Agnieszka Golec de Zavala, and Mateusz Olechowski. 2015. "'They Will Not Control Us': Ingroup Positivity and Belief in Intergroup Conspiracies." *British Journal of Psychology* 107 (3): 556–576.
Connor, Walker. 1994. *Ethnonationalism. The Quest for Understanding*. Princeton University Press.
Curtis, Paula. 2021. "Ramseyer and the Right-Wing Ecosystem Suffocating Japan." *Tokyo Review*, 30 May. https://www.tokyoreview.net/2021/05/ramseyer-and-the-right-wing-ecosystem-suffocating-japan (accessed 20 October 2021).
Dale, Peter. 1986. *The Myth of Japanese Uniqueness*. London: Routledge.
Evans, Richard. 2000. *In Defence of History*. New York: W. W. Norton.
Evans, Richard. 2002. *Lying About Hitler. History, Holocaust, and the David Irving Trial*. New York: Basic Books.
Evans, Richard. 2020. *The Hitler Conspiracies: The Third Reich and the Paranoid Imagination*. London: Allen Lane.
Freud, Sigmund. 1991. *Civilization, Society and Religion* (Penguin Freud Library 12). London: Penguin.
Fuchs, Eckhardt, Sven Saaler, and Tokushi Kasahara, eds. 2018. *A New Modern History of East Asia*. 2 vols. Göttingen: V&R Unipress.
Fukuyama, Francis. 2018. *Identity: The Demand for Dignity and the Politics of Resentment*. New York: Farrar Straus & Giroux (Kindle Edition).

Furedi, Jacob. 2016. "Bank of America Analysts Think There's a 50% Chance We Live in the Matrix." *The Independent*, 22 April 2023, https://www.independent.co.uk/tech/bank-of-america-the-matrix-50-per-cent-virtual-reality-elon-musk-nick-bostrom-a7287471.html.
Gellner, Ernest. 1983. *Nations and Nationalisms*. Oxford: Blackwell.
Giddens, Anthony. 1985. *The Nation-State and Violence* (A Contemporary Critique of Historical Materialism, v. 2). Cambridge: Polity Press.
Golec de Zavala, Agnieszka. 2011. "Collective Narcissism and Intergroup Hostility: The Dark Side of 'In-Group Love'." *Social and Personality Psychology Compass* 5 (6): 309–320.
Golec de Zavala, Agnieszka, and Aleksandra Cichocka. 2012. "Collective Narcissism and Anti-Semitism in Poland: the Mediating Role of Siege Beliefs and the Conspiracy Stereotype of Jews." *Group Processes and Intergroup Relations* 15 (2): 213–229.
Golec de Zavala, Agnieszka, Aleksandra Cichocka, Roy Eidelson, and Nuwan Jayawickreme. 2009. "Collective Narcissism and its Social Consequences." *Journal of Personality and Social Psychology* 97 (6): 1074–1096.
Golec de Zavala, Agnieszka, Karolina Dyduch-Hazar, and Drottya Lantos. 2019. "Collective Narcissism: Political Consequences of Investing Self-Worth in the Ingroup's Image." *Advances in Political Psychology* 40 (1): 37–74.
Golec de Zavala, Agnieszka, and Dorottya Lantos. 2020. "Collective Narcissism and Its Social Consequences: The Bad and the Ugly." *Current Directions in Psychological Science* 29 (3): 273–278.
Greenfeld, Liah. 1993. *Nationalism: Five Roads to Modernity*. Harvard University Press.
Hall, Jeffrey J. 2021. *Japan's Nationalist Right in the Internet Age: Online Media and Grassroots Conservative Activism*. London: Routledge.
Hashimoto, Akiko. 2015. *A Long Defeat: Cultural Trauma, Memory, and Identity in Japan*. Cambridge, MA: Oxford University Press.
Hobsbawm, Eric and Terrence Ranger, eds. 1983. *The Invention of Tradition*. Cambridge University Press.
Iwabuchi Koichi. 2002. "'Soft' Nationalism and Narcissism: Japanese Popular Culture Goes Global." *Asian Studies Review* 26 (4): 447–469.
Lipset, Seymour Martin. 1996. *American Exceptionalism: A Double Edged Sword*. New York: W. W. Norton.
Lipstadt, Deborah E. 1994. *Denying the Holocaust: the Growing Assault on Truth and Memory*. New York: Plume.
McNeill, David. 2021. "An ultranationalist school, a suicide and a wife on a quest for the truth." *The Irish Times*, 27 June, online: https://www.irishtimes.com/news/world/asia-pacific/an-ultranationalist-school-a-suicide-and-a-wife-on-a-quest-for-the-truth-1.4605015 (accessed 31 July 2021).
Mill, John Stuart. 1958. *Considerations on Representative Government*. Edited by Currin V. Shields. New York: The Liberal Arts Press.
Mosse, George. 1990. *Fallen Soldiers: Reshaping the Memory of the World Wars*. Oxford University Press.
Mosse, George. 2001. *The Nationalization of the Masses*. New York: H. Fertig.
Müller, Jan-Werner. 2016. *What Is Populism?* University of Pennsylvania Press.
Osaki, Tomohiro. 2017. "Former Trump Strategist Steve Bannon Praises Abe's Nationalist Agenda," *The Japan Times*, 17 December. https://www.japantimes.co.jp/news/2017/12/17/national/politics-diplomacy/former-trump-strategist-bannon-praises-abes-nationalist-agenda (accessed 6 January 2022).
Saaler, Sven. 2005. *Politics, Memory, and Public Opinion. The History Textbook Controversy and Japanese Society*. München: Iudicium.
Saaler, Sven. 2014. "Bad War or Good War? History and Politics in Post-War Japan." In *Critical Issues in Contemporary Japan*, edited by Jeff Kingston, 135–146. London and New York: Routledge.
Saaler, Sven. 2016a. "Nationalism and History in Contemporary Japan." In *Asian Nationalisms Reconsidered*, edited by Jeff Kingston, 172–85. London and New York: Routledge, 2016.
Saaler, Sven. 2016b. "Nationalism and History in Contemporary Japan." *Asia-Pacific Journal/Japan Focus*, 14/20 (7). https://apjjf.org/2016/20/Saaler.html (accessed 12 February 2022).
Saaler, Sven. 2018. "Introduction: Japanese-German Mutual Images from the 1860s to the Present." In *Mutual Perceptions and Images in Japanese-German Relations, 1860–2010*, edited by Sven Saaler et al., 1–63. Leiden and Boston: Brill.
Saaler, Sven. 2020. *Men in Metal. A Topography of Public Bronze Statuary in Modern Japan*. Leiden und Boston: Brill.

Saaler, Sven. 2021a. "Japan's Soft Power and the 'History Problem'". In *Remembrance – Responsibility – Reconciliation*, edited by Lothar Wigger and Marie Dirnberger, 45–56. Berlin: J. B. Metzler.
Saaler, Sven. 2021b. "Heisei Historiography: Academic History and Public Commemoration in Japan, 1990–2020." In *Heisei Japan*, ed. Tina Burrett, Jeff Kingston, Noriko Murai. London and New York: Routledge.
Smith, Anthony D. 1999. *Myths and Memories of the Nation*. Oxford University Press.
Smith, Anthony D. 2004. *The Antiquity of Nations*. Cambridge: Polity.
Staub, Ervin, and Howard Lavine. 1999. "On the varieties of national attachment: Blind versus constructive patriotism." *Political Psychology* 20: 151–174.
Trump, Donald J. 2020. *Mount Rushmore Speech*. Online: https://www.rev.com/blog/transcripts/donald-trump-speech-transcript-at-mount-rushmore-4th-of-july-event (accessed 31 July 2021).
Warren, Muriel P., and Attilio Capponi. 1996. "The role of culture in the development of narcissistic personality disorders in American, Japan and Denmark." *Journal of Applied Social Sciences* 20 (1): 77–82.
Weaver, Eric Beckett. 2006. *National Narcissism: The Intersection of the Nationalist Cult and Gender in Hungary*. Frankfurt and Bern: Peter Lang.
Weber, Eugen. 1976. *Peasants into Frenchmen: The Modernization of Rural France, 1870–1914*. Stanford, CA: Stanford University Press.
Weiner, Tim. 2008. *Legacy of Ashes: The History of the CIA*. New York: Anchor.
Williams, Brad. 2020. "US Covert Action in Cold War Japan: The Politics of Cultivating Conservative Elites and its Consequences." *Journal of Contemporary Asia* 50 (4): 593–617.
Yamaguchi, Tomomi. 2020. "The 'History Wars' and the 'Comfort Woman' Issue: Revisionism and the Right-wing in Contemporary Japan and the U.S." *Asia-Pacific Journal/Japan Focus* 18 (6): 5381. https://apjjf.org/-Tomomi-Yamaguchi/5381/article.pdf.

Japanese-language references

Abe Shinzō. 2007. *Utsukushii kuni e* (*Towards a Beautiful Country*). Tokyo: Bungei Shunjû.
Abe, Shinzō and Hyakuta Naoki. 2013. *Nihon yo, sekai no man-naka de saki-hokore* (*Oh, Japan, blossom with pride in the center of the world*). Tokyo: Wakku
Abe, Shinzō and Sakurai Yoshiko. 2021. "Tôkyô gorin, shingata korona, wakuchin sesshu, Suga-sôri, Shū Kinpei, Jieitai, Taiwan, jiki sôri sôsai, sôsenkyo—dokusen 90fun, subete o katarô" (Tokyo Olympics, new corona virus, vaccination, prime minister Suga, Xi Jinping, the SDF, Taiwan, the next LDP president, general elections—exclusive 90 minutes interview about everything). *Hanada* 8: 34–53.
Aoki, Tamotsu. 1990. *'Nihonbunkaron' no henyō* (*The Transformation of 'Japanese Culture Discourses'*). Tokyo: Chūō Kōronsha.
APA. 2021. *Shin no kingendaishi-kan kenshō ronbun* (Prize for the Best Article on the True View of Modern History). https://ajrf.jp/ronbun/index.html (accessed 14 March 2021).
Befu, Harumi. 1987. *Ideorogī toshite no Nihonbunkaron* (*Japanese Culture Discourse as Ideolgy*). Tokyo: Shisō no Kagakusha.
Fujiwara, Akira. 2001. *Gashi shita eirei-tachi* (*The Heroic Souls that Starved to Death*). Tokyo: Aoki Shoten.
Kasahara, Tokushi. 2007. *Nankin jiken ronsōshi* (*History of the Controversy about the Nanjing Incident*). Tokyo: Heibonsha (second, enlarged edition, 2018).
Nakamura, Hideki. 2012. *Senkaku shotō-oki kaisen* (*The Naval Battle on the Shores of the Senkaku Islands*). Tokyo: Ushio Shobô Kôjin Shinsha.
Suga, Yoshihide. 2019. "Reiwa no jidai—seiji o mae ni!" (The Era of Reiwa—Politics to the front). *WiLL* 8: 28–34.
Takahashi, Shirô. 2015. "'Nankin, ianfu' no detarame" (The Fakes of Nanjing and Comfort Women). *Rekishitsū* 15 November: 158–162.
Takahashi, Yūichi and Kadoda Ryūshō. 2021. "'Gorin yamero!' Jama suru hannichi riberaru no shôtai" ("Stop the Olympics!" The Truth about the anti-Japanese liberals). *WiLL* 8: 32–44.
Takayama, Masayuki and Mabuchi Mutsuo. 2020. "Toranpu shikkyaku undō no genkyō wa Jōji Sorosu (The Villain behind the Movement to Overthrow Trump is George Soros). *WiLL* 9: 121–126.
Tanaka, Masaaki. 1987. *Nankin jiken no sōkatsu* (*Summary of the Nanjing Incident*). Tokyo: Kenkōsha.
Watanabe, Shōichi. 2012. "Kankoku no eiyū wa terorisuto bakari" (Korean heroes are all Terrorists). *Rekishitsū* 11: 30–37.

16
ABE'S FECKLESS NATIONALISM

Jeff Kingston

Introduction

The July 2022 assassination of Abe Shinzo (2012–2020; 2005–2007), Japan's longest serving prime minister, sent shockwaves through the nation, triggering divisive debate over his legacy. He became a Diet member in 1993 with a rightwing nationalist agenda of revising the Japanese Constitution and rewriting Japan's wartime history. He failed to achieve constitutional revision, acknowledging his inability to gain public support for this quest and saying this was his greatest regret when he announced in August 2020 that he would step down. However, on Abe's watch, reference to the comfort women was purged from most secondary school textbooks and moral education was revived, a subject tainted by association with pre-1945 militarism (Bamkin 2018). In addition, at his behest the government mandated Patriotic Education (2006). During his long tenure, he empowered rightwing groups, pundits and activists who helped transform political discourse about Japan's shared history with Asia and with his support took the offensive against individuals and media organizations that favor a more contrite and critical perspective on the wartime and colonial past. To take the measure of Abe's nationalism, this essay also explores other issues aside from revisionist history and constitutional revision that highlight his empty posturing and the limited appeal of his agenda to overturn the postwar order. To that end, we examine his record on immigration, territorial disputes, the US alliance, freedom of expression and the 2020 Tokyo Olympics. Overall, he was more feckless than resolute, achieving relatively little on his nationalist agenda despite his ruling coalition's dominance in the Diet. Moreover, the disappointing results of Abenomics, numerous scandals involving cronies, his downsizing by the COVID-19 pandemic and the surprising revelations about his extensive ties with the Unification Church, popularly known as the 'Moonies', define his legacy more than his abortive efforts to infuse national identity with patriotic fervor.

Immigration?

Nationalist discourse is often about blood and ethnic purity, focusing on not only "who we are" but also "who we are not." This othering is endemic in Japan where the concept of "pure Japanese" is mainstream and widely accepted even as some contest it. The example of Europe is often invoked to illustrate the risks of having enclaves of unassimilated "foreigners" and why this should be avoided. One potential policy response to Japan's aging society and labor shortages is increased immigration, but reflecting Abe's nationalist reservations about an influx, he only adopted some limited half-measures that will have a little impact on these problems. In many nations, immigration is strongly opposed and highly politicized by nationalists, but not in Japan. During Abe's tenure, the number of non-Japanese residents in Japan increased from 2.09 million in 2012 to 2.93 million in 2019, accounting for 2.3% of the population. Despite this surge, there has been no popular nationalist backlash and no political party runs on an anti-immigrant platform. There was a doubling of overseas students from 2007 to 2017 to 267,000; they are eligible to work 28 hours per week, often staffing convenience stores, restaurants and other high visibility service sector establishments. Abe has also presided over a quiet process of boosting migrant workers arriving under the Technical Intern Training Program (TITP), from about 150,000 in 2012 to over 400,000 by 2019 (Tran 2020). In addition, in 2018, he passed legislation that provides visas to medium- and low-skilled workers in 14 designated sectors (Milly 2020). These visas are subject to limited periods of duration, so they are ostensibly migrant worker programs as distinct from immigration. In practice, such a distinction may be wishful thinking, but it does provide useful political cover. In announcing the 2018 plan, Abe made clear this distinction to reassure conservative supporters that he was not facilitating a permanent influx of foreigners and agreed in Diet deliberations to cap the number of migrants under the scheme at 345,000 over five years down from the original proposal of one million.

In opening the door for workers in sectors that have been hardest hit by labor shortages, Abe was responding to business groups while he managed potential political fallout by imposing limits on duration of stay and the number of migrants allowed in. However, he did nothing significant to facilitate assimilation for non-Japanese or to promote a more inclusive and welcoming environment so that Japan can benefit from growing diversity in its population (Liu-Farrer 2020). In that sense, Japan remains in denial about increasing reliance on non-Japanese workers and providing better working and living conditions for them.

The situation is especially acute for elderly care as many discouraged foreign caregivers return home within a few years of arriving, a waste of the money invested in recruiting and training them that leaves a graying Japan woefully understaffed. The scale of the agreements with sending countries for caregivers is ludicrously small, hundreds instead of tens of thousands, and the entire system seems designed to dissuade them from staying. There have been some small adjustments in qualifications testing but set against the need for some 300,000 more elderly caregivers by 2025, tweaking this program offers no relief. Abe's 2018 migrant worker program targets 60,000 caregivers by 2025, but even with this inadequate target, there are no signs of the government committing sufficient resources for their recruitment and training.

In assessing Abe's overall record on migrant workers, he tried to finesse his nationalist base but the adjustments he introduced are inadequate for a labor market of some 65 million workers and will do little to boost the nation's economy. Ironically, public opinion polls suggest that the public is not especially xenophobic and relatively positive about foreign workers, but the ruling conservative elite regularly invokes their imagined opposition to justify its exclusionary policies and strict limits (Pew 2018, *Nikkei* 2020). So if foreigners can't raise nationalistic hackles, what about hallowed land?

Territorial disputes

Japan has longstanding territorial disputes with Russia, South Korea and China over islands, islets and rocks that are hotly contested and threaten regional peace and make difficult any improvement in relations. Historical narratives can be adjusted, but once made, territorial claims are hard to concede, and compromise is difficult. These disputes are framed as an affront to national dignity and subject to intense politicization that limits the space for diplomacy.

Russia

PM Abe found out just how difficult such diplomacy can be in his sustained efforts to seek compromise with Russian President Vladimir Putin over the Northern Territories, four islands Russia has controlled since 1945 off the coast of Hokkaido. Abe met with Putin more than any other world leader to persuade the Russian leader to part with at least two of the islands but came away empty-handed. During this time, Russia beefed up fortifications on the islands and otherwise made Abe's undertaking appear delusional. It is hard to escape the conclusion that Putin played Abe and was more interested in driving a wedge between Washington and Tokyo than in cutting a deal. So why did Abe persist against the odds? Actively asserting Japan's claims played well to Abe's nationalist base and reflected his belief in personal diplomacy. Certainly, there was more smoke than fire, but Abe appeared resolute and domestically there was no downside because expectations of success were limited. Abe could count on the Japanese media to portray this as further evidence that Russia was not trustworthy, and Putin unreasonable, thus in that sense his posturing carried little political risk. It was also a gambit appreciated by nationalists because it is one of the rare instances of Tokyo not taking its cues from Washington, defying the US efforts to isolate Moscow and carving out an independent foreign policy. In essence, striding the world stage to regain lost territory was pure showmanship and decent PR, especially because it was a quixotic quest.

South Korea

There was also no headway in the dispute with South Korea over the Takeshima/Dokdo islets in the East Sea/Sea of Japan, but Abe made no effort to shift the status quo. Seoul's perceived intransigence over the comfort women and forced labor issues reinforced negative perceptions toward Koreans that prevail in contemporary Japan. These disputes dominated the diplomatic bandwidth and generated domestic support for his dismissive stance toward S. Korea, a nation that is portrayed in Japan as playing the history card to gain advantage. Abe dutifully agreed to a deal regarding the comfort women, something few expected him to do, because the US insisted, but when that unraveled following the impeachment of President Park in 2017, he could simply ignore her successor Moon Jae-in with impunity. Oddly enough, Abe claimed the moral high ground in the comfort women dispute, using the derailment of the 2015 agreement to project a reasonable image and painting Moon, and Koreans in general, as unreasonable.

China

Relations with China got off to a rocky start and President Xi Jinping made clear his distaste for Abe, initially fending off repeated requests for a meeting and then when they first met in 2014 on the sidelines of APEC, made a sour face when he briefly shook Abe's hand. The reason for the rancor was Japan's nationalization of the disputed Senkaku/Diaoyu islets in 2012 under Abe's predecessor, PM Noda Yoshihiko from the Democratic Party of Japan (DPJ). The deterioration in bilateral relations and regional security that ensued helped Abe and the Liberal Democratic Party (LDP) to regain power because the DPJ had alienated Washington and the alliance had weakened (Murphy 2014). A rising China with regional hegemonic ambitions made Abe's hawkish nationalist credentials more appealing to voters. China saw Abe as a strong leader who would nurture better relations with the US, boost defense spending, take a hardline on territorial issues and in addition was unrepentant on history issues. For Chinese nationalists, Abe was made to order, a Japanese leader everyone could agree to hate who could be relied on to stoke anti-Japanese sentiments with his gestures, speeches and policies. To the extent that Abe could provoke hostility in China (and Korea), Japanese nationalists also gained momentum domestically while Abe reaped stature and political capital.

Due to President Donald Trump's erratic diplomacy and trade sanctions, there was a limited thaw in the permafrost of bilateral Sino-Japanese relations as both leaders had a common interest in insulating their economies from the damage. There were plans for a Tokyo summit in 2020, but the pandemic forced cancellation. Even so, the saber rattling over the Senkaku persisted and there were continual Chinese incursions into the territorial waters as Beijing seeks to normalize its claims and not accede to Japan's 2012 overturning of the informal accord to shelve the sovereignty dispute that prevailed since the late 1970s.

Impasse

Thus, with Moscow, Seoul and Beijing, Abe made no significant headway on any of his regional disputes, a failing his biographer harshly criticizes (Harris 2020). What Abe did was to enshrine these islands as national core interests in secondary school textbooks, transforming them into talismans of national pride for younger Japanese who can now visit a small museum in downtown Tokyo where Japan's claims are promoted and validated. Thus, rather than managing regional tensions, Abe has fanned the nationalist flames of discord, emulating his neighbors' dead-end policies instead of exercising statesmanship. The dreary calculus is that tensions are beneficial to nationalists in the region, but only so long as the antagonism doesn't spin out of control.

Constitutional revision

Conservatives are united in seeking to modify and overturn the postwar reforms initiated by the US during the Occupation between 1945 and 1952 (Mullins 2016) For Abe, the American-drafted 1947 Constitution symbolizes Japan's humiliating subordination to the US and revising it remains unfinished family business. His grandfather, Prime Minister Kishi Nobusuke (1957–1960), also wanted to revise it but was ousted from power before he could do so. This ignominious downfall was due to his strongarming a renewal of the US-Japan Security Treaty through the Diet by literally having opponents carried out of the chamber before the vote (Kapur 2018). That authoritarian move sparked widespread protests by those who believed the treaty unconstitutional and overly provocative toward the Soviet Union. Ironically, Kishi, a Japanese conservative once jailed by the US as a Class A war crimes suspect, became prime minister just ten years after his release, heading the LDP that the CIA helped establish in 1955 and funded thereafter. The LDP was created to consolidate conservative forces to preserve the alliance and safeguard the US military presence, a somewhat awkward agenda for nationalists. A Cold War-focused Washington saw Japan as essential to its efforts to contain Soviet expansionism and was anxious about widespread opposition to the alliance and US bases in Japan (McCormack 2007).

In Article 9 of the Constitution, Japan renounces the right to wage war and maintain military forces and it has become a cherished symbol of Japan's commitment to pacifism among the Japanese people. This enduring support explains why Abe's efforts to revise that article never gained traction. Furthermore, Abe ruled in a coalition with Komeito, a Buddhist-affiliated party that opposed Abe's agenda, making it necessary for Abe to gain support from other party's lawmakers to secure the two-thirds support in both houses of the Diet required in Article 96 to revise the constitution. This proved elusive because support for the idea of revision confronted the reality of sharp differences over what to revise and the wording of revisions, even among members of his own party. Moreover, even among the public that supported revision, a majority opposed it happening under Abe, highlighting the distrust he generated even among conservatives sympathetic to his agenda (*Jiji Press*, 2017). Here too, Abe's nationalism resonated with the sound of one-hand clapping.

Back in 2012 the LDP published a draft new constitution that attracted widespread criticism for weakening civil liberties and overhauling Article 9 (Repeta 2013). After regaining power, Abe incrementally whittled down his proposal for modifying Article 9, in the end settling for adding a line about declaring the Self Defense Forces constitutional, but the harder and longer he pushed, opposition stiffened. Abe also backed efforts to revise Article 96 of the Constitution to lower the threshold for revision and making it easier to amend a document that has never been modified. This effort also failed to gain political support.

Collective self-defense

In 2014, Abe unilaterally overturned the longstanding government position that Japan had the right to collective self-defense (CSD), but not to actually exercise it (Kingston 2014). On the 60th anniversary of the establishment of the SDF, Abe announced a cabinet decision that reinterpreted Article 9 of the constitution to allow Japan to exercise CSD (Liff 2017). This constitutional reinterpretation (kaishaku kaiken) was decried as a stealth revision of the constitution without consulting the Diet, an extraordinary move given how entrenched and widely supported the official ban on exercising CSD had been for six decades.

The following April, he signed the 2015 US-Japan Defense Guidelines that greatly increases Japan's commitments to provide military support for the US without any limit on the geographical scope of such actions. These commitments were backed up by CSD legislation the Diet passed later that summer despite intense public opposition, massive demonstrations and the shared opinion of the two constitutional experts summoned by the LDP who testified that the legislation was unconstitutional (Kingston 2015; Gupta 2015; Kyodo 2015). Critics called it "war legislation" as a rebuke to Abe's branding his security policy "proactive pacifism" (Stockwin 2015).

Cumulatively, these changes in Japan's security posture are dubbed the Abe Doctrine and characterized as potentially transformational by Hughes (2015), while Liff (2017) argues that the implications are limited. Both are right. Abe's CSD legislation and the new defense guidelines overturned the minimalist Yoshida Doctrine and allow Japan to embrace a more assertive security role despite conditions that potentially make it harder to exercise CSD. In the end, Abe was forced to agree to some constraints, but the criteria necessary for invoking CSD are vague and leave much up to the prime minister's discretion. The conditions Abe accepted for exercising CSD are "(1) Japan's 'national survival' (kuni no sonritsu) must be threatened by a 'clear danger' (meihakuna kiken), (2) no alternative means of addressing the threat can exist, and (3) whatever force Japan uses must be limited to the minimum necessary" (Liff 2017, 161).

Thus, Abe did what he could to appease Washington and tried to exorcise the ghosts of unilateral pacifism that left Japan weak and subordinate, but in the end made concessions due to strong domestic opposition that resulted in a limited version of CSD. Those limitations were on full display in early 2020 when PM Abe decided against joining a US-led allied convoy patrolling the Straits of Hormuz even though a Japanese oil tanker had recently been attacked in the vicinity and the threat to Japan's access to Middle East oil was a potentially grave national risk that seemed to meet the criteria for invoking CSD. In fact, in 2015, Abe cited a blockade of the Straits of Hormuz as an example of a "survival threatening situation" that would justify invoking CSD (Gupta 2015). In the event, Abe dispatched a single destroyer to the Gulf safely distant from the Straits of Hormuz, with the promise that it would stay in contact with the convoy. This very limited show of force happened against the backdrop of the US assassination of Iranian General Qasem Soleimani on January 3, 2020, and expectations that Tehran might retaliate.

Avoiding CSD was crucial at this juncture because Abe still harbored hopes of revising Article 9 and knew that if anything went wrong, it would scupper any chances of gaining two-thirds support in the Diet and majority public support in a national referendum. Hence, a leader known as a hawkish nationalist eager to do whatever was needed to strengthen the US alliance shrugged off a direct request from the Trump Administration due to pragmatic domestic political calculations. Abe's lack of political will to act on an issue in which he invested so much political capital raises doubts that his successors would do more, but now they have the legal basis for doing so if they choose to act; that is transformational. Abe hit the ineffectual sweet spot of promising too much to the US and downplaying those promises to the Japanese, sowing seeds of possible discord. The three conditions he accepted provide an excuse for his successors to balk at exercising CSD. Washington has long been frustrated by Tokyo invoking Article 9 as a reason it could not do more on security and now faces the prospect of being warded off by the amulet of three conditions. Again, Abe didn't follow through on his nationalist principles.

Revising history

As Saaler (2016) details, Abe has been actively involved in efforts to rehabilitate Japan's wartime past and shared history with Asia. In his book *Towards a Beautiful Country* (*Utsukushi Kuni e*), Abe (2007) makes clear that his support for historical revisionism – efforts to minimize, deny, relativize and shift responsibility for Japan's wartime atrocities and excesses – is motivated by his desire to clear the family name and to nurture national pride. He greatly admires his grandfather Kishi Nobuske and believes that Japan has embraced a masochistic history that unduly tarnishes the nation's honor and unfairly condemns wartime leaders by accepting the so-called "victor's justice" narrative that emerged from the International Military Tribunal for the Far East (1946–1948). Until the 1990s, secondary school textbooks in Japan avoided controversial issues and were circumspect about the devastating consequences of Japan's 15-year war in Asia (1931–1945). This whitewashing was facilitated by the Ministry of Education's role in vetting textbooks and imposing revisions. Ienaga Saburo challenged this censorship in a series of lawsuits from the 1960s because he felt that government efforts to impose a collective amnesia about Japan's wartime record were counterproductive, tarnishing the nation's dignity overseas by downplaying the suffering of Japan's victims and misleading the public about the sacrifices Japan endured in a reckless and unjustified war (Ienaga 2001). Improbably, the textbooks emphasized Japan's role as a victim and minimized its role as a perpetrator, what was suffered rather than inflicted, focusing more on the atomic bombings than the millions of Asians killed in a conflict Japan initiated to subjugate the region and mobilize its resources for Japan's advantage (Dower 1999; Goto 2003).

Revisionists prefer to justify Japan's imperial aggression as a defensive war fought under the banner of Pan-Asian liberation, a conceit that does not bear scrutiny (Saaler 2007).

Revisionist organizations such as the *Atarashi Rekishi Kyokasho Tsukurukai* and *Nippon Kaigi* were established from the mid-1990s in response to the more forthright reckoning about the wartime past that began to emerge following Emperor Showa's death in 1989, the posthumous regnal name for Hirohito under whose auspices the Holy War was waged. Suddenly, in the early 1990s, the inglorious past cascaded out of the crypt as Japanese scholars began to take the measure of what the nation had done (Yoshimi 1995, 2002). Many Japanese were unprepared for this new self-critical narrative that beamed a light into the dark corners of Japanese depredations across Asia.

Comfort Women

Perhaps no issue was as emotive as the comfort women regarding young females from all over Asia who were kept in wartime brothels on military bases and improvised battlefront huts to provide sex to Japanese soldiers (Soh 2007). The 1993 Kono Statement acknowledges the role of the Japanese military and state in establishing this system and coercively recruiting women and girls into sexual servitude and remains a bête noire for revisionists:

> The then Japanese military was, directly or indirectly, involved in the establishment and management of the comfort stations and the transfer of comfort women. The recruitment of the comfort women was conducted mainly by private recruiters who acted in response to the request of the military. The Government study has revealed that in many cases they were recruited against their own will, through coaxing coercion, etc., and that, at times, administrative/military personnel directly took part in the recruitments. They lived in misery at comfort stations under a coercive atmosphere.
>
> *(Kono Statement 1993, August 4)*

The Kono Statement also offers an apology and promises to teach this history. Subsequently, the government established and provided most of the funding for the Asia Women's Fund (1995–2007) that offered solatia and apologies to former comfort women, but only 363 accepted, highlighting how this initiative never gained traction or much credibility. Partly, this was because advocate organizations in Japan and South Korea were critical of the government's arms-length involvement intended to preserve its argument that legally all such issues with South Korea were already resolved in the 1965 Basic Treaty of normalization between Tokyo and Seoul. This calibrated position conveyed a half-hearted effort to resolve a deep bilateral trauma, falling well short of a grand gesture of reconciliation. In terms of Kono's promise to teach young Japanese about the comfort women, by the end of the 1990s, all secondary school textbooks covered the comfort women issue. The revisionists, however, became ascendant in government from the early 2000s and currently the comfort women have disappeared from almost every secondary school textbook. Schools that adopted the sole junior high school text that covers the comfort women have been subject to orchestrated campaigns of harassment.

Japan's longest serving Prime Minister Abe gave the revisionists' exculpatory and valorizing narrative considerable momentum. The fin de siècle rightward shift in Japan's political center of gravity created political space for rightists and trolls to harass and target those who oppose this whitewashing of history (Nakano 2016). In the Diet in 2014, Abe failed to condemn threats of violence against a former Asahi reporter Uemura Takashi for articles that he wrote (and some he didn't) about the comfort women and instead vented his ire on the Asahi (Yamaguchi 2017a). Abe's protégé, Inada Tomomi, conducted a Diet inquiry intended to discredit the Kono Statement that Abe had long criticized. It was only under pressure from the US that Abe promised not to repudiate the mea culpa. Such pressure from the Obama Administration (2009–2017) on history did not always bear fruit. For example, despite sustained lobbying exhorting him to refrain, Abe visited Yasukuni Shrine at the end of 2013, prompting a sharp rebuke from Washington due to concerns that this gesture to nationalist constituents might derail efforts to improve trilateral security cooperation with Seoul and unnecessarily provoke Beijing. A few weeks later, Abe gave a speech at Davos that invoked the specter of WWI, suggesting that Japan and China might be sleepwalking toward war like Germany and the UK a century earlier, an analogy that drew harsh media criticism for its apparent bellicose tone. His spin doctors insisted that this was a misinterpretation of his remarks based on a poor translation, but the shadow of his Yasukuni pilgrimage lingered, tarnishing his international image, and leaving pundits assuming the worst.

Further pressured by Washington, in 2015, Abe reached an agreement with S. Korean President Park Geun-hye (2013–2017) to "finally and irreversibly" resolve the comfort women issue, but this deal proved abortive and only stoked mutual recriminations as it ineluctably unraveled (MOFA 2020. Park's impeachment not long after only reinforced negative sentiments among Koreans toward a deal that never enjoyed much public support. Problematically, the agreement was conducted in secret without consulting key stakeholders, a dubious process compounded by the lack of a public apology by Abe; there was only a second-hand report that he apologized in a phone call to Park and no transcript of the conversation was provided. Abe was criticized by some in the Diet who felt that he had conceded too much and gotten nothing but empty promises in exchange. Yen 1 billion was paid to a newly established foundation to distribute the money to surviving comfort women with what Tokyo thought was a commitment by Seoul to remove the comfort women statue across the street from the Japanese Embassy. The South Korean government maintained that it only promised to make best efforts to do so but had not guaranteed removal. Moreover, part of the agreement was not to engage in international diplomacy related to the comfort women, but Abe's MOFA violated this understanding by submitting an amicus curae to the Supreme Court in California supporting an appeal by local revisionists trying to compel the city of Glendale to remove a memorial to comfort women. In 2017, the Supreme Court of California decided not to review the decisions by the district and superior courts dismissing the lawsuit. The saga of the escalating statue wars under Abe is revealing about how his nationalist blinders on history tarnished Brand Japan.

Revisionists tarnish brand Japan

Toward the end of 2014, Japanese diplomats visited the offices of McGraw-Hill in New York City to pressure the publisher to remove passages covering the comfort women issue from one of its textbooks. This high-profile intervention was preceded in early 2012 by Japanese diplomats lobbying the town hall of Palisades Park, New Jersey to remove a comfort women memorial that had been installed in 2010 (Semple 2012). These diplomatic interventions drew negative media coverage because it seemed that the Japanese government was in denial about its wartime past. Overlooking the testimony of survivors, and impugning their integrity, revisionists asserted that the comfort women were prostitutes who willingly engaged in sex for money.

Statue wars

In December 2011, the Statue of Peace depicting a comfort woman was installed in Seoul across the street from the Japanese Embassy, amplifying festering tensions over Japanese colonial rule. Japan's diplomats failed badly in not understanding that in the twenty-first century, it is not possible or productive to simply bury a history of egregious human rights violations and ignore heightened concerns about women in war and gender issues. But following these blunders, MOFA escalated the statue wars, and in doing so drew more negative attention. MOFA would have been better off in just ignoring the statues, but instead put them and Japanese denialism on the global radar screen. Informally, Abe's envoys lobbied US academics and pundits to support their removal campaign, a tone-deaf and counterproductive effort. These interventions melted Japan's Gross National Cool, but the Abe government continued to escalate the statue wars, ensuring that more would be built.

In 2018, on the eve of departing for his new post as Abe's appointed ambassador to the US, Sugiyama Shinsuke insisted that his number one priority would be removal of all the comfort women statues and memorials in the US (*Nikkei* 2018). This was a curious primary issue because the Japanese Embassy in Washington has such a wide range of bilateral security and economic issues to manage. Given the importance of the US Alliance, and the prime minister's control over top bureaucratic appointments (George-Mulgan 2017), it is inconceivable that Abe did not back this anti-comfort women statue campaign.

History wars escalate

This ill-considered quest is consistent with Abe's notorious track record of comfort women denial and minimization (Yamaguchi 2017a). He quibbled in the Diet on March 1, 2007 when he was prime minister about the degree of coercion involved in recruiting comfort women, remarks that coincided with South Korean celebrations of the 1919 uprising against Japanese colonial rule. Subsequently, under strong pressure, he offered a vague apology on an April visit to the US, ensuring that he did not defuse the issue (Onishi 2007). Even so, this was a stunning stand down because Japan hires high paid lobbyists and powerbrokers to promote government interests in the US and to rally US lawmakers' support. But Abe's views on the comfort women were politically toxic, making it awkward for politicians to back him on this high-profile issue (Kingston 2016). As a result, in the summer of 2007, the US House of Representatives passed a nonbinding resolution calling on the Japanese government to "formally acknowledge, apologise and accept historical responsibility in a clear and unequivocal manner" for the sexual enslavement of as many as 200,000 "comfort women" (McCurry 2007).

When Abe returned to power in 2012, he persisted in his revisionist agenda of rewriting textbooks and conducting an international campaign in what the rightwing newspaper *Sankei* termed "The History Wars." From 2014, *Sankei* ran a series of columns titled "History Wars" and published a book with the same title in English that was distributed to Japan specialists and journalists focusing on Japan by the Global Alliance for Historical Truth (GAHT) (*Sankei* 2017). It is a poorly researched and unconvincing jeremiad expressing rightwing concerns that Japan was losing the PR battle to South Korea and China over East Asia's shared wartime and colonial past in the US. The book is credited to Komori Yoshihisa, a rightwing ideologue who writes for the *Sankei* newspaper and has aggressively gone after critics of Abe and revisionism (McNeill 2006). The polemical arguments are specious and unpersuasive, begging the question of why go to the expense and trouble of distributing this book, and another telling Koreans to just get over the past, with the endorsement of LDP Upper House member Inoguchi Kuniko? Yet again, the revisionist meddling only stoked critical scrutiny rather than boosting support for Abe's nationalist narrative.

Internationally, historical revisionism has been an epic own goal for Japan, conveying a lack of contrition about wartime atrocities and abuses and an unseemly enthusiasm to sweep this sordid history under the national tatami mat. Denialism is undignified because it tramples on the memories of nations and people victimized by Japanese aggression and dishonors the three million Japanese who were sacrificed by reckless wartime leaders. At home, the Abe government empowered revisionists and they have made some headway in rehabilitating the wartime record in textbooks and public discourse, but this attempt to rebury already exhumed and acknowledged history is contested effectively in the media and academia. Revisionism provides a convenient escape from historical responsibility and atonement that some Japanese may find appealing, but this shirking of the burdens of history is resisted by many Japanese and draws global condemnation. Revisionists try to scapegoat Japan's liberal media for harming Japan's international reputation by reporting about the comfort women but are themselves the indelible stain.

Stifling freedom of expression

Threats of violence by *uyoku* (internet ultranationalists) targeting those with differing opinions in Japan are a significant threat to freedom of expression. It is a sign of the times that the Japanese government failed to unequivocally condemn such threats against an art exhibit at the 2019 Aichi Triennale (McNeill 2019). In the exhibit *After "Freedom of Expression?"* organizers displayed some 20 transgressive works, including a comfort woman statue that incensed Japanese conservatives because it drew attention to the Japanese military's system of sexual slavery in the 1932–1945 period. As discussed above, a similar statue is located across the street from the site of the Japanese Embassy in Seoul that Tokyo wants removed, along with others around the world that reproach Japan over its inadequate contrition and efforts to downplay the comfort women issue. Japan's culture wars escalated in early August 2019 over this art exhibit, as some netizens made threats to set fire to the venue, sent hundreds of menacing emails and harangued exhibition staff over the phone. In response, organizers shut down the exhibit just three days after it opened, mindful of the arson attack on Kyoto Anime the previous month that killed 35 employees. The decision to close the exhibit due to this intimidation resonated with irony, given that the *After "Freedom of Expression"* exhibit was intended to challenge such efforts to stifle this freedom. In the end, the rightwing trolls prevailed.

Unintentionally, the curator succeeded in highlighting how an ideologically charged public discourse under Abe has increased intolerance and censorship. Plans to revive the show in 2021 were stymied by similar threats of violence imparting a whiff of what life must have been like under the wartime militarists when censorship was widespread and dissent dangerous. There are numerous other instances of media harassment, intimidation, censorship and self-censorship that undermine freedom of the press and influence how the news is reported (Kingston 2017). Abe's administration engaged in various media muzzling initiatives, including the appointment of a crony with no media experience to head NHK who began his tenure in 2014 by downplaying the comfort women issue and proclaiming that the nation's most influential broadcaster could not say left if the government said right (Fackler 2014).

Curbing academic freedom

The application by George Washington University scholar Celeste Arrington for an Abe fellowship in 2015 illustrates how academic freedom suffered during Abe's tenure. Frank Baldwin (2019) details why her application was rejected despite an excellent evaluation from a panel of eminent scholars that reviewed the proposals. The Abe fellowship program is jointly administered by the Center for Global Partnership (CGP) in Tokyo and the Social Science Research Council (SSRC) in New York City. The CGP was established in 1991 as part of the Japan Foundation with a large grant from MOFA. To ensure the integrity of the program, and ward off Japanese government meddling, the SSRC insisted on an independent selection committee it named to review proposals and the final say on scholarship recipients.

Arrington is a respected scholar with a solid track record of research in Japan and South Korea. She is not a firebrand on the history issues that trouble revisionists. In 2014, however, she presented a paper related to litigation and Japanese wartime atrocities, including the comfort women, at a US conference funded by the CGP. The CGP abruptly disassociated itself from the symposium when it learned that her presentation referred to the comfort women system as "sexual slavery."

Subsequently, Arrington applied for an Abe Fellowship in 2015 and her proposal, "Lawyers and Litigation in Japanese and Korean Politics," was deemed exceptional and the strongest by the peer review committee. Her proposal had nothing to do with comfort women or hot button history issues. According to Baldwin, the CGP pressured the SSRC to reject Arrington's proposal because of the 2014 paper. The SSRC capitulated and Arrington was sent a standard rejection notice, unaware of the intense behind-the-scenes politicking.

Make such a big deal over one scholarship may seem excessive but the Abe Administration was prickly about any criticism, especially in the US, and inclined to muzzle critics and promote its revisionist views. For the CGP, running a program honoring PM Abe's father created special circumstances. Moreover, in 2015, the government tripled the public diplomacy budget, and subsequently waged a public relations blitz aimed at cultivating positive views of Japan overseas. Ranging from infomercials on CNN and hiring Washington lobbyists to endowing chairs in Japanese studies and establishing Japan Houses in London, Los Angeles and São Paulo, PM Abe's government sought to nurture positive perceptions and counter negative narratives.

Undiplomatic interventions

MOFA, especially during the second Abe Administration (2012–2020), became more aggressive on history issues. For example, consular officials would attend Japan Foundation-funded programs and engage in insidious tactics, leveling critical broadsides against presentations that did not align with their views but ducking debate. Scholars specializing in Japan around the world came to understand that they were being monitored and assume that this might affect future funding, fellowships and awards. This more confrontational stance also caused panic at the SSRC/CGP, dependent as they were on the government's goodwill.

This more interventionist approach escalated in 2018 at a conference commemorating the 150th anniversary of the Meiji Restoration hosted by Tel Aviv University. As the Japan Foundation doesn't have an office in Israel, the Japanese Embassy there administered the grant funding the conference. Well past the deadline for applying, organizers reported that embassy staff insisted they include two Japanese participants associated with revisionist organizations. It was a large gathering with attendees from all over the world, a chance to showcase lively scholarly discussions about the Meiji era but the two imposed participants made a spectacle of themselves by heckling other presenters and giving presentations unrelated to the conference theme. Instead, they offered revisionist diatribes that were debunked by attending scholars. These revisionists were wined and dined by the Embassy and treated as special guests, but the effort backfired as those who attended the conference witnessed Japan at its worst, embracing a glowering nationalism that sent a message of intolerance and little consideration for scholarly standards.

Given the stiff competition for funding, Japanologists understand what is at stake, but if conferences and publications are a barometer of academic freedom, the Japanese government's efforts to stifle debate and criticism have been remarkably ineffective. The fabulist revisionist history promoted by Abe and others aligned with Nippon Kaigi (Japan Conference) that downplays, denies and shifts responsibility for wartime atrocities has come under sustained criticism by Western scholars and journalists as unsubstantiated assertions and wishful thinking. Nippon Kaigi is a small rightwing group of less than 30,000 members but includes a high proportion of Diet members (Tawara 2017). Under Abe, members held about 80% of cabinet posts.

The awkward Emperor

Emperor Akihito (1989–2019) is greatly admired as the nation's chief emissary of reconciliation in Asia and as the consoler-in-chief at home. He visited battle sites across the region to pray for the war dead and offered gestures and expressions of atonement to nations that suffered from Japanese aggression. He attended to the unfinished business of Emperor Showa's reign when Japan's Asian rampage occurred, and compassionately conveyed the nation's sorrow about the horrors and indignities Japan inflicted on fellow Asians.

Emperor Akihito spent much of 2015 repudiating "Abenesia," making pointed comments about the need to address wartime history with persistence and humility. There was a striking contrast between the 70th anniversary statements by Abe and Emperor Akihito in 2015 about how the nation got to where it is today. Regarding the death of three million Japanese in the war, Abe dog-whistled: "The peace we enjoy today exists only upon such precious sacrifices. And therein lies the origin of postwar Japan." This assertion that wartime sacrifices begot contemporary peace is a revisionist trope, suggesting that the horrors endured during a reckless war of aggression were somehow worthwhile.

Abe was also vague where he needed to be forthright – on colonialism, aggression and the "comfort women" – and came up short in expressing contrition by invoking apologies made by predecessors without offering his own. Abe also expressed perpetrator's fatigue, calling for an end to apology diplomacy. As a result, the Abe statement represented significant backsliding from those issued by former prime ministers Murayama and Koizumi in 1995 and 2005, which helped Japan and its victims regain some dignity while promoting reconciliation. In swearing off further apologies, Abe was yet again out of synch with public opinion as an NHK poll at that time indicated that only 15% of the country opposed apology, while 42% supported such gestures (Suzuki 2015). Apology is certainly not the magic wand of regional reconciliation, but it is naïve to think that it doesn't matter. Revisionists complain that Japan has already apologized numerous times, but they overlook the fact that prominent conservatives publicly repudiate every apology, thereby keeping Japan behind the eight ball of history.

Emperor Akihito offered a veiled rebuke on August 15, 2015, when he said, "Our country today enjoys peace and prosperity, thanks to the ceaseless efforts made by the people of Japan toward recovery from the devastation of the war and toward development, always backed by their earnest desire for the continuation of peace." Peace and prosperity, in the emperor's view, did not come from treating the Japanese people and other Asians like cannon fodder during the war, but rather was based on their postwar efforts to overcome the needless tragedy inflicted by the nation's militarist leaders. During his reign, Akihito forcefully advocated a pacifist identity as the foundation for today's Japan, one that still resonates widely in Japan, challenging Abe's agenda of transforming Japan into a so-called "normal nation," free from constitutional constraints on the military.

In serving as the conscience of Japan and articulating the early 1990s consensus that it was time for a more forthright reckoning, Akihito gained unquestioned moral authority and showed compassion to those victimized by the war waged in his father's name. But a tectonic shift in Japan's war memory in the twenty-first century rendered Akihito an inadvertent symbol of opposition to revisionist's selective amnesia and their patriotic boosterism. He remained steadfast in contrition, while the political elite lurched rightward in reimagining and rehabilitating the wartime era. In terms of national identity, based on public support when they stepped down, it seems that more Japanese embraced Akihito's vision than the feckless nationalism Abe offered. The public warmed to the modest persona of the Emperor and grew tired of Abe's arrogance, scandals and his empty promises for Abenomics and womenomics.

After Akihito's three-decade reign, public support for the imperial family hovered around 80%, a record high (CBS 2019). In contrast, an unhealthy and discredited Abe left office under a cloud of scandals (Nakano 2020) with a support rate of just 33% (*Jiji Press* 2020). For a leader committed to nurturing national pride, his misconduct and poor judgment offered little to celebrate, while his biographer Tobias Harris (2020) concluded that he achieved very little during eight years of numerous missed opportunities.

Olympic follies

In March 2020, Abe reluctantly agreed to postpone the Tokyo 2020 Summer Olympics a year due to the global pandemic. At the time there was guarded optimism that the pandemic would fade away before 2021, but in August 2020 Abe resigned knowing his Olympic dream was in jeopardy.

While the 1964 Summer Olympics signaled Japan's return to the comity of nations and promoted its high-tech prowess and recovery from war, the 2020 branding suffered from a series of setbacks. Instead of showcasing the nation's many strengths, including its design prowess, superb infrastructure and social capital, the runup to the postponed Games highlighted various shortcomings, especially the gap between global norms and values, and Japan's conservative elite on diversity, sustainability, transparency and gender. In February 2021, former Prime Minister Mori Yoshiro was ousted as the president of the Tokyo 2020 Olympics Organizing Committee in 2021 for blatantly sexist remarks that earned a gold medal for sexism from Human Rights Watch. Previously, in 2019, the nation learned that the Japan Olympic Committee (JOC) made illicit payments to secure the bid. After French authorities announced that JOC president Takeda Tsunekazu was under formal investigation on suspicion of "active corruption," he resigned (McCurry 2019). This followed cancellation of the original stadium design, replacement of the plagiarized logo and massive cost overruns. This was not the showcase gala Abe had in mind when he appeared at the Rio Olympics in 2016 dressed up as Super Mario (Kingston 2020).

Originally dubbed the "reconstruction Olympics" aimed at stimulating Japan's post-Fukushima rebound, the media focused on the grimmer realities about the delayed decommissioning of the stricken reactors and diversion of resources from Tohoku, the region hit hardest by the 3.11 triple disasters – earthquake, tsunami and reactor meltdowns. Olympic scrutiny has also raised doubts about Japan's green credentials with the 2020 decision to dump large volumes of Fukushima's tainted water into the ocean, a reminder of just how absurd PM Abe's reassurances to the IOC were in 2013 when he asserted that contaminated water leaks from the crippled reactors were "under control."

Downsized

Japan suffered just over 1,000 deaths from the pandemic as of August 2020, but PM Abe did not benefit politically because very few people credited him for this relatively successful outcome. Typically, Japan's low death toll is attributed to the public taking sensible precautions, wearing masks to impede transmission, staying home and observing social distancing guidelines.

PM Abe's decision to declare a national emergency on April 8, 2020 drew widespread criticism for being too late. Abe's woes continued to mount during the second wave of the outbreak after the national emergency was lifted in late May 2020. By July, according to a Mainichi poll, only 17% thought highly of Abe's pandemic response, while 60% did not (*Mainichi* 2020). On the eve of announcing his resignation on August 28, NHK reported that his support rate fell to 34%, the lowest since he returned to power in 2012 (NHK 2020).

Why did the public judge Abe so harshly? In early February, when the Diamond Princess cruise ship docked at Yokohama and became a coronavirus incubator due to botched quarantine procedures, Japan had a wake-up call. But Abe did not provide any crisis leadership and was slammed on social media for being missing in action. The image of a decisive and competent leader nurtured since Abe returned to power in 2012 evaporated as his aptitude for crisis management came under withering scrutiny.

Moreover, a cascade of scandals implicating Abe in cronyism, coverups, corruption and data tampering further eroded public trust, especially the vote-buying allegations implicating his former Justice Minister Kawai Katsuyuki. Additionally, the 2017 Moritomo Gakuen scandal involving a sweetheart land deal implicating Abe roared back to life in 2020 when the wife of a Finance Ministry official released her husband's suicide note citing pressures to cover up the wrongdoing. In the aftermath, former Prime Minister Koizumi Junichiro who was once Abe's mentor called on him to resign and take responsibility for his role in the scandal (UPI 2020).

Conclusion: dubious legacy

Abe had some impact on national security policy and increased the power of the kantei (Office of the Prime Minister), but the revamp he most yearned for, sweeping constitutional revision, remained elusive because the public was wary of his agenda and distrusted him. He was the most ideological Japanese leader since his grandfather Kishi, but seemed fainthearted in pursuit of his nationalist goals, and did more posturing than achieving. Significantly, public support was always lukewarm; in NHK's monthly polls from 2013 to 2020 among those who supported him, typically 15% did so for his leadership qualities, 15% for his policies, while about half acknowledged that support for him was due to a lack of viable alternatives, hardly a resounding endorsement. Moreover, during campaigns, Abe trumpeted Abenomics rather than his ideological agenda, perhaps because he understood that his nationalist priorities evoked little enthusiasm. This was the lesson from 2007 when he led the LDP to a drubbing in upper house elections because he was out of touch with public concerns and was dubbed KY-kuuki yomenai (unable to read the situation as in clueless). Five years on, Abenomics was more like a product relaunch than a well thought out economic strategy, initially garnering positive global media coverage until it sputtered. It seems that Abe and his advisors understood that the public appetite for revising the constitution and history was limited and thus he campaigned in a series of elections on Abenomics because it generated a buzz about the issues people cared about. This meant downplaying the issues he was really concerned about, running on the economy then claiming a mandate for constitutional revision and the Abe Doctrine, an artful tactic that eventually caught up with him as an often deferential (rightwing) and intimidated (liberal) media turned negative due to scandals involving cronies and ultranationalists linked to him. There was a recrudescence of reactionary nationalism and patriotic boosterism during the Abe era, but this has been a top-down phenomenon that did not ignite grassroots support (Yamaguchi 2017b). For a while, Abe helped dispel the doom and gloom consensus about Japan's future that prevailed when he took office; yet, few Japanese believe that he made Japan safer, established a sustainable economic recovery or mitigated gathering demographic challenges. Indeed, Prime Minister Kishida Fumio (2021-) has been dismissive of Abenomics, asserting it accentuated disparities and did not establish the basis for sustainable growth while doing nothing to boost household income.

Strengthening the US alliance will be remembered as Abe's major diplomatic achievement, but in doing so he reinforced the client state relationship, ignored the democratic voice of the Okinawan people, gained the unflattering distinction of being Donald Trump's closest friend among world leaders, while also increasing the possibility of putting Japan's troops in harm's way.

In the wake of his assassination in 2022, there were detailed revelations about his close ties with the Unification Church and how he and the LDP helped promote its conservative social agenda. (Kingston 2022) The assassin said he killed Abe to avenge the coercive fundraising tactics of the Unification Church that left his family destitute. The media reported that Abe's grandfather Kishi Nobusuke had helped the Unification Church get established in Japan and members there became the organization's largest source of funds. By the time of Abe's death, some 30,000 formal legal complaints had been filed by households against the Unification Church for its high-pressure fundraising tactics, but authorities failed to crack down, generating suspicion that it enjoyed political protection. Abe's deep connection with the so-called "Moonies", an organization best known for conducting mass weddings and fleecing members, soured the public mood towards him, casting a dark shadow over his political career.

Overall, his flawed record and policy shortcomings diminished his legacy, and limited his ability to transform national identity and nurture ardent nationalist sentiments. Questions about his character, and irresolute inclinations, doomed his agenda. As Japan's longest serving prime minister and master campaigner, Abe was a political giant who disappointed and left a shallow imprint.

References

Abe, S. 2007. *Towards a Beautiful Country.* New York: Vertical.
Baldwin, F. 2019. "Book Burning in Japan," In *AAUP Journal of Academic Freedom.* Vol. 10, https://www.aaup.org/sites/default/files/Baldwin.pdf.
Bamkin, S. 2018. "Reforms to Strengthen Moral Education in Japan: A Preliminary Analysis of Implementation in Schools," *Contemporary Japan* 30 (1): 78–96.
CBS. 2019. "Japan's Emperor Akihito officially announces abdication," April 30, https://www.cbsnews.com/news/emperor-akihito-japanese-abdication-rituals-today-2019-04-30/
Dower, J. 1999. *Embracing Defeat.* New York: WW Norton.
Fackler, M. 2014. "Japan's Public Broadcaster Faces Accusations of Shift to the Right," *New York Times*, January 31, https://www.nytimes.com/2014/02/01/world/asia/japans-public-broadcaster-faces-accusations-of-shift-to-the-right.html.
George-Mulgan, A. 2017. *The Abe Administration and the Rise of the Prime Ministerial Executive.* Abingdon: Routledge.
Goto, K. 2003. *Tension of Empire.* Athens: Ohio University Press.
Gupta, S. 2015. "Abe's new security legislation doubles-down on the US alliance" *East Asia Forum.* September 20. https://www.eastasiaforum.org/2015/09/20/abes-new-security-legislation-doubles-down-on-the-us-alliance/
Harris, T. 2020. *The Iconoclast: Shinzo Abe and the New Japan.* London: Hurst.
Ienaga, S. 2001. *Japan's Past, Japan's Future.* Lanham, MD: Rowman & Littlefield.
Jiji Press. 2017. "Nearly 70% against 2018 Constitution Revision Proposal: Jiji Poll," *Jiji Press*, December 15.
Jiji Press. 2020. "Nearly 70% Say Abe Bears Responsibility for Ex-Justice Chief's Arrest," *Japan Times*, July 17.
Kapur, N. 2018. *Japan at the Crossroads.* Cambridge, MA: Harvard University Press.
Kingston, J. 2014. "PM Abe Overturns Japan's Pacifist Postwar Order," *Friedrich-Ebert-Stiftung, Tokyo Office*, July. http://library.fes.de/pdf-files/bueros/japan/11282.pdf.
Kingston, J. 2015. "Abe's security laws nothing like same sex marriage," *Japan Times*, August 8. https://www.japantimes.co.jp/opinion/2015/08/08/commentary/abes-security-laws-nothing-like-sex-marriage/
Kingston, J. 2016. "The Japan Lobby and Public Diplomacy," *Asia-Pacific Journal Japan Focus* 14 (9): 4884 (May 1), https://apjjf.org/2016/09/Kingston.html.
Kingston, J., ed. 2017. *Press Freedom in Contemporary Japan.* Abingdon: Routledge.
Kingston, J. 2020. "Diversity Olympics Dogged by Controversy," *Asia-Pacific Journal Japan Focus* 18 (4): 5343, https://apjjf.org/-Jeff-Kingston/5341/article.pdf.
Kingston, J. 2022. "Abe Leaves Behind a Toxic Legacy," *Global Asia* 17(3), September. https://www.globalasia.org/v17no3/focus/abe-leaves-behind-a-toxic-legacy_jeff-kingston
Kono Statement. 1993 (August 4), https://awf.or.jp/e6/statement-02.html.
Kyodo. 2015. "Abe's Security Bills Baffle 81% of the Public: Survey," *Japan Times*, May 31. https://www.japantimes.co.jp/news/2015/05/31/national/politics-diplomacy/81-say-state-explanations-controversial-security-bills-insufficient-poll/.
Liff, A. P. 2017. "Policy by Other Means: Collective Self Defense and the Politics of Japan's Postwar Constitutional Reinterpretations" *Asia Policy* July.
Liu-Farrer, Gracia. 2020. *Immigrant Japan: Mobility and Belonging in an Ethno-nationalist Society.* Ithaca NY: Cornell University Press.
Mainichi. 2020. "Q&A for July 2020 Mainichi Poll on Abe Cabinet Support, Japan's Coronavirus Response," *Mainichi*, July 24. https://mainichi.jp/english/articles/20200723/p2a/00m/0na/013000c.
McCormack, G. 2007. *Client State.* New York: Verso.
McCurry, J. 2007. "Japan Rejects US Calls for Apology over 'Comfort Women'," *Guardian*, July 31. https://www.theguardian.com/world/2007/jul/31/usa.japan.
McCurry, J. 2019. "Japanese Olympic Chief to Quit Amid Corruption Allegations Scandal," *Guardian*, March 19. https://www.theguardian.com/world/2019/mar/19/japan-olympic-committee-president-tsunekazu-takeda-to-resign-corruption-allegations-scandal.
McNeill, D. 2019. "Freedom Fighting: Nagoya's Censored Art Exhibition and the 'Comfort Women' Controversy," *Asia Pacific Journal Japan Focus* 17 (20): 5320, https://apjjf.org/2019/20/McNeill.html.
McNeill, D. 2006. "The Struggle for the Japanese Soul: Komori Yoshihisa, Sankei Shimbun, and the JIIA Controversy," *The Asia Pacific Journal Japan Focus* 4 (9): 2212, https://apjjf.org/-David-McNeill/2212/article.pdf.

Milly, D. 2020. "Japan's Labor Migration Reforms: Breaking with the Past?" *Migration Information Source*, https://www.migrationpolicy.org/print/16694#.
MOFA 2020. "The Issue of Comfort Women: Press Announcement December 28, 2015," *Diplomatic Blue Book*, Ministry of Foreign Affairs of Japan, https://www.mofa.go.jp/policy/other/bluebook/2020/html/references/r0101.html
Mullins, M. 2016. "*Neonationalism*, Religion, and Patriotic Education in Post-disaster *Japan*." *Asia Pacific Journal: Japan Focus* 14(20): 5 (October 15), https://apjjf.org/2016/20/Mullins.html
Murphy, R. 2014. *Japan and the Shackles of the Past*. Oxford: Oxford University Press.
Nakano, K. 2016. "Contemporary Political Dynamics of *Japanese Nationalism*." *Asia Pacific Journal: Japan Focus* 14(20): 5, October 15, https://apjjf.org/2016/20/Nakano.html
Nakano, K. 2020. "Shinzo Abe is quitting and leaving a trail of scandals," *New York Times*, August 30, https://www.nytimes.com/2020/08/30/opinion/shinzo-abe-resign-japan.html
NHK. 2020. "NHK Poll: Cabinet Approval Rate Falls To 34%", *Japan Bullet*, August 12. https://www.japanbullet.com/news/nhk-poll-cabinet-approval-rate-falls-to-34.
Nikkei. 2020. "Nearly 70% of Japanese Say More Foreigners Are 'Good': Survey," *Nikkei*, October 5, https://asia.nikkei.com/Spotlight/Japan-immigration/Nearly-70-of-Japanese-say-more-foreigners-are-good-survey.
Nikkei. 2018. "Japan's new US envoy eyes removal of 'comfort women' statues" *Nikkei Asia*, February 16, https://asia.nikkei.com/Politics/International-relations/Japan-s-new-US-envoy-eyes-removal-of-comfort-women-statues
Onishi, N. 2007. "Abe only partly successful in defusing 'comfort women' issue," *New York Times*, April 29, https://www.nytimes.com/2007/04/29/world/asia/29iht-abe.1.5487927.html
Pew. 2018. "Perceptions of Immigrants, Immigration and Emigration" *Pew Research Center*, November 12. https://www.pewresearch.org/global/2018/11/12/perceptions-of-immigrants-immigration-and-emigration/.
Repeta, L. 2013. "Japan's Democracy at Risk," *Asia Pacific Journal Japan Focus* 11 (28): 3969, https://apjjf.org/2013/11/28/Lawrence-Repeta/3969/article.html.
Saaler, S. 2016. "Nationalism and History in Contemporary Japan" *Asia Pacific Journal: Japan Focus* 14(20): 5, October 15, https://apjjf.org/2016/20/Saaler.html
Saaler, S. and J. Koschman, eds. 2007. *Pan-Asianism in Modern Japanese History*. Abingdon: Routledge.
Sankei. 2017. *History Wars, Japan—False Indictment of the Century*. Translation directed by Komori Yoshihisa. Tokyo: Sankei.
Semple, K. 2012. "In New Jersey, Memorial for 'Comfort Women' Deepens Old Animosity," *New York Times*, May 18, https://www.nytimes.com/2012/05/19/nyregion/monument-in-palisades-park-nj-irritates-japanese-officials.html
Soh, C.S. 2007. *The Comfort Women*. Chicago: University of Chicago Press.
Stockwin, A. 2015. "Japan's defence and diplomacy heading in the wrong direction," *East Asia Forum*, August 1, https://www.eastasiaforum.org/2015/08/01/japans-defence-and-diplomacy-heading-in-the-wrong-direction/
Suzuki, S. 2015. "Will Japan's war apologies ever satisfy China?," *East Asia Forum*, November 5, https://www.eastasiaforum.org/2015/11/05/will-japans-war-apologies-ever-satisfy-china/
Tran, B.Q. 2020. "Vietnamese Technical Trainees in Japan Voice Concerns Amidst COVID-19," *Asia Pacific Journal Japan Focus* 18 (18): 5748, https://apjjf.org/2020/18/Tran.html.
Tawara, Y. (2017), "What Is the Aim of Nippon Kaigi, the Ultra-Right Organization that Supports Japan's Abe Administration?" *Asia Pacific Journal Japan Focus* 15 (21): 5081 (November 1), https://apjjf.org/2017/21/Tawara.html.
UPI. 2020. "Junichiro Koizumi Suggests Japan's Abe Resign Following Scandals," *UPI*, March 31. https://www.upi.com/Top_News/World-News/2020/03/31/Junichiro-Koizumi-suggests-Japans-Abe-resign-following-scandals/1861585669109/.
Yamaguchi, T. 2017a. "Press Freedom under Fire: 'Comfort Women,' the Asahi Affair and Uemura Takashi." In *Press Freedom in Japan*, edited by J. Kingston, 135–151. Abingdon: Routledge.
Yamaguchi, T. 2017b. "The 'Japan Is Great!' Boom, Historical Revisionism, and the Government" *The Asia Pacific Journal Japan Focus*, 15:6:3 (March 15, 2017), https://apjjf.org/2017/06/Yamaguchi.html.
Yoshimi, Y. 1995. *Jūgun ianfu*. Tokyo: Iwanami.
Yoshimi, Y. 2002. *The Comfort Women*. New York: Columbia University Press.

17
COMMERCIAL NATIONALISM AND COSMOPOLITANISM

Advertising production and consumption of (trans)national identity in Japan

Koji Kobayashi

Introduction

Nationalism and cosmopolitanism are often regarded antithetical to each other. In many ways, either of them may not be fully understood without a consideration of the other. This chapter in particular draws an attention to commercial representations of national and cosmopolitan identities that are produced and consumed through Japanese advertising. Japan exists as a unique space of cultural economy where domestic advertising agencies, media organisations and other business entities dominate the production and circulation of commercial messages. This structural arrangement, underpinned by local cultural idiosyncrasies, serves as a basis for the centrality of Japanese language, settings and actors used within advertising. It is in this sense that the production and consumption of national identity through advertising contribute to the formation and reinforcement of 'commercial nationalism'. In contrast, what this chapter also identifies is that the globalisation of business, goods and services made it possible for Japanese consumers to aspire to emulate Westerners and become global citizens through what I refer to as 'commercial cosmopolitanism'. Thus, this chapter is set out to explore the mediated construction of national and cosmopolitan representations and the relations of their mutual influences.

In terms of how this chapter is organised, it begins by reviewing key concepts to discuss nationalism with a particular focus on its development in Japan. This is then followed by explanations of commercial nationalism and cosmopolitanism as the theoretical framework of this study. After this, this chapter goes on to draw on a few examples of commercial nationalism and cosmopolitanism and examine these two contrasting phenomena as manifested within the context of Japanese advertising production and consumption. Lastly, this chapter concludes with a summative discussion and a suggestion for future research.

Nation, nationalism and Japan

One of the key ideas with respect to the nation and nationalism is Benedict Anderson's (1983) 'imagined community' which does not always resonate with the territory, sovereignty and control of the state. For Anderson (1983), the nation is "*imagined* because members of even the smallest nation will never know most of their fellow-members, meet them, or even hear of them, yet in the minds of each lives the image of their communion" (15, emphasis in original). This 'image of communion', according to Anderson (1983), was only made possible by the invention of modern mass printing technology and the (re-)production of shared national history, culture and identity through circulation of the print media. The development of the print technology and capitalism enabled the modern nation-state system to be first formed out of Europe, thereby placing European nation-states at the top of 'the word order' and as the vanguard of 'civilisation' (Smith 1991). In this context, the state elites articulated the idea of 'the nation' and mobilised a mass to share and promote the sense of unity in the form of what we now call nationalism—which is defined by Smith (1991) as "an ideological movement for attaining and maintaining autonomy, unity and identity on behalf of a population deemed by some of its members to constitute an actual or potential 'nation'" (73, emphasis removed).

From this view, national culture is considered less as an organically emerging collective way of life than as a cultural-political formation of discourses. As Hall (1992) elaborates:

> Instead of thinking of national cultures as unified, we should think of them as constituting a *discursive device* which represents difference as unity or identity. They are cross-cut by deep internal divisions and differences, and 'unified' only through the exercise of different forms of cultural power... One way of unifying them has been to represent them as the expression of the underlying culture of 'one people'. Ethnicity is the term we give to cultural features – language, religion, custom, traditions, feeling for 'place' – which are shared by a people. It is therefore tempting to try to use ethnicity in this 'foundational' way. But this belief turns out, in the modern world, to be a myth. Western Europe has no nations which are composed of only one people, one culture or ethnicity. *Modern nations are all cultural hybrids.*
>
> *(297, emphasis in original)*

As such, it is suggested that there is no benign formation of a nation-state because these internal divisions and differences "were only unified by a lengthy process of violent conquest – that is, by the forcible suppression of cultural difference" (Hall 1992, 296). The formation of Japan as a modern nation-state is no exception to this.

For Japan, the unwelcomed visit of the 'black ships' led by Commodore Matthew Perry from the U.S.A. in 1853 symbolically marked the turning point towards modernisation or by another name Westernisation. Threatened by superior military forces of the West, the Tokugawa feudal government at the time was urged to open its trade relations with foreign countries and eventually ended its over 200 years of isolation policy. After the feudal government was overthrown by the oppositional *samurai* groups mainly consisting of those from two regional domains (Satsuma and Choshu), the Meiji government was subsequently established by mobilising the Emperor as a sovereign and symbol of state's legitimacy in 1868. Before the period of modernisation, it is fair to say that there was a lack of consciousness of Japan as a political unity and collective cultural identity within the general public because, in the pre-modern, insular society, people had stronger identifications with regional domains (e.g., Satsuma and Choshu) and classes (e.g., warrior, peasant, artisan and merchant). As such, the Meiji government centralised its cultural-political control to transform the nation into an economic and military superpower through the re-definition and reconstruction of history, space and identity of modern Japan.

One of the principal philosophies of Japanese modernisation was "encapsulated in the implicitly glocalist aphorism, *wakon yōsai* ('Japanese spirit, Western learning')" (Giulianotti and Robertson 2007, 180, emphasis and macron added). This philosophy represents the ways in which Japan actively adopted the Western systems, science and technology while simultaneously raising a national consciousness of Japan across different local communities or former domains. In this context, the discursive practices were mainly undertaken and guided by the national leaders most of whom were warrior-class men from Satsuma and Choshu. In other words, this group, consisting of a dominant minority, was privileged to advance their own interests and cultural politics in the selection, reproduction and naturalisation of discourses of Japan as a homogeneous society—thereby obscuring a diversity of ethnicities, languages, religions, cultures, customs and values across a range of localities. The modern myth of Japan as a homogeneous society lingered on into the post-war essentialist construction of *nihonjinron* (discourse of Japanese-ness), which continues to undermine and underrepresent the existence of ethnic minorities such as Ainu, Ryukyuan/Okinawan, *zainichi* (residing in Japan) Koreans and ethnically diverse populations (Cho and Kobayashi 2019). The philosophy and practice of *wakon yōsai* also nurtured the general perception of civilisational—and racial—hierarchy in which Europeans and white are constructed as more developed, modern and civilised and therefore placed higher than Asians and non-white. As such, modern Japan sought to cultivate its own unique position of superiority by denouncing the West for its selfish individualism, materialism and decadence via 'Occidentalism' (Robertson 1990) and Asia for its primitivity, irrationality and backwardness via 'Oriental Orientalism' (Iwabuchi 2002). However, this modern construction of Japanese identity has been called into question since the rise of other Asian economies that forced Japan "to come to terms with the increasingly visible gap between a discursively constructed 'backward Asia' and the rapidly developing economic power of geographically specific Asian nations" (Iwabuchi 2002, 16).

Another important aspect of cultural politics during the Meiji period was the signification of spirit, morals, virtues and values of the Japanese warriors—*bushi* or *samurai*. As a means of transforming a mass population into military forces, *bushidō* (way of the *samurai*) was promoted as the discipline of Japanese men and an important part of education for Japanese youth. According to Kusaka (2006, 21), *bushidō* is characterised by "an emphasis on the moral excellence of Confucianism, a fighting spirit which was influenced partly by Zen-Buddhism, and a consciousness of shame". The philosophical and corporeal embodiment of these Eastern cultural characteristics has been most commonly found in *budō* or Japanese martial arts such as judo, karate and kendo, and more generally school physical education and extracurricular sport activities called *bukatsudō* (Kobayashi 2012b). Thus, it is no coincidence that views of *bushidō* as the ideal of Japanese masculinity were popularised, romanticised and mobilised to reinforce the discourses of cultural nationalism particularly at the times of the Sino-Japanese War, Russo-Japanese War and later Second World War. In the post-war context, the Confucian-inspired values and practices have been largely maintained and clearly manifested, for instance, within the discourse of 'salaryman' (*sararīman*) that is constructed as the normative figure of a Japanese middle-class, white-colour male employee who is extremely hardworking and loyal to his company (Kobayashi and Jackson 2020). The discourse of salaryman exists in relation to the Confucian cultural code of obligational—rather than contractual—relationship between an employee and a company, which is often viewed analogous to the reciprocal obligation that *bushi* had with his *ie* or traditional extended family structure (Bhappu 2000). Furthermore, the distinctive characteristics assigned to the salaryman have been informed by a wider context of Japanese economic, industrial and cultural arrangements, including lifetime employment, seniority-based hierarchy and enterprise union (Kobayashi et al. 2010). In this sense, the Japanese way of economic life, social relations and cultural practices continues to underlie the contemporary reproduction of national identity.

As in the West, the modern mass print media was instrumental in shaping and re-shaping a national consciousness in Japan. Clearly, the national governments over generations played a central role in promoting a sense of belonging and pride among their citizens through (re-)production of shared memories, histories and sensibilities. However, with the further advancement of media technology and global expansion of consumerism, it is evident that the 'image of communion' has been increasingly reconstructed through commercial spaces and relations or what can be described as 'commercial nationalism'. To delineate how the cultural politics operates within commercial production and consumption, I now turn to a theoretical framework that illuminates understanding of how commercial signs are articulated with certain meanings of national and cosmopolitan identities.

Commercial nationalism and cosmopolitanism

In the era of 'flexible specialisation' often recognised as the post-Fordist mode of production since 1970s (Amin 1994), it has been said that there are increased demands of consumers for a variety of choices to suit their specific needs, tastes and styles. These choices provide consumers with a sense of distinction in symbolising their wealth, social status and cultural identity (Bourdieu 1984). Among an array of collective configurations (e.g., gender, sexuality, race, ethnicity, social class and age), national identity or belongingness has proven to be a potent source of appeal to consumer sensibility. This is not only restricted to overtly assertive commercial messages such as 'Buy American' and 'Made in Japan' but also implicitly embedded within the language, actors, locations and behaviour as commonly featured by a majority of Japanese advertising. It is in this sense that nationalism is perhaps most prevalently reproduced, reinforced and naturalised through the realm of commercial culture. To denote this phenomenon, the choice of the term 'commercial nationalism' is a strategic one. As there have been varied understandings of the term as well as various other terms that denote similar conceptualisation, this section first offers a broad, and by no means definite, definition that is used for the rest of this chapter to interpret and frame the phenomena under investigation.

Building on Smith's (1991) definition of nationalism, this chapter primarily deploys the term 'commercial nationalism' to refer to an ideology that is *commercially* produced, represented and consumed "for attaining and maintaining autonomy, unity and identity on behalf of a population deemed by some of its members to constitute an actual or potential 'nation'" (73, emphasis removed). This commercial form of nationalism differs from more orthodox forms of ethnic and civic nationalism as it locates commercial actors and activities central to the (re)construction of 'the nation' within today's increasingly global capitalist and consumerist society. In the previous literature, commercial nationalism has been most rigorously deployed and developed by the scholars of 'nation branding'—that is, the nation-state government's promotion of its national images and attractiveness as a means of attaining soft power (Volcic and Andrejevic 2011; see also Volcic and Andrejevic 2015 for an edited collection on this topic). While not too dissimilar to their use—as Volcic and Andrejevic (2011, 613) recognise the role of commercial entities selling nationalism "as a means of winning ratings and profits", my deployment of the term is rooted in and derived from the traditions of cultural studies, and in particular Hall's (1992) early revelation that

[c]ultural flows and global consumerism between nations create the possibilities of 'shared identities' – as 'customers' for the same goods, 'clients' for the same services, 'audiences' for the same messages and images – between people who are far removed from one another in time and space.

(302)

In this context of globalisation, according to Hall (1992), "differences and cultural distinctions which hitherto defined identity become reducible to a sort of international *lingua franca* or global currency into which all specific traditions and distinct identities can be translated" (303, emphasis in original). In turn, national identity, as one such example, has been increasingly translated into a commercial sign that is produced, represented and consumed through the ongoing transformation of our everyday lived experience on a global scale.

Similar ideas have been expressed, captured and framed by other concepts such as 'corporate nationalism' (Silk et al. 2005), 'brand nationalism' (Iwabuchi 2015) and 'consumer nationalism' (Castelló and Mihelj 2018). Indeed, it is a shared premise with these other concepts that commercial activities and representations—whether it be produced or consumed by corporations, brands, governments or consumers—are central to the contemporary construction of 'the nation'. Elsewhere, I have conducted a series of studies on corporate nationalism with respect to how sings of national identity were incorporated within corporate marketing and advertising (Kobayashi 2012a, 2012b; Kobayashi et al. 2019). One of the key findings from these studies was that advertising agencies, and creatives in particular, were located at the centre of creative processes and practices for encoding advertisements with meanings and affective connotations (Kobayashi et al. 2018). The centrality of advertising agencies in reproducing and reconstructing 'the nation' is not limited to corporate marketing and advertising but also found in the promotions created by nation-state governments and NGOs/NPOs (Volcic and Andrejevic 2011). Furthermore, the corporate representations of national identity can be embraced, negotiated or resisted by consumers to suit their political or cultural preferences via consumer nationalism (Castelló and Mihelj 2018) or adopted and reinforced by prosumers who are actively involved in reproduction of these symbolic meanings through direct or indirect association with corporations and advertising agencies (Baruk 2019). Given the complex power relations among actors and organisations within the 'regime of mediation' (Cronin 2004) and the remarkedly reduced distance between producers and consumers through digitalisation, the concept of commercial nationalism has a merit in capturing the entirety of how signs of national identity are produced, represented and consumed *commercially* by a range of actors and organisations, including governments, corporations, not-for-profit organisations, advertising agencies and consumers. Although there is a risk of losing sight of micro and meso power relations with this holistic approach, commercial nationalism does provide a framework to focus on the macro-level interaction and interpenetration among state, market and civil society. The concept can also be heuristically contrasted with commercial cosmopolitanism in constituting a comparative framework to take both into account for understanding each of them fully as they are mutually constitutive of each other.

The comparative framework of commercial nationalism and cosmopolitanism was inspired by Calhoun's (2008) analysis of nationalism and cosmopolitanism. Although the original formulation of cosmopolitanism was based on Kantian ethics and philosophy, it is now, according to Stevenson (2003), more "concerned with the transgression of boundaries and markers and the development of a genuinely inclusive cultural democracy and citizenship for an information age" (332). Likewise, Calhoun (2008) identifies that the contemporary discourses of cosmopolitanism are oriented towards both being transnational in transcending the local and being multicultural in appreciating the diversity within a particular locality. Since the 1990s, the word 'cosmopolitan' has been turned into a popular stylistic signifier that is epitomised by metropolitan tastes, fashion and lifestyle of transnational mobile elites. It is in this sense that cosmopolitanism has been reduced to a consumerist tool of self-expression through purchase of certain commercial signs that bring the most pleasure and gratification. As Calhoun (2008) points out, "cosmopolitanism commonly reflects the experience and perspective of elites and obscures the social foundations on which that experience and perspective rests" (441). As such, cosmopolitan identity today has been constructed less in claiming the moral righteousness as a citizen of the world than in attaining a commercial marker of difference and individuality as the emerging cultural capital of (trans)national elites (Kobayashi et al. 2018). Subsequently, commercial cosmopolitanism in this chapter is set out to be heuristically contrasted with commercial nationalism, which therefore enables analysis of contestation, negotiation and mutation between the contrasting ideological formations of the global (i.e., cosmopolitanism) and the local (i.e., nationalism) from both ends of spectrum.

Advertising production and consumption of (trans)national identity in Japan

Commercial nationalism in Japan

In contrast to many other Asian nations where American and British advertising agencies dominated their markets, Japanese advertising agencies have largely managed to resist and outperform their foreign competitors within the domestic industry and market (Moeran 2002). In particular, the Japanese advertising industry has been dominated by only two agencies, Dentsu and Hakuhodo, both of which are highly ranked among world's top agencies in global sales (Kawashima 2006). Part of the reason why Dentsu and Hakuhodo have been world-class advertising agencies, despite their lack of a successful record on international business, resides in the fact that Japanese advertising agencies nurtured domestic business environment and practice to allow for handling competing accounts from the same industrial categories (e.g., Toyota, Honda, Subaru, Mercedes and Ford from the automobile industry) (Johansson 1994; Moeran 2002). Additionally, these giant agencies have established interlocking connections with a range of media outlets, especially with the domestic television stations, thereby exercising sustained and rarely challenged media buying power over both foreign and local competitors (Kawashima 2006). Thus, Japan exists as a distinctive symbolic and cultural space with respect to its advertising industry, whereby two major agencies vie for control of the marketplace. An implication of this structural arrangement is that advertising messages and representations tend to be relatively similar to each other across a variety of brands and industries. It is therefore no surprise that there has been a tendency in Japanese advertising to promote and reinforce a particular view of Japanese ethnicity, culture and identity as dominant and legitimate (Kunihiro 2004).

One of the illustrative examples that have historically and consistently reproduced the ideology of Japanese cultural nationalism is the energy drinks industry. Lipovitan-D was released as the first energy drink in Japan in 1962 and has been the market's most recognisable product to date. This was soon followed by other companies introducing similar products such as Oronamin-C and Yunker. The rise of popularity in consumption of energy drinks coincided with Japan's post-war economic growth that helped construct and maintain the image of Japanese hardworking 'salaryman'. In both reflecting and constructing the social norms at the time, energy drinks were promoted with advertising messages and representations that are "predominantly male in orientation and masculinist and middle-class in composition" (Roberson 2005, 369). Lipovitan-D, in particular, is known for a long history of deploying the same visual format, composition and storyline for its television commercials that typically depict male actors engaging in outdoors or adventurous activities, overcoming crisis moments and exclaiming the brand slogan 'Fight! One shot!' (Faito! Ippatsu!). As Roberson (2005) contends, this series of commercials for Lipovitan-D reinforces the ideals of Japanese masculinity by positioning athletic or muscular male actors at the centre of action in outside (as opposed to inside home) environments, thereby creating "the association of their energy- and strength-providing products with the strength of the men in their commercials" (377). The most iconic, or certainly memorable, commercial message that signified the masculinist salaryman ideology was produced for Regain in the late 1980s. It was the period in which Japan was still enjoying the fruit of its post-war economic ascendancy, and this was reflected in the positive and assertive tone of the commercial song which asked, "Can you fight for twenty-four hours?" (nijūyojikan tatakaemasuka?) and ended with a phrase "Business man, business man, Japanese business man" (bijinesuman, bijinesuman, japanīzu bijinesuman). This commercial song was received so fervently by the public for its wit and catchy sound that it was then turned into a music CD to be sold nationwide. Around the same time, another popular product, Gronsan, was promoted with the advertising message "Gronsan for men after five" (gojikara otoko no Guronsan), which signified the social expectation of male employees to work overtime into the evening and even night. With the economic collapse of 1990 that led to the decade-long recession and the public concerns over an increase in cases of karōshi or death by overwork, these commercial campaigns and messages for energy drinks were criticised and, in turn, adjusted to better reflect the realities of many who lost their jobs or generally struggled to make ends meet. Despite these recent changes made in response to cosmopolitan sentiments, it is fair to say that the energy drinks advertising has represented the masculinist and nationalist ideology at a particular time. In this sense, energy drinks are constantly and continuously promoted as a source of energy and power in (over-)charging 'salarymen' (and now salarywomen to be more frequently featured in their advertising) to cope with the long-hour and stressful working conditions instead of taking time off and achieving the life-work balance.

The unique structure and arrangement of the Japanese advertising industry have served as a significant barrier to foreign brands when entering the market. In order to overcome this, they have often been left with no choice but to cooperate or collaborate with local workers or organisations for production and distribution of their advertisements in Japan. In terms of advertising representations, the use of Japanese language, symbols, actors and locations is found crucial for foreign brands to appeal precisely to the local identity, reality and sensibility. This strategy of a multinational corporation to adapt to local conditions of production and consumption is commonly known as 'glocalisation' (Robertson 1995). The key to glocalisation for foreign brands in Japan is to establish a certain form of relationship—whether it be cooperation, collaboration, alliance or partnership—with their local subsidiaries, business partners or advertising agencies that can translate and mediate the cultural differences (Kobayashi 2012a, 2012b, 2016). The prevalence of foreign brands' glocalisation entails that they often end up collaborating with the same Japanese advertising agencies such as Dentsu and Hakuhodo, especially when distribution of television commercials is required because these agencies dominate contracts with local television stations (Kawashima 2006). In my previous studies, for example, Nike—an American sporting goods company—mostly delegated the production and distribution of local marketing campaigns to local teams at its subsidiary and advertising agency, Nike Japan and Wieden+Kennedy Tokyo (Kobayashi 2012a, 2012b, 2016). These studies found that Japanese workers at both organisations played a central role in generating and authenticating the meanings associated with the Japanese extracurricular school sport activities (bukatsu), which were then incorporated as signifiers of local physical cultural practice and identity within the ads. One of the implications from these studies is that even with foreign brands, products and services becoming readily available, local cultural intermediaries such as marketers, advertising professionals and media distributors have a strong hold of control over the advertising industry and largely maintain their power to keep shaping the commercial culture in Japan. Consequently, this configuration with the dominance of a few Japanese advertising agencies and the centrality of local actors and organisations in promoting products and services is most likely to reproduce a sense of national pride, prestige and belongingness, thereby fostering the production and consumption of commercial nationalism.

Commercial cosmopolitanism in Japan

Given the level of power and control that Japanese advertising agencies and cultural intermediaries hold over the space of domestic commercial production, it may come as a surprise to many that foreigners as racial Others have been over-represented in Japanese advertising—for instance, Prieler (2010) identified that white people accounted for less than 1 per cent of Japan's demography but were featured by 14.3 per cent of the ads from his analysis. Many of the previous literatures consider that the frequent appearances of foreigners and racial Others in Japanese advertising are directly linked to the construction and re-imagining of the national self because the Otherness can help defining its distinctive characteristics (Creighton 1995). As such, the over-representation of foreigners functions to remind domestic consumers of the clear distinction between the Japanese as 'us' and foreigners as 'them' while simultaneously reproducing the imagined homogeneity of Japanese ethnicity, culture and identity (Hagiwara 2004; Kunihiro 2004). In reference to advertising for energy drinks, for instance, Roberson (2005) points out that foreign others are predominantly represented as white and set out to be defeated by Japanese salarymen with a help of power and strength from these energy drinks. It has been also known from the previous literature that Japanese advertising has been reflective, and constitutive, of Japanese cultural nationalism that operates through dual forces of differentiation from the West via Occidentalism (Robertson 1990) and other non-Western nations via Oriental Orientalism (Iwabuchi 2002). In this Japanese context of racial hierarchy and classifications, Hagiwara (2004) identified from his study that the advertising representations featured 72.9 per cent of 'foreigners' (gaikokujin) as 'white people' (hakujin) while linking 'white people' with luxury goods such as automobiles and consumer electronics, 'black people' (kokujin) with sport and health, and 'other Asian people' (tōyōjin) with food and drinks. Although the high proportionality of white people to represent foreigners in Japanese advertising suggests that they serve as a major reference figure of racial Others, another interpretation exists—that is, the representation of white people and Western imageries as a proxy vision for attaining cosmopolitan character, taste and lifestyle.

Over decades, European and American luxury brands and products have been articulated with the social status of wealth and power in Japan, and the acquisition of these powerful signs has been managed in a way not to threaten the core constituents of national identity but to connote a particular view of cosmopolitan culture and lifestyle that may co-exist. As such, it is perhaps less surprising to find frequent appearances of white people and European imageries as stylistic signs of cosmopolitan tastes and identity within ads by Japanese multinational corporations in the automobile and consumer electronics industries. Since Japanese advertising relies heavily on the use of celebrities in catching an instant attention rather than creating an inspirational storyline than Western counterparts (Mueller 1992), these signs of commercial cosmopolitanism have been more than often personified by these individual celebrities, especially Hollywood stars who are identified as white, Caucasian or Anglo-Saxon. In its publication in English in 1978, Dentsu, for instance, stated that "[t]he foreign label is very much the symbol of prestige and quality, despite the availability of domestic products of comparable quality. To lend a sense of foreignness, many Japanese products are advertised using Caucasian models" (cited in Mueller 1992, 18). One of the illustrative examples that has naturalised the conflation between whiteness and cosmopolitanism in Japan is the cosmetics industry. Japanese cosmetic companies have long promoted products for skin whitening through the concept of bihaku (美白) or 'beautiful white' as "the normative and aspirational ideal of physical beauty" (Russell 2017, 31). In assessing how the understanding of whiteness is constructed in Japan, Russell (2017) further suggests that there are Japanese people who consider their own skin colour as white—a perception that enables the conflation because "whiteness is referenced but not registered; it is a transparency that permits Japanese to see beyond race and toward the normative (read Americo-Eurocentric) cosmopolitanism" (31).

Nevertheless, cosmopolitanism is not always linked with an overt desire to emulate the bodies and lifestyles of Western celebrities. Sometimes, another interpretation of cosmopolitanism—that is, the quality of being a global citizen—does make a rare appearance in Japanese advertising from time to time. NGOs and NPOs working to alleviate global humanitarian crises are well-known for appealing to this cosmopolitan sentiment and using ads to solicit donations. For an example from Japanese companies, Nissin's *No Border* advertising campaigns in 2004 and 2005 are worthy of particular attention. Nissin Food Products Company is a Japanese food manufacturer and best known for inventing the world's first instant ramen noodle, Cup Noodle, which is now sold across more than 80 countries. The *No Border* campaigns were said to reflect on the founder's philosophy of 'no food, no world peace' (shokusoku sehei, 食足世平) and aimed at sending the company's wish that "there won't be no border in people's mind like there is no border in how food tastes good" (Nissin Food Holdings Co., Ltd 2005, translated by the author). The 2004 campaign featured a series of television commercials depicting foreign settings of wars or conflict zones in which Cup Noodle was used to mediate the tensions and bring about peace. For instance, one of the commercials depicts a boy at a border in a war-torn foreign land with the border being formed by a line of countless cups of Cup Noodle. The boy, who apparently seems tormented by the symbolic separation, then picks up one of the cups in an attempt to remove the border. The commercial ends with a scene of an old man from the other side of the border joining the boy for eating Cup Noodle together. Another commercial in the series depicts a boy holding a rifle and checking the security at a coastline of an imagined conflict zone. The boy was then approached by a girl, which brought a smile on his face. The commercial ends with a scene of the boy and the girl eating Cup Noodle together and smiling to each other. The last scene was accompanied by a message on the screen: "There are more than 300,000 child soldiers in the world. What can we do for them? http://cupnoodle.jp" (translated by the author). It is noteworthy that this particular commercial was withdrawn shortly after its release in response to public criticisms as it was interpreted by some to affirm the existence of child soldiers (Shogakukan, Inc. 2016). Analytically, what is important to recognise from this series of commercials is the absence of Japanese people, spoken language and locations.

The portrayal of foreign lands and settings as sites of wars and conflicts, which are only mediated by consumption of Cup Noodle, conversely signifies the safety, peacefulness and material wealth, including food in Japan. In this sense, the cosmopolitan compassion for saving have-nots on the other side of the world is inherently linked to the construction of the national self. The 2005 series of *No Border* campaigns offered a different twist and demonstrated the company's aspiration of creating an even more universal food product that can be consumed outside of the Earth. The commercial was set in outer space and featured Russian astronaut Sergei Krikalv eating 'Space Ram'—microgravity-friendly noodle that Nissin created in collaboration with the Japan Aerospace Exploration Agency. Arguably, Nissin's re-imagining of the universe as cosmopolitan space literally without national borders and for humanities to come together through sharing of its food product could not be more transnational.

Conclusion

This chapter has offered and deployed a comparative framework of commercial nationalism and cosmopolitanism in order to understand the construction of both national and cosmopolitan identities through Japanese advertising. By way of concluding this chapter, I would like to highlight potential contributions of this framework to the body of knowledge about nationalism and potential areas for future research. To begin with, it is clear that Japanese advertising, and mass media more generally, has remained in serving as a main vehicle of nation-centric ideas, views and sentiments due to the insularity of their domestic industries and the centrality of Japanese actors and organisations within the context of cultural production. The dominant use of Japanese languages, locations, celebrities and people in advertising reinforces a parochial view of the world and nationalist discourses as exemplified by the promotion of energy drinks in association with the salaryman ideology. This form of commercial nationalism through everyday consumption and embodiment of national identity is powerful in normalising and naturalising the homogeneity of Japanese ethnicity, culture and identity. In this context of Japanese advertising, foreigners are actually over-represented and often used as symbolic markers of racial Others to signify the difference and distinctiveness of the national self. On the other hand, cosmopolitan identity is reduced to a commercial sign of stylistic taste and lifestyle as often represented by foreign, especially Hollywood, celebrities featured in advertisements. From the analysis of commercial cosmopolitanism, Nissin's *No Border* campaigns stand out as a rare incident of signification with respect to its embracement of cosmopolitanism as the ideal of transcending parochialism and uniting humanity as a whole. Conversely, the fact that such advertisements have been rarely found points to the difficulty of cosmopolitan and transnational imaginings within the current nation-centric environment and conditions of advertising production and consumption. As the sample of chosen ads for analysis was rather random though purposive, future research may conduct a systematic review of ads in terms of their national and cosmopolitan representations. Also, further investigations could illuminate the ways in which advertising agencies differentiate the use of emphasis on either national or cosmopolitan sentiments in a variety of global-local situations.

Given the strong hold of commercial nationalism in Japan, it is unlikely to see a plethora of advertisements promoting cosmopolitan ethics and philosophy in the foreseeable future. However, the studies of nationalism would benefit from further insight into cosmopolitanism for the following reasons. First, it is important to explore a potential imagining of an alternative spatial identity that may threaten, complement or influence national identity, and cosmopolitanism can provide a theoretical and philosophical basis for such an alternative. Second, as the forces of globalisation necessitate individuals to constantly re-assess their relationships with the world, cosmopolitan representations and practices—such as humanitarian assistance by global NGOs and NPOs and the United Nations' initiatives for the Sustainable Development Goals—are becoming more visible and prominent. Third, perhaps as a result of the second point, cosmopolitanisation is increasingly incorporated within the process of nation re-building today or what is referred to as 'cosmopolitan nationalism' (Beck, 2006). This is often found when nation-state governments compete to promote its cosmopolitan outlook in order to brand their nations as desirable and attractive destinations for investments, businesses and tourists internationally. In this sense, although I separated the cases of commercial nationalism and cosmopolitanism for the analytical purpose in this chapter, these two contrasting ideas are often integrated in practice—for instance, within the same advertisement and its production process that mediate complex consumer preferences to attain both national belongingness and global symbols (see Kobayashi et al. 2018). Thus, future research would benefit from understanding the dual process of how nationalism is cosmopolitanised (i.e., the nation's adoption of the *universal* principles) and how cosmopolitanism is nationalised (i.e., a *localised* interpretation of cosmopolitanism).

References

Amin, Ash, ed. 1994. *Post-Fordism: A Reader.* Oxford: Blackwell Publishers.
Anderson, Benedict. 1983. *Imagined Communities: Reflections on the Origin and Spread of Nationalism.* London: Verso.
Baruk, Agnieszka Izabela. 2019. "The Effect of Consumers' Ethnocentric Attitudes on Their Willingness for Prosumption." *Heliyon* 5 (7): 1–9.
Beck, Ulrich. 2006. *Cosmopolitan Vision.* Translated by Ciaran Cronin. Cambridge: Polity Press.
Bhappu, Anita D. 2000. "The Japanese Family: An Institutional Logic for Japanese Corporate Networks and Japanese Management." *The Academy of Management Review* 25 (2): 409–415.
Bourdieu, Pierre. 1984. *Distinction: A Social Critique of the Judgement of Taste.* R. Nice, Trans. Cambridge: Harvard University Press.
Calhoun, Craig. 2008. "Cosmopolitanism and Nationalism." *Nations and Nationalism* 14 (3): 427–448.
Castelló, Enric, and Sabina Mihelj. 2018. "Selling and Consuming the Nation: Understanding Consumer Nationalism." *Journal of Consumer Culture* 18 (4): 558–576.
Cho, Younghan, and Koji Kobayashi. 2019. "Disrupting the Nation-Ness in Postcolonial East Asia: Discourses of Jong Tae-Se as a Zainichi Korean Sport Celebrity." *The International Journal of the History of Sport* 36 (7–8): 681–697.
Creighton, Millie R. 1995. "Imaging the Other in Japanese Advertising Campaigns." In *Occientalism: Images of the West*, edited by James G. Carrier, 135–160. Oxford: Clarendon Press.
Cronin, Anne M. 2004. "Regimes of Mediation: Advertising Practitioners as Cultural Intermediaries?" *Consumption, Markets and Culture* 7 (4): 349–369.
Giulianotti, Richard, and Roland Robertson, eds. 2007. *Globalization and Sport.* Malden, MA: Blackwell Publishing.
Hall, Stuart. 1992. "The Question of Cultural Identity." In *Modernity and Its Futures*, edited by Stuart Hall, David Held, and Anthony McGrew, 273–325. Cambridge: Polity Press.
Hagiwara, Shigeru. 2004. "Nihon no terebi kōkoku ni arawareru gaikoku ime-ji no dōkō (The Trend in Representations of Foreign Images in Japan's Television Advertising)." *Keio Media and Communications Research* 54: 5–26.
Iwabuchi, Koichi. 2002. *Recentering Globalization: Popular Culture and Japanese Transnationalism.* Durham: Duke University Press.
Iwabuchi, Koichi. 2015. *Resilient Borders and Cultural Diversity: Internationalism, Brand Nationalism, and Multiculturalism in Japan.* Lanham: Lexington Books.

Johansson, Johny K. 1994. "The Sense of 'Nonsense': Japanese TV Advertising." *Journal of Advertising* 23 (1): 17–26.

Kawashima, Nobuko. 2006. "Advertising Agencies, Media and Consumer Market: The Changing Quality of TV Advertising in Japan." *Media, Culture & Society* 28 (3): 393–410.

Kobayashi, Koji. 2012a. "Corporate Nationalism and Glocalization of Nike Advertising in 'Asia': Production and Representation Practices of Cultural Intermediaries." *Sociology of Sport Journal* 29 (1): 42–61.

Kobayashi, Koji. 2012b. "Globalization, Corporate Nationalism and Japanese Cultural Intermediaries: Representation of *Bukatsu* through Nike Advertising at the Global–Local Nexus." *International Review for the Sociology of Sport* 47 (6): 724–742.

Kobayashi, Koji. 2016. "Taking Japan Seriously Again: The Cultural Economy of Glocalization and Self-Orientalization." In *Global Culture: Consciousness and Connectivity*, edited by Roland Robertson and Didem Buhari-Gulmez, 193–210. Farnham: Ashgate.

Kobayashi, Koji, John M. Amis, Richard Irwin, and Richard Southall. 2010. "Japanese Post-Industrial Management: The Cases of Asics and Mizuno." *Sport in Society* 13 (9): 1334–1355.

Kobayashi, Koji, and Steven J. Jackson. 2020. "Neoliberalism Without Guarantees: The Glocality of Labor, Education and Sport in Japan from the 1980s to the 2000s." In *Challenges of Globalization and Prospects for an Inter-Civilizational World Order*, edited by Ino Rossi, 551–571. New York: Springer.

Kobayashi, Koji, Steven J. Jackson, and Michael P. Sam. 2018. "Multiple Dimensions of Mediation within Transnational Advertising Production: Cultural Intermediaries as Shapers of Emerging Cultural Capital." *Consumption Markets & Culture* 21 (2): 129–146.

Kobayashi, Koji, Steven J Jackson, and Michael P Sam. 2019. "Globalization, Creative Alliance and Self-Orientalism: Negotiating Japanese Identity within Asics Global Advertising Production." *International Journal of Cultural Studies* 22 (1): 157–174.

Kunihiro, Yoko. 2004. "Terebi CM ni miru nihonjin no jiishiki: Tanitsu minzoku shakai no shinwa to "gaikokujin" kategorii o megutte (The Representation of Japanese Identity in Television Commercials: Examining the Myth of Homogeneous Society and the Category of Foreigners)." *Keio Media and Communications Research* 54: 27–42.

Kusaka, Yuko. 2006. "The Emergence and Development of Japanese School Sport." In *Japan, Sport and Society: Tradition and Change in a Globalizing World*, edited by Joseph Maguire and Masayoshi Nakayama, 19–34. London: Routledge.

Moeran, Brian. 2002. "Japanese Advertising Discourse: Reconstructing Images." In *Exploring Japaneseness: On Japanese Enactments of Culture and Consciousness*, edited by Ray T. Donahue, 385–398. Westport, Connecticut: Ablex Publishing.

Mueller, Barbara. 1992. "Standardization vs. Specialization: An Examination of Westernization in Japanese Advertising." *Journal of Advertising Research* 32 (1): 15–24.

Nissin Food Holdings Co., Ltd. 2005. "*Konohoshi ni 'BORDER' nante nai* (There is no BORDER on this planet)." Released October 31. https://www.nissin.com/jp/news/929

Prieler, Michael. 2010. "Othering, Racial Hierarchies and Identity Construction in Japanese Television Advertising." *International Journal of Cultural Studies* 13 (5): 511–529.

Roberson, James. 2005. "Fight!! *Ippatsu*!!: 'Genki' Energy Drinks and the Marketing of Masculine Ideology in Japan." *Men and Masculinities* 7 (4): 365–384.

Robertson, Roland. 1990. "Japan and the USA: The Interpenetration of National Identities and the Debate about Orientalism." In *Dominant Ideologies*, edited by Nicholas Abercrombie, Stephen Hill, and Bryan S. Turner, 182–198. London: Unwin Hyman.

Robertson, Roland. 1995. "Glocalization: Time-Space and Homogeneity-Heterogeneity." In *Global Modernities*, edited by Mike Featherstone, Scott Lash, and Roland Robertson, 25–44. London: Sage Publications.

Russell, John G. 2017. "Replicating the White Self and Other: Skin Color, Racelessness, Gynoids, and the Construction of Whiteness in Japan." *Japanese Studies* 37 (1): 23–48.

Shogakukan, Inc. 2016. "Nissin Cup Noodle CM hōei chūshi: Watashitachi wa nani ni rakutan subekika (The cancellation of Nissin Cup Noodle's commercials: A lesson for what we should be disappointed)." *News Post Seven*. Released April 9. https://www.news-postseven.com/archives/20160409_401958.html/2

Silk, Michael L, David L Andrews, and C. L Cole, eds. 2005. *Sport and Corporate Nationalisms*. Oxford: Berg.

Smith, Anthony D. 1991. *National Identity*. Reno: University of Nevada Press.
Stevenson, Nick. 2003. "Cultural Citizenship in the 'Cultural' Society: A Cosmopolitan Approach." *Citizenship Studies* 7 (3): 331–348.
Volcic, Zala, and Mark Andrejevic. 2011. "Nation Branding in the Era of Commercial Nationalism." *International Journal of Communication* 5: 598–618.
Volcic, Zala, and Mark Andrejevic, eds. 2015. *Commercial Nationalism: Selling the Nation and Nationalizing the Sell*. New York: Palgrave Macmillan.

18
NATION, NATIONALISM AND IDENTITY DISCOURSES IN NORTH KOREAN POPULAR CULTURE

Udo Merkel

Introduction

The Democratic People's Republic of Korea (DPRK) remains one of the most isolated and secretive countries in the world. Governed by the Kim dynasty since its foundation in 1948, North Korea is one of the least globalised and poorest countries on this planet. It occupies the Northern part of the Korean peninsula with the Republic of Korea (ROK) taking up the Southern half.

Although ethnicity plays a vital role in the nationalist fabric of both countries, there are several other properties that contribute to a distinctive sense of national identity in the two Korean states. In the north, the vast majority of these are linked to the short political history of the country, its rulers, and fundamental and very distinctive socio-economic and political principles. Therefore, a brief contextualisation is deemed to be necessary in order to fully understand the complex construction of the North Korean nation and corresponding identity narratives. Subsequently, those concepts and theories that shape and underpin this chapter will be explained. The next part will then analyse the national identity discourses in staged, spectacular and extraordinary events and celebrations as well as the mundane, everyday and ubiquitous cultural practices of the North Korean people. Focussing on these two cultural fields was partly inspired by Tim Edensor's convincing book on *National Identity, Popular Culture and Everyday Life* (2002) and the absence of examples from North Korea in this influential publication. It goes without saying that the division of the Korean people makes this process of identity construction more complicated than in many other countries, as pan-Korean identity discourses that focus on the unity of all Koreans continue to be promoted by both Korean governments. However, this chapter will only touch on this issue as its focus is on the essence and 'ingredients' of North Korea's state-endorsed sense of national identity, which is most obvious and explicit in public festivities. The conclusion will then draw the main observations together.

This chapter will largely ignore North Korea's attempts at nation branding in international environments, particularly through the participation in global sports events as a means to increase the country's global recognition and, ultimately, Soft Power (Nye 2004 and 2008) as these have been discussed elsewhere (Merkel 2014 and 2019). Instead, it aims to answer the following three questions: First, what defines the North Korean nation? Second, what are the most essential elements and symbolic signifiers of the people's sense of national identity? Third, which tools, devices and mechanisms are used by the political regime to promote a sense of 'we', shared destiny, belonging and collective memories among its citizens?

The socio-economic and political context

The Korean nation's existence in the twentieth century has largely been shaped by outside forces and global tensions. Japan's ruthless colonialism, at the beginning of the twentieth century, led to the annexation of the Korean peninsula and suppression of its people from 1910 to 1945. At the end of World War II, Soviet and American troops terminated Japanese rule and occupied the country. After unification talks failed, the Cold War rivals backed the formation of governments sympathetic to their respective leaders and ideologies, which resulted in the current political division and the existence of two Korean states: The ROK in the south, founded on 15 August 1948, hosting a population of almost 52 million, and the DPRK in the north, established three weeks later on 9 September 1948, with currently approximately 25 million people. Shortly after the Soviet Union and the USA withdrew most of their armed forces, North Korea invaded the South, in 1950, in order to unify the country. Although an armistice agreement brought an end to the hostilities in July 1953, both countries have yet to sign a peace treaty, which would officially end the Korean War. The subsequent creation of a heavily fortified Demilitarised Zone (DMZ), along the 38th parallel, has divided the two countries since then (Blair 1987; Cumings 2004).

For almost three-quarters of a century, Koreans in the DPRK and the ROK have led separate and very different lives. South Korea's fast and successful economic development is well researched (Hwang 1993). The country followed the Japanese model of export-oriented growth and became quickly one of the most affluent in the world. Despite severe economic problems following the Asian financial crisis in the late 1990s, South Korea continues to have a solid and healthy economy (Cumings 2005, 299–341). The country is globally well known and highly respected for its openness in terms of trade and tourism. It has also developed a large number of Soft Power resources, for example, K-Pop, staging mega sports events, Korean food, cinema and highly successful sports teams and athletes all of them assuring a continuous and confident presence on a global stage.

In sharp contrast, North Korea's post-World War II political, economic and cultural development was heavily influenced by the Soviet Union and China. The country hardly engaged with the outside world (Cumings 2005, 404–447) continues to be economically, politically and culturally isolated and is therefore frequently referred to as the 'Hermit Kingdom'. Over the last three decades, the country's poverty has grown significantly, particularly since the collapse of the Soviet Union in the early 1990s. The absence of modern technologies and the inadequate management of the centrally planned economy have led to severe food shortages. Furthermore, natural disasters have hit North Korea frequently and have caused severe famines. Cautious estimates by aid agencies suggest that up to two million people have died since the mid-1990s because of acute food shortages. Due to these extremely difficult economic circumstances, it became ever more important for the state to foster strong bonds between its citizens in order to unify the population, legitimise the government, avoid political dissent and mobilise people to engage in various economic recovery programmes.

Largely responsible for laying the foundations of these developments is Kim Il-sung, North Korea's founding father and 'Eternal Leader'. His leadership and political ambitions were driven by the search for an outdated Korean ideal, an autarkic and self-sufficient nation-state. When Kim Il-sung died in 1994, his son, Kim Jong-il, replaced him. The idea of ideological, political, economic and military independence, self-sufficiency and self-reliance, *Juche*, remained one of the most important cornerstones of the state's ideology. *Juche* is often seen as a philosophical concept describing a state of self-reliance (Cumings, 2004, 158–160). Although Kim Jong-il did not introduce any significant ideological changes during his reign from 1994 to 2011, his slightly more pragmatic policies led to the establishment of full diplomatic ties with a large number of European countries, Canada, Australia and several others.

After Kim Jong-il's death in December 2011, his youngest son, Kim Jong-un, quickly took over. North Korea's ruling party finalised his ascension with the transfer of all powers to the 'Great Successor' in April 2012. Since then, Kim Jong-un repeatedly confirmed and upheld the long-standing and fundamental ideological principles that his father and grandfather had pursued. He also continued their strategy of sending mixed messages to the outside world. After suspending long-range missile tests, in early 2012, in exchange for large amounts of US food aid, he announced the launch of a rocket carrying a satellite into orbit. Disagreements with the outside world partly generated and exacerbated by the country's nuclear ambitions and frequent testing of ballistic missiles helped to rally the powerful military apparatus and people behind the young leader. Although he frequently re-enacts his grandfather, he has also been keen to project an image that stresses youth, vitality and more political openness, and develop his own leadership style (Lorenz 2012, 19). He surprised the world by his frequent television appearances and his occasional endorsement of American, in particular Hollywood, manufactured, cultural icons as well as appreciated South Korean cultural products.

Kim Jong-un's three fruitless meetings with the previous US president Donald Trump in 2018 (Singapore) and 2019 (Hanoi and the DMZ) attracted global media interest. So did North Korea's participation in the 2018 Winter Olympics hosted by the South Korean city of Pyeongchang. As on several occasions before, the two Koreas marched under one flag at the opening ceremony and even fielded a joint women's ice hockey team. However, Kim Jong-un's sister, Kim Yo-jong, attracted even more media and political interest. She was the first member of the Kim dynasty to visit South Korea and was charged to deliver a personal message to the country's president, Moon Jae-in, inviting him to visit her brother in the north. That indeed happened and since then both men have met three times. These meetings produced historical images but no substantive outcomes apart from various declarations and statements of intention. And yet, there was, briefly, a sense that the usually tense mood on the Korean peninsula was shifting, that diplomatic channels had been reopened and that a foundation for further inter-Korean engagement had been laid. That did not last for very long, as in 2019 North Korea discontinued the political dialogue with the South. The country did not participate in the Tokyo Summer Olympics in 2021 and, thus, South Korean hopes of reviving diplomacy through contacts at the Games were crushed. It, once again, showed how delicate the relationship between the general political climate on the divided Korean peninsula and sport diplomacy is (Bridges 2012; Choi 2002; Jonsson 2006; Merkel 2008).

Theoretical considerations

There is little doubt that nationalism is a modern phenomenon. And yet, Anthony Smith (1991, 1996 and 1998) has convincingly shown that many modern nations have premodern origins. He also argues that ethnicity has played an important role in the making of modern nation-states. According to Smith, the core of many nation-states is the ethnicity of its citizens who share – among many other things – very often a common language, historical memories, customs and traditions, sacred places and rituals, festivals and celebrations. Smith's most valuable contribution to academic discussions is his distinction between *civic* and *ethnic* forms of nations and nationalism. The latter is of particular significance for an understanding of the identity discourses in the divided Korean peninsula. There appears to be a general consensus in both popular and academic discourses that the Korean nation's sense of self is largely underpinned by the firm belief that Koreans share a common ancestry, are ethnically homogenous, have a pure bloodline and a very distinct and unique culture that dates back hundreds (if not thousands) of years. Although, after World War II, this notion of ethnic nationalism was abandoned in many countries such as Germany and Japan, in Korea, several social scientists continue to investigate the Korean nation's 'unique racial and cultural heritage' (Pai 2000, 6) and argue that this is the most influential resource in the people's sense of national identity.

The most refined and detailed analysis of this issue certainly derives from Gi-wook Shin's seminal work on *Ethnic Nationalism in Korea*. He concludes that

> Koreans maintain a strong sense of ethnic homogeneity based on shared blood and ancestry, and nationalism continues to function as a key resource in Korean politics and foreign relations. This is even more pronounced in North Korea, which has been stressing the importance of ethnic national identity in their struggle for regime survival.
>
> *(Shin 2006, 232)*

Shin thoroughly traces the roots, politics and legacy of Korean ethnic nationalism, which extensively draws on the sense of a shared bloodline and ancestry, and links these to North Korea's political system.

In their persuasive essay on *Communism, Nationalism and Political Propaganda in North Korean Sport*, Jung-woo Lee and Alan Bairner (2009, 390–410) confirm the existence of ethnic-nationalist discourses in the world of North Korean sport. They argue that 'nationalistic sporting practice appears to be less a response to globalization than an extension of the North Korean communist movement' (Lee and Bairner 2009, 406). They also trace and account for the historical 'development of the national consciousness in North Korean politics' and suggest that there are three clearly identifiable 'stages: the first period of Marxist-Stalinist ideology, the second period of *Juche* (self-reliance) ideology and the third period of *Chosun minjok cheil juui* ("Korea is best" nationalism)' (Lee and Bairner 2009, 393). This chapter is mainly concerned with the last phase that commenced in the late 1980s and contemporary developments.

Although Lee and Bairner's research is focussed on the significance of sport, it constitutes a fruitful starting point as some of their insights can also be applied to the world of popular culture, in particular the DPRK's extensive events calendar that will be analysed later. However, doing this will also demonstrate that the key ingredients of national identity discourses in North Korea are slightly more complex and multi-layered. While the core of North Korea's identity narratives certainly focusses upon the sense of a shared and pure bloodline and ancestry, there are several other layers that demonstrate the distinctiveness of the North Korean nation, particularly in comparison and contrast to their Southern neighbours. It is these very distinctive North Korean characteristics that this chapter is mostly concerned with.

As this chapter pays particular attention to both the staged, often spectacular performances of North Korea's national identity and the very ordinary and ubiquitous signifiers,

Michael Billig's work on *Banal Nationalism* (1995) is also of utmost relevance. Among many other things, his research has clearly shown how cultural practices in everyday environments produce and reproduce representations of the nation in very subtle and sublime ways often being part of an obscure background. Such practices are often unnoticed due to their prevalence, ubiquity and constant repetition. Billig (1995) suggests that these less obvious signifiers of modern nationalism make it a very powerful ideology as they remain unchallenged. Examples of banal nationalism include the use of flags in everyday contexts, symbols on money, the *national* news and the *national* weather, specific colour combinations and songs, sporting events and so on. What all these signifiers have in common is that they can be found, and are usually deeply embedded, in the realms of everyday life and ordinary as well as spectacular cultural practices.

Finally, the concept of performativity underpins chapter. It has its roots in various social-scientific subdisciplines and is most frequently linked to the work of Erving Goffman (1969), Richard Schechner (1985), Victor Turner (1988) and Judith Butler (1993 and 1997). They share the view that performances are central to social arrangements and dynamics, and all human beings put on, and are part of, performances. Focussing on these enables us to assess the ways people act and react in social environments and allows us to make sense of how people situate themselves and others in the world.

Goffman (1969) introduced and applied the metaphor of the theatrical performance, and the front- and backstage, to the analysis of human interaction. He considers people to be actors on a 'social stage' where they continuously create, manage and make sense of impressions. We all play various roles and, in Goffman's terms, put on a variety of 'fronts' depending on the social environment we find ourselves and other actors in, and through these performances we are able to attach meaning to social situations. Both Schechner (1985) and Turner (1988) focussed on the performative nature of societies around the world. Their ethnographic studies showed how events, festivals and rituals (as well as daily life) were all governed by a code of performance. In addition to her ground-breaking work on the social construction of gendered identities, Butler's (1993) work is of particular relevance for this chapter as she developed the concept of performativity. She defines it as 'that reiterative power of discourse to produce the phenomena that it regulates and constrains' (Butler 1993, XII). This concept can be applied to a variety of social and cultural phenomena, for example, identity construction processes. One of the key characteristics of performativity is repetition, which is, of course, typical for annual ceremonial performances, events, rituals and celebrations that the next section of this chapter considers.

Constructing the nation in everyday, mundane environments and the grand spectacles

More than a decade ago Tania Branigan (2010, 25) offered a detailed journalistic description of life in North Korea that was implicitly underpinned by the notion of performativity. It can be succinctly summarised as full of repetitive, symbolic practices, prescriptive and participatory rituals and scripted, thoroughly choreographed and rehearsed performances that display and celebrate the uniqueness of this political community, its successes, a sense of national identity, unity and purpose. Branigan's summary of everyday life in North Korea also exemplifies what Clifford Geertz (1980) meant with the term 'theatre state'. It refers to countries that have a very keen interest in staging dramatic and ritualised performances, elaborate ceremonies and celebrations and, most importantly, impressive spectacles. The concept features prominently in Heonik Kwon and Byung-Ho Chung's book *North Korea: Beyond Charismatic*

Politics (2013) that is primarily concerned with the public display of power in North Korea. The combination of both concepts, 'performativity' and the 'theatre state', constitutes a helpful device to make sense of identity discourses, particularly of those that focus on the nation. In North Korea, people are not just consuming what the authoritarian state offers but millions usually actively participate in the performances as directors, actors, extras and other staff, which, in some cases, involves weeks and/or months of practising and rehearsing.

There are almost 40 public holidays, celebrations and commemorations per year in North Korea. A handful are internationally recognised and also important occasions in many other countries around the world such as New Year's Day, Labour Day and International Women's Day. However, the overwhelming majority of these public holidays mark and reinforce distinctive components of the autocratic political system and people's sense of national identity. These annual ceremonial performances are rather unique and only make sense in the North Korean context as the following short selection (in chronological order) shows:

- *Military Foundation Day* (8 February; until 2014 marked on 25 April);
- *Day of the Shining Star* (16 February, the birthday of Kim Jong-il);
- *Day of the Sun* (15 April, the birthday of country's first leader, Kim Il-sung, the 'Eternal President of North Korea');
- *Day of Victory in the Great Fatherland Liberation War* (27 July, remembering the end of the Korean War in 1953);
- *National Liberation Day of Korea* (15 August, commemorating the end of Japanese occupation in 1945);
- *Day of Songun* (25 August, emphasising the elevated position of the armed forces in Korean society);
- *Day of the Foundation of the Republic* (9 September 1948);
- *Party Foundation Day* (10 October, referring to the establishment of the WPK (Workers' Party of Korea) in 1945);
- *Constitution Day* (27 December, marking approval of the country's constitution in 1972).

All of these are public holidays, and offices, banks, government institutions, schools, universities and retail outlets are closed for at least one day. The most important annual celebration is without any doubt the *Day of the Sun* on 15 April, the birthday of North Korea's founder and leader (1948–1994) Kim Il-sung, followed by Kim Jong-il's birthday in February and the *Foundation of the Republic Day* in September. It is only since 2012, the year following Kim Jong-il's death, that his birthday is called *Day of the Shining Star*. Before, that is between 1982 and 2012, the day was known as *The Spring of Humanity*. While the *Day of the Shining Star* actually lasts for two days, his father's birthday celebrations, the *Day of the Sun*, are followed by two days of rest, turning it into a three-day holiday. However, festivities of all different kinds take place throughout the whole month of April. The two-month period between the *Day of the Shining Star* and the *Day of the Sun* is known as the *Loyalty Festival Period* and various celebrations occur throughout.

Although all these festivals have different names and mark distinctively different occasions, they have, at least, four characteristics in common: First, they can all be described and are intended to be, National Days, that David McCrone and Gayle McPherson define as 'commemorative devices in time and place for reinforcing national identity' (2009, 1). The case studies they have put together in their compelling book clearly show how diverse National Days are. A large number of National Days across the world appear to be rather unstable symbolic signifiers, several are very low-key celebrations, others have experienced significant changes over time in order to adjust to changing socio-economic, cultural and political circumstances, and some have been contested, argued over, abandoned, reclaimed and reinvented. None of this, however, applies to North Korea, where National Days are taken very seriously. Most of them have their roots in the very short political history of the country and are explicitly linked to the country's past and present rulers, the Kims. They are significant markers in the young nation's biography, comprehensively celebrated and able to mobilise millions of people. Although the matter of these celebrations, the people's national identity, is, of course, an abstract phenomenon, the way they are celebrated, in particular the people's involvement and the activities surrounding them, turns them into memorable and visceral experiences.

Second, all the above-mentioned events occur frequently and on exactly the same day as in the year before. Edensor argues that 'repetition is essential to a sense of identity, for without recurrent experiences and unreflexive habits there would be no consistency given to experience, no temporal framework within which to make sense of the world' (Edensor 2002, 96). Furthermore, they tend to follow exactly the same pattern or structure as the events in the previous year.

Third, all the above-mentioned events can be categorised as what Eric Hobsbawm calls 'invented traditions'. He defines these as cultural practices usually 'governed by overtly or tacitly accepted rules and of a ritual or symbolic nature, which seek to inculcate certain values and norms of behaviour by repetition, which automatically implies continuity with the past' (Hobsbawm 1999, 1). Of course, the emergence of two (very different) Korean states and societies in 1948, which involved a change in borders, population, social structures and political system, made a large number of cultural traditions obsolete. Therefore, the North Korean rulers had to start from scratch and new traditions had to be designed in order to achieve social stability. Interestingly, the extensive celebrations of Kim Il-sung's birthday (in 1912) de facto increase the length of North Korea's past considerably.

Finally, the format, dramaturgy and choreography of all these commemorative devices are very similar. 'Round' dates, that is, anniversaries that end in 0 and 5, are, of course, celebrated more extensively and lavishly than others. Apart from that, the festive arrangements hardly differ. They usually contain several of the following ingredients: Political speeches; military demonstrations and large-scale parades occasionally showcasing new weapons; fly-overs; people's parades cheering their leader and performing living mosaics; torchlight marches; seminars focussing on fundamental political ideas such as *Juche* and *Songun*; exhibitions such as art and flower displays; an art and theatre festival with live performances; dance and music performances; choral singing and, of course, a wide variety of local national and even international sport events such as the Pyongyang Marathon that is usually held in April. It goes without saying that there are hardly any ludic and playful elements in these celebrations, except for, perhaps, the mass dances in the evenings in public spaces, music performances and the very popular informal picnics of families in local parks.

The main roads are usually decorated with flags, banners and posters containing political messages and slogans. Many North Koreans commemorate these holidays by visiting places that have an explicit connection with their past leaders such as the hundreds of Kim Il-sung and Kim Jong-il statues in Pyongyang, where North Koreans turn up in their best attire, lay flowers, wreaths and bouquets, and bow for several seconds. These statues of the country's leaders are also very popular as background for wedding photos. Members of the armed forces prefer to pose in front of military monuments. In the evenings, there are mass dancing parties and live music performances. Occasionally, there are evening firework displays, most frequently in Pyongyang in the context of the *Day of the Sun*.

Loyalty and commitment to the Kim family are one of the most important elements of North Koreans' sense of identity. Bradley K. Martin (2006) has analysed this personality cult in great detail and compares it to a religion that offers a comprehensive belief system surrounding, maintaining and justifying the exalted and sacrosanct position of the Kim dynasty. His very detailed analysis shows how Kim Il-sung and Kim Jong-il have successfully managed to portray North Korean society as a large family with the respective rulers being the father and all North Korean citizens the children. That is certainly one of the most striking features of North Korean discourses about the nation. Framed by Confucian ideas about the family, such a set-up, of course, requires loyalty, allegiance, devotion, obedience and uncritical adherence from the North Korean people. In fact, their treatment of the Kims shows all the characteristics of religious worshipping. Martin (2006) further argues that the unequivocal following of, and devotion to, the Kims is based on the systematic and relentless indoctrination of the population that starts in early childhood and never ends. In addition to all the traditional school subject areas such as Korean, Mathematics, Physics, Music and Physical Education, there is one in North Korean schools that is exclusively devoted to the Kims. It is called 'The lives of the Great Leaders'.

Furthermore, Kim Il-sung and Kim Jong-il are omnipresent in people's everyday lives through imposing statues, large monuments, gigantic murals on house walls and elaborate paintings in public spaces, such as underground stations. All of these portray the two men as the fatherly, enigmatic and yet strict rulers that the North Korean people identify with and look up to. The display of their portraits in offices, factories, workshops, museums, schools, shops, restaurants, public buildings, train stations, hotel lobbies and many other venues is compulsory. Every private household in North Korea is required to display framed portraits of the two previous heads of state. All newlywed couples receive a set of framed photos from the state. Since these photos are powerful and universal symbols of the idolisation of the Kim family and, of course, their omnipresence, there are strict rules surrounding the treatment of these portraits. Inside, for example in flats or shops, they must be hung on walls with nothing else on them, in a prominent position and high enough so that they cannot be covered by a person. They must be cleaned every few days and dust must be prevented from settling on the frames. Outside, cyclists have to dismount from their bikes and look at the portraits. Car drivers have to slow down. Passers-by must turn to gaze at the images. At night, in Pyongyang, these portraits are lid. Folding or crumbling a newspaper with the images of Kim Il-sung and Kim Jong-il is strictly forbidden. Equally mandatory are the small red metal badges that show the faces of the two Kims. All North Korean citizens must wear them across their left breast near the heart, preferably on the lapel. These badges have been around since the late 1960s and suggest that North Korea's leaders are always with the people and that the people belong, and are loyal, to the leaders. But most importantly, the above-mentioned Kim Il-sung and Kim Jong-il statues, monuments, murals on house walls, portraits, mosaics and paintings are ubiquitous and daily reminders to the public of the paramount role of the Kim dynasty in their country's history and people's lives.

In addition, there are several other symbolic signifiers that the state promotes as key elements of the country's national identity. These include, and that is also reflected in the country's annual (events) calendar, historical events, such as the Korean War, officially, in the North, referred to as 'The Fatherland Liberation War', and contemporary phenomena, such as the country's military might with a standing army of around one million soldiers. The exalted and central position of the 'Korean People's Army' (KPA) is justified by the previously mentioned *Songun* policy, the military-first principle, which prioritises the country's armed forces. The *Songun* principle is inseparable from the *Juche* policy as the former is based on and predicated by the latter. According to this dictum, the armed forces must be supported wholeheartedly and by all means and never allowed to be vulnerable as they are the guardians of the North Korean people. The allocation of enormous national resources to the military apparatus, despite severe shortages throughout the country, is the logical and inevitable consequence. When Kim Jong-un delivered his first public speech at a military parade, in April 2012, he promised to continue his predecessors' domestic and foreign policies, in particular the *Songun* policy.

The importance of both the Korean War and the armed forces is further evidenced by the existence of the massive 'Victorious Fatherland Liberation War Museum', in the centre of Pyongyang, and the celebration of *Victory Day* on 27 July, which marks the end of the Korean War in 1953. *Military Foundation Day*, on 8 February, offers another opportunity to praise the country's one million soldiers. Like many other buildings in Pyongyang, the 'Victorious Fatherland Liberation War Museum' is a fascinating place that displays war-damaged military hardware, such as tanks, planes, torpedo boats, trucks, cars, rifles and ammunition. In its over 80 exhibition rooms, it also displays vivid illustrations and dioramas of key battles in the Korean War that serve to maintain collective memories.

All these elements of North Korea's official national identity can also be found in Pyongyang's monumental architecture and the most famous, often colossal, landmarks. As in other communist societies, the physical and spatial surroundings play a significant role in the creation of a new social order, political system, a sense of pride and national identity (Portal 2005, 138–149). As the Korean War destroyed large parts of Pyongyang, the incoming rulers had a clean slate to rebuild North Korea's capital. The most remarkable buildings and sights include the 170-metre tall '*Juche* Tower', the giant bronze statue of Kim Il-sung at Mansu Hill with an abundance of North Korean flags and figures depicting the war and revolutionary struggle, the 'Revolutionary Martyrs Cemetery', the 'Victorious Fatherland Monument', built in 1993 to mark the 40th anniversary of the end of the Korean War and the 'Reunification Monument'. The latter was constructed in 2001, is 30 metres high and constitutes a massive arch that shows two Korean women in traditional dresses holding a map of Korea. It can be found south of Pyongyang over the motorway to Panmunjom. This grand monument, of course, is part of the other identity narrative, which attempts to maintain a sense of pan-Koreanness. International sports events, in particular the Asian and Olympic Games, have also frequently be used to publicly confirm, celebrate and demonstrated Korean unity (Merkel 2014).

Kim Jong-un's birthday is not (yet) a public holiday, although he is closely associated with the relatively new *Songun Day* as he awarded this day official status in 2013. According to Adam Cathart, 'the function of this commemoration is actually to reinforce Kim Jong-un's legitimacy to rule, confirm the principle of very early succession and young leadership, and emphasize the preternatural military abilities of the sons in the Kim family' (2015). Kim Jong-un appears to be keen to be associated with his grandfather as he is frequently copying his Kim Il-sung's demeanour, often wears the kind of tunic suit and straw hat his grandfather was regularly seen in and even has the same hairstyle.

Having said this, since he came to power, he has been performing a delicate balancing act that tries to find an equilibrium between continuity and innovation. For example, he has been keen to improve the leisure, sport and entertainment infrastructure of North Korea. In addition to building the high-profile Masikryong ski resort in order to boost international tourism, which was widely reported in the international press, he has also pushed for the construction of new amusement and water parks, particularly in Pyongyang. However, even there, local visitors are unable to escape explicit references to the country's previous and present leaders. In the capital's most modern amusement park near the 'Arch of Triumph', a commemorative sign in front of one of the attractions reads: 'The Swing Boat that Kim Jong-un kindly rode on April 25, 2010'. There is nothing unusual about this as there are thousands of such plaques all over the country in factories, on farms, in offices, shops, hospitals, army barracks, educational establishments, squares, parks and many other places commemorating the visit of one of the Kims. The Munsu Water Park east of Pyongyang that hosts indoor and outdoor swimming pools, several slides, playing fields for volleyball and basketball, a rock-climbing wall as well as a café, bar and restaurant was opened in November 2013. There, a life-sized statue of Kim Jong-il can be found in the entrance area of the indoor swimming pool.

His state funeral in December 2011 provided the North Korean rulers with another opportunity to put on a spectacular show. It confirmed that North Korea takes exceptional and unique political spectacles very seriously. The planning, choreography and execution of Kim Jon-il's funeral was meticulous and full of symbolism. It was meant to cement Kim Jong-il's legacy and introduce his youngest son, Kim Jong-un, as his legitimate political heir. The funeral proceedings lasted for two days. The first day was without doubt the more spectacular, full of coded but unambiguous political messages and rich in symbolisms. It was dominated by the funeral procession slowly moving through the streets of Pyongyang against a backdrop of snowfall. Despite freezing temperatures, the streets were lined by tens of thousands of grieving mourners, many of them appearing to be members of the armed forces. Further down the route, women in civilian clothes shook with grief. During the three-hour procession, Kim Jong-un walked at the front with his hand on the black limousine bearing his father's casket on the roof, while a senior general walked on the other side. That set-up answered the most important questions about the country's future political leadership and demonstrated a smooth transition of power suggesting that fears of a political vacuum were unsubstantiated. Ahead of the hearse were cars carrying a large wreath draped with black ribbons and an enormous portrait of a smiling Kim Jong-il in his trademark khaki outfit. About a dozen of black Mercedes Benz cars and a larger fleet of white luxury vehicles followed the hearse. Later, a 21-gun salute marked the end of the proceedings.

One of the most popular, sophisticated and impressive spectacles that North Korea hosts regularly are the mass games. They usually take place in Pyongyang's striking May Day Stadium, which has a 150,000 capacity, and offer an alternative form of physical culture. The actual performance comprises three distinctive parts: First, a floorshow of complex and highly choreographed group routines performed by tens of thousands of gymnasts, dancers and athletes with large artificial flowers, flags, hoops, balls, ropes and clubs, acrobats with poles, ladders, springboards, trampolines and huge metal-framed wheels, and dancers. Second, the backdrop, a giant human mosaic generating detailed and rich panoramas of historical and contemporary scenes, landscapes, architecture, portraits of individuals, such as Kim Il-sung and Kim Jong-il, slogans and cartoons. More than 20,000 school children hold up coloured cards that are part of a 200-page book and change them so quickly and precisely that these images appear to be animated. Third, the music that links the mass performances in the centre of the May Day stadium and the backdrop (Merkel 2010, 2467–2492).

Such mass performances of sport and physical culture with an explicit political agenda have a long history and go back to Stalinist Russia in the late 1920s and throughout the 1930s where mass events were an omnipresent and integral element of cultural and political life. They were meant to forge a socialist consciousness among the people and strengthen their loyalty to party, state and leader. According to Roche, 'during this distinctive period of transformation ... there were determined strategies to develop propaganda and cultural policy in general, and to construct extra-ordinary, compelling and memorable experiences in mass publics as part of these strategies by means of the staging of mass cultural events' (2001, 494). The Soviet Union regarded itself a progressive society, qualitatively very different from Capitalist societies, and rejected the Capitalist concept of sport as it was considered to be an alienating experience for the individuals involved due to the exaggerated importance of competitiveness, the achievement principle, individualism, winning and the centrality of hierarchies – all embodying the spirit of Capitalism. Like the political elite of the former Soviet Union, the North Korean regime has always taken great 'great pride in its truly awesome choreographed mass marches through the great central square in Pyongyang, with literally a million people marching in step in fifty parallel columns' (Cumings 2004, 137).

Since 1946, the country has also more or less regularly staged mass gymnastic games. However, since the beginning of this millennium, these shows have grown grander, more lavish and prominent, and have attracted international media and tourist attention. 'True to the North's way of doing nothing by half, it dwarfs anything seen even during the heyday of the far more prosperous communist regimes of the former eastern bloc' (Watts 2002). It was very much the 'Arirang Festival' (2002–2013) that made the mass games famous. After a five-year break, the mass games returned in September 2018 with a new edition entitled 'The Glorious Country'. It celebrated the 70th anniversary of the foundation of the DPRK. This show also provided the background for an emotional speech that Moon Jae-in, South Korea's president, gave during his three-day visit of Pyongyang. Subsequently, the heads of both Korean states watched the mass games performance, which had been slightly modified to please the South Korean delegation. In 2019, the latest edition entitled 'The People's Country' was performed from June to October. Such a long run clearly indicates the popularity of this event among locals. A cautious estimate suggests that several millions of North Koreans watched the performance, which is, of course, free for locals. These shows are breath-taking spectacles that 'offer an alternative to modern sport since they have reinvigorated an outdated form of physical culture that involves the masses and falls outside the dominant "high, stronger, faster" philosophy' (Merkel 2010, 2486) of modern commercialised international sport. More importantly, however, they are 'joyous celebrations of the pure-bloodedness and homogeneity' (Myers 2010, 83) of the North Korean people.

I have offered a detailed analysis of the contents, choreography and political significance of the 'Arirang Festival' in relation to North Korea's national identity narratives, nation branding and foreign policy elsewhere (Merkel 2010, 2012, 2013, 2014) and will therefore only provide a quick summary before identifying a small number of changes in the 2018 and 2019 editions of this spectacle.

As in everyday life and many other events, the 'Arirang Festival' reiterated the sacrosanct, supreme and elevated position of the Kim dynasty. The backdrop frequently offered images of Kim Il-sung and Kim Jong-il showing both men in different environments and portraying them as paternal and protective figures, wise leaders, enlightened teachers and the ultimate saviours of the Korean nation. There is little doubt that this show underpins the religious cult of the country's rulers (Ryall 2011). It also featured all of the previously mentioned components of the North's national identity, such as the ethnic homogeneity of the Korean people, the *Juche* philosophy and the *Songun* principle. The latter is very conspicuous and appears in various segments, for example, in the context of martial arts routines, in particular taekwondo movements, and images that are part of both the floorshow in the centre of the stadium and the backdrop. Furthermore, the division of the Korean people and the reunification theme played important roles in the 'Arirang Festival'.

Like its predecessor, 'The Glorious Country' edition in 2018 offered a colourful and spectacular representation of the country's national identity while simultaneously trying to awe and inspire. There were several noteworthy technological improvements and upgrades. The show sketches North Korea's vision of its past and present, and continues to promote key political ideas and principles. However, it came across as less militaristic and more forward-looking. Images of missiles had totally disappeared, and the image of the atom was no longer part of the military section but featured in the context of technology and science. The show appeared to reflect Kim Jong-un's perspective, namely that his grandfather built and rebuilt North Korea, while his father, Kim Jong-il, successfully steered the Korean people through difficult times. Now, Kim Jong-un is paving the way into an optimistic and promising future through economic reforms.

Kim Jong-un appeared only once in the show but in a very powerful and highly emotional context. The backdrop showed him with South Korea's president, Moon Jae-in, referring to their above-mentioned historic meeting in Pyongyang in 2018. The final chapter was exclusively devoted to the country's international relations, in particular China, and even contained a few messages and slogans in English.

Despite these changes, the mass games continue to be a unique and grandiose ideological spectacle that offers North Korean-style entertainment, provides a highly selected summary of North Korean history, celebrates the questionable achievements of the political system, stresses the importance of key political dictums and promotes the religious cult of the Kim dynasty. Furthermore, the mass games demonstrate another fundamental ideological principle of North Korean society, namely that success is based on the subordination of the individual to the group and that a single, unified collective will and effort is above any individual desires or self-interest.

All the above-mentioned annual celebrations and commemorations, cultural events and festivals, and artistic spectacles have in common that they constitute symbolic practices through which North Korea domestically asserts its identity (and sovereignty to the outside world). At the same time, they demand and call for respect and loyalty from the country's citizens. Furthermore, these events are meant to establish national cohesion, symbolise membership in the national community, legitimise the existing power structures and socialise new members into North Korea's norms and values system, which, of course, includes fundamental philosophies and policies of the state.

Conclusion

This chapter set out to make a contribution to wider social-scientific, particular political, debates about the complex relationship between popular culture and national identity discourses with particular reference to North Korea's extensive list of public celebrations and festivities. In general, popular culture often offers people plenty of opportunities for communal bonding and developing and experiencing a sense of collective identity. In the context of North Korea, however, popular culture must not be understood as 'a form of entertainment that is mass produced or is made available to large numbers of people' (Street 2007, 7). Quite the opposite. More than in many other countries, North Korea's ruling regime has developed an extensive set of cultural tools particularly for nation-building purposes that underpin the country's claims to national distinctiveness and help its citizens to make sense of who they are as a nation against the wider context of the two Koreas being a divided society.

In addition to the ethnic basis of the (whole) Korean nation, key elements of the people's sense of national identity in North Korea derive from the short biography of this young nation-state, fundamental socio-economic and political principles such as the *Juche* philosophy and *Songun* policy and their familial relationship with the ruling Kim dynasty. The latter is of particular importance and partly helps to explain the continuity of the DPRK despite the dissolution and collapse of states with similar political systems in the early 1990s such as the Soviet Union and many Eastern European countries. E.J.R. Cho describes this phenomenon as 'familial nationalism' and North Korea as a 'family state' (2017, 594–622). It is therefore no surprise that the state and official North Korean media outlets employ the terms (North-) *Korean nation* and *Kim Il-sung nation* interchangeably.

In addition to an abundance of conventional signifiers of North Korea's national distinctiveness such as official flags and state symbols, anthems and songs, political posters, national news, home-grown heroes and heroines, traditional dresses and food, there are dozens of elaborate annual ceremonial performances, commemorations, rituals and celebrations that can be categorised as National Days as they focus on the nation and inform national narratives. These events make significant contributions to North Korean's sense of national identity and are in fact able to mobilise millions of people to take part. Therefore, this chapter was largely framed by the notion of performativity. It was not only applied to ubiquitous, everyday routines and deeply ingrained, widespread cultural practices but also to several annual celebrations, rituals, ceremonies, festivals and spectacles.

Sociologically, the latter are seen as symbolic cultural, social and political spaces, in which the performers, participants and attendees create, confirm and reinforce shared meanings. Such events continue to be 'the most obvious and recognisable ways in which national identity is performed [...] when the nation and its symbolic attributes are elevated in public display' (Edensor 2002, 72). They are highly politicised devices that are meant to cement the stability and continuity of the political system. The choreography and dramaturgy of many of these events show a high degree of similarity. They enable North Koreans to extract, and make sense of, the symbolic practices that signify the people's sense of nation and nationalism and contribute to their sense of national identity and belonging.

There is little doubt that national identities are, generally, relatively stable over time, but they are not written in stone. To some extent, they tend to be dynamic and often developing. They can be subject to contestation and alterations in response to changing socio-economic, cultural and political conditions and circumstances. That is a reflection and the result of the multitude of influences in an increasingly global environment. None of this, however, applies to North Korea where national identity discourses have been, to a very large extent, persistent and durable.

There is a simple reason for this. The impact of outside influences, for example, global cultural trends and political developments, is minimal in North Korea due to the country's self-imposed isolation. Access to modern information technologies remains the privilege of the ruling cast of the country. They have succeeded in restricting the population's contacts with the outside world over the last seven decades and continue to do so. Furthermore, almost all cultural products and practices such as the above-mentioned events, festivals and spectacles are state-sponsored. They are designed and strictly controlled by the rulers of the DPRK and primarily used as devices to maintain existing power relations. Since Kim Jong-un came to power in 2011, he has approved a few minor modifications in order to present himself as an innovator and has frequently used these as photo opportunities. Famous Disney characters, such as Mickey Mouse and Winnie the Pooh, featured prominently as a visual backdrop at a gala in honour of the country's new ruler in 2012, which also featured an all-female band playing Western rock and pop music (Lorenz 2012). In April 2018, Kim Jong-un attended a rare concert of South Korean pop musicians and performers, including the well-known K-Pop girl band Red Velvet, in Pyongyang. But these are token gestures and do not reflect any substantial changes in the regime's hostile attitude towards foreign cultural products and practices. Indeed, in December 2020, North Korea's Supreme People's Assembly agreed a batch of new laws (including draconian punishments for breaking them) to fight foreign ideological and cultural influences, in particular those originating in South Korea. There is little doubt that Kim Jong-un considers the influx of South Korean media products and cultural practices a threat to North Korea's power structures, the fabric of the state-sponsored culture and the cohesion of the North Korean people. Knowledge about the outside world, in particular about South Korea's wealth in comparison to the North's poverty, constitutes a serious threat to the regime's legitimacy and its ideological base.

Having said that, on a very small number of occasions, the North Korean government also promotes a pan-Korean identity that emphasises the strong ethnic ties and common cultural heritage of the Korean people on the divided peninsula. That, of course, is a delicate balancing act but keeps the issue of reunification in the public discourse without the need to engage in complex and difficult political negotiations. One event, that celebrates a distinctive North Korean identity and, at the same time, frequently offers an emotional and sentimental reminder of pan-Korean unity and integrity, are the mass games. They, of course, contain all the above-mentioned constituents of North Koreans' sense of national identity and also promote 'an extreme form of ethnocentric Korean nationalism […] that expresses pride and self-esteem based on the greatness of the Korean nation' (Lee and Bairner 2009, 394). In comparison to the other events and celebrations that have been mentioned before, the mass games are also intended for an international audience as they provide the North Korean rulers with a rare and unrivalled opportunity to present the usually secluded country to the rest of the world and to showcase the strength and vigour of its socialist system. Furthermore, they are part of the country's foreign policy and marketing strategy and a nation branding tool in order to increase the country's global recognition.

References

Billig, Michael. 1995. *Banal Nationalism*. London: Sage.
Blair, Clay. 1987. *The Forgotten War: America in Korea, 1950–1953*. New York: Times Books.
Branigan, Tania. 2010. "The Cultural Life of North Korea." *The Guardian*, October 15: 25.
Bridges, Brian. 2012. *The Two Koreas and the Politics of Global Sport*. Leiden/Boston: Global Oriental.
Butler, Judith. 1993. *Bodies that Matter: On the Discursive Limits of Sex*. New York/ London: Routledge.
Butler, Judith. 1997. *Excitable Speech: The Politics of the Performative*. New York/ London: Routledge.
Cathart, Adam. 2015. "'Day of Songun' and the Ongoing Succession Process in North Korea." https://adamcathcart.com/2015/08/25/day-of-songun-in-north-korea/
Cho, E.J.R.. 2017. "Nation Branding for Survival in North Korea: The Arirang Festival and Nuclear Weapons Tests." *Geopolitics* 22 (3): 594–622.
Choi, Dae-souk. 2002. "Building Bridges: The Significance of Inter-Korean Sports and Cultural Exchange." *East Asian Review* 14 (4): 107–115.
Cumings, Bruce. 2004. *North Korea – Another Country*. New York and London: The New Press.
Cumings, Bruce. 2005. *Korea's Place in the Sun – A Modern History*. New York: W.W. Norton and Company.
Edensor, Tim. 2002. *National Identity, Popular Culture and Everyday Life*. Oxford: Berg.
Geertz, Clifford. 1980. *Negara: The Theatre State in Nineteenth-Century Bali*. Princeton: Princeton University Press.
Goffman, Erving. 1969. *The Presentation of the Self in Everyday Life*. London: Allen Lane.

Hobsbawm, Eric. 1999. "Introduction: Inventing Traditions". In *The Invention of Tradition,* edited by Eric Hobsbawm and Terence Ranger, 1–14. Cambridge: Cambridge University Press.

Hwang, Eui-gak. 1993. *The Korean Economies.* Oxford: Clarendon Press.

Jonsson, Gabriel. 2006. *Towards Korean Reconciliation: Socio-Cultural Exchanges and Cooperation.* Aldershot: Ashgate.

Kwon, Heonik and Byung-ho Chung. 2013. *North Korea: Beyond Charismatic Politics.* Lanham: Rowman & Littlefield Publishers.

Lee, Jung-woo and Alan Bairner. 2009. "The Difficult Dialogue: Communism, Nationalism and Political Propaganda in North Korean Sport." *Journal of Sport and Social Issues* 33 (4): 390–410.

Lorenz, Andreas. 2012. "Kim Jong-un Sends Cautious Signals of Reform", *Der Spiegel*, 12 July: 19.

Martin, Bradley K. 2006 *Under the Loving Care of the Fatherly Leader – North Korea and the Kim Dynasty.* New York: Thomas Dunne Books.

McCrone, David and Gayle McPherson, eds. 2009. *National Days – Constructing and Mobilising National Identity.* Basingstoke: Palgrave.

Merkel, Udo. 2008. "The Politics of Sport Diplomacy and Reunification in Divided Korea: One Nation, Two Countries and Three Flags." *The International Review for the Sociology of Sport* 43 (3): 289–312.

Merkel, Udo. 2010. "Bigger than Beijing 2008: Politics, Propaganda and Physical Culture in Pyongyang." *The International Journal of the History of Sport* 27 (14–15): 2467–2492.

Merkel, Udo. 2012. "Sport and Physical Culture in North Korea: Resisting, Recognizing and Relishing Globalization." *Sociology of Sport Journal – Special Issue: "Glocalization of Sports in Asia"* 29 (3): 506–524.

Merkel, Udo. 2013. "'The Grand Mass Gymnastics and Artistic Performance Arirang' (2002–2012): North Korea's Socialist-Realist Response to Global Sports Spectacles." *The International Journal of the History of Sport – Special Issue: "The New Geopolitics of Sport in East Asia"* 30 (11): 1247–1259.

Merkel, Udo. 2014. "The Politics of Sport and Identity in North Korea." *The International Journal of the History of Sport – Special Issue: The Politics of Sport and Identity is Asia* (edited by Fan Hong and Lu Zhouxiang) 31 (3): 376–390.

Merkel. Udo. 2019. "Nation Branding in the Divided Koreas: Soccer, Status and Soft Power: Lessons for Xi Jinping?" In *Soccer, Soft Power, Supremacy – The Chinese Dream,* edited by J.A. Mangan, Peter Horton and Christian Tagsold, 209–230. Bern: Peter Lang Publishers.

Myers, Brian Reynolds. 2010. *The Cleanest Race: How North Koreans See Themselves – And Why It Matters.* Brooklyn, NY: Melville House Publishing.

Nye, Joseph. 2004. *Soft Power – The Means to Success in World Politics.* New York: Public Affairs.

Nye, Joseph. 2008. "Public Diplomacy and Soft Power." *The Annals of the American Academy of Political and Social Science* 616 (1): 94–109.

Pai, Hyung-il. 2000. *Constructing "Korean" Origins: A Critical Review of Archaeology, Historiography, and Racial Myth in Korean State-Formation Theories.* Cambridge: Harvard University Press.

Portal, Jane. 2005. *Art under Control in North Korea.* London: Reaktion Books.

Roche, Maurice. 2001 "Modernity, cultural events and the construction of charisma: Mass cultural events in the USSR in the interwar period." *International Journal of Cultural Policy* 7 (3): 493–520.

Ryall, Julian. 2011. "North Korea's Bizarre Personality Cult and Why It has Worked So Far." *The Telegraph*, January 31: 31.

Schechner, Richard. 1985. *Between Theatre and Anthropology.* Philadelphia: Pennsylvania University Press.

Shin, Gi-wook. 2006. *Ethnic Nationalism in Korea: Genealogy, Politics, and Legacy.* Stanford, CA: Stanford University Press.

Smith, Anthony. 1991. *National Identity.* London: Penguin.

Smith, Anthony. 1996. "Culture, Community and Territory: The Politics of Ethnicity and Nationalism." *International Affairs* 72 (3): 445–458.

Smith, Anthony. 1998. *Nationalism and Modernism.* London: Routledge.

Street, John. 2007. *Politics and Popular Culture.* Cambridge: Polity Press.

Turner, Victor W. 1988. *The Anthropology of Performance.* New York: PAJ Publications.

Watts, Jonathan. 2002. "Despair, Hunger and Defiance at the Heart of the Greatest Show on Earth – Surreal North Korean Party Opens Isolated State to the World." *The Guardian.* May 17: 22.

19
TAEKWONDO
A symbol of South Korean nationalism

Udo Moenig

Introduction

Taekwondo, the recently declared official national sport of the Republic of Korea, was accepted as a formal Olympic sport in the year 2000 and recognised as a leading symbol of Korean culture and identity around the world. In 2018, the South Korean National Assembly passed legislation giving it flagbearing national sport status (Giles 2018). Despite typically being portrayed as a 2,000-year-old indigenous Korean martial art, taekwondo is in reality largely an offspring of Japanese karate. Its historical formation is rooted in the post-Korean War period, a time of chaos and confusion which led to the rise of the military government under General Park Chung Hee (Pak Chŏng-hŭi, 1917–1979) in 1961. Korean nationalism and militarism were defining characteristics of the time, and the formation of taekwondo has to be seen in this context.

The term 'nationalism' in this study refers to a movement that draws people together through a common consciousness of shared history, ethnicity and religious, cultural and political heritage. The portrayal of a group's or nation's history is a vital element in their shared sense of identity; therefore, invented histories and traditions are equally suited to reinforcing these sentiments, as extensively discussed in Eric Hobsbawm and Terence Ranger's classic work of historiography, *The Invention of Tradition* (1983).

With this in mind, the Park regime utilised sport as a tool to manipulate the population by installing proud nationalistic sentiments. In particular, taekwondo became a means to showcase the Korean nation abroad and to inspire patriotic feelings in young Koreans, with Park declaring taekwondo a 'national sport' in 1971. Under these circumstances, the Korean taekwondo establishment and leadership gradually invented a 2,000-year-old indigenous Korean tradition for taekwondo.

This chapter attempts a critical analysis of the historical formation of taekwondo, its roots and purposes, linking it to the broader social, political and nationalistic environments of the time. It will initially provide some background information by describing the early formation process of taekwondo, followed by an analysis of the role Korean nationalism played in the decision to elevate taekwondo to the national sport of South Korea. Lastly, it will describe the formation of modern taekwondo in the light of Korean politics and nationalism.

The early formation of taekwondo

The origins of taekwondo can be traced to the period of Korea's liberation from Japanese colonial rule at the end of the Second World War. Its forerunners were a variety of martial arts styles and fighting methods taught in five martial arts schools in Seoul called *kwan* (館 –literally 'hall' or 'house', but referring to a martial arts gymnasium, school, style or organisation), all established between 1944 and 1946. The taekwondo establishment later designated these *kwan* as 'founding schools of taekwondo'. The *kwan* were disunited and had different teaching methods; their founders had learned from a variety of different karate instructors in Japan, though the *Shōtōkan* karate style of Funakoshi Gichin (1869–1957, often called the father of *karate-dō*) featured most prominently. A couple of the founders also had some Chinese *kwŏnbŏp* (拳法: *quanfa* or 'fist method') experience, though this played an insignificant role in the formation of taekwondo. The lack of unity between the different *kwan* was actually a problem inherited from karate, which lacked unified teaching methods, organisation and leadership. However, the historical origin of taekwondo, which remains a much disputed subject, is not the focus of this chapter.[1]

A few years later, during the Korean War (1950–1953), several *kwan* founders went missing and some of their students consequently established their own gymnasiums and styles. Disputes among members were another reason for branching out and founding new schools. In fact, a *kwan* could consist of several gymnasiums in different parts of the country.

The first attempt to establish an umbrella martial arts organisation for these different *kwan* took place during the Korean War. During the Communist North Korean onslaught on South Korea, the defenders, under the command of the UN with the U.S. as the principal force, had to retreat to the Pusan (Busan) Perimeter in the far south. Pusan was never occupied by Communist forces and thus served for some time as a temporary capital for the Republic of Korea. As a result, the city hosted refugees from all over the country, including practitioners and leaders of the martial arts community. Some of them established branches of their *kwan* during their stay in Pusan and tentatively launched an umbrella organisation, the Korea Kongsudo Association,[2] in 1950. However, before long a couple of *kwan* leaders renounced their membership because of their exclusion from the leadership. Nevertheless, this short-lived organisation was not completely dissolved and lingered on.

After the most pressing hardships of the Korean War were alleviated and life had tentatively returned to normal, the leadership of the martial arts community returned to Seoul and the idea of a unified martial arts association was revived. However, rather than unification, the fragmentation of schools, in fact, accelerated in the second half of the 1950s, due to power struggles among the various leaders.

During this period, the different *kwan* used various terminologies for their martial arts styles: *tangsudo*, *kongsudo* and *kwŏnbŏp*. This last term, which points towards Chinese origins, was also widely used as a karate term in Okinawa and Japan (Japanese: *kenpō*),[3] while the first two terms point more clearly to Japanese origins. *Tang-su-do* (唐手道 'way of the Tang hand', referring to the Chinese Tang Dynasty) and *kong-su-do* (空手道 'way of the empty hand') are both Korean transliterations of the Japanese term *kara-te-dō*. The first character in both sets has the same *kun* reading[4] (*kara*) in Japanese. The term *tangsudo* was more popular among Koreans, since it invoked Chinese associations through the *tang* (唐) character.

The use of martial arts terms was often influenced by nationalism and anti-Japanese sentiments. As a result, some leaders aimed to distance themselves from their karate past through the creation of a new name. Choi Hong Hi (Ch'oe Hong-hŭi, 1918–2002) invented the name taekwondo[5] in 1955, replacing *tangsudo* in his military-based *Odo Kwan* (Oh Do Kwan, founded in 1954). However, other than in his school and the closely related civilian *Ch'ŏngdo Kwan* (Chung Do Kwan), the new name was not popular or recognised by others.

In 1959, due to his power as a military general and his relationship with the administration of Rhee Syngman (Yi Sŭng-man, 1975–1965, first South Korean president, in office 1948–1960), Choi was able to secure the support of the Ministry of Education and the Korea Amateur Sports Association; with their help, he forced several of the important *kwan* to join an umbrella organisation under his leadership, the Korea Taekwondo Association (Kang and Lee 1999, 29–31; Gillis 2011, 54). However, this was short-lived due to President Rhee's forced resignation the following year (1960), caused by his authoritarian rule and massive political corruption within the ruling party (Han 2011, 43).

Against a general backdrop of social and political instability, protests and unrest, Park Chung Hee, a South Korean general, seized the opportunity to remove the short-lived government of the Second Republic (1960–1961) through a military coup d'état in 1961. By means of martial law, amid a purification campaign that purged political opposition and rival generals, social unrest and political chaos begun to subside and order returned (Han 2003, 51–57).

The new military government forced changes in all walks of life, and the martial arts community was no exception. The different *kwan* were urged to unite under a single umbrella organisation, since the Ministry of Education would no longer tolerate different organisations registered with the Korea Amateur Sports Association. This period marked the beginning of heavy-handed government involvement in the martial arts community. After much wrangling for position, the *kwan* leaders settled once again on a new official name for the martial art: *tae-su-do* (跆手道). This was a compromise – it used the first character of the recently invented term *tae-kwon-do* (跆拳道), the second character of the karate terms *tang-su-do* and *kong-su-do*, and the common character *do* (道 'way' or 'method'), attached to almost all the modern Japanese and Korean martial arts. Alongside this, a newly united martial arts organisation was founded in 1961: the Korea Taesudo Association (KTA) (Figure 19.1).

Figure 19.1 Park Chung Hee (centre) during the military coup, 1961
Source: Public domain

Choi Hong Hi tentatively supported the military coup in 1961, but held conflicting positions, in addition to a personal animosity towards Park Chung Hee. Consequently, the Park regime removed Choi from his military role by appointing him the ambassador to Malaysia in 1962 (Gillis 2011, 56–61). With no military position and his physical absence from Korea, Choi's power and influence in the martial arts community diminished rapidly. However, after his tenure in Malaysia was suddenly terminated, possibly due to embezzlement, he was recalled to Korea in 1964 (Chong Woo Lee, as cited in Yook 2002, 303) and lobbied to become the president of the new KTA. After skilful political manoeuvring, Choi succeeded, and unilaterally changed the names back to taekwondo and the Korea Taekwondo Association in 1965.

The unpopular Choi and his actions were perceived as authoritarian and arrogant by large segments of the martial arts community. Within a year, he had been once and for all expelled from the Korea Taekwondo Association (Kang and Lee 1999, 49; Gillis 2011, 76–78), and as a result founded the International Taekwondo Federation (ITF) as a rival organisation in 1966. Subsequently, Choi's taekwondo and the taekwondo of the KTA parted ways in both technical and organisational terms. Choi, the principal name-giver of taekwondo, thereafter had no influence over the course and technical direction of the KTA style, which would later become Olympic taekwondo. Despite his removal, the unifying name was retained and the sport is still known as taekwondo.

Taekwondo becomes the national sport

Martial arts training was popular among Korean police forces and the military. The Vietnam War provided a great boost for its international proliferation, since many South Korean military taekwondo instructors were sent to train South Vietnamese soldiers in hand-to-hand combat. Partly conceived as repaying a debt to the U.S. for its role in the Korean War, the Park regime supported the Vietnam War by providing manpower and logistical support, but also demanded extensive financial compensation in return. Taekwondo instructors were among the first troops to be dispatched to Vietnam in 1962, receiving extensive public exposure and media coverage. Seemingly exaggerated reports of Korean soldiers using lethal hand-to-hand fighting in battles against the Vietcong surfaced at the time; in reality, Korean soldiers had a notorious reputation as being among the most ruthless and brutal in the conflict. As a result of exposing great numbers of South Vietnamese soldiers to taekwondo, taekwondo training (still mostly referred to as *tangsudo* at that time) also became very popular among American servicemen, who started inviting Korean instructors to teach on their bases and subsequently also in the U.S. (Gillis 2011, 64–69; Ku 1999).

The image and purpose of taekwondo also began to change during that time, with its principal function as a means for self-defence gradually replaced by the goal of training for sporting contests in the form of sparring competitions. Taekwondo, called *taesudo* at the time, was registered with the Korea Amateur Sports Association, and after strong lobbying by the *Chido Kwan* (Jido Kwan) was admitted as a demonstration sport in the annual National Sports Festival (Moenig 2015, 92)[6] in 1962. The following year, *taesudo* was recognised as an official sport. This admission to the nationwide sporting event helped raise its status and general recognition, and was the beginning of taekwondo as a competition sport which would soon come to be strongly supported by the Park Chung Hee regime for a variety of reasons.

The Park regime, which came to power during that time, regarded the establishment of a Korean cultural identity as a primary policy objective. Consequently, it introduced a policy of cultural revival under the catch-phrase 'Cultural Korea' (*Munhwa Han'guk*) (Park 2010, 74–78).

Due to the general perception and often repeated narrative (both then and now) of national victimisation, humiliation and loss of identity at the hands of the Japanese, the regime's goal was to install in Koreans a sense of identification with their nation, and a belief in their culture as unique and distinctive; ultimately, Koreans should feel proud of being Korean.

However, contrary to the anti-Japanese sentiment running deep in the general population, Park, ideologically shaped by his time in the Japanese military, admired the Japanese and wanted to turn South Korea into a 'second Japan' (Im 2011, 234). He followed the model for social and political reengineering provided by Japan's Meiji Restoration (1868), and as the base for South Korea's economic advance, he chose the *Chaebol* system of large family controlled corporate groups, modelled after the Japanese *Zaibatsu* structure that emerged during the Meiji period. In the political arena, Park's *Yusin Constitution*, inaugurated in 1972, was also modelled after the Japanese Meiji Restoration and had similar goals, such as catching up economically with the West and building a strong, self-reliant military (Kim and Vogel 2011).

By and large, there existed a general desire for Koreans to emulate Japan; this was (and is) contradicted by their nationalistic and emotional rejection of Japan, linked to Korea's complicated colonial past. This paradox also extended into the realm of martial arts when karate was transplanted into Korea towards the end of the colonial period and reincarnated as a supposedly 2,000-year-old indigenous Korean martial art named taekwondo.

The Park regime started to indoctrinate the population through a variety of mass movements and mobilisation campaigns, forms of social, cultural and ideological reengineering mostly based on pre- or post-war Japanese prototypes. For instance, the aim of the well-known New Village Movement (*Saemaŭl Undong*), modelled largely after the Japanese postwar New Life Movement (*Shin Seikatsu Undō*), was to modernise the countryside; but it was also perceived, according to Park Chung Hee, as a spiritual movement for moral and patriotic restoration of the rural population (Park 2010, 78–79).

Sport fitted particularly well into this scheme of patriotic indoctrination through mass events and large-scale spectacles such as the Olympic Games, featuring 'nationalistic symbols, images, [and] rhetoric' (Capener 2016, 71). In addition, watching these events was a form of entertainment and distraction from the regime's suppressive politics, social hardships and realities of life.

Another aspect of sport was that it provided a practical tool of physical exercise to increase the discipline and health of the nation's youth. Martial arts, with its military-style training culture and roots, were particularly suited to reinforcing discipline and authority. The Korean combat sports favour military-style synchronised ceremonies, formations and training methods, with a military-like hierarchy among students and instructors inherited from the Japanese martial arts. Taekwondo lessons and events (demonstrations, tournaments and promotion tests) also came to incorporate rituals of nationalism (Park 2010, 80), such as saluting the Korean national flag or pledging verbal allegiance to the nation, also adopted from the Japanese imperial era (Empire of Japan, 1871–1945).

These training methods and customs remain a part of taekwondo tradition. The peculiar ritual of bowing or saluting the Korean national flag when entering or exiting a *dojang* ('place of *do*', a training hall or gym), before and after workouts, is also expected from non-Korean taekwondo students around the world. In a sense, taekwondo exported Korean nationalism; according to Kim Yong-ok, a well-known Korean philosopher, it succeeded in gaining the respect of Westerners where general politics had failed (Kim 1990, 130–132).

At the beginning of the nineteenth century, the Japanese incorporated judo (*jūdō*) and kendo (*kendō*) into the general public education system (*karate-dō* was incorporated officially only in the Okinawan school system and therefore played a lesser role). These martial arts were also promoted as physical training activities in the Imperial Japanese Army. In addition to increasing the physical strength and discipline of students and conscripts, martial arts served as a tool for nationalistic indoctrination. On an ideological level, *bushidō* (武士道 'way of the warrior'; in Korean *musado*), "an obscure literacy term before the 1890s… ha[d] become a broad descriptive word for Japanese samurai thought and behavior" (Benesch 2014, 4). Subsequently, evolving imperial *bushidō* was tied to cultural chauvinism and ideological militarisation, mutating into a cult of ethnic superiority, self-sacrifice and loyalty to the emperor, who was elevated to represent the core of the nation, resulting in 'total war' (Benesch 2014, 4).

During Korea's colonial period (1910–1945), the Japanese promoted the *bushidō* doctrine, along with judo and kendo, in a similar fashion in Korea. Park Chung Hee, as a former officer in the Imperial Japanese Army, had similar ideas about taekwondo when it was introduced as a mandatory training exercise in the Korean military during the 1960s (having been pioneered by Choi Hong Hi in his army unit in the 1950s) and made part of the Korean public education system during the early 1970s. The military-style order and discipline of taekwondo training lessons suited the general militarisation of society (Figure 19.2).

On an ideological level, the Japanese *bushidō* doctrine was reincarnated in Korea as the *hwarang* spirit[7] of the Silla (57 BCE–935 CE) warriors which featured strongly in South Korean military symbolism and taekwondo philosophy (Rutt 1961, 30; Moenig 2015, 15; 157–158). The *hwarang* spirit promoted the ideals of sacrifice and loyalty to the nation, and served as an example for unification and glory by means of military conquest,[8] a hint of the regime's preferred resolution in its dealings with the Communist North. This was a period

Figure 19.2 The victorious ROK Army Taekwondo Team, 1973: Taekwondo became part of South Korean military training

Source: Courtesy of Greg S. Kailian (back row)

when "mythological narratives have undergone a slow process of historicization" (Sintionean 2013, 268), and taekwondo's nationalistic historical narrative matured during this period as well (Capener 2016).

In addition to exploiting sport as a tool for nationalistic ends, Park Chung Hee also used it to market Korea internationally through sporting achievements, with the goal of enhancing national prestige abroad (Capener 2016, 73). Sport functioned as a means of displaying Korean cultural and racial superiority in international competition, bearing similarities with many authoritarian regimes of the twentieth century.[9] In this context, taekwondo, an increasingly internationally recognised sport, had great potential to showcase Korea. The regime therefore invested heavily in training professional athletes and taekwondo trainers to be sent overseas, in addition to lobbying to host international sporting events, which often served as a springboard for taekwondo's inclusion in international sporting events.

In this political environment, President Park Chung Hee advocated taekwondo under the slogan 'Physical strength is national power' and "often referred to the role of sports and martial arts in building a strong nation" (Park 2010, 79–80; Capener 2016, 73). Therefore, similarly to *budō* (武道 'martial ways') sports[10] in Imperial Japan, Park designated the martial art *kukki taekwondo* (國技跆拳道, 'national sport taekwondo') in 1971. This coincided with the appointment of a powerful new president of the KTA, Kim Un Yong, who would strongly press for taekwondo's promotion as an international sport.

Formation of modern taekwondo in the context of Korean politics and nationalism

Following Park Chung Hee's rise to power in 1961, taekwondo became increasingly institutionalised under the control of the Ministry of Education. Moreover, ruling party political figures were often appointed to the KTA presidency despite having a limited practical background in martial arts, or even none at all. These political leaders brought fundraising powers and recognition of the standing of taekwondo within Korean society. Taekwondo has been entangled in the politics of South Korea ever since.

After declaring it a national sport, the Park regime could not leave taekwondo in the hands of individuals who spent most of their time quarrelling over leadership and personal gain. They needed a trustworthy and reliable leader who would work foremost in the interest of the Park regime. As a result, the regime gave its blessing to Kim Un Yong (Kim Un-yong, 1931–2017), who despite minimal practical martial arts background was invited to become the new president of the KTA in 1971. Kim Un Yong is neatly described by the Kukkiwon, the so-called World Taekwondo Headquarters, as a "diplomat who worked at the Korean Embassy in the United States" before his appointment to the KTA (Kukkiwon n.d., 30).[11]

In a report to the U.S. House of Representatives in 1978, which was investigating the lobbying efforts and illegal activities of the South Korean Unification Church (nicknamed the Moonies) in connection with the so-called Koreagate (a 1976 political lobbying scandal entailing South Koreans influencing members of Congress), Kim Un Yong and taekwondo were implicated along with the religious cult and the Korean Central Intelligence Agency (KCIA). According to the report, Kim Un Yong, alias Mickey Kim, was a former aide of Kim Jong Pil (Kim Chong-p'il, 1926–2018),[12] one of the "principal participant[s] in the 1961 military coup" and subsequent founder of the KCIA. The report detailed that Kim Un Yong, a 'KCIA officer', was appointed 'counselor' at the Korean Embassy in Washington and later "served as an aide to… [the] head of the Presidential Protective Force" (Report of the Subcommittee on International Organizations of the Committee on International Relations

U.S. House of Representatives, 1978, quotes in following order: 363; 76 and 356; 445).[13] This shows that Kim Un Yong, a former officer of the fierce KCIA, had the blessing of the most powerful people in the country, on top of retaining his position in the Presidential Protective Force during his early tenure in the KTA.

From the onset, Kim Un Yong had big, forward-looking plans for taekwondo's development. After assuming office, his most immediate task was to establish an authoritative taekwondo headquarters that would become a symbolic centre recognised throughout the divided community. On a more practical note, the KTA needed its own space to conduct events such as promotions, tests and competitions. Therefore, construction of the KTA's Chungang Dojang ('Central Gymnasium') – soon renamed the World Taekwondo Headquarters, or Kukkiwon – began the same year.

The name Kukkiwon (國技院 *Kukkiwŏn*, 'Gymnasium of the National Sport'), and likely also the idea, was borrowed from the Japanese national sport *sumō* and its headquarters, the *Ryōgoku Kokugikan* (両国国技館, 'Gymnasium of the National Sport'), (Moenig 2015, 52; Capener 2016, 86–87).[14] In the term Kukkiwon, the final character *kwan* (館 Japanese: *kan*, 'house, hall') with the very similar in meaning character *wŏn* (院 'compound, institution, hall'), thereby avoiding association with the individual, disunited *kwan* that Kim Un Yong longed to suppress.

The Kukkiwon is on an elevated location on a small hill south of Seoul, in Kangnam, which was chosen to highlight the Kukkiwon's symbolic significance. Mountains have always played a central role in Korean mythology, native Shamanistic beliefs and Buddhism – higher ground symbolises enlightenment and spirituality. According to Kang and Lee, in an attempt to convey Korean philosophy, culture and tradition, the architecture of the building incorporated elements of popular Korean and Chinese symbolism of yin and yang (陰陽, a theory of dualistic-monism) and the eight trigrams of the *Yi-Ching* (易經 *Book of Changes*) (Kang, and Lee 1999, 82; Kukkiwon n.d., 22–26). The *T'aegŭk p'umsae* (*T'aegŭk* forms) introduced during the same period were named after and related to the same principles. However, rather than being the product of deep philosophical deliberation, it probably reflected simple, popular Korean nationalism, since the symbols mirror the South Korean national flag, the *T'aegŭkki* (*T'aegŭk* flag).

Association with the *t'aegŭk* (太極 Chinese: *taiji*, 'supreme ultimate') symbolism gave taekwondo and the Kukkiwon a mystical Oriental sense that resonated well with many Westerners fascinated by the esoteric and theatrical aspects of the martial arts. In short, as a centre of devotion for the taekwondo community, the name Kukkiwon needed to carry a spiritual quality in addition to representing the unification of the *kwan* and the consolidation of central power. In accordance with the choice of the name, the KTA style of taekwondo has since then often been referred to as *kukki taekwondo* ('national sport taekwondo'), to convey legitimacy in contrast to other organisations. The leaders of *kukki* taekwondo also further systematised and reinforced uniform technical standards, training elements and promotion requirements, as well as universal use of terminology and in 1972 introduced a new set of forms (patterns), the previously mentioned *Taegŭk p'umsae* (Kukkiwon n.d., 34–35).

In parallel with the construction of the Kukkiwon, Kim Un Yong strongly focused on globalisation. In contrast to Choi Hong Hi's internationally established ITF, the KTA lacked a global organisation. Therefore, under Kim's direction, an official international body, the World Taekwondo Federation (WTF), was inaugurated during the First World Championships, held at the Kukkiwon in 1973. In addition to the leadership of the KTA Kim assumed the presidency of both the Kukkiwon and the WTF. The second-tier leaders were also shuffled around in a cozy relationship, alternately holding posts in these three organisations over the years. The previously mentioned U.S. government report states:

[Kim Un Yong] also became head of the World Tae Kwando [sic.] (Karate) Association. KCFF [Korean Cultural Freedom Foundation, a foundation established by the Unification Church] records revealed a number of payments to Mickey Kim and his karate association. KCFF accounting records referred to his being helpful to the KCFF in unspecified ways (Report of the Subcommittee on International Organizations… 1978, 363).

This suggests that taekwondo's expansion into foreign countries had been supported by various secretive and possibly illicit activities by the KCIA and other dubious organisations, such as the Unification Church (Gillis 2011, 103–104).

Oddly, after completion of the Kukkiwon in 1972, the KTA, the supposed beneficiary of the project, never moved into the building. Instead, it began housing the newly founded WTF. The South Korean government and taekwondo leadership seem to have realised the immense potential of taekwondo in promoting Korea internationally. Therefore, from this time onwards, taekwondo was exported globally through a state-sponsored promotion campaign with an eye on the Olympics.

And as with so many modernisation projects and movements under the Park-regime taekwondo's quest for the Olympics seems to have been directly inspired by a Japanese model. After judo gained successful admission to the 1964 Tokyo Olympics, it was recognised as an official Olympic sport in 1972. As a result, South Korean officials emulated Japan by lobbying for international sporting events such as the 1986 Asian Games and the 1988 Olympics to be held in Seoul, as a springboard for taekwondo's introduction to the Olympics.

According to Kim Un Yong, Korean officials contemplated applying to host the Olympics after successfully hosting the World Shooting Championships in 1978 (Olympic Story n.d.); the unacknowledged main motivation was likely the desire to catch up with Japan and become the second Asian nation to host the prestigious event. The 1988 Seoul Olympics was an opportunity to showcase Korea's economic progress, in its desire to join the developed nations – Japan being the only Asian country seen in those terms at the time. Moreover, it was taekwondo's debut as an Olympic demonstration event, after the WTF was recognised by the IOC in 1980.

When Kim's former superior in the Presidential Protective Force, Park Chong Kyu [Pak Chong-kyu], died of cancer in 1985, Kim Un Yong was promoted to fill his post at the IOC, heralding his debut in the Olympic movement (Jennings and Simson 1992, 126). Subsequently, due to his unconditional support of Juan Antonio Samaranch (in office 1980–2001), the acting IOC President, Kim, assumed the presidency of the General Assembly of International Sports Federation (GAISF), "and within two years Samaranch shepherded Mickey [Kim] on to the IOC's executive board" in 1988 (Jennings 1996, 104).

It is customary for the host country of the Olympics to introduce a demonstration sport to the Games, hence taekwondo's admission. However, during the 1988 Seoul Olympics (when Koreans won every men's taekwondo gold except in the heavyweight division), taekwondo was not seriously considered as a future official sport – it looked like a purely Korean undertaking, since almost all the national coaches, in addition to the referees, were Korean. Despite this, after intense lobbying by Kim, taekwondo was again "against all Olympic precedents" a demonstration sport at the 1992 Barcelona Olympics (Jennings 1996, 106).

Due to the continuing domination of Koreans, Kim skilfully manipulated perceptions by limiting the participation of taekwondo competitors from any single nation, meaning that Koreans could only potentially win half of the weight divisions. In the ongoing struggle for official Olympic representation in rivalry with karate's World United Karate Organisation (WUKO), and despite the opposition of Choi Hong Hi (who represented the ITF, sponsored by North Korea), taekwondo was chosen by the IOC – amidst accusations of extensive nepotism and corruption – to finally become an official sport in the 2000 Sydney Olympics (Jennings 1996, 106–109; Gillis 2011, 147–166; Kukkiwon n.d.).

Kim Un Yong held a wide range of domestic and international sporting posts over the years, and rose to become perhaps the most powerful individual in Asian sport. He was even considered the foremost candidate to become the future president of the IOC. Until forced to resign all his positions, Kim held the posts of South Korean National Assembly member, IOC Executive Committee member, President of the Korea Amateur Sports Association and President of the Korean Olympic Committee, in addition to leadership positions in the taekwondo organisations. The lobbying process that led to taekwondo gaining access to the Olympics was a drama in itself, full of accusations of bribery and corruption and ending with Kim's downfall and incarceration in 2004. The success of taekwondo was foremost the result of his power and influence, enabling political lobbying and favouritism in the IOC, an organisation which reportedly continues to feature a culture of deep-seated corruption and nepotism (Gillis 2011, 147–150; Jennings and Simson 1992; Jennings 1996).

Conclusion

On a domestic level, sport often evokes tribal sentiments, such as when football teams compete against each other and fans root for their teams. In the international domain, sport and nationalism are commonly blended in many ways, such as the display of national flags and the playing of national anthems at events like the Olympic Games. Spectators root for their country's teams and athletes, often with uncontrolled outbursts and nationalistic emotions. However, taekwondo in particular has been intertwined with Korean nationalism on multiple levels in Korean society and recent history.

Strong nationalistic tendencies were evident from very early on. Most Korean martial arts leaders preferred to use the terms *tangsudo* or *kwŏnbŏp* rather than *kongsudo*, in order to obscure the Japanese origins. The formation of taekwondo happened during the turbulent decades after Korea's liberation from colonial rule; the ensuing fraternal war with the Communist North, in the wider context of the Cold War, resulted in widespread social chaos and poverty that eventually gave rise to the military regime of Park Chung Hee. The general atmosphere of those times was one of ultra-nationalism and militarism; taekwondo became an instrument for the authoritarian regime, and benefited in terms of support and development.

The Park-regime used sport as a tool to control the population during its drive for national spiritual, moral and cultural restoration. Moreover, sporting achievements and the hosting of international sporting events served to advance Korea's image as an economically developing, modern nation. The Park-regime realised the potential of taekwondo not only as a form of physical exercise to increase the discipline and health of its youth and soldiers, but also as a way to present a 'uniquely Korean' sport to the world. As a result, taekwondo was designated a national sport of South Korea in 1971.

Related to this event, the new KTA leader, Kim Un Yong, had strong ties to the highest political leadership and the KCIA; taekwondo was always tied to a certain degree to political suppression and intimidation, in addition to gangsterism. In terms of reputation, taekwondo instructors have always struggled with a contradictory image abroad and at home. Abroad, they have referred to themselves as masters or grandmasters with an aura of Oriental wisdom, often in a cult-like fashion; at home in Korea, they have been associated with low-class ruffians and gangsters. Lee Chong Woo (Yi Chong-u, 1929–2015), an early taekwondo pioneer who held many important posts in the taekwondo institutions, stated: "Taekwondo instructors were perceived as being like gangsters during the 1960s. Myself... I didn't get married until I was 42. At that time, no decent family would let their daughter marry a man who used his fists" (as cited in Yook 2002, 293). In fact, taekwondo has yet to completely shed this image in South Korea.

Under Kim Un Yong's leadership, taekwondo was basically a purely Korean enterprise, with its institutions until recently directed and controlled by a selected group of leaders who rose to power during the 1960s and 1970s. The Korean government also provides financial and political support in various forms and degrees, thereby influencing taekwondo's direction and projecting international power through 'taekwondo politics'. Direct financial gain through taekwondo tourism, related industries, employment of instructors overseas and reputational benefits for 'Brand Korea' are deciding factors in the pursuit of 'keeping taekwondo Korean'. The Korean taekwondo community and public regard taekwondo as a sort of Korean national property, with its leaders therefore expecting extraordinary privileges in decision-making, controlling rights and direction. These sentiments are compounded by lingering nationalistic attitudes in regard to taekwondo's origins and history.

However, taekwondo's role in Korean nationalism is only one example of nationalism in connection with indigenous martial arts in Asian countries. The Japanese invented the *budō* and *bushidō* mythos at the beginning of the twentieth century, linked with the rise of Imperial Japan and ultra-nationalism, and this nationalistic martial arts tradition was a model for taekwondo. The Chinese also invented many traditions for their modern martial arts, most of which are not ancient, but only a few hundred years old or products of the twentieth century. The Chinese government is also very protective of their martial arts, which it considers part of the nation's cultural tradition and heritage. Korea is far from unique in the general presentation of Asian martial arts in association with heritage and nationalism.[15]

Note on Romanisation

The Romanisation of words has been conducted according to the McCune-Reischauer system for Korean, Hepburn for Japanese and Pinyin for Chinese. However, the spellings of names of well-known individuals in the West, such as Park Chung Hee, have been left according to their popular use. Korean and Japanese names in the main text are presented according to tradition, with family names first.

Acknowledgements

This chapter is partly based on an article by Udo Moenig and Minho Kim: 'A Critical Review of the Historical Formation of Olympic-Style Taekwondo's Institutions and the Resulting Present-Day Inconsistencies', *The International Journal of the History of Sport* 34, 12 (2017), 1323–1342. There are also some similarities to the book chapter by Udo Moenig and Minho Kim: 'In Search of a Tradition for Taekwondo', in *The Routledge Handbook of Sport in Asia*, eds. Fan Hong and Lu Zhouxiang (New York: Routledge, 2021), 83–95. I would also like to thank Dr Gregory S. Kailian for his helpful advice, comments and corrections.

Notes

1 Compare the 'official' historical narrative of the Korea Taekwondo Association KTA (accessed 26.9.2021) to leading alternative publications, such as Capener 1995; Kang and Lee 1999, 2–29; Madis 2003; Hŏ 2008, 39–108; and Moenig 2015. The former World Taekwondo Federation (WTF) featured similar content, but the recently renamed World Taekwondo (WT) removed all historical content from its homepage a few years ago.
2 韓國空手道協會 *Han*會3; *Kongsudo Hyygsud*, which basically means 'Korea Karate-dō Association'. See the ensuing discussion in the main text regarding the terms *kongsudo* and *tangsudo*.

3 In addition, during the late 1950s, the ancient Chinese term *subak* (手搏 Chinese: *shoubo,* 'hand fighting') was introduced, but mainly only used by Hwang Kee (Hwang Ki, 1914–2002), the founder of *Mudŏk Kwan*.
4 The *kun*-reading (*kunyomi*) is the native Japanese reading associated with the meaning of a *kanji* (adopted logographic Chinese character). Funakoshi replaced the 唐 character with the 空 character during the mid-1930s, to distance karate from any Chinese associations.
5 The term *tae-kwon-do* (跆拳道) is derived from three Chinese characters. The first (跆) was described by Choi (1965, 14) in the following way: "*Tae* literally means to jump or kick or smash with the foot." Choi's invented definition, or a very close one, has remained in all later taekwondo literature. In fact, the character *tae* has the meaning of 'step on' or 'trample'. *Kwon* (拳) means 'fist', and *do* (道) literally means 'way'. Regarding the choice of the name, see Moenig (2015, 48–49).
6 The Korean Sports Festival (*Chŏson Ch'eyuk-hoe*) was reintroduced under the colonial rule in 1948, reorganised and renamed the National Sports Festival (*Chŏn'guk Ch'eyuk-taehoe*).
7 *Hwarang* (花郎 'flower boys'): There are other possible translations for the term based solely upon language.
8 Silla conquered the Paekche and Koguryŏ kingdoms during the seventh century, creating what is often considered the first unified Korean kingdom.
9 For example, the Nazi regime tried to prove German racial superiority during the 1936 Berlin Olympics, and the Soviets (also modern-day Russia) attempted to demonstrate superiority through sport.
10 Japanese *budō* sports include *judō, kendō, karate-dō* and several others.
11 However, the Kukkiwon's historical account is generally inadequate.
12 Kim Jong Pil was very influential in South Korean politics and a long-term National Assembly member. He was the Prime Minister from 1971 to 1975 and headed the United Liberal Democrats until his retirement in 2004.
13 The report also says: "Kim Un Yong was involved in a number of activities significant to Korean-American relations" (76, footnote 85). Moreover, according to the report, some Korean taekwondo instructors in the U.S., such as Jhoon Rhee, were implicated in dubious activities with the Unification Church and the KCIA (377). Furthermore, taekwondo instructors were also reportedly involved in various other illegal activities, such as abductions of Korean dissidents by the KCIA (Gillis 2011, 79–85; 88–102; 105–107; 114–115).
14 The Ryōgoku Kokugikan was built in 1901l; Ryōgoku is the name of the Tokyo neighbourhood where it is located. The first character in *Kuk-ki-wŏn* and *Koku-gi-kan,* 國 and 国, is the same. The former is the traditional Chinese character (used in Korea and Taiwan), and the latter is the simplified version (used in mainland China and Japan). The first two characters in *Kuk-ki-wŏn* (國技院) are the Korean transliteration of the first two characters of the Japanese term *Koku-gi-kan* (国技館).
15 See, for example, Guttmann and Thompson (2001); Nakajima and Thompson (2012); Tan (2004); Moenig and Kim (2018). Regarding China, for example, Xu Xiadong encountered problems with the Chinese authorities after soundly defeating, and humiliating, traditional Chinese martial artists in public. See "MMA VS Kung Fu Xu Xiaodong Defeat Tai Chi, Wing Chun… Challenging Fake Kung Fu" (2019).

References

English-language references

Benesch, Oleg. 2014. *Inventing the Way of the Samurai*. Oxford: Oxford University Press.
Capener, Steven D. 1995. "Problems in the Identity and Philosophy of *t'aegwondo* and Their Historical Causes." *Korea Journal* 35 (4): 80–94.
Capener, Steven D. 2016. "The Making of a Modern Myth: Inventing a Tradition for Taekwondo." *Korea Journal* 56 (1): 61–92.
Choi, Hong Hi. 1965. *Taekwondo – The Art of Self-Defence*. Seoul: Daeha Publication Company.
Giles, Thomas. 2018. "Taekwondo Designated as South Korea's Flagbearing National Sport." *Inside the Games,* April 4. Retrieved from www.insidethegames.biz/articles/1063449/taekwondo-designated-as-south-koreas-flagbearing-national-sport
Gillis, Alex. 2011. *A Killing Art – The Untold History of Tae Kwon Do*. Toronto: ECW Press.
Munhwasa.Guttmann, A., and L. Thompson. 2001. *Japanese Sports: A History*. Honolulu: University of Hawaii Press.

Han, Yong-Sup. 2011. "The May Sixteenth Military Coup." In *The Park Chung Hee Era – The Transformation of South Korea*, edited by Byung-Kook Kim and Ezra F. Vogel, 35–57. Cambridge: Harvard University Press.

Im, Hyug Baeg. 2011. "The Origins of the Yushin Regime: Machiavelli Unveiled." In *The Park Chung Hee Era – The Transformation of South Korea*, edited by Byung-Kook Kim and Ezra F. Vogel, 233–64. Cambridge: Harvard University Press.

Jennings, Andrew, and Vyv Simson. 1992. *The Lord of the Rings*. Transparency Books.

Jennings, Andrew. 1996. *The New Lords of the Rings*. London: Simon & Schuster.

Hobsbawm, Eric and Terence Ranger. eds. 1983. *The Invention of Tradition*. Cambridge: Cambridge University Press.

Kim, Byung-Kook, and Ezra F. Vogel. eds. 2011. *The Park Chung Hee Era – The Transformation of South Korea*. Cambridge: Harvard University Press.

Kim, Yong-ok. 1990. *Principles Governing the Construction of the Philosophy of Taekwondo*. Seoul: T'ongnamu.

Korea Taekwondo Association (KTA). "History of Taekwondo". Retrieved from www.koreataekwondo.co.kr/d002.

Ku, Su Jeong. 1999. "The Secret Tragedy of Vietnam." *Hankyoreh21* 273, September 2. Retrieved from http://legacy.h21.hani.co.kr/h21/vietnam/Eng-vietnam273.html

Kukkiwon, *Kukkiwon 40 Years History* (n.d.). Retrieved from www.kukkiwon.or.kr/ebook/40year_eng/eng.html

Madis, Eric. 2003. "The Evolution of Taekwondo from Japanese Karate." In *Martial Arts in the Modern World*, edited by Thomas A. Green and Joseph R. Svinth, 185–209. Westport: Praeger Publishers.

Moenig, Udo. 2015. *Taekwondo – From a Martial Art to a Martial Sport*. London: Routledge, 2015.

Moenig, Udo, and Minho Kim. 2018. "The Japanese and Korean Martial Arts: In Search of a Philosophical Framework Compatible to History." *The International Journal of the History of Sport* 35 (15–16): 1531–1554.

"MMA VS Kung Fu Xu Xiaodong Defeat Tai Chi, Wing Chun… Challenging Fake Kung Fu." YouTube, July 26, 2019. Retrieved from www.youtube.com/watch?v=QrkkewDC54g.

Nakajima, T., and L. Thompson. 2012. "Judo and the process of nation building in Japan: Kanō Jigorō and the formation of Kōdōkan judo." *Asia Pacific Journal of Sport and Social Science* 1 (2–3): 97–110.

Olympic Story. "History." Accessed 12 January 2014. Retrieved from http://eotem5.eowork.co.kr/02/his00.php

Park, Sang Mi. 2010. "The paradox of postcolonial Korean nationalism: State-sponsored cultural policy in South Korea, 1965-present." *The Journal of Korean Studies* 15 (1): 67–94.

Report of the Subcommittee on International Organizations of the Committee on International Relations U.S. House of Representatives, *Investigation of Korean-American Relations*. Washington: U.S. Government Printing Office, 31 October 1978. Retrieved from https://babel.hathitrust.org/cgi/pt?id=pur1.32754077064610;view=1up;seq=9

Rutt, Richard. 1961. "The Flower Boys of Silla (Hwarang)." *Royal Asiatic Society* 38 (October): 1–66.

Sintionean, Codruta. 2013. "Heritage practices during the Park Chung Hee era." In *Key Papers on Korea*, edited by Andrew David Jackson, 253–274. Kent: Global Oriental.

Smith, Anthony D. 2001. *Nationalism: Theory, Ideology, History*. Cambridge: Polity Press.

Tan, K. S. 2004. "Constructing a Martial Tradition: Rethinking a Popular History of Karate-Dou." *Journal of Sport and Social Issues* 28 (2): 169–192.

Yook, Sung-chul. 2002. [Interview with Chong Woo Lee]. "Kukkiwon Vice President Chong Woo Lee's shocking confession of Olympic competition result manipulation!" *Shin Dong-A*, translated by Soo Han Lee, April 2, 290–311.

Korean-language reference

Han, Pyŏng-ch'ŏl. 2003. *Kosu rŭl Chachsŏ* (*In Search of the Master*). Seoul: Yŏngwŏn.

Kang, Won Shik, and Kyong Myong Lee. 1999. *T'aegwŏndo hyŏndae sa* 태권도現代史 (*A Modern History of Taekwondo*). Seoul: Pokyŏng Munhwasa.

Hŏ, In-uk (허인욱).태권도형성사 [*Taekwondo's formation history*]. Kyŏngki-Do: Hanguk Haksul Ch'ŏngbo, 2008. [In Korean only] Kim Yong-ok (김용옥). 태권도철학의구성원리 *Principles governing the construction of the philosophy of taekwondo*. Seoul: T'ongnamu, 1990. [In Korean only] Yook, Sung-chul [Yuk Sŏng-ch'ŏl](육성철).이종우국기원부원장의 '태권도과거'충격적고백! "Kukkiwon Vice President Chong Woo Lee's shocking confession of Olympic competition result manipulation!". Trans. Lee Soo Han. *Shin Dong-A*, (2002, April). 290–311.

20
SOUTH KOREA'S POSTDEVELOPMENTAL NATIONALISM

Charles R. Kim

Introduction

On August 15, 1998, Kim Dae Jung (1998-2003) addressed South Koreans on the day that marked the fifty-third year since Korea's liberation from Japanese rule and the fiftieth anniversary of the establishment of the Republic of Korea. The first-year president used the occasion to lay out his government's program, a veritable "second nation building" that represented a "historic decision to save the nation from crisis and develop it anew." Aiming for a speedy recovery from the devastating economic crisis that had hit the country a year earlier, Kim promised an 'overall reform of national policy and a people's movement to fully develop democracy and a market economy based on our proven strength for advanced industrialization and democratization' (Lee 1998).

In his 2008 inaugural address, President Lee Myung-bak (2008-2013), a staunch conservative, emphasized that his presidency marked a clear departure from the liberal reformism of Kim and of Roh Moo-hyun (2003-2008). Nonetheless, Lee echoed Kim's 1998 speech in gesturing toward still another new beginning for the South Korean nation:

> As the President of this great nation, at this juncture when we are beginning another 60 years of the Republic, I hereby declare the year 2008 as the starting year for the advancement of the Republic of Korea. I do declare our solemn start towards a society that cherishes the fruit of democratization and industrialization, with each of its members doing their bits voluntarily in collaboration for the general welfare and towards a country that abounds in wealth, caring, and dignity. (Lee 2008)

A sense of the political differences between Kim and Lee can be gathered from the two snippets above. For example, where the former democracy fighter Kim had infused his speech with the idiom of grassroots participation, the former corporate CEO Lee opted for a top-down posture in which people would make their 'bit' contributions to a larger, nationwide program of renewed economic growth. Yet the two speeches share notable similarities. Both leaders invoked the nation's post-1945 achievements in industrialization and in democratization to herald the start of a new era of advanced development. In particular, they projected confidence that in spite of recent setbacks, South Korea would continue its role as an economic, technological, democratic, and cultural exemplar in the globalized world. Political differences notwithstanding, the speeches of the liberal Kim and the conservative Lee fit within the framework of South Korea's postdevelopmental nationalism.

The notion of postdevelopmental nationalism implies that there was a form of nationalism that preceded it. This precursor was South Korea's developmentalist nationalism, which was dominant during the era of authoritarian nation building (1948–1980s). In a broad view, both forms are distinct, historically shaped manifestations of a modern Korean nationalism that revolves around a narrative cycle in which the Korean nation is confronted with and strives to overcome collective crisis. The overcoming of successive crises across historical periods from antiquity to recent times forms the basis of the Korean nation narrative. Developmentalist nationalism, a nation-centered discourse set in the context of anticommunist decolonization, focused on realizing a collective rebound from colonial subjugation (1910–1945), national division (1945–1948), and the Korean War (1950–1953). It was a future-oriented discourse that was animated by an aspirational narrative of national ascent by way of "late" capitalist industrialization.

Postdevelopmental nationalism, which began to coalesce in the 1980s, is built upon developmentalist nationalism. The current form emerged at a key juncture in which South Korea had begun to show notable progress toward key economic and political aims of the earlier form. Postdevelopmental nationalism retains a forward-looking orientation insofar as it aspires to the nation's continuing advancement. However, this newer form centers on public memory of South Korea's developmental successes, especially those achieved in the rapid authoritarian industrialization of the 1960–1980s. In this regard, postdevelopmental nationalism is a triumphal discourse in which national self-understanding is defined first and foremost in terms of South Korea's recovery from the major national crises of the twentieth century, through its post-1948 achievements in political and especially economic development.

The aim of this chapter is to lay out the basic contours of South Korea's postdevelopmental nationalism. I do this by providing a descriptive account of the shift to postdevelopmental nationalist discourse in the late 1980s to the early 2000s. Since this is a single chapter, my account, of necessity, briefly examines selected episodes and processes to illustrate this shift: the democratic transition of 1987; the Seoul Olympics of 1988; the financial crisis of 1997–1998; the 2002 Korea-Japan World Cup; and, in terms of processes, South Korea in neoliberal globalization. I wish to illustrate how across much of the political spectrum, the country's post-1948 industrialization and democratization take pride of place in postdevelopmental nationalism. And yet, this triumphal self-understanding is shot through with underlying anxieties concerning South Korea's continued advancement and the maintenance of its position on the world stage.

Commentators, intellectuals, or government leaders do not commonly refer to postdevelopmental nationalism, nor do people identify as postdevelopmental nationalists. Instead, I use the term to refer to a widely used set of common-sense assumptions and narratives about the (South) Korean nation-state, its historical trajectory, its current place in the world, and its desired direction into the future. In this regard, it is a hegemonic discourse that is produced and reproduced by a broad range of conservative, liberal, and (to a lesser extent) progressive actors in government, journalistic and entertainment media, and mainstream academia, as well as by countless ordinary South Korean citizens.

Postdevelopmental nationalism is used to make appeals for personal sacrifice on behalf of the nation, reflecting deeply ingrained patterns from the colonial and the developmentalist past. The discourse obtains popular consent through appealing images, narratives, and sentiments about South Korean triumphs, past and present. But even as postdevelopmental nationalism make claims to collective unity on behalf of the nation's betterment, it lends support, as a hegemonic discourse, to the perpetuation of the socioeconomic status quo, with its structures of inequality and inequity. As such, popular consent is never total but is imbued with skepticism toward the interests, intentions, and systemic privilege of political and economic elites. The brief presidential quotes above, one from a liberal and the other from a conservative, point up the central importance of the triumphs of industrialization and democratization, while evincing traces of these characteristic tensions between pride and uneasiness and between unity and stratification. This chapter takes into account the hegemonic, cross-partisan, multiply produced qualities of postdevelopmental nationalism.

It is important to note that postdevelopmental discourse has been shaped historically by domestic and international events and processes. At the domestic level, this chapter will show the evolution of earlier phases of postdevelopmental nationalism by selectively considering transitional uses of the discourse during the events of 1987–1988, 1997–1998, and 2002. At the international level, I take into consideration ways in which South Koreans' participation in the interrelated processes of neoliberal globalization and the end of the cold war was mediated through the evolving discourse of postdevelopmental nationalism. To put it differently, even as postdevelopmental nationalism looks inward in heralding developmentalist triumphs and aspiring for further national advancement, the discourse has also been utilized by various actors to make sense of and respond to neoliberal globalization and the transition to the post-cold war order.

In terms of the former, macrolevel process, the economy-first focus of postdevelopmental nationalism is a pertinent example. Economy-firstism, economic growth as the nation's top priority, was a core component of developmentalist nationalism. In the transition to the postdevelopmental form, economy-firstism was adapted seamlessly by leaders, commentators, and ordinary citizens as a dominant modality for understanding and engaging with the competitive exigencies of neoliberal globalization. Relatedly, the trope of postcolonial "late development" evolved from the pre-1980s period into a postdevelopmental emphasis on the need for South Korea to maintain its "national competitiveness." These and related continuities across developmentalist and postdevelopmental nationalism reflect the path dependency of South Korea's economy-first proclivity. This deeply ingrained propensity is rooted in the formative mid-century juncture in which Japanese rule in 1945 gave rise to a bipolar political settlement on the Korean peninsula (1945–1953), with an anticommunist developmentalist state (1948–1988) holding power in the South.

With respect to the post-cold war turn, postdevelopmental nationalism adapted to the realities of the dissolution of the communist bloc and the end of the bipolar global order in several salient ways. First, at the most apparent level, beginning in 1989, the South Korean state forged new ties with former cold-war enemy states, including Russia and China, as a way to enhance its prestige as an emerging middle power and to pursue economy-first national objectives within the neoliberal globalist paradigm.

Second, postdevelopmental nationalism, which centers on a narrative of capitalist triumph in a non-Euro-American/Asian postcolony, dovetailed with the global narrative of capitalism's "victory" over communism. From the late 1980s on, South Korea's capitalist and liberal-democratic accomplishments—and its eclipsing of North Korea's postcolonial developmental project—have provided strong ideological support for global capitalist triumphalism. In addition, the South Korean success story resulted in the further marginalization of North Korea in post-1945 historical memory and, paradoxically, in the further effacement of North Korean realities from South Korea's postdevelopmental nationalism, despite it being a discourse on the Korean ethnic nation. In concrete terms, these shifts solidified the entrenched view that South Korea is the "authentic" locus of modern Korean historical and contemporary experience. With the cementing of this view, North Korean experiences were regarded internationally and within South Korea as anomalous and outside the "normal" currents of modern world history. In postdevelopmental nationalist discourse, the equation of the Korean ethnic nation with the South Korean nation and the marginalization/elision of North Koreans are indicated in this essay by the term (South) Korea.[1]

Third, the post-cold war turn and the dominant view of "Korea" as (South) Korea coincided with a relative weakening of anticommunism in South Korea. In the triumphal discourse of postdevelopmental nationalism, the Democratic People's Republic of Korea no longer warrants concern as a legitimate ideological rival, and the issue of South-North unification has lost urgency, both marking significant shifts away from developmentalist nationalism. In the post-cold war era, the North Korean state remains an enemy state and the most important national security concern of the South Korean state. But the strident anticommunism of the 1940s–1980s has given way to a less adversarial—and in some cases, non-adversarial—stance vis-à-vis the North, as well as growth and diversification in (South) Korean ethnic nationalist cultural representations that point up the potential for common ground and reconciliation between North Koreans and South Koreans.

Even while triumphal postdevelopmental nationalism affords somewhat more ideological latitude with respect to North Korea, the discourse does maintain the anticommunist foundations of developmentalist nationalism. Anticommunist, anti-North Korean assumptions and rhetoric remain pervasive in conservative and extreme right public discourse. In addition, following the democratic transition of 1987, the country's conservative political reform process resulted in the preservation of authoritarian instruments of coercive power, such as the National Security Law, as well as the creation of new techniques of disciplinary control. Such post-authoritarian aspects of the present-day ruling system constitute a salient area in which cold war authoritarian vestiges remain embedded in post-cold war South Korea—and are supported, usually in tacit ways, by the anticommunist underpinnings of postdevelopmental nationalism.

Finally, with respect to national Others, it should also be noted that the uneasy national pride embedded in postdevelopmental nationalism has been the source of intermittent enactments of South Korean national identity, expressed in opposition to the discursive notions, and actual policies and actions, of the United States, Japan, and other international allies. This late cold war/post-cold war development was an outgrowth not only of the dissolution of the bipolar cold war, but also of the heightened competition of neoliberal globalization and the emergent qualities of memory politics in East Asia and in other regional contexts.

Developmentalist nationalism, 1948–1980s: a brief overview

South Korea's developmentalist nationalism was a variant of the modern Korean nationalism that emerged at the turn of the twentieth century as Koreans grappled with the competitive and exploitative realities of global capitalist modernity (Schmid 2002). Modern Korean nationalism was built on the assumption that history was a process of linear-progressive development in which Koreans needed to "catch up" to the standards of advanced nations. At the same time, it was premised on a narrative frame wherein the Korean nation moved through a recurring cycle of crisis that was met with resistance/perseverance, which, in turn, led to the realization of a collective triumph. Developed by turn-of-the-century intellectuals, this frame was used to narrate national history extending back to antiquity. After 1948, two competing versions of the recurring crisis-to-triumph narrative were disseminated and obtained widespread purchase among North Koreans and among South Koreans

Built upon this narrative cycle, South Korea's developmentalist nationalism of the cold war era addressed twin postcolonial crises of national division and underdevelopment. Developmentalist nationalism was the ruling ideology of the authoritarian government of Rhee Syngman (1948–1960) as well as the military regimes of former generals Park Chung-hee (1961–1979) and Chun Doo-hwan (1980–1988). Among these presidents, it was Park Chung-hee who put forth the most systematic expression of developmentalist nationalism, in rhetoric and in policy, through his program to "modernize the fatherland" (choguk kŭndaehwa).

Park, who rose to power through a military coup, laid out a state-led path to industrialization. To fortify his weak legitimacy, Park extended a promise to the people. In exchange for their sacrifice, hard work, perseverance, and loyalty, his government would lead the nation out of the mid-century crisis to a modern, prosperous, independent, democratic future as an "advanced nation" (sŏnjinguk) (Kim 2012, 83). Park's promise was a central tenet of his economy-first developmentalist program, which prioritized South Korea's industrialization and export-led growth within the capitalist, "free world" bloc. Political democratization and national unification were to be postponed in favor of growth, until economic conditions allowed for the expansion of political freedoms and for the ROK's future absorption of North Korea. Dissent was blocked, often brutally, in the name of anti-communism and the preservation of national security.

To mobilize the productive capabilities of the people, the Park regime, in 1962, instituted the first in a series of five-year economic plans that targeted key industries based on a two-pronged approach of import substitution and export promotion (Lee SC 2003, 81). In 1972, implementation of the third five-year plan marked the earnest start of the country's "heavy-chemical industry drive," which included expansion into new strategic sectors, such as petrochemicals and shipbuilding. Park's developmentalist model relied on the symbiosis of the state and *chaebol* business conglomerates. The former granted preferential loans and various government subsidies to incentivize the coordination of new chaebol ventures with the state's macroeconomic policies (Lee BC 2003, 34). This symbiosis was at the core of a sociopolitical system that enabled state and chaebol elites to aggrandize power and wealth, and that engendered new patterns of socioeconomic injustice and inequity.

Tangible economic improvements lent credence to Park's economy-first nation building promise. However, popular support for the developmental state was never total. For much of his tenure, Park dealt with criticisms and outcry over his regime's authoritarian excesses, especially with respect to state violence, the miscarriage of constitutional democracy, and socioeconomic inequality. Contrary to his inaugural pledge, economic progress was not giving way to political reform, and the problem of uneven distribution remained. Reacting to the strong showing of opposition presidential candidate Kim Dae Jung in 1971, Park promulgated the Yusin Constitution, which dissolved the National Assembly, disbanded political parties, and suspended presidential elections. A series of nine emergency decrees imposed in 1974–1975 expanded the state's repressive powers. In spite of the risks, growing numbers of students, workers, religious leaders, journalists, and intellectuals carved out ways to voice their dissent against Park and his draconian Yusin system (Chang 2015). In 1979 Park was assassinated amid mounting public backlash against the continuing repression and inequality.

Many hoped that Park's death would usher in a new, democratic constitution and pave the way for the election of a civilian administration. Within weeks, however, General Chun Doo-hwan staged his December 1979 military coup. This was the initial act of a "creeping coup" that culminated in Chun's rise to the presidency less than a year later (West 1997,

90–93). While minor changes were made to the Yusin system, Chun's military regime inherited the state's repressive capabilities, and the electoral structure continued to tilt strongly in favor of the ruling party. Coming out of the Yusin period, South Koreans did not welcome the prospect of prolonging authoritarian developmentalism. The widely reviled Chun sought to keep iron-fisted control of political power, while creating the impression that in the areas of society and culture, South Korea was liberalizing—and thus making progress away from austerity and dictatorship. During his eight-year term, Chun struggled to maintain this delicate balance between maintaining control and allowing a modicum of liberal reforms.

Challenging the Chun regime, 1980–1987: *Minjung* nationalism

This section briefly shifts away from the dominant developmentalist nationalism to examine the counter-discourse of *minjung* nationalism (Lee 2007). Left-progressive minjung nationalism is relevant because it was central to the democratic breakthrough of June 1987. Subsequent to that key development, certain elements of the counter-discourse were co-opted into postdevelopmental nationalism, especially by liberal reformers. At the same time, the conservatives' economy-first approach continued beyond the developmentalist era, evolving in concert with the shift to neoliberal globalism.

In the 1970s, critically minded students, politicians, labor activists, intellectuals, and religious leaders, made increasingly urgent calls for democratic and socioeconomic reform. Direct challenges to the foundations of state legitimacy were avoided. This changed during the Chun regime. The Gwangju Movement of 1980—in which Chun twice dispatched military forces to suppress civilian protests with brute force—spurred the reconfiguration of dissident thought. Hundreds, likely thousands, of civilians were killed in Gwangju. After the Gwangju massacre, a crucial act in Chun's creeping coup, progressive-left intellectuals and activists expanded and deepened the counter-discourse of *minjung* nationalism based on a comprehensive rethinking of the historical and structural factors behind domestic injustice and inequality. Their aim was to effect the implementation of systematic political, social, and economic reforms that would constitute Korea's substantive decolonization, centered on the interests of the nation's subaltern masses, or minjung.

Such transformative change would correct South Korea's historical path by resolving the national issues rooted in the undemocratic post-1945 political settlement on the Korean peninsula. With respect to South Korea, many figures in the ruling class had collaborated with the Japanese colonial state and imperial military-industrial complex. Utilizing the protective support of the anticommunist US military government (1945–1948), former collaborators to the south of the 38th parallel generally avoided serious consequences for their colonial pasts (Cumings 1981, 135–178). Many of these people became a part of the anticommunist ruling elite and capitalized on the formation of asymmetrical relations between the Republic of Korea and the United States. From the US point of view, South Korea, like Japan and Taiwan, was an important cold war geopolitical bulwark, especially after the Korean War. As long as some semblance of political and economic stability was maintained, the Rhee, Park, and Chun regimes could depend on the backing of the United States.

In June 1987, minjung nationalist groups spearheaded massive antigovernment protests in Seoul and in other cities. They were the latest expression of indignation over the Chun regime's ongoing authoritarian abuses and, by implication, the unjust configuration of political and economic power endemic in the nation's modern history. On June 29, the ruling party was forced to make major concessions in an eight-point democratization plan that included constitutional reform to instate direct presidential elections (Lee and Kim 2016,

294–306). To achieve this breakthrough, minjung forces were joined in an expansive but ephemeral coalition that consisted of conscientious religious leaders, journalists, academics, political dissidents, and liberal opposition politicians. The coalition received widespread popular support from urban poor, small business owners, housewives, white-collar workers, and other non-activist segments of the population. Broad-based people power secured the country's transition to democracy.

However, the antigovernment coalition had adopted a narrow stance that consisted of immediate demands to "overthrow the dictatorship" and "abolish the protection of the [undemocratic] constitution" (Lee and Kim 2016, 294). Minjung nationalist aspirations for fundamental, decolonizing reforms were excluded so as to avoid alienating opposition liberals, middle-class citizens, and other moderate elements, as well as to effect convergence on the cause of securing direct elections. While this strategy was necessary to achieve the June 1987 breakthrough, it also prefigured the consolidation of a political system that remained fundamentally conservative.

The June 1987 breakthrough gave way to the passage of limited constitutional revisions in October 1987 (Choi 2012, 100–103). The ruling party, by making significant concessions in the June 29 Declaration, was able to take the central role in the revision process, seating four members on the revision committee. The other four members were opposition party elites. Progressive minjung nationalists—and their reform agenda—were left out of the negotiations. The constitutional revisions resulted in a switch to direct presidential elections, the reduction of presidential powers, and the creation of a constitutional court. However, the state's repressive capabilities were left intact, and the nexus of political-business power unaffected (Kim 2016, 41). Democratic consolidation had furnished opposition liberals with a somewhat fair seat at the political table. But the table itself remained elite-centered and economy-first.

In essence, the opposition liberals abandoned their coalition with minjung nationalists, and ruling-party conservatives co-opted the accomplishment of the minjung-led June 1987 democratic transition. The ruling party also capitalized on the June 1987 breakthrough when their candidate Roh Tae-woo, another former general and a long-time crony of Chun, defeated the center-right Kim Young Sam and the center-left Kim Dae Jung in the December 1987 presidential election, as well as far-right conservative Kim Jong-pil. The post-June 1987 rebound of the conservative establishment continued through the 1988 parliamentary elections, in which center-liberal opposition parties were outperformed by the ruling party and the opposition conservative party (Kim 2016, 42). The conservative nature of the country's democratic consolidation preserved the economy-first course that had been established in the mid-century political settlement and set the conditions for postdevelopmental and post-authoritarian trends in subsequent years.

The Seoul Olympics and the turn to postdevelopmental nationalism

To offset his weak legitimacy, Chun had instituted modest social and cultural liberalization measures that included the lifting of curfew and an unofficial "3S" policy. The latter policy entailed loosening restrictions and opening up new outlets in the areas of "sports, sex, and screen" (Davis 2011, 113–114). But underneath these measures, the authoritarian foundations of his "new military regime" remained in place. Difficulties in maintaining balance between control and liberalization gave rise to the June 1987 breakthrough. However, the toppling of authoritarian rule ultimately expedited the transition from developmentalist nationalism to a postdevelopmental nationalism that was friendly to conservative economic interests. The Seoul Olympics was an important early step in this transition.

Hosting the 1986 Asian Games and the 1988 Olympics formed the centerpiece of Chun's cultural policy. Because many citizens perceived the mega-events to be projects of the regime, popular compliance with the impositions and intrusions that came with preparations was often ambivalent. But the exigency of improving the country's image abroad helped tip many South Koreans toward positive investments in the events (Bridges 2008, 1945).

Each of the three "East Asian Olympics," held in Japan, South Korea and China, served as a national "coming out party," in which the host country showcased to the world its modern attainments, in accordance with Euro-America-centered developmental norms (Collins 2011, 2241). Successfully hosting the Olympics, South Koreans understood, was a golden opportunity to supplant the images of war devastation and of political turbulence that shaped international perceptions of the country. These were to be replaced by visions of a modern, economically ascendant nation with a vibrant, welcoming culture that fused indigenous tradition with Euro-American modernity. This globalist message was captured in the 1988 Olympic themes of "Harmony and Progress" and "Seoul to the World, the World to Seoul." The Seoul Olympic Organizing Committee (SLOOC), an appendage of the Chun regime, oversaw the production of the nation's new image for international and domestic audiences. Leading up to and even following the event, domestic corporations also connected to this new image in marketing their high-tech or contemporary lifestyle products, which usually included a Hodori logo or other Seoul Olympic symbol. Direct associations with the ROK state were in large part omitted from the imagery of an emergent modern Korea. Reservations for Chun notwithstanding, most South Koreans embraced the cultural representations of the Seoul Olympics, and their own parts in the representational process, which included the mobilization of over 250,000 temporary employees and volunteers (Cho and Bairner 2012, 278).

The Asian Games in 1986 had served as a valuable rehearsal for the presentation of the country to international audiences. But with the Olympics came a marked increase in the scale of popular interactions with people from across the world as well as an unprecedented level of national exposure in the international media. Citizens were well aware that foreign visitors and journalists would be scrutinizing, among other things, the country's infrastructure, level of stability, and cultural competence. In Asian host nations, the equation of an Olympiad (or other mega-event) with the country's level of historical development is often the source of an "uneasy nationalism." Historian William Tsutsui describes the phenomenon as "swelling national pride" intermixed with "an acute sense of anxiety… driven by a history of marginalization in a world sporting culture and a global political order long (and still) dominated by the West" (Tsutsui 2011, 8). Undergirding uneasy nationalism is the reality, born of unequal power relations, that the international community, and especially Euro-American observers, are the ultimate arbiters in the assessment of a mega-event's degree of success. This assessment, in turn, directly informs the overall international perception of the non-Euro-American host country.

In South Korea, uneasy nationalism underlay popular investment in the project of national image-making. At one level, feelings of national pride were connected to the state's developmentalist nationalism. Revolving around the central narrative of debilitating crisis, courageous (anti-Japanese, anticommunist) resistance, tenacious recovery, and present/future triumph, postdevelopmental nationalism served as the primary discursive framework through which South Koreans rendered the prevailing meaning of the event as a proud, hard-won milestone. Seoul Olympic imagery projected an appealing hybrid cultural identity of traditional harmony and modern progress. But these representations corresponded to a collective story of grit, hustle, and perseverance. Midway through the Olympics, aspects of the American TV network NBC's coverage of the event, and the disorderly conduct of a number of American athletes, triggered public expressions of outrage and of anti-Americanism that were dismissed by international and some domestic observers as the outcome of Koreans' cultural oversensitivity. For many citizens, though, the issues symbolized American disregard for their country's momentous occasion (Kim 1989, 756).[2]

The uneasy nationalist public tied the dominant story line of national redemption to extra-state understandings of Korean peoplehood. Many harbored popular resentments shaped by the realities of the unequal Korea-US relationship, made evident in the everyday experience of the US military presence, as well as in intermittent US interventions in national affairs. Significantly, in the years leading up to the Olympics, minjung critiques of US neoimperialism that emerged from the suppression of the Gwangju Movement had opened up new space for the public expression of anti-American sentiments (Kim 1989, 761). In addition, even though many South Koreans had pulled their support from progressives who were agitating for further reform, the expression of popular pride and resentment drew on the vestigial undercurrent of antigovernment people power from June 1987.

While people chafed at instances of cross-cultural insensitivity, most still gave considerable credence to external assessments, Americans' included. As the international consensus view of a successful Seoul Olympics materialized in its final days, domestic anxieties gave way to a sense of relief and satisfaction over having hosted the event—at once a symbolic developmental milestone and in itself a new, confidence-building achievement.

Experienced through such feelings as pride, joy, indignation, anxiety, relief, and satisfaction, the popular nationalist feelings that surrounded the Seoul Olympics were more effective than the state's older developmentalist nationalism in producing popular consent to the nation-centered projects surrounding and subsequent to the mega-event. The relatively diverse sources for national identity production, which encompassed statist, business, and grassroots discourses, partially obscured the event's linkages to the existing power structure. Further, national identity production was not confined to the dynamics of domestic politics and development, but occurred in large part through popular, athletic, and media interactions with other countries.[3] The production of the (South) Korean people—and of postdevelopmental nationalism—from a variety of angles reduced skeptical sentiments toward the now post-authoritarian government. Moreover, it set the pattern by which the emerging hegemonic postdevelopmental discourse made appeals to and obtained consent from the majority of the population.

Crisis, rebound, and the 2002 World Cup

The Seoul Olympics turned out to be an international publicity coup for government and big business. Following the cold war boycotts of the 1980 and 1984 Olympiads, South Korea had successfully facilitated cross-bloc cultural diplomacy between the capitalist "west" and the communist "east," under the self-orientalizing banner of "harmony and progress." While Cuba did join North Korea in boycotting the 1988 Olympiad, the participation of major North Korean allies, including China and the Soviet Union, contributed to the dominant perception of ROK's cold war victory over the DPRK. As president, Roh Tae-woo parlayed the country's 1980s successes into further improvements in the nation's image and, by extension, new opportunities for economic growth. Under its Northern policy, the Roh administration normalized diplomatic relations with a number of former adversaries of the dissolving communist bloc, including Hungary (1989), the Soviet Union (1990), and China (1992), thereby connecting South Korea to new foreign markets (Kim 2020, 136).

That the Korean peninsula had for decades been regarded as an experimental lab for competing cold war ideologies, and that the North was in a deepening economic funk, made South Korea an especially compelling poster country for the sequential process of economic and political development laid out in US modernization theory. The collapse of the socialist bloc soon after the Seoul Olympics solidified the international view that South Korea was a postcolonial exemplar of liberal-capitalist modernization, providing support for the post-cold war "end of history" thesis (Cumings 2002, 11).

As cold war structures began to decompose in the 1990s, the framework for the pursuit of economy-first objectives turned from state-guided, protectionist developmentalism to a nation-centered neoliberal globalism that featured the strengthening of chaebol autonomy in relation to the state's macroeconomic policies (Kwon 2010, 1–12; Cho 2013, 14). In conjunction with this shift, emphasis was placed on fostering further development in high-tech industries and on the enhancement of the nation's soft power in order to catapult South Korea to "advanced nation" status. This uneasy, postdevelopmental quest was continued under the subsequent administrations of conservative Kim Young Sam and liberal reformers Kim Dae Jung and Roh Moo-hyun, as well as more recent administrations. Notably, it allowed for the maintenance of the chaebol-centered, economy-first system that had taken root during the developmentalist era.

Domestically, under Kim Young Sam and Kim Dae Jung, neoliberal policies and initiatives were usually referred to as economic liberalization—that is, the movement away from the multifaceted restrictions of the authoritarian era toward the realization of greater freedoms and, presumably, more economic prosperity (Lee 2019a, 21–22; Lee 2019b, 17–18). It connoted linear and inevitable historical "Progress" not only in economy but also in politics, the media, social norms, cultural practices, and other areas. The semantics of liberalization helped to facilitate the introduction of neoliberal economic reforms by the two Kim administrations. Domestically, the postdevelopmental economy-first imperative was the chief factor behind these reforms. But in implementing them, the two presidents were also acceding to pressures exerted by the United States, the Organisation for Economic Co-operation and Development (OECD), the World Trade Organization, and other international bodies to reduce trade barriers, deregulate financial markets, and so on.[4]

Under the Kim Young Sam administration (1993–1998), carelessly instituted neoliberal globalist reforms gave rise to ballooning chaebol debt and a solvency crisis that in 1997 escalated into a nationwide economic crisis. Months before the end of his term, the International Monetary Fund (IMF) granted a massive $57 billion bailout package that included stringent restructuring conditions. The incoming Kim Dae Jung administration (1998–2003) largely complied with the conditions imposed by the IMF and the World Bank and, in doing so, greatly accelerated the neoliberalization of economy and society (Lee 2010, 35–38).

Kim Dae Jung's assumption of the presidency marked the country's first-ever peaceful transfer of power to an opposition leader. Although there were skeptics among minjung and other progressives, Kim's reputation as a long-time champion of democracy underlay general public trust that his reforms would ultimately lead toward a fairer, more just society. Promising a "bottom-up," "participatory" process, the new president appropriated the memory of 1980s people power.[5] However, his liberalizing rhetoric served as a Trojan horse for neoliberal policies that would bring detrimental, even grave, effects to many South Koreans.

In 2001, the country finished paying off its bailout loans three years ahead of schedule and by the following year, the economy appeared to be in good shape. Although many South Koreans were still coping with the effects of the crisis, the 2002 World Cup, co-hosted with Japan, doubled in South Korea as a jubilant celebration of the country's progress since the late

1990s. During the month-long tournament, hundreds of thousands of fans gathered in the Gwanghwamun area of central Seoul to exult in each step of the South Korean team's Cinderella run to the semifinals. In spirit, if not in person, the Red Devils were joined in ecstatic expressions of peoplehood by fellow citizens of all ages and social backgrounds. Compared to the anxiety-tinged Seoul Olympics, the 2002 World Cup represented an unbridled moment of collective effervescence.

Known as the "Red Devils," the young, passionate masses were an extension of the national team, the Reds, whose athletes constituted the on-the-field embodiment of the ethnic nation. Of the two, Red Devils revelry on the streets was the more striking visual manifestation of non-state peoplehood. They expressed sheer joy and newfound confidence over the football victories and over their own grassroots participation in collective self-representation, through which they projected an image of their nation as fun and exuberant, yet peaceful and orderly, as well as technologically advanced, culturally ascendant, and the equal of other advanced countries (Cho Han 2004, 9–12). In contrast to the older generations' uneasiness during the 1988 Olympics, the Red Devils proudly embraced South Korea's moment on the global stage.

Similar to the 1988 Olympics, popular expressions of Korean peoplehood were structured, in part, by the central narrative of postdevelopmental nationalism, most readily apparent in the prevalence of Taegukgi imagery and collective chants of "Taehan minguk!" ([Go] Republic of Korea!). In addition, the Korean team's scrappy, underdog triumphs were metaphors for the country's unexpected economic ascent. Collective identification was also shaped by dominant and popular memories of colonialism, suggested in the use by some fans of the precolonial English spelling, "Corea." While the Red Devils incorporated selected aspects of the earlier nationalist form, their confident expressions of peoplehood contained an inclusive and egalitarian streak that reflected underlying hopes for a fuller break with the developmentalist past. Nonetheless, the selective use of triumphal elements rendered the street revelry of the Red Devils, and the football performance of the Reds, subject to ready subsumption into the dominant definition of the 2002 World Cup as the cultural manifestation of the country's globalizing achievements. This postdevelopmental nationalist message was conveyed in the official slogan for the event, "Dynamic Korea."

In the final weeks of 2002, scores of young citizens gathered in the streets again, this time to raise direct questions about South Korea's relationship with the United States. While the World Cup was in progress, two middle-school girls, Sin Hyosun and Sim Misŏn, had been tragically killed by a large, armored US Army vehicle, as it barreled through a residential neighborhood to the north of Seoul. According to the US-ROK Status of Forces Agreement, the investigation of and criminal procedures for the killings did not fall under South Korea's jurisdiction. As a result, the two American military personnel responsible for the lethal accident were tried in a US military court.

In late November, upon news of the soldiers' acquittals, tens of thousands of citizens held a series of candlelight vigils in Seoul and in other cities. The solemn memorials quickly developed into sites of critical expression. At issue were the unwillingness of South Korean leaders to pursue the problem with the United States, and the asymmetrical US-ROK alliance that was the source of the deaths and their unsatisfactory resolution (Kang 2016, 48–64). The demonstrations, which extended into January, consisted of seasoned activists and a high proportion of non-activists in their teens and twenties, many of whom had also taken part in World Cup street spectatorship. In December, half a year after the World Cup, this re-galvanization of young citizens played an instrumental role in the election of liberal reformer Roh Moo-hyun to the presidency.

Postdevelopmental anxieties

Inspired by a vigorous digital grassroots campaign, young voters willed longshot candidate Roh Moo-hyun to office. While the World Cup had truly been a nationwide celebration, the communitarian effort that boosted him to the top political office was more specifically representative of liberal and progressive political stances and of under-40 voters. Roh, a self-made labor rights lawyer, inspired hopes for substantive progress away from inequality and discrimination, and toward a fairer, more just society.

With respect to the deaths of Hyosun and Misŏn, the Nosamo (Love Roh) movement was sparked by critical sentiments toward the United States that consisted, on the one hand, of former 1980s activists' older, left-nationalist views on decolonization. On the other hand, there were newer, and in some cases inchoate, understandings common among under-40 supporters who believed that contemporary South Korea deserved to stand on equal ground with the United States; they regarded the unequal US-ROK alliance to be a post-authoritarian anachronism of the cold war era. Their assertions of equality were also rooted in recent examples of US arrogance and unilateralism (Kang 2016, 48–50).[6]

In terms of domestic issues, even though economic recovery had been dubbed a success, work insecurity, financial hardship, and youth unemployment remained widespread. Seeking new paths for advancement in career and in life, supporters saw in Roh a principled political outsider who would squarely address these postdevelopmental problems and break up the closed, elite networks that had dominated politics, economy, and society since the authoritarian era (Song 2003, 113–114). Although these optimistic, grassroots feelings of peoplehood proved instrumental in the 2002 election, Roh was not able to live up to the expectations that had boosted him to office. His administration retained the economy-first focus of the dominant nationalism.

Like Kim Dae Jung's "Government of the People," Roh's "Participatory Government" was faced with the complex challenge of achieving more equitable distribution while simultaneously ensuring robust economic growth. The latter exigency was accentuated by public anxieties stoked by conservatives in politics and in the national media, who were quick to take advantage of any shortfall, real or perceived, in economic performance. During the ten years of reform liberal leadership, decent rates of annual GDP growth were achieved, but the problems related to distribution actually worsened.

With respect to the economy-first imperative, the Kim and Roh administrations forged ahead on the postdevelopmental quest to improve national competitiveness and attain advanced nation status (Sŏ and Kim 2013, 168–175). They banked on continuing progress in well-established industries, such as semiconductors, automobiles, and consumer electronics, while emphasizing the need for further expansion in the IT and service sectors. Like their conservative predecessors, both leaders deemed the chaebol to be indispensable to achieving these objectives. Under Kim, at the height of the crisis, big business was forced to accept strict restructuring regulations and forced mergers. Yet, despite their culpability in the financial meltdown, the Kim administration stopped short of fully dismantling conglomerates or decentering their place in the economy. Under Roh, the country's biggest chaebol found new ballast by adapting to post-1997 realities (Lim and Jang 2012, 175; Suh et al. 2012, 832–833).

Roh's signature growth initiative aimed at transforming South Korea into the business hub of Northeast Asia, a long-term project that included the completion of a free trade agreement with the United States. Free trade and chaebol-driven growth, Roh claimed, would be beneficial for the "national citizens' economy" (Sŏ and Kim 2013, 174). However, the reality was that conglomerates were family run multinational enterprises that, as a consequence of the IMF restructuring, had become increasingly reliant on global finance capital. While good chaebol performance had a salutary effect on the nation brand, the tangible benefits for ordinary South Koreans were hard to find (Lee 2010, 36–40). Meanwhile, a number of government policies under Kim Dae Jung and under Roh, including labor flexibilization and the deregulation of consumer lending, institutionalized new structures of hardship that had begun to crystallize during the crisis, with mass layoffs of blue- and white-collar workers. In addition, further global integration brought on by the US-South Korea FTA, which was later ratified in 2011, would increase the vulnerability of social groups that were already struggling to get by. It is important to note that under Kim and Roh, post-authoritarian repressive strategies were employed against labor and anti-FTA struggles (Kim 2011, 256–262; Kwon 2014). These are some of the salient contours of the liberal reformers' approach to postdevelopmental nationalism.[7]

As neoliberalization proceeded, South Koreans saw a number of disturbing trends that included growing rates of temporary labor, the deepening of wealth inequality, and stark increases in household debt (Lee 2010, 38–40). Connected to these trends were a marked decline in birth rates and a stark rise in the incidence of suicide (OECD 2021a; OECD 2021c). Under these conditions, the Kim and Roh administrations introduced significant new programs to the social welfare system, but the economy-first imperative and reliance on neoliberal approaches forestalled a more generous expansion (Park 2007, 8–16). At the end of Roh's term, welfare spending remained meager, ranking quite low among OECD nations, both in per capita and as a percentage of GDP (OECD 2021b). Conversely, economy-firstism and neoliberal instrumentality combined to limit the extent of gender and family reforms (Ma et al. 2016, 629–645). The curtailment of this reform process and the post-1997 problem of economic precarity only worsened under the conservative administrations of Lee Myung-bak (2008–2013) and Park Geun-hye (2013–2017).

Conclusion

At the outset of this chapter, I characterized postdevelopmental nationalism as a multiply produced, cross-partisan hegemonic discourse that is based on triumphal memories of (South) Korea's economic and political development. In the sections that followed, I have sought to illustrate these aspects by examining selected episodes and processes in the shift from developmentalist to postdevelopmental nationalism, with attention to how the discourse was adapted to the domestic conjuncture of 1987–1988 as well as the global processes of neoliberal globalization and the ending of the cold war. In particular, I have paid attention to liberal uses of postdevelopmental nationalism under the administrations of Kim Dae Jung and Roh Moo-hyun. By way of closing, I will briefly examine neoconservative uses of postdevelopmental nationalism, following the end of Roh's presidency in 2008. For starters, a quick look at how the decade of liberal government ran its course is instructive.

Alongside their economic and social policies, the Kim and Roh administrations instituted left-of-center reforms on selected issues of national history and politics that had been derived from the pre-1987 struggles for democracy and decolonization. Examples include a policy of engagement with North Korea (1998–2008) aimed at economic cooperation and the gradual integration of the two countries' economies; the passage of an act to restore the honor of, and provide compensation to, democracy activists whose lives had been adversely affected by political repression (1999); the creation of the Committee to Investigate the Truth of Pro-Japanese Anti-National Activities (2005), which oversaw research on the pre-1945 era that identified figures who had collaborated in Japanese colonialism or imperialism; and the formation of a Truth and Reconciliation Commission (2005–2010), tasked with investigating state violence committed during the colonial era, the period of national division and the Korean War, and the authoritarian era (Cho 2002; Kim DC 2015; Kim JC 2015; Lee and Moon 2020).[8]

The simultaneous institution of economy-first, redistributive, and historico-political reforms left Roh and his party, as well as centrist liberals overall, vulnerable to criticism from multiple angles. For example, progressives and liberal segments felt betrayed by Roh's push for a US-South Korea FTA and by his failure to implement policies that would ameliorate socioeconomic conditions for ordinary people. A botched opportunity to repeal the National Security Law in 2004 added to their disappointment. Conversely, conservative leaders and pundits invoked the anxieties woven into postdevelopmental triumphalism by blaming popular difficulties on the putative underperformance of the national economy during the "ten lost years" under Kim and Roh. Conservatives also criticized Kim and Roh's engagement policy with North Korea as being ineffectual, overly accommodating, and even pro-communist. The decline in public faith in reform liberals was made clear in the 2007 presidential election, won handily by conservative Lee Myung-bak (Doucette 2010, 22–30).

With regard to postdevelopmental nationalism, two points are noteworthy about the conservatives' return to power. First, they capitalized on "restorative nostalgia" for the developmentalist past (Boym 2001, chap. 4). A salient aspect of contemporary conservatism, developmentalist nostalgia originated in sympathetic public memories of the Park Chung Hee era that had emerged during the Kim Young Sam administration (Lee 2019b, 25–33). Nostalgia for Park's resolute style of leadership gathered strength, especially among older voters, in reaction to the liberal leadership of Kim Dae Jung and Roh Moo-hyun, as well as to the postmaterialist political and cultural sensibilities of younger cohorts. With respect to Lee Myung-bak, prior to his presidential campaign, he had become a household name through his infrastructure and redevelopment projects as the mayor of Seoul (2002–2006). But the former chair of Hyundai Construction was also a throwback to the halcyon growth years of the 1960s–1980s. Unsubtly nicknamed the "Bulldozer" during his time at the major conglomerate, Lee offered a semi-atavistic brand of splashy, neoliberal growth that promised trickle-down benefits to the people. His postdevelopmentalist program was captured in his "747 pledge" that under his pragmatic leadership, South Korea would achieve a 7% annual growth rate, reach a per capita GDP of US$40,000, and become the world's seventh-largest economy (Doucette 2010, 23). Lee fell short of reaching these goals.

Second, economy-first nostalgia obtained support in "New Right" discourse. This neoconservative ideology, which coalesced in the mid-2000s, equipped developmentalist nostalgia with an intellectual platform that justified South Korea's path-dependent economy-first history, through a reinterpretation of colonial-era collaboration and pre-1987 authoritarian rule. Touting this reinterpretation of the national past, New Rightist politicians, commentators, and academics called for the pursuit of unfettered economy-firstism (Lee 2019b, 34–37). The neoconservative discourse also supported the return to a more adversarial approach to ROK-DPRK relations. Developmentalist nostalgia and New Right ideology are evident in the Taegukgi assemblies that have become commonplace in recent years.

Influenced by the New Right, Lee turned to an assertively pro-business orientation that cast aside any real consideration of mitigating socioeconomic disparities. He also rolled back the mnemonic reforms and the North Korea engagement policies of his two predecessors, while shifting to a post-authoritarian "politics of public security" that relied on state agencies to "stifle dissent and criticism." This disconcerting trend escalated under the conservative Park Geun-hye administration (2013–2017) (Doucette and Koo 2014).

Developmentalist nostalgia also helped propel Park, the daughter of Park Chung-hee, to the presidency. In 2016–2017, the living Park was impeached from office in the face of scorching public outcry. Most immediately, it was a corruption scandal and other abuses of power, as well as widespread dissatisfaction over her ineffectual leadership, that impelled millions of citizens of all ages to take to the streets for massive candlelight demonstrations. But also embedded in the 20 weeks of these peaceful assemblies, which built on the tradition of the 2002 candlelight vigils for Sin Hyosun and Sim Misŏn, were emergent "structures of feeling" rooted in systemic patterns of economic hardship, downward social mobility, and gender and other forms of social discrimination (Lee 2019a, 23–31; Williams 1977, 128–135).

In 2017, the election of liberal Moon Jae-in in the wake of this collective outburst heralded the beginning of a new chapter in the continuing story of South Korea's hegemonic postdevelopmental discourse.

Notes

1 Embedded as a core assumption of postdevelopmental nationalism, this claim to authenticity is ingrained in standard South Korean language, in words such as "Hanguk" ((South) Korea) and "Hangul" (the (South) Korean script). This fundamental assumption was also embedded in South Korea's developmentalist nationalism and dates back to the establishment of rival Korean nation-states in 1948. An analogous assumption is also ingrained in standard North Korean language, in words such as "Choson" ((North) Korea) and "Chosongul" (the (North) Korean script).
2 National sensitivity was also a part of the 1964 Summer Games in Tokyo and the 2008 Summer Games in Beijing (Tsutsui 2011, 8–10).
3 South Korea's fourth-place finish in the medal count, its outpacing of larger countries such as China, Japan, and West Germany, and the many strong performances of Korean athletes were additional sources of collective pride.
4 It is worth noting that international pressures to neoliberalize the South Korean economy, and other Asian economies, had begun building since the Chun regime (Shin 2010, 13).
5 A prominent example of the invocation of people power was the nationwide gold collection campaign proposed by president-elect Kim Dae Jung in December 1997 and launched soon afterward in 1998 by the national public broadcaster KBS. During the four-month campaign, 3.5 million citizens donated $2.1 billion in gold to contribute to the country's payment of the IMF loan.
6 Examples include: the view that the United States was behind the IMF's imposition of economic restructuring in 1997–1998; President George W. Bush's inclusion of North Korea in his "axis of evil," in his 2002 State of the Union address; and the controversy surrounding the disqualification of a South Korean short-track speedskater, which enabled American athlete Apolo Ohno to win a gold medal at the 2002 Winter Olympics (Kang 2016, 36–41).
7 So Chongmin and Kim Hyunjun focus on a distinct but related phenomenon, which they term "nationalist neoliberalism" (minjokchuŭijŏk sinjayujuŭi) (Seo 2013, 179). Roh Moo-hyun himself was known to refer to his economic policies as a form of "leftist neoliberalism" (Suh et al. 2012, 838).
8 The Truth and Reconciliation Commission was relaunched in 2020.

References

English-language references

Boym, Svetlana. 2001. *The Future of Nostalgia*. New York: Basic Books. Kindle.
Bridges, Brian. 2008. "The Seoul Olympics: Economic Miracle Meets the World." *The International Journal of the History of Sport* 25 (14): 1939–1952.
Chang, Paul Y. 2015. *Protest Dialectics: State Repression and South Korea's Democracy Movement, 1970–1979*. Stanford: Stanford University Press.
Cho, Hee-Yeon. 2002. "Sacrifices Caused by State Violence under Military Authoritarianism and the Dynamics of Settling the Past during the Democratic Transition." *Korea Journal* 42 (3): 163–193.
Cho, Hee-Yeon. 2013. *Contemporary South Korean Society: A Critical Perspective*. Abingdon: Routledge.

Cho Han, Hae-joang. 2004. "Beyond the FIFA's World Cup: An Ethnography of the 'Local' in South Korea around the 2002 World Cup." *Inter-Asia Cultural Studies* 5 (1): 8–25.

Choi, Jang Jip. 2012. *Democratization After Democracy: The Korean Experience*. Stanford: Walter H, Shorenstein Asia-Pacific Research Center.

Cho, Ji-Hyun, and Alan Bairner. 2012. "The sociocultural legacy of the 1988 Seoul Olympic Games." *Leisure Studies* 31 (3): 271–289.

Collins, Sandra. 2011. "East Asian Olympic Desires: Identity on the Global Stage in the 1964 Tokyo, 1988 Seoul and 2008 Beijing Games." *The International Journal of the History of Sport* 28 (16): 2240–2260.

Cumings, Bruce. 1981. *The Origins of the Korean War: Liberation and the Emergence of Separate Regimes, 1945–1947*. Princeton: Princeton University Press.

Cumings, Bruce. 2002. "Civil society in West and East." In *Korean Society: Civil society, democracy and the state*, edited by Charles K. Armstrong, 9–32. Abingdon: Routledge.

Davis, Lisa Kim. 2011. "Cultural Policy and the 1988 Seoul Olympics: '3S' as Urban Body Politics." In *The East Asian Olympiads, 1934–2008: Building Bodies and Nations in Japan, Korea, and China*, edited by William M. Tsutsui and Michael Baskett, 106–119. Leiden: Global Oriental.

Doucette, Jamie. 2010. "The Terminal Crisis of the 'Participatory Government' and the Election of Lee Myung Bak." *Journal of Contemporary Asia* 40 (1): 22–43.

Doucette, Jamie, and Se-Woong Koo. 2014. "Distorting Democracy: Politics by Public Security in Contemporary South Korea [UPDATE]." *The Asia-Pacific Journal: Japan Focus*, February 24, 2014. https://apjjf.org/2014/12/8/Jamie-Doucette/4078/article.html.

Kang, Jiyeon. 2016. *Igniting the Internet: Youth and Activism in Postauthoritarian South Korea*. Honolulu: University of Hawai'i Press.

Kim, Alice S. 2011. "Left Out: People's Solidarity for Social Progress and the Evolution of *Minjung* after Authoritarianism." In *South Korean Social Movements: From Democracy to Civil Society*, edited by Gi-Wook Shin and Paul Y, Chang, 245–269. Abingdon: Routledge.

Kim, Dong-Choon. 2015. "Critical Assessments of the South Korean Truth and Reconciliation Commission." In *Routledge Handbook of Memory and Reconciliation in East Asia*, edited by Mikyoung Kim, 144–159. Abingdon: Routledge.

Kim, Jeong-Chul. 2015. "On Forgiveness and Reconciliation: Korean 'collaborators' of Japanese colonialism." In *Routledge Handbook of Memory and Reconciliation in East Asia*, edited by Mikyoung Kim, 159–171. Abingdon: Routledge.

Kim, Jinwung. 1989. "Recent Anti-Americanism in South Korea: The Causes." *Asian* Survey 29 (8): 749–763.

Kim, Jongtae. 2012. "The West and East Asian National Identities: A Comparison of the Discourses of Korean *Seonjinguk*, Japanese *Nihonjinron*, and Chinese New Nationalism." In *Globalization and Development in East Asia*, edited by Jan Nederveen Pieterse and Jongtae Kim, 80–97. Abingdon: Routledge.

Kim, Ki-jung. 2020. "Korean foreign policy: A historical overview." In *Routledge Handbook of Korean Politics and Public Administration*, edited by Chung-in Moon and M. Jae Moon, 129–143. Abingdon: Routledge.

Kim, Sun-Chul. 2016. *Democratization and Social Movements in South Korea: Defiant institutionalization*. Abingdon: Routledge.

Kwon, Heonik. 2010. *The Other Cold War*. New York: Columbia University Press.

Kwon, Jong Bum. 2014. "Forging a Modern Democratic Imaginary: Police Sovereignty, Neoliberalism, and the Boundaries of Neo-Korea." *Positions: Asia Critique* 22 (1): 71–101.

Lee, Byeong-cheon. 2003. "The Political Economy of Developmental Dictatorship: A Korean Experience." In *Developmental Dictatorship and the Park Chung-hee Era: The Shaping of Modernity in the Republic of Korea*, edited by Lee Byeong-cheon, 3–48. Paramus, New Jersey: Homa & Sekey Books.

Lee, Chang-sup. 1998. "Kim Proposes S-N Dialog Panel." *Korea Times*, August 15, 1998. Proquest Historical Newspapers.

Lee, Kang-Kook. 2010. "Neoliberalism, the Financial Crisis, and Economic Restructuring in Korea." In *New Millennium South Korea: Neoliberal Capitalism and Transnational Movements*, edited by Jesook Song, 29–45. Abingdon: Routledge.

Lee, Myung-bak. 2008. "Inauguration Speech of President Lee Myung-bak." Accessed May 10, 2021. https://www.mofa.go.kr/eng/brd/m_5676/list.do.

Lee, Namhee. 2007. *The Making of Minjung: Democracy and the Politics of Representation in South Korea.* Ithaca: Cornell University Press.
Lee, Namhee. 2019a. "Discourses of De-Democratization and Transformatory Politics in South Korea." *Public Jurist* (November 2019): 18–36.
Lee, Namhee. 2019b. "Social Memories of the 1980s: Unpacking the Regime of Discontinuity." In *Revisiting Minjung: New Perspectives on the Cultural History of 1980s South Korea*, edited by Sunyoung Park, 17–45. Ann Arbor: University of Michigan Press.
Lee, Namhee, and Kim Won, eds. 2016. *The South Korean Democratization Movement: A Sourcebook.* Seongnam: The Academy of Korean Studies Press.
Lee, Sang-cheol. 2003. "Industrial Policy in the Park Chung-hee Era." In *Developmental Dictatorship and the Park Chung-hee Era: The Shaping of Modernity in the Republic of Korea*, edited by Lee Byeong-cheon, 80–107. Paramus: Homa & Sekey Books.
Lee, Sangkeun, and Chung-in Moon. 2020. "Korean Unification Policy." In *Routledge Handbook of Korean Politics and Public Administration*, edited by Chung-in Moon and M. Jae Moon, 177–192. Abingdon: Routledge.
Lim, Hyun-Chin, and Jin-Ho Jang. 2012. "Whither Democracy? South Korea under Globalization Revisited." In *Globalization and Development in East Asia*, edited by Jan Nederveen Pieterse and Jongtae Kim, 166–181. Abingdon: Routledge.
Ma, Kyoung Hee, Seung-Kyung Kim, and Jae Kyung Lee. 2016. "Work and Family policy Framing and Gender Equality in South Korea: Focusing on the Roh Moo-hyun and Lee Myung-bak Administrations." *Development and Society* 45 (3): 619–652.
OECD. 2021a. "Fertility Rates (Indicator)." Accessed April 25, 2021. https://data.oecd.org/pop/fertility-rates.htm.
OECD. 2021b. "Social Spending (Indicator)." Accessed April 25, 2021. https://data.oecd.org/socialexp/social-spending.htm.
OECD. 2021c. "Suicide Rates (Indicator)." Accessed April 25, 2021. https://data.oecd.org/healthstat/suicide-rates.htm.
Park, Yong Soo. 2007. "Revisiting the Welfare State Regime in Korea." *Asia Pacific Journal of Social Work and Development* 17 (2): 7–17.
Schmid, Andre. 2002. *Korea between Empires, 1895–1919.* New York: Columbia University Press.
Shin, Kwang-Yeong. 2010. "Globalization and social inequality in South Korea." In *New Millennium South Korea: Neoliberal Capitalism and Transnational Movements*, edited by Jesook Song, 11–28. Abingdon: Routledge.
Song, Ho Keun. 2003. "Politics, Generation, and the Making of New Leadership in South Korea." *Development and Society* 32 (1): 103–123.
Suh, Jae-Jung, Sunwon Park, and Hahn Y. Kim. 2012. "Democratic Consolidation and Its Limits in Korea: Dilemmas of Cooptation." *Asian Survey* 52 (5): 822–844.
Tsutsui, William M. 2011. "Introduction." In *The East Asian Olympiads, 1934–2008: Building Bodies and Nations in Japan, Korea, and China*, edited by William M. Tsutsui and Michael Baskett, 1–22. Leiden: Global Oriental.
West, James. 1997. "Martial Lawlessness: The Legal Aftermath of Kwangju." *Pacific Rim Law and Policy Journal* 6 (1): 85–168.
Williams, Raymond. 1977. *Marxism and Literature.* Oxford: Oxford University Press.

Korean-language reference

Sŏ, Chong-min (Seo, Jung Min), and Hyŏn-jun Kim (Kim, Hyeon Jun). 2013. 신주유주의 대한민국? 경쟁력 있는 국가개념과 한국의 정치경제 (Neoliberal Republic of Korea? The idea of national competitiveness and the political economy of South Korea). *Hyŏndae chŏngch'i yŏngu* 6, no. 2: 157–186.

21
THE EMERGENCE OF CALCULATED NATIONALISM IN SOUTH KOREA IN THE TWENTY-FIRST CENTURY

Gil-Soo Han and David Hundt

Introduction

Ethnic nationalism was prevalent in South Korea until the 1990s. It was commonly believed that South Koreans shared the same ancestors with North Koreans, as part of the Dangun mythology. Following the Independence from Japanese colonialism (1910–1945), the Korean War (1950–1953), the 'April 19 Revolution' which toppled the despotic Rhee Syngman regime in 1960, and the *coup d'état* of May 1961 which brought Park Chung-Hee to power, South Korean society went through rapid urbanization and industrialization under authoritarian leadership. A society that had been characterized by *Gemeinschaft* started shifting towards *Gesellschaft*, i.e., from being generally oriented on the community to individuals. South Korea's cataclysmic experiences in the twentieth century created the impetus for a transition from ethnic nationalism to an individualist-oriented form of nationalism which we refer to as *calculated nationalism*.

The key elements of nationalism, in its classical definition, are 'the preservation of the cultures, customs, governance, and identity,' which are deemed essential for establishing and maintaining a sovereign state (Stacey 2018, 8). Nationalism refers to a sense of 'belonging to a common nation, which is defined by citizenship in the same nation-state' (Stacey 2018, 8). Nationalism is also an ideology that is in pursuit of a nation's 'independence, self-reliance, integration and glory' (Y.-M. Kim 2016, 230). Stacey acknowledges nationalism as an ideology as well as an affective sense of belonging to a sovereign nation (p. 8). So the definition of nationalism also includes 'a network of attitudes, norms, and actions that provide the necessary political, social (including moral), and cultural value to a nation or national identity, while simultaneously providing obligations for members of the nation to maintain and develop' (Stacey 2018, 8).

In ethno-nationalism, a nation was understood as 'a self-conscious ethnic group' (Connor 1973, 3). This form of nationalism, which is closely associated with the Alt-Right and the rise of Donald Trump, typically does not support globalism or multiculturalism (Stacey 2018, 9; Volcic and Andrejevic 2016). For ethno-nationalism, national identity is based on ethnicity and one's 'adopted national identity is superior to all others' (Stacey 2018, 11). It emphasizes a shared heritage and common language (p. 11) and a shared sense that the members of a nation are akin to an extended family (Muller 2008, 20), which is sometimes known as pureblood nationalism (Han 2016).

This chapter illustrates how and why calculated nationalism has (re)emerged in South Korean society. In the process of shifting from *Gemeinschaft* to *Gesellschaft*, South Koreans are increasingly finding their worth and value as the proprietors of their own tradeable skills and capacities. Koreans are becoming more individualized and this is increasingly reflected in their relations with the state. At the same time, the rise of the individualist form of nationalism does not imply a transition to civic nationalism. Most Koreans see themselves as a mono-ethnic community. Older Koreans either under authoritarian or democratic regimes were prepared to endure personal struggles and suppress their personal benefits since they were in solidarity to bring about an affluent nation-state for all Koreans. However, today Koreans of all ages are reluctant to make personal sacrifices for the greater good. They are happy to contribute to national development as far as there are likely to be personal benefits. Therefore, individuals commit to the nation based on calculated benefits at the individual level as well. Calculated nationalism can emerge in any modern state and as such it is not unique to Korea. It is beyond the scope of this chapter to compare the practice of nationalism in South Korea with the experience of other societies, but intuitively we might expect a similar process in East Asian comparators such as Taiwan, Japan, and China, which have all had their own debates about how the relationship between the state and citizen should be renegotiated under late capitalism.

Calculated nationalism

Calculated nationalism, this chapter argues, is a localized outcome in an affluent South Korea of a wider renegotiation of the relationship between states and their citizens since World War II. The blurring of the boundaries of the nation-state and new forms of political action have put the notion of citizenship in flux. For example, Donati (2016, 41) argues that 'a transmodern (societal) citizenship is currently springing from a nascent global civil society rather than from the nation-state.' Citizenship is not a matter to be granted '*from above*,' but an actual experience, i.e., 'the result of a *bottom-up* approach … originating in the subjects' wills' (Donati, 2016, 64, emphasis added). Subjects are not only governed by nationalism in particular times and places but form and 'practise' their own kinds according to their calculated needs.

Various groups of people see their civil activities as essential to citizenship, but it is becoming less common to base citizenship on the rights and duties required for the maintenance of a nation-state. For example, when the South Korean nation-state was built on ethnic nationalism, Koreans understood their relationship with the state in similar terms. However, the influx of 'new Koreans' into the body politic and the expansion of national boundaries have significantly changed the context of Korean nationalism. The reunification of the two Koreas, because of their blood relations, makes less sense to the younger generation than the older one. In this respect, the younger generation's nationalism is much more calculated than that of the older generation (Han 2018).

The emergence of calculated nationalism in politically free and economically affluent South Korea is no accident. C. Brough Macpherson's concept of 'possessive individualism' sheds light on this form of nationalism (Cohen 1996; Macpherson 1964).

> … the individual as essentially the proprietor of his own person or capacities, owing nothing to society for them. The individual was seen neither as a moral whole, nor as

part of larger social whole, but as an owner of himself. ... Society consists of exchange between proprietors.

(Macpherson 1962, 3)

The rights and duties attached to citizenship have undergone change especially in Europe and North America since the end of World War II (Donati 2016). From the viewpoints of a nation-state, on the one hand, a 'smooth operation of the citizen's rights and duties through a relational management' has become an urgent and ongoing issue for most nations under the influence of globalization (p. 54). On the other hand, how an individual citizen perceives their civil, political, social, human (p. 56), and economic rights are achieved and how they can relatively easily meet their duties is a serious matter. When citizenship was largely based on ethnic nationalism, South Koreans were more willing to cede their rights but meet their duties. However, they now see their nation-state to be politically, economically, and internationally 'competent' and their expectations of the nation have changed in terms of their rights and duties.

South Korea's calculated nationalism has been increasingly evident in the twenty-first century. The 2008 Candlelight vigil was a turning point for South Korean civil movements due to their frustration over their immediate personal concerns, e.g., the consequence of consuming the beef affected by foot and mouth disease (Hong 2017), which implies that civic movements before 2008 mainly focused on national concerns. The 2016/17 Candlelight Revolution was unique insofar as it resulted from the combination of calculated personal as well as national concerns. Noh Hyeong-Il and Yang Eun-Kyeong (2017, 16, cited in Jung 2017, 261–262) go as far as to argue that the candlelight demonstrations were an effort to search for identity and were motivated by individualistic benefits. Other examples include the formation of a unified women's Hockey team from North and South Korea during the 2018 Pyeongchang Winter Olympics. The North Korean team joined the games only weeks before the official opening, and the unified team was agreed upon in the interests of promoting better relations between the two Koreas. Young South Koreans, however, responded negatively to the removal of South Korean players from the team so that North Koreans could be included. The South Korean players' hard work and right to participate in the games, young people thought, was more important than advancing inter-Korean relations. Furthermore, Seon Dong-Ryul, the baseball team coach for the 2018 Asian Games, faced severe criticism for selecting a playing squad on criteria other than merit. South Koreans have become intolerant of these and other instances of what they perceive to be unfairness.

Calculated nationalism, therefore, has much in common with Emma Campbell's 'globalized cultural nationalism,' which she argues can explain young Koreans' adoption of universal values such as modernity and transnationalism (Campbell 2016, Ch.4). We contend that contemporary Koreans consider their individual economic interests are as important as cultural values and that calculated nationalism applies to all age groups, in that national interest is not discarded but personal gains take a disproportionate prominence.

Calculated nationalism and the emergence of new Koreans since the 1990s

The transition to calculated nationalism in South Korea has not been entirely smooth or frictionless. 'New Koreans' have been most severely impacted by this transition. South Korean immigration policy has been revised to allow for new citizens to be incorporated into the body politic, but there is still a strong emphasis on protecting the fabric and essence of Korean society (Hundt 2016, 488). Claims about the alleged superiority of the Korean ethnicity have often been made in terms of culture and ideology rather than 'natural' or biological differences (McLelland 2008). Such claims have long been part of Korean culture and offered Koreans a way to set themselves apart from non-Koreans. These claims are deeply embedded in the national psyche, but recent studies confirm that the Koreans are less homogeneous than 'pureblood' nationalism would suggest. A substantial number of foreigners have settled and naturalized in Korea throughout history (C.S. Kim 2011, xiv; Yi 2008), and there is evidence that 'over the course of 2,000 years various groups entered the peninsula and found a niche in the mosaic of a developing complex society' (Nelson, 1993, 163). Increasingly, South Koreans themselves have become less convinced about the notion of pureblood nationalism and believe that it is anachronistic (Hundt 2016; Hundt, Walton, and Lee 2019).

These older ideas of pureblood nationalism need to be understood in the context of the harsh Japanese colonialization of Korea (1910–1945). The 'racial' inferiority and the dislike of Japanese resonate deeply with Koreans, and were passed on from generation to generation through socialization and education (Pak 2002; Kim 2021, 105–113). It is no surprise that 'Korean school textbooks still show what critics call "an anachronistic misconception" that Korea is ethnically and racially homogeneous' (*Korea Herald*, June 23, 2008, cited in C.S. Kim 2011, 67). In the decades since independence, South Korea has developed a sophisticated capitalist economy, but one in which non-citizens and new citizens have sometimes been subject to exploitation. In this 'nouveau-riche nationalism' (Han, 2016), Koreans have developed a sense of superiority in regard to 'who is included' and/or 'who is excluded' (see Brubaker 2009).

Even when non-Koreans are naturalized and become Korean citizens, there is some evidence of a 'hierarchy of citizenship' in South Korea, whereby some new Koreans are treated better and differently than others (Hundt 2016). Koreans, for instance, demonstrated more favourable attitudes towards the possibility of naturalization by Americans and less favourable attitudes towards Chinese, Korean-Chinese, Japanese, Southeast Asians, and Mongolians (Choe 2007, 159). Historically and genealogically, Koreans have close ethnic affiliations with the latter group, but Koreans often express the most discriminatory attitudes against these fellow Asians mainly because of what Koreans perceive as the relatively poor economic performance of their countries of origin.

A survey of attitudes towards multiculturalism conducted by Seoul National University in 2011 asked foreign brides: 'What are the key grounds on which foreigners are discriminated in Korea?' More than one third (36.6 per cent) of respondents said: 'country of origin.' Nguyen Ba Thanh, a Vietnamese migrant worker who arrived in Korea in 2008, said: 'When I am mistreated simply because of my Southeast Asian origin, I feel like leaving Korea which is my second home country' (*Kyeongin Ilbo* 2013). The mistreatment of Southeast Asian women became so severe in the early 2000s that Cambodia reintroduced a ban on local women marrying Korean men, and the governments of Vietnam and the Philippines warned local women about the possibility of violence and abuse should they become marriage migrants in South Korea (Hundt et al 2019, 445).

Son Jeong-A, a human rights counsellor, found that female migrant workers are exposed to low wages, unsafe work conditions, and sexual assault by male colleagues and employers. Even after being assaulted by their employers, female workers often returned to work due to the fear of deportation. Son contends that deportation is the worst fear for these women since they often pay large sums to reach and work in Korea. Many incidents of abuse go unreported, she claims (*Daejeon Ilbo* 2013). The key reason for those women's assaults is due to their poor backgrounds. Being a woman from a Southeast Asian country immediately puts them in a highly vulnerable position (Jo 2009, 116). Marriage brokers, meanwhile, have a superiority complex and feel entitled to 'misbehave' with these women because the brokers are members of a relatively well-off nation.

Mukul Basu, an Indian who became a Korean citizen in 2000, had a similarly disturbing experience. He is an English teacher in a private academy. According to Basu, 'Koreans are kind-hearted like Indians but double-minded. They are kind amongst them and towards Westerners. However, Koreans are readily discriminatory and disrespectful to coloured people.' He was bashed up and verbally abused on several occasions because of his dark skin (*Gwangju Ilbo* 2013). While diversity is a feature of South Korea's calculated nationalism, testimony such as Basu's indicates that Koreans are reluctant to share their wealth with those from less well-off countries.

Analogies have been drawn between the fate of migrants in other countries and the case of South Korea. *Chungcheong Today* reported that discriminatory exclusion or unilateral assimilation policy in France and Germany was problematic, and consequently led to riots by Muslim immigrants in France. Just as some French migrants have become a permanent underclass who are often blamed for crime and accused of being unwilling to work, the newspaper reported, so too have crimes involving foreign workers in Korea met with an upsurge in verbal abuse, discrimination, and exclusion (*Seoul Kyungje* 2013).

Other analyses support these claims about the precarity of new Koreans amid calculated nationalism. Chang Sun-Mi, an advocate for multiculturalism, claims that discrimination and exclusion of migrant workers will result in the formation of an underclass and lead to social conflict (*Jugan Dangjinsidae* 2013). *E-Today* argued that the treatment of migrant workers as potential criminals will limit their life opportunities and they will fall into the category of 'the newly created poor' in competitive Korea, which will create the seeds for social conflict (*E-Today* 2013). An analysis of media narratives about multiculturalism in South Korea illustrated that there is an idealized version of the incorporation of new Koreans into the body politic, most commonly through marriage migration. The lived reality of new Koreans, however, is quite different, and they often struggle to secure gainful and satisfying employment, affordable homes, and happy lives (Hundt et al 2019).

Shirking the costs of reunification

A separate but related challenge for calculated nationalism in South Korea is to incorporate North Korean refugees as fully fledged citizens. Surveys in the twenty-first century have indicated that sentiment towards North Koreans has cooled considerably, and there is less support for the idea that they should be automatically included as citizens (Hundt 2016). Likewise, interest in reunification has also declined in the two decades. Limited public awareness of the complexity of reunification and geopolitics remain as obstacles (Han 2019, Ch.3). A lot of South Koreans want reunification, but are unwilling to pay its costs.

South Koreans differ in how they want to contribute to reunification. Some are willing to make significant sacrifices. For instance, a group of elderly people from Goheung Town, Jeollanam-do province, raised $22,000 by accumulating the 30 cents that they would otherwise spend on a cup of coffee from a vending machine. Each person saved up to $9 per month, for a period of four years. Some members also raised money by selling vegetables. These older people dreamed of passing down a reunified Korea to the next generation and they were determined to continue to accumulate their savings until their dream came true (*Joongang Ilbo* 2012). The vast majority of Koreans, however, are unwilling to pay their share of the costs of reunification: they agree that reunification is important and also that a tax might be needed, but over 90 per cent of respondents to a 2014 survey wanted to contribute less than $100 per year to this cause. This phenomenon has been called 'Not Out of My Pocket' (*Seoul Kyungje* 2014).

At the time of the 2018 North-South Korea Summit, more than 70 per cent of respondents to another survey said that they were willing to play a role in reducing the gap in living standards in the North and South. But they thought this would be best achieved through an increase in the stock market, which was expected to boom in the event of reunification. That is, a lot of Koreans view reunification as a form of economic stimulus rather than a national imperative in its own right (*Seoul Sinmun* 2018). Another survey, in early 2019, found that nearly half (47.3 per cent) of respondents opposed reunification, which was an increase from 36 per cent in 2016. Opposition was especially strong for people in their 20s and 30s. About 30 per cent (29.2 per cent) said that reunification may be possible after 20 years and 26 per cent said it would never happen (*Joongang Ilbo* 2019a).

One reason for this declining public support for reunification is that political leaders are unwilling to publicly promote it. Politicians' passive approach and the public's reluctance to pay the costs of reunification, in turn, are affected by the ongoing economic uncertainty and slowdown since the high-growth era of the 1970s and 1980s. The media's sensationalizing of the sluggish economy and negative reports about the possible impact of reunification also play a role (Han 2019, Ch.3). Germany's experience of costly unification seems to have a negative impact on South Korean perceptions of reunification. As noted, most ordinary Koreans see the benefit for the nation, but not for themselves. According to Hong Yong-Pyo, the Minister of Reunification (2015–2017), the attitude of young people is: 'As I live a comfortable life with a good job, I don't see a point of seeking the reunification' (*Kookmin Ilbo* 2015). Hana Financial Management Research Institute suggested that a way to prepare for the costs of reunification was through a Reunification Lottery, which had the advantage of not requiring a new tax (*Digital Times* 2015). This is the epitome of calculated nationalism in the context of a free market, as it represents the willingness of people to donate only if there is a personal benefit to them.

Karl Friedhoff in the Asan Institute for Policy Studies points out that Koreans in their 20s regard themselves as 'citizens' rather than as part of an ethno-national group. Observing North Korea's aggressions such as the attacks on the ROKS Cheonan Corvette and Yeonpyeongdo Island, they ask, 'Why should we try so hard to reunify with those who threaten us with death' (*MBC* 2014)? Similarly, Emma Campbell (2016) sees little prospect for reunification due to younger Koreans' adoption of individualism rather than continuing collective and communal values to embrace fellow North Koreans. Meanwhile, a survey of primary, middle, and high school students conducted at the time of the Inter-Korea Summit, in April 2018, found that one of the biggest attractions of reunification was the prospect of taking a railway trip through North Korea, China, Russia, and on to Europe (*Hankook Kyungje* 2018). Notably, a lot of those in their 20s/30s and 50s/60s share this somewhat indifferent attitude to reunification and complacency about the status quo (*Maeil Kyungje* 2013). This declining interest in reunification is increasingly evident in the public discourse.

The legacy of Japanese imperialism and Japan's trade restrictions

'No Abe, No Japan' was a Korean grassroots social movement that emerged in 2019 to boycott Japanese products and also Japan as a tourist destination. The movement was a response to the announcement by Japanese Prime Minister Abe Shinzo that trade restrictions would be implemented against South Korea, specifically through restrictions on the export of three chemicals (fluorinated polyimide, resist, and hydrogen fluoride) which were critical for manufacturing semiconductors and display screens. With the intention of supporting the South Korean government's reluctance to accept these restrictions, this Korean social movement launched its own campaign against the Abe government (*CNBC* 2019). The 'No Japan Movement 2019–20' illustrated that just as strong anti-Korean sentiment persisted in Japan, so too did anti-Japanese sentiment persist in Korea. This anti-Japanese sentiment resurfaced during the trade dispute, and the case illustrated how such sentiment can be managed, concealed, or surfaced depending on the state of bilateral relations.

The trade restrictions sparked a nationwide reaction in Korea. Many local governments felt pressured to go along with the grassroots campaigns. The *Minjung* Party (renamed *Jinbodang* on 20 June 2020) in Ulsan City and local citizens who opposed Abe's actions produced 130 banners reading 'No Abe; Japanese Collaborators Out.' The banners were displayed at the sides of two streets in Ulsan, which became known as 'No Abe Streets' (*Kyungsang Ilbo* 2019). Another banner was placed in front of the Whale Museum in Ulsan City, a major tourist attraction for Japanese visitors (*Money Today* 2019a).

The anti-Japanese sentiment affected relations between local authorities in the two countries. Every Korean province and most major cities have established sisterhood relations with counterparts in Japan for regular exchange programmes (*Kyungnam Domin Ilbo* 2019). Choongcheongnam-do province's Seosan City and Nara prefecture's Tenri City, for instance, had maintained sister relationships since 1991, but Seosan informed its counterpart that it was cancelling plans to welcome a group of visiting students from Tenri (*Money Today* 2019b). Goseong Town decided to proceed with its planned Youth Exchange Program that involved a group of Japanese students (*Kyungnam Domin Ilbo* 2019), but many other such arrangements were suspended. Some local governments in South Korea even explored the possibility of establishing new relationships with counterparts in China (*Segye Ilbo* 2019a).

Bilateral sports exchanges were also cancelled. Chooncheon City Hall's Women's Curling Team cancelled its participation in the 2019 Hokkaido Bank Curling Classic that was scheduled for early August in Sapporo (*Hankyoreh Sinmun* 2019). Gangreung City had planned a friendly game of Curling in August 2019, involving teams from China and Japan (*Kangwon Domin Ilbo* 2019). The city first said that it would not pay an honorarium to the Japanese team for participating, and then later completely withdrew the invitation (*Younhap News* 2019). The cancellation of cultural and sports exchanges such as these raised significant concerns at all levels. Yi Hae-Chan, the leader of the Democratic Party, contended that bilateral exchanges had to continue despite the trade dispute (*Seoul Kyungje* 2019).

Some local governments took the initiative in the 'No Japan, No Abe' campaign, arguing that Koreans needed to show a united front to Japan (*Chosun Ilbo* 2019a). However, social movements opposed the involvement of the central and local governments in the boycott. Seoul's Junggu district office decided to display more than 1,000 banners in the Myongdong, Euljiro, and Namsan neighbourhoods, which attract many tourists. Social activists, local traders, and social commentators protested against the government-made banners because local workers were displaying their own. A petition against the banners appeared on the President's Bulletin Board. The grassroots social movements responded to the local government's plans to display banners, arguing that, 'The business of boycotts should be left with people and any government's intervention in the movement will tarnish its essence. … The banners in the middle of downtown will speed up the deterioration of the Korea-Japan relationships' (*Kookmin Ilbo* 2019a).

Ordinary Koreans agreed with this stance. Park Jeong-Hun, a 29-year-old salaryman, said that the district office had gone too far and that citizens were handling the boycott well by themselves. Others said that the District office's clumsy actions would hurt local traders, and that there was nothing to gain by treating Japanese visitors badly (*Money Today* 2019c).

There was some support for the local government's involvement in the boycott, but the prevailing view was that the banners should not be displayed (*Chosun Ilbo* 2019a).

The grassroots social movements demonstrated a significant degree of maturity in their approach to the boycott. Thus, calculated nationalism is not simply self/individual-oriented but sophisticated and nuanced. Following the district office's withdrawal of its 'No Japan' banners, the 'People's Diplomacy' section of the Korean Ministry of Foreign Affairs offered a special welcome to Japanese students from Kaisei High School. The students were visiting as part of a bilateral exchange programme organized by the Korean Embassy in Japan. Despite the bilateral tensions, Korean governments and social movements were adamant that people-to-people relations must remain strong. They hoped that people's diplomacy would enhance mutual understanding of culture and history, which would contribute to improving bilateral relations (*Chosun Ilbo* 2019b). According to *Money Today*, South Koreans recognized the importance of people's diplomacy and many Japanese tourists continued to visit areas such as Myongdong. Most Koreans welcomed them and continued to treat them hospitably (*Money Today* 2019d). The grassroots social movements criticized the role of local governments in the boycott and in discouraging cultural, sports, and arts exchanges (*Kookmin Ilbo* 2019b). It was heartening that two Japanese children's soccer teams held friendly matches with teams in Gyungju City in late August 2019. In addition to presenting souvenirs to the Japanese teams, Koreans prepared supportive banners for and cheered on the visiting players. Yun Seok-Jun, one of the Koreans who cheered on the Japanese players, said the visit was a wonderful event, but continued to take part in the 'No Abe' movement (*Gyungju Sinmun* 2019).

According to Kim Ui-Young, a professor of political science and diplomacy, Koreans participating in the boycott were not protesting against Japan or the Japanese, but against Prime Minister Abe. Koreans boycotted Japanese products and travel to Japan but wanted to preserve exchange programmes with Japan (*Joongang Ilbo* 2019b). Korean grassroots movements told local and central governments not to hinder efforts to cultivate better bilateral relations (*KBS News* 2019). Political leaders began to take a more positive as well as confident approach to sports and cultural exchanges and travel to Japan (*Kwangju Ilbo* 2019), and toned down the campaign from 'No Japan' to 'No Abe' (*Segye Ilbo* 2019b).

People's diplomacy was possible due to the efforts of grassroots social movements in Korea as well as Japan. When the Statue of Peace was under threat from Japanese political leaders and extreme activists in 2019, peace activists were at the forefront of protecting the statue, demonstrating in the streets, and releasing a statement. According to *Munhwa Ilbo*, many Japanese tourists continued to visit Korea because they did not support Abe's trade restrictions (*Munhwa Ilbo* 2019).

The hashtag movement brought some Koreans and Japanese together. A Japanese Twitter user uploaded photos of Koreans campaigning to support the victims of the earthquake in East Japan in 2011 and argued that many Japanese appreciate Koreans and agree with them despite their government's dislike of Korea. Others shared stories about their trips to Korea, including instances when Koreans helped them when they got lost. A Japanese group held an anti-Abe rally in Tokyo in early August 2019 (*Segye Ilbo* 2019c). Five thousand intellectuals, including Wada Haruki, an emeritus professor of Tokyo University, released and signed a statement against the trade restrictions (*Joongang Ilbo* 2019b). Shiraishi Takashi, who is part of Japan's Alliance of Hope, noted that the Supreme Court of Korea had ruled on the payment of reparations for the forced labour induced by Japanese corporations during World War II and that the Japanese government's rejection of this ruling was ignoring a verdict reached by the independent Korean judiciary, which was a sign of immaturity in Japanese democracy (*Kyunghyang Sinmun* 2019).

Grassroots social movements provided a constructive approach to the boycott, and offered a path forward for the government. Just as social movements did not interfere with the government's effort to have the issue of forced labour resolved, nor did they want the government to interfere with their campaign. Social movements wanted to continue people's diplomacy, including by businesses that sold goods to Japanese tourists. These activities were an example of calculated as well as mature nationalism.

Concluding remarks

This chapter has discussed the emergence of calculated nationalism in Korea in recent decades. It has illustrated how calculated nationalism plays out in South Korea's treatment of ethnic minorities, in its views of reunification, and in relations with Japan.

First, the influence of ethno-nationalism has waned as South Korea has witnessed economic development, a large influx of immigrants, and young people's pursuit of individualism. In its place, calculated nationalism has become the prevailing force in the South Korea in the twenty-first century. Ethnicity, however, remains influential when Koreans deal with newly settled Koreans or foreigners. Calculated nationalism has been entrenched in South Korea, but multiculturalism has yet to be firmly established.

Second, calculated nationalism has influenced how South Koreans see reunification and what they were willing to sacrifice for it. With the passage of time, this chapter showed, most South Koreans have become indifferent to reunification. They anticipate the benefits of reunification, including its potential to stimulate the sluggish economy and the possibility of travelling by train to China, Russia, and Europe, but are reluctant to pay the costs of unifying with North Korea. Nationalism based on shared ancestry is not extinct, but it is becoming less significant compared to personal benefits.

Finally, calculated nationalism is evident in South Korean attitudes to relations with Japan. As this chapter argued, the grassroots movement against Abe Shinzo called for constructive bilateral relations through people's diplomacy, which led to the slogan of 'No Abe rather than No Japan.' The maturity of Korean social movements rejected a blind protest against Japan despite the brutal colonial period. Koreans made clear that they want co-prosperity and peace with Japan, but they vehemently protested against Abe's trade restrictions. This was the epitome of calculated nationalism.

Acknowledgement

This work was supported by the Laboratory Programme for Korean Studies through the Ministry of Education of the Republic of Korea and Korean Studies Promotion Service of the Academy of Korean Studies [AKS-2018-LAB-2250001].

References

English-language references

Brubaker, Rogers. 2009. 'Ethnicity, Race, and Nationalism.' *Annual Review of Sociology* 35: 21–42.
Campbell, Emma. 2016. *South Korea's New Nationalism: The End of 'One Korea'?* Boulder, CO: FirstForumPress.
CNBC. 2019. 'The Japan-South Korea Dispute Could Push up the Price of Your Next Smartphone', 22 July, https://www.cnbc.com/2019/07/23/japan-south-korea-dispute-impact-on-semiconductor-supply-chain-prices.html, accessed 17 November 2020.

Cohen, Anthony P. 1996. 'Personal Nationalism: A Scottish View of Some Rites, Rights, and Wrongs.' *American Ethnologist* 23 (4): 802–815.
Connor, Walker. 1973. 'The Politics of Ethnonationalism.' *Journal of International Affairs* 27 (1): 1–21.
Donati, Pierpaolo. 2016. 'On the Social Morphogenesis of Citizenship: A Relational Approach.' SocietàMutamentoPolitica 7 (13): 41–66.
Han, Gil-Soo. 2016. *Nouveau-riche Nationalism and Multiculturalism in Korea: A Media Narrative Analysis.* Abingdon: Routledge.
_____. 2018. 'Time to make two Koreas one again: Korean Christians' self-reflection and diakonia duties.' *International Journal for the Study of the Christian Church* 18 (4): 296–314.
_____. 2019. *Funeral Rites in Contemporary Korea: The Business of Death.* Singapore: Springer.
Hundt, David. 2016. 'Public opinion, social cohesion and the politics of immigration in South Korea.' Contemporary Politics 22 (4): 487–504.
Hundt, David, Jessica Walton, and Soo-Jung Elisha Lee. 2019. 'The politics of conditional citizenship in South Korea: An analysis of the print media.' *Journal of Contemporary Asia* 49 (3): 434–451.
Jo, Seong-Su. 2009. 'Chabyeoljeok damunhwajuuiwa simingwon -3 (Discriminatory multiculturalism and civil rights -3).' *Jachi Baljeon (Self-relying Development)* (September): 114–121.
Kim, Choong Soon. 2011. *Voices of Foreign Brides: The Roots and Development of Multiculturalism in Korea.* Lanham: AltaMira Press.
Macpherson, C. Brough. 1962. *The Political Theory of Possessive Individualism: Hobbes to Locke.* New York: Oxford University Press.
_____. 1964. 'Post-liberal Democracy.' *Canadian Journal of Economics and Political Science* 30: 485–498.
McLelland, Mark. 2008. '"Race" on the Japanese Internet: Discussing Korea and Koreans on "2-channeru".' *New Media & Society* 10 (6): 811–829.
Stacey, Hershey. 2018. *Nationalism, Social Movements, and Activism in Contemporary Society: Emerging Research and Opportunities.* Hershey: IGI Global.
Volcic, Zala, and Mark Andrejevic. eds. 2016. *Commercial Nationalism: Selling the Nation and Nationalizing the Sell.* London: Palgrave MacMillan.

Korean-language references

Choe, Hyeon. 2007. '한국인의 다문화 시티즌십 (Korean Perception of Multicultural Citizenship: With Reference to Awareness of Multiculturalism).' 시민사회와 *NGO (Civil Society and NGO)* 5 (2): 147–174.
Chosun Ilbo. 2019a. '서울 도심에 "No재팬" 깃발 내건 중구청, "관제 반일 논란" 커지자 뒤늦게 철거 ("No Japan" Banners in the Centre of Seoul: A Bureaucratic Influence Accused and the Banners Removed).' 6 August, https://www.chosun.com/site/data/html_dir/2019/08/06/2019080601147.html, accessed 28 January 2021.
Chosun Ilbo. 2019b. '한일戰 격화되는 와중에도…외교부 청사 찾은 日고교생들 (Some Japanese Students Visit the Korean Ministry of Foreign Affairs in the Middle of Korea-Japan Conflict).' 6 August, https://www.chosun.com/site/data/html_dir/2019/08/06/2019080601959.html, accessed 29 January 2021.
Daejeon Ilbo. 2013. '약자중의 약자 이주여성인권 (The Weakest of the Weak: Female Migrant Workers' Human Rights).' 30 October. http://www.daejonilbo.com/news/newsitem.asp?pk_no=1088940, accessed 26 May 2021.
Digital Times. 2015. '하나금융경영연구소: 통일자금 복권사업으로 충당 가능 (Hana Finance Management Research Institute: Lottery Ticket Business Can Meet the Reunification Costs).' 7 July, http://www.dt.co.kr/contents.html?article_no=2015070702109958739005, accessed 23 April 2021.
E-Today. 2013. '철학 필요한 다문화정책 (A Philosophy Is Required for Multicultural Policy).' 29 March, https://www.etoday.co.kr/news/view/710748, accessed 29 March 2013.
Gwangju Ilbo. 2013. '외국인 노동자도 우리이웃' (Migrant Workers Are Our Neighbours, Too), 31 October, http://www.kwangju.co.kr/read.php3?aid=1383145200509665028, accessed 26 May 2021.
Gyungju Sinmun. 2019. '일본유소년축구단 올린 유석준씨 (Yu Seok-Jun in Support of the Japanese Boys' Soccer Team).' 29 August, http://m.gjnews.com/view.php?idx=65670, accessed 30 January 2021.
Hankook Kyungje. 2018. '초중고교생 73%, 통일 긍정적으로 인식… 90%가 남북정상회담으로 남북관계 개선됐다고 생각 (73% of Primary, Middle and Highschool Students Perceive Reunification to be Positive… 90% of Them Think the Inter-Korea Relations have Improved).' 18 May, https://www.hankyung.com/society/article/201805188410i, accessed 29 April 2021.

Hankyoreh Sinmun. 2019. '전국 시민, 사회단체, 지자체 등 일본 경제 도발에 강력 대응 (Citizens, Social Organizations, Local Governments Strongly React against the Japanese Economic Provocation).' 4 August, http://www.hani.co.kr/arti/area/yeongnam/904440.html, accessed 27 January 2021.

Hong, Seong-Min. 2017. '감정구조와 촛불혁명: 2008년과 2016년 (Emotional Politics and Candle Revolution).' 시민사회와 *NGO* (*Civil Society & NGO*) 15 (1): 79–110.

Joongang Ilbo. 2012. '통일기금 2200만원 모은 고흥 노인 33인 (Goheung's 33 Older Koreans: Saving a Reunification Fund of $22,000).' https://news.joins.com/article/8013742, accessed 22 April 2021.

Joongang Ilbo. 2019a. '통일해야 한다, 인식 50.8%…2년새 11%p 하락 (50.8% Agree Reunification Is Essential… 11% Decrease in 2 Years).' https://news.joins.com/article/23592865, accessed 23 April 2021.

Joongang Ilbo. 2019b. '[중앙시평] 일본 사람들의 마음을 사자 (Let Us buy the Japanese Minds).' 9 August, https://news.joins.com/article/23547724, accessed 1 February 2021.

Jugan Dangjinsidae. 2013. '다문화정책 이대로 좋은가 (Examining Korean Multiculturalism).' 15 March. http://www.djtimes.co.kr/news/articleView.html?idxno=49507, accessed 26 May 2021.

Jung, Byungkee. 2017. '68혁명운동과 비교한 2016/2017 촛불 집회의 비판 대상과 참가자 의식 (The Consciousness of the Participants in the South-Korean Candlelight Rally in 2016/2017 in Comparison to the European May 1968).' 동향과 전망 (*Journal of Korean Social Trends and Perspectives*) 101: 261–291.

Kangwon Domin Ilbo. 2019. '체육계부터 맘카페까지 "NO 재팬" 확산 (Sport Clubs and Mum's Internet Cafes All Join "No Japan" Movement).' 7 August, http://www.kado.net/news/articleView.html?idxno=981654, accessed 27 January 2021.

KBS News. 2019. '성숙하고 신중하게…도 넘은 반일에 균형 잡은 시민의 힘 (Mature and Cautious… Citizens Show Balanced Ways against Reckless Ways).' 9 August, https://mn.kbs.co.kr/news/view.do?ncd=4259215, accessed 1 February 2021.

Kim, Sang-Jun. (2021). 붕새의 날개: 문명의 진로 (The Wings of the Legendary Bird: The Roads of Civilization). Paju, Akanet.

Kim, Yung-Myung. 2016. '한국 민족주의의 쟁점: 개념과 과제 (The Concepts and Tasks Concerning Korean Nationalism).' 한국정치외교사논총 (*Journal of Korean Political and Diplomatic History*) 38 (1): 217–247.

Kookmin Ilbo. 2015. '통일 논의 가능하다면 남북 정상회담도 가능, 홍용표, 지뢰도발로 北대화제의 시간 걸릴듯 (If the North and South Are Willing to Discuss Reunification, the Inter-Korea Summit Should Be Possible as Well; Minister Hong Yong-Pyo Says, the North's Minecraft Provocation to Make Their Response Slow to the South's Request for a Dialogue).' 16 August, http://news.kmib.co.kr/article/view.asp?arcid=0009755532&code=61111111&sid1=i, accessed 23 Apri 2021.

Kookmin Ilbo. 2019a. '명동에 "노 재팬" 깃발 걸겠다는 중구… 시민들 "오버 말라" 질타 (Citizens Accuse the Local Government Wishing to Display 'No Japan' Banners).' 6 August, http://news.kmib.co.kr/article/view.asp?arcid=0013573865, accessed 28 January 2021.

Kookmin Ilbo. 2019b. '여행업계, 與에 쓴 소리 "한일 민간교류 막지 말라"' (The Tourism Industry and the Voice: "Do not Block Private Exchanges between Korea and Japan), 7 August, http://news.kmib.co.kr/article/view.asp?arcid=0013581056&code=61111511&sid1=i, accessed 29 January 2021.

Kwangju Ilbo. 2019. '지도부, 올림픽 보이콧·여행 금지 등 반일 정서 과열 제동 (Leaders Rightly Oppose Boycotting the Olympic and Trip to Japan).' 9 August, http://www.kwangju.co.kr/print.php?aid=1565293800673541004, accessed 1 February 2021.

Kyeongin Ilbo. 2013. '다문화를 말하다 (Talking about Multiculturalism).' 4 September, http://www.kyeongin.com/main/view.php?key=765444, accessed 26 May 2021.

Kyunghyang Sinmun. 2019. '[인터뷰]시라이시 다카시 희망연대 대표 "아베 폭주 막지 못해 죄송…한국 민주주의 배워야" (Shiraishi Dakashi of Hope Solidarity from Japan: Sorry for Not Being Able to Stop Abe's Provocation & We Should Learn from Korean Democracy).' 8 August, http://news.khan.co.kr/kh_news/khan_art_view.html?art_id=201908081657001, accessed 2 February 2021.

Kyungnam Domin Ilbo. 2019. '자매도시 어찌할꼬 고민에 빠진 지자체 (Local Governments under a Torment Regarding their Sister Cities).' 26 July, https://www.idomin.com/news/articleView.html?idxno=703742, accessed 27 January 2021.

Kyungsang Ilbo. 2019. '울산지역 일본 불매운동 확산…동구에, NO 아베 거리 (Spread of Boycotting Japan in Ulsan… No Abe Street in the Eastern District).' 1 June. http://ksilbo.co.kr/news/articleView.html?idxno=710195, accessed 26 January 2021.

Maeil Kyungje. 2013. '2030 vs 5060 인식 비교해보니 (People in their 20s and 30s vs. 50s and 60s: A Comparison of Their Perception of Reunification).' 7 January, https://www.mk.co.kr/news/economy/view/2013/01/12613/, accessed 29 April 2021.

MBC. 2014. '한국 20대, 통일이 필요하다는 인식 약해져 (Koreans in 20s Now Perceive of the Less Need for Reunification).' 9 May, https://imnews.imbc.com/news/2014/world/article/3459983_31662.html, accessed 28 April 2021.

Money Today. 2019a. '노(NO) 아베 거리에, "일본인 요금 815만원" 현수막도… ($8,500, an Admission Charge for Japanese—A Banner in the Street of No Abe).' 2 August, https://news.mt.co.kr/mtview.php?no=2019080213454024529&MRH_P, accessed 27 January 2021.

Money Today. 2019b. '[日, 경제도발]日 언론, 한 달새 35건 한일교류 중단 (Japanese News: 35 Korea-Japan Exchanges Halted in a Month).' 2 August. https://news.mt.co.kr/hotview.php?no=2019080215423240164&type=1&sec=O&hid=201908021731472936&hcnt=69&vgb=hot, accessed 27 January 2021.

Money Today. 2019c. '명동 한복판에 "노 재팬" 깃발…"너무 나갔다" vs "시의 적절" ("No Japan" Banners in the Centre of Myongdong: "Gone Too Far" vs. "Appropriate").' 6 August, https://news.mt.co.kr/mtview.php?no=2019080609124858931, accessed 28 January 2021.

Money Today. 2019d. '日 관광객 배척? 이런 때 일수록 더 환영해야 (Really the Time to Welcome the Japanese Tourists Rather than Unwelcoming them).' 7 August, https://news.mt.co.kr/mtview.php?no=2019080715370261134&type=2&sec=society&pDepth2=Stotal&MSC_T, accessed 29 January 2021.

Muller, Jerry. 2008. 'Us and Them: The Enduring Power of Ethnic Nationalism.' *Foreign Affairs* 87: 9–14.

Munhwa Ilbo. 2019. '日 관광객마저 내쫓는 지자체 (Mad Local Governments Driving away Japanese Tourists).' 9 August, http://www.munhwa.com/news/view.html?no=2019080901071303025001, accessed 1 February 2021.

Nelson, Sarah M. 1993. *The Archaeology of Korea*. Cambridge World Archaeology. Cambridge and New York: Cambridge University Press.

Pak, Noja. 2002. '한국적 근대만들기 -1, 우리사회에 인종주의는 어떻게 정착되었는가? (Achieving Korean Modernisation I, the Settlement of Racism in Korean Society).' 인문과 사상 *(People and Thoughts)* 45 (1): 158–172.

Segye Ilbo. 2019a. '충남도, 중국 지린성과 자매결연 체결 (ChoongcheongNamdo, Signing a Sister Relationship with Jilin Sheng, China).' 22 August, http://www.segye.com/newsView/20190821513790?OutUrl=google, accessed 27 January 2021.

Segye Ilbo. 2019b. '與, 反日 수위 조절… 野, 외교적 해결 촉구 (Leading Party Hopes the Control of the Level of Protesting Japan…Opposition Party Wants a Diplomatic Solution).' 8 August, http://m.segye.com/view/20190808511760, accessed 2 February 2019.

Segye Ilbo. 2019c. '한일 경제대립 속 일본 국민들은 "좋아요_한국" (Many Japanese tweet "Like_Korea" amidst Korea-Japan Economic Conflict), 10 August, http://www.segye.com/newsView/20190809506048, accessed 2 February 2019.

Seoul Kyungje. 2013. '한국도 다문화갈등 전초단계 진입 (Korea Entering an Early Stage of Potential Riots).' 25 June, https://cjdthdrhtps.tistory.com/entry/한국도-다문화-갈등-전초-단계-진입, accessed 25 June 2013.

Seoul Kyungje. 2014. '통일세 연 10만원 이하가 적당 (Reunification Tax, about $100 is the Right Amount).' 4 September, https://www.sedaily.com/NewsView/1HSFQKU1TZ, accessed 22 April 2021.

Seoul Kyungje. 2019. '노 재팬 대신 노 아베, 與, 反日공세 수위조절 (No Abe Instead of No Japan, the Leading Party Adjusts the Wording).' 8 August, https://www.sedaily.com/NewsVIew/1VMW2YLFMH, accessed 28 January 2021.

Seoul Sinmun. 2018. '통일 인식 달라져… 30~50대 더 적극 (Perception of Reunification Is Changing… People in 30s to 50s Are More Interested than Others).' 10 May, http://www.seoul.co.kr/news/newsView.php?id=20180510005002, accessed 23 April 2022.

Yi, Hui-Geun. 2008. 우리안의 그들: 섞임과 넘나듦 그 공존의 민족사 *(Those Who Live with Us: Ethnic History of Biological Mixing, Crossing Back and Forth and Symbiosis)*. Seoul: Neomeo Books.

Younhap News. 2019. '한일관계 악화에…강릉 컬링친선전서 일본 제외 (Korea-Japan Relationship Deteriorates…Gangreung Friendly Curling Games to Exclude Japan).' 5 August, https://www.yna.co.kr/view/AKR20190805128100007, accessed 28 January 2021.

22
THE BIRTH AND TRANSFORMATION OF JAPANESE-KOREAN NATIONALISM

Masaki Tosa

Introduction

Nationalism pushes the human mind to extremes—either total denial or narcissistic assertion. It is extremely difficult to assess its significance within a moderate framework, and nationalism in East Asia is no exception. The combination of the colonial rule of Japan and the postcolonial authoritarian regimes of the new Asian states elevates this problem in the region. For example, Korean nationalism is born out of complex interactions with Japanese nationalism. Thus, criticising one side usually contributes to glorifying the other. There is no safe terrain to objectively analyse one country's nationalism by detaching it from the other. This study attempts to find an alternative path based on a relational viewpoint and deal with both these nationalisms as a unit, hereby referred to as the 'Japanese-Korean nationalism'. This is the first aim of this chapter.[1]

Second, this chapter will rely on the 'nationalism trilogy' of Liah Greenfeld for the theoretical framework in order to enrich the interpretation of Japanese-Korean nationalism. It is challenging to understand East Asian nationalisms in Greenfeld's framework, but I believe that it is theoretically worthwhile. My attempt resonates with some previous works in postcolonial historiography, particularly the perspective of 'colonial modernity' (Shin & Robinson 1999; Miyajima et al. 2004), and will contribute to a theoretical advancing.

Nationalism trilogy

One of the distinctive features of Greenfeld's perspective comes from reconsidering the relationship between modernity and nationalism. Major theorists of nationalism argue that the birth of nationalism is subordinate to the context of modernity. The focus of analysis ranges from print capitalism (Anderson 1983), and industrialisation (Gellner 1983), to world capitalism (Giddens 1995). They share the same conjecture that modern conditions provide the seedbed for nationalism, that is, no modernity, no nationalism. Nationalism is a recent creation in human history, a product of specific historical conditions that emerged in nineteenth-century Western Europe. Greenfeld accepts the special relation between modernity and nationalism, but her causality points to the other way round—no nationalism, no modernity. She particularly pays attention to sixteenth-century England to explore this historical evidence.

According to Greenfeld, the semantic transformation of a 'nation' showed an irregular pattern in history, and the last one that took place in the early sixteenth century was the most crucial because after that, a nation came to signify 'a unique sovereign people', which is consistent with today's definition. This semantic transformation legitimised social mobility, enabled people to develop with effort and education, and radically changed the image of social reality. The birth of the nation preceded the birth of capitalism, industrialisation, and democracy. Thus, Greenfeld's theoretical focus moves from defining 'nationalism by its modernity' to 'modernity defined by nationalism' (Greenfeld 1992: 18).

She extends her analysis based on the England's history with France, Russia, Germany, and the Unites States. Three general elements are particularly highlighted from her comparative study of nation as the essential idea that constitutes nationalism:

1 equality (and liberty)
2 self-definition (identity)
3 secularism

Equality, or more accurately, secular equality, is most crucial for the nation. Many religious doctrines include the idea of equality given in 'the other world' like heaven. Secular equality was a new idea in human history. The nation, once created on the idea of secular equality, provided a strong foundation for collective development. Greenfeld's second volume deals with the relationship between nationalism and modern economic development (Greenfeld 2001), while her third volume seeks another trajectory of nationalism—the spread of madness in society (Greenfeld 2013).

Greenfeld's 'nationalism trilogy' is an extensive endeavour to explore nationalism with massive discursive evidence from multiple perspectives. This chapter is a modest attempt to test the applicability of her thesis to East Asia.

In the late nineteenth century, the modern Western civilisation arrived in East Asia with several 'gifts', such as science, technology, legal system, and capitalism. However, before people could enjoy the fruits of modernisation, they needed to quickly protect themselves to fight against Western imperialism with nationalism. In East Asia too, it is more convincing to place nationalism before modernity. This chapter will focus on the major features of the history of Japanese-Korean nationalism to argue that Greenfeld's thesis is helpful for deeper understanding.

Origin of nationalism

The term 'nation' is translated into Japanese as kokumin or minzoku, and into Korean as kungmin or minjok. The existence of two words testifies to the difficulty of interpreting this new Western idea. Many modern Western concepts were translated into Japanese using Chinese characters, which then spread to China and Korea. The concept of nation followed the same trajectory.

Andre Schmid specifies how the interpretation of nation began in East Asia. When Kato Hiroyuki, a legal scholar and politician, translated Johann Kasper Bluntschli's *The Theory of the State* (*Allgemeines Staatsrecht*) into Japanese and published it in 1872, he 'rendered Bluntschli's threefold distinction of "staat, volk, and nation" with the character combinations of "kokka, kokumin, and minzoku"' (Schmid 2002: 315). This interpretation was passed on to China and Korea. The correspondence of volk and nation contradicts today's usage, but the idea of nationalism was still in flux in Germany at the time, as well as in East Asia.

The character combination 民族 literally means a 'people group'. It is pronounced minzoku in Japanese, minzu in Chinese, and minjok in Korean. Although this word has its roots in Chinese classic texts, its meaning experienced radical transformation in East Asia inspired by the encounter with the West. The degree of change was the most radical in Korea.

At the turn of the twentieth century, when Korea was agonising over identity, 'pan-Asianism was more salient than nationalism as an ideology of Korean independence and security' (Shin 2006: 27). Minjok was equivalent to race (injong) in this context, for instance, the phrase 'eastern race' (tongbang mijok) versus 'white race' (paegin minjok). Minjok was used in a leading newspaper as 'a racial unit transcending Korea to incorporate all the peoples of East Asia' (Schmid 2002: 173). Many intellectuals sought the pan-Asian solidarity based on the concept of minjok to fight against Western imperialism. Such perspective collapsed after 1905, when Korea was virtually colonised by Japan based on the Japanese Protectorate Treaty. The loss of the independent state challenged Korean intellectuals to seek a unique identity, a spiritual one, to release Korea from imperial powers, such as the West, Japan, Russia, and China. The idea of minjok was introduced to meet this demand; the scope of minjok was limited to people within the Korean Peninsula. The spiritual transcendence of ethnic identity was brought to the fore.

Shin Chaeho (1880–1936) was a representative intellectual who sought such spiritual exploration. He was born in a ruling family (yangban), and had received classical education at the most renowned institution, Seonggyungwan in Seoul. However, he tried to acquire knowledge and fashion of the new age. As an editor of two Korean newspapers, he repeatedly expressed his opinion on minjok to introduce this new idea to the Korean audience, and had a great influence on the trajectory of Korean nationalism.

For Shin, minjok was indivisible from history, particularly archaic history being the origin of minjok. History was regarded as a process of struggle between 'us' and 'them'. The state was an extension of the family; an organic body integrated by the ethnic spirit. But minjok was a more transcendental entity than the state. He believed that even if the state as a form collapsed, minjok could survive as long as the state as a spiritual entity was sound.

In 1910, just before Japan annexed Korea, Shin left his country and migrated to Vladivostok, Shanghai, and then lived in Beijing in exile. He engaged in the independence movement and undertook a philological investigation of the archaic history of Korean minjok. He wrote many articles to explore ethnic glory in ancient Manchuria and Balhae as the uncontaminated origin of Korean minjok. His romantic discourse encouraged activists of the independence movement. In the monumental statement, 'Declaration of Korean Revolution' (1923), he addressed the fellows as follows:

> Minjung (people) are the foundation of our revolution. Violence is the only weapon of our revolution. We must go to people, shake hands with them, and defeat the rule of burglar Japan with invincible violence, assassination, destruction, and riots. We must reform the Japanese imperial system that is insensitive towards our life. We must construct an ideal Korea where humankind does not suppress humankind, and society does not exploit society.
>
> *(Kim 2011: 163)*

Minjung, which was equivalent to minjok in this context, translated as the entity of nation. The idea of nation showed an extreme form of development in the colonial context. It meant equal sovereign people, but at the same time, it was a tight bond essentialised by ethnicity, and a tool mobilised for revolution. This left Shin Chaeho in dilemma. He felt disappointed with actual activism and became inclined towards anarchism. Minjok, stripped of equality and liberty, came close to an iron collective identity with uplifted self-respect. His eccentricity was often observed by his fellows and his depression peaked during his exile. Later in his life, he lost his rationalist stance and even applauded a magical curse as the only weapon of the weak (Cho 2007: 46–48).

Here it is worth mentioning another prominent individual, Fukuzawa Yukichi (1835–1901), who engaged in the birth of nationalism in Japan at the threshold of the new age, and paved a different path of nationalism in contrast to Shin Chaeho.

Fukuzawa was born into a low-ranking samurai family, and became a leading journalist and advocate of new ideas, including nationalism. One of his early writings, *Gakumon no Susume (An Encouragement of Learning)*, published between 1872 and 1876, became a national bestseller and contributed to spreading the idea of the nation to a wide audience. The nation was translated as kokumin. Jinmin (people) was an equivalent term that was used more often. There was no mention of minzoku in those texts.[2] His understanding of the nation was entirely rationalist and secular. He stressed the equality of all in the nation, and understood it as a basis for fair competition, not as a guaranteed result. That is why he encouraged people to learn. He believed that anyone who endeavoured to learn and acquire the necessary knowledge was meant to climb up the social ladder. He thought that national strength and independence could be accomplished through personal strength and independence; as a person-to-person relation was equal, a nation-to-nation relation should also be equal. This last ideal of his experienced a brief shift as he engaged with Korea more deeply.

Although Fukuzawa first ignored Korea as an underdeveloped country, he later felt sympathetic towards the confusion of the neighbour and tried to support some Korean reformist intellectuals. For example, Kim Ok-gyun (1851–1894), a leading activist and politician, visited Japan, met Fukuzawa, and acquired new knowledge at Fukuzawa's private school to reform Korea. Kim attempted a coup, which came to be known as the Gapsin coup, with the help of the Japanese government in 1884, but failed because of Chinese interference; in 1894 he was eventually killed by a Korean assassin in Shanghai. The failure of the Gapsin coup and the assassination of Kim became a significant factor that led to the First Sino-Japanese War. Fukuzawa restored his disregard for Korea, and gave up his idea to help the neighbouring countries.

The contrast between Shin Chaeho and Fukuzawa Yukichi symbolises a crossroad of the understanding of nationalism in the two countries. Korea developed ethic nationalism after abandoning pan-Asian solidarity. Shin represented this tendency; after him, ethnicity became an extreme weapon to divide the enemy from 'us'. Fukuzawa sought a rationalist and self-sufficient model of nationalism. But this path led to another extremity. He tried to justify the war against China as a battle between civilisation and savagery. This shift from isolationism to expansionism became increasingly drastic after Fukuzawa's death. Japan continued to expand its territory as a new imperial power. Since Japan included various people in its territory, it could not build on a singular idea of nationalism based on ethnicity. Thus, in contrast to Korea's ethnic nationalism, it is possible to characterise Japanese nationalism as state nationalism. This contrast, or polarisation, can be observed till today.

During the colonial period (1910–1945), Korean people belonged to the nation of imperial Japan. They were the same koumin/shinmin (imperial people), or kokumin, along with many different ethnic people in the territory of Japan. Many Koreans tried to assimilate into Japanese in order to participate in the modernisation project. Education and entrepreneurship provided a chance of social mobility. However, Korean people were subjected to poor treatment and discrimination. The colonies were beyond the jurisdiction of the constitution of the Empire of Japan. Korea was supposed to be a part of Japan, and a different place at the same time. This duality contributed to breeding the extreme character of Korean nationalism.

The distinction between Japanese and Korean nationalism was a practical problem for the colonial government. Korean people were regarded as Japanese when contrasted with Westerners, but as non-Japanese when contrasted with the Japanese living in mainland Japan. This dual treatment came from circumstantial and expedient policies (Oguma 1998: 155). As Japan needed to undertake a war economy in the 1940s, it had to prioritise the state over ethnicity in order to mobilise different people in the territory. The colonial government in Korea applauded the idea of inter-ethnic harmony based on eastern spirit, which it believed, should supersede the Western ethnic nationalism. According to this ideology, the state should transcend ethnicity; the state should destruct and create ethnicity according to its will (Oguma 1998: 425). Therefore, Japanese nationalism was also distorted through the historical process.

Postcolonial nationalism

The colonial situation provided a peculiar condition for the birth and development of Japanese-Korean nationalism. They were like twins, who negated each other and tended to polarise each other. This legacy still looms large. Both Japan and Korea endeavoured to negate the colonial history to create postcolonial nationalism. However, they showed different modes of negation.

Japan tried to erase the history of colonialism through collective amnesia, either feigned or unintentional. During the colonial period, both colonisers and colonised constituted the same nation, despite some discriminatory treatment. However, those colonised, including Korean and Taiwanese, experienced disparate discriminatory treatment in post-war Japan. They suddenly became 'ethnic minorities'. The Treaty of San Francisco signed in 1951 endorsed a new position of Japan in the world. The Japanese government invalidated the Japanese nationality of the Koreans and Taiwanese living in Japan, and gave them a Special Permanent Resident status instead. The political turmoil in East Asia was well-suited for Japan's expediency. Korea was divided into two countries, and both North and South Korea showed expedient behaviour. They sometimes tried to subsume as many people as possible, both at home and overseas, for national propaganda, but tended to neglect fellow people living overseas.

From the Korean standpoint of ethnic nationalism that asserted the permanence of ethnicity, the colonial history should never have existed. As compared to Japan's expedient amnesia of its own colonial past, it took more effort for postcolonial Korea to accomplish the erasure of history. Denial in a psychological sense is an appropriate term to describe this process (Pells 1998). It can be defined as a subconscious attempt to minimise or annihilate Japan in order to reinvent the past and the real. There is no division between North and South Korea in this respect. The case of South Korea shall be focused upon from here.[3]

Postcolonial South Korea could not develop without the support of Japan in many sectors of its society. Even if Japan could forget about Korea, Korea could not forget Japan. So, anti-Japanism played an important role to deny the considerable influence of Japan. It functioned not only to exaggerate the importance of the resistance movement during the colonial period, but also to minimise the role of Japan that it played in the postcolonial development.

Japan normalised diplomatic relations with South Korea in 1965. Thereafter, Japanese capital and technology contributed to the rapid economic development in Korea, but this was a delicate issue and thus kept secret. The colonial legacy of Japanese legislation, education, administration, business, and culture survived and was disguised to be non-Japanese. Such symbolic manipulation was most evident in the field of mass culture. Plagiarism of Japanese culture was rampant in any genre such as music, drama, movies, anime, and novels. It was a convention that every weekend, television producers visited Busan, where Japanese television broadcast could be received; Korean producers watched and imitated these Japanese programmes to make their own. South Korea did not defend itself from Japanese influence; instead, plagiarism and piracy used to be rampant in Korean culture.

Figures 22.1 and 22.2 show a typical example of cultural piracy. Figure 22.1 came from the first pages of the famous Japanese manga, *Garasu no kamen* (*Glass Mask*), by Suzue Miuchi. Figure 22.2 shows its pirated version, but it is not a simple replica. The setting, Yokohama, is changed to Busan, and the Japanese kimono is transformed into an unidentified archaic costume. The original first volume was published in Japan in 1976. The pirated version was published in South Korea in 1993, by the author who impersonated a Korean (Tosa 2004: 135–138).

This was a typical way of consuming Japanese cultural commodities in Korea. Japanese pop culture was officially banned in South Korea up until 1998. But many manga and anime texts were imported and consumed after erasing 'waesaek' (Japanese elements). Many Japanese television programmes were plagiarised and broadcast as Korean ones. Japanese pop songs were recompiled, dubbed in cassette, and sold on the Korean streets. So, the ban did not protect from exposure to Japanese culture, but pushed it underground, and encouraged piracy. As the infringement of copyright was criticised by the United States (US) and the General Agreement on Tariffs and Trade (GATT), the Korean government needed to change this inconsistent policy and halt its piracy culture.

Japan, on the contrary, could do without Korea. Many Japanese were not at all interested in their neighbour. The colonial past represented a dark phase they wished to forget, and the current military regime of South Korea also looked like a darkness to turn away from. Furthermore, it is true that some people contributed to the development of postcolonial Korea due to a remorse for the past. Even they could not sense that the same nation had been divided. They simply showed sympathy for the poor neighbour. Such an imbalanced relationship continued up until the late 1980s.

Along with negating the past, the belief in the 'homogeneous nation state' or 'state of unitary nation' ('tan'itsu minzoku kokka' in Japanese, and 'tanil minjok kukka' in Korean) supported the creation of a new form of nationalism in both countries. This ideology became an official version of postcolonial nationalism. Since imperial Japan was a multiethnic state, the 'homogeneous nation state' was an obvious fiction. Japan still included many former colonial subjects from Korea and Taiwan, not to mention other minorities like Okinawan and Ainu. Korea was put in a better position to claim the ideology of ethnic unity, because the Allied Powers forced most Japanese, over six million, to repatriate from its colonies, including one million from Korea (Watt 2009). But the influence of Japan in postcolonial

Figure 22.1 Garasu no kamen (*Glass Mask*) by Suzue Miuchi

Figure 22.2 Pirated version of *Garasu no kamen*

South Korea was far greater than the other way around. Consequently, the new nationalism based on ethnic unity worked excellently both in Japan and in South Korea.

It was observed in both countries that the government-led plan involved and mobilised people to achieve rapid economic development. A vast crowd of people migrated from the countryside to cities to provide necessary labour, and their next generations climbed up the social ladder to form a large middle class. They became the substance of a nation, and this new nationalism, with the legacy of transcendental ethnic unity, promoted the real development of the state and society. The 'economic miracle' occurred in Japan from the mid-1950s to the mid-1970s, and in South Korea from the late 1960s to the 1980s. This parallel phenomenon is a good testimony to prove the thesis that nationalism provides the conditions for capitalism.

Max Weber claimed that modern capitalism could grow only in a special cultural environment epitomised by the Protestant ethic. Greenfeld acknowledged this thesis, but for her, it is nationalism that prepares necessary conditions of capitalism. Nationalism promotes social mobility and competition by equal people, and thus reifies the obsession with sustained growth (Greenfeld 2001). The economic competition was a substitute of war for both countries. For Japan, it was a war against the West after it failed in the Second World War. For Korea, it was a war against its coloniser, Japan, and the West. But ironically, it was the West, particularly the US, that helped the economic development of both countries. The US played an ambivalent role, as an adversary and as a benefactor, to sustain the nationalism of both the countries. Japan played a similar role with respect to South Korea. The nationalism of 'homogeneous nation state' contributed to the great success in both countries during the Cold War period, but with many side effects. The negation of history created a distortion of perception, one of whose aftereffects is a continuous dispute surrounding the awareness of colonial history.

Past and future of ethnonationalism

There have been two radical watersheds for Japanese nationalism. The first turning point can be identified between the 1870s and 1880s when the idea of nation spread, and the modern political and economic system started to take off. The scope of the nation was extended following the imperialist expansion and by absorbing different people. In this framework, Japan prioritised state nationalism over ethnic differences, and suppressed ethnic nationalism in its colonies. After 1945, particularly in the 1950s, Japan experienced the second transformation of nationalism. It abandoned imperial ideology and reinstated ethnic nationalism to seek economic development.

Korea experienced similar historical transformations with significant differences. The gap between the premodern worldview and the inception of modern nationalism was far greater. Korea developed a unique ethnocentrism during the 500-year rule of the Chosun dynasty (1392–1897). Although it abided by the Sinocentric worldview, its basic policy was seclusion. It had diplomatic relations only with China and Japan. But it was confined mostly to ritual dimension, particularly with Japan. While the Korean government dispatched a diplomatic mission 12 times during the Edo period (1603–1868), and their parade was welcomed as a great pageant by the government and local people; the Japanese envoy, however, was not welcomed and was stopped at Busan. This was partly the aftermath of the Japanese invasions (1592–1598), but the more essential motivation was to protect their ethnocentric idea of a Confucian state, which provided a seedbed to accept and develop the modern idea of ethnonationalism. Premodern Korea neglected the economic advance of Japan, and believed in its moral superiority over Japanese based on the Confucian ideology. As a result, the impact of colonisation was even more shocking.

Japan also developed its own ethnocentric worldview based on faith in the 'divine land' in the premodern context. These proto nationalisms characterised the articulation of modern nationalism in struggling with the radical world change (Smith 1995), and through the interaction of two countries. Korean premodern worldview was overthrown by colonisation and transformed into a more complexly deformed ethnocentrism. This hedgehog-type nationalism was maintained even in the postcolonial regime. Thereafter, in my view, South Korea experienced the second turning point in the 1990s.[4]

It is possible to argue that South Korea did not fundamentally change its state system even after decolonisation. It continued to develop society in a top-down manner using the authoritarian system just like the colonial government. The significant difference lied in the actuality of nationalism. Imperial Japan tried to subsume colonial subjects as the same nation (koumin) to promote modernisation. But it could involve only a section of the people, and the reward was the birth of extremist ethnonationalism. Postcolonial South Korea was successful in mobilising the majority of people as a nation (kungmin). It could accomplish the state-led economic development, and the reward was the building of the equal nation that sustained social integration. However, even during this period, the anti-government movement did not wane, and it was in the 1990s that the dissidents took hold of the social mainstream.

This began in 1987 when the military government announced the agenda of democratisation to tame the intensified demonstrations. The government successfully hosted the 1988 Seoul Olympic Games to debut as a member of the global community. The junta ended in 1993. Those are the major events that marked the transition from the old regime to a new one. The government stopped to censor and control mass culture, and its policy was redirected to promoting the cultural industry. South Korea was once a society that just imitated Japanese and American culture, and eventually transformed itself into a creative society that continued to transnationally produce popular dramas and songs for the Asian audience. The authoritarian government-led society was transformed into a society to be improved at the grassroots level.

It is not a linear change of the total society, but a patchy process that has been observed in South Korea (Tosa 2004). The new wave was intermingled with old elements, and the hybrid process went back and forth in unpredictable ways. It was precisely in the 1990s when anti-Japanese nationalism showed its extreme expression in mass culture, along with the rapid advancement of globalisation. Novels and nonfiction books that abused and antagonised Japan sold as record bestsellers. Anti-Japanese dramas and films were welcomed enthusiastically. In hindsight, it can be interpreted as paired with the phenomenon that was observed a decade later in Japan. Anti-Korean books started to occupy shelves of bookstores. After Lee Myung-bak abruptly visited the disputed isle of Dokdo in 2012 as the first President of South Korea, hate speech became rampant on the streets in Tokyo and Osaka.

This is just one facet of the vicious cycle that has been reinforced through the interaction of both nationalisms. It looks as if the Japan-South Korean relationship has recently worsened through the never-ending dispute over colonial issues such as comfort women, and conscripted labour.

But such hysteresis obscures the real change that has taken place in both countries. The case of South Korea shall be focused upon as it has shown a more radical change since the 1990s.

I have mentioned the transition of political power from the junta to a more democratic regime, and the change of the cultural policy that marked the official lifting of the ban on

Japanese culture in 1998. The real reason for such regulation was concerned not only with the control of Japanese culture but also with the control of total domestic culture through censorship. The concern of the invasion of Japanese imperialist culture was a pretext to protect the interests of the domestic cultural industry that had poor competitive attraction under government control. However, lifting the ban did not lead to an assault of the Korean market by the Japanese cultural industry, but a sudden outflow of Korean culture to the overseas market. The record of the annual exports evidently shows that Korean movies and TV programmes had no overseas presence up to 1998, and suddenly boomed since then (Berg 2015). It is not a simple effect of the policy change, but of the complex transformation of total society. The implications of the Korean Wave, or Hallyu, have already been analysed by many scholars (Cho 2011; Lie 2012; Schulze 2013).

After the 2000s, South Korea showed another dimension of radical social change, that is, human migration. The degree of Korean diaspora has been an overt phenomenon since the late nineteenth century. The colonisation process accelerated the population outflow, but what characterises the Korean diaspora is that the outflow never ended after the decolonisation, or even now. Each time a poll is carried out by various nongovernment bodies, a large proportion, usually over 60 per cent, professes the will to migrate. The main reason used to be an economic one, but recently, this has changed to concern about the over competitive educational environment. According to the Ministry of Foreign Affairs of South Korea, there are about 7.5 million overseas Koreans as of 2019. Although this number includes naturalised Koreans based on ethnicity, it is surprising to know that the degree of Korean diaspora exceeds 10 per cent of the total population. Korean people have been one of the most mobile ethnic groups on the global scale.

The outflow of migration met the sudden inflow growth in the 2000s. In tandem with decolonisation, South Korea became one of the most homogenous countries in the world. All the Japanese left for the home country except for thousands of Japanese women married to Koreans; even the only minority group of Chinese decreased to 20,000 in the early 1990s due to discriminatory treatment. So, it really became a 'homogeneous nation state'. But the situation has completely changed since. As of 2018, the number of foreign residents exceeded 2.5 million—almost 5 per cent of the total population. The proportion is already higher than in Japan, and the pace of change is phenomenal.

The sudden inflow of migrants can be classified into three groups: migrant workers, migrant brides, and overseas Koreans. The main reasons for such growth are concerned with the structural dilemmas of Korean society. The rapid development that accompanied the spread of higher education and the demographic transition has marginalised the status of unskilled labour and peasants. Migrants were needed to satisfy the shortage of labour in the city, and the shortage of brides in the countryside. Most of them came from China and Southeast Asia to seek a better life.

This sudden transition from a homogenous society to a multicultural one caused a lot of conflict. The media covered many shameful incidents such as underpayment and abuse of migrant workers in the late 1990s. Many women from poor countries were arranged to marry peasants and experienced discrimination and unexpected hardship in the countryside. The intermarriage rate of the rural area increased to 40 per cent at its peak in 2008. However, the government has struggled to solve those issues resolutely. Many NGOs have played a significant role in improving the human rights situation.

The most difficult problem is derived from people of the same ethnicity, particularly Chosŏnjok (Koreans in China). South Korea normalised diplomatic relations with China in 1992 following the end of the Cold War. After that, many Koreans in northeast China started to migrate to South Korea to seek a better life. They could easily come to South Korea with an Overseas Korean Visa, and most of them engaged in business or unskilled labour. The number has presumably reached 800,000. They joyously visited their prosperous 'mother country', but their dream quickly turned into disappointment. Even though they supposedly shared the 'same blood' with people in South Korea, in actuality, they were treated as aliens, and even regarded as more alien than other foreigners.

Migrant workers are regarded as temporary residents. The government helps them work in a legitimate condition until they leave after several years. Migrant brides are expected to assimilate into Korean society. Although an intermarried family is called a 'multicultural family', the basic framework of policies is assimilation. Several programmes ranging from language learning to mental consultation are provided for them to integrate into the mainstream society. Since Chosŏnjok are regarded as the same ethnic people who speak Korean, they are left unattended beyond the scope of public aid for migrants. Consequently, disparity and discrimination spur antagonism, and they tend to form their own enclaves in the city.

For instance, Daerim-dong in Seoul became a Chinatown, not for tourists but for Chosŏnjok. The image of Daerim-dong and Chosŏnjok as dangerous villains has been represented in recent dramas and movies, such as *The Yellow Sea* (2010) and *The Outlaws* (2017). Chosŏnjok has become the most difficult 'ethnic minority', too wild to assimilate or integrate. Thus, the concept of nation or minjok is being challenged in a new context.

Nationalism and madness in East Asia

In this final section, the most difficult and controversial question shall be tackled—the relationship between nationalism and madness. Considering the vast scope of this problem, the argument should be confined to a preliminary extent.

Greenfeld defines madness as 'malformation of the mind', that is, 'quite independent of any disease of the brain' (Greenfeld 2013: 28). It is more deeply related to the concept of 'anomie' in Durkheim's sense. The secular concept of equality, unlike religious ideology, drives humans to endless competition, and promotes the prevalence of madness, or social anomie. Premodern society provided an individual with a secure identity based on a fixed status. Modern society makes man free and mentally fragile. But madness was not brought about by modernity or the progress of civilisation. Nationalism is the real culprit. Greenfeld examined extensive discourse and scientific evidence to prove her thesis in five Western countries. The US is ranked at the top, and she warns that the prevalence of madness may ultimately destroy Western civilisation. In contrast, she draws attention to 'the remarkably low rates of the very kind of mental disease that ravages the West in Asia' (ibid. 628). Some major events and indices can be referred to examine Greenfeld's thesis in the East Asian context. The focus is directed to the colonial period and the post 1990s based on my research (Tosa 2018).

Modern psychiatry was introduced to Japan in the 1880s and then to colonial Korea, spreading a new concept of psychosis. Although experts tried to prove that mental illness would prevail in society along with the progress of modernisation and civilisation, they could not find enough evidence. Kure Shūzō (1865–1932), founder of modern psychiatry in Japan, was surprised with the demographic result that the national ratio of psychosis turned out to be 0.075 per cent in 1915, far lower than the average in European countries of 0.2534 per cent. He presumed a part of the reason came from the unreliable statistical processing (Kure and Kashida 2012: 24). But this trend remained relatively unchanged until recently. The endeavour of the experts, however, had a different effect in combination with the police authority. The government modernisation project tried to exclude or reform any uncivilised elements and customs such as wearing a sword, nudity in public places, tattooing, mixed bathing, and nomadic lifestyle. Madness became a symbolic target of social control and exclusion. In particular, as many socialists were executed on the charge of an assassination plot against the Emperor in 1910, the general frame was established that those who defied the Imperial Family and the authorities were psychotic (Inoue 2008). Home detention was the most common treatment for psychotic patients. This social segregation became obligatory in 1908. Psychotic patients were regarded as 'disturbing elements' by the authorities despite the salvation endeavour by medical experts, and finally became the target of sterilisation in tandem with leprosy patients in 1940.

Such framing became more radicalised in colonial Korea. Shamanistic rituals performed to treat psychotic patients were banned as superstition. The media propagated that psychosis should be eradicated for ethnic prosperity (Lee 2013). The birth of Japanese modern psychiatry was greatly influenced by the Kraepelin school. The German medical tradition combined with militarism founded the modern psychiatry in Korea. There was a different genealogy in modern psychiatry in Japan, a more humanitarian one coming from the United Kingdom and the US, but it never arrived in its colonies (Chung et al. 2006). Madness arrived in Korea with forced and marginalised civilisation.

The modern concept of psychosis was used to control society with the police authority and without enough clinical evidence. The urban vogue was another example to examine this problem. Consumer culture started to bloom in the 1920s in Seoul, excluding the great majority of poor peasants in the countryside. Students, intellectuals, bureaucrats, teachers, merchants, and workers appeared as new residents in the city. Japanese houses and stores, Western buildings, hotels, and department stores were constructed along with symbols of the Imperial power, such as the Japanese General Government Building and the head office of the Bank of Korea. The cultural landscape of Tokyo was swiftly transferred to Seoul. The fashion of the Dada movement that started in Switzerland in 1916 was one such example.

The Dada movement that rejected the logic of modern capitalist society and adored irrationality instead, was welcomed by contemporaneous artists and intellectuals in Japan. Two famous artists of the Japanese Dada, Jun Tsuji, who had been hospitalised for temporary psychosis several times and Shinkichi Takahashi, who wrote his own experience of mental disorder in his novel, visited Seoul in 1924 via a Korean Dadaist (Yoshikawa 2014). This vogue disappeared soon, but the criticism of modernity through irrationality influenced many intellectuals at that time.

Colonial intellectuals who read newspapers and magazines not only became the agents of nationalism, but also the adherents of perverse desire. Those who had higher education degrees without enough job opportunities would easily follow such a path. Kim Jinsong attempted a discursive research of major magazines in the 1930s to demonstrate the changing mass consciousness in colonial Korea. He indicates the perverse relationship between knowledge and the subject with the following passage from a magazine article published in 1936:

> Modern pleasure is a kind of masochism, which seeks rapture in pain. So, what modern people demand from a newspaper is not based on knowledge. Even if it provides new knowledge, it is not regarded as a good newspaper unless it gives you a cruel anxiety that acutely thrusts into the nerve.
>
> *(Kim 1999: 131)*

The combination between the ethnic consciousness and the fluid urban lifestyle urged colonial intellectuals to develop a kind of mental disorder. 'Intellectuals would usually suffer from "constipation, pollakiuria, fatigue, weariness, and headache". The morbid and timid personality was the very type of intellectuals. They were quite aware that their condition came exactly from their knowledge' (Kim 1999: 132).

Their mental anxiety was a testimony of a chosen few. But the sick mind that worried about the gap between heightened consciousness and their unrewarded circumstances was destined to become increasingly common, as society continued to develop.

Madness became a major metaphor of a new lifestyle among intellectuals when the consumerist fashion started to rise in metropolitan Tokyo, subsequently in colonial Seoul. In society, however, the prevalence of madness was not evidently observed in Japan or in colonial Korea. The same tendency continued even after the war and decolonisation. According to an exceptional epidemiological survey conducted in a province of South Korea in 1960s, the population ratio of schizophrenia was 0.226 per cent and manic depression 0.208 per cent. The low proportions were interpreted as the effect of the traditional family system (Lee 1972).

The colonial legacy of home detention succeeded in both countries by a long period of hospitalisation as a treatment and social exclusion of psychotic patients. The number of beds in Japan occupied by psychotic patients ranked the top in the world according to the 2001 statistics of the World Health Organisation. South Korea has had the same tendency. However, as this situation began to change, the gap between 'reality' and epidemiology seemed to surface. This chapter will refer to some indices that suggest a more serious mental reality in both countries.

First, various kinds of addictions are alarming in both countries. For instance, the ratios of gambling addiction are much higher than the global average (about 1 per cent). In Japan, the first national survey, conducted by the Ministry of Health, Labour and Welfare in 2007, showed the ratio at 5.6 per cent (Tanaka 2015). In South Korea, a similar survey in 2014 showed the ratio at 5.4 per cent (Fujiwara 2016). Alcoholism indicates a similar statistic (Ishii 2009).

More seriously, the high suicide rates are alarming in both countries; they have been ranked among the top ten globally since the 1990s. Such high suicide rates can be characterised as a symptom of 'suicide anomique' in Durkheim's sense. The social tension and conflict caused by the super competitive environment, long work hours, economic polarisation and low happiness indices have been argued as causes by many scholars. More symptoms can be added to the list that suggests the prevalence of madness in Japan and South Korea. It can be claimed that East Asia is not positioned as exceptional to examine the relationship between nationalism and madness.

One of the essential factors that has hindered seeking this problem is the absence of universalised objective criteria. The epidemiological surveys at the national level are in progress to develop more 'realistic' argument. In Japan, the World Mental Health Japan Survey was conducted between 2004 and 2006 based on the criteria of WMH. According to this result, lifetime prevalence of any mental disorder was 24.4 per cent, and past year prevalence of any mental disorder was 10.0 per cent. The latter proportion turned out to be lower than 26.2 per cent in the US, and higher than 7.0 per cent in China. The Japanese survey list, however, did not include gambling addiction, addictive smoking, and eating disorder (Kawakami 2006). South Korea conducts a national epidemiological survey every five years since 2001. According to the 2011 result, lifetime prevalence of any mental disorder was 27.6 per cent, and past year prevalence of any mental disorder was 16.0 per cent. Although the proportions are higher than Japan, the Korean survey included the questions eliminated from the Japanese survey, and added a unique question of internet addiction disorder (Cho 2011).

The scope of research should be extended as far as it includes major cases of 'malformation of the mind' in both countries, such as repeatedly flaring representations that reproach the other and applause oneself. Since they need detailed and deep cultural analysis for fair assessment, the search for universal criteria continues to be essential. But one may wonder if there is any such possibility of universal survey at all. Many cultural anthropologists will doubt about the universal criteria of madness beyond local differences. Medical scholars will ignore such cultural chatting apart from biological causality. As Arthur Kleinman claimed, we need 'cultural revolution' in psychiatry to overcome the dilemma between cultural analysis and biological reductionism (Kleinman 1991). Some scholars have tried to cope with such dichotomy based on the area study of Japan and South Korea (Kitanaka 2011; Nakamura 2013; Yoo 2016). A theoretical breakthrough may appear soon. So far, it is premature to conclude this problem.

But from many related works and all of my past research, it seems to be a reasonable interpretation to epitomise that Japan and South Korea have engaged in sibling rivalry, precisely because they share the same macroscopic process from the collapse of the traditional society to the birth of a nation in the premodern-colonial situation, to the collective mobilisation and economic growth, and finally to the prevalence of madness. The love-hate relationship is a root metaphor that represents this whole process. The situation may worsen in the future, unless the subjective projection of nationalism is objectified in a multidimensional perspective. Madness, or various forms of social anomie, can be a major syndrome in the future in both countries. So far, madness was delayed in East Asia, along with the delayed realisation of the democratic concept of equality and liberty.

Notes

1 I have been working on the anthropological study of Korean society and culture for over 30 years. My research includes various topics such as pop culture, religion, sports, and food, theoretically focusing on the interaction between nationalism and globalisation. Being conscious of my standpoint as a Japanese scholar, the commitment to the relational perspective seems inevitable. This chapter is a condensed argument of my past works mostly written in Japanese.
2 See https://www.aozora.gr.jp/cards/000296/files/47061_29420.html
3 It is doubtful that postcolonial North Korea has established a nation based on secular equality. In that sense, nationalism is not a pertinent perspective to analyse the interaction between Japan and North Korea.
4 South Korean people do not publicly recognise that post-war Japan has radically changed from a militaristic regime to a democratic country. On the contrary, most Japanese are not aware that South Korea experienced a radical change in the 1990s. This perception gap provides another germ of misunderstanding and conflict.

References

English-language references

Anderson, B. 1983. *Imagined Communities: Reflections on the Origin and Spread of Nationalism*. London: Verso.
Berg, Su-Hyun 2015. "Creative Cluster Evolution: The Case of the Film and TV Industries in Seoul, South Korea." *European Planning* Studies 23 (10): 1993–2008.
Cho, Younghan 2011. "Desperately Seeking East Asia amidst the Popularity of South Korean Pop Culture in Asia." *Cultural Studies* 25 (3, May): 383–404.
Gellner E. 1983 *Nations and Nationalism*. Oxford: Blackwell Publishers

Giddens, A. 1995. "The Nation-State Nationalism and Capitalist Development". In *A Contemporary Critique of Historical Materialism. Vol. 1.* 2nd edition, 182–202. London: Macmillan.

Greenfeld L. 1992. *Nationalism: Five Roads to Modernity.* Cambridge: Harvard UP.

———. 2001. *The Spirit of Capitalism: Nationalism and Economic Growth.* Cambridge: Harvard UP.

———. 2013. *Mind, Modernity, Madness: The Impact of Culture on Human Experience.* Cambridge: Harvard UP.

Kitanaka, Junko 2011 *Depression in Japan: Psychiatric Cures for a Society in Distress.* Princeton: Princeton University Press.

Kleinman, A. 1991. *Rethinking Psychiatry: From Cultural Category to Personal Experience.* New York: Free Press.

Lie, John 2012. "What Is the K in K-pop?: South Korean Popular Music, the Culture Industry, and National Identity." *Korea Observer* 43 (3): 339–363.

Nakamura, Karen. 2013 *A Disability of the Soul.* Ithaca: Cornell University Press.

Pells, R. 1998 *Not Like Us: How Europeans Have Loved, Hated, And Transformed American Culture Since World War II.* New York: Basic Books.

Schmid, A. 2002. *Korea between Empires, 1895–1919.* New York: Columbia UP.

Schulze, Marion 2013. "Korea vs. K-Dramaland: The Culturalization of K-Dramas by International Fans" *Acta Koreana* 16 (2): 367–397.

Shin, Gi-Wook. 2006. *Ethnic Nationalism in Korea: Genealogy, Politics, and Legacy.* Stanford: Stanford UP.

Shin, G.-W., & Robinson, M. eds. 1999. *Colonial Modernity in Korea.* Harvard University Asia Center.

Smith, A. D. 1995. *Nations and Nationalism in a Global Era.* Cambridge: Polity

Watt, L. 2009. *When Empire Comes Home: Repatriation and Reintegration in Postwar Japan.* Cambridge: Polity Harvard University Asia Center.

Yoo, T. J. 2016. *It's Madness: The Politics of Mental Health in Colonial Korea.* Oakland: University of California Press.

Korean- and Japanese-language references

Cho, M. 조맹제 2011. 보건복지부 학술연구 용역사업 보고서2011년도 정신질환실태 역학조사 (Epidemiological Survey of Mental Disorders among Korean Adults) 서울대학교 의과대학.

Cho, Kwanja 趙寬子2007. 植民地朝鮮/帝国日本の文化連環: ナショナリズムと反復する植民地主義 (The Cultural Linkage between Colonial Korea and Japanese Empire.) 有志舎.

Chung, W., N. Lee, and B. Rhi. 鄭元龍, 李那美, 李符永 2006. 서양정신의학의 도입과 그 변천과정 (2)–일제 강점기의 정신의학 교육(1910–1945) (The Introduction of Western Psychiatry into Korea (II) Psychiatric Education in Korea during the Forced Japanese Annexation of Korea (1910–1945)) 醫史學 15 (2): 157–187.

Fujiwara, N. 藤原夏人 2016. 韓国のギャンブル依存症対策 (Measures against Gambling Addiction in South Korea) 外国の立法 No.269、国立国会図書館.

Inoue S. 井上章一 2008. 狂気と王権 (Madness and the Divine Right) 講談社.

Ishii, H. ed. 石井裕正 2009. わが国における飲酒の実態ならびに飲酒に関連する生活習慣病, 公衆衛生上の諸問題とその対策に関する総合的研究 (Comprehensive Study on the Actuality of Drinking, its Lifestyle Diseases, Hygienic Problems, and its Measures in Japan) 厚生労働科学研究成果データベース.

Kawakami, N. 川上憲人 2006. こころの健康についての疫学調査に関する研究 総合研究報告書 (Study on Epidemiological Survey of Mental Health: Report of Comprehensive Study) (https://www.khj-h.com/wp/wp-content/uploads/2018/05/soukatuhoukoku19.pdf)

Kim, J. 김진송 1999 서울에 딴스홀을 허하라 현대성의 형성 (Petition for Dance Halls in Seoul: Formation of Modernity) 현실문화연구.

Kim, Samung 김삼웅 2011. 단재 신채호 평전 2판 (Biography of Shin Chaeho. 2nd edition) 시대의창.

Lee, B. 이방현 2013. 식민지 조선에서의 정신병자에 대한 근대적 접근 (Modern Approach to Treating Mental Patients in Colonial Chosun) 의사학22 (2): 529–577.

Lee, C. 李定均 1972. 韓国における精神障害—講演および質疑応答 (Mental Disorder in South Korea) 精神医学 13 (3): 83–93.

Miyajima, H. et al. eds. 宮嶋博史他編 2004. 植民地近代の視座——朝鮮と日本 (Perspective of Colonial Modernity: Korea and Japan) 岩波書店.

Oguma, E. 小熊英二 1998. ＜日本人＞の境界――沖縄・アイヌ・台湾・朝鮮　植民地支配から復帰運動まで (The Boundary of the Japanese) 新曜社.

Tosa, M. 土佐昌樹 2004. 変わる韓国、変わらない韓国――グローバル時代の民族誌に向けて (Changing Korea and Unchanged Korea) 洋泉社.

Tosa, M. 土佐昌樹2018. 日韓関係とナショナリズムの「起源」III――夢野久作と「狂気」の萌芽 (Japan-Korea Relationship and the 'Origin' of Nationalism III: Yumeno Kyūsaku and an Embryo of 'Madness') *AJ Journal* 13: 59–82.

Kure, S., and G. Kashida 呉秀三・樫田五郎 2012. 精神病者私宅監置の実況 (The Actuality of Home Confinement of Psychotics) 医学書院.

Tanaka, N. 田中紀子 2015 ギャンブル依存症 (Gambling Addiction) 角川書店.

Yoshikawa, N. 吉川凪 2014. 京城のダダ、東京のダダ――高漢容と仲間たち (Dada in Keijo, Dada in Tokyo: Go Hanyong and his Fellows) 平凡社.

PART III

Southeast Asia

Ethnic and religious diversity, local rivalries, and political resistance

Despite changing historical and social contexts, narratives and discourses about the nation have always played an important role in, and since, the formation of modern nation states. The various ideas, concepts, understandings, and interpretations of nationalism can be organized in several distinctive groups; these are described as ethnic, civic, liberal, expansionist, romantic, cultural, and economic, among others. In terms of the function and/or purpose of nationalism, there are, at least, three distinct broad groups: integral nationalism, reform nationalism, and risorgimento nationalism. Integral nationalism develops after a nation has achieved independence and has established a state. On several occasions, this process has been accompanied by radical and extreme ideas, right-wing ideology, and even aggressive-expansionist militarism. It prevailed in Imperial Japan in the first half of the twentieth century. Reform nationalism is more inward-looking and focuses on national salvation and self-strengthening. It tended to emerge 'in an existing state that proved inferior in certain economic, technical and military respects when confronted by Western powers' (Alter 1994, 23). Modern China is a prime example. Risorgimento nationalism can best be compared to a political project that seeks to unite fragmented nations. It 'upheld the principle of solidarity of the oppressed against the oppressors' and 'seeks to create the nation state by fusing together politically divided parts' (Alter 1994, 23). It first emerged in Europe in the mid-nineteenth century as a powerful force that dissolved multinational empires. For example, the national unification and emergence of both Italy (1861) and Germany (1871) were largely due to political and social movements that aimed to end the territorial fragmentation of the Italian and German people, respectively. In the first half of the twentieth century, a parallel form of risorgimento nationalism directed against European colonial rule spread across Southeast Asia and gave rise to revolutions and national liberation movements, transforming a range of 'imperial constructs' in the region into modern nation states (Reid 2009).

According to the historical sociologist Anthony D. Smith's typology of nationalism, which suggests to recognize 'the overall situation in which particular communities and movements find themselves both before and after independence', most of the Southeast Asian nationalisms could also be described as territorial 'anti-colonial' and 'integration' nationalisms. The former 'will seek first to eject foreign rulers and substitute a new state-nation for the old colonial territory' in the pre-independence era; subsequently, the latter intends to 'bring [people] together and integrate them into a new political community often disparate

DOI: 10.4324/9781003111450-26

ethnic populations and to create a new "territorial nation" out of the old colonial state' in the post-independence ear (Smith 1991, 82–83).

Stefan Eklöf Amirell's opening chapter offers a comprehensive overview of the origins and development of nationalism in Southeast Asia during the colonial era when the region was carved up and occupied by France, Portugal, Spain, the Netherlands, the British Empire, the United States, and Imperial Japan. It shows how nationalist ideologies emerged in the Philippines toward the end of the nineteenth century and later in several other colonies, particularly in Burma, Indonesia, and Vietnam. Inspired by nationalist movements in Europe and other parts of Asia, Western-educated Southeast Asian intellectuals began to formulate nationalist ideologies, mixing indigenous traditions with transnational influences, including European and Chinese nationalism and critical Marxist analyses of imperialism. Amirell highlights how anti-colonial resistance was an important building block of nationalism in Southeast Asia. However, he also shows that the nationalists' political agenda was more far-reaching as they did not only seek national independence but also emancipation from traditional forms of inequality, oppression, and injustice, as well as political equality for men and women. Although the efforts to build peaceful, prosperous, and socially just nations were often frustrated after independence, Southeast Asian states have shown a remarkable degree of resilience, primarily fueled by the nationalist ideologies and ambitious visions that were forged in the region during the first half of the twentieth century.

Blackburn (2013, 9) stresses the importance of colonialism in shaping Southeast Asian nationalist movements:

> Its imposition of new state borders helped homogenise some ethnic groups into new nation-states and antagonised others, often with lasting effects. The region thus includes many ethnic groups that almost miraculously came to identify with a nation that had never existed previously, and ethnic groups that were excluded or did not wish to be part of the new nation.

Subsequently, this often led to ethnic tension and conflicts within the newly established Southeast Asian nation states. Enze Han's chapter deals with this issue. He studies the nation building process of multiethnic nation states in the post-colonial era by tracing and comparing the identity construction and ethnic policies and practices of China, Burma/Myanmar, and Thailand. He outlines how China recognizes the existence of 56 ethnic groups and allows the provision of autonomous governments, minority language education, and religious and cultural expression. Myanmar recognizes 135 ethnic groups and established seven ethnic states. However, the long history of military rule in the country has meant that the cultural and political expression of minority ethnic groups has been highly restricted. In Thailand, the national discourse claims that everyone living within the territorial boundaries of the country is Thai. Consequently, the government does not officially recognize ethnic minorities. In addition, Thailand has made irredentist claims to pan-Tai ethnic groups in Myanmar and China. Han then examines different nationalist ideologies and practices on common cross-border ethnic minorities between China and Myanmar, and outlines how Thailand supported the Shan nationalist movements as part of its pan-Tai sentiment. He concludes that 'each state's version of national identity has different degrees of inclusiveness vs exclusiveness, which were partly predetermined by the historical processes of political contestation in the post-WWII periods' (Han 2023, 384).

Despite their governments' attempts at integrating all resident ethnic groups into one nation, whether by force, by negotiation, or through other approaches, many Southeast

Asian states were confronted by problems of ethnic or regional separatism not long after achieving independence from colonial powers. The existing territorial 'anti-colonial' and 'integration' nationalisms soon came to be challenged by the newly emerging ethnic 'secession' and 'diaspora' nationalisms. These seek to 'secede from a larger political unit (or secede and gather together in a designated ethnic homeland) and set up a new political "ethno-nation" in its place' (Smith 1991, 82). By the end of the twentieth century, ethno-nationalist movements were increasingly threatening the integrity and security of several countries in the region, notably Indonesia, Myanmar, the Philippines, and Thailand (May 1990, 28). In the past two decades, Southeast Asia has witnessed several protracted insurgencies where militant groups have resorted to acts of violence, including the use of terrorist tactics to achieve their political objectives. Arabinda Acharya's chapter discusses the extent to which nationalism, ethnicity, and religion have influenced conflicts in contemporary Southeast Asia. He demonstrates how conflicts and violence in the region have strong local roots. Some of the persisting conflicts, such as those in southern Thailand, the southern Philippines, and many parts of Indonesia, are rooted in old-fashioned nationalist or ethno-nationalist movements, while many other conflicts are often layered over communal issues. In many cases, violence is associated with issues of political participation, communal relations, resource competition, identity, and the quest for autonomy. Acharya asserts that Southeast Asia is confronted with a very severe threat from radicalization, which creates the conditions that often lead to terrorism. This is despite the fact that a number of conflicts, especially those involving Islamists in the region, have remained localized, and some of which are being addressed through negotiations.

The next chapters in this section offer an in-depth analysis of nation formation and identity construction in one of the 11 Southeast Asian countries.

In the 1940s, Vietnam, the Philippines, Burma, and Indonesia were the first Southeast Asian countries to achieve independence. Zhifang Song's chapter investigates how concepts of the nation and nationalism have been constantly reshaped in post-colonial Vietnam with particular reference to the Hoa people (ethnic Chinese) who have lived through decades of turmoil in the country. During colonial times, the Hoa people formed communities that were socially and culturally segregated from the local Vietnamese population. After French colonial rule ended, neither of the two post-colonial Vietnamese states tolerated the Hoa people's political and cultural affiliation with China and they were forced to take Vietnamese citizenship. Following reunification in 1975, the government saw all residents of Vietnam as forming a single nation that was composed of 54 nationalities, including the Hoa people. However, in practice, ethnic Chinese were still seen as a threat to the state and therefore denied many civil rights. It was not until some far-reaching reforms in 1986 that restrictions on the Hoa people's rights were gradually lifted. Consequently, they have been increasingly incorporated into the society and have come to be recognized as part of the wider Vietnamese nation.

In his influential work *Nations before Nationalism*, the political scientist John A. Armstrong highlighted that from an anthropological point of view, 'groups tend to define themselves not by reference to their own characteristics but by exclusion, that is, by comparison to "strangers."' It is important to recognize that 'ethnicity is a bundle of shifting interactions rather than a nuclear component of social organization' (Armstrong 1982, 5). The boundaries of identity are based on the perceptions of the individuals forming the group, and the cultural and the biological content of the group may change as long as the boundary mechanisms are maintained. The Hoa people's fate demonstrated how the Vietnamese majority and ethnic minorities interacted, negotiated their identities, and reconstructed the national boundary in the post-independence era.

Chi P. Pham's chapter continues to examine the creation and rise of Vietnamese nationalism and identity through the lens of the 'self' and 'other' nexus by analyzing the portrayals of foreign migrants as national enemies in post-1986 Vietnamese fiction. It reveals that in the Vietnamese literary tradition, writing has been seen as a weapon in the fight against obstacles to the nation's independence and socialist construction since the colonial period. Post-reform Vietnamese literature still provokes nationalist politics typical of the socialist period and plays a distinct role as a cultural strategy in Vietnamese nationalism. It constitutes an ideological instrument for maintaining in the public mind a sense of national democracy and hegemony as the ultimate goal of the post-reform Vietnamese nation building project. Pham concludes that the imagined association in Vietnamese literature of the foreigner with the enemies of the nation – colonialism, capitalism, and imperialism – was formed, and has been maintained, to sustain a vision of the nation that includes only those who share a common negative sentiment about such non-socialist forces.

The modern Philippine nation state developed through the integration process during Spanish and US colonial rules, with a brief Japanese interregnum. Rommel A. Curaming's chapter initially provides an overview of the rise of colonial nationalism, anti-colonial nationalism, and theological nationalism in the Philippines during the late nineteenth and early twentieth centuries. Subsequently, he analyzes the development of populist nationalism in the country by looking at the various ways through which 'the people' have been conceived in Philippine nationalist historiography from the 1880s to the 1980s. His analysis shows how such forms of nationalist writing are populist because of their pro-people, 'us' versus 'them' proclivities, both in form and in aspiration. Curaming argues that parallels exist between the form, aims, context, patterns of and reactions to the development of political populism and populist nationalism in Philippine history writing. The existence of populist scholars and the long tradition of populist scholarship might be factors in the resilience of populism.

While the Philippines has developed into the only Christian nation in Asia as a consequence of centuries of Spanish and US-American colonization, the Burmese successfully maintained their Buddhist tradition during, and despite, British rule from 1824 to 1948. Similar to the theological nationalism in the Philippines, nationalism coined by Buddhist ideas emerged in Burma in the colonial period and has prevailed until today. Niklas Foxeus's chapter studies the symbiosis of Buddhism and nationalism in Burma/Myanmar, which advocates the protection of 'nation/race, religion, and the Buddha's dispensation'. This discourse has been preoccupied with two perceived threats: interreligious and interracial marriages between Burmese Buddhist women and Indian men (later expanded to include Muslim men), and business competition between Indian immigrants and Burmese Buddhists. Foxeus observes that historical narratives of the colonial period of domination, vulnerability, and weakness have created a long-standing sense of collective victimhood and resentment among the Burmese Buddhist majority toward Indian immigrants initially, and later toward Muslims, that has contributed to exacerbating tensions and provoking rioting in contemporary Myanmar.

Foxeus's chapter is complemented by Maitrii Aung-Thwin's contribution which offers a comprehensive overview on diverse forms of Burmese nationalism and various nationalist ideas and groups that prevailed in different historical stages, including the era of imperialism, the era of independence, the era of socialism, and the era of democracy. He points out that the ways Myanmar has been defined as a form of community have varied, influenced by local dynamics' and external influences, institutions and individuals, and by the contingencies and contexts of history. Due to a range of historical, geographic, demographic, political, and cultural factors, the story of Burmese nationalism as it relates to the territorialization (and deterritorialization) of the country has had both a unifying and divisive effect with different ideas of belonging, solidarity, and community being forged simultaneously by competing groups who wish to assert their vision of an independent and modern Myanmar.

Joshua Kueh's chapter focuses on Indonesia, the most populous and geographically largest country in the region. He outlines the ways in which the modern Indonesian nation has been imagined in the twentieth century and identifies the main streams of nationalism that emerged during this time – Pancasila, Islamic, and ethno-nationalism – each competing to become the dominant vision of the state of Indonesia. Indonesians have contemplated and negotiated the values of their imagined political community, giving rise to some dichotomies that have shaped the idea of the nation: national versus regional, religious versus secular, indigenous versus foreign, and modern versus traditional. These oppositional categories have informed how Indonesians have seen their nation and will likely continue to define the conversation on Indonesian nationalism into the future.

Following the first wave of independence movements in Southeast Asia in the 1940s, Cambodia, Laos, Malaysia, and Singapore overthrew French and British colonial rules and gained full recognition of their sovereignty in the 1950s and 1960s.

Kimly Ngoun's chapter examines the journey of Cambodian nationalism from the period of French colonial rule to the present. He explains how nationalism has been used discursively as a political resource by various stakeholders to advance their agenda at different junctures in history, in different contexts, and for different purposes. The French colonial rulers constructed modern concepts of the Cambodian nation to justify their colonial rule. They gave the Khmer people the impression that the French were indeed rescuing the Khmer race from extinction. Cambodian elites then adopted and developed these concepts for their anti-colonial nationalist independence campaigns. In the post-independence era, the Sangkum regime revived old cultural markers, invented traditions, and promoted nationalism to serve the process of nation building. Later on, the communist Khmer Rouge leaders used ethno-nationalism to mobilize popular support for their revolution. In modern Cambodia, Prime Minister Hun Sen has relied on nationalism to counter domestic critics and opposition politicians. Apart from the elites, the abstract concept of nationalism has also started to play a bigger role among ordinary people in Phnom Penh since the outbreak of the Thai-Cambodian Border Conflict in 2008.

The historian and political theorist Miroslav Hroch defined three structural phases in the formation of modern nation states: during Phase A, activists devote themselves to scholarly inquiry into and dissemination of an awareness of the distinctive linguistic, cultural, social, and historical characteristics of their ethnic group; subsequently, in Phase B, additional activists emerge 'to win over as many of their ethnic group as possible to the project of creating a future nation, by patriotic agitation to "awaken" national consciousness among them'; finally, in Phase C, a distinctive set of social structures is established, and the national movement 'differentiated out into conservative-clerical, liberal and democratic wings' (Hroch 1996, 81). Although Hroch's three-phase model was conceptualized with reference to national movements in Europe, to some extent, it coincides with the nation building process of some Southeast Asian countries, notably Laos which, for example, started with the collection of information about the history, language, and customs of the colonized indigenous ethnic group. Ryan Wolfson-Ford's chapter on 'Xāt Lao: imaging the Lao nation through race, history and language' shows how, as early as the 1930s, the Lao elite began inventing a national narrative, incorporating both positive and negative French influences. It paved the way for the formation of national identity and provided the basis for subsequent popular nationalist movements that commenced in the 1940s. After 1945, an alternative multiethnic nationalism, which some Lao had considered, was ultimately abandoned in favor of a stridently nationalist notion of a Lao race. In doing so, Lao intellectuals did not hesitate to distort, evade, and manipulate reality in order to embrace a pure Lao nation. That led to major repercussions for twentieth-century Lao history. Even today there remains a fundamental tension between the aspiration of the Lao People's Democratic Republic (LPDR) to free Laos from foreign influences, and its claim to be a multiethnic nation.

Hroch believed that the transition from one phase of any national movements to the next was a gradual process depending on, and often triggered by, various conditions and socio-economic as well as moral contexts. The transition from Phase A to Phase B is usually triggered by 'a social and/or political crisis of the old order', 'the emergence of discontent among significant elements of the population', and the 'loss of faith in traditional moral systems, above all a decline in religious legitimacy'. To move into Phase C, activists must obtain mass support which is dependent on four conditions and/or circumstances: '(1) a crisis of legitimacy, linked to social, moral and cultural strains; (2) a basic volume of vertical social mobility; (3) a fairly high level of social communication; and (4) nationally relevant conflicts of interest' (Hroch 1996, 85–88). In fact, the nation building process of some of the Southeast Asian countries is more complex than Hroch's three-stage-model. The role of religion in the transition of the three phases, and the rivalry and interaction between different groups of nationalists/activists within a rising ethnic group appears to be quite significant. The aforementioned chapter by Joshua Kueh offers some insights on how different strains of nationalists and nationalism competed for mass support in Phases B and C of Indonesia's nation building process. Ahmad Fauzi Abdul Hamid and Azmi Arifin's chapter continues the discussion of the topic by investigating how Malay nationalism was formed by three rather different political streams: right-wing nationalism, left-wing nationalism, and religious-based nationalism. The only objective all had in common is that they tried to achieve independence from colonial rule and protecting Malay-Muslim rights as an integral part of the national identity. The chapter shows that the 'rightist' stream was more ethnically exclusivist, without totally ruling out inter-ethnic cooperation, while the 'leftist' stream was more open to multiethnic solidarity, without altogether rejecting Malay political and cultural primacy. Both streams incorporated Islam into their agendas, but the nature and extent of their religious co-option differed. The religious stream of Malay nationalism was shaped by the first stirrings of Islamism as a political doctrine that envisioned the establishment of an Islamic state as the ideal mode of governance. Nonetheless, Malay Islamists embraced political collaboration that transcended ideological and ethno-religious identifications. Overall, right-wing nationalism prevailed in independent Malaysia until the United Malays National Organisation (UMNO), which had ruled Malaysia since 1957, lost the general election in 2018.

In the wave of nation state formation across Southeast Asia in the mid-twentieth century, the British colony of Singapore gained internal self-governance in 1959 and joined the Federation of Malaysia in 1963. Two years later, Singapore separated from Malaysia and became a fully independent city-state with the majority of its population being ethnic Chinese. In the following decades, Singapore developed into a major trading hub and one of the most affluent and well-governed countries in the world; a success story in many ways. Michael D. Barr's chapter investigates the process of nation and identity building of Singapore in the post-independence era. He shows how in the mid-1960s, the newly independent Singapore found a nationalist voice in defiant survivalism. It was subsequently transformed into an unabashed expression of triumphalism. Since the 1990s, the nationalist message has been informed, and is underpinned, by four pillars: Singapore as a colonial and Chinese success story; Chinese ethno-nationalism and multiracialism; Singaporean exceptionalism; and gratitude to Lee Kuan Yew as the founder and key driving force of the modernization of Singapore. To this day, national pride and national identity have been built on the back of successful nation building projects. However, the link between politics and nationalism nowadays constitutes an unhelpful burden for national loyalty and patriotism. Barr suggests that reforming and revitalizing the emotional ties that used to bind Singaporeans will require a rethinking of ethnicity, government, and the role of Lee in its national identity – the three decisive elements in Singaporean nationalism.

Brunei and East Timor are the youngest independent countries in Southeast Asia; both achieved full recognition of sovereignty by joining the UN in 1984 and 2002, respectively.

Asiyah Kumpoh and Nani Suryani Abu Bakar's chapter traces the development of Bruneian nationalism in the anti-colonial period (1950s–1980s) and the homogenization period (from 1980s onward). They point out that Bruneian nationalism consists of three overlapping elements: ethnicity, culture, and heritage, represented by Malay, Islam, and Monarchy. Over the years, Brunei has employed the twin strategy of inclusion and exclusion to cultivate Bruneian nationalism, with the objective of preserving state sovereignty, the Monarch, and fostering a collective sense of belonging. Kumpoh and Bakar suggest that Brunei's homogenization and nation building process has probably reached its natural threshold and it is time for the country to embrace diversity by encouraging ethnic minorities to preserve and promote their distinct cultures and identities.

Takahiro Kamisuna's chapter explains how nationalism transcended the existing colonial borders to create a national struggle in East Timor. It demonstrates how the concept of *Rai Timor* (Timor Land) has been historically and spatially transformative. While successive occupations by Portugal and Indonesia created a unique historical trajectory of nationalism between the older and younger generations, East Timor people's different adaptations to international normative discourses transformed their usage of ideological instruments in shaping *Rai Timor*. East Timor's case indicates that the development of nationalism needs to be understood in the context of dynamic national and international transitions, rather than vernacular claims for the emancipation from colonialism.

Among all the countries of Southeast Asia, Thailand is the only one that has never been colonized by a foreign power. It has been ruled by monarchs for centuries and has evolved in recent decades from an underdeveloped agricultural country into the second largest economy in the region. In the last chapter of this section, Jack Fong offers some explanatory and apolitical readings of how the Thai institution of the monarchy has managed to stay in power since the late eighteenth century. Using Max Weber's theory of charismatic authority, Fong discusses how Thai traditional authority has engaged in greater cultural production and nation construction over time and investigates the continuing tensions between Thai nationalism and Thai democracy. He argues that political advantages can be accrued by actors who appropriate and reproduce the historical romance of the Thai nation and leaves open-ended the Weberian understanding that traditional authority fully gives way to rational-legal governance when a nation makes its entry into modernity.

According to the political scientist Partha Chatterjee, nationalism in the non-European world developed through three stages/moments: departure, maneuver, and arrival. The moment of departure starts with the encounters with the West and the awareness that modern Western culture possesses attributes conducive to power and progress. The lack of such attributes, however, in the East was the major cause of its poverty and subjection. The backwardness could be overcome by adopting modern attributes of Western culture in the material domain (economy, statecraft, science, and technology), while the spiritual domain which carries the essential ingredients of cultural identity must be preserved and promoted. The moment of maneuver 'consists in the historical consolidation of the "national" by decrying the "modern", the preparation for capitalist production through an ideology of anti-capitalism'. In the moment of arrival, nationalist thought becomes a discourse of order and the national organization of power. It 'succeeds in glossing over all earlier contradictions, divergences and differences' and becomes a 'passive revolution uttering its own life-history' (Chatterjee 1986, 51). Chatterjee's theory could help us to achieve a better understanding of Southeast Asian nationalisms, especially that of Brunei, Laos, Singapore, Thailand, and Vietnam which did not fully adopt the Western principles, parameters, and conventions. It also makes us rethink how modern Western culture has challenged, informed, and, occasionally, merged with traditional Asian culture to shape Southeast Asian nations and nationalisms, creating unique modern communities and new models of nation states.

Although this handbook is structured according to different regions in Asia, the various case studies in this part clearly show that nation building processes are not inevitably smooth and peaceful processes as they are frequently prone to different forms of contestation. As the following chapters will demonstrate, key issues, and often the reasons for conflicts, are, in particular, the ethnic composition of a nation, the religious diversity of its people, the treatment of minorities, local rivalries, political resistance, and violence. That should not come as a surprise as narratives and discourses about the nation tend to stress commonalities, consensus, unity, and homogeneousness and of its people. All of these attributes, obviously, contradict, or, at least, play down the cultural differences and heterogeneity that can normally be found in large groups of people. Underplaying diversity in nation building processes tends to cause anxieties and fears and can lead to outright opposition and rejection of the project, particularly when, for example, ethnicity, religious orientation, or locality constitute very significant elements of one's social identity. We will have to leave it open whether the challenges to nation building projects are more pronounced in Southeast Asia than in other parts of Asia or whether this is due to the authors' interest in conflicts and tensions, and their chosen theoretical frameworks.

References

Alter, Peter. 1994. *Nationalism*. 2nd Edition. London: Edward Arnold.
Blackburn, Susan, and Helen Ting, eds. 2013. *Women in Southeast Asian Nationalist Movements*. Singapore: NUS Press.
Chatterjee, Partha. 1986. *Nationalist Thought and the Colonial World: A Derivative Discourse*. London: Zed Books.
Han, Enze. 2023. "Comparative Nation-Building in the Borderlands between China, Myanmar, and Thailand." In *The Routledge Handbook of Nationalism in East and Southeast Asia*, edited by Lu Zhouxiang, 375–387. Abingdon: Routledge.
Hroch, Miroslav. 1996. "From National Movement to the Fully-formed Nation: The Nation-Building Process in Europe." In *Mapping the Nation*, edited by Gopal Balakrishnan, 78–97. London and New York: Verso.
Armstrong, John A. 1982. *Nations before Nationalism*. Chapel Hill: The University of North Carolina Press.
May, R. J. 1990. "Ethnic Separatism in Southeast Asia". *Pacific Viewpoint* 31 (2): 28–59.
Reid, Anthony. 2009. *Imperial Alchemy: Nationalism and Political Identity in Southeast Asia*. Cambridge: Cambridge University Press.
Smith, D. Anthony. 1991. *National Identity*. London: Penguin Books.

23
NATIONALISM, COLONIALISM AND DECOLONISATION IN SOUTHEAST ASIA
The rise of emancipatory nationalism

Stefan Eklöf Amirell

Introduction

The origins of nationalism in Southeast Asia can be traced to the colonial period of the nineteenth and early twentieth centuries. Influenced by nationalist sentiments in Europe and other parts of Asia, Western-educated intellectuals in the region began to formulate their own nationalist ideologies based on a combination of indigenous history and cultural traditions and progressive visions for their nation and its place in the modern world.

The nation-states of Southeast Asia are often, explicitly or implicitly, grouped into two main categories. On the one hand, there are the "old nations" of mainland Southeast Asia, where all of the major states today, with some credibility, can claim to be the successors of pre-colonial states and to be centred around long-standing ethno-linguistic affiliations. Cambodia, Myanmar, Thailand and Vietnam all seem to conform to this pattern. On the other hand, in insular Southeast Asia, the modern nation-states seem to be of more recent origin and more dependent on the intervention of modern-day intellectuals, who constructed new nations from the territorial divisions made by the European colonisers. For the most part, these divisions and the borders between them gained their final shape only in the nineteenth or early twentieth century. All major states in insular Southeast Asia, Indonesia, Malaysia and the Philippines, seem to conform to this pattern (Lieberman 2009: 43).

As David Henley has demonstrated, however, this neat division becomes more complex on closer scrutiny. Not only are the lines between the old kingdoms of mainland Southeast Asia and their contemporary successors much less straight than is often assumed, but, conversely, it is also possible to trace the origins of national identity in the Malay world to pre-colonial times (Henley 2013). Moreover, there was nothing historically predetermined about the present nation-states of Southeast Asia, and there is an abundance of unrealised nationalist projects as well as still-ongoing attempts to create new nation-states in the region, including by armed struggles. Some examples of such "nations that could have been" are the early twentieth-century Javanese national movement, the pan-Malay movement of the mid-twentieth century, the attempts to create a Muslim-dominated state in the southern Philippines and the protracted struggles of the Kachin, Karenni (Kayah), Karen, Shan and other ethnic minorities in Myanmar to establish separate nation-states (McIntyre 1973; Majul 1988; Christie 1996; Henley 2013).

Southeast Asia as a whole is characterised by great ethnic, linguistic and religious heterogeneities, but there are significant differences in these respects between the various countries and parts of the region. Indonesia, for example, is both the largest and by far the most ethnically diverse country with more than 1,300 officially recognised different ethnic groups. The Javanese, who make up the largest ethnic group, are still in the minority with currently around 40 per cent of the population (BPS 2015). In Cambodia, by contrast, the Khmers constitute close to 96 per cent of the population according to official statistics (NIS 2020: 25), and the other countries of mainland Southeast Asia are all to a greater or lesser degree dominated by one ethno-linguistic group – Burman, Lao, Thai or Vietnamese – to which between around 55 and 85 per cent of the population belong. However, even though national identity in the mainland Southeast Asian nations in general is more closely linked to the ethnicity of the majority of the population, there are sizeable ethnic minorities in all countries with the exception of Cambodia. In order to deal with this diversity, all the national movements that emerged during the late colonial period, in both mainland and insular Southeast Asia, aimed to a greater or lesser extent, and with varying degrees of success, to include all indigenous Southeast Asian groups of their respective territory, regardless of ethnicity and religion. In addition, Southeast Asian nationalist had to deal with the question of whether and how to include the sizeable groups of more or less recent immigrants to the region, particularly the Chinese, but also Indian, Arab and European populations.

The diversity of Southeast Asia's human geography and history makes it particularly interesting for the comparative study of nationalism. The region also has a long and complex political history, a central position as a cross-road between East and South Asia as well as between Europe and East Asia, and an interesting variety of political systems in the contemporary nation-states. For these reasons, Southeast Asia has been something of a testing-ground for the development of theories about nationalism outside of Europe. In particular, the second, revised edition of Benedict Anderson's seminal book *Imagined Communities*, which appeared in 1991, owed much of its argument to the author's long-standing engagement with Southeast Asian culture and politics. The arguments advanced by Anderson with regard to the character of nationalism, particularly in the non-Western world, are still ongoing (Anderson [1983] 1991; cf. Anderson 1998; Bergholz 2018).

Colonialism and the frameworks for nations

Although European colonial presence in Southeast Asia can be dated back to the sixteenth century, colonial rule in most parts of the region was only established during the nineteenth or early twentieth century. In particular, the period 1870–1910 was a transformative period during which the Western colonial powers – Britain, France, the Netherlands, Spain, Portugal and the United States – divided the region's peoples and territories between them and set about to transform the economy and social fabric of their colonies. In doing so, the imperial powers demarcated new borders throughout Southeast Asia, which in many instances led to the incorporation of formerly autonomous peoples between or on the margins of older centres of power. Although Siam (Thailand), as the only country in Southeast Asia, remained independent, similar processes of integration and modernisation took place there, led by the royal dynasty (Steinberg 1987: 173; Winichakul 1994).

For the most part, the borders established by the colonial powers and Siam were new inventions. This was particularly obvious in maritime Southeast Asia, where the Dutch and Spanish colonisers created vast new political entities, such as the Dutch East India (present-day Indonesia) and the Philippines, that had no obvious historical precedent, despite attempts by Indonesian historians during the post-colonial era to cast the ancient Javanese kingdom of Majapahit as a "proto-Indonesia" (Wood 2005: 41). The colonial borders also cut right through regions that had a long tradition of integration by trade and other forms of contact, such as the so-called Sulu Zone of the southern Philippines and eastern Indonesia (Warren 1981) or the Strait of Malacca, where the British and Dutch colonisers drew a border right through the waterway that was the historical centre of Malay trade and culture.

In mainland Southeast Asia, the kingdoms of Annam (Vietnam), Cambodia, Burma (Myanmar) and Siam could all trace their roots to pre-colonial times, but the borders and administrative divisions between them were nonetheless for the most part new. The traditional kingdoms in the region have been described as mandala states, in which the authority of the king receded with increasing distance from the capital, leaving vast borderlands, particularly the sparsely populated highlands far away from the centres of royal power, largely autonomous. Through these mountainous regions, the colonial powers and the Siamese monarchy drew borders and attempted, with varying success and frequently by means of conquest or coercion, to tie the ethnically diverse populations to one or the other colony or country. In doing so, they intensified a drawn-out process that continues to this day, whereby an increasingly intrusive state tries to gain control over and exploit Southeast Asia's mountainous regions and its populations (Winichakul 1994; Anderson 1991: 170–178; Scott 2009).

Given the lack of historical continuity and weak legitimacy of the colonial states, the political borders of Southeast Asia have proven remarkably persistent, a circumstance that can largely be attributed to the influence of nationalism. Despite several attempts by the post-colonial states in the region to move the borders, the only lasting major changes to the colonial borders to date have been the establishment of Brunei as an independent state when Malaysia was formed in 1962 and the secession of Singapore from the union three years later. Indonesia's failed attempt between 1975 and 1999 to integrate the former Portuguese colony of East Timor illustrates the strength of the colonial legacy when it comes to national borders, as does the failure so far of the West Papua liberation movement to secede from Indonesia after the territory was transferred to the country by the Netherlands in the 1960s (Heidbüchel 2007). Likewise, none of the ethnic movements in Myanmar have to date succeeded in establishing their own nation-state or even autonomous region, despite the weakness of the state (Christie 1996; Reid 2010: 2).

The nineteenth and early twentieth centuries brought unprecedented social and economic change to Southeast Asia, without which the rise of nationalist movements would have been unthinkable. The region was transformed from a reliance principally on self-subsistence agriculture to an export-oriented economy in which agricultural products and natural resources were produced for a global market. The changes set in motion by colonial expansion and exploitation brought about the demise of many traditional forms of economic and social power. New elites – including Europeans as well as Chinese, Indian and indigenous Southeast Asians – emerged, often displacing traditional landlords and aristocracies, which led to the break-down of established, largely reciprocal patron-client relations. The population of the region increased as a result of the economic expansion and particularly from the end of the nineteenth century, a rapid urbanisation took place. Railroads, telegraph lines, harbours and regular shipping services were established, connecting towns and big cities with each other and with the outside world (Elson 1999).

During the period of high imperialism, from around 1870 to 1914, colonial governments created strong, centralised states that provided new models of political authority and greatly extended the reach of the state. The regimes built bureaucracies and imposed laws and regulations across their territories, all of which contributed to strengthen internal cohesion and interdependence among the inhabitants of each colony, particularly those who participated actively in the modern economy. In doing so, colonial governments inadvertently created the frameworks for the new nation-states that intellectuals in the colonies began to envision, first in the Philippines towards the end of the nineteenth century and in other parts of the region – particularly in Burma, Indonesia and Vietnam, some what later, mainly during the inter-war years. Although colonialism did not predetermine the fate of the post-colonial states in the region, it set the nations off on course by integrating the educated elites of each colony and by providing the territorial boundaries and the central institutions for the new nation-states (Steinberg 1987: 173–218; Sidel 2012).

Colonial rule also triggered protests and uprisings, and the rapid social and economic change, paired with the increasingly intrusive character of the state, led to several peasant uprisings throughout Southeast Asia in the nineteenth and early twentieth centuries. It would be misleading, however, to label such uprisings nationalist or even proto-nationalist, despite the attempts of later historians to integrate them in grand national narratives. The peasant uprisings were rural protests and for the most part local affairs whose influence seldom extended beyond the region in which they started. They tended to focus on a particular grievance, such as a burdensome tax or forced labour obligations, rather than seeking to change an exploitative system or to bring about a lasting regime change. The peasant movements thus tended to dissipate after the grievance that had triggered them had been addressed or the uprising been suppressed. Moreover, in contrast to the nationalist ideologies that emerged among the educated urban elites in the twentieth century, peasant movements tended to be more or less reactionary, seeking to restore a previous and often idealised social and political order, whether real or imagined (Benda 1965; Adas 1981).

However, Western colonial expansion during the nineteenth century also led to broader and more sustained armed resistance movements and colonial wars, including in Java (1825–1830), Aceh (1873–1904), Sulu (1876–1913), Burma (1885–1895) and Vietnam (1885–1896). These movements were explicitly anti-colonial and some of them – particularly the Can Vuong ("Help the king") movement in Vietnam following the French invasion – contributed to fostering national, or proto-national, sentiments and identities. Like the peasant uprisings, however, these early anti-colonial resistance movements were looking to restore a deposed or emasculated monarch and envisioned a return to a traditional way of life rather than to establish a new social and political order. In contrast to the national movements that emerged after the end of World War I, the leaders of the earlier anti-colonial resistance movements were for the most part traditional elites, such as princes, aristocrats and religious leaders, who often sought to defend or restore their privileges and position. The leaders of the later nationalist movements that eventually would succeed in establishing independent nation-states in Southeast Asia, by contrast, belonged to a new class of Western-educated intellectuals, who tended to be more mixed in terms of social and family background.

Urbanisation and the rise of national intellectual elites

The breeding grounds for nationalism in Southeast Asia (as elsewhere) were the big cities that grew up as a result of the expansion of the colonial economy and administration. Cities such as Batavia (Jakarta), Manila, Rangoon (Yangon), Saigon (Ho Chi Minh City) and Singapore attracted people from across each colony as well as from abroad and brought together people from different racial, ethnic, religious and social background. The influx of ideas and inspiration from around world through the media, the education system and personal encounters and experiences, combined with the rise of a class of indigenous intellectuals, provided a fertile ground for the rise of new social, political and cultural ideas, including nationalist sentiments.

The big cities were not only hubs of the colonial economy and administration. They were also important as educational centres, where higher education, which seemed to be the key to economic, social and cultural advancement in the age of high imperialism, could be acquired. Towards the end of the nineteenth century, the colonial regimes established schools that provided secondary and tertiary education according to European curricula. The purpose was to provide a white collar work force of indigenous people to staff the lower echelons of the bureaucracy and to implement so-called civilising policies in the fields of, for example, education, health, law and agriculture. In addition, private enterprises also needed educated personnel, such as clerks, overseers and engineers. In relation to the population of the colonies, the number of indigenous people who received higher education was small, but in the big cities they came to form a new intellectual elite, from which the leadership of the nationalist movements would be drawn. Some of those who received higher education in the colonies were members of royal or aristocratic families, but most came from more modest middle class backgrounds, including local officials, petty landowners and traders (Steinberg 261–268). The father of the Vietnamese nationalist leader Ho Chi Minh (1890–1969), for example, was district magistrate, whereas the Burmese nationalist leader Aung San's (1915–1947) father was a lawyer. Indonesia's pivotal nationalist leader Sukarno (1901–1970) came from an aristocratic family but his father worked as a primary school teacher in Java.

Education seemed to provide a ticket to economic and social advancement, but the expectation to find a qualified and well-paid employment after graduation was frequently not met. As put by Nicholas Tarling (1998: 75), by thus providing young men of indigenous origin with education but not opportunity, the colonial regimes inadvertently bred nationalism. The increasingly pronounced racism towards the end of the nineteenth and early twentieth centuries also contributed to discontent with colonial rule and on a personal level, many members of the educated elites felt that they were being discriminated against, professionally as well as socially. The small number of students who received part of the education in the colonial metropoles in Europe, moreover, were often deeply affected by their experience of living in a country that was not colonised – both by being treated, at least in some respects, more like humans than members of an inferior race, and by the realisation that there were serious flaws in the supposedly highly civilised European societies (Steinberg 1987: 265–266). The strong nationalism that flourished in Europe in the early twentieth century stood in sharp contrast to the explicitly anti-nationalist character of the colonial state in Southeast Asia, which aimed to suppress and curtail all expressions of nationalist sentiments, save for expressions of loyalty to the colonial motherland.

The lack of social security and traditional bonds of dependence in the colonial cities led to the establishment of new organisations, particularly self-help organisations and religious and educational societies. Several religious organisations founded in the first decades of the twentieth century, such as the Young Men's Buddhist Association in Burma (founded in 1906) and Muhammadiyah (1912), Sarekat Islam (1912) and Nahdlatul Ulama (1926) in the Dutch East Indies, would play important parts in the national movements.

Another type of modern organisation, with its roots in the Enlightenment, was the learned society, such as the Koninklijk Bataviaasch Genootschap van Kunsten en Wetenschappen, the Malayan Branch of the Royal Asiatic Society, the Siam Society and the Burma Research Society. Their membership was made up of European and Asian literati, and the research activity that they sponsored and encouraged would be crucial for the creation of national identities based on indigenous history and culture (Lewis 2013). Like in many national movements in Europe during the nineteenth century, political nationalism in Southeast Asia was preceded by a great interest in indigenous culture and identity (cf. Hroch 1993), which later provided the moulds for forging national identities.

The shift from cultural to political issues as the focus of interest among indigenous educated elites was often gradual and characterised by substantial disagreement over both the long-term goals and the means by which to achieve them. In the beginning of the twentieth century, to the extent that the nationalists in Southeast Asia raised political demands they mostly concerned increased political influence within the existing colonial structure, for example through the establishment of advisory councils. The mainstream nationalists then often moved to demand some form of political autonomy within the empire, such as had been granted to the white settler colonies of the British Empire in the early twentieth century or earlier. Finally, in the 1920s or 1930s, nationalists – often pushed by the repressive policies of the colonial state – began to demand full independence and focus their efforts on eventually gaining full national sovereignty.

This general course of development contains considerable variation in timing. Nationalist movements developed at very different speed in the Southeast Asian colonies and nationalist ideas and sentiments often failed to travel from one colony to another, particularly when there were linguistic or administrative barriers between them. The Philippine national movement, which was the first to emerge in Southeast Asia, thus emerged already in the 1870s (following the Glorious Revolution in Spain in 1868), whereas nationalism in the neighbouring Dutch East Indies only emerged in the first decades of the twentieth century and around the same time in Vietnam and Burma. In British Malaya, meanwhile, a modern nationalist movement only began to coalesce around the mid-1920s, whereas there was little nationalist sentiment in Laos or Cambodia before the outbreak of World War II.

Consequently, although transnational influences were important in the forging of nationalist movements in Southeast Asia, nationalism until around 1920 was above all shaped by internal conditions and grievances in the colonies. The efforts of the colonial state to modernise and connect the different parts of each colony provided a readily available frame for nationalists. The railroads, regular shipping services, telegraph lines and postal services established by the colonial regimes all served to integrate the different and often far-flung regions in each colony. The new infrastructure improved communications between the big cities, where students and educated indigenous elites were concentrated. Local newspapers, in both European and vernacular languages, were circulated by means of the modern infrastructure and were read by educated members of the new elites. All of these developments stimulated to the emergence of nationalist sentiments within each colony rather than across colonial borders (Cribb 2000: 137–148; Henley 2013).

In other respects, however, international developments and transnational influences were important for the spread of nationalist sentiment and became increasingly central after the turn of the twentieth century. Japan's victory over Russia in the war of 1904–1905 was a major event that resonated across Asia and boosted the moral of nationalists by demonstrating that an Asian nation (or race, in the terminology of the time) was able to defeat a great European power, something that had seemed inconceivable until then. A decade later, the terrifying slaughter of World War I and the political upheaval in its wake in Europe, including the Russian Revolution of 1917, more or less dislodged the colonial discourse about the racial, cultural and moral superiority of European civilisation. The emphasis on national self-determination in Europe in the aftermath of the war and US President Woodrow Wilson's proposal for a new world at the peace conference in Versailles 1919 – which called for a "free, open-minded, and absolutely impartial adjustment of all colonial claims" based on the right to self-determination of the populations concerned – encouraged nationalists to pursue the goal of independence. Freedom from colonial domination also began to look like a more realistic goal after the United States Congress, in 1916, passed an act that promised independence to the Philippines and the colonial regime began to prepare for a transfer of power in the future by swiftly replacing American colonial civil servants with Filipinos.

During the inter-war years, Southeast Asian intellectuals and politicians began to formulate more systematic nationalist ideologies and visions. Their sources of inspiration were eclectic, and they often mixed elements of traditional indigenous culture with contemporary transnational ideologies such as liberalism, socialism and fascism. Armed with their linguistic and analytical skills, Southeast Asian nationalists began both to analyse the colonial regimes from systematic and theoretical-critical perspectives and to formulate alternatives to colonialism, including demands for national independence. In doing so, they saw themselves as part of a broader international community and an international exchange of ideas and critical analyses of imperialism (Osborne 2000: 118; Smith ed. 2018: 241–263; see further below about the ideological sources of inspiration for Southeast Asian nationalists).

Language, finally, played an important but contested role in the forging of nationalism. On the one hand, higher education was given in the language of the colonial power in each colony and the new educated elites were generally highly skilled in one or more European languages, which allowed them both to absorb new ideas, including radical political views, from Europe and other parts of the world and to communicate with educated members from other ethnic and linguistic groups in each colony. For example, the *ilustrados* (the erudite ones) of the Spanish Philippines were fluent in Spanish, which allowed them to get in contact with the nationalist sentiments as well as liberal and radical ideas that flourished in Europe and Latin America in the second half of the nineteenth century. Spanish also provided a means of communication between *ilustrados* with different ethno-linguistic backgrounds and contributed to create a sense of cohesion among the educated members of the indigenous elites in the Philippines, which transcended local and regional divisions.

On the other hand, nationalists were often uncomfortable about adopting the language of the colonisers as their main means of communication or to envision having a foreign language as their official national language. As we have seen, the exploration of indigenous languages and literature was an important aspect of the early cultural nationalism and this effort continued, with increasingly political connotations, as the nationalist movements developed. Newspapers in vernacular languages provided an important arena for the exchange of ideas and debates among nationalists, and by adopting an indigenous language, such as Burmese, Malay or Tagalog, as the national language, nationalists both made a cultural statement aiming to strengthen national unity and pride in indigenous culture, and a political one, aiming to displace the language of the colonisers as the language of the state and facilitating the spread of nationalist sentiments to the great majority of the population who did not speak or understand European languages. In most cases these efforts were eventually very successful, and with the exception of English in Malaysia, Singapore and the Philippines and Portuguese in East Timor, the use of European languages, such as Dutch, French and Spanish, quickly vanished after the end of the colonial era.

Emancipatory nationalism

Discontent with colonialism was a major trigger for the emergence of nationalism in Southeast Asia, but in addition there were several other important dimensions of the early nationalist movements in the region. Consequently, describing Southeast Asian (and other non-European) nationalisms as primarily "anticolonial", "anti-imperial", "anti-Western" or "derivative" (Go & Watson 2019; Eckert 2013; Reid 2010: 8–10; Chatterjee 1986) seems both reductive and misleading. The term emancipatory nationalism, by contrast, serves better to capture the character of the nationalist ideologies and movements that emerged in Southeast Asia (and in many other colonies in Asia and Africa) during the first half of the twentieth century. The term points to the broader goals of these nationalist movements, which went beyond anti-colonialism. Throwing off the yoke of colonialism was not the ultimate goal for the early Southeast Asian nationalist leaders but a step towards realising the emancipatory objectives embedded in the nationalist visions, including nation building and the creation of a modern, harmonious, egalitarian and prosperous society.

This emancipatory and progressive orientation of Southeast Asian nationalisms was not the only thinkable alternative. Just as in Europe there were in many parts of Southeast Asia strong traditional indigenous polities around which retrospective and socially conservative nationalist ideologies could have been built. For example, royal dynasties still commanded considerable loyalty and prestige, not only on the mainland but also throughout much of insular Southeast Asia, for example in Java, the Malay Peninsula, North Borneo and the Sulu Archipelago. At least in theory, royal dynasties, such as the Nguyen dynasty in Vietnam, the Konbaung dynasty in Burma or the sultans of Sulu, Aceh or Yogyakarta, were eligible candidates for Southeast Asian nationalists to rally around. Had Southeast Asia followed a trajectory similar to that of Europe during the nineteenth century in this respect, royal dynasties would have played a prominent role in the nationalist movements. One could, for example, imagine that Burmese nationalists had tried to reinstate King Thibaw Min (or one of his offspring) at the head of an independent constitutional monarchy or that a Javanese nationalist movement in the Dutch East Indies had made the Sultanate of Yogyakarta the focus of their nation-building project.

Emancipatory nationalism, however, was the ideological opposite of such traditional polities with their pompous ceremonies, social inequality and static relations of power, all of which seemed to the new generation of Western-educated nationalists obsolete. Moreover, most of the traditional ruling houses (with the main exception of Siam's Chakri Dynasty) had either lost their former lustre as a result of their defeat at the hands the Westerners or were seen by the new generation of Asian nationalists as too tainted by their complicity in the colonial system to deserve any significant political role in the new nations-to-be. Southeast Asian nationalists were thus not only anti-imperial but also, for the most part, opposed to the rajas and sultans who had been at apex of the pre-colonial societies and who, in many cases, were tainted by collaboration with the colonisers.

Another difference between Southeast Asian and European nationalism during the interwar years – that is, the defining years for most major nationalist movements in Southeast Asia – was that while post-World War I Europe enthusiastically embraced ethnonationalism and dismantled the multi-ethnic empires that had dominated much of the European continent up until the war, Southeast Asian nationalist for the most part envisioned ethnically and religiously diverse nation-states, some of which (particularly Indonesia) in fact resembled empires. Such visions were most pronounced in insular Southeast Asia, but they were also important in some of the colonies of the mainland, particularly in French Indochina, where

Vietnamese nationalists, including the Communist Party, tried – unsuccessfully, as it turned out – to extend the nationalist project to include Cambodia and Laos, as well as the many smaller ethnic minorities that were part of the population of French Indochina (Goscha 1995).

The new nations were to be based on tolerance and harmony between the diverse and sometimes mutually antagonistic ethnic, linguistic and religious groups who lived within the borders of the independent states-to-be. National integration and nation building was a major priority and was to be realised through voluntary and peaceful means, much in contrast to the aggressive and imperialist ambitions of many nationalist leaders in Europe at the time. Neither was hatred or aggression against the colonisers prominent in the nationalist discourses in Southeast Asia, even when nationalists – such as in the Philippines, where the nascent nationalist movement was brutally crushed by the Spanish – had every reason to hate their imperialist oppressors (Anderson 1991: 142; Amirell 2012: 41–42).

The aspiration to peace and harmony was obviously idealistic, and much violence and bloodshed accompanied the process of decolonisation in Southeast Asia, particularly in French Indochina, but also in most of the other colonies and new states, including Burma, Indonesia, Malaysia and the Philippines. The main lines of conflict did not only, and in many cases not even primarily, run between colonisers and colonised, but between different ethnic, religious or political groups made up primarily of people with Southeast Asian origin.

The ideological sources of inspiration for Southeast Asian nationalists were eclectic and transnational. They often mixed ideologies with indigenous cultural and sometimes religious notions. Western influences were obviously important, not only in the form of nationalism, understood as a modern ideology, in itself, but also in the form of radical anti-imperialism. Imperial expansion had been criticised in Europe from the outset and during the nineteenth century, it was particularly prominent in Great Britain and the United States. From the late nineteenth century, however, the critique became more systematic and was often linked to Marxist interpretations of the links between capitalism and imperialism. The English Economist John A. Hobson's book *Imperialism: A Study*, published in 1902 against the backdrop of the Boer War in South Africa, was one of the first serious attempts to critically analyse modern Western imperial domination as a global economic and political system linked to capitalism and international flows of finance and investment. Hobson's analysis became an important source of inspiration for socialist intellectuals in Europe, many of whom now began to give more attention to the global dimensions of class conflict and the potential for socialist revolution in the colonies. Vladimir Lenin's book *Imperialism: The Last Stage of Capitalism*, first published in 1916, became an important source of inspiration for nationalists in Asia as it was translated from Russian to several international languages in the wake of the Russian Revolution. To many Asian nationalist, Lenin's and other socialists' analyses of Western imperialism seemed highly relevant in order to understand the asymmetrical power relations in which the colonies were locked.

Lenin both offered a credible explanation as to why Europeans had come to dominate the rest of the world and highlighted the global economic relations that underpinned the colonial system. Lenin also gave the intellectuals in the colonies a crucial role in mobilising the exploited colonial workers in order to break the imperialist system at what was assumed to be its weakest point. Under his leadership, Russia and the Soviet Union began to actively work to realise this goal. The Third Communist International (Comintern), founded in 1919, helped to establish and support communist organisations throughout Southeast Asia and other parts of the colonised world (Mommsen 1982: 29–65; McLane 1966).

European influences were decidedly important in the forging of nationalist ideologies in Southeast Asia, but there were other important sources of inspiration too. An often overlooked source of both resentment and inspiration for Southeast Asian nationalists came from China. On the one hand, much of the discontent with economic inequality and injustice in the colonies centred on the prominent role of Chinese entrepreneurs, who dominated much of the modern parts of the economy, including trade and finance. Chinese presence in Southeast Asia long pre-dated colonial rule, but the transformations of the nineteenth century led both to a sharp increase in migration of Chinese to Southeast Asia and to increasing prosperity for some Chinese entrepreneurs and merchants, particularly in the towns and cities. Many people saw with envy on the success of the Chinese in business and commerce and concluded that it came at the expense of indigenous Southeast Asians (Reid 2001, 2010: 49–80).

On the other hand, Chinese nationalism provided a model and source of inspiration for Southeast Asian nationalists. The Chinese republican leader Sun Yat-sen looked to overseas Chinese in Southeast Asia for support, particularly after he was expelled from Japan in 1906, and during the subsequent years he visited the region, particularly Singapore and Malaya, numerous times (Khoo 2008). His Three Principles of the People – nationalism, popular rule and social welfare – were taken up by his Chinese sympathisers in Southeast Asia, who, in turn, influenced indigenous nationalists in the region. This influence was strongest in the Philippines, the Dutch East Indies and Vietnam, where leading nationalists such as José Rizal, Sukarno and Phan-boi Chau were inspired by Sun Yat-sen's ideas and nationalist visions (Wells 2001: 171–187).

Sun Yat-sen, like most prominent Asian nationalist leaders – including many who were not self-avowed socialists or members of a Communist organisation – was influenced by Marxist analyses of imperialism and advocated some form of socialism after independence. A central pillar of emancipatory nationalism was the promise of a prosperous society with greater economic equality and social justice, much in contrast to the poverty, exploitation and inequality of both colonialism and traditional indigenous societies (Stuart-Fox 2000; Anderson 2002: 3). George McT. Kahin, an American scholar who personally experienced the mood in Indonesia during the Revolution (that is, the war for independence from the Netherlands) from 1945 to 1949, described the progressive character of Indonesian nationalism as the country stood on the threshold of independence:

> It was not nationalism alone that characterized the citizenry of the Republic during my stay there. Also prominent, but more difficult to define, was another broadly based quality undoubtedly related to the thrust of nationalism. This I think can best be described as a sense of shared purpose – not simply for independence from the Netherlands, but also for far-reaching social change. The nature of this objective was not precisely delineated for many of those who desired this change, nor their way to it clear. But for most of the Republic's leadership there was a strong commitment to greater social justice, and independence was regarded as its indispensable precondition. For nearly all of them the route to that goal was some variant of socialism.
>
> *(Kahin 1997: 23–24)*

Another dimension of the progressive visions for the new nations concerned the legal and political rights of women. The emergence of nationalist movements in Southeast Asia largely coincided with the first wave of feminism in Europe and the Americas, which focused on achieving legal and political rights for women equal to those of men. When the Southeast Asian nationalist movements gained momentum in the 1920s, the struggle for women's suffrage had already been won in most of Europe and North America, and to suggest anything but universal suffrage in the new nation-states in Southeast Asia was unthinkable to most nationalists. Many of them probably also realised that in order for their struggle to have a chance to succeed, they needed to mobilise the whole people regardless of gender. Against that background, the struggle for women's emancipation became an integrated and essential part of the national movements in most Southeast and other Asian colonies (Jayawardena 1986: 8).

There is a significant contrast when it comes to the role of women in the nation between, on the one hand, the emancipatory nationalist movements in Asia and, on the other hand, the political ideologies of the earlier waves of nationalism in Europe and the Americas. Early nationalism in those parts of the world explicitly excluded women from the political sphere, regardless of whether the nation was defined primarily in terms of ethnicity or territoriality, and women only gained political rights after a long struggle (Scott 1996; Pateman 1989: 40–41; Mosse 1985). In the vision of Southeast Asian nationalists, by contrast, women were to have the same political rights as men – although the emancipation for women, for the most part, was limited to the political sphere and did not extend to other spheres of life, such as the social or domestic.

Conclusion

In the 1920s (and in some places, particularly in the Philippines, earlier), nationalist leaders throughout Southeast Asia began to demand independence from colonial rule and to formulate visions for what their nations should look like after independence. In doing so they were inspired both by indigenous culture and history, the exploration of which had preceded the rise of nationalism by several decades, and by transnational political ideologies and movements. Much of the inspiration came from Europe, both in the form of nationalism itself and in the form of radical and critical ideas, particularly anti-imperialism, socialism and the first wave of feminism. China was another important source of influence, particularly the nationalism and political ideas of Sun Yat-sen.

An often overlooked aspect of the nationalist ideologies in Southeast Asia is that most of them had more far-reaching objectives than simply to end colonial domination. Consequently, the common practice of labelling Southeast Asian (and other Asian and African) nationalist movements anti-colonial, anti-imperial or the like obscures many of their central aspects. Criticism of colonial rule and imperialism was certainly important, as was the goal of achieving national independence. The latter, however, was not the ultimate goal of the nationalists, but a step in the nation's development to become a modern, prosperous, harmonious and just society. The nationalist visions thus went further than the anti-colonial resistance which had characterised earlier uprising and proto-nationalist movements. For Southeast Asian nationalists, independence was a milestone rather than the end of the road.

The most prominent feature of Southeast Asian nationalisms, as they coalesced in the inter-war years, was not their anti-colonialism but rather their emancipatory character. At least three aspects of the progressive and emancipatory nationalism that emerged in Southeast Asia can be distinguished. First, and most obviously, they envisioned political emancipation. Such emancipation did not only aim at freedom from colonial rule. It also envisioned emancipation from traditional forms of political domination by indigenous rulers, who often were seen both as obsolete and as morally corrupt due to their collaboration with the colonisers. Second, Southeast Asian nationalists envisioned social and economic emancipation, that is, freedom from both modern, capitalist forms of exploitation and traditional, feudal ones, such as slavery, bondage, forced labour, arbitrary taxation and unjust land lease arrangements. These social and economic goals, it was widely believed, could be realised only after the twin yoke of colonial rule and traditional indigenous oppression had been cast off. Third, Southeast Asian nationalism was emancipatory and progressive with regard to women's political rights. Men and women were to have equal political rights in the new nation-states, much in contrast to the male dominance of the nationalist movements in Europe and the Americas.

These aspirations were not always realised after independence and the attempts to bring about economic, social and political change often met with resistance, for example from landowners, ethnic minorities and conservative religious leaders. The global struggle between socialism and capitalism during the Cold War also made it difficult for the new states to implement the moderate socialism that many nationalist leaders had envisioned. Ethnic, religious and political tensions often led to protracted war, particularly in Vietnam, or armed rebellions.

Despite these difficulties and deviations from the original nationalist projects, however, the Southeast Asian nation-states that gained independence around the mid-twentieth century, based on the territorial divisions of the colonial period, have proven remarkably resilient. That resilience owes a great deal to the nationalist ideologies and visions that were forged in the region, mainly during the first half of the twentieth century.

Acknowledgement

I am grateful to the Linnaeus University Centre for Concurrences in Colonial and Postcolonial Studies for funding research and time for writing this chapter. Thanks also to the member of the Centre's Research Cluster for Colonial Connections and Comparisons for valuable comments and suggestions on the text.

References

Adas, Michael. 1981. "From Avoidance to Confrontation: Peasant Protest in Precolonial and Colonial Southeast Asia." *Comparative Studies in Society and History* 23 (2): 217–247.
Amirell, Stefan Eklöf. 2012. "Progressive Nationalism and Female Rule in Post-colonial South and Southeast Asia." *Asian Journal of Women's Studies* 18 (2): 35–69.
Anderson, Benedict. 1991. *Imagined Communities: Reflections on the Origin and Spread of Nationalism*. Rev. and extended ed. London: Verso.
———. 1998. *The Spectre of Comparisons: Nationalism, Southeast Asia, and the World*. London: Verso.
———. 2002. "Bung Karno and the Fossilization of Soekarno's Thought." *Indonesia* 74: 1–19.
Benda, Harry J. 1965. *Peasant Movements in Colonial Southeast Asia*. New Haven, CT: Yale University, Southeast Asia Studies.
Bergholz, Max. 2018. "Thinking the Nation: *Imagined Communities: Reflections on the Origin and Spread of Nationalism*, by Benedict Anderson." *American Historical Review* 123 (2): 518–528.
BPS (Badan Pusat Statistik). 2015. "Mengulik Data Suku di Indonesia." [Glimpse of data of tribes of Indonesia]. Website of Statistics Indonesia, https://www.bps.go.id/news/2015/11/18/127/mengulik-data-suku-di-indonesia.html (accessed 25 August 2021).
Chatterjee, Partha. 1986. *Nationalist Thought and the Colonial World: A Derivative Discourse*. London: Zed Books.
Christie, Clive J. 1996. *A Modern History of Southeast Asia: Decolonization, Nationalism and Separatism*. London: Tauris Academic Studies.
Cribb, Robert. 2000. *Historical Atlas of Indonesia*. Honolulu: University of Hawaii Press.
Eckert, Andreas. 2013. "Anti-Western Doctrines of Nationalism." In *The Oxford Handbook of the History of Nationalism*, edited by John Breuilly, 56–74. Oxford: Oxford University Press.

Elson, Robert 1999. "International Commerce, the State and Society: Economic and Social Change." In *The Cambridge History of Southeast Asia: Volume 2, Part 1, From c. 1800 to the 1930s*, edited by Nicholas Tarling, 127–191. Cambridge: Cambridge University Press.

Go, Julian, and Jake Watson. 2019. "Anticolonial Nationalism from Imagined Communities to Colonial Conflict." *European Journal of Sociology/Archives Européennes de Sociologie* 60 (1): 31–68.

Goscha, Christopher E. 1995. *Vietnam or Indochina? Contesting Concepts of Space in Vietnamese Nationalism 1887–1954*. Copenhagen: Nordic Institute of Asian Studies.

Heidbüchel, Esther. 2007. *The West Papua Conflict in Indonesia: Actors, Issues and Approaches*. Wettenberg: Johannes Herrmann Verlag.

Henley, David. 2013. "The Origins of Southeast Asian Nations." In *The Oxford handbook of the History of Nationalism*, edited by John Breuilly, 263–286. Oxford: Oxford University Press.

Hobson, John A. 1902. *Imperialism: A Study*. London: James Nisbet.

Hroch, Miroslav. 1993. "From National Movement to the Fully-formed Nation." *New Left Review* 198 (1): 3.

Jayawardena, Kumari. 1986. *Feminism and Nationalism in the Third World*. London and Totowa, NJ: Zed Books.

Kahin, George McT. 1997. "Some Recollections From and Reflections on the Indonesian Revolution." In *The Heartbeat of the Indonesian Revolution*, edited by Taufik Abdullah, 10–27. Jakarta: Gramedia.

Khoo, Salma Nasution. *Sun Yat Sen in Penang*. Penang: Areca Books, 2008.

Lenin, Vladimir I. 1927 [1916]. *Imperialism: The Last Stage of Capitalism*. London: Communist Party of Great Britain.

Lewis, Su Lin. 2013. "Between Orientalism and Nationalism: The Learned Society and the Making of 'Southeast Asia'." *Modern Intellectual History* 10 (2): 353–374.

Lieberman, Victor B. 2009. *Strange Parallels: Southeast Asia in Global Context, c. 800–1830. Volume 2: Mainland Mirrors: Europe, Japan, China, South Asia, and the Islands*. Cambridge: Cambridge University Press.

Majul, Cesar A. 1988. "The Moro Struggle in the Philippines." *Third World Quarterly* 10 (2): 897–922.

McIntyre, Angus. 1973. "The 'Greater Indonesia' Idea of Nationalism in Malaya and Indonesia." *Modern Asian Studies* 7 (1): 75–83.

McLane, Charles B. 1966. *Soviet Strategies in Southeast Asia: An Exploration of Eastern Policy under Lenin and Stalin*. Princeton, NJ: Princeton University Press.

Mommsen, Wolfgang J. 1982. *Theories of Imperialism*. Chicago, IL: Chicago University Press.

Mosse, George L. 1985. *Nationalism and Sexuality*. New York: Howard Fertig.

NIS (National Institute of Statistics). 2020. General Population Census of the Kingdom of Cambodia 2019. https://www.nis.gov.kh/nis/Census2019/Final%20General%20Population%20Census%202019-English.pdf (26 August 2021).

Osborne, Milton. 2000. *Southeast Asia: An Introductory History*, 8. ed. St. Leonards, NSW: Allen & Unwin.

Pateman, Carole. 1989. *The Disorder of Women*. Cambridge: Polity Press.

Reid, Anthony, ed. 2001. *Sojourners and Settlers: Histories of Southeast Asia and the Chinese*. Honolulu: University of Hawaii Press.

Reid, Anthony. 2010. *Imperial Alchemy: Nationalism and Political Identity in Southeast Asia*, Cambridge: Cambridge University Press.

Scott, James C. 2009. *The Art of Not Being Governed: An Anarchist History of Upland Southeast Asia*. New Haven, CT: Yale University Press.

Scott, Joan W. 1996. *Only Paradoxes to Offer: French Feminists and the Rights of Man*, Cambridge, MA: Harvard University Press.

Sidel, John T. 2012. "The Fate of Nationalism in the New States: Southeast Asia in Comparative Historical Perspective." *Comparative Studies in Society and History* 54 (1): 114–144.

Smith, Bonnie G. 2018. *Modern Empires: A Reader*. New York: Oxford University Press.

Steinberg, David Joel, ed. 1987. *In Search of Southeast Asia*. Rev. ed. Honolulu: University of Hawaii Press.

Stuart-Fox, Martin. 2000. "The Nature and Causes of Revolution in Asia." In *Eastern Asia: An Introductory History*, 3rd ed., edited by Colin Mackerras, 163–176. Frenches Forrest, NSW: Longman.

Tarling, Nicholas. 1998. *Nations and States in Southeast Asia*. Cambridge: Cambridge University Press.

Warren, James F. 1981. *The Sulu Zone, 1768–1898: The Dynamics of External Trade, Slavery, and Ethnicity in the Transformation of a Southeast Asian Maritime State*. Singapore: NUS Press.

Wells, Audrey. 2001. *The Political Thought of Sun Yat-sen*. Houndmills, Basingstoke: Palgrave Macmillan.

Winichakul, Thongchai. 1994. *Siam Mapped: A History of the Geo-body of a Nation*. Honolulu: University of Hawaii Press.

Wood, Michael. 2005. *Official History in Modern Indonesia: New Order Perceptions and Counterviews*. Leiden: Brill.

24
COMPARATIVE NATION-BUILDING IN THE BORDERLANDS BETWEEN CHINA, MYANMAR, AND THAILAND

Enze Han

Introduction

How did different nationalist ideologies in China, Myanmar, and Thailand affected the politics of national identity among various ethnic minority groups living along the borders among the three countries? This chapter first reviews the nation-building politics of these three countries. For the People's Republic of China, it officially recognizes 56 ethnic groups, and there is provision of "nominal" ethnic autonomy. It means that the Chinese state, at least on paper, allows institutional provisions of autonomous government, minority language education, and religious, cultural expressions and so forth (Mullaney 2010). For the Myanmar government, it officially recognizes 135 ethnic groups and established seven ethnic states. However, the long history of military rule in the country meant that an ethnic cultural expression has been highly restricted, and ethnic schools continue to be banned. More significantly, the state has heavily repressed its ethnic minority groups in their fight for self-determination. Finally, in Thailand, its national discourse claims that everyone living within the territorial boundaries of Thailand is Thai while not officially recognizing ethnic minorities who live on the kingdom's peripheries. At the same time, at certain points in history, Thailand has made irredentist claims to pan-Tai ethnic groups in Myanmar as well as in China (Walker 2009).

This chapter then compares the implications of different nationalist ideologies and practices on common cross-border ethnic minorities between China and Myanmar (Han 2020). Compared with China, Myanmar's treatment of its ethnic minorities has been much more brutal as the country has been engulfed in more than half a century of civil war. The military campaigns toward various ethnic rebel organizations intensified repression against ethnic minorities in the Kachin and Shan States (South and Jolliffe 2015). During the past three or more decades, the contrast across the China-Myanmar borderland area has been evident in terms of stability as well as economic prosperity on the Chinese side of the border. For many ethnic minority groups across the border, China is often perceived as the place where ethnic minorities are better treated than in Myanmar (Han 2019a).

This chapter also examines how close ethnic linkages between the Shan and Thai manifest in Thailand's interest in supporting the Shan nationalist movements as part of its pan-Tai sentiment (Reynolds 2004, 119). Although since the end of the WWII, Thailand has forfeited all its claims to other Tai territories in neighboring states since the end of WWII, it continues to heavily influence them culturally and religiously. In the Myanmar Shan State, this manifests itself in terms of how culturally the Shan are oriented toward Thailand. Shan monasteries and monks have close ties with their counterparts in Thailand, while Thai pop music is popular among the Shan (Jirattikorn 2008; 2012, 336). Additionally, support by the Thai government and public, although mainly symbolic, is crucial for maintaining Shan nationalism against Myanmar (Jirattikorn 2012, 334).

Three modes of national identity construction

China

Consolidating Chinese territorial integrity in the ethnic peripheral regions was treated as a top priority by the new communist government when it rose to power in 1949. Borrowing from the Soviet Union's model, the Chinese Communist Party (CCP) adopted a political structure granting ethnic minority groups certain rights of autonomy and self-government, promising them rights equal to the majority Han Chinese and allowing them to develop and use their native languages (Han 2013a; Hansen 1999). Beijing set up a list of autonomous areas, such as the five autonomous regions – Guangxi, Inner Mongolia, Ningxia, Tibet, and Xinjiang – that were given provincial status. In the Southwestern province of Yunnan, with its more than 30 ethnic minority groups, several larger ethnic groups were granted autonomy at the prefectural level, while smaller or more scattered groups were granted autonomy at the county or even township level. For example, in the borderland area between China and Myanmar, Dehong and Xishuangbanna (Sipsongpanna), where most of the Chinese Tai/Dai population live, became autonomous prefectures (Hsieh 1989; Santasombat 2011).

The Ethnic Identification Project (minzu shibie), carried out in the mid-1950s, provided the CCP detailed information about the ethnic composition of Chinese society, but also provided a means for the government to better regulate ethnic minority affairs (Mullaney 2010). As a result of this categorization, the modern-day Chinese nation, according to the CCP's categorization, comprises 55 ethnic minority groups in addition to the majority Han Chinese. However, despite accommodation and cooptation of ethnic minority elites in the early years, the communist government's ethnic minority policies turned repressive as domestic politics became radicalized. Particularly during the Cultural Revolution, not only was there significant violence against minorities in the ethnic regions, but the CCP's overall tolerance toward ethnic cultural differences reached its nadir.

The end of the Cultural Revolution led the CCP to make efforts to redress the excesses committed in the ethnic minority areas. The 1982 Constitution, which is still in use today, elaborates a wide range of minority rights to be realized through national and local legislatures (Sautman 1999, 288). The same document also states that ethnic equality is to be cherished and prohibits discrimination against and oppression of any ethnic minority groups.

Beijing passed the Law on Regional Autonomy (LRA, minzu quyu zizhifa) in 1984. The LRA allows ethnic autonomous areas – such as the aforementioned autonomous regions, prefectures, and counties – to adapt, modify, or supplement national law according to local conditions. More power was given to autonomous areas in terms of education, culture, environment, health care, and family planning (Sautman 1998). For example, there is an emphasis on preferential hiring and promotion of ethnic minorities in enterprises, government institutions, and public security forces. The draconian family planning policy was also loosened to allow ethnic minority couples to have two children in urban areas and more in rural areas. In the areas of language use and education, bilingualism is once again permitted and promoted (Han 2013c). Preferential treatment and quotas have also been implemented for minority students for secondary and tertiary schools. Although the actual implementation of the LRA varies by location, and effectiveness of autonomy provisions has been questioned, at least on paper the Chinese nation conceptualized as multi-ethnic and with ethnic minorities granted certain cultural rights has been propagated by the CCP throughout the modern period.

In recent years, in the name of economic development, Han migration to ethnic minority areas has increased, inevitably exerting great demographic pressure on local minority populations, which might dread growing assimilationist pressure and increasing competition in the job market (Han 2013a, 38). Furthermore, the Chinese government has stepped up its effort to promote the teaching of Mandarin Chinese in ethnic minority areas. Language education reform programs have been carried out to limit ethnic language education (Postiglione 1999). Debate has also emerged recently about whether the ethnic autonomy system should be rethought altogether, with some calling for the system to be abolished rather than improving the system or moderating repressive policies. Citing the failure of the Soviet model, many argue that China should learn from the American melting pot model, where "the absence of group-differentiated institutions, laws, or privileges encourages natural ethnic mingling and a shared sense of civic belonging" (Leibold 2013, 21).

Myanmar

Myanmar's national identity formation process has been more contentious. Its colonial history as part of British India resulted in mass migration of people from the South Asian sub-continent, and the prevalence of Indians "gave the appearance of an Indo-British occupation rather than British occupation of Burma" (Chakravarti 1971, 97). Indians dominated the lower administrative positions of the colonial bureaucracy, and more significantly Indian moneylenders, Chettiars, came to control land in the Irrawaddy Delta area and were heavily resented by the Bamar population and thus became the image associated with foreign exploitation (Gravers 1999, 27; Egreteau 2011, 38). In addition to the Indians, ethnic groups such as Karen, Kachin, and Chin, many of whom were converted to Christianity by Western missionaries, were employed disproportionally in the police and military, leading the Bamar people to view the colonial military as a tool through which they became subjugated by these ethnic minority groups (Walton 2013, 8).

Because of such subordination in the land that they believed as solely theirs, Bamar nationalism started on a very strong anti-foreign, xenophobic foundation. The nationalist rallying cry in the 1930s, dobama "our Bamar," was set on an oppositional term against those thudobama, referring to those who dominated Burma during the colonial period (Nemoto 2011, 3). In such a nationalist discourse, the "us vs. them" dynamic set the foundation for post-independence ethnic strife in the country because many ethnic minorities that were prominent in the colonial administration were viewed with disdain and suspected of disloyalty. Buddhism also became associated directly with Bamar nationalism as a result of the Bamar nationalists' perceived threat from Hindus and Muslims migrating from India and from increasingly large numbers of ethnic groups in Burma converting to Christianity (Gravers 1999, 31; Turner 2017).

All these cleavages created by the colonial experience considerably influenced the post-independence Burmese state's approach to nation-building. In the 1948 Burmese Citizenship Act, the Burmese government specified that to be a Burmese citizen, one has to be a descendant from one of the eight "national races (thanyintha)" – Bamar, Chin, Kachin, Karen, Karenni, Mon, Rakhine, and Shan – who were already residents of Burma by 1823, which was a year before the British colonization occurred. Thus, all the Indians, Chinese, and other foreign nationals would have to apply for naturalization as associated citizens, and applicants had to go through "long and sadistic legal processes" (Egreteau 2011, 40). After Ne Win's coup in 1962, the Burmanization of the economy further kicked out many more Indians and Chinese because foreigners were forbidden to own land and barred from many professions (Holmes 1967). Later, the 1982 Citizenship Act made it even more difficult for "foreigners" to acquire Burmese citizenship, targeting mainly the Rohingya in the Rakhine State, who remain stateless (Egreteau 2011, 41; Han 2021).

As the country faced one insurgency after another since the very day of its independence, the Burmese military, on behalf of the Bamar majority, became obsessed with holding the union together at any cost. Thus, particularly since Ne Win's rise to power in 1962, it was military force that held the Union of Burma together, but not a sense of common national belonging. In Joseph Steinberg's words:

> Each government of the Union of Burma has attempted to create this sense of nationhood – a sharing of national values and will amongst all of its diverse people. Yet, each effort has to a major degree been unsuccessful. Although a 'Union of Burma' as a state was titularly created, a union of people as a nation was not.
>
> *(Steinberg 2001, 182)*

Instead of granting ethnic groups autonomy, a unitary state was forced on the ethnic areas that were under control of the Burmese government, with a strong emphasis on unity among ethnic groups under the Bamar hegemony (Walton 2015). Burmese became the national language, and ethnic languages were banned from the school system (Gravers 2007, 21).

The Myanmar government has consistently pushed for an image of all the national races as part of a happy union (Ferguson 2016, 132). However, such overt display of unity and equality among the national races is contradicted by the reality, where the majority Bamar culture is equated with Myanmar national culture, the Burmese language is the official language, and "In order to be considered truly Myanmar (a member of the nation) one must adopt the trappings of Burman culture" (Walton 2013, 12). Furthermore, given the ongoing insurgency by several ethnic groups in the country, non-Bamar ethnic groups have to prove their loyalty to the Myanmar state, while the majority Bamar does not (Walton 2013, 13).

One may also add that the Myanmar national identity is more repressive and exclusionary in practice. The government's constant emphasis on the "indigenous" nature of the national races continues to exclude large chunks of the population from the nation. Thus, while Chinese or Indians might have naturalized as Myanmar citizens, they are nonetheless excluded from the Myanmar nation. The worst case of course is that of the Rohingya, who have never been issued any citizenship documents and continue to be considered illegal migrants from Bangladesh (Parnini 2013). Years of repression by the Myanmar government and society have led to several instances of Rohingya refugees fleeing to Bangladesh, which has recently received significant international media attention (Kingston 2015). It is here that the Myanmar state's arbitrary and exclusive national identity construction shows its ugliest manifestation.

Thailand

In Thailand's case, the priority of the Thai nation-building project since the early twentieth century has been determining how to incorporate into Thai society the sizable overseas Chinese community, which was estimated to be about a quarter of Siam's entire population in the nineteenth century (Chansiri 2008, 48). Centuries of tributary/trading relations between the two brought many Chinese traders to Siam, but migration from Southern China intensified in the late nineteenth century due to domestic political instability caused by the Taiping Rebellion (Skinner 1957; Wang 2002). By this time, overseas Chinese had already occupied a crucial economic role in Siam because of lucrative trading relations with China, but also due to the fact that they were exempted from corvée labor, and many became actively involved in tax farming for the Siamese court (Wongsurawat 2016, 566). In 1909, the Qing government for the first time started claiming Chinese abroad to be under its protection, redefining Overseas Chinese as citizens whose loyalty should be toward China rather than the European colonies in Southeast Asia. A new Law of Nationality was issued that set out a jus sanguinis principle that defined anyone born to either a Chinese father or mother as a Chinese citizen, and also granted dual citizenship to all Chinese and their descendants living abroad (Han 2019b). Given their economic clout in Siam as both Chinese business and labor contributed heavily to its modernization projects, the Siamese court under Rama VI King Vajiravudh was prompted to issue its own Nationality Act of 1911, which was based on a jus soli basis and granted everyone born on Siamese territory as Siamese citizen (Sng and Bisalputra 2015, 270).

However, the rising popularity of republicanism among Overseas Chinese started to alarm the Siamese royalty. In 1912, there was an aborted assassination attempt on Rama VI (Wongsurawat 2016, 560). King Vajiravudh thus started to take on a harsh view to the presence of the Chinese in Siamese society, and published an essay in 1914 that portrayed the Chinese as "The Jews of the Orient," where he denounced the Chinese as "vampires who steadily suck dry an unfortunate victim's life-blood," which was referring to the economic dominant position of the Chinese and the fact that they sent money back to China (Vella 1986, 194). Such negative portrayal of the Chinese was perhaps motivated by the king's anxious desire to prevent the spread of republicanism within Thai society (Wongsurawat 2016, 561).

However, the Siamese government had no intention to exclude the Chinese. Rather, such denunciation should be interpreted as pressure for the Chinese to assimilate and be loyal to the Siamese king. After the fall of the absolute monarchy in 1932, the Phibun government intensified its assimilationist pressure on the Chinese community for fear of their political entanglement in China. A 1939 modification to the Nationality Act demanded that Chinese who want to naturalize must change their Chinese names to Thai ones, and they should send their children to Thai schools, speak Thai, and cut all allegiance to China (Chansiri 2008, 71). Additionally, a series of acts were passed during the 1938–1939 to wrest the Thai economy from Chinese control. The Chinese were prevented from many professions and trading in several popular commodities, restricted from certain residential areas, Chinese schools and presses were closed down, and much more (Skinner 1957, 262–267). Later, in 1943, the Chinese were prevented from buying land (Skinner 1957, 276). The pressure was aimed at non-Thai-citizen Chinese migrants rather than Chinese born in Thailand, who were natural-born Thai citizens, and the ultimate goal was to induce Chinese migrants to naturalize and assimilate.

From 1950 onward, the Thai government also tightened immigration quotas that made it almost impossible for new migration from China. Thus, the Chinese population in the country became increasingly dominated by those born in Thailand, and the assimilation pressure also compelled many to become culturally and linguistically Thai (Skinner 1957, 381). At the Bandung Afro-Asian Conference in 1955, PRC Premier Zhou Enlai proclaimed that China was willing to negotiate with Southeast Asian governments on the nationality and citizenship of Overseas Chinese (Fitzgerald 1972). Subsequently in the Sino-Indonesian Dual Nationality Treaty of 1955, the PRC officially abandoned the jus sanguinis principle, which effectively relinquished its claim over Overseas Chinese in Southeast Asia. Reception of this change in Thailand was positive because it essentially meant that Bangkok could be confident about the loyalties of the Chinese minority in its society (Skinner 1957, 379).

Solving the Chinese question thus consumed Thai government for almost half a century in its nation-building efforts. Throughout all these processes, the Thai state's approach to the meaning of being Thai have overall emphasized three principles of Thainess, that is, loyalty to the nation, religion, and the king (chat, satsana, and phra mahakasat) (Laungaramsri 2003, 155). Thus, implicitly at least, to be Thai, one has to speak the Thai language, be a Buddhist, and be loyal to the monarchy (Chachavalpongpun 2005). Particularly since the 1960s, a series of military governments has promoted the Thai monarchy as symbolizing Thai nationalism, while at the same time encouraging loyalty and obedience toward the authoritarian military regime (Connors 2006, 48–49). Thus, in contrast to the Chinese official policy of the Chinese nation being multi-ethnic, the Thai concept leaves much less room for alternative ethnic and cultural expression, while emphasizing assimilation.

Comparative nation-building at the borderland

One fruitful way to understand the formative logic of each of the three states' nation-building approach to its multi-ethnic society is to look at whether the central government, and the ethnic majority it represents, perceives enough security in the ongoing nation-building projects within its territorial domain. This sense of security or the lack thereof also has to do with whether ethnic minority groups living in these countries are content with their situations. As I have argued elsewhere, for ethnic groups with transnational kin relations, external factors can play a significant role in shaping whether and how an ethnic group is going to mobilize politically against the nation-building project imposed on it by the state. Through comparison with its external kin relations, an ethnic group can evaluate how it has been treated by the national government, which forms the foundation of its political satisfaction or grievance. In addition, the presence of substantial external support would provide the needed opportunity structure and resources for the group's political mobilization to occur (Han 2011a; 2011b). This theoretical framework also fits our understanding of how ethnic groups across the borderland area among China, Myanmar, and Thailand have similarly reacted to changes within and across the national borders.

Although China as a whole continues to face active resistance to its nation-building projects, it mainly occurs in Tibet and Xinjiang (Han 2010), but not along the southwestern border. Given the different dynamics, the Chinese state has tailored its policies toward managing the variations in different groups' political integration (Han and Paik 2017). For many of the ethnic minority groups living in the Southwest borderland area, the frequent comparison they make in terms of political rights, cultural expression, and economic welfare is with their external kin groups in Myanmar. As a result, few groups in the Yunnan borderland area perceive a better alternative in Myanmar, and overall these ethnic groups are content with their current situation as minorities in a multi-ethnic China while negotiating their limited space for cultural autonomy (Han 2013a, 109).

This is the case with the Jingpo and their external kin group in Myanmar, the Kachin. As a small ethnic group numbering only around 150,000, the Jingpo nonetheless have enjoyed relative political significance, because the group titularly shares autonomous status within the Dehong Tai and Jingpo Autonomous Prefecture. During the early years of the PRC, when domestic political radicalization surged during the Great Leap Forward and Cultural Revolution, large numbers of Jingpo crossed the border into Myanmar. However, since the late 1970s, for those who remained or returned, life on the Chinese side of the border has seen more stability and economic development. In particular, the past couple of decades have further demarcated the differences between the two (Han 2016).

Furthermore, increasing control over the Kachin State by the Myanmar central government meant a strong push for Burmanization and strict control of Kachin cultural expression. Perceptions of the degradation of the Kachin State situation and the affinity between the two populations have prompted a movement among Chinese Jingpo to support the Kachin against the Myanmar government as well as offer humanitarian assistance to displaced Kachin (E. L.-E. Ho 2017). Many Chinese Jingpo also expressed their willingness to influence the Chinese government's policy toward the Kachin State (T. Ho 2016, 171). Although the effect these protests by the Jingpo can have on Chinese foreign policy is debatable, one can certainly argue that the Chinese state does not want to antagonize one of its erstwhile loyal minority groups.

A similar case can also be made about the Wa, who likewise straddle the Sino-Myanmar border, particularly because the territorial demarcation of the Wa areas was only finalized in the 1960 border agreement (Fiskesjö 2017). Currently, there are roughly 430,000 Wa living on the Chinese side of the border, while the number in Myanmar is difficult to come by but estimated to be around 600,000. The United Wa State Army (UWSA) has become the largest ethnic rebel group in the country, especially after it fought with the Myanmar government troops to take down the Mong Tai Army (MTA) by Khun Sa in 1996 (Liu 2014, 78). Afterward, the UWSA took over the territories previously occupied by the MTA along the borderland between Myanmar and Thailand, thus adding a new southern division to its previous areas (northern division) along the Chinese border.

Although the Wa speak their own language, Chinese is the lingua franca in the Wa State, with street signs written in Chinese and TV broadcast in Mandarin. The Wa State government also modeled itself on China's, and in many ways it resembles a Chinese sub-provincial entity. While officially the Wa State government claims that it wants high levels of autonomy within a Federated Myanmar, it seems that its ability to maintain that autonomy is substantially greater than that of other ethnic rebels in Myanmar. Given the close ties with China in every aspect, Myanmar's nation-building projects have never even reached into the Wa State.

Even more telling of how crucial comparisons with external kin groups and availability of external support for ethno-nationalist mobilizations are the cases of different Tai/Shan groups across the borderland between China and Myanmar in their relations with Thailand. These groups' reactions toward their incorporation into the respective nation-building projects in China and Myanmar have varied. Such variations can be partly explained through the external dimension. For example, the Tai groups in China have not seen in Myanmar a better alternative to their present situations, nor have they received any international support. However, the Shan nationalist movements in Myanmar do view Thailand as a better alternative and have periodically received support, both materially and symbolically, from Thailand.

China's Sipsongpanna Tai Autonomous Prefecture is such a case in point. Ever since its establishment in 1953, Chinese rule over Sipsongpanna has been secured without many open challenges. The previous political elites of the Tai Lue aristocracy were stripped of their hereditary powers, but have also been coopted into the political system with symbolic titles. Because of the economic interest of the Chinese government in promoting ethnic tourism in Sipsongpanna (or Yunnan in general), Tai cultural expressions have been tolerated. Thus, the Tai cultural resurgence during the past decades has been partially related to the Chinese state's tactful use of it for its own governance purpose (Han 2013b). Although the Tai Lue language is taught mostly in the monasteries, linguistic assimilation with the Han Chinese is also accelerating (Borchert 2008; 2010; Hansen 1999). With improving economic conditions and comparatively better life prospects compared with neighboring Myanmar or Laos, the Sipsongpanna Tai people have overall accepted their Chinese citizenship (Han 2013a, 113; Diana 2009; Sturgeon 2013). There have been efforts to maintain or revive Tai Lue culture, but few if any political claims can be seen in Sipsongpanna that would challenge Chinese rule.

However this is not the case with the Shan in Myanmar. The Shan nationalist insurgencies have been haunted by a lack of cohesion from the start, and what has been observed is a series of fragmentation and regrouping of various nominally Shan rebel groups (Laungaramsri 2006, 72). These groups all held political claims for fighting for independence or autonomy on behalf of the Shan people against the Myanmar government, but at the same time many were embroiled in the illegal trafficking of goods and drugs across the border to sustain their insurgencies (Yawnghwe 2010, 123).

Such fragmentation notwithstanding, one main reason why the variety of Shan insurgent groups could survive for more than half a century had to do with their physical locations close to the porous Thai-Myanmar border, as well as the tolerance and tacit support they received from the Thai government and society. Ever since the mid-1950s, the Thai government has practiced a "buffer zone" policy toward various ethnic rebels along the bilateral border with Burma (Lintner 1995, 72). The policy was first designed to thwart Thailand's historical enemy, Burma, but also served to prevent communist infiltration from the north. Although the Thai state did not offer open support, rebel armies "were allowed to set up camps along the frontier, their families were permitted to stay in Thailand and they could buy arms and ammunition" (Lintner 1995, 74). Thus, from the 1960s to the 1980s, Shan insurgent groups established closely knit networks across the border in Thailand, and the porous borderland facilitated the movement of migrants as well as illicit trade.

The Thai government's "buffer zone" policy toward the borderland with Myanmar changed in the late 1980s when the Chatichai government started to push a new policy to "turn battlefield into marketplace." Not only did the Thai government agree to solve the problems at the border caused by the ethnic rebels, but Bangkok also obtained forest concessions from the Burmese military government in 1988, which turned out to be disastrous for the Shan armed groups because they gradually lost their logging industry. However, the Myanmar government continues to accuse the Thai government of supporting ethnic insurgencies along the border. In the end, Thaksin Shinawatra's government announced Thailand should abolish the "buffer zone" policy and officially ended support for ethnic armed groups in Myanmar in 2003.

The sustainment of the Shan nationalist groups has also to do with the ethnic kin sentiment that many Thais have toward the Shan. The Thai public discourse still considers the Shan as ethnic kin to the Thai (Jirattikorn 2012, 333). In particular, there are Thai intellectuals who romanticized the Shan as maintaining many of the old Tai traditions that the modernized Thai society has foregone (Winichakul 2008). Thus, the Thai domestic discourse has played a role in "constructing a romantic, revolutionary image of the Shan" insurgents in their resistance against the Myanmar government (Jirattikorn 2012, 334).

After the MTA's collapse in 1995, many Shan former insurgents and civilians crossed the border into Thailand. Concentrated in northern Thailand and particularly Chiang Mai, they established exile Shan nationalist organizations (Jirattikorn 2011, 19). These Shan exile groups have utilized newfound resources and freer media spaces in Thailand to disseminate information toward the Shan State, within Thailand, as well as to the international community, regarding the political situation in the Shan State (Ferguson 2013). For example, Shan nationalist materials printed in Chiang Mai were brought back to the Shan States through underground channels (Ferguson 2008). It seems that the Thai state tolerated Shan media production that is otherwise banned in Myanmar, which allowed the exile Shan organizations to be able to disseminate their visions of Shan nationalism (Ferguson 2008). Within Thailand, Thai academics and activists, who are sympathetic toward the Shan, also mobilized domestic media to promote the Shan cause (Jirattikorn 2011, 31–32). Thus, books, songs, TV programming, and movies have been made to showcase the Thai society's support for the Shan (Jirattikorn 2011, 31).

Suffice it to say, the Shan State is still plagued by the continual militarization of various rebel groups and militias, and there is no clear sign how and when these insurgencies would end. Although much of the Shan resistance against the Myanmar government originated from Myanmar's domestic interethnic tensions and history of military repression, it is necessary to recognize the role the neighboring Thailand had providing permissive conditions for successive Shan insurgencies to sustain themselves.

Separately, Thailand itself still has the task of integrating several groups of ethnic minorities in its geopolitical peripheries into the imagined Thai nation. Other than the issue of assimilating the large number of Chinese that we have discussed earlier, one main challenge that the Thai state faced during the Cold War was how to deal with the itinerant hill tribes (*chao kao*) in the northern mountainous regions. Lumping several groups together into this category, the Thai state's official discourse has treated these groups as particularly threatening to the territorial and national integrity of Thailand (Laungaramsri 2003, 164). Partly, this perception of a security threat was based on the migratory practices of these groups across national borders, which the Thai state deemed as evidence of lacking concrete ties with the Thai nation, i.e. the three principles of the Thai nationalism as discussed above. Bangkok has employed a list of bureaucratic measures to regulate the citizenship status of these hill tribes, providing Thai-language education to generate a sense of national belonging, in addition to the use of forest management and other agricultural transformation policies through the Royal Development Projects to territorialize the tribes (Laungaramsri 2003, 165–167).

Although the hill tribes' population in Thailand number less than one million,[1] they have been featured prominently in the Thai state's nation-building projects since the 1960s, particularly since the intensified perception of security threat from communist infiltrations from the north (Safman 2007, 35). Because of porous borders and the migratory nature of these groups, the Thai state designed a complicated ID card system to document and regulate such communities by providing a contingent and layered system of citizenship (McCargo 2011). Indeed, since 1967, the Thai state had offered at least 17 different kinds of ID cards on different groups of people who have entered Thailand at various times so as to certify individual identity and control people's movements across borders (Laungaramsri 2014, 150). However, many of the criteria used to categorize people were arbitrary, and the complex nature of the ID card system only created a strong sense of confusion among the subject population the Thai state aims to regulate while further marginalizing them from the mainstream Thai society (Laungaramsri 2014, 158).

However, in contrast to the Shan/Tai, Kachin/Jingpo, and Wa cases we discussed above, the groups that have been categorized as hill tribes, such as Karen, Hmong, Akha, Lisu, Lahu, Yao, and so forth, none of them have received any substantial external support. At the same time, living conditions in Thailand are overall much better than in Myanmar or Laos due to chronic poverty and warfare in the latter two countries, which explains why migration has still continued. Lacking their own ethno-nationalist aspirations, these groups became the target of the Thai state's extensive development interventions aiming to incorporate them into the Thai nation-state (Gillogly 2004, 116).

Framed within the discourse of counter-insurgency and forest management, the Thai state has extended administrative control over the hill tribes through a few government agencies such as Department of Public Welfare (DPW), the Royal Forestry Department, and the Border Patrol Police (BPP). For example, the DPW's Hill Tribes Relations Program started in 1965, involving sending Thai university students to teach the highlanders in a civilizing mission (Gillogly 2004, 122). The Royal Forestry Department has been heavily involved in opium eradication and ending swidden agriculture among hill tribes, and it has consistently used the rationale of forest and wildlife protection to restrict hill tribe's land use and relocate them (Gillogly 2004, 130).

Furthermore, the BPP has been extremely crucial in enacting state control over the hill tribe in the borderland area, as well as nation-building through its extensive school systems, which "constitute concrete steps toward actualizing a vision of a territorially and psychologically consolidated Thailand by ensuring the national loyalty of border populations" (Hyun 2014b, 342). Crucial emphasis has been put on teaching the Thai language to the hill tribes, as well as spreading the patronage of the royal family through development projects in the borderland area (Hyun 2017; 2014a). Indeed, although many hill tribe people remain stateless in the borderland area, since the end of the Cold War few groups have overtly challenged the Thai state's nation-building projects. In fact, most BPP-built schools have recently been transferred to the Ministry of Education or local level administration, which suggests the decline of the Thai state's security threat perception, and the success of integrating these hill tribes to the Thai society (Ball 2013, 1:116).

Concluding remarks

In this comparative analysis of the intricacies of nation-building among the three countries, we have noted the marked differences in their respective approaches toward the conception of national identity. Each state's version of national identity has different degrees of inclusiveness vs. exclusiveness, which were partly predetermined by the historical processes of political contestation in the post-WWII periods. However, such different versions of national belonging and the international politics of cross-border relations have demonstrated how deeply interrelated the nation-building projects have been in these three countries. Although domestic politics of nation-building in each country has played a major role, it is crucial to recognize how much the external dimension across national borders has exerted different effects on similar sets of ethnic groups.

Note

1 It is difficult to precisely calculate the hill tribe population in Thailand, and many in fact remain stateless. However, according to a major census of hill tribes conducted in 1985–1988, the population was documented to be 554,172 (Vaddhanaphuti 2005, 156).

References

Ball, Desmond. 2013. *Tor Chor Dor: Thailands Border Patrol Police: History, Organisation, Equipment and Personnel*. Vol. 1. 2 vols. Bangkok, Thailand: White Lotus Co Ltd.
Borchert, Thomas. 2008. "Worry for the Dai Nation: Sipsongpannā, Chinese Modernity, and the Problems of Buddhist Modernism." *The Journal of Asian Studies* 67 (1): 107–142.
———. 2010. "The Abbot's New House: Thinking about How Religion Works among Buddhists and Ethnic Minorities in Southwest China." *Journal of Church and State* 52 (1): 112–137.
Chachavalpongpun, Pavin. 2005. *A Plastic Nation: The Curse of Thainess in Thai-Burmese Relations*. Lanham, MD: University Press of America.
Chakravarti, Nalini Ranjan. 1971. *Indian Minority in Burma: Rise and Decline of an Immigrant Community*. London and New York: Oxford University Press.
Chansiri, Disaphol. 2008. *The Chinese Émigrés of Thailand in the Twentieth Century*. Youngstown, NY: Cambria Press.
Connors, Michael Kelly. 2006. *Democracy and National Identity in Thailand*. Revised edition. Copenhagen: NIAS Press.
Diana, Antonella. 2009. "Re-Configuring Belonging in Post-Socialist Xishuangbanna, China." In *Tai Lands and Thailand: Community and State in Southeast Asia*, edited by Andrew Walker. Honolulu: University of Hawai'i Press.
Egreteau, Renaud. 2011. "Burmese Indians in Contemporary Burma: Heritage, Influence, and Perceptions since 1988." *Asian Ethnicity* 12 (1): 33–54.
Ferguson, Jane M. 2008. "Revolutionary Scripts: Shan Insurgent Media Practice at the Thai-Burma Border." In *Political Regimes and the Media in Asia*, edited by Krishna Sen and Terence Lee, 106–121. Abingdon: Routledge.
———. 2013. "Is the Pen Mightier than the AK-47? Tracking Shan Women's Militancy Within and Beyond." *Intersections: Gender and Sexuality in Asia and the Pacific* 33: 3.
———. 2016. "Ethno-Nationalism and Participation in Myanmar: Views from Shan State and Beyond." In *Metamorphosis: Studies in Social and Political Change in Myanmar*, edited by Renaud Egreteau and Francois Robinne, 127–150. Singapore: NUS Press.
Fiskesjö, Magnus. 2017. "People First: The WA World of Spirits and Other Enemies." *Anthropological Forum* 27 (4): 340–364.
Fitzgerald, Stephen. 1972. *China and the Overseas Chinese: A Study of Peking's Changing Policy: 1949–1970*. Cambridge: Cambridge University Press.
Gillogly, Kathleen. 2004. "Developing the 'Hill Tribes' of Northern Thailand." In *Civilizing the Margins: Southeast Asian Government Policies for the Development of Minorities*, edited by Christopher R. Duncan, 116–149. Ithaca, NY : Cornell University Press.
Gravers, Mikael. 1999. *Nationalism as Political Paranoia in Burma: An Essay on the Historical Practice of Power*. Abingdon: Routledge.
———. 2007. "Introduction: Ethnicity against State – State against Ethnic Diversity?" In *Exploring Ethnic Diversity in Burma*, edited by Mikael Gravers, 1–33. Copenhagen: NIAS Press.
Han, Enze. 2010. "Boundaries, Discrimination, and Interethnic Conflict in Xinjiang, China." *International Journal of Conflict and Violence (IJCV)* 4 (2): 244–256.
———. 2011a. "The Dog That Hasn't Barked: Assimilation and Resistance in Inner Mongolia, China." *Asian Ethnicity* 12 (1): 55–75.
———. 2011b. "From Domestic to International: The Politics of Ethnic Identity in Xinjiang and Inner Mongolia." *Nationalities Papers* 39 (6): 941–962.
———. 2013a. *Contestation and Adaptation: The Politics of National Identity in China*. New York and London: Oxford University Press.
———. 2013b. "Transnational Ties, HIV/AIDS Prevention and State-Minority Relations in Sipsongpanna, Southwest China." *Journal of Contemporary China* 22 (82): 594–611.
———. 2013c. "External Cultural Ties and the Politics of Language in China." *Ethnopolitics* 12 (1): 30–49.
———. 2016. "Borderland Ethnic Politics and Changing Sino-Myanmar Relations." In *War and Peace in the Borderlands of Myanmar: The Kachin Ceasefire, 1994–2011*, edited by Mandy Sadan. Copenhagen: NIAS Press.
———. 2019a. *Asymmetrical Neighbors: Borderland State-Building between China and Southeast Asia*. New York and London: Oxford University Press.

———. 2019b. "Bifurcated Homeland and Diaspora Politics in China and Taiwan towards the Overseas Chinese in Southeast Asia." *Journal of Ethnic and Migration Studies* 45 (4): 577–594.
———. 2020. "Neighborhood Effect of Borderland State Consolidation: Evidence from Myanmar and Its Neighbors." *The Pacific Review* 33 (2): 305–330.
———. 2021. "Overconfidence, Missteps, and Tragedy: Dynamics of Myanmar's International Relations and the Genocide of the Rohingya." *The Pacific Review* (October): 1–22.
Han, Enze, and Christopher Paik. 2017. "Ethnic Integration and Development in China." *World Development* 93 (May): 31–42.
Hansen, Mette Halskov. 1999. *Lessons in Being Chinese: Minority Education and Ethnic Identity in Southwest China*. Seattle: University of Washington Press.
Ho, Elaine Lynn-Ee. 2017. "Mobilising Affinity Ties: Kachin Internal Displacement and the Geographies of Humanitarianism at the China–Myanmar Border." *Transactions of the Institute of British Geographers* 42 (1): 84–97.
Ho, Ts'ui-p'ing. 2016. "People's Diplomacy and Borderland History through the Chinese Jingpo Manau Zumko Festival." In *War and Peace in the Borderlands of Myanmar: The Kachin Ceasefire, 1994–2011*, edited by Mandy Sadan, 169–201. Copenhagen: NIAS Press.
Holmes, Robert A. 1967. "Burmese Domestic Policy: The Politics of Burmanization." *Asian Survey* 7 (3): 188–197.
Hsieh, Shi-Chung. 1989. "Ethnic-Political Adaptation and Ethnic Change of the Sipsong Panna Dai: An Ethnohistorical Analysis." Ph.D. Dissertation. Seattle: University of Washington.
Hyun, Sinae. 2014a. "Indigenizing the Cold War: Nation-Building by the Border Patrol Police in Thailand, 1945–1980." Ph.D. Dissertation. Madison: University of Wisconsin-Madison.
———. 2014b. "Building a Human Border: The Thai Border Patrol Police School Project in the Post–Cold War Era." *Sojourn: Journal of Social Issues in Southeast Asia* 29 (2): 332–63.
———. 2017. "Mae Fah Luang: Thailand's Princess Mother and the Border Patrol Police during the Cold War." *Journal of Southeast Asian Studies* 48 (2): 262–282.
Jirattikorn, Amporn. 2008. "'Pirated' Transnational Broadcasting: The Consumption of Thai Soap Operas among Shan Communities in Burma." *Sojourn: Journal of Social Issues in Southeast Asia* 23 (1): 30–62.
———. 2011. "Shan Virtual Insurgency and the Spectatorship of the Nation." *Journal of Southeast Asian Studies* 42 (1): 17–38.
———. 2012. "Aberrant Modernity: The Construction of Nationhood among Shan Prisoners in Thailand." *Asian Studies Review* 36 (3): 327–343.
Kingston, Lindsey N. 2015. "Protecting the World's Most Persecuted: The Responsibility to Protect and Burma's Rohingya Minority." *The International Journal of Human Rights* 19 (8): 1163–1175.
Laungaramsri, Pinkaew. 2003. "Ethnicity and the Politics of Ethnic Classification in Thailand." In *Ethnicity in Asia*, edited by Colin Mackerras, 157–173. Abingdon: Routledge.
———. 2006. "Women, Nation, and the Ambivalence of Subversive Identification along the Thai-Burmese Border." *Sojourn: Journal of Social Issues in Southeast Asia* 21 (1): 68–89.
———. 2014. "Contested Citizenship: Cards, Colors, and the Culture of Identification." In *Ethnicity, Borders, and the Grassroots Interface with the State: Studies on Southeast Asia in Honor of Charles F. Keyes*, edited by John A. Marston, 143–162. Chiang Mai: Silkworm Books.
Leibold, James. 2013. *Ethnic Policy in China: Is Reform Inevitable?* Washington, DC: East-West Center.
Lintner, Bertil. 1995. "Recent Developments on the Thai-Burma Border." *IBRU Boundary and Security Buletin* April: 72–76.
Liu, Xuan. 2014. "United Wa State Army in Myanmar: Origin, Development and Influence (Miandian Wabang Liangejun: Qiyuan, Fazhan Ji Yingxiang)." *Indian Ocean Economic and Political Review (Yingduyang Jingjiti Yanjiu)* 3: 71–93.
McCargo, Duncan. 2011. "Informal Citizens: Graduated Citizenship in Southern Thailand." *Ethnic and Racial Studies* 34 (5): 833–49.
Mullaney, Thomas. 2010. *Coming to Terms with the Nation: Ethnic Classification in Modern China*. Berkeley: University of California Press.
Nemoto, Kei. 2011. "The Concepts of Dobama ('Our Burma') and Thudo-Bama ('Their Burma') in Burmese Nationalism, 1930–1948." *Journal of Burma Studies* 5 (1): 1–16.
Parnini, Syeda Naushin. 2013. "The Crisis of the Rohingya as a Muslim Minority in Myanmar and Bilateral Relations with Bangladesh." *Journal of Muslim Minority Affairs* 33 (2): 281–297.

Postiglione, Gerard A., ed. 1999. *China's National Minority Education: Culture, Schooling, and Development.* Garland Reference Library of Social Science ; Reference Books in International Education, v. 1090. v. 42. New York: Falmer Press.

Reynolds, Bruce. 2004. "Phibun Songkhram and Thai Nationalism in the Fascist Era." *European Journal of East Asian Studies* 3 (1): 99–134.

Safman, Rachel M. 2007. "Minorities and State-Building in Mainland Southeast Asia." In *Myanmar: State, Society and Ethnicity*, edited by N. Ganesan and Kyaw Yin Klaing. Singapore: Institute of Southeast Asian Studies.

Santasombat, Yos. 2011. *Lak Chang: A Reconstruction of Tai Identity in Daikong.* Canberra: Australian National University Press.

Sautman, Barry. 1998. "Preferential Policies for Ethnic Minorities in China: The Case of Xinjiang." *Nationalism and Ethnic Politics* 4 (1–2): 86–118.

———. 1999. "Ethnic Law and Minority Rights in China: Progress and Constraints." *Law & Policy* 21 (3): 283–314.

Skinner, George William. 1957. *Chinese Society in Thailand an Analytical History.* Ithaca, NY: Cornell University Press.

Sng, Jeffery, and Pimpraphai Bisalputra. 2015. *A History of the Thai-Chinese.* Singapore: Editions Didier Millet.

South, Ashley, and Kim Jolliffe. 2015. "Forced Migration: Typology and Local Agency in Southeast Myanmar." *Contemporary Southeast Asia: A Journal of International & Strategic Affairs* 37 (2): 211–241.

Steinberg, David I. 2001. *Burma: The State of Myanmar.* Washington, DC: Georgetown University Press.

Sturgeon, Janet C. 2013. "Cross-Border Rubber Cultivation between China and Laos: Regionalization by Akha and Tai Rubber Farmers." *Singapore Journal of Tropical Geography* 34 (1): 70–85.

Turner, Alicia. 2017. *Saving Buddhism: The Impermanence of Religion in Colonial Burma.* Honolulu: University of Hawai'i Press.

Vaddhanaphuti, Chayan. 2005. "The Thai State and Ethnic Minorities: From Assimilation to Selective Integration." In *Ethnic Conflict in Southeast Asia*, edited by Kusuma Snitwngse and W. Scott Thompson, 151–166. Singapore: Institute of Southeast Asian Studies.

Vella, Walter F. 1986. *Chaiyo!: King Vajiravadh and the Development of Thai Nationalism.* Manoa: University of Hawai'i Press.

Walker, Andrew, ed. 2009. *Tai Lands and Thailand: Community and State in Southeast Asia.* Singapore: National University of Singapore.

Walton, Matthew J. 2013. "The 'Wages of Burman-Ness:' Ethnicity and Burman Privilege in Contemporary Myanmar." *Journal of Contemporary Asia* 43 (1): 1–27.

———. 2015. "The Disciplining Discourse of Unity in Burmese Politics." *Journal of Burma Studies* 19 (1): 1–26.

Wang, Gungwu. 2002. *The Chinese Overseas: From Earthbound China to the Quest for Autonomy,* Cambridge: Harvard University Press.

Winichakul, Thongchai. 2008. "Nationalism and the Radical Intelligentsia in Thailand." *Third World Quarterly* 29 (3): 575–591.

Wongsurawat, Wasana. 2016. "Beyond Jews of the Orient: A New Interpretation of the Problematic Relationship between the Thai State and Its Ethnic Chinese Community." *Positions* 24 (2): 555–582.

Yawnghwe, Chao Tzang. 2010. *The Shan of Burma: Memoirs of a Shan Exile.* Singapore: ISEAS Publishing.

25
NATIONALISM, ETHNICITY, AND REGIONAL CONFLICT IN TWENTY-FIRST-CENTURY SOUTHEAST ASIA

Arabinda Acharya

Introduction

Several aspects of conflicts in Southeast Asia present unique characteristics. To the naked eye, these seem like age-old separatist movements or terrorism, and now, with the advent of Al Qaeda and the Islamic State of Iraq and Syria (ISIS), religio-political conflicts. To be sure, the region has witnessed several protracted insurgencies during which militant groups have resorted to acts of violence, including the use of terrorist tactics, to achieve political objectives. In almost all cases, these conflicts have strong local roots, though their nature differs from country to country. Some of the persisting conflicts, such as in southern Thailand, the southern Philippines, and many parts of Indonesia, are old-fashioned nationalist or ethno-nationalist movements. In many cases, as in southern Thailand and Indonesia – such as in Aceh, Ambon, and Maluku – these are often layered over communal issues. But not all political conflicts or ideological contestations lead to terrorism in the region, and not all are inherently religious, as they have conventionally been made out to be. In many cases, violence is associated with issues of political participation, communal relations, competition for resources, identity, and a quest for autonomy.

Explaining conflict in Southeast Asia

Colonialism

From a historical perspective, many conflicts in the world, especially in the global South, are unwelcome consequences of colonialism. In fact, it is possible to trace the roots of some of the conflicts in Southeast Asia to the period when the colonial powers began to alter the region's social, political, and economic structures in order to consolidate their rule. Among the sweeping changes introduced was the redrawing of the political boundaries of some of the key countries of the region. These essentially artificial boundaries amalgamated diverse groups into new political entities without much regard to their distinct ethnic, religious, cultural, and linguistic roots. An unintended consequence was the dilution of demographic balance and the appearance of new identities which subsequently found themselves at loggerheads. In fact, the reinforcement of the majority and minority dynamic, and identity dissonance, came to define many of the conflicts in Southeast Asia in the post-colonial era, irrespective of the underlying objectives (Acharya 2015).

As Nicholas Tarling argues, the borders drawn up in colonial Southeast Asia were originally intended to prevent the outbreak of war among the rival colonial powers in the region (Tarling 2001, 286), but their retention in the post-colonial era complicated the principles of self-determination and nationality (Tarling 2001, 286). Southeast Asian states did not undergo "the kind of culturally homogeneous national assertiveness that broke up empires in Europe and the Americas under the pressures of industrialization and print capitalism" (Reid 2010, 1). Instead, the territorial and demographic predicament of the post-colonial states, especially the "lack of fit" between territorial boundaries and the ethnic, cultural, and religious composition of new states in Southeast Asia, underpinned the quest of these nations for "national security" (Ayoob, 1995).

Concern for regime survival and the need for consolidation exacerbated this dynamic for the states in the region. Additionally, there was a degree of external pressure on the emerging countries to vigorously defend their new-found sovereignty and territorial integrity (Tarling 2004, 164). In the post-colonial era, Southeast Asian nations – including Thailand, despite never being colonized – were thus confronted with the need to build effective state structures and cohesive national identities, and to accomplish both tasks simultaneously (Henderson and Singer 2000, 278).

However, in multi-ethnic, multi-religious, and multi-cultural societies, attempts at state consolidation also came face-to-face with resistance, often in the form of armed rebellion, from groups seeking self-determination for one reason or another (Horowitz 1986). While the roots of the quest for self-determination varied – from minority concerns over their share in the political space to control over resources – almost all led to political violence and terrorism in the region (Gurr 2001).

History and ethnic nationalism

The historical roots of some of the communities and groups in conflict are also of particular importance in the Southeast Asian context. Many of them – mostly minorities in terms of ethnicity, religion, language, and the like – had previously been proud subjects of independent kingdoms, sultanates, or even colonial powers before being confronted with challenges of integration into much larger, often alien, political entities. Additionally, they had to contend with regimes dominated by majority ethnic and religious groups. As Jack Snyder puts it, such conditions invariably provoke a tendency to define national identity in terms of the dominant (majority) group's values and culture, with other (minority) groups tending to be, or perceiving themselves as, left on the periphery (Snyder 2000, 322–323).

This becomes more problematic when ethnic or religious minorities are seen as potential threats to national integration by the ruling elite, which as mentioned above is drawn from the majority community (Winichakul 1994). Domination, as Snyder points out, works if the power of the dominant group is so overwhelming as to preclude rational resistance, or when it is tolerated by those who are deprived of power but decide that being second-class citizens is better than being first-class rebels (Winichakul 1994). In an ethno-nationalist or religious context, conflict and strife are the outcome if domination fails or is not tolerated by the minority community, as seen specifically in the context of Thailand.

T. Vanham states that there is a strong positive correlation between ethnic conflict and ethnic nepotism, expressed in terms of ethnic heterogeneity (tendency of the majority to appropriate public positions and public goods in exclusion of the minority, for example), albeit in particular contexts, such as in Malaysia and Thailand (Vanham 1999, 55–73). This is also the case when religion is implicated in these conflicts (Reynal-Querol 2002, 29–54). With religious polarization, conflicts tend to become protracted – there can be a perception that the issues are indivisible and hence not amenable to settlement through political means or negotiation (Svensson 2007, 930–949). There are also other factors, not the least being linguistic and cultural diversity and economic disparity, that cut across all these fault lines.

Nation-building and state consolidation

It is also held that minority grievances over a lack of political and civil rights, income inequality, and social and cultural marginalization – perceived or otherwise – are mostly conducive to internal unrest and violent conflicts. In almost all cases, such grievances, especially in newly emerging societies, relate to state consolidation. Though not an exclusive regional issue, state consolidation has an impact on the existing state, society, and institutional arrangements, which in the situation of a minority-majority dynamic invokes uncertainty in the minority about their status, rights, and remedies.

As Holsti notes, there is also a tendency on the part of the state authority to use harsh measures, as leaders entrapped in such situations often experience a "state strength dilemma" (Holsti 1996, 128), in which rather than seeking legitimacy through the political process, there is a preference to achieve assimilation through harsh policies and measures (Poe et al. 2000). This, in turn, provokes even stronger resistance from the minority communities, often leading to civic strife and even terrorism. In the Southeast Asian context, the conflicts in southern Thailand and southern Philippines attest to this logic, though it has also manifested in a milder form in Indonesia and Malaysia, especially in the context of contested political space and resources between people of Chinese and Indian origins and the majority Muslim population (Suryadinata 2004, 18).

Historically, violence has been more common in areas that were not deeply integrated into the former colonies. For example, at the time of independence, East Timor and West Papua were not part of Indonesia, and Aceh was only weakly integrated into the Netherlands East Indies during Dutch colonial rule. After independence, the Acehnese engaged in a campaign to establish an Islamic republic until they were brought into the mainstream through negotiation. There were armed secessionist movements in East Timor before it gained independence, and West Papua has also experienced armed insurgency demanding independence (Gershman).

Sovereignty, survival, and identity

Sensitivity to sovereignty and territorial integrity is a well-established normative consideration among both scholars and political elites of the region, to the extent that protection and preservation of both has become a mantra for the countries of Southeast Asia. Both involve a focus on the security of the state as a territorial entity. Others, especially those belonging to the Copenhagen School, argue however that there is always a tension between a state's striving for security and a society's craving for self-preservation, as both are linked to concern for survival – the survival of the state relies on "maintenance of its sovereignty," whereas the survival of society depends on "maintenance of its identity" (Waever et al. 1993, 24–25). In other words, state security is generally concerned with external threats, while societal security concerns situations when a society perceives threats to its existence and decides to do something about it. As Michael Clarke notes, "If a state loses its sovereignty, it will not survive as a state, while if a society loses its identity, it will not survive as a society" (Clarke 2008, 273).

In this context, governance policies and practices in these states are found to have put ethnic, religious, cultural, and linguistic groups at loggerheads. In many cases, such as southern Thailand, the desire of particular minorities (Malay Muslims) to protect their identity often comes into conflict with the demands of loyalty to a state dominated by the Thai majority. The contradiction in these two desires is the root cause of many conflicts with ethno-religious connotations. In such cases, some minorities also perceive themselves to be in a disadvantageous position vis-à-vis the majority in their state (Yuchao and Dongyan 2006, 25), with threats of political marginalization, economic deprivation, forced assimilation, cultural oppression, and physical oppression, to name a few (Ibid).

Nation-building and demand for national self-determination

Additionally, in some cases, minorities in a particular nation do not perceive their current political status as legitimate, which explains their demand for national self-determination and even their resorting to armed rebellion under particular circumstances (Connor 2002, 37). Such a demand could be due to demographic imbalance as a result of arbitrary demarcation of boundaries, as is the case with the Malay Muslims who find themselves on the wrong side of the Thailand-Malaysia border. It could also be a reaction to the nation-building process of a particular state, such as in China, which however is seen as an exercise of state power dominated by the majority to build a cohesive national identity (Yuchao and Dongyan 2006, 26). In a state-building process, assimilation is often a national demand and minorities' rights and interests are compromised, as they have to be subordinated to the dominant political entity.

Evidently, some policies and commitment of nation-building can be perceived not only as violations of human rights, but also as threats to minority identity. These real or perceived threats generate the discontent of the disadvantaged minorities at the very root level (Yuchao and Dongyan 2006, 26). Thus, to a great extent, the ruthless or indiscriminate pursuit of nation-building, modernization, and legitimacy by many Southeast Asian states, by whatever means, has contributed to the hardening of identities of certain social entities vis-à-vis these states.

Although ethno-nationalist and minority conflicts are usually rooted in the perception of threat and marginalization, such perceptions do not always lead to conflict or terrorism. "Conflicts in which the rights and political/social viability of particular communities are central issues are not evidence of ethnic chauvinism or of hatred for 'the other'," as Ernie Regehr puts it. "Conflicts emerge with intensity when a community, in response to unmet basic need for social and economic security, resolves to strengthen its collective influence and to struggle for political recognition" (Regehr, 2007). Such conflicts are reflections of a more fundamental social distrust borne out of a community's experience of economic inequity, political discrimination, and human rights violations, to name a few factors. In this respect, conflicts in Southeast Asia are no exception.

Tussles over resources and native rights

At the same time, however, not all conflicts involve minority concerns. Southeast Asia also experiences conflicts which involve tussles over resources and what could be termed communal and/or sectarian conflict. To be sure, demands for self-determination have been a major source of conflict in Southeast Asia. This includes demands for independence and/ or significant autonomy. Desire for greater autonomy includes demands by local people for a province or distinct political unit of their own, or the right to choose their leaders without interference from central government; a more generous share in resources; and more importantly, the opportunity to determine how local resources are used, and for whom.

In most cases, these conflicts are associated with concerns about the exploitation of local resources or the unfair distribution of the proceeds. This is manifested in the centralized and elite ownership and control of natural resources, displacement, and transmigration typical of many Southeast Asian countries (O'Connor 2004, 319–333; Pryor 1979; Hardjono, 1977). Grievances over resource allocation and resource use have also often been expressed in violent terms in many other parts of the region, such as in Aceh and Kalimantan.

One of the more recent examples of grievances over exploitation of resources leading to terrorist attacks was the suicide bombings on 17 July 2009 targeting the JW Marriott and Ritz-Carlton hotels in Jakarta. In a statement on 26 July, the mastermind, Noor din Top, claimed that the attack was designed to target the "KADIN Amerika" (US Chamber of Commerce and Industry) – the meeting of top Indonesian functionaries and foreign businesses organized by Castle Asia Group in the Marriott (Noordin M Top 2009). The meeting also featured top Indonesian businessmen, mostly of Chinese origin. The deeply entrenched historical animosity of the majority Muslims toward Indonesians of Chinese origin, due to their relative wealth, is well-known in the region. For example, during the All-Indonesian National Importers Congress in March 1956, a speech entitled "The Chinese Grip on Our Economy" put this hostility in rather stark terms:

> The power of the exclusivist and monopolistic Chinese in the economic field is far more dangerous for the progress of the Indonesian people, but that power is not regulated in any agreement... it has been rooted and entrenched in society for centuries. Therefore, liquidation of this legacy of Dutch colonialism is very difficult. We must face this danger together. The entire people and the government must face it consciously and systematically, as we have struggled to liquidate all other aspects of Dutch colonialism.
> *(Feith and Castles 1970)*

Similar sentiments can be seen in Malaysia, which has a number of policies like preferential treatment of Bumiputras, giving primacy in jobs and business to Muslims, to counter the relative wealth of citizens of Chinese origin (Abrahim 2003, 52–54).

Transmigration and displacement

Transmigration has been particularly problematic in Southeast Asia – in Indonesia and Thailand, to be specific, where population relocation has been a deliberate state policy. The Thai government's Self-Help Land Settlement Project led to mass migration of Thai Buddhists from other regions to the south, which was resented by the Malay Muslim community as a manifestation of cultural colonization by means of deliberate dilution of local demography (Yegar 2002). In Indonesia, transmigration of the Madurese to Kalimantan was part of the national relocation policy from high-density areas of Java to sparsely populated islands (*International Crisis Group* 2001, 14).

The indigenous Dayaks felt threatened by the large migration of the Madurese (Gershman 2002) to Kalimantan. Apart from the dilution of the demographic mix, they were also disturbed by the government's handing out of vast parcels of forest to logging companies, many connected to members of the Suharto family, his cronies or the military. As a result, many forest-dwelling Dayaks were driven from their traditional habitat. A 1979 law mandating uniform structures of local government throughout Indonesia undermined the authority of traditional village leaders and the cohesion of Dayak communities. Accompanying this dislocation was a widespread feeling among Dayaks that they were often looked down on by other communities as backward and uncivilized.

The outcome was large outbreaks of riots in 1987, in which hundreds allegedly died. More ethnic riots also broke out in the 1990s, and in 1999–2000 this area witnessed some of Indonesia's most vicious ethnic killings. The initial conflict had been between Madurese and Malays – both Muslim communities – with the non-Muslim Dayaks joining in later on the Malay side. Only after virtually all Madurese had fled Sambas was order restored (Peterbang and Sutrisno 2000). Whatever the reason, transmigration in Thailand and Indonesia has been implicated in conflicts involving identity and resources.

Democracy in conflict?

Related to these issues is a discourse about democracy, or more specifically democratization of society and politics in Southeast Asia. Prior to 9/11, debates about democratization in Southeast Asia featured the following questions: Is democracy good for development? Are democratic transitions, such as the one unfurling in Indonesia, a catalyst for regional disorder? (Acharya 1999). However, the debate over democratization has undergone a marked shift to focus on two questions: Is a lack of democracy a root cause of conflict? Does democracy limit the ability of states to effectively respond to conflict? (Acharya 2002).

Before his release from prison in September 2004, Anwar Ibrahim, the deposed and jailed Deputy Prime Minister of Malaysia, observed, "Osama bin-Laden and his protégés are the children of desperation; they come from countries where political struggle through peaceful means is futile. In many Muslim countries, political dissent is simply illegal" (Ibrahim 2001). Farish Noor, a Malaysian scholar of Islam, makes a direct link between terrorism and authoritarian politics in Malaysia:

> It is the absence of… democratic culture and practices in the Muslim world in general that leads to the rise of self-proclaimed leaders like the Mullahs of Taliban, Osama bin laden and our own Mullahs and Osama-wannabes here in Malaysia. And as long as a sense of political awareness and understanding of democracy is not instilled in the hearts and minds of ordinary Muslims the world over… we will all remain hostage to a bunch of bigoted fanatics who claim to speak, act and think on our behalf without us knowing so.
>
> *(Noor 2001, 4)*

But democratization has also been seen as part of the problem rather than the solution, especially by the region's political elite. Most blame democratization for the rise of separatist activity in Indonesia. It is argued that the failure of both Indonesia and the Philippines to rein in separatist movements could be due to the absence of legal regimes like the Internal Security Act (ISA), which Malaysia and Singapore have effectively used. Indonesia's efforts to bring the perpetrators of the October 2002 Bali bombings to justice suffered a setback when in July 2004 the Constitutional Court held the retroactive application of Indonesia's antiterrorism law implemented after the bombings to be unconstitutional (Santoso 2012). While safeguards against creation of ex-post facto laws are not uncommon, what was important here was the opinion of the court that bombings such as in Bali could not be classified as extraordinary crimes that warranted retroactive application.

Similarly, after much haggling Manila enacted the Philippines Human Security Act 2007 to deal with terrorism in the country. Even as a large number of safeguards to prevent its abuse have made it virtually toothless (Palma 2013), human rights and advocacy groups in the Philippines argue that the law forms the building blocks of "martial law, widespread political killings, the militarization of Metro Manila" (*Asian Journal Online* 2007).

At the same time, "war on terror" rhetoric has produced support for seemingly draconian legislation feared by pro-democracy voices in the region. The most significant source of this support is the US. For example, after his meeting with then US Attorney General John Ashcroft, Malaysian Legal Affairs Minister Rais Yatim claimed that Ashcroft had "endorsed the significance of the ISA." He explained, "After today's talks, there is no basis to criticise each other's systems. If they do that, they could jeopardise the credibility of the PATRIOT Act" (Roberts 2002).

Democratization in Southeast Asia has thus been implicated in fostering unmanageable dissent, leading to conflicts involving in many instances political violence and terrorism. Theories on democracy highlight the fact that the democratization process is painful and turbulent, which explains the emergence of voices of dissent in various manifestations. For example, many of the structural ills and conflicts in Indonesia are attributed to the country's painful transition to democracy after the Suharto era. Democratic transition is also implicated in the political chaos and impasse in Bangkok and the reluctance of the Philippines government to implement stronger counterterrorism measures, as done in Indonesia. This has also been the case in Malaysia, with the government repealing the ISA, castigated as entailing extreme violations of human rights, liberties, and due process.

With this background, the following sections briefly examine how nationalism and ethnicity define conflict in some of the countries in Southeast Asia.

Indonesia: Splintered identities, dissimilar conflicts

Communal conflicts, secessionist demands, and Islamist terrorism proliferate in Indonesia. Though most conflicts have a religious base, as they primarily involve Muslims, terrorism in Indonesia is also associated with resource competition, political participation, and separatist ambitions (Gershman 2002). Moreover, most of the conflicts overlap.

While these conflicts did not appear overnight, the end of the "New Order" under Suharto's rule (Aspinall and Fealy 2010) and the instability associated with political transitions thereafter seem to have been contributing factors. After the end of the Suharto era, weak government institutions and the absence of charismatic leadership paved the way for dissent and bold secessionist demands. In other words, the democratization process that followed the ouster of Suharto led to open dissent and more assertive articulation of secessionist demands, religious expression and discontent over the sharing of resources (*Human Rights Watch* 2001, 9).

Under the Suharto regime, challenges to the territorial integrity of Indonesia were dealt with primarily through repression. Public discussion of racial, ethnic, and religious issues (termed SARA – *Suku, Agama, Ras, Antar-golongan*) was banned (Clear 2005, 143). After his fall, the legal basis for the banning of opposition parties such as the Indonesian Communist Party (PKI) and Darul Islam (DI) was removed in 1998 with the scrapping of the 1963 Anti-Subversion Law (McBeth 2005). Although this was an important step in the promotion of democratic rights, it nevertheless created a powerful legacy of conflict between the national government and a very broad range of local society, not just small, radical groups. As society became more open after the end of the New Order regime in 1998, the legacy of excess became a powerful mobilizing force for these groups (Gershman 2002).

Demands for self-determination have been a major source of conflict in Indonesia. These include demands for independence or significant autonomy, most pronounced in Aceh, West

Papua, and East Timor. Almost all cases involved armed insurgents fighting the Indonesian security forces. Of these, East Timor was successful in gaining independence after a period of violent struggle (*The World Factbook* 2004). Grievances over resource allocation and usage have also been expressed violently in many regions, especially those that had not been deeply integrated into the former Dutch colonies (Gershman 2002).

Communal conflict in Indonesia runs along lines of ethnicity, religion, and culture, and is distinct from conflicts of self-determination. For example, the violence against the Sino-Indonesian community in Malukus and the Poso in Central Sulawesi does not involve issues of self-determination, but separatist conflicts such as those in Aceh have often been on communal (religious) lines. Both types of conflict nevertheless involve struggles over economic, environmental, and political resources. Locals often complain about the exploitation of regional economic resources by the central government in Jakarta, and there is considerable discontent over the unfair distribution of the proceeds of such resources.

Thailand: Identity conflict at its worst

The conflict in southern Thailand is rooted in the perceived injustice of non-fulfillment of minority (Muslim) needs and interests, preventing their integration (Abuza 2011; Croissant 2005, 21–43; Acharya and Gunaratna 2013, 18–69; True 2004). Bangkok's failure to address the fundamental needs of minority groups, to provide for participation in governance, and to ensure an equitable distribution of resources and benefits has exacerbated this situation (Lederach 1997, 8). Malay Muslims perceive government attempts to promote an integrated polity in southern Thailand through the promotion of Buddhism, the Thai language, and a uniform assimilative education as direct threats to the region's ethno-religious identity (Prathet 1979, 5–6; Alagappa 1987, 204–207). Some analysts believe that the resurgence of violence is the result of government policies that have not only been insensitive to Muslim values, but also repressive and frequently irrelevant.

Two past examples of insensitive and repressive government measures are the 1921 Education Act and the 1939 *Thai Ratthaniyom* (Thai Customs Decree). The Education Act forced Muslims to attend state-run schools that imparted teachings in Buddhist ethics, with monks often serving as teachers (Yegar 2002, 89). The Education Act also mandated use of the Koran in the Thai language, an insult to Muslims. The Customs Decree forced the minority group to conform to a set of common cultural norms (Che Man 1990, 63–64), with Muslims prevented from adopting Muslim names or using the Malay dialect and the Shariah replaced by Thai Buddhist laws of marriage and inheritance (Forbes 1982, 1056–1073). In some cases, Muslims were even forced to participate in the public worship of Buddhist idols, and men were required to wear Western-style trousers (Che Man 1990, 65). Anti-Thai behavior and non-Thai identity were considered unpatriotic and seditious (Reynolds 1991, 6). These measures, taken in the name of national integration, challenged Muslim ethno-cultural and religious identity and led to rebellion against the central government.

Additionally, the southern provinces are marked by fundamental abjection – poverty, unemployment, lack of public infrastructure, lack of capital, low living standards, lack of markets for agricultural products, and environmental disasters (Udomsap 2002, 62–66). Over-reaction by security agencies, abuse of authority, corruption, intimidation tactics, and lack of sensitivity to local religious and cultural values have further aggravated the situation and led to what some analysts call the hardening of identities, through blatant injustice such as torture and abductions inflicted by the security forces (True 2004, 16).

The Philippines: Identity contestation over resources?

The Philippines has a majority Christian population, with Muslims concentrated mostly in the south. While Manila has a grip on political power at the center, in the resource-rich south, there is a sense of discontent over access to power and distribution of wealth. Over the years, particularly through the issue of ownership involving "ancestral domain," this has transformed into armed conflict under the influence of disparate ideologies.

Through the 1990s, Al Qaeda had widespread operations in the Philippines. A number of charities and lawful businesses were set up by Osama bin Laden's brother-in-law Mohammad Jamal Khalifa, most of which diverted money to fund not only local Al Qaeda activities but also regional groups, especially the Moro Islamic Liberation Front (MILF), the Abu Sayyaf Group (ASG), and Jemaah Islamiyah (JI) (Mendoza Jr. 1994, 1–7). JI is also deeply involved in the conflict in the southern Philippines and supports groups like the MILF and the ASG. The MILF hosted training facilities both for Al Qaeda and JI in its sprawling Abu Bakr training complex in Mindanao.

In the Philippines, however, the terrorist experience has been more varied than in other countries in the region, ranging from ethno-nationalist struggles, religious conflicts, and left-wing extremism to pure criminality. The MILF and parent group the Moro National Liberation Front (MNLF) have predominantly ethno-nationalist objectives, though the former strayed for a time into the Al Qaeda-led global jihad during its initial years under the leadership of Hasim Salamat (May 2013). However, the group moderated its objectives in 2003 when Salamat openly reaffirmed his commitment to pursuing negotiations with the Philippines government (Jubair 2007, 205–209). The ASG began as a political group with the objective of establishing an Islamic state, but gradually degenerated into criminality with large-scale kidnappings and extortions (Chalk et al. 2009, 42–43).

The country also faces a significant threat of left-wing insurgency involving the Communist Party of the Philippines/New People's Army/National Democratic Front (CPP/NPA/NDF), which aims to seize political power through violent means and establish communist rule. Over the years, it has succeeded in setting up a web of local, national, and international organizations and linkages to achieve this end. It continues to undermine governance by establishing a parallel administration and collecting taxes in the territories it controls (Chalk et al 2009, 57–63).

Myanmar – Rohingyas without identity or nation

What is happening in Myanmar is there for all to see and analyze. Since the country opened its doors to democracy, it has been plagued by an intense religious conflict involving the Buddhist majority and the Rohingya (Muslim) minority. Rohingyas are a Muslim ethnic minority in Myanmar, but are not recognized as citizens by the state (Cramer 2010, 74). This contested status has led to negative stereotyping, dehumanization, and violently racist attitudes from the Buddhist majority toward the community (Bashar 2012). State persecution has led to mass displacement and a flow of refugees to neighboring Bangladesh and other Southeast Asian countries (Bjornberg 2012).

The situation has become particularly alarming since May 2012, when a wave of violence against Muslims in Rakhine state was sparked by an incident in which a Buddhist woman was reportedly raped and killed by three Muslim men (Holliday 2013, 96). The violence has since spread to Meiktila in the Mandalay region and Shan state in northeastern Myanmar (Hill 2013).

Before 9/11, a number of Rohingya groups had attempted to secede from the state by violent means – the Arakan Rohingya Islamic Front (ARIF), the Arakan Rohingya National Organization (ARNO), and the Rohingya Solidarity Organization (RSO). RSO was in the limelight, as it maintained a training camp in which militants from all over the world trained. This was evident from training videos recovered from Al Qaeda facilities in Afghanistan (Acharya and Gunaratna 2005).

The RSO was formed in the early 1980s when radical elements broke away from the more moderate Rohingya Patriotic Front (RPF) led by Muhammad Yunus. Following the breakup of the ARNO in 1999–2000, three new factions emerged, all reclaiming the name RSO. According to reports, the RSO had linkages to Jamaat-e-Islami and Islami Chhatra Shibir in Bangladesh, Gulbuddin Hekmatyar's Hizb-e-Islami in Afghanistan, Hizb-ul-Mujahideen (HM) in Kashmir in India, and Angkatan Belia Islam sa-Malaysia (ABIM), the Islamic Youth Organization of Malaysia. In the early 1990s, the RSO had several military camps near the Burmese border, where cadres from the Islami Chhatra Shibir were also trained in guerrilla warfare (Lintner 2002).

Having been driven from the country by the ruling junta in Myanmar, none of these groups have the capability to pursue a separatist agenda or threaten the stability of the country. However, the evolving Rohingya crisis in recent years has significant implications for the countries in the region.

First, there are now large numbers of Rohingya refugees in some countries in Southeast Asia, especially Thailand, the Philippines, and Indonesia (Coates 2013). This has not only created a humanitarian crisis of immense proportions, but has also exposed refugees to recruitment by radical groups in the region, similar to what has happened in Bangladesh in the past (Huda 2013). For the displaced and marginalized, the desire to avenge injuries and insults through violent means is an option whose importance cannot be understated.

Islam and identity in Southeast Asia

As Islam is implicated in a number of conflicts involving identity and nationalism, it is useful to discuss the nature of Islam in Southeast Asia. Its spread is attributed to the early reformist movements and Indian Ocean trading networks, in sharp contrast to its spread through violent conquest elsewhere (Karasik and Benard 2004, 434–438). Islam spread in the region slowly and gradually, having taken root in northern Sumatra through the interactions of locals with Muslim traders from India, Persia, and southern Arabia (Houben 2003, 153–154). It is often regarded as peaceful and moderate, having no problem with modernity, democracy, human rights, and other tendencies of the contemporary world (Azra 2003, 45). Islam in Southeast Asia is also very diverse, reflecting the region's "cultural, ethnic and linguistic diversity and the presence of substantial non-Muslim communities, which by and large become accustomed to coexistence with other religious and cultural traditions" (Rabasa 2003, 14).

However, the arrival of colonial powers in the sixteenth century and their eventual dominance of the region created nations that would expand horizontally, erecting new international boundaries that did not exist beforehand, and also vertically, altering indigenous social and political structures. On the whole, Muslim regional and local elites lost out in the process, which explains why many of the anti-Western resistance movements were led by representatives of these communities (Rabasa et al. 2004, 155).

In the post-colonial era, successor states came to impose their own obstacles to Muslims' quest for identity, as the colonizers once did. In Indonesia, the Sukarno and Suharto regimes that ruled the country from 1945 to 1998 essentially continued the Dutch policy of curtailing the political role of Islam (Mutalib 2008, 14). In southern Thailand and the Philippines, the minority Muslims also faced "neglect, low socio-economic status, [and] religious antagonism" (Mutalib 2008, 59), in addition to a suppression of their quest for identity. Malaysia and Singapore, however, had a different structure to the rest of Southeast Asia, having been under British rule. This fed into their post-colonial experiences, though Malaysia later confronted the global wave of Islamization engendered by the Iranian Revolution of 1979 (Mutalib 2008, 26–27).

Southeast Asia has mostly been influenced by local issues – antagonistic state policies, for example – contrary to the notion that Islam in Southeast Asia has been unduly inclined toward the Wahhabi strain, which takes a literal approach and primarily originates from Saudi Arabia (Desker 2002, 384–386). Johan Saravanamuttu argues that there has been a "gradual transformation of the Wahhabi-inspired dakwah-Islam of the late 1970s into new discourses of Islamic civil society undertaken by the emerging middle classes" (Saravanamuttu 2010, 2) within Indonesia and Malaysia, both Muslim-majority countries.

David Wright-Neville has demonstrated that most Islamic organizations in Southeast Asia can be classified as "activist," which is to say that they are "dedicated to altering or replacing the political hierarchy and its policies and to infuse national politics with a more Islamic flavor, but they do not seek to change the principles that underpin existing political and/or democratic frameworks" (Wright-Neville 2004, 32). In Indonesia and Malaysia, there have been Islamic movements seeking to accommodate Muslims into the existing political frameworks of the state, such as the Liberal Islam movement in Indonesia and the Islam Hadhari discourse in Malaysia (Nagata 2015, 24–25).

Even though there has been a gradual shift toward Islamization since the 1980s, this has not led to the integration of Southeast Asian Islam with the pan-Islamic rhetoric that some militant groups, particularly those influenced by the global jihadist movement, have espoused. There is in fact a range of competing influences in the region – Sufi brotherhoods, renewalist/pietistic movements, Islamist parties/groups, charity organizations, *da'wa* groups (Mandaville 2009, 11–12) – which are subject to "internal deliberation, contestation, and dissent" (Mandaville 2009, 17), practices that are either alien to the global jihadist movement or not tolerated.

The argument that the transnational linkages of Islam in Southeast Asia pose an existential threat primarily focuses on the ideological and logistical impact of movements such as Al Qaeda on local conflicts, and on the rather under-articulated influence of radicals or fundamentalists on the political direction of regional Islamist parties/groups. These assessments focus on the flow of effects of transnational Islam in only one direction, largely ignoring the social and cultural diversity of Southeast Asia and the impact of local factors such as ethnicity and nationalism, highlighting the limitations of such a unidirectional approach.

Regional implications of nationalism ethnicity and identity

Regionalism in Southeast Asia is recognized for its inclusiveness and flexibility, and the uniqueness of ASEAN in terms of its decision-making norms and approach to socialization (Acharya 2003). These attributes serve the interests of Southeast Asian countries well, to the extent that their concerns about sovereignty and non-interference in each other's domestic affairs have been adequately addressed.

Southeast Asian regionalism has also been influenced by considerations of identity which have facilitated institution-building and institutional efficacy. The formation of ASEAN, for example, was clearly accompanied by the projection of a Southeast Asian identity. This is in contrast to many other regional organizations, especially in the Asian neighborhood, which have displayed no such identity-building initiatives.

Conclusion

An assessment of the conflicts in Southeast Asia indicates two mutually contradictory key trends. First, the operational threat from the groups in conflict in the region has declined significantly, at least since 9/11. This is due to the securitization of the threat with strong counterterrorism measures, albeit to differing degrees. The threat from JI has in consequence been reduced and largely localized, though it continues to revitalize itself and be reincarnated in various forms.

Second, and unfortunately, the region is confronted by a very severe threat of radicalization. This is due to the influence of the Internet and social media, though in certain countries like Indonesia, the print media is also heavily implicated (*International Crisis Group* 2008). Additionally, differing perceptions of the threat of terrorism and different responses to it by individual countries have created an enabling environment for radicalization to spread in the region.

Though radicalization itself is not a precursor of terrorist violence, it definitely creates the conditions that have often led to terrorism. This is despite the fact that a number of conflicts, especially those involving Muslims in the region, have remained localized. Few of these are being addressed through negotiation, or broadly through "hearts and minds" approaches as in the Philippines and Thailand.

Additionally, the nature of Islam in the region is different to that in the Middle East or in parts of South Asia; it does not provide enough space – in terms of both numbers and scope – for radical Islam to entrench itself and expand. The willingness to negotiate in itself demonstrates the disdain that the majority of the groups in conflict have toward a radical Islamist discourse.

The nationalist fervor of the conflicts is also apparent from the punishment that groups receive for any marked deviation from their stated cause. For example, an ASG defector said that he quit the movement because it had lost its original reason for being and moved toward criminality and personal gratification (Torres Jr. 2001, 41).

Moreover, implementation of Sharia where permitted – in Aceh in Indonesia and in Malaysia, where Islamic law takes precedence over civil law in certain matters – has not transformed these areas into Taliban fiefdoms. In other words, there is significant internal challenge to radical ideology in the Muslim communities themselves, something which distinguishes Southeast Asia from other regions.

Given the complex composition and history of the polities of Southeast Asia, multiple groups will remain at the margins of society or perceive that they are being exploited. As such, some form of politicized violence will persist for the foreseeable future. The good news is that this violence will not have much of a transnational flavor. The bad news is that political violence as a means of problem-solving will remain attractive at the regional and sub-national levels.

Thus, even as significant successes at operational level have reduced both the domestic and the transnational threats in the short term, the countries in the region must remain prepared for prolonged regional and localized conflict in the years to come.

References

Abrahim, Collin. 2003. *The Naked Social Order: The Roots of Racial Polarisation in Malaysia*. Kuala Lumpur: Pelanduk Publications.

Abuza, Zachary. 2011. *The Ongoing Insurgency in Southern Thailand: Trends in Violence, Counterinsurgency Operations, and the Impact of National Politics (Strategic Perspectives No. 6)*. Washington, DC: National Defense University Press.

Acharya, Amitav. June 1999. "Southeast Asia's Democratic Moment?" *Asian Survey* 39 (3): 418–432.

Acharya, Amitav. September 2002. "One Result: The Retreat of Liberal Democracy." *International Herald Tribune*, September 17.

Acharya, Amitav. 2002. "State-Society Relations: Asia and the World after September 11." In *Worlds in Collision: Terror and the Future of Global Order*, edited by Ken Booth and Tim Dunne, 194–204. London: Palgrave.

Acharya, Amitav. 2003. *Regionalism and Multilateralism: Essays on Cooperative Security in the Asia-Pacific*. Singapore: Eastern University Press.

Acharya, Arabinda, and Rohan Gunaratna. 2013. *The Terrorist Threat in Southern Thailand: Jihad or Quest for Justice*. Washington, DC: Potomac Books Inc.

Acharya, Arabinda, and Rohan Gunaratna. 2005. "The Terrorist Training Camps of Al Qaeda." In *The Making of a Terrorist: Recruitment, Training, and Root Causes*, edited by J.F. Forest. Westport, CT: Praeger Publishers.

Acharya, Arabinda. 2015. *Whither Southeast Asia Terrorism*. London: Imperial College Press.

Alagappa, Muthiah. 1987. *The National Security of Developing States: Lessons from Thailand*. Dover, MA: Acorn House.

"All you can do is pray: crimes against humanity and ethnic cleansing of Rohingya Muslims in Burma's Arakan State." April 2013. *Human Rights Watch*. www.hrw.org/sites/default/files/reports/burma0413webwcover_0.pdf

"Anti-terror law: For bombers only." March 2007. *Asian Journal Online*. http://www.asianjournal.com/?c=186&a=18613

Aspinall, Edward, and Greg Fealy. 2010. *Soeharto's New Order and Its Legacy*. Australia: ANU E Press.

Ayoob, Mohammed. 1995. *The Third World Security Predicament: State Making, Regional Conflict and the International System*. Boulder, CO: Lynne Rienner.

Azra, Azyumardi. 2003. "Bali and Southeast Asian Islam: Debunking the Myths." In *After Bali*, edited by K. Ramakrisha and Andew Tan, 39–57. Singapore: World Scientific.

Bashar, Iftekharul. June 2012. "Rohingyas: A Quest for a Sustainable Solution." *The Nation*. http://www.nationmultimedia.com/opinion/Rohingyas-A-Quest-for-a-Sustainable-Solution-30184813.html

Bjornberg, Anders. 2012. "Displaced Rohingya at the Margins." *South Asia Journal*. 6 October. http://southasiajournal.net/2012/10/displaced-rohingya-at-the-margins/.

Chalk, Peter, Angel Rabasa, William Rosenau, and Leanne Piggott. 2009. *The Evolving Terrorist Threat to Southeast Asia: A Net Assessment*. Santa Monica, CA: RAND Corporation.

Che Man, Wan Kadir. 1990. *Muslim Separatism: The Moros of Southern Philippines and the Malays of Southern Thailand*. Manila: Ateneo de Manila University Press.

Clarke, Michael. 2008. "China's 'War on Terror' in Xinjiang: Human Security and the Causes of Violent Uighur Separatism." *Terrorism and Political Violence* 20 (2): 271–301.

Clear, Annette. 2005. "Politics: from Endurance to Evolution." In *Indonesia: The Great Transition*, edited by John Bresnan, 46–147. Lanham, MD: Rowman & Littlefield Publishers.

Coates, Eliane. February 2013. "Rohingya boat people: A new challenge for SE Asia." *The Nation*. www.nationmultimedia.com/opinion/Rohingya-boat-people-a-new-challenge-for-SE-Asia-30200771.html

"Communal Violence in Indonesia: Lessons from Kalimantan." 2001. *International Crisis Group*. Asia Report No. 19. 27. www.crisisgroup.org/~/media/Files/asia/south-east-asia/indonesia/Communal%20Violence%20in%20Indonesia%20Lessons%20from%20Kalimantan.pdf

Connor, Walker. 2002. "Nationalism and Political Illegitimacy." In *Ethnonationalism in the Contemporary World*, edited by Daniele Conversi, 24–49. New York: Routledge.

Cramer, Tom. 2010. "Ethnic Conflict in Burma: The Challenge of Unity in a Divided Country." In *Burma or Myanmar? The Struggle for National Identity*, edited by Lowell Dittmer. Singapore: World Scientific.

Croissant, Aurel. 2005. "Unrest in South Thailand: Contours, Causes, and Consequences since 2001." *Contemporary Southeast Asia* 27 (1): 21–43..

Desker, Barry. 2002. "Islam and Society in South-East Asia after 11 September." *Australian Journal of International Affairs* 56 (3): 383–394.

Feith, Herbert and Lance Castles. 1970. *Indonesian Political Thinking 1964–1965*. Ithaca, NY: Cornell University Press.

Forbes, Andrew D.W. 1982. "Thailand's Muslim Minorities: Assimilation, Secession, or Coexistence?" *Asian Survey* 22 (11): 1056–1073.

Gershman, John. 2002. "Indonesia: Islands of Conflict." *Asia Times*, October 26. www.atimes.com/atimes/Southeast_Asia/DJ26Ae05.html

Gurr, Ted Robert. 2001. *People versus States: Minorities at Risk in the New Century*. Washington, DC: United States Institute of Peace Press.

Hardjono, Joan M. 1977. *Transmigration in Indonesia*. Kuala Lumpur: Oxford University Press.

Henderson, Errol A., and J. David Singer. 2000. "Civil War in the Post-colonial World, 1946–1992." *Journal of Peace Research* 37 (3): 275–299.

Hill, Cameron. July 2013. "Myanmar: sectarian violence in Rakhine – Issues, humanitarian consequences, and regional responses." *Report prepared for the Parliament of Australia*. http://parlinfo.aph.gov.au/parlInfo/download/library/prspub/2613925/upload_binary/2613925.pdf;fileType=application/pdf

Holliday, Ian. 2013. "Myanmar in 2012: Toward a Normal State." *Asian Survey* 53 (1): 93–100.

Holsti, Kalevi Jaakko. 1996. *The State, War and the State of War*. Cambridge: Cambridge University Press.

Horowitz, Donald L. 1986. *Ethnic Groups in Conflict*. Berkeley: University of California Press.

Houben, Vincent J.H. 2003. "Southeast Asia and Islam." *Annals of the American Academy of Political and Social Science* 588 (July): 149–170.

Huda, Mirza Sadaqat. January 2013. "The Rohingya Refugee Crisis of 2012: Asserting the Need for Constructive Regional & International Engagement." *South Asia Journal*. http://southasiajournal.net/2013/03/the-rohingya-refugee-crisis-of-2012-asserting-the-need-for-constructive-regional-international-engagement

Ibrahim, Anwar. 2001. "Growth of Democracy is the Answer to Terrorism." *International Herald Tribune*, October 11.

"Indonesia: Jemaah Islamiyah's Publishing Industry." February 2008. *International Crisis Group*. Asia Report No. 147. www.crisisgroup.org/~/media/Files/asia/south-east-asia/indonesia/147_indonesia__jemaah_islamiyah_s_publishing_industry.ashx

"Indonesia: Violence and Political Impasse in Papua." July 2001. *Human Rights Watch* 13: 2C. www.hrw.org/reports/pdfs/n/newguinea/papua0701.pdf

Jubair, Salah. 2007. *The Long Road to Peace: Inside the GRP-MILF Peace Process*. Cotabato City, Philippines: Institute of Bangsamoro Studies.

Karasik, Theodore and Cheryl Benard. 2004. "Muslim Diasporas and Networks." In *The Muslim World After 9/11* by Angel M. Rabasa, Matthew Waxman, Eric V. Larson, and Cheryl Y. Marcum. Santa Monica, CA: RAND Corporation.

Lintner, Bertil. 2002. "Religious Extremism and Nationalism in Bangladesh." *Muktomona*. www.mukto-mona.com/Articles/bertil/religious_extremism4.htm

Mandaville, Peter. 2009. "Transnational Islam in Asia: Background, Typology and Conceptual Overview." In *Transnational Islam in South and Southeast Asia: Movements, Networks, and Conflict Dynamics*, edited by Ali Riaz, Alexander Horstmann, Farish A. Noor, Noorhaidi Hasan, Animesh Roul, Dietrich Reetz, Rommel C. Banlaoi, Ahmad Fauzi Abdul Hamid, Joseph Chinyong Liow, and Peter Mandaville. Seattle, WA: The National Bureau of Asian Research.

May, Ron J. 2013. "The Ongoing Saga of Moro Separatism." In *Diminishing Conflicts in Asia and the Pacific: Why Some Subside and Others Don't*, edited by Edward Aspinall, Robin Jeffrey, and Anthony J. Regan, 221–234. London and New York: Routledge.

McBeth, John. October 2005. "Indonesia's Battle with Terrorism: Outlawing JI No Simple Matter." *The Straits Times*.

Mendoza Jr., Rodolfo B. December 1994. "The Islamic Fundamentalist/Extremist Movements in the Philippines and their links with International Terrorist Organizations." Special Investigation Group-Intelligence Command. Philippine National Police.

Mutalib, Hussin. 2008. *Islam in Southeast Asia*. Singapore: Institute of Southeast Asian Studies.

Nagata, Judith. 2015. "Authority and Democracy in Malaysian and Indonesian Islamic movements." In *Islam and Politics in Southeast Asia*, edited by Johan Saravanamuttu, 34–60. New York: Routledge

Noor, Farish. October 2001. "Who Elected You, Mr Osama?" *Malaysiakini.com*. www.worldpress.org/asia/1201malaysiakini.com

O'Connor, C.M. 2004. "Effects of Central Decisions on Local Livelihoods in Indonesia: Potential Synergies between the Programs of Transmigration and Industrial Forest Conversion." *Population and Environment*, 25 (4): 319–333.

Palma, Pelagio V. 2013. "The Problem of Excessive Human Rights Safeguards in a Counter-Terror Measure: An Examination of the Human Security Act of the Philippines." *Ateneo Law Journal* 58: 476.

Lederach, John Paul. 1997. *Building Peace – Sustainable Reconciliation in Divided Societies*. Washington, DC: United States Institute of Peace Press.

Palma, Pelagio V. 2013. "The Problem of Excessive Human Rights Safeguards in a Counter-Terror Measure: An Examination of the Human Security Act of the Philippines." *Ateneo Law Journal* 58: 476.

Peterbang, Edi, and Eri Sutrisno. 2000. "Konflik Etnik di Sambas." *Institut Studi Arus Informasi*. Jakarta.

Poe, Steven C., C. Neal Tate, Linda Camp Keith, and Drew Lanier. 2000. "Domestic Threats: The Abuse of Personal Integrity." In *Paths to State Repression: Human Rights Violations and Contentious Politics*, edited by Christian Davenport, 27. Latham, MD: Rowman and Littlefield.

Prathet, Krasuang Kan-Tang. 1979. *Thai Muslims*. Bangkok: Thailand Ministry of Foreign Affairs.

Pryor, Robin J. 1979. *Migration and Development in South-East Asia: A Demographic Perspective*. Kuala Lumpur: Oxford University Press.

Rabasa, Angel M. 2003. *Political Islam in Southeast Asia: Moderates, Radicals and Terrorists*. Oxford: Oxford University Press.

Rabasa, Angel M., Matthew Waxman, Eric V. Larson, and Cheryl Y. Marcum. 2004. *The Muslim World After 9/11*. Santa Monica, CA: RAND Corporation.

Regehr, Ernie. May 2007. "It's Not Really a Matter of Hate." *Disarming Conflict*. http://www.igloo.org/disarmingconflict/itsnotre

Reid, Anthony. 2010. *Imperial Alchemy: Nationalism and Political Identity in Southeast Asia*. Cambridge: Cambridge University Press.

Reynal-Querol, M. 2002. "Ethnicity, Political Systems and Civil Wars." *Journal of Conflict Resolution* 46 (1): 29–54.

Reynolds, Craig J. 1991. "National Identity and Its Defenders." In *National Identity and its Defenders, Thailand 1939–1989. Monash Papers on Southeast Asia No. 25*, edited by Craig J. Reynolds. Clayton: Monash University Centre of Southeast Asian Studies.

Roberts, John. May 2002. "The Bush Administration Embraces Malaysian Autocrat." *World Socialist Website*. http://pgoh.free.fr/socialist_mahathir.html

Santoso, Topo. 2012. "Anti-terrorism Legal Framework in Indonesia: Its Development and Challenges." 9th Asian Law Institute Conference. National University of Singapore. mimbar.hukum.ugm.ac.id/index.php/jmh/article/viewFile/421/267

Saravanamuttu, Johan. 2010. "Introduction: Majority-Minority Muslim Politics and Democracy." In *Islam and Politics in Southeast Asia*, edited by Johan Saravanamuttu, 17–33. London and New York: Routledge.

"Situs Internet yang Memuat Pernyataan Noordin M Top." 2009. *Tvone*. Trans. Singapore: International Centre for Political Violence and Terrorism Research.

Snyder, Jack. 2000. *From Voting to Violence: Democratization and Nationalist Conflict*. New York: W.W. Norton & Company.

Suryadinata, Leo. 2004. *Chinese and Nation-Building in Southeast Asia*. Singapore: Marshall-Cavendish International.

Svensson, Isak. 2007. "Fighting with Faith: Religion and Conflict Resolution in Civil Wars." *Journal of Conflict Resolution* 51 (6): 930–949.

Tarling, Nicholas. 2001. *Imperialism in Southeast Asia: 'A Fleeting, Passing Phase'*. London and New York: Routledge.

Tarling, Nicholas. 2004. *Nationalism in Southeast Asia: 'If the people are with us'*. London and New York: Routledge.

The World Factbook 2004. Washington, DC: Central Investigation Agency. www.cia.gov/cia/publications/factbook/geos/tt.html

Torres Jr, Jose. 2001. *Into the Mountain: Hostaged by the Abu Sayyaf*. Quezon: Claretian Publications.

True, Linda J. 2004. *Balancing Minorities: A Study of Southern Thailand*. SAIS Working Paper. Washington, DC: Paul H. Nitze Scool of Advanced International Studies.

Udomsap, Prinya et al. 2002. *The Findings to Understand Fundamental Problems in Pattani, Yala and Narathiwat.* Bangkok: National Research Council of Thailand.

Vanham, T. 1999. "Domestic Ethnic Conflict and Ethnic Nepotism: A Comparative Analysis." *Journal of Peace Research* 36 (1): 55–73.

Waever, O. et al. 1993. *Identity, Migration and the New Security Agenda in Europe.* London: Pinter.

Winichakul, Thongchai. 1994. *Siam Mapped: A History of the Geo-Body of a Nation.* Chiang Mai: Silkworm Books.

Wright-Neville, David. 2004. "Dangerous Dynamics: Activists, Militants and Terrorists in Southeast Asia." *The Pacific Review* 17 (1): 27–46.

Yegar, Moshe. 2002. *Between Integration and Secession: The Muslim Communities of the Southern Philippines, Southern Thailand, and Western Burma/Myanmar.* Maryland: Lexington Books.

Yuchao, Zhu, and Blachford Dongyan. 2006. "Ethnic Disputes in International Politics: Manifestations and Conceptualizations." *Nationalism and Ethnic Politics* 12 (1): 25–51.

26
THE MAKING OF HOA IDENTITY
Migrants, nationalism and nation-building in post-colonial Vietnam

Zhifang Song

Introduction

When maritime disputes in 2014 aroused nationwide protests and demonstrations against China in Vietnam, I was worried about my friends of Chinese descent there, as news reported that even Taiwanese-owned factories in the suburbs of Ho Chi Minh City became targets of violent attacks (Hodal and Kaiman 2014; Amer 2015). But when I returned to Vietnam on another field trip the following year, I was glad to find that the local ethnic Chinese were not affected by this wave of Vietnamese nationalism. This situation was in sharp contrast to what happened in the late 1970s and early 1980s, when conflicts between China and Vietnam turned the ethnic Chinese in Vietnam into enemies of the Vietnamese state, forcing many of them to flee the country as refugees (Chan 2011). What does this change mean for the position of the ethnic Chinese in Vietnam? What does this change imply for the Vietnamese nation and nationalism? Answering these questions will help to understand the experience of the ethnic Chinese in post-colonial Vietnam and shed light on the transformation of the nation and nationalism in post-colonial Vietnam.

Nationalism has played and is still playing important roles in shaping the modern world. Theorizing nationalism, however, has been a challenge to scholars, who cannot even come to a consensus on how to define a nation, the loyalty to which nationalism is all about (Day and Thompson 2004; Özkırımlı 2010). In the post-colonial world, the idea of the nation-state often associates a nation with a state that has sovereignty power over a well-defined territory. As few modern sovereign states enjoy cultural and ethnic homogeneity within their borders, a nation needs to be defined in ways that accommodate cultural and ethnic heterogeneity for the stability and prosperity of a nation-state. Benedict Anderson (1991) has argued that nations are "imagined communities" that are historically constructed. From this perspective, nation-building for a post-colonial state is just a process of constructing such an imagined community out of cultural and ethnic heterogeneity often found within the borders of a new post-colonial state.

Despite the lack of consensus over definitions of the nation and nationalism, most people might agree that politics of inclusion and exclusion is an essential part of nationalism. With ethnic and cultural heterogeneity, nation-building for a post-colonial state often involves political manipulations about who are included or excluded and what culture is prioritized or restricted. Thus, the meaning of the nation and nationalism are inevitably shaped and reshaped in the process. Instead of seeking precise definitions and meaning for the nation and nationalism, it is more rewarding to see how boundaries of inclusion and exclusion are shaped in different contexts and how people and their cultures are affected in the process. This essay intends to examine how the changing relationship between the ethnic Chinese and the Vietnamese society has redrawn the boundaries of the Vietnamese nation, and thus transformed the meaning of Vietnamese nationalism.

The last couple of decades has seen increasing research on the Chinese experience of nationalism and nation-building in post-colonial Southeast Asian countries (Wang 2005). As immigrants or descendants of immigrants from South China, the Chinese in most colonies in Southeast Asia enjoyed economic success. They maintained close ties to their ancestral homes and were recognized as Chinese nationals by the Chinese government. In the first half of the twentieth century, Chinese nationalism greatly influenced the Chinese communities (Song 2019). All these features of the Chinese communities were incompatible with indigenous nationalism in most of the post-colonial Southeast Asian states where "the nation is defined in indigenous group terms" (Suryadinata 2007, 95–98). From the perspective of indigenous nationalism, only indigenous people were seen as natural citizens of the new nations and thus given full citizen rights. For example, people of indigenous groups, *pribumi* in Indonesia and *bumiputra* in Malaysia, were seen as inherent members of the new nations and thus enjoyed privileges. Non-indigenous groups only had qualified membership and were denied certain privileges. In other words, membership in these nations was tiered.

Consequently, even after most Chinese lost their Chinese citizenship and became citizens of these countries, they still did not have equal status to the indigenous people. In Malaysia, the *pribumi* were given better economic, educational and occupational opportunities. These privileges were institutionalized by a New Economic Policy in 1970 (Yow 2017). Similar policies also existed in Indonesia (Suryadinata 2007, 232–233). Most Southeast Asian countries adopted cultural nationalism that took indigenous cultures as their national cultures and discriminated in various ways against the Chinese culture (Suryadinata 1997). For example, Indonesia and the Philippines all adopted assimilationist policies, suppressing the Chinese culture. Chinese schools, Chinese media and Chinese organizations, three pillars of the overseas Chinese culture, were either forbidden or restricted. Even in Malaysia where the cultural rights of the Chinese were officially recognized, Chinese culture was not treated as equal to the indigenous culture. For example, the government refused to fund schools that used Mandarin as the teaching language. In short, the Chinese were nationals of these countries legally, but were not treated as full members of the nations in practice. Although things have improved in the new century, many policies favouring the indigenous people still exist today.

The Chinese experience of post-colonial nationalism in Vietnam, however, has rarely been researched. The Chinese in colonial Vietnam shared many features with their counterparts in other parts of Southeast Asia. But several features also set them apart. First, the French colonial administration allowed them to enjoy higher social and political autonomy (Barrett 2012). Second, there has been an anti-China sentiment among the Vietnamese population due to historical and recent conflicts between China and Vietnam (Bui 2017). Third, post-colonial Vietnam has seen much more turmoil than other Southeast Asian countries. The end of French colonial rule in Vietnam gave rise to two competing states, fighting each other in a two-decade bitter war, with the United States, the Soviet Union and China involved in different ways. The country's reunification after the war was followed by a decade of border conflicts with China, which further intensified the anti-China sensation in Vietnamese nationalism.

What impacts did such differences have on the Chinese experience of Vietnamese nationalism in post-colonial nation-building? Most existing research on the ethnic Chinese in Vietnam focuses on the effect of government policy on the Chinese (Amer 2014; Huang 2006; Li 1990; Stern 1985a). But few scholars have paid attention to the nationalist motivations behind such policies. No scholars have examined how the Vietnamese nation and nationalism have also been reshaped by the interactions between the Chinese and the post-colonial Vietnamese states.

Lack of attention to these critical perspectives has prevented a comprehensive understanding of the experience of the ethnic Chinese and the process of nation-building in post-colonial Vietnam. This essay argues that interactions between the ethnic Chinese and Vietnamese states have redefined not only the identity of the Chinese but also the Vietnamese nation and nationalism. The Vietnamese nation has been redefined to include the ethnic Chinese. Seen as part of the Vietnamese nation, the ethnic Chinese were not affected by the recent anti-China protests.

The Chinese, the Vietnamese and nationalism in colonial Vietnam

The French colonization of Vietnam in the late nineteenth century increased trade between Vietnam and the world market, mainly for the benefit of the colonizers. But one side effect of the increase in trade was that more and more traders and labourers from the Southeast Coast of China were attracted to Vietnam, especially the area around Saigon. As a result, the Chinese gradually dominated some trades and became economically powerful (Li 1990, 19–28; Stern 1985b; Xu and Lin 2011, 210–230).

The French colonial authorities gave the Chinese the right to self-governance so long as they paid special taxes and posed no threats to the colonial order. Based on differences in language and place of origin, the Chinese organized themselves into five Bang (congregations), Fujian, Cantonese, Chaozhou, Hainan and Hakka, with successful businessmen elected as their leaders (Barrett 2012). Every Chinese arriving in Vietnam was required to join one of the Bang and thus was subject to the governance of the Bang leaders. Each Bang had a meeting place called Huiguan, which usually had a temple attached to it and served as the social, political and religious centre for its members (Barrett 2012; Xu and Lin 2011, 175–187; Serizawa 2006).

As their population and economic power grew, the Chinese in major urban centres established schools, hospitals and other social service facilities, usually sponsored by Bang groups to serve their members. They also published Chinese newspapers and magazines. As a result, the Chinese communities in Vietnam developed into cultural enclaves socially and culturally segregated from the local society.

The early twentieth century saw a rise of nationalism in colonial Vietnam, both among the Chinese and the Vietnamese. While the French colonial administration relentlessly suppressed Vietnamese nationalist movements, Chinese nationalism was tolerated since it was concerned with the politics of China rather than that of Vietnam and thus posed no threat to French colonial rule. From the 1930s to the 1940s, China's resistance war against Japanese invasion played an essential role in promoting nationalism in Chinese communities in Vietnam. The Chinese raised funds for China's war efforts and helped transport materials badly needed by China. Through these efforts, whether rich or poor and politically left or right, people felt that they were all part of the Chinese nation, whose future depended on their actions (Li 1990, 152–175; Xu and Lin 2011, 348–362).

During WWII, Ho Chi Minh, one of the founders of the Vietnamese Communist Party, organized Viet Minh as a coalition of all Vietnamese nationalists against both the Japanese, the new occupiers, and the French colonial administration. When the Japanese surrendered, he and his Viet Minh entered Hanoi and made a stellar debut by ceremonially declaring the independence of Vietnam and the formation of a provisional national government (Dommen 2002; Duiker 2018). Although Ho and his provisional government soon lost Hanoi to the French, who were determined to restore colonial rule, he firmly established himself as the most prominent leader of the Vietnamese nationalist movement (Anh 2002; Duiker 2018; Moise 1988). He led a war against the French in subsequent years and forced them to end their colonial rule in 1954.

While the Chinese Communist Party provided vital support for Ho's war against the French, most Chinese in Vietnam, especially in South Vietnam, remained aloof from the Vietnamese nationalist movement because they did not see Vietnam as their own country.

Turning the Chinese into Vietnamese: success and failure in the two post-colonial Vietnamese states

The Geneva Accords reached in 1954 put an end to French colonial rule and divided Vietnam into two states, which later developed into the communist Democratic Republic of Vietnam (DRV) in the North and the anti-communist Republic of Vietnam (ROV) in the South. Despite their ideological differences, both Vietnamese states used nationalism as an important instrument to legitimate their governments (Tran 2013). The practice of Vietnamese nationalism might vary through time and between the two regimes, but building a nation based on the Kinh, who formed the majority of the population, was the goal for both states (Tran 2013). Such an indigenous nationalism would not tolerate the existence of Chinese communities that culturally and politically identified with China, be it the People's Republic of China (PRC) or the Republic of China (ROC) on exile in Taiwan. Chinese schools, media, temples and Huiguan had been symbols of Chineseness and upheld Chinese nationalism in Chinese communities. Both states saw them as barriers to building the Vietnamese nation and thus tried to remove them.

North Vietnam had a much smaller Chinese population. But even a small group of residents loyal to a foreign nation was not something that the government would like. Luckily for the North Vietnamese government, the PRC abandoned the *Jus sanguinis* principle of citizenship. Those who had foreign citizenship would no longer be seen as Chinese citizens (Song 2019). In 1955, the communist parties of China and Vietnam reached an agreement that encouraged the Chinese in Vietnam to obtain Vietnamese citizenship voluntarily (Chang 1982b). Beijing gradually relinquished its control over the Chinese in North Vietnam, putting them more under the jurisdiction of the DRV government (Ungar 1987). As a result, open expression of Chinese nationalism gradually diminished among the Chinese in North Vietnam.

In the South, the anti-communist nationalist Ngô Đình Diệm established the ROV. Soon after consolidating his power, Diệm began the efforts to end the social and cultural autonomy of the Chinese. The economically powerful Chinese communities, which were socially and culturally segregated from the local population and politically loyal to a foreign nation, were seen as a barrier to the cultural and political integration of the new state. Thus, from a Vietnamese nationalist perspective, it was deemed necessary to suppress the Chinese culture and assimilate them into the local population.

The first effort he made was to cut off the legal ties of the Chinese to China, converting them from Chinese nationals to Vietnamese citizens (Huang 2007; 2010). From 1955, Diệm's government passed several decrees, forcing the Chinese to adopt Vietnamese citizenship. But few Chinese wanted to take Vietnamese citizenship. Even after the government had made great efforts, only several hundred people registered their Vietnamese citizenship, while 170,000 people reconfirmed their Chinese citizenship with the Chinese Embassy (ROC) in Saigon (Huang 2007; 2010).

The ROV government also used economic measures to force the Chinese to take Vietnamese citizenship (Huang 2007; 2010). From 1955, it reserved the right to some trades only for Vietnamese citizens. The Chinese then had only two options: adopting Vietnamese citizenship or losing their businesses. With all these efforts, more than 900,000 Chinese adopted Vietnamese citizenship by 1963 (Huang 2010: 207). That means the majority of the Chinese population was entirely under the jurisdiction of the South Vietnam government. As a result, their political attachment to China was legally cut off.

It might have been relatively easy to cut off their political ties to China, but cutting off their cultural attachment to China was a more challenging task. But Diệm wanted to get it done. Chinese schools had been the most important venues that cultivated the cultural autonomy of the Chinese community and promoted Chinese nationalism among the younger generation. In the 1950s, all Chinese schools in South Vietnam used the curriculum and textbooks from Taiwan, and teaching was all in mandarin (Huang 2007; 2010). Such education prevented students from identifying with the Vietnamese nation and developing a desire to be part of it.

Diệm wanted to change that. His government made a five-year plan for Chinese schools to gradually change their curriculum to adopt the Vietnamese curriculum by 1962 (Huang 2007; 2010). However, the assassination of Diệm in 1963 and the subsequent political chaos in South Vietnam prevented the ROV government from taking further steps. The new leaders relaxed their efforts in the Vietnamization of Chinese schools. Most Chinese schools adopted the Vietnamese curriculum only in form to meet the government's minimum requirements. In reality, most subjects still more or less followed the curriculum of Taiwan and were taught in Mandarin. The Chinese benefited from the wartime economy and enjoyed unprecedented economic prosperity, which enabled more families to send their children to school. Thus, this period saw a significant expansion of Chinese schools in student numbers.

Benedict Anderson (1991) found that the standardization of language due to the development of printing was essential in creating modern nations and nationalism in Europe. Using Mandarin as the teaching language helped cultivate a cultural attachment to the Chinese nation among the younger generation of the ethnic Chinese. The expansion of Chinese education in the 1960s and the early 1970s left a whole generation of young people well educated in Chinese. Thus, instead of being assimilated as Vietnamese, they were even more Chinese than their parents. When I did my fieldwork in Cholon, I found that many Chinese who grew up in the 1960s and early 1970s could still speak fluent Mandarin. Thus, the efforts of the ROV government to assimilate the Chinese into the Vietnamese nation did not achieve complete success. Legally, the Chinese were Vietnam citizens, but culturally they were far from becoming part of the Vietnamese nation yet.

Enemies of the Vietnamese nation: the Chinese experience of Socialism and nationalism in unified Vietnam

In 1975, the communist troops entered Saigon, the ROV government collapsed, and Vietnam was reunified under the communist regime. But forging a culturally and ideologically unified Vietnamese nation was still a goal yet to achieve, especially because Vietnam had numerous groups of people with cultures and languages different from the Kinh people who formed the majority of the country's population. To address such cultural and ethnic heterogeneity, the Vietnamese Communist Party adapted an ethnic policy borrowed from the Soviet Union and China. It grouped all people in Vietnam into "nationalities." These nationalities together formed a single Vietnamese nation and their rights to their own cultures were supposed to be respected. In 1979, 54 "nationalities" were officially recognized, with most of the Chinese put into the nationality "Hoa" (Keyes 2002; Michaud, Turner, and Roche 2002; Michaud 2009; Pelley 1998; Teng 2017). From then on, Hoa, instead of "Hoa Qiao," was the name used to identify the ethnic Chinese. The difference was not only in words but with many political implications. The Hoa were supposed to be part of the Vietnamese nation and do not identify with China.

Recognizing the Hoa as one of the 54 nationalities and thus part of the Vietnamese nation did not mean that the government would treat the Chinese the same as other people in Vietnam., As the Chinese in South Vietnam had depended much on the capitalist economy and had been culturally attached to China, from the perspective of the government, much efforts were needed to turn them into Hoa, who would be patriotic Vietnamese nationals and loyal citizens of the socialist state. Consequently, the Chinese soon found that the new rulers were much harsher towards them than the ROV government.

Immediately after occupying South Vietnam, the communist regime began to restructure the society. The first targets were the so-called "Comprador Bourgeoisie," who were seen as not only capitalists but also collaborators with foreign powers. In September 1975, the government launched a campaign, sending armed "work groups" to the factories, shops and houses of those identified as "Comprador Bourgeoisie," who were arrested and whose important properties were confiscated (Li and Luo 1989; Li 1990; Chen 2008; Stern 1984; Amer 1996). Nearly all those labelled as "Comprador Bourgeoisie" were Chinese, while almost no Vietnamese businessmen were affected (Li 1990, 199–200). This fact showed that even though such a campaign appeared to be driven by communist ideologies, nationalism was part of the motivation.

While this campaign affected only a few Chinese, who were large business owners, the subsequent socialist restructuring of the economy scathed most of the Chinese. Smaller businesses were taken over by the government, with very little compensation for their owners, who were then sent to remote areas to reclaim wasteland. Markets were closed, and many people who had made a living by trading on the markets lost their jobs. Eventually, even peddlers or roadside stall owners were not allowed to do their businesses (Li 1990, 199–200). As the Chinese had depended much on the private economy, such a reform deprived many Chinese of their means of subsistence.

Besides depriving the Chinese of their wealth, the government also abolished Chinese social organizations and cultural facilities. Immediately after occupying Saigon, the new government summoned the leaders of Huiguan, ordering them to close their temples and offices and turn all Huiguan-owned assets over to the government. Hospitals sponsored by these Huiguan were converted into government-owned hospitals (Huang 2006, 140–144). Chinese schools were also taken over by the government and were renamed to de-emphasize their Chinese ties. They were not allowed to use Mandarin in teaching. Soon, all these schools were no different from other Vietnamese public schools. All Chinese media, including newspapers, magazines, etc., were closed. The only publication in Chinese was the Chinese version of the local government newspaper. Chinese cultural activities, such as the lunar new year parade, were forbidden (Li and Luo 1989; Li 1990; Chen 2008; Stern 1984; Amer 1996).

With their economic power deprived, social organizations disbanded, schools and hospitals taken over, and cultural activities banned, the foundation for the Chinese social and cultural autonomy from the local society no longer existed. Through these measures, the government conveyed a clear message: the Chinese needed to become Vietnamese if they wanted to survive in Vietnam; a Chinese cultural enclave would no longer be accepted.

Such measures met resistance from the Hoa. Some of them took to the street and required the communist government to allow them to regain their Chinese citizenship. Pictures of Mao Zedong were even displayed during the demonstrations (Chang 1982b; Stern 1984). The government saw such actions as evidence of their disloyalty towards Vietnam and suspected that Beijing was behind such protests. The military conflict between Vietnam and China in 1979 further intensified the distrust between the Hoa and the Vietnamese government. Due to the continued border conflicts with China in the 1980s, the government endorsed nationalist discourses that depicted China as the biggest threat to Vietnam's independence since ancient times. These further increased the animosity towards the Chinese in Vietnam (Bui 2017). Government jobs, military positions and other vital occupations were unavailable to the Hoa. Even those who were Communist Party members and had fought the Americans and South Vietnam troops were driven out of the Party or removed from important positions. When the government took complete control over the economy and forbade private businesses, many Chinese were in a desperate situation. Officially, the Chinese were seen as citizens, but practically they were treated as enemies of the Vietnamese nation (Amer 1996; 2014; Chang 1982b; Li 1990; Li and Luo 1989; Stern 1984; 1985a).

Fearing that things would worsen, many Hoa decided to leave the country. They made up a significant part of "the boat people" that fled the country in the early 1980s (Amer 2011; Chan 2011; Chang 1982a; Kumin 2008; Vuong 2011). Many settled in Western countries, but many others perished in the sea. When I did my fieldwork in Ho Chi Minh City, a local friend pointed to a fancy restaurant on one of the main streets of Cholon. He told me that the family of the original owner of that restaurant fled Vietnam in the early 1980s, but the whole family were killed in a shipwreck.

Although the Vietnamese government never had an official policy of evicting the ethnic Chinese, many practices achieved that effect. Chinese were allowed to leave if they could pay a large sum of money. Many Chinese used their last drop of wealth to buy the opportunity to escape. The Chinese joked in private contexts that if the light poles had feet, they would also flee the country. Different sources estimated that one third to half of the Chinese population in Vietnam left after 1976 (Amer 2011; 2013; 2014; Stern 1985a). Even today, the population of the Chinese has not reached the number before 1976.

To sum up, from the fall of Saigon till 1986, the Vietnamese nation was officially redefined as a unit composed of 54 nationalities, including the Hoa. But in practice, the government saw most the Chinese as enemies of both the communist regime and the Vietnamese nation. The government was happy to see them flee the country. Those unable to leave were denied citizen rights.

Contributing to the post-socialist economy: the Hoa becoming a part of the Vietnamese nation

The socialist transformation of the economy of former South Vietnam led to devastating results (Amer 2014). The socialist economy could neither provide enough job opportunities nor produce enough commodities to meet people's needs. Moreover, in the 1980s, the Soviet Union encountered economic difficulties and could no longer give the financial aids that Vietnam badly needed. As a result, the Vietnamese economy further worsened. The Vietnamese Communist Party leaders were forced to change their policy. In 1986, the Vietnamese Communist Party decided to reduce restrictions over private economy and welcome foreign investments (Amer 1996; 2014; Chen 2008; Huang 2006; Xu and Lin 2011).

The eased restrictions enabled the Hoa to use their business skills and overseas connections to achieve economic success (Amer 1996; 2014; Chen 2008; Huang 2006; Xu and Lin 2011). Into the 1990s, when the economy was further liberalized, the Hoa already had some very successful businessmen. Cholon, which covered Districts Five and Eleven of the present-day Ho Chi Minh City, became a hub for small businesses. In subsequent decades, businesses established by the Hoa expanded with further economic liberalization. Some Hoa even hit the Vietnamese rich list.

Zhang Meilan married a man from Hong Kong. Through his connections, they secured funds to invest in Vietnam at the beginning of the post-socialist reform and accumulated enormous wealth in subsequent decades. Shen Pi, who was from a very humble background, became one of the richest men in Vietnam. He once even controlled one of the country's largest bank corporations.

Although few could hit the rich list, and the Hoa might never regain their previous economic dominance, the market-oriented economy has provided opportunities for most Hoa. Numerous small businesses owned by the Hoa sprung up, generating wealth for the country and creating job opportunities for both the Hoa and the whole society. Thus, the Hoa have made no small contributions to the country's economic boom since 1986.

Since the beginning of the economic liberalization, the Vietnamese government has been aware of the value of business skills and overseas connections of the Hoa. Gradual and calculated lifting of social, political and cultural restrictions over the Hoa happened from the mid-1980s onwards. Annual New Year celebrations were restored. Temples were allowed to open, religious activities were permitted and people could worship and pay tributes to the deities housed in these temples. The government also recognized most Hoa temples as cultural heritage sites and permitted the Hoa to form managing boards to manage these temples (Amer 1996; 2014; Chen 2008; Huang 2006; Xu and Lin 2011).

But the government would neither give the Hoa a free hand in reviving their own culture nor allow them to return to the level of social and cultural autonomy they had enjoyed before 1975. The goal to convert the Chinese into Hoa, a part of the Vietnamese nation, has never changed. The aspects of Hoa culture restored are expected to be a part of the Vietnamese national culture. They are not supposed to be used to reconfirm Hoa's cultural ties to China. Thus, the government has monitored the Hoa's cultural restoration closely. Important cultural activities are organized by government offices in collaboration with Hoa organizations. Managing boards of Huiguan are elected from the Hoa communities, but candidates are screened by the government. They are never allowed to participate in the management of schools and hospitals that Huiguan had sponsored before 1975.

Chinese schools and Chinese media, which played an essential role in sustaining a strong sense of Chinese nationalism in colonial times and under the ROV, have never been restored. Although most students in schools converted from former Chinese schools are from Hoa families, Mandarin is not allowed to be used as a language in teaching and learning. Only a few schools are permitted to offer Chinese courses as extracurricular programmes for Hoa students. As Vietnamese is the only language used in education and public communication, Hoa students must learn Vietnamese. Thus, among the younger generation of the Hoa, who have received education after 1975, few can speak fluent Mandarin. Without exposure to Chinese education at school and Chinese media, people of the younger generation identify themselves more as Vietnamese than Chinese (Chan 2018). In this sense, the Vietnamese Communist Party have achieved some success in assimilating the Hoa into the Vietnamese nation.

However, the persecution of the Chinese in the early years of the reunification still left a lot of scars on the older generation. Their trust in the government remains low. Barriers between them and the local population have not disappeared yet. But such a sense of distrust could only be expressed in privacy and should not be expressed in public, especially in the presence of government officials. Many key figures in the Hoa communities belong to this generation. They often have to compromise between their wishes to keep their Chineseness and the practical need for showing their identification with the Vietnamese nation. They do their best to uphold the Hoa culture and protect the assets of the Hoa communities from being taken away. At the same time, they also have to cater to requirements from the government to show their loyalty to the country.

For example, Hoa Buddhist temples have a shortage of religious staff, as the temples cannot recruit and train enough religious personnel from the local Hoa. At the same time, the government does not allow them to hire people from overseas. But those managing the temples were determined not to let Vietnamese monks take the temples over. Although they are now Vietnamese citizens, Chineseness is still more important than Vietnameseness to them. But at the same time, these temples often participated in fundraising events for disasters not affecting the Hoa communities to show their loyalty to Vietnam.

Over the past three decades, many Huiguan have accumulated wealth from donations by wealthy people or contributions by worshippers to deities that their temples house. Besides using the wealth to fund charity programmes for the Hoa, the managing boards actively participated in charity programmes sponsored by the government. Beneficiaries of these programmes were usually not Hoa people. The government granted medals and prizes to the managing boards and their leaders for these efforts. Whether they emotionally identify with the Vietnamese nation or not, they have to show their loyalty to the nation in public. Both the government and the Hoa understand the performativeness of this carefully expressed Vietnamese nationalism, but it is something that both sides can accept.

Such publicly expressed loyalty helped build a working trust between the Hoa and the government, which gave the Hoa more room to retain their culture. For example, in 2013, Yi An Huiguan employed a Chinese corporation to rebuild its temple using materials imported from China. Employing a Chinese corporation was unthinkable ten years before when another Huiguan only dared to use local materials and labour to repair its temple.

Many Huiguan have started to put younger people on their boards in the last few years, as the first generation of board members are getting old and about to retire from active service. Unlike the older generation, who were primarily businessmen, people of the younger generation are more diverse in occupation, including business people and professionals with college degrees. Growing up after 1975, they have been educated in Vietnamese and are less able to speak fluent Mandarin than people of the previous generation. But they are better incorporated into the local society. Compared with the older generation, they are more Hoa than Chinese. With leaders of the younger generation gradually replacing those of the older generation, the Hoa are better integrated into the Vietnamese nation.

Conclusion

Nationalism is about loyalty to nations as "imagined communities" (Anderson 1991). Nationalism in Vietnam is no exception. How to position the ethnic Chinese in the Vietnamese nation was a challenge to Vietnamese nationalists and the post-colonial Vietnamese states. The Chinese nationalism within the Chinese communities made the Chinese's loyalty to the Vietnamese nation questionable to the Vietnamese states. Both South Vietnam and North Vietnam took measures to assimilate the Chinese into the Vietnamese society, with different levels of success. The conflicts between communist Vietnam and China turned the Chinese into enemies of the Vietnamese nation. But the economic needs forced the government to change its economic policy and the policy towards the Chinese. As a result, the Chinese have been more and more incorporated into the Vietnamese nation. That does not mean that people have forgotten the persecutions they suffered. But to survive and prosper in Vietnam, the Hoa had to show the government and the public that they were part of and loyal to the Vietnamese nation. While people of the older generation still have a sense of cultural attachment to China, the younger generation is better incorporated into Vietnamese society. As Chan has found, they take Vietnam as their country land, while seeing China as their ancestral hometown (Chan 2018). The identity of the ethnic Chinese has been redefined as Hoa, and the Vietnamese nation has been reshaped to include the ethnic Chinese, who are now less vulnerable to the anti-China sentiment of Vietnamese nationalism.

References

English-language references

Amer, Ramses. 1996. "Vietnam's Policies and the Ethnic Chinese since 1975." *Sojourn: Journal of Social Issues in Southeast Asia* 11 (1): 76–104.
———. 2011. "Examining the Demographic Developments Relating to the Ethnic Chinese in Vietnam Since 1954." In *Migration, Indigenization and Interaction*, 171–229. Co-Published with Chinese Heritage Centre, Singapore.
———. 2013. "Examining the Demographic Changes of the Ethnic Chinese in Vietnam since 1975." *Malaysia Journal of Chinese Studies* 2 (1): 1–34.
———. 2014. *Ethnic Minorities, Government Policies, and Foreign Relations: The Ethnic Chinese in Vietnam and Ethnic Vietnamese in Cambodia*. Asia Paper Series. Singapore: Institute for Security and Development Policy.
Anderson, Benedict R. O'G. 1991. *Imagined Communities: Reflections on the Origin and Spread of Nationalism*. Rev. and Extended ed. London and New York: Verso.
Anh, Nguyễn Thế. 2002. "The Formulation of the National Discourse in 1940–45 Vietnam." *Journal of International and Area Studies* 9 (1): 57–75.
Barrett, Tracy C. 2012. *Chinese Diaspora in South-East Asia: The Overseas Chinese in IndoChina*. London: I.B.Tauris.
Bui, Nhung T. 2017. "Managing Anti-China Nationalism in Vietnam: Evidence from the Media during the 2014 Oil Rig Crisis." *The Pacific Review* 30 (2): 169–187.
Chan, Yuk Wah. 2011. *The Chinese/Vietnamese Diaspora: Revisiting the Boat People*. Abingdon: Routledge.
———. 2018. "'Vietnam Is My Country Land, China Is My Hometown': Chinese Communities in Transition in the South of Vietnam." *Asian Ethnicity* 19 (2): 163–179.
Chang, Pao-min. 1982a. *Beijing, Hanoi, and the Overseas Chinese*. China Research Monograph, no. 24. Berkeley: Institute of East Asian Studies, University of California, Berkeley, Center for Chinese Studies.
———. 1982b. "The Sino-Vietnamese Dispute over the Ethnic Chinese." *The China Quarterly* 90 (June): 195–230.
Day, Graham, and Andrew Thompson. 2004. *Theorizing Nationalism*. Basingstoke, Hampshire and New York: Palgrave Macmillan.
Dommen, Arthur J. 2002. *The Indochinese Experience of the French and the Americans: Nationalism and Communism in Cambodia, Laos, and Vietnam*. Bloomington: Indiana University Press.
Duiker, William J. 2018. *The Communist Road to Power in Vietnam: Second Edition*. Abingdon: Routledge.
Hodal, Kate, and Jonathan Kaiman. 2014. "At Least 21 Dead in Vietnam Anti-China Protests over Oil Rig." *The Guardian*, May 15, sec. World news.

Keyes, Charles. 2002. "Presidential Address: 'The Peoples of Asia'—Science and Politics in the Classification of Ethnic Groups in Thailand, China, and Vietnam." *The Journal of Asian Studies* 61 (4): 1163–1203.

Kumin, Judith. 2008. "Orderly Departure from Vietnam: Cold War Anomaly or Humanitarian Innovation?" *Refugee Survey Quarterly* 27 (1): 104–117.

Michaud, Jean. 2009. "Handling Mountain Minorities in China, Vietnam and Laos: From History to Current Concerns." *Asian Ethnicity* 10 (1): 25–49.

Michaud, Jean, Sarah Turner, and Yann Roche. 2002. "Mapping Ethnic Diversity in Highland Northern Vietnam." *GeoJournal* 57 (4): 305–323.

Moise, Edwin E. 1988. "Nationalism and Communism in Vietnam." *Journal of Third World Studies* 5 (2): 6–22.

Özkırımlı, Umut. 2010. *Theories of Nationalism: A Critical Introduction*. 2nd ed. Basingstoke and New York: Palgrave Macmillan.

Pelley, Patricia. 1998. "'Barbarians' and 'Younger Brothers': The Remaking of Race in Postcolonial Vietnam." *Journal of Southeast Asian Studies* 29 (2): 374–391.

Serizawa, Satohiro. 2006. "Chinese Charity Organizations in Ho Chi Minh City, Vietnam: The Past and Present." In *Voluntary Organizations in the Chinese Diaspora*, edited by Khun Eng Kuah-Pearce and Evelyn Hu-DeHart, 99–119. Hong Kong: Hong Kong University Press

Sidel, John T. 2012. "The Fate of Nationalism in the New States: Southeast Asia in Comparative Historical Perspective." *Comparative Studies in Society and History* 54 (1): 114–44.

Song, Zhifang. 2019. "Global Chinese Diaspora." In *The Palgrave Handbook of Ethnicity*, edited by Steven Ratuva, 1–17. Singapore: Springer.

Stern, Lewis M. 1984. "Vietnamese Communist Policy toward the Overseas Chinese, 1920–82." PhD Thesis. Pittsburgh: University of Pittsburgh. http://www.nlb.gov.sg/biblio/9841277.

———. 1985a. "The Overseas Chinese in the Socialist Republic of Vietnam, 1979–82." *Asian Survey* 25 (5): 521–36.

———. 1985b. "The Overseas Chinese in Vietnam, 1920–75: Demography, Social Structure, and Economic Power." *Humboldt Journal of Social Relations* 12 (2): 1–30.

Suryadinata, Leo, ed. 1997. *Ethnic Chinese as Southeast Asians*. New York : Singapore: St. Martin's Press; Institute of Southeast Asian Studies.

———. 2007. *Understanding the Ethnic Chinese in Southeast Asia*. Singapore: Institute of Southeast Asian Studies.

Tran, Nu-Anh. 2013. "Contested Identities: Nationalism in the Republic of Vietnam (1954–1963)." PhD Thesis. Berkeley, CA: UC Berkeley.

Ungar, E. S. 1987. "The Struggle over the Chinese Community in Vietnam, 1946–1986." *Pacific Affairs* 60 (4): 596–614.

Vuong, Martina. 2011. "The Impact of the Anti-Chinese Páihuá Policy in Vietnam after Reunification: The Refugees' Perspective." *Vienna Journal of East Asian Studies* 2 (1): 149–170.

Wang, Gungwu, ed. 2005. *Nation Building: Five Southeast Asian Histories*. Singapore: ISEAS–Yusof Ishak Institute.

Willmott, Donald E. 2009. *The National Status of the Chinese in Indonesia 1900–1958*. Singapore: Equinox Publishing.

Yow, Cheun Hoe. 2017. "Ethnic Chinese in Malaysian Citizenship: Gridlocked in Historical Formation and Political Hierarchy." *Asian Ethnicity* 18 (3): 277–95.

Chinese-language references

Chen, Yande 陈衍德. 2008. "从排斥到接纳: 越南华人政策的转变 (From Exclusion to Integration: Changes in Vietnamese Policies towards the Ethnic Chinese in Vietnam)." *World Nationalities*, no. 6: 41–53.

Huang, Chung-ting 黃宗鼎. 2006. "战后越南的華人政策 (Policies towards the Ethnic Chinese in Post-War Vietnam)." Masters. Taipei: National Chengchi University.

———. 2007. "越南共和国之华人政策 (1955–1964)" (The Policies toward Ethnic Chinese of Republic of Vietnam (1955–1964)). *Bulletin of Academia Historica* 11: 189–249.

———. 2010. "1945–70 年代初南越華人之政治景況 (The Political Situation of the Chinese in South Vietnam from 1945 to 1970). *Chinese Southern Diaspora Studies* 4: 202–214.

Li, Baiyin 李白茵. 1990. 越南华侨与华人 *(The Ethnic Chinese in Vietnam)*. Nanning: Guangxi Normal University Press.

Li, Baiyin 李白茵, and Fangming Luo 罗方明. 1989. "越南各个时期的华侨政策 (Policies towards the Ethnic Chinese in Different Historical Periods in Vietnam)." *Dong Nan Ya Zong Heng* 4: 12–17.

Teng Chengda 滕成达. 2017. 越南当代民族问题和民族政策研究 *(Contemporary Ethnic Issues and Ethnic Policies in Vietnam)*. Xiamen: Xiamen University Press.

Xu, Shanfu 徐善福, and Minghua Lin 林明华. 2011. 越南华侨史 *(History of the Ethnic Chinese in Vietnam)*. Guangzhouo 广州: Guangdong Higher Education Press.

27
WRITING NATIONALISM IN POST-REFORM VIETNAM
Portrayals of national enemies in contemporary Vietnamese fiction

Chi P. Pham

Most scholarship on Vietnamese literature in the post-socialist period, marked by the reform in 1986, examines universal, apolitical themes, emphasizing the detachment of this literature from its officially assigned role as the essential ideological tool of modern nation-building. In so doing, this scholarship tends to highlight the relaxation of nationalism, in the sense of socialism and national independence under the Party's leadership. This chapter examines portrayals of foreign migrants as national enemies in some post-1986 fiction, answering the question of how this literature deals with the political references and implications. Specifically, this chapter analyzes how, in post-socialist portrayals of foreign migrants, discursive formulations about "colonial capitalists" and "foreign invaders" echo those in socialist era and anti-colonial Vietnamese literature. The continuity of the anti-colonial, socialist imaginaries of foreigners, both explicit and implicit, in post-reform Vietnamese literature indicates that this literature still provokes nationalist politics typical of the socialist period. This is a way of writing the nation that aims at reminding and retaining in public minds anti-colonial and anti-capitalist sentiments. As such, this chapter suggests prolonged nationalism in post-socialist Vietnam. In other words, this chapter argues that post-socialist Vietnamese literature continues to be an ideological instrument for maintaining in the public mind national democracy and hegemony as the ultimate goal of post-reform Vietnamese nation-building.

Nationalism and the portrayal of foreigners in socialist realist Vietnamese literature

The reform in 1986 officially "untied" Vietnamese writers from obligatory political responsibilities. Their writings were freed from political engagement (Nguyễn 2008a, 1–20; 2008b, 1–10). This historical background may be the reason why most prominent international scholars of Vietnamese literature see the disappearance of national responsibility and social engagements as significant themes in post-reform Vietnamese literature. Montira Rato (2004) addresses this condition as the "decline of socialist realism in post-1975 Vietnamese literature." Phạm Thị Hoài (2004) asserted that "the Renovation literary movement" that began in 1986 included any theme except for politics. Nguyễn (2008a) shares a similar opinion when writing that the force of the free economy and globalization caused the death of socialist realism as a movement and a doctrine in Vietnam after 1986. Dana Healy (2013, 49–50) emphasized post-1986 Vietnamese literature as "a literature in transition," in which the strictly guarded and sheltered rules of socialist realism are abandoned and "the new" and "the unknown" are encouraged.

Recent scholarship about post-reform Vietnamese literature has delved into innovations in writing techniques and transformation in social reflections and ideological positions of this literature as responses by Vietnamese authors to the rapidly developing market economy, globalization, and the rise in new technologies, mass media, and the internet. Dana Healy (2000, 2006, 2007, 2010, 2014), in most of her articles and book chapters, explores non-nationalist politics. These politics include unorthodox creativity, penchant for experiment, resentment of authority, gender, sexuality, love, resignation, cultural disorientation, and war-related traumas. For Healy, in her article "New Voices: Socio-cultural Trajectories of Vietnamese Literature in the 21st Century" (2013, 1), contemporary Vietnamese literature stops being the "servant of revolution" and becomes the "purveyor of entertainment, modernity, and individualism" after Vietnam "embraced the new globalized consumer age." Similarly, Rebekah Lin Collins (2015) emphasizes the "extraordinary everyday" as the dominant aesthetic of contemporary Vietnamese literature. Phan Thi Vang Anh and Pham Thu Thuy (2003, 202–220) examine, in particular, the theme of love and marital freedom as the most definitive evidence of the radical change of post-socialist Vietnamese literature. Although there are discussions about social engagement in this literature, it largely focuses on individual tragedies caused by economic inequalities and political or ideological conflicts. Undeniably, the existing scholarship about the post-socialist Vietnamese literature highlights the political moods and cultural practices in post-reform Vietnam that are separate from anti-colonial nationalism – the ideology that dominated the country before the reform and from the emergence of modern Vietnamese literature in the early twentieth century.

This chapter, as outlined above, provides an alternative perspective on the nationalist engagement of this literature by examining its portrayals of the foreign population in Vietnam. Since the post-socialist transition, initiated with the economic reforms in 1986, the Communist Party-led government has opened Vietnam to investment and intervention from other non-communist countries. As a result, foreign professionals from India, China, France, Germany, Russia, Taiwan, Korea, and the United States have increasingly immigrated to and legally settled down in Vietnam. In public media, the Vietnamese state constantly eulogizes certain foreign migrants (Đảng cộng sản Việt Nam 1993; Minh 2013; Phong 2013). Fiction published after the reform, on the surface, appears to accord with the official line of eulogizing foreigners. Successful businessmen from India, nostalgic and sentimental former soldiers from the United States, and respectful intellectuals from France form the main characters in post-socialist literary works by prominent authors such as Tô Hoài (1920–2014), Hồ Anh Thái (b. 1960), Lê Minh Khuê (b. 1949), and Nguyễn Ngọc Thuần (b. 1972). The positive status of foreigners in the contemporary Vietnamese public sphere is particularly notable, given that in the Vietnamese histories of the socialist era (1945–1985), all foreigners were depicted as either greedy bourgeoisie or aggressive invaders. They were identified as class and national enemies of the democratic and independent revolution of Vietnam, who deserved to be displaced and forced into exile (Võ 1990; Devare 2008; Liu 2019; Cục văn thư lưu trữ nhà nước 2007). Likewise, in socialist realism, the official Vietnamese literature during the socialist era, immigrants were depicted as the other, largely in the form of "bloodsucking" colonial capitalists and ignorant foreign soldiers (Đặng 1944; 1969; Trần 1957; 1960; Phạm 1966). Such socialist realist portrayals of foreigners were intended to provoke fear and hate of capitalism and colonialism in the public mind. In other words, the depiction of foreigners as national and class enemies was part of a tradition in socialist realist Vietnamese literature that engaged with the national democratic revolution promoted by the Communist Party. These presentations of foreigners thus embody the dominance of Marxist-Leninist doctrine in socialist Vietnam, where literature was seen as an ideological instrument in the struggle for national homogeneity, national sovereignty, and social democracy (Pham 2021, 80–101).

Portrayals of foreign businessmen in contemporary Vietnamese literature

A close reading of the portrayal of foreigners in post-socialist Vietnamese literature reveals that they continue to be depicted as the national enemies, the colonial capitalists and exploiters, that formed the central characters of earlier anti-colonial, socialist Vietnamese literature. Thus, the post-socialist Vietnamese literature continues postcolonial nationalism, a form of nationalism that is centered on postcolonial values, including national homogeneity and sovereignty, and on socialism. Tô Hoài (1920–2014), a nationally acknowledged Vietnamese writer, describing the Indian owner of a chain of Indian restaurants in Vietnam in the short story "Qua miền Trung" (1993), raises questions around the return of colonial capitalism to Vietnam in the form of foreign investment. The story centers on the adventures of the narrator through the central provinces of Vietnam; an image of sheep wandering in the Ninh Thuan highland reminds the narrator of curried sheep meat in Indian restaurants at Hồ Gươm and Mã Mây streets in Hanoi. Opening the paragraph about the Indian owner, the narrator uses terms such as *sét ty* (chettiar, an Indian trader) and *tây đen bán vải* (non-white foreigner selling textile). These are terms that were commonly associated with foreign exploitative capitalists or colonial remnants in earlier mainstream Vietnamese writing. The narrator wondered whether this man was a trader, a manager of some trading company, a heavy moneylender, sét ty, or tây đen bán bải at Hàng Ngang and Hàng Đào streets. Although the surface tone of this description is an admiration of the Indian migrants' business success, a reader familiar with mainstream socialist Vietnamese writing would immediately recognize an implicit criticism that is associated with this language and, in particular, the connection of the negative terms sét ty and tây đen bán bải with Hàng Ngang and Hàng Đào streets, which together would evoke in the audience images of the Indians as colonial capitalists and foreign invaders. Socialist realist authors used similar descriptions of Indian migrants in Hanoi to depict them as an invading force that took over property and businesses from the local population. For example, Hoàng Đạo Thúy (1974) describes how greedy Indians increasingly took over the traditional textile business of the native Vietnamese: vivid, colorful silk of Hanoi had fallen out of fashion since the introduction of French cloth that was promoted by Indian textile sellers. At first, there was only one Indian shop selling French cloth in Hàng Đào Street, then

> three, four shops. Then they threw money to rent houses, from one hundred to five hundred and several thousands. They also occupied some dozens of other shops … As a consequence, noble Hanoi people were pushed to go back to countryside or to rent houses in other parts [of Hanoi].
>
> *(1974, 71)*

This paragraph demonstrates the familiar formulaic metaphor and metonym of Indian migrants in socialist Vietnamese literature where the presence and expansion of the Indian community in Vietnam is historically associated with and similar to that of French colonialism.

The narratives in Tô Hoài's story emphasize details that potentially remind the audience of the image of the bloodsucking Indian migrant in colonial Vietnam, who relentlessly pursued capital accumulation. These narratives are that the restaurant's Indian owner never takes a rest, and that he undertakes many tasks at the same time to save money and to make more, including taking food orders, serving customers, cleaning tables, and taking payment. The traditional Vietnamese perception of Indian migrants as the best group at trading occurs in the detail about the sheep meat supply; finding that the sheep meat in the restaurant comes from Calcutta, the narrator, confident of his native knowledge, excitedly tells the Indian owner of his knowledge of sheep sources in Ninh Thuận province and advises him to import sheep meat from there instead of from India. Immediately, the narrator is embarrassed as he realizes that his advice is unnecessary for the Indian, a "wanderer everywhere [to earn money]"; the Indian owner is described as a person who does not need anyone else's advice on how to make money in the most convenient way. He himself explored the sheep sources in central Vietnam long enough to open a curried sheep meat restaurant in Saigon. In the end, the narrator admits that he is wasting his time trying to advise on the matter of capital accumulation to an Indian when they are famous all over the world for their excellence in making money; even Gandhi was described in this story to have wandered the ports of Africa selling textiles when he was a child.

The description here of the Indian's enthusiasm for enriching himself economically echoes familiar discourses about Indian migrants in socialist Vietnamese literature. In *Nhớ và ghi về Hà Nội* by Nguyễn Công Hoan (2004), images of Indians are used as a metaphor and metonym for colonial capitalist exploiters. This socialist realist author describes how Indian businessmen occupied most of the trading and financial streets of old Hanoi before 1945. Hoan particularly focuses on ways through which *sét-ty* occupied the land and other property of the masses: to borrow money from these sét-ty, non-employees had to mortgage their houses and land, while employees had to mortgage their salary for them. Sét-ty, as Hoan emphasizes, took very high interest, "*vay tây đen*" ("borrowing money from a non-white foreigner," the quotation marks are original) was very dangerous as most debtors of moneylending westerners ended up bankrupt and destroyed.

Another depiction of the "Indian capitalists" who formed the old world in Hoan's writings was the *Tây đen bán vải* (the textile selling non-white foreigner). These Muslim textile sellers rented five or six houses in Hàng Đào Street and there was a big Bombay silk shop in Tràng Tiền Street. Many customers were attracted by the elegant, colorful silk from Bombay. The Indian bosses usually hired Vietnamese female laborers to serve Vietnamese customers. In describing Indian textile sellers, Hoan subtly reveals their exploitative nature by inserting details about their bad treatment of native employees. These Muslim businessmen would carefully lock their shops whenever they went out, keeping their employees outside. All employees "had to go out, standing on the streets" in cold weather, while their bosses prayed at their mosques on Fridays.

The image of the Indian restaurant owner relentlessly accumulating his capital belongs to the socialist realism ("Chủ nghĩa hiện thực xã hội") school of literature that had begun in the 1920s and dominated literary and cultural production in Vietnam until the reform in 1986. This literature is commonly described in official Vietnamese histories as the product of the influence of Russian Marxist realism, particularly the work of Maxim Gorky (Hà et al. 1985, 36–37, Lại Nguyên Ân 2004, 254–256). It depicted social conflicts between partisans and farmers on the one side and capitalists and feudal landlords on the other. In socialist realist Vietnamese literature, Indians are commonly depicted as bloodsucking creatures – a metaphor for landlords and colonial capitalists – with the aim of provoking in public minds an image of the ruin supposedly caused by feudalism and colonial capitalism. Readers of Tô Hoài's portrayals of Indians are reminded of the pervasive metaphors of greedy explorative Indians in socialist realistic Vietnamese literary works (Pham 2021 32–56).

The subtle reoccurrence of the formulaic metaphor of Indians as colonial capitalists in Tô Hoài's work potentially provokes public anxiety over the new colonial capitalism and other associated economic and social inequalities in post-reform Vietnam. In other words, the public fear about the increasing visibility of capitalism and increasing social inequality – similar to that experienced under colonialism – is transmitted in the subtle, uncertain echoes of the formulaic metaphor of bloodsucking Indians in Tô Hoài's accounts of present-day Indians. This way of depicting Indians provokes concerns about the Vietnamese government's increasing acceptance of foreign investments (Trần 1–24). Since the early 1990s, the Vietnamese government acknowledges economic partnerships with other countries as important to globalize the nation (Tran 2006). International research on the impact of foreign investment in Vietnam restates the idea that it contributes to reducing poverty and empowers the Vietnamese economy (Tran 2006; World Bank 2000). Tô Hoài's portrayal of Indians suggests to a Vietnamese audience the possibility that colonialist exploitation is embedded in the rising globalization of contemporary Vietnam's economy and culture. Some research does indicate that the growing presence of foreign businesses and the associated economically and educationally powerful social groups of people have been culturally damaging and created more economic, educational, and social inequalities in Vietnam. The prosperity of those who benefit most from foreign investment forms a threat to local economic, cultural, and social unity (Le et al. 2021; Vũ 2014). Vietnamese nation-makers have been conscious of the degeneration in national unity caused by the growing openness to non-socialist economic sectors and partners. Non-materialistic values became a special focus at the eighth Party Congress (1996). This Congress decided that all cultural, literary, and artistic activities "must ... inherit and promote the intellectual and aesthetic values, cultural and artistic heritage of the nation... inheriting and promoting the people's ethical traditions" (*75 Years of the Communist Party of Vietnam* 2005, 983). These cultural aims were intended to eradicate capitalist values such as "money worshipping," "the defiance of morality," and the tendency to glorify "the alien and the profane leading to the loss of one's national roots" (*75 Years of the Communist Party of Vietnam* 2005, 983). The recurrence of the metaphor of bloodsucking capitalists in Tô Hoài's writing seems to aim at awakening and provoking a lasting fear of capitalists and colonialists, who are supposedly the embodiments of materialism, self-interest, and national otherness. As such, his writing suggests to a Vietnamese audience the potential colonialist exploitation that is associated with the rising global, transnational presence in Vietnam's contemporary economy and culture.

Portrayals of former American soldiers in contemporary Vietnamese literature

As such, post-reform Vietnamese literature provokes nationalism by maintaining the public doubt around the growing foreign investment in Vietnam that is seen as threatening the idealized vision of national unity and independence. This nationalist engagement also occurs in portrayals of foreigners coming from the United States, the former imperialist enemy of Vietnam. In recent years, there have been many Vietnamese literary works about former American soldiers coming back to Vietnam and refreshing their memories. One of the prominent novels on this topic is the 130-page *Basic is Sad* (*Cơ bản là buồn*) by Nguyễn Ngọc Thuần (2004). The book is widely respected as a representation of post-Vietnam War trauma. The story opens with the image of X, a mixed-race Vietnamese-American girl, who happens to be a guide for Mr. John, a former American soldier, who has come back to the former battlefields to search for his lost youth that had been forever buried in Vietnam. X knows about her American father only through the vague information provided by her mother – the Vietnamese woman who had a baby by an American soldier. Driven to learn about the sufferings of previous generations, X attempts to support John in re-visiting the battlefields and in connecting him with his former Vietnamese lover. She learns that her mother might have been raped by an American soldier or might have had a love affair with one that caused her to be rejected by her people. John, the former American soldier, recalls what he and his fellow soldiers did to the Vietnamese land and people. He wants to take responsibility for the loss that he and his comrades caused in Vietnam. While on this goodwill mission, the former American soldier realizes that the Americans were in Vietnam not only to bomb and spread toxic chemicals toxic but also to spread their seed among Vietnamese women, resulting in many mixed-race children, many of whom died before being born, some of whom survived to live in a space caught between the past and the present, and some of whom were victims of Agent Orange. The meeting between John and a boy named Hữu Nghĩ (friendship), who is believed to be his abandoned son, is described in an emotional tone. The old soldier quietly sits on the veranda floor in the afternoon shadow; he is confused and anxious when facing the mixed-race boy who is disabled and dumb. As described in the last pages of the novel, John does not find anything beautiful or memorable during his visit to Vietnam. However, the trip helps him to understand that he is not the only one who is suffering from post-war trauma and that many who were not born at the time, and so did not experience the war firsthand, are still affected by the war. They are embodied in the images of X and Hữu Nghị, mixed-race children who were abandoned and continue to live with the legacy of their parentage and the accompanying family and community narratives.

What is noticeable here is that the portrayal of the former American soldier echoes the discursive formulas of "American imperialists" pervading socialist realist Vietnamese literature during the Vietnam War period. In reading Nguyễn Ngọc Thuần, anyone familiar with this literature will immediately recall the ignorant, inhuman foreign invaders in works by revolutionary writers such as Nguyên Ngọc (b. 1932), Hữu Mai (1926–2007), and Anh Đức (1934–2014). Anyone who experienced a high school education in Vietnam should know by heart the lyrics of the "resistance literature" (văn học kháng chiến) or "revolutionary literature" (văn học cách mạng) about the ignorance of the foreign invaders:

> Our homeland from that terrible day
> When the foreign invader pulled up a fierce fire
> Our rice fields became barren
> Our houses were burnt
> Dogs were poisoned
> The invaders' wrenches and swords were covered with blood
>   (Bên kia sông Đuống/Over the Other Side of the River, Hoàng Cầm, 1948)

> A bowl of rice filled with tears
> The invaders still pulled them from my mouth
> The Western invaders, the landlord
> One crushed our necks, the one peeled the skin
>   (Đất nước/Country (1948–1955), Nguyễn Đình Thi)

That year, when the Japanese and the Westerner dominate our country,
They competed to steal our people's rice.
We ran out of rice, sweet potatoes;
even banana tubers, and even cassavas!
   (Đói/Hungry – 1957, Bà Bá Lân)

Only if grasses around the Thap Muoi damp were cleared grass,
Will there no longer be people who want to the Western invaders?
The Eastern sea is full and shallow,
But our haters for imperialism are ever forgotten
The Western guys are so evil.
they hit, they kicked, they raped, they cursed.
   (Folk song)

The recurrence of such traditional portrayals of imperialist foreigners in post-socialist works suggests that the foreign characters are there to remind the public about the endless loss as a consequence of the presence of foreigners in the land. More precisely, images of foreigners in the novel provoke and strengthen the public fear of the presence of foreigners in Vietnam: whatever their reason for being in Vietnam, they cause lasting pain and loss for Vietnamese people of all social classes. As such, the American soldier in the novel by Nguyễn Ngọc Thuần conforms to the tradition of representing foreigners as enemies of the national struggle, suggesting that this struggle is still ongoing as the country opens to the globalized market.

The most haunting image is that of the soul of a dead African-American soldier, who had once served in the American forces during the Vietnam War. In "Anh lính Tony" (Soldier Tony) by Lê Minh Khuê (1997) this soldier appears in the form of a ghost that haunts the sleeping and waking hours of the Vietnamese characters. The story is set in a collective house in Hanoi during the subsidy period (1975–1986) that is tightly filled with people, all of whom are deadly hungry while being jealous and curious about the possession of their neighbors. The focal point of the story is centered on the room of the old man Thiến and his son Thán, residents of the shabby house, who are noted for being stingy, dirty, and rude. As the story is told, Thán had mined for gold for a long time. He comes back to this house with a big and heavy backpack. All the neighbors are excited about the bag; although they do not know what is in it, everyone believes it must be packed with gold. This belief is intensified when Thán takes care of the bag so carefully that even his father, a skillful thief, cannot discover what is inside it. He keeps his eyes constantly on the bag and continuously wanders around with it. In the end, Thán reveals that inside the bag is not gold but something "more valuable than gold. That is an American skeleton [skeleton of a former American soldier]" named Tony. The story details the process of Thán discovering the "real" personality of this ghost of the American soldier; he is a thief.

The description given of the foreigner highlights his physical otherness and strangeness, making him appear completely alien from the locals. The appearance of the foreigner is also described as being terrifying looking. The body of the foreigner is characterized as an alien creature which is both threatening and strange: "the bare white skeleton frame stepped clankingly and threateningly around the room, the skeleton climbed up the bed and the window." His eyes are described as "fearfully staring... from two holes of eyes and the bony mouth." The smell of the foreigner is highlighted as the most distressing: "he (Thán) smelled the stink of rotten flesh and bones that were dug up from tombs." The dark skin color is an especially disturbing element "an American ... is black like tar, whose teeth were white like lime, who was stroking his hair with bony fingers."

Noticeably, the foreign soldier in this story is a ghostly character. He does not talk but moves quietly and keeps following the living native people. More particularly, the portrait of the black American soldier in the novel is in between being factual and imaginary, real and ghostlike, which can be read as an allegory of the lasting fearful obsession with these migrants and their abnormal or inhuman existence. The novel describes how "the corpse just sat in the same position while shaking its head," "the loose bone joints moved, creating clanking sound like music of a jumping house," and "he (Thán) saw through the smoggy scene a very white skeleton looking at him, the blurring skeleton, it was moving lightly and putting its hands on the top of its head." The constant use of the body parts to describe the foreigner's movements (metonymy) provokes fear and disrespect toward the foreigner. The feeling of disrespect and even disgust is more explicit in the narrative: "He (Thán) could see very clearly that the two leg bones were walking around its body, a stinking stench arose which made him feel nausea." The gestures of "smiling" and "calm" denote different meanings, including challenging, stubbornness, and calculating. The simplification of the image of the foreigner into silent acts and the erasure of his voice contributes to the feelings of doubt and anxiety about the foreigner, even though he is already dead.

The most dramatic event, and the one that symbolizes the obsession with the foreigner as a national enemy, is the moment when Thán discovers that he has lost his savings. Without a second thought, he asserts that it is the foreigner's skeleton who has taken his money:

> He suddenly thought, and was dumbfounded by something he hadn't thought of in a long time: It was the black soldier who had stolen the bundle of money. Damn it, no wonder it had not appeared since that day! Such a cheeky boy!

The story ends suddenly, leaving the reader with the feeling that they too have been deceived by the foreign character. It turns out that the long and slow narrative about his silence, his strange appearance, his gaze, and his mechanical movements are to prepare for the last surprise: while the local character, Thán, and the reader are searching for the reason for the silence of the foreign skeleton, it has secretly discovered the place where Thán keeps his money. The narrator leads the reader to believe, as the main character Thán does, that the foreigner's ghost is not harmful, but he then breaks their trust by having it steal all of Thán's savings. In this way, the narrative highlights the cunningness of the foreign character and its eventual betrayal. Moreover, the sudden appearance in the narrative of the stolen money implies a long-lasting prejudice of the locals about the greed and deceitfulness of foreigners.

This characterization is clearly derived from traditional discourses about the black foreigner, named *Chà và* – which mostly refers to the Indian migrants – in older Vietnamese literature. In this literature, the Chà và often appears at first sight as quiet, tranquil, and obedient but are then revealed later in the narratives as harmful outsiders, dangerous in nature. This way of representing Indian migrants pervades colonial-era Vietnamese writing. For instance, Trần Quang Nghiệp's short story "Con của ai" (Whose son is it? 1931) centers around a foreign character who is described as silent and harmless but later turns out to have been deceptive. The whole story is told through the efforts of a local man, Minh, and his family to find medicines for his barren wife. A year passes, and his wife informs him that she is pregnant. Minh happily reports this to his parents and spends all his money taking care of his wife. On the day of her baby's delivery, his parents visit the couple in the hospital. Tragically, as soon as they look at the baby's face, they collapse; the baby has dark skin and energetic looks like "anh Chà" (an Indian). Not until this point does the narrator start talking about this antagonist. More than a year earlier, Minh had befriended an Indian man, his co-worker; seeing this Indian man as an honest person, Minh offered to let him share his house. While living together, Minh had given this man his absolute trust; he is shown as seemingly harmlessly innocent – he just sat in his room reading every day, he was gentle and quiet, and attempted not to disturb the other members of the household. All the details show how Minh offered the Indian a position of trust and accepted him into his Annamese world. When the story returns to the present, it reveals the concealed deceit of the Indian man: in response to Minh's astonishing statement, "this is not my son," his wife, in an indifferent tone, responds, "who had told you this would be your son?" In the end, Minh leaves the hospital quietly without expressing any anger; he just throws his house keys to the Indian man, telling him that the house and his wife now belong to him. Here also, the act of betrayal by the foreigner does not appear until the end of the story.

The recurrence of the image of the silent but untrustworthy foreigner in Lê Minh Khuê's story can be read as suggesting that the locals should never treat the foreigners as insiders for fear that they would lose everything to them. War trauma is very explicit in this story: even in peacetime, the losses caused by the war still haunted people; they lived miserably in poor crowded complexes in increasingly cities; and the relationships among the people became worse due to the lack of money. Nevertheless, the fear of the foreigner is undeniable, the ghostly image of the black soldier presents the native people's lingering distrust of foreigners. Although the American soldiers left Vietnam 50 years ago, in present-day Vietnam, the public caution about the possible losses of the local people caused by their return, as invoked in this story, remains. When it comes to imagining foreigners, contemporary Vietnamese writers, who traditionally self-identify as the mind and conscience of the nation, invoke public anxiety about globalization and engender nationalist sentiments and discourses. In other words, images of the foreigners in the literary narratives act as an indirect way of reminding the public of the possible return to Vietnam of colonial capitalism, colonialism, and imperialism in the form of globalization, a threat to the idealized national identity and socialism of the nation.

National allegory in Vietnamese literary theory and in postcolonial criticism

Such a national allegory is derived from the tradition of indirect, suggestive social criticism in Vietnamese literature. Vietnamese literary theorists have insisted on the social responsibility of the author, who must bear the mission of being a prophet of their time, public educator, and national conscience; the act of writing is seen as an act of engaging with and influencing reality. Nguyễn Văn Trung (1963) asserted that intellectuals, including authors, are embodiments of the national conscience and national mind, thus their writings should accept social criticism as their essential responsibility. Moreover, indirectness is a literary tool that has been a tradition in Vietnamese literature of social criticism. Royal authors expressed their concerns about destructible kingdoms and society through indirect literary expressions such as "*ẩn dụ*" (metaphor) and "*hoán dụ*" (metonymy) (Trần 2005, 35–50). Indirectness also forms a tradition in Vietnamese communication; this tradition refers to the way of addressing one thing in order to mean another thing (Trần 1996, 70–76). This indirectness is expressed in figurative idioms such as "*vòng vo tam quốc*" (meandering [as though running around] three countries) and "*nói bóng gió*" (insinuation). In writing, this tradition is embodied in literary devices such as ẩn dụ and hoán dụ (Hà et al. 1985, 192). Nguyễn Văn Trung (1963) argues that indirect, suggestive presentations form the main literary tool for writers to realize their social responsibility. He asserts that "literary language is always indirect" and "the unspoken is the ultimate target of the spoken."

The indirectness is particularly essential in a society where the government considers literary and cultural activities as ideological instruments of nation-building, and so censors them, either explicitly or more subtly (Thayer 2021). Even at the 6th Party Congress (1986), the congress that initiated the reform policies, the Party asserted that no other ideological form other than literature could effectively foster "healthy sentiment" and "renew people's thinking habit [sic] and way of life" (*75 Years of the Communist Party*, 744). In following government aims for literary and cultural issues, literature is still confined to the responsibility of fighting against any hindrances to the nation's socialist construction and independence (Đảng cộng sản Việt Nam 1993, 54–55; Tô 2009, 13–19; Vũ 2006, 30–36). In general, Vietnamese nation-makers, many of whom are literary theorists, writers, and researchers, continue making literature an instrument for sustaining public memory of the victories in the national and class revolutions, which, in turn, indicates the Party's eminence. The way that contemporary Vietnamese writers use formulaic discourses and old images of foreigners from the anti-colonial, socialist realist literature, is an indirect way of provoking in the public perceptions of colonial capitalism, colonialism, and imperialism, which are imagined as eternal enemies of modern Vietnamese nation-building. In other words, the portrayal of the foreigner as metaphor of national enemies in contemporary Vietnamese literature constitute the double-sided social criticism of this literature: it reflects the increasing acceptance of foreign economic, cultural, and social factors in the officially promoted image of a globalized Vietnam while warning of the potential return of colonial capitalism and imperialism associated with the force of globalization.

Conclusion

In arguing that Vietnamese nationalism as a form of class and national struggle remains vital in post-reform Vietnam, this chapter considers recent discussions about literature and nationalism in postcolonial countries. Imre Szeman (2003) asserts that the use and the appreciation of the national allegory in literature is a "particular kind [s] of cultural strategy" in national struggles. This is because national allegory presents an opportunity for intellectuals in developing countries to provoke hearts and minds toward issues of community – a mental unification that contributes toward the formation and development of nation-states (Culler 2007, 43–72; Anderson 1998, 70; 1991, 1–8). The continuing use of national allegory in postcolonial writing is particularly important in the context of disappearing national identities and collapsing national economies in the face of globalization (Szeman 2001, 817; Krishna 2009, 7–30). In the Vietnamese literary tradition, writing has always been seen as a weapon in the fight against hindrances to the nation's independence and socialist construction since the colonial period. Thus, by examining the presentation of the foreigner as an allegory in contemporary Vietnamese writers' "revolutionary efforts" aimed at strengthening the democratic and hegemonic figure of the nation, this chapter tries to demonstrate that literature continues to play a distinct role as a "cultural strategy" of Vietnamese nationalism in present-time.

As such, this chapter also engages with discussions about nationalism in postcolonial criticism. Postcolonial scholarship critically focuses on examining political betrayals and economic and cultural failures in postcolonial states; it dramatizes the "cacophony of bourgeois triumphalism" and marginalizes the common people, including working classes, women, and ethnic minorities (Guha 1997; Spivak 1988; 1999; Chatterjee 1993; Parry 2005). Lazarus (1993, 70–71) argues that there is a clear and profound hostility toward nationalism among these postcolonial discourses: nationalist discourse, seen as "coercive, totalizing, elitist, authoritarian, essentialist, and reactionary," is disparaged as "a replication, a reiteration, of the terms of colonial discourse itself." Noticeably, the discursive pessimism about the stability of nationalism in developing-world countries seems to complement popular ideas of the inevitable collapse of the nation-state as the result of the global expansion of capitalism. In general, from the postcolonial view, postcolonial states exist in a vulnerable, volatile space. They are evanescent; sooner or later, the project of postcolonial liberation will fade. The continuity of the metaphor of the foreigner as national enemy in contemporary Vietnamese literature, as examined in this chapter, suggests the continuity of postcolonial nationalism in Vietnam. The continuity of Vietnamese nationalism is more in the form of what Fanon (1968) calls national consciousness – the combined revolutionary efforts of an oppressed people that aim at liberating the country and creating a nation-state. Vietnamese intellectuals form this national consciousness by constantly extolling Vietnamese people's triumphs over colonialism and capitalism – triumphs that are allegorized in metaphors of the foreigner as national enemy. Moreover, Vietnamese intellectuals maintain such national consciousness by constantly reminding their public of the exploitation of colonialism and capitalism, which in Vietnam is traditionally associated with the image of the foreigner. To be precise, the imagined association of the foreigner with the enemies of the nation – colonialism, capitalism, and imperialism – in Vietnamese writing was formed and has been maintained to sustain a possibility of the formation of a nation, a nation that usually includes only those who share the common negative sentiment about such non-socialist forces in the nation state (Culler 2007, 72).

Acknowledgment

Dr. Tran Tinh Vy contributed to this chapter with the quoted poems. Dr. Do Hai Ninh suggested about contemporary Vietnamese literary works to be examined.

References

English-language references

75 Years of the Communist Party of Vietnam (1930–2005): A Selection of Documents from Nine Party Congresses. 2005. Hanoi: Thế giới Publishers.
Anderson, Benedict. 1991. *Imagined Communities: Reflections on the Origins and Spread of Nationalism.* London: Verso.
Anderson, Benedict. 1998. *The Spectre of Comparisons: Nationalism, Southeast Asia, and the World.* London: Verso.
Chatterjee, Partha. 1993. *The Nation and Its Fragments, Colonial and Postcolonial Histories.* Princeton, NJ: Princeton University Press.
Collins, Rebekah Linh. 2015. "Vietnamese Literature after War and Renovation: The Extraordinary Everyday." *Journal of Vietnamese Studies* 10 (4): 82–124.
Culler, Jonathan. 2007. *The Literary in Theory.* Stanford: Stanford University Press.
Devare, Sudhir. 2008. "Rising India and Indians in Cambodia, Laos and Vietnam." *Rising India and Indian Communities in East Asia*, edited by K. Kesavapany, A. Mani, and P. Ramasamy, 287–300. Singapore: Institute of Southeast Asian Studies.
Fanon, Frantz. 1968. *The Wretched of the Earth.* New York: Grove Press.
Guha, Ranajit, ed. 1997. *A Subaltern Studies Reader 1986–1995.* Oxford: Oxford University Press.
Healy, Dana. 2000. "'Homosapiens A' and 'Homosapiens Z': Love, Resignation, and Cultural Disorientation in Phạm Thị Hoài's novel Thiên sư." *South East Asia Research* 8 (2): 185–203.
Healy, Dana. 2006. "Of Victims and Cowards: Recasting the Peasants in Nguyễn Minh Châu's Story Phiên chợ Giát." *Annalen der Hamburger Vietnamistik* 2 & 3: 53–77.

Healy, Dana. 2007 "Negotiating Gender and Sexuality in Contemporary Vietnamese Literature." *Archív Orientální* 75 (1): 39–59.
Healy, Dana. 2010 "From Triumph to Tragedy: Visualizing War in Vietnamese Film and Fiction." *South Asia Research* 18 (2): 325–347.
Healy, Dana. 2013. "New Voices: Socio-Cultural Trajectories of Vietnamese Literature in the 21st Century." *Asian and African Studies* 22 (1): 1–30.
Healy, Dana. 2014 "Cultural Policies and Literary Legacies of Vietnamese Renovation." *Archív Orientální* 82 (1): 117–140.
Healy, Dana. 2013. "Literature in Transition: An Overview of Vietnamese Writing of the Renovation Period" In *The Canon in Southeast Asian Literature: Literatures of Burma, Cambodia, Indonesia, Laos, Malaysia, Philippines, Thailand and Vietnam*, edited by David Smith, 41–50. New York: Routledge.
Hồ, Anh Thái. 1998. *Behind the Red Mist*. Willimantic, CT: Curbstone Press.
Krishna, Sankaran. 2009. *Globalization & Postcolonialism. Hegemony and Resistance in the Twenty-First Century*. Lanham: Rowman & Littlefield Publishers.
Lazarus, Neil. 1993. "Disavowing Decolonization: Fanon, Nationalism, and the Problematic of Representation in Current Theories of Colonial Discourse." *Research in African Literatures* 24 (4): 69–98.
Lê, Minh Khuê. 1997. "Anh lính Tony." Lê Minh Khuê, những ngôi sao, trái đất, dòng sông. Hà Nội: NXB Phụ nữ. 140–161
Le, Quoc Hoi, Quynh Anh Do, Hong Chuong Pham, and Thanh Duong Nguyen. 2021. "The Impact of Foreign Direct Investment on Income Inequality in Vietnam." *Economies* 9 (1): 27. https://doi.org/10.3390/economies9010027.
Nguyễn, Tuấn Ngọc. 2008a. *Socialist Realism in Vietnamese Literature: An Analysis of the Relationship between Literature and Politics*. Saarbrücken, Germany: VDM Verlag.
Nguyễn, Võ Thu Hương. 2008b. *The Ironies of Freedom: Sex, Culture, and Neoliberal Governance in Vietnam*. Seattle: University of Washington Press.
Parry, Benita. 2005. *Postcolonial Studies: A Materialist Critique*. Abingdon: Routledge.
Pham, Chi P. 2021. *Literature and Nation-Building in Vietnam: The Invisibilization of the Indians*. Abingdon: Routledge.
Pham, T. Hoài. 2004. "The Machinery of Vietnamese Art and Literature in the Post-Renovation, Post-Communist (and Post-Modern) Period." *UCLA: Center for Southeast Asian Studies*. Retrieved from https://escholarship.org/uc/item/79z98070.
Phan, Thi Vang Anh, and Pham Thu Thuy. 2003. "Let's talk about love: Depiction of Love and Marriage in Contemporary Vietnamese short fiction." In *Consuming Urban Culture in Contemporary Vietnam*, edited by Lisa Drummond and Mandy Thomas, 202–220. Abingdon: Routledge.
Rato, Montira. 2004. "Land Reform in Vietnamese Literature." *Asia Review*, 17: 1–24.
Spivak, Gayatri Chakravorty. 1988 "Can the Subaltern Speak?" In *Marxism and the Interpretation of Culture*, edited by Cary Nelson and Lawrence Grossberg, 271–313. Urbana: University of Illinois Press.
Spivak, Gayatri Chakravorty. 1999. *A Critique of Postcolonial Reason: Toward a History of the Vanishing Present*. Boston: Harvard University Press.
Szeman, Imre. 2001. "Who's Afraid of National Allegory? Jameson, Literary Criticism, Globalization." *The South Atlantic Quarterly* 100 (3): 803–827.
Szeman, Imre. 2003. *Zones of Instability: Literature, Postcolonialism, and the Nation*. Baltimore, MD: Johns Hopkins University Press.
Thayer, Carlyle A. 2021. "Vietnam: Censorship No Joking Matter." Available at http://www.scribd.com/doc/77405369/Thayer-Vietnam-Censorship-No-Laughing-Matter
Trần, Đình Lâm. Foreign Direct Investment in Vietnam, 1–24. Available at https://www.bot.or.th/Thai/MonetaryPolicy/NorthEastern/DocLib_seminar56/Tran%20Dinh%20Lam--Foreign%20Direct%20Investment%20in%20Vietnam.pdf. Accessed December 12, 2021.
Tran, Trong Hung. 2006. Impacts of Foreign Direct Investment on Poverty Reduction in Vietnam. Available at https://www.grips.ac.jp/vietnam/VDFTokyo/Doc/18TTHungPaper.pdf. Accessed December 12, 2021.
Vo, Nhan Tri. 1990. *Vietnam's Economic Policy after 1975?* Aldershot: Ashgate Pub Co.
Vũ, Văn Hậu. 2006. "Objectivation on the Impact of Globalization on the Religious Life in Vietnam." *Thông tin khoa học xã hội* 8: 30–36.
Vũ, Văn Phúc. 2014. "Reform Policy of the Communist Party of Vietnam after Nearly 30 Years of Renewal." *Communist Review* (December). Available at http://english.tapchicongsan.org.vn/

Home/Politics/2014/765/Reform-policy-of-the-Communist-Party-of-Vietnam-after-nearly-30-years.aspx. Accessed May 2, 2017.

World Bank. 2000. "World Development Report 2000/2001: Attacking Poverty." Washington, DC: World Bank.

Vietnamese-language references

Cục văn thư lưu trữ nhà nước. *Hà Nội sự kiện, sự việc 1945–1954 qua tài liệu lưu trữ*. Hà Nội: Nhà xuất bản Quân đội nhân dân, 2007

Đảng cộng sản Việt Nam. 1993. *Văn kiện hội nghị lần thứ tư Ban chấp hành Trung ương, khóa VII* [Documents of the Fourth Meeting of the Central Committee, 7th Term]. [Hà Nội]: Lưu hành nội bộ.

Đặng, Thai Mai. 1944. *Văn học khái luận*. Hà Nội: Hàn Thuyên.

Đặng, Thai Mai. 1969. *Trên đường học tập và nghiên cứu: phê bình và tiểu luận*. 3 Vols. Hà Nội: Văn học.

Hà, Minh Đức, Bá Hán Lê, Phương Lựu. 1985. *Cơ sở lý luận văn học*. Hà Nội: Đại Học và Trung Học Chuyên Nghiệp.

Hoàng, Đạo Thúy. 1974. *Phố phường Hà Nội*. Hà Nội: Sở văn hóa thông tin Hà Nội.

Lại Nguyên Ân. 2004. "Chủ nghĩa hiện thực phê phán."*Từ điển văn học*. Ed. Đỗ Đức Hiểu. Hà Nội: Nhà xuất bản thế giới. 254–256

Lê, Minh Khuê. 2019. *Tuyển tập truyện ngắn và vừa*. Tp Hồ Chí Minh: NXB Trẻ.

Minh, Phương. 2013. "30 năm nghĩa tình của ông Shantanu với Việt Nam." *Tin tức* October 4, 2013. *Tin tức* is an information channel of the government; it is published by Thôn tấn xã Việt Nam.

Nguyễn, Công Hoan. 2004. *Nhớ và ghi về Hà Nội*. Hà Nội: Nhà xuất bản trẻ.

Nguyễn, Văn Trung. 1963. *Lược khảo văn học*. 3 tập. Sài Gòn: Nam Sơn.

Phạm, Cao Dương. 1966. *Thực trạng của nông dân Việt Nam dưới thời Pháp*. Saigon: Khai Tri.

Phong Vân. 2013. "Ông Shantanu kỉ niệm 30 năm gắn bó với đất nước Việt Nam." *Sài gòn giải phóng*. October 4.

Tô, Hoài. 1993. "Qua miền Trung" *Tập truyện ngắn Tô Hoài*. Hà Nội: NXB Lao động.

Tô, Huy Rứa. 2009. "Tiếp tục khơi dậy và phát huy tiềm năng, năng lực sáng tạo của đội ngũ văn nghệ sĩ giàu tâm huyết và tài năng của đất nước." *Tính dân tộc và tính hiện đai trong văn học nghệ thuật Việt Nam hiện nay*. Ed. Hội đồng lý luận phê bình van học nghệ thuật trung ương. Hà Nội: Nhà xuất bản chính trị quốc gia Hà Nội.

Trần, Đình Sử. 2005. *Thi Pháp văn học trung đại Việt Nam*. Hà Nội: Nhà xuất bản Đại học quốc gia Giáo dục.

Trần, Huy Liệu. 1957. *Tài liệu tham khảo lịch sử cách mạng cận đại Việt Nam*. Vol 6. Hà Nội: NXB Văn Sử Địa.

Trần, Huy Liệu. 1960. *Lịch sử thủ đô Hà Nội*. Hà Nội: Sử học.

Trần Ngọc Thêm. 1996. *Tìm hiểu về bản sắc văn hóa Việt Nam*. Hồ Chí Minh City: Nhà xuất bản tổng hợp thành phố Hồ Chí Minh City.

28
POPULIST NATIONALISM IN PHILIPPINE HISTORIOGRAPHY

Rommel A. Curaming

Introduction

"Populism" or "populist" is a terminology that used to be confined to the hifalutin academic discourses. In recent decades, however, it has become a buzzword even in the public sphere, particularly since the Brexit and the startling election of Donald Trump in 2016. Being a slippery concept, it evades clear definition, prompting one observer to title her article as "'Populism' is Meaningless" (Serhan 2020). What is unequivocal is the often-negative subtexts it implies whenever used, in both academic and popular platforms. Serhan (2020) was not off the mark when she observed that "populism has simply been reduced to a political shorthand to describe *that which we do not like*" (emphasis original).

When paired with another term—nationalism—that also easily conjures negative images among many scholars, particularly from Europe and the United States (US), populist nationalism doubly evokes sinister vibes (Fukuyama 2019; Gamble 2021; López-Alves and Johnson 2019). While nationalism in many Asian and other postcolonial societies seldom elicits negative associations, the term populist nationalism also often carries pejorative undertones (Yu 2014; Oates 1985). This probably owes to the tacit preference for civic nationalism common in the liberal-dominated academia.

The negativities that surround populism emanate from the supposed danger it poses to democracy, liberalism, rationality, inclusivity, diversity, decency, civility and obeisance to law and other long-standing norms (Eatwell and Goodwin 2018; Abts and Rummens 2007; Riker 1982; Canovan 2002). Many observers claim that politicians like Trump, Bolsonaro, Modi and Duterte embody populism. Labelled as demagogue, they allegedly manipulate hopes, fears and desires of the common people for their own political interests. Fukuyama characterises populist nationalist leaders as ones who create a narrow and anti-elite conception of "the people", formulate policies and ideas favourable to them, and present themselves (leaders) as ones who listen, understand, protect and fight for "the peoples'" interests (Fukuyama 2019).

While the theatrics of the so-called populist leaders received constant attention, the activities of what may be called "populist scholars" and the intellectual underpinning of populism as a movement or an ideology remain insufficiently examined. This is the case both in the Philippines and beyond. The close association of populism with anti-elitism and anti-intellectualism blindsides observers to its possibly fundamental roots in daily intellectual exercise. By examining nationalist history writing in the Philippines, which has over a century of provenance, this chapter aims to foreground the long-standing practice of intellectual populism.

This chapter shows that the three characteristics identified by Fukuyama (2019), as noted above, parallel what scholars in the Philippines have done in conceptualising "the people" in writing Philippine nationalist history. In both cases, "the people" need somebody more powerful and daring to speak on their behalf, nurture their identity and represent or fight for their interests. Because of limited space here, I cannot fully discuss the push back against, and the varying support received by, populist nationalist scholars in the Philippines, but the idea should be clear that such receptions are functionally analogous to the simultaneously harsh critiques of, and strong popular support received by, populist leaders like Trump, Duterte and others. The scale and intensity are, of course, different, as scholarly debates hardly received public attention to the extent similar to populist leaders. However, the fundamental logic of contested power relations, of "power games" as Fuller (2018) puts it, is similarly operative in the two cases. I should emphasise at the outset: in drawing parallelism between political and scholarly populism, I have no intent to trivialise the political or ethical implications they carry. I intend to draw out, on the contrary, significant political implications of this analytic exercise. Also, I do not wish to impute moral equivalence between what populist leaders and populist scholars do. I leave to the readers whatever judgement they might have on their (populists') behaviour and the consequences of their actions. I must note though that unethical attributes are not inherent to populism. What is inherent in populism is the privileging of the people's standpoint, regardless of the definition of "the people". By foregrounding the deep intellectual roots of populism, it would help dispel sources of misunderstanding its nature. It includes populism's supposed antithetical relationship with democracy, elitism and intellectualism. Rather than opposites, I argue that they are among populism's constitutive elements. We do not see them in that way because of unrecognised perspectival biases that blindside us.

Overview of Philippine nationalism

The modern Philippine nation-state developed through the integration process during almost four centuries (1565–1946) of colonial experience under Spain and the US, with a brief Japanese interregnum. Standard accounts of the history of Filipino nationalism trace its development to the secularisation controversies that aggrieved Filipino priests since the 1850s. This partly paved for the Cavite Mutiny and the tragic execution in 1872 of the three priests (Gomez, Burgos and Zamora, popularly known as Gom-Bur-Za) and the rise of the generation of *ilustrados* (or the enlightened) in the 1880s represented by Jose Rizal and other Propagandists (Agoncillo 1974; Schumacher 1981; 1991). It culminated in 1896 in the revolution against Spain and extended into the war against the US in 1899–1902 (Agoncillo 1956; Silbey 2013). Hitherto reformist but developed in the last decades of the nineteenth century into being fiercely anti-colonial in action and aspiration, Filipino nationalism underwent fragmentation and transformation under four decades of colonial experience under the US (1901–1946). As generations of Filipinos grew to appreciate the English language, public education, democracy, among other American legacies, what Abinales (2002) calls "colonial nationalism" developed and flourished. Colonial nationalism upholds the centrality of the nation as a sovereign bounded territory to define for whom and what is important, just like anti-colonial nationalism, but it acknowledges, nay, even celebrates, rather than reject as anti-colonial nationalism does, the role of colonial experience in shaping positive characteristics and images of the nation.

Both anti-colonial and colonial nationalisms noted above conceived of the people in abstraction, as an undifferentiated mass of people called Filipinos. They are both made up largely by elite-led discourses, ideology and movements. By elite, it did not mean just politico-economic elites, but intellectual elites as well. It also did not mean being truly powerful, rich and highly educated in absolute terms, but relative to the multitude of people during that time. Through the early decades of the twentieth century, these nationalisms paralleled and often opposed each other. Alongside these streams, another discernible current emanated from the supposedly Christian-identity of the Filipino nation. This identity derived from centuries-long experience being the only Christian nation in Asia (before Timor Leste became independent) (Francisco 2014). In history writing, the father-daughter tandem of Gregorio and Sonia Zaide who wrote widely used textbooks, well represent this current. Aptly, Cornelio (2020) labels it "theological nationalism". Long-standing and mutually reinforcing relationship exists between these strands of nationalism enabled by the long history of Christianity in the Philippines and the ensuing close ties forged between the Church and the various elite groups of both anti-colonial and colonial nationalist shades. However, the recurrent tensions between segments of these elites and the Catholic Church that flared up, say, in the Propagandists' critiques of the Church since the late 1800s (Schumacher 1991) and the quarrelsome debates on the Rizal Bill in 1956 (Schumacher 2011) and on the Reproductive Health Law (RH Law) in 2011–2012 (Leviste 2016), serve as a reminder of the multilayered and contested character of Philippine nationalisms as they continually evolved up to now.

To elaborate, the opening up of the Philippines to world trade in the 1850s and the education reforms of the 1860s paved for the rise of generations of Filipino *ilustrados* ("enlightened" ones) or educated class that challenged the long-standing hierarchies in colonial relationship, including the hegemonic clout of the Catholic Church. Besides spiritual influence that held the people psychologically captive, the Church had a bureaucratic presence in remote places, much wider, more enduring and more penetrating than the government. The abuses by Church officials appeared rampant, and they were clearly depicted in Jose Rizal's novels (*Noli Me Tangere* and *El Filibsterismo*), at least part of which were based on cases Rizal had a personal knowledge of. Other intellectuals in Rizal's generation, collectively called the Propagandists, also wrote about abuses by priests and other church and government officials. Theirs were the bitterest and most trenchant critiques of the corruption and abuses in the Philippines during that time. Being largely confined to the emergent community of intellectuals and those who actively participated in the 1896 revolution to expel the Spaniards, the long-term impact of their critiques on the rest of the society seemed limited. Despite the strong anti-Church sentiments that fuelled the 1896 revolution and the inroad of Protestantism under the American rule from 1900s to 1940s, the country remained in the stranglehold of Catholic influence long after Spain had left.

An instance that tested the lingering influence of the Catholic Church happened in the 1950s. The postwar years saw the rising tide of anti-colonial nationalism in Asia and the Third World more broadly. Nationalist lawmakers pushed for a bill in the Congress to require the reading of the unexpurgated version of Rizal's novels in high school and the university, so the younger generations would not forget Rizal and his ideas. Aware of Rizal's unsavoury depictions of Catholicism and Church functionaries in the novels, the Catholic Church threw its weight to block the proposed bill (Schumacher 2011). The rancorous debates that ensued between supporters of both sides showed the complex texture of the growing

Filipino nationalism in the 1950s (Ileto, 2010). At stake in this confrontation was the question of whether, and to what extent the competing secular and religious forces would prevail in shaping Filipino identity in the future. The law that was eventually passed, Republic Act 1425, popularly known as the Rizal Law, was an outcome of a compromise. It limited the requirement of reading the unexpurgated version of the novels to university-level students and it allowed exemption for students who, on religious ground, ask for it. Despite being watered down, it was a victory for secular strands of Filipino nationalism, but the vigorous fight put up by the Church and its supporters, and their subsequent moves to dilute, delay or derail its full implementation showed the enormous institutional power that it could wield.

The echoes of this acrimonious episode reverberated half a century later in the debates on Reproductive Health Bill in 2010–2012. Seeking to promote the use of contraceptives and sex education, among others, the Church strongly opposed it on moral, legal and doctrinal grounds (Leviste, 2016). Just like in the 1950s, the debates polarised politicians and the country more broadly. This time, however, the Church stance was clearly defeated, but not after the president exerted all efforts and political resources at his disposal. While this episode has shown further weakening of the Church's political influence, it remains a political force to be reckoned with up to now.

Anti-colonial nationalism sees nationalism largely from the political and/or economic standpoint, colonial nationalism from both political and socio-cultural perspectives, while theological nationalism is from a religious viewpoint. As a basis for typology-building, these are no doubt useful. However, their being top-down or elite-driven, consciously promoted, and their assumed unity of the nation as a category, conflating it with society and state, set the limit to types of nationalism that they can cover. An approach that accommodates a more broad-based, fluid, people-oriented, bottom-up, fragmentary, banal and everyday form of nationalism (Billig 1995; Skey and Antonsich 2017) is needed.

Populist nationalism closely relates to, but is not the same as banal or popular nationalism that Billig (1995) and many other scholars have examined. They are both society- or people-oriented rather than nation- or state-centric. They highlight the "people" in its various conceptions as object of and subject in analysis. However, while the popular or taken-for-granted, everyday nationalism may be simultaneously of-, for- and by-the-people, populist nationalism may be, but not necessarily of- and for-the-people. Also, it is definitely not by-the-people. Just as the "subalterns cannot speak" (Spivak 1988), someone else or certain groups, such as scholars, speak on their behalf. The next section examines how key Filipino historians have conceptualised the *populus* or "the people" as an object of analysis and as the subject in the development of Philippine nationalism.

From colonial to Filipino viewpoint

The birth of the nation and the nationalist historiography go hands in gloves (Deletant and Hanak 1988; Palti 2001). The early stirrings of this process manifested in the 1880s when Rizal and other Filipino intellectuals challenged the Spaniards' bipartite view of Philippine history, which located the period before Spain's arrival as the "age of darkness" supposedly supplanted by the "age of enlightenment" during the period of Spanish colonisation. Rizal and other Propagandists eschewed this framing and offered a tripartite view of Philippine history. They inverted the valuation of the pre-Hispanic period into the "golden" age while the three centuries of Spanish colonisation, the "age of darkness". In addition, they envisioned the post-Spanish colonial era as an opportunity for redemption, or the beginning of a new golden age (Salazar 1983).

This clear-cut differentiation makes up the sharp demarcation between the colonial and the Filipino viewpoints. The rise of generations of Filipino scholars in the early decades of 1900s, who appreciated colonial legacies while upholding the Filipino viewpoint, blurred this distinction. Gregorio Zaide, for example, along with Leandro Fernandez (1919; 1925) and Conrado Benitez (1926), was branded as a colonial historian for his appreciative assessment of both Spanish and American legacies. He also promoted a Filipino viewpoint that is continuous with Propagandists', in that it anchored on the question of what was beneficial for Filipinos. In "The Rewriting of Philippine History", Zaide expunged the Filipino viewpoint of anti-foreign bent, asserting that, "One can really love his fatherland without hating other nations. One can glorify the achievements of his nation without denigrating the achievements of other nations. And one can praise his own people without slandering other peoples" (Zaide 1973, 174).

Teodoro Agoncillo gave a different slant to Filipino viewpoint when he provocatively declared that "there was no Philippine history before 1872" (Agoncillo 1958). By this, he meant that much of what writers or scholars wrote before (and even after) 1872 was a history of Spain in the Philippines, not Philippine history. Written from the perspective of the Spaniards, Filipinos as actors in the unfolding history were hardly visible. In his view, Filipinos ought to be at the foreground of historical narrative and anything that has nothing to do with the formation of Filipino nation did not deserve to be included in the writing of Philippine history (Agoncillo 1958). While for the Propagandists and Zaide, the primary determinant of Filipino viewpoint was whether things were favourable for Filipinos, for Agoncillo the extent to which Filipinos were accorded a place in narrative and their relevance to the formation of Filipino nation were key. The scholarly effort that paved for the crystallisation of Filipino viewpoint in history, in opposition to or in the consonance with the colonial perspective, was crucial for the conception of "the Filipino people" as distinct from other peoples.

The pre-Second World War decades also witnessed the growth of radical politics in the Philippines as indicated by recurrent revolts and pro-labour and pro-peasant social movements such as Partido Komunista ng Pilipinas (PKP), Communist Party of the Philippines (CPP), Sakdal and Hukbalahap (Fuller 2007; Kerkvliet 2002; Richardson 2011; Terami-Wada 1988). This continued in the postwar decades with the establishment of the CPP and New People's Army (NPA) in the late 1960s (Weekley 2001). Radical ideas infused the intellectual atmosphere during this period. It proved fertile for the reformulation of the Filipino viewpoint in favour of social justice and politico-economic equity, rather than mere citizenship or the abstract collectivity of the "Filipino people". Teodoro Agoncillo's *Revolt of the Masses: The Story of Bonifacio and the Katipunan* (1956) exemplified this push to fragment this collectivity by claiming that the 1896 revolution was a handmade of the "masses". Previously, the revolution was understood as a collective national effort or that it was led by the elites. Agoncillo, in effect, put the common people at the vanguard of the pivotal episode in the nation's history. The book could have been published soon after it won an award in 1948, but arousing concerns from certain influential quarters of the political and intellectual communities in the country, it did not come out until 1956 (Ileto, 2011). Critics branded the book as communistic or Marxist, revolutionary, biased and flawed, among other invectives (Hernandez and Del Rosario 1956; May 1991; Zafra 1956). Criticisms and counter-criticisms persisted decades after its publication in the 1950s, which showed the unresolved tensions and issues among competing groups (May 1991).

Renato Constantino (1975; Constantino and Constantino 1978) extended the logic of Agoncillo's argument to cover not just the 1896 revolution but the entire stretch of the

Philippine colonial and postcolonial history. Doing so, he elevated the "masses" as prime movers or engine of history change. If for Agoncillo the main test of historical relevance and inclusion in Filipino viewpoint lies in one's role in the formation of Filipino nation, for Constantino, it was whether one can help the "masses" resist the colonial and neo-colonial oppression (Constantino 1975, 9).

Constantino explicitly rejected the "big men's" history or "history from above" that relegates the masses to the background, if seen at all. For all his championing of people's history, however, it is striking that the people in his historical accounts (Constantino 1975; Constantino and Constantino 1978) are muted: they hardly speak, think and feel by and for themselves, as a perceptive observer has noted (Ileto 1979, 5). Members of the elite classes have had to do these for them. This may be due largely to the type of archival sources commonly used by historians, which are mostly produced by the literate and dominant classes. Aware of the limits of archival sources, historians mulled if and how the authentic voices of "people" can be heard in the pages of historical documents.

Reynaldo Ileto's *Pasyon and Revolution* (Ileto 1979) was a path-breaking effort that sought to address precisely this challenge. It has shown that notwithstanding inherent bias of archives towards historical sources produced by educated classes, it remains possible to write history where the voices of the subaltern classes can be heard. It used non-conventional sources like poems, songs, prayers and *pasyon* or an epic poem about Jesus Christ's life and death, to extrapolate the *mentalité* of the marginalised and inarticulate communities. Doing so allows the underpinning logic of their worldview to be understood in its own terms. Rather than seeing it as deviant, presupposing the givenness of the elite mindset and categories derived from it, we may acknowledge it as simply different, not necessarily inferior.

Despite its landmark achievement, Ileto's *Pasyon and Revolution* had more than a fair share of critics who saw problems in, among other things its claim to capture the *mentalite* or worldview of the peasants in Tagalog societies in the late nineteenth and early twentieth centuries using alternative historical sources. These include Milagros Guerrero's "Understanding Revolutionary Mentality" (Guerrero 1981) and the most trenchant, Joseph Scalice's (2018) *Reynaldo Ileto's Pasyon and Revolution Revisited, A Critique*. Both complained about the conceptual imprecision of the Ileto's category of "masses". But more damaging is Scalice's argument that Ileto's reading of the unconventional sources was elitist and it had no discernible connection to the supposed consciousness or worldview of the peasants.

The cultural relativistic logic that underpins Ileto's approach was developed on a much grander scale by, for lack of a better term, the *Pantayong Pananaw* (PP) school in Philippine historiography. This school developed since the late 1960s or early 1970s from efforts of historians at the University of the Philippines led by Zeus Salazar. Limited space here prevents fuller discussion of PP. I provide a critically appreciative assessment of PP elsewhere (Curaming 2016). In addition, several works that explain PP in detail are available (Guillermo 2009; Navarro et al. 1997; 2015; Reyes 2002; Salazar 2000). In Tagalog, "we" has two equivalents: *tayo* and *kami*. *Tayo* is used when both the speaker and the spoken-to, along with others in the imaginary or real group where both belong, have a discourse. It is, in short, a marker of in-group. Combined with *pan*, which in Tagalog is a prefix for "for", *pantayo* means by-us/for-us. *Kami*, on the other hand, is used when the one spoken to is deemed excluded from the in-group. Prefixed with *pang*, which also means "for", *pangkami* means by-us/for-others. This simple differentiation has far-reaching historiographic implications, which are germane to the conception of populist history. For one, it clearly specifies who makes or from whose standpoint a historical account is made and to whom it is addressed: simply, the in-group where the historian belongs. It is also clear about whom history is written for and for what purpose: history is for a specific in-group and it is to promote mutual understanding among members, to unify the collective and strengthen it. In PP's formulation, the in-group can be calibrated to varying scales, say, from as small as a local community to as encompassing as nation, multi-national region and civilisation, but in the current form, it's mainly concerned about nation and region. In other words, PP is explicit about the purposiveness and situatedness of historical interpretation. It foregrounds people as an active participant in historical process, both as actors and as writers of history, as the historians are viewed as one of, not detached from, the people, not dissimilar to Gramsci's notion of organic intellectuals. PP sheds off pretence of universal applicability, objectivity or impartiality. Instead, it foregrounds relevance to and fairness for the "people" who belong to the in-group. By defining clearly the "us" and the "them", the fragmentary nature of discursive communities is acknowledged, and the interests of the in-group vis-à-vis the out-group's are duly justified. These are among the fundamental features of populism, which it shares with nationalism (Singh 2021).

The "people" in PP, Agoncillo's, Constantino's and Ileto's accounts are conceived as non-congruent with the population of the Philippine nation-state. What sets PP's approach apart from the three others is the flexibility in scale and membership it allows for forming collectivity. For Agoncillo, Constantino and Ileto, people are the "masses" who are socio-economically and culturally apart from the "elites". While Salazar's formulation heavily emphasises the "great cultural divide" that ensued from colonial experience, it is merely one of the fault lines that separates one group from another. Theoretically, PP allows the envisaging of the collectivity of people that cuts across socio-economic, cultural, linguistic and religious divides, and for a scale not necessarily co-terminus with the nation-state boundary.

This conception of the people as potentially fragmentary of the population within the nation-state boundary is distinguishable from the strictly integrative approaches employed by earlier historians like Fernandez (1919; 1932), Benitez (1926; 1954) and Zaide (1949). The state-sponsored project, *Tadhana: A History of Filipino People* (Marcos 1976), is similarly integrative in approach. As it shared with PP the formative years of development, with one of Tadhana's progenitors being the founder of PP, I shall discuss this project in the next section to illuminate the shared and the divergent elements in the two approaches. More importantly, it exemplifies the intertwined relationship between history and scholars, on the one hand, and the state, on the other, in the process of "people-making" and nation-building. As a nationalist history that is populist in orientation, this project also illustrates the case of populism that is state-sponsored. With limited space, discussion here is limited in scope and depth. For an in-depth analysis and detailed account, see Chapters 2, 3 and 6 of my book *Power and Knowledge in Southeast Asia: Scholar and State in Indonesia and the Philippines* (Curaming 2020).

The "people" in the Tadhana project

Ferdinand Marcos, the president of the Philippines from 1966 to 1986, initiated in the early 1970s a very ambitious project in partnership with some of the best Filipino scholars to write a 21-volume comprehensive history of the country. One of the brilliant scholars who agreed to participate was Zeus Salazar. As noted above, he pioneered the approach which in due time would be known as the PP school. Salazar was with the project roughly from 1974 to late 1979, the formative years, and he spearheaded it, being one of the two chief designers of *Tadhana*. Along with Samuel Tan, Zeus Salazar conceptualised and drew up the detailed outline of the project and much of the ideas that underpinned the Pantayo-approach found its way into the design (see Marcos 1976). These include, among several others, the idea that runs counter to commonly and widely held understanding of the determinate role of colonial experience that ran for over three centuries in the development of the Filipino nation and the Philippine state. In both PP and Tadhana, the over three centuries of colonisation constituted merely a "thin flake" on top of over 1,000 years of development of the foundational base culture of the Filipinos and other Malayo-Polynesians. This means that underneath the very glaring differences among modern-day Christian Filipinos and Muslim Malays and Indonesians, one would find shared deep-seated cultural characteristics. The decentring of colonial period as a keystone in historical development and the search in the very distant past for the origins of Filipino nation and culture overlap in PP and Tadhana. It is a mark of Salazar's contribution. This formulation allowed PP and Tadhana to envision the common people with low or no education and with limited adaptation to Western culture as the "true" repositories of "authentic" Filipino culture.

An important diverging point between PP and Tadhana, which is crucial in defining the "people", reflected the contribution of Samuel Tan, who co-designed Tadhana with Salazar. In his article "A Historical Perspective for National Integration" (1976), he took variance with Salazar's unitary approach based on the presumed underlying unity provided by the supposed common base-culture and affinity to Malayo-Polynesian language family. From Tan's view, this search for a "common thread in the maze of ethnic diversities and complexities" is problematic as "there are indefinite numbers of events or circumstances in the historical process which do not necessarily form into an inter-related whole" (1976, 5). Furthermore, in the pre-Hispanic period, communities existed autonomously and apart from each other. Cohesion was externally imposed and was political in nature. As an alternative, he conceived of the idea of "tri-sectoral communities" comprising the Christians, Muslims and *lumads* (various non-Christian and non-Muslim indigenous groups) that co-existed in the archipelago for centuries. This idea addressed the long taken-for-granted bias in Philippine history writing towards the lowland Christianised communities. Arguably, Tadhana constituted among the earliest acknowledgement in Philippine historiography that the Filipino nation-in-the-making was inherently multi-cultural and multi-religious. In short, while PP views the highly visible cultural diversity as superficial and looks for the deepest past for the ultimate unifying roots, Tadhana, via Tan's contribution, takes it constitutive of, rather than an obstacle to nation-formation.

The tensions that are discernible in Salazar's unitary and Tan's pluralist-integrative approaches are echoed in other areas in Tadhana, including the simultaneously top-down (indigenous state-centric) and bottom-up (people-oriented) framework that informed historical narrative and analysis. What stands out, however, is the penchant to integrate or synthesise and smoothen out potential conflicts. Tadhana's interpretation of the 1896 revolution, which sits atop the totem pole of Philippine nationalism as its birthing moment, exemplifies this point. For a work that developed in the 1970s and 1980s, when left-leaning politics and anti-colonial nationalist sentiments engulfed the country, it was rather unusual for Tadhana scholars to run counter to the hegemonic view (within the progressive circles) that upholds Agoncillo's "revolt of the masses thesis" and Constantino's Marxist class analysis. But as a state-sponsored history, it did not surprise that Marcos and his scholar-partners framed it in that manner.

Tadhana endeavours to create a creative synthesis of the "mass" and the "elitist" elements in the 1896 revolution. It argues that the revolution was a "product both of ilustrado and mass ideologies" and thus was an "expression of the national community" (Marcos 1976, 38). While Agoncillo and Constantino underscored the sharp distinction between the supposedly "merely" reformist aims of the Propaganda Movement and the revolutionary aspirations of the *Katipunan*, Tadhana downplays the difference using *La Liga Filipina* to provide a smooth transition and blur the separation. Notwithstanding *La Liga Filipina*'s short-lived existence, owing to the arrest and exile of its founder to a very remote place in Mindanao, Tadhana regarded it as a "milestone in the effort of the reformers to link the *ilustrados* with the masses" and that it represented the "marriage of strong social forces in a new dynamic ideology of national community" (Marcos 1982, 1:432). It insisted that the incipient national ideology was fed both by liberal ideas promoted by the *ilustrados* and by "populist-messianic sentiments of the masses" (Marcos 1982, 58). The Tadhana thus claims:

> Where Rizal and del Pilar represented the *ilustrado* reaching the masses in a common struggle against the frailocracy,[1] Bonifacio stood for the masses struggling from below to reach the ear of the *principalia-ilustrado* (emphasis original).
>
> *(Marcos 1982, 437)*

In other words, the "revolution represented the convergence of all the classes in Philippine society" (Marcos 1982, 438). Rather ironically, Tadhana re-instated the interpretation of the Philippine revolution that was common in colonial historiography of the early decades of the 1900s.

Conclusion

Academic debates among proponents of various conceptions of the "people" or "Filipino people" are usually framed within the strictures of scholarly imperatives. There were also instances when patently political factors were at play, and thus invited public reactions, such as in the caustic early reactions to Agoncillo's and Constantino's works. In the latter case, one can see its parallelism to the virulent critiques of populist leaders like Trump and Duterte in that both pairs transgressed the long-accepted liberal norms, ideas and practices. Upon gaining scholarly and political platforms, respectively, for being published and being elected as presidents, they propagated their ideas and gained even more followers. By the 1970s–1980s, Agoncillo-Constantino became the orthodoxy in Philippine historiography, at least within certain very influential sectors of the liberal and left-leaning academia represented by the University of the Philippines. Beyond this sphere, their critics—both silent and vocal—remain many, but the hegemonic position of the University of the Philippines in the country's intellectual sphere ensures the longevity and relevance of Agoncillo-Constantino's populist ideas. Similarly, Duterte and Trump were previously ignored or dismissed as viable presidential candidates. When they won, to the consternation of the largely liberal press and intelligentsia in the Philippines and the US, they have been criticised for both valid and questionable reasons internationally and in their own countries. While in power, the bulk of their fanatic supporters at home swelled enabling their resilience: Duterte keeps his persistently high approval ratings (70–80%) despite his many dubious antics and coercive policies, while Trump just narrowly lost in his re-election bid in 2020 and may win again in 2024.

Observers may find this parallelism absurd or even repulsive, but that is precisely the point: many are loath to consider the possibility that the scholarly and the political may be logically and functionally analogous, rather than oppositional as commonly believed, and that any populist move, in the sense of taking the cudgel for "the people", be it scholarly or political in form and aims, elicits counter-reactions perhaps proportionate to the threat it poses to the established elite-dominated order, also in scholarly or political senses. I drew out the latter point—about proportion of counter-reaction—from the fact that conceptions of the people that are integrative of and co-terminus with the whole population of the nation-state elicited little disapproving reactions unlike the fragmentary and class-conflicting ideas of Agoncillo and Constantino. Examples are many from the cases I referred to earlier: the Propagandists', Fernandez's, Benitez's, Zaide's, Salazar's, Tan's and Tadhana's. I should note that the strong pushback against Tadhana owed to Marcos's ghost authorship and the Marcos-scholars partnership that made it possible, not because of its populist conception of the people.

Similarly, not all populists in the political sense are equal: some are more despised than others. The likes of Trump and Duterte are among the most loathed internationally and domestically as well; Indonesia's Joko Widodo of Indonesia is among the least disliked, even liked ones. What is important is to not elide the question, who despises or favours them, and why they do so? Populists have their own base of support from the broad swathe of population and while it seems easy to dismiss their supporters as manipulated or gullible, the even rising wave of populism in some of the largest countries (the US, Brazil, Russia, India and Indonesia) forces us to take populism more seriously. The existence of populist scholars and scholarship, as discussed in this chapter, indicates that populism may have another well-spring: the long-existing pro-people intellectual or scholarly traditions. This should make us less surprised and less bewildered by the continuing rise of populism.

Note

1 Frailocracy or friarocracy refers to the rule of the Spanish friars. It seems to be used only in the Philippine academic discourse. A search on the web reveals that only sites related to the Philippines contain this word. Dictionaries also do not recognise it.

References

Abinales, Patricio. 2002. "American Rule and the Formation of Filipino 'Colonial Nationalism'." *Southeast Asian Studies* 39 (4): 604–621.
Abts, Koen, and Stefan Rummens. 2007. "Populism versus Democracy." *Political Studies* 55 (2): 405–424.
Agoncillo, Teodoro. 1956. *The Revolt of the Masses: The Story of Bonifacio and the Katipunan*. Quezon City: University of the Philippines.
———. 1958. "Our History under Spain." *Sunday Times Magazine*, August 24.
———. 1974. *Filipino Nationalism, 1872–1970*. Quezon City: R. P. Garcia Pub. Co.
Benitez, Conrado. 1926. *A History of the Philippines*. Boston: Ginn and Co.
———. 1954. *History of the Philippines: Economic, Social, Cultural, Political*. Revised edition. Boston: Ginn and Co.
Billig, Michael. 1995. *Banal Nationalism*. London: Sage.
Canovan, Margaret. 2002. "Taking Politics to the People: Populism as the Ideology of Democracy." In *Democracies and the Populist Challenge*, edited by Yves Mény and Yves Surel, 25–44. London: Palgrave Macmillan UK.
Constantino, Renato. 1975. *The Philippines: A Past Revisited*. Quezon City: Tala Pub. Services.
Constantino, Renato, and Letizia R. Constantino. 1978. *The Philippines: The Continuing Past*. Quezon City: Foundation for Nationalist Studies.
Cornelio, Jayeel. 2020. "Claiming the Nation: Theological Nationalism in the Philippines." In *What Does Theology Do, Actually? Observing Theology and the Transcultural*, edited by Matthew Robinson and Inja Inderst, 149–165. Leipzig: Evangelische Verlagsansta.
Curaming, Rommel A. 2016. "Postcolonial Studies and Pantayong Pananaw in Philippine Historiography: A Critical Engagement." *Kritika Kultura*, 27: 63–91.
———. 2020. *Power and Knowledge in Southeast Asia: State and Scholars in Indonesia and the Philippines*. Rethinking Southeast Asia. Abingdon: Routledge.

Deletant, Dennis, and Harry Hanak. 1988. *Historians as Nation-Builders: Central and South-East Europe.* https://public.ebookcentral.proquest.com/choice/publicfullrecord.aspx?p=5643963.
Eatwell, Roger, and Matthew J. Goodwin. 2018. *National Populism: The Revolt against Liberal Democracy.* London: Pelican an imprint of Penguin Books.
Fernandez, Leandro Heriberto. 1919. *A Brief History of the Philippines.* Boston: Ginn and Co.
———. 1925. *Philippine History Stories.* Manila and NY: World Book Co.
———. 1932. *A Brief History of the Philippines.* Boston, New York: Ginn and Co.
Francisco, Jose Mario. 2014. "People of God, People of the Nation Official Catholic Discourse on Nation and Nationalism." *Philippine Studies: Historical & Ethnographic Viewpoints* 62 (3/4): 341–375.
Fukuyama, Francis. 2019. *Identity: Contemporary Identity Politics and the Struggle for Recognition.* London: Profile Books.
Fuller, Ken. 2007. *Forcing the Pace: The Partido Komunista ng Pilipinas: From Foundation to Armed Struggle.* Quezon City: University of the Philippines Press.
Fuller, Steve. 2018. *Post-Truth: Knowledge as a Power Game.* New York: Anthem Press.
Gamble, Andrew. 2021. "Making Sense of Populist Nationalism." *New Political Economy* 26 (2): 283–290.
Guerrero, Milagros. 1981. "Understanding Philippine Revolutionary Mentality." *Philippine Studies* 29: 240–256.
Guillermo, Ramon. 2009. *Pook at Paninindigan: Kritika Ng Pantayong Pananaw.* Diliman, Quezon City: University of the Philippines Press.
Hernandez, Jose, and Simeon del Rosario. 1956. *The Revolt of the Masses : The Story behind Agoncillo's Story of Andres Bonifacio.* Manila: JM Hernandez.
Ileto, Reynaldo. 1979. *Pasyon and Revolution: Popular Movement in the Philippines, 1840–1910.* Quezon City: Ateneo de Manila University Press.
Ileto, Reynaldo. 2010. "Heroes, Historians, and the New Propaganda Movement, 1950–1953." *Philippine Studies* 58 (1/2): 223–238.
Ileto, Reynaldo. 2011. "Reflections on Agoncillo's The Revolt of the Masses and the Politics of History." *Southeast Asian Studies* 49 (3): 496–520.
Kerkvliet, Benedict J. 2002. *The Huk Rebellion: A Study of Peasant Revolt in the Philippines.* Lanham, MD: Rowman & Littlefield.
Leviste, Enrique Niño. 2016. "In the Name of Fathers, In Defense of Mothers: Hegemony, Resistance, and the Catholic Church on the Philippine Population Policy." *Philippine Sociological Review* 64 (1): 5–44.
López-Alves, Fernando, and Diane E. Johnson, eds. 2019. *Populist Nationalism in Europe and the Americas.* Abingdon: Routledge.
Marcos, Ferdinand. 1976. *Tadhana Outline: History of the Filipino People.* Manila: Ferdinand Marcos.
Marcos, Ferdinand E. 1982. *Tadhana: Two-Volume Abridgement of the History of the Filipino People.* Abridged [ed.]. Vol. 1. 2 vols. S.l.: s.n.
May, Glenn. 1991. "Agoncillo's Bonifacio: The Revolt of the Masses Reconsidered." *Pilipinas* 17: 51–67.
Navarro, Atoy, Mary Jane Rodriguez-Tatel, and Vic Villan. 1997. *Pantayong Pananaw: Ugat at Kabuluhan: Pambungad sa Pag-Aaral ng Bagong Kasaysayan.* Mandaluyong: Palimbagang Kalawakan.
Navarro, Atoy, Mary Jane Rodriguez-Tatel, and Vicente Villan, eds. 2015. *Pantayong Pananaw: Pagyabong Ng Talastatasan, Pagbubunyi Kay Zeus A. Salazar.* Quezon City: Bagong Kasaysayan Inc. (BAKAS).
Oates, Leslie. 1985. *Populist Nationalism in Prewar Japan: A Biography of Nakano Seigo.* Sydney: Allen Unwin.
Palti, Elías José. 2001. "The Nation as a Problem: Historians and the 'National Question.'" *History and Theory* 40 (3): 324–46.
Reyes, Portia L. 2002. "'Pantayong Pananaw and Bagong Kasaysayan in the New Filipino Historiography: A History of Filipino Historiography as an History of Ideas." PhD thesis. Bremen: University of Bremen.
Richardson, Jim. 2011. *Komunista: The Genesis of the Philippine Communist Party, 1902–1935.* Quezon City: Ateneo de Manila University Press.
Riker, William H. 1982. *Liberalism against Populism: A Confrontation between the Theory of Democracy and the Theory of Social Choice.* Long Grove, IL.: Waveland Press.

Salazar, Zeus. 1983. "A Legacy of the Propaganda: The Tripartite View of Philippine History*." In *Ethnic Dimension: Papers on Philippine Culture, History and Psychology*, edited by Zeus Salazar, 107–126. Cologne: Counselling Center for Filipinos, Caritas Association for the City of Cologne.

———. 2000. "The Pantayo Perspective as a Discourse Towards Kabihasnan." *Southeast Asian Journal of Social Science (Now Asian Journal of Social Science)* 28 (1): 123–152.

Scalice, Joseph. 2018. "Reynaldo Ileto's Pasyon and Revolution Revisited, a Critique." *Sojourn: Journal of Social Issues in Southeast Asia* 33 (1): 29–58.

Schumacher, John. 2011. "The Rizal Bill of 1956: Horacio de la Costa and the Bishops." *Philippine Studies: Historical & Ethnographic Viewpoints* 59 (4): 529–553.

Schumacher, John N. 1981. *Revolutionary Clergy: The Filipino Clergy and the Nationalist Movement, 1850–1903*. Book, Whole. Quezon City, Metro Manila: Ateneo de Manila University Press.

———. 1991. *The Making of a Nation: Essays on Nineteenth-Century Filipino Nationalism*. Manila: Ateneo de Manila University Press.

Serhan, Yasmeen. 2020. "'Populism' Is Meaningless." *The Atlantic*. March 14. https://www.theatlantic.com/international/archive/2020/03/what-is-populism/607600/.

Silbey, David J. 2013. *A War of Frontier and Empire: The Philippine-American War, 1899–1902*. New York: Farrar, Straus and Giroux. https://www.overdrive.com/search?q=FF817E63-8995-4DED-B2A3-21A238BD6EDB.

Singh, Prerna. 2021. "Populism, Nationalism, and Nationalist Populism." *Studies in Comparative International Development* 56 (2): 250–69. https://doi.org/10.1007/s12116-021-09337-6.

Skey, Michael, and Marco Antonsich, eds. 2017. *Everyday Nationhood: Theorising Culture, Identity and Belonging after Banal Nationalism*. London: Palgrave Macmillan.

Spivak, Gayatri. 1988. "Can the Subaltern Speak?" In *Marxism and the Interpretation of Culture*, edited by Cary Nelson and Lawrence Grossberg, 271–316. Urbana and Chicago: University of Illinois Press.

Tan, Samuel K. 1976. "A Historical Perspective for National Integration." *Solidarity: Current Affairs, Ideas and the Arts* 10 (2): 3–17.

Terami-Wada, Motoe. 1988. "The Sakdal Movement, 1930–34." *Philippine Studies* 36 (2): 131–150.

Weekley, Kathleen. 2001. *The Communist Party of the Philippines, 1968–1993: A Story of Its Theory and Practice*. Quezon City: University of the Philippines Press.

Yu, Haiyang. 2014. "Glorious Memories of Imperial China and the Rise of Chinese Populist Nationalism." *Journal of Contemporary China* 23 (90): 1174–1187. https://doi.org/10.1080/10670564.2014.898907.

Zafra, Nicolas. 1956. "The Revolt of the Masses: Critique of a Book." *Philippine Studies* 4 (4): 493–514.

Zaide, Gregorio. 1973. "The Rewriting of Philippine History." *Historical Bulletin* 17 (1–4): 162–177.

Zaide, Gregorio F. 1949. *Philippine Political and Cultural History*. 2 vols. Manila: Philippine Education Co.

29
BUDDHIST NATIONALISM IN BURMA/MYANMAR
Collective victimhood and ressentiment

Niklas Foxeus

In most periods of rapid social, political, and economic changes since the colonial period in Burma/Myanmar, Buddhist nationalist discourse has emerged calling for protection of *amyou-bhāthā-thāthanā*, "nation/race, religion, and the Buddha's dispensation," three emotion-laden and inextricably linked signifiers fueling a sense of victimization of the majority group. The number of Buddhist nationalist movements that emerged during the second parliamentarian period (2011–2021) in post-independence Burma/Myanmar, and the extent and frequency of Buddhist nationalist preaching attracting huge audiences, and the impact of their preaching on society were unprecedented in Burma's history. During this period, many Buddhist nationalist movements, the most well-known of which were the 969 movement and Ma Ba Tha, emerged that were led by monks but included laypeople. They disseminated an anti-Muslim discourse aiming to protect and defend their nation, Buddhism, and their country from the Muslim minorities.

These Buddhist nationalist movements emerged in response mainly to (1) structural transformation (social, political, and economic); and (2) Buddhist-Muslim riots in the Rakhine State. As for structural change, uncertainty and fear were brought about by the political shift in 2011 after a long period of military dictatorships (1962–2011). In 2010, the military-backed party Union Solidarity and Development Party (USDP) won an election that was neither free nor fair, and Thein Sein, a former general and prime minister in the military dictatorship SLORC-SPDC (1988–2011), was elected the president. That semi-civilian and semi-democratic government initiated a process of democratization and political liberalization, and further implementation of liberal capitalism (see Egreteau 2016; Lall 2016). The liberalization of the economy entailed the reappearance of the stereotype of the successful Muslim businessman. It bred fears about a Muslim dominance of the economy, and their alleged use of money to entice Buddhist women into interreligious marriages. The riots in the Rakhine State in Western Burma/Myanmar broke out between Buddhists and Muslims (especially Rohingyas) in 2012 and were followed by riots in other parts of the country in 2013–2014, including Mandalay and Meiktila in central Burma. Most of the victims were Muslims (ICG 2013; Green, McManus, and Venning 2015).

Besides structural change, Buddhist nationalist discourse has, since the colonial period, been an additional factor that has contributed to exacerbate tensions and instigate riots between Buddhists and Indians (later Muslims). It has been disseminated by nationalist monks and laypeople through sermons, speeches, journals, newspapers, and today through social media. This chapter demonstrates that there is a discursive continuity within Buddhist nationalist discourse from the colonial period until today, in the form of two recurrent and interrelated issues: the perceived dangers posed by interreligious marriages and by the successful Indian (later, Muslim) businessman to Burmese nation/race, and the Buddha's dispensation.

Based on Buddhist nationalist sermons, publications, interviews, and fieldwork, this chapter argues that the sermons and the agendas of these contemporary movements gained popularity because they resonated with and made sense to the people. Historical narratives of the colonial period of domination, vulnerability, and weakness have created a long-standing sense of collective victimhood and *ressentiment* among the Burman Buddhist majority population toward initially Indian immigrants and later the Muslims. These fears have created a concern, if not a paranoia, regarding the imminent weakening and, ultimately, destruction of the Burmese nation/race, religion, and the Buddha's dispensation (*amyou-bhāthā-thāthanā*). In the post-independence period starting in 1948, these narratives came to be linked to anti-Muslim conspiracy theories (Foxeus, 2019, 2022).

I have interviewed about 90 people (2016, 2017, and 2019) in semi-structured interviews within Ma Ba Tha and other Buddhist nationalist organizations. The majority were monks, but some were laypeople, and a few were "nuns" (*thīla-shin*). Almost all of them belonged to the Burman majority population. Most of my interviews were conducted in Upper Burma, especially in Mandalay but also in smaller cities there, and some in the Yangon area (2016 and 2017). I have also conducted fieldwork and socialized with the monks in Mandalay area and in Yangon using participant observation as a method. All translations from Burmese into English are, if not otherwise indicated, made by the author.

Buddhist nationalism, *ressentiment*, and collective victimhood

A Buddhist nationalist discourse emerged during the colonial period in Burma that was shaped by bitterness, envy, and hatred (*ressentiment*) toward especially the Indian immigrants (Hindus and Muslims) and a sense of inferiority, and vulnerability created by the colonial situation in which the Buddhist majority population experienced themselves as a minority under siege – that is, a sense of collective victimhood – fearing the disappearance of the Buddha's dispensation and the Burmese nation/race. Narratives shaped by such sentiments (first a "colonial threat narrative" and later anti-Muslim conspiracy theories) have later been reproduced and perpetuated in social memory, education, nationalist pamphlets, articles, sermons, and the like until today and have been instrumental in creating tensions and in inciting riots between Buddhists and Muslims (see Foxeus 2019, 2022).

The sociological concepts of collective victimhood and *ressentiment* deal with similar socio-psychological conditions and dynamics. These concepts are overlapping and complementary. They are useful to employ in the case of Burma/Myanmar because they highlight a specific kind of social and psychological sources of conflict and tension that brought about Burmese Buddhist nationalist movements and nationalist discourse in the early twentieth century. The concept of collective victimhood refers, according to Bar-Tal et al. (2009), to a mindset shared by group members, and results from a perceived intentional harm (oppression, humiliation, and the like) inflicted by another group. As this harm is felt to be undeserved, unjust, and immoral, the responsibility is ascribed to the out-group. This generates negative feelings toward them such as anger, and self-pity that often leads to a desire to take revenge. Past injustice can be maintained in the collective memory through generations. Members of the collective perceive themselves to be morally superior, and innocent victims. Such groups tend to view themselves as victims also in new situations, in which the collective victimhood serves as a cognitive frame for interpretation (Bar-Tal et al. 2009, 236–239, 241).

As a philosophical concept, *ressentiment* was coined by Friedrich Nietzsche (1996 [1887]). According to Max Scheler, who developed his concept into a sociological concept, *ressentiment* is a "self-poisoning of the mind" and a "lasting mental attitude, caused by the systematic repression of certain emotions and affects." *Ressentiment*, Scheler explains, can only emerge if emotions such as vengefulness, hatred, malice, and envy are strong and are not immediately acted out but are suppressed because of the fear that an immediate reaction would lead to defeat. This inability to act them out leads to frustration, which is a suppressed state, in which the emotions turn into *ressentiment* that poison and embitter the personality (Scheler 1998 [1915], 31). It should be noted that *ressentiment* is most likely to emerge in a modern society characterized by competition and in which there should be equality between social groups (Scheler 1998 [1915], 32, 36–38; Frings 1998), which should have been the case with the British colonial subjects in colonial Burma.

The concept of *ressentiment* has been developed in theories about nationalism, as being an integral element of a certain form of ethnic nationalism that David Brown (2008, 778) calls "ressentiment nationalism." That is an intolerant form of nationalist response among a majority population against a perceived threat posed by minorities.[1] At the same time, this is an identity-building process based on *ressentiment* drawing a distinct boundary between the in-group and the out-group, the dominating Other, the antagonistic Other, that is, a polarization between us versus them (see Jaffrelot 2005, 11; Greenfeld and Chirot 1994; Brown 2008).

Dominated and powerless people who feel marginalized, humiliated, and frustrated because they are incapable of acting out their vengefulness and envy, who must suppress such sentiments, may take recourse to what Nietzsche called an "imaginary revenge." That entails creating collectivist stereotypes and portraying the oppressing Other as evil and wicked enemies and the own group as the virtuous ones. This moral condemnation is the imaginary revenge that serves as a substitute for real revenge (Nietzsche 1996 [1887], 22–28; see also Brown 2008, 778). In this way, the *ressentiment* can be overcome by such stereotyping, moral condemnation, and demonizing in nationalist ideology (Greenfeld 1992, 254–255; Brown 2008). In Burmese Buddhist nationalist discourse, such moral condemnation and stereotyping of Indians began during the colonial period and came to be almost exclusively focused upon Muslims since around the 1980s. However, as noted above, these sentiments have also been a contributing factor in the outbreak of riots.

Burmese Buddhist nationalism and national identity

In Burma, a Buddhist nationalist discourse evolved during the colonial period in the early decades of the twentieth century. In Burmese Buddhist nationalism, an ethnic identity has been intrinsically intertwined with a Buddhist identity and came to be shaped by developments during the colonial period. Buddhist-Muslim stereotypes can be traced back to that period, although they have developed throughout the years. Thereby, a construction of incompatible religious identities shaped by Orientalism and the major colonial taxonomic categories of "race" and religion imposed by the British colonial administration evolved. Under the impact of such British bureaucratic taxonomies, religious and ethnic identities that previously had been rather fluid became more ossified. Moreover, ethnicity came to be viewed as biological and immutable "races." Such essentialized religious and "racial" identities evolved in colonial Burma, with Buddhists being stereotyped as tolerant and Indians (Muslims and Hindus) as intolerant (Turner 2019; see also Ikeya 2011). The alleged Buddhist tolerance became an integral part of Buddhist nationalist discourse in the early twentieth century. It was perceived as a weakness that made Buddhists more liable to be overrun by intolerant Indians (Turner 2019). This Buddhist tolerance is today perceived as an essential aspect of Buddhist national identity. Buddhist nationalist discourses are permeated by positive and negative stereotypes of Buddhists and Indians (later Muslims). These stereotypes came to develop more in pamphlets with anti-Muslim conspiracy theories in the 1950s and the 1980s onward, and especially after 2011, all of which were shaped by *ressentiment* and a sense of collective victimhood. These two features have remained persistent aspects of Buddhist nationalist discourse since the colonial period until today, even though the Buddhist majority population has not lived under domination after the achievement of independence in 1948. Buddhists portrayed as mild, filled with loving-kindness, propagating non-violence, and practicing meditation is a recurrent stereotype within contemporary Buddhist nationalist sermons, with Muslims stereotyped as evil, violent, egoistic, and libidinous (Foxeus 2022). Although nationalist monks have disseminated anti-Muslim hate speech in their sermons that have inflamed tensions and incited riots between Buddhists and Muslims, they have nevertheless denied responsibility insisting that they are filled with loving-kindness and have merely warned the Buddhists (see Walton and Hayward 2014; Foxeus 2022). In recent decades, the old nationalist slogan that to be a Burmese is to be a Buddhist has even become the norm at Immigration offices, where a Burman Buddhist identity is fabricated by bureaucratic procedures. When applying for ID cards, on which "race" and "religion" are registered, mainly Muslims, including Burman Muslims, are required to either select an origin foreign to Burma/Myanmar, such as India, Bangladesh, Pakistan, and the like, or such an exogenous ethnicity combined with an indigenous ethnic group. Thereby, they are turned into people of "mixed blood" (*thway-hnaw*) or "mixed race" (*kapyā*) of lesser status (fieldwork, Mandalay, 2016–2019; Nyi Nyi Kyaw 2016, 2015).

Burmese Buddhist nationalist discourse, in which a national identity consisting of a hybrid of ethnic and religious identity is implied, is intimately linked to two issues: interreligious marriages and business competition with Indians (later Muslims). These two issues are closely related: wealthy Indians were accused of using their wealth to persuade and lure Burmese Buddhist women into marriages with them, whereby they would be converted to Islam. Thereby, Burmese Buddhist race/nation would decline, and their race would be diluted and finally disappear. This discourse began during the colonial period and was revitalized in the second parliamentarian period (2011–2021). Women were perceived as the weakest point of the nation through whom it will be corrupted (mixed race/blood) and ultimately be destroyed and wiped out through the "incursions" (*kyū-kyaw*) by the Muslims.

The colonial period: Buddhist nationalist movements

Since the colonial period, Buddhist nationalist movements have been framed by a discourse of victimization and have been mobilized by a sense of bitterness, hatred, and envy (*ressentiment*) toward Indians and later Muslims and that have been reproduced through social memory. The signifiers to which that felt injustice and victimhood have been linked are the three words *amyou-bhāthā-thāthanā*, nation/race, language (today, religion), and the Buddha's dispensation (Phyo Win Latt 2020; Foxeus 2019; Nyi Nyi Kyaw 2016). The aim of protecting *amyou-bhāthā-thāthanā* seems to have emerged within the Buddhist lay association Bouddha-bhāthā Kalyāṇa Yuwa Athin known as the Young Men's Buddhist Association

(YMBA), which also included *pyinnyā*, "education" in its fourfold slogan (see Maung Maung 1980, 3; Schober 2011; Phyo Win Latt 2020, 72–73).

YMBA and other Buddhist lay associations emerged to protect the Buddha's dispensation and *amyou* (race, nation, ethnicity, etc.) against the perceived threats to them posed by the British colonization, its colonial policies, modernization projects, and implementation of a capitalist economy, as well as the British abolishment of the Burmese monarchy in 1885. Formerly, the Buddhist king had been the main agent assuming the duty to protect and promote the Buddha's dispensation (Smith 1965; Turner 2014). In the absence of a Buddhist king, that responsibility now shifted to the Buddhist laypeople, and hundreds of Buddhist lay associations were founded between 1890 and 1920 (Turner 2014). YMBA was founded by a Western-educated Burmese elite and began as a kind of cultural nationalist organization seeking to cultivate and promote Burmese religion, *amyou* (see below), culture, language, and to prevent them from disappearing during the British colonial rule when local culture and religion were perceived to be weakening and disappearing. In the first issue of the *Burman Buddhist*, the mouthpiece of YMBA, one of the aims of the organization was to preserve the "Burman national character," and the "conservation of those characteristics and tendencies which have frequently led to the definition of a 'Burman' as a 'Buddhist'" (*The Burman Buddhist* 1908 1(1): 2). At the same time, YMBA and many other Buddhist lay associations engaged in a variety of social, educational, and religious activities that created a sense of Buddhist community protecting the Buddha's dispensation in the religious diversity that characterized Rangoon and other larger cities in colonial Burma (Turner 2014). In 1916, YMBA turned into a more political nationalist organization with its campaign known as the shoe question and it raised demands on the British colonial government. In 1920, YMBA became the General Council of Burmese Associations (GCBA) and came to be more involved in nationalist political activities and mobilizing (Turner 2014; Smith 1965; Maung Maung 1980).

Since this period until today, there has been a recurrent Buddhist nationalist discourse on the decline of *amyou* and the Buddha's dispensation. The word *amyou* is a polysemic concept of belonging. It can connote "kind," "sort," "species," "lineage," "relative," etc. (see Stewart and Dunn 1969, 252–253).[2] In the pre-colonial period, an important meaning of *amyou* was a descent group or kinship and implied a common origin. At some point in the first decades of the twentieth century during the British colonial period, *amyou* came to denote "nation" in the modern sense, and the modern Western concept of biological "race" (see Stewart and Dunn 1969, 252; Ikeya 2011; Phyo Win Latt 2020, 55–57; Taylor 2015).

Indian immigration: *ressentiment*, collective victimhood, and riots

Two factors serve as the sociological basis or the structural conditions for the development of *ressentiment* in nationalist discourse: first, the fundamental comparability and equality between the subject and the object of envy. Second, an inequality has emerged between them, but is regarded as unfair (Greenfeld 1992; Greenfeld and Chirot 1994, 84–85; see also Scheler 1998 [1915], 32, 36–38). The main target of the Burmese Buddhist response was the Indian immigrants, especially because of their dominance within the commercial business sector, and in the colonial administration, on the one hand, and the intermarriages between them and Burmese Buddhist women, on the other. Moreover, the British colonial administration regarded Burmese as being too backward for equal treatment with the Indians (Charney 2009, 23). Burmese nationalists felt themselves to have been colonized twice: first by the British, and second by the Indians (Taylor 2015, 4; see also Chakravarti 1971). The

British army that invaded Burma and forced it into subjugation consisted predominantly of Indians. This gave the impression, Chakravarti explains, not of a British but an Indo-British occupation of Burma, with Indians being perceived as a part of the occupying colonial force (Chakravarti 1971, 96–97). As one newspaper wrote in 1937, "since the dawn of history, Indians have been the leaders of attack against the Burmans on behalf of the white faces…" (Riot Inquiry Committee 1939a, 36).

Burmese nationalism originated first as an anti-Indian response (Hindus, Muslims, etc.; see Chakravarti 1971, 101), and that slightly later turned anti-colonial. In 1922, the nationalist monk U Ottama accused "foreigners of having hypnotized the Burmese into believing that they are an inferior race" (Mendelson 1975, 223). The background of this response and these rising tensions was a concern among Burmese about the unregulated immigration and the disproportionate political, economic, and social influence of the Indians and that were favored by the British colonizers. Indians came to occupy a dominant position vis-à-vis the Burmese (Egretau 2011, 36; Phyo Win Latt 2020; Khin Maung Kyi 1993, 627–628). The British encouraged Indians to migrate to Burma to work in the colonial administration. An elite among the Indians were offered the most prestigious positions, while the Burmese were unprivileged and mostly assumed subordinate positions and fared poorly in business. In the larger cities, Burmese people constituted a minority that occupied the lowest rung in the colonial hierarchical order, while the Indians were the majority situated in the middle position, and the British were at the top (see Charney 2009, 28–30; Khin Maung Kyi 1993). Indian businesses dominated the economy in Burma, not only in major cities but in smaller cities too. They predominated in almost every line of business, including merchanting, brokerage, banking, shopkeeping, moneylending, and the like (Khin Maung Kyi 1993, 628). In Rangoon in 1931, the Indian population was 212,929 or 53% and the Burmese population (predominantly Burman) was 127,582 or 32%. More than 66% of Rangoon's population was composed of immigrants (see Chakravarty 1971, 19–20). There was a similar ratio in other larger cities (Khin Maung Kyi 1993, 634). Likewise, English was the lingua franca in administration and education, Hindi dominated the commercial sector, and Burmese language was marginalized (Charney 2009: 23–24).

The humiliating second-rate status of Burmese people, and the marginalization of their language and culture, brought about *ressentiment* toward Indians. This experience of marginalization and minority position among the Burman Buddhist majority population have created a lasting sense of collective victimhood, vulnerability, and of being under siege that can be described as a majority with a minority complex (see Foxeus 2019, 2022).

Following the unrestricted immigration of labor from India to Burma that increased in the latter half of the nineteenth century, many Indians married Burmese Buddhist women. Although some men were Hindus, most of the cases were concerned with Muslim Indian men. Many Burmese Buddhist women who married Indian men reportedly believed that they were married with them, according to Burmese customary laws, but were – from the point of view of, for instance, Islamic law – legally merely a kind of mistress without any inheritance rights. They could not legally marry Hindu men due to cast-regulations, and to legally marry Indian Muslim men they first had to convert to Islam, which many did but that was not always sufficient for the marriage to be legally valid (Chakravarti 1971; Cady 1958; Ikeya 2011; Smith 1965, 109; Khin Yi 1988, 96; Mazumder 2014). The intermarriage problem was made into a racial problem of "mixed races" (*kapyā*) and dilution of the Burmese race, and it brought fears of the extinction of the Burmese race and their nation (Mazumder 2014, 500; see also Ikeya 2011). In the early 1920s and especially in the 1930s, an alarmist discourse emerged in media and among Burman nationalist leaders in the legislature that Burma was being "swamped" and "swallowed" by Indians and that their race or nation was being extinguished (see Ikeya 2011; Chakravarty 1971, 19; Mazumder 2014; Phyo Win Latt 2020; Nyi Nyi Kyaw 2020). In the newspapers, Indians were frequently referred to as "the Indian peril" (Riot Inquiry Committee 1939a, 35). Fears emerged among nationalists that Buddhism, Burmese race, and local culture would imminently be wiped out (see Chakravarti 1971; Smith 1965; Cady 1958; Turner 2014; Charney 2009), thereby bringing about an "Indophobia" (Egreteau 2011). This fear of extinction of Burmese race is what Nyi Nyi Kyaw (2020) has called the "myth of deracination."

Since the colonial period, Burmese Buddhist nationalism has been gendered. The Burmese Buddhist woman has served as a metaphor of the nation that must be protected from foreign intrusion, violation, and insults. Already in the late 1910s up to 1927 (when the Buddhist Marriage and Divorce Bill was introduced in the Legislative Council), YMBA and later the GCBA, as well as related women organizations, lobbied to have an intermarriage law enacted for Burmese Buddhist women and foreign men, especially Indians. It was not enacted until 1939. It was called the Buddhist Women's Special Marriage and Succession Act (see Ikeya 2011; Mazumder 2014; Phyo Win Latt 2020).

Being in a subordinate and minority position in the urban setting, Burmese Buddhists utilized cultural means to take their imaginary revenge shaped by *ressentiment*. In the vernacular press, especially in the 1920s and 1930s, there was a recurrent anti-Indian discourse that exacerbated tensions. It was encountered in newspapers, short stories, cartoons, and novels. It criticized, ridiculed, accused, and demonized the Indian immigrants claiming that they are destroying their race/nation, religion, and the Buddha's dispensation (Phyo Win Latt 2020; Ikeya 2011; Mazumder 2014). The newspapers were seen by the colonial authorities as playing a significant role in inflaming Burmese anti-Indian sentiments before and during the 1938 Indo-Burmese riots (Phyo Win Latt 2020, 136; Riot Inquiry Committee 1939a, 33–43). In a popular Burmese song from the late 1930s, it was claimed about Indians that they are, "Exploiting our economic resources and seizing our women, we are in danger of racial extinction" (Khin Yi 1988, 96–97). In a poem from 1939, the following was stated regarding the immigrants:

> These *Kala* [Indians] and *Tayoke* [Chinese] never cease coming in throngs
> This makes our country's future a grave concern
> Poor Burmans are trampled underfoot and made to kowtow
> While our dignity and glory are no more now
> Are the aliens cahooting to destroy our *Amyo* [race/nation]? […].
> (transl. in Phyo Win Latt 2020, 143–144; square brackets added)

In 1920, Ledi Pandita U Maung Gyi wrote about how the women are the main source of the decline of *amyou* because of intermarriages with foreigners. Here, *amyou* clearly refers to "race," as such unions is claimed to entail "mixed blood." Women were exhorted to love and protect their race by refraining from marrying men from other races (Phyo Win Latt 2020, 80). He wrote the following regarding protection of Burmese race:

> Women are the root cause of the decline of *Amyo* [race]. If a Burmese *Amyothamee* (woman) is married to a Burmese man, their *Amyo* will still exist through their posterities. However, if she is married to an *Amyokwe* (people from a different *Amyo* or people of other blood or faith), her descendants' *Amyo* will disappear or be ruined.
> (transl. in Phyo Win Latt 2020, 83; square bracket added)

The first anti-Muslim moral panic emerged during the 1938 Indo-Burmese riots that were specifically anti-Muslim and left 240 dead (Riot Inquiry Committee 1939b, 281). These riots broke out in the tense situation of the 1937 partition from India, economic depression; indebtedness of peasants to Indian Chettiyar moneylenders who became landlords; and social turmoil (see Cady 1958; Smith 1965). Marriages between Buddhist women and Indian men, and economic exploitation were identified as important causes to the riots (Riot Inquiry Committee 1939a, 11–14, 28–33, 1939b). The riots were preceded by anti-Muslim articles appearing in the Burmese press due to a pamphlet written by a Muslim that allegedly insulted Buddhism.³ One monk said that Muslims have "taken possession of the wealth of the Burmese people and also their daughters and sisters" (Riot Inquiry Committee 1939b, 8). At a meeting at Shwedagon Pagoda attended by more than 10,000 people, including 1,500 monks, speeches were delivered constituting "a bitter attack on Muslims." Monks resolved that "steps would be taken to treat Muslims as enemy No. 1" and to "bring about the extermination of the Muslims and the extinction of their religion" if the British failed to meet their demands, including the enacting of a marriage law for Buddhist women (Riot Inquiry Committee 1939b, 12–13, Appendix II). This riot seems to have set a precedent for later ones, with interreligious marriages, business competition, and insults to Buddhism as causing tensions in unstable socioeconomic conditions, as well as involving anti-Muslim monastic mobilization (see Foxeus 2022).

Anti-Muslim conspiracy theories: fearing a Muslim takeover

The "colonial threat narrative" of elimination of Burmese race (*amyou*) and the Buddha's dispensation that created a sense of collective victimhood and bitter *ressentiment* shaped narratives and discourses in the post-independence period too (see Foxeus 2022). In the 1950s, there was a widespread anti-foreigner climate and there was a recurrent discourse in the vernacular press of blaming women for being unpatriotic and for destroying Burmese race and religion by marrying foreigners and exhorting them to marry people only of the same race and religion (Tharapi Than 2014, chap. 6). Buddhist nationalist publications appeared that were more sinister than those preserved from the colonial period.⁴ An anti-Muslim conspiracy theory about a Muslim takeover of Burma and the entire world during the twenty-first century through business and interreligious marriages appeared. It was similar to the anti-Semitic conspiracy theory called the "Protocols of the Learned Elders of Sion" that was fabricated in 1903 and that was appropriated by the Nazis (see Bronner 2000). The Burmese conspiracy theory is most well-known through the anonymous and undated pamphlet *Amyou-pyauk-hmā-sou-kyauk-sayā*, "Fearing that the Nation/Race will Disappear," that – according to my sources – was distributed from around the late 1980s.⁵ In that pamphlet, allegedly secret documents intended for circulation among Muslims alone were reproduced stating that Muslims should mark their shops with 786; they should make business only among themselves; and they should marry Buddhist women to expand their group.⁶ According to the documents, their aim is to achieve Islamic supremacy throughout the world, including Burma, during the twenty-first century (7 + 8 + 6 = 21). Moreover, rewards would be given to Muslim men who managed to marry indigenous Buddhist women (*Amyou-pyauk-hmā-sou-kyauk-sayā*, p. 78–82; see also Marshall 2013).⁷ In that pamphlet, it is, furthermore, stated that Muslims wiped out Buddhism from India, Afghanistan, Indonesia, and Malaysia. That historical narrative was frequently elaborated in sermons delivered in 2012–2015 to provide evidence of the evil intentions of the Muslims. Muslims are claimed to have a plan to "swallow" (*wā-myou*) other nations/races and religions. Pamphlets with similar content have been disseminated in times of social unrest and instability since at least the 1980s (see Fink 2001; Selth 2004; *Human Rights Watch* 2002). In sermons delivered in 2012–2015, nationalist monks reproduced the abovementioned Islamophobic conspiracy theory of secret plan to turn Burma into an Islamic State in the twenty-first century. Likewise, in the early SLORC period, that is, the military dictatorship that seized power in 1988, a series of articles about the disappearance of their race/nation (*amyou-pyauk-hmā sou-kyauk-hla-pa-thi*, "We greatly fear that our race/nation will disappear"), claiming that Buddhism is under threat from Islam and Muslims (especially the Rohingyas), appeared 1989 in the state-controlled newspaper *Working People's Daily* (Nyi Nyi Kyaw 2016, 194). Around this period, according to Renaud Egreteau (2011), the Indophobia of the colonial period largely shifted into Islamophobia.

As in the 1930s, such imaginary revenge on the Indians (here Muslims) through Buddhist nationalist discourse have exerted disastrous social impact, including riots, especially in periods of rapid social and political change, and economic hardship. Conditions worsened for people of Indian descent after General Ne Win's military coup in 1962. Indians and other people of foreign descent were barred from political positions of authority according to the 1974 Constitution. The 1982 Citizenship Law of unequal citizenship turned Indians and other people of foreign descent into second-class citizens (see Taylor 1993). Ne Win's rationale for that law was motivated by distrust (Ne Win 1982). This could be read as a *ressentiment*-tinged revenge for the humiliating situation for Burman Buddhists during the colonial period (see above).

Contemporary Buddhist nationalist movements: the 969 movement and Ma Ba Tha

In the Buddhist nationalist movements that emerged after 2012 in Burma/Myanmar, the key issues were basically the same as during the colonial period: interreligious marriages and business competition. Before the general elections in November 2015, the Buddhist nationalist movements were tacitly supported by the government led by President Thein Sein, and the military-backed party USDP (see Marshall 2013; Klinken and Su Mon Thazin Aung 2017). In the political liberalization, with abolishment of the censorship board, permissions to organize demonstrations, and strikes, a telecommunication revolution, with access to mobile phones and social media to anyone, a social and political space was opened up that enabled the Buddhist nationalist movements to gain unprecedented influence and popularity in Burma's history (see Foxeus 2022; Egreteau 2016; Lall 2016). A globalized Islamophobia linked to extremist, violent forms of Islam like Islamic State (IS) was an additional factor that shaped the contemporary Buddhist nationalist discourses. Muslim businesses were frequently rumored to receive financial support from abroad, especially Saudi Arabia (see Foxeus 2022).

In response to the 2012 riots in Rakhine State, many Buddhist nationalist movements, networks, and organizations were formed. The 969 movement was a monastic network established in late October 2012 in Lower Burma. It was especially known for its buy Buddhist campaign, boycott of Muslim-owned businesses, and its marry Buddhist campaign (see Nyi Nyi Kyaw 2016; Walton and Hayward 2014; Marshall 2013). On June 27, 2013, this movement largely morphed into a larger and better structured organization, *Amyou-bhāthā-thāthanā-saung-shauk-yay-ahpwe*, the "Organization for Protecting Nation (Race), Religion, and the Buddha's Dispensation" (Ma Ba Tha). While incorporating the agenda of the 969 movement, Ma Ba Tha came to focus on its four family laws protecting nation and religion (*amyou-saung-upaday*) that would, for instance, make it more difficult for Muslim men to marry Buddhist women. In contrast to the 969 movement,

Ma Ba Tha was led by senior, well-respected, and venerated monks, which increased the impact and broadened the support of the nationalist movement (see Foxeus 2022). As a lobby group, Ma Ba Tha persuaded the government under President Thein Sein to enact the four nationalist family laws in the parliament in 2015, including an intermarriage law for Buddhist women. These laws were similar to the 1939 Buddhist Women Marriage and Inheritance Act that was re-enacted and amended in 1954 (see Phyo Win Latt 2020; Ikeya 2011; Mazumder 2014). The aim of the contemporary Buddhist nationalist movements was to protect the Buddhist nation and the sovereignty of the state of Myanmar against the perceived threat of a Muslim expansion.

When Ma Ba Tha was founded, the words in its name (*amyou-bhāthā-thāthanā*) struck a chord among Buddhists and that contributed to the organization's initial popularity throughout the country and support by monks, "nuns," and laypeople, as these signifiers resonated with their sense of concern for Buddhism and their national heritage. The monks exerted considerable influence over the laypeople due to the authority attributed to monks in Burmese Buddhist culture (see Walton and Jerryson 2016; Nyi Nyi Kyaw 2016; Foxeus 2022).

The numbers 969 represent Buddha, Dhamma, and Sangha, the Three Gems. The movement urged Buddhists to mark their shops with stickers with that symbol to identify their shops and restaurants as Buddhist. It was used as a retaliation against the practice among Muslims to mark their businesses and restaurants with 786, which mainly aim to signal that they serve *halal* food.[8] However, Buddhist nationalists interpreted 786 in accordance with the conspiracy theory mentioned above claiming that these numbers, when tallied up, amount to 21 and that number referred to their alleged plan to take over Burma and turn it into an Islamic country during the twenty-first century (see Foxeus 2022). In 2012–2013, this Buddhist nationalist campaign led to a widespread boycott of Muslim-owned businesses.

The 969 movement was frequently accused by the media of having incited riots with their anti-Muslim sermons, although the monks have consistently denied any responsibility (see Walton and Hayward 2014; see also Marshall 2013). Although the sermons did not justify violent action and did not exhort or encourage Buddhist laypeople to attack Muslims, the recurrent themes of the sermons (see below) were strongly inflammatory and likely to exacerbate existing tensions and intensify hatred toward Muslims. For that reason, their sermons did, in all likelihood, contribute to incite riots in 2013–2014 (see Foxeus 2022). The nationalist monk U Wirathu, who was not the leader of the 969 movement but rather its most well-known public face, delivered many 969 sermons of that kind in 2013 (later, he became a leading monk within Ma Ba Tha). On July 1, 2013, U Wirathu appeared on the cover of *Time* under the headline of "The Face of Buddhist Terror." The article was banned in Burma/Myanmar due to the injured feelings among the Burmese Buddhist public and the authorities (see Schearf 2013; Vrieze and Htet Naing Zaw 2013). As noted above, an integral feature of Buddhist national identity is that Buddhists are perceived to be essentially non-violent, peaceful, friendly, and filled with loving-kindness. The title was therefore an anomaly, an oxymoron, for most Burmese Buddhists. For Buddhist nationalists (and others), the real terrorists (*akyan-hpek-thamā*) were the Muslims, which they made clear in sermons, nationalist journals, books, pamphlets, and on social media.[9] In a 969 pamphlet issued in the fall of 2013, U Wirathu, in response to the accusations of having incited violence, claims that the 969 movement is not about terror/violence, oppression, being blood-thirsty, instigating riots due to race/nation, religion, and politics, and is not about discriminating against other religious and ethnic/racial groups, but is rather about living peacefully together, protecting the rights of women, and loving-kindness and compassion, and so forth (Wirathu 2013d).[10]

Buddhist nationalist sermons

The examples from sermons in 2013–2015 below are from 969 and Ma Ba Tha sermons. The main difference between them is that the former dwelled more on the alleged economic dominance of the Muslims and the related buy-Buddhist campaign. Both focused on the perceived Muslim incursion into the Buddhist community through the Buddhist women. The difference is slight, as the money from success in business was suspected to be used to persuade Buddhist women to marry Muslims.

In their sermons, many nationalist monks retold a kind of horror stories about women who got married to Muslims that serve to demonize Muslims and to create an anti-Muslim moral panic (see Foxeus 2022). These stories about domestic violence constitute accusations claiming that Muslims force Buddhist women to convert to Islam and to step on Buddha images; that they beat, mistreat, and torture or even kill them, and that they rape Buddhist women, especially underaged girls and even children. In accordance with the conspiracy theory, it is typically claimed that Muslims pretend to be in love with Buddhist women but are merely strategically using them as an instrument for breeding and implementing their plan to expand their group to take over the country (see Foxeus 2022).

In a 969 sermon, Ashin Pyinnyā Wara (2013) replicated the conspiracy theory mentioned above saying that the Muslims have a plan to take over Burma in the twenty-first century symbolized by the number 786. Wrongly claiming that the Muslim population was 22% in 2012, he predicted that the Muslim population will use strategic marriages and business to decrease the Buddhist population, and, finally, wage violent Jihad war through which Buddhism and all Buddhists in Burma will be wiped out before the end of the twenty-first century. In a Ma Ba Tha sermon, Ashin Thawpaka (2015) explained that a "different religion" (Islam) uses various methods to "swallow" other religions. First, they "swallow people by people" by high rates of reproduction and by marriages with Buddhist women. Second, they use persuasion, for instance, when Muslims become strong in business, they manipulate and swallow those who are poor and ignorant. Third, they use terrorism as method like the IS to swallow other nations and religions. Fourth, Muslims seek to seize the power of the state. Thereby, Myanmar will lose its sovereignty, and their country, nation, religion, and the Buddha's dispensation will disappear.

In a 969 sermon delivered on May 18, 2013, in the city of Muse, Shan State, U Wirathu (2013c) brought up the alleged dangers of buying from shops owned by Muslims. Having told the audience to mark their shops with the symbol 969, he provided the rationale for that practice:

> If the Buddhists help themselves in that manner, would their money fall into the hands of the enemy? Would the money fall into the hands of a different religion [Islam]? If that would happen, could they [Muslims] draw up plans to swallow our race/nation (*lū-myou*) by using that money? Could they implement their plan? Having spent this money on young (Buddhist) Myanmar girls, can't they be persuaded? Could they [Muslims] force them to convert into their religion in an unlawful manner? Could they take over Buddhist fields, houses, and land with that money? If that is the case, will Buddhists exist as long as the world exists? Will Myanmar race/nation be without dangers? Will Buddhists be without dangers? Will the country Myanmar be without dangers? […] If people buy at any shop, don't they put their profit into their hand? Wouldn't [their profit] fall into the hands of strangers [Muslims]? If the business of strangers would flourish, […] couldn't they use that money to swallow our race/nation? Couldn't they destroy our religion? Couldn't they destroy the Buddha's dispensation? Couldn't they

invade (*kyū-kyaw*) our country? Therefore, don't every Buddhist need to protect our race/nation, religion, and the Buddha's dispensation (*amyou-bhāthā-thāthanā*)? Don't they need to be loyal to them?

In another 969 sermon, delivered on January 30, 2013, in the city Paleik near Mandalay, U Wirathu (2013b) claimed that:

> If their population grow [the Muslims], won't they attack and be violent against us with their hordes as in the Rakhine State? Won't they become a great danger? Should you put your profit into the hands of people who are a great danger to our country, race/nation, religion, and the Buddha's dispensation, that is, into the hands of people who will become our enemies? [...] If you buy the things that you want at any shop [a Muslim shop], wouldn't that amount to buying a knife to cut your own throat? Aren't there reasons to be scared?

A recurrent theme in Buddhist nationalist sermons (for instance, Wirathu 2013a; Pyinnyā Wara 2013), publications, and in my interviews, is that Muslims do not pose a danger as long as they are weak and poor, but that they will seek to achieve dominance and take over the country if they become stronger. That was one explicit reason why Buddhists should discriminate against Muslim-owned businesses. Thereby, they would remain weak, poor, and powerless and cannot implement their alleged plan. The best way to protect Buddhism was therefore to ensure that Muslims remain poor and weak. This could be read as a faint echo of the colonial period, at which time Burmese Buddhists felt that Indians were taking over, as they were the majority in the cities and dominated most positions of authority and economic influence. Boycott by Buddhists of Indian-owned businesses began already during the colonial period.[11] It was an extension of the Gandhi-inspired boycott of British products carried out by GCBA under the influence of the nationalist monk U Ottama, and other nationalist organizations in the 1920s onward (see Smith 1965; Maung Maung 1980; Chakravarty 1971).

The 969 campaign was strongly discriminatory against Muslims. Buddhists should cut all social relationships with Muslims and should only have social and business dealings among themselves (see also Walton and Hayward 2014; Nyi Nyi Kyaw 2016). In 2013, U Wirathu urged Buddhists to adopt a nationalist view (*amyou-thā-yay-amyin-ne*) in whatever they did, including buying and selling a house, education, looking for a job, employing staff, political activities, marriage, and the like (Wirathu 2013a). This is also a *ressentiment*-tinged revenge against the Muslims. That idea of adopting a nationalist view in all everyday activities – a kind of everyday discriminatory nationalism – was a recurrent theme in Ma Ba Tha's Buddhist nationalist publications too.

The contemporary Islamophobic Buddhist nationalist discourses still articulate distrust toward Indians/Muslims and a concomitant fear of economic domination, as well as elimination of Burmese Buddhist race/nation and the Buddha's dispensation through the women, as in the colonial threat narrative or the myth of deracination (Foxeus 2022; Nyi Nyi Kyaw 2020), which are based on a sense of collective victimhood and *ressentiment* toward Muslims. Although the contexts of the colonial period and contemporary Burma/Myanmar are very different, the discourses are surprisingly similar.

Locally, Muslims dominate some smaller and medium-sized businesses. As many Muslims are businessmen, shop keepers, owners of hotels, bus companies, construction companies, and the like, it may give the impression that they dominate the economy, and they have often been targeted in periods of economic hardship (see Selth 2004; Egreteau 2011; Fink

2001, 218–219, 225–226; *Human Rights Watch* 2002; Marshall 2013). However, at a macro level, the economy is dominated by the military and its business corporations, and military-allied capitalist cronies (the majority of whom are Buddhists), but also by the Chinese (see Jones 2014; Marshall 2013). In contemporary Burma/Myanmar, the Muslims consist of various minorities, between some of which there are tensions (especially between "Indian" Muslims in Yangon and indigenous Burman Muslims in Upper Burma), and they do not constitute a homogenous community (Yegar 1972; Selth 2004; interviews, Mandalay, 2016, 2017). As for the statistics, it is, in fact, the Christian community that has increased the most since 1973 (Table 29.1):

The number of Muslims was 4.3% in 2014, which is a minor increase of that population since 1973. The highest increase between 1973 and 2014 of a particular religion was thus Christianity, not Islam. Some nationalists claimed that there were 22% Muslims in 2013. At that time, it was generally believed that their numbers were higher than they turned out to be.[12] There was thus no reason for alarm. Although the number of Christians had increased the most between 1973 and 2014 (1.6%), they were not targeted in Buddhist nationalist sermons delivered between 2013 and 2015. Although there are tensions between different religious communities in Burma/Myanmar, including Christians and Buddhists, the main fault line in Burmese society is that between Buddhists and Muslims (see Ware and Laoutides 2018, 61–63), which is reflected in the 969 movement, Ma Ba Tha, and in my interviews with nationalist monks and laypeople. Many Buddhist nationalists even sense a kind of affinity between Buddhism and Christianity, but Islam remains a dangerous outsider. It is the Other.

The contemporary discrimination and demonization of Muslims should rather be understood as scapegoating that has been a recurrent theme in Burma's history (see also McArthy and Menager 2017; Fink 2001): whenever Burma/Myanmar has undergone rapid structural change (political, economic, and social), that is, periods characterized by uncertainty and fear, the Muslims have frequently been attacked. They have served as a more concrete, manageable, personalized target representing more complex, vague challenges and problems the country has faced in different periods: the 1938 riots, which occurred in a kind of "transition period" of social distress and economic hardship, after Burma was separated from British India in 1937; in the early post-independence period; during the uprising 1988 against the socialist dictatorship; in other periods of social distress and economic hardship; and in the so-called transition period after 2011. In such periods, Muslims have been blamed for felt grievances whereby collective victimhood has served as a cognitive frame to interpret events. In that way, *ressentiment* and collective victimhood tend to intensify in periods of social distress and uncertainty. Many Burmese Buddhists (and others) have a propensity to develop anti-Muslim sentiments that otherwise mostly recede into the background, but that can turn into an active mode during periods of social distress, especially in connections to rumors of a rape of a Buddhist woman by Muslims, which have frequently served as a catalyst for riots (see Fink 2001; McArthy and Menager 2017; Foxeus 2022).

Table 29.1 Changes of Christian, Buddhist, and Islam communities between 1973 and 2014

National Census	Buddhism (%)	Christianity (%)	Islam (%)
1973 census	88.8	4.6	3.9
1983 census	89.4	4.9	3.9
2014 census	87.9	6.2	4.3

Source: Ministry of Labour, Immigration and Population (2016, 5).

Conclusion

Since the colonial period, Buddhist nationalism has mainly been concerned with protecting and defending *amyou-bhāthā-thāthanā*, "Burmese race/nation, religion, and the Buddha's dispensation." From the colonial period until the second parliamentarian period (2011–2021), Buddhist nationalist discourse has been preoccupied with two perceived threats to the referents of these three signifiers, namely interreligious and interracial marriages between Burmese Buddhist women and Indian men (later, Muslims), and business competition by Indian immigrants with Burmese Buddhists, As we have seen, these two "threats" were interrelated, as the profit would – according to the accusations by the Buddhist nationalists – be used to lure Burmese Buddhist women into marriages with Muslim men, whereby they would be forced or persuaded to convert to Islam. This discourse is the essence of Burmese Buddhist nationalism since the colonial period. It originated in colonial Burma as a response characterized by a sense of *ressentiment* and collective victimhood. This phenomenon can also be described as a majority with a minority complex because Burmese Buddhist nationalists still tend to behave as if they are an endangered minority.

During the colonial period, Burmese Buddhists were dominated not merely by the British colonizers but also by the Indian immigrants – at least by the elite among them – and were marginalized in urban areas. This domination within the colonial order created the structural, social, and psychological conditions for the development of *ressentiment*, that is, a deep bitterness, frustration, and humiliation, as well as envy, vengefulness, and hatred toward the Indian immigrants. Mainly the Indian immigrants were blamed on moral grounds for this situation, and a fertile soil for taking imaginary revenge in a compensatory manner in nationalist discourse, in the form of stereotyping the Indian out-group as an evil, immoral Other and the Buddhists, the in-group, as the virtuous ones. At that time, it was mainly articulated in the popular press, nationalist publications, and the proposed marriage law. These portrayals were strongly shaped by Orientalist and colonial stereotypes of Buddhists, Muslims, and Hindus, depicting the Buddhists as tolerant – an inherent weakness but also a moral virtue – and the other two groups as intolerant (and therefore immoral). Although Burmese Buddhists have assumed a dominant position toward the Indians since the post-independence period, the *ressentiment* toward the Indians have been perpetuated by social memory, anti-Muslim conspiracy theories, books, education, and the like. It has also been maintained by the fact that Indians (Muslims) tend to dominate smaller and medium-sized businesses on the local level and have been targeted in times of economic hardship. This perceived domination and threat was further intensified during the second parliamentarian period (2011–2021), with globalization and rumors that local Muslim businesses received financial support from Muslim countries abroad. The sense of collective victimhood shaped by *ressentiment* has served as a cognitive frame to interpret events and have, during periods of rapid change and uncertainty, contributed to incite riots since the colonial period until today. It has also shaped the 1982 Citizenship Law, the discriminatory procedures regarding ID cards at immigration offices, and the like.

This Buddhist nationalist discourse has been preoccupied by the threats to Buddhism rather than cultivating a Buddhist national identity. The nature of the latter is mostly taken for granted, and that is assumed to be acquired through the socialization process. This naturalized identity may not be subject to conscious reflection and goes at least back to YMBA, meaning that to be a Burmese is to be a Buddhist. In Buddhist nationalist discourse, this Buddhist identity is mostly understood by negation. The nature of Buddhists tends to be the opposite of the Muslims, the Other, and tends to be interpreted in normative, positive stereotypical terms: Buddhists are friendly, tolerant, hospitable, filled by loving-kindness, peaceful, engage in meditation, and charity work, whereas Muslims are mostly stereotyped in negative terms as their very opposite: violent, aggressive, intolerant, egoistic, and libidinous. Similarly, the conspiracy theories reveal that Indians/Muslims were and are perceived as being greedy, cunning, plotting to displace Burmese Buddhists, unpatriotic, and loyal merely to their own group. That has been a recurrent discourse about the Indians from the colonial period, via Ne Win's 1982 Citizenship Law and his rationale for it, until today, especially within the 969 movement and Ma Ba Tha.

Acknowledgment

The research for this chapter was supported by the Swedish Research Council (Vetenskapsrådet) under Grant number 2019–02601. Part of the empirical research for this chapter was conducted when the author was a Royal Swedish Academy of Letters, History and Antiquities Research Fellow. The fieldwork was funded by travel grants from the Royal Swedish Academy of Letters, History and Antiquities; Margot and Rune Johansson's Foundation; and Helge Ax:son Johnson's Foundation.

Notes

1 Ethnic nationalism is understood as a nation based on a sense of community which focuses on birth, myths of common decent that are perceived to be confirmed by contemporary similarities of physiognomy, language, or religion. This identity is ascriptive, exclusive, and collectivist (Brown 2000, 49–50; Greenfeld 1992, 12–13; Greenfeld and Chirot 1994, 82–83).
2 For a comprehensive examination of the various meanings of that concept, see Phyo Win Latt (2020, 57–71).
3 For more on this pamphlet, see Phyo Win Latt (2020, chap. 4).
4 Some publications were banned due to their inflammatory content and are not available any longer (see Phyo Win Latt 2020).
5 It was illegal during the SLORC-SPDC period (1988–2011) but it seems to have been widespread at the time, and it was disseminated from hand to hand. It was in circulation also in the anti-Muslim riots in 2001 (see *Human Rights Watch* 2002). Many, if not most, Burmese Buddhists are familiar with that pamphlet.
6 For the meaning of 786 for Muslims, see Nyi Nyi Kyaw (2016).
7 That Burmese, anti-Muslim conspiracy theory also appeared, verbatim, in an undated pamphlet entitled *Koudaw-karuṇa*, the "Compassion of the Monk" (n.d.: 37–38), which was claimed to be a reproduction of three articles by the movie director Shwe Done Bi Aung published in 1953 in a journal. I have different copies of the undated pamphlet. There were colonial precursors to this conspiracy theory. In 1938, the newspaper the *Sun* claimed to summarize a book from Delhi saying that Islam should be propagated in Burma by means of marriages by Muslims with Burmese women (Riot Inquiry Committee 1939b, 8). Cartoons from the colonial period were also comparable to the conspiracy theory, albeit made in a joking mode but nevertheless shaped by *ressentiment*. Such cartoons could depict Indians as scheming to displace Burmese in business and take away their women (see Phyo Win Latt 2020, 150–151). In some short stories from 1920s–1930s, Indians were "portrayed as scheming, manipulative, monopolistic, and always planning to seduce young Burmese women" (Phyo Win Latt 2020, 138).
8 For more on the meaning of the symbols 969 and 786, see Nyi Nyi Kyaw (2016).
9 For instance, in a 2014 nationalist pamphlet called "The Origin of Terror" (Naung Daw Lay 2014), there are vivid and gruesome illustrations of the atrocities of Muslim extremist organizations (especially al-Qaeda and the Islamic State), with terrorist acts against civilians (such as the 9/11), violent treatment of women, opposition to democracy, the 2001 destruction of the Bamiyan Buddha statues in Afghanistan, opposition to human rights, and so forth. It also includes numerous extracts from the *Quran*. I received this pamphlet from a Ma Ba Tha monk in 2016, as providing part of the reasons to why he joined Ma Ba Tha.

10 I obtained a copy of this pamphlet from U Wirathu in September 2013.
11 Boycotting Indian-owned businesses was described in a novel from the late 1910s (Phyo Win Latt 2020); in the Dobama Asiayoun's, "We Burman's Association's," first manifesto from 1930 (see Khin Yi 1988, 2–3; see also Nyi Nyi Kyaw 2016); and in connection with the 1938 Indo-Burmese riots (see Riot Inquiry Committee 1939b, 9, 13).
12 The results of the 2014 census regarding the numbers of religions were not publicized until 2016 after the 2015 general elections. If the results had been made official earlier, it had probably eased the tensions. The Thein Sein government under USDP probably had political reasons for delaying the official announcement of the results.

References

Bar-Tal, D., L. Chernyak-Hai, N. Schori, and A. Gundar. 2009. "A Sense of Self-Perceived Collective Victimhood in Intractable Conflicts." *International Review of the Red Cross* 91 (874): 229–258.
Bronner, S. E. 2000. *A Rumor about the Jews: Reflections on Antisemitism and the Protocols of the Learned Elders of Zion*. New York: St. Martin's Press.
Brown, David. 2000. *Contemporary Nationalism: Civic, Ethnocultural and Multicultural Politics*. Abingdon: Routledge.
———. 2008. "The Ethnic Majority: Benign or Malign?" *Nations and Nationalisms* 14 (4): 768–788.
Cady, J. F. 1958. *A History of Modern Burma*. Ithaca, NY: Cornell University Press.
Chakravarti, N. R. 1971. *The Indian Minority in Burma: The Rise and Decline of an Immigrant Community*. London: Oxford University Press.
Charney, M. 2009. *A History of Modern Burma*. Cambridge: Cambridge University Press.
Egretau, Renaud. 2011. "Burmese Indians in Contemporary Burma: Heritage, Influence, and Perceptions since 1988." *Asian Ethnicity* 12 (1): 33–54.
———. 2016. *Caretaking Democratization: The Military and Political Change in Myanmar*. Oxford: Oxford University Press.
Fink, C. 2001. *Living Silence: Burma under Military Rule*. Bangkok: White Lotus.
Foxeus, N. 2019. "The Buddha was a Devoted Nationalist: Buddhist Nationalism, *Ressentiment*, and Defending Buddhism in Myanmar." *Religion* 49 (4): 661–690.
———. 2022. "Buddhist Nationalist Sermons in Myanmar: Anti-Muslim Moral Panic, Conspiracy Theories, and Sociocultural Legacies." *Journal of Contemporary Asia*: 1–27. https://doi.org/10.1080/00472336.2022.2032801.
Frings, Manfred S. 1998. "Introduction." In *Ressentiment*. Transl. Lewis B Coser and William W. Holdheim, 1–21. Milwaukee, WI: Marquette University Press.
Green, Penny, Thomas McManus, and Alicia de la Cour Venning. 2015. *Countdown to Annihilation: Genocide in Myanmar*. London: International State Crime Initiative.
Greenfeld, Liah. 1992. *Nationalism: Five Roads to Modernity*. Cambridge: Harvard University Press.
Greenfeld, Liah, and Daniel Chirot. 1994. "Nationalism and Aggression." *Theory and Society* 23 (1): 79–130.
Human Rights Watch. 2002. "Crackdown on Burmese Muslims: July 2002." https://www.hrw.org/legacy/backgrounder/asia/burmese_muslims.pdf.
ICG (International Crisis Group). 2013. "The Dark Side of Transition: Violence against Muslims in Myanmar." *Asia Report No. 251*. Brussels: Belgium.
Ikeya, C. 2011. *Refiguring Women, Colonialism, & Modernity in Burma*. Honolulu: University of Hawai'i Press.
Jaffrelot, Christophe. 2005. "For a Theory of Nationalism." In *Revisiting Nationalism: Theories and Processes*, edited by Alain Dieckhoff and Christophe Jaffrelot, 10–61 New York: Palgrave Macmillan.
Jones, Lee. 2014. "The Political Economy of Myanmar's Transition." *Journal of Contemporary Asia* 44 (1): 144–170.
Khin Maung Kyi. 1993. "Indians in Burma: Problems of an Alien Subculture in a Highly Integrated Society." In *Indian Communities in Southeast Asia*, edited by K. S. Sandhu and A. Mani, 624–665. Singapore: ISEAS.
Khin Yi. 1988. *The Dobama Movement in Burma: Appendix*. Ithaca, NY: SEAP.
Klinken, G. van, and Su Mon Thazin Aung. 2017. "The Contentious Politics of Anti-Muslim Scapegoating in Myanmar." *Journal of Contemporary Asia* 47 (3): 353–375.
Lall, M. 2016. *Understanding Reform in Myanmar: People and Society in the Wake of Military Rule*. London: Hurst and Company.

Maung Maung. 1980. *From Sangha to Laity: Nationalist Movements of Burma 1920–1940*. Delhi: Manohar.
Mazumder, Rajashree. 2014. "'I Do Not Envy You': Mixed Marriages and Immigration Debates in the 1920s and 1930s Rangoon, Burma." *The Indian Economic and Social History Review* 51 (4): 497–527.
McCarthy, G., and J. Menager. 2017. "Gendered Rumours and the Muslim Scapegoat in Myanmar's Transition." *Journal of Contemporary Asia* 47 (3): 396–412.
Mendelson, E. Michael. 1975. *Sangha and State in Burma: A Study of Monastic Sectarianism and Leadership*. Ithaca, NY: Cornell University Press.
Ministry of Labour, Immigration and Population. 2016. *The 2014 Myanmar Population and Housing Census. The Union Report: Religion*. Naypyidaw: Department of Population.
Naung Daw Lay. 2014. *akyan-phek-hmu-tou-myic-phyā-khan-yā* ["The Origin of Terror"]. Yangon: Amyou-thā-yay-athan Sā-pay.
Ne Win. 1982. "Translation of the Speech by General Ne Win." *The Working People's Daily*, 9 October. Accessed August 7, 2021. http://www.burmalibrary.org/docs6/Ne_Win%27s_speech_Oct-1982-Citizenship_Law.pdf.
Nietzsche, Friedrich. 1996 [1887]. *On the Genealogy of Morals*. Transl. Douglas Smith. Oxford: Oxford University Press.
Nyi Nyi Kyaw. 2015. "Alienation, Discrimination, and Securitization: Legal Personhood and Cultural Personhood of Muslims in Myanmar." *The Review of Faith & International Affairs* 13 (4): 50–59.
———. 2016. "Islamophobia in Buddhist Myanmar: The 969 Movement and Anti-Muslim Violence." In *Islam and the State in Myanmar: Muslim-Buddhist Relations and the Politics of Belonging*, edited by Melissa Crouch, 183–210. New Delhi: Oxford University Press.
———. 2020. "The Role of Myth in Anti-Muslim Buddhist Nationalism in Myanmar." In *Buddhist-Muslim Relations in a Theravada World*, edited by Iselin Frydenlund and Michael Jerryson, 197–226. Singapore: Palgrave Macmillan.
Phyo Win Latt. 2020. "Protecting Amyo: The Rise of Xenophobic Nationalism in Colonial Burma, 1906–1941." PhD Dissertation. Singapore: National University of Singapore.
Riot Inquiry Committee. 1939a. *Interim Report of the Riot Inquiry Committee*. Rangoon: Supdt., Govt. Printing and Stationery, Burma.
Riot Inquiry Committee. 1939b. *Final Report of the Riot Inquiry Committee*. Rangoon: Supdt., Govt Printing and Stationery, Burma.
Schearf, Daniel. 2013. "Burma Objects to Time Magazine Criticism." *VOA*, June 24.
Scheler, Max. 1998 [1915]. *Ressentiment*. Transl. Lewis B. Coser and William W. Holdheim. Milwaukee, Wis: Marquette University Press.
Selth, A. 2004. "Burma's Muslims and the War on Terror." *Studies in Conflict and Terrorism* 27: 107–126.
Shwe Done Bi Aung. n.d. *Koudaw-karuṇā* [The Compassion of the Monk].
Smith, Donald Eugene. 1965. *Religion and Politics in Burma*. Princeton: Princeton University Press.
Stewart, J. A. and C. W. Dunn. 1969. *Burmese-English Dictionary*, Part V, revised and edited by Hla Pe, A. J. Allott and J. W. A. Okell. London: School of Oriental and African Studies.
Taylor, Robert H. 1993. "The Legal Status of Indians in Contemporary Burma." In *Indian Communities in Southeast Asia*, edited by K. S. Sandhu and A. Mani, 666–682. Singapore: ISEAS.
———. 2015. "Refighting Old Battles, Compounding Misconceptions: The Politics of Ethnicity in Myanmar Today." *ISEAS Perspective* 12: 1–16.
Tharapi Than. 2014. *Women in Modern Burma*. Abingdon: Routledge.
Turner, Alicia. 2014. *Saving Buddhism: Moral Community and the Impermanence of Colonial Religion*. Honolulu: Hawai'i University Press.
———. 2019. "The Violence of Buddhist Tolerance: Genealogies of Religious Difference in Colonial Burma." Paper presented at the workshop, *Land, Law, and Nationalism in Myanmar*, Royal Swedish Academy of Letters, History and Antiquities, Stockholm, April 24–26.
Vrieze, Paul, and Htet Naing Zaw. 2013. Govt, Local Media Condemn Time Magazine's Cover of U Wirathu." *Irrawaddy*, June 24.
Walton, M. J., and S. Hayward. 2014. *Contesting Buddhist Narratives: Democratization, Nationalism, and Communal Violence in Myanmar*. Policy Studies No. 71. Honolulu: East-West Center.
Walton, M. J., and Michael Jerryson. 2016. "The Authorization of Religio-Political Discourse: Monks and Buddhist Activism in Contemporary Myanmar and Beyond. *Politics and Religion* 9: 794–814.
Ware, A., and C. Laoutides. 2018. *Myanmar's "Rohingya" Conflict*. London: Hurst and Company.
Wirathu, U. 2013d. *969-mū-wāda* ("969 Policy").
Yegar, Moshe. 1972. *The Muslims of Burma: A Study of a Minority Group*. Wiesbaden: Harrasowitz.

Sermons

Pyinnyā Wara, Ashin. 2013. *Bhawa-lan-khwe-tayā-daw* [*A Sermon about Different Paths of Life*]. In the city Bhīlin, Mon State, January 14.
Thawpaka, Ashin. 2015. *Amyou-bhāthā-thāthanā-ne-amyou-saung-upaday* [*Nation, Religion and Sāsana, and the Law Protecting the Nation*]. September 12, Mawlamyine.
Wirathu, U. 2013a. *Amyou-thā-yay paw-paw-ma-tway-ne-tayā-daw* [*Don't Think Lightly about Nationalism!*]. Yangon, January 15, 2013.
———. 2013b. *Nyī-nyut-hma ngyein-khyan-myi* [*Only If There Is Unity, Will There Be Peace*], Paleik, Mandalay region, January 30.
———. 2013c. *Hpyū-sin-myat-nou-969-tayā-daw* [*A Pure and Cherished 969 Sermon*], May 18, Muse.

30
NATIONALISM IN COLONIAL AND POSTCOLONIAL MYANMAR

Solidarities, discordance, and the crisis of community

Maitrii Aung-Thwin

Introduction

At its core, nationalism in Myanmar, like in other settings across Southeast Asia, is an expression of belonging, self-referencing, and affiliation (Cooper 2005). Brought about by "homogeneities of readership, education, language, work-place and eventually imagination", nationalism might be regarded as a form of communicating notions of solidarity, unity, or coherence (Reid, 2009). Viewed over the span of the twentieth and twenty-first centuries, nationalism has meant different things to different communities living within and traversing across the territorial boundaries of what today is referred to as Myanmar.

Nationalism in Myanmar has come to refer to a variety of forms: a collection of discourses, images, experiences, processes, and actions that represent a vision for collective action, a common affiliation, a shared space, or aspirations. Articulated through a variety of media, performances, or activities, nationalism can be understood as the stories, discourses, or narratives that people create and refer to express or assert affiliation to a particular place, people, culture, history, experience, language, doctrine, or future. Conventionally connected to the bounded space of the nation-state, nationalism can also be understood as the ways particular members of society comprehend, construct, or give meaning to a particular place. From this perspective, nationalism can be considered as a rationale behind territorialization or the manner in which a particular space is delineated, defined, and demarcated. As such, it is possible to consider nationalism as one genre of place-making and community formation that has emerged in Southeast Asia (and elsewhere) over its long history.

Locating Myanmar nationalism

The ways Myanmar has been defined as a form of community have varied, influenced by local dynamics and external influences, institutions, and individuals, and certainly by the contingencies and contexts of history. The history of Myanmar reveals that nationalism was regarded as a kind of self-referencing by people professing to represent those ideas associated with a collective identity and territory. As part of this process, elites borrowed from different models of developing and governing societies that were circulating in the colonial and postcolonial world, attempting to fit them into how they saw the needs, shortcomings, and potential of the country. In many cases, how different groups interpreted, modified, and applied these social models differed and often clashed, creating different political positions under the same ideological banner. This discussion suggests that deep differences over what "anti-colonialism", "independence", "socialism", or "democracy" meant to "nationalists" over the course of the twentieth and twenty-first centuries hindered a more shared sense of community from developing.

Nationalism in the era of imperialism (1885–1942)

The origins of nationalist sentiment, ideas, and activities can be regarded as an outgrowth of the British annexation of the country that began in 1824 and ended in 1885 with the capture of King Thebaw and the royal court in Mandalay. The legacies of the wars, the dismantling of the monarchy, and the establishment of the Province of Burma under British Indian authority created a crisis for many elites and their followers whose welfare was tied to the Burmese throne.

Some elites, mainly princes and other claimants related to the king, sought to restore the old regime, and attempted to rally followers around the colors of the former Konbaung court against the British. Protracted rebellions seeking to resurrect the monarchy relied on personal networks that were limited in scope and scale, often based at traditional centers of power and authority in Upper Burma. While these attempts were eventually overcome by the colonial army, they represent a vision of the country that was associated with the old order, a system based on Brahmanic-Buddhist notions of kingship, power, and authority. Attempts at restoring the monarchy was an early response to colonial rule that sought in vain to rally followers based on the possibility of a returning king. While certainly not the sole basis for later nationalism, the destruction of the crown in Mandalay—with its association as a protector of religious institutions and society's secular well-being more broadly—would become a rallying cry for social reformers a generation later (Sarkisyanz, 1965).

Community through cultural loss

The dismantling of the monarchy had profound psychological and socio-economic effects, creating noticeable changes to life's rhythms that were associated with both spiritual and everyday aspects of society. These issues of social-welfare that included the decline in the support of Buddhist temples, monasteries, and education resulted in the formation of associations and other organizations to fill in the role normally administered by the monarchy. Led by elites who had access to Western forms of organization and mobilization, these groups organized schools and programs to help educate the public using Christian curricular models. Groups like the Young Men's Buddhist Association and the Burma Research Society engaged in bringing matters of heritage, religion, and culture into the public sphere, though much of its early activities and audiences were limited to the educated elite. The contributions to the study of history, custom, language, and literature of the country led to the eventual connection of the place—Burma/Myanmar—to the civilizational heritage being studied by the Burma Research Society and promoted by the YMBA (Turner, 2014).

Both collectives (and several others like them) contributed to the process of constituting what Burma/Myanmar meant in the wake of new values and symbols being promoted by the colonial authorities. These efforts to create a parallel, if complimentary, understanding about British Burma's heritage provided an expression of solidarity based on a broadly conceived "shared" sense of cultural heritage amongst local communities, one that was developed in reference to the British. Although not yet deeply politicized, the efforts of groups such as the YMBA provided later reformers and activists with the cultural vocabulary to connect political aspirations with discourses of solidarity. Coping with what was perceived as cultural decline in British Burma was an important source of inspiration for the development of heritage discourses that promoted solidarity across community lines, especially as a response to British colonial values, standards, and civilizational discourses that were associated with the British Indian Empire. The monarchy may have been dismantled, but the traditions, responsibilities, and patronage it once oversaw were now being evoked and administered by local elites.

Early nationalist organizations

The growth of solidarity movements across Asia and in British Burma was connected to the growing educational opportunities for colonized subjects. While early Western-educated elites had been reserved at the turn of the century for existing members of Burmese upper classes (who were often represented by ethnic minority groups), by the end of World War I, a younger generation had emerged under colonial education systems. These new groups began to pursue more politically oriented issues. By 1916, the General Council of Buddhist Associations (GCBA) was formed, a combination of several branches of the previous YMBA that had emerged around the country. In the years following the end of World War I, the group began to focus more directly on political issues, highlighted by the "no-footwear" controversy that saw the group pressure the colonial government to ban the wear of shoes by Europeans in Buddhist religious sites. What was important about this campaign was the way in which activists identified a cultural norm (removing one's shoes in religious spaces) and used the issue to forge connections across society in a way that transcended class, linguistic, and geographical divisions. Urban-based nationalist groups would adapt this strategy of looking to perceived shared cultural-historical traditions to create solidarity around symbols and figures that could represent a "culmination of grievances" brought on by the colonial state (Cady, 1958).

The GCBA eventually changed its name to the General Council of Burmese Associations, emphasizing a connection that extended membership beyond religious conceptions of belonging in favor of a vaguely shared notion of Burmese-ness. The GCBA became the most powerful umbrella organization that connected a whole range of members to its ranks. There were groups that continued to see cooperation with the colonial authorities as the way to move reforms forward and there were also younger, more action-oriented members who joined the GCBA in order to promote a more politically focused agenda through more direct means. These groups were often drawn from the student ranks who took part in the 1920 demonstrations over the Education Act that seemed to change the standards for university entry. Exposed to Marxist/Leninist readings and eager to consider the situation in Burma via socialist ideas, this younger generation of political activists considered the possibility of a future of the country without the British. Their objectives, tactics, and operational approaches were much different from the older generation of reformers who still sought to work closely with the colonial authorities (Maung Maung, 1980).

Nationalist solidarities

By the 1920s, different ideas about political mobilization, action, and objectives began to form amongst (for the most part) urban elites into three groups. The first group consisted of older reformists who were embedded within the colonial system and saw working through the system set up by the British as a preferred pathway to their socio-political objectives. For them, the British offered opportunities, security, and expertise that would benefit their communities, many of whom were ethnic and religious minorities. Many of these groups included those who began to articulate their sense of belonging via ethnic distinctions and notions of community that missionaries and colonial personnel used to organize Burmese society. Reworking the colonial system from within, these legislators, lawyers, writers, and business leaders used their international networks, new communication platforms, and access to capital to encourage modest change through available socially allowable channels.

A second generation of students and union leaders used the models of political campaigns in India to issue more substantive reforms, but still within the framework of the law. They formed trade associations, women's associations, and organized debates around issues such as "Separation" from India, a major administrative change that would decouple British India from British Burma. Focusing on colonial policy issues, they sought to promote political reform through the system, joining the Burma Legislative Council, or more indirectly by provoking debate and discussion through print media.

A third group, many of them coming out of the ranks of the GCBA, felt dissatisfied with these two options and saw few options working with the colonial authorities or even with local elites who often remained somewhat aloof from needs of the urban and rural poor. Energized with revolutionary rhetoric circulating across Asia, as well as solidarity movements stressing a common "Asian" experience, these groups began to develop ideological foundations that stressed their differences—cultural, political, and historical—with the West. They also saw the need to mobilize the countryside and began to connect with village leaders to create *wunthanu athin* (patriotic associations), to serve as units of a grass-roots network that could connect rural constituents with urban activists and create an administrative architecture to rival the colonial state's bureaucratic structures. In the Burmese context, it was this third group—considered the most "radical" by colonial authorities—that was quick to spread throughout the countryside, emerging as a valuable asset for urban political organizations. Sharing a sense of solidarity with political monks (discussed below) who sought to mobilize the countryside, this younger generation of political activists would infuse a revolutionary zeal with a more militant rhetoric that set it apart from the English-educated elite a generation earlier.

Religion as nationalism

The rise of urban-based social-welfare groups and political organizations that emerged in response to colonial rule was mirrored by attempts by monks and laypersons attached to or affiliated with Buddhist institutions to promote self-help and self-governance. Monks concluded that Buddhism was under threat if foreign rule continued, amplifying what earlier reformers had hinted about a decade earlier. The General Council of Sangha Sammeggyi (GCSS) was a key umbrella organization that brought together groups of monks across the countryside who were more committed to engaging in public affairs. A key pillar of anti-colonial mobilization, the GCSS had powerful influence, even competing with the GCBA for influence over the countryside, given that its communication strategy was more focused than its secular counterpart. Designated simply as "political" or sometimes as "wondering" monks by the colonial authorities, these monks spoke publicly about reform, social conditions, anti-colonialism, and action using Buddhist idioms, symbols, and teachings to articulate the challenges under colonial rule that were being faced by everyday Buddhists (Maung Maung, 1980).

Touring the countryside, they supported the formation of local Buddhist councils and village protection organizations, while also serving as conduits through which village grievances could be communicated and connected to urban political strategic plans. This access to the countryside and their role in the local education campaigns empowered the GCSS to play a greater role in anti-colonial mobilization, eventually aligning with leading figures in the "secular" General Council of Burmese Associations. Some monks who drew the attention of the colonial authorities because of their growing followers transcended their role within the Buddhist community and became symbols of political mobilization. Monks like U Wisara (1888–1929), who died while in prison, became symbols of resistance to the colonial state for generations to come (Schober, 2011).

Monks also became influential beyond the domestic context and contributed to the linking of Myanmar's anti-colonial campaigns to broader, trans-Asian anti-colonial conversations. U Ottama (1879–1930), who was described as a political agitator in a monk's robe, was noted for aggressively promoting a cultural dimension to the nationalist politics of the day. Educated in Calcutta and politicized in the anti-colonial atmosphere of Bengal, U Ottama represented a more mobile segment of Myanmar's politicized population that circulated in and out of the colony (sometimes undercover) and contributed to its connectedness with other Asian political networks. His travels took him to different urban centers in South and East Asia. Returning to Burma in 1921, he was involved in the organization of strikes, boycotts, and other forms of resistance. At the same time, he was also a part of the more domestic dhammakatikas movement of Buddhist political monks who used their status within Buddhism to reach out to the masses. Stressing the threat toward Buddhism, his speeches urged a younger generation of monks and followers to rise up for Home Rule via strikes, boycotts, and other public forms of dissent that were being practiced across the colonial world. Through figures like U Ottama, Myanmar's nationalism was very much shaped by mobilization strategies and ideological influences from beyond its borders (Schober, 2011).

Militant nationalism

By the 1930s, a new generation of students and union leaders began to express solidarity through a more assertive patriotism of community, language, and place. Calling themselves Dobama Asiayone ("Our Burma Association") but also known as the Thakin Party, this somewhat disparate group of students, shopkeepers, lecturers, and lab assistants sought to create a movement that might enable its members to transcend the divisions over message and method that plagued previous generations of activists by focusing on the basic goal of independence and self-rule (Daw Khin Yi, 1988). Rather than limiting their campaign to protecting traditional culture (that alienated elites) or delving too deeply into policy issues (that alienated the masses), the Dobama Asiayone promoted a sense of belonging based on a shared culture, language, and place.

Arguably more cognizant of the importance of place as a unifying discourse, the emphasis on Bama as "our country" suggested a fundamental shift in how collective solidarity was being imagined and asserted. At the same time, they attempted to apply radical critiques of other colonial situations at the time into their own setting, including communist literature and those who would promote a more National Socialism (Daw Khin Yi, 1988). Adopting the practice of addressing each other as "Thakin", an honorific previously used to address a European, the group introduced new tactics of recruitment, messaging, and coalition building that emphasized a more confident sense of community identity in reference to the colonial authorities. Through newspaper op-eds, song recitals, rallies, boycotts, demonstrations, and cross-country railway tours, the group positioned itself more directly in opposition to the colonial government. The Dobama Asiayone dominated the political space, marginalizing more moderate political organizations that continued to cooperate with the British.

Rebellion as nationalism (1930–1932)

The combination of a more radicalized political generation in the cities, the increasing presence of the colonial state into rural lives, and the worldwide depression of 1930 culminated in a breakdown of social order in the countryside as cultivators, grass-roots activists, monks, and bandits rose in armed rebellion. What appeared to be a local uprising in the rice-producing districts of Lower Burma soon erupted into two years of open rebellion. Armed attacks against colonial installations, public property, colonial personnel, and village headmen (who were appointed by the colonial authorities) typified the two years of civil unrest. Cases of arson, robbery, and murder amongst villages also increased as general security of the countryside disintegrated as the authority and capacity of the state receded (Cady, 1958).

Rangoon authorities initially claimed that the uprising was an attempt by traditionalist fanatics hoping to install their leader as the new king. The blame would soon be redirected against the wunthanu athins that were accused of using their village networks to hide their capacity for rebellion. Pro-British urban elites denounced the rebellion, while security forces comprising mainly Indian troops and other ethnic minorities led the counter-insurgency effort. Alleged ties of the rebellion's leadership to the GCBA compelled urban politicians and activists to denounce it as well, though many offered sympathetic statements of support in the press (Herbert, 1982).

Lasting officially for over two years, what was called the Burma Rebellion (and later the Saya San Rebellion after the alleged leader) was the largest case of rural dissent since the Anglo-Burmese wars of the nineteenth century. Ardent anti-colonial politicians at the time and nationalist scholars would characterize the violence as an expression of nationalist sentiment, a collective demonstration of rural dissent and protest of the conditions living under colonialism. Subtle references to Burmese kingship and restoring Buddhism would lead a later generation of scholars to interpret the uprising as a Buddhist millenarian movement (Sarkisyanz, 1965). Authorities downplayed statements made by detainees at special rebellion trials that economic motivations, relentless taxation, and the loss of access to forest and fishery products (due to privatization) were amongst the motivating factors for joining the rebellion. In the end, the rebellion was deemed to be political in nature and an expression of early nationalist sentiment. Given the fragmented nature of society at the time, the intra-village violence, and wide range of activities associated with uprising, the Burma Rebellion was probably less an expression of collective nationalist sentiment and more likely an expression of local dissatisfaction and economic grievances (Brown, 2005).

Nationalism in wartime (1942–1945)

The more assertive form of nationalism that developed under the *Wunthanu Athins*, the All Student League, and *Dobama Asiayone* continued to do so under the Japanese, who swiftly overran minimal British defenses in March 1942 and took administrative control of the country. Imprisoning pro-British politicians and releasing various ultranationalists who the British had imprisoned altered the political landscape dramatically and set into motion a series of developments that would shape the course of the country in the decades to come. The Japanese declared Burma "Independent" and set up the Burma *Baho* Government, inserting into the new administration members of the Burma Independence Army (including Colonel Aung San, the future leader of independent Burma) and staunch anti-British politicians who had formed the "Freedom League" party. The Japanese encouraged an anti-colonial nationalism that also embraced Burmese cultural forms, language, and social practices as a way of demoting British cultural prestige that had been associated with colonial power. The Thakins' "Burma for the Burmans" mantra, which was well in circulation before the outbreak of World War II, found new life in Japan's "Asia for the Asiatics" rhetoric, once again connecting notions of territory with identity and Southeast Asian ideas with those from East Asia. Collectively, these measures reinforced thinking about solidarity through cultural idioms and in opposition to the colonial state, a template that later generations would continue to reference (Cady, 1958).

At the same time, those communities that had associated themselves with the colonial state, the English language, Christianity, and British cultural norms regarded both the Japanese and the Thakins as threats to their own livelihoods and future. Pro-Japanese Burma Independence Army troops were undisciplined and exercised unchecked authority in the countryside, intimidating villagers and ethnic minorities while stoking already existing flames of mistrust between those who were regarded as British sympathizers and those who saw themselves as liberators. To Anglophile communities during the occupation, it was the highly nationalist Thakins who were to be feared—less so than the Japanese—because the colonial state to which many of these minorities pledged their allegiance was the very entity that was being dismantled under the Japanese. Wartime experiences and the memory of intra-community violence would deepen the commitment of separate solidarities by minority groups (Callahan, 2004).

The importance of the Japanese to the broader story of nationalism in Myanmar was both institutional and ideological. The role of the Japanese in the formation of the Burma Independence Army, the elevation of an anti-colonial, culturally based rhetoric of solidarity, and the persecution of pro-British communities and the Burma Communist Party helped set the stage (and the terms of debate) for a confrontation amongst these stakeholders for control of the post-war state. Elites (mainly ethnic minorities) and the Communist Party—many of whom were also ultranationalist Thakins—expressed their notions of solidarity in reference to the British but through an explicitly different set of ideas and aspirations. During the context of the war, many of these groups would come together to form the Anti-Fascist People's Freedom League (AFPFL), once it became clear that their expectations of independence would not come to fruition replacing one imperial power with another, albeit an Asian one. The occupation by the Japanese brought together Thakins, the communists, the Burma National Army (the former BIA), peasant and worker associations, and even Karen and other ethnic regiments into a tenuous, but united coalition. While these groups had different notions of solidarity and visions of a future Burma, the common experience of war, hardship, and resistance brought these different stakeholders into temporary collaboration until the eventual Japanese surrender to the Allies in 1945 (Taylor, 2009).

While unified temporarily via the AFPFL, these competing notions of community resurfaced after the war—especially when it became clear that the British were no longer going to be part of the political future of the country. The ultranationalist, anti-colonial rhetoric that was initially directed toward the British and their local clients did not provide the assurances nor political space for communities to bridge these different understanding of solidarity. Nor was there a strong enough appeal in communist visions of the future to accommodate the different communities whose livelihoods were connected to international commercial interests. Nationalism and supporting discourses of solidarity in the ensuing decades of independence would be expressed by post-war leaders through a grammar of cultural, linguistic, and religious distinctiveness, originally conceived in opposition to or in support of the West. In this new context of nation-building, the focus of nationalism would shift from coping with imperialism and asserting independence from Britain to questions over what type of nation the Union of Burma would be and for whom.

Nationalism in an era of independence (1945–1962)

The fall of the Japanese left the AFPFL as the leading political organization in post-war Burma. As a wartime coalition, it had managed to draw into its ranks representatives across the political spectrum. Except for the communists, the AFPFL included it its leadership social democrats, a large contingent of the Burma National Army, representatives from the All Burma Youth League, the Karen Central Organization, and the Maha Sangha (representing four of the major Buddhist sects in the country). Following a nearly two-year process of separating from Britain, Burma's leaders faced the challenge of forging a new government and keeping the country's minority groups and other political stakeholders from breaking away to form their own respective states. The lack of a fully functioning state bureaucracy, a decimated economy, an armed countryside, and a war-torn infrastructure left the new government in a vulnerable position with limited capacity to run the country. The assassination of Aung San and most of his cabinet in 1947 further weakened the AFPFL government, barely before it could get the country moving. Differences within the AFPFL over policies, politics, and personal rivalries further constrained the government from expanding its authority beyond the city limits of Rangoon.

Different forms of nationalism re-emerged during this period, reflecting the range of visions concerning the political direction of the country and the capacity of the postcolonial state to adapt to what was fast becoming a crisis of national proportions. Connecting political identity with ethnic or religious designations became the preferred template for many groups seeking to carve a place in or from the new nation-state. Left with little experience on how to define community beyond historical, ethnic, or religious criteria, political groups began to fix notions of who they were and where they believed they should live. Spatial expressions of community—where certain groups lived and claimed authority—were also asserted by different political stakeholders, straining the already tenuous boundaries that held the union together. Karen nationalists had even envisioned an autonomous "Karenland" that claimed a large part of the Lower Burma delta that would have clashed with Burma' national borders that had been inherited by the colonial state (Cady, 1958).

Internal competition over who should lead, whether to continue or discontinue colonial governance structures, and what principles would define the nation, became ongoing flash points for political stakeholders. Not merely an intellectual issue, post-World War II leaders had to deal with policy questions concerning what defined the national community, who belonged in it, and what system could best generate and accommodate the different answers to these questions? With the British gone, colonial-era intra-group rivalries and mistrust resurfaced, deepening already political wounds that emerged during the Japanese period. One of the key challenges facing the new government, now led by the socialist Thakin U Nu, was finding a way to bridge these differences and communicate solidarity in a situation where few of the players envisioned community and solidarity in the same way.

Part of the challenge for the U Nu government and subsequent state managers was finding the right message to promote; most nationalist groups had been born and bred as opposition resistance groups during the colonial era. The independence government and ultranationalist factions within it were committed to reducing the legacy of the West as a demonstration of their nationalist credentials. Yet, the terms and themes that were based on differentiating indigenous groups from those who were deemed "foreign" were no longer suitable since the British were no longer on the scene. Furthermore, the symbols and narratives used by nationalists such as the GCBA, the *Dobama Asiayone*, and other nationalist groups did not appeal to groups that defined themselves through different criteria. What might have worked in reference to the British was not applicable to the postcolonial situation; anti-colonial nationalism (even if deployed as a message of solidarity) was regarded as threating to groups whose notions of solidarity and community were based on references to the British.

Nationalism in an era of socialism (1962–1988)

In some respects, the era of socialism began at independence as the U Nu government had already begun to nationalize the economy, assert state ownership of industry, and expand social services. The problem was that the socialists themselves were not terribly united. Matters of policy, ideology, and personality divided the broader Marxist-Leninist wing of the political landscape and resulted in the split of the AFPFL. Due to the ongoing instability of the civilian-led government, the increasing threat of a full-blown ethnic insurrection, and U Nu's religion policies (making Buddhism a state religion), the military, led by General Ne Win, took over the reins of government via two separate coups in 1958 and again in 1962 (Steinberg, 1982).

Ne Win was a Thakin who had served in the Burmese Independence Army alongside Aung San during the War. He established military rule and created a Revolutionary Council (of mainly military and a few civilian leaders) to manage the transformation of the former colonial administration and its post-independence version into a socialist-oriented state. The premise of the new state would be based on nationalism and socialism, replacing not only the British quasi-parliamentary system that had been inherited and continued after World War II, but the ideological rationale governing state and society relations (Taylor, 2015). The basis for the new system, entitled "the Burmese Way to Socialism" was in some respects the culmination of anti-colonial, nationalist impulses that emerged during the 1920s. From a broader perspective, the change could also be seen as an attempt to answer a far older question about how to approach modernization without the political presence of a Western power.

In many ways, the decoupling of the country from the international market system, the emphasis on self-reliance, and a commitment to populism was a deliberate move away from both the colonial state under the British and its post-World War II incarnation under the U Nu-led AFPFL. At the same time, there continued to be debate within the Revolutionary Council on matters concerning the role of private enterprise for socialist ends, reflecting deeper differences about socialism meant and how it could be achieved. Nationalization of businesses, major industries, trade, banking, commodities, and the reduction of the private sector more generally was followed by a concerted effort to promote the agricultural sector and the millions of rural cultivators whose livelihood depended on it. The military-led government sought to control the economy while expanding the role of the state, reversing in some respects the institutional context that supported the laissez-faire approach under the British while attempting to address the absence of the state in the social-welfare of rural communities. At the same time, the move was also an attempt to compete with the communists, whose ideological appeal and focus on the agricultural sector needs had weakened the prestige of the previous U Nu government. Institutionally speaking, Ne Win was pursuing *towhlanyei* (revolution), an aspiration that would become an important ingredient in the way nationalism would be narrated by state managers (Nakanishi, 2013).

Under the Burma Socialist Programme Party, a socialist inflected form of nationalism developed as the state attempted to reorient, rebuild, and expand its role in society. The population was divided into workers or peasants and organized into corresponding associations that were managed by elected executive committees. These associations penetrated the countryside and served as a conduit between central authorities and village members. People's Councils were elected at the local level. The Lansin Youth Organization was founded in 1985 and served to educate and indoctrinate its members on the Party spirit on the model of the Boy Scouts (Taylor, 2009).

With ethnically designated minority groups still in rebellion and the ongoing communist insurgency drawing the attention of the military, ideas of preserving the union, stability, equality, and order were very much part of official state rhetoric. Attempts to transcend broad cultural differences with ethnic groups were constructed via the recognition of national races. The seven groups corresponded to seven territories and reinforced via heritage sites, museum exhibits, histories, and parks over the decades under the BSPP. The celebration of Union Day, meant to champion ethnic diversity, was instituted amongst other forms of recognition. These efforts and the emphasis on "equality" by Ne Win would be criticized by commentators for generations to come as an attempt to subsume the country's diverse communities into a single ethnic identity through the controversial process of "Burmanization" (Taylor, 2015).

Nationalism in an era of democracy

By the 1980s, Myanmar's economy was in shambles with little hope of generating the type of development and investment needed to improve its status of a Least Developed Country by the World Bank. It became clear that the socialist revolution envisioned by Ne Win and the BSPP did not provide the path toward self-reliance and prosperity. Ne Win's eventual decision to step down as party chairman and call for a referendum on the prospect for future multiparty elections signaled the end of the Burma Socialist Program Party and the socialist revolution. Residents in Rangoon and other urban centers had already lost their patience and trust in the government, especially when the local currency was demonetized for the second time despite Ne Win's promise not to do so. When local police officials failed to manage a student brawl at a teahouse, students from the Rangoon Institute for Technology and other educational institutions directed their protests toward the local BSPP offices and the central government. The demonstrations soon expanded to engulf most of Rangoon as workers, students, civil servants, public intellectuals, shop owners, and office workers took to the streets, many of them calling for "democracy". The heavy-handed response by the security forces that led to thousands of arrests and causalities resulted in condemnation from the world, especially as countries in other parts of Asia seemed to be embracing a wave of democratic transitions. With the security forces focused on the streets, ethnic armed organizations began to initiate military maneuvers to enhance their positions. With the threat of disintegration once again sweeping across the country, Ne Win declared martial law, and established the State Council for Law and Order Restoration Council, formally ending the experiment with socialism.

For many observers, the military's actions on the streets of Rangoon in August 1988 and the nullification of the 1990 constituent assembly elections marked the beginning of a national struggle for democracy against an antiquated military elite that sought simply to hold on to power. Indeed, the rise of the National League for Democracy (NLD) as a political player was reminiscent of the anti-colonial nationalist movements during the British era; only this time their efforts were directed against an indigenous military state. A new language of resistance based on liberal democratic aspirations, human rights, and the rule of law brought the new political party in line with post-Cold War international governance models and expectations. Daw Aung San Suu Kyi, the daughter of the former nationalist general Aung San, became the "face" of this nationalist struggle in Myanmar, representing both the hopes of a younger generation and the need for political change that seemed to be sweeping across Asia in South Korea, Taiwan, Timor, and the Philippines. A massive international movement of foreign governments, transnational activist organizations, philanthropies, media organizations, and multi-lateral institutions mobilized in support of the NLD, ethnic organizations, and other grass-roots organizations.

What complicated matters was the announcement in 2003 that the military planned to launch a "Road-map to Disciplined-flourishing Democracy". It represented a different pathway to pursuing democracy than that being pursued by the NLD and other opposition groups. The "Roadmap" emphasized the writing and approving a constitution first, establishing the institutional foundations for the state, and then holding general elections—all under the military's supervision. This vision of democracy was a top-down, managed process of building democracy, following a template that was reminiscent of how new governance systems were established during the colonial, wartime, and independence eras. In many respects, the vision put forth by the State Peace and Development Council (the former SLORC caretaker government) expressed similar nationalistic themes that the previous AFPFL and BSPP governments had articulated under U Nu and Ne Win—unity, social order, and sovereignty—only this time it was done through the vocabulary and tropes of liberal democracy. For many domestic and international critics, this plan did not represent (their vision of) democracy; it only affirmed the accusation that the military only sought to retain power under the disguise of democratic change.

By the mid-2000s, the military organized and convened its constitutional convention, prompting the NLD to boycott the process. A few political parties and representatives of ethnic groups did join the convention, complicating what constituted "the people of Myanmar" that was being referred to by all the stakeholders involved. When the constitution was completed and ratified by referendum controversially in the aftermath of Cyclone Nargis, few outside the military and its domestic allies placed much hope in the document or the government's assurances that a "Burmese Way" to democracy would amount to anything more than the perpetuation of military rule. The 2010 elections, that brought the military's civilian party, the Union Solidarity and Development Party, to lead the government under the new constitution did little to change these views given that Daw Aung Suu Kyi was still under house arrest.

The new Thein Sein administration and the liberalization program it pursued surprised most stakeholders and observers. The sweeping reforms to domestic and foreign policy challenged expectations about how democracy could be implemented in a Southeast Asian context. The state withdrew much of its presence over society in areas such as education, media, and the economy, de-centralizing administrative machinery that had once been tightly controlled by an ineffective socialist agenda. While stability, sovereignty, and unity were still themes that the new government expressed, it was done so alongside rhetoric that included references to democracy, the rule of law, human rights, liberalization, and freedom. The release of Aung San Suu Kyi, her eventual election into the parliament and the NLD's inclusion into the political system was regarded as progress. When she and her party won a landslide victory in the 2015 elections, only then did external observers start to accept that the military had indeed instituted the foundations of a workable—yet imperfect—democratic system of governance.

Between the years 2015 and 2020, the Aung San Suu Kyi administration pursued a national agenda that called for a recalibration of the 2008 constitution, particularly the clause that reserves 25 percent of the parliamentary seats for the military. This vision of a reduced presence for the military fundamentally clashed with the armed forces' own version of democracy, which sees themselves as part of that system, protecting the integrity of the 2008 constitution and the institutional system it authorizes. While very much a rivalry between civilian and military elites for control of the country (a dynamic that has been in play since the colonial period), in the current context this is also a competition over which "democracy" shall prevail and who will be in charge to implement it.

In the years since her election in 2015, the Suu Kyi administration embarked on their own version of integration and national reconciliation, choosing to evoke the memory of the 1947 Panglong Agreement that her father secured as a symbol of future intra-ethnic reconciliation. While mirroring the previous administration's attempts at securing a national ceasefire agreement in pursuit of national integration and ending the over half-century of fighting, Suu Kyi's government did not convince the key armed ethnic organizations to de-militarize and work within the national fold. Many of these ethnic designated communities continue to express their own form of nationalism and territorial sovereignty as separate from those of the Myanmar state, emboldened by the same liberal democratic concepts and vocabulary that both the military and the NLD draw upon to assert political identity. The continuing presence of competing nationalisms, often based on fixed cultural and religious distinctions, was incompatible with the equally essentialized forms of nationalism being promoted by successive Naypyidaw administrations.

Moreover, marginalized and persecuted communities seeking recognition were being targeted by ultranationalist groups who found their voice through new social media platforms and a more liberal communication space no longer regulated closely by the state authorities. Growing discrimination against the Rohingya began to increase with the rise of Buddhist right-wing nationalists in the 2010s who began to hold rallies to spread ideas about future threats to the country being tied to the Muslim community. Paralleling the political monks of the 1920s and 1930s, these extremists revived a form of nationalism that was predicated on culturally frozen imaginings of what constituted Myanmar. Deadly violence between Rakhine Buddhists and Muslims erupted in 2017, creating a humanitarian crisis that, according to international observers, was caused by the Myanmar military. With the outbreak of the Rohingya crisis, the reactionary emergence of an Arakanese nationalist movement, and the apparent refusal of the Suu Kyi administration to take responsibility for the crisis, the prospect of forging solidarities amongst Myanmar's many communities seems a long way off.

Conclusion

To speak of nationalism in Myanmar suggests that there is a particular type or form that emerged within the territorial boundaries of the nation-state. In some respects, this is true; the type of solidarities, identity politics, divergent priorities, and discordant worldviews that informed different expressions of nationalism in Myanmar is a product of the country's particular geographies, social structure, ethno-linguistic diversities, classes, ideologies, and colonial/postcolonial historical experiences. The anti-colonial nationalism that emerged in the 1920s and 1930s was very different from the nationalism—broadly construed—that emerged in British Malaya/Singapore for a range of reasons that had as much to do with the nature of the pre-colonial state as it did with British colonizers.

At the same time, it is possible to view the history of nationalism that developed in Myanmar as part of a broader story of coming to terms with the West as many societies were compelled to do in the nineteenth and twentieth centuries across the colonized world. From this vantage point, the different forms of nationalism that emerged within Myanmar might be seen to reflect attempts by different generations of political actors to experiment with the prevailing models of governance/ideology at the time. These experiences were not confined to the boundaries of colonial Burma or independent Myanmar but were also transnational in origin and reflected Myanmar's connectedness to Asia and to other parts of the globe. The anti-colonial nationalism that emerged in British Burma was very much connected to and inspired by political actors in British India, Communist China, and Imperial Japan. Myanmar's political intellectuals interacted with individuals and networks that circulated across the Indian Ocean, Straits of Melaka, and South China Sea and were therefore part of a broader political conversation of what constituted "Asia" as much as the concern was for what might be understood as "Myanmar". The development of anti-colonialism in Myanmar had as much to do with interactions with India, China, and Japan as it was developed in reference to Britain. The engagement by young students with Marxist-Leninist ideas by a young Aung San and his brother-in-law Than Tun reflected an attempt by a generation of students to modernize through foreign models while retaining political sovereignty, an aspiration that would be central to leaders of the country from independence till this day. As such, it is possible to regard more contemporary competition for the state, rivalry between civilian and military elites, and ideological battles over democracy as part of this longer attempt to find a model of governance that will be able to bridge these deeply embedded divisions within Myanmar society.

The recent move by the military in 2021 to suspend the 2008 constitution, nullify the 2020 elections, and evoke Emergency Law (a move that is highly contested) has raised questions as to whether Myanmar's "experiment" with democracy is over after a ten-year run. The brutal way the military responded to the rise of a robust "civil disobedience movement" in protest of the "coup" would seem to suggest that the days of democracy as a template for governance in Myanmar are over. Yet, the military asserts that it will reconvene elections soon and reboot the 2008 constitutional system that placed itself and its political opponents in a power-sharing scenario. Meanwhile, the National Unity Government, the exile government made up of 2020 election members of parliament, civil service officials, activists, and ethnic political party representatives, counter that there is no going back to the 2008 constitution, preferring instead to write a new constitution that reflects its own version of democracy. Whether that alternative version of democracy, one that may not involve the military, will enable the various political stakeholders in Myanmar to overcome their differences of community that have divided the country since 1948 remains to be seen.

References

Brown, I. (2005). *A Colonial Economy in Crisis: Burma's Rice Cultivators and the World Depression of the 1930s*. Abingdon: Routledge.
Cady, J. (1958). *A History of Modern Burma*. Ithaca: Cornell University Press.
Callahan, M.P. (2004). *Making Enemies: War and State Building in Burma*. Ithaca: Cornell University Press.
Cooper, F. (2005). *Colonialism in Question: Theory, Knowledge, History*. Berkeley: University of California Press.

Herbert, Patricia (1982). *The Hsaya San Rebellion (1930-1932): Reappraised*. Melbourne: Centre of Southeast Asian Studies, Monash University.

Maung Maung, U. (1980). *From Sangha to Laity*. Manohar: Australia National University.

Nakanishi, Y. (2013). *Strong Soldiers, Failed Revolution: The State and Military in Burma, 1952–1988*. Singapore: NUS Press.

Reid, A. (2009). *Imperial Alchemy: Nationalism and Political Identity in Southeast Asia*. Cambridge: Cambridge University Press.

Sarkisyanz, E. (1965). *Buddhist Backgrounds of the Burma Revolution*. The Hague: M. Nijhoff.

Schober, J. (2011). *Modern Buddhist Conjunctures in Myanmar: Cultural Narratives, Colonial Legacies, and Civil* Society. Honolulu: University of Hawaii Press.

Steinberg, D.I. (1982). *Burma: A Socialist Nation of Southeast Asia*. Boulder: Westview Press.

Taylor, R.H. (2009). *The State in Myanmar*. Singapore: NUS Press.

Taylor, R.H. (2015). *General Ne Win: A Political Biography*. Singapore: NUS Press.

Turner, A. (2014). *Saving Buddhism: The Impermanence of Religion in Colonial Burma*. Honolulu: University of Hawaii Press.

Yi, Daw Khin (1988). *The Dobama Movement in Burma (1930-1938)*. Ithaca: Cornell University Press.

31
COMPETING NATIONALISMS
Shifting conceptions of nation in the construction of Indonesia in the twentieth century

Joshua Kueh

Introduction

This chapter traces the origins of the idea of Indonesia and competing conceptions of the nation of Indonesia, an archipelagic state with borders that mirror those of the Netherlands East Indies at the height of its territorial claims. During the twentieth century, various groups began to see each other in community within the boundaries of the colonial state: Muslim merchants who saw Islam as a focal point for identity in opposition to Dutch rulers and non-Muslim Chinese merchants; communists who saw the inhabitants of the colony as workers and sought to overthrow imperialists; proponents of an Indonesian Islamic state called the Negara Islam Indonesia; and others who envisioned an Indonesian nation based on the principles of the Pancasila, which became the dominant discourse on nation. Each of these competing nationalisms bound large groups of people together but also marginalized many – Chinese, Acehnese, and Papuans, among others. High Modernist programs sought to remake the Republic in the image of the center, based on the island of Java, and stirred up conflicts between ethnic groups. As the long years of the Suharto New Order regime gave way to the years of reform (reformasi) at the end of the twentieth century, Indonesians once again found themselves reimagining the nation. The history of nationalism in Indonesia for the last 100 years or so suggests that nationalism, like any hegemonic discourse, is subject to ongoing negotiation.

This negotiation became most visible when the national model of Indonesia was contested. Jacques Bertrand (2004, 4) explains that the

> principles that come to define the nation or relations between nations– that is, the national model – establish inclusion/exclusion of its members and the terms of inclusion. Members might be included within a national model with conditions…that imply the shedding of group identities or the acceptance of a particular hierarchy of ethnic relations.

This chapter sees three critical periods for the national model of Indonesia:

1   ca. 1910–1950: These years saw the rise of various nationalist movements in Indonesia – ethno-nationalists, Islamic nationalists, and those who saw an archipelago-wide state

united by civic principles. The period culminated in an independent unitary state which experimented with liberal democracy – an experiment that ended in 1957.
2   1957–1968: This period witnessed the abandonment of liberal democracy and the introduction of authoritarian rule, first under Sukarno's Guided Democracy, and then under Suharto's New Order. The vision of Indonesia formed during these years was imposed by the center and relied heavily on the military. Its vision of a modern Indonesia was an all-encompassing one that did not permit ideas deemed disruptive to the national project. This "integralist" imagining of Indonesia exacerbated tensions in regions like Aceh, Papua, and East Timor and marginalized ethnic minorities like the Chinese.
3   1998: With the resignation of Suharto in May 1998, the New Order collapsed and ushered in a period of uncertainty and ethnic conflict but also reform. Indonesians called for reformasi (reform), seeking a more democratic form of government and more local autonomy.

This chapter will examine negotiations during these periods to reveal the major conceptions of "Indonesia" formed during the twentieth century. Additionally, this chapter delves into the origins of the term "Indonesia," outlining its evolution from an ethnographic and geographic term to a political one, underlining the constructed-ness of the idea. At different times, "Indonesia" has meant different things to different people. As Benedict Anderson (2016, 4) famously argued:

> Nationality…nation-ness, as well as nationalism, are cultural artefacts of a particular kind. To understand them properly we need to consider carefully how they have come into historical being, in what ways their meanings have changed over time, and why, today, they command such profound emotional legitimacy.

1850–1950: origins to independence

The idea of Indonesia as a political community is little more than a 100 years old. By the early 1920s, "Indonesia" was ubiquitous in the names of nationalist organizations and newspapers, such as the Indonesische Vereeniging (Indonesian Association) – a rebranding of the organization Indische Vereeniging (IV; Indies Association) in 1922, becoming the Perhimpunan Indonesia (Indonesian Union) in 1925; Partai Komunis Indonesia (Indonesian Communist Party or PKI), until 1924 the Perseikatan Komunis India (Indies Communist Union); the Indonesian Study Club; Persatuan Muslimin Indonesia (Union of Indonesian Muslims); and the newspaper Indonesia Merdeka. While the political sense of Indonesia developed a century ago, its origins predate this period by about 50 years.

Prior to the late nineteenth century, when Dutch rule over the islands and peoples of the archipelago established the boundaries of what would become Indonesia, there was no conception of an Indonesian nation or state. In that sense, Indonesia was born out of colonialism; unrelated groups came to share the same legal status within the colonial hierarchy, creating a sense of a common connection and cause. Dutch education (extended to a small group of elites) provided opportunities for the educated to engage with each other and with modern ideas such as nationalism and socialism within the larger space of the Netherlands East Indies.

Beyond the experience of Dutch rule, the hajj was another contributor to identity formation. An increasing number of Muslims from all over the archipelago came together in Mecca where they were exposed to the worldwide community of Muslims. In Mecca, those from the archipelago and Malay-speaking world were known as Jawi. The Jawi, like other pilgrims, had a tradition of staying in the region to exchange ideas and knowledge. There were about 5,000 Jawis in Mecca at the end of the 1800s. With the capture of Mecca by Ibn Saud, supported by Abd al-Wahab, who were seen as opposed to the form of Islam practiced in Asia, Jawis relocated to Cairo, where they encountered Islamic modernism, discussed independence from "infidel" colonial rule and the possibility of establishing a transnational Islamic state (Formichi 2010, 126–7).

Despite Dutch rule and the experience of the Jawis, before the twentieth century, there was no conception of Indonesia as various peoples with a shared destiny within the confines of a sovereign state. The Dutch colonial state itself was still only in formation in the late nineteenth century. While the Dutch had been engaged in trade with Southeast Asia since the late 1500s, they only had a sustained presence centered in Batavia on Java. It was not until the 1800s that the Dutch began to expand their rule into the outer islands (from their perspective) of the archipelago, with Papua being the last area to come under Dutch occupation in the late nineteenth century (Ricklefs 2008, 161–180). It was only around 1910 that the areas that constitute the Republic of Indonesia were united under Dutch rule. Given this history, a conception of an archipelago-wide imagined political community only came about in the early twentieth century. Within a few decades, on 17 August 1945, the independence of Indonesia was declared. So how did the idea of Indonesia gain ground and become a reality so quickly? To understand this historical process, an excavation of the term "Indonesia" will help.

The word "Indonesia" comes from a term invented by the Englishman, George Windsor Earl. In volume IV of Journal of the Indian Archipelago, published in 1850, Earl wrote:

> Nevertheless the time has arrived when a distinctive name for the brown races of the Indian Archipelago is urgently required, and it should be made to accord as closely as possible with the terms by which the portion of the world is most generally known, namely 'Indian Archipelago' or 'Malayan Archipelago'. By adopting the Greek word for 'islands' as a terminal, for which we have a precedent in the term 'Polynesia', the inhabitants of the 'Indian Archipelago' or 'Malayan Archipelago' would become respectively Indu-nesians or Malayu-nesians.
>
> *(quoted in Jones, 1973, 102)*

This was the first occurrence of the word "Indu-nesians," although Earl himself preferred "Malayu-nesians" (quoted in Jones 1973, 102).

It was James Logan who first embraced "Indonesia" as a geographical term. In the article "Ethnology of the Indian Archipelago: Embracing enquiries into the Continental relations of the Indo-Pacific Islanders," Logan borrowed from Earl saying:

> Mr. Earl suggests the ethnographical term Indunesians but rejects it in favour of Malayunesians, ...I prefer the purely geographical term Indonesia, which is merely a shorter synonym for the Indian Islands or the Indian Archipelago. We thus get Indonesian for Indian Archipelagian or Archipelagic, and Indonesians for Indian Archipelagians or Indian Islanders, ... The term has some claim...to be located in the region, for in the slightly different form of nusa it is perhaps as ancient in the Indian Archipelago as in Greece.
>
> *(quoted in Jones, 1973, 103)*

The term was slow to catch on. It was not widely used as a geographical and ethnographical term until the 1880s, owing in part to its usage by the famous German ethnographer Adolf Bastian, and the Dutch ethnologist and former Indies official G.A. Wilken.

By the early 1900s, "Indonesia" began to be used beyond academic discussions more widely. In 1917, the Indonesisch Verbond van Studeerenden (IVS; Indonesian Association of Students) was established in Leiden by Indonesian and Dutch Indology students, the first instance of "Indonesia" appearing in the title of a society (Jones 1973, 109). "Indonesia" soon acquired a political connotation with Mohammad Hatta writing that "With indefatigable zeal since 1918 we have carried on propaganda for 'Indonesia' as the name of our motherland" (Jones 1973, 109).

The entrance of "Indonesia" into political discourse necessitated a discussion of the scope of "Indonesians." In 1917, in the monthly journal *Hindia Poetra* (Sons of the Indies), the musicologist R.M.S. Suryoputro used "Indonesian" to communicate the oneness of the peoples of the archipelago, "an Indonesian consciousness of race" (Elson 2008, 23). This nativist conception of Indonesia as a homeland of those seen as indigenous to the islands would become a recurring theme in Indonesian politics. From the earliest days of Indonesian nationalism, an ethnic formulation of the imagined Indonesian community sowed tension between migrant and indigenous communities, foreshadowing the discourse of "pribumi" and "non-pribumi" inhabitants of Indonesia.

The ethno-nationalism of Suryoputro, which posited the existence of an "Indonesian" race, was perhaps a reflection of the social hierarchy of The Netherlands East Indies: "Europeans" at the top, "Foreign Orientals" such as the Chinese and Arabs in the middle, and "Native" populations at the bottom (Van der Meer 2020, 113). This classification scheme, which colonial authorities used in 1920, stemmed from an older organization introduced in the colony's Constitutional Regulation of 1854: "on the one hand, Europeans and those 'deemed to be alike' (gelijkgesteld) European in status, and on the other hand, natives and those categorized as gelijkgesteld natives, which included Chinese, Arabs and other foreign Orientals" (Djalins 2015, 230). These colonial categories obscured nuances within groups, movement between them, and the advantages of the elite of each group within colonial society. Nonetheless, the lumping together of autochthonous populations stimulated a sense of kinship in the face of shared oppression. This is not to say that autochthonous peoples in the Netherlands East Indies did not see themselves as Javanese, Minangkabau, or Acehnese; indeed, there were strong ethno-nationalist movements in Indonesia at different points over the last century.

Many Javanese aristocrats chose to develop a form of Javanese, rather than Indonesian, nationalism and were among the earliest nationalists founding the Boedi Oetomo (Glorious Endeavor) in 1908, the first indigenous political organization in the Netherlands East Indies. Javanese nationalists of aristocratic background like Soetatmo Soeriokoesoemo did not put stock in the new idea of "Indonesia" but focused on rejuvenating Javanese culture and retaining their position in society rather than a revolutionary rethinking of the political order (Fakih 2012, 423).

Related to ethno-nationalism was religious nationalism, specifically the political vision of Indonesia as a nation under Islam. Muslims on the hajj met with ideas concerning independence from colonial rule and the establishment of a transnational Islamic state. These ideas were encapsulated in a political concept called "pan-Islamism" in the late nineteenth century. Espoused by the Young Ottomans, pan-Islamism was an attempt to unify Muslims under the Ottoman Sultan (Formichi 2010, 129). Over time, this ideology focused on how Muslims should work together for independence from infidel rule and unite under one spiritual and political leader. The implications of this vision were debated in al-Azhar University's periodical al-Manār and reached the Netherlands East Indies through pilgrims and students in the Middle East, who, in turn, continued the conversation in local newspapers like Seruan

Azhar and al-Irshad (Formichi, 129). In Indonesia, historical circumstances would affect how Muslim leaders understood pan-Islamism and imagined the boundaries and aims of an Islamic Indonesian state. Chiara Formichi explores this changing relationship in the writings of S.M. Kartosuwiryo between 1928 and the 1950s (2010, 128–146). As a prominent Muslim leader who advocated for an Islamic conception of the nation-state, Kartosuwiryo was a member of the first Islamic nationalist party in Indonesia, Partai Sarekat Islam (PSI), which had developed from the Sarekat Dagang Islam (Islamic Trade Association), founded in 1905 to protect the interests of Muslim batik traders. As a journalist for the PSI newspaper Fadjar Asia, and later one of its main leaders, Kartosuwiryo's views on the pan-Islamic ideal varied as the shifting political situation from the 1920s to the 1960s shaped the limits of what he saw as possible.

In the 1920s, with the Dutch in power, Kartosuwiryo presented pan-Islamism as a rallying point for independence and a theory of internationalism. By the 1930s, with the Indonesian nationalist movement suffering serious setbacks, he began calling for a worldwide unification of the ummah, an outcome beyond the reach of the colonial state. Japanese occupation in the 1940s offered new possibilities. Within their vision of a Greater Asia Co-Prosperity Sphere, Kartosuwiryo saw an opportunity to create a new Islamic world in East Asia. The Japanese surrender in 1945 ended this outlook. The declaration of Indonesian independence drew Kartosuwiryo's attention to the national project and he fought to ensure a role for Islam in the nation-state. However, the Renville agreement in January 1948, which put West Java in Dutch hands, changed his goal to an Islamic state in West Java. When the federal state of Indonesia was agreed in 1949, implying a rejection of an Indonesia under Islamic law, Kartosuwiryo declared an Indonesian Islamic state (Negara Islam Indonesia). His vision spread to Aceh, South Sulawesi, and South Kalimantan, and would persist as a challenge to the Republican view of Indonesia until his arrest and execution in 1962 (Formichi 2010, 125–146).

If pan-Islamism formed one facet of political Islam in Indonesia, Islamic Socialism was another. H.O.S. Cokroaminoto was a proponent of this school of thought. Drawing heavily from the ideas of Mushir Hosein Kidwai, a scholar born in India's United Provinces in 1878 who studied law in England, Cokroaminoto authored Islam dan Socialisme (Islam and Socialism) in 1924. Following Kidwai's arguments, which were built on Quranic sources and Islamic history, Cokroaminoto argued for socialism as a religious system and argued that Muhammad's socialism was spiritual and moral, whereas secular socialism was materialistic. Cokroaminoto also agreed with Kidwai that "true Islamic teachings led to a kind of socialism in which all Muslims (and later all humanity) would work together to help one another, uphold the dignity of humanity, and run society in accordance with God's laws" (Fogg 2019, 1746). At a time when Sarekat Islam had just shed many of its communist members and was in competition with other secular nationalist groups (Fogg 2019, 1747), Islam dan Socialisme laid out Cokroaminoto's views regarding social justice and distinguished Sarekat Islam's platform from those of the communists and secular nationalists. Islamic Socialism became "a leading political idea for several decades and a jumping-off point for both secular and religious political thinkers moving forward" (Fogg 2019, 1761), including Kartosuwiryo and Sukarno.

Islamic nationalism, with its connection to socialism and pan-Islamism, would prove to be a constant in Indonesian political life. Its main challenger would be a conception of the state that included all inhabitants as one people and one nation. This conception of Indonesia can be traced back to thinkers like E. F. E. Douwes Dekker (also known as Setiabuddhi). Dekker was of mixed European and indigenous heritage and founded the Indische Partij

(Indies Party) in 1912. Dekker re-conceptualized the Indies in the "first great breakthrough in Indonesian thinking about the nation and the shape it should take" (Elson 2008, 15). Douwes Dekker dared to imagine "only one people, one 'nation in the making'" (Elson 2008, 15). Two Western-educated Javanese joined Dekker in proclaiming an archipelago-wide nationalism with independence as its goal – Dr. Tjipto Mangunkusumo, decorated by the Dutch for his work in combating the plague, and the Javanese aristocrat Suwardi Surjaningrat (later called Ki Hadjar Dewantara). In 1913, the Dutch exiled them to the Netherlands.

In the Netherlands, the three nationalists would push the IV to become more political. Founded in 1908, the IV aimed "to promote the common interests of the Indiërs in the Netherlands and to keep in touch with the Netherlands East Indies. By Indiërs is understood the native inhabitants of the Netherlands East Indies" (Elson 2008, 9). The arrival of Douwes Dekker, Tjipto, and Suwardi saw the association become politically engaged. Tjipto sought to get the association to support popular movements such as Sarekat Islam. In 1916, Suwardi began editing *Hindia Poetra* as a journal "not only of the 'Indiërs' studying in the Netherlands, but also of prominent people in the Indies-native world" and to promote "the harmonious development of the Indies people" (Elson 2008, 23). Publication stopped due to lack of funds but was revived in 1918 by the IVS, "a group of Indonesian and Dutch Indology students who planned careers of service in the Indies" (Elson 2008, 23). The IVS sought to bring various like-minded organizations together, including the IV and the Sino-Indonesian student association Chung Hwa Hui (Chinese Association). Under the IVS, *Hindia Poetra* became a political publication. Suwardi, as an editor, did not lose sight of the vision of an Indonesia where "anyone who considered the Indies or Indonesia as his fatherland, irrespective of whether he was pure Indonesian, or whether he has Chinese, Dutch or general European blood in his veins" would be understood as Indonesian (quoted in Elson 2008, 25).

We can glimpse in Suwardi's conception of Indonesia a type of civic nationalism based not on ethnic or religious criteria but on loyalty to the state. In its attempts to implement this third conception, the Indonesian government drove religious and ethno-nationalisms to the margins, but these imaginings of the nation continued to influence civic nationalism and resurfaced when ideas about the nation were renegotiated.

During the 1920s, Islamic and ethno-nationalism began to be overshadowed by growing calls for freedom through unity. Sukarno championed the view that the various streams of Indonesian political thought had to come together for the purpose of freeing Indonesians, whom he conceived as all the people of the archipelago regardless of their ethnic affiliation. In his 1926 tract "Nationalism, Islam and Marxism," Sukarno argued that "the ship that will take us to a Free Indonesia is the Ship of Unity!" He asked:

> …Nationalism, Islam, or Marxism. Can these spirits work together in a colonial system to form one Great Spirit, the Spirit of Unity?...In colonial territories can the Nationalist movement be joined with Islamic movement, which essentially denies the nation? Can it be allied with Marxism, which proclaims an international struggle?

Sukarno responded in the affirmative: "There is nothing to prevent Nationalists from working together with Moslems and Marxists" (Soekarno 1970, 36–40).

While there was consensus on the need for unity against colonialism to achieve freedom, what was less clear was how to achieve and implement such unity. Japanese rule in Indonesia accelerated the conversation surrounding this topic.

In the closing months of the Second World War, the Japanese military government announced the establishment of a Committee for the Investigation of Independence (Badan

Untuk Penyelidik Usaha-usaha Persiapan Kemerdekaan or BPUPK) tasked with agreeing the basis of an Indonesian state. The solution put forward reflected its composition: "territorial nationalist rather than Islamic, Java-centric in orientation if not necessarily in ethnicity...conservative in temper, authoritarian in disposition and, by the standards of the day, aged" (Elson 2008, 105). The solution was Sukarno's five principles or the Pancasila:

1   The enduring unity of the Indonesian nation
2   Internationalism/Humanitarianism
3   Representative democracy
4   Social justice
5   Belief in the One Supreme God

Those who envisioned a leading role for Islam in the state pushed for inclusion of a preamble (called the "Jakarta Charter") that all Muslims had to follow Islamic law. This and a requirement that the president be a Muslim were removed from the draft Constitution due to threats from eastern Indonesian delegates to secede. The word for God was also switched from "Allah" to "Tuhan," which was not as linked to Islam. Notwithstanding Islamic nationalist dissatisfaction, the revised Constitution was adopted. Citizenship was given only to "native Indonesians" as a matter of right, but those seen as of foreign ancestry, such as the Dutch, Chinese, and Arabs, could be citizens by law (Elson 2008, 113–114).

The principles of Pancasila were broad enough to admit divergent points of view, but they did not provide direction on where Indonesia was going politically, nor on how the country should be ruled. Despite this, the formulation of a basis for the Republic of Indonesia at the end of a period of intense politicization speaks to a changed ideological landscape – one where a return to the colonial status quo was unacceptable.

When the Dutch attempted to restore their rule in Indonesia, they found themselves on a collision course with Indonesian revolutionaries. These revolutionaries were internally divided, but they united against colonial rule and forged a strong Indonesian identity that ensured that, despite their differences, they would "find their solution in the context of one nation" (Reid 1974, 172).

The Dutch struggled to grasp the idea of an independent Indonesian nation. Their illusion that the Republic represented "only a gang of collaborators without popular support" was shattered by the ferocity and great cost of the Battle of Surabaya in late 1945 when 6,000 British Indian troops went to Surabaya to evacuate internees (Ricklefs 2008, 254). Despite the many deaths on both sides, the Dutch persisted with a conception of their mission as one of restoring control and order in their colony for the good of the masses, whom they saw as wanting the Dutch back.

Tessel Pollmann, analyzing novels that appeared in the 1940s and early 1950s written by Dutch soldiers who served in the Indies during the late forties, argues that most Dutch believed that the ordinary Indonesian wanted them back, and this myth made it possible to portray the brutal war as "a 'police action' devoted to the poor and powerless" (2000, 94).

Dutch policy makers continued to operate from a colonial understanding of Indonesia as a space where the Dutch were arbiters in an archipelago-wide realm of ethnically based polities ruled by elites. This is evident in the Dutch insistence on federal states organized along ethnic lines or with ethnic representation in mind, such as the Great Dayak semi-autonomous administrative unit in Kalimantan. In the Linggadjati agreement of 1946, the Dutch agreed to recognize the Republic as the de facto authority in Java, Madura, and Sumatra within the framework of a federal United States of Indonesia, which would include other sovereign states in a Dutch-Indonesian union with the Dutch queen as the symbolic head. While there was support for local autonomy in areas outside Java, the Dutch failed to grasp the depth of feeling for an independent Indonesia throughout the archipelago. As late as December 1948, the Dutch tried to persuade Sultan Hamengkubuwono IX to become a leader of a new Javanese state, something the Sultan rejected.

As negotiations to maintain a Dutch presence in Indonesia faced stiff resistance, the Dutch turned to violence in the shape of so-called police actions, bloody campaigns to crush the Republic. While these seemed to bring the Dutch closer to their goal of conquest, the international geopolitical situation turned against them.

In December 1948, the Dutch launched their second police action. The Republican government allowed itself to be captured, correctly calculating that world opinion would turn against the Dutch. The UN Security Council was outraged, and the United States was angered, particularly because it saw the Republican government as significant in the fight against Communism. To understand this perception, some background on the Communist Party of Indonesia (PKI) is needed.

The PKI, founded in 1920, was the first communist party in Asia. From its beginnings until its violent demise in 1965, it played an active role in Indonesian politics and as an influence on leftists. Amir Sjariffudin, a founder of the Indonesian People's Movement (Gerindo), leader of the Partai Socialis (Socialist Party), and prime minister from 1947 to 1948; and Tan Malaka, proponent of "national Communism" (the idea that Indonesia should seek its own path toward a socialist state) and founder of the Persatuan Perdjuangan (Struggle Front) that aimed at 100 percent merdeka (independence) and opposed concessions to the Dutch. During the years of the Revolution, the arena in which the PKI operated had many left-leaning individuals and groups. In addition to the Struggle Front and Amir's Partai Socialis – made up of the Indonesian Socialist Youth (Pesindo or Pemuda Socialis Indonesia) and supporters of Sutan Sjahrir, a socialist who served as Indonesia's prime minister from 1945 to 1947 – there was an organization launched by a lawyer called Yusuf that went by the name PKI but operated independently of the historic PKI. Harry Poeze explores the intricacies of this complicated scene in "The Cold War in Indonesia, 1948" (2009, 497–517), focusing on the role of Muso, a veteran PKI leader with close ties to Moscow, in precipitating the showdown between Republican forces and the PKI.

In August 1948, Muso arrived in Yogyakarta from the USSR. Before that, the PKI had kept a low profile and focused on working with leftist organizations and individuals. In 1948, Yugoslavia's refusal to subordinate itself to Stalin's orders resulted in a shift in Moscow's thinking. Cooperation with non-communist nationalist entities was to be repudiated. Muso, based in the USSR for 23 years, was sent back to Indonesia to discipline the PKI and chart a new path. Under Muso's leadership, the PKI sought to take charge of the national revolution. There was to be no room for compromise with "bourgeois" leaders like Sukarno in the struggle against imperialists.

Muso's rise culminated in open warfare between pro-PKI and pro-Republican forces. Pro-PKI units gathered in the city of Madiun and took over strategic points, killing pro-Republican officers, and announcing a new National Front government led by Muso and other PKI leaders. Sukarno denounced the Madiun rebels over radio and issued a call for Indonesians to rally to him and Hatta. Muso responded by saying that he would fight to the end. Military units had to choose between Muso and Sukarno. Many chose to back the Republic, which opened the way for pro-Republican forces to defeat the pro-PKI forces. On 31 October 1948, Muso was captured and killed. Defeat of Muso and the PKI encouraged American support for the Republic within its global strategy of containing communism, which in 1948 appeared to be gaining ground with the Berlin blockade, the communist coup d'état in Czechoslovakia, the communist insurrection in Malaya, and communist advances in China. "Within this framework, the Indonesian Republic had shown itself to be anti-communist and hence worthy of American support" (Ricklefs 2008, 267).

When the Dutch launched their second police action, the Americans threatened to withdraw aid needed for reconstruction after the Second World War. The Dutch were forced to back down and ultimately hand over power in Indonesia (except Papua) to the federal United States of Indonesia on 27 December 1949. This federal state was short-lived; on 17 August 1950, it was replaced by a new unitary Republic of Indonesia, notwithstanding opposition in East Sumatra and East Indonesia.

The Revolution did not resolve regional problems, but it did settle one important issue – Indonesia was no longer a Dutch colony. The Revolution "destroyed a colonial polity controlled from the other side of the world, with its racial castes, its anachronistic, powerless rajas, its rigid social categories. It released tremendous energies and aspirations..." (Reid 1974, 171).

1950–1998: "Western" democracy, Guided Democracy, and the New Order

Independence allowed Indonesians to contest what Indonesia should be. From 1950 to 1957, the country was pulled in different directions. The historic first national elections of 1955 did little to resolve the disagreements and inability to realize the goal of a modern and prosperous Indonesia. Following seemingly unending political gridlock, regionalist rebellions during 1956–7, and discontent with Jakarta's exchange rate policies that negatively affected exports from regions outside Java (Bertrand 2004, 36), Sukarno's patience with party politics and liberal democracy was wearing thin. In early 1957, Sukarno concluded that "we have used a wrong system, a wrong style of governance, a style which we call Western democracy" (Elson 2008, 181).

Instead of Western democracy with its system of competition between political parties, Sukarno presented a conception of Indonesia that emphasized consensus and unity under a leader who could discern the will of the people – Guided Democracy. Guided Democracy would be based on the principle of family, with "the Nation of Indonesia...as one family, large, whole not fractured into many pieces. ...What I propose to you, brothers and sisters, is...the principle of family-ness (kekeluargaan), the principle of mutual assistance" (quoted in Elson 2008, 182).

This new way entailed a new structure in governance. The leader of the country – Sukarno – would be advised by an extra-parliamentary Working Cabinet (Kabinet Karya) based on the principle of mutual assistance, and hence made up of all the major factions, including the PKI. There would also be a National Council of representatives made up of functional and regional representatives, including armed forces chiefs. This new structure created an alternative to parliament and moved power away from elected representatives to the executive.

This new system of governance gave the army – headed by Nasution – a legal basis for participation in politics and weakened political parties, giving the army reason to back it. As Elson observed, what the army wanted "was a powerful national executive government to harness the diffuse sources of power, end the demoralizing ideological bickering, instability and corruption of a civilian government, and discipline the country to achieve its promised future" (Elson 2008, 183).

Guided Democracy was not without its critics, the strongest challenge coming from the Revolutionary Government of the Republic of Indonesia (Pemerintah Revolutioner

Republik Indonesia – PRRI) in Sumatra, proclaimed in 1958. The PRRI sought the removal of the Sukarno government, which it saw as Java-centric, excessively leftist, and corrupt. It was also highly critical of the Sukarno government's refusal to grant autonomy to the "Outer Regions." The CIA backed the PRRI, which galvanized Jakarta to act swiftly and firmly; troops from Java were sent to put down the PRRI, which was compromised by its ties to a foreign agency (Elson 195–196).

Following the suppression of the PRRI, Sukarno suspended the Constituent Assembly in 1959 and decreed a reversion to the Constitution of 1945 with Pancasila as the basis of the state. In 1960, parliament was dissolved and replaced with an appointed parliament. Sukarno and the army attempted to resolve debates on the idea of an Indonesian Islamic state and autonomy in certain regions by force. Initially, the opposition had no reply that could seriously challenge Sukarno's vision of Indonesia.

Having relied on force to establish Guided Democracy, Sukarno found that he was dependent on the military. He tried to counterbalance them by cultivating a closer relationship with the PKI. As PKI influence began to grow and infiltrate various sectors of society and the armed forces, particularly the air force, the army pushed back.

Events on the night of 30 September 1965 allowed Suharto, an army general who commanded the Army Strategic Reserve (KOSTRAD), to destroy the PKI. These events are often called the 30 September Movement (Gerakan September 30) or Gestapu (Gerakan September Tiga Puluh) to note the night when a battalion of the palace guard killed six army generals, ostensibly to protect Sukarno from a coup by a group of high-ranking generals allegedly connected to the CIA (Ricklefs 2008, 319). The motivations behind the 30 September Movement have been much debated, but what is clear is that it gave Suharto a chance to eliminate the PKI, remove Sukarno from power, and introduce his New Order.

Suharto's New Order built upon ideas Sukarno had outlined for Guided Democracy. However, it

> greatly modified its institutionalization. His New Order regime was based on a united nation coinciding with a unitary state, guided by the Constitution of 1945 and Pancasila as its foundation. He extended the core institutions of Guided Democracy, centralized political control, and curtailed opposition. By 1968, most of the elements of the political system were in place.
>
> *(Bertrand 2004, 38)*

From the early 1970s, the state began to impose its vision of "Integralist Indonesia" (Elson 2008, 246). Suharto saw the contradictory conceptions of the nation and political competition about them as the major problem faced by Indonesia. As Suharto remarked:

> With the one and only road already there, why must we have so many cars, as many as nine? Why must we have wild speeding and collisions?...It is not necessary to have so many vehicles. But it is not necessary to have only one. Two or three is fine.
>
> *(quoted in Elson 2004, 247)*

Suharto's reflection on politics suggests that he already had a clear conception of Indonesia in his mind (with the one and only road already there), and that politics should be managed, with only a limited number of ideas or choices that were unlikely to cause collisions permitted. The goal was the development of Indonesia and the way to get there, in Suharto's words, was through "unity and integrity of the strongest kind between all layers, all groups, all circles and all generations of the Indonesian nation" (quoted in Elson 2002, 187).

To achieve this unity and integrity, the state weeded out competition and imposed a standardized ideology and organization. For example, in 1974 and 1979, the central government introduced a uniform government bureaucracy across all regional and village governments. These laws remade local structures to conform to one pattern. To minimize friction between workers and owners, unions were organized by sector and united in a federation of unions controlled by the government. Similarly, journalists, civil servants, and other groupings in society were organized to be uniform and easily controlled (Bertrand 2004, 38–39; Elson 2008, 249–253). These efforts served the Archipelago Concept (Wawasan Nusantara), which saw "the whole National Territory with all its contents and resources" as "one Territorial Unity, one place, one sphere of life and unity of norms of the whole of the People, and be the asset and property of the People" (quoted in Elson 2008, 254).

Wawasan Nusantara, and the efforts of the Indonesian state under Suharto, could be characterized as "high modernist," a term used by James Scott. High Modernist ideology, Scott explains, is

> a strong, one might even say muscle-bound, version of the self-confidence about scientific and technical process, the expansion of production, the growing satisfaction of human needs, the mastery of nature (including human nature), and above all, the rational design of social order commensurate with the scientific understanding of natural laws.
>
> *(Scott 1998, 4)*

In a state that sought to control social order, diversity was seen as a potential threat to harmony. Nationals of foreign descent were to be assimilated by removing elements that could cause lack of harmony with "indigenous" Indonesians (Elson 2008, 253–4). Chinese in Indonesia found themselves and their culture the target of this push for uniformity and control; they faced pressure to change their names to more indigenous sounding ones, had to show their letter of proof of Indonesian citizenship (SBKRI) for all matters related to the bureaucracy, and had a special symbol on their identity cards (Dahana 2004, 58). This suggests that Chinese were to be made part of the Indonesian nation by removal of markers of their non-indigenous ethnicity (their Chinese names) but were still not accepted as truly Indonesian and were to be marked as such. While these methods of control were modern and aligned with New Order thinking, one can also point to deeper roots for the treatment of the Chinese.

It is likely that perceptions and historical tensions from the colonial period shaped the way the state perceived the Chinese. Adrian Vickers has pointed out that "Java has had a history of strong anti-Chinese racism, marked by periodic anti-Chinese riots at times of general unrest" (2022, 5). Vickers draws attention to the period from 1811 to 1830 when Dutch colonial policies separated the Chinese into primarily economic roles such as tax farming and moneylending, roles which the Chinese continued to hold into the period of the cultivation system of 1830–1870. These did not endear the Chinese to the Javanese population (Vickers 2022, 5). Philip Kuhn observed that Indonesia's "Chinese problem" stems from "long-nurtured feelings of status humiliation and resentment among indigenous Indonesians, feelings that have survived the fall of colonialism" (2008, 291). If New Order thinking on the Chinese was shaped by these experiences and set Chinese apart from indigenous Indonesians, we can glimpse within the civic nationalism of the New Order an underlying layer of ethno-nationalism.

While marginalization of Chinese in Indonesia during the New Order was linked to not being fully admitted into the nation, East Timor and Papua's marginalization had to do with being forced into Indonesia against their will.

East Timor was integrated into Indonesia in 1975, even though it did not identify with Indonesia. Its incorporation was by way of an invasion and ongoing military action. During the initial years of occupation, populations suspected of supporting the resistance organized by the Revolutionary Front of Independent East Timor (Fretilin), a socialist organization that enjoyed the backing of many East Timorese, suffered execution or relocation into camps where they could be monitored.

In addition to military measures, the New Order imposed measures to bring East Timor in line with its totalizing vision. For example, a new governmental structure was introduced to East Timor that mirrored the model used throughout Indonesia. At the village level, the new expectations and responsibilities of village heads had little resonance in East Timor, as they followed the structure of Javanese villages (Bertrand 2004, 141). Local norms had to give way to the national model.

In schools, uniformity was encouraged by implementing a curriculum taught in the Indonesian language, where previously schools had used Portuguese or Tetum. Children were taught the Pancasila and learned about Indonesian heroes, symbols, and common culture, with an emphasis on Javanese culture. To implement this policy, hundreds of teachers were brought in from other regions, especially from Java and Sulawesi (Bertrand 2004, 140).

Accompanying the teachers were many other migrants, who came either independently or as part of a government-sponsored transmigration program. They came for government jobs and to conduct business. Over time, the main towns of Dili and Baucau were populated by non-Timorese majorities (Bertrand 2004, 140). This migration had the effect of making East Timor appear more like the rest of New Order Indonesia, at least in the towns.

The New Order also introduced a policy of population control in East Timor. East Timor received 20 percent more family planning agents per person than other parts of Indonesia. Injectable contraceptives were promoted as vaccines against tetanus and were used at much higher rates than elsewhere in Indonesia (Bertrand 2004, 140). This approach to population control suggests the state's determination to impose itself in the face of local resistance.

These government programs and the presence of the Indonesian military marginalized the local population and created a strong sense of nationhood in opposition to Indonesia. In 1999, when given a choice to be independent or part of Indonesia, East Timorese overwhelmingly chose independence.

Papua was likewise absorbed by Indonesia against the wishes of its people. After Indonesian independence, Papua remained in Dutch hands. However, in 1963, following negotiations between the Dutch and Indonesians, the region was integrated into Indonesia. The Papuans were not a party to these negotiations. In 1969, a plebiscite called the "The Act of Free Choice" was held to ascertain whether Papuans preferred integration or self-determination. Papuan delegates chose integration but there were allegations that the process was not free since delegates were either selected or intimidated by Indonesians to cast their vote in favor of joining Indonesia (Bertrand 2004, 144–149).

As in East Timor, the military had a central role to play in integrating Papua into Indonesia. The military punished dissent brutally, burning houses and subjecting civilians to torture, kidnappings, and shootings. In addition to military measures, the Indonesian government encouraged transmigration to Papua. In 1977, it had a target of 1.7 million migrants to Papua, which would have made migrants the majority in the province (the estimated population of indigenous Papuans was 1.2 million). Migration changed the demographics of Papua and served to make it more like other parts of Indonesia.

Papuan culture was perceived by the state to be an obstacle to becoming proper, modern citizens of Indonesia. The government sought to change this culture through campaigns targeting Papuan culture, such as a campaign in the Papuan highlands to persuade people there to abandon their koteka (penis-sheaths) and wear clothes considered modern. A clear indication of the government's goal of cultural assimilation can be found in a statement made by Foreign Minister Mochtar Kusmaatmaja on Australian television:

> Culture is a changing thing, and I think it's a mistake to want to preserve a certain culture and freeze it at a certain time...What we are doing in Irian Jaya is to introduce the Irianese, which are admittedly of a different cultural level, into the mainstream of Indonesian life...They will be part of the Indonesian nation.
>
> (quoted in Bertrand 2004, 153)

By setting Indonesian norms and expectations as the standard that Papuans had to measure up to, the Indonesian state came to act like a colonial regime. Through movements like the OPM (Organisasi Papua Merdeka/Free Papua Organization), Papuans rejected the marginalization of their culture and resisted being forced to integrate. Papuan nationalism, stimulated by earlier Dutch policies in the 1950s and early 1960s that aimed at cultivating an elite to put Papua on the path to self-determination, and strengthened by Indonesian rule, took the form of an ethno-nationalist movement.

The cases of East Timor and Papua show the limits of the idea of Indonesia. The means of integration chosen by the Indonesian state – primarily military repression – reinforced the conceptions of the East Timorese and Papuan nations.

As in East Timor and Papua, marginalization led to an ethno-nationalist movement in Aceh. Acehnese nationalists supported the idea of an Indonesian nation from the outset and continued to imagine themselves as part of the Republic even after their vision of an Islamic Indonesia was sidelined. They settled for local autonomy where they could at least be a part of Indonesia on their own terms. When that too was removed as an option, the Indonesian project lost its appeal. In 1976, the separatist Gerakan Aceh Merdeka (GAM; Free Aceh Movement) appeared in Aceh. Its leader, Hasan Tiro, saw Indonesia as a "cloak to cover up Javanese colonialism" (quoted in Elson 2008, 268). GAM did not have much support among the local population in the 1970s, perhaps because it barely mentioned Islam and did not have the backing of clerics; its main grievances had to do with exploitation of national resources by the center and use of military force to maintain control (Bertrand 2004, 171). Aceh remained part of the Republic, tied to the center by Acehnese elites who rose to high positions in the government and military.

However, from the early 1970s, economic exploitation of Aceh's natural gas resources by Jakarta and foreign investors without tangible benefits accruing to Aceh increased tensions with the center. The continued presence of troops in Aceh to protect industrial plants heightened these tensions. When GAM reappeared in 1989, it had much wider support but was still not a widespread armed insurgency. The disproportionate response of the ruling regime, sending thousands of troops to Aceh to put down the rebellion, pushed the Acehnese away from a broader Indonesian national identity. Throughout the 1990s, Indonesia maintained troops in Aceh and arbitrary killings reinforced the sense of injustice and separate identity felt by the Acehnese. In Aceh, as in East Timor and Papua, state violence spurred an ethno-nationalist response. The military had held the Republic together for decades, but it eventually tore it apart.

The dual function (dwi fungsi) that Suharto saw for the military as "an armed tool of the state and as a functional group to achieve the goals of the revolution" (quoted in Elson 2008, 258) betrayed the fatal flaw in the New Order. It was a conception of Indonesia that required coercion, and one that could not be maintained without it.

1998: collapse of the New Order

For all its faults, the New Order did deliver a period of sustained economic growth for Indonesia. This period of growth saw the rise of a middle class that sought to participate in the political process. From the late 1980s, new NGOs began to campaign for more rights. Suharto was caught between these liberalizing forces and a military that opposed changes that threatened its role in the New Order. Realizing that Indonesian society was changing, Suharto began to build connections with civilian groups and sought to disassociate the Golkar (Partai Golongan Karya/Party of Functional Groups) from military influence. These efforts did not stop the calls for more freedom and a rethinking of the basis of the New Order. When the Asian currency crisis struck in 1997, it shook the New Order to its core. The economic crisis focused attention on the failings of the state. Amidst an atmosphere of discontent, Suharto still managed to win the elections in 1997. However, he lost credibility when he appointed a cabinet packed with his family and cronies. He still held on, but the end was in sight. The shooting of Trisakti University students at a peaceful protest was the last straw. It sparked violent riots, notably in Jakarta and Surakarta. Suharto family enterprises and Chinese were the primary targets. Over a thousand people died in Jakarta in the riots. On 21 May 1998, Suharto publicly resigned, and the long years of the New Order came to a violent and ignominious close (Ricklefs 2008, 380–381). At the end of the twentieth century, Indonesians once again found themselves having to reimagine the nation.

Conclusion

This chapter has sought to outline the ways in which the Indonesian nation has been imagined in the twentieth century. The main streams of nationalism that emerged during this time – Pancasila, Islamic, and ethno-nationalism – competed to become the dominant vision of the state of Indonesia. Each of these nationalisms was in both competition and conversation with the others. Historical circumstances and ideas shaped the possibilities and limits of Indonesian nationalisms. At critical points in the twentieth century, Indonesians have contemplated and negotiated the values of their imagined political community. At these times, some dichotomies that have shaped the idea of the nation in Indonesia have emerged: national versus regional, religious versus secular, indigenous versus foreign, and modern versus backward. These oppositional categories have informed how Indonesians have seen their nation and will likely continue to define the conversation on nationalism in Southeast Asia's largest and most populous state.

References

Anderson, Benedict. 2016. *Imagined Communities: Reflections on the Origin and Spread of Nationalism.* London: Verso.
Bertrand, Jacques. 2004. *Nationalism and Ethnic Conflict in Indonesia.* Cambridge, UK; New York: Cambridge University Press.

Dahana, A. 2004. "*Pri* and Non-*Pri* Relations in the Reform Era: A *Pribumi* Perspective." In *Ethnic Relations and Nation-building in Southeast Asia: The Case of the Ethnic Chinese*, edited by Leo Suryadinata, 45–65. Singapore: ISEAS.
Djalins, Upik. 2015. "Becoming Indonesian Citizens: Subjects, Citizens, and Land Ownership in the Netherlands Indies, 1930–37." *Journal of Southeast Asian Studies* 46 (2), 227–245.
Elson, R.E. 2002. "In Fear of the People Suharto and the Justification of State-sponsored Violence under the New Order." In *Roots of Violence in Indonesia: Contemporary Violence in Historical Perspective*, edited by Edited by Freek Colombijn and J. Thomas Lindblad, 173-196. Leiden: KITLV Press; Singapore: ISEAS.
Elson, R.E. 2008. *The Idea of Indonesia: A History*. Cambridge, UK; New York: Cambridge University Press.
Fakih, Farabi. 2012. "Conservative Corporatist: Nationalist Thoughts of Aristocrats: The ideas of Soetatmo Soeriokoesoemo and Noto Soeroto." *Bijdragen tot de Taal-, Land- en Volkenkunde* 168 (4): 420–444.
Fogg, Kevin W. 2019. "Indonesian Islamic Socialism and its South Asian Roots." *Modern Asian Studies* 53 (6): 1736–1761.
Formichi, Chiara. 2010. "Pan-Islam and Religious Nationalism: The Case of Kartosuwiryo and Negara Islam Indonesia." *Indonesia* 90 (October): 125–146.
Jones, Russell. 1973. "Earl, Logan and 'Indonesia.'" *Archipel* 6: 93–118.
Kuhn, Philip A. 2008. *Chinese among Others: Emigration in Modern Times*. Lanham: Rowman and Littlefield Publishers, Inc.
Poeze, Harry A. 2009. "The Cold War in Indonesia, 1948." *Journal of Southeast Asian Studies* 40 (3): 497–517.
Pollmann, Tessel. 2000. "The Unreal War: The Indonesian Revolution through the Eyes of Dutch Novelists and Reporters." *Indonesia* 69 (April): 93–106.
Reid, Anthony. 1974. *The Indonesian National Revolution: 1945–1950*. Hawthorn, Victoria: Longman.
Ricklefs, Merle Calvin. 2008. *History of Modern Indonesia since c. 1200*. Stanford: Stanford University Press.
Scott, James. 1998. *Seeing like a State: How Certain Schemes to Improve the Human Condition Have Failed*. New Haven: Yale University Press.
Soekarno, 1970. *Nationalism, Islam and Marxism*. Translated by Karel H. Warouw and Peter Weldon. Ithaca: Modern Indonesia Project, Southeast Asia Program, Dept. of Asian Studies, Cornell University.
Van der Meer, Arnout. 2020. *Performing Power: Cultural Hegemony, Identity, and Resistance in Colonial Indonesia*. Ithaca: Cornell University Press.
Vickers, Adrian. 2022. "Erasing and Re-inscribing Chinese into Indonesian History." *Asian Ethnicity* 24 (1): 78–92. https://www.tandfonline.com/doi/full/10.1080/14631369.2022.2069083.

32

A JOURNEY THROUGH CAMBODIAN NATIONALISM

Political, elite and popular

Kimly Ngoun

Introduction

Cambodian nationalism has made a long journey from the period of French colonial rule to the present. It was first constructed by the colonial rulers as an ideology to justify their colonialism, the so-called "civilising mission" (Edwards 2007). It was subsequently adopted and adapted by circles of Cambodian political, educated and religious elites, who exploited printing and broadcasting technologies to shape and construct notions of modern Cambodian nationhood and nationalism.

During the colonial period and Prince Norodom Sihanouk's Sangkum Reastr Niyum [Popular Socialist Community] regime (1955–1970), Cambodian nationalism was largely cultural nationalism, with the reviving of old cultural markers and tradition, particularly the symbolism of the ancient Angkorian temples, and the attachment of new nationalist meanings to those cultural icons to serve the colonial and post-colonial political projects (Edwards 2007; Ngoun 2018).

Cambodian nationalism as an ideology became predominantly an issue of race when a small group of Cambodian political elites with communist revolutionary tendencies started their struggles for political power. Saloth Sâr, known to the world as Pol Pot, dreamed of building a utopian Cambodia based on an authentic or pure Khmer race with communist revolutionary ideas and ideals. His Khmer ethno-nationalism influenced his regime's policies when he came to power in April 1975 and began the reign of terror, causing the death of nearly two million people. Pol Pot's Democratic Kampuchea (DK) regime controlled the country for less than four years before it was ousted from Phnom Penh on 7 January, 1979.

A new Vietnam-backed regime, the People's Republic of Kampuchea (1979–1989), was established and throughout the 1980s, notions of the Cambodian nation and nationalism were caught up in the bloody civil war and Cold War contexts. Cambodian warring factions propagated and interpreted nationalist discourses of defending the Khmer race and territory against their factional and foreign enemies, to give a nationalist framework to their political and military struggles.

After the Paris Peace Agreements in 1991, followed by the UN-administered general elections in 1993 which led to the establishment of a democratic constitution enshrining a multi-party political system, Cambodian nationalism became a political resource in electoral politics and party politics, mobilising popular support to win elections. Opposition political parties often propagated a nationalism discourse portraying the ruling Cambodian People's Party (CPP) as serving foreign interests and failing to defend border territories. They amplified issues of race, border territories and Vietnamese immigrants as their main electoral strategy to challenge the legitimacy of the CPP.

The CPP countered those narratives by promoting its achievements for the Cambodian nation in liberating the people from Pol Pot's murderous regime, building peace and developing public infrastructure and the economy. Throughout the 1990s and 2000s, print and broadcast media were the means by which those political parties promoted their nationalist narratives and crafted nationalist images for their parties and leaders.

2008 was a watershed year for Cambodian nationalism. Between 2008 and 2011, Cambodia and Thailand had a dispute over Preah Vihear Temple and a few other Khmer ancient temples on the Cambodia-Thailand border, leading to clashes and a tense military stand-off. The Cambodian state invested heavily in nationalist projects over the border temple dispute, to enhance the state elites' legitimacy and mobilise mass participation and support of the government's campaign against the Thai "aggressor" (Ngoun 2016). The Cambodian state-led nationalist campaign triggered the explosion of widespread participatory popular nationalism in the country, especially in Phnom Penh and provincial cities.

Before 2008, discussions and exchanges of views about politics and national affairs among the general public were limited due to fear of political repercussions, and tended to divide along the lines of political parties. However, with the opening created by the Preah Vihear border dispute, ordinary people throughout Phnom Penh and provincial cities became empowered to confidently talk about national matters. During the border conflict, people in a plethora of places discussed, exchanged views and updated each other on the conflict with Thailand. Some even took action to materialise their nationalist sentiment, using their own resources to participate in the defence of their Cambodian nation.

This participatory popular nationalism did not end when Cambodia and Thailand managed to end the conflict and restore relations in 2011; it has continued to evolve and manifest in various forms of civic engagement, such as medical nationalism, sporting nationalism and environmental nationalism. Aided by the widespread use of smartphones, the internet and social media, and by the country's young population, Cambodia's popular nationalism has become multifaceted and manifests not only in physical settings but also online.

This chapter aims to provide an account of the journey through Cambodian nationalism, from the colonial era to the present. It examines discursive notions and discourses of nationalism and the purposes of different stakeholders relying on nationalism, such as the French colonial rulers, Cambodian political elites and ordinary urban people in Phnom Penh. This chapter argues that different stakeholders in Cambodia have used nationalism as a political resource together with other resources, or as an alternative political resource when other resources are constrained, to augment their power and realise their varied political, social and economic needs and visions for the Cambodian nation.

The research for this chapter followed qualitative methods. It relied on published and unpublished materials, online sources, the author's observations and interviews carried out in Phnom Penh between 2012 and 2014. Following this introduction, this chapter has five sections: Nationalism as (alternative) political resource, Political nationalism, Elite nationalism, Popular nationalism and Conclusion.

Nationalism as an (alternative) political resource

To understand Cambodian nationalism, I propose to study it as an (alternative) "political resource". Using this concept, I frame nationalism as a political resource that is relatively available and accessible to a wide range of people, elites and non-elites, who may rely on it to obtain their political objectives (when access to other available resources is constrained or lacking). Nationalism is a resource that can be tapped by the powerful and the weak alike to augment power and achieve desired political outcomes. As a mode of influencing others by appealing to what is shared in common, its effects are achieved through means as varied as discourses, symbolism, propaganda, images, campaigns, performances and enactments.

So why is nationalism powerful and appealing to different stakeholders? Why do many people identify with it? Anderson (1983) elegantly argues that nationalism's appeal to modern people lies in its evocation of sentiments of commonality or identification. Smith (1991) grounds his analysis of the political appeal of nationalism as deriving from its representation of shared experience, or "collective cultural phenomena". Greenfeld (2006, 205) argues that nationalism has potency because it is based on "the principles of popular sovereignty and egalitarianism". For Hutchinson (2003, 71), the nation, whose shadow is nationalism, is a powerful notion because of its wide recognition as "the hegemonic cultural and political unit of the modern period".

In searching for the reason for nationalism's appeal, it is also beneficial to study nationalism as a political resource. Briefly, I would argue that politics is a negotiation for control over available resources (Stoker 1998; Deutsch 1961). The resources are diverse, including material, financial, coercive, ideological, symbolic, communicational and organisational power (see, for example, Giddens 1981; Brady et al. 1995). Access to these resources is available through a variety of political strategies: seizure of the state in coups or elections; mass mobilisation politics (Deutsch 1961; Lipsky 1968); patron-client politics (Scott 1972); informal politics (Chatterjee 2004; Bayat 1997); network-based politics (McCargo 2005); politics of gift (Hughes 2006); money politics (Kang 2002; Weiss 2016); populist politics (Calhoun 1988; Weyland 2001); political legitimacy (Beetham 1991; Barker 2004); weapons of the weak or everyday resistance (Scott 1985) and everyday politics (Kerkvliet 2005).

However, these political strategies all have their limits, in that access to resources remains socially situated and unevenly distributed in relation to one's capacity and socio-economic situation (Mann 1984; Brady et al. 1995). Moreover, desire for such resources is situationally constructed: resources may be differently valued in relation to one's particular social position, desires, needs and concerns (Bourdieu 1990; Yuval-Davis 2006).

Therefore, no matter how advantaged a social actor might be, in the negotiation over control for resources, political ambitions are frequently frustrated. A well-connected elite may lack a constituency over which to exert influence; a leader who seizes power may be unable to gain approval; materially well-off people may be frustrated by a lack of control or sense of belonging; geographically or socially marginal groups may be excluded from access to services. In these circumstances, nationalism presents itself as an alternative means for mobilising, controlling or attracting desired resources. In this sense, I regard nationalism as an (alternative) political resource, one which individuals or groups may resort to when their ambition to obtain control over resources by other available political means is thwarted.

This conceptual framework is highly appropriate for the study of the politics of nationalism in Cambodia. It helps us to understand the discursive contexts of individuals or groups who identify with national symbols, identities and imagery. We can also gain better insights into the nuances of what nation and nationalism mean for different political, social and spatial segments of Cambodia. In contemporary Cambodia, where access to financial, organisational and institutional resources and other mechanisms is constrained, political elites and non-elites alike often employ nationalism as an (alternative) political resource in their pursuit of political, social and economic empowerment.

Political nationalism

Cambodge: a French construction

Cambodia became a French protectorate in 1863 and gained independence in 1953. Notions of the Cambodian nation and nationalism as an ideology derived from their construction by the French colonial rulers in order to justify their "civilising mission". The French promoted Angkor, studied Cambodia's past and constructed important monuments such as the Grand Palace, the National Museum and the Buddhist Institute in Phnom Penh.

Extensive, ground-breaking work by Penny Edwards in her book *Cambodge: The Cultivation of a Nation: 1860–1945* investigates the contexts, processes, discourses and actors during the French colonial period that gave rise to notions about the Cambodian nation that remain politically influential to this day (see Edwards 2007). The book places great importance on the roles of the French colonial officials, architects, artisans and engineers in modernising Phnom Penh. They oversaw many construction projects that greatly transformed the city's spatial landscape, and some of their constructions and urban landscaping, such as the Naga Bridge and Wat Phnom, integrated Angkor's architectural style, conjuring up imagery of a link between Phnom Penh and Angkor. The French thus effectively situated the power of Angkor in Phnom Penh in order to justify their colonial presence in Cambodia (ibid., 44–50).

Moreover, the French constructed an official national narrative for Cambodia, with the promotion of Angkor as the pre-eminent national symbol and the Khmer as a declining race rescued from extinction by the French. While this constructed notion of the Cambodian nation was a political resource serving French colonial interests, it started to influence a small group of Cambodian elites educated in French schools in Phnom Penh, Saigon and Paris. They started to imagine the cultural "geo-body" of their country and their race as a nation, with Angkor Wat as the symbol of Cambodian national and cultural sovereignty (Edwards 2007, 44–50; Osborne 2008, 87–89).

Anti-colonial nationalism

Colonial encounter led to the imagining of a nation in Cambodia, as elsewhere in Southeast Asia (Anderson 1998), which gave rise to anti-colonial nationalist movements for independence. The abstract discourses of the Cambodian nation were further promoted by the Phnom Penh Khmer vernacular nationalist newspaper Nagara Vatta (Nokor Wat/Angkor Wat), established by nationalists Son Ngoc Thanh and Pach Chhoeun in 1936. They were also propagated by the Buddhist Institute's monthly publications of the Khmer-language journal *Kambuja Surya*. Chandler (1986, 83) writes that Nagara Vatta's weekly circulation of 5,000 copies shows that it was widely read. The publication of the newspaper and the journal in Khmer vernacular language spread the seeds of nationalism more widely and brought to light more terms and notions related to the nation and nationalism.

Observers of Cambodian history suggest that nationalism flourished in Phnom Penh in the 1930s and 1940s. Several school clubs, newspaper groups and literary associations were established, with their members representing different segments of urban society, especially the emerging class of neak-cheh-doeng [intellectuals] (see Edwards 2007, 15, 210–241). In other countries as well, the intelligentsia is widely known to have contributed significantly to nationalist projects in colonial and post-colonial societies (see Shils 1960; Chatterjee 1993, 35). Their bilingual literacy allowed them access to various foreign ideas of state, culture, nation and nationalism (Anderson 1983, 116–119), which they could copy or localise to suit their country's conditions. Their bilingualism also enabled them to see their own language as integral in protecting their cultural realm from the colonial rulers (Chatterjee 1993, 7).

Anti-colonial nationalism in Cambodia was also heightened during the above-mentioned periods by domestic and global events – Thailand's reoccupation of Battambang and Sisophon, the decline of French military influence in Indochina, and Japan's expanding imperialism into Southeast Asia. There were public protests in Phnom Penh and resistance against French colonial rule in the countryside. Notably, a demonstration in 1942 in Phnom Penh saw hundreds of Buddhist monks joining with thousands of other demonstrators calling on the French to release two Cambodian nationalists, Achar Hem Chieu and Nuon Duong – the protest was called the "Umbrella War" because of the umbrellas the monks carried. Cambodia finally achieved independence from France in 1953.

Genocide nationalism

Cambodian nationalism became an issue of race when a small group of Cambodian political elites with communist revolutionary tendencies started their struggle for political power. When they controlled the country, the Khmer Rouge labelled people in different categories, with urban residents as "new people" and rural people as "base people" [neak moultanh] (Kiernan 2002, 485–486). The urban residents were not considered to represent the authentic Khmer race and the revolutionary ideal. Therefore, the Khmer Rouge DK treated them cruelly, and under its rule over 1.5 million of Cambodia's eight million people died from execution, overwork, starvation and disease (Kiernan 1996; Hinton 1998a, 93–94). Approximately, 650,000 of these were "new people" (Kiernan 2002, 486).

The DK regime was led by a group of educated Cambodian elites educated in Phnom Penh, Paris and Bangkok who intended to turn Cambodia into a utopian, egalitarian agrarian society. How did these intellectuals become ultra-nationalists and perpetrators of such heinous crimes? Edwards (2007, 1–12) suggests that their ideas were rooted in the authenticity discourse of Khmerness, with an emphasis on glorification of the Angkorian period. DK leaders believed that they could restore Cambodia to its past grandeur by eliminating anything and anyone not considered to be authentically Khmer.

Barnett (1990) and Kiernan (2001) emphasise Cambodian historical and nationalist discourses. The country was seen to have once occupied vast areas of land covering much of present-day Thailand, Laos and southern Vietnam; it had been greatly reduced in size due to annexation of its territory by Thailand and Vietnam. Looking at a modern map of Cambodia and its immediate neighbours, Khmer Rouge leaders must have felt sad and angry about lost territories, and at the same time fearful that Thailand and particularly Vietnam would continue to swallow up the remainder of Cambodia's land.

The new regime, as a result, pursued irredentism by waging war against Vietnam in the hope of restoring Kampuchea krom [lower Cambodia]. They also purged a huge number of people working for the regime whom they accused of acting as spies for Vietnam and other countries. Hinton (1998a) and Hinton (1998b) argue that DK leaders' ultra-nationalism and brutality originated from a "Cambodian cultural model of disproportionate revenge" and Cambodian socio-cultural beliefs related to "face and honour".

While I generally agree with these arguments, I think attention should also be paid to the roles of cities in influencing and shaping the Khmer Rouge leaders' perspectives of Khmer ethnicity and nation. The urban spaces of Phnom Penh and Paris enabled the young communist-educated elites to establish connections, meet like-minded people and empower their movement. If Saloth Sar, whom the world came to know as Pol Pot, had not pursued his studies in Phnom Penh and Paris, the views of Khmer ethnicity and nationhood which informed his policies when he came to power would have been different, and perhaps he would not have been able to rise to political prominence.

Pol Pot and several other DK leaders were born in the provinces but moved to cities to pursue their studies in their youth. Pol Pot was born Saloth Sar in Kampong Thom province; Ieng Sary and Son Sen in Kampuchea krom; Khieu Samphan in Svay Rieng; and Nuon Chea in Battambang. Pol Pot became friends with Ieng Sary when they were students in Phnom Penh; their wives, sisters Khieu Ponnary and Khieu Thirith, were also students at Lycée Sisowath, as was Khieu Samphan. Pol Pot, Ieng Sary and Khieu Samphan further pursued their studies in Paris in the 1950s and became active in the Khmer Students' Association there. As for Nuon Chea, he attended Thammasat University in Bangkok, where he became involved with the Thai communist movement (see Chandler 1992; Heder and Tittemore 2001; Kiernan 2004).

The experience of being away from rural villages and encountering urban culture must have had some degree of influence on the young Saloth Sar and other future Khmer Rouge leaders, and must have led them to compare life and culture in their villages with what they saw in these new places. This may have led them to redefine their own identities in relation to the broader identities of space, ethnicity, culture and nation to which they were exposed in the urban setting. They may have found the ethnic and cultural diversity of Phnom Penh alien and contaminated, less authentically Khmer than rural peasants. Put succinctly, urban living may have engendered an identity crisis that led them to adopt extreme views of what did and did not constitute Khmer cultural, ethnic and national identity. There is a literature documenting similar cases elsewhere – young people from rural areas becoming fundamentalists after encountering urban modernity and feeling uprooted from their own traditions (see, for example, Pye 1956; Muzaffar 1987).

The social spaces of the Lycée Sisowath in Phnom Penh and dormitories and universities in Paris allowed Saloth Sar to find other students from rural areas who shared similar views. Through their networks and associations, their shared views gained amplitude and they started to think of rescuing the nation. They began to exploit the urban space to proclaim themselves defenders and saviours of the Cambodian nation and to recruit people into their political movement.

Elite nationalism

Prince Norodom Sihanouk: cultural nationalism for post-colonial nation-building

Like other leaders of post-colonial states, Prince Norodom Sihanouk took great pride in attaining independence for his country; he proudly referred to himself as the Father of Cambodia's national independence. He aspired to build the Cambodian nation and to achieve a similar level of political and economic progress and modernity to that of those "civilized" states in the West. Sihanouk's immediate political priority after independence, to build the nation, was also driven by the fact that he needed a nation that would provide him with a new framework or an arena to work with, in order to rule Cambodia. He could not go backwards; he could not adopt the pre-colonial political order or state system, because the colonial encounter had altered the political relationship between the ruler and the ruled and introduced new concepts of power, politics, state and nation. Besides, post-independence countries were set in forward motion. That meant he needed to work with the notion of nation in order to define Cambodia's place in the world of nation-states.

However, Prince Sihanouk's modern nation-building aspirations soon faced the typical major constraints of post-colonial states. First, he was unable to forge peaceful relationships with Cambodia's neighbours, Thailand and South Vietnam. Sihanouk was deeply suspicious and disdainful of Thai Prime Minister Field Marshal Sarit Thanarat and South Vietnamese President Ngo Dinh Diem, who likewise disliked the Cambodian leader and accused him of being "a stalking-horse for communism in the region" (see Osborne 1994, 151–152). Sihanouk accused both leaders of being behind the unsuccessful assassination attempts and coup plots against him in 1959 (Ibid, 108–111).

The second major challenge to Sihanouk's nation-building was political fragmentation among the Cambodian political elites. His political authority was challenged by other political groups vying for control of post-independence Cambodia. The political forces that presented formidable hurdles to Sihanouk's rule were the Democratic Party, Khmer communists with links to communist North Vietnam, and Son Ngoc Thanh's Khmer Serei [Free Khmer] movement (for details, see Osborne 1994, 108–111).

The third major constraint was the repositioning of Cambodia's foreign policy in the new international political context of the Cold War and tension between the world's superpowers. He adopted neutrality and non-alignment as his guiding foreign policy principle – a middle path of being neither ally nor enemy to the two competing political blocs. However, he found it increasingly difficult to maintain this path as the domestic, regional and international political situation grew increasingly complex and fluid. As a result, his foreign policy veered off course. As leader of a small, politically fragile state surrounded by unfriendly neighbours, Sihanouk had limited space and resources to manoeuvre between the superpowers.

Caught between his aspiration to build a modern nation and the constraints on his political leadership, Prince Sihanouk had to rely on, among other things, nationalism as one of the important (alternative) political resources to achieve his political objectives. Geertz (1973, 237) notes that ruling elites in post-colonial countries relied greatly on nationalism for nation-building. Nationalism became "normalized as a universal project in the post-colonial world" (Gupta 1998, 14).

Prince Sihanouk made use of the cultural politics of representing the nation to help imagine it in ways that suited his political purposes. His Sangkum regime sponsored various projects and activities to invent Khmer national identity, from linking it with Angkor to co-opting disparate popular cultural fragments, reproducing them and according them new national meanings. Urban planners designed the Phnom Penh urban landscape, monuments and buildings in such a way as to invoke a sense of the city's continuity and links with Angkor. Government officers in the arts sector were tasked to go to various provinces and remote parts of Cambodia to collect and document local popular dances, music, folklore, arts and crafts, and rituals, as part of the state's project of promoting and preserving Khmer cultural practices and traditions, so prevent them from becoming extinct. This project was institutionalised and promoted through the newly established state-owned Royal University of Fine Arts and various state-affiliated troupes of performers (Daravuth and Muan 2001).

These reinvented and reinterpreted cultural symbols were an integral part of image-making and the face of Sihanouk's Sangkum. State officials and media compared samai Sangkum Reastr Niyum [the period of the Sangkum regime] to the Angkorian period, which the Cambodians widely consider their country's golden era and thus a significant source of national pride.

Phnom Penh was a favourite site for Sihanouk's cult of nation-building – the face of his new nation-state. Landmarks like the Independence Monument, the Olympic National Stadium, Chatumuk Conference Hall and several universities were constructed there during the Sangkum period. Traditional Khmer architectural concepts were integrated into several of those buildings as part of the creation of modern concepts of building, space and people (see Daravuth and Muan 2001, 3–23). Wide, orderly parks adorned with flowers and lined trees were also integrated into the regime's urban landscaping.

Those grand urban public buildings and beautiful parks, and the concept of an orderly city, allowed Sihanouk to communicate a nation-building narrative which portrayed his Sangkum regime as restoring the nation to its former pride and splendour. The urban spatial transformation was publicised as a representation of a high level of national achievement comparable to that of the Khmer Empire of Angkor. In this context, nationalism was an alternative political resource for the prince's nation-building and embodiment of the Cambodian nation.

Prime Minister Hun Sen: nationalism for political legitimacy

Rising to power from a non-elite background after the fall of Pol Pot's DK regime in 1979, Prime Minister Hun Sen's political legitimacy has relied greatly on the narrative of his government's important role in liberating the country, saving the people from the horrendous Khmer Rouge regime, and preventing DK from coming back to power. However, as Cambodia has gone through major political and socio-economic transformations since the early 1990s, the prime minister has been facing new challenges to his right to rule, requiring him to carefully construct and reconstruct his political legitimacy.

The first major constraint took place during Cambodia's transition from one-party state to multi-party electoral democracy in the early 1990s, when Hun Sen's CPP lost the 1993 general election to the royalist Funcinpec Party of Prince Norodom Ranariddh, King Norodom Sihanouk's son. Realising that Funcinpec's election victory derived largely from capitalising on Sihanouk's mass popularity, and that his own political legitimacy needed to rely on electoral popular support, Hun Sen began to establish reciprocal relations with rural people, in a similar fashion to Sihanouk during the Sangkum regime. Through his own and his party's financial sponsorship of various rural and agricultural development projects, Hun Sen managed to turn rural areas into a strong CPP electoral base. He used the launches or inaugurations of those projects to present himself as a guarantor of peace and builder of post-conflict Cambodia, which became major sources of his political legitimacy.

When Hun Sen, at the time the second prime minister, ousted first prime minister Prince Ranariddh in 1997, some critics alleged that this was illegitimate and disrespected the royal family. To defend his action, Hun Sen declared that the CPP was also a royalist party, going even further to sponsor and propagate a narrative depicting himself as the reincarnation of sixteenth-century King Kân, a commoner who usurped the throne, suggesting that he also came from a royal background (see Norén-Nilsson 2013). In Cambodian society, the monarchy represents not only moral authority but also culture and tradition; therefore, having royal connections or representing the monarchy enhances a leader's political legitimacy.

However, as argued by White (2005, 4), that legitimacy is "partial, never total". Prime Minister Hun Sen remains vulnerable to political challenges and criticism from political opponents and critics, who have long accused his government of being submissive to the Vietnamese government. The rise of Hun Sen and many senior members of his government to power under Vietnam's patronage in 1979, after the Vietnamese army had helped overthrow Pol Pot's DK regime, has given rise to such allegations. According to this anti-government nationalist narrative, Hun Sen is not a nationalist and cannot defend Cambodia's national borders. Allegations that the prime minister is a puppet of Vietnam or has been ceding border territories to Vietnam have appeared in newspapers affiliated with opposition political parties, and on well-known anti-government nationalist online blogs such as KI-Media, Khmerisation and Sacravatoons.

Before the eruption of the Preah Vihear border conflict with Thailand in 2008, Hun Sen was vulnerable on nationalist grounds, despite being overwhelmingly popular at the time due to his patronage politics. Critics frequently pointed to the nationalist question as his Achilles heel, and in the decade leading up to the border conflict he was relentlessly portrayed as a servant of Vietnam rather than of the Cambodian people. Since the early 2000s at least, Hun Sen's opponents have concentrated almost exclusively on his lack of nationalist credentials as their mass mobilisation strategy to contest elections, while he has been constrained in vigorously countering that perception by the fear of damaging relations with neighbouring countries.

The eruption of the Preah Vihear border dispute was a perfect opportunity for Hun Sen to counter domestic critics and opposition politicians, and at the same time construct political legitimacy as a nationalist and staunch defender of Cambodia's national borders and heritage against Thai aggression. His government made a massive nationalist investment in the defence of the Preah Vihear border (see Ngoun 2016), with wide support from segments of the Cambodian population. His CPP won a resounding election victory that year, winning 90 out of 123 National Assembly seats. In this context of political legitimation, nationalism has proved a valuable (alternative) political resource for the leader to use to deal with constraints to his rule, bolster his political legitimacy and mobilise popular support for his government.

In addition to enhancing domestic political legitimacy, the Hun Sen government has relied on nationalism to bolster its international legitimacy, through nation rebranding to build a positive international image of Cambodia. This is still to some extent tarnished by the legacy of the genocide, violence and war of the recent past, undermining government diplomacy and efforts to attract foreign tourists and investment. A positive new image is therefore significant. However, as a small developing country, Cambodia does not have many resources to invest in enhancing international soft power and nation rebranding. This therefore relies largely on two important projects, cultural diplomacy and peace diplomacy, the country's main resources.

As a cradle of the ancient civilisation of the Khmer Empire of Angkor, Cambodia has a rich cultural heritage on which to capitalise in order to enhance its international image through international cultural cooperation. The government has been promoting Cambodia as a "cultural corridor" of the Mekong region, connecting with cultures and civilisations of other regions to promote international cooperation for peace and progress. For example, the Asian Cultural Council (ACC), an institutional umbrella of the International Conference of Asian Political Parties (ICAPP), was established in January 2019 and based in Cambodia to promote cultural exchange and cooperation for peace and sustainable development.

Moreover, Cambodia has been successful in coordinating international efforts to safeguard world heritage sites. It hosts the International Coordinating Committee for the Safeguarding and Development of the Historic Site of Angkor (ICC – Angkor) and the International Coordinating Committee for Safeguarding and the Development of Preah Vihear (ICC – Preah Vihear). The government has recently even promoted culinary diplomacy through a cookbook called *The Taste of Angkor*, distributing it widely among the diplomatic community and requiring Cambodian diplomats and spouses to attend a cooking class before being posted overseas (Chheang 2022, 33–34).

Peace diplomacy is also essential to Cambodia's nation rebranding, promoting an international image as a peace-loving nation and contributor to international peace. Cambodia used to be a war-torn country – between 1991 and 1993 it hosted more than 10,000 UN peacekeeping personnel, the largest such deployment in UN history, to restore peace and administer the 1993 general election. However, since 2006, Cambodia has instead become a UN Peacekeeping Operations (UNPKO) contributing country. As of December 2020, it has sent more than 7,000 troops, including women, to nine war-torn countries (Chheang 2022, 35). Among other benefits, sending troops to join UNPKO allows the Cambodian government to gain national pride and build a positive international image of the country's transformation from a recipient of UN peacekeeping to a state contributing to international peace (Hing 2020, 112).

In these contexts of cultural diplomacy and peace diplomacy, nation rebranding enables Prime Minister Hun Sen's government to bolster its international legitimacy, and international recognition of the government's achievements in cultural and peace diplomacy can be translated into national pride. Therefore, nationalism is a valuable (alternative) political resource allowing the Cambodian leader to enhance both domestic and international legitimacies for his regime.

Popular nationalism

Whitmeyer (2002, 322) calls the nationalism of ordinary people "popular nationalism", in contrast to elite nationalism. Therefore, I use the term throughout this chapter to refer to the nationalism of the ordinary people, though I recognise that there are many differences among them. The dynamics of popular nationalism in Cambodia at present have developed from the outburst of widespread popular nationalism in Phnom Penh during Cambodia's Preah Vihear border conflict with Thailand. It is thus imperative that this section examines urban nationalism in Phnom Penh during the border conflict, to offer a framework for understanding contemporary popular nationalism in Cambodia.

The Preah Vihear border conflict (2008–2011) was an interesting moment to observe popular nationalism in Phnom Penh, with the general tone of urban nationalism high at that time. According to one survey, 97 per cent of Cambodian respondents regarded the Preah Vihear Temple conflict as an important issue (International Crisis Group 2011). Many urban residents participated in a nationalist movement to defend Preah Vihear Temple and to express their support for the defence of Cambodia's national borders. As one motorbike repairman stated during an interview: "I am a peace lover. However, we must defend our temple and border at any cost, even through war with Thailand". This sentiment was also expressed by other people during interviews and informal conversations. Many city residents expressed their anger at Thailand. A security guard said, "Preah Vihear Temple belongs to Khmers. The Khmers built it. I am really angry that they want to take it away from us". Urban residents also discussed and exchanged views about the conflict widely and intensively with people in their networks. A motor-taxi driver said, "I followed the news about the conflict from various sources. My fellow *moto dop* [motor-taxi drivers] and neighbours also paid close attention to it. We talked about it almost every day".

The movement to defend Preah Vihear among Phnom Penh residents was an interesting example of urban nationalism. Although it did not manifest in the form of demonstrations against Thailand, it took other forms, such as widespread discussion of the conflict in public places and in families, and donations to government-managed border defence funds. Moreover, there were cases of individuals and groups of people in the city who went beyond mere expressions of sentiment to materialise their nationalist ideas through concrete action. They organised trips, mobilised and spent their own resources to travel to the region and distribute donations to Cambodian soldiers there. Their actions were self-organised and self-planned, completely independent of the Cambodian government.

I will highlight a few, as insights into popular nationalist responses to the border dispute. A young woman working for a local NGO in Phnom Penh stated during an interview:

> You know? If we don't defend our nation, who will defend it for us? I therefore collected contributions from people in my NGO. We collected 670 dollars. We spent 250 on hiring a van to Preah Vihear and the rest on buying instant noodles, medicines, dried fish and mosquito nets. My colleagues and I distributed our donations to our poor soldiers there. We were so happy that our donations reached their hands.

University students in Phnom Penh also organised trips to Preah Vihear Temple during the border dispute. I interviewed a young man who had organised such a trip. He said:

> I was in my third year at the university in 2008 when the conflict took place. My classmates and I were shocked to see Thailand still intent on grabbing more Khmer land although it was already in the twenty-first century when countries were working with each other through institutional frameworks of ASEAN and the United Nations.

He added:

> My classmates and I agreed that we had to do something in response. We were not going to fight against them, but we wanted to show them that we love our Preah Vihear Temple and land. Thus we decided to organize a trip to the temple in September 2008. The road to the temple was very bad. However, soon after we arrived we were overwhelmed with excitement and pride. We brought dried food and pure drinking water for our soldiers.

It was not only the young urban educated elites who took action; certain groups of ordinary city dwellers also did so based on ideas of nation and national heritage. This was the case with Toul Tom Poung Market vendors. A female vendor aged 39 stated during an interview that she and seven other market vendors went to visit the temple during the border tension:

> When I saw Preah Vihear Temple on TV, it was so beautiful. I only started to know what the temple looked like when the dispute occurred. My friends in the market and I felt pain to see Thailand wanting to snatch it away from us. We arranged a trip to the temple a few months later. We wanted to see the beauty of the temple with our own eyes, and we wanted to tell Thai soldiers that ordinary Cambodian people loved peace.

Observing the dynamics of this popular nationalist phenomenon, I wanted to understand why these Phnom Penh people expressed their support for the defence of the nation's territorial integrity and national cultural heritage site. Why did city people demonstrate and mobilise to express their support for the nation's territorial integrity?

This was not the first time that Phnom Penh residents had expressed such nationalist sentiment. Nationalism has been present as a powerful force at various junctures in modern Cambodian history. However, the nationalist feeling that erupted during the border conflict was unprecedented in the city, in that it was relatively spontaneous. Furthermore, it developed into a widespread but largely uncoordinated nationalist movement for defending and rescuing the nation. This urban nationalist movement was independent and autonomous of the Cambodian state, and was expressed through channels that differed from the official nationalism described in the previous sections.

What important underlying factors have made urban nationalism in Phnom Penh emerge as a significant political force? In other words, what were the contexts for these kinds of autonomous nationalist attitudes and sentiments? A conventional analysis would suggest that urban nationalist responses to the Preah Vihear conflict derived from a sense of belonging to the imagined community of Cambodia. They imagined that their country was being invaded, so they had to react. However, a close analysis revealed that the widespread nationalist attitudes among city people were deeply rooted in their frustration with Cambodia's political system, and in individual disaffection, as they had to deal with various types of constraints in their everyday life as a consequence of Phnom Penh's recent rapid spatial, social, economic and political transformations.

Change in Phnom Penh over the last two decades has been taking place at a dizzying rate, transforming not only the cityscape but also urban society, culture, politics and economy. Signs of concentration of wealth in the city are clear, especially in construction, banking and services and among the rich and the expanding middle class. Cambodia's economy has grown at an annual average of 7.7 per cent for the last two decades, making it the sixth fastest growing country in the world (World Bank 2014). Much of this economic growth is concentrated in urban areas, especially Phnom Penh.

More and more Phnom Penh residents now spend their leisure time with families, friends and colleagues at modern shopping malls and global franchised cafés and restaurants. Young men and women from rural areas who work in garment factories in Phnom Penh and its suburban areas also aspire to catch up with these symbols of modernity, globalisation and new lifestyles, as reflected in their hairstyles, clothes and new taste for Korean pop music.

To sum up, contemporary Phnom Penh has already moved beyond the post-conflict stage of city-building, to the stage of increasing integration into the global system; and in terms of livelihood, urban residents have also generally moved beyond the stage of trying to meet basic survival needs, as seen in the 1980s and 1990s, to an exploration of new lifestyles with new expectations.

While these transformations have created opportunities and benefited many Phnom Penh residents, the people of the city now face a wide range of new (collective) issues, such as high housing and land prices, traffic congestion, inadequate public sanitation, poor and inadequate public health and education facilities, mismanagement of urbanisation, and food containing high levels of chemical substances that pose health risks. The government has appeared ineffective in solving these problems, and these issues have therefore become discourses of public criticism of the government and the basis for new forms of urban social, political and nationalist activism.

At the time of the Preah Vihear Temple conflict, city people felt frustrated and powerless, and they viewed the problems as damaging to the Cambodian nation. Their sense of powerlessness and frustration as individuals and citizens prompted them to create their own popular discourses and actions to rescue and empower the nation. In light of these disaffections and constraints, it did not come as a surprise that diverse individuals and groups of Phnom Penh residents moved patriotically to defend the Preah Vihear Temple and the border.

To these people, the Thai assaults on Preah Vihear were a confrontational symbol of the collective humiliation experienced by Khmers, and fed into their own disparate experiences of frustration and powerlessness. Joining a popular movement to defend this Cambodian temple and its surrounding territory against foreign aggression was a way for them to restore their power and dignity. By taking part in a movement to rescue the nation, they could gain a sense of agency and control over their own circumstances and affirm and enforce standards of conduct which they believed should be observed in all aspects of life. The people took pride in the nation, and also in themselves for defending the temple and the border. In this context, their autonomous nationalist actions served as an alternative political resource, allowing urban people to communicate their shared views of grievances and national decline, and inspiring them to take individual and collective action to restore the well-being and dignity of the citizens and the nation.

The autonomous popular nationalism manifested during the Preah Vihear conflict has lived on and developed into various types of participatory popular nationalism, such as medical nationalism and environmental nationalism. There have been many cases of ordinary people raising funds or making donations to Kantha Bopha Children's Hospital and in the campaigns against the COVID-19 pandemic. There are also individual and collective efforts to protect and restore the environment. Such activities are normally posted on social media and come with captions expressing pride in making contributions to fixing the issues faced by the country and enhancing national well-being. Further academic studies should be conducted in order to understand the dynamics of this emerging and increasingly established trend of popular nationalism in Cambodia.

Conclusion

This chapter on the journey through Cambodian nationalism shows that nationalism has been used discursively, as a political resource to advance their agenda, by various stakeholders at different junctures of history, in different contexts and for different purposes. The French colonial rulers constructed modern concepts of the Cambodian nation to justify their colonial rule and give Khmer people the impression that the French were reviving ancient Khmer culture and rescuing the Khmer race from extinction. Borrowing these modern concepts from the French, some Cambodian elites developed them further and used them for their anti-colonial nationalist campaigns for national independence.

In post-independence Cambodia, Prince Sihanouk skilfully used nationalism for his politics of nation-building. His Sangkum regime revived old cultural markers, invented tradition and designed Phnom Penh's urban landscape in such a way to evoke the comparison of his regime with the Angkorian era, a period widely believed among Cambodians to be their country's golden era.

The communist Khmer Rouge leaders, primarily Pol Pot, used ethno-nationalism by creating and interpreting nationalist discourses based on notions of authentic Khmer race and Khmer peasants to mobilise popular support for their revolutionary struggle to control Cambodia. When they came to power, this led to the categorisation of people and elimination of those whom the regime considered not to be pure Khmer – those who did not have a peasant or proletariat background, as well as those betraying the revolution or serving foreign interests.

As for Prime Minister Hun Sen, he has relied on nationalism to counter domestic critics and opposition politicians who allege that his regime is indifferent to protecting national borders and interests. His nationalist investment in defending the Preah Vihear border against Thailand was an important political resource bolstering his political legitimacy. At present, his government is embarking on nation rebranding based on cultural and peace diplomacy, in order to enhance Cambodia's small state diplomacy and the regime's soft power, national pride and international legitimacy.

Apart from the elites, nationalism has also been widely demonstrated among ordinary people in Phnom Penh since the outbreak of the Preah Vihear border conflict. Current urban nationalism is embodied by diverse individuals and groups, originates from diverse sources and is used for different reasons. It manifests in actions taken by individuals and groups to secure control over their environment and materialise their visions of social, economic and political well-being. In these ways, nationalism can be seen as a political resource on which various urban people rely to communicate their grievances, model conduct and enact a better society. It is a form of collective action rooted in individual frustration and civic idealism. Nationalism can help people from diverse backgrounds overcome differences and is a material idiom for expressing and experiencing collective agency. It provides city residents with a degree of empowerment and is a basis for making claims of a more far-reaching kind.

Acknowledgements

In preparing the draft for this chapter, the author has benefited from discussion with Professor Philip Taylor.

References

Anderson, Benedict. 1983. *Imagined Communities: Reflections on the Origin and Spread of Nationalism.* London: Verso.
Anderson, Benedict. 1998. *The Spectre of Comparisons: Nationalism, Southeast Asia and the World.* London: Verso.
Barker, Rodney. 2004. *Legitimating Identities.* Cambridge: Cambridge University Press.
Barnett, Anthony. 1990. "Cambodia Will Never Disappear." *New Left Review* 180: 101–125.
Bayat, Asef. 1997. "Un-Civil Society: The Politics of the 'Informal People'." *Third World Quarterly* 18 (1): 53–72.
Beetham, David. 1991. *The Legitimation of Power.* New York: Palgrave Macmillan.
Bourdieu, Pierre. 1990. *In Other Words: Essays toward a Reflexive Sociology.* Translated by Matthew Adamson. Stanford, CA: Stanford University Press.
Brady, Henry E., Sidney Verba, and Kay Lehman Schozman. 1995. "Beyond Ses: A Resource Model of Political Participation." *The American Political Science Review* 89 (2): 271–294.
Calhoun, Craig. 1988. "Populist Politics, Communications Media and Large-Scale Societal Integration." *Sociological Theory* 6 (2): 219–241.
Chandler, David P. 1986. "The Kingdom of Kampuchea, March-October 1945: Japanese-Sponsored Independence in Cambodia in World War II." *Journal of Southeast Asian Studies* 17 (1): 80–93.
Chandler, David P. 1992. *Brother Number One: A Political Biography of Pol Pot.* North Sydney, NSW: Allen and Unwin.
Chatterjee, Partha. 1993. *Nationalist Thought and the Colonial World: A Derivative Discourse.* London: Zed Books.
Chatterjee, Partha. 2004. *The Politics of the Governed: Reflections on Popular Politics in Most of the World.* New York: Columbia University Press.

Chheang, Vannarith. 2022. "Cambodia's Changing Public Diplomacy and Nation Branding." In *Winning Hearts and Minds: Public Diplomacy in ASEAN*, edited by Sue-Ann Chia, 32–39. Singapore: World Scientific.

Daravuth, Ly, and Ingrid Muan. 2001. *Culture of Independence: An Introduction to Cambodian Arts and Culture in the 1950's and 1960's*. Phnom Penh: Reyum Publishing.

Deutsch, Karl W. 1961. "Social Mobilization and Political Development." *The American Political Science Review* 55 (3): 493–514.

Edwards, Penny. 2007. *Cambodge: The Cultivation of a Nation, 1860–1945*. Honolulu: University of Hawaii Press.

Geertz, Clifford. 1973. *The Interpretation of Culture: Selected Essays by Clifford Geertz*. New York: Basic Books.

Giddens, Anthony. 1981. *A Contemporary Critique of Historical Materialism*. Stanford, CA: Stanford University Press.

Greenfeld, Liah. 2006. *Nationalism and the Mind: Essays on Modern Culture*. Oxford: Oneworld Publications.

Gupta, Akhil. 1998. *Postcolonial Development: Agriculture in the Making of Modern India*. Durham, NC and London: Duke University Press.

Heder, Steve, and Brian Tittemore. 2001. *Seven Candidates for Prosecution: Accountability for the Crimes of the Khmer Rouge*. Washington, DC: War Crimes Research Office, Washington College of Law, American University and Coalition for International Justice.

Hing Vandanet. 2020. "Peacebuilding and Development Implications of Cambodia's Peacebuilding Operation." *Journal of Peacebuilding & Development* 15 (1): 111–116.

Hinton, Alexander. 1998a. "Why Did You Kill? The Cambodian Genocide and the Dark Side of Face and Honor." *The Journal of Asian Studies* 57 (1): 93–122.

Hinton, Alexander. 1998b. "A Head for an Eye: Revenge in the Cambodian Genocide." *American Ethnologist* 25 (3): 352–377.

Hughes, Caroline. 2006. "The Politics of Gifts: Tradition and Regimentation in Cambodia." *Journal of Southeast Asian Studies* 37 (3): 469–489.

Hutchinson, John. 2003. "Nationalism, Globalism, and the Conflict of Civilisations." In *Nationalism and its Futures*, edited by Umut Ozkirimli, 71–92. New York: Palgrave Macmillan.

International Crisis Group. 2011. *Waging Peace: ASEAN and the Thai-Cambodian Border Conflict. Asia Report No. 215*. Bangkok/Jakarta/Brussels: International Crisis Group.

Kang, David C. 2002. "Bad Loans to Good Friends: Money Politics and the Developmental State in South Korea." *International Organization* 56 (1): 177–207.

Kerkvliet, Benedict. 2005. *The Power of Everyday Politics: How Vietnamese Peasants Transformed National Policy*. Ithaca, NY: Cornell University Press.

Kiernan, Ben. 1996. *The Pol Pot Regime: Race, Power and Genocide in Cambodia under the Khmer Rouge, 1975–1979*. New Haven, CT: Yale University Press.

Kiernan, Ben. 2001. "Myth, Nationalism and Genocide." *Journal of Genocide Research* 3 (2): 187–206.

Kiernan, Ben. 2002. "Introduction: Conflict in Cambodia, 1945–2002." *Critical Asian Studies* 34 (4): 483–495.

Kiernan, Ben. 2004. *How Pol Pot Came to Power: Colonialism, Nationalism, and Communism in Cambodia, 1930–1975*. New Haven, CT: Yale University Press.

Lipsky, Michael. 1968. "Protest as a Political Resource." *The American Political Science Review* 62 (4): 1144–1158.

Mann, Michael. 1984. "The Autonomous Power of the State: Its Origins, Mechanisms and Results." *European Journal of Sociology* 25 (2): 185–213.

McCargo, Duncan. 2005. "Network Monarchy and Legitimacy Crisis in Thailand." *The Pacific Review* 18 (4): 499–519.

Muzaffar, Chandra. 1987. *Islamic Resurgence in Malaysia*. Petaling Jaya, Malaysia: Fajar Bakti.

Ngoun, Kimly. 2016. "Narrating the National Border: Cambodian State Rhetoric vs Popular Discourse on the Preah Vihear Conflict." *Journal of Southeast Asian Studies* 47 (2): 210–333.

Ngoun, Kimly. 2018. "From a Pile of Stones to a National Symbol: Preah Vihear Temple and Norodom Sihanouk's Politics of Postcolonial Nation-Building." *South East Asia Research* 26 (2): 194–212.

Norén-Nilsson, Astrid. 2013. "Performance as (Re)Incarnation: The Sdech Kân Narrative." *Journal of Southeast Asian Studies* 44 (1): 4–23.

Osborne, Milton. 1994. *Sihanouk: Prince of Light, Prince of Darkness.* St. Leonards, NSW: Allen & Unwin.
Osborne, Milton. 2008. *Phnom Penh: A Cultural and Literary History.* Oxford: Signal Books.
Pye, Lucian W. 1956. *Guerrilla Communism in Malaya: Its Social and Political Meaning.* Princeton: Princeton University Press.
Scott, James C. 1972. "Patron-Client Politics and Political Change in Southeast Asia." *The American Political Science Review* 66 (1): 91–113.
Scott, James C. 1985. *Weapons of the Weak: Everyday Forms of Peasant Resistance.* New Haven, CT: Yale University Press.
Shils, Edward. 1960. "The Intellectuals in the Political Development of the New States." *World Politics* 12 (3): 329–368.
Smith, Anthony D. 1991. *National Identity.* London: Penguin Books.
Stoker, Gerry. 1998. "Governance as Theory: Five Propositions." *International Social Science Journal* 50 (1): 17–28.
Weiss, Meredith. 2016. "Payoffs, Parties, or Policies: 'Money Politics' and Electoral Authoritarian Resilience." *Critical Asian Studies* 48 (1): 77–99.
Weyland, Kurt. 2001. "Clarifying a Contested Concept: Populism in the Study of Latin American Politics." *Comparative Politics* 34 (1): 1–22.
White, Lynn. 2005. "Introduction–Dimensions of Legitimacy." In *Legitimacy: Ambiguities of Political Success or Failure in East and Southeast Asia,* edited by Lynn White, 1–28. Singapore: World Scientific.
Whitmeyer, Joseph M. 2002. "Elites and Popular Nationalism." *British Journal of Sociology* 53 (3): 321–341.
World Bank. 2014. *Cambodia Overview.* Washington, DC: World Bank.
Yuval-Davis, Nira. 2006. "Belonging and the Politics of Belonging." *Patterns of Prejudice* 40 (3): 197–214.

33
XĀT LAO
Imagining the Lao nation through race, history and language

Ryan Wolfson-Ford

Introduction

The notion of *Xāt Lao* (ຊາດລາວ) engrossed the minds of the Lao elite at the very moment they envisioned the Lao nation (Katay 1953, 9). In this line of thinking, there existed Lao people divided up and living under the rule of Thai, French, Vietnamese, Cambodian, Burmese and Chinese states. They inhabited lands formerly ruled by Lan Xang (1353–1707), the Lao kingdom which disintegrated for centuries after 1707. While scholars have seen it in spatial terms, this Greater Laos (ລາວໃຫຍ່) was based on modern notions of a Lao race (Ivarsson and Goscha 2007). In pre-colonial Laos, ethnicity was relatively plastic, but after over half a century of French colonial rule (1893–1945), itself predicated on racial hierarchy, Lao elites no longer perceived ethnicity as changeable (Wolfson-Ford 2017). They saw instead the world divided up among mutually antagonistic races locked in a struggle for survival for land and resources. This eventually crystallized into the virulently nationalist idea of a Lao race that shaped the first post-colonial Lao state amid the Cold War as both the Royal Lao Government (RLG) (1945–1975) and the Pathet Lao fought to free the country from foreign forces. This chapter examines the influence of race on Lao nationalism. Contrary to existing scholarship, Laos did not suffer from a lack of nationalism, but from an overabundance of it, to the point that armed groups emerged fighting to rescue the nation (ກູ້ຊາດ). This chapter explores competing forms of nationalism – exclusionary and inclusive – and why the exclusionary form, centering on a Lao race, won out.

The idea of a Lao race greatly influenced Lao nationalist thinking, signified by the word *Xāt*, which in the twentieth century meant both "race" and "nation." As early as the 1930s, the Lao elite invented the nation, with both positive and negative French influences, which formed the basis for popular nationalist movements since the 1940s. After 1945, an inclusive multiethnic nationalism was gradually abandoned for a virulently nationalist notion of a Lao race. In doing so, Lao intellectuals made distortions, evasions and manipulations to embrace a purely Lao nation, which had serious repercussions for decades. While the elite's invention of the nation was creative and served to unite the country, some Lao elite papered over their own diverse backgrounds. The national culture they forged drew from non-Lao sources (Thai, Khmer, the West). Alongside these intellectual processes, were intense nationalist feelings generated by rivalry and hatred of Vietnamese, French and Thai, at the root of which lay a fear of impending Lao racial extinction.

There was also a precarious, hybrid identity rising to mediate with the West. The French-Lao identity was fraught with difficulties – cultural alienation and cultural dislocation – but it nonetheless represented different ways of being Lao unique to the period. Homi K. Bhabha wrote that such hybrid identities can disrupt colonialism (1994). Lao who were French-educated grew incensed when relegated to subordinate roles in the colony by the French, fueling anti-colonial desire. The contradiction between a stridently nationalist Lao race and a multiethnic French-Lao identity was only resolved after a lengthy process of intellectual searching to bring many diverse signs under the unitary sign of "Lao." Rejecting cultural alienation, the idea of a Lao race won out over more inclusive notions of Lao nationalism better suited to the country's ethnic diversity. Nationalism came to Laos as questions of identity affecting real people as their lives were shaped by dramatic, global events. Culture, ideas and politics met at a powerful juncture in history. While separated in time, the French-Lao identity parallels the Lao People's Democratic Republic's (LPDR) (1975–) own brand of multiethnic nationalism and suggests the ways in which the contradiction between the two poles of Lao identity has never been resolved (Tappe 2013). This inclusive nationalism too fragile, even its adherents could not resist the appeal of Xāt Lao, mirroring the decline of multiethnic nationalism (and reassertion of ethnic Lao hegemony) in Laos today.

The idea of Xāt Lao captured the minds of the Lao elite at a crucial turning point in the development of Lao nationalism in the 1930s–1940s. In their writings, Lao elite used a word with some ambiguity, Xāt – ຊາດ, but in their French and English writings, they always used the word "race." In fact, race and nation were so linked in Lao thinking that when writing in French the elite often wrote "our nation, our race"; they truly could not separate the two. French colonialism stressed the idea that the Lao racial declining, threatened with extinction, and must be saved (Ivarsson 1999). It traced back to the first French explorations of the Mekong when French marveled at decaying Lao ruins (destroyed by Thai). Lao were on the verge of extinction as Jules Harmand saw it: "we can count upon the Annamites… to colonize a great deal of the valley of the [Mekong] river to our benefit, and where they will quickly supplant the left-overs of the decrepit races which inhabit it" (Gunn 2017). One French historian claimed Lao racial decline began in the seventeenth century:

> The Laotian feeling protected by a feared sovereign [Soulinyavongsa, r.1638–1694], cultivated his native carelessness resulting both from the moderation of his desires and from the fertility of his soil. Living without needs, for him everything was a matter of joy.
> *(LeBoulanger 1930)*

This invited invasion and rule by Thai, Burmese and Vietnamese. France used this trope to assert racial superiority and justify colonialism. However, Lao already had their own ideas of ethnic superiority, especially vis-à-vis ethnic minorities. There are signs Lao ethnonationalism began emerging in 1890s northern Laos. Western notions of race overlapped with the existing pre-colonial Lao political order. Race was also introduced by American missionaries who opened a printing press in 1892 in Chiang Mai. They disseminated huge volumes of tracts; one was recently rediscovered at the Library of Congress. Since it was written in Tham script – used in Lao and Northern Thai manuscripts – it was a unique vehicle to disseminate Western thinking, including the notion of a world divided into races (Wolfson-Ford 2019).

Western notions of race cast a long shadow over twentieth-century Lao history. As the Lao elite attended French schools in ever greater numbers, they became deeply exposed to these ideas. France used the narrative of racial decline to legitimize colonial rule, claiming that they had saved the Lao from extinction. Yet, the Lao elite appropriated this narrative to prefigure a Lao nation politically and culturally. They wrote of their race and nation seeking to redeem it from French racist myths of lazy and docile Lao. They appealed to the notion of a Lao race to engender an imagined unity which was crucial for preparing a new political union. Simultaneously, they generated and unified a single Lao history, culture and language from diverse sources, inventing a Lao tradition. And, intriguingly, some Lao elite were so enamored by the idea of a Lao race they set aside their own diverse backgrounds to embrace the new identity. Finally, rewriting history and questions of language became pronounced after 1945, in the wake of the Issara, the Lao independence movement. Using Lao elite writings, this chapter considers the elite's background before examining the invention of a Lao tradition in the 1930s and considering key developments after 1945.

While not as well-known, a greater Lao race is comparable to the greater Thai race prevalent in Thailand at the time (Barmé 1993). Likewise, Lao nationalist fears of racial extinction at the hands of powerful neighbors parallel Cambodia (Kiernan 2008). But until recently, scholars thought Lao nationalism was insignificant, if not non-existent. Some saw Laos as nothing more than a collection of tribes, utterly devoid of nationalism (Brown and Zasloff 1985). If anything, Laos did not suffer from a lack of nationalism, but an overabundance of it. Recent research has provided an increasingly more complex picture. Geoffrey Gunn wrote the first monograph studying Lao nationalism but did not see it as a force before 1945 (1988). Soren Ivarsson investigated Lao national awakening during World War II among Francophone Lao elites via a French-sponsored Lao Renovation Movement (Ivarsson 2008). Simon Creak expanded on this by revealing the movement concerned not just the mind, but the body, too (2015). Both noted the prevalence of a racial discourse in different ways. Yet, most scholars take Xāt to only mean nation, when it also meant race; by neglecting both senses of the word, one misses crucial dimensions of Lao nationalist thinking. Moreover, Lao nationalism did not suddenly arise in 1941. As this chapter shows, the elite had already been working on it behind the scenes for over a decade. Their works provided the blueprint for Lao Renovation and other 1940s mass popular nationalist movements. While neglected, the 1930s was a crucial time when Lao intellectuals first cultivated the idea of a nation, influenced by French education. It was when a distinctly Lao language, history, poetry, calendar and Buddhism were first articulated.

In previous works, Lao agency has not been fully appreciated, while historians were too wedded to French sources appearing to show French playing a leading role in creating Lao nationalism. This chapter argues that it was the Lao elite who played the leading role in fashioning Lao nationalism, in both its cultural and political forms, in the 1930s–1940s. Proper appreciation of Lao agency can recast Lao history so that Lao are active participants. In this regard, Chairat Polmuk has undertaken a sophisticated study of literature in the development of nationalism in the 1940s, involving a careful analysis of multiple genres of texts (2014). Chairat allows us to enter the mental world of key nationalist Lao intellectuals at a pivotal moment. Yet, Lao elite cultural works had both positive and negative French influences, as they admired and reviled being taught exclusively French history and culture. They drew from many sources when articulating a standard Lao culture. Their insight was to link their cultural works to political claims. The Lao elite were not limited by the constraints of French empire as they envisioned the nation, especially in light of its racist, repressive nature which often excluded and oppressed them.

After 1945, these issues culminated in the clash of the Issara's stridently nationalist, anti-colonial and anti-French writings with loyalist (those who supported France's return after August 1945) writings struggling with identity questions. Loyalists rapidly developed a unique hybrid French-Lao identity, embracing inclusive views, but struggled with how to be Lao in a society still dominated by France. As they learned French, they lost fluency in Lao. And they debated whether to say "Lao" or "Laos," the final "s" aligning with French pronunciation. Confronting difficulties, multiethnic nationalism was discarded for the alluring Xāt Lao, even among loyalists. Meanwhile, Issara authored the first nationalist account of Lao history by interrogating Auguste Pavie's colonial myth of the "Conquest of Hearts," denouncing it as a lie, claiming that Pavie had engineered Luang Prabang's destruction in 1887. The Ho (overland Chinese) were reviled by Lao nationalists for this act, but the Issara redirected that feeling against French. In the process they fought to free Lao history from control by French scholars. The Issara introduced strong anti-French elements to Lao nationalist thinking (later taken up by Pathet Lao). Events in the 1930s and 1940s reveal the pivotal role of intellectual processes in Lao nationalism's development and the Lao elite's central role as they seized the opportunity to steer events in a new direction.

School days in colonial Laos

French schools were a locus of nationalism in colonial Laos. There, the elite could begin to imagine the Lao nation. Many came from diverse backgrounds: a Lao-Cambodian, Pierre Somchine Nginn, a Lao(-Vietnamese?), Katay Don Sasorith, an Isan-born Lao-Thai, Sila Viravong. But all embraced a single national culture with dreams of sovereignty in the wings. The first generation of French-Lao also included Prince Phetsarath Rattanavong, King Sisavang Vong, Thao Nhouy Abhay, Prince Souvanna Phouma and Prince Souphanouvong. They were the first to mediate with the West while remaking their traditions to conjure the nation. They traveled across Laos, Indochina and France for education gaining exposed to Western culture, which was greatly influenced by racism, fascism and on the verge of World War I even as their worldview broadened encountering communism, democracy and diverse people. It was a uniquely generative moment for modern Lao history. Considering elite backgrounds, one can see how some manipulated their identities to conform with an idealized form of the Lao nation embodied by the idea of a Lao race.

Phetsarath was the first to receive a French education. In 1897, his father, Chao Boun Khong, sent him to study at a French school, in Luang Prabang, before continuing in Saigon ("3349" 1978). Many other elites followed, where they witnessed lively politics and a freer press than in Laos (where no press was allowed). Sisavang Vong came two years later before going on to the École Colonial in Paris in 1900. In Saigon, Phetsarath studied, with French students, separately from Vietnamese. In 1905, he went to the École Colonial where he confronted his French teachers whose instruction was inappropriate for Lao students. In 1907, he began studying English, and next year spent the summer in England. He became enamored with England, returning many times, with trips to London. Studying in Europe for nearly a decade changed Phetsarath. When he briefly returned to Laos, he recalled ordaining as a monk as "sheer suffering." In 1914, he returned to work for the French, becoming the highest-ranking Lao official. In his duties he traveled widely, being one of the first to envision the new Lao nation spatially. Phetsarath was the leading force in convening an assembly in 1923 of Lao from all regions, which one French official said was the first of its kind since 1707. His growing influence led to a cadre of followers coalescing around him. By the 1930s, he viewed the Vietnamese as "the 'cruelest of imperialists' who 'sought to exterminate the Lao race'" (Gunn 1988).

Phetsarath's path contrasts with "Pierre" Somchine Nginn. Nginn's father, a Cambodian man, worked for Auguste Pavie before settling in Luang Prabang and marrying a Lao woman. Nginn wrote his name multiple ways, but complained that Lao heard his given name and assumed that it meant "mixed with Chinese" (Nginn 1971). He retained his nickname, "Pierre," from a Paris lycée all his life. He too attended the first French school in Luang Prabang in 1897 before going to study in Vientiane in 1901. Nginn fondly recalled his teachers' praise and still knew by heart French poetry at the age of 79, suggesting the deep impression his education made on him. He continued studying in Saigon in 1905 at the Collège Chasseloup-Laubat before going to France in 1906. He was given a scholarship to study at the École Colonial by Pavie. While there, he, Phetsarath and other elites studied the same evening courses as future French colonial administrators in addition to their regular courses in the day. When traveling to France, Nginn wanted to write his parents, but could only write them in French, for he had never studied Lao in school. Confronting this conundrum, he went on to become a Lao language instructor for decades afterward. In his memoirs, he wrote at length about the wonderful sights across France, but said little about school beyond the fact that "we were well housed and well fed. We could go out on Saturday night and all day on Sunday" (Nginn 1972). Being in France deeply influenced him. He kept in contact with people he met for years after, including a woman that "had considered me in France as her own child." He recalled his affection for France: "despite nearly forty years of separation, its memory and its image are still in my heart and my thoughts."

Katay Sasorith was not as forthcoming about his heritage. He saw himself as Lao even though his father, who ran a bistro serving French, was reportedly Vietnamese. Katay even wrote disparagingly of "little Annamite school boys," like most Lao nationalists of his time (Katay 1958). He recalled French boyhood friends speaking Lao better than French, who became thoroughly Lao in some ways – perhaps to overcome his heritage. He and his Lao and French friends founded the first football team in Pakse. Despite close bonds with French, Katay did face discrimination. His school did not allow French students. He flaunted his superiority in French, teasing Frenchmen about grammar in ways echoing his own trials. He criticized French but saw beyond their ethnicity to see their shared humanity. While noting French brutality, he also recalled deep attachments with others. He dedicated his memoir to his French teacher. He was illiterate until the age of 10 when, meeting a new teacher, he learned to read French, but Lao as well, using Thai textbooks since there were no Lao ones. Katay played a key role in the anti-colonial movement by co-founding the Lao Issara. He wrote prolifically, so his writings came to embody the movement. As noted below, Katay's rewriting of Lao colonial history created the first truly nationalist history. Like others, he espoused the idea of a Xāt Lao, which mirrored his own embracing of his identity as Lao. He quoted approvingly a French scholar who wrote of a pure Lao race: "The Laotian (Lao)… is of all the Thais the one who has preserved the purest [blood], with however a proportion of Aryan blood much more considerable than in the other varieties…" (Katay 1948b). In the same work, Katay divided the country into Lao, "Kha" and "Meo," which was the same racial classification used in RLG statistics. In 1958, the ultra-nationalist Committee for the Defense of National Interests also praised the purity of the Lao race.

Inventing tradition at the Vientiane Buddhist Institute

Lao elite first envisioned a cultural nation – prefiguring a political one – at the Vientiane Buddhist Institute. This library and Pali school opened in February 1931 under the leadership of Prince Phetsarath Rattanavongsa assisted by Sila Viravong, who never went to Europe for education, unlike his peers. It created a modern cultural nationalism holding sway even to the present in some respects. As Creak observes, Laos, like Ireland, had to realize its own independent culture before it could seek political independence (2015). The cultural works produced provided a blueprint for mass movements, including Lao Renovation, which was permitted by French authorities as they warily lifted the political repression that had kept such pent-up feelings hidden below the surface.

Lao elites were concerned, for the first time, with creating a distinct Lao history, literature, grammar, poetry, calendar, religion, architecture and language. They reacted against their French education which taught them French history, culture and language, but not their own. They created a standardized culture uniting many diverse conceptions under the nation, thereby paving the way for popular nationalism. Lacking mass media, which undergird Lao Renovation, elites in the 1930s wrote the overarching cultural script that was distilled and popularized in the 1940s. Their works, appearing in journals and monographs, were the antecedent to the first popular nationalism witnessed during Lao Renovation.

Phetsarath actively participated in the invention of Lao tradition, writing the first modern Lao astrology textbook, which explained how to calculate calendars according to Lao methods (2011 [1951]). His project contained serious tensions, revealing central problems in the elite's cultural nationalist project: nationalists might revive culture, but only in a distorted fashion in which the original was irrevocably lost. For example, the "Lao" calendar Phetsarath sought to revive was itself based on an earlier Mon system. Phetsarath's project rejected the French calendar and wider colonial project of assimilation. Yet, Phetsarath had Western influences. In England, he stayed with an astronomy teacher:

> Mr. Lemon knew that I was interested in astronomy and often took me up on the roof to look at the sky and to see the movements of the planets through his large telescope. My great interest in astronomy after returning to Laos was the product of Mr. Lemon's advice about these matters.
>
> *("3349" 1978)*

Phetsarath was driven to revive Lao astrology, yet drew on diverse sources. In his preface, he claimed that astrology was a lost science. No one could be found who knew it anymore, which he linked to the decline of Laos since the fall of Lan Xang. Phetsarath faced a serious problem: how could he revive Lao astrology if there was no one left to teach him?

> When I did see the difficulties to make oneself a new calendar and the lack of understanding in calendar texts like this, then [I] had even more of an interest, wanting to study the science of ancient astrology more greatly. But were [one] to seek a teacher, a person who understands this science, [they] were rare, or [one] might even say that there was not any [teacher] at all. I thus needed to seek, research [and] learn by myself, according to the texts of the Lao, Khmer and Thai ancestors. These texts also might bear good fruit. Yet, in these texts there was no explanation for the basis of various principles. Anyhow, I still hold that the texts of the three races [Lao, Khmer, Thai] are good teachers for me.
>
> *(2011 [1951])*

Striving to recover a distinctly Lao calendar, Phetsarath found that he was too late. What he was searching for was already lost. Filling in the gaps, he relied on Thai and Cambodian works. Phetsarath was not simply recovering old Lao traditions, nor merely preserving them, but recreating and re-inventing them. Before modern times, no Lao had ever thought of making a "Lao" calendar, only a Buddhist one. Phetsarath carved out a Lao Buddhism in the process, transitioning from a universal religion to a national one, a uniquely nationalist endeavor. An authentic Lao culture, where it had been lost, was created by cultural geniuses among the elite.

Sila Viravong, Phetsarath's secretary, wrote the first Lao grammar in 1935, thereby staking a claim to the independence of the Lao language. He also wrote a treatise codifying Lao poetry, explaining it distinctiveness from Thai poetry. Like Phetsarath, Sila did not have any teacher when he codified the rules of Lao poetry and had to make up the verse rules, inevitably drawing from Thai (Koret 1999). By then Sila was becoming an important intellectual among the Lao elite, but this was not inevitable. Born in Roi-et, Northeast Thailand, to a farming family, he trained to become a Thai judge before quitting after being racially abused in Bangkok for being Lao. He recounted this pivotal episode:

> I read a book called… "The Suppression of the Rebellion of Ai Anou of Vientiane"… [where] they called King Anou "Ai" Anou and his wife Queen Khamporng was called "Ee" Khamporng. [Finishing] this story, I felt extremely hurt and angry, and the idea of national liberation arose very strongly. From that time on, I urged my fellow monastics… to form a group to liberate Laos, even though we had no power or knowledge of politics, only anger and resentment.
>
> (2004)

Ai (ໄອ່) means "bastard" or "fool," so the offense Sila felt is obvious. It is also how adults address children, portraying Lao as helpless wards of Thai. Westerners in Bangkok recorded that speaking Lao would cause Thai to call them monkeys. The Lao Renovation newspaper printed political cartoons mocking Thai as monkeys. Such antagonism was formative in the development of Lao nationalism. Until this point, Sila tried to assimilate to the dominant Thai culture, but after being subjected to racist abuse awakened to the cause of Lao nationalism, in youthful anger.

Tradition was invented by the Lao elite at the Vientiane Buddhist Institute for political purposes. The nationalist movement would have been impossible, or very different, without it, but it also drew on diverse sources. French sponsored elite cultural works, but they suppressed any political element or emerging Lao nationalism. French colonialism maintained divisions within Laos, especially north and south, while assimilating Lao and denying any political rights, and even largely excluding Lao from the administration, employing Vietnamese instead. Some French suggested that Lao use Thai script or that Vat Sisaket be made into a museum, arousing opposition from Phetsarath, who was never a docile colonial subject.

Elite cultural nationalism cannot be separated from the mass popular nationalism promoted by the Issara independence movement (1945–1949), among others. Elsewhere, such a dichotomy may have existed, but in Laos, Phetsarath led the Vientiane Buddhist Institute and the Issara. Illustrating the connection, Issara printed broadsides on the back of Lao Renovation papers. Finally, according to Katay, a close follower, in the 1930s, Phetsarath already dreamed of an independent Laos as he "saw taking shape the future Lao state of which he passionately wanted independence and of which he molded the foundations with his hands" (*Lao Hakxa Sat* 1959). While Lao nationalism first took shape as cultural works, those working in the 1930s were not apolitical, and had serious differences with France that became all too obvious after World War II.

Loyalists: multiethnic nationalists?

World War II (1939–1945) was a pivotal moment when the French-sponsored Lao Renovation (1941–1945) spread nationalism to the masses for the first time. While the French tried to steer it to imbue loyalty to France, it unleashed nationalist forces that could not be controlled. One participant recalled, "we were well disciplined which gave us the feeling that Lao can rule themselves rather than the French or the Vietnamese" (Halpern 1964). After the War, the Issara declared independence, establishing the first post-colonial Lao state. Sisouk Na Champassak wrote, "the first awakening of a true Lao consciousness dates from 1945" (1961). On March 9, 1945, the uneasy truce between Japan and France ended in Indochina. Japanese jailed the French, while some Lao nationalists responded positively as others sided with France. The co-founders of Lao Renovation, Katay Sasorith and Nhouy Abhay, cooperated with Japan and joined the Issara. Nhouy ran a newspaper calling for "yellow races" to unite against the white race. Both he and Katay feared Vietnamese in Lao cities seeking to unite with a resurgent Vietnam.

When the Lao Issara emerged (1945–1946), Lao nationalists split between those loyal to France, the loyalists and those seeking immediate independence, the Issara. The resulting struggle lent a partisan edge to questions of nationalism. The Issara embraced the idea of an exclusionary Lao race seeking unity against France, while some loyalists espoused a multiethnic nationalism. Among loyalists, Nginn and Nhouy Abhay (who joined the loyalists in 1946) produced many works on Lao culture. When not publishing in *France-Asie* or *Sud-est*, they wrote in *Kinnari*, a French-Lao cultural review. Yet, their vision of nationalism confronted serious problems of cultural alienation and questions of identity. This raised doubts among loyalists and ultimately led them to reject the nascent inclusive nationalism in favor of the exclusionary one.

Loyalists were more likely to champion cross-cultural currents of their time. They did not often invoke Xāt Lao, as the Issara did, but spoke of a multiethnic country, as an anonymous author writing under the pseudonym "Lao Blood" (ເລືອດລາວ) did:

> Since ancient times a country might have people of the same race [Xāt], but in the present it is not like that because communication connects [peoples] back and forth together easily. Clever countries that have exceedingly powerful weapons can collect small, tiny countries to unite them and keep [them] with itself. Therefore, in the present [one] does not see any country at all in the world that may be entirely of a single race living together.
>
> *(1947)*

This inclusive view, while perhaps a product of a colonial discourse legitimizing foreign domination, promised an inclusive, albeit fragile nationalism compared to the idea of a single Lao race and nation. This nationalism addressed the multiethnic realities of the country far better than the ultra-nationalist Issara who tended to deny any minorities even existed.

Loyalists are demonized for promoting French culture at the expense of their own. Some LPDR history works have even referred to this period as one of French "cultural pollution" (Souneth et al. 2000). Loyalists were perceived as forgetting their culture in their fascination with the West. Their willingness to transgress cultural boundaries was reviled by Issara, who felt themselves so deeply Lao. In one appeal to loyalists, Issara went so far as to say, "never forget you are Lao" (Katay 1948a). Issara were Westernized too, but their political demands buttressed by anti-colonialism delineated important boundaries which loyalists lacked. Loyalists confronted deep contradictions. Could one support French rule and still be nationalist? Could one speak French fluently and still promote Lao language and culture?

Loyalists feared that Issara were too close to the Vietnamese. Both were strongly anti-Vietnamese. They resented that their cities and colonial administration were dominated by Vietnamese to the point they felt like second-class citizens in their own country. But Issara strategically allied with Vietminh to resist French rule. Loyalists feared that Issara would deliver Laos to Vietnam and sought French protection. Loyalists had their own brand of nationalism regardless of political entanglements with France and belief that Laos was not ready for immediate independence. Yet, loyalists still maintained a French-Lao Friendship trope to frame their works. Cultural studies appearing in Kinnari exhibited French influence. Kinnari contributors were proud heirs of French culture and learning, but tensions remained. The name of the magazine suggested this. Maha Phoumy Chitaphong referred to a *kinnari* as a being whose "head is Vietnamese, chest is Lao, body is French…one may not say with certainty, truly what it is" (1946). Loyalists faced tensions between essentialist notions of Lao nationalism juxtaposed with more transgressive views. They raised questions suggesting the limits of multiethnic nationalism. They debated whether to call the country "Lao" or "Laos" while questions of identity emerged from French-Lao pupils.

Writing about learning French, a Lao pupil raised profound questions about French-Lao identity. To him, a true meeting of Lao and French was impossible, each isolated, unable to access the other; and those who tried became dislocated and lost. His experiences showed limits for any nascent French-Lao identity. They suggest why so many Lao of his time sought out an essentialist, virulently nationalist idea of a Lao race, which promised an antidote to the rising cultural alienation among French-Lao who wrestled with questions of identity. In "Will Lao Be Learned?" Phouvong (Phimmasone?) gave a stark account of his experiences as a student in a French school (1947). He described the difficulty of studying in a bilingual context, torn between two languages:

> I feel a great difficulty to express myself in French, it not being my mother tongue. I often would like to write. I take the pen. I make effort to construct phrases. Ideas come to me, but vocabulary and ease I lack to make a useful work. Why then not write in Lao? The difficulty is still greater, when it comes to translating Lao thought by a truly Lao mind. For a Lao out of French-Lao schools, it is the habit to envision things according to the French mind. To express his ideas, he is obliged to make two efforts: to express himself first in French, then translate his ideas expressed in French into Lao. The task is not easy. We spend to this effect, twice the time.

Phouvong faced the unexpected dilemma of being unable to express himself in Lao as he became more exposed to French. He was not alone, as 36,716 Lao students entered French schools in 1949 (Kingdom of Laos 1961). If Phouvong spoke for the experiences of emerging French-Lao, it was an identity fraught with difficulties.

Phouvong's difficulties led to becoming alienated from his culture and language. Rendering his thoughts into a meaningful expression became difficult, even impossible, to express to Lao not touched by French learning:

> The translation of a French text to Lao is not often faithful. The ideas distort themselves more or less. One could maintain the French thoughts, but the Lao expression becomes defective and perfectly unintelligible for those who have not received French instruction.
> *(1947)*

If the French-Lao identity was distinct, then it is distinguished by alienation from other Lao:

> We learn to speak Lao correctly, avoid the habit, that seems a little ridiculous in the eyes of foreigners, of speaking gibberish mixing Lao with French. We speak French among Lao, we use French words to express certain ideas, because most often the Lao word does not come spontaneously to mind, [by] lack of frequent use. We joke, we mock ourselves. We search [for] means to remedy it.

Phouvong doubts whether French-Lao identity might ever become whole.

> The French mind does not conceive an idea [in] the same manner as the Lao mind. I cite an example: "d'où revenez-vous?" [Where are you coming from?] CHAO PAY SAI MA (you – to go – where – to come). It is a clear example of the phenomenon in question. Of the two sides, in French like in Lao, the notion of return (*render*) – that of return (*retour*) is the same …[while] French pay particular attention to the idea of the return (*retour*), Lao adopt on the contrary a different method, the chronological walk. [Lao] notions render one following the other in a chronological order. "Where is-you go for to return?" One could render the same idea by the same words: Chao Kap Ma Te Say (you return from where?). But it is bad Lao. This example shows that this is a general case, Lao and the French languages render the same ideas, not only by different words, but also by a difference of construction and by a different order, resulting in the difference of operations of the mind.

Phouvong's years of study led him to see many gaps between the two cultures. He no longer held the optimism that comes from naively regarding possibilities for cross-cultural contact. In his study, he had to give up his Lao mind, where it was incompatible with the French mind, to express himself in the new language. But doing so lost full access to his native tongue, leaving him stranded between two cultures, speaking utterly unintelligible pidgin phrases with un-Francophone-Lao. Finally, it was not a matter of different vocabulary or even grammar but of a different mind entirely, or as he put it "the Lao mind, to conceive things, follows a different route from that employed by Westerners."

The dilemmas confronting loyalists to bolster French-Lao identity was revealed by another author, T. N. Singharaj, who debated the issue "should we say *Laotien* or Lao?" (1947). First, Singharaj explained the French impact on Laos: "the first French [who] came to Laos would have certainly said the 'country of Laos,' but this did not affect Lao discourse until later." To find the original, authentic form, Singharaj went back to before French colonialism while marking how deeply it impacted Lao, symbolized by the addition of the "s" to their country's name. "Here it is, in a word, the origin of 'Laos', [of] purely French origin…" To Singharaj, the French, by adding the "s" and obscuring the true form, then introduced a question of authenticity, as many variants were introduced (Laocien, Laosien). France's arrival to the country introduced confusion and ambiguity about terminology, but to loyalists, it struck deeper to question their identity, symbolized by the cloud of uncertainty surrounding the proper appellation. This rupture introduced what could only be described as an identity crisis felt among loyalist Lao. Singharaj felt that it must be addressed.

Singharaj believed that Lao discourse remained unaffected by French, or even Thai: "Whatever this term 'Laos' be imposed in the administrative and international milieu, it does not prevent the Lao and their neighbors of the right bank of the Mekong of saying between them and always 'MUONG LAO' (country of Laos)." To him, Lao remained unaffected after being colonized and divided up to live under numerous states. He saw an eternal, unchanging identity, a Xāt Lao which survived, immutable and expressed in the local vernacular, not elite but popular, which excluded French, Thai, Vietnamese and Chinese. Its appearance in Kinnari suggests its ubiquity in Lao thought of the time. Singharaj continued:

> It is right therefore for a new Laos that is organized and to which the liberating French come to grant generously democratic liberties, to fix, for all time, the choice of the one or the other term. SHOULD WE SAY LAOTIEN OR LAO?

He concluded: "Finally, the wish dearest of all, this would be to see used only the term 'Lao' to designate the inhabitants of Muong Lao, both by the [French] as by foreign nations..."

The dilemma was for Lao to accommodate French, and submit to using Laotien, or for French to follow Lao usage. Raising the question was a subtle way to query whose interests would predominate after 1945? Singharaj called for Laos to be called Lao, embracing the idea of a single Lao race, which did not address the problem of inclusivity in a multiethnic state. Singharaj was too concerned with confronting foreign powers to consider a more inclusive form of nationalism, much less worry about non-Lao minorities living within the territorial boundaries. This was a common mistake made by many Lao nationalists of the time who were concerned with resisting foreign power at the cost of thinking through the implications their conception of the nation had for the one of the most diverse countries in the region. Some loyalists called for a more inclusive vision of the nation. They also raised serious questions about the prominence and spread of French culture. Simply because they decided to remain in Laos after French reconquest, and to participate in the postconquest government, did not preclude them from expressing anti-French views. Thus, even loyalists embraced the idea of Xāt Lao while struggling with questions of identity and cultural alienation in a cosmopolitan milieu.

The appeal of Issara anti-colonial nationalism

The Issara embrace of Xāt Lao by the anti-colonial route was rather easier. They resisted French influence. Writing in exile (1946–1949), they sought to reclaim their history from French colonial historians. This produced the first nationalist Lao history ever written. The loyalists were not the only ones to continue the cultural studies started in the 1930s. The Issara in exile, having broken from France, charted a new direction in cultural nationalism, going beyond what was possible living under French rule, yet clearly building on earlier experiences. Rather than working in the spirit of French-Lao friendship, the Issara, led by Katay, began to seriously question the role of the French in Lao history. The works of French colonial historians, whom the loyalists cited approvingly, were mercilessly interrogated by Katay, who wrote many Issara works. The Issara sought to decolonize the mind and culture of the Lao. They saw that it was not just a matter of getting the French to physically leave the country, but that Lao, to safeguard true independence, must view themselves differently than they had under French rule. To them, the idea of a Lao race was a clarion call to unite the country and throw out the foreign invader.

Issara questioned the founding myth of colonial Laos, Auguste Pavie's so-called "Conquest of Hearts" (Katay 1948a). In this event, Pavie traveled to Luang Prabang in 1887 to serve as the French vice-consul, and while there, reputedly saved King Oun Kham from an attack on the palace led by the son of the ruler of Muang Lai, Deo Van Tri (who killed the Luang Prabang Viceroy among others). Afterward, Pavie said that the King asked for French protection. Katay was the first to question this account and was critical of the "commonly accepted version" given by French colonial historians. He knew of the event's importance because it was repeatedly invoked by French to legitimate their rule. Moreover, in the "Conquest of Hearts" story, Lao were portrayed as willing subjects of France, since it was the King himself who had called for protection. The myth portrayed all French-Lao relations under the halo of "friendship," casting France as unassailably benevolent. Katay complained that even French anti-colonists were won over by Pavie's "Conquest of Hearts," thereby insidiously concealing French domination. His revisionist views were aptly conveyed in the pamphlet's title:

> The truth of the sack of Luang Prabang by Deo Van Tri in June 1887 – the Machiavellian role of Auguste Pavie in this historic event which decided the fate of Laos, by bringing the country under the protection of France.

Katay alleged that Pavie was responsible for engineering the attack on Luang Prabang, which positioned him to "save" the Lao king, thereby winning a foothold in Laos for French colonialism. He questioned the "commonly accepted account" which "only comes from the account of Auguste Pavie" and which no historian has tried "to verify." He presented a "second version" of events based on investigations by the princes of Luang Prabang, who collected information from the family of Deo Van Tri and the people of Muang Lai. He also questioned the "old people" of Luang Prabang about Pavie's version of events. He tried to "examine objectively and impartially the facts, to reconcile" the different versions and concluded that the version given by Pavie was "strongly subject to caution."

Katay investigated Pavie's own accounts, especially as he recorded them in the *Mission Pavie*. By doing so, Katay re-read the colonial-era documents to create a counter-narrative of events. He quoted Pavie's journal where Pavie wrote: "the idea, which I am enamored – to make Laos – a French country…" to claim Pavie was an imperialist. He went beyond colonial records, relating that many people in Luang Prabang were already suspicious of Pavie ("*thane nam oy*," or "Mr. Sugar Cane") even before the disaster. He pointed to entries in Pavie's journal which he said proved that Pavie planned to destroy Luang Prabang, such as an entry from days before the attack recording a Thai official in the city accusing Pavie of arming Deo Van Tri's men. In other places, Katay outright denied certain entries in Pavie's journal, such as Pavie's claim to have offered to defend the town before the impending attack, saying "this assertion is formally denied by the old people of Luang Prabang."

The most serious accusations focused on Pavie's activities leading up to the attack in April–May, when Pavie toured the Nam Ou valley and Muang Ngoi, which were both on the invasion route taken by Deo Van Tri. Katay accused Pavie of contacting Deo Van Tri to plot the attack. Katay alleged that even though Pavie was warned of the danger of bandits in the area, he still traveled north with some unspoken goal. Katay suggested that Pavie wanted "precise information" on Deo Van Tri's troops. Katay focused on a ten-day period Pavie spent at Muang Ngoi, when Pavie was already returning to Luang Prabang. Katay observed that Pavie's journal was kept so "meticulously," yet gave no reason for his stay there nor what he did in the intervening time. In other places, Katay openly accused Pavie of inciting Deo Van Tri to attack Luang Prabang:

> It would be at the instigation of Auguste Pavie that Deo Van Tri undertook the sack of Luang Prabang. Auguste Pavie had said (or made to be said) to Deo-Van-Tri that his brothers and brother-in-law were taken in secret to Luang Prabang to the house of the

Phaya Muang Saen (an official of the court), [and] that he must hasten to free them if he did not want to see them taken to Bangkok, that the city of Luang Prabang, emptied of all its young elite…was no longer able to defend itself, that it contained treasures sufficiently important to cover the cost of an armed expedition etc.

When the final attack came, Pavie's assistant was "miraculously" ready to intervene to succor the King in a boat ready and waiting. This assistant woke up early in the morning and waited near the palace. Katay called this a "well planned scenario."

Katay noted further that Pavie never returned to Laos after he left in September 1895. To Katay, it showed that Pavie never really cared about the country, but only saw it as a gift to bestow to imperial France. Katay even suggested that Pavie did not return because he was ashamed and feared that Lao would figure out his deception. At any rate, "many Lao, young and old, are convinced" of the truth of Pavie's role in the destruction of Luang Prabang. The Issara did not limit itself to writing critiques. Even before gaining power in 1945, they boasted of having torn down a statue of Pavie in Vientiane "the day after the entry of Japanese troops." Later, they destroyed another Pavie statue in Luang Prabang when seizing it in November 1945. The statue in Vientiane had stood in the garden of the Résident-Supérieur's residence since 1932 to commemorate Pavie's death. Katay concluded that it was likely that Pavie had incited the attack of Deo Van Tri and thus, "the French occupation of Laos is vicious in its origin. So that the 'unanimous consent of Laos to place themselves under the protection of France' does not arise in truth from a will freely determined…" Katay argued that the colonial bond was never based on anything but deception and violence. He saw the French not as saviors of Lao, but as enemies of the nation. Finally, a new nationalist sentiment was visible in Katay's writings that could not be openly expressed under the French as his work was dedicated: "To the memory of all those who heroically fell for the Cause of Lao National Independence." Katay's veneration for the unknown soldier sought to inculcate a willingness to die for the nation which is nationalism par excellence.

Conclusion: two visions of Lao nationalism

Modern Lao nationalism has been haunted by two visions: a virulently nationalist Lao race symbolized by Xāt Lao or a more inclusive multiethnic form of nationalism. Even today there remains a fundamental tension between the founding of the LPDR to free Laos from foreign influence, and its claim to a multiethnic Lao nation. The very act of rooting out foreign influence to purify the nation inevitably raises questions about who belongs in the nation and who is foreign. This risks tearing at the fabric of an ethnically diverse society like Laos. The French-Lao, as much as they are vilified by LPDR histories, presaged LPDR multiethnic nationalism founded on the "multiethnic Lao people" in as much as at times they saw themselves not just as a single race, but as an inclusive, multiethnic nation. To the degree that the LPDR fails to live up to promises of ethnic equality, it too has been captured by the hyper-nationalist idea of a Lao race just as had its old foe, the RLG. Pride in Lao culture and history can quickly devolve into ethnic chauvinism in Laos, like anywhere else in the world. But between these two poles of identity, it must be admitted that the Lao elite played a leading role in crafting their vision of the nation.

Nationalism did not suddenly appear in 1941 with the French-sponsored Lao Nhay campaign. Indeed, it reached back to the 1890s when ethno-nationalism first appeared. It developed in many stages. One key formative stage was the invention of a Lao tradition at the Vientiane Buddhist Institute. While this was a French colonial institution, the French were both positive and negative influences on Lao nationalism; positive as a model, and negative as racist, oppressive and denying equality or political freedom to Lao. One did not need to be a communist to be anti-French. At a time when communism in Laos was almost entirely a Vietnamese affair, the Lao elite developed unique forms of nationalism. Even though multiethnic nationalism failed to hold Lao attention, study of its failure is important for revealing how and why Lao nationalism developed as it did; and how it became captured by Xāt Lao – a virulently nationalist idea of a Lao race.

References

"3349." 1978. *Iron Man of Laos: Prince Phetsarath Ratanavongsa*, trans. John B. Murdoch, ed. David Wyatt. Ithaca: Cornell SEAP.
Barmé, Scott. 1993. *Luang Wichit Wathakan and the Creation of a Thai Identity*. Singapore: National University of Singapore, Institute of Southeast Asian Studies.
Bhabha, Homi K. 1994. *The Location of Culture*. Abingdon: Routledge.
Brown, MacAlister, and Joseph Zasloff. 1985. *Apprentice Revolutionaries: The Communist movement in Laos, 1930–1985*. Stanford: Hoover Institute Press.
Creak, Simon. 2015. *Embodied Nation: Sport, Masculinity, and the Making of Modern Laos*. Honolulu: University of Hawai'i Press.
Gunn, Geoffrey. 1988. *Political Struggles in Laos, 1930–1954*. Bangkok: Editions Duang Kamol.
Gunn, Geoffrey. 2017. "The Invention of French Laos." *Engaging Asia: Essays on Laos and Beyond in Honour of Martin Stuart-Fox*, edited by Desley Goldston, 144–181. Copenhagen: NIAS Press.
Halpern, Joel. 1964. *Government, Politics and Social Structure in Laos: A Study of Tradition and Innovation*. New Haven: Yale University Southeast Asia Studies.
Ivarsson, Soren. 1999. "Toward a new Laos: *Lao Nhay* and the campaign for a national "reawakening" in Laos, 1941–1945." In *Laos: Culture and Society*, edited by Grant Evans, 61–78. Chiang Mai: Silkworm Books.
Ivarsson, Soren. 2008. *Creating Laos: The Making of a Lao Space between Indochina and Siam, 1860–1945*. Copenhagen: NIAS Press.
Ivarsson, Soren, and Christopher Goscha. 2007. "Prince Phetsarath (1890–1959): Nationalism and royalty in the making of modern Laos." *Journal of Southeast Asian Studies* 38 (1): 55–81.
Katay, Sasorith. 1948a. *Contribution à l'histoire du mouvement d'Independence nationale Lao*. Bangkok: editions Lao-Issara.
(Thao) Katay, Sasorith. 1948b. *Le Laos*, n.p.: Editions Lao Issara.
Katay, Sasorith. 1953. *Le Laos: Son évolution politique et sa place dans l'Union française*. Paris: Editions Berger-Levrault.
Katay, Sasorith. 1958. *Souvenirs d'un ancien écolier de Paksé*. N.p.: éditions Lao Sédone.
Kiernan, Ben. 2008. *The Pol Pot Regime: Race, Power and Genocide in Cambodia under the Khmer Rouge, 1975–1979*. New Haven: Yale University Press.
Kingdom of Laos. 1961. *Annuaire Statistique du Laos: Quatrième Volume, 1953 à 1957*. n.p.: Kingdom of Laos.
Koret, Peter. 1999. "Books of Search: The Invention of Traditional Lao Literature as a Subject of Study." In *Laos: Culture and Society*, edited by Grant Evans, 226–257. Chiang Mai: Silkworm Books.
"Lao Blood." 1947. ເລືອດລາວ ["Principles of Democracy"], *Kinnari*, no. 5, July.
Lao Hakxa Sat. 1959. November 16.
LeBoulanger, Paul. 1930. *Histoire du Laos française: Essai d'une étude chronologique des principautés laotiennes*. Paris: Librairie Plon.
Nginn, Pierre Somchine. 1971. "Les mémoires de M. Nginn." *Bulletin des amis du Royaume Lao*, no. 4–5.
Nginn, Pierre Somchine, 1972. "Les mémoires de M. Nginn (II)." *Bulletin des amis du Royaume Lao*, no. 7–8.
Pavie, Auguste. 1947. *A la conquête des cœurs: le pays des millions d'éléphants et du parasol blanc*. Paris: Presses universitaires de France.
(Prince) Phetsarath, Rattanavongsa. 2011 [1951]. ໂຫຣາສາດລາວ [*Lao Astrology*]. Vientiane: Dokked.
(Maha) Phoumy Chitaphong. 1946. "ກິນນະຣີ [Kinnary]." *Kinnari*, November.
Phouvong. 1947. "Apprendra-t-on le Laotien?" *Kinnari*, no. 6, November.

Polmuk, Chairat. 2014. "Invoking the Past: The Cultural Politics of Lao Literature, 1941–1975." MA Thesis. Ithaca: Cornell University.
(Maha) Sila Viravong. 2004. ຊີວິດຜູ້ຂ້າ [*My life*]. Vientiane: Manthathurat Publishing House.
Singharaj, T. N. 1947. "*Faut-il dire Laotien ou Lao?*" *Kinnari*, July, 1–2.
Sisouk Na Champassak. 1961. *Storm over Laos*, New York: Praeger.
Souneth, Photisane et al. 2000. ປະຫວັດສາດລາວ ["History of Laos"]. Vientiane.
Tappe, Oliver. 2013. "Facts and Facets of the Kantosou Kou Xat – the Lao 'National Liberation Struggle' in State Commemoration and Historiography." *Asian Studies Review* 37 (4): 433–450.
Wolfson-Ford, Ryan. 2017. "Strangers in the hills: Social disruption and the origins of Lao nationalism (1873–1911)." *South East Asia Research* 25 (4): 412–430.
Wolfson-Ford, Ryan. 2019. "Tai Manuscripts and Early Printed Books at the Library of Congress." *Journal of the Siam Society* 107 (2): 135–154.

34
DIFFERENT STREAMS OF MALAY NATIONALISM FROM THE LATE COLONIAL TO CONTEMPORARY ERAS

Ahmad Fauzi Abdul Hamid and Azmi Arifin

Introduction

This chapter discusses debates on various facets of Malay nationalism that developed in the Malay Peninsula or Malaya from the late colonial epoch to more contemporary times. It does not take into account-related discourses on Malay nationalism which conceive of a broader geographical notion of 'the Malay' as encompassing the several groups that constitute the Malay *ethnie* in present-day Indonesia, southern Thailand, Myanmar, the Philippines, Brunei, Singapore, Sri Lanka, Madagascar, South Africa and the Malaysian states of Sabah and Sarawak in Borneo island (Milner 2008), the existence of genealogical links connecting the vast expanse of the putative Malay world notwithstanding. Neither does this chapter discuss other forms of Malay nationalism that incorporate elements of non-Malay nationalistic impulses in the Malay Peninsula, such as a racially transcending Malayan nationalism that sought to marry the interests of Malay, Chinese, Indian and Orang Asal or aboriginal communities in singular political movements (Wang 1962; Kheng 1985; Mauzy 2006). The present authors' research focuses exclusively on the political awakening and struggle of indigenous Malay political activists, whose ethno-religious identity is marked by such common traits as profession of Islam as their religion, use of Malay as their quotidian language, practice of Malay custom in their daily lives and a moderate phenotype in physical built and skin complexion. The existence of such generalities does not however deny sociological developments that may affect the nature and definition of 'the Malay' from time to time (Ismail 1985; Milner 2008).

The limited ethno-nationalist scope above is compounded by the circumscribed periodisation of this study. Without denying the links that obtain among Malay nationalist currents of different colonial periods, this chapter focuses on the development of Malay nationalism from the Second World War until the early years of Malaya's independence, with occasional references to contemporary developments wherever and whenever relevant.

This chapter argues that the local historiography of Malay nationalism has been unduly influenced by local historians' ideological inclinations and biases, particularly in its binary positioning of a pro-establishment 'rightist' variant as against an anti-establishment 'leftist' variant. While the former is more racially exclusivist without ruling out inter-ethnic cooperation, the latter is generally more open to multi-ethnic solidarity without however rejecting altogether Malay political and cultural primacy. Both the rightist and leftist streams incorporate Islam into their agendas, but the nature and extent of their religious cooptation differ. Right-wing Malay nationalism held sway over independent Malaysia's Malay-Muslims until May 2018, when for the very first time the United Malays National Organisation (UMNO) was removed from power after losing in the country's 14th general elections.

Finally, this chapter acknowledges the vast contributions made by revisionist accounts of Malayan history of the 1945–1957 period. By conceiving of the history of Malay nationalism in a more all-encompassing and long-term manner, revisionist historians have aptly located the emergence of both right-wing and left-wing variants of Malay nationalism to emergent Islamists of the early twentieth century.

The splintered discourse of Malay nationalism

Any discussion on Malay nationalism will have to deal with three major issues that have occupied not only historians of the subject but also contemporary stakeholders such as politicians, civil society activists and educationists until today. The first issue is concerned with the timeline of the emergence of Malay nationalism, in particular, when did it appear as a significant factor in national politics? Second, what were and are its aims? Was Malay nationalism a movement to liberate Malays from not only colonial but also monarchical rule, or was it a tool of defence against encroachment of foreigners, as how the migrant Chinese and Indian communities were perceived before they were accepted as full citizens of the country under the Federation of Malaya Agreement 1948. Third, who were the primary activists who led Malay political re-awakening via their championing of Malay nationalism?

In tackling the above issues, local historians and political scientists are divided into several camps. Interestingly, these scholarly camps generally reflect the ideological segmentation of Malay nationalists themselves. Academically speaking, the historiography of Malay nationalism has been closely aligned to distinct activist streams of Malay nationalism (Arifin 2014). In other words, the historical trajectory of Malay nationalism has been strongly influenced by contemporary developments in Malaysian politics; Malaysia here being understood as the nation-state that was founded on September 16, 1963, out of the merger of Malaya or Peninsular Malaysia as it is known today, with Sarawak and Sabah on Borneo island, and Singapore; Singapore later leaving the federation in August 1965. Malay nationalism has been instrumentalised to attract sympathy, strengthen ideological leanings and immortalise a particular political party's contributions in the fight for independence and the quest for nation-building. Differences that transpire between scholarly camps owe less to conceptual variations in the understanding of Malay nationalism itself, but more to the intellectual gulf separating scholars and activists of Malay nationalism as conditioned by their diverse experiences and thought processes (Kratoska 1985; Arifin 2014).

On the first issue – periodisation of the advent of Malay nationalism, studies of a generic nature conventionally pinpoint the years immediately following the Second World War, or more specifically in tandem with the departure of Japanese occupiers, as its beginning (Silcock and Aziz 1953; Bamadhaj 1975; Akashi 1985). This era witnessed a culmination of Malay political consciousness arising from changes in colonial policies and ever-increasing risks posed by a burgeoning immigrant population. Within such a context, some researchers argue for the mid-1940s as the moment of Malay nationalism's arrival, marked by the convergence of its rightist and leftist streams in standing up in unity against the British plan to embark on full-fledged colonial rule via its Malayan Union scheme. This sudden outpouring of anti-colonial activism gave birth to UMNO in 1946 (Kheng 1988; Omar 1993).

Other scholars have postulated a later emergence of Malay nationalism. For example, Pluvier (1967–1968, 1974) and Wang Gungwu (1981) dispute the concepts of nation and nationalism as contributing to the rise of anti-colonial activities in the 1940s, and instead settle on the 1950s as the decade in which a more multi-ethnic form of Malayan nationalism began taking shape on the national stage.

A putative view which later entered the national discourse as more or less official history, as crystallised in secondary-level history textbooks of independent Malaysia, was put forward by Soenarno (1960) and Roff (1967). They generally divided Malay political consciousness of immediate pre-independent and post-independent Malaya into three categories, namely religious, socio-economic and political. They trace the germination of political awakening of the Malays as a nation to the reformist Kaum Muda (Young Faction) movement from the cusp of the twentieth century through the 1930s. The Kaum Muda socio-religious revivalist impulse was however stifled by the prevalence of tradition-bound 'feudalism' among the Malay community, which resulted in intellectual stagnation of the Malay masses (Soenarno 1960).

In his doctoral thesis widely regarded today as a classic, *The Origins of Malay Nationalism* (1967), Roff dismisses the Kaum Muda as representing rising nationalist consciousness among the Malays that was of any widespread political significance. Their mouthpiece, Al-Imam (The Leader) (1906–1908), modelled on the Arabic newspapers *Al-Manar* (The Lighthouse) and *Al-Urwat al-Wuthqa* (The Indissoluble Link), focused disproportionately on religious issues and relegated social and political discussions to the periphery. To Roff, the Kaum Muda were to all intents and purposes British loyalists whose mixed descent – many of them being of Arab-Malay and Indian-Malay extraction and active in the Colonial Office-controlled Straits Settlements – drew them further apart from the Malay masses living under monarchical rule or *kerajaan* in the various Malay states. Malay elites in these various states, many of whom had increasingly benefited from Western education in Malay schools, were unprepared to conceive the Malays as a cohesive nation beyond the borders of the states, hence the formation of different state-based Malay associations scattered throughout Malaya. A modern inclusive nation-state was far from their national imagination. Even among the Malay literati as per their discussions in newspapers of the day, Malay political consciousness was conceived more as a response to the non-Malay rather than colonial threat:

> Chauvinist, or ethnicist, rather than politically nationalist, the Malay Associations professed complete loyalty to the traditional Malay establishments, on the basis of the separate state structure, and an almost equal enthusiasm for British colonial rule, as the bulwark for the time being of Malay interests against the rapacious demands of Malayan-domiciled aliens.
>
> *(Roff 1967, 324)*

Inheriting such a dichotomised framework, the historiography of Malay nationalism has since the end of the Japanese occupation (1941–1945) revolved around the binary interpretations of right-wing against left-wing nationalism. Both these streams gradually built up support among the scholarly community in the post-Second World War era. While the dichotomous state of affairs has largely persisted, it is the role of ruling party, UMNO, which ruled Malaysia as part of the Perikatan (Alliance) and Barisan Nasional (BN: National Front) coalitions continuously from 1957 until 2018, that has pre-occupied participants of the debates on Malay nationalism. Styling itself as the paragon of Malay nationalism, UMNO is taken to represent its right-wing or rightist stream as opposed to an assorted bloc of left-wing or leftist Malay parties, of which the Pan-Malayan Islamic Party (PMIP, today known as the Islamic

Party of Malaysia or PAS) has served as a rival except for brief periods of reconciliation in 1973–1977 and 2019–2022.

Essentially an elite conservative Malay party, UMNO's struggle has been equated with championing Malay interests to the exclusion of non-Malay communities. This encompasses realising through governmental authority constitutional clauses which seek to defend Malay and other native or Bumiputera (sons of the soil) privileges such as the sanctity of Islam and the Malay language, and preferential access to educational scholarships and civil service quotas. Right-wing nationalists accuse left-wing nationalists of being liberal in matters of citizenship and fluidity of ethnic identity, as obtained in the ten-point Perlembagaan Rakyat (People's Constitution) proposals struck between the Malay-dominated Pusat Tenaga Ra'ayat (PUTERA: Centre for People's Power) and the non-Malay All-Malayan Council of Joint Action (AMCJA) in 1947 (Abdul Hamid 2007). In the worldview of right-wing Malay nationalism, there always lurks the shadow of a non-Malay threat to Malay primacy in national political, economic and social affairs. This privileging of Malay categories in defining the identity of Malaysia as a nation-state has since the 1980s been captured by the term *ketuanan Melayu*, i.e. Malay supremacy (Chin 2016).

Due to its pre-dominant position in successive Perikatan-BN governments for more than 60 years (1957–2018), it is UMNO's version of the independence struggle that has prevailed in official repositories of history such as school textbooks, archives, museums and the pro-government printed media. In such a version, UMNO elite figures such as its first President Onn Jaafar (1895–1962) and second President Tunku Abdul Rahman (1903–1990) are invariably raised to the status of political icons and even founding father of the country in the case of the latter. The national-level struggle for independence is portrayed as having been the painstaking concerted efforts of right-wing Malay elite leaders assisted by moderate non-Malay figures from the Malayan (later Malaysian) Chinese Association (MCA) and Malayan (later Malaysian) Indian Congress (MIC), both of which together with UMNO made up the Perikatan governing coalition from 1955 to 1969. Although right-wing Malay nationalism had in actual fact appeared on the national scene since the 1920s through the sporadic founding of Malay associations, it is UMNO's emergence in 1946 – the outcome of the state-based Malay associations forming a united front – that official history prefers to identify as the cradle of Malay nationalism. The choice of the timing is linked to the manifestly anti-colonial character of the UMNO-led agitation against the Malayan Union, whereas the reality is that during most other times, the right-wing Malay nationalists' posture with respect to the British was more conciliatory.

This official version of history fails to acknowledge the contributions of left-wing Malay nationalists in UMNO's struggle, especially the critical phases of its establishment and changing of its slogan from 'Hidup Melayu' (Long Live the Malays) to 'Merdeka' (Freedom) (Hussain 2004; Arifin 2014). The UMNO-centric version of history depicts its right-wing protagonists of Malay nationalism as moderates as opposed to the radical left-wing Malay nationalists. In truth, placements along the moderate-radical spectrum depended on the extent of a particular group's anti-colonial disposition. While outwardly displaying anti-colonial fervour during the Malayan Union protests of 1946, UMNO never wavered in its attitude of looking up to the British as a protector of the Malays against the non-Malay threat and as a benign colonial power (Khoo 1991). Claiming the full credit for achieving independence of Malaya on August 31, 1957, UMNO and like-minded right-wing Malay nationalists and writers relegated by default left-wing Malay nationalists, non-Malay interest groups, and *madrasah* (Islamic school)-based Islamic activists to the periphery of the independence struggle narrative. Worse still, virtually all of these left-wing cohorts were lumped together under the 'communist' or at least 'communist-influenced' category, without denying that fascination of communist ideology did exist among some quarters of leftist nationalist activists broadly understood. In an age when there was no competitor against the colonial government's propaganda via printed media, such demonisation worked perfectly, justifying in the eyes of the public the clampdown on leftist activism in 1948, as exercised via large-scale detentions without trial authorised by the Emergency Regulations Ordinance, precursor of the Internal Security Act (ISA) 1960.

It was not until the late 1990s that the official history above was contested. Buoyed by contemporary political economic developments which saw a devastating economic slump engulfing Malaysia in 1997–1998, which was aggravated by widespread protests arising from then Prime Minister Dr Mahathir Mohamad's unceremonious dismissal of his deputy Anwar Ibrahim from all his government and party posts, scholars long supportive of Anwar rose to the occasion with more nuanced accounts of historical events and personalities. Anwar, a long-time icon of left-wing Malay nationalism during his student days at Universiti Malaya in the late 1960s and early 1970s, was brought into the government by Dr Mahathir to help with his 'assimilation of Islamic values' programme in the 1980s. During Anwar's tenure as the Minister of Education (1986–1991), history was made a compulsory subject at secondary level in 1989. The period in which Anwar participated as a member of the UMNO-led government coincided with the zenith of the *dakwah* (propagation) movement amidst a global Islamic resurgence spurred by such galvanising events as the Iranian revolution and the Soviet invasion of Afghanistan in 1979. *Dakwah* in the Malaysian context was manifested most vigorously in the flourishing of Islam as a 'way of life' beyond mere rituals, as promoted by a host of Islamist organisations such as the Angkatan Belia Islam Malaysia (ABIM: Muslim Youth Movement of Malaysia), the Jemaah Islah Malaysia (JIM: Society of Islamic Reform), Jamaat Tabligh and Darul Arqam (Nagata 1984; Abdul Hamid 2003).

The premature sacking and eventual imprisonment of Anwar (1999–2004) on charges of corruption and sexual misdemeanour all but dashed hopes of a 'reform from within' with respect to UMNO and government administration, but by then a new generation of teachers, educators, scholars and intellectuals had been nurtured in Malaysian educational institutions, determined not to stay silent over historical fallacies committed by the powers that be and state-connected gatekeepers of history. Many of these new cohorts of Malay intelligentsia were former cadres of the *dakwah* movements mentioned above, or at the very least had participated in various *dakwah* programmes conducted in schools and institutions of higher learning throughout the 1970s–1980s. *Dakwah* and Islamist ideals had injected new vitality and ambitions into their professional activities.

Risking accusations of whitewashing atrocities committed by the Malayan Communist Party (MCP), revisionist accounts of Malay nationalism present more inclusive narratives of the independence struggle by recognising the efforts of wide-ranging segments of Malay society such as the nobility, the *ulama* (religious scholars), the schoolteachers and grassroots community leaders united by their refusal to cooperate with and abide by terms given by the British. Within the context of anti-colonial Malay nationalism, the authors locate its genealogy as stemming from the struggle of various Malay warriors against British incursions on behalf of their capitalist interests as part of its forward movement into Malay states following the signing of the Anglo-Perak Pangkor Treaty of 1874. In the annals of the Malay anti-colonial struggle, names of such fighters as Dato' Bahaman (b. 1838) of Pahang, Dato' Dol Said (1773–1849) of Naning, Tok Janggut (1853–1915) of Kelantan and Abdul Rahman Limbong (1868–1929) of Terengganu have been immortalised in official and oral histories as the epitomes of anti-British Malay heroic rebels. The lineage continues through the Kaum Muda reformists whose focus was on educational renaissance rather than physical insurrection. Such reformism had morphed into left-wing Malay activism by the late 1930s through efforts of such fervent nationalists as Dr Burhanuddin Al-Helmy (1911–1969). As Khoo (1991) explains, the Malay leftist movement was a motley group represented by activists of distinct stripes, including Islamists – meaning those whose political vision centred around the formation of an Islamic state which implemented the *sharia* (Islamic law) as law of the land, but who were united by an anti-UMNO disposition. According to this revisionist version of history, the Malay left were betrayed by right-wing Malay nationalists who had the defence and maintenance of their privileges and rights as their foremost concerns, and who thus colluded with the British. Crackdown on and witch-hunting of left-wing Malay activists by the colonial authorities forced some of the insurrectionists underground, and into the clutches of the MCP. For these extremist elements of the Malay left, their platform was MCP's all-Malay Tenth Regiment (Mohammed Salleh 2015). But the entire gamut of Malay leftists were united in their view that UMNO were traitors to the Malays, and left-wing Malay nationalists personified the true struggle for Malayan independence (Abdul Hamid 2007; Ali 2018; Hishamuddin 2020).

Political reformation and exegetical changes of Malay nationalism narratives

Spurred on by cries of *Reformasi* (Reformation), referring to the widespread demand for all-encompassing political and socio-economic reforms championed by Anwar Ibrahim, all of which were throttled by his sudden deposition from the corridors of power on September 2, 1998, massive street protests erupted in a gallant show of defiance against the UMNO-led government in 1998–1999. Widely regarded as having been the victim of political conspiracy, Anwar was consequently found guilty of corruption and sodomy – allegations which his supporters regarded as trumped-up charges whose culpabilities had been decided on by corrupt ruling elites acting in cahoots with an emasculated and biased judiciary. Righly or wrongly, Anwar instantly became the icon of *Reformasi*, euphoria about which resonated among Malaysian communities worldwide, with messages of sympathy and encouragement pouring in from the political leaderships of Indonesia, the Philippines and the United States of America (USA), among others. Although Anwar and his political compatriots either left or were ejected from the UMNO-controlled ruling establishment during subsequent purges, many outwardly politically neutral professionals remained in the bureaucracy or government-linked companies (GLCs) while growing disenchanted with the humiliating treatment meted out to the former Deputy Prime Minister. UMNO-related themes swiftly fell into disrepute among pockets of Malay communities especially in urban areas. In the educational sphere, this disorientation extended to a history syllabus seen as too UMNO-centric or even outright right-wing nativistic propaganda that marginalises both the roles of non-Malays and non-UMNO Malays alike in nation-building. Such propaganda was perpetuated through a whole set of nationalist paraphernalia, the BN-controlled mass media and national-level commemorative ceremonies during occasions of countrywide importance. The stage had thus been set, on the cusp of the new millennium, for revisionist interpretations of Malaysian history to take hold.

Since 1999, diverse sections of Malaysian society have become disillusioned with UMNO's depraved stewardship of the nation. The official version of history which had hitherto marginalised the roles of anti-UMNO elements in the struggle for independence started to be rivalled by an alternative version which showed greater appreciation for the country's unsung heroes. These included anti-colonial warrior fighters of the 1870s, religious reformists and Islamists of the 1900s–1930s and left-wing nationalists of the 1940s–1950s. The arrival of internet blogs quickly raised the popularity of such alternative narratives, many of which, in contrast to the erudite nature of official history, were written in simple and comprehensible enough language designed to capture a popular audience. However, not everything about the revisionist versions of history was trailblazing. For example, in many ways, they were still unable to free themselves from the stereotype, inherited from colonial and Western historians (cf. Furedi 1991, Stockwell 1993), that the Malay leftist-Islamist stream was simply another manifestation of the communist movement, disguised in religious garb to conceal its more sinister motives.

On the one hand, among the generation who entered the labour force when Anwar Ibrahim was Deputy Prime Minister in the 1990s, an urgent need was felt to re-define history in a mould that gave due justice to fighters whose contributions to the independence struggle had been unjustly neglected by the UMNO-dominated regime. There was also more openness to admit the grim fact that UMNO's early leaders were British collaborators, hence generating debates on whether this amounted to betrayal or not. Among Malays who grew up under the shadow of the New Economic Policy (1971–1990), there was increasing albeit belated admission that a multi-cultural Malaysian rather than just Malay nationalism needed to be recognised on the nation-building path. Calls henceforth emerged for greater recognition for a host of left-wing organisations that mushroomed in the period between the end of the Second World War and independence. These included the Malay Nationalist Party (MNP, also known by its Malay acronym PKMM: Parti Kebangsaan Melayu Malaya), PUTERA, Angkatan Pemuda Insaf (API: Aware Youth Corps), Angkatan Wanita Sedar (AWAS: Aware Women Corps), Kesatuan Ra'ayat Indonesia Semenanjung (KRIS: Union of Peninsular Indonesians) and the non-Malay AMCJA. Such demands for more inclusivity were gradually incorporated into the secondary school syllabus as UMNO, weakened by poor performances at the national polls in 2008 and 2013, tried to adapt to the younger generations' sentiments. Although the move towards greater inclusivity in independence narratives had started under the oversight of BN-controlled education ministries, it was the Pakatan Harapan (PH: Pact of Hope) administration (2018–2020) that was to bear the brunt of attacks from right-wing Malay groups which accused it of influencing changes in the Kurikulum Standard Sekolah Menengah (KSSM: Secondary School Standard Curriculum) such as to vindicate the communist struggle in the Year 4 official history textbook (Ramlah 2020). In truth, being denied a specific chapter focusing on itself, UMNO's role was apparently marginalised in the book, in contrast to a whole chapter devoted to discussing the communist threat and the 1948 Declaration of Emergency (Hasan et al. 2019).

On the other hand, to those scholar-activists and politicians on the centre-left spectrum of the political divide, the piecemeal acceptance of leftist nationalist discourses amidst the post- *Reformasi* euphoria was a welcome development to which they later contributed via semi-academic or scholarly pieces of work. Among these academics-cum-politicians were Syed Hussein Alatas (1928–2007) – founder of the multi-racial Parti Gerakan Rakyat Malaysia (GERAKAN: Malaysian People's Movement Party) and former Vice-Chancellor of Universiti Malaya (1988–1991); Syed Husin Ali (b. 1936) – former Sociology professor at Universiti Malaya, former President of Parti Rakyat Malaysia (PRM: Malaysian People's Party) (1990–2003) and former Deputy President of Parti Keadilan Rakyat (PKR: People's Justice Party) (2003–2010); and Chandra Muzaffar (b. 1947) – former political scientist at both Universiti Sains Malaysia and Universiti Malaya and former Deputy President of Parti Keadilan Nasional (KEADILAN: National Justice Party) (1999–2001), the precursor of PKR.

On the party political front, among vocal spokesmen for centre-left positions on nationalism, besides Anwar Ibrahim himself, were Mohamad Sabu (b. 1954) – former Deputy President of PAS, present President of Parti Amanah Negara (AMANAH: National Trust Party) and former Minister of Defence in PH's short-lived government, and Ronnie Liu (b. 1958) – a loquacious Democratic Action Party (DAP) politician who has legally landed in hot soup several times for his seemingly pro-communist statements. Research and publications articulating leftist orientations have been the forte of independent publishing houses such as the Strategic Information and Research Development Centre (SIRD), Gerak Budaya and Pusat Sejarah Rakyat (People's History Centre). However, brushes with the authorities cannot be avoided when this alternative version of the 'people's history' dangerously occupies liminal spaces between social democracy, socialism and communism (cf. Zainudin 2020). A purported association with the communist movement has perennially been used against advocates of this alternative history.

Their anti-UMNO strand and vindication of left-wing Malay nationalism serve as points of convergence among the several variants of 'people's history' proffered by revisionists (Arifin 2014; 2019a). In these versions, elitist UMNO-centric themes, while not being discarded altogether, have been diluted in significance, giving way to more adventurous discussions of anti-UMNO nationalists from the likes of organisations hitherto portrayed as 'radical' such as Kesatuan Melayu Muda (KMM: Young Malays Union), MNP, API, AWAS, PUTERA-AMCJA, Hizbul Muslimin (HM) and even MCP. According to this revisionist narrative, leftist-Islamist factions of Malay nationalists were prime targets of harassment from UMNO and the British colonial authorities. The peak of such harassment was the Emergency Declaration of 1948, which authorised a drastic swoop of all left-wing activists under ISA-like detention laws. The crackdown was legitimised on the pretext of defeating the communists, who were alleged to have penetrated post-bellum left-wing organisations in their bid to wrest power when the time was ripe. MCP, a dreaded force then given the contemporary rise of global communism under the patronage of Soviet Union and the People's Republic of China, served as a convenient scapegoat that enabled the British to paralyse once and for all manifestations of leftist nationalism. This immensely benefited UMNO, the colonial authorities' chosen representative to negotiate independence on behalf of the Malays (Arifin 2014; 2019b).

Polemical debates that arose among historiographers of Malay nationalism reflect the wide gulf that separates the rightist and leftist schools of thought and that aligns broadly with the gap dividing right-wing and left-wing politicians and civil society activists. This chasm owes to several issues. First, at dispute is the extent to which the different streams of nationalism wanted full independence from the British. Among a significant portion of right-wing Malay nationalists, pessimistic attitudes prevailed concerning the prospects of completely severing relations with the British at a time of rising non-Malay demands. Those aligned to UMNO's first President Onn Jaafar, for instance, feared that independence would merely open the floodgates for non-Malays to exact greater stakes in the country's political and socio-economic affairs, besides exposing gaps that could be exploited by the communists (Stockwell 1977; Stockwell 1995). The fact of the matter was that a fairly large number of right-wing nationalists were beneficiaries of colonial-mandated favours such as privileged access to English medium schools for their children and to civil service positions. To them, the British played a useful 'protector' role in withstanding pressure from the increasingly demanding non-Malays. What frightened these rightist nationalists especially was open non-Malay questioning of Malay privileges and traditional Malay institutions such as the monarchy (Mohamed Nordin 1976; Stockwell 1977; Ramlah 1998).

The second fault line emerges over the rightist and leftist nationalists' differential responses towards societal maladies, which, in turn, generated distinct reactions from the Malay community. Right-wing nationalists, elitist as they were, took full advantage of British preferential treatment of them to create a Malay upper middle class that worked hand in glove with the colonial authorities and Malay royalty in administering the political economy of the Malay states. Detached from the Malay masses, by the 1920s leading figures of this newly emerging class of brown-skinned Anglophiles founded a string of state-based Malay associations to claim leadership of the Malays. Yet, their demands were meek in contrast to the agendas of left-wing nationalists such as KMM and MNP, whose criticisms of the powers that be extended to censure of their ethnic brethren from among Malay ruling and administrative elites. Viewed as radical and subversive by the colonial state and its Malay allies, it was from the leftist stream that the first attempt to break down the racial barrier separating Malay and non-Malay nationalists materialised in the form of the Perlembagaan Rakyat of 1947 (Mandal 2003). Left-wing nationalists were more grounded in society, but except for communist-inclined activists who looked up to China, they lacked a patron inasmuch as their right-wing rivals had the British as their protector. The furthest they looked to for guidance was neighbouring Indonesia, from where many trace their ancestors too (Saat 2019). When both wings of Malay nationalism decided to work together rallying the Malays against the Malayan Union proposal in 1946, the British were momentarily taken aback. UMNO – product of originally concerted efforts between right-wing and left-wing Malay nationalists, upon the exodus of its left-wing supporters shortly after the British backed down on the Malayan Union proposal – regressed into a purely right-wing organisation echoing ethnocentric programmes.

The third issue of contention on which right-wing and left-wing Malay nationalists were at loggerheads was on the identity of those who could be truly regarded as genuine independence fighters. This matter arose in response to the distorted narratives employed to vilify the whole range of left-wing Malay nationalists, encompassing KMM, MNP, PUTERA-AMCJA, HM and MCP. These groups were demonised as being agents of non-Malays, Indonesia and communists. The framework used by scholars writing in this mould did not diverge from how UMNO perceived left-wing Malay nationalists as a whole. Onn Jaafar, for instance, was on record for warning Malays against danger coming from 'the jungle,' 'mountain' and 'ashore,' which were proverbial references to the communists, the Kaum Muda reformists and the Indonesian-influenced nationalists (Ibrahim 1978).

Contestations over which version of Malay nationalist history is the most legitimate have thus acquired not only historical but also political importance. In their bitter rivalry for over 60 years of independence, the UMNO-imposed version is what we invariably see in textbooks, pre-internet media and official narratives as read out and reified during national-level celebrations. But deep down, grassroots forces and civil society were gradually rebelling against this official version as the findings of more serious historical studies of the era came to light. A new generation of Malaysians born since independence slowly discarded UMNO's version; such new ways of thinking penetrated mainstream society and official institutions through new cohorts of civil servants, educationists and politicians who went to university in the 1980s–1990s. By 2018, when UMNO and BN for the first time conceded defeat at the national polls, the right-wing narrative, while still in existence if only in compartments, has been seriously challenged by a revisionist version which gives more credence to left-wing nationalist voices in the 'road to independence' storyline. BN-UMNO's epistemic influence over the Malays has been eroded to a significant extent, and although their parliamentarians were jolted back into power when the PH government crumbled in February 2020 due to defections, they are still far from regaining the primacy BN-UMNO once held in Malaysian politics. Their version of Malay nationalist history, while not totally destroyed, is far from intact, having to accommodate discourses which better appreciate Malay left-wing nationalists' contributions in the fight for independence and nation-building endeavours. It is not the extreme left 'people's history' desired by socialists and communists, as alleged by right-wing Malay extremists, either.

The centrist position in the historical exegesis of Malay nationalism

As our discussion unfolds, it becomes clear that the historiography of Malay nationalism has seen bitter rivalry between proponents of the right-wing and left-wing streams, both at the scholarly and activist levels. The historical division broadly impinges on contemporary politics by influencing the discursive framework and language of modern Malaysian politicians. Yet, occupying the liminal space between both ends of the nationalist spectrum is a centrist position, which has elements of both left-wing and right-wing nationalism but could not be collapsed into either due to the existence of unique features of its own. This centrist stream, we argue, is the Islamist stream, which has been either marginalised by scholars influenced by the post-Second World War academic trend of dismissing religion as an important factor in contemporary social sciences, or taken for granted as playing subordinate roles within the larger rightist or leftist grouping.

In other words, the Islamist stream is discursively denied an identity of its own. Khoo (1991) and Abu Talib (2008), for example, describe its members as 'Islamic-left,' pointing out how figures such as Dr Burhanuddin Al-Helmy played leading roles in the leftist MNP, KRIS and PUTERA before assuming the Presidency of PAS in 1956. Due to prevailing circumstances of the time, whether by accident or careful planning, Islamists found it strategically more rewarding to be directly involved in left-wing or right-wing organisations, such that in formal communique the 'Islamist' or 'Islamic' tag more often than not eludes them. We seek here to argue that the time has come for systematic studies of the Islamist faction of Malay nationalism be undertaken as separate research from both its right-wing and left-wing nationalism strains, the presence of overlapping traits among them notwithstanding.

An important thread tying together Islamists among the early Malay nationalists was their common educational background. Most of them were grounded in traditional Islamic education during their childhood, before progressing to Islamic boarding schools known as *pondok* (lit: huts) for the traditionally oriented and *madrasah* for the reformist-oriented students. A typical educational sojourn overseas would then take one to the Haramayn, i.e. Mecca and Medina for the traditionally oriented scholar or alternatively Cairo. Once Mecca and Medina fell under Saudi occupation, Cairo overtook the Haramayn as Malay students' preferred destination in search of religious knowledge (Shiozaki 2015). Their activism continued back home in their capacity as teachers, independent preachers, entrepreneurs, newspaper columnists, members of socio-political associations such as Persaudaraan Sahabat Pena (PASPAM: Brotherhood of Pen Friends) and MNP and later activists of Malay political parties (Abdullah 1976; Soh 1999). Kaum Muda *madrasahs* were suspected by the colonial authorities as being havens for leftist Malay nationalists following the post-War crackdown ostensibly to curb the communist threat. Left-wing Islamism never really recovered from the clampdown; existing MNP, HM and anti-UMNO activists then flocked to PAS, transforming the Islamic party from adopting a broadly right-wing stance and whose membership overlapped with that of UMNO into espousing a more leftist version of Islamism (Funston 1976). Some MNP members, especially of the 'transient leftist' variety, joined

UMNO directly, as was the case with Abdul Ghafar Baba (1925–2006), who later rose to become Deputy President of UMNO (1987–1993) and Malaysia's Deputy Prime Minister (1986–1993) (Abu Talib 2008).

During Dr Burhanuddin's leadership of PAS (1956–1969), Islam and Malay nationalism became twin pillars of its Islamist ideology. As far as he saw it, there was no contradiction between the two concepts; it is the Malay nationalists' creative ability to effect such doctrinal fusion that has confused foreign scholars and colonial policy-makers who could not imagine a leftist orientation that did not embrace socialism if not outright communism (Abu Talib 2008). The present authors are inclined to believe, based on credible evidence, that a large number of these Islamists were not thoroughbred leftists. However, despite being anti-communists at heart, they were not averse to tactical cooperation with communists towards the larger end of expelling the British colonialists from Malaya, preferring to delay the question of what to do in the eventuality of a communist triumph (Abdullah 1976; Ismail 2009; Arifin 2019b). In arguing our case, we recognise nevertheless the fact that some early nationalists of the Islamist variety did end up on the extreme right or left of the political spectrum, for instance, MCP stalwarts Musa Ahmad (1921–1995) and Shamsiah Fakeh (1924–2008).

Until today, PAS vacillates between foregrounding either the leftist or rightist variants of its ideology as it accommodates Islamists of both doctrinal inclinations. After Dr Burhanuddin's era, PAS veered towards right-wing Islamism under the leadership of Mohd Asri Haji Muda from 1969 to 1982 – a period which included PAS's brief stint in a newly formed BN (1973–1977). From 1999 to 2001 and again from 2008 to 2015, PAS's direction was steered towards left-wing Islamism as it tied its electoral fortunes to the Barisan Alternatif (BA: Alternative Front) and Pakatan Rakyat (PR: People's Pact) coalitions, respectively. Both BA and PR were alliances that included Anwar Ibrahim's Malay leftist parties KEADILAN (1999–2003) and PKR (2003–present day), and the multi-racial but Chinese-dominated DAP, whose ideology is best described as 'social democracy' as transmuted from its original tenet of 'democratic socialism' (Abdul Hamid and Johari 2019, 234). Since its break-up with PH, however, PAS's current President Haji Hadi Awang has steered the party back into the direction of right-wing Islamism, cooperating with UMNO via a Muafakat Nasional (MN: National Concord) signed in September 2019 and participating as an official member of the Perikatan Nasional (PN: National Alliance) governing coalition. In the federal government led by Prime Minister Muhyiddin Yassin (March 2020–August 2021), three cabinet ministers and five deputy ministers were from PAS.

The point here is that, being centrist in their ideological leaning, Islamist nationalists have been flexible enough, according to time and circumstances, to project either a leftist or rightist face. They have commonly navigated somewhere between both extreme paths, preferring moderate over extremist positions, without denying that some Islamists have fallen for extremist postures until Islamic sensibility brings them back along the middle path. Their loyalty is not towards ideology as such, but to Islam – understood as a comprehensive way of life encompassing multi-faceted aspects of managing society in accordance to God-laid rules and regulations. If the situation beckons, moderate Islamists can always cooperate with non-Islamist allies on a political basis, as have been demonstrated many times in history not only in Malaysia but also in other Muslim countries. The arrival of such political alliances does not mean jettisoning Islamic principles that have all along been the pillars of Islamist parties. Unfortunately, harbouring the pre-conceived notion of Islamism as a dogmatic and power-crazy ideology, many observers fail or simply refuse to acknowledge the skilful manoeuvring abilities of Islamists in the service of Islam. This extends to political collaboration with non-Muslim parties, civil society organisations and individuals, in the national interest, as has been courageously attempted in the 1946–1957 period as Malaya verged towards independence (Saat 2010).

Concluding remarks

Through this chapter, the authors have called for a historiographic shift: that the cohort of Malay nationalists known to have formed the religious wing of Malay nationalism be afforded a distinctive treatment of its own in sync with its *sui generis* characteristics outside the shadows of both right-wing and left-wing Malay nationalism. In line with contemporary terminology in the field of political Islam, we argue that the emergence of this religious stream formed, in Malaya at least, the first stirrings of Islamism as a political doctrine that envisions the establishment of an Islamic state as its ideal mode of governance. Nonetheless, unavoidable circumstances and pragmatic considerations persuaded these pioneering Islamists to embrace political collaboration that transcended ideological and ethno-religious identifications.

Although Kaum Muda reformists formed an important segment of these early Islamists, post-Second World War Islamism in reality reflected a curious synergy between Islamic reformism, with which the Kaum Muda activists were identified, and Islamic neo-traditionalism. Among prominent neo-traditionalist scholars who carved a name as one of the founders of PAS was Sheikh Muhammad Fadhlullah Suhaimi (1886–1964), who represented the Kaum Tua (Old Faction) in a memorable debate against leading Kaum Muda proponent Ahmad Hassan Bandung (1887–1958) in 1953 in Penang. While the Kaum Muda thrived in the modernist *madrasahs* that sprouted throughout Malaya from the 1920s onwards, the neo-traditionalists were typically *pondok* graduates fortunate enough to have travelled widely and undergone some form of overseas education that exposed them to nationalist currents sweeping the early twentieth-century *ummah* (global Muslim community). These neo-traditionalists must be differentiated from Kaum Tua traditionalist apologists who were conservative defenders of the religious status quo and unwavering supporters of Malay royalty and aristocracy – the type of *ulama* Roff (1967, 85–86) reprovingly notes as 'hawkers of religion,' obstacles to progress and pawns of the Malay ruling class.

The omission of the Islamist category from the ranks of pre- and post-Second World War Malay nationalists reflects the broader trend then of marginalising religion as a mobilising factor in the social sciences and humanities. In line with the Western-dominated intellectual spirit of the post-War era, modernisation was deemed to go hand in hand with secularisation, which amounted to relegation of religious and metaphysical categories to the periphery if not to outright oblivion (Abdul Hamid 2012). It was not until the 1980s, encouraged by such developments as the global Islamic resurgence and growth of Christian evangelicalism that religion made a paradigmatic comeback to the scholar, and courses on 'religion and politics' and 'sociology of religion' began to gain popularity in higher learning institutions worldwide.

Acknowledgements

Both authors would like to acknowledge the State Government of Penang, Malaysia, who funded research leading to this chapter via a grant from its think-tank, the Penang Institute, 10, Brown Road, George Town, Penang (project collaboration number: FY2021/FG_001). The project is titled 'The Roles of Islamist Movements and Islamism in the Political and Independence Struggle of Malaya, 1945–1957.' The proposal for this study was originally rejected by the Fundamental Research Grant Scheme operated by the Ministry of Higher Education, Kuala Lumpur, testifying to the immense difficulties scholars face in proffering alternative perspectives which run against the flow of official history. Both authors were granted access to Penang Institute's research facilities through their appointments as its Visiting Fellows (History and Regional Studies) from July 1, 2021 until June 30, 2022.

References

Abdul Hamid, Ahmad Fauzi, and Zairil Khir Johari. 2019. "Secularism and Ethno-religious Nationalist Hegemony in Malaysia." In *Secularism, Religion and Democracy in Southeast Asia,* edited by Vidhu Verma, 213–249. New Delhi: Oxford University Press.

Abdul Hamid, Ahmad Fauzi. 2003. "The Maturation of *Dakwah* in Malaysia: Divergence and Convergence in the Methods of Islamic Movements in the 1980s." *IKIM Journal* 11, no. 2 (July/December): 59–97.

Abdul Hamid, Ahmad Fauzi. 2007. "Malay Anti-Colonialism in British Malaya: A Re-appraisal of Independence Fighters of Peninsular Malaysia." *Journal of Asian and African Studies* 42, no. 5 (October): 371–398.

Abdul Hamid, Ahmad Fauzi. 2012. "Religion, Secularism and the State in Southeast Asia." In *Thinking International Relations Differently,* edited by Arlene B. Tickner and David L. Blaney, 253–274. Abingdon: Routledge.

Abdullah, Nabir Haji. 1976. *Maahad Il Ihya Assyariff Gunung Semanggol, 1934–1959.* Bangi: History Department, Universiti Kebangsaan Malaysia.

Ahmad, Abu Talib. 2008. "Aliran Kiri Dalam Nasionalisme Melayu, 1946–57: Satu Pemerhatian." [The Leftist Stream in Malay Nationalism, 1946–57: An Observation] *Malaysia Dari Segi Sejarah* 36: 24–51.

Akashi, Yoji. 1985. "The Japanese Occupation of Malaya: Interruption or Transformation?" In *Southeast Asia under Japanese Occupation,* edited by Alfred W. McCoy, 54–70. New Haven: Yale University Southeast Asia Studies Monograph Series, no. 22.

Ali, Syed Husin. 2018. *A People's History of Malaysia: With Emphasis on the Development of Nationalism.* Petaling Jaya: Strategic Information and Research Development Centre and Pusat Sejarah Rakyat.

Arifin, Azmi. 2014. "Local Historians and the Historiography of Malay Nationalism 1945–57: The British, the United Malays National Organization (UMNO) and the Malay Left." *Kajian Malaysia: Journal of Malaysian Studies* 32, no. 1 (April): 1–35.

Arifin, Azmi. 2019a. "Book Review: *Sejarah Rakyat Malaysia (Khususnya Perkembangan Nasionalisme)* by Syed Husin Ali. Petaling Jaya: Strategic Information and Research Development Centre dan Pusat Sejarah Rakyat, 2017, 200 pp." *Kajian Malaysia: Journal of Malaysian Studies* 37, no. 1 (April): 149–156.

Arifin, Azmi. 2019b. "Darurat atau 'Perang Kolonial' 1948 di Tanah Melayu: Satu perbahasan berdasarkan beberapa aliran pemikiran dan perspektif." [Emergency or 'Colonial War' 1948 in Malaya: A Debate Based on Several Schools of Thought and Perspectives]. *KEMANUSIAAN: The Asian Journal of Humanities* 26 (2, October): 53–80.

Bamadhaj, Halinah. 1975. "The Impact of the Japanese Occupation of Malaya on Malay Society and Politics." M.A. Thesis, Department of History, University of Auckland, New Zealand.

Chin, James. 2016. "From *Ketuanan Melayu* to *Ketuanan Islam*: UMNO and the Malaysian Chinese." In *The End of UMNO? Essays on Malaysia's Dominant Party,* edited by Bridget Welsh, 171–212. Abingdon: Routledge.

Funston, John. 1976. "The Origins of Parti Islam Se Malaysia." *Journal of Southeast Asian Studies* 7, no. 1 (March): 58–73.

Furedi, Frank. 1991. *Colonial Wars and the Politics of Third World Nationalism.* London: I.B. Tauris.

Hasan, Ridzuan bin, Sharifah Afidah binti Syed Hamid, Muslimin bin Fadzil, and Subramaniam a/l Raman. 2019. *Sejarah Tingkatan 4* [Form 4 History]. Kuala Lumpur: Dewan Bahasa dan Pustaka.

Hishamuddin, Rais. 2020. "Komunis dan Sejarah Kiri." [Communists and Leftist History]. *Malaysiakini,* January 8 (https://www.malaysiakini.com/columns/506296, accessed August 15, 2021).

Hussain, Mustapha. 2004. *Malay Nationalism before Umno: The Memoirs of Mustapha Hussain* (Trans. by Insun Sony Mustapha & edited by Jomo K.S.). Kuala Lumpur: Utusan Publications & Distributors Sdn Bhd.

Ibrahim, Safie bin. 1978. "The Islamic Elements in Malay Politics in Pre-Independent Malaya, 1937–1948." *Islamic Culture* 52, no. 3 (July): 185–195.

Ismail, Abdul Rahman Haji. 1985. "Takkan Melayu Hilang Di Dunia: Suatu Sorotan tentang Nasionalisme Melayu" [Never Will the Malay Vanish: An Account of Malay Nationalism]. In *Isu-Isu Pensejarahan: Esei-Esei Penghargaan Kepada Dr. R. Suntharalingam* [*Issues of Historiography: Essays Dedicated to Dr. R. Suntharalingam*], edited by Abu Talib Ahmad and Cheah Boon Kheng, 36–53. Penang: Universiti Sains Malaysia Press.

Ismail, Abdul Rahman Haji. 2009. "1948 and the Cold War in Malaya: Samplings of Malay Reactions." *Kajian Malaysia: Journal of Malaysian Studies* 27, nos. 1–2 (April/October): 155–175.

Kheng, Cheah Boon. 1985. "Asal-Usul dan Asas Nasionalisme Malaya." [The Origin and Basis of Malayan Nationalism]. In *Nasionalisme Melayu: Satu Tinjauan Sejarah* [*Malay Nationalism: A Historical Survey*], edited by R. Suntharalingam and Abdul Rahman Haji Ismail, 81–101. Petaling Jaya: Penerbit Fajar Bakti.

Kheng, Cheah Boon. 1988. "The Erosion of Ideological Hegemony and Royal Power and the Rise of Postwar Malay Nationalism, 1945–46." *Journal of Southeast Asian Studies* 19, no. 1 (March): 1–26.

Khoo, Kay Kim. 1991. *Malay Society*. Petaling Jaya: Pelanduk Khoo Publications.

Kratoska, Paul. 1985. "Nasionalisme dan Ahli-Ahli Sejarah dan Nasionalisme dalam Sejarah." [Nationalism and Historians and Nationalism in History]. In *Nasionalisme Melayu: Satu Tinjauan Sejarah* [*Malay Nationalism: A Historical Survey*], edited by R. Suntharalingam and Abdul Rahman Haji Ismail, 18–33. Petaling Jaya: Penerbit Fajar Bakti.

Mandal, Sumit K. 2003. "Transethnic Solidarities in a Racialised Context." *Journal of Contemporary Asia* 33, no. 1 (February): 50–68.

Mauzy, Diane K. 2006. "From Malay Nationalism to a Malaysia Nation." In *After Independence: Making and Protecting the Nation in Postcolonial and Postcommunist States*, edited by Lowell W. Barrington, 45–70. Ann Arbor: University of Michigan Press.

Milner, Anthony C. 2008. *The Malays*. Oxford: Wiley-Blackwell.

Mohamed Nordin, Sopiee. 1976. *From Malayan Union to Singapore Separation: Political Unification in the Malaysia Region 1945–1965*. Kuala Lumpur: University Malaya Press.

Mohammed Salleh, Lamry. 2015. "A history of the Tenth Regiment's struggles". *Inter-Asia Cultural Studies* 16, no. 1 (March): 42–55.

Nagata, Judith A. 1984. *The Reflowering of Malaysian Islam: Modern Religious Radicals and their Roots*. Vancouver: University of British Columbia Press.

Omar, Ariffin. 1993. *Bangsa Melayu: Malay Concepts of Democracy and Community, 1945–1950*. Kuala Lumpur: Oxford University Press.

Pluvier, Jan M. 1967–1968. "Malayan Nationalism: A Myth." *Journal of the Historical Society Universiti Malaya*: 26–40.

Pluvier, Jan M. 1974. *Southeast Asian from Colonialism to Independence*. Kuala Lumpur: Oxford University Press.

Ramlah, Adam. 1998. *Kemelut Politik Semenanjung Tanah Melayu* [*Political Troubles of the Malay Peninsula*]. Kuala Lumpur: Dewan Bahasa dan Pustaka.

Ramlah, Adam. 2020. "Buku teks sejarah agungkan PKM?" [History textbook glorifies MCP?], *Utusan Malaysia*, October 9 (https://www.utusan.com.my/rencana/2020/10/buku-teks-sejarah-agungkan-pkm/, accessed August 13, 2021).

Roff, William R. 1967. *The Origins of Malay Nationalism*. New Haven: Yale University Press.

Saat, Ishak. 2010. "Caturan Politik Pelbagai Kaum di Tanah Melayu 1946–1957." [Multi-Communal Political Arrangements in Malaya 1946–1957]. *Jebat: Malaysian Journal of History, Politics, and Strategic Studies* 37: 68–85.

Saat, Ishak. 2019. *Radikalisme Melayu: Mendepani Politik Malaysia* [*Malay Radicalism: Facing Malaysian Politics*]. Inaugural professorial lecture delivered on February 27, 2019, Tanjung Malim: Universiti Pendidikan Sultan Idris.

Shiozaki, Yuki. 2015. "The Historical Origins of Control over Deviant Groups in Malaysia: Official *Fatwa* and Regulation of Interpretation." *Studia Islamika: Indonesian Journal for Islamic Studies* 22, no. 2 (September): 205–232.

Silcock, Thomas Henry, and Ungku Abdul Aziz. 1953. "Malayan nationalism." In *Asian Nationalism and the West*, edited by William L. Holland, 269-345. New York: Macmillan.

Soenarno, Radin. 1960. "Malay Nationalism, 1896–1941." *Journal of Southeast Asian History* 1, no. 1 (March): 1–28.

Soh, Byungkuk. 1999. "Some Questions about the Impact of Japanese Occupation (1942–45) on the Development of Malay Nationalism: With Special Reference to the Kesatuan Melayu Muda." *International Area Studies Review* 2, no. 1 (March): 19–42.

Stockwell, Anthony John. 1977. "The Formation and First Years of the United Malays National Organization (UMNO)." *Modern Asian Studies* 11, no. 4 (October): 481-513.

Stockwell, A. J. 1993. "A widespread and long-concocted plot to overthrow government in Malaya'? The origins of Malayan Emergency." *Journal of Imperial and Commonwealth History* 21, no. 3 (September): 66–88.

Stockwell, Anthony John. ed. 1995. *The Malayan Union Experiment 1942–1948*. London: Her Majesty's Stationary Office.

Wang, Gungwu. 1962. "Malayan Nationalism." *Journal of the Royal Central Asian Society* 49, nos. 3–4 (July/October): 317–328.

Wang, Gungwu. 1981. *Community and Nation: Essays on Southeast Asia and the Chinese*. Singapore: Heinemann Educational Books (Asia).

Zainudin, Faiz. 2020. "Cops Raid PJ Publisher over Controversial Book Cover." *Free Malaysia Today*, June 30 (https://www.freemalaysiatoday.com/category/nation/2020/06/30/cops-raid-pj-publisher-over-controversial-book-cover/, accessed August 15, 2021).

35
SINGAPORE'S NATIONAL NARRATIVE

Ripe for renewal

Michael D. Barr

Introduction

Singapore is in its sixth decade as an independent republic and has yet to see a change in government. In 1963, the Peoples' Action Party (PAP) government led Singapore out of colonialism and into membership of the Federation of Malaysia, and in 1965, it led Singapore out of Malaysia to independence. The PAP has henceforth woven and imposed a distinctive identity for the young nation, built on a seemingly unbreakable link between the PAP, its leading family and the country's impressive level of material success and social stability. It started as defiant survivalism in the face of a hostile world, but since the 1990s, it has morphed into a much more overt and strident nationalism, headlined by increasingly immodest claims of Singaporean exceptionalism – to the point where Singapore's leadership has offered its creation as a 'model' of success to the world (Ortmann and Thompson 2020). In 2013, then Deputy Prime Minister Lee Hsien Loong expressed this triumphalism thus: 'We are today, exceptional. And if we are not exceptional, we are ordinary…' His father, former Prime Minister Lee Kuan Yew, separately argued that Singapore differentiates itself from its neighbours 'in a positive way' (Barr 2015, 1). More recently, Deputy Prime Minister Heng Swee Keat declared that 'Staying exceptional is how we survived' (*Australian Financial Review*, 16 February 2021). The claim of exceptionalism provides the core feature of Singapore's nationalist narrative as it now stands: the zenith and meeting point of several other strands of the national mythology, all of which have a common feature of serving partisan ends as readily as national pride.

In the 1960s and 1970s, there was no national mantra of exceptionalism. Premature claims of 'success' were in fact present even before independence (Lee 1959–1990, 22 March 1964 and 15 October 1965), but they were not yet sufficiently credible to become a major theme. In those days, the main nationalist messaging was centred on a collective determination that tiny, independent Singapore would survive in the face of the hostility of its nearest neighbours, Malaysia and Indonesia: 'an Israel in a Malay-Muslim sea' as Lee Kuan Yew put it at the time (Wilairat 1975, 47); or 'a Chinese island in a Malay sea' as he put it in his memoirs (Lee 1998, 23).

At all times the government has been surprisingly comfortable celebrating a century-and-a-half of colonialist achievements, and arguing that this provided the foundations of a strong foundation and a successful future for Singapore, but it was not until the 1980s that the mantra of independent Singapore as a success story was actively promoted in the mainstream (Drysdale 1984; Sandhu and Wheatley 1989; Fernandez 1992 [1985]). At about the same time, a meta-narrative of the beneficent colonial heritage reached full voice in school history textbooks (Curriculum Development Institute of Singapore 1984; 1985) though the origins of this colonialist narrative were already discernible in the immediate aftermath of independence; when Prime Minister Lee Kuan Yew decided to retain the colonial-era statue of Sir Stamford Raffles, the British 'founder' of Singapore (Barr 2021a). Immediately following full sovereign statehood, the Singapore government began developing a national mythology based on a forward-looking drive to achieve success in the face of adversity, but from day one it rested that messaging on a presumption that independent Singapore's successes had their origins in Britain's colonial rule, which began with Raffles in 1819.

Today's government-generated national mythology of exceptionalism still rests on the foundations set by the government in the late 1960s and 1970s, with the original rags-to-riches story easily identifiable through the various iterations of nation-building projects (Cheng 2019, 78–79) and school history textbooks (Barr 2021b), but there are signs that it is starting to wear thin. While a 1999 school history textbook could unblushingly talk of 1819 as 'the beginnings of Singapore' and say how it was going to explain how 'our pioneering immigrant forefathers came here to help build a town and a port' (Ministry of Education 1999, iii), more recent school textbooks place the success of colonial Singapore itself in the context of its pre-colonial history as a naval and commercial port, though they do so without yet abandoning the post-1819 'rags-to-riches' motif (Ministry of Education 2014). Not only is the foundation story of Singapore's success approaching the point of being unviable, but other elements of Singapore's nationalist mythology are also under pressure. Most vulnerable to challenge is the current and most pivotal mantra of Singaporean 'exceptionalism', thanks to nearly two decades of political and administrative underperformance by the government (Barr 2020a).

With Singapore's national mythology fraying at both its historical foundations and its contemporary claims of performance legitimacy, the entire edifice seems to be undergoing a revision, though where it will end up is far from certain.

Foundation, twice over

In 1969, four years after Singapore declared itself an independent republic, the Singapore government hosted perhaps the most awkward of all nationalist celebrations: the sesquicentenary of the planting of the British flag on the island in 1819. And it was a fulsome celebration of colonialism, not the mere marking of a historical turning point. As the 1969 Singapore Year Book tells us:

> The celebrations were held throughout the year, with exhibitions, displays, cultural shows and parades. ... Other events were the Festival of Sports, the exhibition on Singapore's "150 Years of Development" ... and procession of forty illuminated floats illustrating Singapore's progress.
>
> *(Ministry of Culture 1970, 2–3)*

The Singapore International Chamber of Commerce joined with one of the government's favoured publishers to release a mammoth celebratory volume called *The First 150 Years of Singapore* (Moore and Moore 1969). President Yusof bin Ishak reflected the official messaging as he memorialised the country's founding fathers: 'A hundred and fifty years ago, Singapore began its history as a multi-racial society. Sir Stamford Raffles, its founder [was] a man of great vision and tenacity...' (Ministry of Culture 1970, 3). President Ishak also provided the necessary nuance that contextualised the government's paean to colonialism: fulsome praise for the masses of immigrants who flooded British Singapore and who 'left behind for us a throbbing, dynamic and prospering city' (Ministry of Culture 1970, 3).

This state-driven narrative of immigrant success under benign British rule was readily accepted by the immigrant Chinese population who comprised 74.4 per cent of the population (Ministry of Culture 1970, 64). Their newspapers lauded 1969 as an occasion for a 'double celebration' – 150 years since the foundation of British Singapore and four years since the foundation of independent Singapore Ministry (*Nanyang Siang Pau*, 9 August 1969; *Sin Chew Jit Poh*, 9 August 1969). Such presumption was nevertheless contentious among the indigenous Malays, who comprised 14.5 per cent of the population. Haji Ahmad Taff, head of a Malay political party (PKMS or Singapore National Malay Organisation), declared that the decision to celebrate the arrival of Raffles in 1819 as the 'foundation' of Singapore was an 'insult'. 'The people of the republic should realise that Raffles was more of an agent of the British imperialists', he said (*Utusan Melayu*, 12 August 1969). Two weeks later, Taff reiterated his concern about the government's 'insult', and convinced the Central Executive of PKMS to make a formal protest over the sesquicentenary celebrations (*Utusan Melayu*, 28 August 1969). In 1970, when the Ministry of Education published new history textbooks that echoed and reinforced the government's narrative about Raffles, the leader of the PKMS Youth Wing, Inche Yahya Mohd. Noor, burnt copies of them outside party headquarters, claiming that the history

> humiliates the Malays, distorts Singapore's historical facts, idolizes Raffles and some Chinese traders as creators of Singapore's history, makes fun of the history of Temasek before the arrival of Raffles by treating it as mere legend, and deals with Singapore's history as though it commenced from the time of Raffles.
>
> (*Utusan Melayu, 3 March 1970*)

The political challenge posed by PKMS had little impact because it was easily silenced by a government that had no compunction about intimidating and censoring opposition voices (*Utusan Melayu*, 28 August 1969; Rajah 2012, Chapters 3 and 4). Indeed, the Kuala Lumpur-based newspaper that exclusively reported this episode had been banned in Singapore just two weeks earlier, on 22 February 1970 (*Utusan Melayu*, 28 February and 2 March 1970).

1965 – A nation launched in trauma

The mainstream nationalist narrative that depicts Raffles launching a colony of high-achieving and mainly Chinese immigrants became by default the dominant theme of the national mythology (Barr 2021b). It was odd to see a post-colonial, nationalist government adulating colonialists, but not so strange if we regard Singapore's Chinese 'immigrant pioneers' as partners of the colonialists – which was indeed how they were portrayed at the time of independence and for decades thereafter (Barr 2021b). Thus, the emerging national narrative was effectively a 'colonial settler' mythology, more commonly associated with 'white' former colonies like Australia and New Zealand (Rahim 2009, Chapter 2; Knapman 2021).

Beyond the convenience of presenting a colonial settler history in a more palatable form, the government later acknowledged a different motive for starting Singapore's history in 1819. It was trying to avoid legitimising any discussions that might – to use the words of Foreign Minister S. Rajaratnam – 'turn Singapore into a bloody battleground for endless racial and communal conflicts' (Kwa 2006, 252–253). To understand the origins of this somewhat dramatic expression of concern, we have to realise that when Chinese-majority Singapore was granted independence in August 1965, it had just spent two difficult years as a constituent state of the Malay-dominated Federation of Malaysia, and the government had spent that time telling Singaporeans that they were Malaysians and should be proud of it. Then, at 4.30 p.m. on 9 August 1965, TV Singapura broadcast Singapore Prime Minister Lee Kuan Yew's press conference recorded at 10 a.m. that morning – a broadcast that retained the full drama of Lee pausing the session because he was shedding tears as he announced that Singapore had been expelled from Malaysia (*The Straits Times*, 10 August 1965; Cheng 2019, 17–19).

The republic was thus born in tears and trauma, and the video of that press conference has entered the national lexicon as the quintessential dramatisation of that trauma (Cheng 2019, 18–19). In fact, the story was a concoction: Lee and his Minister for Finance, Goh Keng Swee, had initiated Singapore's withdrawal from Malaysia, and spent weeks secretly negotiating the terms (Tan 2007, 116–123), but it suited all the key parties on both sides to make it look like an expulsion. The false story of Singapore's expulsion was accepted by scholars and the public alike for the next three decades until Goh Keng Swee revealed the truth in a limited-edition book published in 1996 (Chew 1996, 147). It is a tribute to the government's capacity to control the release of inconvenient facts that ordinary Singaporeans had to wait until 2015 before the mainstream press reported this 'new' revelation to a stunned public (*The Straits Times*, 22 December 2015; 21 August 2015). Lee Kuan Yew's memoirs (published after 1996) and even supposedly serious history books written for university students all perpetuated the mythology of the Malaysian Prime Minister 'casting Singapore out' (Lee 1998, 628–631; Lee 2008, 260). Significantly, even in 2021, the false story was still being taught to school children and recommended to teachers, and is being reinforced in nationalist comic books and illustrated reading primers (Yeoh c.2010; Yee 2015; Nabeta and Fujiwara 2016).

It seems that regardless of the facts, the moment of Singapore's launch as an independent country will always be remembered as being drenched in trauma (and tears). That trauma was, in turn, embedded in the racial-cum-communal politics that brought the government of Singapore and the central government in Malaysia to divorce. The political contestation between Lee Kuan Yew (in particular) and the Malay leadership in Kuala Lumpur had been drenched in the language of race and communalism for more than a year before separation: ever since April 1964, when Lee's PAP unwisely and fruitlessly contested parliamentary seats on the peninsula in the Malaysian Federal elections, contrary to an agreement Lee had made with Malaysian Prime Minister Tunku Abdul Rahman. Lee belatedly recognised his 1964 election campaign as the turning point in his relations with the government in Kuala Lumpur, but only after the damage was done (Lee 1965). Over the next 16 months, an escalating war of words between the mainly Chinese leadership in Singapore and the mainly Malay leadership in Kuala Lumpur sent a relentless message to both populations that the political contest between the Singapore government and the central government was in fact a communal contest between Chinese and Malays (Chew 1996, 167).

Chinese–Malay relations were thus central to the creation of independent Singapore and were viewed by the Singapore government as a contentious territory. This perception subdued any tendency the government may have had to play up either ethnic identity or any history that would draw attention to ethnic identity. By the start of the 1970s,

Singapore's public historiography rested almost unthinkingly on the base provided by the British colonial 'settler' narrative, whereby Singapore's development had been the product of collaboration between British wisdom and Chinese enterprise (Rahim 2009, Chapter 2). This account lent itself to the presentation of a seamless transition from a colonial success story under the British to a modern success story under the PAP (Barr 2020b, Chapter 1), but after the book burning of 1970, the government was afraid that the risks of highlighting ethnically tinged narratives outweighed any advantages, so it actively discouraged reflection on the past (including the teaching of History in school). Instead, it reinforced the already-established idea of Singapore as a tolerant multiracial (and multilingual, multireligious) society, and made it a central element of national identity (Moore 2000). Yet, the contrary idea – also well-established – of Chinese having a special place in Singapore was never very far below the surface, and much of the country's public policy operated on this sublimated racist assumption (Rahim 1998; Barr and Skrbiš 2008). Hence, the government supplemented multiracialism with the promotion of materialistic and exclusively forward-looking ambition, a message that was directed at all communities. Currents of ethnic and historical contention remained, but as a mere background, neither abandoned, nor highlighted. This status quo survived until roughly the beginning of the 1980s, whereupon a newly confident Lee Kuan Yew unleashed a cultural tsunami that broke through all the reticence of the previous decade.

1980s – continuity with change

There were two decisive and closely connected developments in the 1980s that ended the ambiguities of the 1970s. The first was Lee Kuan Yew's personal Chinese 'turn', which prompted him to restructure Singaporean nationalism around a central pillar built from Chinese ethnonationalism (Barr 2019). The second was the full-throated embrace of the 'settler' national mythology, complete with a new generation of school History textbooks enthusiastically embracing the narrative of Singapore's success being built upon a combination of British rule and Chinese labour and enterprise (Barr 2021a; 2021b). The embrace of a settler narrative was the least surprising: it merely dispensed with the reticence of the 1970s and moved what had been background into the foreground. The other development – the embrace of Chinese ethnonationalism – was revolutionary. While throughout most of the 1970s championing ethnic Chinese identity or language risked severe sanction (Seow 1998), beginning in 1978, Lee started deploying government resources to generate a Chinese cultural and educational revival that permeated every corner of society (Barr 2019). The government revived and reconfigured old Chinese schools as vibrant centres of Chinese language learning and cultural celebration; Confucianism was resourced as a subject in school; Speak Mandarin Campaigns became annual celebrations of Chinese culture; special funding and privileges were doled out for teaching Chinese pre-schoolers; and school students who mastered Mandarin at matriculation were given bonus points when applying for university (Barr 2008, 92–93). In the 1980s, primary school reading primers began providing explicit lessons in racialising and stereotyping children by dress, hair and skin colour. In the world of the hand-drawn characters through which the books taught grammar and vocabulary, Chinese children are studious, well behaved, and grow up to become teachers or wealthy business owners; Indians are tempestuous and argumentative; Malays are playful, lazy and end up as bus drivers or the like (Barr 2019, 115). The hegemony of Chinese identity in society eventually reached the stage where non-Chinese politicians at Cabinet and Presidential levels were learning Mandarin in an effort to fit in (Barr 2008, 100). Non-Chinese

Singaporeans found themselves living in a condition that I once characterised as 'incomplete assimilation':

> ... having established its ideal vision of a Chinese Singaporean, the government has, since the early 1980s, been using this as the template and the standard of its ideal Singaporean. Thus, if members of a minority race want to go further than merely meeting the minimum requirements of acceptance and actually prosper in this society, then they need to internalise 'Chinese virtues' and become 'like the Chinese' in subtle but important ways, even as they are excluded from full participation in this ethno-national project in vital ways. This is what we mean by the term, 'incomplete assimilation' – a balancing act between the imperative that minority members need to strive to act 'like Chinese' in order to succeed and the insistence that at the end of this process they will continue to be relegated to a minority status.
>
> (Barr and Skrbiš 2008, 98)

This new phase of 'multiracialism' highlighted ethnic identity per se, privileged the already-dominant Chinese identity within Singapore's ethnic mosaic and at the same time taught minority communities to accept their relative marginalisation as a natural and acceptable cost of living in a successful Chinese society. Scholars sympathetic to the regime identified these developments benignly – as an even-handed and uplifting exploration of ethnic identity within the bounds of a Singaporean version of multiculturalism (Vasil 1993) – but in fact only Chinese Singaporeans felt very uplifted. In 1990, Lee Kuan Yew actually criticised an opposition politician of Indian extraction for being 'un-Chinese' and contrasted his performance with that of opposition politicians of Chinese extraction, who were 'at least on the same side of the river' as himself. In May 1991, Lee declared his satisfaction that the physical interspersion of the Malays throughout Chinese-dominated housing estates had 'helped increase competitiveness in the Malay community by example and interaction' (Barr 2019, 116).

1990s – National Education and The Singapore Story

These twin trajectories continued with little deviation until the mid-1990s, when both were overtaken by and absorbed into an upgraded variant of the national narrative based explicitly on Lee Kuan Yew's forthcoming autobiography. Known formally as National Education, it soon settled into its more commonplace nomenclature as 'The Singapore Story', which was the title of Lee's two-volume set of personal memoirs (Lee 1998; 2000). These memoirs were pivotal to the new direction being set by National Education, because in three words they claimed that Lee's personal biography and the history of Singapore were indistinguishable. While the post-1980s national memory foregrounded colonial achievements, the new linkage of Singapore's national history and Lee's personal biography naturally shifted attention away from colonial history and made Lee himself the centre of attention. The first volume was very much a justification of his actions leading up to Singapore's independence, but the second volume traced out the direction of Singapore's next stage of nationalism. Lee explicitly denied that it is a 'how-to' book on governance (Lee 2000, 13), but it reads very much like one, and is certainly a showcase of achievement in which there is no effort to distinguish Lee's life from that of 'his' nation.

Singapore's nationalist trajectory was substantially transformed at this point, though not with full consistency. The centrality of Chinese ethnonationalism continued unchanged, since Lee's personal success story was implicitly a Chinese story in any case. Yet with the full title of the second volume – *From Third World to First: The Singapore Story: 1965–2000. Memoirs of Lee Kuan Yew* – he also purported to have taken the country 'from third world to first'. He was effectively restarting Singapore history with his own life story, thus side-stepping the inadequacies inherent in grounding national identity on colonial foundations. But the suggestion that Singapore was a third world country rather than a successful colonial port city when Lee took over flatly contradicted the established narrative of colonial Singapore as a roaring success. If Lee's Singapore Story had been fully embraced by educationists and myth makers, this contradiction would have required a full reversal of the established mythology. In fact, the school textbooks and comparable outlets of nationalist messaging grafted The Singapore Story seamlessly onto the earlier historiography, without showing any sign that anyone had noticed a contradiction – and without any local scholars pointing it out. Thus, National Education was able to perpetuate what Aaron Koh has called 'the cultural memory of Raffles' founding spirit' so that it could be 'celebrated, romanticised and glorified as virtues to be emulated', even as it 're-imagine[d] and construct[ed] a [new] sense of Singapore's nationhood and national identity' (Koh 2005, 81, 84). The National Education textbooks continued the colonial settler 'immigrant pioneer' messaging of earlier generations, albeit at shorter length, but it extended the success story with two new messages: jingoistic pride in Singapore's post-independence achievements; and gratitude to Lee Kuan Yew for those achievements (Ministry of Education 1999; Barr 2016; Abdullah 2018). Central to the emotional and jingoistic messaging was a series of didactic national 'days', each complete with parades and shows and literature targeted at school children. Thus, Total Defence Day (15 February), Racial Harmony Day (21 July), International Friendship Day (Term 2 in the Singapore school calendar) and National Day (9 August) each entered the school curriculum through National Education (Koh 2005, 82).

Over the following decades, litanies of Singaporean achievements and tokens of recognition offered by overseas entities emerged as standard fare in nationalist discourse (Barr 2020a), supplementing the lashings of 'banal' nationalism (posters, slogans, flags, campaigns and other red-and-white motifs) adorning the residential estates, libraries, buses, trains and shopping centres across the island (Cheng 156–157; Barr and Skrbiš 2008, Chapter 12). Thanks to the omnipresent messaging of The Singapore Story, a new narrative of Singapore exceptionalism was being linked inseparably with the person of Lee Kuan Yew, the fruits of which were on display in the twin 'celebrations' of 2015: the sombre 'celebration' of Lee's life upon his death at the age of 91 and the national celebration of the 50th anniversary of Singapore's independence (SG50) a few months later.

Both 'celebrations' reached new heights of triumphalism, but more significantly for this account of the evolution of Singapore's nationalism, they blended into each other and also blended with the PAP's election campaign in the 2015 General Election (GE), which followed a matter of weeks after the SG50 celebrations. The PAP had suffered its worst result since independence in the previous (2011) GE, but this time it regained most of the ground it had lost (in terms of votes; though not seats), substantially on the back of the narrative of The Singapore Story: it was Prime Minister Lee Kuan Yew who took Singapore 'from third world to first' and now Prime Minister Lee Hsien Loong, his son, was asking for their votes. It seemed that the Lee family had become a brand, and was able to be passed from father to son (Barr 2016).

A new century: disrupting the myths

Despite the apparent seamlessness and success of Singapore's state-driven nationalist meta-narrative, and its successful deployment for partisan political ends, below the surface challenges had been emerging and gaining ground since the turn of the century. As of the time of writing in the early 2020s, three contemporary elements of the narrative are fraying under pressure from below: the twin narratives of 1819 and the British-cum-Chinese success story; the twin narratives of ethnic essentialism and Chinese achievement; and the narrative of exceptionalism.

1819 and the colonial narrative

We opened this chapter considering the enigma of the sesquicentenary celebrations of Singapore's 'foundation' in 1819. In most settler colonies, such as Australia or Canada, such anniversaries have generally been laced with ambiguity of late, as histories of colonial and post-colonial (usually white) 'progress' and achievement have been confronted by claims of dispossession by First Nations. And so it was in Singapore by 2019 when it was time to celebrate the bicentenary of 1819. To the surprise of many – and contrary to earlier public indications (*The Straits Times*, 22 May 2017) – the official 'bicentennial celebrations' overtly challenged the orthodoxy that Singapore had no history prior to 1819: in public seminars, scholarly books and museum displays, the mention of the bicentenary of 1819 was little more than a starting point for a sustained focus on Singapore's earlier history (Barr 2021b). The official Bicentennial Committee's '1819 turn' was a pivotal development in the nationalist narrative, and it was the direct outcome of years of revisionist historical scholarship by historians working both in Singapore and in overseas universities that challenged the denial of the island's pre-colonial history and the hagiographical veneration of Raffles (Abdullah 2018; Barr 2021b; Kwa 2019; Kwa 2021; Sa'at et al. 2021).

It is not that the '1819 turn' has yet been fully embraced in official nationalist mythology. Even revisionist national histories that highlight pre-colonial history still sometimes 'restart' their story in 1819 so that the colonialist success story is not disturbed (Kwa et al. 2019). Also missing from the new histories is a fulsome reassessment of the role of non-Chinese Asians in Singapore's colonial success story. There are hints of such a development among revisionist scholarship (Barr 2021a), but it has yet to gain traction.

A taste of the lines of analysis that might result from avoiding 'restarting' history in 1819 was evident in a rather pointed question asked at a high-profile public seminar during the official Bicentennial celebrations in 2019. Following two scholarly accounts of Singapore's history as a busy centre of business and as a naval base in the centuries before 1819, Zainul Abidin Rasheed (a retired diplomat and veteran Malay politician aligned with the PAP) offered this thought:

> I want to thank both professors for … unequivocally debunking [the myth of] the 'sleepy fishing village' pre-Raffles and by the same token, the myth of the 'lazy native'.
>
> Right now, we 'know' that Singapore is so bustling, so dynamic, and so successful because of the 75 per cent Chinese that we have in Singapore. Because of the drive, the business, and the culture in them.
>
> But what was it like pre-Raffles, when Singapore, both of you said, was very bustling too, was very successful too? What was the composition of Singaporeans then like, how cosmopolitan were they, and what brought about the drive and the bustling Singapore then?
>
> *(Institute of Policy Studies 2019, at 79 minutes)*

Zainal Abidin's references to the 'sleepy fishing village' and the 'bustling Chinese' are drawn straight from Lee Kuan Yew's standard repertoire, so his contribution was more of a debating point or a pointed barb than a question, all the more so since it was asked in the presence of Deputy Prime Minister Heng Swee Keat, who was also on the schedule of speakers.

Chinese ethnonationalism and ethnic essentialism

The account of Zainul Abidin's provocative question brings us to the second element of the nationalist narrative that is under stress: Chinese ethnonationalism and overt ethnic essentialism. The push-back against these elements of the nationalist agenda has been much less complete than that against the colonial 1819 narrative, but its base is much broader and more heterogenous, reaching throughout the coffee shops and housing estates.

This field of contestation was forced open in the late 1990s and 2000s by intensely critical scholarship that confronted the standard narratives about the management of ethnicity (Rahim 1998; Moore 2000; Lai 2004; Barr and Skrbiš 2008). Parallel with these initiatives, less confrontational contributions probed the limits of mainstream scholarship (Goh 2010; Tan 2018; Kwen 2016; Chua et al. 2016; 2019). The process has now reached the stage where scholarly indifference to the government's racist agenda is the exception rather than the norm.

The response of ordinary Singaporeans ('heartlanders' in the local vernacular) is, however, more varied – at least in so far as we can judge from elections, coffee shop talk, social media, inter-marriage figures, etc. Many Singaporeans are clearly uncomfortable with Singapore's heightened consciousness of ethnic identity, but there is also incontrovertible evidence that many fully embrace xenophobia and racism. One very public incident stands out as evidence of the first reaction: the grassroots hostility to the government's decision in 2018 to change the constitution so it could 'reserve' the presidency of the country for a Malay in the following election. Prime Minister Lee Hsien Loong justified this move by saying that it had been a long time since the Malays had had a 'turn' at being president (Rodan 2018). Yet, this position stood in stark contrast to his earlier statement that Singaporeans are 'not ready' for a non-Chinese prime minister, even though every prime minister to date had been Chinese (Barr 2019, 122). Some of the popular reactions gave voice to ethnic Chinese resentment of special treatment for Malays, but much more widespread was rejection of ethnic identity per se as a key factor in public life. Significantly, the move did not even garner much enthusiasm among the Malays, who seem to have generally regarded it as tokenism. Such negative and indifferent reactions were helped along by widespread cynicism about the government's manipulation of ethnic identity for political purposes: it was well-known that Lee was keen to stop a particular Chinese politician (Dr Tan Cheng Bock) from contesting the presidency, whereas he was just as keen to exclude a particular Indian Cabinet colleague (Deputy Prime Minister Tharman Shanmugaratnam) from becoming prime minister (Barr 2019, 122–123).

Unfortunately, the contrary impulse is illustrated by even stronger evidence: a swarm of overtly racist and xenophobic incidents caught on camera by smart phones and shared on social media (e.g., *The Straits Times*, 10 May, 7 June and 23 June 2021; *Channel NewsAsia*, 4 June 2021). Prime Minister Lee acknowledged racism a problem in his 2021 National Day Rally speech and is trying to manage it through new government regulation and social policing without acknowledging any government responsibility or the existence of Chinese privilege (*Today*, 29 August 2021). It is tempting to think that racism is a new phenomenon in Singapore, but it is not. When Viswa Sadasivan was chairing government-sponsored 'Feedback Unit' sessions in the 2000s, he found that the loudest arguments among the (hand-picked, mostly pro-government) participants were over racial issues and followed ethnic communal lines (Viswa 2011). In fact, he feared on one occasion that his meeting of grassroots leaders and leading citizens was going to descend into a fistfight. This historical report suggests that racial xenophobia is not so much a new problem, as an old problem newly under the spotlight, thanks to the ubiquity of phone cameras and social media.

The new vocalisation of racism also points to another line of analysis in the changing dynamics of Chinese ethnonationalism: the increasing unwillingness of the minority communities – mainly the Malays and Indians – to silently accept their subordinate place in Singapore society and the Singapore economy. The reality of this sea-change is visible both at the imprecise level of coffee shop and social-media talk, and at the more verifiable level of elite politics, where such concerns were singled out by Prime Minister Lee in his 2021 National Day Rally Speech (*The Straits Times*, 29 August 2021). It should also be noted that in sharp contrast to a generation ago, today's opposition parties are spoiled for choice when recruiting high-quality candidates from minority ethnic communities. Indeed, the official Leader of the Opposition – the Workers' Party's Pritam Singh – is an uncomfortable reminder to the government that its social compact with Singapore's ethnic minorities requires immediate attention. Successfully bringing the ethnic minority communities along on a Chinese-inflected nationalist journey has always been one of the more problematic elements in Singapore's nationalist agenda – requiring constant nurturing and adaptation to changing circumstances – so perhaps it is not so surprising that this feature has emerged as a front-line problem for the government.

Both Chinese privilege and ethnic essentialism are still alive in Singapore, but between being rejected by much of the population and embraced a little too enthusiastically by others, it is apparent that the government has lost control of the agenda. While the government is unquestionably genuine in its stated goal of deploying ethnic identity as a benign tool for building social harmony, it has unwittingly (though predictably) opened a pandora's box of stereotyping and prejudice that threatens the very harmony it aims to sustain.

Singaporean exceptionalism

Of all the elements of Singapore's nationalist narrative in the first quarter of the twenty-first century, Singaporean exceptionalism is both the most central and the one that has suffered the most damage. The primary line of degradation is the most obvious: the claim is based on the performance of the government and the Singapore 'system' more broadly, but the failures and shortcomings of both of those entities are too publicly on display for any serious observer to take claims of exceptionalism seriously. This Handbook is not the place to repeat the detailed litany of failures, but suffice to say that the most public turning point came during the 2011 GE when Prime Minister Lee Hsien Loong issued a public apology for letting a terrorist escape prison through a toilet window, for allowing flooding in the city's main retail strip, for shortages in housing and shortcomings in public transport, along with 'other mistakes' (Barr 2016, 8). This was followed over the next two years by a regular flow of ministerial-level apologies for more failures (Barr 2020a). No matter what other achievements might be notched up, this is not much of a basis for a claim of exceptionalism. And then, over 2019–2021, Singaporeans watched agog as Deputy Prime Minister Heng Swee Keat – Lee Hsien Loong's designated and hand-picked successor – imploded in very public display of ineptitude that exposed him to international ridicule (*Australian Financial Review*, 10 July 2020). The widespread sense of relief at the news that Heng had stepped aside and would never be prime minister could not dissipate the wonder that he could have been considered in the first place (*The Economist*, 8 and 17 April 2021).

Yet, mere administrative failures and a new culture of ordinariness in government are only part of the story. Beyond these headline spectacles, the reception of the 'exceptional

Singapore' message has suffered from a widespread sense that it is disconnected from the lives of ordinary people. In earlier decades, Singaporeans shared a sense of ownership over individual and collective wins, awards and breakthroughs – that a new Singapore was being built through a collective effort, and for the benefit of most of its people. Today, however, there is little sense that such achievements have anything to do with ordinary people living in the housing estates. In part, this sense of disconnection is the logical result of the government's messaging, which relentlessly adulates high achievers (both as individuals and as collectives) to the point that ordinary Singaporeans are left with little role beyond that of an applauding audience. Improvements in standards of living and public goods used to be so tangible and visible that there was a widespread acceptance that 'all boats were rising' with the incoming tide of achievement. Today, it is commonplace to hear scepticism about the spread of social benefits in coffee shop talk, in social media and in election campaigns. Furthermore, serious scholarly analysis of outcomes mostly validates the common view (Rahim and Yeoh 2019). From the 1960s to perhaps the 1990s, social mobility used to be on such a strong upward trajectory that high achievers had often risen from humble backgrounds. They might have been your neighbours once. By contrast, the winners and builders of today's Singapore are more likely to be seen as atas (Singapore slang for 'upper class' and 'uppity') products of elite schools and elite neighbourhoods, having little or no connection with ordinary folk (Koh 2014; Chua et al. 2016; Chua et al. 2019). The government appears to be conscious of this disconnection and has taken to programmatically depicting the life stories of ordinary people in its messaging, with special attention to didactic stories about ordinary people making good in the face of adversity (Cheng 2019). Perhaps this move will help rebuild bridges between the nationalist narrative of achievement and the ordinary folk, but it seems like it has a long way to go.

The Lee Kuan Yew story

One element of the old nationalism that appears to be secure in the public mind is the constructed memory of Lee Kuan Yew as the builder of modern Singapore. If anything, this mythology has taken on new life as Singaporeans contrast rose-coloured 'memories' of Singapore's founding prime minister with the less impressive performance of his son. The restoration of the PAP vote on the back of the Lee brand arguably saved the PAP in the 2015 GE, but then the PAP lost all those gains and more in the following (2020) GE, suggesting that the political dividend from three decades of National Education and The Singapore Story might not be as transferable as hoped.

The problem the PAP faces is that the constructed memory of Lee Kuan Yew is intimately linked to Singaporean exceptionalism, and if contemporary performance is anything less than stellar, it risks highlighting the government's inadequacies. A case in point was the 2020 GE campaign, when the memory of Lee Kuan Yew was invoked against the PAP by a new political party, Tan Cheng Bock's Progress Singapore Party (PSP), which targeted seats in the PAP's heartland. Tan had been a long-term PAP Member of Parliament and a personal friend of Lee's. During and before the campaign, he identified himself with Lee's legacy and attacked the PAP for having forgotten its roots – a message that the government could not confront without drawing even more attention to Tan's shared history with Lee and the PAP (*The Straits Times*, 5 August 2019; *AsiaOne*, 7 July 2020). Just for good measure, Prime Minister Lee's younger brother campaigned for the PSP (*Today*, 24 June 2020). Tan personally led the PSP team in a multimember constituency where nearly four out of five voters usually vote PAP. He achieved a 26 per cent swing against the government and came within 1.7 per cent of winning five seats in one swoop (*The Straits Times*, 11 July 2020). Such is the ongoing strength (and political capriciousness) of the Lee Kuan Yew brand.

Role reversal

In a sea of mostly incremental changes in Singapore's nationalist agenda, one of the most profound has arguably been the relationship between nationalism and politics. Until about the turn of the century, national pride and to a considerable extent national identity were assets created in the wake of the government's regime legitimation. Government and national achievements were plentiful and the population in the housing estates readily accepted narratives in which the PAP took much of the credit. Nationalism was the net winner of the emotional element of this exchange.

That was then. For the last two decades, the two partners in this relationship have been silently swapping roles. Today, rather than the credibility of politicians underpinning national pride, incumbent politicians are relying on waves of national pride to retain their partisan support. The situation has not yet reached a tipping point, but the linkage between politics and nationalism is now imposing an unhelpful burden on national loyalty and patriotism. It seems likely that the next decades will see newer and less homogenous expressions of nationalism, national pride and national identity emerge to rival the centralised, top-down and highly politicised narratives that have dominated thus far.

Ripe for renewal

The first half-century of Singapore's life as an independent republic has seen nationalism morph through several iterations, becoming increasingly shrill and forceful as it has aged. Beginning with a rather modest set of claims that drew mostly on the narrative of Britain's colonial success story, Singapore has grown in its own imagination to be a beacon of hope based on the talent of a multiracial population and social (i.e., government) systems that cultivate, train and channel that talent.

At all stages, this national self-imagery has been fraught with tensions, particularly over issues of race, the relationship between the government and Singapore society, and the special place of the person and family of its self-styled founding father, Lee Kuan Yew. Indeed, I suggest that these three elements – race, government and the Lees – have been the most decisive elements in the shaping of Singaporean nationalism through its phases, and also the most critical points of weakness in the current iteration. These fault lines reflect the emergence of new social realities wherein today's Singaporeans are looking at these key headline elements of the national vision, only to find them unconvincing and unappealing. Reforming and revitalising the emotional ties that used to bind Singaporeans will require a major rethink – possibly even a full decoupling – of the place of these three elements in Singaporean nationalism.

References

Abdullah, Walid Jumblatt. 2018. "Selective History and Hegemony-Making: The Case of Singapore." *International Political Science Review* 39 (4): 473–486.
AsiaOne:
    7 July 2020. "GE2020: PSP's Tan Cheng Bock Recalls How Lee Kuan Yew Shot Down His Wish to Put Singaporeans First."
Australian Financial Review:

16 February 2021, "Singapore's Economy Tipped to Roar Back to Life."
10 July 2020, "How Singapore's Family Feud Coloured an Election."
Barr, Michael D. 2021a. "Background Figures in a British Portrait: The Johor Royal Family in Nineteenth-Century Singapore." *History Australia* 18 (2): 283–301. doi:10.1080/14490854.2021.1917302.
Barr, Michael D. 2021b. "Singapore Comes to Terms with its Malay Past: The Scholarship and Politics of Crafting a National History." *Asian Studies Review* 46 (2): 350–368.
Barr, Michael D. 2020a. "The Singapore School: Technocracy or Less." In *China's 'Singapore Model' and Authoritarian Learning*, edited by Stephan Ortmann and Mark R. Thompson, 54–71. Abingdon: Routledge.
Barr, Michael D. 2020b. *Singapore: A Modern History*. London and New York: Bloomsbury.
Barr, Michael D. 2019. "Ethno-nationalism travels incognito in Singapore." In *Civic Nationalisms in Global Perspective*, edited by Jasper M. Trautsch, 110–128. Abingdon: Routledge.
Barr, Michael D. 2016. "The Lees of Singapore: A quality brand." *South East Asia Research* 24 (3): 341–354.
Barr, Michael D. 2015. "Ordinary Singapore: The Decline of Singapore Exceptionalism." *Journal of Contemporary Asia. Journal of Contemporary Asia* 46 (1): 1–17.
Barr, Michael D., and Zlatko Skrbiš. 2008. *Constructing Singapore: Elitism, Ethnicity and the Nation-Building Project*. Copenhagen: Nordic Institute of Asian Studies.
Channel NewsAsia:
  4 June 2021. "Jail for Man Who Spat at Woman on a Bus, Claiming She Brought 'Coronavirus' from China."
Cheng, Nien Yuan. 2019. "The Storytelling State: Performing Life Histories in Singapore." PhD Thesis, University of Sydney.
Chew, Melanie, ed. 1996. *Leaders of Singapore*. Singapore: Resource Press.
Chua, Vincent, Eik Leong Swee, and Barry Wellman. 2019. "Getting Ahead in Singapore: How Neighborhoods, Gender, and Ethnicity Affect Enrollment into Elite Schools." *Sociology of Education* 92 (2): 176–198.
Chua, Vincent, Mathew Mathews and Yi Cheng Lo. 2016. "Social capital in Singapore: Gender differences, ethnic hierarchies, and their intersection." *Social Networks* 47: 138–150.
Curriculum Development Institute of Singapore. 1984. *Social and Economic History of Modern Singapore 1*. Singapore: Longman.
Curriculum Development Institute of Singapore. 1985. *Social and Economic History of Modern Singapore 2*. Singapore: Longman.
Drysdale, John. 1984 (1996 reprint). *Singapore: Struggle for Success*. Singapore: Times Editions.
Fernandez, George J. 1992 [1985]. *Successful Singapore: A Tiny Nation's Saga from Founder to Accomplisher*. Singapore: SS Mubaruk and Brothers.
Goh, Daniel P. S. 2010. "Multiculturalism and the Problem of Solidarity." In *Management of Success: Singapore Revisited*, edited by Terence Chong, 561–578. Singapore: Institute of Policy Studies.
Knapman, Gareth. 2021. "Settler Colonialism and Usurping Malay Sovereignty in Singapore." *Journal of Southeast Asian Studies* 52 (3): 418–440. doi:10.1017/S0022463421000606.
Koh, Aaron. 2014. "Doing Class Analysis in Singapore's Elite Education: Unravelling the Smokescreen of 'Meritocratic Talk'." *Globalisation, Societies and Education* 12 (2): 196–210.
Koh, Aaron. 2005. "Imagining the Singapore 'Nation' and 'Identity': The role of the media and National Education." *Asia Pacific Journal of Education* 25 (1): 75–91.
Kwa, Chong Guan, ed. 2021. *1819 & Before: Singapore's Pasts*. Singapore: ISEAS-Yusof Ishak Institute.
Kwa, Chong Guan. 2019. "Editorial Foreword: The Singapore Bicentennial as public history." *Journal of Southeast Asian Studies* 50 (4): 469–475.
Kwa, Chong Guan. 2006. *S. Rajaratnam on Singapore: From Ideas to Reality*. Singapore: World Scientific and Institute of Defence and Strategic Studies.
Kwa, Chong Guan, Derek Heng, Peter Borschberg and Tan Tai Yong. 2019. *Seven Hundred Years: A History of Singapore*. Singapore: National Library Board and Marshall Cavendish Editions.
Kwen, Fee Lian, ed. 2016. *Multiculturalism, Migration and the Politics of Identity in Singapore*. Singapore: Springer.
Lai, Ah Eng, ed. 2004. *Beyond Rituals and Riots: Ethnic Pluralism and Social Cohesion in Singapore*. Singapore: Eastern Universities Press by Marshall Cavendish for the Institute of Policy Studies.
Lee, Edwin. 2008. *Singapore: The Unexpected Nation*. Singapore: Institute of Southeast Asian Studies.

Lee, Kuan Yew. 2000. *From Third World to First: The Singapore Story: 1965–2000. Memoirs of Lee Kuan Yew.* Singapore: Singapore Press Holdings and Times Editions.
Lee, Kuan Yew. 1998. *The Singapore Story: Memoirs of Lee Kuan Yew.* Singapore: Prentice Hall.
Lee, Kuan Yew. 1965. "Secret Letter to Sir Robert Menzies, Prime Minister of Australia," 20 April. Available in National Archives of Australia: https://www.naa.gov.au/learn/learning-resources/learning-resource-themes/war/cold-war/olympic-athletes-communist-countries-secret-letter-prime-minister-robert-menzies.
Lee, Kuan Yew. 1959–1990. *Prime Minister's Speeches, Press Conferences, Interviews, Statements, etc.*, Singapore: Prime Minister's Office.
22 March 1964. Address to a Mass Rally at Suleiman Court, Kuala Lumpur.
15 October 1965. The Prime Minister Mr Lee Kuan Yew Speaks to Civil Servants.
Ministry of Culture. 1970. *Singapore 1969.* Singapore: Ministry of Culture.
Ministry of Education. 2014. *Singapore: The Making of a Nation-State, 1300–1975.* Singapore: Curriculum Planning and Development Division, Ministry of Education and Star Publishing.
Ministry of Education. 1999. *Understanding Our Past: Singapore from Colony to Nation.* Singapore: Curriculum Planning and Development Division, Ministry of Education and Marshall Cavendish.
Moore, Donald, and Joanna Moore. 1969. *The First 150 Years of Singapore.* Singapore: Donald Moore Press in association with the Singapore International Chamber of Commerce.
Moore, Quinn R. 2000. "Multiracialism and meritocracy: Singapore's approach to race and inequality". *Review of Social Economy* 58 (3): 339–360.
Nabeta, Yoshio, and Yoshihide Fujiwara. 2016. *The LKY Story. Lee Kuan Yew: The Man Who Shaped a Nation.* Singapore: Shogakukan Asia.
Nanyang Siang Pau (cited in *Mirror of Opinion*, the Ministry of Culture's weekly summary of the non-English press):
9 August 1969. "Double Celebration of the Republic of Singapore."
Ortmann, Stephan, and Mark R. Thompson. ed. 2020. *China's 'Singapore Model' and Authoritarian Learning.* Abingdon: Routledge.
Rahim, Lily Zubaidah, and Yeoh Lam Keong. 2019. "Social Policy Reform and Rigidity in Singapore's Developmental State." In *The Limits of Authoritarian Governance in Singapore's Developmental State*, edited by Lily Zubaidah Rahim and Michael D. Barr, 95–130. Singapore: Palgrave Macmillan.
Rahim, Lily Zubaidah. 2009. *Singapore in the Malay World: Building and Breaching Regional Bridges.* Abingdon: Routledge.
Rahim, Lily Zubaidah. 1998. *The Singapore Dilemma: The Political and Educational Marginality of the Malay Community.* Oxford; Singapore; New York: Oxford University Press.
Rajah, Jothie. 2012. *Authoritarian Rule of Law: Legislation, Discourse and Legitimacy in Singapore.* Cambridge, UK and New York: Cambridge University Press.
Rodan, Garry. 2018. "Singapore's Elected President: A Failed Institution." *Australian Journal of International Affairs* 72 (1): 10–15.
Sa'at, Alfian, Faris Joraimi, and Sai Siew Min. 2021. *Raffles Renounced: Towards a Merdeka History.* Singapore: Ethos Press.
Sandhu, Kernial Singh and Paul Wheatley (eds). 1989. *Management of Success: The Moulding of Modern Singapore.* Singapore: Institute of Southeast Asian Studies.
Seow, Francis T. 1998. *The Media Enthralled: Singapore Revisited.* Boulder and London: Lynne Rienner.
Sin Chew Jit Poh (cited in *Mirror of Opinion*):
9 August 1969. "Celebrating Singapore's National Day and 150th Anniversary."
Singapore Bicentennial Conference, 2019, 30 September. Available at: https://www.youtube.com/watch?v=TT-KsfsJ3A8. Accessed 16 June 2020.
South China Morning Post:
26 July 2019. "'I Didn't Change, the PAP Did': Singapore Opposition Politician Tan Cheng Bock Pledges to Ask Government Tough Questions."
Tan, Kenneth Paul. 2020. *Singapore: Identity, Brand, Power.* Cambridge, UK: Cambridge University Press.
Tan, Siok Sun. 2007. *Goh Keng Swee: A Portrait, Singapore.* Editions Didier Millet.
The Economist:
17 April 2021, "Singapore's Ruling Clique Loses Its Reputation for Predictability."
8 April 2021, "Singapore's Prime-Minister-in-Waiting Gives Up the Job."
The Straits Times:
29 August 2021. "National Day Rally 2021: 7 Highlights from PM Lee Hsien Loong's Speech."

23 June 2021. "Woman Who Shouted Racist Abuse on Bus Jailed for 4 Weeks."
7 June 2021. "Police Investigating Incident in Which Racist Remarks Were Made to Interracial Couple."
10 May 2021. "Police Investigating Man Accused of using Racial Slur and Kicking 55-Year-Old Woman."
11 July 2020. "GE2020 Results: PAP Holds on to West Coast GRC with 51.69% of Votes against PSP."
5 August 2019. "'It Saddens Me To See How Tan Cheng Bock Has Lost His Way': ESM Goh Chok Tong."
22 May 2017. "Bicentennial of S'pore's Founding Offers Teachable Moment."
22 December 2015. "Secret Documents Reveal Extent of Negotiations for Separation."
21 August 2015. "Separation 1965."
10 August 1965. "Singapore is out."

Today:
24 June 2020. "'I believe Tan Cheng Bock's vision will build a better S'pore': Lee Hsien Yang on why he joined PSP."
29 August 2021. "NDR 2021: Here's what you need to know".

Utusan Melayu (cited in *Mirror of Opinion*):
12 August 1969. "Ahmad Haji Taff Criticises the 150th Anniversary Celebration of the Founding of Modern Singapore."
28 August 1969. "150th Anniversary Celebrations to Commemorate the Founding of Modern Singapore 'Do Not Portray the Existence of Malays in the Republic' – PKM."
28 February 1970. "Sending *Utusan Melayu* by Post Is Also Prohibited by Government."
2 March 1970. "Rafeah Buang Longs for *Utusan*. 'A Day Is Like a Year…' She Says."
3 March 1970. "History Book on Singapore Burnt".

Vasil, Raj. 1993. *Asianising Singapore: The PAP's Management of Ethnicity*. Singapore: Heinemann Asia.
Viswa Sadasivan. 2011, January 19. Research interview.
Wilairat, Kawin. 1975. *Singapore's Foreign Policy: The First Decade*. Singapore: Institute of Southeast Asian Studies.
Yee, Patrick. 2015. *The Legacy of Lee Kuan Yew: Harry Builds a Nation*. Singapore: Epigram Books.
Yeoh, Joe. c.2010. *To Tame a Tiger: The Singapore Story*. Singapore: Wiz-Biz.

36
EXCLUSION AND INCLUSION

Melayu Islam Beraja and the construction of Bruneian nationalism and national identity

Asiyah Kumpoh and Nani Suryani Abu Bakar

Introduction

Brunei, also known as Brunei Darussalam, is situated on the north-eastern coast of Borneo in Southeast Asia, neighboring the fellow ASEAN nations of Malaysia, Indonesia, and Singapore. With an area of 5,675 square kilometers and a population of 430,000 (Department of Economic Planning and Statistics 2022), it is divided into four districts: Brunei-Muara, Belait, Tutong, and Temburong.

Brunei is a multi-ethnic society with seven ethnic groups recognized as indigenous: Brunei, Tutong, Belait, Dusun, Kedayan, Murut, and Bisaya. A larger constitutional framework of Malaynization, which will be discussed later, brings these ethnic groups together under the broad umbrella of Malay ethnicity. This constitutional development has been concomitant to Brunei's nation-building efforts, the country's main political agenda since the 1950s.

Brunei is ruled by one of the world's oldest monarchies. Official narratives point to its emergence as a Muslim sultanate in 1368, under Sultan Muhammad Shah. Before the nineteenth century, it controlled expansive territories in the north-west and north-east of Borneo, covering the present-day Malaysian states of Sarawak and Sabah (previously known as North Borneo). However, foreign powers – the Brookes and the British North Borneo Chartered Company (BNBCC) – aggressively took territory to form their own government in Sarawak and North Borneo. By the beginning of the twentieth century, Brunei had been reduced to its present-day size, Temburong District dangling on its own, pushing the nation to the verge of extinction.

The establishment of the British Residency in 1906, following the signing of the Supplementary Agreement between Britain and Brunei, to a great extent saved Brunei from dissolution. However, the appointment of a British Resident whose advice should be taken and acted upon did not sit well with the sultan or nobles. There were instances when the sultan disregarded the Resident's advice and instead took the side of his people, leading him to be threatened with dethronement. When Sultan Omar Ali Saifuddien III (SOAS III) ascended to the throne in 1950 as the 28th Sultan of Brunei, the political tension between him and the British Resident became more palpable.

Analyzing the narratives of Brunei's political turbulence in the nineteenth century and the first half of the twentieth century, Kumpoh and Abu Bakar (2021, 85) argue that Brunei has always fought to protect the crown, the monarchical tradition – "the most potent symbol of Brunei's sovereignty and nationhood" – and to keep the sultan's pledge to protect his people. Such a fight is "a demonstration of nationalistic sentiment and a persistent demonstration of a strong sense of belonging" (ibid.). They see protection of state sovereignty and a sense of belonging as the key themes of Bruneian nationalism.

The last five decades have witnessed an extraordinary proliferation of works on nationalism, further broadening its definitional contours. Smith (1972) defines modern nationalism as an ideological movement supporting people's ambition to become an independent nation, whereas Gellner (1983) theorizes nationalism as a doctrine of political legitimacy, an outcome of capitalist modernization. Anderson (2006, 6), drawing on his study of the historical experience of nationalism in Southeast Asia, argues that nationalism should be defined as a powerful expression of an imagined political community that creates a sense of solidarity and sovereignty.

There is also an expanding body of literature that identifies and explores how the subject of inquiry influences the definition and characters of nationalism (Derichs and Heberer 2006; Norbu 1992; Jung and Morris-Suzuki 2011). Significantly, Norbu (1992, 9) cogently argues that the functions of nationalism are shaped by "certain objective conditions" which eventually make the characteristics of one's nationalism highly contextually distinctive. He was also increasingly prepared to argue (1992, 21) that the characteristics of Eastern nationalism would and should not replicate those of Western nationalism, which warranted growing out of the Eurocentric theory of nationalism and paying more attention to the specific conditions leading to the rise of nationalism in the East (ibid, 5–6).

Attending to the relationship between the conditions of society and the form of its nationalism is essential to comprehending the definitions and character of Bruneian nationalism. As shown throughout this chapter, Bruneian nationalism is distinctive and unique. It is primarily shaped by the country's long monarchical tradition and heritage, and the prominence of Islam and Malayness in its past history. The monarchy, Islam, and Malayness are the foundational elements of Bruneian nationalism.

Interestingly, the same tripartite foundation was adopted as the integral tenets of Melayu Islam Beraja (MIB), or Malay Islam Monarchy, which was declared to be Brunei's national philosophy or national ideology when it gained independence from the UK in 1984. MIB bears a striking resemblance to Indonesia's Pancasila and Malaysia's Rukun Negara in its aim to achieve collective social and cultural solidarity among the population (Derich and Heberer 2006, 9). However, with its overarching ideological character, MIB also "serves as a moral and ethical framework for all aspects and levels of domestic governance in the country" (Salbrina and Mabud 2021, 45–46). It will become clear in the discussion below that MIB has also been increasingly identified and embraced as Bruneian nationalism since its promulgation in 1984.

The discussion on Bruneian nationalism has also been enriched by the growing identification of two key themes that embody it: the persistent demonstration of, and fight for, sovereignty; and the forging of a collective sense of belonging. Indeed, these play a central role in nation-building processes and ultimately define the distinctive characteristics of Bruneian nationalism.

The periodization of Bruneian nationalism is equally unique, in line with Gupta's (2007, 269) assertion that the stages or periodizations of nationalism should vary from one context or society to another. Ahmad (2004, 2) studied the rising consciousness of anti-colonial (anti-British) sentiments in Brunei from the 1930s to the 1960s. Dissatisfaction with colonial dominance and keenness to make efforts to bring people together for national development were sentiments repeatedly expressed by young nationalists during the period (Ahmad 2004, 5–7). A similar study of anti-colonial nationalism was carried out by Osman et al. (1995) in the context of the post-war period; they further elaborate (1995, 61) on Bruneian nationalism during the struggle to retrieve power from the British and return it to the monarchical system. This demonstrates a distinctive character of Bruneian nationalism as both an anti-colonial nationalism and a fight to preserve the traditional Malay monarchical system. Menon (1987, 91) subsequently called this "indigenous, non-traditional nationalism" emerging after the promulgation of Brunei's 1959 Constitution.

One can discern that Brunei from the 1980s onward has primarily worked on forging and strengthening the collective sense of belonging among its people – the homogenization period. When Brunei gained independence in 1984, the new nation declared MIB to be the state philosophy. Through *Titah* (decrees), MIB continues to shape and give meaning to national strategies and agendas (Phan et al. 2021, 418). Previous works on MIB also demonstrate how this state philosophy acts as "the country's national adhesive and a key source for social stability" (Phan et al. 2021, 417).

With a solid foundation laid by the Brunei Constitution and the passing of the Nationality Law in 1959 and 1962, the homogenization process, also known as the Malaynization strategy, commenced in the 1980s. As part of state efforts, with a greater emphasis on the three foundational elements of monarchy, Islam and Malay, the strategy aimed

> to homogenise the seven state-recognised ethnic groups into the mainstream Malay society and accordingly into an image of a strong and cohesive nation, which, over time, had essentially caused the ethnic boundaries of the Malay ethnic group to soften, allowing the integration of the different ethnic groups into the mainstream society.
> *(Kumpoh 2011, 12)*

As MIB substantially defines the image of Brunei as a Muslim-Malay nation with one of the oldest existing monarchical systems in the world, it has naturally become the main pillar of Brunei's national identity. It is well-documented that Islam, Malay, and monarchy represent cultural, ethnicity, and heritage elements in the Bruneian national identity. We can argue that this national identity is a natural outcome of Bruneian nationalism, as MIB has further cemented these three elements as the cornerstones of national identity.

Periodization and inclusion-exclusion strategies

As discussed, Bruneian nationalism essentially embodies two key themes: the preservation of state sovereignty (which also means the preservation of the monarchy) and the fostering of a collective sense of belonging. Two broad periods of Brunei nationalism have also been identified: the anti-colonial period and the homogenization period.

To further examine the distinctive nature of Brunei nationalism and the ways heritage, ethnicity, and culture intersect to characterize it, and consequently the national identity, the following discussion explores the ways Bruneian nationalism employs inclusion and exclusion strategies to fulfill its central role of nation-building. The anti-colonial period (1950s–1980s) saw an exclusion strategy aimed at removing British interference and involvement in state administration. In comparison, a holistic and transformative inclusion strategy prevailed during the homogenization period (from the 1980s onward). Through the official declaration of Malay, Islam, and monarchy as the three integral elements of the state philosophy, and the expansive definition of Malay to include all constitutionally recognized ethnic groups under one larger ethnic framework, a collective sense of belonging among the people has been generated. Siddique (1985, 108) perceives MIB explicitly as the "Bruneian concept of nationalism".

The anti-colonial period (1950s–1980s)

Brunei first came under British rule as a protectorate in 1888, as an outcome of the Protectorate Agreement between Brunei and Great Britain, with Article 1 stipulating that "the State of Brunei shall continue to be governed and administered by the said Sultan… as an independent State under the protection of Great Britain…" (Hussainmiya 1995, 392). However, the British failed to fulfill the protection clause and Brunei's survival and sovereignty were increasingly threatened by the aggression of the Brookes and the BNBCC, the British powers occupying the neighboring states of Sarawak and North Borneo, respectively, and eyeing Brunei's remaining territory.

The Brookes forcefully annexed Limbang in 1890, splitting Brunei into two and leaving present-day Temburong District dangling on its own. This led Sultan Hashim, the 25th Sultan of Brunei, to insist on better protection from the British, leading to a 1905 addendum to the Protectorate Agreement requiring the appointment of a British Resident in Brunei to assist the sultan in any matters related to state administration, except those pertaining to religion. This Supplementary Agreement sustained the British presence in Brunei until independence in 1984.

As discussed, the political and administrative imposition of a British Resident was initially welcomed by the sultan, as the new administration "bolstered the status and authority of the Sultan when… the fiscal and land rights of the Brunei nobles were stripped" (Hussainmiya 2003, 275). However, over time the British Resident's advice and rulings became less likely to be listened to and acted upon as planned. Instead there was growing suspicion toward, and resentment of, British domination and administrative interference in local affairs. Time and again, the sultan cautioned the British Resident not to interfere with local customs and traditions, demonstrating his protection of the rights of the people and ultimately state sovereignty (Kumpoh and Abu Bakar 2021, 86).

Relative to the rest of Southeast Asia, an early manifestation of nationalism in Brunei can be detected after the Second World War, partly due to the political impact of the Japanese occupation, which awakened local political and cultural sensibilities (Hussainmiya 2003, 286). Hussainmiya (1995, 80) regards the immediate post-war years as the "genesis of nationalism". Moreover, growing resentment toward the British presence in Brunei inevitably led to emergent nationalist voices slowly coming to the fore.

In 1946, a nationalist movement called Barisan Pemuda (Youth Front), or BARIP, emerged, catching the attention of the local people and the British. Unlike some quasi-political organizations formed during the pre-war period, BARIP was conspicuously nationalistic and made it clear to British officials that it demanded the return of Brunei's sovereignty to the sultan (Jibah 1994, 195). When it became evident that BARIP was attempting to align itself with the anti-colonial spirit of the Indonesian revolution, and its growing influence and popularity attracted the attention of neighboring Malaysian states (Ahmad 2004, 7–8), the British took a firm stand that led to BARIP's demise in 1948.

In 1956, Partai Rakyat Brunei (People's Party of Brunei), or PRB, was formed with the precise aim of opposing any form of colonialism while preserving the reputation of the sultan and his heirs (Ahmad 1987, 96). This anti-colonial advocacy was similarly upheld by Ahmad Boestamam's Partai Ra'ayat Malaya (Malaya's People's Party) and Harun Mohd Amin's

People's Party of Singapore, which both wielded notable political influence (Jibah 1994, 198). At its first congress in 1957, the PRB once again clearly stated its detestation of any form of colonialism while declaring allegiance to and support for the sultan (Osman et al. 1995, 124). This clear anti-colonial political stance caused uneasiness among British officials.

Alongside the growing popularity of the PRB was the constitutional plan laid out by SOAS III, who had ascended to the throne in 1950. There was no secret as to why he initiated the constitutional process: to determine the political future of Brunei, specifically its constitutional status, including the succession laws of the Brunei sultans, and to reorganize Brunei's State Council with appropriate legislative arrangements (Hussainmiya 2000, 16). Furthermore, often noted are SOAS III's frequent expressions of his national vision to bring modernize Brunei and make concerted efforts for the benefit of the Brunei people (Kumpoh and Abu Bakar 2021, 87). This motivation and vision were fundamentally an implicit language of anti-colonial nationalism, which later took on more definition as SOAS III steadily carried forward the constitutional plan.

The materialization of the constitutional plan was not in any way smooth. The Brunei Constitution Advisory Committee, Tujuh Serangkai, was tasked to ascertain and report on public opinion on the plan. More importantly, it functioned as an advisory body to SOAS III in drafting the Constitution. At the same time, taking advantage of the British-created District Council and State Council, increasingly politically active Bruneians began to put checks on the power of the British Resident, to the point that he came to consider their voices and actions obstructive (Hussainmiya 1995, 153). Nationalistic slogans such as "Brunei for Bruneians" were also increasingly echoed by the educated vernacular intelligentsia who dominated the State Council (Hussainmiya 1995, 145).

Unlike this latter group, SOAS III's expressions of nationalism were somewhat tacit and deeply embedded in his poems. During the constitutional process, he composed Syair Perlembagaan Negeri Brunei (the Negeri Brunei Constitution Poem), which contains repeated references to his political frustration with the British Resident as "the misfortune of hardship" (Al-Sufri, 2010, 78). Damit (2013, 101) also interprets the sultan's words as expressions of his growing impatience with the British Resident and his displeasure with the Resident's advisory role. SOAS III was adamant that he meant "to win back the effective sovereignty of the Brunei Ruler from the hands of the British overlordship" (Hussainmiya 2011, 21).

The struggle against British domination in Brunei culminated with the promulgation of Brunei's first written constitution in September 1959. This without doubt indicated the reclamation of the sultan's power, authority, and legitimacy from the British (Zawawi 2017, 51). The Constitution deployed an exclusionary strategy in order to retrieve state sovereignty and internal independence. By reinstating the executive and legislative authority of the monarchy, Brunei effectively excluded the British from playing any further significant role in the internal administration of the state. The Constitution clearly stipulated the appointment of a Mentri Besar (Chief Minister) who "shall be responsible to the Sultan for the exercise in the State of all executive authority" (Perlembagaan Negeri Brunei 1959, 35). The Chief Minister was to be appointed by the sultan, as were other key positions in the government such as Setia Usaha Kerajaan (State Secretary), Peguam Negara (Attorney-General), and Pegawai Kewangan Negara (State Financial Officer) (ibid.). The Constitution also declared Islam and Bahasa Melayu (Malay language) to be the national religion and language (Perlembagaan Negeri Brunei 1959, 33; 122).

There is no doubt that the Constitution's exclusionary clauses effectively serve its main purpose: to reclaim internal sovereignty from British rule. The return to Brunei's historical roots, with a particular emphasis on the ethnic-culture-heritage nexus as constitutional provisions, provided a sound justification for reinforcing the monarchical system, subtly challenging British control over the state for the previous 50 years. It is also worth noting that the return of the sovereign right to rule to the sultan and local administration, and the constitutional declaration of Bahasa Melayu and Islam, laid the foundation for the formulation of the national identity of Brunei in the coming decades (Kumpoh and Abu Bakar 2021, 88).

The concerted effort to retrieve full sovereignty and attain independence continued in the next three decades, the 1960s, 1970s, and 1980s. Concomitant to such a process was the creation of symbols of nationhood – a national flag and anthem. As bearers of national symbols and meanings, these are critical to bolstering the nation-building process and solidifying a sense of collective belonging.

Brunei's National Anthem was officially adopted in 1952, during the early years of SOAS III's reign. Composed by prominent Bruneians Awang Haji Besar bin Sagap and Pengiran Haji Mohamed Yusof bin Pengiran Haji Abdul Rahim, it was first disseminated in several vernacular schools to introduce and promote familiarity with the emergent representative of nationalism.

Brunei's national flag, however, has had a series of modifications since the signing of the Supplementary Agreement in 1906. Starting with a plain yellow, then the addition of black and white stripes to represent the traditional colors of the monarch and the principal Wazir (viziers), the national crest was added after the promulgation of the Brunei Constitution. The Arabic inscription means "Always render service by God's guidance". A red ribbon below the crescent has a Jawi inscription: "Brunei Darussalam".

Since the second half of the twentieth century, flag-hoisting ceremonies and mass singing of the national anthem have become ubiquitous when marking national celebratory events. One must say that such strategic use of the national symbols is as powerful as the voices of nationalists, both equally emphasizing the promotion of unity and a collective sense of belonging. It is interesting to observe how Bruneian society in the second half of the twentieth century somewhat resembled Anderson's (2006) imagined community, and how it has transformed into a cohesive and inclusive society demonstrating national solidarity, particularly in times of national crisis, including the recent COVID-19 pandemic.

What happened next is equally interesting to examine. Once full sovereignty had been returned to the monarchy (thus strengthening the monarchical system), Brunei needed to pave a broader way for development and modernization, for the benefit of the people and subsequently a collective sense of belonging, another key theme in Bruneian nationalism. This was the start of the homogenization period, during which Brunei delicately transitioned from an exclusionary strategy to a welcoming inclusionary strategy for the sole purpose of nation-building.

Homogenization period (1980s onward)

Of the two periods of Bruneian nationalism, the homogenization period is the most critical, due to its substantial contribution to the nation-building role of Bruneian nationalism. We can also observe during the period a much stronger emphasis on and inculcation of the elements of Bruneian nationalism: ethnicity, culture, and heritage in the form of Malay, Islam, and monarchy.

As mentioned above, the homogenization period has employed an inclusionary strategy to ensure the continued implementation of nation-building policies. This is essentially supported by the promulgation of the 1959 Brunei Constitution and the 1961 Nationality Act, as an addendum and clarification to the loose specification of the citizen of Brunei and the subjects of the monarch in the Constitution (Perlembagaan Negeri Brunei 1959, 20). The more urgent push to pass the Nationality Act came from the PRB's demand that the government sort out the citizenship issue so that eligibility of voters for the District Council Elections could be determined (Ahmad 2004, 52).

The Nationality Act 1961 defines subjects of the sultan by law as those who belong "to one of the following indigenous groups of the Malay race, namely, Belait, Bisayah, Brunei, Dusun, Kedayan, Murut or Tutong" (Brunei Nationality Act n.d., 4). It is worth mentioning that there are significant religious and cultural differences between these indigenous or ethnic groups, with the Belait, Bisaya, Dusun, and Murut mainly non-Muslim, and thus crucial that the Nationality Act set out a new classification that constitutionally recognized the seven ethnic groups as Malay. In other words, the Malay race had expanded to include these ethnic groups, particularly those professing religions other than Islam and whose mother tongue is not Bahasa Melayu.

Examining this Malay race classification in the context of local politics and the full independence gained in 1984, the Nationality Act is without doubt an inclusionary strategy to create a mainstream Malay society and promote ethnic integration that advocates political consolidation and nation-building (Kumpoh et al. 2017, 11). Equally important is that the redefinition of Malay as encompassing the seven ethnic groups gave more substantial political relevance in Bruneian nationalism to Malay ethnicity, an integral element of Bruneian national identity. This lends further support to the earlier argument that Bruneian national identity has been defined by the notion of nationhood and nationalism, rather than purely ethnicity.

It is worth noting that the ability to bestow official citizenship through the passing of the Nationality Act also demonstrates state sovereignty, a core theme of Bruneian nationalism. The Act was without doubt one of the key milestones achieved by Brunei in its nation-building efforts, fulfilling the ideal of nationalism.

The attainment of state sovereignty was further embodied in the proclamation of independence made by His Majesty Sultan Hassanal Bolkiah, the 29th Sultan of Brunei, on 1 January 1984. In the proclamation, he also declared Brunei a sovereign, democratic, independent Malay Muslim monarchy that would observe the Ahli Sunnah Waljamaah School of the Islamic faith. This was also a declaration that MIB was the state philosophy upon which subsequent political, economic, religious, and social development should be modeled.

This period witnessed the construction of a new nation-state through accommodative means to overcome social, cultural, religious, and linguistic divides. One method used was the promulgation of MIB as Brunei's national ideological concept. As discussed, similarly to Indonesia's Pancasila and Malaysia's Rukun Negara, Brunei's MIB pursued a collective, imaginary solidarity among different ethnic groups, ensured basic living standards, and clarified the relationship between the state (the government of the day) and the nation (Derich and Heberer 2006, 9). Furthermore, it consolidated a collective sense of belonging and identity in the form of Malay-Muslim ethnicity (Kumpoh et al. 2017, 20; Adriani et al. 2021, 203). Thus, one can safely argue that since the 1980s, Bruneian nationalism has increasingly constituted a political ideology – the MIB.

The implementation of MIB led to the strengthening of Malaynization, a demonstrably inclusionary strategy of nationalism. This process reflects a strong ethnic nationalism through the persistent emphasis on Malay, Islam, and monarchy. Putri et al. (2017) argue that ethnic nationalism typically suggests the exclusion of those who do not belong to the dominant ethnic group. However, in the case of Bruneian nationalism, Malaynization has been orientated in the opposite direction by expanding the definition of Malay to include all seven ethnic groups.

The national education system has played a critical role in supporting the Malaynization strategy. Since the 1960s, Bahasa Melayu has been implemented as the national language "in a renewed spirit of nationalism" (Hj-Othman 2005, 70). It was the main medium of instruction in the school system from the 1960s to the 1980s. When Brunei introduced the Bilingual Education Policy in 1985, which places equal emphasis on Bahasa Melayu and English as the preferred languages of school instruction, the former increasingly became the mother tongue of non-Malay and non-Muslim ethnic groups, due to the "visible shift away from ethnic languages to the Malay Language" (Hj-Othman 2005, 71).

Similarly, Islamic Religious Knowledge (IRK) was also introduced as a school subject at various academic levels. When the 21st Century National Education System (SPN21) was introduced in 2008, Bahasa Melayu was retained as a compulsory subject, with IRK a compulsory complementary subject at primary and lower secondary levels.

Growing proficiency in Bahasa Melayu and increasing familiarity with Islam led to a strong sense of recognition of Bahasa Melayu, Islam, and MIB, as well as a subtle emulation of the Muslim-Malay way of life (Kumpoh 2011, 27). Thus, by the 1990s, it had become increasingly clear that the Malaynization strategy had broken down religious, cultural, and social boundaries between different ethnic groups. King (1994, 86) contends that it is difficult nowadays to distinguish between the original Brunei Malays and Muslims, and other ethnic groups.

The homogenizing effects of the education system were further strengthened by incorporating other school subjects that acted as continual reminders of nationhood, nationalism, and national identity, such as History and MIB. On the History syllabus, historical narratives are communicated to the young generation; while MIB is compulsory in tertiary education. Both subjects carefully construct historical narratives of the country's past to frame state sovereignty, reinforce national unity and consolidation, and ultimately promote a distinctive sense of Bruneian nationalism and national identity.

Apart from the education system, local historiography has also played a critical role in the nation-building and homogenizing processes, and the formulation of national identity. The writing of the history of Brunei has always been instrumental in defining the historical character and contours of the country (Davies 1996, 2). Thus, when Brunei gained independence in 1984, the production of local historiography focused on narratives of nationhood and nation-building. Among the themes in Brunei history which have been exhaustively studied are the origin and the rise of Brunei as a Muslim sultanate, and the arrival of Islam. Publication of what is known as national and autonomous history became a main government agenda in order to support and justify national identity and the conceptualization of MIB (Kumpoh et al. 2023).

The critical roles of local actors in contributing to strengthening, developing, and sustaining national development have also been increasingly highlighted in local historical accounts. SOAS III is one of the most studied figures, particularly regarding his contributions to Brunei's development in the second half of the twentieth century. The volume of work on SOAS III considerably increased after His Majesty Sultan Hassanal Bolkiah fondly referred to his father as the architect of modern Brunei (Kumpulan Titah 2017, 97), specifically referring to his nation-building projects and related programs. This led to an increase in historical research and publication on his reign, including the drafting process and promulgation of the Constitution (Duraman 1995; Abdullah 1993; Hussainmiya 1995) and the introduction and development of the modern education system (Jibah 1983; Mail 2006).

Moreover, in 1985, the establishment of Brunei's premier university, Universiti Brunei Darussalam (UBD), further spurred publication of books and articles on the transformative changes experienced by Brunei during the reign of SOAS III. Similarly, government bodies such as the Museum Departments and Brunei History Centre, established in 1965 and 1982, respectively, also directly contribute to the active production of Brunei historiography through the introduction and management of academic journals that showcase the research efforts of both local and foreign experts.

Narratives of national identity

National history has also been extensively utilized in constructing the inclusionary and official narratives of national identity. National identity is often derived from a shared past, and as discussed, Brunei's national identity has been historically conditioned. Keillor and Hult (1999) argue that the notion of national identity is commonly based on ethnicity, culture, and heritage, and Brunei well exemplifies this argument through Malay, Islam, and monarchy, as MIB has been increasingly and synonymously defined as Brunei's overarching national identity (Saunders 1994, 187).

Local historiography thus accordingly justifies the historical conceptualization and legitimization of MIB as both state philosophy and national identity (Hamid 1992; Umar 1993). More authoritative and official publications on MIB and its historical connection to Brunei's past have also emerged to offer further support and justification for the relevance and preservation of its three integral elements (Umar 1993; Serudin 1998; Ibrahim 1994). In addition, there has also been an increasing amount of original research on Brunei's independence and national identity. For instance, Ismail's (1991) work on the re-emergence of Brunei as a sovereign nation studies the political conditions leading to independence and contributing to its distinctive identity as a Malay-Muslim sultanate.

A survey of the current literature demonstrates that Bruneian national identity is a deliberate creation to support the nation-building process (Talib 2002; Derichs and Heberer 2006; Tey 2007; Fanselow 2014). As one of the requirements of the processes, MIB was formulated as a common and collective ideology articulating desirable ideals and values palatable to Bruneian society. The historical roots of MIB are emphasized to demonstrate an unbroken link with the common past, necessary to fulfill the homogenizing role of national identity. In this respect, MIB has a dual function of providing a concept of both nationalism and national identity.

The homogenizing role of MIB as national identity is further activated in the face of cultural conflicts, mainly to ward off threats against Bruneian culture and tradition. Majlis Tertinggi Melayu Islam Beraja (MTMIB, the Supreme Council of Melayu Islam Beraja) strives to maintain and express Bruneian society's national identity, particularly for the new generation, against the background of aggressive waves of globalization (Melayong 2019).

It is also worth pointing out that in the Bruneian context, national identity is not merely an elite-constructed identity representing national character and sentiments. As a national identity, the quotidian expression of the Bruneians has always embodied values of virtue, morality, and manners that intrinsically belong to and represent the values and practices of MIB. This set of values, referred to as *Kebruneian* (Bruneianness), essentially comprises significant values such as responsibility, trustworthiness, generosity, humility, respect, and reverence. One can argue that MIB, as the national identity, successfully permeates the Bruneian way of life (Phan et al. 2021, 418). At the same time, however, these values were actually embedded in the fabric of people's lives long before the promulgation of the national philosophy in 1984 (Ibrahim 2003, 21; Umar 1993, 16). They are so distinctive and strongly identifiable within Bruneian culture that they ultimately frame the expression and articulation of Bruneian national identity.

Similarly, common cultural expressions of national identity are not initially elite-constructed expressions. Starting with local people whose articulation and expression of national identity are commonly derived from the historical past, it is common nowadays for Kampong Ayer (the Water Village), *kain tenunan* (traditional textiles), and certain types of local cuisine to be considered contemporary depictions of Bruneian national identity. This is consistent with a more authoritative affirmation of national identity demonstrated through national events and celebrations such as the National Day, His Majesty's Birthday, the anniversary of the Royal Brunei Armed Forces, and important dates in the Islamic calendar.

Conclusion

The above discussion demonstrates that MIB essentially defines and represents Bruneian nationalism and national identity. Its historical and contemporary functions demonstrate its continued relevance in dealing with the competing forces and nuances of the globalized world. The discussion also points out that Brunei historiography plays a critical role in defining the meaning of nationalism and consequently facilitating the formation of national identity.

It is also fair to argue that the homogenization process undertaken in the last 40 years has probably reached a natural threshold. With the demonstrably strong and homogenized social, cultural, and even religious character of present-day Bruneian society, the country can now afford to pursue diversity. There have been calls for ethnic groups to preserve their distinct culture, identity, and heritage, and during the National Day parade in 2022, the announcer omitted the term "Malay" in introducing the seven ethnic groups to attendees and the public.

The articulation of nationalism has always been made by institutions and leadership, with somewhat minimal consideration of how ordinary people actually appreciate and articulate notions of nationalism and national identity in their everyday life. Hobsbawm (1990, 10) calls for the examination of nationalism from below, capturing "the assumptions, hopes, needs, longings, interests of ordinary people, which are not necessarily national or still less nationalist". Such an approach to studying nationalism remains under-explored in the context of Brunei. Hence, further research should assess the people's appreciation and understanding of nationalism and national identity. It would also be interesting to study how the institutional nurturing of nationalism and national identity has affected and defined the local understanding of the two terms.

References

English-language references

Adriani, Nour, M. Labibatussolihah, Mohammad Refi Omar Ar Razy, and Andi Suwirta. 2021. "The Land of Complexity: 19th and 20th Century Northern Borneo Socio-Demographic History: A Review." *Jurnal Sosial Humaniora* 14 (2): 193–207.

Ahmad, Haji Zaini. 1987. *The People's Party of Brunei: Selected Documents*. Kuala Lumpur: INSAN.

Al-Sufri, Jamil. 2010. *Royal Poet: Al-Marhum Sultan Haji Omar 'Ali Saifuddien Sa'adul Khairi Waddien* (translated by Datin Hajah Masni binti Haji Ali). Bandar Seri Begawan: Brunei History Centre.

Anderson, Benedict. 2006. *Imagined Communities: Reflections on the Origin and Spread of Nationalism*. Second Edition. New York: Verso.

"Brunei Nationality Act." n.d. Accessed March 21 2021. www.agc.gov.bn/AGC%20Images/LAWS/ACT_PDF/cap015.pdf

Davies, Putu. 1996. "Introduction." In *Constructing a national past: National history and historiography in Brunei, Indonesia, Thailand, Singapore, the Philippines, and Vietnam. A collection of conference papers from the International Workshop on National History and Historiography*, edited by Putu Davies, 1–30. Bandar Seri Begawan: Universiti Brunei Darussalam.

Department of Economic Planning and Statistics, 2022. "Population." Accessed 2 February 2022. https://deps.mofe.gov.bn/SitePages/Population.aspx

Derichs, Claudia, and Thomas Heberer. 2006. "Introduction: Diversity of Nation-building in East and Southeast Asia." *European Journal of East Asian Studies* 5 (1): 1–13. https://doi.org/10.1163/157006106777998061.

Fanselow, Frank. 2014. "The Anthropology of the State and the State of Anthropology in Brunei." *Journal of Southeast Asian Studies* 45 (1): 90–112.

Gellner, Ernest. 1983. *Nations and Nationalism*. Ithaca, NY: Cornell University Press.

Gupta, Akhil. 2007. "Imagining Nations." In *A Companion to the Anthropology of Politics*, edited by David Nugent and Joan Vincent, 267–281. Carlton, Victoria, Australia: Blackwell Publishing Ltd.

Hamid, Haji Hashim. 1992. "Melayu Islam Beraja: Satu Kesinambungan Sejarah Brunei." *Jurnal Darussalam* 1: 77–87.

Hj-Othman, Noor Azam. 2005. "Changes in the Linguistic Diversity of Negara Brunei Darussalam: An Ecological Perspective." PhD dissertation. Leicester: University of Leicester.

Hobsbawm, Eric John. 1990. *Nations and Nationalism since 1870. Programme, Myth, Reality*. Cambridge: Cambridge University Press.

Hussainmiya, Bachamiya Abdul. 1995. *Sultan Omar Ali Saifuddin III and Britain: The Making of Brunei Darussalam*. Kuala Lumpur: Oxford University Press.

Hussainmiya, Bachamiya Abdul. 2000. *The Brunei Constitution 1959: An Inside History*. Bandar Seri Begawan: Brunei Press.

Hussainmiya, Bachamiya Abdul. 2003. "Resuscitating Nationalism: Brunei under the Japanese Military Administration (1941–1945)." *Senri Ethnological Studies* 65: 273–300.

Hussainmiya, Bachamiya Abdul. 2011. *Brunei: Traditions of Monarchic Culture and History, R.H. Hickling's Memorandum upon Brunei Constitutional History and Practice*. Bandar Seri Begawan: Yayasan Sultan Haji Hassanal Bolkiah.

Ismail, Mohd Eusoff Agaki. 1991. "Brunei Darussalam: Its re-emergence as a sovereign and independent Malay-Muslim Sultanate (1959–1983)." MA dissertation. Hull: University of Hull.

Jung, Kang Sang, and Tessa Morris-Suzuki. 2011. "Tunneling through Nationalism: The Phenomenology of a Certain Nationalist." *Asia-Pacific Journal – Japan Focus* 9(36): 2.

Keillor, Bruce, and Tomas M. Hult. 1999. "A Five-Country Study of National Identity: Implications for International Marketing Research and Practice." *International Marketing Review* 16 (1): 65–84. https://doi.org/10.1108/02651339910257656.

King, Victor Terry. 1994. "What Is Brunei Society? Reflections on a Conceptual and Ethnographic Issue." *South East Asia Research* 2: 176–186.

Kumpoh, Asiyah. 2011. "Conversion to Islam: The case of the Dusun ethnic group in Brunei Darussalam." PhD dissertation. Leicester: University of Leicester.

Kumpoh, Asiyah, Siti Norkhalbi Wahsalfelah, and Noor Azam Hj-Othman. 2017. "Socio-cultural Dynamics in Bruneian Society." In *Comparative Studies in ASEAN Cultures and Societies*, 1–44. Bangkok: Semadhma Publishing House.

Kumpoh, Asiyah, and Nani Suryani Abu Bakar. 2021. "The Bruneian Concept of Nationhood in the 19th and 20th centuries: Expressions of State Sovereignty and National Identity." *The Brunei Museum Journal*: 79–94.

Kumpoh, Asiyah, Stephen Druce, and Nani Suryani Abu Bakar. 2023. "Brunei Historiography." In *The Routledge Handbook of Contemporary Brunei*, edited by Ooi Keat Gin and Victor Terry King, 118–142. London: Routledge.

Melayong, Mohd Hadi. 2019. "Young Helping Share Brunei's Culture, Tradition." *Borneo Bulletin*, 3 June 2019. Accessed 5 May 2021. https://borneobulletin.com.bn/youth-helping-share-bruneis-culture-traditions

Menon, K. U. 1987. "Brunei Darussalam in 1986: In Search of the Political Kingdom." *Southeast Asian Affairs*: 85–101. https://doi.org/10.1355/9789812306777-008.

Norbu, Dawa. 1992. *Culture and the Politics of Third World Nationalism*. London and New York: Routledge.

Phan, Le Ha, Asiyah Kumpoh, and Keith Wood. 2021. "Wrap Up to Move Forward." In *Globalisation, Education, and Reform in Brunei Darussalam*, edited by Phan Le Ha, Asiyah Kumpoh, Keith Wood, Rosmawijah Jawawi, and Hardimah Said, 415–429. Switzerland: Palgrave Macmillan.

Putri, Idola Perdisi, Ellisha Nasruddin, and Juliana Abdul Wahab. 2017. "Defining the Concept of National Identity in Post Modern Society." In *3rd International Conference on Transformation in Communications 2017 (IcoTiC 2017)*, 175–180. Atlantis Press.

Salbrina, Sharbawi, and Shaikh Abdul Mabud. 2021. "Malay, Muslim and Monarchy: An Introduction on Brunei Darussalam and Its National Identity." In *Globalisation, Education, and Reform in Brunei Darussalam*, edited by Phan Le Ha, Asiyah Kumpoh, Keith Wood, Rosmawijah Jawawi, and Hardimah Said, 45–66. Switzerland: Palgrave Macmillan.

Saunders, Graham. 1994. *A History of Brunei*. Singapore: Oxford University Press.

Siddique, Sharon. 1985. "Negara Brunei Darussalam: A New Nation but an Ancient Country." *Southeast Asian Affairs*, 99–108.

Smith, Anthony David. 1972. *Theories of Nationalism*. New York: Harper and Row.

Talib, Naimah. 2002. "A Resilient Monarchy: The Sultanate of Brunei and Regime Legitimacy in an Era of Democratic Nation-states." *New Zealand Journal of Asian Studies* 4 (2): 134–147.

Tey, Tsun Hang. 2007. "Brunei's Revamped Constitution: The Sultan as the Grundnorm?" *Australian Journal of Asian Law* 9 (2): 264–288.

Zawawi, Majdey. 2017. "Manoeuvring Power Dynamics: The Brunei Constitution 1959." *The Journal of Islamic Governance* 3 (1): 51–67.

Malay-language references

Abdullah, Muhammad Hadi. 1993. "Cabaran-cabaran ke arah pembentukan Perlembangan Negeri Brunei 1959." *Beriga* 38: 33–77.

Ahmad, Haji Zaini. 2004. *Pertumbuhan Nasionalisme di Brunei (1939–1962)*. Brunei Darussalam: Asia Printers.

Damit, Yusop. 2013. "Pembentukan Perlembagaan Negeri Brunei 1959: Dasar British dan Respons Brunei." In *Survival Negara Bangsa: Himpunan Kertas Kerja Seminar Serantau*, edited by Haji Rosli bin Haji Ampal and Yus Sa'bariah binti Haji Adanan, 87–112. Bandar Seri Begawan: Pusat Sejarah Brunei.

Duraman, Haji Sulaiman. 1995. "Perlembagaan Negeri Brunei 1959, Suatu Tinjauan Umum Mengenai Proses Pembentukannya." *Jurnal Darussalam* 2: 142–153.

Hamid, Haji Hashim. 1992. "Melayu Islam Beraja: Satu Kesinambungan Sejarah Brunei." *Jurnal Darussalam* 1: 77–87.

Jibah, Matassim. 1983. "Perkembangan Persekolahan Melayu di Brunei dalam Pentadbiran Sistem Residen 1906–1959." *The Brunei Museum Journal* 5 (3): 1–26.

Jibah, Matassim. 1994. "Perkembangan Politik Brunei 1945–1962." In *Brunei di Tengah-Tengah Nusantara. Kumpulan Kertas Kerja Seminar Sejarah Brunei*, edited by Muhammad Latif, Hashim Noor, and Rosli Ampal, 191–202. Bandar Seri Begawan: Jabatan Pusat Sejarah.

Ibrahim, Haji Abdul Latif. 1994. "Melayu Islam Beraja dari Perspektif Perbandingan." A paper presented at the International Seminar on Brunei Malay Sultanate in Nusantara, organized by Yayasan Sultan Haji Hassanal Bolkiah and the Academy of Brunei Studies, International Convention Centre, Brunei Darussalam, 13–17 November 1994.

Ibrahim, Haji Abdul Latif. 2003. *Melayu Islam Beraja: Pengantar Huraian*. Bandar Seri Begawan: Universiti Brunei Darussalam, Akademi Pengajian Brunei.

Kumpulan Titah Kebawah Duli Yang Maha Mulia Paduka Seri Baginda Sultan Haji Hasssanal Bolkiah Mu'izzadin Waddaulah, Sultan dan Yang Di-Pertuan Negara Brunei Darusssalam Tahun 1984, 1985, 1986, dan 1987. 2017. Bandar Seri Begawan: Borneo Printers.

Mail, Haji Asbol. 2006. *Sejarah Perkembangan Pendidikan di Brunei 1950–1985*. Bandar Seri Begawan: Pusat Sejarah Brunei.

Osman, Sabihah, Mohd Hadi Abdullah, and Sabullah Hj Hakip. 1995. *Sejarah Brunei Menjelang Kemerdekaan*. Kuala Lumpur: Dewan Bahasa dan Pustaka Malaysia.

Perlembagaan Negeri Brunei. 1959. Brunei: Jabatan Perchetakan Kerajaan.

Serudin, Zain. 1998. *Melayu Islam Beraja: Suatu Pendekatan*. Bandar Seri Begawan: Dewan Bahasa dan Pustaka.

Umar, Haji Awang Abdul Aziz. 1993. Melayu Islam Beraja Negara Brunei Darussalam. In *Melayu Islam Beraja*. Gadong: Universiti Brunei Darussalam.

37
NATIONALISM IN TRANSITION
Construction and transformation of Rai Timor

Takahiro Kamisuna

> FRETILIN deeply believes in the people of East Timor. They are the dynamic force of the life of the nation. Only those who don't believe in the people and their creative and transformative power would accept integration in Indonesia...
>
> *(The Campaign for independent East Timor 1974, 4)*

> We learnt Indonesian, we had lessons about Indonesian history, we had PMP or Pendidikan Moral Pancasila [Education in Pancasila Morality], we had to learn by heart the words, "freedom is the right of all nations", taken from Indonesia's declaration of independence.
>
> *An interview with an East Timorese youth, Rogerio A.P. (TAPOL 1987, 5)*

Introduction

No single account of nationalism explains the transitional path of East Timorese nationalism. The different struggles against colonialism and occupation by Portugal and Indonesia shaped nationalist aspirations in different ways between the Generation of 75 (*Geração '75*) and the New Generation (*Geração Foun*) (Bexley and Tchailoro, 2013; Kamisuna, 2020). While conventional scholarship has explained nationalism as vernacular aspirations to ultimately create a single nation-state (Geertz 1973; Smith 1986), such theories fail to capture transformative features of the nationalist movements between the generations.

In contrast, the study of East Timorese nationalism potentially offers theoretical implications for the development and transformation of nationalism. In East Timor, occupation by Portugal and Indonesia created a unique historical trajectory for nationalism between the older and younger generations; their different adaptations to international normative discourse transformed their usages of ideological instruments in shaping *Rai Timor* (Timor Land). While *Geracao '75* ('75 Generation) sought to 'translate' the right to self-determination into their local language of Maubereism in order to emancipate themselves from the colonial *exploração* (exploitation) (cf. Rafael 2005), *Geracao Foun* (New Generation) was able to 'translate' *terus* (suffering) into the international language of universal human rights by Indonesianising and universalising their struggle.

On the one hand, the geographical notion of East Timor is historically malleable (Tsuchiya 2019), and thus the concept of *Rai Timor* does not necessarily rest on territorial boundaries. Different experiences of *exploração* and *terus* under Portuguese colonialisation and Indonesian occupation further created two distinct generations of struggle (Kamisuna 2020). While *Geração '75*'s nationalism rested on the traditional claim in the developing world of self-determination to participate in the nation-state system, *Geração Foun* displayed a transnational form of nationalism in which East Timorese youths actively worked with Indonesian pro-democracy activists.

On the other hand, East Timorese nationalism in the Cold War period had to borrow external ideological foundations to legitimatise its claim against Indonesia. Thus, the nationalist claim of the East Timorese was presented as hinging on the international transition from the right of self-determination to universal human rights. While the earlier development of East Timorese nationalism devoted tremendous efforts into translating international discourses on human rights into indigenous language (Webster 2013), the subsequent transition reflects the global transition in human rights discourse between the 1980s and 1990s.

This chapter provides a parallel explanation of how East Timorese nationalism transformed in national and international contexts. The first part provides a brief overview of the existing arguments concerning East Timorese nationalism. The second examines the emergence and transformation of this nationalism by analysing the political education of earlier East Timorese nationalists and the youth struggle of *Geração Foun* in Indonesia. By contextualising the transitional independence struggle of East Timorese within the global transition of human rights, this chapter provides a nuanced explanation of the development of nationalism over the two consecutive generations of struggle.

Nationalism in transition

Since the rise of the East Timorese nationalist movement in the 1970s, scholars have studied the East Timorese struggle for colonial emancipation extensively in order to understand its unitary ideological foundations (Jolliffe 1978; Nicol 1978; Matsuno 2002; Hill 2002; Dunn 2003). In contrast, recent scholars have examined diversity and discrepancy among different nationalist groups within and beyond *Rai Timor* (Bexley 2007; Bexley and Tchailoro 2013; Arthur 2018; Tsuchiya 2017, 2019; Damaledo 2018, Kamisuna 2020). As a whole, the existing literature has unpacked the distinctive differences between *Geração'75* and *Geração Foun*. While *Geração'75* incorporated Portuguese culture as an integral part of national identity in order to distinguish itself from Indonesia (Hill 2002), *Geração Foun* was culturally more affiliated with Indonesia, as the new generation had studied in Indonesia's schools and spoke the Indonesian language more fluently than they did Portuguese (Bexley and Tchailoro 2013). Hence, the two generations relied on different cultural weapons in articulating their East Timorese nationalism, though both shared the same pursuit for independence.

Perhaps the cultural difference between the two generations derived from divergent colonial language policies between Portugal and Indonesia towards East Timor. The literacy policy in Portuguese Timor was a part of cultural missionary work intended to enlighten 'uncivilised' East Timorese natives (Taylor-Leech 2009). Indeed, colonial exploitation entailed a minimal level of assimilation, including fluency in Portuguese (Anderson 1962). Hence, Portuguese literacy policies incorporated a limited number of indigenous leaders into the colonial enterprise, but socially excluded the rest of the population. As a result, colonial rule produced a handful of indigenous elites who were later involved in the anti-colonial independence movement. By contrast, Indonesia's language policy aimed to socially and ideologically control the masses, not only East Timorese but ordinary Indonesians from different parts of the islands (Taylor-Leech 2009). In line with the creation of *imagined communities* (Anderson 1983), Indonesia's literacy policy aimed to create a nation-state, whereas, for the Portuguese, a literacy policy was introduced to civilise the indigenous people.

The internal cultural and social transformations do not, however, solely explain the transition in East Timorese nationalism. Focusing on the transitional international discourse from post-Second World War decolonisation to post-Cold War universal human rights provides a different analytical scope. Arguably, nationalist claims for independence in East Timor changed their ideological justification in light of international discourse. Therefore, the de-territorialisation of nationalism could offer a better explanation for the initial development and the subsequent divergent trajectories of East Timorese nationalism. While this study examines the internal development of East Timorese nationalism, it further reveals that the change in the international normative narrative from the right of self-determination in the period of decolonisation (1950s–1970s) to that of universal human rights in the post-Cold War period (the late 1980s–1990s) accelerated the transformation of East Timorese nationalism (Cmiel 2004; Burke 2002).

In practice, this involves analysing the earlier political education of the first East Timorese nationalists in Fretilin (*Frente Revolucionária de Timor-Leste Independente*, Revolutionary Front for an Independent East Timor) and other political movements by Indonesian-educated East Timorese youths in Renetil (*Resistência Nacional dos Estudantes de Timor-Leste*, East Timorese Students National Resistance). While *Geração '75*'s nationalists' popular education internalised the imaginative notion of *Rai Timor*, Renetil's nationalists from *Geração Foun* made great efforts towards externalisation of East Timorese nationalism by linking themselves to Indonesia and the international community.

The construction of East Timorese nationalism

The wave of nationalism arrived late to Portuguese colonies, compared with other Western colonies in Asia and Africa. The 1974 April Revolution in Portugal, which led to democratisation following Salazar's dictatorship, accelerated political movements in the colonies. Following the revolution, the Portuguese administration proposed three possible options for the decolonisation of East Timor: maintaining the link to Portugal with autonomy, integration with Indonesia, and full independence (Jolliffe 1978). In response to this, three major political parties were formed by the East Timorese: the UDT (Timorese Democratic Union), the ASDT (Timorese Social-Democratic Association, which later became Fretilin), and the APODETI (Timorese Popular Democratic Association). The UDT sought integration within a Portuguese-speaking community, while the ASDT supported independence from Portugal with the communist orientation. The APODETI was a pro-Indonesian party in favour of integration with Indonesia with autonomy though the support to this party is relatively limited. Each party represented a different national vision based on their respective cultural and social positions. Indeed, the emergence of the three political parties, before Indonesia's invasion, reflected the reality and idealism of the East Timorese nation. The disagreement between the parties concerning the nation's vision resulted in an anti-communist coup against Fretilin by the UDT in August 1975, which led to civil war. Indonesia's government saw the civil war as a communist insurgency by Fretilin and began its invasion of East Timor on November 28, 1975. The coup was suppressed by Fretilin and, together with President Xavier do Amaral, it promptly declared the independence of East Timor as

Indonesia's armed forces were approaching Dili. In the ceremony, Xavier do Amaral read the Declaration of Independence as follows:

> Expressing the highest aspirations of the people of East Timor and to safeguard the most legitimate interests of national sovereignty, the central Committee of FRETILIN decrees by proclamation, unilaterally, the independence of East Timor, from 00.00 hours today, declaring the state of the Democratic Republic of East Timor, anti-colonialist and anti-imperialist. Long live [*Viva*] the Democratic republic of East Timor! Long live [*Viva*] the people of East Timor, free and independent! Long live [*Viva*] FRETILIN!
>
> *(Hill 2002, 169)*

Thus, the independence of the Democratic Republic of East Timor was proclaimed as a consequence of emancipation from the long-lasting colonial exploitation by the Portuguese empire.

On the same day, Xavier do Amaral delivered his inauguration speech defining the idea of the nation-state for the people of East Timor:

> From all this, one concludes that the nationalist spirit has always been alive in the people of East Timor. It was not ASDT/FRETILIN that instilled in the minds of the *Maubere* people the idea that one day [they] would come to rule their own land. ASDT/FRETILIN's mission was, is and will always be to indicate the "*modus governandi*," in other words the manner of how the people will govern their land without exploitation of man by man
>
> *(Fretilin 1975)*

The speech expresses the right to self-determination of the people of East Timor through emancipation from colonial exploitation. The decade of the 1960s, when some of the first nationalist leaders spent their lives in former Portuguese colonies, was the moment of the end of colonialism and the advent of the nation-state system in the developing world. Self-determination emerged as a crucial agenda of human rights within the body of international law (Burke 2002). The efforts of Fretilin's old leaders, therefore, reflected the translation of the right of self-determination into their local language.

Vicente Rafael's *The Promise of the Foreign* (2005) illuminates this 'translation' of normative discourses between international and local paradigms. While Rafael explained that the indigenous efforts of the translation into Spanish as the common language accelerated the earlier development of Filipino nationalism, the belated development of East Timorese nationalism in the 1970s needed to 'translate' the universal language of decolonisation into their own local language, Tetun. In this respect, the Tetun term *Maubere* is politically salient. During the Portuguese colonial period, *Maubere* was used to disparage local Timorese as illiterate, ignorant, and impoverished people in the under-developed colony (Hill 2002). Fretilin re-created this term as an integral part of East Timorese national identity associated with struggle and resistance against colonial rule, by using terms like '*Maubere* brother' or 'the warriors of *Maubere*' (*Maubere asuwain*) (Hill 2002, 73; McWilliam and Traube 2011, 15).

Nonetheless, the destiny of *Maubere* people was forcefully suppressed by Indonesia's dictatorship and again the nation suffered during 24 years of struggle for independence. Indonesia's occupation not only disrupted but also altered the process of creating a national identity for *Maubere* people. McWilliam and Traube (2011, 15) argue that East Timorese suffering under Indonesia's military occupation created a 'new forms of imaginative connection to land and landscape, especially around the idea of the "homeland": *Rai Timor.*' Hence, the invention of

Maubere provided a new cosmology of place between East Timorese spatial belonging and their cultural homeland through their suffering under the occupation. In this respect, analyses of Fretilin's political and literacy manuals are revealing as they demonstrate how Fretilin's leaders attempted to create imaginative connections between the people and land.

The creation of *Rai Timor* entailed an ideological foundation in representing the differences between East Timorese and Indonesians. The earlier ideological foundation of Fretilin's nationalism was primarily reported and analysed by Australian scholars and journalists (Jolliffe 1978, Hill 2002). According to their studies, it was a unique combination of Marxism for economic emancipation and grassroots developmentalism for local development. Leaders who spent time in African Portuguese colonies, such as Mari Alkatri, were part of the Marxist/leftist stream, while Nicolau Lobato, who had stayed in East Timor and was involved in agricultural and economy policy, was a grassroots developmentalist. Such divergent ideological streams rested on the narrative of decolonisation that had been internationally recognised from roughly 1950 to 1970.

East Timor's first nationalists absorbed the spirit of decolonisation of their African counterparts who had gained independence in the 1960s. Emancipation from colonial rule ultimately led to the right to self-determination (Hill 2002). Fretilin's nationalist elites, however, needed to translate 'self-determination' into their local language. In this respect, Fretilin's political education built on the unique ideological basis in crystallising the self-image of *Maubere*.

Analysis of Fretilin's literacy and political manuals

Alongside the national agendas of Fretilin, *consciencialização politica* (political awareness) was a primary method of transforming *Maubere* into East Timorese. The literacy manual *Rai Timur Rai Ita Niang* (Timor is Our Country) was developed by Antonio Carvarinho, Francisco Borja da Costa, and others when they were in Lisbon and was widely distributed during the process of decolonisation (Leach 2017). The manual was based on the ideas of Brazilian educator Paulo Freire, who had worked on literacy development with local peasants in Northeast Brazil (Hill 2002). Indeed, Freire's pedagogy (1970) aimed to *awaken* the oppressed peasants to be emancipated from the naïve view. East Timorese leaders resonated with this awakening of peasants in (re)creating *Maubere*. Since illiteracy had hampered the political aspirations of indigenous East Timorese under Portuguese colonialism, independence from colonial rule could eradicate the prevailing illiteracy among the peasants. A manual outlining the political programme published and distributed by Fretilin in East Timor in 1974 explains the struggle against illiteracy as such:

> The people must be informed so that they can decide about their own life. The people cannot be allowed to remain ignorant, so that people can abuse that ignorance and exploit them. . . The high rate of illiteracy in our country is an obstacle to the development of the culture of our people. . . To build our country, to build a truly free and independent East Timor, it is imperative that everyone without exception learn to read and write. FRETILIN therefore will begin a widespread campaign of anti-illiteracy with a system of education that truly liberates our people from 500 years of darkness
>
> *(Fretilin 1974, 5)*

It is crucial to note that the manual was written in the East Timorese local language Tetun, rather than the official language, Portuguese. Fretilin leaders made an enormous effort to develop the East Timorese national language, Tetun, and spread the language throughout the entire population. Since East Timorese traditional societies were divided into multiple language groups, the first task of Fretilin in making *Maubere* was to establish a common language among the people in order to imagine their national community (Anderson 1983). In this respect, the invention of the literacy manual was the first *lingua franca* policy by Fretilin under the occupation. Through the literacy campaign, Fretilin attempted to emancipate *Maubere* from its own definition of illiteracy and ignorance in order to gain their own *ukun rasik aan* (self-determination or independence).

Researchers have previously studied the contents and roles of this booklet and identified several features crucial to national identity-making (Hill 2002, da Silva 2011; Leach 2017, Cabral 2019). Antero da Silva identifies 50 words accompanied by illustrations in the manual. These are basic Tetun words used in a peasant's ordinary life, including *batar* (corn), *foho* (mountain), *hare* (rice), and *kuda* (horse) (da Silva 2011, 137). The next part of the literacy manual recounts the East Timorese history of struggle. In this part, some words introduced in the previous section appear and are used to connect the lives of the people and their history of suffering. The story is titled *Timor Oan Sei Hamutuk Hodi Ukun Rasik ita nia Rain* (Timorese will be united to rule our land).

Against this backdrop, the manual explicitly sets the people's interests against the economic exploitation by the coloniser. The explanation of the manual by Leach (2016) that follows illuminates how the people's interests (*osan*, or money) could be secured by uniting people from all districts against the colonial ruler:

> On page 12 a *malai* (foreigner) is represented carrying a bag of money "Osang $$$" away, while East Timorese warriors fight each other with traditional weapons. The accompanying text declared "in the past colonialists entered our land because our ancestors fought amongst each other" (12–13). The following page returned again to the map, this time showing East Timorese from different districts holding hands, with the text "Timorese came together to free our land" (14–15).
>
> *(Leach 2016, 64)*

Here, the visual creation of *Rai Timor* illustrates the unity of *Maubere* in preserving indigenous interests against colonial exploitation. Through this, Fretilin's urban intellectuals were able to link their vision of the nation to local interests. The earlier form of East Timorese nationalism was, therefore, an effort of the political leadership to visualise their nation by mobilising indigenous populations.

Another influential tool for nation-making was the *Manual e Programa Políticos* (Political Manual and Program) published by Fretilin in 1974. This manual was used for political education, to make East Timorese people understand the role of Fretilin and the purpose of the independence struggle. Although the manual is written in Tetun and Portuguese, a recent study by Kisho Tsuchiya (2021) reveals that the contents are different between the two languages, since each language targeted specific readers. According to Tsuchiya, the Tetun version was written for the rural population of East Timor, while the Portuguese manuscript aimed to present Fretilin's vision abroad. For this reason, this chapter analyses the manuscript written in Tetun to understand how Fretilin attempted to inculcate the notion of territory and independence as a sovereign state to the rural East Timorese.

In the manual, Fretilin explains how the people's rural lives will be changed by independence:

> We simply achieved our INDEPENDENCE—self-rule—however, only a few people will benefit as it is in the present time. The large majority of the people will continue to be poor.

> FRETILIN wants to achieve true independence for Timor land [*Rai Timor*] with the Timorese... Ridding colonialism from our land means transferring the power to the Timorese. Only Timorese will govern [*Ukun*] Timor land [*Rai Timor*]
>
> (Fretilin, 8)

Fretilin further needed to unite the entire population of East Timor in making the nation-state. Here, 'land' [*rai*] is linked to the people of East Timor in explaining independence:

> A number of political parties have appeared. However, we the sons of Timor have not achieved our independence yet. We only found the political parties in the country that already gained its independence. Nowadays, many parties will only divide us. Thus, they are provoking the Timorese calling some of them Kaladi and others Firaku. But we all have only one land and only children of Timor alone. Now, we all together could have power to be independent
>
> (Fretilin, 5)

The political manual explains to the people that they must be united to rule themselves (*ukun an*) within the One land (*rai ida*).

The terms *Rai Timor* and *timur oan* (Children of Timor) do not, however, correspond with the actual territory of 'East' Timor. Kisho Tsuchiya provides a nuanced analysis of the cosmology of East Timorese people and land as such:

> Fretilin's official political manual and the party anthem did not emphasise the colonial territorial arrangement or even 'East Timor'. 'The collective term for the Timorese was *timor oan* (children of Timor)' and the conception of their land was Timor rather than East Timor (or *Timor Lorosae*).
>
> (Tsuchiya 2019, 379)

Here, *Rai* (land) does not refer to any administrative territory; rather, the emphasis is on tangible benefits for the people of East Timor. Independence further aimed to elevate people's standard of living, including agriculture, schooling, and health (Fretilin, 1974, 10); for instance, the political manual explains:

> Tilling the land for crops, in order for people to become better, means we search first to grow various crops in order to produce an abundance of food, so that East Timor people would not be starving anymore. Colonialism only seeks something that brings about more money for colonisers. In this manner, you see that they seek to plant only coffee, rubber and vanilla. They do not seek to grow food that people can eat. Therefore, we see the two types of hunger in the land of East Timor
>
> (Fretilin, 15)

The political education by Fretilin nationalists was a mixture of anti-colonialism and rural developmentalism. While emancipation from colonial rule resonated with decolonisation struggles of Portuguese colonies in Africa, such as Angola and Mozambique, the political education served to translate claims of self-determination into the emancipation from long-lasting hunger and poverty under colonial exploitation. Fretilin, therefore, believed that *ukun raik aan* brings about emancipation from hunger and poverty.

In short, the reconceptualisation of *Maubere* is an illustration of the political leverage of Fretilin's urban elites in transplanting the modern definition of *Maubere* to rural populations. In doing so, the old nationalist leaders were able to internalise their claims of self-determination into emancipation from colonial exploitation, i.e., *ukun raik aan*. Hence, the nationalism of the *Geração* '75 aimed to shape the form of East Timor by translating the norms of decolonialisation into tangible benefits for rural people. Nevertheless, their vision of nationalism did not successfully attract international attention. The ideology of self-determination of the 1950s and 1960s had already come to seem old-fashioned by the 1970s and 1980s. The next decade, the 1990s, witnessed a more inclusive form of human rights, which consequently brought the younger generation opportunities to enhance their East Timorese nationalism.

Geração Foun: Indonesianess and youth nationalism

The earlier East Timorese nationalism of the mid-1970s was the creation of a unique translation of the right of self-determination into localised *ukun raik aan*. In creating *Maubere*, the leaders of *Geração* '75 made efforts to link the universal struggle of decolonisation with emancipation from economic exploitation. Nevertheless, the development of East Timorese nationalism was non-linear. Indeed, the incorporation into Indonesia's authoritarian state created a new generation of nationalists, the *Geração Foun*. *Geração Foun,* schooled under the Indonesian occupation, culturally experienced an exclusion and inclusion between East Timor and Indonesia (Bexley and Tchailoro 2013). While *Geração* '75 experienced *esplorasaun* (exploitation) under Portuguese colonialism, the experience of Indonesia's occupation for *Geração Foun* was characterised as *terus* (suffering). The life stories of most of the prominent activists of *Geração Foun* began with suffering in the jungle during their childhoods (de Carvalho 2015). Hence, the struggle of *Geração Foun* was the articulation of the collective memories of *terus* among the youth.

Meanwhile, the nationalist movement of *Geração Foun* was *Indonesianised*, meaning that it worked more closely with Indonesian pro-democracy activists supportive of their independence struggle (Kamisuna 2020). Their movement was also internationalised in the sense that the suffering of the youth was situated within the context of international solidarity for universal human rights protection. In Indonesian society, as well as throughout the international community during the 1990s, universal human rights became a strong political instrument for pro-democracy activists in the fight against dictatorships. Hence, East Timorese youths who were politically active in Indonesia gained strong support from pro-democracy and human rights activists there.

Renetil was the most prominent student-led clandestine East Timorese youth organisation active in Indonesia. Founded in Bali, Indonesia in 1988, Renetil had initiated a unique political movement, *Indonesiação do Conflito de Timor-Leste* (Indonesianisation of conflict in East Timor), which aimed to *Indonesianise* their independence struggle by incorporating Indonesia's pro-democracy movement into the East Timorese independence struggle (Saky 2013). This inclusion within Indonesia brought a new current of national aspiration to East Timorese nationalism, which shared the common goal of independence with the old generation but intended to achieve it with different political and historical instruments. The following section will demonstrate how the nationalism of *Geração Foun* transcended the existing space of *Rai Timor*, linking itself with the pro-democracy movement and the struggle for human rights in Indonesia and beyond.

From the Indonesianisation of the East Timorese to Indonesiação do Conflito de Timor-Leste

The 'integration' of East Timor into Indonesia in 1975 was part of the larger project of the Indonesianisation of Indonesia's archipelago. Indonesia's Soeharto regime intended to Indonesianise Indonesians (Moertopo, 2003). *Pancasila*, seen as the supreme moral principle of the Indonesian nation, was widely taught in Indonesian schools to construct a 'national personality' for the Indonesian people, including the East Timorese (Tsuchiya 1995, 280). In this respect, *Pancasila* was the New Order regime's political instrument to 'Indonesianise Indonesians' or 'mak[e] Indonesians truly Indonesian' (Moertopo 2003, 111). Hence, the incorporation of the East Timorese into Indonesia's society was an extension of the Indonesianisation of Indonesians.

For the East Timorese during the occupation, the New Order's Indonesianisation was equated with modernisation (Kamisuna 2020). An English booklet published by the Indonesian government in 1977, for instance, clearly claimed that the Indonesian effort to modernise East Timor would provide necessary social services and basic infrastructure 'long denied them by colonialism' (Department of Information Republic of Indonesia 1977, 47).

Against this backdrop, East Timorese youths shared an ambivalent political culture between East Timor and Indonesia, which alienated them from their elders. As a result, the old generation pejoratively dubbed the young generation the *Generasi Supermi* (Supermi generation), likening their soft and inconsistent attitude towards the independence struggle to the popular Indonesian instant noddle *Supermi* (Bexley 2007). Nonetheless, the spirit of East Timorese youngsters did not vanish amid the cultural assimilation.

Rather, they were Indonesianised in terms of their political struggles through interactions with pro-democracy youths and intellectuals in Indonesia. Through the initial interaction with Indonesian youths, the prominent leaders of Renetil imagined that *terus* in struggles against Suharto's authoritarian rule would be a common experience for both (Alve 2014; Araújo 2015). Such an experience gradually crystallised into a counter-ideological discourse against the Indonesianisation of the East Timorese, *Indonesiação do Conflito de Timor-Leste* (Indonesianisation of Conflict in East Timor) movement. Indeed, the movement of *Indonesiação do Conflito de Timor-Leste* was an eclectic creation of East Timorese youth nationalism in which they articulated the independence of East Timor in the context of Indonesia's political culture. Against the cultural incorporation under the New Order rule, the central mission of the East Timorese youths became the Indonesianisation of their independence struggle. Demetrio do Amaral de Carvalho, a former secretary general of Renetil, for instance, explained Indonesianisation as a strategy to 'expand the East Timorese conflict to Jakarta' (de Carvalho 2015). They attempted to fight Indonesia's regime by using all available resources from Indonesia, including Indonesia's own history of struggle against Dutch colonial rule (Kamisuna 2020). Such activism began with clandestine communication with Indonesian pro-democracy youths at universities during the 1980s. Following the integration, East Timorese youths were allowed to study at universities in major cities in Indonesia such as Jakarta, Bali, Yogyakarta, and Surabaya, which Indonesia's regime expected to make them truly Indonesian.

Renetil member Lucas da Costa, who invented the idea of *Indonesiação do Conflito de Timor-Leste*, explained the motivation of that movement to work with Indonesian youths in line with the common experience of suffering between East Timorese and Indonesian youths:

> We had strongly believed young Indonesian intellectuals were seeking a way to democratise the country. Because, under the Suharto rule with its very strong dictatorship,

young Indonesian intellectuals were not very free to prosecute the objective of the nation. [. . .] Taking this situation into account, we established contact with some Indonesian intellectuals on campus. But, systematically, we went up to contact students as well. [. . .].

(da Costa 2014)

Hence, universities became not only epicentres of youth struggle for East Timorese and Indonesian students but a common platform that connected two different nationalist movements.

Apart from clandestine activities, Renetil's political aspirations extended to the more radical front of the movement. East Timorese youths in Indonesia organised a protest at the US Embassy in Jakarta in December 1994, when Indonesia was hosting the APEC summit. Twenty-nine East Timorese activists scaled a fence, broke into the US Embassy, and occupied it for 14 days (*Inside Indonesia* 1994). Surprisingly enough, the fence-scaling action at the US Embassy was successfully executed despite the strict surveillance and control of the New Order regime, under which none of the Indonesian students or NGOs could actively protest (Wagstaff 1994). Benedict Anderson described this *coup de théâtre* as 'another sign that "History" is now on the youngsters' side' (Anderson 1998, 138). This one action by East Timorese youth in the heart of the New Order regime brought new political momentum, not only to the East Timorese movement but to the Indonesian one (Alve 2014). Indeed, Indonesian pro-democracy activist Wilson, a founder of the Indonesian Student Solidarity for Democracy (SMID), appreciated the impact of Renetil's *aksi massa* (mass action) on the Indonesian pro-democracy movement (Wilson 2010). Crystallised with the audacious *aksi massa*, *Indonesiação do Conflito de Timor-Leste* movement enabled Indonesian youths to 'shar[e] the spirit of the struggle' with East Timorese youngsters (Alve 2014).

Significantly, Indonesian pro-democracy activists were able to share the spirit of the struggle not because of programmatic motivations to use the East Timorese struggle to fight against the New Order regime but, rather, because the *suffering* of East Timorese youth was politically salient in Indonesian history. Indonesian youths were able to project their past of colonial struggle against the Dutch onto the independence struggle of East Timor. Indonesian pro-democracy figures articulated the impact of the East Timorese struggle on the Indonesian pro-democracy movement.

Wilson reconceptualised an alternative version of nationalism against the New Order's territory-oriented nationalism through interactions with the East Timorese independence movement:

[The] East Timorese did have an impact on the definition of nationalism, specifically from conservative to progressive nationalism. Some radical groups tried to give a new definition to Indonesian nationalism because of East Timor.

(Wilson 2015)

Wilson himself projects the struggle of the East Timorese onto Indonesia's own independence struggle against Dutch colonialism. The following excerpt from a letter that an imprisoned Wilson sent to his East Timorese comrade, Puto (Naldo Rei), indicates his reflections on *pemuda* (Indonesian youth) and the *jeventude* (East Timorese youth) struggle.

... since I came to know Puto and his history of struggle, I feel like I am living in the past, at a time when the colonialism of the western countries was still in full swing, fifty years ago. And through Puto's story, I have become embarrassed at my own country;

that a country that had won freedom through a long struggle against colonialism was now taking the same position as its colonial masters in that previous era . . . . Maybe such a person as this had existed in Indonesia during the nationalist struggle against the colonialism of the Dutch and Japan. It was true. Puto had reversed the wheels of my political history to the former colonial period.

(Rei 2007, 309)

For radical youth figures such as Wilson, the struggle of East Timor's *jeventude* exemplified a genuine form of nationalism for emancipation of the nation from suffering under state oppression, similar to that which Indonesia had undergone in the 1940s against the Dutch colonial rule. The *Indonesiação do Conflito de Timor-Leste* movement was able to transcend the spirit of nationalism through the struggle of youth beyond the existing colonial boundaries.

Perhaps Indonesian youths were able to situate the struggle of East Timorese youths within their national history of *pemuda* (youth) struggle. For Indonesian nationalists, the term *pemuda* assumed a political salience in the national history, and thus it was often translated as 'politicised youth' (Lee 2011). Doreen Lee explains that the narrative of *pemuda* could be attributed to the successive generations of youth who had emerged in every single moment of national aspirations and insurgencies in Indonesia's political history, from the *pemuda* of 1908, 1928, 1945, 1966, 1974, 1978, 1989, until 1998.

The *Indonesiação do Conflito de Timor-Leste* movement enabled Indonesian youths to imagine the struggle of East Timorese youths in the historical constellation of *pemuda* struggles, including the independence struggle against Dutch colonial rule in 1945.

Beyond Rai Timor: universal human rights

The *Indonesiação do Conflito de Timor-Leste* movement was further able to link the East Timorese struggle to Indonesia's long struggle for human rights protections. As Geoffrey Robinson puts it, the East Timorese struggle successfully 'combined demands for human rights and national self-determination, and employed both the rhetoric of revolutionary war and the discourse of human rights morality' (Robinson 2014, 34). Former Indonesian student activist and the chair of *PIJAR* (Centre for Information and Action Network for Democratic Reforms) Rachland Nashidik explains the impact of East Timorese struggles as such:

> There was a long struggle conducted by generations of Indonesian activists trying to overthrow the dictator. But, we always failed . . . . [B]efore we were acquainted with the East Timorese struggle, we did not realise that international pressure was so effective. You know, to push for the openness of Indonesian politics in Indonesia, we admit that only by using the East Timorese struggle, Indonesian politics could be opened up.

(Nashidik 2015)

In this respect, the Santa Cruz massacre in 1991 was a 'trigger' in promoting youth struggles in the international community (Kamisuna 2020, 85). The incident in East Timor, resulting in the deaths of at least 250 youths, demonstrated the human right abuses by Indonesia's military of East Timorese youths. The contemporary development of international norms of human rights in the 1990s coincided with this incident. By attracting international attention towards the abuses of Indonesia's military regime, East Timorese youth realised that demonstrations were the most effective instrument to emancipate themselves.

Rachland Nashidik describes the transnational dimension of suffering between East Timor and Indonesia in terms of their struggle for human rights protection:

> After a long struggle to promote human rights, we were helped, ironically enough, by the suffering of the East Timorese . . . . It was really because of the East Timorese struggle for independence that we became aware that the democratic movement in Indonesia should, or must, go side by side with the East Timorese struggle for independence because we faced the same enemy: the dictator.
>
> (Nashidik 2015)

Here, the contemporaneity of East Timorese and Indonesia's youth struggles resonated with changes in world history. The transition from the Cold War's ideological contestation to the triumph of liberalism accelerated regional struggles against human right abuses under authoritarian regimes (Cmiel 2004). The international community witnessed humanitarian crises in Rwanda, Kosovo, Iraq, the West Bank, and East Timor in the post-Cold War period. Hence, the normative form of human rights had gradually transformed from exclusive forms of self-determination to more inclusive forms of universal human rights in accommodating individual rights through the acceleration of modernisation from the 1970s to the 1990s. Jack Donnelly (1998) provides a cogent framework for this transition. He explains how the norms of self-determination are inclusive but narrowly negative in substance in such a way that it provides only the minimum requirements of sovereign states in the international community ('Hobbesian'). In contrast, the concept of universal human rights is more positive and inclusive, accommodating the rights of individual citizens ('Lockean'). The East Timorese generational transition from the claim of self-determination to universal human rights, or in other words, from *exploitation* to *suffering*, therefore, hinged on the transition of the human right discourse from self-determination to universal human rights in international history.

Indonesia's Catholic communities also played a crucial role in consolidating Indonesia-East Timor solidarity within Indonesia, a country with a Muslim majority. A Catholic religious leader and former member of Solidamor (*Solidaritas untuk Penyelesaian Damai Timor-Leste*, Solidarity for East Timor Peace Settlement), Yusuf Bilyarta Mangunwijaya, for instance, held a mass for East Timorese activists before a demonstration at Indonesia's Ministry of Foreign Affairs on July 12, 1998 (Saky 2013). Mangunwijaya also wrote to his former schoolmate President Habibie hoping to persuade him to support the referendum for East Timor (Mangunwijaya 1998). In the letter, he referenced the spirit of the preamble to the 1945 Constitution of Indonesia that recognised 'the right of all nations to be independent' (Kamisuna 2020, 98). Under the global norm of human rights protection, the religious community had the political power to make the East Timor issue a part of Indonesia's domestic political agenda.

John Sidel's study of social revolution in Southeast Asia (2021) informs us of a broader ideological paradigm for explaining nationalist struggles. He demonstrates diverse patterns of national revolutions beyond elite nationalist and vernacular claims. The great revolutions in Southeast Asia utilised the power of the ideological instruments of Islam and communism as political bases for revolutionary mobilisations during the post-Second World War period. While such cosmopolitan origins of national revolutions have consistently held true in the modern history of revolutions, the international community after the Cold War witnessed an ideological transition to universal human rights.

The series of international social solidarity movements among youths in the Asia-Pacific region provided more powerful ideological tools for social change and against dictatorships.

In 1993, for instance, NGOs from the Asia-Pacific region came together in Bangkok to make a declaration on human rights to the United Nations General Assembly (Coalition for Peace and Development 1993). In 1994, a conference of the Asia-Pacific Timor Coalition was held in Manila in the Philippines. Over 500 participants attended, including over 130 accredited delegates from East Timor support groups. The coalition aimed to consolidate the Asia Pacific coalition in East Timor (Indonesia Solidarity Action 1994). Indonesian activist Rachland Nashidik spoke at the conference, saying that '[w]e are here in this conference because we cannot refuse to see that East Timor is part of the democratic and human rights struggle in Indonesia' (Indonesia Solidarity Action 1994, 4). Indeed, the 1990s discourse of universal human rights accelerated the struggle of East Timorese and Indonesian youths in articulating their rights of democracy and independence.

The *Indonesiação do Conflito de Timor-Leste* movement not only brought a new political agenda to the Indonesian pro-democracy community from East Timor but enabled Indonesians to claim universal human rights in the international arena, by linking their struggles for human rights to East Timorese *terus*. The movement crystallised in a series of coalitions and joint actions with Indonesian pro-democracy youths as the People's Democratic Union (*Partai Rakyat Demokratik*, PRD) in Indonesia created the Indonesian People's Solidarity Struggle with the Maubere (East Timorese) People (*Solidaritas Perjuangan Rakyat Indonesia untuk Maubere*, SPRIM) in March 1995. Under this youth coalition, a series of joint demonstrations were conducted at the Russian and Dutch embassies in Jakarta, which eventually led to large demonstrations at the People's Representative Council and the Ministry of foreign affairs in 1998. The 1990s witnessed an amalgamation of youth activism between Indonesia and East Timor amid the gradual transition in the narrative of human rights at the global level.

Conclusion

This chapter has elucidated the malleable concept of *Rai Timor* through analysis of the transformation of East Timorese nationalism from both national and international perspectives. While occupations by Portugal and Indonesia created a unique historical trajectory of nationalism between the older and newer generations, their different adaptations to international normative discourse transformed their usages of ideological instruments in shaping *Rai Timor*. While *Geracao '75* sought to 'translate' the right of self-determination into their local language of Maubereism in order to emancipate themselves from the colonial *exploração* (cf. Rafael 2005), *Geracao Foun* was able to 'translate' *terus* into the international language of universal human rights by Indonesianising and universalising their struggles. Overall, this chapter provides a framework to understand the transformation of nationalism in both domestic and international historical contexts. Further empirical research may reveal more diverse and unique forms of nationalism beyond colonial borders within and outside of Asia.

References

Anderson, Benedict. 1983. *Imagined Communities: Reflections on the Origin and Spread of Nationalism*. London and New York: Verso Books.
Anderson, Benedict. 1998. *The Spectre of Comparisons: Nationalism, Southeast Asia and the World*. London and New York: Verso.
Anderson, Perry. 1962. "Portugal and the End of Ultra-Colonialism 2." *New Left Review* 16 (1): 88–123.
Arthur, Catherine. 2018. *Political Symbols and National Identity in Timor-Leste*. Cham: Palgrave Macmillan.
Bexley, Angie. 2007. "Seeing, Hearing and Feeling Belonging: The Case of East Timorese Youth." *The Asia Pacific Journal of Anthropology* 8 (4): 287–295.

Bexley, Angie, and Nuno Rodrigues Tchailoro. 2013. "Consuming Youth: Timorese in the Resistance against Indonesian Occupation." *The Asia Pacific Journal of Anthropology* 14 (5): 405–422.

Burke, Roland. 2002. *Decolonization and the Evolution of International Human Rights*. Philadelphia: University of Pennsylvania Press.

Cabral, Estêvão. 2019. "Timor-Leste 1974–1975: Decolonisation, a Nation-in-waiting and an Adult Literacy Campaign." *International Journal of the Sociology of Language* 259: 39–61.

Cmiel, Kenneth. 2004. "The Recent History of Human Rights." *The American Historical Review* 109 (1): 117–135.

Coalition for Peace and Development. 1993. *Bangkok NGO Declaration on Human Rights*. Geneva: United Nations General Assembly.

Damaledo, Andrey. 2018. *Divided Loyalties: Displacement, Belonging and Citizenship among East Timorese in West Timor*. Canberra: ANU Press.

da Silva, Antero. 2011. "FRETILIN Popular Education 1973–1978 and its Relevance to Timor-Leste Today." Unpublished PhD thesis, University of New England.

Department of Information Republic of Indonesia. 1977. *Decolonization in East Timor*. Jakarta: Department of Information Republic of Indonesia.

Donnelly, Jack. 1998. "Human Rights: a New Standard of Civilization?" *International Affairs* 74 (1): 1–23.

Dunn, James. 2003. *East Timor: A Rough Passage to Independence*. Double Bay, New South Wales: Longueville Books.

Freire, Paulo.1970. *Pedagogy of the Oppressed*. New York: Continuum.

Fretilin. 1974. *FRETILIN/Manual e Programa Políticos*. AMRT, Pasta: 05005.002

Fretilin. 1975. "Discurso do Presidente da República por Ocasião da Investidura." *Timor-Leste Jornal do Povo Mau Bele*, December 4.

Geertz, Clifford. 1973. *The Interpretation of Cultures*. New York: Basic books.

Hill Hellen. 2002. *Stirrings of Nationalism in East Timor: Fretilin 1974–1978: The Origins, Ideologies and Strategies of a Nationalist Movement*. Otford, NSW: Otford Press.

Indonesia Solidarity Action. 1994. *Suara Aksi*, July 6.

Inside Indonesia. 1994. "Timor: No Longer a Sideshow." *Inside Indonesia* 41, December 7.

Jolliffe, Jill. 1978. *East Timor: Nationalism and Colonialism*. St Lucia: University of Queensland Press.

Kamisuna, Takahiro. 2020. "Beyond Nationalism: Youth Struggle for the Independence of East Timor and Democracy for Indonesia." *Indonesia* 110 (1): 73–99.

Leach, Michael. 2016. "The FRETILIN Literacy Manual of 1974–75: An Exploration of Early Nationalist Themes." In *Timor-Leste: The Local, the Regional and the Global, Volume II*, edited by Sarah Smith, Nuno Canas Mendes, Antero B. da Silva, Alarico da Costa Ximenes, Clinton Fernandes and Michael Leach, 60–68. Hawthorn: Swinburne Press.

Leach, Michael. 2017. *Nation-building and National Identity in Timor-Leste*. Abingdon: Routledge.

Lee, Doreen. 2011. "Images of Youth: On the Iconography of History and Protest in Indonesia." *History and Anthropology* 22 (3): 307–336.

Mangunwijaya, Yusuf B. 1998. *Menuju Indonesia Serba Baru: Hikmah Sekitar 21 Mei 1998*. Jakarta: Gramedia Pustaka Utama.

Matsuno Akihisa. 2002. *Higashi Timōru Dokuritsu-shi*. Tokyo: The Waseda University Press.

McWilliam, Andrew, and Elizabeth Traube. 2011. *Land and Life in Timor-Leste: Ethnographic Essays*. Canberra: ANU Press.

Moertopo, Ali. 2003. "Indonesianising Indonesians." In *Indonesian Politics and Society: A Reader*, edited by David Bourchier and Vedi R. Hadiz, 110–112. Abingdon: Routledge.

Nicol, Bill. 1978. *Timor: A Stillborn Nation*. Camberwell and Victoria: Widescope International Publishers.

Rafael, Vicente L. 2005. *The Promise of the Foreign: Nationalism and the Technics of Translation in the Spanish Philippines*. Durham and London: Duke University

Rei, Naldo. 2007. *Resistance: A Childhood Fighting for East Timor*. Brisbane, Queensland: University of Queensland Press.

Robinson, Geoffrey. 2014. "Human Rights History from the Ground Up: The Case of East Timor." In *The Human Rights Paradox: Universality and its Discontents*, edited by Steve J. Stern and Scott Straus, 31–60. Wisconsin: University of Wisconsin Press.

Saky, Carlos. 2013. *Renetil—Iha Luta Libertasaun Timor-Leste: Antes sem Titulo, do Que sem Patria!* Dili: CV. Primaproint.

Sidel, John. 2021. *Republicanism, Communism, Islam: Cosmopolitan Origins of Revolution in Southeast Asia*. Ithaca: Cornell University Press.

Smith, Anthony D. 1986. *The Ethnic Origins of Nations*. Oxford: Basil Blackwell.

TAPOL. 1987. "Growing up in an Indonesian Colony." *TAPOL Bulletin* No. 82 (August 1987).

Taylor-Leech, Kerry. 2009. "The Language Situation in Timor-Leste." *Current Issues in Language Planning* 10 (1): 1–68.

The Campaign for Independent East Timor. 1974. *What is Fretilin?* Sydney: The Campaign for Independent East Timor.

Tsuchiya, Kenji. 1995. *Indoneshia: Shisō no Keifu* [*Indonesia: Its Genealogy of Thought*]. Tokyo: Keisō shobō.

Tsuchiya, Kisho. 2017. "Awkwardly Included: Portugal and Indonesia's Politics of Multi-culturalism in East Timor, 1942 to the early 1990s." *Asian Review* 30 (86): 79–102.

Tsuchiya, Kisho. 2019. "Representing Timor: Histories, Geo-bodies, and Belonging, 1860s–2018." *Journal of Southeast Asian Studies* 50 (3): 365–386.

Tsuchiya, Kisho. 2021. "Southeast Asian cultural landscape, resistance, and belonging in East Timor's FRETILIN Movement (1974–75)." *Journal of Southeast Asian Studies* 52 (3): 1–24.

Wagstaff, Jeremy. 1994. "Dissent Just a Rumble as Suharto Bangs APEC Gong." *Reuters*, November 11.

Webster, David. 2013. "Languages of Human Rights in Timor-Leste." *Asia Pacific Perspectives* 11 (1): 5–21.

Wilson. 2010. *A Luta Continua!: Politik Radikal di Indonesia dan Pergerakan Pembebasan Timor Leste*. Jakarta Selatan: Penerbit Tanah Lapang.

Interviews

Araújo, Fernando de. 2015. Interview, January 7, 2015. Dili, East Timor.
Alve, Domingos Saramento. 2014. Interview, December 26, 2014. Dili, East Timor.
da Costa, Lucas. 2014. Interview, December 12, 2014. Dili, East Timor.
de Carvalho, Demetrio do Amaral. 2015. Interview, January 5, 2015. Dili, East Timor.
Nashidik, Rachland. 2015. Interview, January 27, 2015. Jakarta, Indonesia.
Wilson. 2015. Interview, January 22, 2015. Jakarta, Indonesia.

38
THE ROUTINIZATION OF CHARISMA IN THAI NATION CONSTRUCTION

A Weberian reading of Thai royalism, nationalism, and democracy

Jack Fong

When one approaches Thailand's recent political problems related to governance and liberal democracy, observers invariably highlight the tension-filled relationship between the country's monarchistic and rational-legalistic institutions. As axes that underpin the architecture of the Thai state's legitimacy, scholars are not incorrect in resurrecting these two pillars for continued analyses when desiring to offer a "reading" of Thailand's political climate in the twentieth and twenty-first centuries. I am not an exception in such an effort. Indeed, this chapter intends to revisit the tensions between Thailand's monarchist and rational-legal institutions at the theoretical level, one inflected by classical sociologist Max Weber and his typology of power systems (1947; 1978). It aims to illuminate the social construction of the Thai nation in the spirit of Hobsbawm and Ranger's *Invention of Tradition* (1983) and Anderson's *Imagined Communities* (1991), inflected from the traumas and hopes of all Thais across the present and across time. The work should thus be seen as polemical and theoretical, allowing the voices of as many Thai historians as is feasible, and to the best of my ability, to convey indigenous conceptions of stress that reframes attributes of charismatic leadership through kings and queens in the preindustrial period. Our figures will be situated in this temporal expanse to such extent that the delimitations of a chapter in an edited collection allow, so as to provide a reworking of how proto-nationalism of yesteryear can offer cautious extrapolations about Thai political dynamics in the twenty-first century.

Max Weber's theory on power, specifically the trinity of charismatic, traditional, and rational-legal authority, has become a legendary typology for social scientists seeking to understand expressions of social power. Yet, Weber's major theoretical shortcoming is his linear view on social progress, a commonly held orientation during the empiricism that defined the dynamics of industrial and scientific Europe. With these considerations, Weber's theory essentially predicted that a world of kings and queens would give way to a world of politicians, with activists/revolutionaries holding accountable the leader and pundits of both spheres through time. For Weber, society exhibits social conditions that will invariably move from a more irrational state of existence to greater degrees of rationality, made possible by the establishment and embeddedness of institutions and their bureaucracies. Weber was resigned to this rationality industrial complex, if I may, that would configure social action and structure modern social relations. However, Weber gave charismatic power players a wide breadth, pointing to their revolutionary potential in toppling tyranny in both traditional and rational-legal systems. Pride of place will be given to Weber's discussion of charismatic authority and its routinization as explicated in the *Theory of Social and Economic Organization* (1947), a section of his seminal *Economy and Society* (1978).[1] For Weber, the charismatic individual and the person's supporting institutions exhibit attributes that endear the revolutionary system to supporters. Weber "took for granted that a charismatic bureaucracy is merely a less developed form of bureaucratic organization" (Costas 1958, 404). Nonetheless, Weber himself notes how followers perceive the charismatic actor as

> endowed with supernatural, superhuman, or at least specifically exceptional powers or qualities...not accessible to the ordinary person, but are regarded as of divine origin or as exemplary, and on the basis of them the individual concerned is treated as a leader.
> *(1947, 359)*

This ideal type rendering is pertinent for understanding the role of Thai charismatic actors in the centuries leading toward *fin de siècle* Siam, for Weber notes how charismatic authority expresses its power "specifically *outside* the realm of *everyday routine and the profane spheres* [emphases added]" (1947, 361). In its rawest conceptualization, charismatic authority can be understood to be anti-systemic, subversive, and in many instances even authoritarian in that this "genuine prophet...preaches, creates, or demands *new* obligations" that are "recognized by the members of the religious, military, or party group" (1947, 361). Weber acknowledges the coterie of supporters or disciples that uphold the legitimacy and seemingly metaphysical quality of the charismatic leader. He makes much reference to the symbiotic relationship between those who desperately want to reproduce the staying power of charismatic persons and the charismatic person themselves, for such persons have embraced the task of repudiating the "past" and thus is a "revolutionary force" (1947, 362). Elsewhere, Weber further points to the charismatic leader's subversive power and describes how charisma expressed in such historical periods can become the "greatest revolutionary force" (1947, 363). However, Weber notes that such a character can only remain elevated "as long as it receives recognition and is able to satisfy the followers or disciples. But this lasts only so long as the belief in its charismatic inspiration remains" (1947, 362). Yet, comparatively less-explored is Weber's discussion of the routinization of charisma, the process by which charismatic leadership is rendered stable, institutionalized, and predictable for constituents who defer to the authority of the charismatic leader/s. Weber notes how the power of charismatic authority stems only from the act of originating, and as such, authority from such a social force "cannot remain stable, but becomes either traditionalized or rationalized, or a combination of both" (1947, 364). Such an outcome is significant for Weber since his discussion of charisma is "heavily oriented toward its stabilization and routinization" (Friedland 1964, 19). For Weber, the understanding is that a routinized charisma, one made possible when the charismatic leader is integrated into the state apparatus, tempers if not eliminates the revolutionary zeal of the charismatic actor. Yet in such a process, Weber remains unclear as to whether routinization conclusively tames charisma into *in*efficacy. The consideration fielded in this chapter is how Thailand—the only country in Asia never colonized by a European power during the *fin de siècle*—managed to ensure that its traditional authority system remained intact by appropriating from its historical chronology inspirational charismatic leaders that were kings, queens, lords, ladies, and villagers. Buddhism amplified the process of narrative generation for their exploits, imbuing in such leaders semi-divine attributes that are celebrated and reproduced as cultural values. By the twentieth century, Thai nationalism had, by design, political power plays, and court/political intrigue, equated charismatic authority as the primary expression of its monarchs, if not the institution of monarchy. The narrative of the Thai nation, then, *empowers* routinized charisma in the long chronology of Siamese history.[2] It is this history, in a condensed format, that I hope to employ for framing the processes of routinization as strategically prudent for pro-monarchy nationalists and political entrepreneurs. For scholars such as Ake, the utility of charismatic authority for analyses can only be enhanced with history since the "theory of charismatic legitimation shows little sense of history," and this was "a fault of inherited from Weber" (1966, 7). Ake echoes an earlier and more critical view by Blau, who notes how Weber's theory "encompasses only the historical processes that lead from charismatic movements to increasing rationalization and does not include an analysis of the historical conditions that give rise to charismatic eruptions in the social structure" (1963, 309).

My discussion considers how Thai monarchs, its nobility, as well as the common folk who sacrifice for their nation, can be seen as bona fide charismatic actors embedded in externally imposed systems. The rationale for such a perspective is drawn from the number of monarchs in Thai history that have had to rely on exceptional qualities to lead followers toward some semblance of liberation from belligerents that existentially threatened the Thai nation. Drawing from chroniclers and scholars of Thai history, I reinforce such a view by making operative Weber's charismatic leadership as expressions of nation construction, one that celebrates the vanquishing of historical enemies which have meted out tyranny upon the Thais. Such Thai actors were "revolutionary" in that they were compelled to overturn a society imposed upon them from the outside. In our case, Thailand's historical nemesis Burma,[3] and to a certain extent, European machinations, will be discussed in a condensed format, with pride of place given to the former.

To Thai nationalist scholars of the late nineteenth and early twentieth centuries, Burma was the main belligerent responsible for the destruction of Siamese society, specifically through its second invasion of Siam in a total war between the two hegemons. This culminated in the destruction of the Ayutthaya Kingdom in 1767, one already weakened when influential European officials serving the Ayutthayan King Narai (1632–1688; reigned 1656–1688) were attempting to proselytize Christianity as well as engage in court intrigue to forward Western interests.[4] The 1767 destruction of Ayutthaya, however, did not prevent the Thonburi and Bangkok periods from revitalizing a monarchy, Buddhism, and nation construction that glorified the sacrifices of Thai ancestors, with the Bangkok Era (1782–present) pivotal in ensuring that "intellectual leaders such as learned monks" constructed the Burmese as a "dangerous enemy of Buddhism" (Chutintaranond 1992, 92–93).[5] Burma and its role in shaping Siamese/Thai history was integral in generating a series of charismatic responses through resistances offered by its great Siamese kings and queens, with unequivocal support offered by their constituents. Even in contemporary Thai films such narratives resurface in epics, especially centering on Ayutthaya, Siam's second capital before the founding of Bangkok, with recent examples seen in Chatri Chalerm Yukol's the *Legend of Suriyothai* (2001), his six-part epic *Kingdom of War* (2007–2015), and Tanit Jitnukul's *Bang Rajan* (2000). Yet, it would be during the founding of Bangkok when Ayutthayan survivors and descendants explicitly constructed Burma as an antipode to the Thai nation. For historian Sunait Chutintaranond,

Ayudhya chroniclers, unlike Bangkok's, did not seriously consider wars conducted against the Burmese as being more important than other historical events. In actual practice, the Ayudhya rulers were more concerned with military expeditions into the territories of Sukhothai and Chiang Mai in the north, Cambodia in the east, Tavoy, Mergui, and Tenasserim in the west, and Malaya in the south, but not into the heartland of Burma.

(1992, 89; see also Chutintaranond 1988)

In the post-Ayutthaya period, Thai nation construction thus bestowed charisma to those who defended the Thai nation, for it had become subjugated, requiring national liberation. Such a prescription neutralizes the belligerent status of a charisma that revolutionizes itself toward power *within* nation, to a social force that is seen to overturn tyranny *between* nations. Making operative charisma in a geopolitical context thus renders the concept and those who uphold the epithet easily routinized, since such actors already have their raison d'être: the epic to ensure sovereignty thus becomes an existential goal given the systemic crises meted out to them by tyrannical forces. By the Bangkok Era, Ayutthaya's downfall was harnessed to indict Burma's hegemonic expansionism as exhibiting diabolical and ignoble attributes. Thus, in *Suriyothai*'s concluding scenes, the eponymous queen of sixteenth-century Ayutthaya engages in a battle against the Burmese invaders as it attempted to raze the walled city (see Figure 38.1).

In the film's crescendo, Suriyothai and the princess climb atop their war elephants and go off to battle for their king and nation, with both cut down in the melee. In *Kingdom*, Thai historical accounts point to how the Ayutthayan King Naresuan (1555–1605; reigned 1590–1605) engages a Burmese prince, Mingyi Swa, in elephant combat and slays him (see Figure 38.2), thus preventing yet another invasion by Burma.[6] In *Bang Rajan*, Thai peasants

Figure 38.1 Prince Narisara Nuwattiwong's 1887 painting "Queen Suriyothai Elephant Combat" depicting the queen (center with weapon) defending King Maha Chakkraphat (right with weapon) from the Burma's Viceroy of Prome (left with weapon) before she was slain (public domain)

express their love of nation, ultimately sacrificing their lives to stifle attempts by the Burmese to invade Ayutthaya.[7] For Chutintaranond,

> The image of the Burmese as an archenemy of the Thai gradually emerged in Thai historiography and literary works after the kingdom of Ayutthaya fell to the Burmese armies in 1767. Prior that tragic incident, Thai chroniclers were not anxious to record any historical event concerning wars between Siam and Burma.
>
> *(1992, 89)*

The historian Prince Damrong Rajanubhab, often referred to as the "father of Thai history," wrote the most famous historical text during this period, the important *Thai Rop Phama* (Our Wars with the Burmese) (2001) first published in 1917. In the work, Damrong chronicled with much granularity "almost every fighting episode that appeared in the Thai chronicles and foreign records" (Chutintaranond 1992, 96). In the work, Damrong's sacralized nationalism was martial and justified revanchism when it came to the Burmese. He enables the terrain of resistance for a routinization of charisma to function as aspirational and liberatory, so as to contest Burma's wars with Siam. There were many:

> According to...the history of Siam, when Ayutthaya was the capital of Siam, the Siamese fought with the Burmese twenty-four times. Subsequently when...Thonburi and... Bangkok...were the capitals of Siam, we fought with the Burmese twenty times, in all

Figure 38.2 The 1593 elephant combat between Mingyi Swa (left with weapon) and Naresuan (right with weapon). In Thai accounts, the former is slain by the latter in the duel. Based on a Siamese painting from the seventeenth–eighteenth century (Collection of Maurice Collis, public domain)

forty-four times. In the forty-four times mentioned, sometimes the Burmese invaded Siam and sometimes the Siamese invaded Burma.

(2001, 3)

Elsewhere Damrong notes:

> Hostilities began because the Burmese conquered the Mon country and they consequently carried the war into Siam. For this reason, the war which the Siamese carried into Burmese territory, though it was the initiative of the Siamese, was only a reprisal for what the Burmese had done to the Siamese territory on previous occasions.
>
> *(Damrong 2001, 6)*

Through the Thai retelling of Burma, the urgency of a society being destroyed becomes the greatest urgency, one where the routinization of charisma can be seen to offer a functional *and* normative benefit: to ensure stability and continuity of resistance through the charismatic leader who upholds the values of the Thai nation—seen in the guise of a noble, villager, chief, king or queen. Such a charismatic actor will save the nation in crises from external oppressors, thus "othering" Burma as a malevolent force to be repulsed in the Thai nation-building narrative. An attempt at rendering a power trinity whereby charismatic authority is seen as a separate axis with its own political staying power is untenable in the Thai example. Charismatic leaders embraced by Thai heroes and heroines, and later, pro-royal nationalists, are located historically, often in the scenario of total war, experiencing systemic and existential crises, yet still able to lead the Thais toward freedom with the fervor of their adherents and royalists.

Although the process of transitioning from an absolute to constitutional monarchy in 1932 subsumed a modern and ostensibly weaker monarchy under the constitution of a modernizing Thai state, one that changed its name from Siam to Thailand 1939,[8] the cultural production performed by royalist imaginations continue to exhibit a romanticized and sacralized sense of the Thai people, nation, religion, and monarchy as one. The notion of Thai nationalism thus harks back toward proto-nationalistic tendencies seen in the exploits of Thai monarchs such as Narai, Naresuan, Taksin, and Queen Suriyothai, to name but a few, and how they informed the construction of a Thai nation before modernity. The extrapolation offered thus far is that a Thailand modernity that historically has only ever experienced intermittent democracy will still allow its political actors to harness the romance of how the Thai nation was constructed by their kings, by royalist historians like Damrong, and by royalists today that counter reformist movements against royalism. Moreover, such a process of nation construction also acts as important primordial counterpoints to Western and Orientalized framing of Thailand since its sixteenth-century contact with the West and other nations in Asia and the Pacific. As such, unlike a Weberian framing of the charismatic leader that suggests it is able to withstand for some time forces they contest, Siam's sacralization of monarchy in a manner that conflates it with history, nation, paternalism, and maternalism, along with a Buddhist-inflected rendering of a supernatural validation of the monarch, quickly routinizes charisma, and makes it yield to the exigencies of traditional authority, an efficacious process that is still sloganeered in a transcendent manner today. In the case of Thai nation construction through its royalism, one that informs twenty-first-century Thai politics, it will be helpful to thus consider the staying power of such a formulation when it was first employed to counter external belligerents—the cultural and ethnic/racialized "other," especially in the guise of Burma, and to a certain extent the Europeans who attempted to subjugate Siam.

The aim of this chapter is not to take a stance in support or refutation of political actors on all sides of Thailand's power continuum, one which has a long chronology inflected by traditional authority, with its rational-legal institutions only a modern but nonetheless vociferous arrival to the Thai political arena. I hope to offer conceptualizations and cautious extrapolations on the staying power of Thailand's traditional authority system—one which, in contrast to Weber's conceptualization—has atavistically remained intact even though the Thai state's monarchist system transitioned from an absolute to constitutional monarchy in 1932. Extrapolating from Weber's perspective, such a process should have seen the weakening of traditional authority as rational-legal systems of the modern state apparatus embed themselves in the Thai lifeworld. However, Thailand's institution of monarchy has remained entrenched in the psyche of many Thais, ensuring that the institution survive challenges posed by rational-legal iterations of modernity that have influenced the country and its civil societies during the twentieth and twenty-first centuries. Thus, the thrust of this chapter is to consider how the Thai institution of monarchy remains empowered through its appropriation of the nation's raison d'être. Such a construction requires making visible key tenets of Weber's notion of the routinization of charisma as well as cautiously extrapolating upon its utility in understanding the continuing embeddedness of the monarchist system in Thai society today.

To undertake this task, one could begin an examination of Thailand's monarchistic history with the conventionally accepted founding of the Thai nation through the Sukhothai Kingdom that spanned the thirteenth and fifteenth centuries. However, our chapter begins its examination of Thailand's epic with the founding of Bangkok in 1782, or what Thais informally refer to as *Krung Thep*, or "City of Angels," because it was the resurrection of the Thai nation via post-Ayutthaya kings that generated the nationalist hindsight necessary to capture the historical travails of the Thai people leading up to the establishment of their new city of Bangkok, which remains the capital of Thailand today. Additionally, much English-language content of the Sukhothai and Ayutthaya periods have already been addressed elsewhere (see Chutintaranond 1992; Wyatt 1982; Wyatt 2003; Winichakul 1994; Baker and Phongpaichit 2005; Terwiel 2005; Chaloemtiarana 2007; Aphornsuvan 2009; and Chachavalpongpun 2020 to name but a few).

The approach adopted in this chapter is to minimize attribution of outcomes to actors in ways that require extensive biographical framing. As a work that employs a sociological imagination inflected by Weberian themes, focus will be to embed dynamics of actors within Weber's theoretical formulation so as to further inform how one can approach Thailand's traditional authority system as it transitioned from absolute to constitutional monarchy, a period that also saw a proto- and nascent Thai state engage if not repulse, the indoctrination and pieties introduced by European states with imperialist and faith-based interests. It is hoped that such an effort will illuminate more clearly the breadth of political tensions seen in the country today between the royalists with political staying power due to their status as being the source of charisma, and those who envision a liberal democracy that ensures its system is politically accountable to new truths as it moves Thailand toward a more progressive future.

Founded by the Thai polity that survived Burma's 1767 devastation of the former capital of Ayutthaya, the soon to be Bangkok Era (1782–present) was preceded by the short-lived Thonburi Kingdom led by King Taksin (1734–1782; reigned 1767–1782) before his overthrow and execution, a development that ushered in the Chakri Dynasty, one which remains with us today. It also ushered in a new nominal reference to the period as the Rattanakosin Era, one led by kings with the honorific appellation of "Rama" to signify their status as the nation's sovereign. The Chakri Dynasty remained intact in Bangkok's development at a time when, crucially, Western colonial powers were seizing territories for their imperialist agendas as they coveted markets, resources, and territories of South and Southeast Asia. It was also in this period that Burma was constructed as a historical rival of the Thai nation:

> In actual practice, the Ayudhya rulers were more concerned with military expeditions into the territories of Sukhothai and Chiang Mai in the north, Cambodia in the east, Tavoy, Mergui, and Tenasserim in the west, and Malaya in the south, but not into the heartland of Burma.
>
> *(Chutintaranond 1992, 89)*

Yet, the destruction of Ayutthaya in 1767 ushered in a national wound exploited by nationalists, one that reflected how the "annihilation of Ayudhya in 1767 brought the Thai a great deal of damage, both physically and spiritually" (Chutintaranond 1992, 90).

The process of routinizing charisma can thus be considered a desirable outcome for Thai royalists or the Thai people who, through auspicious signs or perceived Buddhistic intervention, become fervently impassioned to defend nation. The charismatic leader who now serves the nation is thus bestowed with resources, history, a military, and "destiny," nullifying the wherewithal in the person to stand as an independent axis of power or a novel source of new values hitherto unheard. Such persons would engender social change that is beneficial for the nation. The earliest kings of post-Ayutthaya, King Taksin and King Rama I (1737–1802; reigned 1782–1809) had set into motion the creation of the "other" in the guise of a Burmese nemesis, with the latter even studying Burmese military strategies translated into Thai, while King Rama II (1767–1824; reigned 1809–1824) commissioned the military to "compile all necessary information concerning war routes lying between Siam and Burma" for the sole purpose of intercepting the "Burmese army understood to be coming to attack Bangkok in 1820" (Chutintaranond 1992, 91). More dramatically, King Rama III (1788–1851; reigned 1824–1851), presciently anticipating encroaching European imperialism of the *fin de siècle*, remarked on his deathbed:

> There will be no more wars with Vietnam and Burma. We will have them only with the West. Take care, and do not lose any opportunities to them. Anything that they propose should be held up to close scrutiny before accepting it; do not blindly trust them.
>
> *(Wyatt 1982, 180)*

By the time of the precocious King Chulalongkorn (Rama V; 1853–1910; reigned 1868–1910), son of the legendary King Mongkut (Rama IV; 1804–1868; reigned 1851–1868) had ascended the throne and visited Europe in 1897 and later in 1907 and warmly received with much fanfare, the United Kingdom had already seized India and Burma (the latter of which was seized after the three Anglo-Burmese Wars) as well as set up the Federated Malay States. The French had already established French Indochina, seizing the northeast areas of the Siamese Kingdom in the Franco-Siamese War of 1893, an act that would ultimately result in the relinquishing of Laos, while Cambodia, desiring to wrestle free from Siam's hegemony, allied itself with French interests, becoming its protectorate as far back 1867. It would be in the reign of Chulalongkorn where the geopolitics that would directly affect Siam's territorial ambitions came to the fore, a process which refined his acumen for interacting with the West in ways that likely prevented the future Thai state from becoming a client or constabulary state of the imperial powers (see Figure 38.3).

Indeed, as far back as the mid-seventeenth century, the Dutch and its subsidized trading company, the *Vereenigde Oost-Indische Compagnie* (VOC), were already mediating in dynastic disputes between different rulers on various islands of the Indonesian archipelago, further embedding, if not entangling its presence within local politics and social change. With violent characters like Governor General Jan Pieterszoon Coen razing the early Jakarta to build Batavia as the capital of the Dutch East Indies, as well as instigating the Banda Massacre that killed thousands of Bandanese, by the time Chulalongkorn made his second visit to Europe in 1907, much of Asia had been punctured by the combined ideological and industrial forces of imperialism, its jingoisms, its conflagrations, as well as indigenous conceptions of stress that resulted in mutinies, uprisings, and rebellions against colonial rule across what would one day become the Third World—but only if it first became a graveyard for European imperialisms. Such a notion would not be lost by members of the Thai court and the people. Therefore, a view that Siam had at some point in its history suffered a similar status of being semi-colonialized is unfounded, namely because there was never an establishment of macro-level institutions from the belligerent state into the country that is reinforced by a perennial standing army. These forces Siam withstood when seen in the late nineteenth century as *Indochine* was established by the French (although with then Siamese-occupied Laos ceded by the Siamese), while concomitantly Burma lost its territories after its trio of Anglo-Burmese Wars. Moreover, Siam's "loss" of then a section of what is today's Laos cannot even historically be interpreted, initially, as a proto-nationalist gain, given the powerful Lan Xang kingdoms had suffered dismemberment at the hands of the Burmese by the late eighteenth century. Moreover, Lan Xang's southern kingdom of Champasak was suzerain to Siam only in name against which Vietnam would later encourage its rebellion (Askew et al. 2006). Bangkok was never razed by the likes of a Jan Pieterszoon Coen in a manner that Ayutthaya was razed by Burma's King Hsinbyushin.

It was during this stretch of chronology that Aphornsuvan (2009) notes that Siam engaged with notions of modernity as it encountered Western ideals (or at the very least, non-Thai or non-Buddhistic ideals), trade practices, different atavisms of Christianity, and Europeans and Americans coveting territory and/or souls for Christian salvation. For Aphornsuvan (2009), it would be Chulalongkorn's father and predecessor, King Mongkut, where the Siamese court and the people continued to be confronted with imported notions of modernity and civilization, a situation that contributed to tensions between Thai royalists and Western missionaries and diplomats. Such interactions, for Aphornsuvan, convinced the Siamese aristocracy the merits of ensuring the survivability of monarchy by adopting from other cultures ideas and values that can benefit Thailand's *royalized* approach toward modernity. Urgency drove such an approach toward nation construction: those doing the bidding of their imperialist nations—missionaries included—had over time "became more aggressive in their relations with the court and they competed fiercely for economic domination in Siam in the late seventeenth century" (Aphornsuvan 2009, 405). Such an orientation toward the Thai court only convinced monarchs over time that they needed to be directly engaged with the modernization of the kingdom from within, a view held by King Mongkut and his scions (Aphornsuvan 2009, 409). For Mongkut, these developments would be undertaken through adjustments of domestic or cultural policies—a different tact from his son and successor, Chulalongkorn, who engaged Siam with world powers on a world stage, heralding Siam's geopolitical presence for the Occident.[9]

Most notably during the rule of Mongkut and later, Chulalongkorn, catalysts of social change began to find traction in Thai society: "Western" or "modern" ideals—especially those related to trade, culture, and faith—began to contest the Buddhistic worldview so

Figure 38.3 The "Ruling Monarchs" postcard printed by Rotary Photographic Co Ltd. in 1908. Chulalongkorn is first at the top left (public domain)

carefully nourished and propagated by centuries of traditional authority rule. Mongkut had to repulse attempts by Christian missionaries from France, Germany, the United Kingdom, and the United States to influence the Thai social order. He was cognizant and prescient enough to realize these same imperialistic states with their moral supremacist views frequently enforced traumatic policies of regime change around the world in spite of their sloganeered pieties of hailing from democracies or "civilized" Christian cultures. However, having learned geography, physics, chemistry, astronomy (even predicting an eclipse), French, and Latin through characters such as French Bishop Pallegoix who arrived in 1830, Mongkut thus ensured that Siam remained lenient—if only grudgingly—toward missionaries whose goal it was to steer Thailand toward Christendom. Such tact was adopted because Mongkut's familiarity with the Occidental framework tempered his nativism. Moreover, Mongkut was privy to how missionaries frequently employed Siam only as a stopover point for their most coveted destination for evangelical work, China. Through the tolerance of Mongkut and his court, Aphornsuvan notes that Christian or Western worldviews introduced by the exploits of such arrivals became "pivotal in the formation of modern ideas in Siam and its perception of the modern world" (2009, 409) even though "these missions failed in their attempts to convert the Siamese people to Christianity" (2009, 408).

Mongkut and Chulalongkorn's prescience ensured that Thailand remained a sovereign state vis-à-vis the empire building engaged by European powers. Thus, Mongkut and Chulalongkorn are credited for respectively introducing the idea of the "unified state," as well as establishing "the idea of Thailand being a nation state belonging to the Thai people with Bangkok as its center" (Chutintaranond 1992, 94). Sequencing Thai history between Mongkut and Chulalongkorn reveals how both, but especially the former, realized that the system of Christianity—in spite of its sloganeered pieties—was, and has always been insofar as imperialism is concerned, an oblique if not explicit agent of regime change. Indeed, during the missionary period when modern printing allowed for early attempts at dismantling the architecture of Thailand's Buddhistic worldview and zeitgeist, Western knowledge and its worldviews were concomitantly disseminated to commoners and wider audiences in schools and universities. Here, Aphornsuvan's incisive observation remains timely and relevant in that many Americans had "built many denominational 'colleges' and schools that still exist in Thailand today" (2009, 410). Such clarity in understanding the agenda of colonial empires abroad can be credited to the synergy and synchronization of perspectives between Mongkut, who essentially brought the West to Siam, and Chulalongkorn, who brought Siam to the West (Huen 2009; Aldrich 2015).

In spite of the comparative openness Siam and Thailand exhibited toward non-Thais, but especially toward Europeans and their Occidental metaphysics and spirituality during the *fin de siècle*, ideological diacritica sloganeered as advancement and civilization were unable to contest the longer chronology that a Buddhistic traditional authority system had infused into the institution of monarchy. This nation-building resource, what I term as "chronological capital"—the perceived depth of historical time, replete with its own metaphysics and epics, the latter of which inform the nationalist genre—has successfully allowed the institution of monarchy to command *into* nation construction the romance of Thai primordialism. Political entrepreneurs operating outside of such contexts of power do so at a disadvantage while those within its highly formalized in-groups prevail. Aphornsuvan notes how such a Buddhist-king concept predates the Ayutthaya period and was conceived in the era of the Sukhothai Kingdom (2009). Moreover, the seventeenth-century Ayutthayan monarch, King Narai, mined from Khmer history the conceptualization of empire as stemming from "the Hindu concept of kingship in which the monarch was conceived as a God-king with unlimited power over his subjects" (Aphornsuvan 2009, 407). Even the post-Ayutthaya King Taksin fused Buddhist ethics into his proto-nationalism, proclaiming before battle with the Burmese at Bang Khao province in 1774 that

> the reason I have spent my life on battlefields up to the present is not because I am concerned about my own fortune and advantage. I choose to live harshly because I want to uphold Buddhism, priests, Brahmins, and the people in my kingdom.
> *(cited in Chutintaranond 1992, 91)*

By the Rattanakosin Era, Prince Vajirañana, the Supreme Patriarch serving under King Vajiravudh (Rama VI; 1881–1925; reigned 1910–1925), formally proclaimed that the "primary duty of the kings was to protect the welfare of the Buddhist religion, of the kingdom and of the people from external intrusion" (cited in Chutintaranond 1992, 92).

With the sense of nation under existential threat from the supposedly enlightened West, nations and states like Siam and Thailand, respectively, had little recourse but to harness a more glorious and doctrinal history for cultural production, for imagining communities as conveyed by Benedict Anderson (1991). In this capacity, King Vajiravudh himself emphasized the "significance of the three elements, nation, religion, monarch" as crucial components for the construction of a Thai identity; he further emphasized: "Allegiance to any one of the three meant loyalty to all three; disloyalty or disobedience or disrespect toward one meant disrespect toward all" (cited in Chutintaranond 1992, 95). Primordialism and Buddhism are given their flow into Thai nation construction with Vajiravudh's view. In such a worldview, Thai nation construction conveyed by its charismatic monarchs and institution of monarchy blur the lines between the natural and supernatural, between the physical and metaphysical, as they fended off historical atavisms of oppression meted out to Siam, and later Thailand. Even by the twentieth century when progressive forces in Thailand tamed the country's absolute monarchy and transitioned the system into a constitutional variant, its narrative of nation as exhibiting secular, modernist, and proto-fascist and pro-socialistic undertones—perhaps the profane world of Durkheim's persuasion—can still be seen as a disruptor of an idealized and romanticized Thai history.

Rendering the survival and resurrection of its people by envisioning the Thai nation as led by righteous monarchs and their faithful over a long chronology, allows its imagined, yet romanticized communities to appropriate the nation's historical epics, from which charismatic warriors, kings, queens, chiefs, and villagers—through the institution of monarchy and its royalists—employed traditional authority experiencing duress to routinize charisma for the sake of preserving nation. By envisioning the charismatic revolutionary not as an undesirable political malcontent but a liberator from invasion and occupation—as in the case of King Naresuan and his "declaration of independence" from Burma as told by Damrong (2001), for example—Thailand's institution of monarchy thus reframe the ideal charismatic actor to self-actualize *during* routinization and *within* Thailand's traditional authority system. Such a process draws on historical epics where Thais fought against tyranny, whether it emanated from a hegemonic *fin de siècle* Burma, or from modernity's profane lifeworld of *gesellschaft*, all for the sake of revitalizing traditional authority in the midst of a nation's existential crises, be it from Burmese invasions, the Haw wars, the hubris and Orientalisms of Anna Leonowens, or European militarization to engender regime change during the *fin de siècle*, as in the Franco-Siam War and the later Franco-Thai War, to name but a few examples.

More importantly, such metaphysics informed and continues to inform the Rattanakosin Era as it experienced its transition from absolute monarchy toward that of a constitutional monarchy by 1932. Led by the "Promoters" of the *Khana Ratsadon* (People's Party), Pridi Banomyong (conventionally referred to as "Pridi") and Plaek Phibunsongkhram (conventionally referred to as "Phibun"), a bloodless coup ended the absolute reign of King Prajadhipok (Rama VII; 1893–1941; reigned 1925–1935), the first Chakri monarch to transition into a constitutional role as king, as well as the first to abdicate. The end of King Prajadhipok's absolute reign can be seen to validate Weber's linear view of historical progression where traditional authority gives way to rational-legal authority, for alas, is not such an abdication a victory for rational-legal authority systems promoted by twentieth-century Thai nationalists—one that envisions a better modernity and future, a process that only needs to tokenistically include narratives, if at all, from outmoded diacritica of traditional authority?

A more incisive observation, however, behooves us to make operative Max Weber's additional observations on power dynamics to explain the staying power of the Thai monarchist system. Yet, adopting a linear perspective to frame Thai political tensions between its monarchistic and rational-legalistic power centers would only offer inaccuracies in explaining the staying power of the country's monarchy. As such, the idea of charismatic leadership will need to be reexamined in uniquely Thai contexts, especially as Thailand continues to pivot from the *fin de siècle* period into a modernity that may not be of its own making. Seen in such a fluid context, my chapter attempted to illuminate how Thai history envisions charismatic leadership as one that supports the staying power of monarchy under duress, even though Thailand's transition from absolute to constitutional monarchy has seen geopolitical intrigue, machinations, and even revanchist policies meted out against the nascent Thai state by European powers and industrializing Japan during the transitional sweep from the nineteenth into the twentieth centuries. This chapter attributes to the institution of monarchy its capacity to routinize charismatic actors *for* traditional authority as desirable and "revolutionary," a process that encourages resistance for a dynamic and existential defense of nation. Such a process legitimates the aura and primordial relevance of Thailand's great monarchs, their dynasties, great chiefs, and villagers who repulsed, conquered, and/or led the Thais toward freedom during periods of acute historical duress. Thus, a routinization of charisma in the Thai context does not appear to be a political deficit that would detract from Thai nation construction, but one that can still through the country's monarchistic system, serve as a conduit to a past greatness and a *persevering* present, even in a globalized age replete with social discontents. As such, rational-legal authority systems derived from modernist social movements that informed the *Khana Ratsadon*—in spite of the efforts of its influential leaders such as Pridi and Phibun, do not have the chronological capital to effectively legitimate the Thai nation without the comforts of epic and victorious history, reproduced and sublimated through the continuing staying power of Thailand's monarchy system.

The lack of chronological capital for a globalized age, along with Western ideals that desire hegemony over indigenous conceptions of stress, can still be envisioned as a counterpoint to royalism in Thailand today, with the most recent example seen in how the cosmopolitan mogul, former prime minister Thaksin Shinawatra, and later his family and associates, were systematically purged from the Thai political machine by the country's military during the first two decades of the twenty-first century. Atavisms of Thaksin's modernist, quasi-progressive yet entrepreneurial ideals manifesting in Thai political circles had little traction against a highly primordialized and romanticized backdrop of nation. By monopolizing the power of charisma and integrating it into a historical narrative of kings and queens who were revolutionary in that they repulsed the yoke of tyranny imposed upon them from outsiders, an elevated legitimation of charisma from "outside" this royal framework is unlikely. Modern progressive political entrepreneurs can always be framed as newcomers that threaten the sacralized process of Thai nation construction with king as head of state. Arguably, such an outcome befell Phibun, Pridi, and later Thaksin, while pro-royalists generals like Sarit Thanarat explicitly upheld the sanctity of monarchy through his support of King Bhumibol Adulyadej, the most revered Thai monarch in recent times, and one who reigned for 70 years (Rama IX; 1927–2016; reigned 1946–2016) (see Chaloemtiarana 2007; Fong 2009; 2019) after succeeding his brother King Ananda Mahidol (Rama VIII; 1925–1946; reigned 1935–1946) who died in a gun accident at the age of 20, an event that traumatized the nation.

Although key revolutionary and rational-legal charismatic leaders such as Pridi and Phibun, as well as the rank and file of the *Khana Ratsadon*, to name but a few, have explicitly served as key agents of social change for Thai society, the cultural production set into motion by our modernists does not exhibit the level of depth as those who desire to preserve tradition. Moreover, it overlooks later military characters that explicitly embrace Thai royalism, such the aforementioned Sarit Thanarat who celebrated the monarchy through the media, going as far as reviving traditional cultural ceremonies with the king as head of state that hark back to Siam's absolutist history as well as eliminating key enemies of the state such as Khrong Chandawong and Thongphan Suthimat (see Figure 38.4) (Baker and Phongpaichit 2005; Chaloemtiarana 2007; Fong 2009). One can imagine the narrative that emerges through the aura of monarchistic Thailand as it employs its "sacred nationalism," one whose trajectory of sacralized and Buddhistic nation construction descend to the secular/profane lifeworld to attend to politicians and their petty minutiae and ideological whimsies (Fong 2009). In this manner, the sense of the Thai nation—one indivisible from kingship—is more intoxicating, certainly more primordial, because of its capacity to appropriate the sacralized and long chronology of the Thai nation. The consequence of this is that the machinery of Thai democratic politics arrived stunted to the debate regarding the merits of constitutional monarchy versus monarchy reform. Even during the later decades of the twentieth century, royalism has successfully attributed to Rama IX, for example, the repulsion of communism that endeared him to Western sensibilities, namely in how the Thai state escaped the predicted outcomes of a domino theory that saw states such as Vietnam, Laos, and Cambodia subscribe to communism. The propagation of royalism into a perennial transcendent force of nation-building, then, remains embedded even during the political discontents and intrigues of Thai modernity, be it domestic or international in nature.

In such an elegiacal rendering, the rational-legal authority systems established since 1932, be they from the "left" or "right," be they from the current politically tense binary seen in the "red" versus "yellow" shirt contestations to construct nation—are unable to at this juncture duplicate a history that is rooted in kingship and royalism, and its perseverance and triumph in the wake of invasions by Burma, colonial forces, and the violent geopolitics of the twentieth and internal strife of the early twenty-first centuries. In essence, a *gesellschaft* modernity and their political actors have yet to historically "age" enough. Thus, my chapter notes how Thailand's traditional authority system successfully routinized charisma without debilitating the potency of its royalist charismatic actors' attempts at liberatory social change, one that reestablishes collective sovereignty in the guise of nation that is attributed to pre-modern dynamics of nation construction. The cultural production of Thai identity thus remains within the influence of monarchy since it legitimates the historical endurance of a nation's trials and tribulations over a long chronology to be the source of national empowerment. What thus remains an incontrovertible fact is that the promises of Thai democracy will remain an *unresolved* issue in the terrain of modern Thai politics and in the people's conceptualization of democratic freedoms vis-à-vis the romance of nation.

Figure 38.4 Khrong Chandawong (right) and Thongphan Suthimat (left) being led to their execution by firing squad (Baker and Phongpaichit 2005, 174)

Now that Thailand has again welcomed to the throne King Vajiralongkorn (Rama X; 1952–present; reign 2016–present) tensions have resurfaced between pro-royalist and liberal democratic camps that maneuver or are ushered in and out of the country's parliament depending on political climate, with the most recent coup in 2014 embedding a former general and royalist, Prayuth Chan-ocha, in power. He remains prime minister at the time of this writing, one that toes the line where the king is head of state, going as far as dissolving in 2020 the *Phak Anakhot Mai* (Future Forward Party) formed to contest the role of the military in Thai politics. The dated webpage of *Phak Anakhot Mai* at the time of this writing still harbors photographs and videos of its English-speaking founder Thanathorn Juangroongruangki, hailing from Thailand's "left" university, Thammasat University, as well as from the University of Nottingham. The site also continues to aspirationally profess its democratism by profiling its supporters and their views, with the website's landing page at the time of this writing proclaiming on its banner that "The future we aspire to is a future where the ultimate power truly belongs to the people." As recently as late 2021, attempts at reforming the power of royalism by democracy activists have encountered setbacks even though a bill advocating for the repealing of the draconian *lese majeste* was signed by over 100,000 supporters with verifiable identities. Prayuth reiterated his rejection of such attempts, noting that the Thai government "runs the country by adhering to the principles of nation, religion and the monarchy," while a defrocked Buddhist monk and ultranationalist, Suwit Thongprasert, defended the institution of monarchy as Thailand's bedrock for arts, culture, and traditions—the latter subsequently submitted a list of 222,928 counter-signatories to the government (*Bangkok Post* 2021). During the same period, three pro-democracy activists, Panusaya Sithijirawattanakul, Arnon Nampa, and Panupong Jadnok calling for the reform of monarchy were accused by Thailand's Constitutional Court for advocating the *toppling* of monarchy, sparking hundreds to protest in Bangkok (*Al Jazeera* 2021). Arnon and Panupong are currently being held in pre-trial detention at the time of this writing (*CNN* 2021). Yet, resistances once impossible under Rama IX have begun to express themselves as in some

Thai theatergoers refusing the hitherto expectation to stand for the national anthem played at the beginning of every film, one that displays imagery of the king and queen and their benevolent exploits. As 2021 draws to a close, "more and more people are opting to stay seated" rather than pay respect to Rama IX's son, King Maha Vajiralongkorn, "whose short time on the throne has seen unprecedented protests calling for reform of the monarchy" (Thanthong-Knight 2021).

Weber's routinization of charisma begs further elaboration in twenty-first-century Thailand, especially how such processes are now primed by intra-state political conflicts unlike those shaped by regional empire building seen in the Siamese, Burmese, Khmer, Lanna, or Lan Xang varieties, to name but a few regional hegemons that were unfurling their expansionism in the preindustrial period under examination in the early part of this chapter. Specifically, we will need to examine whether one can draw a definitive conclusion about royalist efficacy of charismatic authority when it experiences routinization vis-à-vis intrastate dynamics, and how an expertly constructed primordialism by traditional authority—infused with the ideals, iconography, and the pageantry that validate such a leader—can maintain the romance of the charismatic actor even after such routinization. The linearity with which Weber saw authority systems transition from its traditional authority variant toward that of rational-legal authority does not theoretically detract from charismatic leaders their purpose if the routinization process frames belligerents, as my paper argues, as existing outside the system in a nation-to-nation conflict. However, in the post-Cold War twentieth and twenty-first centuries, Thainess is now the protagonist *and* antagonist that is confronting itself. That Weber assumed charismatic authority to be "unstable in the extreme" and that "charisma must necessarily transform itself" (Costas 1958, 401) offer scholars of Thai Studies ample cues for reinvigorated discussions on the royalist dimension of charismatic power and its future influence upon Thailand's civilian politics and their development. As it stands, the royalists have had a head start through its longer chronology, one being challenged perennially by opposition groups that are finding greater and more vociferous purpose in the post-Rama IX era. The future of Thai democracy and political reform, then, hinges on how realistic the promotion of its ideals will be, a process that, if conflated with idealism, will be to its detriment. That is, Thai political actors that continue to proselytize the merits of democracy must establish consistent definitional clarity about what Thai democracy can be in the machinery of practice, and not in its idealism which can be easily and eloquently sloganeered by debonair politicians. Indeed, during the global COVID-19 pandemic that has devastated Thailand's economy, inciting protests that express an amalgamation of frustrations about inefficacious dispatch of pandemic mitigation and views of a political establishment that has not rectified the inequalities further exacerbated by the pandemic, the Thai state may soon experience a reckoning between those who believe in the fairy tale of kings and queens and those who believe that kings and queens belong in fairy tales.

It is not enough that Thai protestors at the time of this writing express a three-finger salute in honor of Burma's Aung San Suu Kyi when she had long transitioned away from being a democracy activist to that of a politician who acquiesced to the brutal military regime of the country, ignoring the plight of the Rohingya Muslims in the country's west, an act that drew criticism from the international community and resulted in her fall from political grace. Moreover, those seeking to reform Thailand's traditional authority, or more rather disentangle different systemic ideals from one another, must confront with brutal clarity a glaring weakness inherent in the democratic system itself, namely that democratic processes, when they exist, cannot be assumed to by default ensure good governance (*Foreign Policy* 2006). History already teaches us that malfunctioning democracies replete with unbridled constituent angst have placed psychopaths in power. The most current example can be seen in 2016 in the United States when its democracy placed the conservative authoritarian and "habitual liar" Donald Trump in power, one whose nature exhibits "ignorance, emotional instability, demagogy...and vindictiveness," according to fellow conservative Peter Wehner at the right-leaning American think tank, the Ethics and Public Policy Center (Wehner 2020). Unfortunately, these same attributes inspired Trump's sycophants to violently storm the United States Capitol, the bastion of American democracy, when he was unequivocally defeated after serving only one term. Yet, a more pertinent example for closing our chapter—and I believe without the risk of digression—pertains to Germany's first parliamentary democracy, the Weimar Republic (1918–1933), where Max Weber himself fulfilled his role as a "political thinker in action" (Baehr 1989, 20). An enthusiastic and idealistic draftee of the Weimar Constitution in which he advocated for a president to be "elected directly by the people" (Baehr 1989, 21), his death in 1920 due to the devastating 1918 Influenza Pandemic spared him the horrors of confronting how the 1933 demise of Weimar Germany "elected" Adolf Hitler as a chancellor.

Notes

1. The publishers of the former note, however, that the volume is "relatively self-contained...to appear suitable for separate publication in translation" (1947, v).
2. The notion of "long" conveyed herein should be seen only as a heuristic concept for the conceptualization of time and its relationship to nation construction; it is thus not operationalized in this chapter.
3. Burma, by the sixteenth century, had established the largest empire in Southeast Asian history (see Lieberman's excellent 2003 account). Its first campaign against Siam during the fifteenth century resulted in the death of Queen Suriyothai mentioned herein.
4. King Narai's death in 1688 was preceded by Thai royalist that purged the French from the Thai court. Narai had become amenable to French machinations, prompting a coup by the fervently anti-French court councilor Phra Phetracha. Constantine Phaulkon, Narai's trusted minister, his half-brothers Prince Apaithot and Prince Noi, and his adopted son Phra Pi were all tortured and executed by Phetracha. For further reading, see Damrong Rajanubhab's *Thai Rop Phama* (2001) and Thanet Aphornsuvan's "The West and Siam's Quest for Modernity" (2009).
5. Thai authors writing in Thai script are cited by first and then last name. However, Thai authors writing original works in the English language are cited by employing surname and then first name. In the case of films, since its originators produced films first for the Thai market, they are treated as producing works in the Thai language and are thus referred to by their first and last names in sequence.
6. For Chutintaranond, the Burmese were seen by King Naresuan as the demon *Mara*, a being who symbolizes forces that block one's path to enlightenment. King Naresuan was depicted by chroniclers "as the Lord Buddha who, after defeating *Mara*, successfully attained *nirvana*—an extraordinary achievement in itself" (1992, 93).
7. Regardless of the historiographic accounts of the 1593 duel, what is confirmed is that following Naresuan's victory, Burma would be on the defensive until it reinvigorated its wars again with Ayutthaya, ultimately causing the demise of the latter in 1767. Between 1700 and 1800, the Burmese empire fielded its best warriors, repulsing four invasion attempts by China's Qing Dynasty, although it suffered a catastrophic defeat in the Burmese-Siamese War of 1785 when Burma failed in its invasion of the recently promulgated Bangkok Kingdom.
8. Thailand renamed itself Siam between 1946 and 1948, only to again transition back to Thailand when Plaek Phibunsongkhram, one of the nationalists that ensured the downfall of absolute monarchy in 1932, returned to being Prime Minister in 1948. An interesting discussion can be seen in Preecha Juntanamalaga's 1988 article "Thai or Siam?"
9. A well-traveled individual, Chulalongkorn visited Java, Western Europe, Russia, India, and Burma. In Europe, he famously met with different monarchs and political players. He traveled to the Malaya Peninsula on more than ten occasions, visiting Singapore, Johor, Penang, Malacca, Taiping, and Kulim as well as the Dutch East Indies; see also Huen (2009) and Aldrich (2015).

References

Ake, Claude. 1966. "Charismatic Legitimation and Political Integration." *Comparative Studies in Society and History* 9 (1): 1–13.

Aldrich, Robert. 2015. "France and the King of Siam: An Asian King's Visits to the Republican Capital," *French History and Civilization* 6: 225–239.

Al Jazeera. 2021. "Thai Protesters Call for Royal Reforms Again after Court Ruling." November 14. Retrieved November 18, 2021. https://www.aljazeera.com/news/2021/11/14/thai-protesters-call-for-royal-reforms-after-court-ruling.

Anderson, Benedict. 1991. *Imagined Communities*. New York: Verso.

Aphornsuvan, Thanet. 2009. "The West and Siam's Quest for Modernity: Siamese Responses to Nineteenth Century American Missionaries." *South East Asia Research* 17 (3): 401–431.

Askew, Marc, Colin Long, and William Logan. 2006. *Vientiane: Transformations of a Lao Landscape*. Abingdon: Routledge.

Baehr, Peter. 1989. "Weber and Weimar: The 'Reich President' Proposals." *Politics* 9 (1): 20–25.

Baker, Chris, and Pasuk Phongpaichit. 2005. *A History of Thailand*. Cambridge: Cambridge University Press.

Bangkok Post. 2021. "Royal Insult Law Repeal Draws Over 100,000 Supporters." November 6. Retrieved December 4, 2021. https://www.bangkokpost.com/thailand/politics/2210819/royal-insult-law-repeal-draws-over-100-000-supporters.

Blau, Peter. 1963. "Critical Remarks on Weber's Theory of Authority." *American Political Science Review* 57: 305–316.

Chachavalpongpun, Pavin. 2020. "Constitutionalizing the Monarchy." *Journal of International Affairs* 73 (2): 163–172.

Chaloemtiarana, Thak. 2007. *Thailand: The Politics of Despotic Paternalism*. Ithaca, NY: Cornell Southeast Asia Program Publications.

Chatri Chalerm Yukol. 2001. *The Legend of Suriyothai*. Bangkok: Sahamongkol Film International, Sony Pictures Classics, and American Zoetrope.

———. 2007–2005. *The Legend of King Naresuan*. Bangkok: Sahamongkol Film International.

Chutintaranond, Sunait. 1988. "Cakravartin: Ideology, Reason and Manifestation of Siamese-Burmese Kings in Traditional Warfare (1546–1854)." *Crossroads: An Interdisciplinary Journal of Southeast Asian Studies, Special Burma Studies Issue* 4 (1): 46–53.

———. 1992. "The Image of the Burmese Enemy in Thai Perceptions and Historical Writings." *Journal of the Siam Society* 80 (1): 89–103.

CNN. 2021. "Thai Court Rules Protesters Sought to Topple Monarchy as Kingdom Defends Royal Insults Law at UN." November 10, 2021. Retrieved November 14, 2021. https://www.cnn.com/2021/11/10/asia/thailand-student-protest-insult-monarchy-intl-hnk/index.html.

Costas, Helen. 1958. "Max Weber's Two Conceptions of Bureaucracy." *American Journal of Sociology* 63 (4): 400–409.

Damrong, Rajanubhab. 2001. *Our Wars with the Burmese*. Bangkok: White Lotus Press.

Fong, Jack. 2009. "Sacred Nationalism: The Thai Monarchy and Primordial Nation Construction." *Journal of Contemporary Asia* 39 (4): 673–696.

———. 2013. "Political Vulnerabilities of a Primate City: The May 2010 Red Shirts Uprising in Bangkok, Thailand." *Journal of Asian and African Studies* 48 (3): 332–347.

———. 2019. "Mourning a Late King through Portraiture: Articulations of the Sacred and Profane in the Primate City of Bangkok." *Journal of Asian and African Studies* 54 (2): 229–247.

Foreign Policy. 2006. "Failed States Index." May/June.

Friedland, William H. 1964. "For a Sociological Concept of Charisma." *Social Forces* 43 (1): 18–26.

Hobsbawm, E. and T. Ranger. 1983. *The Invention of Tradition*. Cambridge: Cambridge University Press.

Huen, Patricia Lim Pui. 2009. *Through the Eyes of the King: The Travels of King Chulalongkorn to Malaya*. Singapore: Institute of Southeast Asian Studies.

Juntanamalaga, Preecha. 1988. "Thai or Siam." *Names: A Journal of Onomastics* 36 (1–2): 69–84.

Lieberman, Victor. 2003. *Strange Parallels: Volume 1, Integration on the Mainland: Southeast Asia in Global Context, c.800–1830*. Cambridge: Cambridge University Press.

Tanit Jitnukul. 2000. *Bang Rajan*. Bangkok: Film Bangkok, Magnolia Pictures, and Kyivnaukfilm.

Thanthong-Knight, Randy. 2021. "Movie Theaters Show Quiet Resistance to Thai Monarchy Is Growing." *Bloomberg*, November 7, 2021. Retrieved November 13, 2021. https://www.bloomberg.com/news/articles/2021-11-07/movie-theaters-show-quiet-resistance-to-thai-monarchy-is-growing.

Terwiel, B. J. 2005. *Thailand's Political History: From the Fall of Ayutthaya to Recent Times*. Bangkok: River Books.

Weber, Max. 1947. *Theory of Social and Economic Organization*. Mansfield Centre, CT: Martino Publishing.

———. 1978. *Economy and Society: An Outline of Interpretive Sociology*. Berkeley, CA: University of California Press.

Wehner, Peter. 2020. "The Trump Presidency Is Over." *The Atlantic*, March 13. Retrieved June 27, 2020. https://www.theatlantic.com/ideas/archive/2020/03/peter-wehner-trump-presidency-over/607969/.

Winichakul, Thongchai. 1994. *Siam Mapped: A History of the Geo-Body of a Nation*. Honolulu: University of Hawaii Press.

Wyatt, David K. 1982 "The 'Subtle Revolution' of King Rama I of Siam." In *Moral Order and the Question of Change: Essays on Southeast Asian Thought*, edited by David K. Wyatt and Alexander Woodside, 131–174. New Haven, CT: Yale University, Southeast Asia Studies.

———. 2003. *Thailand: A Short History*. New Haven, CT: Yale University Press.

INDEX

Note: **Bold** page numbers refer to tables; *italic* page numbers refer to figures and page numbers followed by "n" denote endnotes.

Abe Shinzô 104, 240, 242, 243–246, 250–264, 330, 332, 333; collective self-defense 254–255; comfort women 256–257; constitutional revision 253–255; curbing academic freedom 260; downsized 263; dubious legacy 263–264; history wars escalate 258–259; Olympic follies 262–263; revising history 255–256; revisionists tarnish brand Japan 257–258; statue wars 258; stifling freedom of expression 259–261; territorial disputes 252–253; undiplomatic interventions 260–261
Abinales, Patricio 430
Abu Bakr 396
Abu Sayyaf Group (ASG) 396, 399
academic freedom: and Abe 260; curbing 260
Achar Hem Chieu 492
Act of Annates (1532) 3
Act of Appeals (1533) 3
Act of Supremacy (1534) 3
advertising production in Japan 272–277
Afro-Asian Solidarity Conference (AASC) 123
Agoncillo, Teodoro 433, 434, 435, 436
Aguinaldo, Emilio 64
Ahmad, Abu Talib 528
Aichi Triennale 259
Ajia no Chugakusei no Tomo eno Tegami 219
Akihito, Emperor 261–262
Alatas, Syed Farid 42
algorithmic mechanics and digital designs 175–176
Ali, Syed Husin 525
Alibaba 174
al-Irshad 476–477

Allison, Graham 159, 162
Al-Manar (The Lighthouse) 521
Alptekin, Erkin 204
Al Qaeda 197, 208–209, 388, 396, 398
Alter, Peter 1
Al-Urwat al-Wuthqa (The Indissoluble Link) 521
al-Wahab, Abd 475
American Narcissism (Caldwell) 235
"America's Pacific Century" (Clinton) 162
Ananda Mahidol, King 589
Anderson, Benedict 1, 15, 23–24, 27, 30, 49–50, 51, 53, 74, 109, 170, 213–214, 267–268, 362, 404, 408, 474, 490, 550, 554, 576
Anderson, Bridget 40
Anderson, Perry 94
Andrejevic, Mark 270
Angkatan Belia Islam sa-Malaysia (ABIM) 397
Anglo-Boer War 125, 127
Anglo-Japanese Alliance 70
Anglo-Saxon dialects 4
Anh Đức 421
Anthropocene 79
anti-colonial nationalism 491–492
Anti-Fascist People's Freedom League (AFPFL) 465–467, 469
anti-imperialism 65, 101, 131, 133, 182, 184, 192, 369, 371
Anti-Japanese War 147
anti-Muslim conspiracy theories 448–449, 455n7
anti-racist pedagogies 36
Anti-Rightist policy (*fanyou douzheng*) 205
Anti-Subversion Law 394
Aphornsuvan, Thanet 584, 586

APODETI (Timorese Popular Democratic Association) 563
Arakan Rohingya Islamic Front (ARIF) 397
Arakan Rohingya National Organization (ARNO) 397
Aristotle 75
Armstrong, John A. 4, 15, 21, 23, 355
Army Strategic Reserve (KOSTRAD) 482
Arrington, Celeste 260
artificial intelligence (AI) 83–84, 174
Asahi Shinbun 243–244
Ashar, Meera 40, 42
Ashcroft, John 394
Asia: British Empire and its influence on 91–92; community of shared future for mankind 99; hegemonic system 89; Legal Orientalism and construction of 96–98; nationalism and pan-Asianism 94–96; nationalism in 8–9; nation building in 8–9; nations, construction of 89–99; resistance from 94–96
Asia as Method (Chen) 37
Asian-African Conference in Bandung, Indonesia 72
Asian Cultural Council (ACC) 496
Asian Infrastructure Investment Bank (AIIB) 159
Asianism 66–72
Asian Monroe Doctrine 65, 69, 70, 71
Asia-Pacific War 104, 213, 215, 216–219, 228, 243
Asia Women's Fund 256
Association of Southeast Asian Nations (ASEAN) 85, 96, 99, 399
Atarashi Rekishi Kyokasho Tsukurukai 256
Athens Olympics 190
Atlanta Olympics 190
Atsumaro, Konoe 64
Awang Haji Besar bin Sagap 554
Azar, Alex 162
Azhar, Seruan 476–477

Baba, Abdul Ghafar 529
Bagehot, Walter 128
Bahasa Melayu 554–557
Baidu 174
Bairner, Alan 283
Baldwin, Frank 260
Ba Maw 64
banal nationalism 105, 284
Banal Nationalism (Billig) 284
Bandung Conference of 1955 96
Bang Rajan (Jitnukul) 578
Bannon, Steve 240
Barcelona Olympics 190
Baren incident 207
Barker, Eddie 97
Barnett, Anthony 492

Bar-Tal, D. 442
Basic Treaty (1965) 256
Bastian, Adolf 475
Basu, Mukul 329
Bauman, Zygmunt 237
Beijing Olympics 190–191
Beiyang 117, 142, 147
Beiyang Women's Medical Bureau 141
Belgian Revolution of 1830 7
Belt and Road Initiative (BRI) 17, 85, 159
Benitez, Conrado 433, 435, 438
Bertrand, Jacques 473
Bhabha, Homi K. 505
Bhumibol Adulyadej, King 589
Biden, Joe 43, 162
Big Nationalism 103
Bilibili 172–173
Billig, Michael 105, 284, 432
bin Laden, Osama 396
Blackburn, Susan 354
Black Lives Matter 43
Blair, Tony 81–82
Bluntschli, Johann Kasper 111, 114, 338
Böckenförde dilemma 74
Boer War 369
Bogd Khanate of Mongolia 118
Bohr, Niels 76
Bokura no Taiheiyo Senso 214, 219, 223, 227
Boniface VIII, Pope 3
Border Patrol Police (BPP) 384
'bourgeois' modernizers 6
Bovingdon, Gardner 207
Boxer Rebellion 69, 115
Branigan, Tania 284
Brass, Paul 26–27
Braudel, Fernand 38–39, 77, 78
Bretton Woods system 93
Breuilly, John 23, 25–26, 51, 56
BRICS 85
British Empire 7; and its influence on Asia 91–92
British imperialism 70
British-Myanmar treaty 65
British Privy Council 98
Brookes and the British North Borneo Chartered Company (BNBCC) 549
Brown, David 443
Brunei: anti-colonial period 552–554; homogenization period 554–557; national identity 557–558; overview 549–551; periodization and inclusion-exclusion strategies 551–557
Bruneian nationalism 549–558
Brunei Darussalam *see* Brunei
Buddhism 57, 210n2
Buddhist nationalism: anti-Muslim conspiracy theories 448–449; Buddhist nationalist movements 444–445; Buddhist nationalist

sermons 451–453; in Burma/Myanmar 441–455; Burmese Buddhist nationalism 443–444; Burmese national identity 443–444; and collective victimhood 442–443, 445–448; colonial period 444–445; Indian immigration 445–448; Muslim takeover, fearing 448–449; the 969 movement and Ma Ba Tha 449–450; and *ressentiment* 442–443, 445–448; and riots 445–448
Buddhist nationalist movements: the 969 movement and Ma Ba Tha 449–450; colonial period 444–445; contemporary 449–450
Buddhist nationalist sermons 451–453
Bunmeiron no Gairyaku (Yukichi) 126
bureaucratic incorporation 22
Burma/Myanmar: Buddhist nationalism in 441–455; Konbaung dynasty in 368; national identity construction 377–378; nationalism in colonial 459–471; nationalism in postcolonial 459–471; Rohingyas without identity or nation 396–397
Burma Rebellion 464
Burma Socialist Program Party 468
Burrett, Tina 15
Butler, Judith 284
Buzan, Barry 199–200
Byung-Ho Chung 284

calculated nationalism: and emergence of new Koreans 327–329; Japan's trade restrictions 330–333; legacy of Japanese imperialism 330–333; overview 326–327; shirking the costs of reunification 329–330; in South Korea 325–333
Caldwell, Wilber 235
Calhoun, Craig 271–272
Cambodge: The Cultivation of a Nation: 1860–1945 (Edwards) 491
Cambodian nationalism: anti-colonial nationalism 491–492; *Cambodge: The Cultivation of a Nation: 1860–1945* 491; cultural nationalism for post-colonial nation-building 493–495; elite nationalism 493–497; genocide nationalism 492–493; Hun Sen 495–497; nationalism as political resource 490–491; overview 488–489; for political legitimacy 495–497; political nationalism 491–493; popular nationalism 497–500; Prince Norodom Sihanouk 493–495
Cambridge Townsmen Association (England) 97
Campbell, Emma 330
Caodaism 64
Carr, E. H. 237–238
Celestial Kingdom 62
Center for Global Partnership (CGP) in Tokyo 260
Central Midwifery Education Committee 144

Chakrabarty, Dipesh 37, 40
Chakravarti, N. R. 446
Chakri Dynasty 582–583
Changlu Women's Medical School 141
Chang Sun-Mi 329
Chao Boun Khong 507
Charlemagne 4
Chatterjee, Partha 15, 50, 112, 359
Cheah, Pheng 40
Chen, Kuan-Hsing 37, 43
Chen Gongbo 129
Cheng-Zhu school 57
Chiang Kai-shek 95, 117, 118, 143
Chiang Mai 383
China: "A Community of Shared Future for Mankind" 96, 99; adoption of Western medicine in 139–140; Belt and Road Initiative (BRI) 17, 85, 96, 159; commercial actors in digital political economy 174–175; concepts of the nation 109–114; digital nationalism 167–178; ethnonationalism 542–543; and Japan 252–253; Japan-China Joint Statement (1972) 225–226; Ministry of Health 144; national identity construction 376–377; and nationalism in colonial Vietnam 406–407; rise and major challenges 159–162; and socialism and nationalism in Vietnam 408–410; Song dynasty 16; Taiwan issue 152; *Tianxia* 101; US-China-Taiwan military expenditure **161**; and Vietnamese 406–407; volatile US-China-Taiwan relations 162–163
China Can Say No 189
China National Amateur Athletic Federation (CNAAF) 182
China Revolutionary Alliance 64
China's Destiny (Chiang Kai-shek) 95
'China Should Train Midwives Today' 143
Chinese Civil War 152
Chinese Communist Party (CCP) 66, 152, 170, 172, 174, 202, 376
Chinese Exclusion Act 43
Chinese Jingpo 381
Chinese Muslim Educational Association (Shanghai) 202
Chinese Muslim General Association (Jinan) 202
Chinese Muslim Young Students Association (Nanjing) 202
Chinese nationalism 52, 101; beginning of the end 116–117; Chinese concepts of the nation 109–114; culturalism and nationalism 111–112; homogenisation and synchronisation 114–115; and imagination of new world order 125–129; internationalism 129–131; in late Qing times 108–119; *minzu* and *minzu zhuyi* 124–125; nationalism in Chinese context 156; nationalism in Chinese revolution 131–134;

nationalism in practice 114–117; overview 108–109; Qing as constitutional monarchy 115–116; rising 156–158; and Taiwanese identity 151–163; trend of 157–158; types of nationalism 156–157; Western and Chinese roots 112–114
Chinese Nationalists Party (KMT) 102
Chinese Olympic journey: criticisms of gold medal fever 188–189; Liu Changchun's one-man Olympics 181–184; and nationalism 181–193; nationalism and Olympic strategy 185–188; Olympics and China's rise 189–191; sports patriotism debate 191–192; two Chinas 184–185
Chinese Revolution 17, 131–134
Chin-Hao Huang 159
Cho, E.J.R. 292
Choi Hong Hi 296, 298, 300, 302, 303
Ch'ŏngdo Kwan (Chung Do Kwan) 297
Chosŏn Korea 51, 54
Chosun dynasty 344
Chou, Cynthia 37
Chou Tsu-yu 167, 169
Christian Byzantine Empire 3
Christian Filipinos 436
Chulalongkorn, monarch of Siam 583–586
Chun Doo-hwan 312–315
Chungcheong Today 329
Chung Hwa Hui (Chinese Association) 478
Chun regime: challenging 313–314; South Korea 313–314
Chuo Koron 217
Circulatory Histories (Duara) 37
Citizenship Law (1982) 449, 454, 455
Clarke, Michael 199, 390
The Clash of Civilizations and the Remaking of World Order (Huntington) 189
classic nationalism theories: applying to East and Southeast Asia 19–32; economic approaches 23–25; ethnosymbolist and cultural approaches 20–23; political approaches 25–27
Clausen, Søren 157
Clement V 3
Clericis laicos (Boniface VIII) 3
Clinton, Hillary 162
Coen, Jan Pieterszoon 584–586
Cohen, Anthony 30; 'personal nationalism' 30
Cokroaminoto, H.O.S. 477
Cold War 8, 63, 72, 96, 102, 159, 197, 254, 281, 304, 344, 346–347, 372, 469
collective narcissism: historical revisionism and 238–240
collective self-defense 254–255
collective victimhood: and Indian immigration 445–448; and *ressentiment* 442–443
Collins, Randal 57

Collins, Rebekah Lin 417
colonial empires 62–72; from semi-colony to 66–72
colonialism 55, 74; and frameworks for nations 362–364; Southeast Asia 388–389
colonial subjugation 309
comfort women 256–257
Comintern 65–66
commercial actors in China's digital political economy 174–175
commercial cosmopolitanism in Japan 274–276
commercial nationalism: and cosmopolitanism 270–272; in Japan 272–274
Common Culture Association 69
Communism, Nationalism and Political Propaganda in North Korean Sport (Lee and Bairner) 283
Communist International 62, 65
communist movement 62–66
The Communist Movement in China (Chen Gongbo) 129
Communist Party of Indochina 65
Communist Party of Indonesia 66
Communist Party of Korea 65
Communist Party of Myanmar 65
comparative nation-building: at borderland 380–384; in borderlands between China/Myanmar/Thailand 375–384
complexity theory 29–31
conflict: and democracy 393–394; and international relations theory 197–198
conflict in Xinjiang: government policies and Uighur identity 204–207; human security perspective 198–199; identity and security 199–200; international relations theory and conflict 197–198; overview 196–197; protests or acts of terrorism 208–209; threats to identity 200–202; Uighur identity, construction of 202–204; unrest in Xinjiang and Beijing's response 207–208
Confucianism 57, 67
Confucian tradition 55
Congress of Vienna 7, 61
Connor, Walker 23
Constantino, Renato 433, 435, 436
constitutionalism 109
constitutional monarchy 115–116
constructivists 27–29
consumption of (trans)national identity in Japan 272–277
contemporary nationalism theories: applying to East and Southeast Asia 19–32; complexity theory approaches 29–31; constructivist approaches 27–29
Cooppan, Vilashini 38
Cortes, Doroteo 64
cosmopolitanism, and commercial nationalism 270–272

COVID-19 pandemic 43, 156, 158, 162, 167, 169, 177, 250, 500, 554, 591
Cronin, Mike 181
'crowdsourced nationalism' 30
culturalism and nationalism 111–112
cultural nationalism 493–495
Cultural Revolution 185, 203, 205, 376, 381
cyber-nationalism 168, 169; and digitally enabled nationalist activism 169–170; and mobilization 169–170
cyber-sovereignty: and China 168–169; and nationalist policy 168–169

Dagong Daily 182
Dalai Lama 26
Darul Islam (DI) 394
Darwin, John 91
Da Silva, Antero 566
Datsu-A Ron 90
Davies, Norman 4–5
Day of Songun 285
Day of the Foundation of the Republic 285
Day of the Shining Star 285
Day of the Sun 285–286
Day of Victory in the Great Fatherland Liberation War 285
The Decline of the West (Spengler) 92
decolonialising Southeast Asian nationalism 35–44
decolonial methodologies 40–42
decolonial pedagogy 42–43
decolonial theory 36–40
decolonized nationalism 93
Decolonizing the Mind (Ngugi Wa) 41
de facto censorship 216–218
Déloye, Yves 29
Demilitarised Zone (DMZ) 281
democracy: in conflict 393–394; Western 481–486
Democratic Party of Japan (DPJ) 253
Democratic People's Republic of Korea (DPRK) 280–281, 283
Democratic Republic of Vietnam (DRV) 407
Deng Xiaoping 96, 159, 186, 187, 203, 205
Dentsu 272–273, 275
Derivative Discourse (Chatterjee) 15
De Sousa Santos, Boaventura 39
Destined for War (Allison) 159
The Destiny of China Being Divided (Hata) 130
Deutsch, Karl W. 1–2, 15
developmentalist nationalism: 1948–1980s 311–313; brief overview 311–313
Diệm, Ngô Đình 407
digital designs and algorithmic mechanics 175–176
digitally enabled nationalist activism/ mobilization 169–170

digital nationalism 168, 170; China 167–178; cyber-nationalism 169–170; and cyber-sovereignty 168–169; digital designs and algorithmic mechanics 175–176; digitally enabled nationalist activism/mobilization 169–170; digital political economy 174–175; nationalist discourses in online spheres 169; and nationalist policy 168–169; official actors 172–174; online nationalism 169; organizational inputs into 171–175; Party and state contributing to 172–174; and socio-technical systems 170–171; techno-nationalism 168–169; user-generated discourse and practice 176–177; working of 168–171
Dikötter, Frank 139
The Discovery of India (Nehru) 95
displacement: and transmigration 392–393
'Divine Right of Kings' 5–6
Dobama Asiayone 464
Do Hai Ninh 426
Donnelly, Jack 572
Douwes Dekker, E. F. E. 477–478
Douyin 172–173
Dowager Cixi, Empress 115–116
Dowager Longyu, Empress 117–118
Duara, Prasenjit 37, 43
Durkheim, Émile 42, 347, 349
Dutch East India (Indonesia) 363, 365
Duterte, Rodrigo 429–430, 437, 438

Eagleton, Terry 229
Earl, George Windsor 475
East Asia: bringing order into things 79–80; classic nationalism theories 19–32; conceptual framework 51–52; contemporary nationalism theories 19–32; diffusionist view 49–51; Great East Asian War/the Imjin War 54–56; internationalism in 74–87; nationalism and madness in 348–350; nationalism in 48–58, 74–87; nation and nationalism 51–52; post-colonialism in 74–87; regional conditions and rise of nationalism 62–66; rise of Kokugaku in Tokugawa Japan 56–58; Song dynasty 52–54
East Asia Association 69
East Asia Common Culture Association 69
East Asian Unionism 95
East Timorese nationalism: construction of 563–565; Fretilin's literacy and political manuals 565–568; *Geração Foun* 568; *Indonesiação do Conflito de Timor-Leste* (Indonesianisation of Conflict in East Timor) movement 569–571; Indonesianess and youth nationalism 568; Indonesianisation of East Timorese 569–571; nationalism in transition 562–563; overview 561–568; Rai Timor 571–573; universal human rights 571–573

East Turkistan Islamic Movement (ETIM) 196–197, 208, 209
Economy and Society (Weber) 577
Edensor, Tim 280
Edo period 344
Education Act (1921) 395
Edward I, King of England 3
Edward III, King 4
Edwards, Harry 186
Edwards, Penny 491
Ehrentraut, Stefan 37
Eight-Power Allied Forces 69
Einstein, Albert 76
Eisenstadt, Shmuel 48, 50, 51
El Filibsterismo (Rizal) 431
elite nationalism 493–497
emancipatory nationalism 361–372
embryonic national consciousness 2–6
Engels, Friedrich 6
English Act (1362) 5
English Civil War 6
English Revolutions 6
Enlightenment 24, 57, 110, 365; Scottish 92
Espiritu, Yến Lê 39
ethnic essentialism 542–543
ethnicity: and 'ethno-preneurs' 28; Khitan 53; regional implications of 398–399
ethnic nationalism 455n1; history and 389–390; Southeast Asia 389–390
Ethnic Nationalism in Korea (Shin) 283
ethno-nationalism 110; Chinese 542–543; past and future of 344–347
Eurocentrism and traditional colonialism 91–92
European colonialism 96
European hegemony 89
European Union (EU) 89
Evans, Richard 238
exceptionalism 57; Singaporean 543–544
Explication de l'Arithmétique Binaire (Leibniz) 83

Facebook 173
Fairbank, John K. 113
Fan Hon 305
Fanon, Frantz 426
feckless nationalism 250–264; immigration 250–251; overview 250; territorial disputes 252–253
female body: and strength of nation 141–143
female hygiene system: construction of 143–146; national rejuvenation and 143–146
Fernandez, Leandro 433
Fernandez, Leandro Heriberto 433, 435, 438
Filipinos 430–431, 436
The First 150 Years of Singapore (Moore) 535
First Sino-Japanese War 63, 67, 69, 109, 115, 124
First World Championships 302
First World War 7, 61, 62, 63, 65, 67, 70, 71, 141

Fitzgerald, John 112
Five Dynasties 52
Five-Power Treaty 70
'Five Races Under One Union' 141
Floyd, George 43
Fong, Jack 359
Foreign Interference (Countermeasures) Act of 2021 98
Formichi, Chiara 477
frailocracy (friarocracy) 438n1
France-Asie or *Sud-est* 511
Francis I, King of France 5
Franco-Siamese War 583, 587
Franco-Thai War 587
Frankopan, Peter 92
freedom of expression 259–261
Freire, Paulo 565
French Revolution 6–7, 17
FRETILIN 565–566
Freud, Sigmund 235
Friedhoff, Karl 330
From Third World to First: The Singapore Story: 1965–2000. Memoirs of Lee Kuan Yew 540
Fujioka Nobukatsu 243
Fukuda Tsuneari 218
Fukuyama, Francis 81, 240, 430
Fukuzawa Yukichi 67, 126
Fuller, Steve 430
Fulton, Mary H. 140
Funü shibao 143
Fu Yuanhui 193

Gakumon no Susume (An Encouragement of Learning) 340
Games of the Newly Emerging Forces (GANEFO) 185
Gandhi, M.K. 40
Garasu no kamen (Glass Mask) 342
Gartner, Scott 159
Geertz, Clifford 284, 494
Gellner, Ernest 1, 15, 23, 24–25, 28, 122, 237, 550
General Agreement on Tariffs and Trade (GATT) 342
General Assembly of International Sports Federation (GAISF) 303
General Council of Buddhist Associations (GCBA) 461, 464
General Council of Burmese Associations (GCBA) 445
General Council of Sangha Sammeggyi (GCSS) 462–463
genocide nationalism 492–493
Geração Foun 568
Gerakan Aceh Merdeka (GAM; Free Aceh Movement) 485
Ge Zhaguang 53–54

Ghosts of War in Vietnam (Kwon) 40
Giddens, Anthony 51
Gilbert, Kent 243
Global Alliance for Historical Truth (GAHT) 259
globalization 9; and new hegemonic system 92–94; taking seriously 81–82
Gluck, Carol 231n9
Goethe, Johan Wolfgang von 77
Goffman, Erving 284
Goh, Beng-Lan 43
Goh Keng Swee 537
Golec de Zavala 239–240, 246
"Good-bye Asia" movement 68
Goode, J. Paul 27
Gorky, Maxim 419
government policies and Uighur identity 204–207
Great Asianism 95
Great East Asian War/the Imjin War (1592–1598) 54–56
Greater East Asia Co-Prosperity Sphere (GEACPS) 66–72, 90
Great Japan Association 69
Great Leap Forward 202–203, 205, 381
The Great Principles of Education (Japan) 67
Greenfeld, Liah 2, 3, 23, 52, 106, 337–338, 344, 347, 490
Gregg, David 140
Grosby, Steven 59n1
Grosfoguel, Ramón 39
Großraum (great space) 71
Guangming Daily 188
Guangzhou Asian Games 192
Guerrero, Milagros 434
Guided Democracy 481–486
Gunn, Geoffrey 506
Guo Moruo 134
Gupta, Akhil 550
Gützlaff, Karl Friedrich August 124
Gwangju Movement 313, 316

Haboush, JaHyun Kim 55
Hagiwara, Shigeru 274
Hagström, Linus 239
Haji Mohamed Yusof bin Pengiran Haji Abdul Rahim 554
Hakuhodo 272–273
Hall, Stuart 268, 270–271
Hamengkubuwono IX, Sultan 480
Han Chauvinism 132
Han Chinese 111, 210n4
Hao Gengsheng 182
Harootunian, Harry 57
Harper, Tim 37, 40–41
Harris, Tobias 262
Has China Won? (Mahbubani) 159

Hassanal Bolkiah, Yayasan Sultan 555–556
Hastings, Adrian 23
Hata, Nakajima 130
Hatta, Mohammad 65, 476
Health Bimonthly 145
Healy, Dana 417
Hechter, Michael 24–25; theory of nationalism 24
hegemonic system and globalization 92–94
Heidegger, Martin 75
Hekmatyar, Gulbuddin 397
Helly, Denise 204
He Long 185
Heng Swee Keat 534, 542, 543
Henley, David 361
Henry VIII, King 3
Herrmann, Peter 16
Hideyoshi, Toyotomi 54–55
Hindia Poetra (Sons of the Indies) 476
Hinton, Alexander 492
Hirohito, Emperor 215–216
"A Historical Perspective for National Integration" (Tan) 436
historical revisionism: and collective narcissism 238–240; as global phenomenon 236–238; main triggers for historical revisionists **241–242**; in twenty-first-century 234–246; in twenty-first-century Japan 234–246
History of the Vietnamese (Taylor) 40
Hitler, Adolf 592
Hizb-e-Islami 397
Hizb-ulMujahideen (HM) in Kashmir 397
Hoa, and Vietnamese nation 410–412
Hồ Anh Thái 417
Hobsbawm, Eric 15, 26, 27, 105, 186, 286, 295, 576; theory of 'invented traditions' 27
Hobson, John A. 369
Hồ Chí Minh 63, 65, 365, 404, 406, 410
Hồ Gươm 418
Holocaust 236
Holsti, Kalevi 197
Holy Roman Empire 3
homogenisation: Chinese nationalism 114–115; and synchronisation 114–115
Honda Katsuichi 216, 231n8
Honda Koei 104, 214, 216–228, 230, 231n8, 232n22; attack on 218; conservative intellectuals and MOE 218; graduation and continuation 226–228; letters of the 1971–1972 classes 218–219; more parental criticism 224; parental responses 221–224; student responses to parental criticism 224–225; students' conducting research by visiting foreign embassies 221; teaching about Asia-Pacific War 216–218
"Hong Kong Extradition Bill" 161
Hong Yong-Pyo, Minister of Reunification 330
Hroch, Miroslav 15

Huang Xingtao 124
Huawei 193
Hughes, Caroline 254
'Hundred Flowers Campaign' 204
The Hundred-Year Marathon (Pillsbury) 159
Hun Sen 357, 495–497, 501
Huntington, Samuel 189
Hutchinson, John 22, 139, 490
Hữu Mai 421
The H-Word: The Peripeteia of Hegemony (Anderson) 94

Ibn Affan, Uthman 202
Ibn Khaldun 42
Ibn Saud 475
Ibrahim, Anwar 393, 526
Ichijo, Atsuko 16–17
identity: regional implications of 398–399; Rohingyas without 396–397; and security 199–200; in Southeast Asia 397–398; and sovereignty 390–391; threats to 200–202
Identity (Fukuyama) 240
Identity in the Shadow of a Giant (Gartner and Chin-Hao Huang) 159
Ienaga Saburo 214, 255
Ileto, Reynaldo 434–435
Imagined Communities (Anderson) 15, 23, 362, 576
Imjin War *see* Great East Asian War
imperialism 62; British 70; and Myanmar nationalism 460; Western 70
Imperialism, the Highest Stage of Capitalism (Lenin) 62
Imperialism: A Study (Hobson) 369
Imperialism: The Last Stage of Capitalism (Lenin) 369
Indian immigration: and collective victimhood 445–448; and *ressentiment* 445–448; and riots 445–448
Indian nationalism 95
Indian National Revolt 91
Indonesia 473–486; 1850–1950 474–481; 1950–1998 481–486; collapse of New Order 486; Guided Democracy 481–486; and New Order 481–486; origins to independence 474–481; splintered identities, dissimilar conflicts 394–395; Western democracy 481–486
Indonesição do Conflito de Timor-Leste (Indonesianisation of Conflict in East Timor) movement 569–571
Indonesian Communist Party (PKI) 394
Indonesianess and youth nationalism 568
Indonesian Genocide 8
Indonesianisation of the East Timorese 569–571
Indonesian Student Solidarity for Democracy (SMID) 570

Indonesian Study Club 474
Indonesische Vereeniging (Indonesian Association) 474
Indo-Pakistani wars 8
Internal Security Act (ISA) 523
International Conference of Asian Political Parties (ICAPP) 496
internationalism 74; in East and Southeast Asia 74–87; nationalism in context of 129–131
The International Journal of the History of Sport 305
International Monetary Fund (IMF) 317
International Olympic Committee (IOC) 184
international relations theory: and conflict in Xinjiang 197–198
International Taekwondo Federation (ITF) 298
International Women's Day 285
Invention of Tradition (Ranger) 295, 576
Iranian Revolution 398
Iran–Iraq War 8
Irving, David 236
Islam 196, 198; introduced to China 202; in Southeast Asia 397–398; traditionalist 202; and Uighur identity 204, 206–208
Islamic Association of China (Zhongguo Yisilanjiao Xiehui) 202
Islami Chhatra Shibir 397
Islamic Movement of Uzbekistan (IMU) 197
Islamic State movement 8
Islamic State of Iraq and Syria (ISIS) 208–209, 388
Israeli-Palestinian conflict 8
Issara anti-colonial nationalism 514–516
Ivarsson, Soren 506
Izvestiya 205

Jackson, Robert H. 133
Jacques, Martin 159
Jamaat-e-Islami 397
James, Patrick 159
James I, King of Scotland 6
Japan: Asianism 64; *Basic Outline of National Policy* 70; and China 252–253; commercial cosmopolitanism in 274–276; commercial nationalism in 272–274; Greater East Asia Co-Prosperity Sphere 95; historical revisionism and collective narcissism 238–240; historical revisionism as global phenomenon 236–238; historical revisionism in twenty-first-century 234–246; Japan-China Joint Statement 225–226; narrating nation in postwar 214–216; nationalism and 267–270; nation and 267–270; Pan-Asianism 64; revisionists tarnish brand 257–258; and Russia 252; and South Korea 252; students visiting foreign embassies 221; territorial disputes 252–253
Japanese Communist Party 242, 243–244

Index

Japanese Constitution 104
Japanese Doctrine 69
Japanese Embassy 257
Japanese imperialism: and Japan's trade restrictions 330–333; legacy of 330–333
Japanese Invasion of Korea *see* Great East Asian War
Japanese *Kokuryū-kai* (Black Dragon Society) 64
Japanese-Korean nationalism: birth and transformation of 337–351; nationalism and madness in East Asia 347–350; nationalism trilogy 337–338; origin of nationalism 338–341; overview 337; past and future of ethnonationalism 344–347; postcolonial nationalism 341–344
Japanese Kwantung Army 70
Japanese nationalism 56; formation of 66–72
Japan Olympic Committee (JOC) 262–263
Jawi 474–475
Jazeel, Tariq 36
Jemaah Islamiyah (JI) 396
Jesus Christ 434
Jiang Zemin 190
Jin Baoshan 144
Jin Yunmei 141
Jitnukul, Tanit 578
Juche philosophy 292
Judeo-Christian cosmology 58
Juguo Tizhi 188, 190

Kada no Azumamaro 57
"KADIN Amerika" (US Chamber of Commerce and Industry) 392
Kahin, George McT. 370
Kailian, Gregory S. 305
Kai Zhi Lu 128
Kambuja Surya (Chandler) 491
Kang Youwei 69, 108, 109, 115–116
Kant, Immanuel 83, 89
Kaoru, Inoue 67
Kaoru Yasui 71
Kartosuwiryo, S.M. 477
Katay Sasorith 508, 511
Kato Hiroyuki 338
Kawai Katsuyuki 263
Kazutami, Ukita 113
Kedourie, Elie 1, 15, 48, 50, 108
Khalifa, Jamal 396
Khan, Genghis 26
Khieu Ponnary 493
Khieu Thirith 493
Khin Maung Kyi 446
Khitan ethnicity 53
Khmer Rouge 25, 357
Kidd, Benjamin 128
Kidwai, Mushir Hosein 477
Kiernan, Ben 492

Kim Dae Jung 308, 312, 314, 317, 319–320, 321
Kim dynasty 282, 290, 291–292
Kim Il-sung 281–282, 285, 286, 287, 288, 290
Kim Jinsong 348
Kim Jong-il 282, 285, 287, 289, 290, 291
Kim Jong-pil 301, 314
Kim Jong-un 282, 288, 289, 291, 292–293
Kim Ok-gyun 340
Kim Ui-Young 332
Kim Un Yong 301, 302, 303, 304, 305
Kim Yo-jong 282
Kim Yong-ok 299
Kim Young Sam 314, 317, 321
Kingston, Jeff 246
Kirch, Patrick Vinton 38
Kishida Fumio 264
Kishi Nobusuke 242, 253, 255, 264
Kiyoshi, Inoue 216
Kleinman, Arthur 350
Koh, Aaron 540
Kohn, Hans 6, 15, 110
Koizumi Junichiro 263
Kokugaku in Tokugawa Japan 56–58
Kokusui Shugi (School of National Essence) 68
Komori Yoshihisa 259
Konbaung dynasty (Burma) 368
kong-su-do 296
Konoe Atsumaro 69
Kono Statement 256–257
Korea: colonial period 300
Korea Amateur Sports Association 298
Korea Kongsudo Association 296
Korean Central Intelligence Agency (KCIA) 301
Korean Cultural Freedom Foundation (KCFF) 303
Korean nationalism 56, 58, 106; and politics 301–304; and taekwondo 301–304
'Korean People's Army' (KPA) 287
Korean politics: and nationalism 301–304; and taekwondo 301–304
Korean Royal Army 55
Korean War 26, 184, 288, 296, 309
Korea Taekwondo Association (KTA) 298, 302, 305n1
Korea Taesudo Association (KTA) 297
Kosaka Masataka 218
Kozyo Satakichi 124
Kranzberg, Malvin 175
Krasner, Stephen D. 133
Krikalv, Sergei 276
Kuhn, Philip 483
Kuomintang (KMT) party 117
Kure Shūzō 347
Kurikulum Standard Sekolah Menengah (KSSM) 525
Kusmaatmaja, Mochtar 485

Index

Kuwabara Jitsuzô 113
Kwon, Heonik 37, 40, 284

Labour Day 285
La Liga Filipina 437
Lansin Youth Organization 468
Lao nationalism: two visions of 516–517
Lao People's Democratic Republic (LPDR) 358, 505
Lao Renovation Movement 506
Laos 505–506; Issara anti-colonial nationalism 514–516; multiethnic nationalists 511–514; school days in colonial 507–508; Vientiane Buddhist Institute 508–510
Latin American Common Market 99
Laurel, José Paciano 64
The Law of Nations (Wheaton) 62–63
Lazarus, Neil 425
League of Nations 70
Lee Chong Woo 304
Lee Hsien Loong 534, 540, 542, 543
Lee Jung-woo 283
Lee Kuan Yew 91, 97, 98, 99, 359, 534–535, 537, 538–539, 540, 544–545
Lee Myung-bak 308, 320, 321, 345
Legal Orientalism: case of Singapore 96–98; and construction of independent Asia 96–98
Legal Profession Act 98
Legend of Suriyothai (Yukol) 578
Legg, Stephen 37
Leibniz, Gottfried 83
Lemberg, Eugen 1
Lê Minh Khuê 417, 422, 423
Lenin, Vladimir 62, 63, 114, 369
Levenson, Joseph 111–113
Liang Qichao 63, 64, 69, 103, 108, 109, 110, 111, 113, 114, 115, 124, 125, 127–128, 138, 140–141
Liberal Democratic Party (LDP) 225, 245, 253–254
liberalism 109
Li Dazhao 63, 130–131
Li Hongzhang 63
Lin Chao 173
Lindholm, Helena 200
Linggadjati agreement 479
Lipovitan-D 272–273
Lipstadt, Deborah 236
Literature Daily 189
Liu, Lydia H. 123
Liu Changchun 181–184, 187, 190
Liu Hailong 177
Liu Ruiheng 144
Liu Shipei 108, 109
Liu Xiang 190
Logan, James 475
London Naval Treaty 70

longue durée 21, 35, 38–39
Lord Guan Yu (Chinese God of War) 182
Louis XIII, King of France 5
Lowe, Lisa 35, 43
Loyalty Festival Period 285
Lucian Pye 153
Luxemburg 114
Lu Zhouxiang 305

Ma Ba Tha 441, 449–450, 453, 455
Mabuchi Mutsuo 244
Macpherson, C. Brough 326
"Made in China 2025" strategic plan 161–162
Maha Vajiralongkorn, King 591
Mahbubani, Kishore 159
Mai Menghua 127
Mainichi Shinbun 224
Maintenance of Religious Harmony Act 98
Malaya Agreement 1948 520
Malay nationalism: centrist position in historical exegesis of 528–530; overview 519–520; political reformation and exegetical changes of 524–528; splintered discourse of 520–524
Malay Youth Association 65
Mã Mây 418
Management Rules for Traditional Midwives 145
Manchu-Mongolian Independence Movement 70
Manchu Qing Dynasty 108
Mandal, Sumit 38
"Mandala system" 61
Mangunkusumo, Tjipto 478
Manichaeanism (Mongolia) 210n2
Man'yōshū 57
Mao Zedong 95, 131, 134, 188, 410
Marcos, Ferdinand 435
Marhaenism 24
Martin, Bradley K. 287
Martin, William 62
Marx, Karl 6, 42, 129–130
Marxism 24
Ma Wanfu (1849–1934) 202
May Fourth Movement 138, 141–142
Ma Ying-jeou 154
McCrone, David 285
McCune-Reischauer 305
McNally, Thomas 57
McPherson, Gayle 285
The Mediterranean and the Mediterranean world in the Age of Philip II (Braudel) 38
Meiji Reforms 115
Meiji Restoration 26, 63, 64, 261, 299
Meirokusha (Meiji Six Society) 67
Meiroku Zasshi magazine 67
Melayu Islam Beraja (MIB) 550
Mengqi Wang 28
methodological nationalism 77
Middle Ages 4, 5

Index

Mignolo, Walter 35, 37, 42
militant nationalism 463–464
militarism 101
Military Foundation Day 285, 288
military revolution 5
Milk Tea Alliance 29
Mill, John Stuart 234
Ming China 54
Ming Dynasty 202
minjung nationalism 313–314
minzu 124–125
minzu zhuyi 124–125
Misŏn, Sim 318, 322
Miyake Setsurei 68
modern hegemonism 89–99
Modernity and the Holocaust (Bauman) 237
Modernity-Coloniality-Decoloniality (MCD) 37
modernization 9
modern Olympic movement 181
MOFA 257–258, 260
Mohamad, Mahathir 523
monarchy, constitutional 115–116
Monbu Jiho 218
Money Today 332
Mongol Border Land 118
Mongolian People's Republic 118
Mongols 114, 118
Mong Tai Army (MTA) 381
Monroe Doctrine 99
Moon Jae-in 290, 291, 322
More, Thomas 87n1
Morey, Daryl 167, 169
Mori Yoshiro 262
Moro Islamic Liberation Front (MILF) 396
Moro National Liberation Front (MNLF) 396
Morris-Suzuki, Tessa 39
Mottley, Mia Amor 84
Mullaney, Thomas 38
multiethnic nationalists 511–514
Munhwa Ilbo 332
Munsu Water Park 289
Muzaffar, Chandra 525
Myanmar nationalism: in an era of democracy 468–470; in an era of independence 466–467; in an era of socialism 467–468; colonial 459–471; community through cultural loss 460–461; early nationalist organizations 461; in the era of imperialism 460; locating 459–466; militant nationalism 463–464; nationalism in wartime 464–466; nationalist solidarities 461–466; postcolonial 459–471; rebellion as nationalism 464; religion as nationalism 462–463

Nagara Vatta 491
Nairn, Tom 24–25
Naitō Konan 52
Nanjing National Government 144, 145
Naoki, Hyakuta 244
Napoleonian expansionism 7, 125
Narai, Ayutthayan King 578, 583
Nashidik, Rachland 572, 573
Nasser, Gamel Abdul 95
nation: Chinese concepts of 109–114; colonialism and frameworks for 362–364; described 51–52; female body and strength of 141–143; and Japan 267–270; and responsibility of every woman 140–141; rise and fall of 140–141; Rohingyas without 396–397
National Identity, Popular Culture and Everyday Life (Edensor) 280
national identity construction: China 376–377; Myanmar 377–378; Thailand 379–380; three modes of 376–380
national intellectual elites 364–367
nationalism 74, 109; anti-colonial 491–492; in Asia 8–9; and China's Olympic journey 181–193; in Chinese context 156; in Chinese revolution 131–134; communist narrative 129–131; competing 473–486; in context of internationalism 129–131; culturalism and 111–112; described 51–52; in East and Southeast Asia 48–58, 74–87; elite 493–497; genocide 492–493; and imagination of new World Order 125–129; and Japan 267–270; and madness in East Asia 347–350; militant 463–464; in Myanmar 459–471; and Olympic strategy 185–188; origin of 338–341; and pan-Asianism 94–96; political 491–493; for political legitimacy 495–497; as (alternative) political resource 490–491; popular 497–500; and portrayal of foreigners in Vietnamese literature 416–418; postcolonial 341–344; in practice 114–117; rebellion as 464; regional conditions for the rise of 62–66; regional implications of 398–399; religion as 462–463; rise of 6–8; socio-technical systems behind contemporary 170–171; in transition 562–563; trilogy 106, 337–338; types of 156–157; in wartime 464–466; *see also specific types*
nationalist discourses in online spheres 169
Nationalist/ Kuomintang (KMT) 152–154
nationalist policy and cyber-sovereignty 168–169
National League for Democracy (NLD) 469
National Liberation Day of Korea 285
national rejuvenation and female hygiene system 143–146
National Security Law 311, 321
national self-determination: nation-building and demand for 391
National Unity Government 471
nation-building: in Asia 8–9; cultural nationalism for post-colonial 493–495; and

demand for national self-determination 391; and state consolidation 390
nation states, rise of 6–8
NATO 8, 89, 189
Nehru, Jawahar Lal 95
neo-Confucianism 57
New Culture Movement 138
New Economic Policy 405
Ne Win 449, 467, 468, 469
New Life Movement 299
New Silk Road 85
Newspaper and Printing Presses Act 98
New Testament 5
Newton, Isaac 76
New Village Movement 299
new world order: imagination of 125–129; and nationalism 125–129
New Year's Day 285
Nginn, Somchine 508
Ngoc Thanh's Khmer Serei (Free Khmer) movement 494
Ngo Dinh Diem 494
Nguyen Ba Thanh 328
Nguyễn Công Hoan 419
Nguyen dynasty in Vietnam 368
Nguyễn Ngọc Thuần 417, 421, 422
Nguyễn Văn Trung 424
Nhớ và ghi về Hà Nội (Nguyễn Công Hoan) 419
Nietzsche, Friedrich 443
Nightingale, Florence 42
Nihonshugi journal 69
Nike 273
Nike Japan 274
Ninety-Five (Luther) 5
Ninh Thuận 419
Nippon Kaigi 256
Nippon Kaigi (Japan Conference) 261
Nishi Amane, 67
Nishimura Shigeki, 67
Nkrumah, Kwame 95
Noh Hyeong-Il 327
'No Japan Movement 2019–20' 331
Nomos of the Earth (Schmitt) 94
NonAligned Movement (NAM) 96, 185
non-Western-centric world order: political subjectivity under 48–58
Norinaga, Motoori 57
North Atlantic modernity 37
Northern Expedition 65
Northern Song era 53
North Korea: Beyond Charismatic Politics (Heonik Kwon and Byung-Ho Chung) 284–285
North Korean popular culture: constructing nation in everyday 284–291; mundane environments and grand spectacles 284–291; socio-economic and political context 281–282; theoretical considerations 282–284

Nosamo (Love Roh) movemen 319
Nosco, Peter 57
Nuon Chea 493
Nuon Duong 492
Nursi, Said 42
Nyi Nya Kyaw 447

Obama, Barack 162, 257
October Revolution 62, 63
Odo Kwan 296
Office for the General Management of Affairs Concerning the Various Countries 62
Okinawa Prefecture 231n7
"Okuma doctrine" 69, 70
O'Leary, Brendan 23
Olympics: and Abe 262–263; and China's rise 189–191; Liu Changchun's one-man 181–184; Seoul Olympics 314–316; strategy 189
Ômura Hideki 244
Onabe Teruhiko 218
online nationalism 168; nationalist discourses in online spheres 169
'On the Development of Imperialism and the Future of the twentieth Century World' 128
On the Protracted War (Mao Zedong) 95
Open Door Policy in China 65
Opium Wars 62, 101, 109, 139
OPM (Organisasi Papua Merdeka/Free Papua Organization) 485
Organisation for Economic Co-operation and Development (OECD) 317
Orientalism 97
Oriental Youth Association 64
"The Origin of Terror" (Naung Daw Lay) 455n9
The Origins of Malay Nationalism (Roff) 521
Oronamin-C 272
The Other Cold War (Kwon) 37
Ottoman Empire 62, 63
The Outlaws 347
An Outline of A Theory of Civilization (Fukuzawa) 67–68
Oxford Dictionaries 238

Pacific War 220
pan-Arabism 95
pan-Asianism 61, 64, 65, 93; nationalism and 94–96
Panglong Agreement 470
Pan-Malayan Islamic Party (PMIP) 521–522
Parent-Teacher Association (PTA) 224
Paris Peace Agreements 488
Park Chong Kyu 303
Park Chung Hee 106, 295, 297, 298–299, 300, 301, 304, 312, 321
Park Geun-hye 257, 320
Park Jeong-Hun 331

Partai Komunis Indonesia (Indonesian Communist Party or PKI) 474
Partai Sarekat Islam (PSI) 477
Party Foundation Day 285
Pasyon and Revolution (Ileto) 434
Peace of Westphalia 52, 90
pedagogy 42–43
Pegawai Kewangan Negara 553
Peguam Negara 553
Peking National First Midwifery School 144
People's Armed Police Force (PAPF) 208
People's Daily 188–191
People's Republic of China (PRC) 124, 151, 167–169, 171, 173, 176, 184–185, 202, 225–226
perpetual peace (Kant) 89
Perry, Matthew 268
Persatuan Muslimin Indonesia (Union of Indonesian Muslims) 474
Perseikatan Komunis India (Indies Communist Union) 474
Persian Constitutional Revolution 61
'personal nationalism' 30
Phạm Thi Hoài 416
Phạm Thu Thuy 417
Phan Bội Châu 64, 127, 370
Phan Thi Vang Anh 417
Philip IV, of France 3, 5
Philippine historiography: from colonial to Filipino viewpoint 432–435; "people" in the Tadhana project 435–437; populist nationalism in 429–438
Philippines: identity contestation over resources 396; nationalism 430–432
Philippines Human Security Act 2007 393
Pillsbury, Michael 159–160
Ping-Pong Diplomacy 185
Plato 238
political nationalism 491–493
political subjectivity and non-Western-centric world order 48–58
Pollmann, Tessel 479
Pol Pot 488
popular nationalism 497–500
populist nationalism: in Philippine historiography 429–438
post-colonialism 75; in East and Southeast Asia 74–87
postcolonial nationalism 341–344
post-colonial Vietnam: Chinese and nationalism in colonial Vietnam 406–407; enemies of Vietnamese nation 408–410; post-socialist economy 410–412; success and failure in post-colonial Vietnamese states 407–408
postdevelopmental anxieties 319–320
postdevelopmental nationalism 308–322, 322n1; and Seoul Olympics 314–316

Power and Knowledge in Southeast Asia: Scholar and State in Indonesia and the Philippines (Curaming) 435
Prasad, Vijay 96
Prayuth Chan-ocha 590
Prince Charles 91
Prince Chun 116–117
Prince Damrong Rajanubhab 580
Prince Narisara Nuwattiwong 579
Prince Norodom Ranariddh 495
Prince Norodom Sihanouk 493–495
Prince Ranariddh 495
Prince Sihanouk 493–495, 500
Prince Vajirañāna 587
Pro-Japanese Anti-National Activities (2005) 320
The Promise of the Foreign (Rafael) 564
Prophet Mohammed 202
'Prosperity and Power Begin with Hygiene' 140
Provincialising Europe (Chakrabarty) 37
Public Order Act of 2009 98
Purchasing Power Parity (PPP) 159
Putin, Vladimir 251
Pyinnyā Wara, Ashin 451
Pyongyang Marathon 286

Qing Dynasty 64, 111, 181–182, 202; as constitutional monarchy 115–116
Qing Empire 108, 109, 113, 114–117, 132
Qingyi Bao 127
Quijano, Aníbal 36–37, 39
Qu Jun 143

Rafael, Vicente 564
Raffles, Sir Stamford 535–536, 541
Rai Timor 571–573
Raja, Yossi 91
Rama II, King 583
Ramos, Jose A. 64
Ranger, Terence 295, 576
Rasheed, Zainul Abidin 541–542
rebellion as nationalism 464
Red Devils 318
Reeves, Keanu 238
Regehr, Ernie 391
Regional Comprehensive Economic Partnership (RCEP) Agreement 72
Reich 71
Rekishi Kyoikusha Kyogikai (History Educationalist Conference in Japan) 227
Rekishitsû 243, 244
religion as nationalism 462–463
Renan, Ernest 2
Renville agreement 477
Reproductive Health Law (RH Law) 431–432
Republic Act 1425 432
republicanism 109

Republican period (1912–1949) 202
Republic of China (ROC) 167, 177; adoption of Western medicine in China 139–140; female body and nation 141–143; national rejuvenation and female hygiene system 143–146; rise and fall of the nation 140–141; *see also* China
Republic of Korea (ROK) 280–281, 295
Republic of Mongolia (1991–today) 118
ressentiment: and Buddhist nationalism 442–443; and collective victimhood 442–443; and Indian immigration 445–448
revisionists and brand Japan 257–258
Revolt of the Masses: The Story of Bonifacio and the Katipunan (Agoncillo) 433
Reynaldo Ileto's Pasyon and Revolution Revisited, A Critique (Scalice) 434
Rhee Syngman 312
Rightwing nationalism
rightwing nationalists 231n5
Rio Olympics 263
River Elegy (TV series) 188
Rizal, José 42, 370, 430–433, 437
Rizal Bill 431–432
Rizal Law 432
Roach, Joseph 36
Rohingya Patriotic Front (RPF) 397
Rohingya Solidarity Organization (RSO) 397
Rohingyas without identity or nation 396–397
Roh Moo-hyun 308, 317, 318–321
Roh Tae-woo 314
Rossabi, Morris 54
Royal Development Projects 383
Royal Forestry Department 384
Royal Lao Government (RLG) 504
Russia and Japan 252
Russian Revolution 61, 245, 366
Russia-Ukraine war 8
Russo-British "Great Game" 63
Russo-Japanese War 61, 65, 67, 269
Ryōgoku Kokugikan 306n14
Ryukyu Kingdom 63

Sabaratnam, Meera 41
Said, Edward 39
Sakai, Naoki 38
Sakurai Yoshiko 244
Salamat, Hasim 396
Salazar, Zeus 434–435, 436, 438
Saloth Sâr 488
Samaranch, Juan Antonio 303
Sankei newspaper 258–259
Saravanamuttu, Johan 398
Sarekat Dagang Islam (Islamic Trade Association) 477
Sarekat Islam 365
Scalice, Joseph 434

Schechner, Richard 284
Scheler, Max 443
Schell, Orville 158
Schmitt, Carl 71, 94
School of Europeanization 67, 71
School of Kokusui Shugi 71
Scott, James 483
Second Sino-Japanese War (1937–1945) 183
Second World War 7, 17, 64, 65, 72, 269, 296, 344, 478, 481, 520, 552
security: identity and 199–200
Self-Strengthening Movement/ Westernization Movement 139, 182
semi-colony 66–72
Seoul Olympic Organizing Committee (SLOOC) 315
Seoul Olympics and postdevelopmental nationalism 314–316
Seton-Watson, Hugh 4, 20
shamanism 210n2
Shanghai Municipal Health Bureau 145
Sheftall, Bucky 246
Sheikh Muhammad Fadhlullah Suhaimi 530
Shen Siliang 182, 183
shidafu (literati) class 53
Shiga Shigetaka 68
Shin, Gi-wook 283
Shin Chaeho 339–340
Shirk, Susan 158
Shokichi, Umeya 64
Sidel, John 572
Sihanouk, Norodom 488
The Silk Roads (Frankopan) 92
Singapore 96–98; 1819 and colonial narrative 541–542; Chinese ethnonationalism 542–543; continuity with change 538–539; disrupting the myths 540–545; ethnic essentialism 542–543; Lee Kuan Yew 544–545; National Education 539–540; national narrative 534–545; as nation launched in trauma 536–538; ripe for renewal 545; role reversal 545; Singaporean exceptionalism 543–544
Singaporean exceptionalism 543–544
Sin Hyosun 318, 322
Sino-Japanese Joint Declaration 225
Sino-Japanese War 269
Sjariffudin, Amir 480
Small Nationalism 103
Smith, Anthony D. 15, 21–23, 27, 234, 268, 270, 282–283, 353, 490, 550
Snyder, Jack 198, 389
social constructs 74–75
Social Darwinism 101
Social Science Research Council (SSRC) in New York City 260
Sociological Theory beyond the Canon (Alatas and Sinha) 42

socio-technical systems and nationalism 170–171
Soekarno 24
Soenarno, Radin 521
Soleimani, Qasem 255
Song dynasty 52–54
Song elite 54
Song Junfu 182–183
Songun policy 287–288, 290, 292
Son Jeong-A 328
South China Sea 94
Southeast Asia: Belt and Road Initiative and BRICS 85; bringing order into things 79–80; colonialism and frameworks for nations 362–364; colonialism in 361–372; decolonisation in 361–372; democracy in conflict 393–394; emancipatory nationalism 368–371; explaining conflict in 388–393; history and ethnic nationalism 389–390; Islam and identity in 397–398; national intellectual elites 364–367; nationalism in 361–372; nation-building and self-determination 391; nation-building and state consolidation 390; post-colonialism, nationalism and internationalism in 74–87; pre-world society 82–84; resources and native rights 391–392; sovereignty/survival/identity 390–391; transmigration and displacement 392–393; and urbanisation 364–367
Southeast Asian nationalism: decolonialising 35–44; decolonial methodologies 40–42; decolonial pedagogy 42–43; decolonial theory 36–40; overview 35–36
South Korea: calculated nationalism in 325–333; Chun regime 313–314; crisis, rebound, and World Cup (2002) 316–318; and Japan 252; and Japan's trade restrictions 330–333; legacy of Japanese imperialism 330–333; *minjung* nationalism 313–314; postdevelopmental anxieties 318–320; postdevelopmental nationalism 308–322; Seoul Olympics and postdevelopmental nationalism 314–316
sovereign states: formation of 2–6
sovereignty: and identity 390–391; and survival 390–391
Spectral Nationality (Cheah) 40
Sport Daily 186
sports patriotism debate 191–192
The Spring of Humanity 285
Stalin, Joseph 114
state consolidation and nation-building 390
state-nationalism 110
statue wars 258
Stavrianos, L. S. 3
Stevenson, Nick 271
Stockholm International Peace Research Institute (SIPRI) 160

Strategic Information and Research Development Centre (SIRD) 526
Suga Yoshihide 243
Suharto 398; New Order 474
Sukarno 65, 365, 370, 398; Guided Democracy 474
Sukhothai Kingdom 586
Suku, Agama, Ras, Antar-golongan (SARA) 394
Sultan Omar Ali Saifuddien III (SOAS III) 549
Sun Yat-Sen 64, 70, 95, 108, 109, 117, 127, 132, 138, 141, 142, 147, 370, 371
supranationalism 74
Suryoputro, R.M.S. 476
Sustainable Development Goals 277
Sutan Sjahrir 480
Sutherland, Claire 17
Suu Kyi, Aung San 365, 466, 469, 470, 471, 591
Suu Kyi, Daw Aung 469
Su Xiaokang 188
Suzue Miuchi 342
SWIFT system 93
synchronisation: and Chinese nationalism 114–115; and homogenisation 114–115
Syngman, Rhee 297
Szadziewski, Henryk 208
Szeman, Imre 425

Tackett, Nicolas 53
Tadhana: A History of Filipino People 435
Tadhana project 435–437
taekwondo: early formation of 296–298; formation of modern 301–304; and Korean politics and nationalism 301–304; as national sport 298–301; overview 295
Taff, Haji Ahmad 536
Tagore, Rabindranath 40
Taidong Daily 182
Taiheiyo Senso o Kangaeru 224
Tai Lue culture 382
Taiping Rebellion 379
Taiwan: issue, brief history of 152; US-China-Taiwan military expenditure **161**; volatile US-China-Taiwan relations 162–163
Taiwanese identity: changing 152–156; and rising Chinese nationalism 151–163
Taiwan Travel Act (TTA) 162
Takeda Tsunekazu 263
Taksin, King 582
Tale of Genji 57
'tamed nationalism' 101
Tan, Samuel 435, 438
Tanaka Kakuei 225
Tan Cheng Bock 544
Tang Dynasty 52, 202
Tang-su-do 296
Tan Malaka 480
Tarling, Nicholas 365, 389

Taro Ohai 64
The Taste of Angkor 497
Taylor, Keith 40
Technical Intern Training Program (TITP) 251
techno-nationalism 168; cyber-sovereignty 168–169; nationalist policy 168–169
Tencent 174, 193
Ten Kingdoms Period 52
Teschke, Benno 77
Thailand 576–592; identity conflict at its worst 395; national identity construction 379–380
Thai nation construction 576–592
Thai Ratthaniyom (Thai Customs Decree) 395
Thakin U Nu 466
Thaksin Shinawatra 382
Than Tun 471
Thawpaka, Ashin 451
Thebaw, King 460
Thein Sein 450
Theory of Social and Economic Organization (Weber) 577
The Theory of the State (Bluntschli) 338
Third World nations 96, 133
threats to identity 200–202
'Three Principles of the People' (Sun Yat-sen) 142, 147
Tianxiaism 101
Tibetans 114, 118
Tô Hoài 417, 418
Tôjô Hideki 242
Tok Janggut 523
Tokugawa Japan: in the eighteenth century 56–58; Kokugaku in 56–58
Tokugawa Mitsukuni 57
Tokugawa Shogunate 56, 67
Tokyo Tribunal 231n5, 231n20
Tomomi, Inada 257
Tony Marano 243
Towards a Beautiful Country (Abe) 242, 255
Townsend, James 112
traditional colonialism 89–99; Eurocentrism and 91–92
traditional empires 62–66
trans-Asia democratic movement 29
transmigration: and displacement 392–393; and Southeast Asia 392–393
transnationalization 208
Tran Tinh Vy 426
Treaty of Shimonoseki 109
Treaty of Tianjin 62
Treaty of Wanghia 65
Treaty of Westphalia 77
trend of Chinese nationalism 157–158
tricontinental solidarity movement 134
Trump, Donald 81, 161–162, 236–237, 240, 253, 264, 282, 326, 429, 430, 437, 438
Tsai Ing-wen 156, 162

Tsutsui, William 315
Tuck, Eve 37
Tunku Abdul Rahman 537
Turkic Muslims 114, 118
Turkic nomadic societies 210n2
'Turkish Empire' 124
Turkistan Islamic Party (TIP) 196
Turner, Victor 284

Uemura Takashi 257
Uighur identity 210n2; construction of 202–204; early years 202–203; going forward 203–204; and government policies 204–207
Ulama, Nahdlatul 365
ummah (global Muslim community) 530
Underground Asia (Harper) 37
"Understanding Revolutionary Mentality" (Guerrero) 434
Unequal Treaties 109
UNESCO 28
Unfinished Empire (Darwin) 91
UN-General Assembly 85
Union Solidarity and Development Party (USDP) 441
United Malays National Organisation (UMNO) 358, 520, 524
United States (US): hegemony 89, 90, 93–94; Monroe Doctrine 71, 99; US-China-Taiwan military expenditure **161**; volatile US-China-Taiwan relations 162–163
United Wa State Army (UWSA) 381
Universal Bulletin 141
universal human rights 571–573
Unthinking Mastery (Singh) 42
urbanisation and rise of national intellectual elites 364–367
US-American legal system 17
user-generated discourse and practice 176–177
US-Japan Defense system 254
US-Japan Security Treaty 94, 253
US-Mexico-Canada Agreement 99
US-Philippines Defense Treaty 94

Vajiravudh, King of Thailand 66
Vandalism Act 98
Van den Berghe, Pierre L. 8
Verdery, Katherine 29
Vereenigde Oost-Indische Compagnie (VOC) 584
'vernacular mobilisation' 22
Vickers, Adrian 483
Victorious Fatherland Liberation War Museum 288
Vientiane Buddhist Institute 508–510
Vietnam: Chinese and nationalism in colonial 406–407; Chinese experience of Socialism and nationalism in 408–410; enemies of 408–410; Vietnamese and nationalism in

colonial 406–407; writing nationalism in post-reform 416–426
Vietnamese Communist Party 411
Vietnamese literature: national allegory in Vietnamese literary theory 424–425; and nationalism 416–418; portrayal of foreigners in socialist realist 416–418; portrayals of foreign businessmen in 418–420; portrayals of former American soldiers in 420–424; postcolonial criticism 424–425
Vietnamese nationalist movement 407
Vietnam War 8, 39, 215
Villers-Cotterets 5
Viravong, Sila 510
Vua Bảo Đại 64

Wada Haruki 332
Waever, Ole 199–200
Wahhabi-inspired reform movements 202
wakon yōsai ('Japanese spirit, Western learning') 269
Walker, Gavin 38
Wang Jingwei 95, 108, 109
Wang Kangnian 124
Wang Meng 187
Wang Zhengting 182
War of the Spanish Armada 54
Warsaw Pact countries 8
wartime: nationalism in 464–466
Washington-based Uyghur Human Rights Project 208
Washington Conference 70, 71
Weber, Max 42, 75, 344, 359, 576–578, 591, 592
Weber, Nicolas 39
Wehner, Peter 592
Weibo, Sina 172–173
Wei Jizhong 192
Weiss, Jessica Chen 158
Wenhui Daily 188
Western centricity 51, 58
Western colonial empires 61
Western colonialism 55, 60, 71, 95
Western democracy 481–486
Western hegemony 56
Western imperialism 70
Western medicine: adoption in China 139–140
Western nationalism 61
Westphalian order 49, 58
Wheaton, Henry 62
When China Rules the World (Jacques) 159
The White Man's burden (Kipling) 41
Whitmeyer, Joseph M. 497
Widodo, Joko 438
Wieden+Kennedy Tokyo 274
Wilken, G.A. 475
WiLL 243–244, 246

Wilson, Woodrow 62, 70, 367; *Fourteen Points* 63
woman: rise and fall of nation is responsibility of 140–141
'Women's Magazine' 142
Working People's Daily 449
World Cup (2002): and crisis 316–318; South Korea 316–318
World Health Organisation 349
World Mental Health Japan Survey 349
World Shooting Championships 303
World Taekwondo Federation (WTF) 302, 305n1
World Trade Organization 317
World Uighur Congress (WUC) 197
World United Karate Organisation (WUKO) 303
World War I 244, 257, 364, 366, 368, 461, 507
World War II 30, 54, 89, 95, 237, 242, 245, 246, 281, 283, 327, 332, 375–376, 384, 406, 465, 466, 467, 510–511
World Wide Web consortium 85
Wright-Neville, David 398
writing nationalism: in post-reform Vietnam 416–426
Wunthanu Athins 464
Wu Zhenchun 144

Xāt Lao: appeal of Issara anti-colonial nationalism 514–516; inventing tradition at Vientiane Buddhist Institute 508–510; loyalists: multiethnic nationalists 511–514; overview 504–507; school days in colonial Laos 507–508; two visions of Lao nationalism 516–517
Xavier do Amaral 563–564
Xiao Zhan 177
Xi Jinping 158, 163, 170, 172
Xinhai Revolution 116
Xinjiang Uygur Autonomous Region (XUAR) 203, 206, 208
Xuantong Emperor Puyi 116

Yaacob, Ibrahim HJ 65
Yahoo China 192
Yan Fuqing 144
Yang, K. Wayne 37
Yang Chongrui 144–145, 148
Yang Du 108, 109, 113, 140
Yang Eun-Kyeong 327
Yang Ming 191
Yatim, Rais 394
The Yellow Sea (2010) 347
Yeo Bang Hsiao 97
Yi An Huiguan 412
Yi Hae-Chan 331
Yihewani *see* Wahhabi-inspired reform movements

Yitan Li 159
Yoshida Doctrine 254
Yoshihiko, Noda 253
Yoshio, Kodama 242
Yōsuke Matsuoka, 71
Young Men's Buddhist Association 365, 445, 454
Young Turk Revolution 62
Youth League 172
youth nationalism: Indonesianess and 568
YouTube 173
Yuan Shikai 70, 116–117, 141
Yuan Weimin 192
Yukol, Chatri Chalerm 578
Yunus, Muhammad 397
Yusin Constitution (Park) 299
Yusof bin Ishak 535
Yu Xiwei 182

Zaide, Gregorio 431, 433, 435, 438
Zaide, Sonia 431
Zaitian, Guangxu Emperor 115–116
Zen-Buddhism 269
Zhang Gong 143
Zhang Guoji 131
Zhang Guowei 193
Zhang Meilan 411
Zhang Taiyan 64, 108, 109, 113, 114
Zhang Xueliang 182
Zhao Yu 188–189
Zhejiang Chao 125
Zheng Chenggong 61
Zheng Zhaokui 191
Zhongde Midwife School 145
Zhou Enlai 95–96, 134, 184, 380
Zi Qiang 128
Zou Rong 108, 109